Microsoft Excel 2013
Inside Out

Mark Dodge
Craig Stinson

PUBLISHED BY
Microsoft Press
A Division of Microsoft Corporation
One Microsoft Way
Redmond, Washington 98052-6399

Library of Congress Control Number: 2013935730
ISBN: 978-0-7356-6905-5

Printed and bound in the United States of America.

First Printing

Microsoft Press books are available through booksellers and distributors worldwide. If you need support related to this book, email Microsoft Press Book Support at mspinput@microsoft.com. Please tell us what you think of this book at http://www.microsoft.com/learning/booksurvey.

Microsoft and the trademarks listed at http://www.microsoft.com/en-us/legal/IntellectualProperty/Trademarks/EN-US.aspx are trademarks of the Microsoft group of companies. All other marks are property of their respective owners.

The example companies, organizations, products, domain names, email addresses, logos, people, places, and events depicted herein are fictitious. No association with any real company, organization, product, domain name, email address, logo, person, place, or event is intended or should be inferred.

This book expresses the authors' views and opinions. The information contained in this book is provided without any express, statutory, or implied warranties. Neither the authors, Microsoft Corporation, nor its resellers or distributors will be held liable for any damages caused or alleged to be caused either directly or indirectly by this book.

Acquisitions Editor: Rosemary Caperton
Developmental Editor: Valerie Woolley
Project Editor: Valerie Woolley
Editorial Production: Curtis Philips, Publishing.com
Technical Reviewer: Rozanne Whalen; Technical Review services provided by Content Master, a member of CM Group, Ltd.
Copyeditor: Roger LeBlanc
Indexer: William Meyers
Cover: Twist Creative • Seattle

Contents at a glance

Table of contents

Part 1: Examining the Excel environment

What do you think of this book? We want to hear from you!

Microsoft is interested in hearing your feedback so we can continually improve our books and learning resources for you. To participate in a brief online survey, please visit:

microsoft.com/learning/booksurvey

Part 3: Formatting and editing worksheets

Part 5: Creating formulas and performing data analysis

Part 6: Creating charts

Part 8: Using Excel collaboratively

Part 9: Automating Excel

Part 10: Integrating and extending Excel

Appendixes

What do you think of this book? We want to hear from you!

Microsoft is interested in hearing your feedback so we can continually improve our books and learning
resources for you. To participate in a brief online survey, please visit:

microsoft.com/learning/booksurvey

Introduction

MICROSOFT EXCEL 2013 has evolved from being a robust grid-based number-cruncher, to becoming the world's most robust grid-based number-cruncher that also happens to be pretty good at text manipulation, graphics, and many other things that were barely imaginable back in the days of Excel 1.0.

Excel is a tool that can be applied to many business tasks, including statistics, finance, data management, forecasting, analysis, inventory, billing, business intelligence, even word processing and graphic design. Excel is also one of the world's most popular programs for keeping all kinds of business and personal lists, from professional contacts to family addresses to home inventories.

There are a lot of great features to learn about, so let's get started.

Who this book is for

This book offers a comprehensive look at the features most people will use in Excel 2013 and serves as an excellent reference for users who need to understand how to accomplish what they need to do. In addition, this book goes a step or two further, providing useful information to advanced users who need to understand the bigger picture.

Assumptions about you

The *Inside Out* series is designed for readers who have some experience with Excel and are pretty comfortable finding their way around the program. You don't have to be a power user or an Excel developer.

How this book is organized

This book gives you a comprehensive look at the various features you will use. This book is structured in a logical approach to all aspects of using and managing Excel 2013.

Part 1, "Examining the Excel environment," covers the new features in the 2013 release, and also discusses the basics of using Excel.

Part 2, "Building worksheets," covers the details of how to construct and organize worksheets, and how to work with multiple sheets and workbooks.

Part 3, "Formatting and editing worksheets," covers all aspects of editing text and data, and applying cosmetics to make your worksheets more user-friendly.

Part 4, "Adding graphics and printing," describes how to work with Excel's full-featured graphics tools and how to prepare your worksheets for printing.

Part 5, "Creating formulas and performing data analysis," explains in detail how to construct formulas, and how to use Excel's sophisticated analysis tools.

Part 6, "Creating charts," shows how to get the most out of Excel's robust charting tools.

Part 7, "Managing databases and tables," covers the special properties of tables and Pivot-Tables, and describes how to work with external data.

Part 8, "Using Excel collaboratively," discusses issues surrounding the use of Excel workbooks and worksheets on the Internet and with email systems, and also covers Office 365.

Part 9, "Automating Excel," covers recording and debugging macros and creating custom functions.

Part 10, "Integrating and extending Excel," discusses the use of hyperlinks, the sharing of data among Office programs, and more.

Does your ribbon look different?

The screen images shown in this book were captured at the screen resolution, magnification, and text size that are optimum for publication purposes. The ribbon on your screen might not look the same as the one shown in the book. For example, you might see more or fewer buttons in each of the groups, the buttons you see might be represented by larger or smaller icons than those shown, or the group might be represented by a single button that you click to display the group's commands.

About the companion content

We have included this companion content to give you an opportunity to gain hands-on experience with some of the concepts explored in this book. You can download this book's companion content from the following page:

http://aka.ms/Excel2013InsideOut/files

The companion content includes sample Excel workbooks and other sample content referred to in the text.

Acknowledgments

We are lucky to have the best editorial team in the business, making authors look better than they deserve and facing inevitable issues with grace and thoughtfulness. Many thanks to project manager and shepherd-in-chief Curtis Philips; eagle-eye tech editor Rozanne Whalen; our copy editor, the incessantly nit-picky Roger LeBlanc; our proofreader and last line of defense, Andrea Fox; and the intrepid Valerie Woolley and Rosemary Caperton, cranking the big ol' book-making machine at Microsoft Press. It's always a pleasure to play with the A-team.

Support and feedback

The following sections provide information on errata, book support, feedback, and contact information.

Errata & support

We've made every effort to ensure the accuracy of this book and its companion content. Any errors that have been reported since this book was published are listed on our Microsoft Press site at oreilly.com:

http://aka.ms/Excel2013InsideOut/errata

If you find an error that is not already listed, you can report it to us through the same page.

If you need additional support, email Microsoft Press Book Support at *mspinput@microsoft.com*.

Please note that product support for Microsoft software is not offered through the addresses above.

We want to hear from you

At Microsoft Press, your satisfaction is our top priority and your feedback our most valuable asset. Please tell us what you think of this book at

http://www.aka.ms/tellpress

The survey is short, and we read every one of your comments and ideas. Thanks in advance for your input!

Stay in touch

Let's keep the conversation going! We're on Twitter: *http://twitter.com/MicrosoftPress*

What's new in Microsoft Excel 2013

C ONSIDERING recent computing history, including the advent of Microsoft Windows 8 and the increasing ubiquity of tablets and touch interfaces, the modest but impor-tant improvements made to Microsoft Excel 2013 might seem like a relative island of calm in rough digital seas. In 2007, there was truly a paradigm shift in Microsoft Excel and Office, and Office 2010 was a significant refinement. The 2013 version represents a fur-ther refinement, a "flatter" appearance, and an increased presence of the Office brand. Web Apps have been available for years now, becoming ever more capable, and are available to anyone with even a free Microsoft account. You can run Office apps on Windows phones, and Microsoft Surface tablets come with Office installed. More people are using Excel in more places. We're happy to say, it's better than ever.

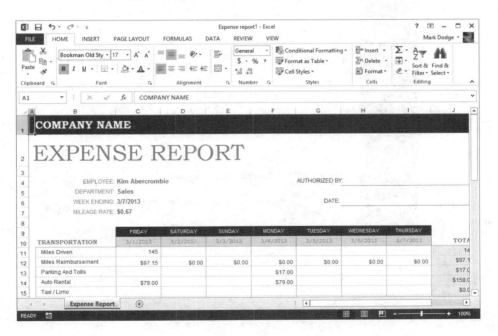

New and improved for 2013

First, we'll highlight the new features in the 2013 release of Microsoft Excel. Later, we'll talk about features that have been retired from the program and summarize the features that will be new to you if you skipped the last upgrade or two.

New templates

It seems as if templates have always been a bit of an afterthought—as if someone slapped together some generic sheets quickly, after everything else was done. No more. Excel 2013 has a new interface for templates, as shown in Figure 1-1, and now it offers some of the most sophisticated and useful prepackaged workbooks you've ever seen. They succeed in banishing the typical wall of numbers from your desktop, while delivering a lot of useful, well-thought-out functionality. These templates are useful, and what's more, you can learn from them. For more information, see "Creating workbooks" in Chapter 2, "Exploring Excel fundamentals."

Figure 1-1 The New command on the File tab reveals a wealth of sophisticated templates.

Quick analysis

If you select more than one nonempty cell, the new Quick Analysis tool appears at the lower right corner of the selected range. Clicking it displays a context-sensitive toolbar containing tabs and controls applicable to the contents of the selected cells. As you move the pointer over icons on the Quick Analysis toolbar, as shown in Figure 1-2, a live preview is applied to the selected data on the worksheet. Just click the icon to make it stick. For more information, see "Using the Quick Analysis tool" in Chapter 2.

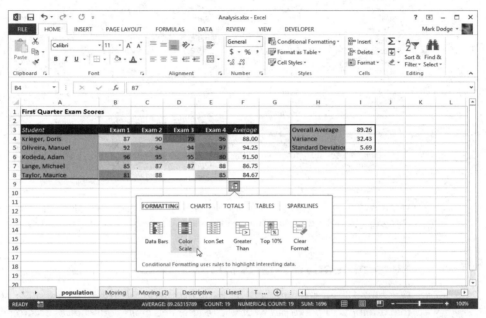

Figure 1-2 Select a range and click the Quick Analysis button to display sets of applicable tools.

Flash Fill

Microsoft describes Flash Fill as a "data assistant that finishes your work for you." Perhaps it's more like "finishing your sentences for you," but as it turns out, Flash Fill is an impressive feature that might better be described as a live concatenation function. As you type data into cells, Excel compares it to data in adjacent cells, and if a pattern is detected, Flash Fill offers a solution, such as the list of full names in column H, shown in Figure 1-3. For more information, see "Automatic parsing and concatenation using Flash Fill" in Chapter 8, "Worksheet editing techniques."

	A	B	C	D	E	F	G	H	I
1	Last Name	First Name	Date of Hire	Date of Birth	Sex	Salary	Age		
2	Nadav	Yinon	6/17/86	11/29/62	M	96000	50	Yinon Nadav	
3	Abrus	Luka	6/22/86	5/15/49	F	32000	63	Luka Abrus	
4	Kopac	Barbara	8/16/86	11/2/59	M	46000	53	Barbara Ko	
5	Bouraima	Herve	10/15/86	5/3/60	M	42000	52	Herve Bou	
6	Seidler	Joachim	10/21/86	12/15/76	M	82000	36	Joachim S	
7	Weinfurter	Walter	11/20/86	10/17/49	M	100000	63	Walter We	
8	Overeem	Pascaline	11/30/86	5/10/76	M	26000	36	Pascaline	
9	Gil	Enrique	1/20/87	3/4/58	M	63000	54	Enrique Gi	
10	Amireh	Kamil	1/23/87	10/22/56	F	94000	56	Kamil Ami	
11	Ozolins	Gatis	2/4/87	4/26/58	F	51000	54	Gatis Ozo	
12	Tuntisangaroon	Sittichai	2/19/87	10/13/78	M	82000	34	Sittichai Tu	
13	Krenthaller	Elisabeth	2/21/87	3/26/76	M	53000	36	Elisabeth	
14	Park	Dan	2/24/87	11/14/74	M	58000	38	Dan Park	
15	Sario	Esko	5/4/87	6/24/73	M	82000	39	Esko Sario	
16	Riis	Bjarne	6/23/87	10/12/51	M	68000	61	Bjarne Riis	
17	Madigan	Tony	6/30/87	6/16/77	M	100000	35	Tony Madi	
18	Wacker	Roland	8/11/87	12/4/70	M	84000	42	Roland Wa	
19	Sasaki	Rie	8/24/87	9/4/67	M	77000	45	Rie Sasak	
20	Cletus	Christian	8/26/87	12/3/69	M	92000	43	Christian C	
21	Marques	Leonor	10/15/87	1/16/78	M	57000	35	Leonor Ma	
22	Belishky	Kostadin	11/15/87	9/27/63	M	63000	49	Kostadin B	
23	Paturskis	Leonids	12/1/87	12/26/60	M	70000	52	Leonids Pa	
24	Ran	Yossi	1/2/88	11/8/65	M	82000	47	Yossi Ran	

Data

Figure 1-3 Typing one full name into cell H2 was all the information Flash Fill needed to correctly guess the desired results, which were suggested after only one letter was typed into cell H3.

Recommended charts

Like Flash Fill, the Recommended Charts button on the Insert tab is another brainy feature that attempts to figure out what you're after and limits your choices accordingly, rather than presenting you with every available option. When the active cell is in a table, clicking the Recommended Charts button displays the Insert Chart dialog box, as shown in Figure 1-4, which now opens to a special tab containing thumbnails of your data displayed in Excel's selected chart types. If you still need more options, the All Charts tab is just a click away. For more information, see "Creating a new chart" in Chapter 19, "Designing charts."

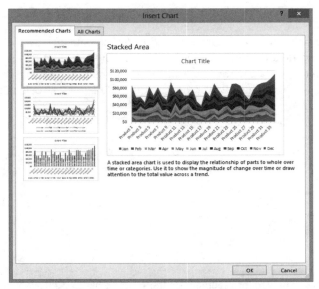

Figure 1-4 Recommended Charts analyzes your data and suggests a few appropriate charts.

New chart-formatting controls

After you create a chart, it is now easier than ever to modify it. The Chart Elements and Chart Styles buttons appear to the right of a chart when it is selected, offering instant chart-formatting gratification, as shown in Figure 1-5. Click options to add or remove elements in the chart, or change the chart's styles and colors. For more information, see "Adding, editing, and removing a chart title" in Chapter 19.

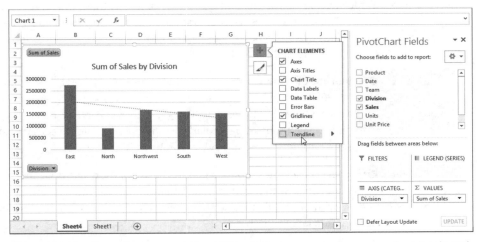

Figure 1-5 The Chart Elements and Chart Styles buttons appear whenever a chart is selected.

Timeline

You might call the new Timeline feature a *date slicer*. If your data includes dates, as in Figure 1-6, you can include a Timeline with your PivotTable or PivotChart that is used to limit the displayed data to any date range you want—in days, months, quarters, or years. For more information, see "Creating a Power View report" in Chapter 24, "Using PowerPivot."

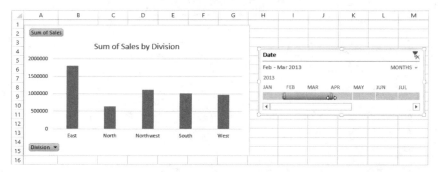

Figure 1-6 You can click any month segment on the Timeline bar to display only that month's data, or drag a handle to include as many months as you want.

Other improvements

Here are more upgrades and enhancements you'll find in Excel 2013:

- **Recommended PivotTables**   Similar to the Recommended Charts feature, Recommended PivotTables analyzes the selected data and offers appropriate suggestions. For more information, see Chapter 24.

- **Table slicers**   Slicers were introduced in 2010, but they worked only with Pivot-Tables. The interface has been upgraded for 2013, and you can now use slicers with other kinds of data tables as well. For more information, see "Creating a Power View report" in Chapter 24.

- **One workbook, one window, one worksheet**   New workbooks contain a single sheet in 2013, not three. And previously, all open workbooks were enclosed within a single Excel window. Now, each workbook is its own window, making it easier to work with multiple workbooks, particularly for multiple-monitor users. For more information, see Chapter 7, "How to work a workbook."

- **Rich chart data labels**   Data labels in charts are more customizable in 2013. You can create labels with text that updates automatically, you can apply rich formatting, and you can display text inside shapes. For more information, see "Adding and positioning data labels" in Chapter 19.

- **Animations**   As you work in Excel 2013, you'll notice subtle animations in various situations, including updating charts, inserting data, and copying and pasting. For example, when you insert a row, the rows below the new row appear to scroll downward. This was formerly referred to as *visceral feedback*, which is a clue to its true value. The animations are not exactly essential, but they help illustrate the changes incurred by your actions.

- **Standalone PivotCharts**   Now, your Pivot Charts do not need to remain tethered to a PivotTable; you can copy and paste them as you wish, without the baggage. For more information, see "Creating PivotCharts" in Chapter 23, "Analyzing data with PivotTable reports."

- **New functions**   There are always new functions, and this time, most of them are meant to increase compatibility with the Open Document format.

- **The Excel Data Model**   Some of the power from the PowerPivot add-in that was introduced in Excel 2010 has now been incorporated into Excel as the Excel Data Model, which you can use to address multiple tables of data from within Excel. For more information, see Chapter 24.

- **Power View**   This new feature leverages the power of the Excel Data Model, which you can use to construct elaborate presentation-ready reports that include graphics and data from multiple tables or external data sources. For more information, see "Creating a Power View report" in Chapter 24.

Does your ribbon look different?

In this book, we provide instructions based on traditional keyboard and mouse input methods. If you're using Excel on a touch-enabled device, you might be using a stylus or your finger to give commands. If so, substitute a tapping action any time we instruct you to click a user interface element. Also note that when we tell you to enter information in Excel, you can do so by typing on a keyboard, tapping an on-screen keyboard, or even speaking aloud, depending on your computer setup and your personal preferences.

Retired in 2013

These are features whose services were no longer required this time around:

- **Save Workspace**   Because of the new "One workbook, one window" interface, the Save Workspace command lost most of its reason to exist.

- **Window Split box**   Near the vertical scroll bar, lived a little box you could double-click to split the worksheet into panes. Although you can do the job using the Split button on the View tab, the box was inexplicably removed—perhaps another casualty of the "one workbook, one window" interface.

If you missed the last upgrade

Just in case you leapfrogged a software upgrade and missed the last big Microsoft Office release, here is a brief description of a few features that are essentially new to you but were introduced in the previous release:

- **Backstage view**   The File tab opens what Microsoft calls *Backstage view,* a single location where you find essential controls and information about your documents and where most of Excel's behind-the-scenes options and settings reside. The traditional File menu commands are here, too—for opening, saving, and creating new files; using templates; printing; and sharing information with others.

- **Ribbon customization**   Users of the static ribbon in Excel 2007 will be happy to know they can now freely rearrange command groups; change the order and position of tabs; remove groups; create custom commands, groups, and tabs; and show or hide existing tabs.

- **Sparklines**   Sparklines are tiny charts that fit within a cell and give you a visual summary alongside your data.

- **Paste Preview**   In Excel, you now can preview how copied information will look before you paste it. When you copy and then click the Paste menu (on the Home tab in the Clipboard group), hovering over the option buttons displays what each one will do on the worksheet if and when you actually click it.

- **Improved picture editing**   Now when you want to insert a picture in a workbook, you can edit it directly in Excel—you no longer need to prepare it in advance using a photo-editing program.

- **Office Web Apps**   Providing a familiar Microsoft Office experience when you are away from your computer, Office Web Apps allow you to work with Excel, Word,

PowerPoint, and OneNote files from just about anywhere, offering browser-based viewing and lightweight editing.

- **Slicers**   Slicers provide an easy way to filter large PivotTables so that you can see exactly the data you need without being distracted by data you don't need.

- **Improved conditional formatting**   New conditional formatting options let you quickly visualize and comprehend data. You will find more styles, icons, and data bars, and you now have the ability to highlight specified items (such as the maximum or minimum value) in a few clicks.

- **New functions and functional consistency**   Microsoft added a number of statistical and financial functions that extend or refine existing functionality. Most of the new functions are statistical distribution functions. For example, in addition to the existing COVAR function, a measure of deviation between data sets, you can now choose COVARIANCE.P or COVARIANCE.S, which applies to an entire population of data (P) or a representative sample (S).

- **Improved math equation support**   Create and display math equations with a rich set of equation-editing tools.

- **Improved charting capacity**   Two-dimensional charts in Excel 2007 were limited to 32,000 data points per series. Chart series are now limited only by system memory.

- **Additional SmartArt graphics**   Incorporate great-looking graphics into your professional documents without a large consulting team or time commitment.

- **64-bit edition**   Excel 2010 introduced 64-bit scalability for the Excel guru or analyst working with massive, memory-intensive datasets.

- **Office Mobile**   Microsoft Office Mobile brought Office tools to the mini screen of your mobile device.

If you missed the last two upgrades

If you are one of the people clinging to Excel 2007 and managed to hang in there all this time, well . . . hey, it's time to upgrade. Here is a summary of the things that were changed in Excel 2007:

- **Results-oriented user interface**   The old toolbars and menu bar have been replaced by a single toolbar and a new dashboard called the *ribbon,* which has a task-oriented structure and easily recognizable tools. Most of the old menus have been reborn as tabs.

- **Graphics enhancements** Excel has improved greatly over the years as a platform for graphics and design, and the 2007 release incorporated a few subtle enhancements, including a robust SmartArt feature; improvements to conditional formatting, shapes, and charting; and new document themes and cell styles.

- **Improved formatting** Microsoft built a lot more intelligence into the formatting features of Excel 2007—including themes, cell styles, and galleries. You can use Live Previews to rest the pointer on an item in a palette of options to see what will happen when and if you click.

- **Page Layout view** Really more than a view, Page Layout view became a working mode with rulers and page previews in which you have full editing functionality and control over the appearance of your documents.

- **Increased capacity and speed** The new XML file format and other internal improvements gave Excel 2007 greatly increased capacities in just about every specification—for example, spreadsheets that can hold more than one million rows of data, 64 levels of nesting in formulas, and built-in support for multicore processors and multithreaded chipsets. Other major specification changes included

  - The total number of available columns: 16,384 (was 256).

  - The total number of available rows: 1,048,576 (was 65,536).

  - The total amount of computer memory: Excel can now use the maximum allowed by Windows (was 1 gigabyte).

  - The number of unique colors allowed in a single workbook: 4.3 billion (was 56).

  - The number of conditional format conditions on a cell: Limited only by available memory (was 3).

  - The number of levels of sorting you can perform on a range or table: 64 (was 3).

  - The number of items allowed in the Filter drop-down list: 10,000 (was 1,000).

  - The total number of unique cell formats in a workbook: 64,000 (was 4,000).

  - The maximum number of characters allowed in formulas: 8,000 (was 1,000).

  - The number of levels of nesting that Excel allows in formulas: 64 (was 7).

  - The maximum number of arguments allowed to a function: 255 (was 30).

○ The maximum number of items returned by the Find command: 2 billion (was 64,000).

○ The number of rows allowed in a PivotTable: 1 million (was 64,000).

○ The number of columns allowed in a PivotTable: 16,000 (was 255).

○ The maximum number of unique items within a single PivotTable field: 1 million (was 32,000).

○ The maximum length of the MDX name for a PivotTable item, the string length for a relational Pivot Table, the caption length, and the field label length: 32,000 (was 255).

○ The number of fields that a single PivotTable can have: 16,000 (was 255).

○ The number of array formulas that can refer to another worksheet: Limited only by available memory (was 65,000).

○ Limit to the number of rows that you can refer to in an array formula: None (was 64,000).

○ The number of categories allowed for custom functions: 255 (was 32).

○ Excel now supports multicore processors and multithreaded chipsets.

- **Better and easier tables**   Excel 2007 introduced a more robust table feature, incorporating PivotTable-like intelligence with easier formatting and editing. New features included the Table Styles gallery, structured referencing, the Remove Duplicates feature, and more.

- **Improved PivotTables and PivotCharts**   Excel 2007 added a few key improvements to PivotTable filtering, design, and layout. The greatly improved appearance of the charting features enabled more compelling PivotCharts.

- **Better database connectivity**   Along with better PivotTables, Excel 2007 provided built-in access to SQL Server Analysis Services and included support for the Unified Dimensional Model (UDM), as well as for online analytical processing (OLAP) browsers and key performance indicators (KPIs).

- **Formula AutoComplete**   Typing functions in formulas became a little easier in Excel 2007. When you type an equal sign (=) followed by any letter, you get a drop-down list of functions that start with that letter, along with a ScreenTip description of the highlighted function. Type another letter, and the list is filtered again. If you have defined cell range names in your workbook, these appear in the list as well.

- **Tools for creating formulas**   In Excel 2007, the formula bar became manually resizable to let you display or hide lengthy formulas. This allowed you to enter longer formulas than before, with more levels of nesting (parenthetical expressions within expressions). The Name Manager dialog box provided greater organization and editing possibilities. In addition, Excel 2007 included many small improvements in the way it works internally, including improvements in subtotals and regression formulas.

- **Built-in Analysis Toolpak functions**   The trusty statistical functions of the venerable Analysis Toolpak were fully integrated into the program in 2007.

- **Enhanced charting features**   Excel 2007 included lots of new chart types, updated graphics, and a new set of Chart Tools contextual tabs, all of which made experimentation and modification a whole lot easier. Microsoft Office PowerPoint 2007 and Office Word 2007 started using the same charting engine as Excel.

- **XLSX file format**   The Microsoft Office Open XML file formats (with the extension .xlsx in Excel) provided better integration with external data sources and resulted in significantly smaller file sizes.

- **Improved sorting and filtering**   The Sort command, which previously allowed only three levels of sorting at a time, was improved to allow 64 levels in Excel 2007. The Filter feature was improved, and the Remove Duplicates button helped make managing database information easier, letting you specify in which columns to look for duplicate information.

- **Enhanced security features**   Microsoft added a number of new features in Excel 2007, including the Trust Center and a digital signatures interface to help secure documents you share with others.

Moving onward with Office 2013

The improvements made in Microsoft Office and Excel 2013 are solid, and the release is significant, considering the new intelligent features and the new platforms supported, including Microsoft's first computer, Surface. If you skipped the 2010 release, you'll find some nice new surprises. If you skipped the 2007 release, you have a lot of catching up to do. Read on!

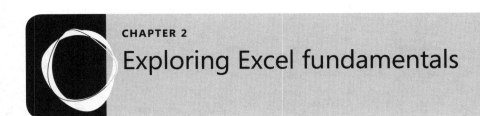

CHAPTER 2

Exploring Excel fundamentals

B EFORE you can get the feel of the controls, you need to know where they are and what they do. This chapter discusses the essential commands, controls, tools, and techniques you need to operate the Microsoft Excel 2013 machine.

Examining the Excel 2013 workspace

This section takes you on a tour of not only the dashboard of Excel 2010 but also the trunk and the glove compartment. We might even slip on some gloves and take a peek under the floor mats.

Facts about worksheets

Here are some tidbits of information about the grid called the *worksheet*, shown in Figure 2-1:

- Column letters range from A through XFD. (After column Z comes column AA, after column ZZ comes column AAA, and so on, up to XFD.) Row numbers range from 1 through 1,048,576.

- The currently selected cell is referred to as the *active cell*. When you select a range of cells, only the cell in the top-left corner is considered the active cell. The reference of the active cell appears in the Name box on the left end of the formula bar.

- The headings for the columns and rows containing selected cells are highlighted, making it easier to identify the location of selected cells.

- With 16,000 columns and 1,048,576 rows, your worksheet contains more than 16 billion individual cells. Before you try to unravel the mysteries of the universe on a single worksheet, however, remember that the number of cells you can use at one time is limited by the amount of memory your computer has. Although Excel allocates memory only to cells containing data, you might have trouble actually using all the cells on one worksheet, no matter how much memory you have.

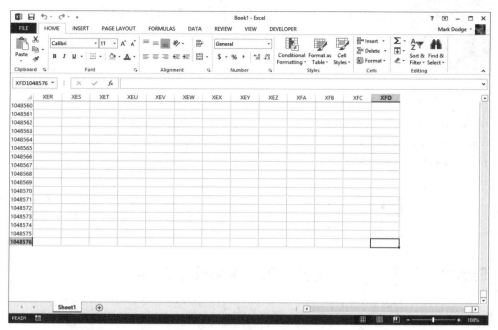

Figure 2-1 There is a huge amount of available space on a worksheet.

The porthole window

The workbook window is like a porthole through which you can see only a portion of a worksheet. To illustrate, suppose you were to cut a small, square hole in a piece of cardboard and place the cardboard over this page. At any given time, you could see only a portion of the page through the hole. By moving the cardboard around the page, however, you could eventually read the entire page through the window in your piece of cardboard. Viewing worksheets in Excel is much the same. You can also open another window to view different sections of the same worksheet simultaneously.

Using the workbook window

A new workbook, shown in Figure 2-2, originally consists of a single worksheet; you click the New Sheet button to add more sheets. This is a change from previous versions, in which new workbooks contained multiple sheets.

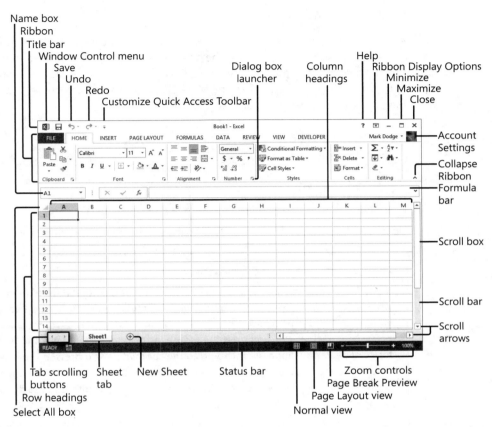

Figure 2-2 Workbooks initially comprise a single sheet, but you can add as many as you need.

For more information about using workbooks, see Chapter 7, "How to work a workbook."

Workbooks are great organizational tools. For example, you can keep in the same work-book all the documents that relate to a specific project, department, or individual. Workbooks can eliminate a considerable amount of clutter on your hard disk. The more documents you have to manage, the more valuable workbooks become. You can use workbooks as a multiuser management tool. For example, you can organize worksheets in groups for individual tasks or individual users. You can also share a workbook so that more than one person can work on it at the same time.

If you routinely create folders on your hard disk to contain groups of related files, you can think of workbooks as folders where you can keep all related worksheets.

For more information about using and sharing workbooks, see Chapter 26, "Collaborating on a network or by email."

Getting around in the workbook

At the bottom of the workbook window are controls you can use to move from sheet to sheet in a workbook. Just click any sheet tab to activate it, but if there are too many tabs to fit across your screen at once, sheet-navigation controls appear to help you get around, as shown in Figure 2-3. Note that the More Sheets (ellipsis …) buttons will not appear until there are too many sheets to display at once.

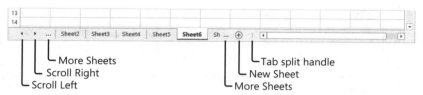

Figure 2-3 Use the workbook navigational controls to move among undisplayed worksheets.

If you have a wheel mouse

If you have one, you can use the wheel on your Microsoft IntelliMouse (and most other wheeled pointing devices) to scroll through your worksheet. Turn the wheel toward you to scroll down or away from you to scroll up. To scroll left or right (called *panning*), press the wheel button, and drag the mouse in the direction you want to move. A gray four-headed arrow appears, anchored to the spot where you pressed the wheel button. The speed of panning depends on how far you drag away from the anchor. As you press the button down and drag, a black arrow appears, pointing in the direction you're dragging:

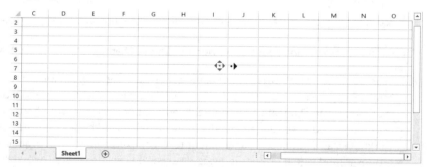

You can change the default behavior of the wheel from scrolling to zooming. To do so, click the File tab and then click Options. In the Advanced category, below Editing Options, select the Zoom On Roll With IntelliMouse check box. For more information, see "Zooming worksheets" in Chapter 6, "How to work a worksheet."

Workbook navigation tips

Many features and controls can help you navigate through the rows, columns, and worksheets in a workbook. Here are the highlights:

- Use the sheet tab navigation buttons to view all the sheet tabs in your workbook; click a tab to view the contents of that worksheet.

- Drag the tab split handle to the right if you want to see more sheet tabs at the expense of the horizontal scroll bar's width. To return to the usual tab display, double-click the tab split handle.

- Press Ctrl+Page Down to activate the next worksheet in the workbook; press Ctrl+Page Up to activate the previous worksheet.

- Press Ctrl+Home to jump to cell A1 from anywhere on a worksheet.

- Right-click any scroll bar to display a shortcut menu dedicated to scrolling actions, as shown in Figure 2-4.

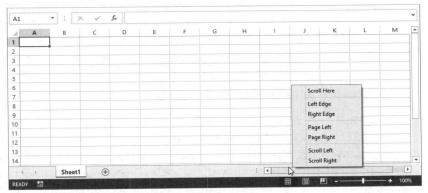

Figure 2-4 Right-click a scroll bar to display a shortcut menu of navigational commands.

- Drag the scroll box (also known as the *scroll thumb*) to move around the worksheet. Click the scroll bar anywhere outside the scroll box to move one screen at a time in the direction in which you clicked.

- The size of the scroll box changes depending on the size of the scrollable area. For example, the scroll boxes shown in Figure 2-4 are more than half as large as the scroll bars themselves, indicating there is little more to see in the active area of the worksheet—nothing, in fact, because this is a blank worksheet. As you add data to more columns and rows than can appear on a single screen, the scroll boxes get proportionally smaller, giving you immediate feedback about the size of the worksheet. A tiny scroll thumb indicates a huge worksheet.

- Using the scroll arrows at either end of the scroll bars, you can move through the worksheet one column or row at a time.

- The Name box at the left end of the formula bar always displays the active cell reference, regardless of where you scroll the window.

- To scroll the worksheet without changing the active cell, press Scroll Lock. For example, to scroll to the right one full screen without moving the active cell, press Scroll Lock and then press Ctrl+Right Arrow.

> **Note**
>
> The active area of a worksheet is simply the rectangular area that encompasses all the data the worksheet contains. So, if you have just three rows and columns of actual data in the top-left corner of the worksheet, the active area would be A1:C3. If, on the same worksheet, a stray character (even a space) happens to be in cell AB1299, the active area would be A1:AB1299. On a new blank worksheet, however, Excel considers the default active area to be roughly what you can see on the screen, even before you enter any data.

Working with workbook windows

In Excel 2013, workbook windows behave differently than in any previous version. Previously, there was one Excel window that contained all open worksheets, which appeared as separate windows within the Excel *workspace*. (Even the term "workspace" has been retired for 2013.) Each workbook appears as a separate *instance* of Excel in the 2013 version. If you have three workbooks open, there will be three windows, each with a complete Excel interface, including ribbon tabs, a formula bar, a status bar, and other such items.

So workbook windows now behave like any other windows in Windows. At the right end of each title bar are the familiar Minimize, Maximize/Restore, and Close buttons. After you maximize a window, a button with two small boxes—the Restore button—takes the place of the Maximize button. Clicking the Restore button changes the maximized window into a floating window.

INSIDE OUT   See more rows on your screen

You can set the Windows taskbar at the bottom of the screen to automatically hide itself when not in use. Right-click the taskbar to display the shortcut menu, click the Properties command, and on the Taskbar tab of the Taskbar Properties dialog box select the Auto-Hide The Taskbar check box and then click OK. Now the taskbar stays hidden and opens only when you move the pointer to the bottom of the screen.

When you click the Minimize button (the one with a small line at the bottom), the window collapses and is relegated to an icon in the Windows taskbar, which you can click at any time to restore the window to its previous configuration. You can also drag the borders of any window to control its size.

Because you can open multiple windows for the same workbook, you might find it convenient to view different parts of the workbook, or even different parts of an individual worksheet, side by side in separate windows, rather than switching between worksheets or scrolling back and forth in one large window.

For more information, see "Opening multiple windows for the same workbook" in Chapter 7.

INSIDE OUT   Microsoft and the SDI

What is SDI? The single document interface (SDI) initiative that Microsoft implemented in its Office programs several versions ago was only an option in Excel 2010, but now... it's the law! Prior to SDI, regardless of the number of documents you had open, the applications were individual; if you had three Excel workbooks open, only one instance of Excel was visible in the Windows taskbar.

Microsoft's SDI initiative now dictates that each document now generates its own window, each of which becomes a separate item on the Windows taskbar. Open three Excel workbooks, and three items appear on the taskbar. This is arguably a more realistic way to handle documents, which is why Microsoft did it in the first place. Multiple-monitor users rejoice!

So in 2013, multiple document interface (MDI) is no more; long live the SDI. By the way, you won't see these terms used very much—for good reason: "multiple" DI creates a single window, and "single" DI creates multiple windows. Geek double-speak!

Exploring the ribbon

After you get the raw data into Excel by whatever means, you'll spend a lot of time using the ribbon to massage and beautify your data. The ribbon was introduced in Microsoft Office 2007 and was one of the most sweeping user interface (UI) changes ever implemented, redefining the workflow in every Office program. By this time—the third generation of the ribbon—the dust has settled, and even grumpy, old Excel users have come to terms with it. Figure 2-5 shows the ribbon at rest.

Figure 2-5 The ribbon dominates the top of the Excel window.

Does your ribbon look different?

The screen images shown in this book were captured at the screen resolution, magnification, and text size that is optimum for publication purposes. The ribbon on your screen might not look the same as the one shown in the book. For example, you might see more or fewer buttons in each of the groups, the buttons you see might be represented by larger or smaller icons than those shown, or the group might be represented by a single button that you click to display the group's commands.

The ribbon comprises a number of tabs, each containing several ribbon groups, which in turn contain sets of related controls: commands, buttons, menus, galleries, and dialog box launchers. The hierarchy within and among ribbon tabs is designed to approximate a general workflow model, with the most-often-used features and options stacked more or less from left to right within and among tabs. For example, the Home tab contains commands you need when you create a new worksheet and start performing tasks such as cutting and pasting, formatting, and sorting, while the Review tab contains commands related to documents that are more or less complete, addressing issues such as verifying spelling and protecting the document.

Note

The 2007 version of the ribbon was not customizable; thankfully, this was remedied in Excel 2010 and continues to be customizable in 2013. Die-hard toolbar-modification aficionados such as your friendly Excel book authors were thrilled. This is explored in detail in "Customizing the ribbon" in Chapter 3, "Custom-tailoring the Excel workspace."

The ribbon speaks

For years now, many of us in the computer-book-writing business have been anticipating early retirement due to the expected advent of stunningly simple user interfaces and the holy grail of "self-documenting" software. In reality, this goal has proven as elusive as the "paperless office," so we've kept pretty busy. But Office 2013 represents another fine attempt at rendering our jobs obsolete. You can gain helpful information about your immediate surroundings simply by brandishing your pointer. For example, the left side of Figure 2-6 shows the ScreenTip that opens when you rest the pointer anywhere in the Number Format drop-down list. The right side of Figure 2-6 shows what happens when you click the Number Format drop-down list.

The icons representing the various options in the Number Format drop-down list shown in Figure 2-6 are another step in the right documentation direction, although further exploration might be required to discover the meaning of items such as the cryptic "12" icon for the Number format. (See "Using Accounting formats" in Chapter 9, "Worksheet formatting techniques.") And, as always, you can press F1 at any time to open the Excel Help window and gain additional insight.

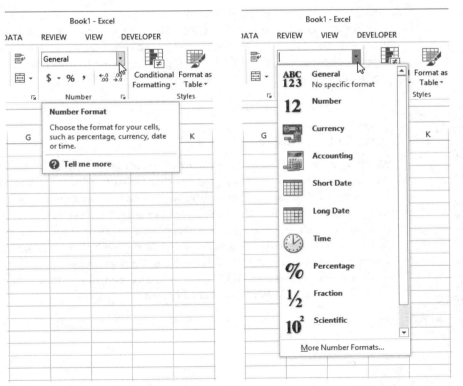

Figure 2-6 Rest your pointer on an object on the ribbon to display an explanatory ScreenTip. Click any arrow on the ribbon to display a menu, list, or gallery of options.

> **Note**
>
> If you need to maximize your worksheet area, you can temporarily hide the ribbon by double-clicking the active tab. Once it is hidden, clicking any tab puts the ribbon back into view.

Drop-down lists and dialog box launchers

The Number group on the Home tab, shown in Figure 2-6, contains the aforementioned Number Format drop-down list, four regular buttons, and a menu button (the $ sign), which acts like any other button when you click the button proper, but when you click the arrow next to it, it displays a drop-down list of alternate actions for that button. Anytime you see an arrow directly to the right of a button or a box on the ribbon, clicking the arrow reveals more options. (Just to confuse the issue a bit, the Increase Font Size and Decrease Font Size buttons in the Font group display arrows that are identical to the menu arrows but are actually part of the button images and don't invoke drop-down lists.)

Many groups display a tiny button in the bottom-right corner called a *dialog box launcher* (labeled for your convenience in Figure 2-2). This is a visual cue telling you there is more you can do there. When you rest the pointer on a dialog box launcher, a ScreenTip opens with details about its function; click the dialog box launcher to display the promised result, as shown in Figure 2-7.

INSIDE OUT   Just pin it

Whether you have Windows 7 or Windows 8, Excel lives in similar surroundings. In Windows 8, Excel runs on the desktop, which is similar to Windows 7, but without a Start button. This means that there is no Start menu with programs pinned to it, and no All Programs menu, either. If you are on the Windows 8 Start screen, click the Excel tile, which activates the desktop and starts Excel. But if you're on the desktop, you have to go back to the Start screen to start Excel. Or you can pin it to the taskbar. The taskbar is standard equipment in both Windows versions. On the Windows 8 Start screen, right-click the Excel tile, and then click the Pin To Taskbar icon. In Windows 7, right-click the Excel icon and click the Pin To Taskbar command.

Figure 2-7 Rest the pointer on a dialog box launcher for an explanation of its function; click it to open the corresponding dialog box.

Sometimes dialog box launchers actually launch dialog boxes, as shown in Figure 2-7; other times, clicking the dialog box launcher displays a task pane on the side of the window, as shown in Figure 2-8. In the latter case, the dialog box launcher acts as a toggle—that is, clicking it opens the task pane, and clicking it again closes the task pane.

Another way to access advanced options relegated to dialog boxes is to look for commands sporting an ellipsis (...) at the bottom of menus and galleries. For example, at the bottom of the Number Format drop-down list shown in Figure 2-6 is a command called More Number Formats. Just as you can with the dialog box launcher, you can click this command to display the Format Cells dialog box. As was the case in previous versions of Excel, an ellipsis adjacent to the name of a command indicates that clicking that command displays a dialog box with additional options rather than immediately issuing the command.

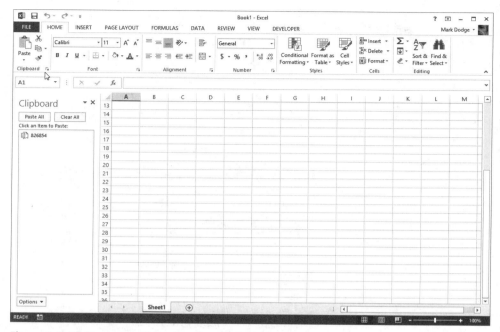

Figure 2-8 Clicking some dialog box launchers causes a task pane to open, docked to the left or the right of the worksheet.

Galleries and live preview

The concept of galleries goes way back. The idea is to provide a visual clue about what's going to happen when you click something, besides just the name of a command or button. Microsoft has done this with fonts for some time now. When you click the Font menu or drop-down list, each font name appears in its own font. Excel 2013 includes a bunch of other galleries that provide similar visuals and adds nifty functionality called *live preview*. Taking the same example one step further, Figure 2-9 shows the Font drop-down list displaying the available fonts in situ. With live preview, you simply rest the pointer on the font name to momentarily cause selected cells to display that font. (In the figure, the entire worksheet is selected.) Helpfully, the selection highlight temporarily disappears while you are previewing fonts.

As you can see in Figure 2-9, Berlin Sans FB Demi is perhaps a questionable choice for a table of sales totals, but it's easy to get a look at a lot of options this way. And helpfully, although you need to select the cells you want to format, the selection highlight goes away temporarily while you are live-previewing. The cell contents are not affected; this is simply a way to visualize what would happen if you actually commit by clicking. Have some fun by dragging the pointer up and down the list of fonts, and watch the cell contents change almost as fast as you can drag.

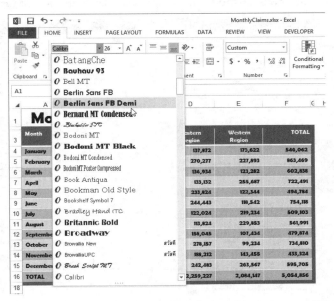

Figure 2-9 Not only are font names displayed in their respective fonts in the drop-down list, but simply resting the pointer on a font name temporarily displays that font in selected cells. (All cells are selected here.)

> ## Note
>
> Not all of the seemingly gallery-like items on the ribbon exhibit live preview behavior. For example, you might think the Number Format drop-down list would be an excellent application of live preview, but it doesn't work that way. As we explain features in detail throughout the book, we'll point out any live preview opportunities.

The omnipotent Excel Options dialog box

The dialog box that opens when you click the File tab and then click Options is probably the most important dialog box in Excel. The Excel Options dialog box controls nearly every aspect of Excel, including general settings such as how many sheets appear in a default workbook and the name and point size of the default font:

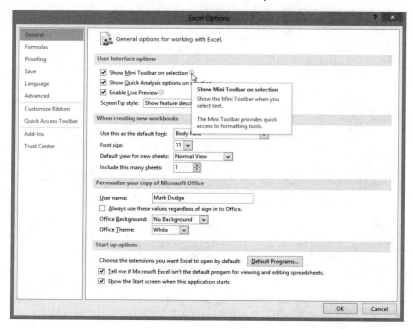

You'll see little *i* (for information) icons adjacent to many of the items shown in the dialog box; rest the pointer on them to display ScreenTips. The Excel Options dialog box also provides special settings for default file-saving formats, worksheet-level and workbook-level display settings, and many other hard-to-classify options. If you take a moment to click each category on the left side of the dialog box and look through the options available, you'll get an idea of the scope of the program as well as the degree of control you have over your workspace. If you're unsure about what a particular setting or option does, simply click the Help button (the question mark icon) in the title bar of the dialog box to open the Help system.

Understanding contextual tool sets

Microsoft has been dancing with context sensitivity for several releases now. In Office 2000, Excel shipped with default "learning" menus and toolbars that modified themselves based on usage patterns, which turned out to be somewhat unpopular because commands would tend to "disappear" with lack of use. Some of this functionality carried through to Excel 2003, with a somewhat better implementation. Since the 2007 release, context sensitivity is smarter and, best of all, does not take little-used items away like the previous approaches—in fact, the ribbon and its normal contents remain steadfast, while additional context-triggered tools appear on ribbon tabs that are displayed only when needed. Figure 2-10 shows what happens when you click a chart object.

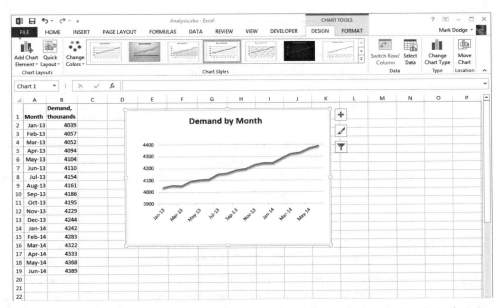

Figure 2-10 When you select an object, tabs appear containing tools that apply only to that object. Here, two tabs of chart tools appear on the ribbon when you select a chart.

Not only do two new tabs appear on the ribbon in Figure 2-10—Design and Format—but a higher-level heading, entitled Chart Tools, is displayed above the new tabs. Headings like this appear over sets of contextually triggered tabs to define their overall function. Chart objects are complex enough that clicking one triggers several tabs' worth of contextual tools; other objects might generate only one tab. This functionality helps reduce clutter in the interface, taking groups of task-specific tools out of the way until you need them.

Using the Quick Access Toolbar

It's hard not to think of the ribbon as a toolbar, especially if you skipped a couple of upgrades. The ribbon is not a toolbar according to Microsoft, and only one "real" toolbar is left. It's at the top of the screen, and it's called the Quick Access Toolbar, as shown in Figure 2-11.

Figure 2-11 The Quick Access Toolbar sits atop the Excel workspace unless you move it under the ribbon.

> ### Note
>
> To suit your work style, you can add buttons and even entire ribbon groups to the Quick Access Toolbar. For more information, see "Customizing the Quick Access Toolbar" in Chapter 3.

The Quick Access Toolbar is pretty much like toolbars as you knew them, with a few exceptions. You can dock it in only two locations—either above or below the ribbon—unlike previous toolbars that could "float" over the worksheet or be docked at the top, bottom, or sides of the screen. And you cannot close or hide the Quick Access Toolbar.

INSIDE OUT Toolbar and ribbon customization

Some of us have spent a lot of time modifying the UI of pre-2007 versions of Excel by changing and adding toolbars and menus. Since Excel 2007, there has been only one toolbar, and you cannot create new ones. Perhaps not surprisingly, 98 percent of the Excel-using public will not miss this functionality. (This statistic was gleaned from usability surveys.) Those of us in the other 2 percent can customize the Quick Access Toolbar, and since 2007, we have been able to tweak the ribbon as well. Hooray! See "Customizing the Quick Access Toolbar" in Chapter 3 for more information.

Accessing commands with the keyboard

When you press the Alt key, Excel activates keyboard command mode and displays little pop-up labels adjacent to each tab and toolbar button, as shown at the top of Figure 2-12.

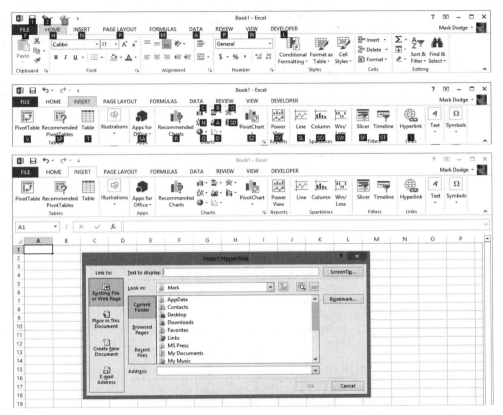

Figure 2-12 Press the Alt key to activate keyboard command mode and display pop-up labels showing you the keys you can press to activate the respective tab, button, or command.

For example, after you press the Alt key to activate the pop-up labels, you can press the N key to display the Insert tab and add pop-up labels to the commands it contains. Then, press the H key—the pop-up letter adjacent to the Hyperlink button—to display the Insert Hyperlink dialog box, as shown in Figure 2-12. So, instead of reaching for the mouse, simply pressing Alt, N, H gets you there. This makes for extremely fast command access after you learn the right keys for tasks you do often.

> ## Keyboard command activation options
>
> You can use the slash (/) key just like the Alt key to access the Excel command structure. But you can alternatively set a different key to activate menus. Click the File tab, click Options, select the Advanced category, scroll way down to the Lotus Compatibility options, and then type a different character in the Microsoft Excel Menu Key text box.

The joy of shortcut menus

Shortcut menus contain only those commands that apply to the item indicated by the position of the pointer when you activate the menu. Shortcut menus provide a handy way to access the commands most likely to be useful at the pointer's location and to help minimize mouse movements (which are hard on wrists!).

To access a shortcut menu, right-click. The menu opens adjacent to the pointer, as shown in Figure 2-13.

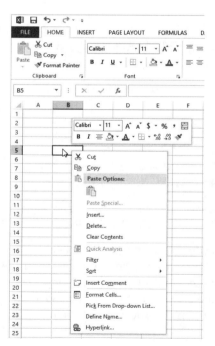

Figure 2-13 Right-clicking almost anywhere displays a shortcut menu with pertinent commands.

Shortcut menus can contain many combinations of commands, depending on the position of the pointer and the type of worksheet. For example, if you display a shortcut menu when the pointer is on a cell rather than a column heading, some of the commands change to ones specific to cells rather than columns.

Belly up to the mini-bar

A small floating toolbar opens along with the shortcut menu whenever the selected object might contain any kind of text, as you can see in Figure 2-13. You can control whether the Mini toolbar appears by using the Excel Options dialog box. Click the File tab, and click Options. Then, in the General category, select or clear the Show Mini Toolbar On Selection check box.

Using the Quick Analysis tool

The top 2013 addition to the Excel cavalcade of context-sensitivity is the Quick Analysis tool, which pops up in the lower-right corner of the selected range any time you select more than one non-empty cell. The Quick Analysis tool takes some of the most sophisticated features of Excel and puts them right near the action. One reason this is helpful is that, often, menus and palettes on the ribbon drop down and obscure the cells you are trying to format. Putting the Quick Analysis tool in the lower-right corner of the range allows you to position the selection on the screen so that you can see more of the cells you are modifying. For example, in Figure 2-14, we selected the totals in cells B4:E15, scrolled the worksheet down a bit to allow room below the table, and clicked the Quick Analysis tool. Resting the mouse pointer over any icon displays a live preview.

The Quick Analysis tool is like a mini-ribbon; across the top are categories (tabs) you click to reveal different sets of icons. The type of data you select determines the tools that are active and available for application. You can use the Quick Analysis tool to apply and remove formatting, insert formulas and tables, create charts and PivotTables, and more.

Chapter 2

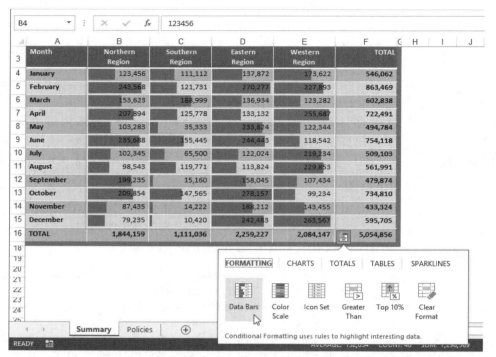

Figure 2-14 Click the Quick Analysis tool to display a context-sensitive "ribbon" with "tabs" containing appropriate actions you can apply to the selected cells.

Meet the formula bar

Worksheet cells are the building blocks of Excel. They store and display the information you enter on an Excel worksheet so that you can perform worksheet calculations. You can enter information directly in a cell, or you can enter information through the formula bar, as shown in Figure 2-15.

The contents of the active cell appear in the formula bar, and the address of the active cell appears in the Name box at the left end of the formula bar. The formula bar split handle and the Insert Function button are always available, but the other two formula-editing buttons are active only while you are entering or editing data in a cell, as shown in Figure 2-15. Click the Cancel button to cancel the current action in the cell, which is the same as pressing the Esc key. Click the Enter button to consummate the current action in the cell, which is the same as pressing the Enter key.

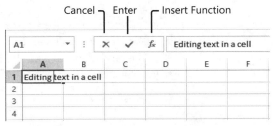

Figure 2-15 The formula bar displays the contents of the active cell.

> **Note**
>
> When you press Enter, Excel finishes the action in the active cell and moves the selection down one cell. You can change this behavior by clicking the File tab, clicking Options, and clicking the Advanced category. If you clear the After Pressing Enter, Move Selection check box, the active cell does not change after you press Enter. Or leave the option selected and choose a different direction (Up, Right, or Left) from the drop-down list.

You can drag the formula bar split handle to the left to make more room for formulas, or to the right to increase the size of the Name box; double-click it to return to the default position. Clicking the Insert Function button displays a dialog box that helps you construct formulas. For information about creating formulas and using the Insert Function dialog box, see Chapter 12, "Building formulas."

> **Note**
>
> By default, Excel displays the formula bar in your workspace. If you prefer to hide the formula bar, click the View tab and clear the Formula Bar check box in the Show group. To redisplay the formula bar, simply reverse this process.

Excel allows you to expand and contract the formula bar to display or hide long formulas. The formula bar split handle helps a bit, but for really long formulas the formula bar is vertically expandable, as shown in Figure 2-16.

When you select a cell containing a long formula, you see only part of the formula in the formula bar. If there is more of the formula to be seen, Excel displays a set of up and down arrows at the right end of the formula bar that you can use to scroll through the formula one line at a time. At the far right end of the formula bar is the Expand Formula Bar button (down arrow), which when clicked expands the formula bar as shown in Figure 2-16. If you need to see more, drag the bottom border of the formula bar as far as you need to. (This particular 100-cell formula is good for illustrating the expanding formula bar, but failure to use the SUM function in this situation might get you drummed out of the Sensible Formulas Guild.) The next time you click the Expand Formula Bar arrow, the bar expands to the last size you specified.

Figure 2-16 The formula bar expands and contracts to show or hide long formulas.

To return the formula bar to its regular size, click the Collapse Formula Bar button. (The Expand Formula Bar button changes its name when the formula bar is expanded.) Note that in the bottom screen shot in Figure 2-16, the pointer turns into a double-headed arrow when you position it over the lower border of the formula bar. You can also drag this border to expand the formula bar.

> **Note**
>
> Functions are the Clydesdales of Excel—they do most of the heavy work. To learn all about them, see Chapter 13, "Using functions."

Facts about the status bar

The status bar, located at the bottom of the Excel window, displays information about what's happening in your workspace. For example, most of the time, Excel displays the word *Ready* at the left end of the status bar. When you type, the status bar displays the word *Enter*; when you double-click a cell that contains data, the status bar displays the word *Edit*.

Several items appear at the right end of the status bar: a few buttons, a slider, and a display area for various purposes—including summary information, keyboard modes, page numbers, and much more—any of which you can turn on or off. Right-click the status bar anywhere to show the Customize Status Bar shortcut menu filled with options, as shown in Figure 2-17.

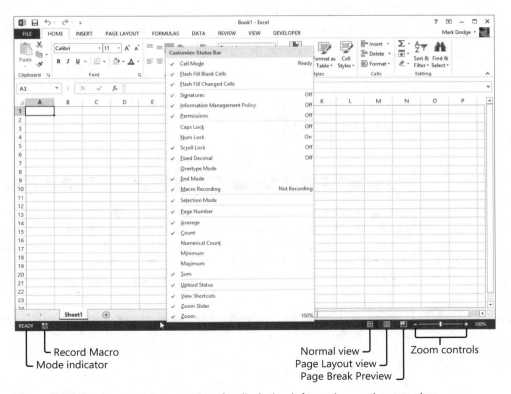

Figure 2-17 You have numerous options for displaying information on the status bar.

All the commands on the Customize Status Bar menu with check marks adjacent to them are turned on by default. Most of the commands on this menu control the display of different types of information, depending on what is selected. Cell Mode refers to the aforementioned Ready/Enter/Edit indicators when working in cells. The icon that looks like a worksheet with a dot, shown in Figure 2-17 on the left side of the status bar, is a record button for macros. The Macro Recording command controls its display. (If any macros are available, a Play arrow appears next to the icon, the display of which is controlled by the Macro Playback command.) The last three commands on the menu control the display of items on the right end of the status bar. View Shortcuts turns on or off the display of the three buttons (Normal View, Page Layout View, and Page Break Preview) visible next to the Zoom percentage and the Zoom slider, which also have corresponding commands controlling their display. Drag the Zoom slider to change the percentage, or click the percentage indicator to display the Zoom dialog box for more precision.

For more information about keyboard modes, see "Navigating regions with the keyboard" in Chapter 6. For more about views, see Chapter 11, "Printing and presenting." For more about macros, see Chapter 28, "Recording macros."

Quick totals on the status bar

When you select two or more cells that contain values, Excel displays summary information using those values on the status bar:

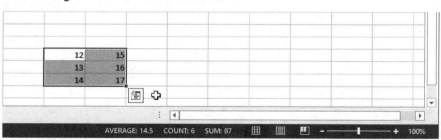

This is the AutoCalculate feature. The status bar normally displays the sum and average of the selected values, as well as the number of cells selected that contain any kind of data (blank cells are ignored). As you can see in Figure 2-17, additional AutoCalculate options are available, including Minimum and Maximum values in selected cells and Numerical Count, which counts only cells containing numbers and ignores cells containing text.

Introducing Backstage view

At first, when you begin working with one of the "ribbon versions" of Excel (starting with Excel 2007), it looks like the old menus are still there across the top of the screen—until you start clicking and you see that no menus are dropping down. Even more interesting if you have been using Excel 2007 is that the File menu, which had been removed, came back in Excel 2010 (and remains in 2013) as a tab, and the Office Button, which was where the File menu used to be, is gone. Now, when you click the File tab, what you see is not so much a menu or a dialog box, but a screen full of information and options that Microsoft calls *Backstage view*. Here you can find the familiar File menu commands, and Backstage view also serves as the access point for most of Excel's "behind-the-scenes" commands and settings.

Clicking the File tab on the ribbon reveals the default Info screen in Backstage view, as shown in Figure 2-18.

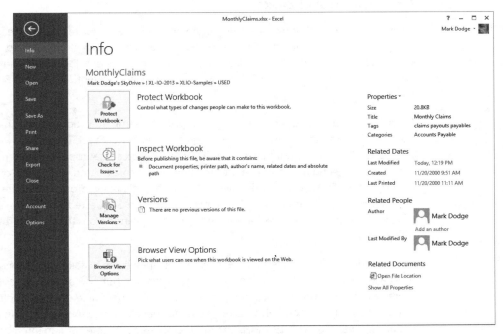

Figure 2-18 Click the File tab to open Backstage view, which includes the old File menu commands; click the arrow button in the upper-left corner to return to the worksheet.

As you can see, many of the old File menu commands are still here as clickable items on the left side of the screen, and the right side of the screen provides additional clickable items. Clicking Info, New, Open, Save As, Print, Share, Export, or Account controls the content visible on the right side of the screen, which offers pertinent options and commands. Clicking Save, Open, Close, or Options launches a separate dialog box.

You can use the new Account command to change settings for your Microsoft account, including connected services such as SkyDrive, and to select a common theme. There is also a Background menu you can use to personalize the appearance of your Office programs using selected designs that appear in the title bar area.

You'll be seeing more of Backstage view and all of its "children" throughout this book.

Exploring file-management fundamentals

One of the advantages of working with computers is the convenience of electronic files. In this section, we describe both the usual and unusual ways you can manage your Excel files.

Creating workbooks

To create a new workbook, click the File tab and then click New to display the screen shown in Figure 2-19. Click the arrow at the top left of the New screen at any time to return to the worksheet. Click Blank Workbook, and a fresh workbook opens. Each new blank workbook you create during the current Excel session is numbered sequentially: Book1, Book2, and so on.

Excel 2013 offers a staggering array of sophisticated templates representing hundreds of hours of thought and effort, and revealing the potential of Excel. There are a lot of helpful templates you can use right away. And if you ever need some inspiration, open a template you find interesting and examine it to see how it was constructed. There is a lot to learn just by looking. Templates are continually added to the online inventory, so be sure to use the search box to see what's new and available on the web. Suggested Searches are clickable links that display categories of available templates gleaned from the Microsoft website at the moment.

Excel is more web connected than ever. Some templates are installed on your system, but most are in the cloud. This not only saves space for you, but also makes it possible to offer more templates, more complex templates, and a constant source of new templates. Keeping templates in the cloud also makes it easy for developers to fix problems and make enhancements. Figure 2-19 shows the nifty templates available with an Internet connection. Figure 2-20 shows the search box disabled and the selection of relatively Spartan (but equally useful) templates that are available when your computer is offline.

Figure 2-19 Click the File tab and then click New to display a selection of available templates, both installed and online.

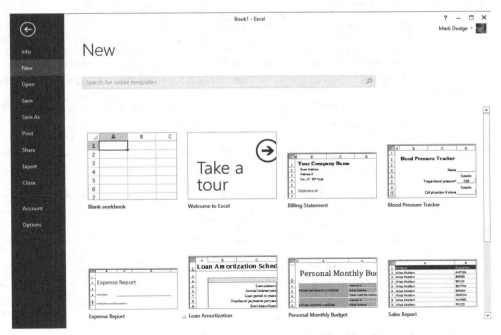

Figure 2-20 The selection of available templates narrows considerably when no Internet connection is available.

Installing your own templates

Creating your own templates is a great idea for worksheets you use a lot. The steps involved are a little different in Excel 2013 than in previous versions. First, organize and format a workbook the way you want (minus the data). Then when you're ready to save the template, click the File tab, click Save As, click Computer, and then click Browse to display the Save As dialog box. Click the Save As Type box and select *Excel Template (*.xltx)* from the list, and the destination folder immediately changes to the Custom Office Templates folder, as shown in Figure 2-21.

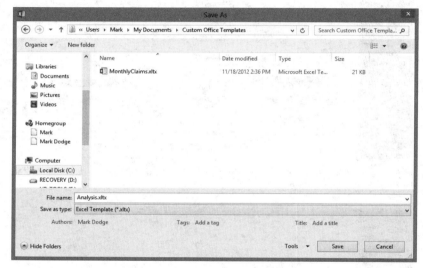

Figure 2-21 Choosing the Excel Template file type activates the Custom Office Templates folder.

When you click the Save button, your new template is installed. You can find this folder in the following locations:

- **Windows XP**   C:\Documents and Settings\<*your name*>\Application Data\Microsoft\Custom Office Templates

- **Windows 7 or Windows Vista**   C:\Users\<*your name*>\AppData\Roaming\Microsoft\Custom Office Templates

- **Windows 8**   C:\Users\<*your name*>\My Documents\Custom Office Templates

Templates in this folder appear on the New screen in the Personal category, as shown in Figure 2-22. The two categories, Featured and Personal, appear only after you save a template for the first time.

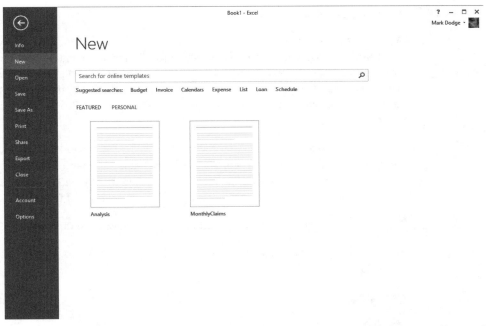

Figure 2-22 When you save a template, two new categories appear on the New screen, Featured and Personal; in this figure, the Personal category is active.

INSIDE OUT   Hidden Windows folders revealed

You probably have to change a Windows setting to find the AppData folder (Application Data in Windows XP) because it is normally hidden. To reveal it, navigate to the folder that bears your name in File Explorer (or Windows Explorer in Windows 7, Windows Vista, or WIndows XP), as shown in the previous paths. Then, in Windows 8, click the View tab and select the Hidden Items option in the Show/Hide group. In Windows 7, click the Organize menu (the Tools menu in Windows XP), click Folder And Search Options, and on the View tab, select Show Hidden Files And Folders. Note that *<your name>* is the user name you use when logging on to Windows.

Saving files

Arguably, the most important function of any computer application is preserving data. In Excel, you can save your files in many ways, including by clicking the Save, Save As, Share, or Export command. You can also click the Close command or click the Windows Close button (X) and you'll be prompted to save, if you have made any changes. The easiest way to save is either by clicking the Save button on the Quick Access Toolbar or by pressing Ctrl+S on the keyboard.

One other command that saves your workbooks is the Share Workbook command in the Changes group on the Review tab. When you click this command, you save your workbook in shared mode. Besides saving the file, this command makes the workbook available to others on a network, who can then open it and make changes of their own.

For more information, see "Sharing workbooks on a network" in Chapter 26.

The first time you save a file, the Save As screen appears in Backstage view, as shown in Figure 2-23.

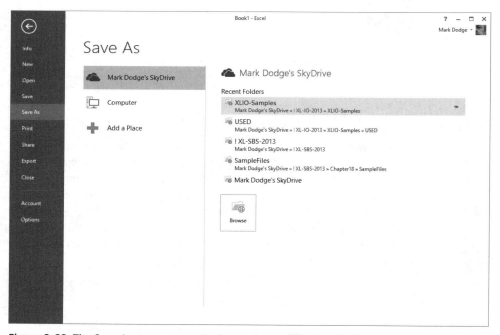

Figure 2-23 The Save As screen appears when you save a file for the first time.

> **Note**
>
> If you use the same folder most of the time, you can specify that folder as the default location that the Open, Save, and Save As dialog boxes use when you first open them. Click the File tab, click Options, select the Save category, and type the full path and file name for the folder you want to use in the Default Local File Location text box.

The Save As screen offers another set of choices, including SkyDrive and your computer. The most recent folders used in the location selected on the left are shown on the right. If the one you want is not listed, click the Browse button, which displays the Save As dialog box, as shown in Figure 2-24.

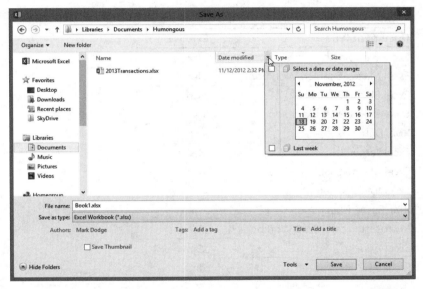

Figure 2-24 When you select a destination or click Browse, the Save As dialog box appears, which you can use to specify a date or date range, if desired.

The Save As dialog box (along with other dialog boxes that are provided by the operating system, including Save and Open) has a sophisticated file interface that includes a number of useful features, such as the ability to find files by using a date range you specify using a calendar, as shown in Figure 2-24. For details, click the Help button (the question mark icon) in the Save As dialog box to display the corresponding Windows Help file.

Rules for file naming

File names in Excel can have up to 218 characters. They can include any combination of alphanumeric characters, spaces, and special characters, with the exception of the forward slash (/), backslash (\), greater-than sign (>), less-than sign (<), asterisk (*), question mark (?), quotation mark ("), pipe symbol (|), colon (:), and semicolon (;). Although you can use any combination of uppercase and lowercase letters, keep in mind that Excel does not distinguish case in file names. For example, to Excel the names MYFILE, MyFile, and myfile are identical.

The old familiar MS-DOS-style file name extensions (which are usually four characters these days, not three) help identify your Excel files, and they are added automatically when you save a file. Table 2-1 lists Excel extensions in the order in which they appear in the Save As dialog box's Save As Type list.

TABLE 2-1 The Excel file extensions

Document type	Extension
Excel Workbook	.xlsx
Excel Macro-Enabled Workbook	.xlsm
Excel Binary Workbook	.xlsb
Excel 97-2003 Workbook	.xls
XML Data	.xml
Excel Template	.xltx
Excel Macro-Enabled Template	.xltm
Excel 97-2003 Template	.xlt
XML Spreadsheet 2003	.xml
Microsoft Excel 5.0/95 Workbook	.xls
Excel Add-In	.xlam
Excel 97-2003 Add-In	.xlm

INSIDE OUT   Hidden file name extensions revealed

File name extensions might not appear with Windows file names, depending on your settings. To display file name extensions in Windows 8, click the File Explorer, click the View tab, and select the File Name Extensions option. In Windows 7, click the Start button, click Computer (Control Panel in Windows XP), click the Organize menu, select Folder And Search Options and on the View tab, and then scroll down and clear the Hide Extensions For Known File Types check box.

Chapter 2

File formats

In addition to providing the file name and location, you can specify a different file format in the Save As dialog box. Click the Save As Type drop-down list, which expands to reveal all the formats in which you can save your files.

The default format is Excel Workbook (*.xlsx), and you'll almost always use this option. If you want to export an Excel file to another program, however, you can use one of the other options to convert the file to a format that is readable by that program.

For more information about the Excel export formats, see "Importing and exporting text files" later in this chapter.

Ensuring file compatibility with previous versions of Excel

When you open a workbook in Excel 2013 that was created in a previous version of Excel, it automatically opens in Compatibility mode, a condition that is indicated in the Excel title bar, as shown in Figure 2-25. You can always tell by looking at the title bar whether you've converted a file to the new format.

Figure 2-25 Files created by any previous version of Excel open in Compatibility mode.

You can work normally with Compatibility mode, and when you save the file, it remains in the old file format. If, however, you make any changes using features that are not compatible with the older version, the Excel Compatibility Checker intervenes when you save and displays a dialog box like the one in Figure 2-26.

The Compatibility Checker lets you know exactly what is causing the problem, so you can click Cancel and rework your worksheet using a different approach or save it anyway. Clicking the Copy To New Sheet button adds a new worksheet to the current workbook titled Compatibility Report, containing a copy of the information displayed in the dialog box—sort of a compatibility paper trail. If you clear the Check Compatibility When Saving This Workbook check box, this dialog box no longer opens when you save the current workbook. You might prefer this if you plan to repeatedly edit and save without updating the workbook to the new file format.

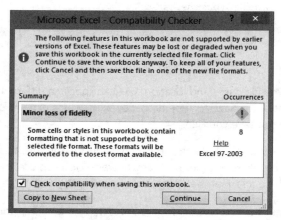

Figure 2-26 The Compatibility Checker opens when you try to save an old-format workbook containing features not supported by the older version of Excel.

But fear not, you can always look for problems at your convenience. Click the File tab, click the Info command, click Inspect Workbook, and click Check Compatibility to display the same dialog box shown in Figure 2-26.

INSIDE OUT   What doesn't work in Compatibility mode?

When Compatibility mode is on, Excel disables a number of features that produce results that cannot be transferred to older versions of Excel. You can still click disabled commands, but when you do, Excel displays a ScreenTip explaining why you can't use them. For example, sparklines were introduced in Excel 2010. If you are working on a workbook saved as an Excel 97-2003 workbook (.xls), Excel displays a ScreenTip when you hover the pointer over one of the sparklines buttons:

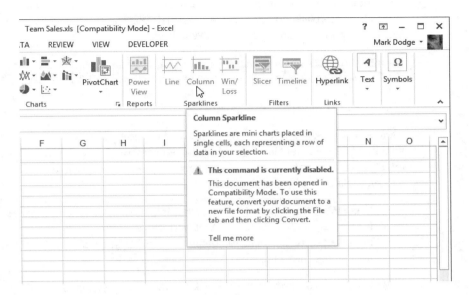

Here are some of the things that can trigger compatibility error messages:

- A workbook contains too many rows, columns, or both

- A formula exceeds the maximum allowed number of characters

- A formula exceeds seven nested levels

- A formula exceeds the maximum number of arguments in a function

- A formula contains more than 40 operands

- A workbook contains too many cross-sheet array formulas

- A workbook has more than 4,050 unique cell formats

- A PivotTable field has more than 32,500 unique items

- A PivotTable item has a string length greater than 255 characters

- A PivotTable caption has more than 255 characters

- A PivotTable field list has more than 1,024 fields

In case you're wondering how to get out of Compatibility mode, all you have to do is use the Save As command to save the workbook in one of the new file formats, such as XLSX or XLSM, and then close and reopen the new converted file you just saved.

If you need to save files in other formats, the Save As Type drop-down list in the Save As dialog box includes a number of special formats you can select, including Excel 97-2003 Workbook and Microsoft Excel 5.0/95 Workbook.

For more information about the newer, less-restrictive limitations of Excel, see "If you missed the last two upgrades" in Chapter 1, "What's new in Microsoft Excel 2013."

Understanding the "XL" formats

Although Microsoft trimmed some of the lesser-used file formats from the last release, the volume of native Excel file formats has swelled somewhat, largely due to accommodating *legacy* file formats—that is, file formats employed in previous versions of Excel. We'll explain the major differences here:

- **Excel Workbook (XLSX)**   This is the default Excel 2013 (and Excel 2010 and 2007) file format, which is based on XML and uses ZIP compression for reduced file size and increased security. Unlike the default file format in older versions of Excel (XLS), this format does not support VBA or XLM macro code.

- **Excel Macro-Enabled Workbook (XLSM)**   Microsoft created a completely separate XML-based file type to be used for workbook files containing VBA or XLM macro code. This increases security by making it impossible to inject macro code into non-macro-enabled workbooks and makes for easier identification of files containing code.

- **Excel Binary Workbook (XLSB)**   This is a lean and mean file format designed for the fastest possible loading and saving. It supports all the features of Excel 2013 and also supports macro code, but it is not XML based, does not use compression, and is less secure than XML-based formats.

- **Excel Template (XLTX)**   This is the template version of the Excel 2013 (and Excel 2010 and 2007) file format. This format does not support VBA or XLM macro code.

- **Excel Macro-Enabled Template (XLTM)**   This is the template version of the Excel 2013 (and Excel 2010 and 2007) file format that does allow VBA and XLM macro code.

- **Excel 97-2003 Workbook (XLS)**   This is a legacy file format used by previous versions of Excel.

- **Microsoft Excel 5.0/95 Workbook (XLS)**   This is a legacy file format used by previous versions of Excel.

- **Excel 97-2003 Template (XLT)**   This is a legacy template format used by previous versions of Excel.

- **Excel Add-In (XLAM)**   This is a special type of VBA-enabled workbook that can be loaded as a supplemental program in Excel.

- **Excel 97-2003 Add-In (XLM)**   This is a legacy type of VBA-enabled workbook that can be loaded as a supplemental program in Excel.

In addition to these "XL" file types, there are two XML file types that are somewhat related. XML Spreadsheet 2003 (XML) is the previous XML file format provided as an option in Excel 2003. Another format, XML Data (XML), shares the same extension but produces entirely different results. This format is a proprietary XML format that requires specific programmatic data maps to be present before you can even save the file. You'll know if you need it.

INSIDE OUT   What is XML?

The Excel 2013 (and Excel 2010 and 2007) file format is based on XML, which was created as a way for structured data to be interpreted and was originally envisioned for use on the web. Excel 2003 introduced XML as an optional file format; Excel versions from 2007 through 2013 use XML as their default format, indicated by the file name extension *.xlsx*. Based on a file format specification called *SpreadsheetML*, Microsoft's implementation of XML has undergone significant improvements since being introduced. At first, the format didn't have, shall we say, sufficient language skills to interpret all of what Excel could do, including objects such as charts and graphics. Now, SpreadsheetML can handle everything Excel can dish out and does so in a much more efficient manner than the old XLS format, resulting in significantly smaller file sizes. The new XML formats also provide improved recovery of damaged files and better overall security. And because SpreadsheetML is part of an overall extensible Open XML format initiative, it's easier for developers to create ways to hook things together.

For some additional information about XML, see "Working with XML files" in Chapter 25, "Working with external data."

Specifying the default file format

Usually when you save a new workbook, you save it in the Excel Workbook format (XLSX). You can specify a different format as the default for saving files. This might be helpful, for example, if you share files regularly with users of Excel 2003. To do so, click the File tab, click Options, and select the Save category, shown in Figure 2-27.

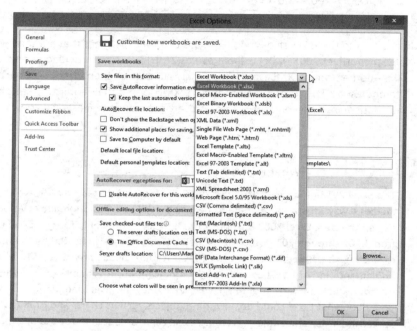

Figure 2-27 You can specify the default format to use when saving.

The Save Files In This Format drop-down list contains all the same file formats as the Save As Type drop-down list in the Save As dialog box.

Creating automatic backup files

You can have Excel create a duplicate copy of your file on the same disk and in the same folder as the original every time you save. Click the File tab, click Save As, click Tools at the bottom of the Save As dialog box, and click General Options to display the dialog box shown in Figure 2-28. Then select the Always Create Backup check box.

The backup file is a duplicate file that carries the same name as your original, but the name is preceded by "Backup of" and has the file name extension *.xlk*.

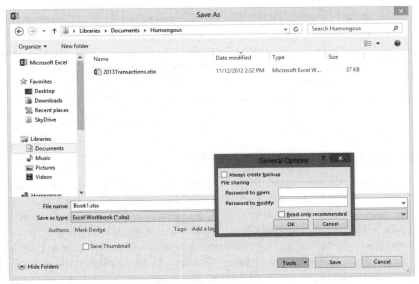

Figure 2-28 To display the General Options dialog box, click the File tab, click Save As, and then click Tools, General Options.

Protecting files

You can password protect your files by using options in the General Options dialog box shown in Figure 2-28. Select from two types of passwords: Password To Open and Password To Modify. Passwords can have up to 15 characters, and capitalization matters. Thus, if you assign the password *Secret* to a file, you can't reopen that file by typing *SECRET* or *secret*.

- **Password To Open**   Excel prompts you to supply the password before reopening the file.

- **Password To Modify**   Anyone can look at the file, but they need the password to edit it.

- **Read-Only Recommended**   This politely suggests that the user open the file as read-only.

INSIDE OUT   Create a better password

Although Microsoft has tightened the under-the-hood security measures of Excel over the years, some people delight in finding new and better ways to crack passwords. You can help by simply building better passwords. Make sure your password is eight or more characters long—the longer, the better—and try to use a healthy mix of upper-case and lowercase alphanumeric characters and nonalphanumeric characters. Never use birthdays, anniversaries, or the names of your children or pets as passwords.

Adding summary information to files

When you click the File tab, the Info screen that first appears includes a short list of properties on the right. The Properties heading is a button; click it and a menu appears. Click Show Document Panel to display the Document Properties panel, which appears below the ribbon, as shown in Figure 2-29. Use this to record general information about the active workbook. If you juggle a lot of files, getting into the habit of adding properties can make it a lot easier to find something later. Windows looks at these property values when you use the Search command to locate files on your computer.

You can quickly view properties for the active workbook by clicking the File tab and looking on the right side of the Info screen. Several properties are displayed there. Click Properties, and then click Advanced Properties to display the Properties dialog box, as shown in Figure 2-30. Most of the information visible on the Document Properties panel is available and editable on the Summary tab.

Exploring file-management fundamentals

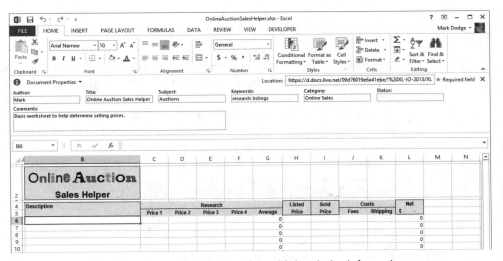

Figure 2-29 Use the Document Properties panel to add descriptive information you can use later when looking for that needle in a file stack.

Figure 2-30 View properties about any file before you open it.

Linking custom properties to cells

You can link your own custom-built properties to named cells on your worksheet. When you do, the value of the custom property becomes whatever the named cell contains and changes whenever the value in the cell changes. First you must name a cell. (See "Rules for naming" in Chapter 12.) Then click the File tab, click Properties, and then click Advanced Properties. On the Custom tab in the Properties dialog box, selecting the Link To Content check box displays the workbook's defined names in the Value box (which changes to a drop-down list named Source when linking content), as shown in Figure 2-31.

Figure 2-31 Use named cells to create dynamic properties based on worksheet cells.

Select or create a name for the custom property in the Name box. (The Type drop-down list becomes unavailable when you're linking to content.) When you've specified a source (the named cell to which you want to link), click Add, and the custom property appears in the Properties list.

If the link is broken (the defined name is later deleted, for example), the Properties dialog box stores the last value recorded for that property.

If the name defines a range of cells, only the value in the cell in the upper-left corner of the range appears as the property value.

Opening files

Only slightly less basic than saving files is opening them. Click the File tab, and click Open to display the Open screen in Backstage view, shown in Figure 2-32.

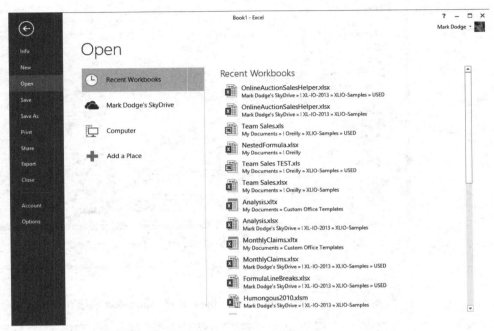

Figure 2-32 Click the Open command, and select a location or a recent workbook.

Click one of the icons on the left side of the dialog box to display the corresponding files on the right side. Recent workbooks are displayed when you first click the Open command. If you click one of the other locations, the recent folders are displayed. If you need something that is not recent, click the Browse button to display the Open dialog box, as shown in Figure 2-33.

The drop-down list to the right of the File Name text box at the bottom of the Open dialog box determines which files are available for selection. The default option is All Excel Files, which displays file names whose extensions begin with *xl*. You can display specific file types or all files by clicking the arrow to the right of the text box.

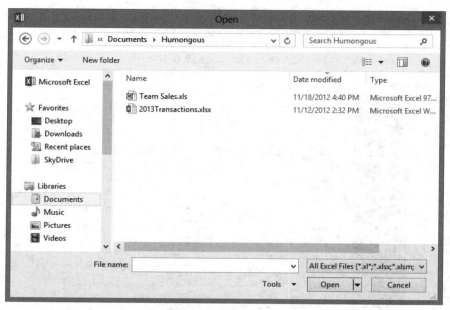

Figure 2-33 Click the Browse button to display the Open dialog box.

> **Note**
>
> **To open several files at once, press the Ctrl key and select each file you want to open.**

Notice that headings appear at the top of the file list in the Open dialog box. When you click one of these headings, you sort the files in order, based on that heading. For example, if you click the Date Modified heading, you sort the files in date order. Click the same heading again to re-sort in reverse order. You can further refine your quest by using the hidden menus adjacent to each heading. When you rest the pointer on a heading, a downward-pointing arrow appears to the right of the heading; click it to display a menu of additional options pertinent to that heading.

> **Note**
>
> **You can right-click most files listed in the Open and Save As dialog boxes to display a shortcut menu that contains commands you can use with the selected file. For example, you can delete a file displayed in the Open dialog box by using this shortcut menu.**

Each heading has its own menu of options, some of which are based on the actual files contained in the current folder. For example, when you click the menu arrow for the Type heading, you can select from a list of file types contained in the folder.

Special ways to open files

To the right of Open at the bottom of the Open dialog box is a small arrow. Clicking this arrow displays a menu containing the following options:

- **Open Read-Only**   This opens the file so that you cannot save any changes made to it without renaming it.

- **Open As Copy**   This creates a duplicate of the selected file, adds the words *Copy of* to the file name, and leaves the original untouched.

- **Open In Browser**   This applies only to HTML documents and opens the selected file in your default web browser.

- **Open In Protected View**   This opens the document for viewing but not editing. All active content is disabled, including any kind of macro or HTML code. Once you have established the bona fides of the file, you can click the Enable Editing button to carry on.

- **Open And Repair**   This is a powerful feature you can use to try opening corrupted files. For more information, see "Recovering corrupted files" later in this chapter.

Opening files when you start Excel

If you have files you need to work on every day, you can store them in a special folder called XLStart. Every time you start Excel, any files in the XLStart folder automatically open. The XLStart folder is created when you install Excel (or you can create it yourself) and is located in the following place:

- **Windows 8, 7, or Vista**   C:\Users\<*your name*>\AppData\Roaming\Microsoft\ Excel\XLStart

- **Windows XP**   C:\Documents and Settings\<*your name*>\Application Data\ Microsoft\Excel\XLStart

If you want to start Excel and simultaneously open files that are in a folder other than the XLStart folder, you can specify an alternate startup folder. Click the File tab, click Options, and select the Advanced category. Scroll down to the General category, and in the edit box labeled At Startup, Open All Files In, type the full path of the folder. This feature is particularly useful if your computer is connected to a network and you want to open files from a shared folder.

Recovering corrupted files

Figure 2-33 shows the Open dialog box, where you can find the Open Options menu (click the arrow next to the Open button) containing the Open And Repair command. This command gives you a fighting chance at either repairing a corrupted file or extracting the data from it if it doesn't respond to a repair attempt. When you select a file and click the Open And Repair command, the message box shown in Figure 2-34 opens.

Figure 2-34 The Open And Repair command gives you a ray of hope for recovering lost data.

Try the Repair button first, and if Excel still has no luck opening the file, try the Extract Data button, which displays the message box shown in Figure 2-35.

Figure 2-35 The Extract Data button offers two ways to recover your data.

You'll have to make a judgment call here—if you think your formulas will be OK after extraction, click Recover Formulas; otherwise, click Convert To Values. Recovering formulas will probably work unless the formulas include references to cells that were lost in corruption. Whatever you select, the Extract Data feature pulls all the data from your workbook, including all worksheets and tabs, in the same order in which they appear in the original file. Unfortunately, the recovery process ignores all formatting, charts, and other objects—you can recover only the actual cell contents (the important stuff).

Note that unless the part of the file that became corrupted was the part storing passwords, you probably won't be able to use this technique to retrieve data from a password-protected file.

INSIDE OUT   Recover data using links

You can try to recover data from a corrupted workbook by using another trick. It is essentially the same trick used by the Excel Open And Repair command, but it still might be worth a try if Open And Repair fails.

First, open two new workbooks. Select cell A1 in one of the workbooks, and then press Ctrl+C to copy. Activate the second workbook, and right-click cell A1. Click Paste Special, and then click the Paste Link button. Next, click the File tab and click Edit Links To Files on the Info screen (this command is in tiny type at the bottom of the shaded area on the right), click Change Source, and locate the corrupted workbook. Click OK, and then click Close to close the Edit Links dialog box.

If luck is with you, data from cell A1 in the lost workbook appears in cell A1, thanks to the linking formula. If it does, press F2 to activate Edit mode, and press F4 three times to change the absolute reference $A$1 to its relative form, A1. Finally, copy the formula down and across until you can see all the data you need to retrieve. Repeat for each worksheet in the workbook. You lose the formatting and formulas, of course, and zeros appear in every blank cell, but at least you can get at the important stuff. Although you can save this worksheet with linking formulas, you might consider converting all the formulas to their underlying values, just in case the original corrupted file has any further degradation. To do so, select all the cells containing the formulas you just created, click Ctrl+C to copy, right-click, click Paste Special, select Values, and then click OK.

For more information about document recovery, see "Recovering from crashes" later in this chapter. For more information about passwords, see "Hiding and protecting workbooks" in Chapter 7.

Importing and exporting files

Excel gracefully accepts proprietary data created in many other applications. Excel also makes it easy to import data from text files and helps you parse it into worksheet columns.

Note

Mountains of very specific, sleep-inducing technical details are available about importing and exporting files. If you need details, you should consult Microsoft Office Online (*office.microsoft.com*). Also, for information regarding sharing data with other Microsoft Office 2013 applications and working with external databases, see Chapter 32, "Integrating Excel and Word," and Chapter 25, "Working with external data."

Importing and exporting files

To import a file from another application or from an earlier version of Excel, click the File tab, click Open, select a location, and click Browse to open the Open dialog box. Then to specify the file type you want to import, use the drop-down list adjacent to the File Name box. If you're not sure, select All Files (*.*), or select a file type and only files of that type are displayed.

To export an Excel file to another application or to an earlier version of Excel, click the File tab and click Export. Then select either Create PDF/XPS Document or Change File Type, as shown in Figure 2-36.

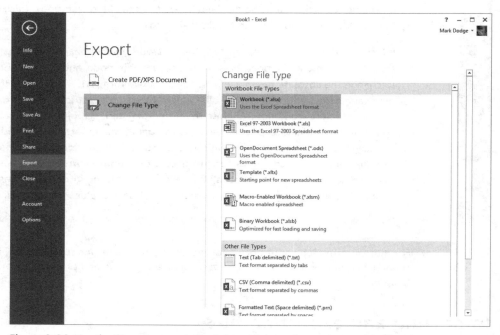

Figure 2-36 Use the Export screen in Backstage view to change to another file type.

Portable Document Format (PDF) and XML Document (XPS) are formats that allow accurate visual representations of documents to be easily shared across platforms by using free and easily obtainable web-based viewers.

Sharing data with Excel for the Macintosh

Excel for the Macintosh since 1998 has been using the same file format as Windows versions of Excel from Excel 97 through Excel 2003. You can share these files with Macintosh users by simply transferring files from one computer to the other. (Note that you cannot share Excel files containing macros—.xlsm files—with Macintosh Excel versions through 2011.)

To save an Excel 2013, 2010, or 2007 file to share with someone using the Macintosh version of Excel, click the File tab, click Save As, select a location, and click the Browse button. You can save it as a regular Excel Workbook (*.xlsx) file when sharing with users of Macintosh Excel 2011, or for greater compatibility, select the Microsoft Excel 97-2003 Workbook (*.xls) option in the Save As Type drop-down list.

To import Macintosh files to your PC, you first need to transfer the file to your PC via a cable, a disk, a thumb drive, a network, an email attachment, a website, or a software tool such as MacOpener. Exporting files from a Windows version of Excel to the Macintosh version is just as easy as importing Macintosh files. Simply transfer the file from the Windows computer to the Macintosh using your method of choice, and then use the Open command to load it into Excel.

Adjusting date values

Although the Windows and Macintosh versions of Excel share many characteristics and capabilities, they might not use the same date system. In the Windows version of Excel, the base date is January 1, 1900. Macintosh Excel 2011 uses the same date system as all Windows versions, so you can share these files as you will. In Macintosh Excel version 2008 and earlier, the base date is January 2, 1904. When you transfer files either to or from the Macintosh, Excel maintains the date type by selecting or clearing the Use 1904 Date System check box in the When Calculating This Workbook area in the Advanced category in the Excel Options dialog box. This technique is usually acceptable, but it can cause problems when a date from a Macintosh file is compared with a date from a Windows file. For this reason, we suggest you use the same date setting on all your machines.

Chapter 2

Sharing data beyond Excel

Yes, some people don't use Excel, and you might meet one someday. Seriously, plenty of reasons exist for making Excel-based data accessible outside the program, whether or not Excel is available at the destination. Posting data to a website or creating data sets for proprietary analysis software are two possible applications where you might want data that can fly free, independent of the Excel mother ship.

Office Web Apps

Office Web Apps give you a familiar Office experience when you are away from your Office applications on your computer. With your Office files uploaded to a web storage location such as your own website or Windows Live SkyDrive, you don't need your own computer or software to view and perform light editing of Word, Excel, PowerPoint, and OneNote files. You just need a computer running a popular Web browser.

For more information about Office Web Apps, see Chapter 27, "Working in the cloud."

Using web file formats

Two options in the Save As Type drop-down list in the Save As dialog box produce files you can use as webpages: Web Page (HTM, HTML) and Single File Web Page (MHT, MHTML). They produce essentially the same result, the important difference being that the Web Page format saves not only a main HTML file but also a folder containing supporting files that must travel with the main file. As you might expect, the Single File Web Page format manages to cram it all into a single file without using the supporting folder. Single File Web Page has the advantage of being more portable, but Web Page gives you more control over individual elements. A separate cascading style sheet is created using the Web Page format, along with individual HTML files for each worksheet in the workbook. Figure 2-37 shows the contents of the supporting folder that is created after saving a five-sheet workbook named Team Sales using the Web Page file format.

If you are an HTML aficionado, you can open the supporting files in other programs. For example, if the original workbook contains graphics, Excel saves them as separate image files (JPEG, PNG, or GIF) you can modify with an image-editing program. Or you can change the fonts used by editing the cascading style sheet with a text editor such as Notepad. This is not work for the timid, of course. The slightest editing error in the HTML code for any of the files has the potential to render them all unusable.

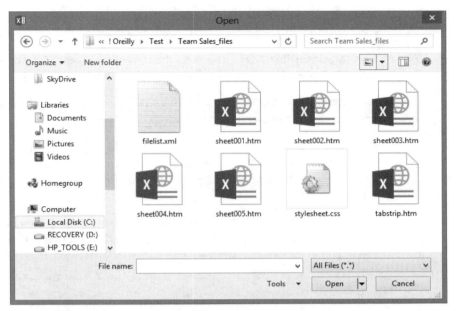

Figure 2-37 The Web Page file format creates a folder full of supporting files to go with the main webpage.

Importing and exporting text files

To export an Excel file as a text file, select one of the following eight text formats from the Save As Type drop-down list in the Save As dialog box. In all of these formats, Excel saves only the current worksheet. Number formatting is preserved, but all other formatting is removed.

- **Formatted Text (Space Delimited) (*.PRN)**   This creates a file in which column alignment is preserved by adding space characters to the data in each column so that each column is always filled to its maximum width.

- **Text (Tab Delimited) (*.TXT)**   This separates the cells of each row with tab characters.

- **Unicode Text (*.TXT)**   This is a worldwide standard text format that stores each character as a unique number; Unicode defines a number for every character in every language and on any computer platform.

- **CSV (Comma Delimited) (*.CSV)**   This separates the cells of each row with commas. Comma-delimited text files are preferable to tab-delimited files for importing into database management programs. (Many database management programs can accept either form of text file, but some accept only .csv files.) Also, many word-processing applications can use .csv files to store the information for mail merge operations.

- **Text (Macintosh) (*.TXT)**   This saves the current worksheet as a tab-delimited text file using the Macintosh character set.

- **Text (MS-DOS) (*.TXT)**   This saves the current worksheet as a tab-delimited text file compatible with the character-based MS-DOS interface.

- **CSV (Macintosh) (*.CSV)**   This saves a comma-delimited text file using the Macintosh character set. The differences between the normal, Macintosh, and MS-DOS variants of each file type have to do only with characters that lie outside the normal 7-bit ASCII range.

- **CSV (MS-DOS) (*.CSV)**   The MS-DOS options use the IBM PC extended character set. (You might see this referred to also as *OEM text*.) Select one of these options if you intend to import your text file into a non-Windows-based application.

> ### Note
>
> Excel 2013, 2010, and 2007 use a file format that is incompatible with previous Excel versions. Excel versions 97 through 2003 share a file format that is incompatible with even older versions. However, you can use the Save As command and Save As Type list to export Excel 2013, 2010, and 2007 workbooks using two formats that play nicely with older versions of Excel: Excel 97-2003 Workbook and Microsoft Excel 5.0/95 Workbook.
>
> If you regularly share files with colleagues using different vintages of the program, you might want to read "Ensuring file compatibility with previous versions of Excel" earlier in this chapter.

Other file formats

You can use a few other file formats, most of which you won't even need unless you have a particular program with which you want to share data. Data Interchange Format (DIF) is a legacy format that allows the specification of data in rows and columns, saves only the active worksheet, and does not process graphic content. Symbolic Link (SYLK), a format that dates back to the days of VisiCalc and Multiplan, is a sort of "rich-text format" for spreadsheets that saves only the active worksheet and does not process graphic content.

Using the Help system

Excel was a powerful program right out of the starting gate way back in 1985. Over the years, Excel has developed into an extremely complex and sophisticated application. It's so complex that most people need to learn only about 20 percent of its capabilities. Many people turn to books like this one to help them make sense of it all. But almost every Excel user turns to the Help system; all Excel users should. After years of working out the kinks, Microsoft has made the Help system more "helpful," less obtrusive, more comprehensive, and much easier to use.

Help on the surface

Although the mythical, magical, space-age vision of easily understood, self-documenting software has yet to be fully realized, Microsoft is taking steps in the right direction. Dynamic pop-up labels called ScreenTips have been around for quite a while providing visual clues to elements in the interface. Many of these ScreenTips have increased in size considerably over the years, and they contain more and better information. Simply rest the pointer on any button or command on the ribbon or the Quick Access Toolbar to display a ScreenTip, as shown in Figure 2-38.

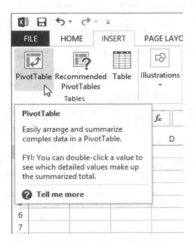

Figure 2-38 Rest the pointer on any command or button on the ribbon or the Quick Access Toolbar to display a ScreenTip.

Help in the form of ScreenTips is also available for many items in dialog boxes such as Excel Options. (To open this dialog box, click the File tab and then click Options.) In this context, look for the little *i* (for *information*) icons next to items in the dialog box, which indicate more information is available. Just rest the pointer on the icon to display the ScreenTip, as shown in Figure 2-39.

Chapter 2

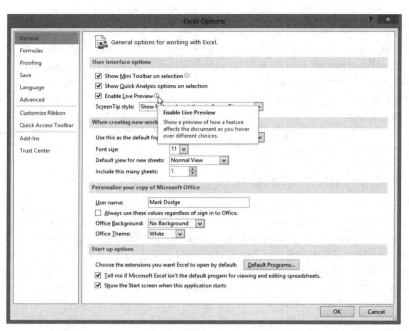

Figure 2-39 A little circle icon containing an *i* means you can see more information by simply resting the pointer on the icon.

Help in depth

When you need more information than a ScreenTip can provide, it's time to invoke the Help dialog box. Simply click the Help button (the question mark icon) that is always available in the upper-right corner of the screen (or any dialog box) to display the Help dialog box. When you first open the dialog box, it attempts to connect to the Microsoft Office Online website, as shown on the left in Figure 2-40. If you are connected to the Internet, the dialog box should quickly display an opening menu of topics, similar to the one shown on the right in Figure 2-40. As mentioned previously, one of the beauties of web-based Help is that it can be continually updated, so it is quite possible this opening screen will change in content and appearance over time; more and more Help topics should be added as well.

As long as you have the Help dialog box open and your Internet connection remains active, web-based Help continues to be available. If you lose your Internet connection, Excel stops trying to connect to the web and displays the "offline" Help system—that is, only those Help topics installed on your computer. You can also do this manually by clicking Connected To Office.com at the bottom of the Help dialog box and clicking Show Content Only From This Computer.

Figure 2-40 Your Help system works best when you're connected to the web.

> **You can prevent Excel from automatically trying to connect to the web by using the Trust Center dialog box. See "Privacy options" in Chapter 4, "Security and privacy."**

You'll find that not much good information is available if you're not connected to the web. The few search results shown on the left in Figure 2-40 are simple Excel menu-to-ribbon command references. The help content is all on the web now, but it's robust with procedures, templates, samples, interactive quizzes, tutorials, introductions, references, live samples, and more as time goes by.

You'll notice that the Help dialog box has a tiny toolbar with controls that look—and act—similarly to the controls on your web browser's toolbar. The first two buttons are Back and Forward, which operate like their browser counterparts—they move you to the next or previous topic in your history list. The Home button returns you to the opening Help screen, and the Print button prints the current topic. Clicking the Use Large Text button is a toggle; click to make the text a bit larger, and click again to return to normal.

The pushpin button in the Help dialog box is Keep On Top. It is set to Keep On Top by default. When the pushpin is horizontal, the dialog box behaves like a normal window, giving way to the active window when you click outside the dialog box. When the pushpin button is vertical, the window stays on top of the Excel workspace, allowing an unobstructed view of the Help window while you work. This button is a toggle; repeated clicking changes the pushpin's ScreenTip from Keep Help On Top to Don't Keep Help On Top. Whatever setting was active when you close the dialog box persists the next time you open it.

> **Note**
>
> Most dialog boxes include a Help button located in the title bar (identified by a question mark icon). Clicking this button displays a Help topic describing the function of and options within that dialog box. If you click the Help button in a tabbed dialog box, you'll see information pertaining to that particular tab.

INSIDE OUT   A user-assistance odyssey

The implication of the term *online Help* has changed somewhat over the years. It used to mean that in addition to the primary source of user assistance—the printed manual—how-to topics and explanations of commands and features were available right on your computer by pressing F1. What a concept! Today, Help really is online, and an Internet connection is almost essential—preferably broadband.

Those who write user-assistance topics and implement the Help system historically had to limit the amount of actual assistance they could provide, being constrained by the amount of space allocated for Help files on the installation CDs (or floppy disks!). Over the past few Office releases, the need for Help files actually shipped on CD has decreased because of the new user-assistance paradigm: web-based Help. This offers tremendous advantages over in-the-box Help. First, instead of having to cram increasing amounts of information into a finite amount of space on a CD, keeping Help files on the web allows virtually unlimited information to be made available. Second, it allows information to be more up to date, which is actually an incredible understatement.

Consider that under the old paradigm, Help content had to be written early and sent through the editorial pipeline many weeks prior to shipping the software—often before developers were finished tweaking features. (Add another month or so for printed manuals! Remember those?) With the constraints on disk space, tough decisions often were made regarding helpful topics and useful aids such as videos and presentations that would simply have to be eliminated to save room. No wonder Help systems have historically been dissed for being inaccurate and incomplete. Under the new "truly online" Help paradigm, topics that would never have made it onto the CD are instead available on the web, and user-assistance writers can update and add more Help topics, videos, presentations, and templates long after the product ships.

Recovering from crashes

In the past, *crash recovery* largely involved an initial flurry of expletives followed by a brisk walk around the office and perhaps a couple of aspirin. Excel 2013 provides something beyond comfort and sympathy for digital mishaps—an actual mechanism that attempts to tuck away open files before the program comes screeching to a halt. And it works pretty well. If Excel encounters a problem, it attempts to save any files that are open at the time the problem occurs, before bad things happen to them when the program crashes and burns.

Understanding AutoRecover

Over the years, Excel has greatly improved its ability to recover lost work after a crash. By default, all unsaved workbooks are backed up automatically every 10 minutes, storing what Excel calls AutoRecover information. This is not the same as saving your workbook, because Excel stores AutoRecover information in a different place with a cryptic file name. You might lose a few minutes worth of work, but you can change the time interval anywhere from 1 to 120 minutes. If Excel or your system crashes, the AutoRecover feature presents a list of rescued versions of all files that were open when the crash occurred the next time you start Excel.

To change settings or turn off AutoRecover, click the File tab, select Options, and select the Save category to display the dialog box shown in Figure 2-41.

AutoRecover File Location is set to a subfolder buried deep in your hard disk—this is OK because you should save the real files elsewhere rather than cluttering up your working directories with recovery files. If you want, you can easily change the location. You can also choose to disable AutoRecover for specific workbooks without having to turn it off and on manually. You can use the AutoRecover Exceptions For area in the dialog box to do this. Just select a workbook in which you want to disable AutoRecover from the drop-down list displaying all the currently open workbooks, and select the Disable AutoRecover For This Workbook Only check box. You can do this separately for any open workbook.

Chapter 2

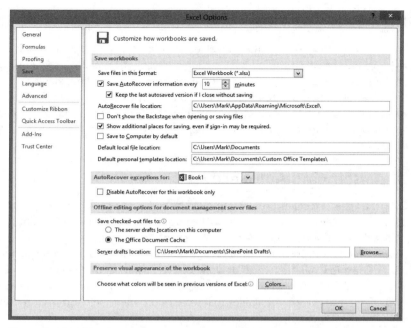

Figure 2-41 With AutoRecover, you can specify how often Excel automatically saves your work.

Managing versions

The AutoRecover feature essentially stores a copy of each unsaved workbook every 10 minutes (unless you specify otherwise). So what happens to these copies? Excel stores one copy of each file you work on—and fail to save—for four days, deleting older copies automatically. Luckily, Excel provides access to these copies. Click the File tab, click Info, click Manage Versions, and click Recover Unsaved Workbooks to display the dialog box shown in Figure 2-42, a version of the Open dialog box, which automatically opens to the specified AutoRecover location.

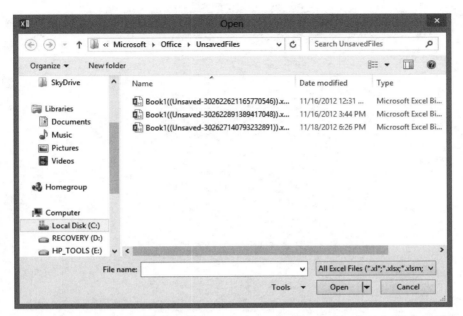

Figure 2-42 You can recover recent versions of your workbooks by using the Recover Unsaved Workbooks command.

When you open an unsaved workbook, it opens in read-only format, and Excel displays "Unsaved File" in the message bar, along with a handy Save As button in the warning area above the formula bar. If you do nothing, the previously scheduled four-day deletion schedule remains and the draft is removed. Clicking Save As displays the dialog box of the same name, open to your normal documents folder.

CHAPTER 3

Custom-tailoring the Excel workspace

Customizing the ribbon. 75

Customizing the Quick Access Toolbar 84

Controlling other elements of the Excel 2010
interface. 95

Enhancing accessibility 99

Installing apps. 101

Y OU NEEDN'T settle for the way the Microsoft Excel 2013 command and control system is organized. You can customize the Quick Access Toolbar and the ribbon, so if you feel that the Microsoft interface designers didn't exactly have you in mind, you can make a lot of adjustments to Excel 2013.

Customizing the ribbon

When the ribbon was introduced in Office 2007, it was fixed—you couldn't modify the user interface unless you were conversant in VBA or XML. In Office 2013, the ribbon is open for interpretation; you can freely rearrange command groups; change the order and position of tabs; remove groups; and create custom commands, groups, and tabs. The bad news: you cannot add or delete commands from existing groups, and you cannot delete existing tabs. But this really isn't much of a problem; a truly dedicated customizer can create a whole new set of tabs and stick them in front, forcing the default tabs off the screen, or simply hide all the default tabs.

Start by right-clicking anywhere on the ribbon and selecting the Customize The Ribbon command on the shortcut menu that appears. This opens the Excel Options dialog box with the Customize Ribbon category selected (saving you several mouse clicks), as shown in Figure 3-1.

Does your ribbon look different?

The screen images shown in this book were captured at the screen resolution, magnification, and text size that is optimum for publication purposes. The ribbon on your screen might not look the same as the one shown in the book. For example, you might see more or fewer buttons in each of the groups, the buttons you see might be represented by larger or smaller icons than those shown, or the group might be represented by a single button that you click to display the group's commands

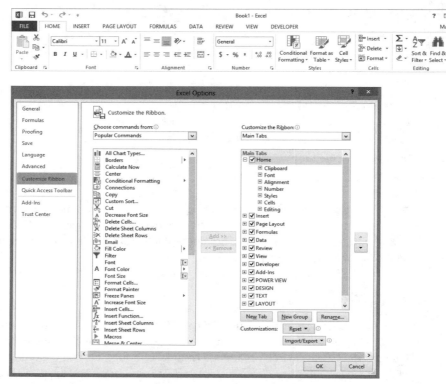

Figure 3-1 The outline on the right side of the dialog box controls the ribbon's structure.

The Customize Ribbon category in the Excel Options dialog box displays two scrollable lists. The Choose Commands From list on the left displays commands you can use to create your own command groups and tabs. The list on the right shows the current contents of the ribbon as a collapsible outline, making it easy to see the ribbon's structure. The first level of the outline represents tabs, and the second level of the outline represents command groups, corresponding to the labels at the bottom of each group (Clipboard, Font, Alignment, and so on) on the ribbon. Click the plus sign icons to reveal the subordinate groups and commands. Many groups have additional plus signs that expose another level of commands. For example, Figure 3-2 shows the outline for the Font group fully expanded. There are a lot of commands in this one group—more than you can see at once.

> **Note**
>
> Some items in the outline might be wider than can be displayed in the dialog box at its default size. Just drag any border of the dialog box to make it wider or deeper. The next few figures were created after making the dialog box a bit larger for ease of viewing.

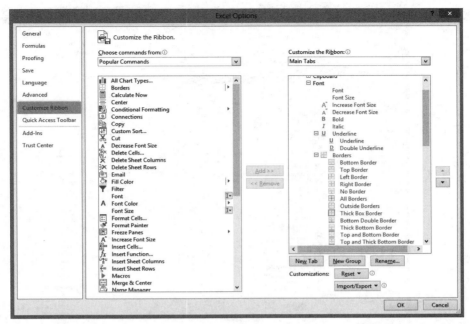

Figure 3-2 The list on the right is a collapsible outline listing the current contents of the ribbon.

The drop-down list boxes above each list contain categories you use to filter the list of displayed commands. For example, Figure 3-3 shows the drop-down list with one of the more interesting categories selected: Commands Not In The Ribbon. This category is fun to browse just to see what you've been missing.

> **Note**
>
> You can clear the check box next to a tab in the outline to hide it on the ribbon; select it to display it. Note that many tabs are dynamic, such as the Add-Ins tab in Figure 3-1, and all of the Tool tabs in Figure 3-3. Even if they are selected in the outline, they do not appear on the ribbon until they're needed.

On the right side of the dialog box in Figure 3-3, the Tool Tabs option is selected in the drop-down list. This displays a wealth of hidden tabs and groups on the ribbon that are normally invisible but that appear dynamically when the appropriate object or tool is selected.

Chapter 3

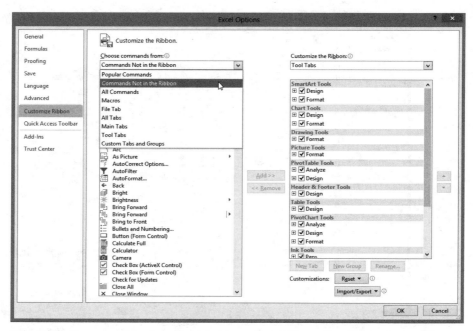

Figure 3-3 Choose options from the drop-down lists above to filter the contents of the scrollable lists below.

Identifying items in the Customize Ribbon and Quick Access Toolbar categories

Most of the items you can see in the command list on the left side of the Customize Ribbon category in the Excel Options dialog box are buttons. That is, clicking the command button on the ribbon executes the associated command immediately. You can see that some items also have a small icon to the right of the command name in the dialog box. These are called *command modifiers*, and they tell you that although the item might still be a button, it is also something more, as detailed in Table 3-1. (Note that this also applies to the Quick Access Toolbar category in the Excel Options dialog box. The controls are almost identical to those in the Customize Ribbon category.)

The Quick Access Toolbar is discussed later in "Customizing the Quick Access Toolbar."

If you want a little more information about the commands in the command list, rest the pointer on any command to display a ScreenTip.

TABLE 3-1 Command modifiers

Item	Description	Image
Drop-down list	A control that displays a menu or palette from which you select an option, such as the Conditional Formatting button on the Home tab	▸
Split button	A two-part item—one side looks and acts like a button, and the other side has a small arrow that displays a drop-down list, such as the Font Color button on the Home tab	▏▸
Edit control	A control you can type into—for example, the Font drop-down list on the Home tab	𝐼▾

Creating a custom ribbon tab

You can add custom groups to existing tabs, but if you have limited screen real estate, creating your own tabs might make more sense. To do so, first right-click the ribbon, click Customize The Ribbon, and then click the New Tab button. This creates a new top-level outline item provisionally titled New Tab (Custom). Select New Tab (Custom), and then click the Rename button to display the dialog box shown in Figure 3-4. The new tab is inserted below the selected tab in the outline.

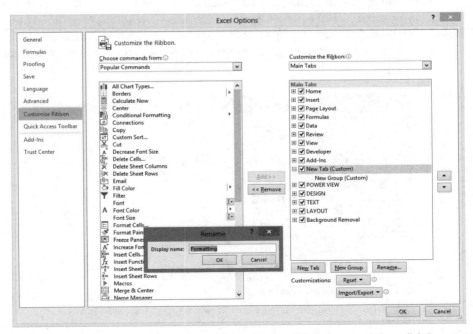

Figure 3-4 Create a new ribbon tab by clicking the New Tab button, and then click Rename to give it a sensible moniker.

After you create a tab, you need a group, because commands can be added only to groups. Helpfully, a custom group is created automatically whenever you create a custom tab, as shown in Figure 3-4. Even after you rename a tab or a group, (Custom) continues to appear, appended in the outline to any title you provide, which helps to quickly identify your own tabs and groups.

You can reposition any tab or group in the outline by simply dragging it to a new location, or you can select it and click the arrow buttons located to the right of the list box. You cannot reposition commands within preset groups, but you can move groups around from tab to tab all you like.

> **Note**
>
> The first tab in the Customize The Ribbon outline—even a custom tab—becomes the default tab that is active every time you start Excel.

Creating a custom command group

Creating custom command groups is similar to creating custom tabs. First, select the tab where you want the custom group to live, and then click the New Group button in the Excel Options dialog box. (If you created a new tab, a new group already appears on the new tab.) Select your new group, and click the Rename button to display the dialog box shown in Figure 3-5.

Figure 3-5 Clicking the Rename button with a group selected allows you to select an icon for the group as well.

As you can see, you can rename your new group and also assign an icon to it, which is visible only when you add the group to the Quick Access Toolbar. If you look at the Home tab on the ribbon, you'll notice that most of the commands do not have labels displayed; they appear as buttons. For example, there are no command labels visible at all in the Font group. The ribbon shown at the top of Figure 3-6 displays a custom Formatting tab populated with border-specific commands with their command labels visible. If you want to create a tab filled with other kinds of Formatting commands, you'll need a lot more space, and hiding the labels helps a lot.

To hide command labels, right-click the ribbon, select Customize The Ribbon, and then right-click any custom group in the outline and select Hide Command Labels. Note that this command appears on the shortcut menu only when you select a custom group. You cannot change the command labels of default groups. The ribbon shown at the bottom of Figure 3-6 shows the result—now there is plenty of space left on the custom Formatting tab for more groups. Notice that hiding the command labels does more than what the command's name implies; the button icons become considerably smaller as well.

Figure 3-6 It is a good idea to hide the command labels when you create new groups.

After hiding the command labels so that they are not visible on the ribbon, you can still easily see the command names by resting the mouse pointer over the buttons.

Adding existing command groups to custom tabs

When constructing custom tabs, you can take advantage of predefined command groups. Microsoft decided to make the built-in groups noncustomizable partly because a lot of sweat and tears went into creating them as they are today. Decades of usability studies and real-world usage of menus and command trees went into the design of the ribbon, and as such it makes sense for 80 percent of our needs. But we're talking about the other 20 percent here. Because you can create your own groups anyway, there is no harm in having the default groups fixed—and plenty of good reasons for you to take advantage of them.

Right-click the ribbon, and then click Customize The Ribbon. In the Choose Commands From drop-down list, click All Tabs to display an outline of all the predefined command groups, as shown in Figure 3-7.

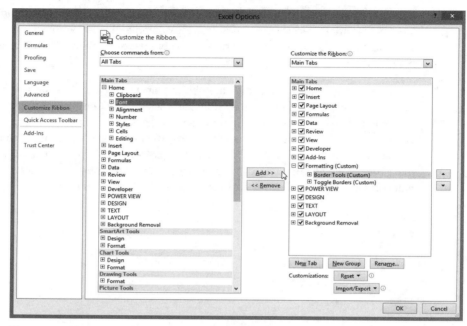

Figure 3-7 Displaying All Tabs reveals all the predefined command groups.

First, select a tab or group in the outline on the right below which you want to insert a pre-set group. Next, in the All Tabs list on the left, click the plus sign icons to expand the outline and locate the group you want. Select it, and click the Add button to insert the group into the outline on the right. If you decide you want your inserted groups somewhere else, you can always move them up and down the outline by using the arrow buttons. A well-populated custom Formatting tab is shown in Figure 3-8, along with the outline in the Excel Options dialog box that created it.

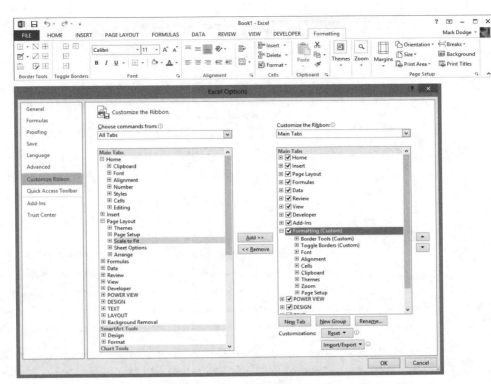

Figure 3-8 The modified outline in the Customize The Ribbon list and its custom tab.

Resetting and recycling your customizations

When you customize the ribbon, it stays customized; everything is still there the next time you start Excel. But if you ever joke about "hitting the reset button," well, now you actually have one. In the Customize Ribbon category in the Excel Options dialog box, the Reset button does the eponymous trick, discarding your customizations and returning the ribbon and the Quick Access Toolbar to their original states. The button is also a menu, offering the dual options of resetting only the selected tab (if one is selected) or resetting all customizations (which resets both the ribbon and the Quick Access Toolbar). Before you reset either, though, you might want to save your customization work so that you can retrieve it later. Below the Reset button, the Import/Export button allows you to reuse and recycle your work. This button is also a menu from which you can choose to import or export a special file containing all your customizations. Figure 3-9 shows a version of the File Open dialog box that appears when you select Import Customization File from the Import/Export menu, with a couple of saved customization files. The first file—Excel Customizations. exportedUI—is the rather clunky default name offered. The proprietary extension for the resulting file—.exportedUI—is appended to any file name you supply.

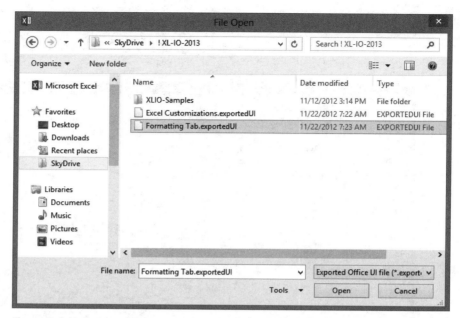

Figure 3-9 You can export any number of ribbon customization files for retrieval later.

Using these exported customization files and a web storage location such as Microsoft SkyDrive, you can store your custom tool sets as well as your workbooks, making them available from any Internet-connected computer in the world running Office 2013.

Customizing the Quick Access Toolbar

The Quick Access Toolbar might be small, but you can pack a lot of tools onto it. If you are stuck using a small screen, or if you prefer an uncluttered workspace, you can set up the Quick Access Toolbar as a sort of "ribbon lite" to help free up some screen real estate.

Positioning the toolbar

When you first start Excel, the Quick Access Toolbar appears above the ribbon, as shown in Figure 3-10. You can change this so that the toolbar appears below the ribbon. Click the Customize Quick Access Toolbar button (the little arrow at the right end of the toolbar), and click Show Below The Ribbon. If you click the Collapse The Ribbon button, as shown in Figure 3-11, you can reveal several more rows of worksheet.

Figure 3-10 The Quick Access Toolbar usually appears above the ribbon on the title bar.

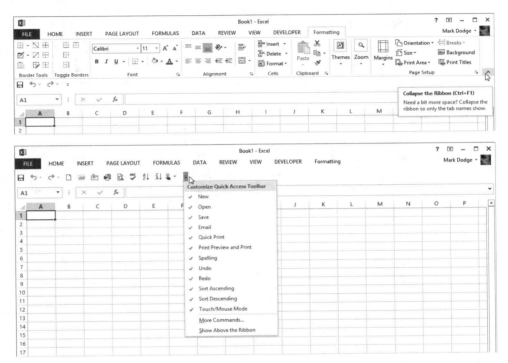

Figure 3-11 You can collapse the ribbon and move the Quick Access Toolbar below it.

Moving the Quick Access Toolbar below the ribbon offers you a couple of advantages: it's closer to the action on the worksheet, and more space is available for additional tools, which we discuss in depth next in "Adding tools to the toolbar." Conversely, the advantage of leaving it at the top of the screen is that it can occupy unused space on the title bar.

Chapter 3

Adding tools to the toolbar

You get three tools to start with on the Quick Access Toolbar: Save, Undo, and Redo. These are undeniably heavily used commands, but you perform other tasks often too and might like to have them just a click away, readily available regardless of which ribbon tab is currently visible. It's easy to customize the toolbar, and you have a couple of ways to do it.

Adding tools as you work

If you find yourself continually returning to the same tab on the ribbon and using a particular command, you might consider adding it to the Quick Access Toolbar. The easiest way to do this is to right-click the command to display the shortcut menu shown in Figure 3-12.

In Figure 3-12, we added the Switch Windows command to the Quick Access Toolbar by right-clicking the command and clicking Add To Quick Access Toolbar. A button then appears on the toolbar that looks similar to the command on the ribbon. Each new button you add appears to the right of the previous button. Not all toolbar buttons are easy to identify, but you can always rest the pointer on a button to display a ScreenTip explaining its function, as shown at the bottom of Figure 3-12. If you add a lot of buttons, these ScreenTips are indispensable.

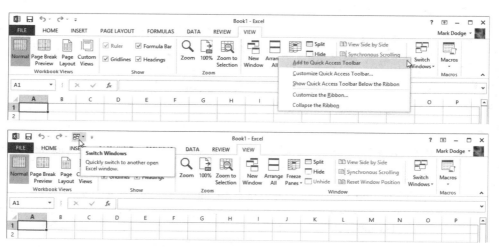

Figure 3-12 Right-click any command or group, and you can add it to the Quick Access Toolbar.

Removing tools

You can remove tools from the Quick Access Toolbar by using the same technique you use to add them. Right-click any tool on the toolbar, and click Remove From Quick Access Toolbar.

Adding and organizing tools

You can add virtually any command or group to the Quick Access Toolbar by using the right-click technique, but if you want to dig in and really create an organized toolbar, you should use the Excel Options dialog box. Right-click the toolbar, and click Customize Quick Access Toolbar to open the Quick Access Toolbar category in the Excel Options dialog box, shown in Figure 3-13.

As you can see in Figure 3-13, the list on the right shows the buttons currently visible on the toolbar. The controls here work just like the Customize Ribbon category—select any item on the left side, and then click the Add button to add it to the list on the right. Select any item on the right side, and click the Remove button to get rid of it; when you select an item, you can click the up and down arrows to reposition the item in the list. You can always click the Reset button if you want to discard all your changes and return to the original configuration.

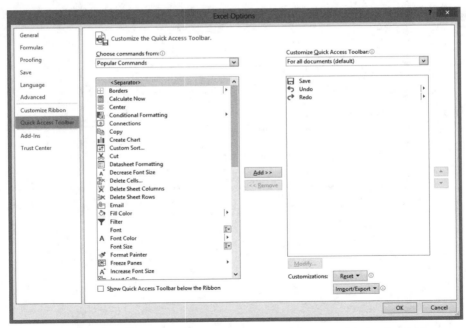

Figure 3-13 The Quick Access Toolbar category in the Excel Options dialog box is the command center for the Quick Access Toolbar.

Notice in Figure 3-13 that *Separator* is the first item in the list on the left. This item is first in each command category, and with it you can insert small vertical bars on the Quick Access Toolbar to visually separate groups of related commands. You can add separators and move them up and down the list on the right side of the dialog box, just as you do with commands. (This item is not available for ribbon customization because you create groups first instead of using separators.)

The items in the Choose Commands From drop-down list include an eponymous item for each of the command tabs visible on the ribbon, plus all the other contextual tabs that appear on the ribbon only when an object is selected, as shown in Figure 3-14. Select any item from the drop-down menu, and the corresponding list of commands appears in the list below.

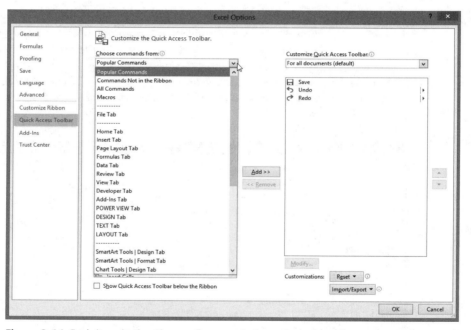

Figure 3-14 Each item in the Choose Commands From drop-down list corresponds to a tab on the ribbon.

INSIDE OUT   Create a mini ribbon

Here is a trick you can use if it just seems like too much bother to click those tabs at the top of the ribbon, or if you just want to maximize screen space. Saving a click here and there can make quite a difference if you do a lot of repetitive work. The following illustration shows the Quick Access Toolbar displayed below the ribbon (which is minimized) and loaded with buttons that correspond to every group on every default tab on the ribbon:

The toolbar shown here includes only buttons that correspond to the command groups (not individual commands) on every default tab. Notice that clicking the Tables button displays a drop-down list of commands identical to those in the ribbon group of the same name on the Insert tab. To customize the toolbar this way, use the Excel Options dialog box. Although you can build a similar toolbar using the right-click approach, using the dialog box offers the advantage of being able to insert separators between groups of buttons.

 You'll find the Ribbon Group Toolbar.xlsx file on the companion website.

Too many tools?

It is certainly possible to load more buttons onto the Quick Access Toolbar than can fit across the screen, even if you move the toolbar below the ribbon. If this happens, a More Controls button appears at the right end of the toolbar, looking like a fast-forward button (>>). As shown in Figure 3-15, clicking More Controls displays the hidden controls on a drop-down toolbar.

Figure 3-15 If you add more buttons than can be displayed, click the More Controls button.

Note that when the More Controls button appears, the Customize Quick Access Toolbar button (the downward-pointing arrow) that usually appears at the right side of the toolbar moves to the "overflow" area of the toolbar.

Creating your own buttons

Right-click any button on the ribbon, click Customize Quick Access Toolbar, and click the Choose Commands From drop-down list. You'll see a special option listed there: Macros. *Macros* are sequences of commands you can create to help perform repetitive tasks. When you select the Macros option, nothing appears on the left side of the dialog box unless you have opened a macro-enabled workbook and the workbook actually contains macros. All the macros available appear here. Figure 3-16 shows the Customize Quick Access Toolbar list containing a single macro that has been added to the toolbar.

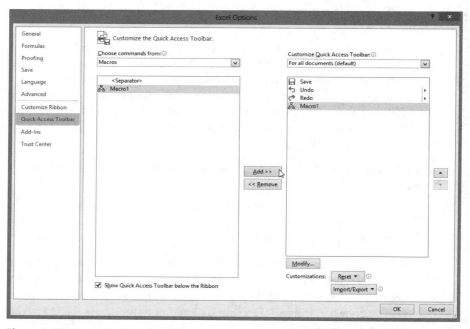

Figure 3-16 You can add custom buttons to run macros in macro-enabled workbooks.

You might notice that the Modify button below the list is active when you add a macro to the list on the right side of the dialog box. By clicking it, you can modify the button image displayed on the toolbar if the default image doesn't do it for you. In case you are wondering, you can modify only custom macro buttons, which is why the Modify button is not available when you select built-in commands. When you click the Modify button, the

Modify Button dialog box appears, as shown in Figure 3-17, and you can use it to select a different image.

For more information about macro-enabled workbooks, see "Saving files" in Chapter 2, "Exploring Excel fundamentals." For more information about macros and VBA, see Chapter 28, "Recording macros."

Figure 3-17 You can change the default button image for your custom macro-driven buttons.

Saving and resetting your custom Quick Access Toolbar

In the Quick Access Toolbar category of the Excel Options dialog box, the default setting in the Customize The Quick Access Toolbar drop-down list is For All Documents. In this case, Excel saves the configuration of the Quick Access Toolbar when you exit the program. If you want to go back to the way things were, click the Reset menu and select Reset Only The Quick Access Toolbar or Reset All Customizations (which resets both the ribbon and the Quick Access Toolbar).

If you want to save your custom toolbar so that you can use it again later, there are two ways to do it. The Import/Export button allows you to save or retrieve a special file containing all your customizations (both toolbar and ribbon). Figure 3-9 earlier in this chapter shows a version of the File Open dialog box that appears when you click Import Customization File from the Import/Export menu, displaying files with the extension *.exportedUI*.

The second way to save a custom toolbar is to attach it to a workbook. To do so, right-click any button or tab, and click Customize Quick Access Toolbar. In the Excel Options dialog box, click the Customize Quick Access Toolbar drop-down list, as shown in Figure 3-18.

You'll find both a customizations file—MiniRibbon.exportedUI—and a file with an attached toolbar—Ribbon Group Toolbar.xlsx—with the other examples on the companion website.

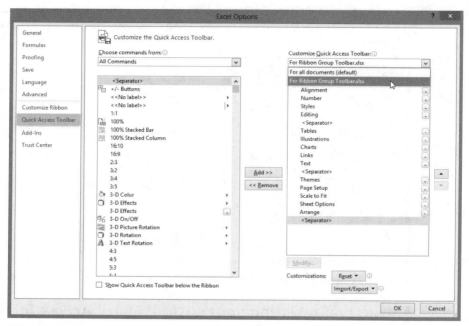

Figure 3-18 You can configure a custom version of the Quick Access Toolbar that travels with a workbook.

The drop-down list shows two items: For All Documents and For <the active workbook name>. If you select the active workbook, the command list starts out blank, and you can begin adding items from the list on the left. (Even though the list starts out blank, the default tools—Save, Undo, and Redo—always appear at the left end of your custom bar.) Any commands you add to the active workbook's toolbar are relevant only to the active workbook; they are saved with the workbook and reappear on the toolbar the next time you open the workbook. To remove a custom toolbar configuration from a workbook, select its name in the Customize Quick Access Toolbar drop-down list and click the Reset button.

Restoring the toolbar

Now that you've thoroughly scrambled the Quick Access Toolbar, perhaps you're experiencing a bit of remorse. Don't worry—it's easy to return it to normal:

- **Restoring the toolbar** Select Quick Access Toolbar in the Excel Options dialog box, click the Reset button, and select either Reset Only Quick Access Toolbar or Reset All

Customizations (which also resets the ribbon). Click Yes to confirm the restoration, and then click OK.

● **Removing individual buttons**   On the Quick Access Toolbar, right-click the button you want to remove and then click the Remove From Quick Access Toolbar command, as shown in Figure 3-19.

Figure 3-19 You can easily remove any button from the Quick Access Toolbar.

INSIDE OUT   What happened to my custom toolbars?

Custom toolbars you created and attached to workbooks in versions of Excel prior to 2007 are still accessible, though you might not think so at first glance. If you open an old workbook with attached toolbars, the toolbars won't appear on the screen. But look at the Add-Ins tab on the ribbon. You might not have seen the Add-Ins tab before, but click this tab, and there they are—your custom toolbars. The following graphic shows an example of having way too many custom toolbars on the Add-Ins tab:

So all your hard work creating custom toolbars is not lost—provided you attached them to workbooks. After you open a workbook containing attached toolbars, the toolbars continue to appear on the Add-Ins tab each time you start Excel. To get rid of them, right-click each toolbar (each row of buttons is a toolbar on the Add-Ins tab) and close it by using the Delete Custom Toolbar command. When you delete the last custom toolbar, if it is the only item on the Add-Ins tab, the Add-Ins tab disappears as well.

Chapter 3

Exploring other toolbar and ribbon options

The following are a few more customization options that are quite helpful. Unless otherwise noted, you can find these options by clicking the File menu, clicking Options, and then selecting the General category:

- **Show Mini Toolbar On Selection**   Controls the display of the Mini toolbar whenever you right-click a cell or object where its formatting tools are applicable, as shown in Figure 3-20.

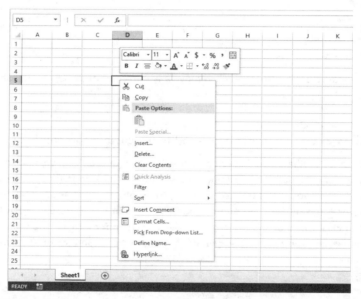

Figure 3-20 You can control whether the Mini toolbar appears when you right-click cells or relevant objects.

- **Enable Live Preview**   Allows you to simply rest the pointer on many palette items to show what the effect would look like, without even clicking.

- **Office Background**   Offers several optional "skins;" that is, background graphics that appear in the title bar, formula bar, Quick Access Toolbar, ribbon, sheet tabs, scroll bars, and headings.

- **Office Theme**   Applies your choice of three color schemes to window frames and other interface elements: White, Light Gray, or Dark Gray.

- **ScreenTip Style**   Offers three options that apply to the pop-up label that appears when you rest the pointer on any item on the toolbar or the ribbon. You can choose to see only a small label with the name of the item, a larger ScreenTip that includes a description, or no label at all. (For more information, see "Enhancing accessibility" later in this chapter.)

For more information about fonts and formatting and live preview, see Chapter 9, "Worksheet formatting techniques."

Controlling other elements of the Excel 2010 interface

In several important locations in Excel, you can control the way your worksheets appear on the screen. These include the View tab on the ribbon, shown in Figure 3-21, and the General and Advanced categories in the Excel Options dialog box. Some options, such as Gridline Color, are self-explanatory; here we'll talk about options with "issues."

Figure 3-21 The View tab on the ribbon contains commands you can use to control the appearance of your workbook.

The Show group on the View tab controls the display of the formula bar as well as the appearance of gridlines, column and row headings, and the ruler (which is active only in Page Layout view). These are the options that are most often used, which is why they appear on the ribbon. But you'll discover more ways to tweak your UI when you click the File menu and then click Excel Options.

For more about Page Layout view, see Chapter 11, "Printing and presenting." For more about security issues, see Chapter 4, "Security and privacy."

The Advanced category in the Excel Options dialog box contains three groups of options, shown in Figure 3-22 (you'll need to scroll down a bit), that control different display behaviors for the program in general and for workbooks and worksheets in particular.

The Display area, shown scrolled to the top of the dialog box in Figure 3-22, offers display options for the program itself. The options in the Display Options For This Workbook area affect only the workbook selected in the drop-down list, which lists all the currently open workbooks; these options do not change the display of any other workbooks, and they do not affect the way the worksheets look when you print them. Similarly, the options in the Display Options For This Worksheet area apply only to the worksheet you select in the drop-down list.

Chapter 3

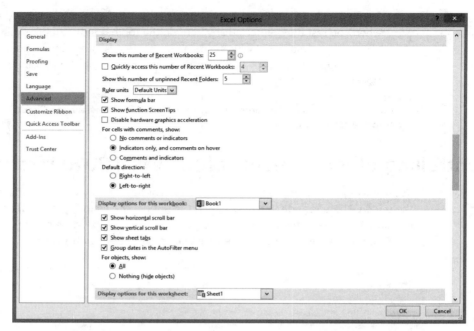

Figure 3-22 The Advanced category in the Excel Options dialog box includes a number of display options.

Displayed vs. printed gridlines and headings

Normally, Excel displays a grid to mark the boundaries of each cell on the worksheet and also displays row and column headings, but these are not printed unless you say so. The grid and headings are usually helpful for selecting and navigating, but you might not want them displayed all the time. The options for these items on the View tab control your screen display, but they do not affect whether these elements will be printed. You can control both display and printing on the Page Layout tab. In the Sheet Options group, select or clear the View and Print check boxes under Gridlines or Headings. For convenience, the View check boxes under Gridlines and Headings on the Page Layout tab are linked to the Gridlines and Headings check boxes on the View tab.

For more about printing a document, see Chapter 11.

Displaying underlying formulas

Usually, cells containing formulas display the results of that formula, not the formula itself. Similarly, when you format a number, you no longer see the underlying (unformatted) value displayed in the cell. You can see the underlying values and formulas only by selecting individual cells and looking at the formula bar or by double-clicking the cell. But what if you want to see more than one formula at once?

Click the File tab and click Options. In the Advanced category of the Excel Options dialog box, scroll down to the Display Options For This Worksheet group and select the Show Formulas In Cells Instead Of Their Calculated Results check box. This displays underlying values and formulas, only for the worksheet you select in the Display Options For This Worksheet drop-down list. As you can see in the worksheet view shown at the bottom of Figure 3-23, the underlying contents of each cell appear, as in the sum formulas in rows 6 through 10, and all the cells are left aligned. (Excel ignores any alignment formatting when you select the Show Formulas check box.) In addition, the width of each column on the worksheet approximately doubles to accommodate the underlying formulas. (The actual width of the columns remains unchanged; columns appear wider only on the screen.) When you clear the Show Formulas check box, Excel restores all columns to their former widths.

> **Note**
>
> You can quickly display and hide formulas in your worksheet by pressing Ctrl+` (accent grave), which is located on the tilde (~) key on most keyboards. To redisplay values, press Ctrl+` again.

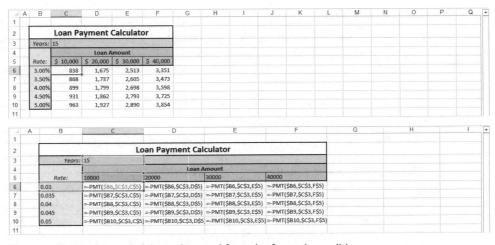

Figure 3-23 Display underlying values and formulas for easier auditing.

> **Note**
>
> If you click the New Window command on the View tab to create two or more windows in which to view the same workbook, you can use different display options in each window. For example, you can display formulas in one window and see the results of those formulas (the usual view) in another window.

The Show Formulas check box is particularly helpful when you need to edit a large worksheet. You can see your formulas without having to activate each cell and view its contents on the formula bar. You can also use the Show Formulas check box to document your work: After you select the Show Formulas check box, you can print your worksheet with the formulas displayed for archiving purposes.

Hiding zeros

Usually, zeros entered in cells, or the results of formulas that produce zero values, display on your worksheet. Sometimes, especially for presentation purposes, it is helpful to eliminate the clutter of excessive zero values on a worksheet. Under the heading Display Options For This Worksheet in the Advanced category of the Excel Options dialog box, clearing the Show A Zero In Cells That Have Zero Value check box causes any such cells to appear as blank cells on the worksheet. The underlying entries are unaffected, of course. If you edit an entry or if the result of a formula changes so that the cell no longer contains a zero value, the value immediately becomes visible. If the Show Formulas check box is also selected, clearing the Show A Zero In Cells That Have Zero Value check box has no effect on the display.

> **CAUTION!**
>
> If you hide zero values, be careful when editing your worksheet. What appears to be an empty cell might actually contain a formula.

> **Changing the display font**
>
> The display font is not only used for all text and numbers you enter in a workbook, but it also determines the font used in row and column headings. You can select fonts to be used when creating new workbooks with the Use This Font As The Default Font and Font Size drop-down lists in the General category in the Excel Options dialog box. The default display font is Body Font, which uses the font defined as such in the current theme. The new display font does not become active until you exit and restart Excel. When you do, the new font is used in all new workbooks you create. You can learn a lot more about formatting and themes in Chapter 9.

Enhancing accessibility

Excel 2013 and all other Microsoft Office 2013 programs support the Microsoft Active Accessibility (MSAA) specification. This makes various accessibility aids more effective, including screen readers and screen enlargers. For more information, visit the Microsoft Accessibility website at *www.microsoft.com/enable/*.

The following is a list of built-in features that, either by design or by default, enhance the accessibility of Excel:

- **The Accessibility Checker**   The most visible accessibility feature appears on the Info screen in Backstage view, and Microsoft calls it the *Accessibility Checker*. Click the File tab, select Info, click the Check For Issues button, and then click Check Accessibility to display the task pane shown in Figure 3-24. This task pane lists all the problematic items identified by the Accessibility Checker in the active workbook; click any item to display an explanation, as shown in Figure 3-24.

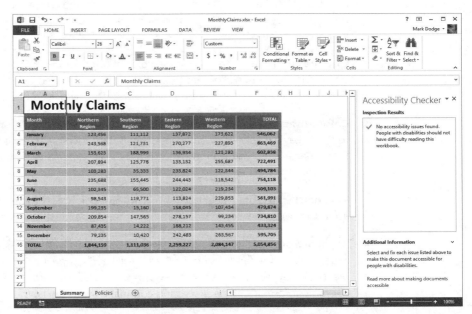

Figure 3-24 The Accessibility Checker lists all the issues found in the current workbook.

- **ScreenTips**   These are the little descriptive labels that appear under toolbar buttons and ribbon controls when you rest the pointer on them. Select one of three display options from the ScreenTip Style drop-down list in the General category in the Excel Options dialog box. For more information, see "Exploring other toolbar and ribbon options" earlier in this chapter.

- **Audio feedback**   The Advanced category in the Excel Options dialog box contains the Provide Feedback With Sound option. Using this option, you hear sounds where you might not expect them, such as when you click the Undo or Redo button. Note that if you select the sound option, you might be prompted to download an add-in from the Microsoft Office website that requires you to exit and restart Excel.

- **Function ScreenTips**   This is a type of pop-up label that displays the syntax and arguments for functions as they are entered or selected on the formula bar or in cells. Select the Show Function ScreenTips check box in the Advanced category of the Excel Options dialog box in the Display group. For more information, see Chapter 13, "Using functions."

- **Cell value AutoComplete**   When entering data in a column, the AutoComplete feature automatically inserts entries in the same column that match the current entry. This option saves keystrokes, for example, when you are repeatedly typing the same entry. In the Advanced category in the Excel Options dialog box, select the Enable AutoComplete For Cell Values check box in the Editing Options group. For more information, see "Letting Excel help with typing chores" in Chapter 8, "Worksheet editing techniques."

- **Gridline color**   You can change the color of gridlines on individual worksheets. Under Display Options For This Worksheet in the Advanced category in the Excel Options dialog box, click the Gridline Color drop-down list and then select a color.

- **Colored sheet tabs**   You can apply color to a single worksheet tab to make it easier to find a key worksheet, or you can assign different colors to each tab. Right-click the worksheet tab you want to color, point to Tab Color, and then click the color you want from the palette.

- **Keyboard shortcuts**   Keyboard shortcuts give you access to any command in Excel using the keyboard. For more information, see Appendix B, "Keyboard shortcuts."

- **Keyboard access**   Pressing the Alt key activates keyboard access, allowing you to issue ribbon commands using the keyboard. Labels appear adjacent to each command, displaying the key you need to press on the keyboard to select that command. For more information, see "Accessing commands with the keyboard," in Chapter 2.

- **Scroll and pan**   If you have a Microsoft IntelliMouse pointing device, you can scroll through a worksheet simply by turning the wheel in the direction you want to scroll. If you press the wheel and drag the mouse, you can pan the worksheet in any direction.

- **Zoom**   You can enlarge the worksheet display up to 400 percent by using the Zoom slider in the lower-right corner of the Excel window, by using the Zoom commands on the View tab on the ribbon, or by holding down Ctrl and turning the wheel on a Microsoft IntelliMouse pointing device.

Ease of access in Windows 8

Windows 8 (as well as Windows 7 and Windows Vista) includes a number of accessibility options referred to as the *Ease Of Access* options. You can find these by opening the Windows Control Panel and then clicking Ease Of Access Center to display the dialog box shown here:

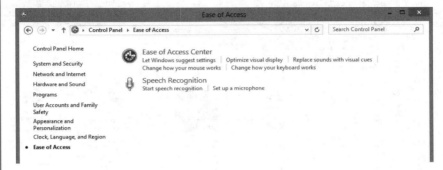

Many of these settings used to be scattered around or available only as add-ins to Windows, so these Ease Of Access options further improve the usability of Excel for folks with varying abilities.

Installing apps

The term "app," which has become ubiquitous, is just another way of saying "program." Programming languages translate human commands into ones and zeros that the computer machine understands. A *program* is the result of the *application* of a particular programming language to make the machine solve a specific problem. While the term "application" never really caught on, the term "app" is so easy and friendly that we now have apps for phones and TVs and tablets. And in 2013 you can download apps for Office applications, too…apps for apps.

Apps live in the cloud, so the first time you click the Apps For Office button on the Insert menu, you'll probably need to click the See All command, which opens the Office Store in your browser, as shown in Figure 3-25.

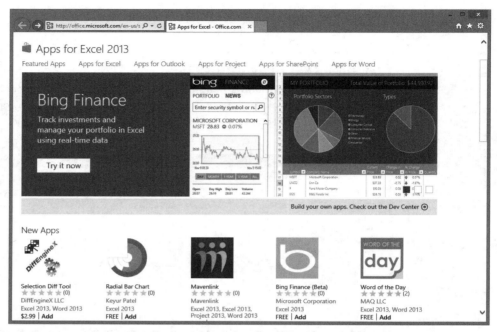

Figure 3-25 Click the See All command to open the Office Store on the web.

Many of the apps listed in the Office Store are free, such as the Radial Bar Chart app shown in Figure 3-25. Click an app to go to a webpage with more information; then if you want it, click the Add button when you're ready. What happens next is...nothing, really. You'll be instructed to go back to Excel and click the Apps For Office button again. This time when you click the See All command, the app you just added is shown in a dialog box, as shown in Figure 3-26.

Select an app in the Apps For Office dialog box, and then click the Insert button to add it to the current worksheet. (You can also click the Featured Apps link in the Apps For Office dialog box to display other apps available from the Office Store.) This is when the actual downloading occurs. Once it is inserted, just follow the app's instructions. After you insert an app, it appears on the Apps For Office menu, as shown in Figure 3-27.

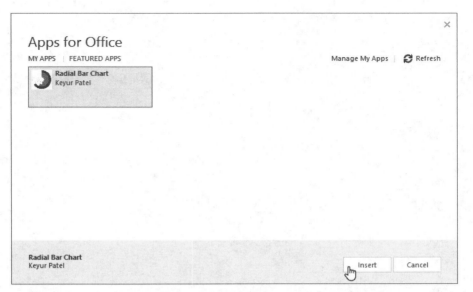

Figure 3-26 After you add an app in the Office Store, it shows up in the dialog box that appears when you click the Office Apps button and click the See All command.

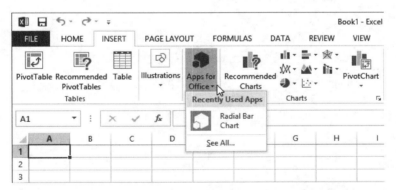

Figure 3-27 After you insert an app, it appears on the Apps For Office menu.

Chapter 3

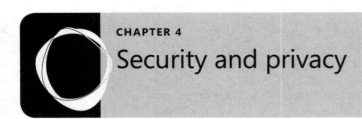

IN THIS CHAPTER, we cover overall system security issues, including ways to help protect your system against malicious software and how to hide your personal information from unwanted scrutiny. We also discuss using digital signatures to both verify incoming files and certify your own outgoing files. Microsoft Excel 2013 has additional security features you can apply within workbooks, worksheets, and even cells. We discuss these features in "Protecting worksheets" in Chapter 6, "How to work a worksheet," and in "Hiding and protecting workbooks" in Chapter 7 "How to work a workbook."

The Trust Center

Microsoft consolidated the kind of security features that are common to many Microsoft Office programs in a dialog box it calls the *Trust Center*. Click the File tab, click Options, and then click Trust Center to display the dialog box shown in the background in Figure 4-1.

This tab in the Excel Options dialog box contains links to disclaimers and declarations on the web. Click the Trust Center Settings button and then click the Trusted Locations category to open the dialog box, as shown in the foreground in Figure 4-1, where the security settings live.

> **Note**
>
> If you work in an organization, the Trust Center might contain default settings specified by your network administrator that you cannot (or should not) modify. Contact your friendly internal administrator for more information.

The settings you can configure in the Trust Center determine how Excel responds when you open a file with active content—that is, any external file that contains links or code used to communicate with another location on the Internet or an intranet. When you open such a file, Excel investigates several measures of trustworthiness. Rules exist by which a publisher attains trusted status. Defined as *reputable developers*, trusted publishers must sign their code by using valid, current digital signatures that are issued by certified certificate authorities (CAs) such as IntelliSafe. If you open a file that does not meet one of these criteria, a security alert appears, and you need to decide whether to run the active content anyway. But even if you add a publisher, unsigned code from that publisher still triggers a security alert. Most of the areas in the Trust Center dialog box deal with issues that directly affect the triggering of security alerts and the ability to run active content.

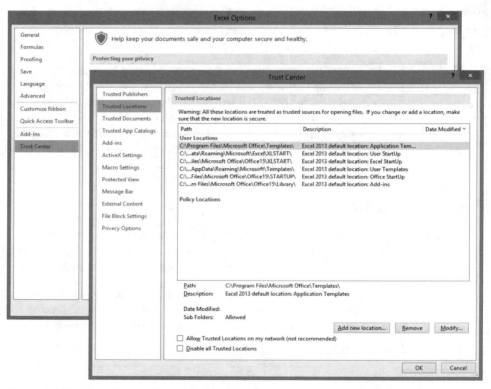

Figure 4-1 The Trust Center dialog box controls many security settings.

When you open a workbook with issues, Excel displays relevant security alerts and messages in the message bar, which appears right above the formula bar, as shown in Figure 4-2. Each message corresponds to a problem lurking within the file, and each includes a button offering a possible resolution. As you can see in Figure 4-2, the message bar can contain more than one message.

For more information about code signing, see "Using digital signatures" later in this chapter.

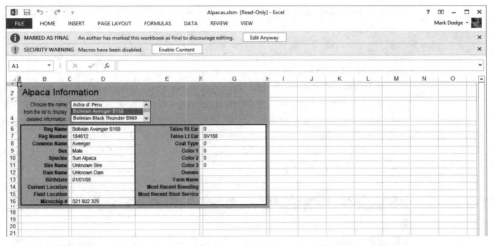

Figure 4-2 Security alerts and messages appear in the message bar.

> **Note**
>
> When you open a workbook with active content or other issues, any unresolved messages or alerts that appear in the message bar also appear in the Info category when you click the File tab.

Trusted publishers, locations, and documents

A *publisher* is a software developer, which can range in relative scale and trustworthiness from a kid with a laptop to Microsoft. You might know the kid, and you might not trust Microsoft. Whatever the case, you can apply your unique level of paranoia by adding or deleting publishers and locations using the first two categories in the Trust Center dialog box: Trusted Publishers and Trusted Locations. Excel populates the Trusted Publishers list whenever you open a macro or add-in for the first time that triggers a security alert. If you decide to enable the content, Excel adds the publisher to the list. Subsequent active content from the same publisher opens without triggering a security alert.

Trusted locations can be folders on your own hard disk or on a network—the more precise, the better. We recommend you designate trusted locations at the subfolder level—even the default Documents folder (a.k.a. The Folder Formerly Known As My Documents) is too broad, particularly if you work in a networked environment. It is better to designate subfolders of Documents—or better yet, use folders outside the Documents folder entirely—to minimize the ease with which others can locate interesting stuff on your computer to steal or to modify. Several trusted locations are installed with Excel, such as subfolder locations for template and startup files, as shown earlier in Figure 4-1 with the Trusted Locations tab displayed.

Each time you open a document that triggers a security alert and enable its content by clicking the Enable Content button in the message bar, you add the name of the document to the Trusted Documents list. The security alert no longer appears on subsequent openings. You can reset the Trusted Documents list (which actually appears nowhere) by clicking the Trusted Documents category in the Trust Center dialog box and clicking the Clear button, shown in Figure 4-3. Here you can also disable Trusted Documents (the feature, not the documents themselves) and choose to allow or deny global "trusted" status to all the documents that exist on your network.

Figure 4-3 You add to the Trusted Documents list when you enable the active content in a document.

App catalogs, add-ins, ActiveX settings, and macro settings

The Trusted App Catalogs, Add-Ins, ActiveX Settings, and Macro Settings categories in the Trust Center, as shown in Figure 4-4, deal with blocking active content. Trusted App Catalogs controls whether or not Excel recognizes Office apps available from specific locations, and it includes a special option for apps from the Office Store. You have only two choices for add-ins: just disable them all or require them to be from a trusted publisher. If you decide on the latter, you can additionally disable the usual message bar notification when an add-in is unsigned.

For more about Office Apps, see "Installing apps" in Chapter 3, "Custom-tailoring the Excel workspace."

Figure 4-4 Using the options in the Trusted App Catalogs, Add-Ins, ActiveX Settings, and Macro Settings categories, you can enable or disable most types of active content you might encounter.

ActiveX controls are more general than add-ins, and they can be designed to run on the web or on your computer, but always within a host application. ActiveX has been the language of choice for many malicious code developers (a.k.a. *hackers*) because it allows nearly unlimited access to your computer. You should never allow ActiveX controls without restriction—the minimum protection option should be Prompt Me Before Enabling All Controls With Minimal Restrictions. The option that mentions Safe For Initialization (SFI) controls refers to a sort of internal code-signing protocol set by the developer to verify its safety. Choosing this option puts code through a few more levels of restriction. The best solution if you want to stay safe yet you need to use certain ActiveX controls is to set up or use a trusted location to store the ActiveX controls you know to be safe.

INSIDE OUT Of web beacons and homograph attacks

The word *exploits*, which used to conjure images of heroic figures and derring-do, has come to describe the actions of malicious software. *Phishing* is a rather clever type of lure used by hackers trolling for data to reel unsuspecting prey into their virtual creels. *Homographs* use the extended international character set to create scam websites with Uniform Resource Locators (URLs) that replace one or more English-alphabet letters in the real domain names with similar ones from another language's character set. You see what you think is a trusted URL, but if you access the site, you might end up sharing information with the phishermen instead of the trusted site. Where homographs are designed to lure you in, *web beacons* might be what you "win" after you get there. These are forms of spyware that infiltrate your system and then just sit there transmitting data—beacons of information—to malicious data-mining operations. These are just a few of the many clever methods being employed to rip you off. The Trust Center addresses some grim realities of this insecure world, but, of course, it shouldn't be your only line of defense. Unfortunately, every Internet-connected computer needs to have an automatically updating antiviral/firewall application installed to fend off current and future exploits.

You can read more about all this in the Help system. The easiest way to get to the relevant topics is to open the Trust Center dialog box and then click the Help button (the little question mark icon in the upper-right corner) to display a Help topic about the currently active category.

Unlike ActiveX controls, macros are application-specific, but they can be destructive when they emanate from a malicious coder. The Trust Center Macro Settings category reveals options that are similar to those of ActiveX controls, as are the recommendations. The Trust Access To The VBA Project Object Model option is for developers only, but it might be desirable in a development environment where a shared Visual Basic for Applications project object model is known to be secure and isolated.

Message bar

The Message Bar category in the Trust Center dialog box simply lets you turn off the display of security alerts in the message bar. It does not turn off the actual security features, just the notifications. The message bar is ordinarily turned on, unless you opt to disable all macros. ActiveX controls still generate their own security alerts.

External content

External content comes in many flavors, and people can use it in many ways to implement malicious intent. The Trust Center dialog box can intercept potential problems by blocking external content such as data connections, hyperlinks, and images, all of which can contain or facilitate malicious code. Figure 4-5 shows the External Content category of the Trust Center dialog box.

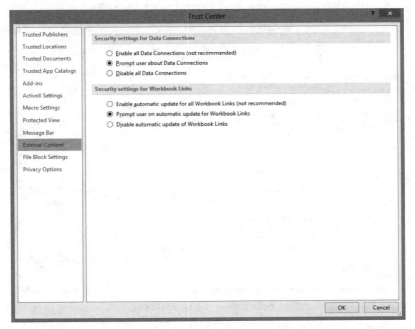

Figure 4-5 The External Content category contains settings that control data connections and links.

The real difference between the two sets of External Content options is that *data connections* are links to data from other programs, such as databases, while *workbook links* are external references used between Excel workbooks. If you do not control or do not have confidence in the linked or connected sources, it's best to go with the default settings, prompting you for a decision whenever external content is encountered. As with most of these Trust Center options, allowing all data connections or workbook links is not recommended.

File block settings

Excel allows you to disable the opening and saving of any individual file type it recognizes. The File Block Settings category in the Trust Center dialog box, shown in Figure 4-6, includes a list of file types that Excel recognizes, each with check boxes you can use to block its opening or saving. Use the options below the list to select the way you'd like Excel to handle the opening of selected file types. You can block a file type by clicking Do Not Open Selected File Types or choose to open the file in Protected View, either read-only or editable.

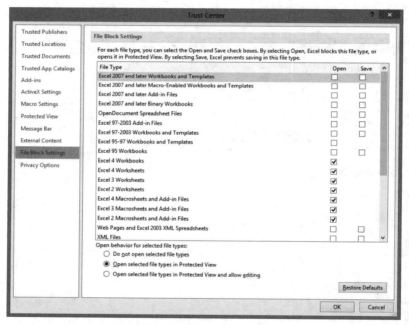

Figure 4-6 You can choose not to allow the normal opening and saving of specific file types.

If you want to restore the default file-block settings, which include the blockage of several old Excel file formats, click the Restore Defaults button. Some of the listed formats do not include a check box to block saving, either because it doesn't work (dBase III/IV) or because several older formats have been subsumed into one newer format (Excel 2 through Excel 4 into Excel 95).

Privacy options

Excel uses the Internet behind the scenes to give you access to all the information you need at a moment's notice. Many people want to know exactly when their computer is retrieving online information, so Microsoft lets you control these interactions by clicking the File tab, clicking Options, clicking Trust Center, and then clicking Trust Center Settings. In the Trust Center dialog box, click the Privacy Options tab to display the dialog box shown in Figure 4-7.

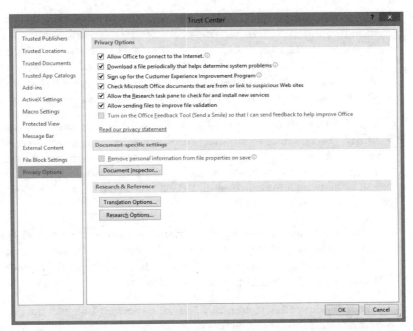

Figure 4-7 If you are uncomfortable with Excel connecting automatically to the web, you can specify that it behave otherwise.

The first set of options you see in Figure 4-7 control whether Excel can automatically communicate and share information over the Internet under various circumstances:

- **Allow Office To Connect To The Internet**   You might prefer to take control of web interactions yourself, for example, if you use a dial-up Internet connection. If you clear this check box, you can still connect to the online Help content from within the Help dialog box. This also controls whether Excel automatically displays web-based templates in the New category on the File menu.

- **Download A File Periodically That Helps Determine System Problems**   You need to decide whether to allow Microsoft to send diagnostic programs to your computer. If you worry about losing data to system crashes, you can select this check box to aid in any future system rehab and recovery efforts.

- **Sign Up For The Customer Experience Improvement Program**   Over the years, Microsoft's on-site usability lab has been instrumental in helping refine products based on how people actually work. The Customer Experience Improvement Program is similar, except that instead of conducting tests in a controlled environment on the Microsoft corporate campus, data is accumulated in a collective "lab" that potentially includes your office. The usage data collected by this program is much more useful than that generated in the artificial environment of a laboratory. This program began with Excel 2003 and has been partially responsible for the changes you see in Excel 2013. It's kind of like installing a Nielsen ratings box on your television—yes, you're sharing information with them, but maybe the TV shows will get better.

- **Check Microsoft Office Documents That Are From Or Link To Suspicious Web Sites**   This option turns on what Microsoft calls *spoofed website detection*. This refers to a homograph-type phishing scheme using web domain names that closely resemble trusted sites. It's often hard to tell the difference with the naked eye, so you can let Excel do it for you. (See the sidebar "Of web beacons and homograph attacks" earlier in this chapter.)

- **Allow The Research Task Pane To Check For And Install New Services**   This option controls whether Excel automatically connects to the web-based resources necessary for the operation of the tools made available by clicking the Research, Thesaurus, or Translate button on the Review tab.

- **Allow Sending Files To Improve File Validation**   If a file fails the built-in, file-format validation process, you're prompted to send file-validation information to Microsoft if this option remains selected.

For all these privacy issues, Microsoft won't collect any personal information and promises that participants remain completely anonymous. You might want to return to the Excel Options dialog box and read the linked information in the Trust Center category before deciding whether to select these check boxes.

INSIDE OUT   Of file format attacks and file validation

Another flavor of malicious exploit is the *file format attack*. Office File Validation helps detect file format attacks, which attempt to insert remotely triggered code bits by modifying the structure of a file. Interestingly, there is a short list of binary file types that are favorites for these attacks, including Excel 97-2003 workbooks and templates and Excel 5.0/95 files. Office File Validation checks these and others on the most-wanted list against a predefined set of rules, or *schema,* that defines the structure of each file type. Validation fails if the file does not conform to the rules. You are prompted to send validation information to Microsoft if a file fails validation. Clear the Allow Sending Files To Improve File Validation option on the Privacy Options page of the Trust Center if you'd rather not share and would rather not see the prompt.

File security

Legions of hackers are seemingly willing to go to any length to gain bragging rights by creating viruses, breaking firewalls, and thwarting password protection. Excel has always had security features, but Excel 2013 raises the ante a bit to help make your workbooks more secure.

For more about workbook security, see "Hiding and protecting workbooks" in Chapter 7.

Removing personal information from your workbooks

It's increasingly important to be sure that you don't leave helpful tidbits of information lying around for others to abuse. Although it's up to you to check that you're not giving away personal information on your worksheets (your password-protected worksheets, of course!), information also lives in places you might forget to look. Excel 2013 includes the Document Inspector, which is designed to look in all the nooks and crannies for you. Click the File tab, click Info, click Check For Issues, and then click Inspect Document to display the dialog box shown in Figure 4-8. (You can also access the Document Inspector by clicking the button of the same name located in the Privacy Options category in the Trust Center dialog box.)

Chapter 4

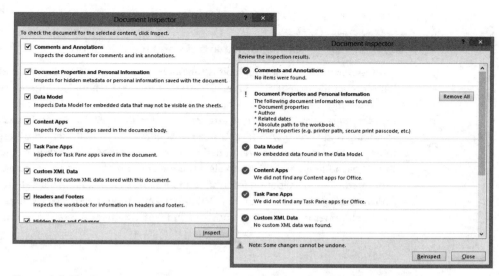

Figure 4-8 The Document Inspector examines the hidden places in your workbooks where personal data can hide.

As you can see in Figure 4-8, data is slippery stuff. The Document Inspector searches and reports on what it finds, as shown on the dialog box on the right of Figure 4-8. You can then click any Remove All button that appears or close the dialog box and edit the area in question. Most of these items are usually perfectly benign, of course. You probably don't want to purge your headers and footers, for example, unless they contain your address or Social Security number. But if you are sharing data with others, the Document Inspector gives you a quick and easy way to find forgotten personal data you might not otherwise have found.

Using digital signatures

Digital signatures are similar to handwritten signatures in that both are intended to provide authenticity to documents. However, although the digital version might include a graphic representation of an actual signature, it also uses cryptography to establish not only a document's authenticity but also the integrity of the file and the identity of the signer. You can add signatures to your own documents and to others' as well. One way to use signatures is to verify that others have read a document (or at least opened it) by adding their signatures.

One important fact about digital signatures is that when you digitally sign a workbook, Excel saves it as a read-only document, preventing you from making further changes. Adding a handwritten signature, being typically the last element you add before sending a letter, in this case ensures that it actually is the last step you perform in a workbook. But don't worry—you can remove and reapply a signature if you need to make changes.

Excel 2013 includes a literal version of a digital signature line that includes a *public key*, a type of digital signature that is generic and temporary. (Search for "digital signature" in Help to learn more.) Like padlocks, these are designed to keep honest people from getting in. They don't protect so much as inform: if the signature is missing or corrupted, you know someone messed with the workbook.

To begin, click the Insert tab and then in the Text group, click Signature Line, and then click Microsoft Office Signature Line to display the dialog box shown in Figure 4-9.

Figure 4-9 You can insert an actual signature line as an object.

After you fill out the dialog box and click OK, Excel inserts a signature block on the worksheet. The signature block is a graphic object, as shown in Figure 4-10. This is a signature block, but it has not yet been signed. To do so, double-click the signature object to display the Sign dialog box, as shown in Figure 4-11.

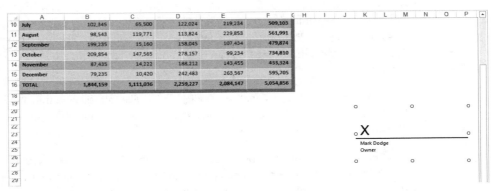

Figure 4-10 The Signature Setup dialog box inserts a signature graphic on the current worksheet.

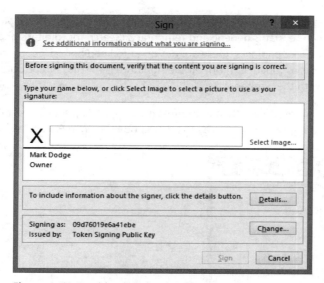

Figure 4-11 Double-click the signature line object to display the Sign dialog box.

You can simply type your name in the Sign dialog box, or you can select a picture to use as your signature. It can be clip art or any picture, perhaps even a scan of your actual signature. You can add information about yourself to the signature by clicking the Details button. Once signed, the document is set to Read-Only; any edits made to the workbook will invalidate the signature, which, of course, is the point. After you apply a signature, a message bar appears in the workbook with a "Marked as Final" message, like the one shown in Figure 4-13.

Creating your own digital signature lets you verify only the authenticity of your own documents, and even then only on your own computer. If you would like to increase the apparent trustworthiness of your workbooks by purchasing a verifiable signature, click the Insert tab, click the Text button, click Signature Line, and then click Add Signature Services. This opens a webpage where you can select and order one from a number of third-party vendors.

You can also add a digital signature by clicking the File tab, clicking Info, clicking Protect Workbook, and then clicking Add A Digital Signature to display the dialog box shown in Figure 4-12.

The Commitment Type list shows four options: None; Created And Approved This Document; Created This Document; and Approved This Document. You can also add a note in the Purpose For Signing This Document box. When you're finished, click the Sign button to sign the workbook.

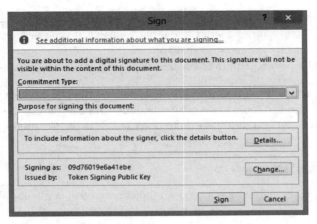

Figure 4-12 The Sign dialog box as it appears when you open it by clicking the File tab, Info, Protect Workbook, Add A Digital Signature command.

This time, no signature line object appears on the worksheet, but it is the same temporary signature type. To view the signature info, click the File tab, click Info, and then click View Signatures to display a Signatures task pane, as shown in Figure 4-13.

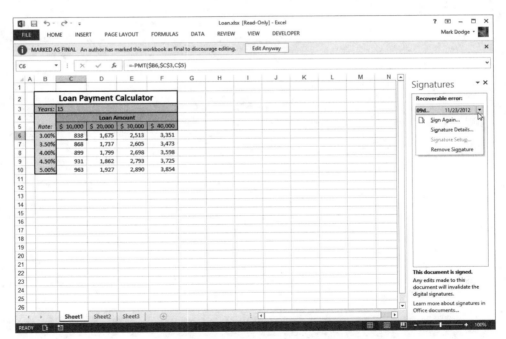

Figure 4-13 The Signatures task pane displays any digital signatures that have been applied.

You'll notice that the Signatures task pane lists our signature as Recoverable Error. This is okay, because it is a temporary signature and is not verifiable. If you select a signature in the task pane and click the menu arrow that appears, the Sign Again, Signature Details, Signature Setup, and Remove Signature commands appear, as shown in Figure 4-13.

After a document is digitally signed, *[Read-Only]* appears in the title bar next to the file name, and a small icon that looks like a certificate ribbon appears next to the word *Ready* in the status bar. You can also click this icon to open and close the Signatures task pane.

Other security features

Several security features in Excel are apropos to topics covered in depth elsewhere in this book:

- For more about worksheet security, see "Protecting worksheets" in Chapter 6.

- For more about workbook security, see "Hiding and protecting workbooks" in Chapter 7.

PART 2

Building worksheets

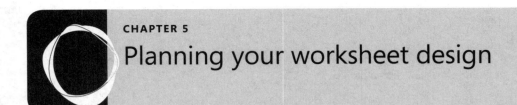

Planning your worksheet design

I N THIS CHAPTER, we pose seven simple questions that might help you greatly when you plan a worksheet. Although it's not necessary to spend time planning every worksheet you create, a little consideration can be helpful when planning worksheets you need to pass on, or share with others.

Which data should be in rows, and which in columns?

Sometimes the answer is rather obvious, but generally speaking, you'll want the data that is most abundant to fill rows rather than columns. Consider the readability of your data when you make this decision. For example, a month-oriented worksheet like the one shown in Figure 5-1 can work well with the month labels either across the top or down the left side of the worksheet. But in this case, having the month labels down the side makes it easier to view the worksheet on the screen and makes it easier to fit it on a printed page. The worksheet in Figure 5-1 contains only four columns of detail data, but if your worksheet has more categories of detail data than the number of months, you might want to run the months in columns instead.

Usually, the detail you accumulate in a worksheet best fits into rows from top to bottom—relatively speaking, a deep and narrow worksheet. It is not unheard of to build a spreadsheet that is shallow and wide (only a few rows deep, with lots of columns), but you might regret it later. A shallow, wide worksheet can be annoying if you must continually pan to the right to find information or if you have to deal with odd column breaks when printing. If you have a wheel mouse, scrolling up and down is extremely easy to do using the wheel, but panning right and left requires clicking and dragging. And after you have the worksheet filled with data, it's time-consuming to change it—especially when you could have designed it differently from the start.

You might also prefer the worksheet to be long rather than wide so that you can use the Page Up and Page Down keys to navigate around the screen. When oriented horizontally, the worksheet shown in Figure 5-1 still works, as shown in Figure 5-2, but you have to scroll to the right to view all the data.

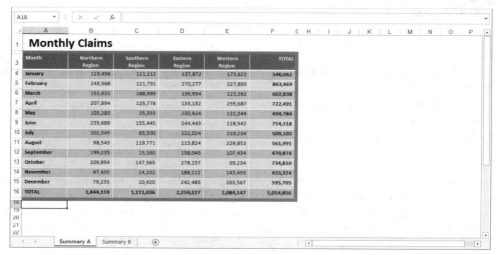

Figure 5-1 Monthly total worksheets are often oriented vertically, as shown here.

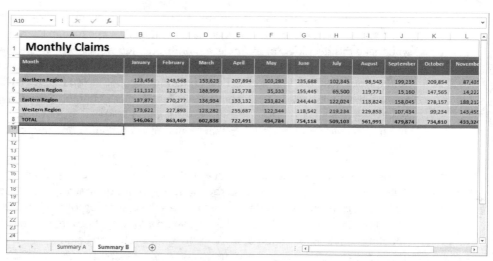

Figure 5-2 Worksheets are often harder to view and print when oriented horizontally.

On the companion website you'll find the BuildingWorksheets.xlsx, TeamSales.xlsx, Alpacas.xlsx, and NorthwindSales.xlsx workbooks.

Will you need to print the worksheet?

Before you start work on a worksheet, you also need to ask yourself whether you will need to print the worksheet. You might realize that you don't need to worry about printing at all—if, for example, you are going to use the worksheet for information storage or reference purposes only.

If you will want to print the worksheet, consider how your data will look and how the worksheet will work on paper. This makes a huge difference to your overall worksheet design. For example, the worksheet in Figure 5-2 requires two pages to print, even if you orient it horizontally (using Landscape Orientation on the Page Layout tab on the ribbon). The second page of the printout contains some of the monthly totals, but you won't see the names of the regions unless you use the Print Titles feature (also on the Page Layout tab) to repeat the headings on each page. For large worksheets in either horizontal or vertical orientation, using print titles is an absolute necessity for intelligible printouts.

For more about page setup and print titles, see Chapter 11, "Printing and presenting."

You also need to consider how you might use the printout. If you're going to use it in a management report, you should try to get the salient information to fit on one page. If it's for a presentation, you might need to distill it further or create smaller, more digestible chunks of data that can be summarized in a small grid of a dozen or so cells so that it fits onto a transparency or a slide. If you have massive amounts of data to start with, you can create summary pages for various purposes, as shown in Figure 5-3, or use outlining to collapse the detail in large worksheets and display only the totals, as shown in Figure 5-4.

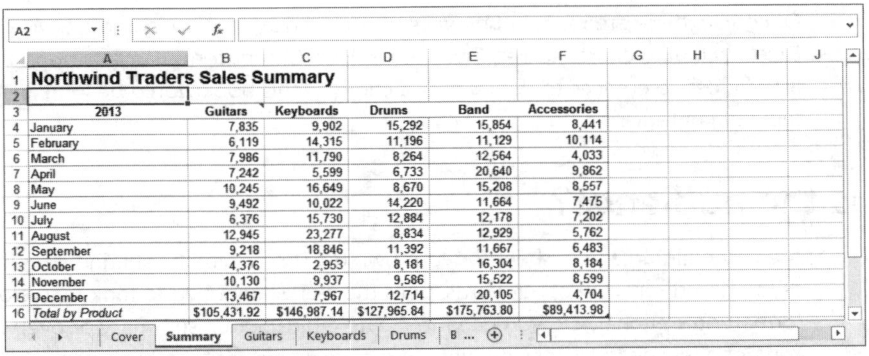

Northwind Traders Sales Summary

2013	Guitars	Keyboards	Drums	Band	Accessories
January	7,835	9,902	15,292	15,854	8,441
February	6,119	14,315	11,196	11,129	10,114
March	7,986	11,790	8,264	12,564	4,033
April	7,242	5,599	6,733	20,640	9,862
May	10,245	16,649	8,670	15,208	8,557
June	9,492	10,022	14,220	11,664	7,475
July	6,376	15,730	12,884	12,178	7,202
August	12,945	23,277	8,834	12,929	5,762
September	9,218	18,846	11,392	11,667	6,483
October	4,376	2,953	8,181	16,304	8,184
November	10,130	9,937	9,586	15,522	8,599
December	13,467	7,967	12,714	20,105	4,704
Total by Product	$105,431.92	$146,987.14	$127,965.84	$175,763.80	$89,413.98

Figure 5-3 If showing all the detail data is too cumbersome, you can create summary sheets for reporting purposes.

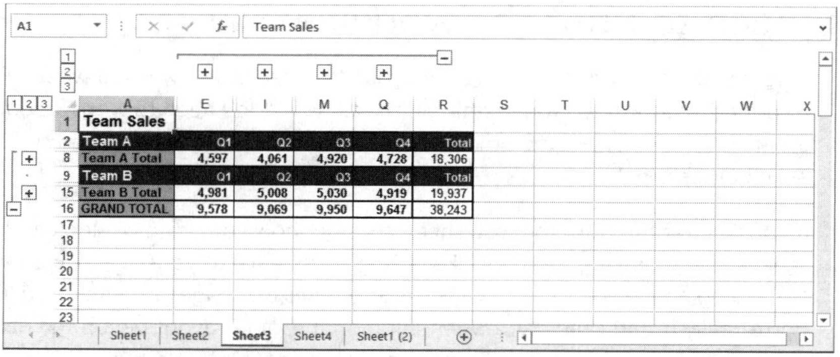

Figure 5-4 You can use outlining to hide the detail for summary purposes.

For information about outlining, see "Outlining worksheets" in Chapter 8, "Worksheet editing techniques."

If the worksheet is for auditing or reference purposes, you probably want to see everything. Orientation is a big issue here. You can print in either landscape (horizontal) or portrait (vertical) format, so design your worksheet accordingly. Sometimes using a landscape orientation helps if you have lots of columns. If you have an inordinate number of columns, you might want to try segmenting your data into an overall system of worksheets—chunks that realistically can be printed without losing context or readability. For example, the sheet tabs at the bottom of the workbook shown in Figure 5-3 give evidence that the displayed summary sheet actually consolidates the data from several other sheets in the same workbook.

Of course, there are many other ways to summarize, analyze, and otherwise distill data in Excel, including charts, tables, PivotTables, PivotCharts, formulas, functions, and more. The list of cross-references to the related sections in this book would be long; just check the table of contents.

Who is the audience?

Are you building a worksheet for your own use, or will you be sharing it with others online or in printed form? In other words, does the worksheet need to look marvelous or is fancy formatting optional? Do you need to create a big-picture summary or overview for others? You definitely need to consider your audience when deciding how your worksheet is going to look.

If you're close to the data in your worksheet—that is, this is your job—you probably think the details are a lot more interesting than others might. You need to think like the people you will be presenting this information to and tell them what they need to know—no more, and certainly no less. If your worksheet contains a lot of data that your audience doesn't really need to see—which is almost always the case—you can create a summary sheet (like the one shown in Figure 5-3) specifically for the purpose of mass consumption. If your worksheet will have more than one type of audience, create different summary sheets for each group, all using the same underlying data.

Would your worksheet survive without you?

If you are creating worksheets that might at some point be used by others, make sure they are understandable and well documented. Most of us don't think about documentation, but every worksheet you create for business or personal use should be created with the possibility in mind that others might need to figure it out someday—possibly without your help. If you change jobs, you will be leaving a good legacy behind for the next person, which reflects well on you. A little documentation goes a long way, as shown in Figure 5-5. You can use the Comment command to add notes anywhere a little explanation is in order.

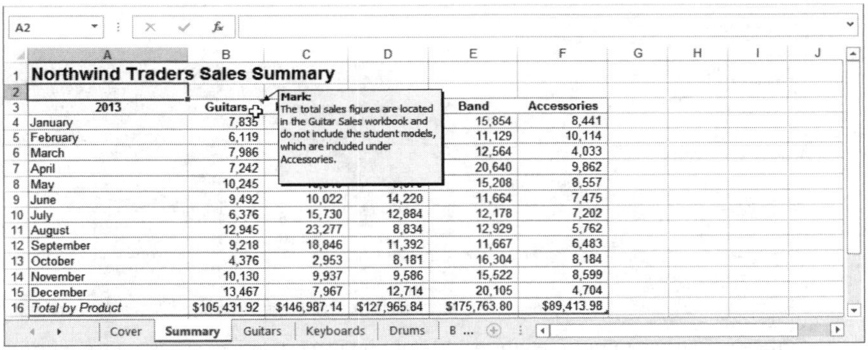

Northwind Traders Sales Summary					
2013	Guitars			Band	Accessories
January	7,835			15,854	8,441
February	6,119			11,129	10,114
March	7,986			12,564	4,033
April	7,242			20,640	9,862
May	10,245			15,208	8,557
June	9,492	10,022	14,220	11,664	7,475
July	6,376	15,730	12,884	12,178	7,202
August	12,945	23,277	8,834	12,929	5,762
September	9,218	18,846	11,392	11,667	6,483
October	4,376	2,953	8,181	16,304	8,184
November	10,130	9,937	9,586	15,522	8,599
December	13,467	7,967	12,714	20,105	4,704
Total by Product	$105,431.92	$146,987.14	$127,965.84	$175,763.80	$89,413.98

Figure 5-5 Make sure critical worksheets are understandable and well documented.

For information about documenting your worksheets, see "Adding comments to cells" in Chapter 8.

You also need to prepare worksheets containing important personal records with survivability in mind. If you were to pass away unexpectedly, you'd want to leave your family with clear financial worksheets.

Does the worksheet rely on imported data?

Many people work with data that is compiled elsewhere as the basis for their worksheet analyses. For example, a database located on your computer or somewhere on a network is often the repository for specific information you extract and analyze. If this is the case, try to make it easy on yourself. Often, people use the ad hoc approach to working—that is, they do it quickly, when it's needed, with no particular attention paid to repeatability. If you gather information from a database, you might be able to construct queries you can execute again and again, on whatever schedule you need, rather than start from scratch each time. This way, you can ensure that the imported data will be structured in the same way each time. Then you might use the structure of the imported data as the basis for your worksheet design. Or it might make sense to keep the imported data on a separate worksheet no one will see and then construct nicely formatted worksheets you can use to extract only the pertinent information. Figure 5-6 shows just such a worksheet. You can see that the raw data is on a separate worksheet behind the information worksheet.

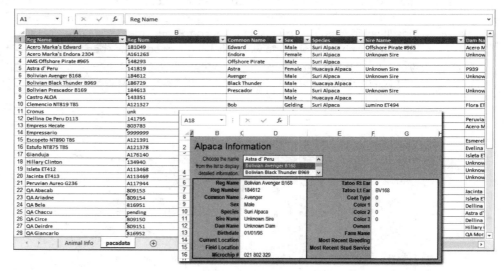

Figure 5-6 You can put raw imported data on its own worksheet and use a formatted worksheet to present the pertinent information.

For information about using information stored elsewhere, see Chapter 25, "Working with external data," as well as the chapters in Part 8, "Using Excel collaboratively."

Databases, fields, and records

Sometimes when you say the word *database*, you can see people's eyes glaze over in anticipation of a barrage of incomprehensible terminology. Although using a database program can be overwhelmingly complex, consider that many of the worksheets you create in Excel (such as the underlying worksheet in Figure 5-6) are actually rudimentary databases. The telephone directory is an example of a database in printed form. In database terminology, each phone listing in the directory is a *record* of the database, and each item of information in a listing (first name, last name, address, and telephone number) is a *field* in the record.

Do you need more than one worksheet?

Spreadsheet programs began as a better way to store, present, and interpret information that previously had been kept on paper and calculated by hand, probably using a 10-key calculator. Often, the first worksheets we created when we were climbing the old Excel learning curve were little more than clean, two-dimensional reproductions of what we used to do on paper. One way to step up from the old, paper paradigm is to use modular design. *Modular design* is a sort of "structured programming" or "object-oriented" approach, where you carve your data into logical chunks that make sense as standalone elements. (The other design approach is called *hierarchical*, where you organize your data for error identification and maximum readability.) Because there's usually no need to keep detail data in any kind of presentable format, why bother? Concentrate your worksheet beautification program on the summary sheets and charts you need to share with others. Design a system of worksheets instead of trying to get everything on a single worksheet. Figure 5-6 shows a rudimentary example of modular design—that is, one worksheet contains data, and another worksheet contains a specific type of analysis. In a complex modular system, you might have dozens of worksheets, each dedicated to a specific task.

Have you allowed room for new data?

It's critical to allow for expansion and editing after you have assembled your worksheet. It's generally a good idea to add a few extra rows and columns to the detail area and to keep totals separate from the detail data by a row or column or two, if possible. One of the most common editing actions you'll perform is inserting new rows and columns. Excel has become a lot smarter about this over the years, making obsolete some of the rules of thumb that we old-timers have collected. But it's still possible to mess up.

A rather famous folkloric tale tells the story of an accounting person who inserted a row at the bottom of a range of cells but forgot to adjust the totals formulas and was fired because his numbers were off by $200,000. The moral: Edit worksheets carefully, and always guard against introducing new errors along the way.

Chapter 5

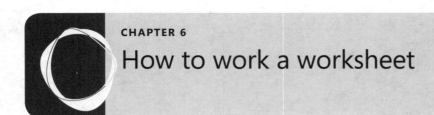

How to work a worksheet

I N THIS CHAPTER, we cover the basics, including moving around within the massive worksheet grid, entering and selecting data, and working with multiple worksheets and protecting their contents. You probably already know many of these techniques, but here you'll also learn alternative methods. You might find a better—or faster—way to do something you do frequently.

Moving around regions

A *region* is a rectangular range of cell entries, or a block of "filled" cells. In Figure 6-1, the range A3:E7 is a region, as are the ranges G3:H7, A9:E10, and G9:H10. (Strictly speaking, cell A1 is a one-cell region, too.) Cell H10 is considered to be within a region, even though it's empty.

The *active area* of the worksheet is the selection rectangle that encompasses all regions—that is, all the filled cells in the active worksheet—which in Figure 6-1 is A1:H10.

The techniques you can use to navigate regions are helpful if you typically work with large tables of data. Getting to the bottom row of a 500-row table is easier when you don't have to use the scroll bars.

> **Note**
>
> The small square in the lower-right corner of the active cell is the *fill handle*. If the fill handle isn't visible on your screen, it means it isn't turned on. To turn it on, click the File tab, click Options, click the Advanced category, and select the Enable Fill Handle And Cell Drag-And-Drop check box.

A3	▼	:	×	✓	f_x	2013			

	A	B	C	D	E	F	G	H	I	J
1	Regional Sales									
2										
3	2013	Qtr 1	Qtr 2	Qtr 3	Qtr 4		Total	Average		
4	Region 1	1000	1050	1100	1150		4300	1075		
5	Region 2	1100	1150	1200	1250		4700	1175		
6	Region 3	1200	1250	1300	1350		5100	1275		
7	Region 4	1300	1350	1400	1450		5500	1375		
8										
9	Total	4600	4800	5000	5200		19600	4900		
10	Average	1150	1200	1250	1300		4900			
11										
12										

Figure 6-1 There are four regions—blocks of "filled" cells—on this worksheet that are separate regions.

Navigating regions with the keyboard

Here is a great way to move around fast without taking your hands off the keyboard. To jump from edge to edge within and between regions, hold down the Ctrl key and then press any of the arrow keys. For example, in Figure 6-1, cell A3 is the active cell; press Ctrl+Right Arrow to activate cell E3. Press Ctrl+Right Arrow again and the active cell jumps to G3, then H3, and finally XFD3—the last available cell in row 3. Just keep pressing Ctrl+Left Arrow to return.

Navigating regions with the mouse

The dark border around the selected cell or cells is called a *selection rectangle*. When you move the plus-sign pointer over the selection rectangle, the pointer becomes a four-headed arrow. When the arrow pointer is visible, double-click to jump from edge to edge among regions—the mouse equivalent of the Ctrl+Arrow keyboard method described earlier. For example, double-clicking the bottom of the single-cell selection rectangle in cell A3, as shown in Figure 6-1, selects cell A7.

The left side of the status bar displays the mode indicators in Table 6-1 when the corresponding keyboard mode is active.

TABLE 6-1 Keyboard modes

Mode	Description
Extend Selection	Press F8 to turn on this mode, which you use to extend the current selection using the keyboard. (Be sure that Scroll Lock is off.) This is the keyboard equivalent of selecting cells by dragging the mouse. Furthermore, unlike holding down the Shift key and pressing an arrow key, you can extend the range by pressing only one key at a time. Press F8 again to turn off Extend Selection mode.

Mode	Description
Add To Selection	Press Shift+F8 to add more cells to the current selection using the keyboard; the cells need not be adjacent. After pressing Shift+F8, click any cell or drag through any range to add it to the selection. This is the keyboard equivalent of holding down Ctrl and selecting additional cells with the mouse.
Num Lock	This mode keeps your keypad in numeric entry mode. This is turned on by default, but its status is not usually displayed in the status bar. However, you can make it do so by right-clicking the status bar anywhere and clicking Num Lock.
Fixed Decimal	To add a decimal point to the numeric entries in the current selection, click the File tab, click Options, select the Advanced category, and select the Automatically Insert A Decimal Point check box in the Editing Options group. Excel places the decimal point in the location you specify in the Places box. For example, when you turn on Fixed Decimal mode, specify two decimal places, and type the number 12345 in a cell, the value 123.45 appears in the cell after you press Enter. Existing cell entries are not affected unless you edit them. To turn off Fixed Decimal mode, return to the Advanced category in the Excel Options dialog box and clear the Automatically Insert A Decimal Point check box.
Caps Lock	Press the Caps Lock key to type text in capital letters. (This does not affect number and symbol keys.) To turn off Caps Lock mode, press the Caps Lock key again. The status of this mode does not usually display in the status bar, but you can make it do so. Right-click the status bar anywhere, and click Caps Lock.
Scroll Lock	Press Scroll Lock to use the Page Up, Page Down, and arrow keys to move the viewed portion of the window without moving the active cell. When Scroll Lock mode is off, the active cell moves one page at a time when you press Page Up or Page Down and moves one cell at a time when you press one of the arrow keys. To turn off Scroll Lock mode, press the Scroll Lock key again.
End	Press the End key, and then press an arrow key to move the selection to the edge of the region in that direction or to the last worksheet cell in that direction. This mode functions like holding down Ctrl and pressing an arrow key, except you need to press only one key at a time. To turn off End mode, press the End key again. End mode is also turned off after you press one of the arrow keys.
Overtype	Click the formula bar or double-click a cell and press the Insert key to turn on Overtype mode (formerly known as Overwrite mode). Usually, new characters you type in the formula bar are inserted between existing characters. With Overtype mode turned on, the characters you type replace any existing characters to the right of the insertion point. Overtype mode turns off when you press Insert again or when you press Enter or one of the arrow keys to lock in the cell entry. The status of this mode does not usually display in the status bar, but you can make it do so. Right-click the status bar anywhere, and click Overtype Mode.

Navigating with special keys

Table 6-2 shows how you can use the Home and End keys alone and in conjunction with other keys to make selections and to move around a worksheet.

TABLE 6-2 Keyboard shortcuts for navigation

Press	To
Home	Move to the first cell in the current row.
Ctrl+Home	Move to cell A1.
Ctrl+End	Move to the last cell in the last column in the active area. For example, in Figure 6-1, pressing Ctrl+End selects cell H10.
End	Start End mode, and then press an arrow key to move around by cell region.
Scroll Lock+Home	Move to the first cell within the current window.
Scroll Lock+End	Move to the last cell within the current window.

Understanding selection

As you will see, there are many ways beyond a simple click-and-drag to isolate the particular types of data, formats, objects, and even blank cells that you need to gather or edit. Here are a few pertinent facts and definitions to start with:

- While a *region* is defined as a rectangular block of filled cells, a *range* is any rectangle of cells, filled or empty.

- Before you can work with a cell or range, you must select it, and when you do, it becomes *active*.

- The reference of the active cell appears in the Name box at the left end of the formula bar.

- You can select ranges of cells, but only one cell can be active at a time. The active cell always starts in the upper-left corner of the range, but you can move it without changing the selection.

- Select all cells on a worksheet by clicking the Select All box located in the upper-left corner of your worksheet, where the column and row headings intersect.

For more about selection, read on.

Selecting with the mouse

To select a range of cells, drag the mouse pointer over the range. Or select a cell at one corner, and then press Shift and click the cell at the diagonal corner of the range. For example, with cells A1:B5 selected, hold down the Shift key and click cell C10 to select A1:C10. When you need to select a large range, this technique is more efficient than dragging the mouse pointer across the entire selection.

Zooming to select large worksheet areas

You can zoom out for a bird's-eye view of a large worksheet, as shown in Figure 6-2. Drag the Zoom slider at the bottom of the screen to the left, or click the Zoom percentage indicator adjacent to the slider to open the Zoom dialog box for more zooming options. The Zoom feature is limited to a range from 10 through 400 percent.

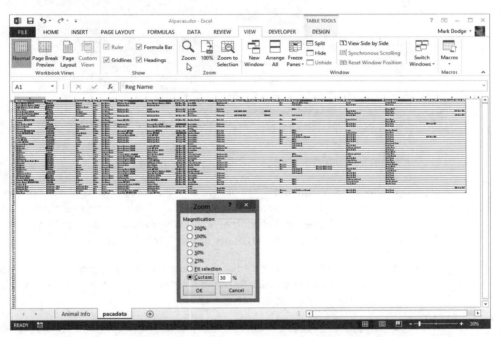

Figure 6-2 Use the Zoom slider or the Zoom dialog box to view large areas of a worksheet for easier selection.

Chapter 6

Selecting columns, rows, and nonadjacent ranges

A *nonadjacent range* (also known as *multiple* or *noncontiguous*) comprises more than one selection rectangle, as shown in Figure 6-3. To select multiple ranges with the mouse, press the Ctrl key and drag through each range you want to select. The first cell you click in the last range you select becomes the active cell. As you can see in Figure 6-3, cell G6 is the active cell.

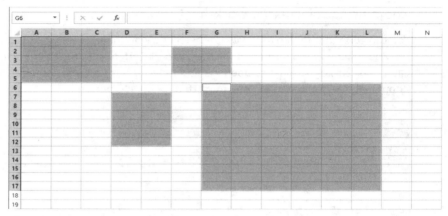

Figure 6-3 Hold down the Ctrl key and drag to select nonadjacent ranges with the mouse pointer.

Use the following methods to select using the mouse:

- To select an entire column or row, click the column or row heading. The first visible cell in the column becomes the active cell. If the first row visible on your screen is row 1000, cell A1000 becomes active when you click the heading for column A, even though all the other cells in the column are selected.

- To select more than one adjacent column or row at a time, drag through the column or row headings, or click the heading at one end of the range, press Shift, and then click the heading at the other end.

- To select nonadjacent columns or rows, hold down Ctrl and click each heading or drag through adjacent headings you want to select.

In Figure 6-4, we clicked the heading in column A and then pressed Ctrl while dragging through the headings for rows 1, 2, and 3.

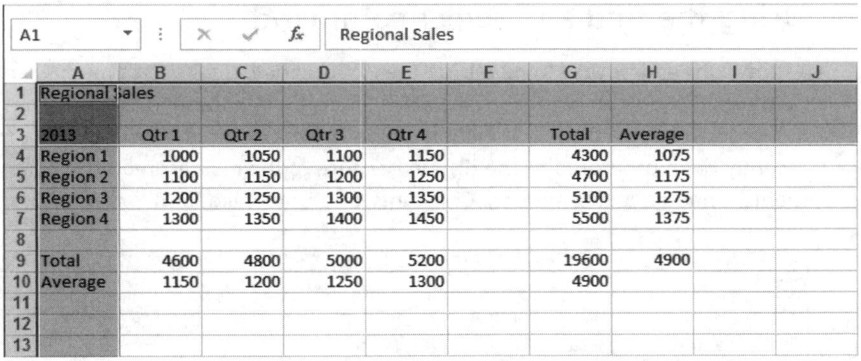

| A1 | ▼ | : | × | ✓ | fx | Regional Sales | | | |

	A	B	C	D	E	F	G	H	I	J
1	Regional Sales									
2										
3	2013	Qtr 1	Qtr 2	Qtr 3	Qtr 4		Total	Average		
4	Region 1	1000	1050	1100	1150		4300	1075		
5	Region 2	1100	1150	1200	1250		4700	1175		
6	Region 3	1200	1250	1300	1350		5100	1275		
7	Region 4	1300	1350	1400	1450		5500	1375		
8										
9	Total	4600	4800	5000	5200		19600	4900		
10	Average	1150	1200	1250	1300		4900			
11										
12										
13										

Figure 6-4 Select entire columns and rows by clicking their headings, or hold down the Ctrl key while clicking to select nonadjacent rows and columns.

Use the following methods to select with the keyboard:

- To select an entire column with the keyboard, select any cell in the column and press Ctrl+Spacebar.

- To select an entire row with the keyboard, select any cell in the row and press Shift+Spacebar.

- To select several entire adjacent columns or rows with the keyboard, select any cell range that includes cells in each of the columns or rows and then press Ctrl+Spacebar or Shift+Spacebar, respectively. For example, to select columns B, C, and D, select B4:D4 (or any range that includes cells in these three columns) and then press Ctrl+Spacebar.

- To select the entire worksheet with the keyboard, press Ctrl+Shift+Spacebar.

Selecting regions

If you hold down the Shift key while navigating regions (as described in "Navigating regions with the keyboard" earlier in this chapter), Excel selects all the cells in between. For example, if cell A3 was the only cell selected in the worksheet shown in Figure 6-4, holding the Shift key while pressing Ctrl+Right Arrow would select the range A3:E3, and then, still holding Shift, pressing Ctrl+Down Arrow would select the range A3:E7.

Chapter 6

Using the find and select commands

At the right end of the Home tab on the ribbon, the Find & Select menu displays several helpful selection commands, as shown in Figure 6-5. In the middle of the menu are five commands that used to be buried in dialog boxes back in the old days, but they've more recently been promoted to the ribbon because of their widespread use: Formulas, Comments, Conditional Formatting, Constants, and Data Validation.

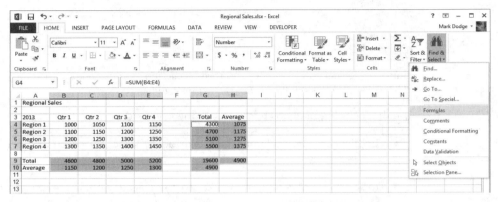

Figure 6-5 Use the Find & Select commands to zero in on specific items.

In Figure 6-5, we used the Formulas command to select all the formulas on the worksheet, which are highlighted by multiple selection rectangles. You can use these specialized selection commands for various purposes, such as applying specific formatting to formulas and constants or auditing worksheets for errant conditional formatting or data-validation cells.

The two Go To commands on the Find & Select menu are also helpful for finding and selecting a variety of worksheet elements. To quickly move to and select a cell or a range of cells, click Go To (or press F5) to open the Go To dialog box; then type a cell reference, range reference, or defined range name in the Reference box, and press Enter. You can also extend a selection using Go To. For example, to select A1:Z100, you can click A1, open the Go To dialog box, type **Z100**, and then press Shift+Enter.

For more about selecting, see "Finding and replacing stuff" in Chapter 8, "Worksheet editing techniques," and "Selecting and grouping objects" in Chapter 10, "Creating and formatting graphics." For more information about defined range names and references, see "Naming cells and cell ranges" and "Using cell references in formulas" in Chapter 12, "Building formulas."

To move to another worksheet in the same workbook, open the Go To dialog box, and type the name of the worksheet, followed by an exclamation point and a cell name or reference. For example, to go to cell A1 on a worksheet called Sheet3, type **Sheet3!A1**. To move to another worksheet in another open workbook, open the Go To dialog box and type the name of the workbook in brackets, followed by the name of the worksheet, an exclamation point, and a cell name or reference. For example, to go to cell H10 on a worksheet called Sheet2 in an open workbook called Regional Sales.xlsx, type **'[Regional Sales.xlsx] Sheet2'!D5**. (Note that because there is a space in the name of the workbook, you must enclose the entire sheet reference in single quotation marks.)

Excel keeps track of the last four locations from which you used the Go To command and lists them in the Go To dialog box. You can use this list to move among these locations in your worksheet. This is handy when you're working on a large worksheet or jumping around among multiple locations and worksheets in a workbook. Figure 6-6 shows the Go To dialog box displaying several previous locations.

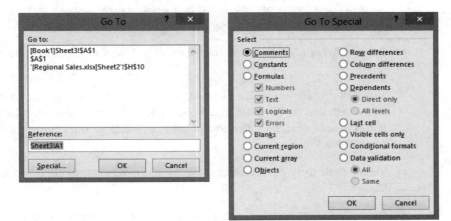

Figure 6-6 The Go To and Go To Special dialog boxes are your selection transporters.

> **Note**
>
> In the Go To dialog box, Excel displays in the Reference box the cell or range from which you just moved. This way, you can easily move back and forth between two locations by pressing F5 and then Enter repeatedly.

Selecting with Go To Special

When you click the Special button in the Go To dialog box (or the Go To Special command on the Find & Select menu), the dialog box shown on the right of Figure 6-6 opens, presenting additional selection options. You can think of the Go To Special dialog box as

"Select Special" because you can use it to quickly find and select cells that meet certain specifications.

After you specify one of the Go To Special options and click OK, Excel highlights the cell or cells that match the criteria. With a few exceptions, if you select a range of cells before you open the Go To Special dialog box, Excel searches only within the selected range; if the current selection is a single cell or one or more graphic objects, Excel searches the entire active worksheet. The following are guidelines for using the Go To Special options:

- **Constants**   Refers to any cell containing static data, such as numbers or text, but not formulas.

- **Current Region**   Handy when you're working in a large, complex worksheet and need to select blocks of cells. (Recall that a *region* is defined as a rectangular block of cells bounded by blank rows, blank columns, or worksheet borders.)

- **Current Array**   Selects all the cells in an array if the selected cell is part of an array range.

- **Last Cell**   Selects the cell in the lower-right corner of the range that encompasses all the cells that contain data, comments, or formats. When you select Last Cell, Excel finds the last cell in the active area of the worksheet, not the lower-right corner of the current selection.

- **Visible Cells Only**   Excludes from the current selection any cells in hidden rows or columns.

- **Objects**   Selects all graphic objects in your worksheet, regardless of the current selection.

- **Conditional Formats**   Selects only cells that have conditional formatting applied. You can also click the Home tab and then click the Conditional Formatting command on the Find & Select menu.

- **Data Validation**   Using the All option, selects all cells to which data validation has been applied; Data Validation using the Same option selects only cells with the same validation settings as the currently selected cell. You can also click the Home tab and then click the Data Validation command on the Find & Select menu, which uses the All option.

For more information about graphic objects, see Chapter 10. For more information about conditional formatting, see "Formatting conditionally" in Chapter 9, "Worksheet formatting techniques."

Navigating multiple selections

Some of the Go To Special options—such as Formulas, Comments, Precedents, and Dependents—might cause Excel to select multiple nonadjacent ranges. But you might want to change the active cell without losing the multiselection. Or you might want to type entries into multiple ranges that you preselect so that you don't have to reach for the mouse. Either way, you can move among cells within ranges, and between ranges, without losing the selection. For example, the worksheet shown here has three ranges selected:

	A	B	C	D	E	F	G
1	Northwind Traders						
2	Startegic Planning Budget						
3							
4		Expenditures					
5		Employee	Brick & Mortar	Merchandise	Advertising	Total	
6	Q1 2013	125000.00	45000.00	510000.00	40800.00	720800.00	
7	Q2 2013	131250.00	56250.00	586500.00	46920.00	820920.00	
8	Q3 2013	143062.50	57937.50	615825.00	49266.00	866091.00	
9	Q4 2013	150215.63	72421.88	708198.75	56655.90	987492.15	
10	Q1 2014	210301.88	108632.81	1026888.19	82151.06	1427973.93	
11	Q2 2014	220816.97	114064.45	1078232.60	86258.61	1499372.63	
12	Q3 2014	231857.82	119767.68	1132144.23	90571.54	1574341.26	
13	Q4 2014	243450.71	125756.06	1188751.44	95100.12	1653058.32	
14	Q1 2015	255623.24	188634.09	1723689.59	137895.17	2305842.08	
15	Q2 2015	268404.41	207497.50	1809874.06	144789.93	2430565.89	
16	Q3 2015	281824.63	228247.25	1900367.77	152029.42	2562469.06	
17	Q4 2015	295915.86	251071.97	1995386.16	159630.89	2702004.88	
18							

To move the active cell through these ranges without losing the selection, press Enter to move down or to the right one cell at a time; press Shift+Enter to move up or to the left one cell at a time. Or press Tab to move to the right or down; press Shift+Tab to move to the left or up. So, in this worksheet, if you press Enter until cell A17 is selected, the next time you press Enter the selection jumps to the beginning of the next selected region—in this case, cell A1. Subsequently pressing Enter selects A2, then B1, then B2, and so on, moving down and across until the end of the region (cell F2), and then to the next region (cell B4).

Selecting precedents and dependents

The Precedents and Dependents options in the Go To Special dialog box let you find all cells that are used by a formula or to find all cells upon which a formula depends. To use the Precedents and Dependents options, first select the cell whose precedents or dependents you want to find. When searching for precedents or dependents, Excel always searches the entire worksheet. When you select the Precedents or Dependents option, Excel activates the Direct Only and All Levels options:

- Direct Only finds only cells that directly refer to or that directly depend on the active cell.

- All Levels locates direct precedents and dependents plus cells indirectly related to the active cell.

Depending on the task, you might find the built-in auditing features of Excel to be just the trick. On the Formulas tab on the ribbon, the Formula Auditing group offers the Trace Precedents and Trace Dependents buttons. Rather than selecting all such cells, as the Go To Special command does, clicking these buttons draws arrows showing path and direction in relation to the selected cell.

For more information, see "Auditing and documenting worksheets" in Chapter 8.

Go To Special keyboard shortcuts

If you do a lot of "going to," you'll want to learn a few of these keyboard shortcuts, which speed things up considerably:

- Press Ctrl+Shift+* to select the current region.

- Press Ctrl+/ to select the current array.

- Press Alt+; to select the visible cells only.

- Press Ctrl+[to select the direct precedents.

- Press Ctrl+Shift+{ to select all the precedents.

- Press Ctrl+] to select the direct dependents.

- Press Ctrl+Shift+} to select all the dependents.

- Press Ctrl+\ to select row differences.

- Press Ctrl+Shift+| to select column differences.

Selecting row or column differences

The Row Differences and Column Differences options in the Go To Special dialog box compare the entries in a range of cells to spot potential inconsistencies. To use these debugging options, select the range before displaying the Go To Special dialog box. The position of the active cell in your selection determines which cells Excel uses to make its comparisons. When searching for row differences, Excel compares the cells in the selection with the cells in the same column as the active cell. When searching for column differences, Excel compares the cells in the selection with the cells in the same row as the active cell.

In addition to other variations, the Row Differences and Column Differences options look for differences in references and select cells that don't conform to the comparison cell. They also verify that all the cells in the selected range contain the same type of entries. For example, if the comparison cell contains a SUM function, Excel flags any cells that contain a function, formula, or value other than SUM. If the comparison cell contains a constant text or numeric value, Excel flags any cells in the selected range that don't match the comparison value. The options, however, are not case-sensitive.

Techniques for entering data

Excel accepts two types of cell entries: constants and formulas. Constants fall into three main categories: numeric values, text values (also called *labels* or *strings*), and date/time values. Excel also recognizes two special types of constants, called *logical values* and *error values*.

For more about date/time values, see Chapter 15, "Formatting and calculating date and time."

Making entries in cells and in the formula bar

In "classic" versions of Excel, all entries and edits happened only in the formula bar; later, in-cell editing was added, and subtle behavioral differences still remain between these modes of entry.

To make an entry in a cell, just select the cell and start typing. As you type, the entry appears both in the formula bar and in the active cell. The flashing vertical bar in the active cell is called the *insertion point*.

After you finish typing, you must press Enter to lock in the entry to store it permanently in the cell. Pressing Enter normally causes the active cell to move down one row. You can change this so that when you press Enter, either the active cell doesn't change or it moves to an adjacent cell in another direction. Click the File tab, click Options, select the Advanced category, and either clear the After Pressing Enter, Move Selection check box or change the selection in the Direction drop-down list. You also lock in an entry when you move the selection to a different cell by pressing Tab, Shift+Tab, Shift+Enter, or an arrow key, among other methods, after you type the entry, as described in Table 6-3.

TABLE 6-3 Keyboard shortcuts for data entry

Press	To
Enter	Activate the cell below the active cell, or whatever direction you have selected for the After Pressing Enter, Move Selection option in the Advanced category in the Excel Options dialog box.
Shift+Enter	Activate the cell above the active cell, or the opposite of the direction set for the After Pressing Enter, Move Selection option in the Advanced category in the Excel Options dialog box.
Tab	Activate the cell one column to the right of the active cell.
Shift+Tab	Activate the cell one column to the left of the active cell.
Arrow Key	Activate the adjacent cell in the direction of the arrow key you press.

When you begin typing an entry, three buttons appear on the formula bar: Cancel, Enter, and Insert Function. When you type a formula in which the entry begins with an equal sign (=), a plus sign (+), or a minus sign (−), a drop-down list of frequently used functions becomes available, as shown in Figure 6-7.

For more about editing formulas, see Chapter 12.

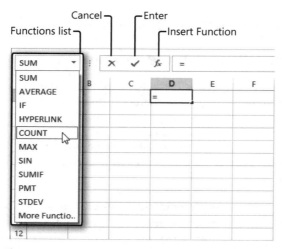

Figure 6-7 When you start entering a formula by typing an equal sign, the formula bar offers ways to help you finish it.

Entering simple numeric and text values

An entry that includes only the numerals 0 through 9 and certain special characters—such as + – E e ( ) . , $ % and /—is a numeric value. An entry that includes almost any other character is a text value. Table 6-4 lists some examples of numeric and text values.

TABLE 6-4 Examples of numeric and text values

Numeric values	Text values
123	Sales
123.456	B-1
$1.98	Eleven
1%	123 Main Street
1.23E+12	No. 324

Using special characters

A number of characters have special effects in Excel. Here are some guidelines for using special characters:

- If you begin a numeric entry with a plus sign, Excel drops the plus sign.

- If you begin a numeric entry with a minus sign, Excel interprets the entry as a negative number and retains the sign.

- In a numeric entry, the characters *E* and *e* specify an exponent used in scientific notation. For example, Excel interprets 1E6 as 1,000,000 (1 times 10 to the sixth power), which is displayed in Excel as 1.00E+06. To enter a negative exponential number, type a minus sign before the exponent. For example, 1E–6 (1 times 10 to the negative sixth power) equals .000001 and is displayed in Excel as 1.00E–06.

- Excel interprets numeric constants enclosed in parentheses as negative numbers, which is a common accounting practice. For example, Excel interprets (100) as –100.

- You can use decimal points and commas as you normally would. When you type numbers that include commas as separators, however, the commas appear in the cell but not in the formula bar. This is the same effect as when you apply one of the built-in Excel Number formats. For example, if you type **1,234.56**, the value 1234.56 appears in the formula bar.

- If you begin a numeric entry with a dollar sign ($), Excel assigns a Currency format to the cell. For example, if you type **$123456**, Excel displays $123,456 in the cell and 123456 in the formula bar. In this case, Excel adds the comma to the worksheet display because it's part of the Currency format.

- If you end a numeric entry with a percent sign (%), Excel assigns a Percentage format to the cell. For example, if you type **23%**, Excel displays 23% in the formula bar and assigns a Percentage format to the cell, which also displays 23%.

- If you use a slash (/) in a numeric entry and the string cannot be interpreted as a date, Excel interprets the number as a fraction. For example, if you type **11 5/8** (with a space between the number and the fraction), Excel assigns a Fraction format to the entry, meaning the formula bar displays 11.625 and the cell displays 11 5/8.

> **Note**
>
> To be sure that Excel does not interpret a fraction as a date, precede the fraction with a zero and a space. For example, to prevent Excel from interpreting the fraction 1/2 as January 2, type 0 1/2.

For more about the built-in Excel Number formats, see "Formatting in depth" in Chapter 9. For more information about date and time formats, see "How AutoFill handles dates and times" in Chapter 8.

Understanding the difference between displayed values and underlying values

Although you can type 32,767 characters in a cell, a numeric cell entry can maintain precision to a maximum of only 15 digits. This means you can type numbers longer than 15 digits in a cell, but Excel converts any digits after the 15th to zeros. If you are working with figures greater than 999 trillion or decimals smaller than trillionths, perhaps you need to look into alternative solutions, such as a Cray supercomputer!

If you type a number that is too long to appear in a cell, Excel converts it to scientific notation in the cell if you haven't applied any other formatting. Excel adjusts the precision of the scientific notation depending on the cell width. If you type a very large or very small number that is longer than the formula bar, Excel displays it in the formula bar using scientific notation. In Figure 6-8, we typed the same number in cell A1 and cell B1; because cell B1 is wider, Excel displays more of the number but still displays it using scientific notation.

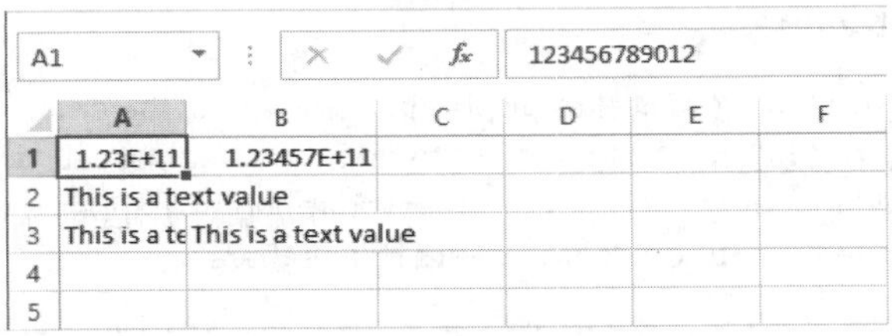

Figure 6-8 Because the number 123,456,789,012 is too long to fit in cell A1, Excel displays it in scientific notation.

For more information about increasing the width of a cell, see "Changing column widths" in Chapter 9.

The values that appear in formatted cells are called *displayed values*; the values that are stored in cells and appear in the formula bar are called *underlying values*. The number of digits that appear in a cell—its displayed value—depends on the width of the column and any formatting you apply to the cell. If you reduce the width of a column that contains a long entry, Excel might display a rounded version of the number, a string of number signs (#), or scientific notation, depending on the display format you're using.

> **Note**
>
> If you see a series of number signs (######) in a cell where you expect to see a number, increase the width of the cell to see the numbers again.

TROUBLESHOOTING

My formulas don't add numbers correctly

Suppose, for example, you write a formula and Excel tells you that $2.23 plus $5.55 equals $7.79, when it should be $7.78. Investigate your underlying values. If you use currency formatting, numbers with more than three digits to the right of the decimal point are rounded to two decimal places. In this example, if the underlying values are 2.234 and 5.552, the result is 7.786, which rounds to 7.79. You can either change the decimal places or select the Set Precision As Displayed check box (click the File tab, click Options, click the Advanced category, and look in the When Calculating This Workbook area) to eliminate the problem. Be careful if you select Set Precision As Displayed, however, because it permanently changes all the underlying values in your worksheet to their displayed values.

Creating long text values

If you type text that is too long for Excel to display in a single cell, the entry spills into adjacent cells if they are empty, but the text remains stored in the original cell. If you then type text in a cell that is overlapped by another cell, the overlapped text appears truncated, as shown in cell A3 in Figure 6-8. But don't worry—it's still all there.

> **Note**
>
> The easiest way to eliminate overlapping text is to widen the column by double-clicking the column border in the heading. For example, in Figure 6-8, when you double-click the line between the A and the B in the column headings, the width of column A adjusts to accommodate the longest entry in the column.

Using text wrapping

If you have long text entries, text wrapping can make them easier to read. Text wrapping lets you enter long strings of text that wrap onto two or more lines within the same cell rather than overlap adjacent cells. Select the cells where you want to use wrapping, and then click the Home tab on the ribbon and click the Wrap Text button, as shown in Figure 6-9. To accommodate the extra lines, Excel increases the height of the row.

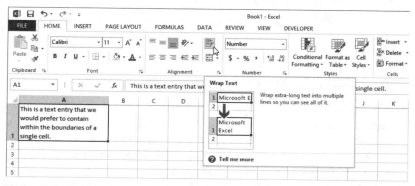

Figure 6-9 Click the Wrap Text button to force long text entries to wrap within a single cell.

For more about wrapping text, see "Wrapping text in cells" in Chapter 9.

Understanding numeric text entries

Sometimes you might want to type special characters that Excel does not normally treat as plain text. For example, you might want +1 to appear in a cell. If you type **+1**, Excel interprets this as a numeric entry and drops the plus sign (as stated earlier). In addition, Excel normally ignores leading zeros in numbers, such as 01234. You can force Excel to accept special characters as text by using numeric text entries.

To enter a combination of text and numbers, such as G234, just type it. Because this entry includes a nonnumeric character, Excel interprets it as a text value. To create a text entry that consists entirely of numbers, you can precede the entry with a text-alignment prefix character, such as an apostrophe. You can also enter it as a formula by typing an equal sign and enclosing the entry with quotation marks. For example, to enter the number 01234 as text so that the leading zero is displayed, type either **'01234** or **="01234"** in a cell. Whereas numeric entries are normally right-aligned, a numeric text entry is left-aligned in the cell, just like regular text, as shown in Figure 6-10.

A5		× ✓ *fx*	'023048								
	A	**B**	**C**	**D**	**E**	**F**	**G**	**H**	**I**	**J**	**K**
1	**Group Policy Summary**										
2											
3	Month	Claims Totals	Column2	Column3	Column4	Column5	Column6	Column7	Column8	Column9	Column10
4	Policy Number	Jan-2014	Feb-2014	Mar-2014	Apr-2014	May-2014	Jun-2014	Jul-2014	Aug-2014	Sep-2014	Oct-2014
5	023048	348.62	6,854.23	710.49	5,454.40	5,333.73	5,305.44	11,452.56	2,943.41	10,166.89	5,272.03
6	004578			4,465.13	5,163.29	10,340.16	3,314.19	9,895.51	6,597.95	2,217.92	8,227.87
7	024589			1,372.33	11,875.26	6,297.04	9,776.26	8,218.69	6,724.23	7,861.23	2,134.41
8	047789			3,086.75	10,596.05	10,433.01	1,745.96	2,490.52	6,575.38	2,675.95	644.96
9	014235			7,509.39	3,268.27	3,281.65	11,255.22	3,017.16	6,173.03	1,621.35	828.13
10	023487			9,402.33	2,272.50	1,027.82	10,958.64	3,729.51	2,497.89	4,838.69	7,466.45
11	123889			8,611.37	11,581.95	2,111.75	2,542.35	9,404.07	7,032.02	6,141.42	12,187.93
12	044512			1,966.89	11,870.83	12,179.69	8,668.29	2,716.95	8,241.95	619.34	11,367.38
13	011347			10,616.99	6,226.22	5,495.64	2,991.71	3,062.91	11,011.04	12,213.95	11,771.73
14	228911			10,806.74	5,655.53	5,433.58	10,677.51	8,032.15	1,784.16	7,271.15	9,120.97
15	023158	6,426.95	1,700.69	2,292.57	646.21	3,677.17	6,985.51	6,138.49	8,036.78	10,213.45	5,748.17
16	011099	9,715.08	12,287.90	9,679.64	9,874.45	9,578.48	3,943.85	8,879.42	2,316.84	4,488.45	12,053.95
17	112899	3,826.44	3,882.25	8,843.21	4,659.34	11,389.01	8,373.12	5,006.37	2.67	4,109.04	1,650.81
18	112345	1,031.12	6,378.98	11,992.86	872.69	5,822.82	6,511.30	2,966.10	10,837.19	8,393.02	2,872.55
19	001234	2,861.41	7,258.49	8,177.16	6,268.16	10,076.80	9,361.12	4,914.66	576.79	860.77	12,265.87
20	002234	6,704.16	8,252.14	1,924.76	5,458.94	506.55	2,382.70	9,327.08	3,993.26	394.55	1,134.24
21	023456	2,338.87	10,909.39	1,510.53	11,140.13	8,427.64	9,550.20	10,167.41	10,389.19	3,422.44	11,331.39
22	123456	1,585.56	7,322.98	12,010.86	4,804.48	4,865.20	8,598.20	5,694.61	6,566.00	9,330.81	3,599.43
23	234567	2,570.89	5,752.81	10,247.15	3,458.66	8,989.34	7,849.81	1,038.36	3,369.83	734.60	7,621.06
24	012345	9,719.31	4,428.72	5,665.96	9,060.82	6,207.50	6,893.91	7,715.61	3,957.67	8,863.96	10,965.81
25	002897	11,476.47	3,135.85	11,370.01	6,935.67	10,420.31	398.37	1,610.70	7,352.24	3,067.38	5,575.70

(Context menu over cells B5:C10: Number Stored as Text / Convert to Number / Help on this error / Ignore Error / Edit in Formula Bar / Error Checking Options...)

Figure 6-10 We typed the policy numbers in column A as text.

Text-alignment prefix characters, like formula components, appear in the formula bar but not in the cell. Table 6-5 lists all the text-alignment prefix characters.

Only the apostrophe text-alignment prefix character always works with numeric or text entries. The caret, backslash, and quotation mark characters work only if Transition

Navigation Keys are turned on. To do so, click the File tab, click Options, select the Advanced category, and then scroll down to the Lotus Compatibility area and select the Transition Navigation Keys check box.

TABLE 6-5 **Text-alignment prefix characters**

Character	Action
' (apostrophe)	Left-aligns data in the cell.
" (quotation mark)	Right-aligns data in the cell. (See the following note.)
^ (caret)	Centers data in the cell. (See the following note.)
\ (backslash)	Repeats characters across the cell. (See the following note.)

You'll find the Humongous.xlsx file with the other examples on the companion website.

When you create a numeric entry that starts with an alignment prefix character, a small flag appears in the upper-left corner of the cell, indicating that the cell has a problem you might need to address. When you select the cell, an error button appears to the right. Clicking this button displays a menu of specific commands. (Refer to Figure 6-10.) Because the apostrophe was intentional, you can click Ignore Error.

> **Note**
>
> If a range of cells shares the same problem, as in column A in Figure 6-10, you can select the entire cell range and use the action menu to resolve the problem in all the cells at the same time. For more information, see "Using custom AutoCorrect actions" in Chapter 8.

Entering symbols

If you ever want to use characters in Excel that are not on your standard computer keyboard, you're in luck. Click the Insert tab on the ribbon, and in the Symbols group, click the Symbol button to gain access to the complete character set for every installed font on your computer. Figure 6-11 shows the Symbol dialog box.

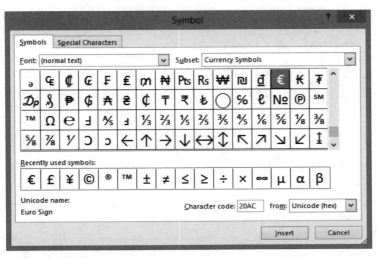

Figure 6-11 You can insert characters from the extended character sets of any installed font.

On the Symbols tab, select the font from the Font drop-down list; the entire character set appears. You can jump to specific areas in the character set by using the Subset drop-down list, which also indicates the area of the character set you are viewing if you are using the scroll bar to browse through the available characters. The Character Code box displays the code for the selected character. You can also highlight a character in the display area by typing the character's code number. You can select decimal or hexadecimal ASCII character encoding or Unicode by using the From drop-down list. If you choose Unicode, you can select from a number of additional character subsets in the Subset drop-down list. The Special Characters tab in the Symbol dialog box gives you quick access to a number of commonly used characters, such as the em dash, the ellipsis, and the trademark and copyright symbols.

Making entries in ranges

To make a number of entries in a range of adjacent cells, first select all of them. Then just begin typing entries, as shown in Figure 6-12. Each time you press Enter, the active cell moves to the next cell in the range, and the range remains selected. When you reach the edge of the range and press Enter, the active cell jumps to the beginning of the next column or row. You can continue making entries this way until you fill the entire range.

Chapter 6

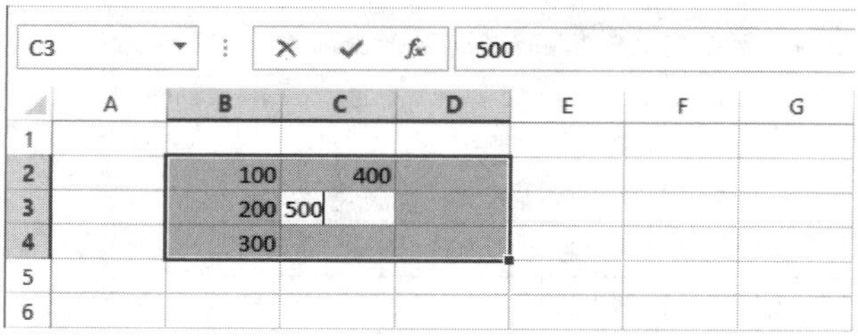

Figure 6-12 You can easily make entries in a range of cells by first selecting the entire range.

> **Note**
>
> To enter the same value in all selected cells at once, type your first entry and then press Ctrl+Enter.

Editing and undoing entries

You can correct simple errors as you type by pressing Backspace. However, to make changes to entries you have already locked in, you first need to enter Edit mode. (The mode indicator at the lower-left corner of the status bar has to change from Ready to Edit.) To enter Edit mode, do one of the following:

- Double-click the cell, and position the insertion point at the location of the error.

- Select the cell, and press F2. Use the arrow keys to position the insertion point within the cell.

To select contiguous characters within a cell, place the insertion point just before or just after the characters you want to replace, and press Shift+Left Arrow or Shift+Right Arrow to extend your selection.

> **Note**
>
> If you don't want to take your hands off the keyboard to move from one end of a cell entry to the other, press Home or End while in Edit mode. To move through an entry one "word" at a time, press Ctrl+Left Arrow or Ctrl+Right Arrow.

If you need to erase the entire contents of the active cell, press Delete, or press Backspace and then Enter. If you press Backspace accidentally, click the Cancel button or press Esc to restore the contents of the cell before pressing Enter. You can also erase the entire contents of a cell by selecting the cell and typing new contents to replace the old. To revert to the original entry, press Esc before you press Enter.

You can always click the Undo button in the Quick Access Toolbar; alternatively, press Ctrl+Z. The Undo button remembers the last 100 actions you performed. If you press Ctrl+Z repeatedly, each of the last actions is undone, one after the other, in reverse order. You can also click the small arrow next to the Undo button to display a list of remembered actions. Drag the mouse to select one or more actions, as shown in Figure 6-13. After you release the mouse, all the selected actions are undone. The Redo button works the same way; you can quickly redo what you have just undone, if necessary.

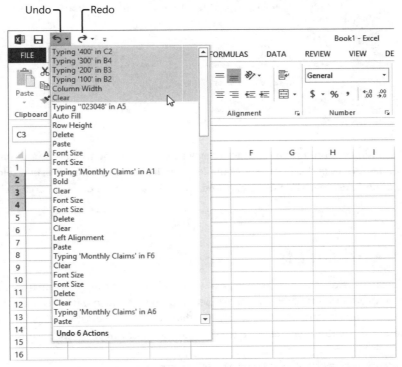

Figure 6-13 Click the small arrow next to the Undo button to select any number of the last 100 actions to undo at once.

Note

You can't undo individual actions in the middle of the Undo list. If you select an action, all actions up to and including that action are undone.

Chapter 6

Floating option buttons

There are several types of "floating" option buttons that appear as you work in Excel. These are provided to give you instant access to commands and actions that are relevant to the current task. Many editing actions trigger the display of an option button. For example, copying and pasting cells causes the Paste Options button to appear adjacent to the last cell edited. If you click the button, a menu offers retroactive editing options:

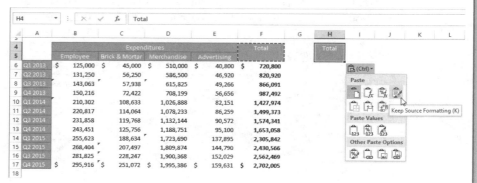

Floating option buttons appear in many situations, so you will hear about them in other places in this book. For examples, see "Tracing errors" and "Pasting selectively using Paste Special" in Chapter 8, and "Entering a series of dates" in Chapter 15.

Managing worksheets

You can have as many worksheets in a workbook as your computer's memory will allow (probably hundreds of worksheets, depending on how much data each contains); consequently, you don't need to try to fit everything onto one worksheet. The following sections present the features you can use to organize your worksheet world.

Inserting and deleting worksheets

To insert a new worksheet into an existing workbook, click the New Sheet button, which you can see at the left of Figure 6-14. The new sheet tab appears to the right of the last worksheet in the workbook. You can also quickly insert worksheets by right-clicking any sheet tab to display the shortcut menu shown at the right in Figure 6-14. Clicking Insert on this menu opens the Insert dialog box, which contains other items you can insert besides blank worksheets, including templates and Excel 4 macro sheets.

 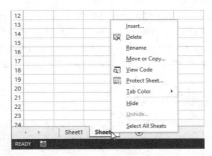

Figure 6-14 To insert a blank worksheet, click the New Sheet button, or right-click any sheet tab to display a worksheet-focused shortcut menu.

In addition to providing a convenient method for inserting, deleting, renaming, moving, and copying worksheets, this shortcut menu contains the Select All Sheets command. As its name indicates, you use this command to select all the worksheets in a workbook, which you need to do to perform certain functions, such as copying or formatting, on all the worksheets at once. The View Code command on this shortcut menu launches the Visual Basic Editor, showing the Code window for the current worksheet.

For more information about the Visual Basic Editor, see Chapter 28, "Recording macros."

> **Note**
>
> As you can see in the shortcut menu shown in Figure 6-14, the sheet tab shortcut menu also contains a Tab Color command. If you are a visually oriented person, you might find color-coding your worksheet tabs to be as useful as changing the worksheet names.

You can also add multiple worksheets to a workbook at the same time (starting with a workbook with multiple sheets in it). To do so, click a sheet tab, press Shift, and then click other sheet tabs to select a range of worksheets—the same number you want to insert—before clicking Insert Worksheet on the sheet tab shortcut menu. (Notice that Excel adds *[Group]* to the workbook title in the window title bar, indicating you have selected a group of worksheets for editing.) Excel inserts the new worksheets in front of the first worksheet in the selected range. Note that this does not copy the selected worksheets; it is just a way of telling Excel how many fresh, blank worksheets you want to insert at once.

For more information about group editing, see "Editing multiple worksheets" in Chapter 8.

Chapter 6

You cannot undo the insertion of a new worksheet. If you do need to delete a worksheet, right-click its sheet tab and click Delete. If you want to delete more than one worksheet, you can hold down Shift to select a range of worksheets, or you can hold down Ctrl and select nonadjacent worksheets, before you click Delete.

CAUTION!

Be careful! You cannot retrieve a worksheet after you delete it.

Naming and renaming worksheets

Notice that Excel numbers the new worksheets based on the number of worksheets in the workbook. If your workbook contains one worksheet, the first worksheet you insert is Sheet2, the next is Sheet3, and so on. If you grow weary of seeing Sheet1, Sheet2, and so on in your workbooks, you can give your worksheets more imaginative and helpful names by double-clicking the tab and typing a new name.

You can use up to 31 characters in your worksheet names. Nevertheless, you should remember that the name you use determines the width of the corresponding sheet tab, as shown in Figure 6-15. Therefore, you might want to keep your worksheet names concise so that you can see more than a couple of sheet tabs at a time.

Figure 6-15 Double-click the sheet tab to type a new name. You might want to keep it short.

Moving and copying worksheets

As you might expect, Excel provides an easy way to move a worksheet from one place to another in the same workbook. In fact, all you have to do is click a sheet tab to select it and then drag it to its new location. Figure 6-16 shows this process. When you drag a worksheet, a small worksheet icon appears, and a tiny arrow indicates where the worksheet will be inserted in the tab order.

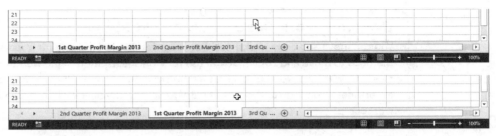

Figure 6-16 Click and drag sheet tabs to rearrange worksheets.

When you move worksheets, remember the following tips:

- If you want to move a worksheet to a location that isn't currently visible on your screen, drag past the visible tabs in either direction. The sheet tabs scroll in the direction you drag.

- You can move several worksheets at the same time. When you select several worksheets and drag, the worksheet pointer icon changes to look like a small stack of pages.

- You can copy worksheets using similar mouse techniques. First, select the worksheets you want to copy, and then hold down Ctrl while you drag the worksheets to the new location.

- When you copy a worksheet, an identical worksheet appears in the new location. Excel appends a number in parentheses to the copy's name to distinguish it from the original worksheet. For example, making a copy of Sheet1 results in a new worksheet named Sheet1 (2).

- You can select nonadjacent worksheets by pressing Ctrl while you click to select the sheet tabs. Then you can click any selected tab and drag to move the group, or click, press Ctrl, and drag to create copies.

- You can click Move Or Copy on the sheet tab shortcut menu to handle similar worksheet management functions, including moving and copying worksheets between workbooks.

Chapter 6

Dragging worksheets between workbooks

You can move and copy worksheets between workbooks by dragging. You use the same methods to move and copy that you use for worksheets in the same workbook. For example, with two workbooks arranged horizontally in the workspace, you can move a worksheet from one to the other by dragging it to the new location in the other workbook:

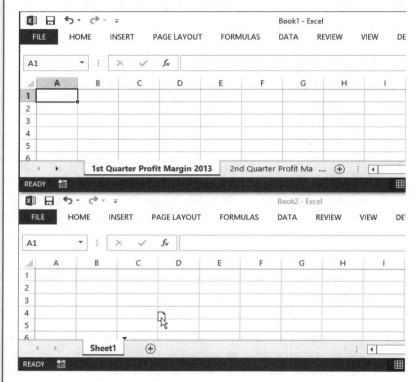

This removes the sheet from the source workbook and relocates it in the destination workbook; to copy it, press Ctrl while dragging. Note that you must arrange the two workbooks together on your screen to allow this to work. To do so, click the View tab on the ribbon, and then click the Arrange All button in the Window group and select an arrangement option (Horizontal in the illustration just shown).

Viewing worksheets

Excel provides a few helpful features you can use to change the way worksheets are displayed. You can set up your workspace for specific tasks and then save the same view settings for the next time you need to perform the same task.

Splitting worksheets into panes

Worksheet panes let you view different areas of your worksheet simultaneously. You can split any worksheet in a workbook vertically, horizontally, or both vertically and horizontally and have synchronized scrolling capabilities in each pane. On the worksheet shown in Figure 6-17, columns B through M and rows 3 through 36 contain data. In Normal view, it's impossible to see all the data at the same time.

B3		✕	✓	f_x	7317						
	A	B	C	D	E	F	G	H	I	J	K
1	**2014 Product Sales Projections**										
2		Jan	Feb	Mar	Apr	May	Jun	Jul	Aug	Sep	Oct
3	Product 1	$7,317	$6,329	$2,110	$1,710	$2,984	$1,100	$2,467	$9,954	$9,696	$11,923	$
4	Product 2	$2,814	$2,336	$9,199	$6,176	$2,842	$1,408	$3,737	$4,543	$4,991	$5,734
5	Product 3	$2,875	$4,107	$5,528	$8,599	$9,769	$5,557	$3,456	$5,467	$2,311	$4,322
6	Product 4	$4,365	$2,202	$5,607	$8,340	$5,832	$2,350	$1,669	$5,094	$3,013	$2,723
7	Product 5	$9,451	$3,398	$3,472	$4,585	$3,453	$8,476	$8,118	$5,796	$8,129	$8,796
8	Product 6	$7,810	$6,982	$7,018	$1,885	$4,336	$6,394	$6,989	$3,333	$4,660	$4,418
9	Product 7	$9,976	$7,267	$5,006	$6,692	$8,388	$9,072	$8,968	$5,923	$6,213	$5,463
10	Product 8	$2,536	$4,100	$6,328	$3,807	$7,850	$1,649	$5,253	$6,754	$5,456	$5,487
11	Product 9	$3,104	$2,467	$5,349	$7,142	$9,305	$2,712	$4,629	$4,453	$2,115	$2,876
12	Product 10	$5,442	$2,783	$1,642	$1,582	$2,456	$5,584	$9,140	$7,915	$11,257	$13,250	$
13	Product 11	$7,816	$8,626	$6,938	$5,200	$8,197	$7,728	$5,955	$5,678	$4,557	$3,624
14	Product 12	$2,786	$6,720	$4,754	$3,556	$2,535	$5,029	$4,740	$7,047	$8,150	$9,474	$
15	Product 13	$7,363	$3,248	$7,295	$9,822	$2,076	$8,372	$1,846	$4,462	$4,347	$4,410
16	Product 14	$9,917	$5,004	$6,873	$8,719	$8,399	$4,204	$8,290	$3,456	$3,402	$2,327
17	Product 15	$6,593	$8,499	$1,404	$1,749	$5,999	$4,398	$9,773	$5,622	$7,509	$7,933
18	Product 16	$2,036	$5,359	$8,656	$4,240	$2,690	$2,211	$4,893	$2,345	$3,447	$3,611
19	Product 17	$733	$5,814	$2,773	$4,464	$2,067	$8,424	$1,337	$3,254	$2,889	$2,536
20	Product 18	$1,831	$1,422	$1,572	$5,771	$6,611	$9,131	$9,121	$6,654	$7,909	$7,921
21	Product 19	$1,533	$2,938	$5,923	$9,180	$7,783	$1,542	$5,745	$5,953	$4,934	$4,805

Sheet1 ⊕

Figure 6-17 You can scroll to display the totals in column N or row 38, but you won't be able to see the headings.

You'll find the 2014Projections.xlsx file with the other examples on the companion website.

It would be easier to navigate the worksheet in Figure 6-17 if it were split into panes. To do so, first select the cell where you want the split to happen, then click the View tab on the ribbon, and click the Split button in the Window group; the window divides into both vertical and horizontal panes simultaneously, as shown in Figure 6-18. When you rest your pointer on a split bar, it changes to a double-headed arrow.

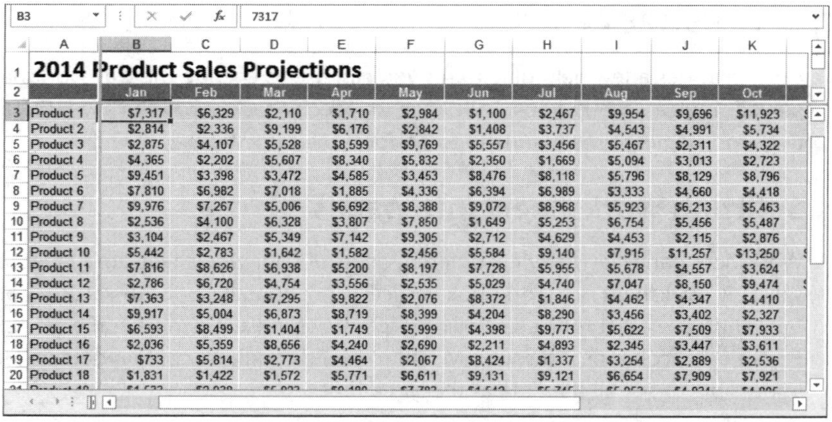

Figure 6-18 With the window split, you can scroll each pane independently.

> **Note**
>
> Before clicking Window, Split or double-clicking one of the split bar icons, select a cell in the worksheet where you want the split to occur. This splits the worksheet immediately to the left or above the selected cell or both above and to the left. If cell A1 is active, the split occurs in the center of the worksheet. In Figure 6-17, we selected cell B3 before choosing the Split command, which resulted in the split panes shown in Figure 6-18.

With the window split into four panes, as shown in Figure 6-18, four scroll bars are available (if not visible)—two for each direction. Now you can use the scroll bars to view columns B through N without losing sight of the product headings in column A. In addition, when you scroll vertically between rows 3 and 37, you always see the corresponding headings in row 2.

After a window is split, you can reposition the split bars by dragging. If you are ready to return your screen to its normal appearance, click the Split button again to remove all the split bars. You can also remove an individual split by double-clicking the split bar or by dragging the split bar to the top or right side of the window.

Freezing panes

After you split a window into panes, you can freeze the left panes, the top panes, or both panes by clicking the View tab on the ribbon, clicking Freeze Panes, and selecting the corresponding option, as shown in Figure 6-19. When you do so, you lock the data in the frozen panes into place. As you can see in Figure 6-19, the pane divider lines have changed from thick, three-dimensional lines to thin lines.

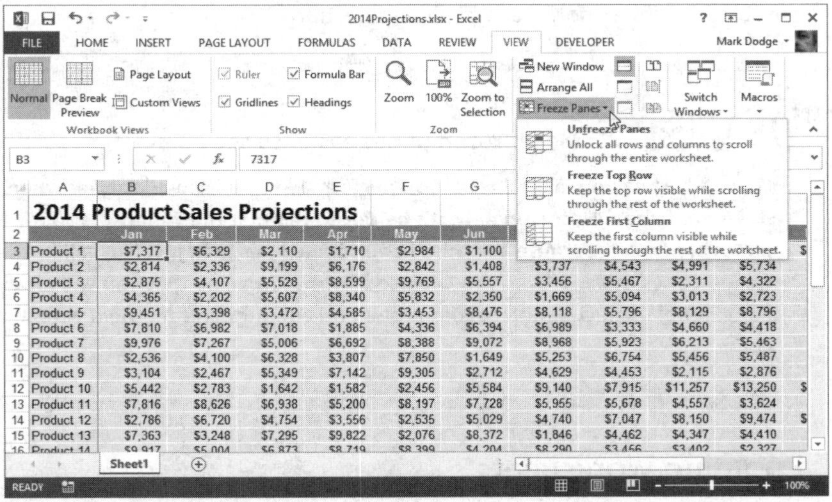

Figure 6-19 Freezing panes locks the top pane, left pane, or both panes of a split window.

> **Note**
>
> You can split and freeze panes simultaneously at the selected cell by clicking Freeze Panes without first splitting the worksheet into panes. If you use this method, you simultaneously unfreeze and remove the panes when you click Unfreeze Panes. (The command name changes when panes are frozen.)

Notice also that in Figure 6-18, the sheet tab is invisible because the horizontal scroll bar is so large. After freezing the panes, as shown in Figure 6-19, the scroll bar returns to normal and the sheet tab reappears.

> **Note**
>
> To display another worksheet in the workbook if the sheet tabs are not visible, press Ctrl+Page Up to display the previous worksheet or Ctrl+Page Down to display the next worksheet.

Chapter 6

After you freeze panes, scrolling within each pane works differently. You cannot scroll the upper-left panes in any direction. In the upper-right pane only the columns can be scrolled (right and left) and in the lower-left pane only the rows can be scrolled (up and down). You can scroll the lower-right pane in either direction.

INSIDE OUT   Make frozen panes easier to see

Generally speaking, all the tasks you perform with panes work better when the windows are frozen. Unfortunately, it's harder to tell that the window is split when the panes are frozen because the thin, frozen-pane lines look just like cell borders. To make frozen panes easier to see, you can use a formatting clue that you will always recognize. For example, select all the heading rows and columns and fill them with a particular color.

Zooming worksheets

Use the Zoom controls in the bottom-right corner of the screen (or click the View tab and use the Zoom button) to change the size of your worksheet display. Clicking the Zoom button displays a dialog box containing one enlargement option, three reduction options, and a Fit Selection option that determines the necessary reduction or enlargement needed to display the currently selected cells. Use the Custom box to specify any zoom percentage from 10 through 400 percent. The Zoom To Selection button enlarges or reduces the size of the worksheet to make all the selected cells visible on the screen. Clicking Zoom To Selection with a single cell selected zooms to the maximum 400 percent, centered on the selected cell (as much as possible) in an attempt to fill the screen with the selection.

Note

The Zoom command affects only the selected worksheets; therefore, if you group several worksheets before zooming, Excel displays all of them at the selected Zoom percentage. For more about grouping worksheets, see "Editing multiple worksheets" in Chapter 8.

For example, to view the entire worksheet shown in Figure 6-17, you can try different zoom percentages until you get the results you want. Better still, select the entire active area of the worksheet, and then click the Zoom To Selection button. Now the entire worksheet appears on the screen, as shown in Figure 6-20. Note that the zoom percentage resulting from clicking Zoom To Selection is displayed next to the Zoom control at the bottom of the screen.

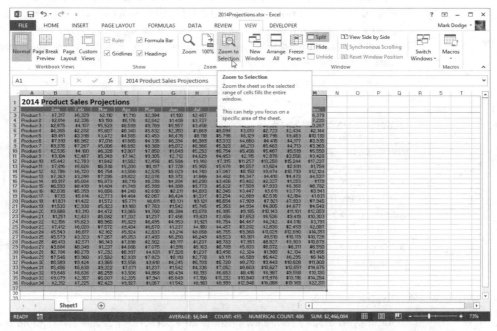

Figure 6-20 Click the Zoom To Selection button with the active area selected to view it all on the screen.

INSIDE OUT   Quick maximum zooming

If you have only one cell selected in the worksheet, the Zoom To Selection button in the Zoom area of the View tab serves as a "Zoom Maximum" button, which enlarges the worksheet to 400%, its maximum possible size.

Of course, reading the numbers might be a problem when your worksheet is zoomed "far out," but you can select other reduction or enlargement sizes for that purpose. The Zoom option in effect when you save the worksheet is the displayed setting when you reopen the worksheet.

Note

The wheel on a mouse ordinarily scrolls the worksheet. You can also use the wheel to zoom. Simply hold down the Ctrl key and rotate the wheel. If you prefer, you can make zooming the default behavior of the wheel. To do so, click the File tab, click Options, select the Advanced category, and select the Zoom On Roll With IntelliMouse check box in the Editing Options area.

Using custom views

Suppose you want your worksheet to have particular display and print settings for one purpose, such as editing, but different display and print settings for another purpose, such as an on-screen presentation. By clicking the Custom Views button on the View tab, you can assign names to specific view settings, which include column widths, row heights, display options, window size, position on the screen, pane settings, the cells that are selected at the time the view is created, and, optionally, print and filter settings. You can then select your saved view settings whenever you need them rather than manually configuring the settings each time.

Note

Before you modify your view settings for a particular purpose, you should save the current view as a custom view named Normal. This provides you with an easy way to return to the regular, unmodified view. Otherwise, you would have to retrace all your steps to return all the view settings to normal.

In the Custom Views dialog box, the Views list is empty until you click Add to save a custom view. All your custom views are saved with the workbook. Figure 6-21 shows the Custom Views dialog box with two views added, as well as the Add View dialog box you use to add them.

 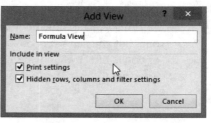

Figure 6-21 Click Add to name the current view and print settings in the Custom Views dialog box.

Protecting worksheets

In addition to password protection for your files, Excel offers several features that you can use to protect your work—workbooks, workbook structures, individual cells, graphic objects, charts, scenarios, windows, and more—from access or modification by others. You can also choose to allow specific editing actions on protected worksheets.

For information about additional security issues in Excel, see Chapter 4, "Security and privacy."

By default, Excel *locks* (protects) all cells and charts, but the protection is unavailable until you activate it. Click the Review tab on the ribbon, and click Protect Sheet to access the Protect Sheet dialog box shown in Figure 6-22. (You can also click the Format button on the Home tab and then click Protect Sheet.) The protection status you specify applies to the current worksheet only.

After protection is turned on, you cannot change a locked item. If you try to change a locked item, Excel displays an error message. As you can see in Figure 6-22, the Allow All Users Of This Worksheet To list contains a number of specific editorial actions you can allow even on protected worksheets. In addition to the options visible in Figure 6-22, you can choose to allow users to sort, use Filter and PivotTable reports, and edit objects or scenarios.

Figure 6-22 The Protect Sheet dialog box gives you pinpoint control over many common editing actions.

Unlocking individual cells

If you click Protect Sheet without specifically unlocking individual cells, you lock every cell on the worksheet by default. Most of the time, however, you don't want to lock every cell. For example, you might want to protect the formulas and formatting but leave particular cells unlocked so that you can type necessary data without unlocking the entire worksheet. Before you protect a worksheet, select the cells you want to keep unlocked, click Format on the Home tab, and click Lock Cell, as shown in Figure 6-23. Lock Cell is selected by default for all cells, so clicking it clears it, unlocking the selected cells.

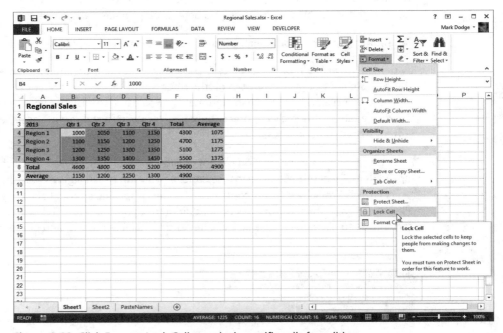

Figure 6-23 Click Format, Lock Cell to unlock specific cells for editing.

You can easily move between unprotected cells on a locked worksheet by pressing the Tab key.

One way to verify the locked status of a cell is to select it and look at the little padlock icon next to the Lock command. If the icon appears to be clicked already, it means that the selected cell is locked, which is the default state for all cells.

> ### Note
>
> You can tell if selected cells are locked by looking at the icon adjacent to the Lock Cell command. If the icon appears to be "pressed" like a button (as shown in Figure 6-23), the cells are locked. Keep in mind that Excel does not provide any other on-screen indication of the protection status for individual cells. To distinguish unlocked cells from protected cells, you might consider applying a specific format, such as cell color or borders.

Protecting the workbook

You can prevent the alteration of a workbook's structure and lock the position of the workbook window. To do so, click the Review tab on the ribbon and click Protect Workbook to display the dialog box shown in Figure 6-24.

For more information, see "Protecting workbooks" in Chapter 7, "How to work a workbook."

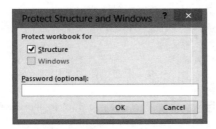

Figure 6-24 Use the Protect Structure And Windows dialog box to set the protection status for the entire workbook.

Allowing password access to specific cell ranges

If you need to do more than protect workbooks or individual worksheets, click Allow Users To Edit Ranges on the Review tab in the Changes group. Use the Allow Users To Edit Ranges dialog box, as shown in Figure 6-25, to provide editorial access to specific areas of a protected worksheet. You can even specify exactly who is allowed to do the editing.

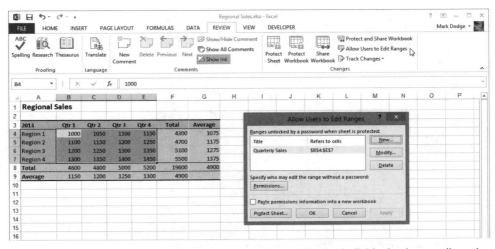

Figure 6-25 You can specify cells that can be edited, as well as the individuals who are allowed to edit them, by using the Allow Users To Edit Ranges dialog box.

When you click New in the Allow Users To Edit Ranges dialog box to add a cell range to the list, the New Range dialog box appears, as shown in Figure 6-26. Type a title for the range of cells you want to allow users to edit. Type a cell range or range name in the Refers To Cells box, or click in the box and drag through the range you want to specify.

Figure 6-26 Use the New Range dialog box to specify ranges you want to allow users to edit.

Selecting the Paste Permissions Information Into A New Workbook check box in the Allow Users To Edit Ranges dialog box is a handy way to keep track of who and what you speci- fied in the Permissions list. Note that you can click the Protect Sheet button for quick access to the Protect Sheet dialog box shown earlier in Figure 6-22. You can click the Permissions button to specify individuals who are allowed to edit each range. When you do so, a dialog box like the one shown in Figure 6-27 appears.

Figure 6-27 Set permissions for individual users by clicking Permissions in the Allow Users To Edit Ranges dialog box.

The Permissions dialog box lists all the users who are authorized to edit the worksheet, as well as whether they need to use a password to do so. For each item in the Group Or User Names list, you can specify password permissions in the box; click Allow or Deny to restrict editing without a password. This lets you, in effect, employ two levels of restriction, because you are restricting editing access to specified users anyway, and you can force even those users to type a password if you want to do so.

> **Note**
>
> You must specify a password in the New Range dialog box (shown in Figure 6-26) or in the identical Modify Range dialog box to turn on the permissions options that you set. If you don't specify a range password, anyone can edit the range.

You can add users and groups to the list in the Permissions dialog box by clicking Add and then clicking Advanced to display the full dialog box shown in Figure 6-28. Click Find Now to locate all the users and groups available to your system. However, if you are connected to a large network, this might take a long time, so you can use the Common Queries area to restrict your search. You can also use the Object Types and Locations buttons to restrict your search further. After you click Find Now, you can select items in the list at the bottom of the dialog box that you want to add. Press the Ctrl key to select multiple items. When you have located the users and groups you want to add, click OK.

> **Note**
>
> To add or change users on your computer, open User Accounts in Control Panel.

Remember, after all this, you still have to activate worksheet protection by clicking Protect Sheet on the Home tab or by clicking Protect Sheet in the Allow Users To Edit Ranges dialog box.

For information about Excel and networks, see "Sharing workbooks on a network" in Chapter 26.

Chapter 6

Figure 6-28 Click Add in the Permissions dialog box, and then click Advanced to select users to authorize.

Hiding cells and worksheets

In a protected worksheet, if you apply the Hidden protection format to a cell that contains a formula, the formula remains hidden from view in the formula bar even when you select that cell. To hide a selected cell or cells, click the Format button on the Home tab, and click Cells to display the Format Cells dialog box. Then click the Protection tab, and select the Hidden option. Formulas in hidden cells are still functional, of course; they are just hidden from view. In any case, the result of the formula is still visible on the worksheet.

For information about hiding numbers, see "The hidden number format" in Chapter 9.

You can also hide rows and columns within a worksheet and even hide entire worksheets within a workbook. Any data or calculations in hidden rows, columns, or worksheets are still available through references; the cells or worksheets are simply hidden from view. To hide a worksheet, click the sheet tab to select the worksheet you want to hide. Then, on the Home tab, click Format, Hide & Unhide, Hide Sheet, as shown in Figure 6-29. Unlike hiding cells, hiding rows, columns, or worksheets happens immediately. Afterward, you can click the corresponding Unhide command to restore the hidden item. However, if you hide a worksheet and then click Protect Workbook on the Review tab, the Unhide command is no longer available, which helps keep the hidden worksheet even better protected.

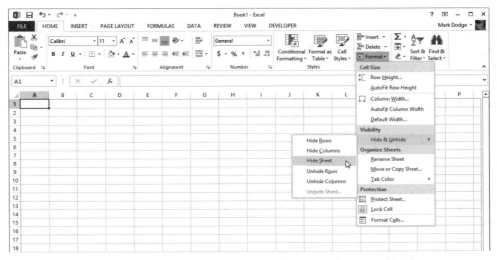

Figure 6-29 Use the Hide & Unhide commands to protect parts of your workbooks.

For more information about workbook protection, see "Hiding and protecting workbooks" in Chapter 7.

Using passwords

When you click Protect Sheet, Protect Workbook, or Protect And Share Workbook on the Review tab, you can assign a password that must be used to disable the protection. You can use unique passwords for each worksheet or workbook you protect.

CAUTION!

> Password protection in Excel is serious business. After you assign a password, you can't unprotect the worksheet or workbook without it. Don't forget your passwords! Remember, capitalization matters.

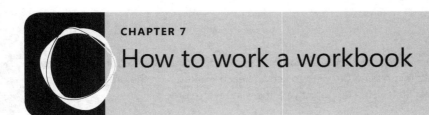

IN EARLY VERSIONS of Microsoft Excel, worksheets, charts, and macro sheets were stored as separate documents. Since Excel 5, however, all these types of data—and more—peacefully coexist in workbooks. You can keep as many worksheets containing as many different types of data as you want in a workbook, you can have more than one workbook open at the same time, and you can have more than one window open for the same workbook. The only limitations to these capabilities are those imposed by your computer's memory and system resources.

Managing multiple workbooks

This chapter describes how to protect workbooks, how to use more than one workbook at a time, and how and why to split your view of a workbook into multiple windows. Generally, when you start Microsoft Excel 2013, a blank workbook appears with the provisional title *Book1*. The only exceptions occur when you start Excel by opening an existing workbook or when you have one or more Excel files stored in the XLStart folder so that they open automatically.

If you start Excel and then open an existing Excel file, Book1 disappears unless you edited it. You can open as many workbooks as you like until your computer runs out of memory.

For more about working with multiple windows, see "Opening multiple windows for the same workbook" later in this chapter. For more information about the XLStart folder, see "Opening files when you start Excel" in Chapter 2, "Exploring Excel fundamentals."

Navigating between open workbooks

If you have more than one workbook open, you can activate a particular workbook in any of the following ways:

- Click its window, if you can see it.

- Press Alt+Tab, which activates the next open window (including any non-Excel windows you have open).

- If you have all your workbook windows maximized, you can shuffle through the open workbooks by pressing Ctrl+Tab to activate each workbook in the order you opened them. Press Shift+Ctrl+Tab to activate them in reverse order.

- On the View tab on the ribbon, click a window name on the Switch Windows menu, which lists as many as nine open workbooks or, if you have more than nine open, displays a More Workbooks command that presents a dialog box listing all the open workbooks.

Arranging workbook windows

To make all open workbooks visible at the same time, click the View tab and click Arrange All. Excel displays the Arrange Windows dialog box, shown in Figure 7-1, which also shows the workbooks arranged in the Tiled configuration with the screen divided into a patchwork of open documents. Figure 7-2 shows the same workbooks in the Horizontal configuration.

You'll find the 2014Projections.xlsx, Humongous.xlsx, Team Sales.xlsx, Regional Sales.xlsx, and NorthwindSales.xlsx files with the other examples on the companion website.

Figure 7-1 Clicking View, Arrange All opens the Arrange Windows dialog box, which gives you a choice of configurations.

If you select the Windows Of Active Workbook check box in the Arrange Windows dialog box, only the active workbook is affected by the configuration setting, and then only if more than one window is open for the active workbook. Excel arranges those windows according to the option you select under Arrange in the Arrange Windows dialog box. This is handy if you have several workbooks open but have multiple windows open for one of them and want to arrange only these windows without closing the other workbooks.

> **Note**
>
> Note that the Save Workspace command, which used to be in the Window group on the View tab, is no longer available in Excel 2013, because of its new single document interface (SDI) behavior. For more information, see the Inside Out tip "Microsoft and the SDI" in Chapter 2.

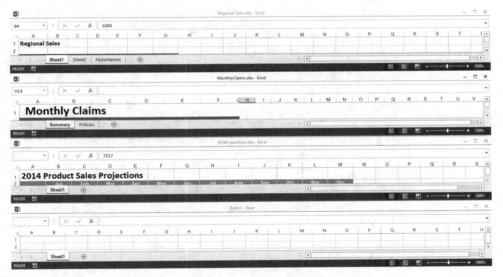

Figure 7-2 These windows are arranged in the Horizontal configuration.

Note that in the horizontal configuration shown in Figure 7-2, Excel hides the ribbons automatically, which is handy, because you would see nothing but the ribbon in each workbook window if it didn't hide them. To reveal a ribbon, double-click the title bar of any of the workbooks.

> **Note**
>
> When you save a workbook, Excel also saves its characteristics, such as the window's size, position on the screen, and display settings. The next time you open the workbook, the window looks the same as it did the last time you saved it. When you open it, Excel even selects the same cells you had selected when you saved the file.

Comparing worksheets side by side

The Arrange All button on the View tab is extremely helpful if you need to compare the contents of two similar workbooks, but another feature makes this task even easier. The View Side By Side button essentially packages the Horizontal window arrangement option with a couple of useful features to make comparison chores a lot easier. The View Side By Side button lives in the Window group on the View tab; it is the top button located to the right of the New Window command, as shown in Figure 7-3.

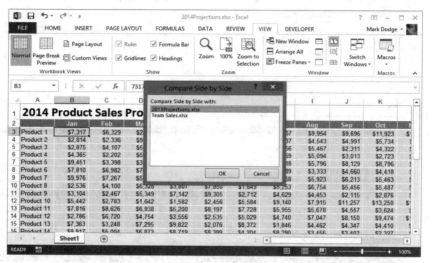

Figure 7-3 If more than two windows are open, select one in the Compare Side By Side dialog box.

> **Note**
>
> The ribbon on your screen might look different from what you see in this book. The ribbon's display adjusts to the size of your screen, its resolution, and the size of the Excel window. For example, the six buttons in the middle of the Window group on the View tab might or might not display adjacent text labels, depending on your screen's size and resolution and whether Excel is maximized.

You can click the View Side By Side button to arrange any two open windows even if they are windows for the same workbook (as described in the next section). But unlike the Arrange button, View Side By Side performs its trick on no more or less than two windows. After you click the button, you see a Compare Side By Side dialog box like the one shown in Figure 7-3 if you have more than two windows open. If so, select the window you want to compare, and click OK; this opens the window and arranges it along with the window that was active when you clicked View Side By Side. (The button name is a little bit misleading because the windows are actually arranged horizontally—not really "side by side," but one above the other.)

After you activate "side-by-side mode," the two buttons below the View Side By Side button become active, as shown here and in Figure 7-4:

The Synchronous Scrolling button locks the two windows together wherever they happen to be; when you scroll in any direction, the inactive window scrolls in an identical fashion. This action is activated automatically when you turn on the View Side By Side feature. The Reset Window Position button puts the active window on top, which is handy. The window that is active when you first click the View Side By Side button is the one that appears on top. If you want the other window on top, click anywhere in the other window, and then click the Reset Window Position button to place it in the top position.

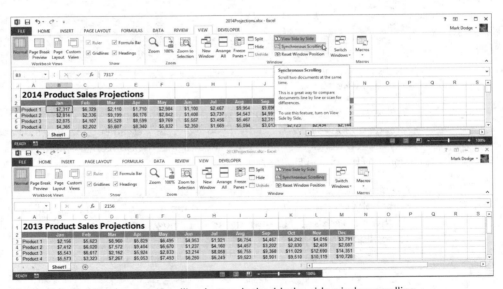

Figure 7-4 The Synchronous Scrolling button locks side-by-side window scrolling.

The View Side By Side button is a toggle. To turn off side-by-side mode and return to Normal view, click the View Side By Side button again. Make sure you turn it off before moving on to other tasks to avoid some odd window behavior.

Opening multiple windows for the same workbook

Suppose you've created a workbook like the one shown in Figure 7-5. You might want to monitor the cells on the summary worksheet while working on one of the other worksheets in the workbook. On the other hand, if you have a large worksheet, you might want to keep an eye on more than one area of the same worksheet at the same time. To perform either of these tasks, you can open a second window for the workbook by clicking New Window on the View tab.

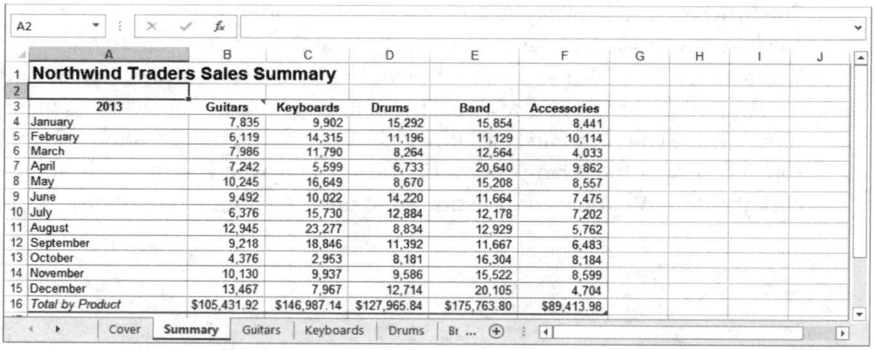

Northwind Traders Sales Summary

2013	Guitars	Keyboards	Drums	Band	Accessories
January	7,835	9,902	15,292	15,854	8,441
February	6,119	14,315	11,196	11,129	10,114
March	7,986	11,790	8,264	12,564	4,033
April	7,242	5,599	6,733	20,640	9,862
May	10,245	16,649	8,670	15,208	8,557
June	9,492	10,022	14,220	11,664	7,475
July	6,376	15,730	12,884	12,178	7,202
August	12,945	23,277	8,834	12,929	5,762
September	9,218	18,846	11,392	11,667	6,483
October	4,376	2,953	8,181	16,304	8,184
November	10,130	9,937	9,586	15,522	8,599
December	13,467	7,967	12,714	20,105	4,704
Total by Product	$105,431.92	$146,987.14	$127,965.84	$175,763.80	$89,413.98

Figure 7-5 We want to view the summary worksheet while working on a supporting worksheet in the same workbook.

To view both windows on your screen, click View, Arrange All and then select any of the Arrange options except Cascade. If you select the Cascade option, you'll be able to view only the top worksheet in the stack. If you select the Horizontal option, your screen looks similar to the one in Figure 7-6.

You might notice that Excel assigned the name NorthwindSales.xlsx:2 to the new workbook window. In addition, it changed the name of the original workbook window to NorthwindSales.xlsx:1. NorthwindSales.xlsx:2 now becomes the active window, and as such, it's positioned on top.

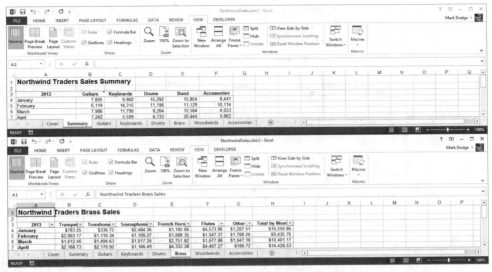

Figure 7-6 After clicking the New Window button to open a second window for the same workbook, select an Arrange option to fit both windows on the screen simultaneously.

> **Note**
>
> Again, if other workbooks are open, but you want to view only the windows of the active workbook, select the Windows Of Active Workbook check box in the Arrange Windows dialog box.

You can view any part of the workbook in any window associated with that workbook. In Figure 7-6, NorthwindSales.xlsx:2 originally displayed the summary worksheet when we first created it, because that was the active worksheet when we clicked the New Window button. Then we clicked the Brass tab in the new window, leaving the summary worksheet visible in NorthwindSales.xlsx:1.

Useful inconsistencies of new windows

When you create multiple windows of the same workbook, anything you do in one window happens in all windows—almost. New entries; formatting changes; inserting or deleting rows, columns, or worksheets; and just about any other editing changes are reflected in the windows. Display characteristics—or *views*—are not. This means that you can zoom in or out and change anything in the Workbook Views and Zoom groups on the View tab as well as use the Split and Freeze Panes commands. View adjustments affect only the active window. You can also click the File tab, click Options, select the Advanced category, and then change the settings in the two Display Options sections: Display Options For This Workbook and Display Options For This Worksheet. You can apply these options differently to windows of the same workbook. Just select the name of the window you want to change in the drop-down list, as shown in Figure 7-7.

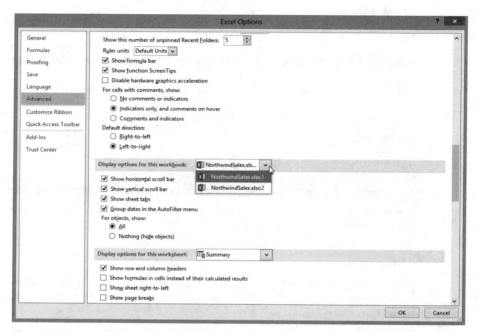

Figure 7-7 You can change the display characteristics of one window without affecting the other.

Figure 7-8 shows a somewhat exaggerated example of worksheet auditing. Formulas are displayed in NorthwindSales.xlsx:1; the worksheet is zoomed in, the ribbon is collapsed; and the formula bar, row and column headings, and gridlines are removed—all in an effort to review the formulas in the summary worksheet to make sure they refer to the proper cells. You can use this technique to audit your worksheets.

If you create a view like NorthwindSales.xlsx:1 in Figure 7-8 and want to be able to re-create it in the future, click the Custom Views button in the Workbook Views group on the View tab to save it. If you want to be able to re-create the entire workspace, including additional windows and their view settings, click the Save Workspace button in the Window group on the View tab.

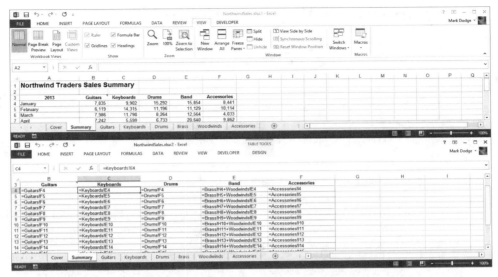

Figure 7-8 You can radically change view options in one window while maintaining a regular view of the same worksheet in another window.

For more information about custom views, see "Using custom views" in Chapter 6, "How to work a worksheet." For more information about the auditing features in Excel, see "Auditing and documenting worksheets" in Chapter 8, "Worksheet editing techniques." For more information about formulas, see Chapter 12, "Building formulas."

INSIDE OUT   Close the default settings window last

When you have two windows open in the same workbook and then close one of them, the "number" of the open window isn't important, but the view settings are. In the example shown in Figure 7-8, if you finish your work and close NorthwindSales.xlsx:2, the modified view settings in NorthwindSales.xlsx:1 become the active view for the workbook. If you then save the workbook, you also save the modified view settings. Be sure you close the windows with view settings you don't want to keep before you close the one with the settings you want to use as the default—don't worry about the window number.

Hiding and protecting workbooks

Sometimes you might want to keep certain information out of sight or protect it from inadvertent modification. You can conceal and protect your data by hiding windows, workbooks, or individual worksheets from view.

For information about protecting individual cells, see "Protecting worksheets" in Chapter 6.

Hiding workbooks

At times, you might need to keep a workbook open so that you can access the information it contains, but you don't want it to be visible, either for convenience or for security. When several open workbooks clutter your workspace, you can click the Hide button on the View tab to conceal some of them. Excel can still work with the information in the hidden workbooks, but they don't take up space on your screen, and their file names don't appear in the Switch Windows menu on the View tab.

To hide a workbook, activate it and then click View, Hide. Excel removes the workbook from view, but the workbook remains open and available in the workspace. To bring the hidden workbook into view, click View, Unhide, and then select the name of the hidden workbook.

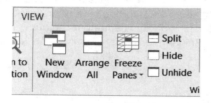

The Unhide command is available only when you have a workbook hidden. The Unhide dialog box, shown in Figure 7-9, lists all the hidden workbooks.

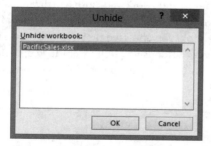

Figure 7-9 The Unhide dialog box lists all the workbooks you currently have hidden.

Clicking the Hide button conceals any open window. However, if you have multiple windows open for the same workbook, clicking the Hide button hides only the active window. The entire workbook isn't hidden. For more information, see "Opening multiple windows for the same workbook" earlier in this chapter.

TROUBLESHOOTING

Nothing happens when I try to open a workbook

If, when you try to open a workbook, you don't see any error messages or dialog boxes but the workbook doesn't appear to open, the window was probably hidden when the workbook was last saved. The workbook is actually open; you just can't see it.

If, in a previous Excel session, you clicked the Hide button on the View tab and then forgot about the hidden window when you exited Excel, you probably saw a message like "Do you want to save changes you made to Book1?" This refers to the hidden file—the change you made was the act of hiding it. The next time you open the file, it appears that nothing has happened, but if you look at the View tab, the Unhide button is active, which happens only when a hidden window is open in the workspace. Click the Unhide button, select the file name to make it visible once again, and then save it before exiting Excel.

Protecting workbooks

Protecting a workbook not only prevents changes to the complement of worksheets contained in the workbook, but it can also prevent modifications to the way the workbook windows are displayed. To protect a workbook, click the Review tab, and click Protect Workbook to display the dialog box shown in Figure 7-10.

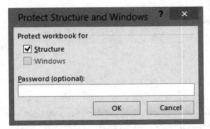

Figure 7-10 Clicking Review, Protect Workbook helps insulate your workbooks from inadvertent modification.

Selecting the Structure check box prevents any changes to the position, the name, and the hidden or unhidden status of the worksheets in the active workbook. When you select the Windows option, the workbook's windows cannot be closed, hidden, unhidden, resized, or moved—in fact, the Minimize, Maximize, and Close buttons disappear. This does not mean you cannot close the workbook; you can still click the File tab and then click Close. However, if you have more than one window open for the workbook, you cannot close any of them individually.

These settings take effect immediately. This command is a toggle—you can turn protection off by clicking Protect Workbook again. If protection has been activated, the Protect Workbook command button is highlighted, or "depressed." If you specify a password in the Protect Structure And Windows dialog box, Excel prompts you to supply that password before it turns off worksheet protection.

Encrypting workbooks

You can provide another level of security for your workbooks by adding encryption. Encryption goes beyond simple password protection by digitally obscuring information to make it unreadable without the proper key to "decode" it. (Therefore, encrypted workbooks can be opened only by Excel.) You apply encryption by clicking the File tab, Info, Protect Workbook, Encrypt With Password. This displays a dialog box that prompts you for a password, as shown in Figure 7-11, and then redisplays itself to confirm the password.

Figure 7-11 Applying a password to encrypt a workbook also turns on protection of the workbook structure.

After encryption, you need the password to open the workbook again; the Protect Structure And Windows dialog box (shown in Figure 7-10) also uses this password to protect the workbook structure. Even if you turn off workbook protection, encryption is still active until you turn it off by clicking the Encrypt Document command again and removing the password from the Encrypt Document dialog box.

Saving workbooks or windows as hidden

Sometimes you might want to hide a particular workbook, perhaps even to prevent others from opening and viewing its sensitive contents in your absence. If so, you can save the workbook as hidden. A hidden workbook is not visible when it's opened. You can save a workbook as hidden by following these steps:

1. Close all open workbooks other than the one you want to hide, and then click View, Hide.

2. Exit Excel.

3. When a message appears asking whether you want to save changes to the workbook, click Save.

The next time the workbook opens, its contents are hidden. To ensure that it cannot be unhidden by others, you might want to assign a password by clicking Review, Protect Workbook before hiding and saving the workbook.

Hiding worksheets

If you want to hide a particular worksheet in a workbook, click the Home tab, and in the Cells group, click Format. On the menu that appears, click Hide & Unhide, and then click Hide Sheet. When you do so, the active worksheet no longer appears in the workbook. To unhide a hidden worksheet, click Unhide Sheet on the same menu. This command becomes active after you have hidden a worksheet. The Unhide dialog box for worksheets is almost identical to the Unhide dialog box for workbooks shown in Figure 7-9. Select the worksheet you want to unhide, and then click OK.

Marking as final

When you need to share your finished workbooks with others rather than distribute them for collaboration, you might be interested in the Mark As Final command. Although anyone can still open a workbook that has been marked as final, the fact that you marked it as final helps your coworkers understand that it is a finished piece of work. Click the Info category on the File tab, and then click the Protect Workbook button to display the menu shown in Figure 7-12.

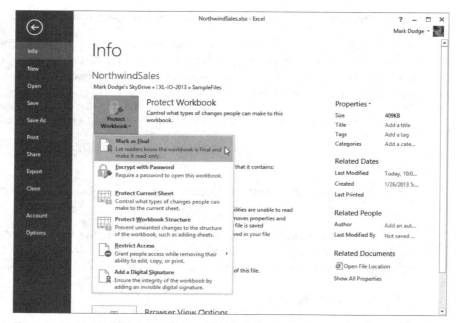

Figure 7-12 Use the Mark As Final command to help prevent others from modifying your finished workbooks.

When you mark a workbook as final, all editing is disabled, the workbook is saved as read-only, and the next time anyone opens it, an alert appears in the message bar revealing that it has been marked as final. Note that this is not intended to be a security feature because you can easily click the Edit Anyway button, as shown in Figure 7-13, to reactivate editing. This is essentially an update of the Read Only Recommended option that was available in versions of Excel prior to 2007.

Note that the Protect Workbook menu shown in Figure 7-12 offers the Protect Current Sheet and Protect Workbook Structure commands, which are equivalent to the Protect Sheet and Protect Workbook buttons on the Review tab. The last two commands, Restrict Access and Add A Digital Signature are Information Rights Management (IRM) features, which are covered in detail in "Controlling document access with Information Rights Management" in Chapter 26, "Collaborating on a network or by email."

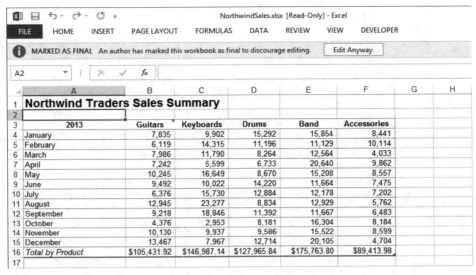

Figure 7-13 After you mark a workbook as final, an alert appears in the message bar.

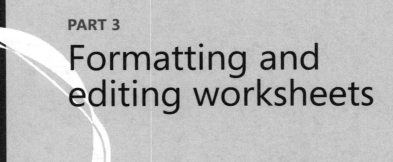

PART 3
Formatting and editing worksheets

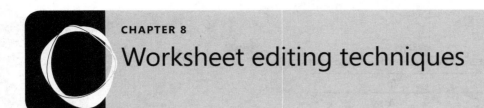

C UT AND PASTE. Insert and delete. Undo and redo. It all seems elementary, but as always in Microsoft Excel 2013, powerful features are hiding beneath the obvious approaches to the simplest tasks; in fact, after reading this chapter, you'll find solutions to problems you probably never even considered. We'll cover all the essential editing techniques, including editing multiple worksheets, checking spelling, selectively pasting entries, filling cells automatically, creating data series, and outlining and auditing worksheets.

Copying, cutting, and pasting

When you copy an item, Excel saves it in memory, using a temporary storage area called the Clipboard. You capture the contents as well as the formatting and any attached comments or objects.

For more information about comments, see "Auditing and documenting worksheets" later in this chapter. For more information about objects, see Chapter 10, "Creating and formatting graphics."

When you copy or cut cells, a *marquee* appears around the cell. (We used to refer to this scrolling dotted line as *marching ants*.) This marquee indicates the area you are copying or cutting. When you cut cells, the marquee disappears after you paste the cells. When you copy cells, the marquee persists after you paste the cells so that you can keep pasting these cells in other places.

The Cut, Copy, and Paste buttons in the Clipboard group on the Home tab are just swell, but you should know the keyboard shortcuts for the quintessential editing commands listed in Table 8-1. You can click the equivalent buttons on the ribbon, but really, if you never learn another keyboard shortcut, learn these. They work in most Windows programs.

TABLE 8-1 Essential keyboard shortcuts

Press	To
Ctrl+C	Copy
Ctrl+X	Cut
Ctrl+V	Paste
Ctrl+Z	Undo
Ctrl+Y	Redo

Copying and pasting

After you copy, you can paste more than once. As long as the marquee is visible, you can continue to paste the information from the copied cells. You can copy this information to other worksheets or workbooks without losing your copy area marquee. The marquee persists until you press Esc or perform any other editing action. The area you select for copying must be a single rectangular block of cells. If you try to copy nonadjacent ranges, you get an error message.

Collecting multiple items on the Clipboard

Although you cannot copy nonadjacent selections, you can use the Collect And Copy feature to copy (or cut) up to 24 separate items and then paste them where you want them—one at a time or all at once. You do this by displaying the Clipboard task pane shown in Figure 8-1 by clicking the dialog box launcher next to the word *Clipboard* on the Home tab on the ribbon.

Ordinarily when copying, you can work with only one item at a time. If you copy several items in a row, only the last item you copy is stored on the Clipboard. However, if you first display the Clipboard task pane and then copy or cut several items in succession, each item is stored in the task pane, as shown in Figure 8-1.

You can change the regular collect-and-copy behavior so that Excel collects items every time you copy or cut regardless of whether the Clipboard task pane is present. To do so, click the Options button at the bottom of the Clipboard task pane (shown in Figure 8-1), and click Collect Without Showing Office Clipboard or Show Office Clipboard Automatically, depending on whether you want the task pane to appear. The latter option activates an additional option, Show Office Clipboard When Ctrl+C Pressed Twice, which is one of the "automatic" methods.

Previewing before you paste

You use the paste preview feature to see what a particular paste option looks like before you commit to actually pasting. After you copy or cut a cell or range, select the destination cell where you want to paste. Click the Paste menu on the Home tab (or right-click and use the Paste Options buttons on the shortcut menu). When you position the pointer over each button, the result of that option is displayed on the worksheet in the specified location. In the following figure, we copied cells A1:A4, right-clicked cell C2 to display the shortcut menu, and then positioned the pointer over the Paste Options buttons:

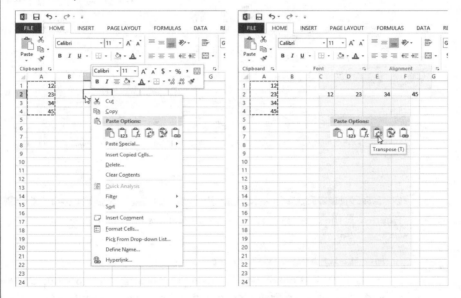

The Paste menu on the Home tab is usually far enough out of the way that it won't obscure the area of the sheet you're working on. And because the shortcut menu appears where you right-click, you would think that it would always be in the way. But as you can see in the figure, it "ghosts" itself when you use the paste preview feature. For more about paste options in general, see "Pasting selectively using Paste Special" later in this chapter, and for information about the Transpose command in particular, see "Transposing entries" later in this chapter.

Each time you copy or cut an item, a short representation of the item appears in the Clipboard task pane. Figure 8-1 shows four items in the Clipboard task pane. You can paste any or all of the items wherever you choose. To paste a single item from the Clipboard task pane, first select the location where you want the item to go, and then click the item in the task pane. To empty the Clipboard task pane for a new collection, click the Clear All button.

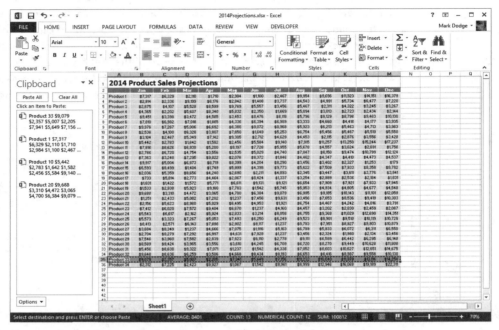

Figure 8-1 The Clipboard task pane stores multiple items that you copy or cut.

Hunting and gathering

You can use the Clipboard task pane to quickly assemble a list. Although the Collect And Copy feature is useful for editing, it can also be a great tool for gathering information. Copy items such as names or addresses from various locations in the order you want them to appear. Then click the Paste All button in the Clipboard task pane to paste all the items you have collected, in the order collected, into a single column.

Pasting multiples

After you copy, press Ctrl+V to paste whatever you copied. It's a no-brainer. However, did you know that if you select a range of cells before pasting, Excel fills every cell in that range when you paste? Figure 8-2 illustrates this.

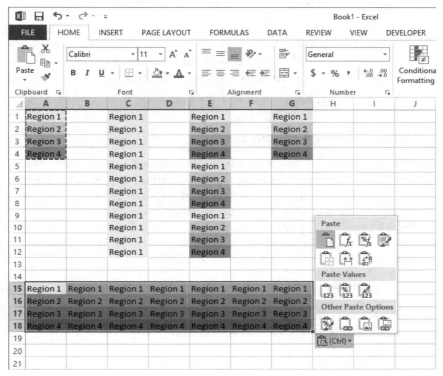

Figure 8-2 Before you paste, select more cells than you copied to create multiple copies of your information.

In Figure 8-2, we did the following:

- Copied cell A1, selected the range C1:C12, and then pasted, resulting in Excel repeating the copied cell in each cell in the selected range.

- Copied Cells A1:A4, selected the range E1:E12, and then pasted, resulting in Excel repeating the copied range within the range.

- Copied cells A1:A4, selected cell G1, and then pasted, resulting in an exact duplicate of the copied range.

- Copied cells A1:A4, selected the range A15:G15, and then pasted, resulting in Excel repeating the copied range in each selected column.

> **Note**
>
> If you select a paste range that contains more cells than the copied range, Excel repeats the copied cells until it fills the destination. However, if you select a paste range that is smaller than the copied range, Excel pastes the entire copied range anyway.

Using the Paste Options button

Notice in Figure 8-2 that we clicked the floating Paste Options button that appears near the lower-left corner of the pasted range. This button appears whenever and wherever you paste, offering actions applicable *after* pasting—a sort of "Smart Paste Special." (Similar floating buttons offering context-triggered options appear after performing actions other than pasting, too.) The best part is that you can try each action in turn. Keep selecting paste options until you like what you see, and then press Enter. The following describes the most interesting items on the Paste Options menu:

- **Formulas**   Pastes all cell contents, including formulas, but no formatting.

- **Formulas And Number Formatting**   Pastes all cell contents, including formulas and number formats, but no text formats.

- **No Borders**   Pastes everything but borders.

- **Transpose**   Flips a column of data into a row and vice versa.

- **Values**   Pastes cell contents and the visible results of formulas (not the formulas themselves) without formatting.

- **Values And Number Formatting**   Pastes cell contents and the visible results of formulas (not the formulas themselves); retains number formats, but not text formats.

- **Values And Source Formatting**   Pastes cell contents and the visible results of formulas (not the formulas themselves), plus all the copied or cut formats.

- **Keep Source Column Widths**   Retains column widths. This option is like normal pasting with the added action of "pasting" the column width.

- **Formatting**   Leaves the contents of the destination cells alone, and transfers the formatting. This works in the same way as the Format Painter button, located in the Clipboard group on the Home tab.

- **Paste Link**   Instead of pasting the contents of the cut or copied cells, pastes a reference to the source cells, ignoring the source formatting.

- **Picture**   Pastes an image of the selected cells as a static graphic object.

- **Linked Picture**   Pastes an image of the selected cells as a dynamic graphic object. If you make any changes to the original cells, the changes are reflected in the graphic object. This is handy for monitoring remote cells.

Cutting and pasting

When you cut rather than copy cells, subsequent pasting places one copy in the selected destination, removes the copied cells from the Clipboard, removes the copied data from its original location, and removes the marquee. When you perform a cut-and-paste operation, the following rules apply:

- Excel clears both the contents and the formats from the cut range and transfers them to the cells in the paste range. Excel adjusts any formulas outside the cut area that refer to the cells that were moved.

- The area you select for cutting must be a single rectangular block of cells. If you try to select nonadjacent ranges, you get an error message.

- Regardless of the size of the range you select before pasting, Excel pastes only the exact size and shape of the cut area. The upper-left corner of the selected paste area becomes the upper-left corner of the moved cells.

- Excel overwrites the contents and formats of any existing cells in the range where you paste. If you don't want to lose existing cell entries, be sure your worksheet has enough blank cells below and to the right of the cell you select as the upper-left corner of the paste area to hold the entire cut area.

- You cannot use Paste Special after cutting. Furthermore, no "floating button" menus appear when you paste after cutting.

Pasting selectively using Paste Special

Paste Special is quite possibly the most useful (and most used) power-editing feature. You can use this feature in many ways, but probably the most popular way is copying the value in a cell without copying the formatting or the underlying formula. After you copy a cell or cells, click the Paste menu on the Home tab, and click Paste Special to display the Paste Special dialog box, shown in Figure 8-3. (You must copy to use Paste Special. When you cut, Paste Special is unavailable.) The most popular Paste Special actions are directly accessible as commands on the Paste menu on the Home tab, as shown on the left in Figure 8-3.

> **Note**
>
> The Paste menu is actually a button with a downward-pointing arrow below it; clicking the button is equivalent to clicking the Paste command. To display the menu shown on the left in Figure 8-3, click the arrow.

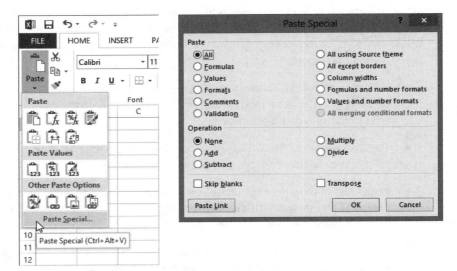

Figure 8-3 Paste Special is probably the most popular power-editing feature, and its most often used options are available as commands on the Paste menu.

> **Note**
>
> You can also open the Paste Special dialog box by right-clicking the cell where you want to paste and then clicking Paste Special.

Here's what the Paste Special options do:

- **All**   Predictably, pastes all aspects of the selected cell, which is the same as clicking the Paste command.

- **Formulas**   Transfers only the formulas from the cells in the copy range to the cells in the paste range, adjusting relative references. This option is also available as a command on the Paste menu.

- **Values** Pastes static text, numeric values, or only the displayed values resulting from formulas. This option is also available as the Paste Values command on the Paste menu.

- **Formats** Transfers only the formats in the copy range to the paste range.

> **Note**
> You can quickly copy and paste formats from a single cell or from a range of cells by using the Format Painter button, next to the Paste menu on the Home tab.

- **Comments** Transfers only comments attached to selected cells.

- **Validation** Pastes only the data validation settings you have applied to the selected cells.

- **All Using Source Theme** Transfers the copied data, and applies the theme from the copied cells.

- **All Except Borders** Transfers data without disturbing the border formats you spent so much time applying. This option is also available as the No Borders command on the Paste menu.

- **Column Widths** Transfers only column widths, which is handy when trying to make a worksheet look consistent for presentation.

- **Formulas And Number Formats** Transfers only formulas and number formats, which is helpful when you are copying formulas to previously formatted areas. Usually, you want the same number formats applied to formulas you copy, wherever they happen to go.

- **Values And Number Formats** Transfers only the resulting values (but not the formulas) and number formats.

- **All Merging Conditional Formats** Transfers cell contents and formats, and merges any conditional formats in the copied cells with those found in the destination range. Copied conditions take precedence if there is a conflict.

For more information about themes, see "Using themes and cell styles" in Chapter 9, "Worksheet formatting techniques." For more about conditional formatting, see "Formatting conditionally" in Chapter 9.

Because the All option pastes the formulas, values, formats, and cell comments from the copy range into the paste range, it has the same effect as clicking Paste, probably making

Chapter 8

you wonder why Excel offers this option in the Paste Special dialog box. That brings us to our next topic—the Operation options.

Pasting using math operators

You use the options in the Operation area of the Paste Special dialog box to mathematically combine the contents of the copied cells with the contents of the cells in the paste area. When you select any option other than None, Excel does not overwrite the destination cell or range with the copied data. Instead, it uses the specified operator to combine the copy and paste ranges.

For example, say you want to get a quick list of combined monthly totals for the Northern and Eastern regions in Figure 8-4. First, copy the Northern Region figures to an empty area of the worksheet, and then copy the Eastern Region numbers; select the first cell in the column of values you just copied and click Paste Special. You then select the Values and Add options in the Paste Special dialog box, and after clicking OK, you get the result shown at the bottom of Figure 8-4.

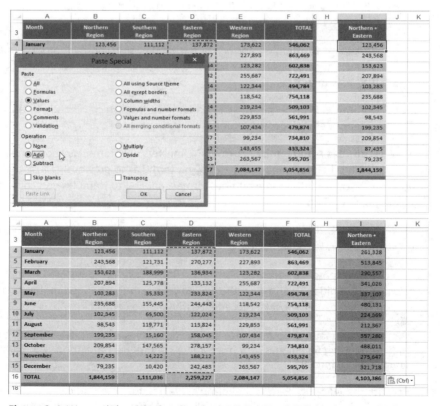

Figure 8-4 We used the Values option in the Paste Special dialog box to add the totals from the Eastern Region to those of the Northern Region.

You'll find the MonthlyClaims.xlsx file with the other examples on the companion website.

The other options in the Operation area of the Paste Special dialog box combine the contents of the copy and paste ranges using the appropriate operators. Just remember that the Subtract option subtracts the copy range from the paste range, and the Divide option divides the contents of the paste range by the contents of the copy range. Also note that if the copy range contains text entries and you use Paste Special with an Operation option (other than None), nothing happens.

Select the Values option when you use any Operation option. As long as the entries in the copy range are numbers, you can use All, but if the copy range contains formulas, you'll get "interesting" results. As a rule, avoid using the Operation options if the paste range contains formulas.

> ## Note
> Excel assigns the value 0 to blank spaces in the copy and paste ranges, regardless of which Operation option you select.

Pasting links

The Paste Link button in the Paste Special dialog box, shown in Figure 8-4, is a handy way to create references to cells or ranges. Although the Paste Special dialog box offers more options, using the Paste Link command on the Paste menu on the Home tab is more convenient. When you click Paste Link, Excel enters an *absolute* reference to the copied cell in the new location. For example, if you copy cell A3, select cell B5, click the Paste menu, and then click Paste Link, Excel enters the formula =$A$3 in cell B5.

If you copy a range of cells, Paste Link enters a similar formula for each cell in the copied range to the same-sized range in the new location.

For more information about absolute references, see "Understanding relative, absolute, and mixed references" in Chapter 12, "Building formulas."

Skipping blank cells

The Paste Special dialog box contains a Skip Blanks check box you can select when you want Excel to ignore any blank cells in the copy range. If your copy range contains blank cells, Excel usually pastes them over the corresponding cells in the paste area. As a result, empty cells in the copy range overwrite the contents, formats, and comments in corresponding cells of the paste area. When you select Skip Blanks, however, the corresponding cells in the paste area are unaffected by the copied blanks.

Transposing entries

One of the often-overlooked but extremely useful Paste Special features is Transpose, which helps you reorient the contents of the copied range when you paste—that is, data in rows is pasted into columns, and data in columns is pasted into rows. (This option is also available as a command on the Paste menu.) For example, in Figure 8-5, we copied the data shown in cells B3:E3, and then we selected cell J3 and clicked Transpose on the Paste menu on the Home tab. This works both ways. If we subsequently select the range just pasted and click Transpose again, the data is pasted in its original orientation.

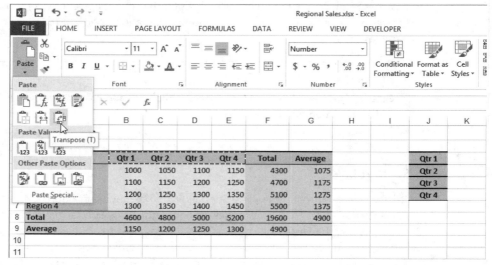

Figure 8-5 We copied cells B3:E3, selected cell J3, and then clicked Home, Paste, Transpose to redistribute the row of labels into a column of labels.

INSIDE OUT   Using paste values with arrays

As with any other formula, you can convert the results of an array formula to a series of constant values by copying the entire array range and—without changing your selection—clicking the Home tab, Paste, Paste Values. When you do so, Excel overwrites the array formulas with their resulting constant values. Because the range now contains constant values rather than formulas, Excel no longer treats the selection as an array. For more information about arrays, see "Using arrays" in Chapter 12.

> **Note**
>
> If you transpose cells containing formulas, Excel transposes the formulas and adjusts cell references. If you want the transposed formulas to continue to correctly refer to nontransposed cells, be sure that the references in the formulas are absolute before you copy them. For more information about absolute cell references, see "Using cell references in formulas" in Chapter 12.

Pasting hyperlinks

The Hyperlink command on the Insert tab has a specific purpose: to paste a hyperlink that refers to the copied data in the location you specify. When you create a hyperlink, it's as though Excel draws an invisible box, which acts like a button when you click it, and places it over the selected cell.

Hyperlinks in Excel are similar to web links that, when clicked, launch a webpage. You can add hyperlinks in your workbooks to locations on the web—a handy way to make related information readily available. You can use hyperlinks to perform similar tasks among your Excel worksheets, such as to provide an easy way to access other worksheets or workbooks that contain additional information. You can even create hyperlinks to other Microsoft Office documents, such as a report created in Microsoft Word or a Microsoft PowerPoint presentation.

Within Excel, you create a hyperlink by copying a named cell or range, navigating to the location where you want the hyperlink (on the same worksheet, on a different worksheet, or in a different workbook), and then clicking Insert, Hyperlink. To create a hyperlink in and among Excel worksheets and workbooks, you must first assign a name to the range to which you want to hyperlink. (The easiest method is to select the cell or range and type a name in the Name box at the left end of the formula bar.) Note that hyperlinks differ from Excel links, which are actually formulas.

For more information, see "Pasting links" earlier in this chapter. For information about defining names, see "Naming cells and cell ranges" in Chapter 12. For more information about hyperlinks, see Chapter 31, "Linking, hyperlinking, and embedding."

When you rest your pointer on a hyperlink, a ScreenTip appears showing you the name and location of the document to which the hyperlink is connected, as shown in Figure 8-6.

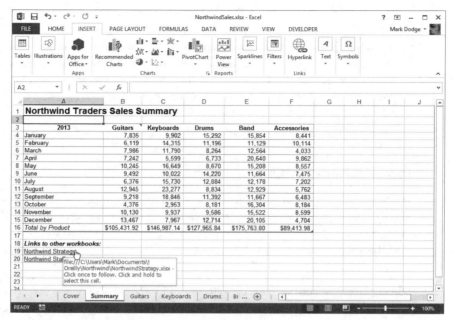

Figure 8-6 We created hyperlinks to supporting workbooks at the bottom of this worksheet.

To use a hyperlink, just click it. To select the cell containing the hyperlink without activating the link, hold the mouse button down until the pointer changes to a cross and then release the mouse button. To edit or delete a hyperlink, right-click it and then click Edit Hyperlink or Remove Hyperlink.

The NorthwindSales.xlsx, NorthwindStaff.xlsx, and NorthwindStrategy.xlsx files are with the other examples on the companion website.

Moving and copying with the mouse

Sometimes referred to as *direct cell manipulation*, this feature lets you quickly drag a cell or range to a new location. It's that simple. When you select a cell or range, move the pointer over the edge of the selection until the four-headed arrow pointer appears, and then click the border and drag the selection to wherever you like. As you drag, an outline of the selected range appears, which you can use to help position the range correctly.

To copy a selection rather than move it, hold down the Ctrl key while dragging. The pointer then appears with a small plus sign next to it, as shown in Figure 8-7, which indicates you are copying rather than moving the selection.

Note

If direct cell manipulation doesn't seem to be working, click the File tab, click Options, and in the Advanced category under Editing Options, check that the Enable Fill Handle And Cell Drag-And-Drop option is selected.

	A	B	C	D	E	F	G	H	I	J	K	L
1	Northwind Traders Keyboard Sales											
2												
3	2013	Hanson	Deloria	Lakes	Total by Month							
4	January	$266.32	$5,523.06	$4,112.45	$9,901.84							
5	February	$7,770.91	$220.37	$6,324.11	$14,315.39					G7:K20		
6	March	$2,577.79	$8,579.42	$632.35	$11,789.56							
7	April	$922.35	$512.38	$4,164.16	$5,598.89							
8	May	$1,358.70	$5,857.58	$9,433.13	$16,649.41							
9	June	$1,777.12	$5,242.94	$3,002.10	$10,022.16							
10	July	$6,524.62	$439.53	$8,765.84	$15,729.99							
11	August	$9,647.00	$5,281.16	$8,349.09	$23,277.25							
12	September	$5,848.97	$4,888.10	$8,108.87	$18,845.95							
13	October	$2,380.42	$187.18	$385.70	$2,953.29							
14	November	$3,356.25	$3,816.38	$2,764.23	$9,936.86							
15	December	$3,936.57	$3,214.41	$815.57	$7,966.55							
16	Total by Product	$46,367.02	$43,762.50	$56,857.62	$146,987.14							
17												
18												
19												
20												
21												

Figure 8-7 Before you finish dragging, press Ctrl to copy the selection. A plus sign and destination reference appear next to the pointer.

You can also use direct cell manipulation to insert copied or cut cells in a new location, moving existing cells out of the way in the process. For example, in the first image in Figure 8-8, we selected cells A6:E6 and then dragged the selection while holding down the Shift key. A gray I-beam indicates where Excel will insert the selected cells when you release the mouse button. The I-beam appears whenever the pointer rests on a horizontal or vertical cell border. In this case, the I-beam indicates the horizontal border between rows 8 and 9, but we could just as easily insert the cells vertically (which would produce unwanted results). You'll see the I-beam insertion point flip between horizontal and vertical as you move the pointer around the worksheet. To insert the cells, release the mouse button while still pressing the Shift key. When you release the mouse button, the selected cells move to the new location, as shown in the second image in Figure 8-8.

For information about using the keyboard for this task, see "Inserting copied or cut cells" later in this chapter.

If you press Ctrl+Shift while dragging, the selected cells are both copied and inserted instead of moved. Again, a small plus sign appears next to the pointer, and Excel inserts a copy of the selected cells in the new location, leaving the original selected cells intact.

You can also use these techniques to select entire columns or rows and then move or copy them to new locations.

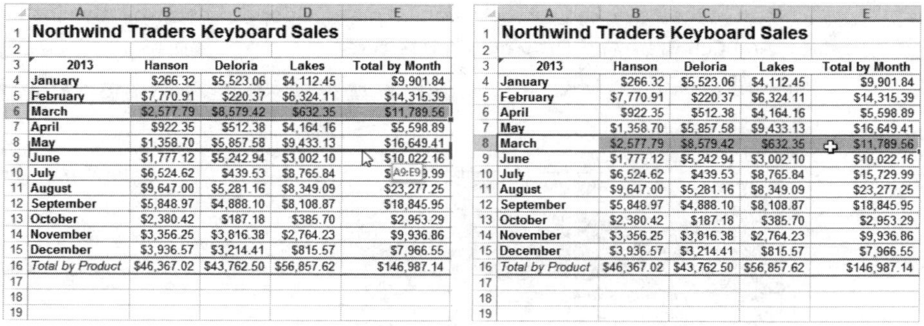

Figure 8-8 The gray I-beam indicates where Excel will insert selected cells.

Inserting and deleting

In the realm of spreadsheets, the complementary actions of inserting and deleting are collectively the second most-used editing techniques. Inserting and deleting rows and columns of information have some nuances that don't exist in the world of word processing, for example, but that you must consider.

Inserting columns and rows

On the Home tab, you can click commands on the Insert menu in the Cells group to add cells, columns, and rows to a worksheet—and even add a new sheet to a workbook. However, when you need to insert entire rows or columns, it's easiest to right-click a column or row heading, which simultaneously selects the whole row or column and displays the shortcut menu shown in Figure 8-9. (You can also drag through several rows or columns and then right-click the selection to insert the same number of columns or rows you selected.) Then just click Insert.

After inserting the column in Figure 8-9, the contents of column D move to column E, leaving the freshly inserted column D blank and ready for new information. The newly inserted cells take on the same formats as the cells in the column to the left, and Excel adjusts the formulas in cells F4:F15 to account for the expanded range.

A floating Insert Options button appears after you insert, which you can use to change the formatting of the inserted cells. Click the button to display the menu shown in the second image in Figure 8-9. If you want to extend a table by inserting a column on its right, for example, you might want to use the Format Same As Right or Clear Formatting option. The default Format Same As Left option works for our example.

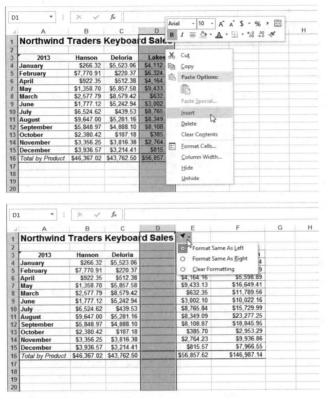

Figure 8-9 Right-click a row or column heading, and click Insert. Click the Insert Options button that appears after you insert for some post-insertion options.

> **Note**
>
> When you insert a row instead of a column, the commands on the Insert Options menu are Format Same As Above (the default), Format Same As Below, and Clear Formatting.

Handy keyboard shortcuts

Some of us are mouse fans; others are keyboard jockeys. If you're a good typist, you might prefer keeping your hands on the keys as much as possible. If so, this table of keyboard shortcuts for typical insertion actions is for you. Note that commas denote sequential keystrokes and plus signs denote additive keystrokes. For example, you press Alt, let go, then press I, let go, then press R to insert a row. But you hold down Shift and press Spacebar to select a row.

Press	To
Alt, I, R	Insert rows
Alt, I, C	Insert columns
Alt, E, D	Delete selected rows or columns
Ctrl+Spacebar	Select columns
Shift+Spacebar	Select rows

Inserting cells

You can insert cells or cell ranges rather than entire rows or columns by using the shortcut menu technique described earlier or by clicking Home, Insert, Insert Cells, which displays the Insert dialog box shown in Figure 8-10.

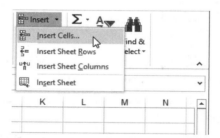 

Figure 8-10 Click the Insert Cells command to choose the direction in which to move existing cells in your worksheet.

Note

The Insert menu is actually a button with an arrow to its right; if you click the button, it is the equivalent of clicking the Insert Cells command, which moves cells either down or to the right, depending on the shape of the selected cell range. To display the menu shown on the left in Figure 8-10, click the arrow.

> ## Note
>
> You can insert multiple nonadjacent cells when you use the Insert command, but only when inserting blank cells. Inserting nonadjacent cut or copied cells is not allowed.

Inserting copied or cut cells

Often, you need to copy or move existing data to the middle of another area of existing data, moving other data out of the way in the process. You can do this the hard way by inserting just the right amount of space in the destination area and then copying or cutting cells and pasting them to the new location. However, it's much easier to click Home, Insert, Insert Copied Cells or Insert Cut Cells because this handles all these actions for you. These commands appear on the Insert menu (or on the shortcut menu) only when you copy or cut some cells. Sometimes it's obvious what needs to happen. For example, if you cut an entire row, you'll surely want to insert the entire row somewhere else. In these cases, Excel employs some common-sense rules and executes the action without hesitation. If Excel needs more information about how to adjust the worksheet, it opens the Insert Paste dialog box shown in Figure 8-11.

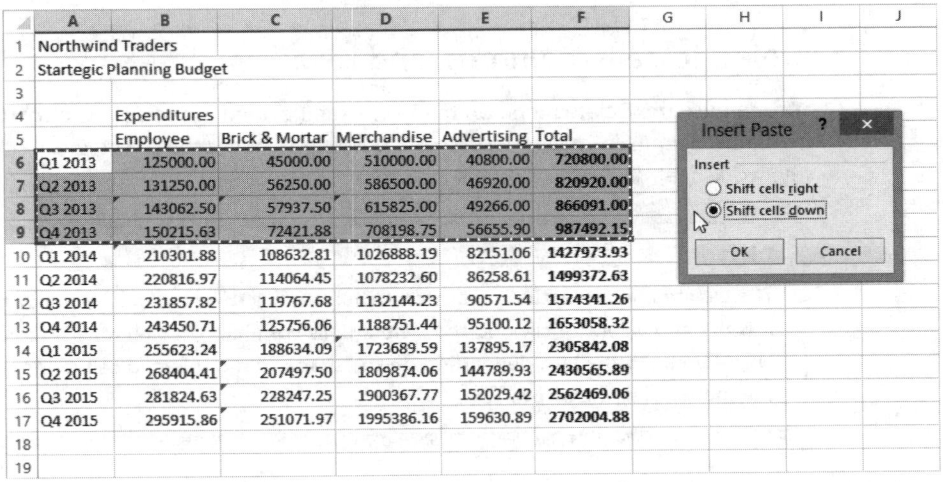

Figure 8-11 When you insert after copying or cutting cells, the Insert Paste dialog box appears.

For example, you can use cutting and inserting to add rows for more data in Figure 8-11 by copying the rows containing 2013 data and editing the contents, thereby saving yourself some unnecessary typing. To do so, select cells A6:F9 and press Ctrl+C to copy the range. Then click Home, Insert, Insert Copied Cells to display the Insert Paste dialog box. Then select the Shift Cells Down option, and click OK. Excel inserts the copied data and moves the rest of the table down to accommodate the insertion, as shown in Figure 8-12.

	A	B	C	D	E	F	G	H	I	J
4		Expenditures								
5		Employee	Brick & Mortar	Merchandise	Advertising	Total				
6	Q1 2013	125000.00	45000.00	510000.00	40800.00	720800.00				
7	Q2 2013	131250.00	56250.00	586500.00	46920.00	820920.00				
8	Q3 2013	143062.50	57937.50	615825.00	49266.00	866091.00				
9	Q4 2013	150215.63	72421.88	708198.75	56655.90	987492.15				
10	Q1 2013	125000.00	45000.00	510000.00	40800.00	720800.00				
11	Q2 2013	131250.00	56250.00	586500.00	46920.00	820920.00				
12	Q3 2013	143062.50	57937.50	615825.00	49266.00	866091.00				
13	Q4 2013	150215.63	72421.88	708198.75	56655.90	987492.15				
14	Q1 2014	210301.88	108632.81	1026888.19	82151.06	1427973.93				
15	Q2 2014	220816.97	114064.45	1078232.60	86258.61	1499372.63				
16	Q3 2014	231857.82	119767.68	1132144.23	90571.54	1574341.26				
17	Q4 2014	243450.71	125756.06	1188751.44	95100.12	1653058.32				
18	Q1 2015	255623.24	188634.09	1723689.59	137895.17	2305842.08				
19	Q2 2015	268404.41	207497.50	1809874.06	144789.93	2430565.89				
20	Q3 2015	281824.63	228247.25	1900367.77	152029.42	2562469.06				
21	Q4 2015	295915.86	251071.97	1995386.16	159630.89	2702004.88				
22										
23										

Figure 8-12 Inserting previously copied or cut cells is faster than inserting cells and then copying or cutting data to fill the inserted range.

Deleting cells, columns, and rows

You can use the Delete menu on the Home tab (located in the Cells group) to remove cells, rows, or columns from your worksheet. Deleting removes the selected cell or range from the worksheet, shifting cells to fill the empty space you create.

> **Note**
>
> The Delete menu is actually a button with an arrow to its right; if you click the button, it is the equivalent of clicking the Delete Cells command, which moves remaining cells either up or to the left, depending on the shape of the selected cell range. To display the menu, click the arrow.

Here are some guidelines for using Delete:

- You can delete multiple nonadjacent rows by pressing Ctrl and clicking each non-adjacent row before clicking Delete. Excel shifts everything below the deleted rows upward and adjusts any formulas accordingly.

- You can delete entire columns by selecting the column heading before clicking the Home tab and then, in the Cells group, the Delete command. Excel moves everything to the right of the deleted columns left and adjusts any formulas accordingly.

- You can delete multiple nonadjacent selections in one operation as long as you delete either entire rows or entire columns. You cannot delete entire rows and columns at the same time, however, because they overlap. The universe would implode.

- You can delete partial rows and columns by selecting a cell or cells and clicking Delete. Excel displays the Delete dialog box shown in Figure 8-13. You can choose the direction you want to shift remaining cells to fill the gap, or you can choose to eliminate the entire rows or columns inhabited by the selected cells.

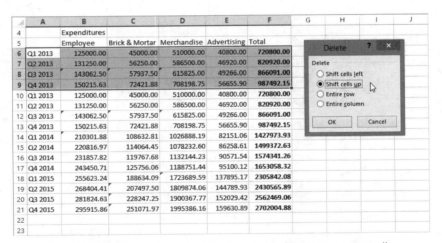

Figure 8-13 Use the Delete dialog box to choose the direction to move cells.

For more information about formulas and cell references, see Chapter 12.

Chapter 8

When you delete (or insert) partial rows or columns, it's easy to misalign data. For example, in Figure 8-14 we deleted cells A6:E9 with the default Shift Cells Up option selected. This eliminated the cells referred to by the formulas in column F, producing #REF errors. In addition, the column F totals in rows 13 through 20 now refer to the data in rows 9 through 16. This is a case where we should have cleared the cell contents rather than deleted the cells.

CAUTION !

Although you can generally use Undo to cancel a deletion, you should take heed of these important points. Before you delete an entire column or row, scroll through your worksheet to be sure you're not erasing important information that is not currently visible. Deleting cells that are referred to by formulas can be disastrous, as Figure 8-14 illustrates. Finally, when you delete a column or row referred to by an argument of a function, Excel modifies the argument, if possible, to account for the deletion. This adaptability is a compelling reason to use functions wherever possible. For more about using functions, see Chapter 13, "Using functions."

	A	B	C	D	E	F	G	H	I	J
4		Expenditures								
5		Employee	Brick & Mortar	Merchandise	Advertising	Total				
6	Q1 2013	125000.00	45000.00	510000.00	40800.00	#REF!				
7	Q2 2013	131250.00	56250.00	586500.00	46920.00	#REF!				
8	Q3 2013	143062.50	57937.50	615825.00	49266.00	#REF!				
9	Q4 2013	150215.63	72421.88	708198.75	56655.90	#REF!				
10	Q1 2014	210301.88	108632.81	1026888.19	82151.06	720800.00				
11	Q2 2014	220816.97	114064.45	1078232.60	86258.61	820920.00				
12	Q3 2014	231857.82	119767.68	1132144.23	90571.54	866091.00				
13	Q4 2014	243450.71	125756.06	1188751.44	95100.12	987492.15				
14	Q1 2015	255623.24	188634.09	1723689.59	137895.17	1427973.93				
15	Q2 2015	268404.41	207497.50	1809874.06	144789.93	1499372.63				
16	Q3 2015	281824.63	228247.25	1900367.77	152029.42	1574341.26				
17	Q4 2015	295915.86	251071.97	1995386.16	159630.89	1653058.32				
18						2305842.08				
19						2430565.89				
20						2562469.06				
21						2702004.88				
22										
23										

Figure 8-14 You can create errors when you delete the wrong cells.

Fixing formula problems

In the following worksheet, notice that the formulas in row 16 have small triangular indicators in the upper-left corner of each cell (they are green on your screen):

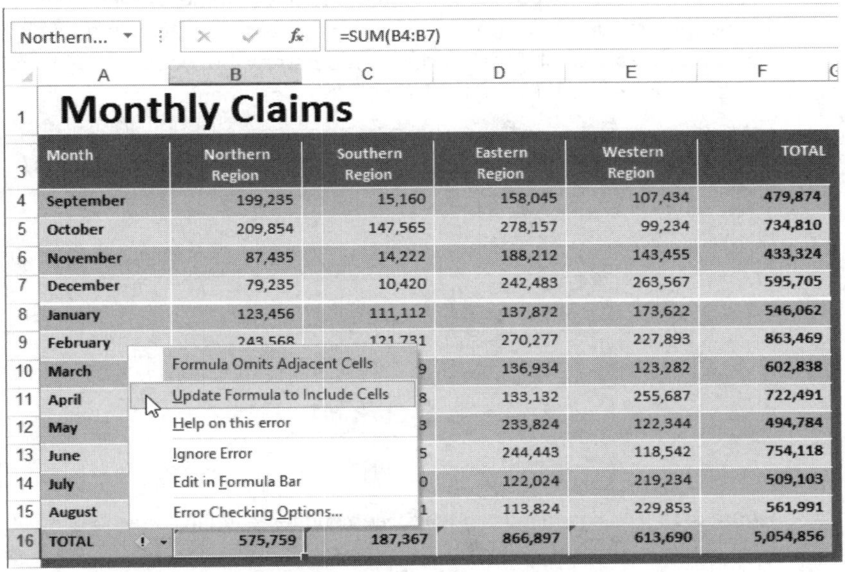

These triangles indicate an anomaly of some kind; in this case, we moved cells around within the table, so the formulas no longer include the cells we moved. Notice in the graphic that the formula bar displays the formula =SUM(B4:B47), omitting cells B8:B15. We used the Insert Cut Cells technique described in this chapter to move the rows containing January through August data from the top of the table to the bottom, which created the problem. When you insert or move rows or columns at the edge of cell ranges referred to by formulas, the formulas might not be able to adjust properly, as is the case here. Excel offers help. As shown here, not only do the little flags appear, but when you select one of the formula cells, a menu appears offering a Formula Omits Adjacent Cells item containing pertinent options.

The Update Formula To Include Cells option works correctly in our example. This is a much easier solution than editing each formula manually.

Clearing cells

The difference between deleting and clearing isn't subtle. Although deleting completely removes selected cells, shifting adjacent cells to fill the void, *clearing* leaves selected cells in place and removes contents, formats, and any comments that might be attached. The Home tab includes a Clear menu, which is one of the buttons in the Editing group. Excel hides the "Clear" label if the window is too narrow, but you can always recognize the button by its eraser icon. Figure 8-15 shows the Clear menu.

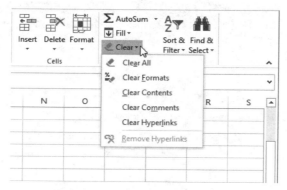

Figure 8-15 The commands on the Clear menu remove the corresponding attributes of selected cells without removing the cells.

The commands on the Clear menu perform the following tasks on selected cells:

- Clear All removes all text, numbers, formulas, formats, borders, and any attached comments.

- Clear Formats removes only formatting and borders.

- Clear Contents removes only text, numbers, and formulas.

- Clear Comments removes only the attached comments.

- Clear Hyperlinks removes only hyperlinks, leaving the formatting intact.

- Remove Hyperlinks removes hyperlinks and formatting.

Inserting, deleting, and clearing cells with the mouse

To perform the next group of operations, you use the fill handle, a tiny black square that appears in the lower-right corner of the *selection rectangle*, which is the bold border that appears around the selected cell or range. If you select entire rows or columns, the fill handle appears next to the row or column heading.

When you select a single cell and drag the fill handle in any direction, Excel copies the contents of that cell to all the cells through which you drag (with exceptions, which you'll learn later). When you select more than one cell, Excel either copies the range or extends a data series in the direction you drag, depending on the cell contents, the shape of the selection, and whether you are holding down Ctrl. Pressing the Shift key while dragging the fill handle lets you insert blank cells into a worksheet.

In the worksheet at the top in Figure 8-16, we selected A7:G7 and dragged the fill handle one row down while pressing the Shift key. The pointer became a double-headed arrow. The worksheet on the bottom in Figure 8-16 shows the newly inserted blank cells.

You use the same technique to insert entire blank rows or columns—just select the row or column headings, or press Shift and drag the fill handle, which appears adjacent to the row or column headings. You can just as easily delete cells, columns, or rows using a similar technique. To delete the cells we inserted in Figure 8-16, select A8:G8, hold down Shift, and then drag the fill handle up one row. The area turns gray, and the pointer changes to a similar double-headed arrow, with the arrows pointing inward this time. When you release the mouse button, Excel deletes the selection.

	A	B	C	D	E	F	G	H	I	J
1	**Regional Sales**									
2										
3	2013	Qtr 1	Qtr 2	Qtr 3	Qtr 4	Total	Average			
4	Region 1	1000	1050	1100	1150	4300	1075			
5	Region 2	1100	1150	1200	1250	4700	1175			
6	Region 3	1200	1250	1300	1350	5100	1275			
7	Region 4	1300	1350	1400	1450	5500	1375			
8	Total	4600	4800	5000	5200	19600	4900			
9	Average	1150	1200	1250	1300	4900				
10										

	A	B	C	D	E	F	G	H	I	J
1	**Regional Sales**									
2										
3	2013	Qtr 1	Qtr 2	Qtr 3	Qtr 4	Total	Average			
4	Region 1	1000	1050	1100	1150	4300	1075			
5	Region 2	1100	1150	1200	1250	4700	1175			
6	Region 3	1200	1250	1300	1350	5100	1275			
7	Region 4	1300	1350	1400	1450	5500	1375			
8										
9	Total	4600	4800	5000	5200	19600	4900			
10	Average	1150	1200	1250	1300	4900				
11										

Figure 8-16 Drag the fill handle while pressing Shift to insert cells.

If you drag the fill handle back over selected cells without pressing Shift, you clear the cell contents instead of deleting the cells. This clears formulas, text, and numbers only. If you hold down the Ctrl key while dragging over a selection, you clear all the cell contents as well as the formatting, borders, and comments.

Fill handles and cell selection rectangles

The *cell selection rectangle* is the heavy black-bordered box that surrounds the currently selected cells. There is only one *fill handle* in a cell selection rectangle, regardless of the number of cells:

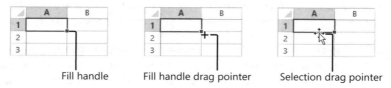

Fill handle   Fill handle drag pointer   Selection drag pointer

Dragging the fill handle extends the selection and performs other feats of prowess, as described in this chapter. Dragging the selection rectangle moves or copies the selection, also as described in this chapter. If the fill handle is not visible, click the File tab, click Options, and then click the Advanced category. In the Editing Options area, select the Enable Fill Handle And Cell Drag-And-Drop check box. The Alert Before Overwriting Cells check box is automatically selected (and recommended).

Dragging with the right mouse button

If you select cells and then drag the selection rectangle using the right mouse button, a shortcut menu appears when you release the button, as shown in Figure 8-17. You can use the options on the shortcut menu to consummate your edit in a variety of ways.

	A	B	C	D	E	F	G	H	I	J
1	**Northwind Traders**									
2	2013		Sales Staff							
3	Name	Units	Sales							
4	Kirwan, Yvette	122.00	28,616.32							
5	Krieger, Doris	41.00	9,616.96		F3:F13					
6	Madigan, Tony	67.00	15,715.52							
7	Hedlund, Magnus	108.00	25,332.48				Move Here			
8	Cools, Kenneth	111.00	26,036.16				Copy Here			
9	Oliveira, Manuel	89.00	20,875.84				Copy Here as Values Only			
10	Stevnsborg, Charlotte	119.00	49,726.72				Copy Here as Formats Only			
11	Mueller, Patrik	98.00	22,986.88				Link Here			
12	Bedecs, Anna	143.00	33,542.08				Create Hyperlink Here			
13	Weiss, Charlotte	184.00	100,626.24							
14			-				Shift Down and Copy			
15	Total	1,082.00	333,075.20				Shift Right and Copy			
16							Shift Down and Move			
17							Shift Right and Move			
18										
19							Cancel			
20										
21										
22										

Figure 8-17 Drag the selection with the right mouse button to display a shortcut menu.

The options on the shortcut menu are as follows:

- **Move Here**   Moves the source cells to the selected destination

- **Copy Here**   Copies the source cells to the selected destination

- **Copy Here As Values Only**   Copies the visible values from the source cells to the selected destination cells but does not copy formulas

- **Copy Here As Formats Only**   Copies the formats of the source cells to the destination cells without affecting the contents

- **Link Here**   Creates linking formulas at the destination that refer to the source cells

- **Create Hyperlink Here**   Creates a web-style link to the source cells in the selected destination

- **The Shift options**   Lets you copy or move the source cells to a location that contains existing data, shifting it out of the way in the selected direction

Undoing previous actions

The word *undo* was never widely used until people started using computers; now it's a verb that we all wish we could apply to more things in life. In Excel, you can click the Undo button, located on the Quick Access Toolbar, or press Ctrl+Z to recover from mistakes.

The Undo button includes a drop-down list of up to the last 100 actions you performed. You can then select and simultaneously undo any number of these actions at once. You display the drop-down list by clicking the small downward-pointing arrow next to the Undo button, as shown in Figure 8-18.

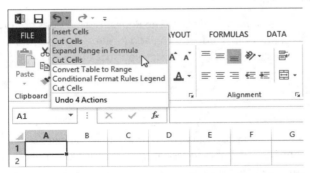

Figure 8-18 Click the arrow next to the Undo button to select and simultaneously undo up to the last 100 actions.

With the drop-down list visible, move your pointer down the list, and select the number of actions you want to undo. When you click, your worksheet reverts to the condition it was in before the selected actions.

Undo reverses the effect of most editing actions and restores any entry in the formula bar. For example, if you accidentally delete a range of data, use Undo to replace the entries. If you edit the contents of a cell and subsequently discover that your changes are incorrect, use Undo to restore the original cell entry. In addition, you can use Undo to reverse formatting and many other types of actions.

Unfortunately, Excel has many actions that Undo can't reverse, such as saving workbooks and deleting worksheets. Closing a workbook erases all the undoable actions displayed in the Undo list. Predictably, actions you cannot undo do not appear in the Undo drop-down list.

Redoing what you've undone

After you use Undo, you can then use Redo, which, unsurprisingly, reverses Undo. You can press Ctrl+Y to redo the last action or click the Redo button on the Quick Access Toolbar, which operates similarly to Undo. Redo also offers a drop-down list with all the undone editing actions. When you redo an action, Excel transfers it to the Undo drop-down list. Redo is valid only if Undo was your last action. After you have redone all the "undos" (up to 100), you're back to the "true" last action—that is, the last action you performed before you used Undo.

You can take advantage of Undo and Redo to see the effects of an editing change in your worksheet. If you edit a cell that is referred to in several formulas, you can use Undo and Redo to get a "before and after" look at the results displayed by the formulas.

Repeating your last action

To repeat the last editing action, press Ctrl+Y. (The Repeat button does not ordinarily appear on the Quick Access Toolbar, but you can add it. See "Customizing the Quick Access Toolbar" in Chapter 3, "Custom-tailoring the Excel workspace.")

Redo and Repeat share the same keyboard shortcut because you can do only one or the other at any given moment. Being able to repeat the last action is a great timesaver and is particularly handy with repetitive chores.

Unlike Undo, Repeat works with most actions. The only exceptions are those actions you can't logically repeat. For example, if you save a file by clicking the File tab and then Save, you can't repeat the action. Whatever the case, Repeat reflects the last repeatable action.

Editing cell contents

You can use the formula bar to edit the contents of a selected cell, or you can perform your editing "on location" in the cell. Excel also includes a few special features you can apply to tasks, such as entering date sequences, which once involved editing each cell but are now semiautomatic if you know where to find the "trigger."

Editing in cells or in the formula bar

While typing or editing the contents of a cell, you can use Cut, Copy, Paste, and Clear to manipulate cell entries. Often, retyping a value or formula is easier, but using commands is convenient when you're working with long, complex formulas or with labels. When you're working in a cell or in the formula bar, these commands work just as they do in a word-processing program such as Word. For example, you can copy all or part of a formula from one cell to another. For example, suppose cell A10 contains the formula =IF(NPV(.15,A1:A9)>0,A11,A12) and you want to type **=NPV(.15,A1:A9)** in cell B10.

> **Note**
>
> You can edit the contents of cells without using the formula bar. By double-clicking a cell, you can perform any formula bar editing procedure directly in the cell.

To do so, select cell A10, and in the formula bar, select the characters you want to copy—in this case, NPV(.15,A1:A9). Then press Ctrl+C, or click the Copy button (located in the Clipboard group on the Home tab). Finally, select cell B10, type = to begin a formula, and press Ctrl+V (or click the Paste button).

> **Note**
>
> Excel does not adjust cell references when you cut, copy, and paste within a cell or in the formula bar. For information about adjustable references, see "How copying affects cell references" in Chapter 12.

When you type or edit formulas containing references, Excel gives you visual aids called *range finders* to help you audit, as shown in Figure 8-19, where we obviously have a problem with our SUM formula. The total should include all the rows of data, so drag a handle on a bottom corner of the range-selection rectangle until it includes all the correct cells.

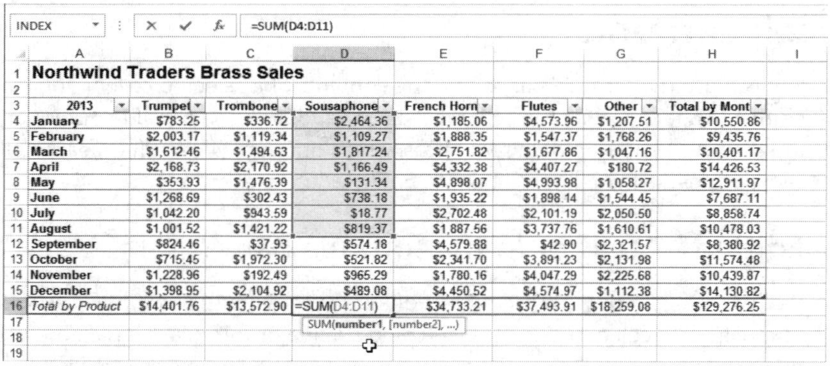

INDEX | =SUM(D4:D11)

	A	B	C	D	E	F	G	H
1	Northwind Traders Brass Sales							
2								
3	2013	Trumpet	Trombone	Sousaphone	French Horn	Flutes	Other	Total by Mont
4	January	$783.25	$336.72	$2,464.36	$1,185.06	$4,573.96	$1,207.51	$10,550.86
5	February	$2,003.17	$1,119.34	$1,109.27	$1,888.35	$1,547.37	$1,768.26	$9,435.76
6	March	$1,612.46	$1,494.63	$1,817.24	$2,751.82	$1,677.86	$1,047.16	$10,401.17
7	April	$2,168.73	$2,170.92	$1,166.49	$4,332.38	$4,407.27	$180.72	$14,426.53
8	May	$353.93	$1,476.39	$131.34	$4,898.07	$4,993.98	$1,058.27	$12,911.97
9	June	$1,268.69	$302.43	$738.18	$1,935.22	$1,898.14	$1,544.45	$7,687.11
10	July	$1,042.20	$943.59	$18.77	$2,702.48	$2,101.19	$2,050.50	$8,858.74
11	August	$1,001.52	$1,421.22	$819.37	$1,887.56	$3,737.76	$1,610.61	$10,478.03
12	September	$824.46	$37.93	$574.18	$4,579.88	$42.90	$2,321.57	$8,380.92
13	October	$715.45	$1,972.30	$521.82	$2,341.70	$3,891.23	$2,131.98	$11,574.48
14	November	$1,228.96	$192.49	$965.29	$1,780.16	$4,047.29	$2,225.68	$10,439.87
15	December	$1,398.95	$2,104.92	$489.08	$4,450.52	$4,574.97	$1,112.38	$14,130.82
16	*Total by Product*	$14,401.76	$13,572.90	=SUM(D4:D11)	$34,733.21	$37,493.91	$18,259.08	$129,276.25
17				SUM(number1, [number2], ...)				
18								
19								

Figure 8-19 Double-click a cell containing a formula to edit it and to display range finders.

For more information about formulas, see Chapter 12. For more about auditing, see "Auditing and documenting worksheets" later in this chapter.

> ### Note
> **You can disable in-cell editing if you want. To do so, click the File tab, click Options, and in the Advanced category, clear the Allow Editing Directly In Cells check box in the Editing Options area.**

Editing options

The Advanced category in the Excel Options dialog box (which you access by clicking the File tab and then Options) contains an assortment of options that control editing-related workspace settings, as shown in Figure 8-20. These options include the following:

- **After Pressing Enter, Move Selection** This locks in the entry and makes the cell below active. To change the direction of the selection after you press Enter, use the Direction drop-down list. When you clear this check box, pressing Enter locks in the entry and leaves the same cell active.

- **Automatically Insert A Decimal Point** For those of us who remember using 10-key calculators, this is equivalent to the "floating point" setting. Ordinarily, you type numbers and decimal points manually. To have Excel enter decimal points for you, select this option, and then select the number of decimal places you want.

For example, when you type **12345** with two decimal places specified, Excel enters 123.45 in the cell. When you apply this option, Fixed Decimal appears in the status bar. This option applies only to entries you make after you select it, without altering existing data. It also applies only when you do not type a decimal point. If you type a number including a decimal point, the option has no effect.

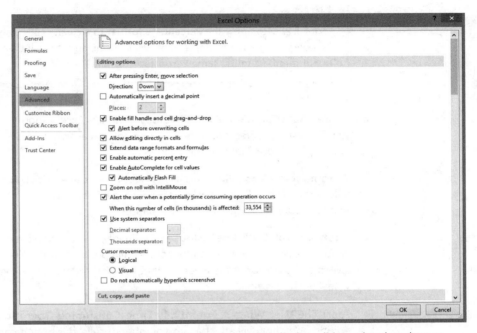

Figure 8-20 Click the File tab, Options, Advanced to display editing-related workspace settings.

- **Enable Fill Handle And Cell Drag-And-Drop**   This is required for the direct manipulation of cells using the mouse. See "Moving and copying with the mouse" earlier in this chapter. Leaving the Alert Before Overwriting Cells option selected is always a good idea.

- **Allow Editing Directly In Cells**   This is required for in-cell editing. See "Editing in cells or in the formula bar" earlier in this chapter.

- **Extend Data Range Formats And Formulas**   This lets Excel apply formatting from existing cells to new cells entered in a list or table.

- **Enable Automatic Percent Entry**   This helps you type values in cells with the Percentage format. When you select this check box, all entries less than 1 are multiplied by 100. When you clear this check box, all entries—including those greater than

1—are multiplied by 100. For example, in a cell to which you already applied the Percentage format, typing either **.9** or **90** produces the same result—90%—in the cell. If you clear the Enable Automatic Percent Entry check box, typing **90** results in the displayed value 9000% (as long as you applied the Percentage format to the cell).

> **Note**
>
> A quick way to apply the Percentage format to a clean cell is to type a number as a percentage. For example, type **1%** in a cell, and the cell then displays subsequent numbers in the same Percentage format.

- **Enable AutoComplete For Cell Values**   This lets Excel suggest cell entries by comparing existing values it finds in the same column as you type. See "Letting Excel help with typing chores" later in this chapter.

- **Automatically Flash Fill**   This lets Excel suggest cell entries by comparing existing values it finds in adjacent columns as you type. See "Automatic parsing and concatenation using Flash Fill" later in this chapter.

- **Zoom On Roll With IntelliMouse**   Ordinarily, if your mouse has a wheel, rotating it causes the worksheet to scroll (or zoom while pressing Ctrl). Select this check box to switch the behavior of the wheel so that the worksheet zooms when you rotate the wheel (or scrolls while you press Ctrl).

- **Alert The User When A Potentially Time-Consuming Operation Occurs**   If an editing operation will affect a large number of cells, this option controls whether you are notified and lets you specify the number of cells it takes to trigger the notification.

- **Use System Separators**   Ordinarily Excel defaults to the designated numeric separators for decimals and thousands (periods and commas, respectively) specified by your Windows system settings. If you want to specify alternative separators, you can do so here.

- **Show Paste Options Button/Show Insert Options Buttons**   This activates the floating button menus that appear after pasting or inserting. Ordinarily, after you perform a paste or an insert operation, a floating button appears, offering a menu of various context-specific actions you can then perform. Clear these options to turn off these features.

- **Cut, Copy, And Sort Inserted Objects With Their Parent Cells**   This is required to "attach" graphic objects to cells. See "Tools to help you position objects on the worksheet" in Chapter 10.

Understanding fixed and floating decimals

The Automatically Insert A Decimal Point option in the Advanced category of the Excel Options dialog box is handy when you need to type long lists of numeric values. (It's equivalent to the floating-decimal feature available on most 10-key calculators.) For example, if you're performing a lengthy data-entry task such as typing multiple dollar values on a worksheet, select the Automatically Insert A Decimal Point option, and click 2 in the Places list. Then just type numbers and press Enter, which saves you an extra keystroke for the decimal point in each entry. If you're entering 1,000 values, typing **295** instead of 2.95 eliminates 25 percent of the keystrokes you would otherwise have to perform. However, you need to be careful to either type trailing zeros or add decimal points to some numbers. For example, you usually type **5** to enter a 5.00 value, but with two fixed decimal places turned on, the same entry becomes 0.05, making it necessary for you to type either **500** or **5.** to correctly place the decimal point.

Chapter 8

Filling cells and creating data series

As described earlier in this chapter, the fill handle has many talents to make it simple to enter data in worksheets. Uses of the fill handle include quickly and easily filling cells and creating data series by using the incredibly useful Auto Fill feature.

Take a look at Figure 8-21. If you select cell B2 and drag the fill handle down to cell B5, Excel copies the contents of cell B2 to cells B3 through B5. However, if you click the floating Auto Fill Options button that appears, right after you drag, you can select a different Auto Fill action, as shown in Figure 8-22 for the range C2:C5.

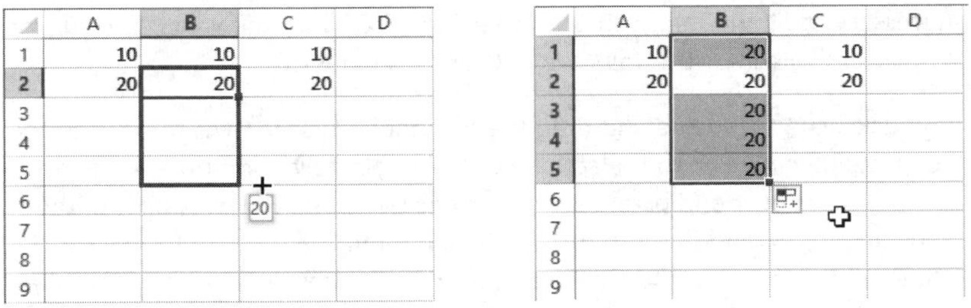

Figure 8-21 Copy the contents of a cell to adjacent cells by dragging the fill handle.

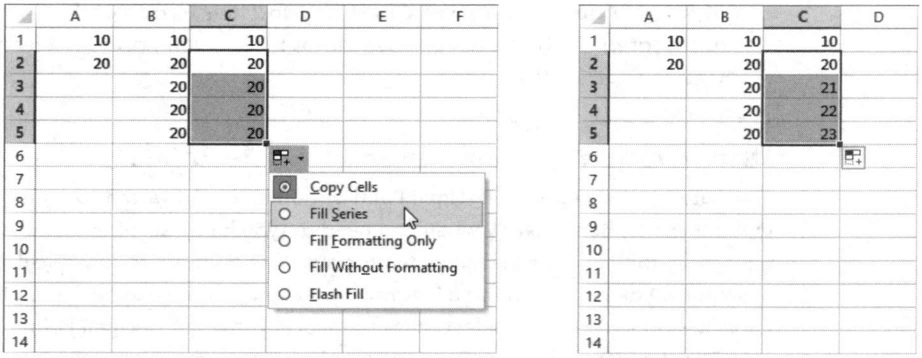

Figure 8-22 Create a simple series by dragging the fill handle and then clicking Fill Series on the Auto Fill Options menu.

INSIDE OUT   Create decreasing series

Generally, when you create a series, you drag the fill handle down or to the right, and the values increase accordingly. You can also create a series of decreasing values by dragging the fill handle up or to the left. Select the starting values in cells at the bottom or to the right of the range you want to fill, and then drag the fill handle back toward the beginning of the range.

If you click Fill Series on the Auto Fill Options menu, Excel creates the simple series 21, 22, and 23 instead of copying the contents of cell C2. If, instead of selecting a single cell, you select the range C1:C2 in Figure 8-22 and drag the fill handle down to cell C5, you create a series that is based on the interval between the two selected values, resulting in the series 30, 40, and 50 in cells C3:C5. If you click Copy Cells on the Auto Fill Options menu, Excel copies the cells instead of extending the series, repeating the pattern of selected cells as necessary to fill the range. Instead of filling C3:C5 with the values 30, 40, and 50, choosing Copy Cells will enter the values 10, 20, and 10 in C3:C5.

If you select a text value and drag the fill handle, Excel copies the text to the cells where you drag. If, however, the selection contains both text and numeric values, the Auto Fill feature takes over and extends the numeric component while copying the text component. You can also extend dates in this way, using a number of date formats, including Qtr 1, Qtr 2, and so on. If you type text that describes dates, even without numbers (such as months or days of the week), Excel treats the text as a series.

INSIDE OUT   Fill series limited to 255 characters

Excel lets you type up to 32,767 characters in a cell. However, if you want to extend a series using Auto Fill, the selected source cells cannot contain more than 255 characters. If you try to extend a series from an entry of 256 characters or more, Excel copies the cells instead of extending the series. This is not really a bug but a side effect of the Excel column-width limitation of 255 characters. Besides, a 256-character entry is not going to be readable on the screen anyway. If you really need to create a series out of humongous cell entries like this, perhaps a little worksheet redesign is in order. Otherwise, you have to do it manually.

Figure 8-23 shows some examples of simple data series created by selecting single cells containing values and dragging the fill handle. We typed the values in column A, and we extended the values to the right of column A using the fill handle. Figure 8-24 shows examples of creating data series using two selected values that, in effect, specify the interval to be used in creating the data series. We typed the values in columns A and B and extended the values to the right of column B using the fill handle. These two figures also show how Auto Fill can create a series even when you mix text and numeric values in cells. Also note that we extended the values and series in Figure 8-24 by selecting the entire range of starting values in cells A3:B12 before dragging the fill handle to extend them, showing how Excel can extend multiple series at once. (We applied the bold formatting after filling to make it easier to differentiate the starting values.)

	A	B	C	D	E	F	G	H
1	**Selected Value**	**Resulting Series**						
2								
3	**9:00**	10:00	11:00	12:00	13:00	14:00	15:00	
4	**1/1/2013**	1/2/2013	1/3/2013	1/4/2013	1/5/2013	1/6/2013	1/7/2013	
5	Qtr 1	Qtr 2	Qtr 3	Qtr 4	Qtr 1	Qtr 2	Qtr 3	
6	Jan	Feb	Mar	Apr	May	Jun	Jul	
7	**January**	February	March	April	May	June	July	
8	**Day 1**	Day 2	Day 3	Day 4	Day 5	Day 6	Day 7	
9	**Mon**	Tue	Wed	Thu	Fri	Sat	Sun	
10	**Product 1**	Product 2	Product 3	Product 4	Product 5	Product 6	Product 7	
11								
12								

Figure 8-23 Create simple data series by selecting a single value and dragging the fill handle.

	A	B	C	D	E	F	G	H
1	Selected Values		Resulting Series					
2								
3	9:00	10:00	11:00	12:00	13:00	14:00	15:00	
4	2013	2014	2015	2016	2017	2018	2019	
5	1/1/2013	2/1/2013	3/1/2013	4/1/2013	5/1/2013	6/1/2013	7/1/2013	
6	1/1/2013	3/1/2013	5/1/2013	7/1/2013	9/1/2013	11/1/2013	1/1/2014	
7	1-Jan	2-Jan	3-Jan	4-Jan	5-Jan	6-Jan	7-Jan	
8	Dec-13	Dec-14	Dec-15	Dec-16	Dec-17	Dec-18	Dec-19	
9	Dec-13	Dec-15	Dec-17	Dec-19	Dec-21	Dec-23	Dec-25	
10	Product 1	Product 2	Product 3	Product 4	Product 5	Product 6	Product 7	
11	Sat	Mon	Wed	Fri	Sun	Tue	Thu	
12	1 1/2	2 3/4	4	5 1/4	6 1/2	7 3/4	9	
13								
14								

Figure 8-24 Specify data series intervals by selecting a range of values and dragging the fill handle.

> **Note**
>
> If you select more than one cell and hold down Ctrl while dragging the fill handle, you suppress Auto Fill and copy the selected values to the adjacent cells. Conversely, with a single value selected, holding down Ctrl and dragging the fill handle extends a series, contrary to the regular behavior of copying the cell.

Extending with Auto Fill

Sometimes you can double-click the fill handle to extend a series from a selected range. Auto Fill determines the size of the range by matching an adjacent range. For example, in Figure 8-25, we filled column A with a series of values. Then, with the values shown in cells B1:B2, we filled cells B3:B5 by selecting the range B1:B2 and double-clicking the fill handle. The newly created series stops at cell B5 to match the adjacent cells in column A. When the selected cells contain something other than a series, such as simple text entries, double-clicking the fill handle copies the selected cells down to match the length of the adjacent range.

> **Note**
>
> You might see the Quick Analysis tool appear adjacent to the fill handle when you select a range of cells. This is a great tool, but not useful for creating fills. You can click the fill handle without disturbing the Quick Analysis tool, but if you prefer, just press the Esc key to dismiss it. For more information, see "Using the Quick Analysis tool," in Chapter 2, "Exploring Excel fundamentals."

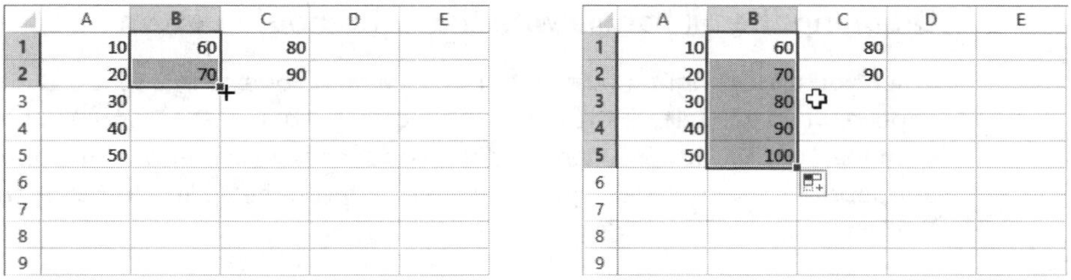

Figure 8-25 We extended a series into B3:B5 by selecting B1:B2 and double-clicking the fill handle.

INSIDE OUT   How Auto Fill handles dates and times

Auto Fill ordinarily increments recognizable date and time values when you drag the fill handle, even if you initially select only one cell. For example, if you select a cell that contains Qtr 1 or 1/1/2013 and drag the fill handle, Auto Fill extends the series as Qtr 2, Qtr 3, or 1/2/2013, 1/3/2013, and so on. If you click the Auto Fill Options menu after you drag, you'll see that special options become available if the original selection contains dates or the names of days or months:

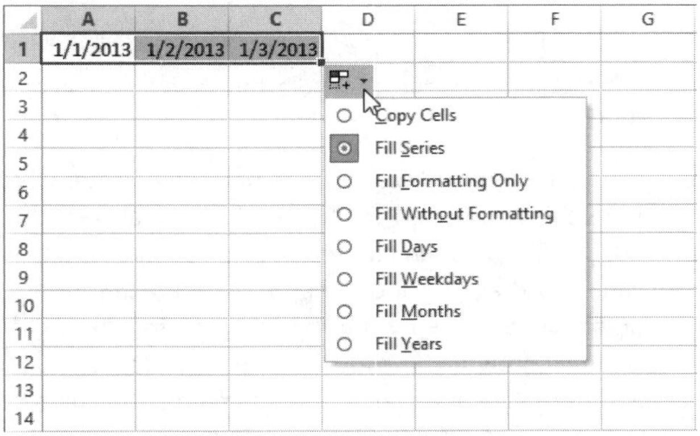

An interesting feature of this menu is Fill Weekdays, which not only increments a day or date series but also skips weekend days. Depending on the original selection, different options might be available on the menu.

Dragging the fill handle with the right mouse button

When you use the right mouse button to fill a range or extend a series, a shortcut menu appears when you release the button, as shown in Figure 8-26. This menu differs somewhat from the Auto Fill Options menu and lets you specify what you want to happen in advance, as opposed to the Auto Fill Options menu giving you the ability to change the action after the fact.

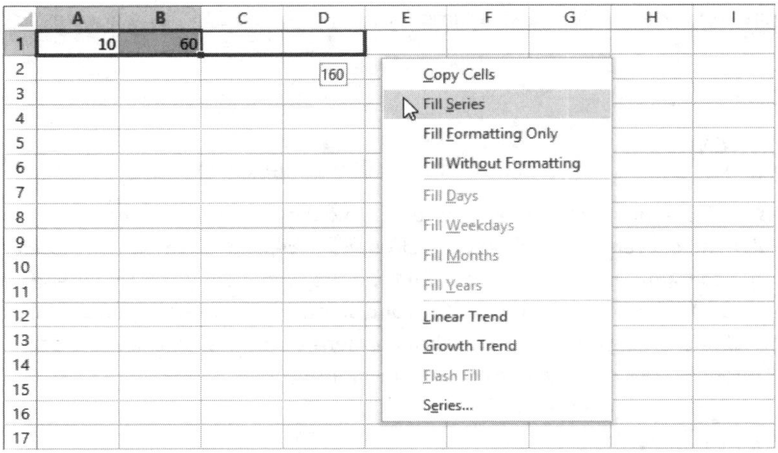

Figure 8-26 If you right-click and drag the fill handle, this shortcut menu appears when you release the mouse button.

The box that appears on the screen adjacent to the pointer indicates what the last number of this sequence would be if we dragged the fill handle as usual (with the left mouse button)—in this case, 160. The Linear Trend command creates a simple linear series similar to that which you can create by dragging the fill handle with the left mouse button. Growth Trend creates a simple nonlinear growth series by using the selected cells to extrapolate points along an exponential growth curve. In Figure 8-27, rows 4 through 6 in column A contain a series created using Linear Trend, and the same rows in column C contain a series created using Growth Trend, starting with the same values.

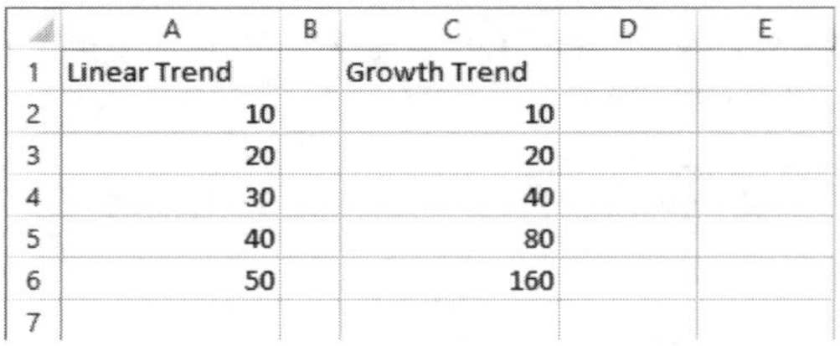

	A	B	C	D	E
1	Linear Trend		Growth Trend		
2	10		10		
3	20		20		
4	30		40		
5	40		80		
6	50		160		
7					

Figure 8-27 We created a linear trend series in column A and a growth trend series in column C.

Using the Series command

On the Home tab in the Editing group, clicking the Fill menu and then Series displays the Series dialog box shown in Figure 8-28, which you use to create custom incremental series. Alternatively, you can display the Series dialog box by selecting one or more cells containing numbers, dragging the fill handle with the right mouse button, and clicking Series on the shortcut menu.

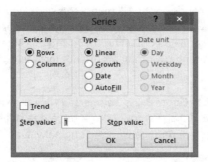

Figure 8-28 Use the Series dialog box for more control when creating a series.

In the Series dialog box, you can specify an interval with which to increment the series (*step value*) and a maximum value for the series (*stop value*). Using this method has a couple of advantages over direct mouse manipulation techniques. First, you do not need to select a range to fill, and second, you can specify increments (step values) without first selecting cells containing examples of incremented values. You can select examples of values if you want, but it is not necessary.

The Rows option tells Excel to use the first value in each row to fill the cells to the right. The Columns option tells Excel to use the first value in each column to fill the cells below. For example, if you select a range of cells in advance that is taller than it is wide, Excel automatically selects the Columns option when you open the Series dialog box. Excel uses the Type options in conjunction with the start values in selected cells and the value in the Step Value box to create your series. If you select examples first, Step Value reflects the increment between the selected cells.

The Linear option adds the value specified in the Step Value box to the selected values in your worksheet to extend the series. The Growth option multiplies the last value in the selection by the step value and extrapolates the rest of the values to create the series. If you select the Date option, you can specify the type of date series from the options in the Date Unit area. The Auto Fill option works like using the fill handle to drag a series, extending the series by using the interval between the selected values; it determines the type of data and attempts to "divine" your intention. Selecting the Trend check box extrapolates an exponential series, but it works only if you select more than one value before displaying the Series dialog box.

For more about typing dates, see "Entering a series of dates" in Chapter 15, "Formatting and calculating date and time."

Using the Fill menu commands

Use the Down, Right, Up, and Left commands on the Fill menu, shown in Figure 8-29, to copy selected cells to an adjacent range of cells. Before clicking these commands, select the range you want to fill, including the cell or cells containing the formulas, values, and formats you want to use to fill the selected range. (Comments are not included when you use these Fill commands.)

Suppose cell A1 contains the value 100. In Figure 8-29, we selected the range A1:K2 and then clicked Fill, Right to copy the value 100 across row 1. With the range still selected, we can click Fill, Down to finish filling the selected range with the original value.

> **Note**
> You can also use keyboard shortcuts to duplicate Home, Fill, Down (press Ctrl+D) and Home, Fill, Right (press Ctrl+R).

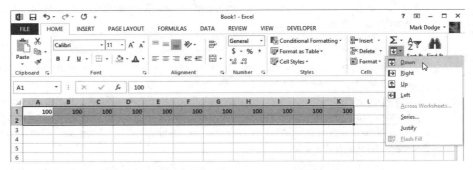

Figure 8-29 Use the Fill menu for quick access to common fill actions.

The Across Worksheets command on the Fill menu copies cells from one worksheet to other worksheets in the same workbook. For more information about using the Across Worksheets command, see "Filling a group" later in this chapter.

Distributing long entries using the Justify command

Clicking Fill, Justify doesn't do what you might think it does. It splits a cell entry and distributes it into two or more adjacent rows. Unlike other Fill commands, Justify modifies the
contents of the original cell.

For information about the *other* justify feature—that is, justifying text in a single cell—see
"Justifying text in cells" in Chapter 9.

For example, in the worksheet on the left in Figure 8-30, cell A1 contains a long text entry.
To divide this text into cell-sized parts, select cell A1 and click Home, Fill, Justify. The result
appears on the right in Figure 8-30.

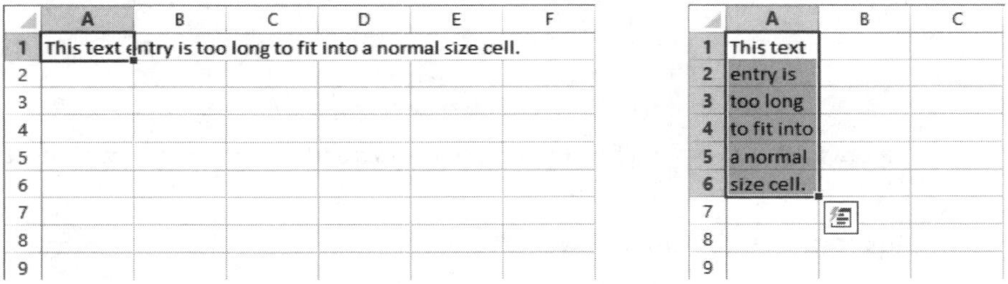

Figure 8-30 Clicking Justify distributes the long label in cell A1 to cells A1:A6.

When you click Justify, Excel displays a message warning you that this command uses as
many cells below the selection as necessary to distribute the contents. Excel overwrites any
cells that are in the way in the following manner:

- If you select a multirow range, Justify redistributes the text in all selected cells. For
  example, you can widen column A in Figure 8-30, select the filled range A1:A6, and
  click Justify again to redistribute the contents using the new column width.

- If you select a multicolumn range, Justify redistributes only the entries in the leftmost
  column of the range, but it uses the total width of the range you select as its guide-
  line for determining the length of the justified text. The cells in adjacent columns are
  not affected, although the justified text appears truncated if the adjacent column's
  cells are not empty.

Creating custom lists

If you find yourself repeatedly entering a particular sequence in your worksheets, such as a
list of names or products, you can use the Excel Custom Lists feature to make entering that
sequence as easy as dragging the mouse. After you create your custom list, you can enter
it into any range of cells by typing any item from the sequence in a cell and then dragging the fill handle. For example, in Figure 8-31 we entered a single name in cell A1 and

dragged the fill handle down. The text in cells A2:A9 was filled in automatically matching the sequence in the custom list we created.

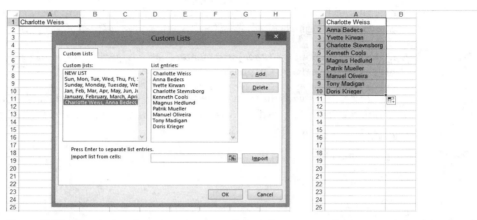

Figure 8-31 You can insert your own custom lists and sequences that you enter by dragging the fill handle.

To create a custom list, follow these steps:

1. Click the File tab, click Options, and click the Advanced category.

2. Scroll all the way to the bottom, and click the Edit Custom Lists button (under General).

3. With New List selected in the Custom Lists box, type the items you want to include in your list in the List Entries box. Be sure to type the items in the order you want them to appear.

4. Click Add to add the list to the Custom Lists box.

5. Click OK to return to the worksheet.

Importing custom lists

You can also create a custom list by importing the entries in an existing cell range. To import the entries shown in Figure 8-31, we selected a cell range containing the list of names before opening the Excel Options dialog box. When you open the Edit Custom Lists dialog box, the address of the selected range appears next to the Import button, which you can click to add the new list. (You can also select the list after opening the dialog box. You need to click in the edit box next to the Import button, and then you can drag on the worksheet to select the cells.)

Automatic parsing and concatenation using Flash Fill

New in 2013, Flash Fill might be the smartest command on the Fill menu. It does tricks that Microsoft refers to as "splitting columns of data" (also known as *parsing*) and "combining text from two or more cells into one cell" (also known as *concatenating*). Flash Fill can also be used to change the case of text.

One of the great things about Flash Fill is that often, you don't even need to click anything; it just happens. For example, the worksheet in Figure 8-32 contains staff names split into separate cells, but suppose you also need full names together in one cell. One full name was typed into column C, and then after typing the first letter of the next name in the second row, Flash Fill displayed what it deduced were the desired concatenated results—in this case, the correct ones.

	A	B	C	D	E
1	**Last Name**	**First Name**			
2	Nadav	Yinon	Yinon Nadav		
3	Abrus	Luka	Luka Abrus		
4	Kopac	Barbara	Barbara Ko		
5	Bouraima	Herve	Herve Bou		
6	Seidler	Joachim	Joachim S		
7	Weinfurter	Walter	Walter We		
8	Overeem	Pascaline	Pascaline		
9	Gil	Enrique	Enrique Gi		
10	Amireh	Kamil	Kamil Ami		
11	Ozolins	Gatis	Gatis Ozo		
12	Tuntisangaroon	Sittichai	Sittichai Tu		
13	Krenthaller	Elisabeth	Elisabeth		
14	Park	Dan	Dan Park		
15	Sario	Esko	Esko Sario		
16	Riis	Bjarne	Bjarne Riis		
17	Madigan	Tony	Tony Madi		

| ◄ ► | Data | **Names** | Custom List | ⊕ |

Figure 8-32 Flash Fill guesses what you want to concatenate and displays its suggestions for the rest of the column in gray.

You'll find the StaffList.xlsx workbook with the other examples on the companion website.

With the gray Flash Fill entries displayed as shown in Figure 8-32, pressing Enter is all you need to do to finish the action and fill the suggested entries down the column. You can also add text to be inserted in each entry, such as adding a comma to create a column of last-name-first entries such as "Nadov, Yinon." Or for example, Figure 8-33 shows the same worksheet with an email address entered in cell C2, which was then re-selected. Then on the Home tab, we clicked the Fill menu in the Editing group, and then clicked Flash Fill, which used the example entry to extrapolate the rest of the entries in the column, as shown in Figure 8-34.

Figure 8-33 You can select an example entry and then click the Flash Fill command to fill the rest of the column for you.

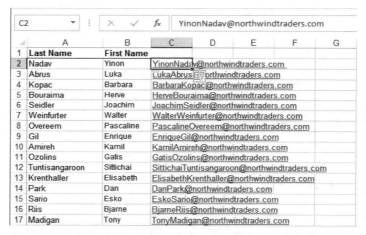

Figure 8-34 Flash Fill can make repetitive work like this a lot easier.

> **Note**
>
> Excel automatically hyperlinks email addresses when you type them in. Two actions occur after you press Enter: the cell entry, and then the hyperlink. This is handy if you want to be able to click and send email directly, but if you'd rather avoid the blue underlined text, click Undo—once—immediately after pressing Enter to undo the hyperlink action.

Flash Fill can go both ways. Suppose you have a column of data where first and last names are already combined, but you need them in separate columns. Figure 8-35 shows such a worksheet, where we used Flash Fill to help parse the last names into column B, and after entering the first letter of the second name in cell C3, Flash Fill intervenes with a complete column of suggested entries.

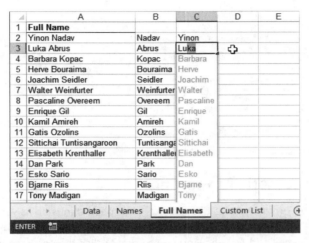

Figure 8-35 Flash Fill can parse as well as it can concatenate.

> **Note**
>
> Flash Fill works well as long as your data is consistent, but even if it isn't, it will probably save you a lot of work. For example, if you have a column containing middle names, but not all of its cells contain data, you might need to edit extra spaces from individual cells after using Flash Fill. (Whether your data is consistent or not, you should always check your results.) If your data is too inconsistent for Flash Fill, try using functions, as described in "Understanding text functions" in Chapter 14, "Everyday functions."

Flash Fill performs another neat trick: changing the case of text. For example, suppose some of your source data is in all caps, such as cells A4, B5, and A8:B8 in the worksheet shown in Figure 8-36. Using the same method of typing in examples, the results shown in Figure 8-36 were suggested by Flash Fill after typing the first letter in the second name.

▲	A	B	C	D	E
1	Last Name	First Name			
2	Nadav	Yinon	yinon.nadav		
3	Abrus	Luka	luka.abrus		
4	KOPAC	Barbara	barbara.kopac		
5	Bouraima	HERVE	herve.bouraima		
6	Seidler	Joachim	joachim.seidler		
7	Weinfurter	Walter	walter.weinfurter		
8	Overeem	Pascaline	pascaline.overeem		
9	GIL	ENRIQUE	enrique.gil		
10	Amireh	Kamil	kamil.amireh		
11	Ozolins	Gatis	gatis.ozolins		
12	Tuntisangaroon	Sittichai	sittichai.tuntisangaroon		
13	Krenthaller	Elisabeth	elisabeth.krenthaller		
14	Park	Dan	dan.park		
15	Sario	Esko	esko.sario		
16	Riis	Bjarne	bjarne.riis		
17	Madigan	Tony	tony.madigan		

Figure 8-36 You can change the case of text with Flash Fill.

Controlling automatic formatting

Excel has several AutoFormat features designed to help speed things up as you work. As you saw in Figure 8-34, in the Flash Fill section, Excel automatically creates a hyperlink when you type in an email address, allowing you to simply click the entry to launch your email program. AutoFormat also adds a hyperlink to any Internet address you type into a cell, which automatically launches your browser when clicked. This is very handy if you want to include one-click access to supporting information in your worksheets—or very annoying if you don't.

Tables also have special AutoFormat skills. If you are working with a table, additional options control the extension of formatting and formulas.

> For more about tables, see Chapter 22, "Managing information in tables." For more about AutoCorrect, see "Fixing errors as you type" later in this chapter.

You might want to turn one or more of these features off—for example, if you want to enter email addresses without hyperlinks. You can control whether or not these features are applied. Click the File tab, click Options, and then select the Proofing category. Click the AutoCorrect Options button to display the AutoCorrect dialog box shown in Figure 8-37. The tab labeled AutoFormat As You Type contains two options pertaining to tables and one that controls whether Excel automatically creates hyperlinks whenever you type recognizable Internet and network paths.

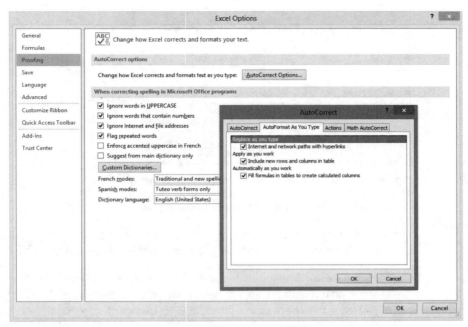

Figure 8-37 The AutoCorrect dialog box controls automatic hyperlinking, and format and formula extension when working in tables.

Finding and replacing stuff

Suppose you built a large worksheet and you now need to find every occurrence of a specific string of text or values in that worksheet. (In computerese, a *string* is defined as any continuous series of characters—text, numbers, math operators, or punctuation symbols.) You can use the Find & Select menu in the Editing group on the Home tab to locate any string, cell reference, or range name in cells or formulas on a worksheet. You can also find formatting with or without strings and then replace what you find with new strings, new formatting, or both.

On the Home tab, in the Editing group, you see the Find & Select button, which is actually a menu. When you click the Find command on the Find & Select menu (or press Ctrl+F), the Find And Replace dialog box appears, as shown in Figure 8-38. (If yours looks different, click Options to expand the dialog box.)

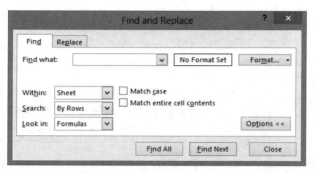

Figure 8-38 Use the Find tab to locate a character string.

Use the options on the Find tab in the following ways:

- **Find What** Type the string of characters you want to find. Be exact. Excel finds exactly what you type, including spaces—nothing more, nothing less.

- **Match Case** Distinguish capital letters from lowercase letters, finding only occurrences that match the uppercase and lowercase characters of the Find What string. If you leave this check box unselected, Excel disregards case.

- **Match Entire Cell Contents** Find only complete and individual occurrences of the string. Ordinarily, Find searches for any occurrence of a string, even if it is part of another string.

- **Within** Choose to search only the active worksheet or the entire workbook.

- **Search** Choose to search by rows or by columns. Unless your worksheet is very large, your search takes place in the blink of an eye, so this option might not be much faster one way or the other. Finding items in a particular order might be desirable, however. When you select the By Rows option, Excel looks through the worksheet horizontally, row by row, starting with the currently selected cell. The By Columns option searches through the worksheet column by column, beginning with the selected cell.

- **Look In** Choose formulas, values, or comments. The default is Formulas, which means all text and numeric entries, regardless of formatting, as well as formulas. When you select Values, Excel searches text and numeric entries and only the displayed results of formulas. When you select Comments, Excel examines only the text attached as a comment to a cell.

> **Note**
>
> If you want to search the entire workbook or worksheet to locate a string of characters (depending on the selection you make in the Within drop-down list), be sure that only a single cell is selected before clicking the Find command. Excel begins its search from that cell and travels through the entire worksheet or workbook. Select more than one cell before choosing Find, and the search is confined to the selected cells.

The nuances of the Look In options, Formulas and Values, can be confusing. Remember that the underlying contents of a cell and the displayed value of that cell are often not the same. When using these options, you should keep in mind the following:

- If a cell contains a formula, the displayed value of the cell is usually the result of that formula.

- If a cell contains a numeric value, the displayed value of the formatted cell might or might not be the same as the cell's underlying value.

- If a cell displays a text value, it is probably the same as the underlying value, unless the cell contains a formula that uses text functions.

- If a cell has the General format, the displayed and underlying values of the cell are usually the same.

For example, if you type **1000** in the Find What text box and select Values as the Look In option, Excel looks at what is displayed in each cell. If you have an unformatted cell with the value 1000 in it, Excel finds it. If another cell has the same value formatted as currency ($1,000), Excel does not find it because the displayed value does not precisely match the Find What string. Because you're searching through values and not formulas, Excel ignores the underlying content of the cell, which is 1000. If you select the Formulas option, Excel finds both instances, ignoring the formatting of the displayed values.

> **Note**
>
> If you close the Find And Replace dialog box and want to search for the next occurrence of the same string in your worksheet, you can press F4, the keyboard shortcut for repeating the last action (of any kind). Later, you can repeat your last search, even if you have performed other tasks since that search, by pressing Shift+F4.

Chapter 8

Finding formatting

Excel provides a way to find cells based on formatting in conjunction with other criteria, and even to find and replace specifically formatted cells, regardless of their content. If you click the Format button in the Find And Replace dialog box shown in Figure 8-39, the Find Format dialog box shown in Figure 8-40 appears. This dialog box has two names—Find Format and Replace Format—depending on whether you clicked the Format button that is adjacent to the Find What text box or the one adjacent to the Replace With text box on the Replace tab. Otherwise, the two dialog boxes are identical. You can select any number of options in this dialog box and click OK when you finish to add them to your criteria.

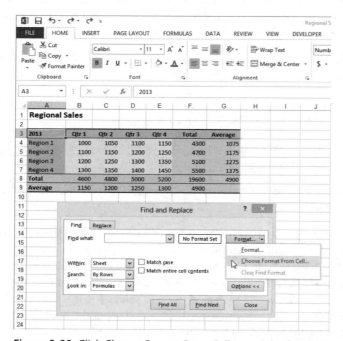

Figure 8-39 Click Choose Format From Cell to use the formatting of a selected cell as search criteria.

If you click the arrow button next to the Format button to display the Format menu, you can click Choose Format From Cell, as shown in Figure 8-39. Choose Format From Cell is also available as a button at the bottom of the Find Format (or Replace Format) dialog box shown in Figure 8-40.

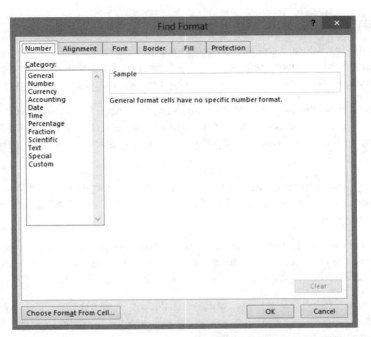

Figure 8-40 Click Format in the Find And Replace dialog box to display the Find Format dialog box.

You'll find the Regional Sales.xlsx file with the other examples on the companion website.

When you click Choose Format From Cell, a small eyedropper appears next to the pointer when you position it over the worksheet area. Click a cell that is formatted the way you want, and the Find And Replace dialog box displays the word *Preview** in the box that otherwise displays the message *No Format Set*. After you set your formatting criteria, Excel will not find any character strings you search for unless the formatting criteria also match. Without a string, Excel searches for the formatting only. For example, choosing the formatting of the selected cell—A3—in Figure 8-39 as the Find What criteria, clicking Find All would result in the selection of all the matching cells on the current worksheet. Or if you search for the word *Sales* and specify bold as a formatting criterion, Excel finds any cells containing the word *Sales*, but only if it is displayed in bold type. The more formatting options you set, the narrower the search.

Here are two things to watch out for. First, make sure the cell you use as an example does not have any nonapparent formatting applied, such as a number format in a cell displaying only text. Second, be sure to click Clear Find Format in the Format drop-down list shown in Figure 8-39 to remove the formatting criteria after you're finished. Otherwise, you might not notice the word *Preview** in the dialog box, and future searches could produce unexpected results.

Specifying variables using wildcard characters

You can use the wildcard characters ? and * to widen the scope of your searches. Wildcard characters are helpful when you're searching for a group of similar but not identical entries or when you're searching for an entry you don't quite remember. Use them as follows:

- The ? character takes the place of any single character in a Find What string. For example, the Find What string 1?0 matches the values 1000, 190, 1900, 100A, Z1R0, and so on. (This finds any entry that contains the search string, even if the entry is part of a larger string.)

- The * character takes the place of zero or more characters in a Find What string. For example, the string 12* matches the entries 12, 120, 125, 1200000, and even 123 Maple Street.

You can use the wildcard characters anywhere within a Find What string. For example, you can use the string *s to find all entries that end with *s*. Alternatively, you can use the string *es* to find each cell that contains the string sequence *es* anywhere in its formula or value.

To search for a string that actually contains a wildcard character (? or *), type a tilde (~) preceding the character. For example, to find the string Who? (including the question mark), type **Who~?** as your Find What text.

Replacing what you find

Replace works much like Find—in fact, they open the same dialog box. When you click Replace on the Find & Select menu on the Home tab (or press Ctrl+H), you see a dialog box like the one in Figure 8-41. (If yours looks different, click Options to expand the dialog box.)

For example, to replace each occurrence of the name Joan Smith with John Smith, type **Joan Smith** in the Find What text box and **John Smith** in the Replace With text box. You can also find and replace formats using the dual Format buttons. For example, you could search for every occurrence of 14-point bold and italic Times Roman and replace it with 12-point, double-underlined Arial.

To replace every occurrence of a string or formatting, click Replace All. Instead of pausing at each occurrence to let you change or skip the current cell, Excel locates all the cells containing the Find What string and replaces them.

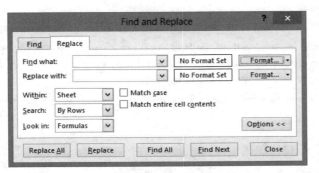

Figure 8-41 You can find and replace character strings and formats by clicking the Replace command on the Find & Select menu.

The expanding dialog box

The Find And Replace dialog box does a neat trick. After you execute a search, the dialog box expands to list all the cells with contents that match your criteria:

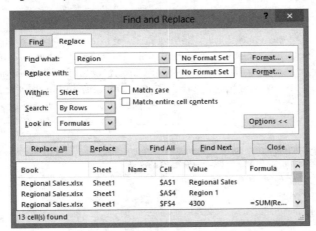

When you select an entry in the list, Excel jumps to that location and selects the cell. You can drag the bottom border of the dialog box to see more of the list. This feature makes it much easier to do extensive find-and-replace tasks because you can see the list at all times; because items remain in the list even after you execute a replacement operation; and because you can keep the dialog box open, change worksheets or workbooks, and use the Undo button while you work.

Chapter 8

> **Note**
> Although you can use wildcards in the Find What box to aid in your search, if you type wildcard characters in the Replace With box, Excel uses a literal ? or * symbol when it replaces each occurrence of your Find What text.

Getting the words right

Worksheets are not all numbers, of course, so Excel includes features to help make typing and editing text easier. AutoCorrect helps you fix common typing errors even before they become spelling problems. For the rest of the words in your worksheets, the spelling checker helps make sure you entered your text according to Webster's. You might even be able to get AutoComplete to do some of the typing for you. And finally, the Research, Thesaurus, and Translate features lend some real clout in your quest for perfect prose.

Fixing errors as you type

Perhaps you have to stop and think "*i* before *e* except after *c*" every time you type *receive*. Perhaps you're a blazing typist who constantly hits the second letter of a capitalized word before the Shift key snaps back. The Excel AutoCorrect feature helps fix many common typing and spelling errors on the fly. Click the File tab, Options, and in the Proofing category, click the AutoCorrect Options button to display the AutoCorrect dialog box, shown in Figure 8-42.

Figure 8-42 You can add your most common typing errors to the AutoCorrect dialog box.

> **Note**
>
> AutoCorrect works when you are entering text in cells, in formulas, in text boxes, on worksheet controls, and in chart labels. AutoCorrect does not work when you're entering text in dialog boxes.

The AutoCorrect tab in the AutoCorrect dialog box contains the following options:

- **Show AutoCorrect Options Buttons**   Controls the display of a menu when Excel detects an error, listing actions you can perform on the affected cell.

- **Correct TWo INitial CApitals**   If a word contains both uppercase and lowercase characters, checks that only one capital letter appears at the beginning of the word. If not, Excel changes subsequent uppercase characters to lowercase. If a word is all caps, Excel leaves it alone (assuming that this was intentional). AutoCorrect does not attempt to modify *mid-cap* words like AutoCorrect, because they have become commonplace.

- **Capitalize First Letter Of Sentences**   Makes sure you use *sentence case* (even if your "sentences" aren't grammatically correct), based on the position of periods.

- **Capitalize Names Of Days**   Recognizes days and applies initial caps. This does not work on abbreviations like *Sat.*

- **Correct Accidental Use Of cAPS LOCK Key**   Scans for this kind of random Shift key mistake.

- **Replace Text As You Type**   Controls the application of the replacement list at the bottom of the dialog box, which lists a number of common replacement items. You can add your own grammatical faux pas to this list using the Replace and With text boxes and the Add button.

In addition to correcting common typing errors, such as replacing *adn* with *and*, Auto-Correct also provides a few useful shortcuts in its replacement list. For example, instead of searching for the right font and symbol to add a copyright mark, you can type **(c)**, and AutoCorrect replaces it with ©.

All these AutoCorrect options use specific rules of order. They use similar logical methods to determine your real meaning. But don't assume that AutoCorrect (or the spelling checker) knows what you mean. Always proofread important work.

> **Note**
>
> If you have other Microsoft Office programs installed, anything you add to the Auto-Correct list in Excel also appears in other Office programs' AutoCorrect lists.

Typing Internet and network addresses

We like to refer to this feature as *AutoAutoFormat*. The AutoFormat As You Type tab in the AutoCorrect dialog box (shown in Figure 8-37 earlier in this chapter) offers the Internet And Network Paths With Hyperlinks option under Replace As You Type. This converts a string recognized as a valid uniform resource locator (URL) or network path into an active hyper-link. As you finish typing it, you can click it immediately to go there.

Using custom AutoCorrect actions

The Actions tab in the AutoCorrect dialog box shown in Figure 8-43 is the repository for customized actions that appear on floating option button menus when appropriate. Excel comes with several of them, and you can download additional actions as they become available on the Microsoft Office Online website (*office.microsoft.com/*).

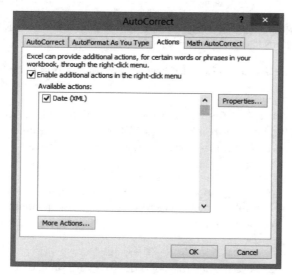

Figure 8-43 The Actions tab in the AutoCorrect dialog box controls the display of special floating option button menus.

The following options are available in the AutoCorrect dialog box:

- **Enable Additional Actions In The Right-Click Menu**   Turns the list of available actions on or off.

- **Available Actions**   Lists the currently installed actions.

- **More Actions**   Connects to the Microsoft Office website to find additional custom actions you can add to the list. You need to be connected to the Internet.

- **Properties**   Tells you more about the action you select in the Available Actions list. You need to be connected to the Internet for this one.

Letting Excel help with typing chores

Often when entering a large amount of data in one sitting, you end up typing the same entries repeatedly. The AutoComplete feature cuts down the amount of typing you need to do. It also increases the accuracy of your entries by partially automating them. Auto-Complete is on by default, but you can turn it off by clicking the File tab, Options, and then Advanced, and then clearing the Enable AutoComplete For Cell Values check box in the Editing Options area.

When you begin typing a cell entry, AutoComplete scans all the entries in the same column and determines as each character is typed whether the column contains a possible match. (This works only when you are typing in a cell adjacent to other entries.) For example, in Figure 8-44, as soon as we typed **W** in cell A14, AutoComplete finished the entry with the unique match found in the same column: Weiss, Charlotte. The text added by AutoComplete is highlighted, so you can either continue typing, if that isn't your intended entry, or press Enter or an arrow key to accept the completion and move to another cell.

	A	B	C
1	**Northwind Traders**		
2	2013		Sales Staff
3	Name	Units	Sales
4	Kirwan, Yvette	122.00	28,616.32
5	Krieger, Doris	41.00	9,616.96
6	Madigan, Tony	67.00	15,715.52
7	Hedlund, Magnus	108.00	25,332.48
8	Cools, Kenneth	111.00	26,036.16
9	Oliveira, Manuel	89.00	20,875.84
10	Stevnsborg, Charlotte	119.00	49,726.72
11	Mueller, Patrik	98.00	22,986.88
12	Bedecs, Anna	143.00	33,542.08
13	Weiss, Charlotte	184.00	100,626.24
14	Weiss, Charlotte		-
15	Total	1,082.00	333,075.20
16			

	A	B	C
1	**Northwind Traders**		
2	2013		Sales Staff
3	Name	Units	Sales
4	Kirwan, Yvette	122.00	28,616.32
5	Krieger, Doris	41.00	9,616.96
6	Madigan, Tony	67.00	15,715.52
7	Hedlund, Magnus	108.00	25,332.48
8	Cools, Kenneth	111.00	26,036.16
9	Oliveira, Manuel	89.00	20,875.84
10	Stevnsborg, Charlotte	119.00	49,726.72
11	Mueller, Patrik	98.00	22,986.88
12	Bedecs, Anna	143.00	33,542.08
13	Weiss, Charlotte	184.00	100,626.24
14	Weiler, Cornelia		-
15	Total	1,082.00	333,075.20
16			

Figure 8-44 Type enough letters to match an existing entry, and AutoComplete finishes it for you. As shown on the right, keep typing to override AutoComplete.

Chapter 8

AutoComplete matches only exact cell entries, not individual words in a cell. For example, if you begin typing **John** in column A of the worksheet, AutoCorrect doesn't intervene because it is not an exact match for any existing entry. Wisely, AutoComplete does not work when you're editing formulas.

Instead of typing, you can right-click a cell and click Pick From Drop-Down List on the shortcut menu to select an entry from the same column, as shown in Figure 8-45. After Excel displays the list, click the entry you want, and Excel enters it in the cell. Of course, you can't add new entries this way, as we did in Figure 8-44; only existing entries in the same column are available in the list.

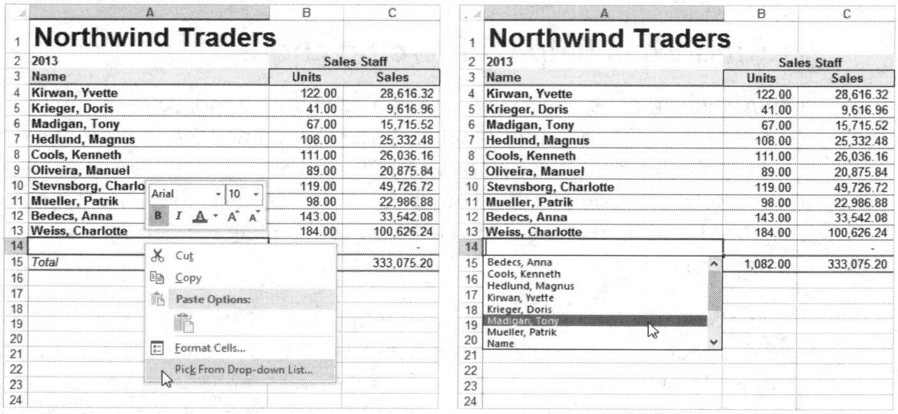

Figure 8-45 Right-click the cell directly below a list, and click Pick From Drop-Down List to display a list of unique entries in the column.

INSIDE OUT   Create your own typing shorthand

You can use AutoCorrect to monitor your own common typing errors and create your own typing shortcuts. Click the File tab, Options, and then click the AutoCorrect Options button in the Proofing category. Add your shorthand entries to the Replace Text As You Type area on the AutoCorrect tab. (Figure 8-42 shows the AutoCorrect tab in the AutoCorrect dialog box.) Type the characters you want to use as the shorthand "code" in the Replace box, type the characters with which you want to replace them in the With box, and finally click Add. For example, you can type **MS** in the Replace box and then type **Microsoft Corporation** in the With box. Thereafter, each time you type **MS**, Excel replaces it with the words *Microsoft Corporation*. Be sure you choose unique codes; otherwise, Excel might apply AutoCorrect to entries you don't want changed.

Cheking yer speling

Click the Review tab on the ribbon, and then click Spelling to check the spelling of an entire worksheet or any part of it. If Excel finds any suspect words, the Spelling dialog box shown in Figure 8-46 appears. Keep the following tips in mind when using the spelling checker:

● If you select a single cell, Excel checks the entire worksheet, including all cells, comments, Excel graphic objects, and page headers and footers.

● If you select more than one cell, Excel checks the selected cells only.

● If the formula bar is active, Excel checks only its contents.

● If you select words that are in the formula bar, Excel checks the selected words only.

● If the range you select for checking the spelling contains hidden or outlined cells that are not visible, Excel checks these as well.

● Cells that contain formulas are not checked.

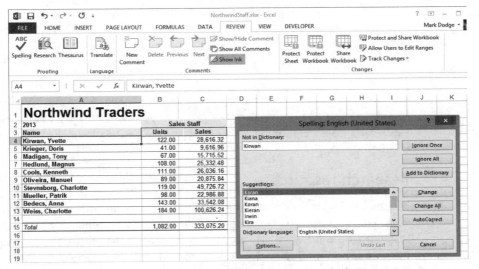

Figure 8-46 Use the Spelling dialog box to review your text and add often-used words to your dictionary.

Click Options in the Spelling dialog box to display the Excel Options dialog box. Click the Proofing category, shown in Figure 8-47. Here you can access the AutoCorrect dialog box, choose dictionaries in different languages, and select special options such as the Ignore Internet And File Addresses check box.

> **Note**
> You can press F7 to instantly begin checking the spelling.

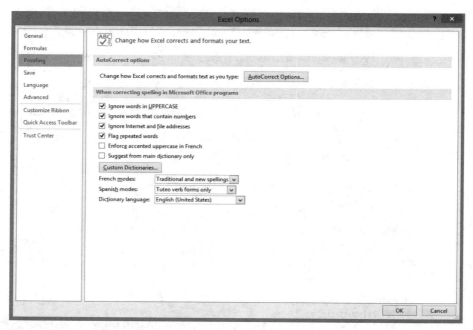

Figure 8-47 Gain more control over spelling with the Proofing tab in the Excel Options dialog box.

Research resources

Besides Spelling, the buttons in the Proofing and Language groups on the Review tab—Research, Thesaurus, and Translate—provide some real horsepower when you are ready to invest time in the word play accompanying your numeric adventures. Clicking any of these three buttons displays a task pane docked to the right side of the screen, as shown in Figure 8-48. Note that only the Research button is a toggle—clicking it a second time closes the task pane. Clicking either of the other two buttons opens the task pane if it is not already visible, but clicking a button again does not close the task pane; it just changes what appears within it.

The cell or range selected when you open the task pane automatically appears in the Search For box. Click the arrow button to the right of the Search For box to execute the search; any search results appear in the main area of the task pane. If you already have the task pane open and you want to change the search text, you can either type it or press Alt while clicking a cell containing the text you want, which then appears in the Search For box.

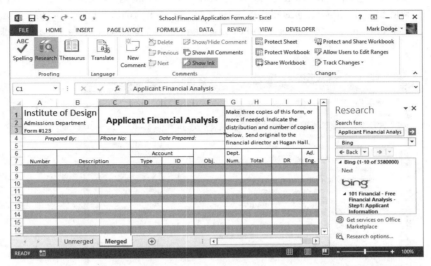

Figure 8-48 The Research, Thesaurus, and Translate buttons on the Review tab open a task pane.

The second box under Search For is a drop-down list that lets you narrow your search to particular resources, as shown in Figure 8-49. As you try different searches in the task pane, click the Back and Next buttons (a.k.a. Previous Search and Next Search) to peruse the various search results.

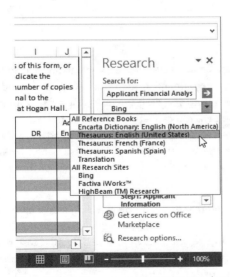

Figure 8-49 You can narrow your search to use specific resources.

You can alter the contents of the drop-down list shown in Figure 8-49 by clicking Research Options, located at the bottom of the task pane, which displays the Research Options dialog box, shown in Figure 8-50. Here you can add places to look to the list, remove places, add to or remove the available options, and specify parental controls (if you are logged on as an administrator). To see the details of a particular service, select it and click the Properties button.

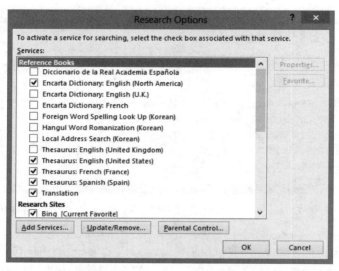

Figure 8-50 Specify the research resources available using the Research Options dialog box.

INSIDE OUT   Task pane tricks

You can reposition or resize the task pane by clicking the small arrow next to the Close button and choosing the appropriate command. Clicking the Move command changes the cursor to a four-headed arrow, letting you drag the task pane away from its docked position on the right side of the screen. You can let it float above the workspace or dock it on the left side if you prefer. After clicking the Size command, drag the mouse (you don't even need to click) to reposition the border of the task pane to make it wider, up to half the screen width when docked. Click when the size of the task pane is to your liking.

In actuality, you don't need these commands at all. You can drag a task pane away from the dock by its title bar at any time. You can drag the borders of the undocked task pane with impunity, making it as large as you like. To restore a floating task pane to its previous docked configuration, double-click its title bar. To remove a task pane from view, click the Close button in its upper-right corner.

At the bottom of the task pane is a Get Services On Office Marketplace link, which connects you to the Microsoft Office website, where Excel then checks to see whether there are any updates to existing services or any new services available that you can add to your research options.

Editing multiple worksheets

If you need to create a bunch of similar worksheets, Excel helps you save some clicks and keystrokes. For example, if the workbook you're creating calls for a separate worksheet for each month, division, product, or whatever, you can save a lot of time by creating them all at once using the techniques described in this section and then tweak each worksheet as needed.

For information about moving and copying worksheets to other workbooks, see "Dragging worksheets between workbooks" in Chapter 6, "How to work a worksheet." For more information about formatting, see Chapter 9.

Grouping worksheets for editing

You can group any number of worksheets in a workbook and then add, edit, or format data in all the worksheets in the group at the same time. Use this feature when you're creating or modifying a set of worksheets that are similar in purpose and structure—a set of monthly reports or departmental budgets, for example.

You can select and group worksheets by using one of these methods:

- Click the sheet tab of the first worksheet in a range of adjacent worksheets you want to work on, hold down Shift, and click the tab of the last worksheet in the range.

- Click the tab of any of the worksheets you want to work on, hold down Ctrl, and click the tabs of each worksheet you want to include in the group, whether or not the worksheets are adjacent.

- Right-click a sheet tab, and click Select All Sheets on the shortcut menu.

To create a workbook containing a separate worksheet for each month, all you need to do is open a new workbook and then click the New Sheet button 11 times, as shown in Figure 8-51.

Chapter 8

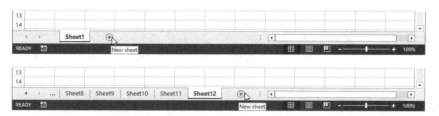

Figure 8-51 Click the New Sheet button to add sheets.

But you can also create new sheets by grouping and copying existing sheets, as we'll show in the following procedure:

1. Click the New Sheet button two times.

2. Click the Sheet1 tab, and then hold down Shift and click the Sheet3 tab. The worksheets are now grouped, as shown in Figure 8-52. Notice that the title bar of the workbook displays [Group] after the worksheet name, and all three sheet tabs are white.

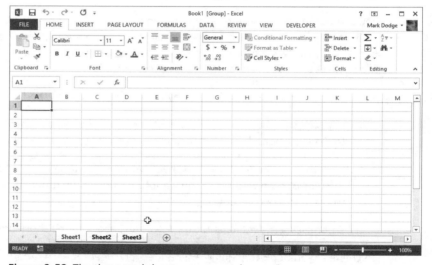

Figure 8-52 The three worksheets are grouped.

3. Right-click any of the selected tabs, and click Move Or Copy on the shortcut menu. In the Before Sheet list in the dialog box that appears, select Move To End. Select the Create A Copy check box, and then click OK. Excel creates three new worksheets, as shown in Figure 8-53.

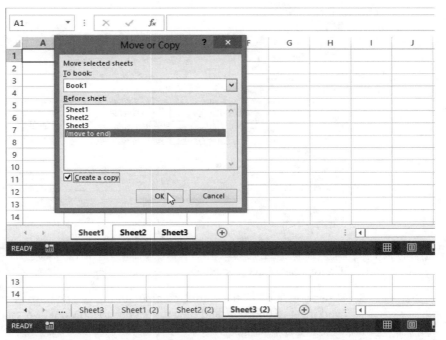

Figure 8-53 Copying a group of worksheets creates the same number of new worksheets.

4. Right-click any tab, and click Select All Sheets on the shortcut menu; then repeat step 3 to create 12 worksheets.

> **Note**
>
> The easiest way to create a new, blank worksheet is to click the New Sheet button. The technique described here is especially useful when you want to create copies of existing worksheets containing data.

5. Rename the worksheets by double-clicking each tab and typing a new name. We used the month abbreviations *Jan* through *Dec.*

6. Group all 12 worksheets by selecting their tabs, as described in step 2. Now, any entries or formatting changes you make in any one of the worksheets are duplicated in all the worksheets in the group.

7. Enter and format the text shown in Figure 8-54.

Figure 8-54 With group editing, Excel applies all edits and formats to all the worksheets.

8. When you finish all the entries, common formulas, and formatting, click any worksheet to ungroup, and then make edits to individual worksheets, such as adding each month's name and entering units and sales data.

You can add formatting, formulas, or any other data to the active worksheet in a group, and Excel modifies all member worksheets simultaneously. Excel transfers any changes you make to column width, row height, view options such as gridlines and scroll bars, and even the location of the active cell to the group.

You'll find the Northwind Brass Sales.xlsx file with the other examples on the companion website.

INSIDE OUT   Group-editing tasks

When you group several worksheets and then click one of the worksheets in the group with the intention of editing it individually, you're still in group-editing mode and could possibly make inadvertent changes to all your grouped worksheets. Keep your eye on the tabs—when they are white, they are all editable. Getting out of group-editing mode works differently, depending on how many worksheets you grouped.

If you grouped all the worksheets in a workbook, clicking any tab except that of the active worksheet exits group-editing mode and removes the [Group] indicator from the title bar of the workbook. However, if you selected some but not all of the worksheets in a workbook, clicking any other grouped sheet tab makes that worksheet active but does not exit group-editing mode. In this case, click any tab *outside* the group to exit group-editing mode.

Besides using the Move Or Copy command to rearrange and duplicate worksheets in a workbook, you can use the mouse to perform the same actions directly. Select a group and drag to move it to a different location. The cursor changes to include a little pad of paper, as shown here at the top:

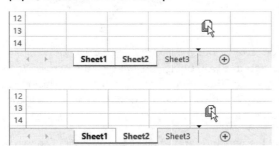

To copy a group of worksheets, drag the group and then press Ctrl before releasing the mouse button. The little pad of paper appears with a plus sign inside it, as shown in the bottom illustration. You can also drag grouped worksheets from one open workbook to another.

What you can do in group-editing mode

Use the Excel group-editing feature to perform the following actions on all member worksheets simultaneously:

- **Entering text**   Whatever you type in one worksheet is entered in all grouped worksheets.

- **Printing**   Using the Print, Print Preview, and Page Setup commands on the File tab affects every worksheet in your group.

- **Viewing**   On the View tab, the Zoom, Workbook Views, Show, and Window options apply to all the selected worksheets. You can even click View, Hide to hide all grouped worksheets.

- **Formatting**   Any formatting you do is applied to all group members at the same time, including row height, column width, font formats, conditional formatting, and cell styles.

- **Editing** This applies all editing actions—including entering formulas, inserting rows and columns, and using Find and Replace—to all worksheets in the group.

- **Page layout** On the Page Layout tab, changes made to themes, page setup options, the Scale To Fit setting, and most sheet options apply to the group.

- **Inserting headers and footers** Using the Header & Footer command on the Insert tab applies to every worksheet in the group.

Filling a group

If you aren't starting from scratch but want to duplicate existing data in one worksheet to a number of other worksheets in a workbook, you can click the Across Worksheets command, located on the Fill menu in the Editing group on the Home tab. This option is available only if you first establish a group. When you click this option, Excel displays the Fill Across Worksheets dialog box, shown in Figure 8-55.

For example, to copy all the text and formatting of the worksheet shown in Figure 8-54 to all the other grouped worksheets in the workbook (if we hadn't already done that using group-editing mode), we could select the range A1:J11 and then click Fill, Across Worksheets. With the All option selected, Excel transfers all text, formulas, and formatting to every other worksheet in the group. If you select the Contents option, Excel duplicates only text and values; the Formats option predictably duplicates only the formats. Using the Fill, Across Worksheets command does not copy row height, column width, or view options, but you can still apply these to the group manually.

Figure 8-55 Use the Fill Across Worksheets dialog box to copy selected data to all the worksheets in a group.

Auditing and documenting worksheets

Excel has a number of powerful and flexible features that help you audit and debug your worksheets and document your work. Most of the Excel auditing features appear on the Formulas tab, in the Formula Auditing group, which is shown in Figure 8-56.

Figure 8-56 The Formula Auditing group on the Formulas tab provides access to most of the auditing features.

Checking for errors

On the Formulas tab, click the Error Checking button to quickly find any error values displayed on the current worksheet and display the Error Checking dialog box if any errors are found, as shown in Figure 8-57. The first erroneous cell in the worksheet is selected, and its contents are displayed in the dialog box along with a suggestion about the nature of the problem.

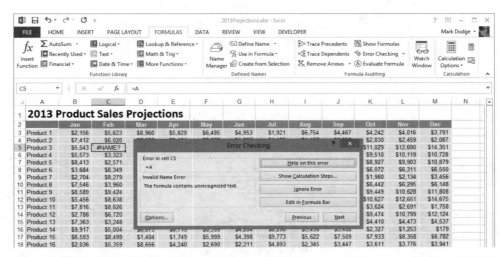

Figure 8-57 The Error Checking dialog box helps you figure out what's wrong with formulas that display error values.

When a problem appears in the dialog box, the following selections are available:

- Help On This Error displays a Help topic related to the problem cell.

- Show Calculation Steps displays the Evaluate Formula dialog box. See "Evaluating and auditing formulas" later in this chapter.

- Ignore Error skips the selected cell. To "unignore" errors, click Options and then click Reset Ignored Errors.

- Edit In Formula Bar opens the selected cell in the formula bar for editing. When you finish, click Resume. (The Help On This Error button changes to Resume.)

Click the Previous and Next buttons to locate additional errors on the current worksheet. Click the Options button to display the Formulas category in the Excel Options dialog box, shown in Figure 8-58. Select or clear the check boxes in the two Error Checking areas to determine the type of errors to look for and the way they are processed. Click the Reset Ignored Errors button if you want to recheck or if you clicked the Ignore Error button in the Error Checking dialog box by mistake.

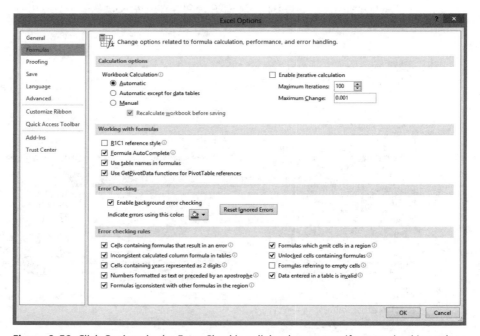

Figure 8-58 Click Options in the Error Checking dialog box to specify error-checking rules.

Evaluating and auditing formulas

Sometimes it's difficult to tell what's going on in a complex nested formula. A formula is *nested* when parts of it (called *arguments*) can be calculated separately. For example, in the formula =IF(Pay_Num<>"",Scheduled_Monthly_Payment,""), the named reference *Pay_Num* indicates a cell that must contain a value in order for the rest of the formula to function. To make this formula easier to read, you can replace this expression with a constant—in this case, 1 (indicating that the expression is TRUE). The formula would then be =IF(1<>"",Scheduled_Monthly_Payment,"").

When you click the Evaluate Formula button on the Formulas tab, you can resolve each nested expression one at a time in complex formulas. Figure 8-59 shows the Evaluate Formula dialog box in action.

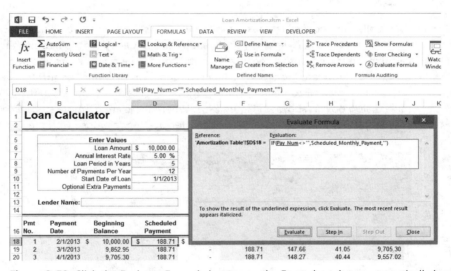

Figure 8-59 Click the Evaluate Formula button on the Formulas tab to systematically inspect nested formulas.

> **For more information about formulas, named references, and arguments, see Chapter 12.**

Click Evaluate to replace each calculable argument with its resulting value. You can click Evaluate as many times as necessary, depending on how many nested levels exist in the selected formula. For example, if you click Evaluate in Figure 8-59, Excel replaces the aforementioned Pay_Num reference with its value. Clicking Evaluate again calculates the next level, and so on, until you reach the end result, which in this case is $188.71, as shown in Figure 8-60.

You'll find the Loan Amortization.xlsm file with the other examples on the companion website.

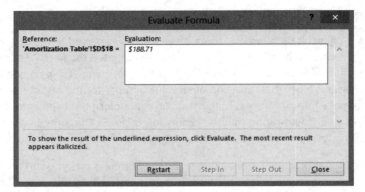

Figure 8-60 Each time you click the Evaluate button, Excel calculates another nested level in the selected formula.

Eventually, clicking Evaluate results in the formula's displayed value, and the Evaluate button changes to Restart, letting you repeat the steps. Click the Step In button to place each calculable reference into a separate box, making the hierarchy more apparent. In our example, the first evaluated reference is to a cell range, which cannot be further evaluated. If the reference is to a cell containing another formula, its address appears in the Evaluate Formula dialog box, as shown in Figure 8-61. Where there are no more steps to be displayed, click Step Out to close the Step In box and replace the reference with the resulting value.

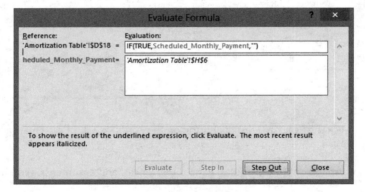

Figure 8-61 Use Step In and Step Out to display calculable arguments separately.

Watching formulas

Sometimes you might want to keep an eye on a formula as you make changes to other parts of a worksheet, or even when you're working on other workbooks that supply information to a worksheet. Instead of constantly having to return to the formula's location to see the results of your ministrations, you can use the Watch Window, which provides remote viewing for any cell on any open worksheet.

Select a cell you want to keep an eye on, and on the Formulas tab, click Watch Window. Then click Add Watch in the Watch Window, as shown in Figure 8-62.

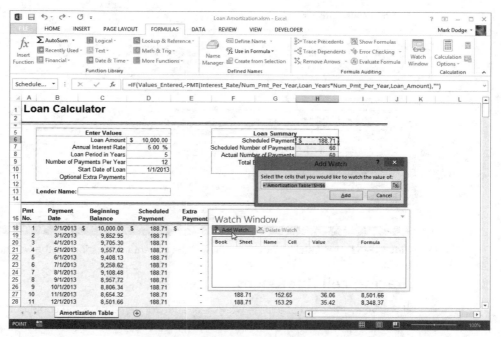

Figure 8-62 Select a cell and click Watch Window to keep an eye on the cell, no matter where you are currently working.

You can click a cell you want to watch either before or after you display the Add Watch dialog box. Click Add to insert the cell information in the Watch Window. You can dock the Watch Window, as shown in Figure 8-63. You can change its size by dragging its borders or drag it away from its docked position.

While your workbook is still open, you can select any item in the Watch Window list and delete it by clicking Delete Watch. The Watch Window button is a toggle—click it again to close the window; or click the Close button at the top of the Watch Window. When you close a workbook, Excel removes any watched cells the workbook contains from the Watch Window list.

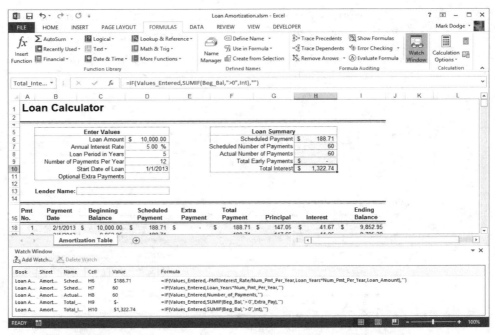

Figure 8-63 The Watch Window displays all the current information for the watched formula.

Tracing cell references

If you've ever looked at a large worksheet and wondered how you could get an idea of the data flow—that is, how the formulas and values relate to one another—you'll appreciate *cell tracers*. You can also use cell tracers to help find the source of those pesky errors that occasionally appear in your worksheets. The Formula Auditing group on the Formulas tab contains three buttons that control the cell tracers: Trace Precedents, Trace Dependents, and Remove Arrows.

INSIDE OUT   Understanding precedents and dependents

The terms *precedent* and *dependent* crop up quite often in this section. They refer to the relationships that cells containing formulas create with other cells. A lot of what a worksheet is all about is wrapped up in these concepts, so here's a brief description of each term:

- Precedents are cells whose values are used by the formula in the selected cell. A cell that has precedents always contains a formula.

- Dependents are cells that use the value in the selected cell. A cell that has dependents can contain either a formula or a constant value.

For example, if the formula =SUM(A1:A5) is in cell A6, cell A6 has precedents (A1:A5) but no apparent dependents. Cell A1 has a dependent (A6) but no apparent precedents. A cell can be both a precedent and a dependent if the cell contains a formula and is also referenced by another formula.

Tracing dependent cells

In the worksheet in Figure 8-64, we selected cell B2, which contains an hourly rate value. To find out which cells contain formulas that use this value, click the Trace Dependents button on the Formulas tab. Although this worksheet is elementary to make it easier to illustrate cell tracers, consider the ramifications of using cell tracers in a large and complex worksheet.

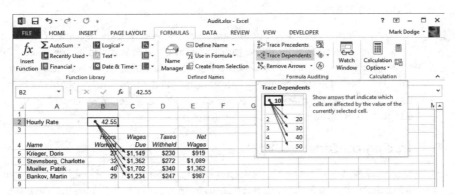

Figure 8-64 When you trace dependents, arrows point to formulas that directly refer to the selected cell.

You'll find the Audit.xlsx file with the other examples on the companion website.

The tracer arrows indicate that cell B2 is directly referred to by the formulas in cells C5, C6, C7, and C8. If you click Trace Dependents again, another set of arrows appears, indicating the next level of dependencies—or *indirect* dependents. Figure 8-65 shows the results.

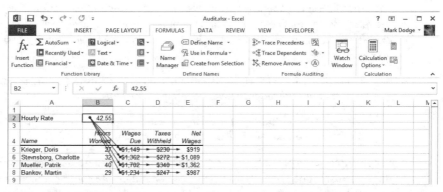

Figure 8-65 When you click Trace Dependents again, arrows point to the next level of formulas, ones that indirectly refer to the selected cell.

One handy feature of the tracer arrows is that you can use them to navigate, which can be advantageous in a large worksheet. For example, in Figure 8-65, with cell B2 still selected, double-click the arrow pointing from cell B2 to cell C8. The selection jumps to the other end of the arrow, and cell C8 becomes the active cell. Now, if you double-click the arrow pointing from cell C8 to cell E8, the selection jumps to cell E8. If you double-click the same arrow again, the selection jumps back to cell C8. If you double-click an arrow that extends beyond the screen, the window shifts to display the cell at the other end. You can use this feature to jump from cell to cell along a path of precedents and dependents.

Clearing tracer arrows

As you trace precedents or dependents, your screen quickly becomes cluttered, making it difficult to discern the data flow for particular cells. To remove all the tracer arrows from the screen, click the Remove Arrows button in the Formula Auditing group. Alternatively, you can click the small downward-pointing arrow next to the Remove Arrows button to display the Remove Arrows menu, where you can be more selective by choosing Remove Precedent Arrows or Remove Dependent Arrows.

Tracing precedent cells

You can also trace in the opposite direction by starting from a cell that contains a formula and tracing the cells that are referred to in the formula. In Figure 8-66, we selected cell E5, which contains one of the net wages formulas, and then clicked Trace Precedents twice to show the complete precedent path.

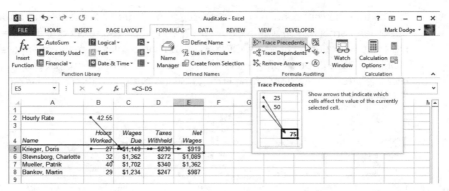

Figure 8-66 When you trace precedents, arrows point from all the cells to which the formula in the selected cell directly refers.

This time, arrows appear with dots in cells B2, B5, C5, and D5, indicating that all these cells are precedents to the selected cell. Notice that the arrows still point in the same direction—toward the formula and in the direction of the data flow—even though we started from the opposite end of the path.

Tracing errors

Suppose your worksheet displays error values like the ones shown in Figure 8-67. To trace one of these errors to its source, select a cell that contains an error, and on the Formulas tab, in the Formula Auditing group, click Trace Error. (Refer to Figure 8-57 earlier in this chapter to see the Error Checking dialog box.)

	A	B	C	D	E	F	G
1							
2	Hourly Rate	42.55					
3							
4	Name		Hours Worked	Wages Due	Taxes Withheld	Net Wages	
5	Krieger, Doris		27	$1,149	$230	$919	
6	Stevnsborg, Charlotte			#VALUE!	#VA	#VALUE!	
7	Mueller, Patrik		40	$1,702			
8	Bankov, Martin		29	$1,234			
9							

Error in Value
Help on this error
Trace Error
Ignore Error
Edit in Formula Bar
Error Checking Options...

Figure 8-67 Cells with error values display an action menu.

Chapter 8

Notice that the cells containing errors display small, green, triangular indicators in their upper-left corners, as shown in Figure 8-67, and when you select one of these cells, a floating Trace Error button appears. Clicking the button displays a menu of applicable actions, including Trace Error, a command you can also find on the menu that appears when you click the arrow to the right of the Error Checking button on the Formulas tab, as shown in Figure 8-68.

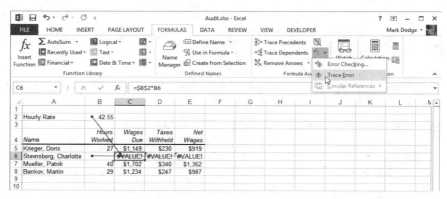

Figure 8-68 Select a cell that contains an error value, and click Trace Error to display arrows that trace the error to its source.

When you click Trace Error, Excel selects the cell that contains the first formula in the error chain and draws red arrows from that cell to the cell you selected, as you can see in Figure 8-68. Excel draws blue arrows to the cell that contains the first erroneous formula from the values the formula uses. It's up to you to determine the reason for the error; Excel takes you to the source formula and shows you the precedents. In our example, the error is caused by a space character inadvertently entered in cell B6, replacing the hours-worked figure. This is a common, vexing problem because cells containing space characters appear to be empty, but a truly empty cell would not have produced an error in this case.

Tracing references to other worksheets

If a cell contains a reference to a different worksheet or to a worksheet in another workbook, a dashed tracer arrow appears with a small icon attached, as shown in Figure 8-69. You cannot continue to trace precedents using the same procedure from the active cell when a dashed tracer arrow appears.

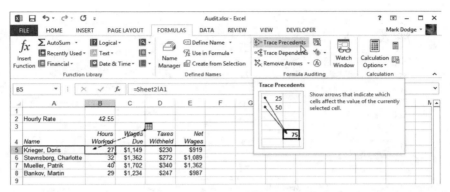

Figure 8-69 If you trace the precedents of a cell that contains a reference to another worksheet or workbook, a special tracer arrow appears.

If you double-click a dashed tracer arrow, the Go To dialog box appears, with the reference displayed in the Go To list. You can select the reference in the list and click OK to activate the worksheet or workbook. However, if the reference is to a workbook that is not currently open, an error message appears.

Adding comments to cells

Someday, someone else might need to use your workbooks, so it's good to be clear and to explain everything thoroughly. You can attach comments to cells to document your work, explain calculations and assumptions, or provide reminders. Select the cell you want to annotate, and then on the Review tab and in the Comments group, click the New Comment button. (The button changes to Edit Comment after you click it.) Then type your message in the box that appears, as shown in Figure 8-70.

When you add a comment to a cell, your name appears in bold type at the top of the comment box. You can specify what appears here by clicking the File tab, Options, and in the Personalize category typing your name (or any other text) in the User Name box. Whatever you type here appears at the top of the comment box followed by a colon. Although you can attach only one comment to a cell, you can make your comment as long as you like. If you want to begin a new paragraph in the comment box, press Enter. When you've finished, you can drag the handles to resize the comment box.

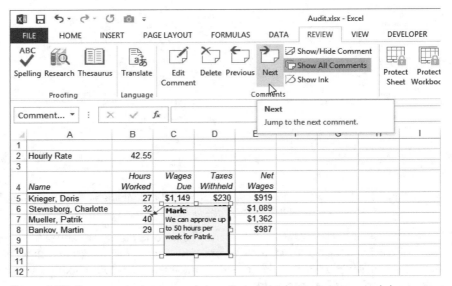

Figure 8-70 You can attach comments to cells to help document your worksheet.

Note

Ordinarily, the presence of a comment is indicated by a small, red triangle that appears in the upper-right corner of a cell. When you rest the pointer on a cell displaying this comment indicator, the comment appears. To control the display of comments, click the File tab, Options, and then the Advanced category. In the Display area, select one of the options under For Cells With Comments, Show.

Tweaking your comments

After you add text to your comments, nothing is set in stone. You can work with comments using the buttons in the Comments group on the Review tab:

- **New Comment/Edit Comment**   Click this button to add a comment to the selected cell. If the selected cell already contains a comment, this button changes to Edit Comment, which opens the comment for editing.

- **Previous and Next**   Click these buttons to open each comment in the workbook for editing, one at a time. Even if your comments appear on several worksheets in the same workbook, these buttons let you jump directly to each one in succession without using the sheet tabs.

- **Show/Hide Comment**   Click this button to display (rather than open for editing) the comment in the selected cell. This button changes to Hide Comment if the comment is currently displayed.

- **Show All Comments**   Click this button to display all the comments on the worksheet at once.

- **Delete**   Click this button to remove comments from all selected cells.

- **Show Ink**   Click this button to show or hide any ink annotations (Tablet PC only).

Printing comments

To print comments, follow these steps:

1. Click the Page Layout tab on the ribbon, and click the dialog box launcher in the Page Setup group (the little icon to the right of the group name).

2. Click the sheet tab, and select one of the options in the Comments drop-down list.

    The At End Of Sheet option prints all the comments in text form after the worksheet is printed. The As Displayed On Sheet option prints comments as they appear on the screen (as text boxes). Be careful, however, because comments printed this way can obscure some contents of the worksheet, and if your comments are clustered together, they might overlap.

3. Click the Print button in the Page Setup dialog box to display the Print dialog box, where you can select additional options before sending your worksheet to the printer.

For more information about printing, see Chapter 11, "Printing and presenting."

Outlining worksheets

Many typical spreadsheet models are built in a hierarchical fashion. For example, in a monthly sales worksheet, you might have a column for each month of the year, followed by a totals column, which depends on the numbers in the month columns. You can set up the rows of data hierarchically, with groups of expense categories contributing to category totals. Excel can turn worksheets of this kind into outlines.

Figure 8-71 shows a table of sales figures before outlining, and Figure 8-72 shows the same worksheet after outlining. To accomplish this, we selected cell B3 in the table (any cell would do), and on the Data tab, clicked the Group menu, and then clicked Auto Outline, as shown in Figure 8-71. (To outline a specific range, select the area before choosing Auto Outline.) Figure 8-72 shows how you can change the level of detail displayed after you outline a worksheet.

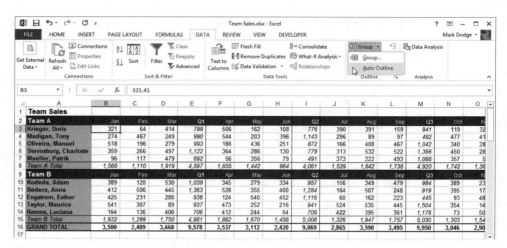

Figure 8-71 Start with a hierarchical worksheet like this one.

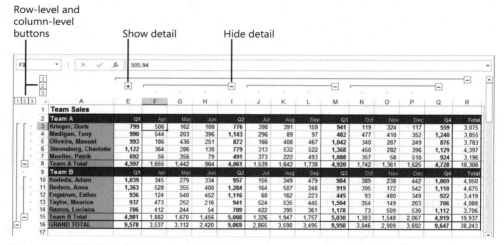

Figure 8-72 The worksheet hierarchies are collapsible using the Excel outlining features.

 You'll find the Team Sales.xlsx file with the other examples on the companion website.

Figure 8-73 shows the outlined worksheet with columns and rows of detail data hidden simply by clicking all the "minus sign" icons. Without outlining, you would have to hide each group of columns and rows manually; with outlining, you can collapse the outline to change the level of detail instantly.

1 2 3		A	E	I	M	Q	R	S	T
	1	**Team Sales**							
	2	**Team A**							
+	8	*Team A Total*	4,597	4,061	4,920	4,728	**18,306**		
	9	**Team B**							
+	15	*Team B Total*	4,981	5,008	5,030	4,919	**19,937**		
−	16	**GRAND TOTAL**	9,578	9,069	9,950	9,647	**38,243**		
	17								
	18								

Figure 8-73 Two clicks transformed the outlined worksheet in Figure 8-72 into this quarterly overview.

Chapter 8

INSIDE OUT   Undoing an outline

Note that after you use the Auto Outline command, you cannot use the Undo command to revert your worksheet to its original state. This is one of the few things within Excel that you can't undo. Instead, click Clear Outline on the Data tab's Ungroup menu to remove the outline, which is a better method anyway because you can do it anytime. Interestingly, after you use the Group command—the other command on the Group menu—Undo works just fine.

Outlining a worksheet with nonstandard layout

The standard outline settings reflect the most common worksheet layout. To change these settings, click the dialog box launcher (the little icon to the right of the group name) in the Outline group on the Data tab to display the Settings dialog box shown in Figure 8-74. If your worksheet layout is not typical, such as a worksheet constructed with rows of SUM formulas (or other types of summarization formulas) in rows above the detail rows or with columns of formulas to the left of detail columns, clear the appropriate Direction check box—Summary Rows Below Detail or Summary Columns To Right Of Detail—before outlining.

Figure 8-74 Use the Settings dialog box to adjust for a nonstandard layout.

When you use nonstandard worksheet layouts, be sure the area you want to outline is consistent to avoid unpredictable and possibly incorrect results; that is, be sure all summary formulas appear in the same direction relative to the detail data. After you select or clear one or both Direction options, click the Create button to create the outline.

Extending the outline to new worksheet areas

At times, you might create an outline and then add more data to your worksheet. You might also want to re-create an outline if you change the organization of a specific worksheet area. To include new columns and rows in your outline, repeat the procedure you followed to create the outline in the first place: select a cell in the new area, and click Auto Outline.

INSIDE OUT   Just say no to automatic styles

In the Settings dialog box, the Automatic Styles check box and the Apply Styles button apply rudimentary font formats to your outline that help distinguish totals from detail data. Unfortunately, this isn't very effective. To ensure that the outline is formatted the way you want, you should plan to apply formats manually.

Hiding an outline

When you outline a worksheet, Excel displays symbols above and to the left of the row and column headings (as you can see in Figure 8-72). These symbols take up screen space, so if you want to suppress them, you can click the File tab, Options; then click the Advanced category, and clear the Show Outline Symbols If An Outline Is Applied check box in the Display Options For This Worksheet area. However, this makes it harder to tell whether there is an outline present on the worksheet.

Collapsing and expanding outline levels

When you create an outline, the areas above and to the left of your worksheet are marked by one or more brackets that terminate in hide detail symbols, which have minus signs on them. The brackets are called *level bars*. Each level bar indicates a range of cells that share a common outline level. The hide detail symbols appear above or to the left of each level's summary column or row. If you have hidden the outline symbols or if you prefer to use the ribbon, you can also use the Show Detail and Hide Detail buttons in the Outline group on the Data tab to collapse and expand your outline.

To collapse an outline level so that only the summary cells show, click that level's hide detail symbol. For example, if you no longer need to see the monthly sales in the outlined worksheet (which is shown in Figure 8-72), click the hide detail symbols above columns E, I, and M. The worksheet then looks like Figure 8-75.

	A	E	I	M	N	O	P	Q	R	S
1	**Team Sales**									
2	**Team A**	Q1	Q2	Q3	Oct	Nov	Dec	Q4	Total	
3	Krieger, Doris	799	776	941	119	324	117	559	3,075	
4	Madigan, Tony	990	1,143	482	477	410	352	1,240	3,855	
5	Oliveira, Manuel	993	872	1,042	340	287	249	876	3,783	
6	Stevnsborg, Charlotte	1,122	779	1,368	450	282	396	1,129	4,397	
7	Mueller, Patrik	692	491	1,088	357	58	510	924	3,196	
8	Team A Total	4,597	4,061	4,920	1,742	1,361	1,625	4,728	18,306	
9	**Team B**	Q1	Q2	Q3	Oct	Nov	Dec	Q4	Total	
10	Kodeda, Adam	1,039	957	984	389	238	442	1,069	4,050	
11	Bedecs, Anna	1,363	1,284	919	395	172	542	1,110	4,675	
12	Engstrom, Esther	936	1,116	445	93	480	349	922	3,419	
13	Taylor, Maurice	937	941	1,504	354	149	203	706	4,088	
14	Ramos, Luciana	706	709	1,178	73	509	530	1,112	3,706	
15	Team B Total	4,981	5,008	5,030	1,303	1,548	2,067	4,919	19,937	
16	GRAND TOTAL	9,578	9,069	9,950	3,046	2,909	3,692	9,647	38,243	
17										

Figure 8-75 When you click the hide detail symbols (–) above Q1, Q2, and Q3, Excel replaces them with show detail symbols (+).

Show detail symbols with a plus sign on them now replace the hide detail symbols above the Q1, Q2, and Q3 columns (columns E, I, and M). To redisplay the hidden details, click the show detail symbols.

Displaying a specific outline level

To collapse each quarter so that only the quarterly totals and annual totals appear, you can click the hide detail symbols above Q1, Q2, Q3, and Q4. The *level symbols*—the squares with numerals at the upper-left corner of the worksheet—provide an easier way, however. An outline usually has two sets of level symbols, one for columns and one for rows. The column level symbols appear above the worksheet, and the row level symbols appear to the left of the worksheet.

You can use the level symbols to set an entire worksheet to a specific level of detail. The outlined worksheet shown in Figure 8-72 has three levels each for columns and for rows. By clicking both of the level symbols labeled 2 in the upper-left corner of the worksheet, you can transform the outline shown in Figure 8-72 to the one shown in Figure 8-73.

INSIDE OUT   Selecting only the visible cells

When you collapse part of an outline, Excel hides the columns or rows you don't want to see. In Figure 8-75, for example, the detail columns are hidden for the first three quarters of the year. Ordinarily, if you select a range that includes hidden cells, those hidden cells are implicitly selected. Whatever you do with these cells also happens to the hidden cells, so if you want to copy only the displayed totals, using copy and paste won't work. Here's the solution: on the Home tab, click Find & Select, Go To Special, and select the Visible Cells Only option. This is ideal for copying, charting, or performing calculations on only those cells that occupy a particular level of your outline. This feature works the same way in worksheets that have not been outlined; it excludes any cells in hidden columns or rows from the current selection.

Ungrouping and grouping columns and rows

If the default automatic outline doesn't give you the structure you expect, you can adjust it by ungrouping or grouping particular columns or rows. You can easily change the hierarchy of outlined columns and rows by clicking the Group and Ungroup buttons on the Data tab.

For example, you could select row 8 in the outlined worksheet shown in Figure 8-72 and click Ungroup to change row 8 from level 2 to level 1. The outlining symbol to the left of the row moves to the left under the row level symbol labeled 1. To restore the row to its proper level, click Group.

Note

You cannot ungroup or group a nonadjacent selection, and you cannot ungroup a selection that's already at the highest hierarchical level. If you want to ungroup a top-level column or row to a higher level so that it appears to be separate from the remainder of the outline, you have to group all the other levels of the outline instead.

Consolidating worksheets

You can use the Consolidate button on the Data tab to combine the values from a set of worksheets in the same workbook or from different workbooks. The Consolidate command lets you assemble information from as many as 255 supporting worksheets in a single master worksheet and displays the Consolidate dialog box shown in Figure 8-76.

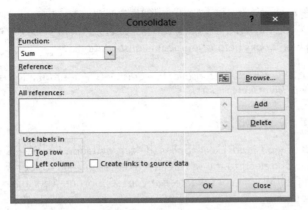

Figure 8-76 The default function in the Consolidate dialog box is Sum.

For example, if you have data for each month in separate worksheets or financial data for several divisions in separate workbooks, you can use the Consolidate command to create a master worksheet that comprises the totals for the corresponding items in each location. You can use the Consolidate command in a number of ways:

- Link the consolidated data to the supporting data so that subsequent changes in the supporting worksheets are reflected in the consolidation worksheet.

- Consolidate the source data on an ad hoc basis, without creating a link.

- Consolidate by position, where Excel gathers information from the same cell location in each supporting worksheet.

- Consolidate by category, where Excel uses column or row labels as the basis for associating worksheets. Consolidating by category gives you more flexibility in the way you set up your supporting worksheets. For example, if your January column is column B in one worksheet and column D in another, you can still gather the correct January numbers when you consolidate by category.

- Use any of the functions listed in the Function list in the Consolidate dialog box, including Count (which corresponds to the COUNTA function), Average, Max, Min, Product, Count Nums (which corresponds to the COUNT function), StdDev, StdDevp, Var, and Varp. As shown in Figure 8-76, the default function is Sum.

  For more information about functions, see Chapter 13 and Chapter 14.

- Consolidate worksheets in workbooks that are currently open or in workbooks that are stored on disk. The workbook containing the worksheet that receives the consolidated data must be open, but supporting workbooks can be closed—provided Excel has the correct locations at which to find each workbook file. (This should not be a problem unless you moved them since you last opened them in Excel.) You must save all supporting workbooks before you begin consolidation.

You can also use PivotTable reports to consolidate worksheets. For information, see Chapter 23, "Analyzing data with PivotTable reports."

Consolidating by position

When you consolidate by position, Excel applies the consolidation function (Sum, Average, or whatever else you select) to the same cell references in each supporting worksheet. By position is the simplest way to consolidate, but your supporting worksheets must have exactly the same layout.

Figure 8-77 shows a simple example of a workbook containing a master worksheet—Consolidated—that matches the layout of 12 supporting monthly worksheets. These worksheets can be consolidated by position because each contains identically structured data.

You'll find the Northwind Brass Sales.xlsx file with the other examples on the companion website.

To consolidate the monthly worksheets in Figure 8-77 into the worksheet named Consolidated, follow these steps:

1. Open the consolidation worksheet, and select the block of cells that will receive the consolidated data. In Figure 8-77, the destination area is the range B5:I10.

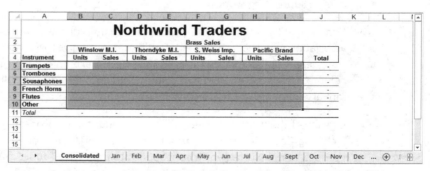

Figure 8-77 All the worksheets in this workbook are identical, which is necessary when you are consolidating by position.

2. Click Data, Consolidate.

3. Select the source range in the first worksheet using the mouse. In this example, we selected B5:I10 in the Jan worksheet.

4. Click Add in the Consolidate dialog box. Excel transfers the reference from the Reference text box to the All References list. Repeat for each worksheet you want to consolidate.

> **Note**
>
> Be sure all supporting workbooks are open when you are building your consolidation worksheet to make it easier to type references. (If a workbook is closed, you must manually type references to it, and you really don't want that.) After you have the consolidation set up and save the workbook, supporting workbooks can stay closed during future consolidations. If you do have to type a reference, you must use the form [File Name]Sheetname!Reference. If the reference is in the same workbook, the file name (and its surrounding brackets) is unnecessary. If you assigned the source range a name, you can use this name in place of Reference (highly recommended). For more information, see "Naming cells and cell ranges" in Chapter 12.

After you add the first range—$B$5:$I$10 in the Jan worksheet—Excel selects the same range in each worksheet when you click its tab. Just click a worksheet tab, and then click Add to add references. Figure 8-78 shows the completed dialog box. Figure 8-79 shows the resulting consolidation.

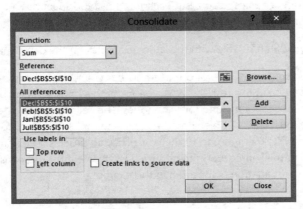

Figure 8-78 The Consolidate command uses the references in the All References list to create the consolidated totals.

> **Note**
>
> After you perform a consolidation, the references you type in the Consolidate dialog box are retained when you save the workbook. The next time you open the workbook and want to refresh the consolidated values, rather than entering the references again, click Consolidate and click OK.

Northwind Traders

Brass Sales

Instrument	Winslow M.I.		Thorndyke M.I.		S. Weiss Imp.		Pacific Brand		Total
	Units	Sales	Units	Sales	Units	Sales	Units	Sales	
Trumpets	14.00	3,283.84	1.00	234.56	11.00	2,580.16	2.00	469.12	6,567.68
Trombones	8.00	2,399.84	8.00	2,399.84	3.00	899.94	12.00	3,599.76	9,299.38
Sousaphones	10.00	4,567.80	6.00	2,740.68	8.00	3,654.24	2.00	913.56	11,876.28
French Horns	10.00	3,456.70	6.00	2,074.02	5.00	1,728.35	10.00	3,456.70	10,715.77
Flutes	5.00	943.90	17.00	3,209.26	6.00	1,132.68	8.00	1,510.24	6,796.08
Other	5.00	499.90	7.00	699.86	3.00	299.94	19.00	1,899.62	3,399.32
Total	52.00	15,151.98	45.00	11,358.22	36.00	10,295.31	53.00	11,849.00	48,654.51

Consolidated | Jan | Feb | Mar | Apr | May | Jun | Jul | Aug | Sept | Oct | Nov | Dec | ...

Figure 8-79 Range B5:I10 in the Consolidated worksheet now contains totals of the corresponding cells in the 12 supporting worksheets.

Consolidating by category

Now let's look at a more complex example. The Northwind Staff workbook contains monthly sales totals for each salesperson, but each monthly worksheet has a few different salespeople and a different number of salespeople, as shown in Figure 8-80.

You'll find the NorthwindStaff.xlsx file with the other examples on the companion website.

The consolidation worksheet we'll use for our example has columns for Units and Sales—each worksheet is the same in this respect. When performing a consolidation by category, your consolidation sheet cannot include row categories. The cells for these categories (salespeople's names) must start out blank on the consolidation sheet. Excel collects the categories (names) and lists them as part of the consolidation process. The names are not consistently arranged in the source worksheets, which is why we must use consolidation by category rather than consolidation by position in this example.

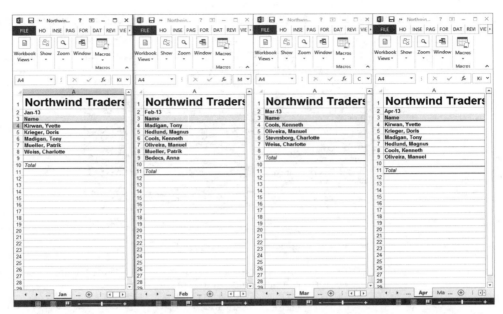

Figure 8-80 Use the categories in the left column of each source worksheet as the basis for this consolidation.

To consolidate by category, follow these steps:

1. Select the destination area. This time the destination area must include the row headings—but how many rows? To answer that, you can look at each source worksheet and determine how many unique line items you have. An easier way, however, is to select a single cell—in this case, cell A4—as the destination area. When you specify a single cell as your destination area, the Consolidate command fills in the area below and to the right of that cell as needed. In the example, to preserve the formatting, we inserted more than enough rows to accommodate the data.

2. Click Data, Consolidate.

3. To consolidate by row categories in this example, select the Left Column check box in the Use Labels In area. Click the default Sum function in the Function drop-down list. (The consolidation worksheet already has column labels.)

4. Each source reference must include the Name, Units, and Sales data. Select these ranges on each monthly worksheet. For example, on the Jan worksheet, we selected $A$4:$C$8. Unlike when consolidating by position, you have to manually select the ranges in each supporting worksheet because Excel selects the last range you added, which will not necessarily be what you need in each worksheet.

5. Click OK, and Excel fills out the Consolidated worksheet, as shown in Figure 8-81.

	A	B	C	D	E
1	**Northwind Traders**				
2	2013	Sales Staff			
3	Name	Units	Sales		
4	Kirwan, Yvette	122.00	28,616.32		
5	Krieger, Doris	41.00	9,616.96		
6	Madigan, Tony	67.00	15,715.52		
7	Hedlund, Magnus	108.00	25,332.48		
8	Cools, Kenneth	111.00	26,036.16		
9	Oliveira, Manuel	89.00	20,875.84		
10	Stevnsborg, Charlotte	119.00	49,726.72		
11	Mueller, Patrik	98.00	22,986.88		
12	Bedecs, Anna	143.00	33,542.08		
13	Weiss, Charlotte	184.00	100,626.24		
14					
15	Total	1,082.00	333,075.20		
16					

◀ ▶ ... Consolidated | Jan | Feb | Mar | Apr | May | Jun | Jul | Aug |

Figure 8-81 The Consolidate command created a separate line item in the consolidation worksheet for each unique item in the source worksheets.

> **Note**
>
> It's important that your categories—in our example, the names of salespeople—are spelled identically on each supporting worksheet. Otherwise, Excel creates a separate line and consolidation for each spelling variation.

Creating links to the source worksheets

The previous examples consolidated numbers with the Sum function, resulting in a range of consolidated constants. Subsequent changes to the source worksheets do not affect the consolidation worksheet until you repeat the consolidation.

You can also use the Consolidate command to create links between the consolidation and source worksheets. To do so, select the Create Links To Source Data check box in the Consolidate dialog box and then consolidate using the same techniques. When you consolidate with links, Excel actually creates an outline in the consolidation worksheet, as shown in Figure 8-82. Each source item is linked separately to the consolidation worksheet, and Excel creates the appropriate summary items. Excel creates additional columns and rows as necessary for each category—one for each unique entry in each worksheet, as shown in rows 27 to 33. Figure 8-82 also shows, in the formula bar, the linking formula for the December units figure in cell C29.

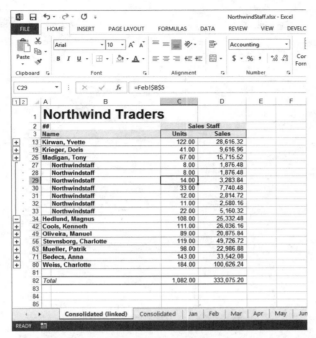

Figure 8-82 When you create links to the source worksheets, the consolidation worksheet is outlined and linking formulas are created in subordinate outline levels.

Note that when you create links, any rows or columns you subsequently add to the source worksheets are not included in the consolidation. However, it is easy to modify the consolidation references. Open the Consolidate dialog box, select the reference you want to change, and click Delete. Then select the modified range, and click Add.

For more information about outlining worksheets, see "Outlining worksheets" earlier in this chapter.

Worksheet formatting techniques

W HEN creating a worksheet in Microsoft Excel, you probably don't ask yourself the question, why use formats? But we'll answer it anyway. Compare Figure 9-1 to Figure 9-2, and we need say no more. Although the data is the same in both worksheets, the worksheet in Figure 9-2 takes advantage of the formatting features available in Excel, and as you can see, it's much easier to read and interpret. In this chapter, you'll learn how to apply basic formatting to help turn your data into information. We also discuss advanced formatting features such as themes, cell styles, and conditional formatting.

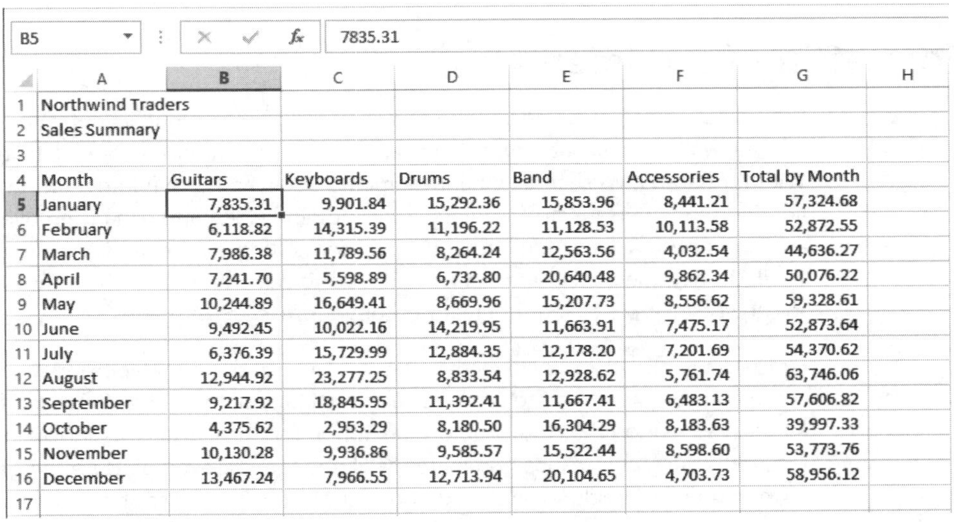

Month	Guitars	Keyboards	Drums	Band	Accessories	Total by Month
January	7,835.31	9,901.84	15,292.36	15,853.96	8,441.21	57,324.68
February	6,118.82	14,315.39	11,196.22	11,128.53	10,113.58	52,872.55
March	7,986.38	11,789.56	8,264.24	12,563.56	4,032.54	44,636.27
April	7,241.70	5,598.89	6,732.80	20,640.48	9,862.34	50,076.22
May	10,244.89	16,649.41	8,669.96	15,207.73	8,556.62	59,328.61
June	9,492.45	10,022.16	14,219.95	11,663.91	7,475.17	52,873.64
July	6,376.39	15,729.99	12,884.35	12,178.20	7,201.69	54,370.62
August	12,944.92	23,277.25	8,833.54	12,928.62	5,761.74	63,746.06
September	9,217.92	18,845.95	11,392.41	11,667.41	6,483.13	57,606.82
October	4,375.62	2,953.29	8,180.50	16,304.29	8,183.63	39,997.33
November	10,130.28	9,936.86	9,585.57	15,522.44	8,598.60	53,773.76
December	13,467.24	7,966.55	12,713.94	20,104.65	4,703.73	58,956.12

Figure 9-1 All entries in this worksheet are displayed in their default formats.

B5	▾	:	✕ ✓	f_x	7835.31		

⊿	A	B	C	D	E	F	G	H
1			**Northwind Traders**					
2			*Sales Summary*					
4	Month	Guitars	Keyboards	Drums	Band	Accessories	Total by Month	
5	January	7,835.31	9,901.84	15,292.36	15,853.96	8,441.21	57,324.68	
6	February	6,118.82	14,315.39	11,196.22	11,128.53	10,113.58	52,872.55	
7	March	7,986.38	11,789.56	8,264.24	12,563.56	4,032.54	44,636.27	
8	April	7,241.70	5,598.89	6,732.80	20,640.48	9,862.34	50,076.22	
9	May	10,244.89	16,649.41	8,669.96	15,207.73	8,556.62	59,328.61	
10	June	9,492.45	10,022.16	14,219.95	11,663.91	7,475.17	52,873.64	
11	July	6,376.39	15,729.99	12,884.35	12,178.20	7,201.69	54,370.62	
12	August	12,944.92	23,277.25	8,833.54	12,928.62	5,761.74	63,746.06	
13	September	9,217.92	18,845.95	11,392.41	11,667.41	6,483.13	57,606.82	
14	October	4,375.62	2,953.29	8,180.50	16,304.29	8,183.63	39,997.33	
15	November	10,130.28	9,936.86	9,585.57	15,522.44	8,598.60	53,773.76	
16	December	13,467.24	7,966.55	12,713.94	20,104.65	4,703.73	58,956.12	
17								

Figure 9-2 The formatted worksheet is easier to read.

You'll find the Table Formats.xlsx workbook with the other examples on the companion website.

Formatting fundamentals

Worksheet *editing* involves creating and modifying the content, layout, and organization of data, while worksheet *formatting* deals with the appearance and readability of that data. With formatting, you can take mind-numbing detail and turn it into information by high-lighting the important stuff, adding visual cues and clues, and enhancing overall readability and organization. Be careful, though—over formatting can be as distracting as using none at all. Usually, the goal of a good worksheet is to call attention to the right information, not to showcase Excel's formatting features (or your mastery of them).

Formatting in Excel is easy: select the cell or range, and use the appropriate buttons and commands on the ribbon to apply formatting. Many of the most often used formatting features appear on the Home tab on the ribbon for quick access, as shown in Figure 9-3. In fact, formatting commands dominate the Home tab; all seven of its ribbon groups include formatting commands (even the Editing group). Figure 9-3 also shows the Format Cells dialog box, which you can access by clicking the dialog box launcher in the Font, Alignment, or Number group on the Home tab on the ribbon. (The dialog box launcher is the small arrow icon to the right of the title in many ribbon groups.)

> **Note**
>
> To quickly access the Format Cells dialog box, press Ctrl+1.

Dialog box launcher

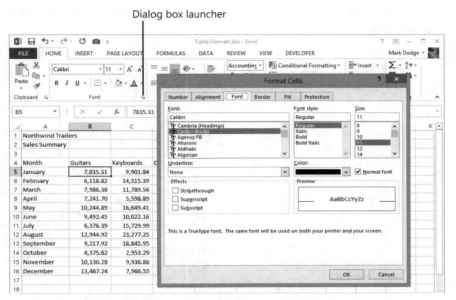

Figure 9-3 The Home tab on the ribbon and the Format Cells dialog box are your formatting toolboxes.

Here are some fundamental rules of formatting in Excel:

- A formatted cell remains formatted until you remove the format or apply a new format.

- When you overwrite or edit a cell entry, you need not reformat the cell.

- When you copy or cut a cell, the formats applied to that cell travel with it.

> **Note**
>
> Build and edit the worksheet first; apply formatting later. Sometimes, the *least* efficient step you can take is to apply your formatting too soon. Applying, removing, and then reapplying formatting is at least three times the work. Trust us, you'll do some reformatting no matter what, so give yourself the freedom to rearrange until the layout becomes clear for your purposes.

Formatting tables

The concept of "tables" in Excel took on fresh meaning with the 2007 release, and it continues through the 2013 release. Tables are special objects in Excel that include many features beyond formatting, but you can use the Format As Table button on the Home tab to apply specific font, border, and fill attributes to all the elements of a table at once. The Format As Table gallery, shown in Figure 9-4, applies predefined combinations of these formatting criteria.

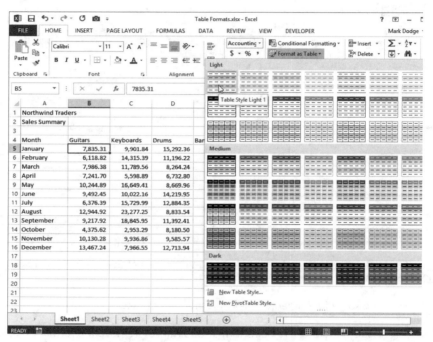

Figure 9-4 The Format As Table gallery offers a selection of predefined formats you can apply with one click.

You can apply the Format As Table command to any *region* of cells (that is, a contiguous block of cells on a worksheet). You select a cell anywhere within the region, click Format As Table, and then select one of the sample table formats from the gallery. When you do, Excel displays the Format As Table dialog box, which lets you adjust the selection, as shown in Figure 9-5.

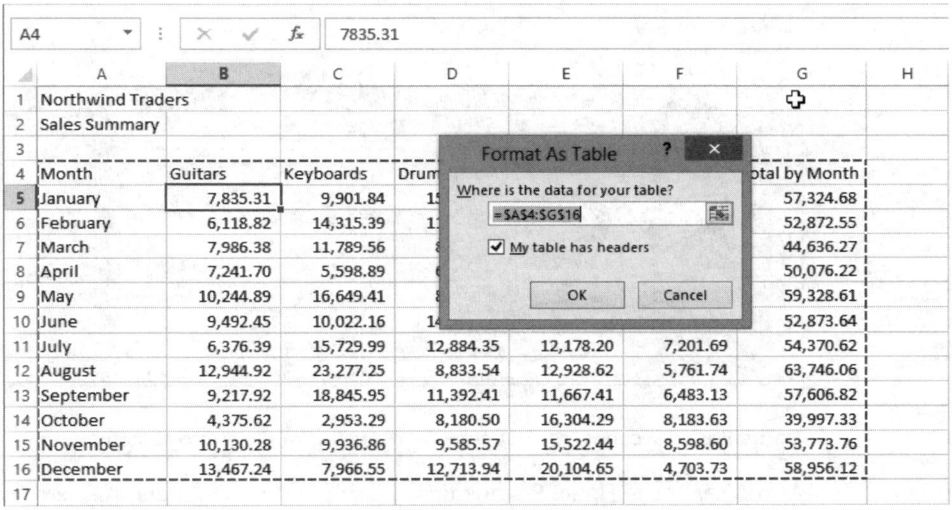

A4	▾	:	×	✓	*fx*	7835.31		

◢	A	B	C	D	E	F	G	H
1	Northwind Traders						✛	
2	Sales Summary							
3								
4	Month	Guitars	Keyboards	Drum			otal by Month	
5	January	7,835.31	9,901.84	1!			57,324.68	
6	February	6,118.82	14,315.39	1:			52,872.55	
7	March	7,986.38	11,789.56	ε			44,636.27	
8	April	7,241.70	5,598.89	(			50,076.22	
9	May	10,244.89	16,649.41	ε			59,328.61	
10	June	9,492.45	10,022.16	14			52,873.64	
11	July	6,376.39	15,729.99	12,884.35	12,178.20	7,201.69	54,370.62	
12	August	12,944.92	23,277.25	8,833.54	12,928.62	5,761.74	63,746.06	
13	September	9,217.92	18,845.95	11,392.41	11,667.41	6,483.13	57,606.82	
14	October	4,375.62	2,953.29	8,180.50	16,304.29	8,183.63	39,997.33	
15	November	10,130.28	9,936.86	9,585.57	15,522.44	8,598.60	53,773.76	
16	December	13,467.24	7,966.55	12,713.94	20,104.65	4,703.73	58,956.12	
17								

Dialog box overlay:

Format As Table   ?   ✕

Where is the data for your table?

=$A$4:$G$16

☑ My table has headers

OK   Cancel

Figure 9-5 The Format As Table dialog box appears after you select a format in the Format As Table gallery.

If your table includes headers (as most do), select the My Table Has Headers check box in the Format As Table dialog box. Excel then selects the entire table automatically and applies the selected table format to it.

Here are a few tips to keep in mind when using Format As Table:

- If you don't like the way something looks, click the Undo button on the Quick Access Toolbar (or press Ctrl+Z).

- The boundaries of a table are defined by blank rows and columns or the edges of the worksheet. Try adding blank columns or rows around your table to effectively fence off areas you don't want Format As Table to touch.

- Select more than one cell before issuing the command, and Format As Table affects only the selected cells.

Chapter 9

Although Format As Table does a pretty good job with simple tables, you usually need to make a few adjustments afterward. For example, starting with the raw data shown in Figure 9-1, we applied the Table Style Medium 20 format. Figure 9-6 shows the result.

▲	A	B	C	D	E	F	G	H
1	Northwind Traders							
2	Sales Summary							
3								
4	Month ▼	Guitars ▼	Keyboards ▼	Drums ▼	Band ▼	Accessories ▼	Total by Month ▼	
5	January	7,835.31	9,901.84	15,292.36	15,853.96	8,441.21	57,324.68	
6	February	6,118.82	14,315.39	11,196.22	11,128.53	10,113.58	52,872.55	
7	March	7,986.38	11,789.56	8,264.24	12,563.56	4,032.54	44,636.27	
8	April	7,241.70	5,598.89	6,732.80	20,640.48	9,862.34	50,076.22	
9	May	10,244.89	16,649.41	8,669.96	15,207.73	8,556.62	59,328.61	
10	June	9,492.45	10,022.16	14,219.95	11,663.91	7,475.17	52,873.64	
11	July	6,376.39	15,729.99	12,884.35	12,178.20	7,201.69	54,370.62	
12	August	12,944.92	23,277.25	8,833.54	12,928.62	5,761.74	63,746.06	
13	September	9,217.92	18,845.95	11,392.41	11,667.41	6,483.13	57,606.82	
14	October	4,375.62	2,953.29	8,180.50	16,304.29	8,183.63	39,997.33	
15	November	10,130.28	9,936.86	9,585.57	15,522.44	8,598.60	53,773.76	
16	December	13,467.24	7,966.55	12,713.94	20,104.65	4,703.73	58,956.12	
17								

The cell reference box shows **B5**, and the formula bar shows **7835.31**.

Figure 9-6 In seconds, you can transform a raw worksheet into something more presentable.

As you can see in Figure 9-6, the title and subtitle in cells A1 and A2 were not part of the table, and therefore were not formatted, so we applied additional formatting manually to arrive at the result shown in Figure 9-2. In addition, we applied number formatting to the cells containing data. Nonetheless, using Format As Table speeds up the formatting process and provides at least one formatting feature that is otherwise unavailable: automatic row and column banding, which was one attribute of the automatic format we applied in Figure 9-6. Another cool part of using Format As Table is the automatic preview feature. After you define a table using the Format As Table command, you can then use the Format As Table gallery to preview other predefined formats. (It doesn't work on raw data.) Rest the pointer on any format in the gallery, and the associated formatting is temporarily reflected in the table you have already created, but it is not actually applied unless you click.

After you create a table, a context-triggered tab appears on the ribbon only when you select a cell or cells within the table. Figure 9-7 shows the Table Tools Design tab.

The Design tab contains formatting commands in the Table Style Options and Table Styles groups. The latter group contains the same gallery as the Format As Table command on the Home tab. In Figure 9-7, we selected both the First Column and Last Column check boxes in the Table Style Options group, which in this particular predefined format applied bold formatting to the fonts in those columns. Also, the Filter Button check box was cleared to unclutter the appearance of the worksheet. (You can always redisplay the filter buttons when you need to massage the numbers; this chapter is all about appearances.) You can select and clear check boxes in this group and view the changes immediately. The Header Row check box actually adds or removes the header row from the table. The Total Row check box adds a double border at the bottom of the table and adds another row containing summary formulas. If you add the summary row, you can select which summary function you want to use by clicking the summary formula in the totals row and then clicking the menu arrow that appears. The menu offers a selection of functions—including Sum (the default), Average, Max, and Min—or you can select More Functions to display the Insert Function dialog box.

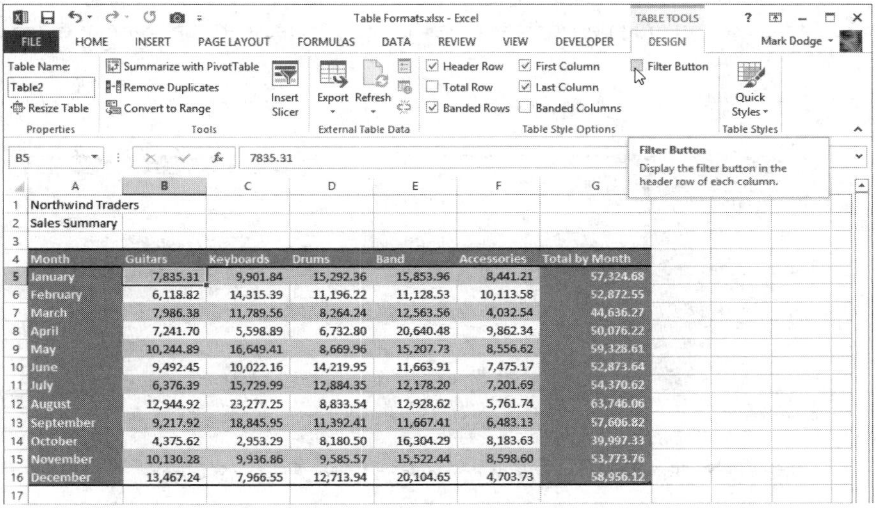

Figure 9-7 The Table Tools Design tab appears on the ribbon whenever you select a cell in a table.

TROUBLESHOOTING

Did your Design tab disappear?

The Table Tools Design tab appears only when you select a cell that is part of a table. When you select any cell outside the table, this context-triggered tab disappears, and the Home tab is activated.

The two "Banded" check boxes on the Table Tools Design tab—Banded Rows and Banded Columns—are useful. In large worksheets, row banding often makes it easier to track long rows of data across a screen or printed page. In previous versions of Excel, banding required you to construct an esoteric conditional formatting formula using the MOD function. Banding is now easier than ever to apply in Excel thanks to these two options, and unlike the old MOD function approach, these table-banding options are smart enough to survive just about any kind of editing, including inserting and deleting rows and columns.

For more information, see "Formatting conditionally" and "Creating conditional formatting rules" later in this chapter.

You can insert and delete rows in a table, even at the edges, and the table automatically does the right thing with formats and formulas. Another great feature of tables is that you can make them bigger just by dragging. As Figure 9-8 shows, the cell in the lower-right corner of the table contains a small triangular indicator (similar to a cell comment indicator) that you can drag horizontally or vertically to increase (or decrease) the size of the table.

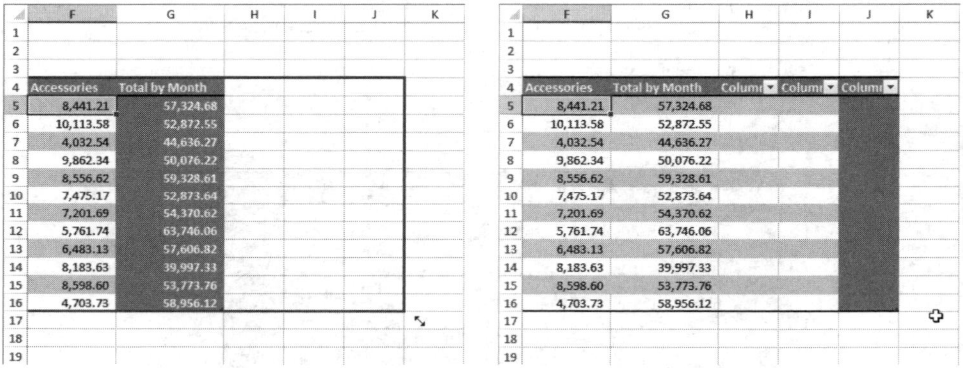

Figure 9-8 Drag the lower-right corner of a table to make it bigger.

Here's another handy feature of tables that makes formatting easier, but also makes it easier to modify the structure of the table, as well. In Figure 9-8, you'll notice that the formatting of the last column moved from column G to column J after dragging the table. Last Column is one of the options on the Table Tools Design tab. When you select this option, it doesn't matter where the last column happens to be located; even if you keep adding and subtracting columns, the last column table format is always applied to the last column in the table. You can turn off the last column format using the eponymous check box on the Table Tools Design tab.

You'll also notice in Figure 9-8 that the Total By Month formulas in column G are now rather ill-placed in the table. Tables help make this an easy fix as well. Simply select cells G4:G16, click the selection border, and drag them to the right. Normally, when moving cells to a new location on a worksheet, you hold down the Shift key while dragging so that they are inserted in the new location rather than pasted over existing data. But when dragging cells around inside a table, you don't need to hold the Shift key, just drag; the selected cells become a large I-beam insertion point, as shown in Figure 9-9. When the insertion point is where you want it, release the mouse button. (You might need to adjust the formulas, however. For more information, see Chapter 12, "Building formulas.")

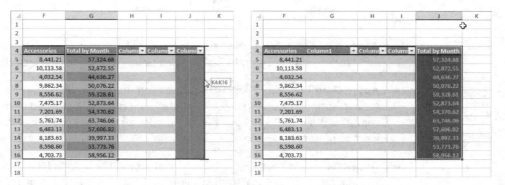

Figure 9-9 You can easily drag complete rows and columns of data around inside a table without disturbing the formatting.

Options for applying table formats

When you right-click an item in the Format As Table gallery, you'll find a few more tools you can employ when you are working with table formats. Figure 9-10 shows the shortcut menu that appears when you right-click a gallery item.

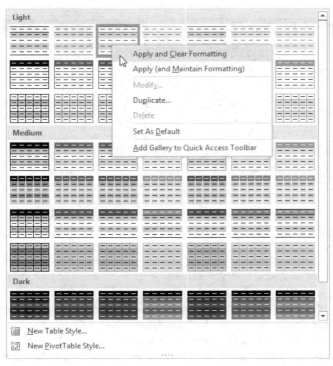

Figure 9-10 Right-click any table format thumbnail to reveal a shortcut menu containing helpful options.

The following are the options:

- **Apply And Clear Formatting** sounds backward, because what really happens is that Excel removes the existing formatting first before applying the selected table format.

- **Apply (And Maintain Formatting)** gives you the option of using the selected table format without disturbing any format attributes previously applied to the selected cells. This is handy if you have special number formats or conditional formats you want to preserve.

- **Duplicate** copies the selected table format; opens the Modify Table Quick Style dialog box (which is identical to the New Table Style dialog box shown in Figure 9-11), letting you make modifications; and places the resulting format in the Custom category at the top of the Format As Table gallery.

Creating custom table formats

If the built-in gallery of table styles doesn't do it for you, you can create your own. To do so, click the Format As Table button on the Home tab, scroll to the bottom of the gallery, and click New Table Style to display the New Table Style dialog box shown in Figure 9-11.

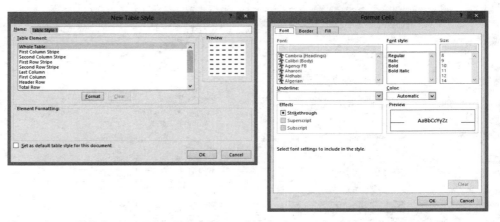

Figure 9-11 Click the New Table Style command in the Format As Table gallery to create your own table styles.

In the New Table Style dialog box, you can assign font, border, and fill formats to each item included in the Table Element list. Select the element you want to format, and click the Format button to display the Format Cells dialog box shown on the right in Figure 9-11. You can click the Clear button to remove the formatting from a selected element; select the Set As Default Table Style For This Document check box to make yours the go-to style whenever you create tables in the current workbook. After you finish specifying formats and click OK, your custom style appears at the top of the Format As Table gallery in the Custom category.

Removing the automatic table features

If you like the formatting you get from tables but don't want or need the special features of a table, click the Convert To Range button in the Tools group on the Table Tools Design tab. When you do so, all the special features applied to the selected table are removed, leaving most of the formatting intact. (Remember, you need to click a cell in the table to display the Table Tools Design tab.) Figure 9-12 shows the message that appears when you click Convert To Range.

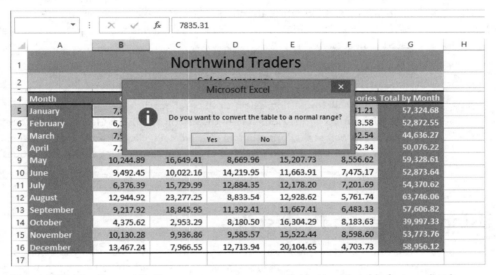

Figure 9-12 The Convert To Range command removes the automatic table features but leaves the formatting.

Convert To Range removes the Filter menus from the selected table, discontinues displaying the Table Tools Design tab, turns off any additional table features (such as automatic cell banding and totals), and relegates the range formerly known as Table to simple "formatted cells" status. Any visible table formatting you applied remains (including the totals row), but the automatic table functionality disappears. Even the banding formats remain, but they are no longer dynamic or automatic. Converting your table in this way makes sense if you don't want to deal with the automatic accoutrements such as Filter menus. This technique is a great way to take advantage of automatic table-formatting features for cell ranges that you just want to format uniformly.

Painting formats

One of the most useful tools on your formatting tool belt is the Format Painter button. The Clipboard group on the Home tab is home to the Format Painter button, which looks like a little paintbrush. Select the cell or range from which you want to copy formatting, and click the Format Painter button. (A small paintbrush icon appears next to the pointer.) Then select the cell or drag through the range of cells to which you want to copy the formatting. It's that simple.

If you copy formats from a range of cells and then select a single cell when you paste, Format Painter selects and formats the same size range—from the selected cell down and to the right. However, if you select a range of cells when you paste formats, Format Painter limits the pasted formats to the shape of the destination range you select. If the range you want to format is a different shape from the copied range, the pattern is repeated or truncated as necessary.

> **Note**
>
> To remove all formatting, select a cell or range, click the Clear menu (located in the Editing group on the Home tab of the ribbon), and click Clear Formats. To remove the values as well as the formatting in selected cells, click Clear All on the menu. For more information, see "Clearing cells" in Chapter 8, "Worksheet editing techniques."

Using themes and cell styles

Excel now offers a couple of ways to format globally—meaning you can perform certain tasks to help standardize the look of your worksheets and create a consistent appearance for all your documents.

Formatting with themes

A *theme* is a set of formatting attributes that apply specifically to the line and fill effects, the color palette, and the fonts that are available when formatting documents. The three buttons that control these attributes—Colors, Fonts, and Effects—appear in the Themes group on the Page Layout tab, shown in Figure 9-13. Themes give individuals or workgroups using Microsoft Office programs (versions 2007 through 2013) the ability to use the same sets of basic design attributes for all the documents they create. You'll find corresponding themes in Microsoft PowerPoint and Microsoft Word as well. You can use themes to standardize all your internal documents, for example, or to maintain a consistent look between pages in a package of presentation handouts.

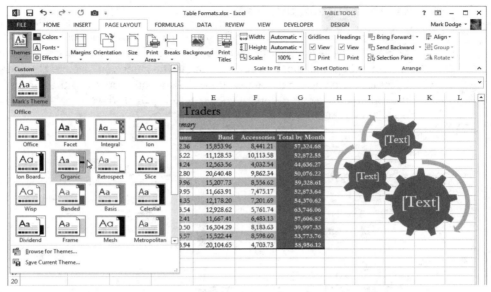

Figure 9-13 Themes control the overall palette of available colors, fonts, and effects. Changing the theme instantly changes the look of all the worksheets in the active workbook.

When you apply a theme using the Themes button, all applicable formats in the active workbook change instantly, including the colors of text, background, accents and hyperlinks, heading and body text fonts, line and fill effects, and even graphics, as shown in Figure 9-13. This happens regardless of the number of cells you selected.

Just as when you choose a theme, changes you make using the Colors, Fonts, or Effects galleries are reflected immediately throughout the workbook. The Colors gallery contains a selection of coordinated color schemes that, when selected, change the available colors in all other galleries where colors are used. The Fonts gallery offers a selection of font sets including two fonts each—one for headings and one for body text. The Effects gallery gives you a choice of graphic "looks," accomplished using various applications of line and fill effects that reflect the current color scheme.

CAUTION!

> Themes have no effect on cells to which you have directly applied font, color, line, or fill formatting using settings that are not part of a theme.

Chapter 9

Creating custom themes

You can save your own themes using the Save Current Theme command at the bottom of the Themes gallery, which you can see in Figure 9-13. Doing so creates a .thmx file and saves it in a special folder on your computer. The name you give the file when you save it becomes the name of the theme, which subsequently appears in the Custom category at the top of the Themes gallery, as shown in Figure 9-14. The Custom category appears only if a custom theme exists.

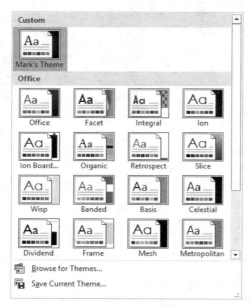

Figure 9-14 The Custom category is created in the Themes gallery when you save a custom theme.

You can use the Browse For Themes button at the bottom of the Themes gallery to load .thmx files from other locations, such as a company theme file on your network.

INSIDE OUT   Mousing around in galleries

Microsoft has gone to great lengths to make features more discoverable and self-explanatory. It crafted a new approach for many of the commands that used to live on menus, transforming them into drop-down galleries containing thumbnail representations of the options they offer. In many cases, these galleries exhibit "live preview" functionality, where you can rest the pointer on items in the gallery to get a live preview in the worksheet of what happens if you actually click. This is a great feature, but it can be finicky. For example, if you convert an older Excel file and try to use the Themes gallery in this way, you might find that not much seems to happen. This can occur when formatting in the old file overrides the default font, color, line, or fill styles controlled by themes. For example, the default font in Excel 2003 is Arial, and the default font in Excel 2013 is Calibri. When you convert an old Excel file, the original fonts carry over as well. Resting the pointer on the Themes gallery might not show any changes in the font, and indeed, applying a theme might not have any effect either.

To get around this problem, you can start with a fresh workbook and type everything again (but who wants to do that?), or you can copy the contents of each worksheet in the old workbook and click Paste, Paste Values (on the Home tab) to add the data to the new workbook. This requires you to redo all the formatting, but that should be a lot easier with the tools in Excel 2013. Another approach is to reformat all the text in the converted workbook using one of the fonts from the current theme. Use the same approach to convert any colors, lines, or fill styles to use current theme styles.

Formatting with cell styles

The comparatively new Cell Styles feature bears little resemblance to the fairly old Styles feature, although the basic idea is the same: applying combinations of formatting attributes all at once to eliminate a lot of time clicking buttons, opening dialog boxes, and choosing individual options. Cell styles help you achieve consistency in formatting, both within a worksheet and across worksheets and workbooks. Using cell styles, you can easily modify the formatting characteristics of many cells at once.

Note

Cell styles are based on the formatting attributes of the current theme. Changing the theme causes the displayed cell styles to update accordingly.

The Cell Styles button appears in the Styles group on the Home tab on the ribbon. Cell styles wield the following formatting attributes: number and fill formatting, cell alignment, fonts, borders, and even cell-level protection settings. Several built-in cell styles have specific purposes, as you can see in Figure 9-15, and you can create your own custom styles (designed in concert with your company theme, perhaps).

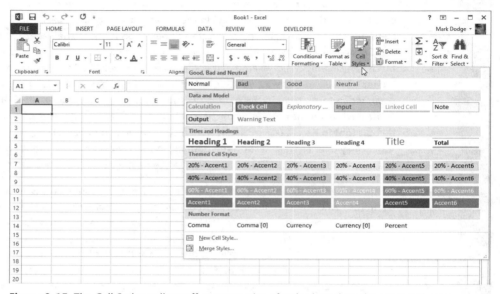

Figure 9-15 The Cell Styles gallery offers categories of styles based on the current theme.

You'll find the following six cell style categories, with individual styles that have uses suggested by their titles and the categories in which they live:

- **Good, Bad And Neutral** If you want, you can use these styles when highlighting good news, bad news, and...just plain old news. The Normal style also lives here, which you can use to "reset" selected cells to default formatting.

- **Data And Model** These styles are intended for specific purposes, such as Input and Output styles for cells that are meant to accept user input or reveal the results of calculations.

- **Titles And Headings** The intended use is self-explanatory, but it's interesting to note that the top three Heading styles include bottom borders of different weights, making them useful for creating color-coordinated column headers in tables.

- **Themed Cell Styles**   These Accent and Emphasis styles are heavily dependent on the current theme colors, offering four graduated percentages of each Accent color for quartile comparisons.

- **Number Format**   Included for continuity, these styles are actually more accessible using the Number buttons on the Home tab on the ribbon.

- **Custom**   This category does not appear in the gallery until you create a custom style. After you do, the Custom category appears at the top of the gallery.

The Cell Styles gallery exhibits "mouse hover" functionality, letting you see a live preview in selected cells on the worksheet when you rest the pointer on an item in the gallery. To apply a style, select the cells you want to format, and click your chosen style in the gallery.

Creating custom cell styles

You can create your own styles using one of two methods: by modifying an existing style or by clicking the New Cell Style command at the bottom of the Cell Styles gallery, which displays the Style dialog box shown in Figure 9-16.

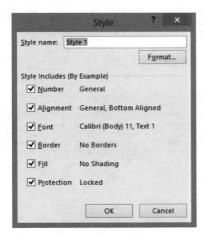

Figure 9-16 Use the Style dialog box to create your own cell styles.

The Style dialog box opens with the attributes of the default Normal style displayed. Styles can have a minimum of one and a maximum of six sets of attributes: Number, Alignment, Font, Border, Fill, and Protection, each with a corresponding check box in the Style dialog box. Select the check boxes to specify the attributes you want for your cell style. For example, you could clear all but the Protection check box to define a style that does nothing more than change selected cells to "unlocked" status, allowing user entries on a protected

Chapter 9

worksheet. Using such a style has no effect on any of the other five style attributes in cells to which it is applied.

To specify style attributes, click the Format button to display the Format Cells dialog box, where you can specify your formatting choices in detail. The Format Cells dialog box contains six tabs corresponding to the six categories of style attributes; you can make as many choices as you want on each tab. When you finish with the Format Cells dialog box, click OK to close it and return to the Style dialog box. Then type a name in the Style Name box, and click OK. Your custom style appears in the Custom category at the top of the Cell Styles gallery, as shown in Figure 9-17, where you can see the Unlocked style we created.

For more information about the Format Cells dialog box, see "Formatting numbers" later in this chapter.

Figure 9-17 Custom styles appear at the top of the Cell Styles gallery.

As you can see in Figure 9-17, you can right-click a cell style to display a shortcut menu you can use to delete, modify, or duplicate the style. Duplication is handy if, for example, you want to create a number of related styles with different fill percentages. Clicking the Duplicate command makes it easier because it copies the other attributes for you—all you have to do is change the fill percentage.

Creating cell styles by example   If you formatted a cell using attributes you want to use often, you can use the style-by-example procedure to encapsulate those attributes in a new style. For example, suppose you format a cell with right alignment and 18-point Arial Black. To make this combination of attributes a new style, follow these steps:

1. Select the cell that contains the formatting you want.

2. On the ribbon, click Home, Cell Styles, New Cell Style.

3. Type a name such as **HeadRight** in the Style Name box.

4. Clear the Number, Border, Fill, and Protection check boxes in the Style Includes area, and click OK. The new style then appears in the Cell Styles gallery.

CAUTION !

The safest way to create a style by example is to select only one cell—one you know has all the attributes you want to assign to the new style. If you select two or more cells that are not formatted identically, the new style assumes only those attributes that all cells in the selection have in common.

Modifying and duplicating cell styles   The principal advantage of using styles is that if you change your mind about the appearance of a particular element in your workbook, you can revise every instance of that element at once by changing the style. For example, if you'd like the font in the custom HeadRight style—which is now 18-point Arial Black—to also be italic, you can redefine HeadRight.

To modify a style definition, follow these steps:

1. Click Home, Cell Styles.

2. Right-click the thumbnail for the style (in this case, HeadRight) in the gallery, and click Modify to display the Style dialog box.

3. Click the Format button to display the Format Cells dialog box, and select the appropriate format options, as shown in Figure 9-18. (For this example, click the Font tab, and select the Italic option in the Font Style list.)

4. Click OK to return to the Style dialog box, and then click OK to confirm your changes.

You can also right-click an existing style and click the Duplicate command, which opens a Style dialog box similar to the one shown in Figure 9-18 and appends a number to the end of the style name. You can then change the name if you like and click the Format button to make adjustments to the formatting attributes. Using Duplicate is helpful when you want to create a number of similar styles or when you want to base a custom style on one of the built-in styles. When you finish defining the style, click OK; your new style appears in the Custom category of the Cell Styles gallery.

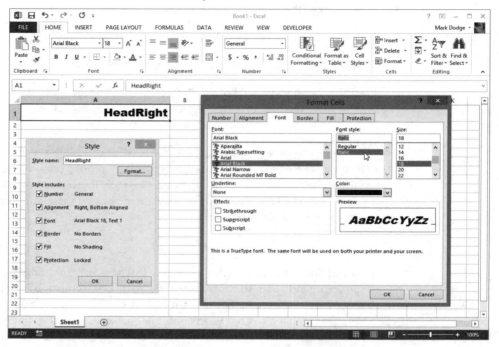

Figure 9-18 Modify an existing cell style by right-clicking its thumbnail in the gallery and clicking Modify.

> **Note**
>
> The predefined Normal style is applied to every cell in every new workbook. Thus, if you want to use the standard set of formatting attributes, you don't need to do anything. If, however, you want to change the default attributes for all cells in a worksheet, you can redefine any or all attributes of the Normal style.

Merging cell styles from different workbooks   To maintain formatting consistency across a group of worksheets, you can keep the worksheets in the same workbook. If this is impractical but you still want to maintain stylistic consistency, you can copy style definitions between workbooks. (Of course, themes are also helpful in this regard and are covered in "Formatting with themes" earlier in this chapter.)

To copy a style from one workbook to another, take the following steps:

1. Open both the source workbook (the one you're copying from) and the destination workbook (the one you're copying to).

2. Click the destination workbook to make it the active window.

3. On the ribbon, click Home, Cell Styles, Merge Styles. Excel displays a dialog box listing all the other open workbooks, as shown in Figure 9-19.

Figure 9-19 Copy cell styles from any open workbook using the Merge Styles command.

4. Select the name of the workbook you want to copy styles from, and click OK.

CAUTION

> If a style in the source workbook has the same name as one already in your destination workbook, a message asks whether you want to merge styles that have the same names. You receive this warning only once, however, no matter how many duplicate style names exist. If you click Yes, the styles from the source workbook override those with the same names in the destination workbook.

Deleting a cell style   To delete a style, click the Home tab, Cell Styles, and right-click the custom style you want to delete. (You cannot delete a built-in cell style.) Then click Delete. Any cells formatted using the deleted style revert to the Normal style.

Formatting conditionally

Conditional formats respond to the contents of cells. They are almost always applied to groups of cells—often rows or columns of totals—if not entire tables. Click Home, Conditional Formatting to display the menu shown in Figure 9-20.

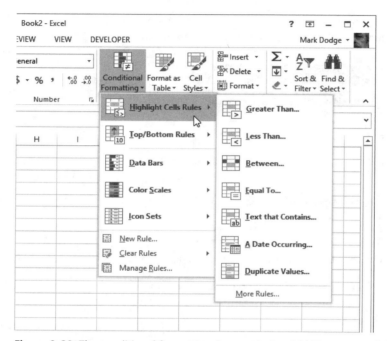

Figure 9-20 The conditional formatting features in Excel 2013 are powerful and easy to use.

Excel 2013 offers five flavors of formatting features you can use for your conditional creations:

- **Highlight Cells Rules**   Formatting you apply to cells that stays "asleep" until the values (numeric or text) the cells contain achieve the specified state. Click Greater Than, Less Than, Between, Equal To, Text That Contains, A Date Occurring, or Duplicate Values to display a dialog box where you can specify the appropriate criteria.

- **Top/Bottom Rules**   Selected formatting applied to all cells in a range that are greater than or less than a given threshold. Click Top N Items, Top N %, Bottom N Items, Bottom N %, Above Average, or Below Average to display a dialog box where you can specify the appropriate criteria.

- **Data Bars**   Gradient fills of color within cells. The bars' lengths indicate the values in the cells relative to all other adjacent cells formatted using the same conditions. Choose from a number of different colors, based on the current theme.

- **Color Scales**   Two-color or three-color formats whose color indicates the values in the cells relative to all other adjacent cells formatted using the same conditions. Choose from a number of different color combinations, based on the current theme.

- **Icon Sets**   Sets of three, four, or five tiny graphic images placed inside cells. The icons' shape or color indicates the values in the cells relative to all other adjacent cells formatted using the same conditions. Choose from a number of different types of icons.

For example, you could apply conditional formatting to a range of cells that contain sales totals, specifying that if any of the totals drops to less than $1,000, the format of the cell changes to stand out from the other cells. To do so, follow these steps:

1. Select the cells you want to format.

2. Click Conditional Formatting, Highlight Cells Rules, Less Than to display the Less Than dialog box shown in Figure 9-21.

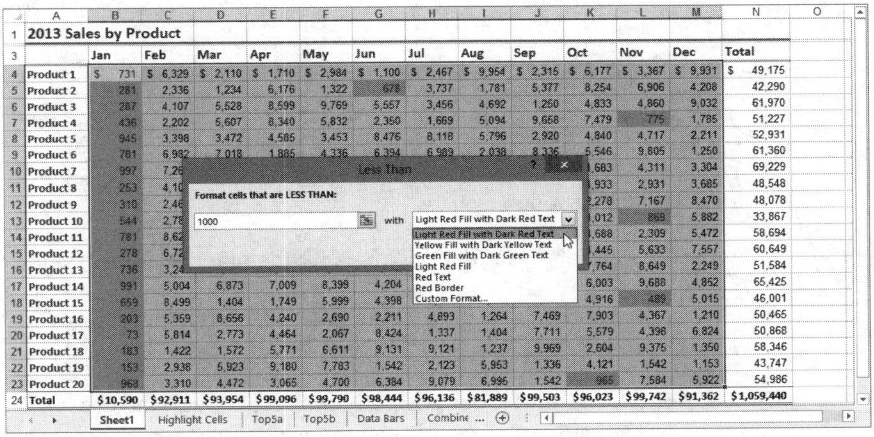

Figure 9-21 Select the Less Than rule on the Highlight Cells Rules menu to create a stoplight chart using conditional formatting.

3. Type the number you want to use as the threshold for this condition; in this case, **1000**.

4. Select one of the options from the drop-down list of available formats.

   Notice that when you select a format option from the Highlight Cells Rules menu, Excel previews it for you on the worksheet. Type a number in the Format Cells That Are Less Than box, select a format option from the drop-down list, and the preview adjusts accordingly. Clicking the Custom Format option at the bottom of the list displays a version of the Format Cells dialog box with the Number, Font, Border, and Fill tabs available.

Chapter 9

5.   Click OK.

Figure 9-22 shows a table after applying conditional formatting. This example was formatted using two highlight cells conditions: one format for numbers greater than 9,000 and a different format for numbers less than 1,000.

	Jan	Feb	Mar	Apr	May	Jun	Jul	Aug	Sep	Oct	Nov	Dec	Total
2013 Sales by Product													
Product 1	$ 731	$ 6,329	$ 2,110	$ 1,710	$ 2,984	$ 1,100	$ 2,467	$ 9,954	$ 2,315	$ 6,177	$ 3,367	$ 9,931	$ 49,175
Product 2	281	2,336	1,234	6,176	1,322	678	3,737	1,781	5,377	8,254	6,906	4,208	42,290
Product 3	287	4,107	5,528	8,599	9,769	5,557	3,456	4,692	1,250	4,833	4,860	9,032	61,970
Product 4	436	2,202	5,607	8,340	5,832	2,350	1,669	5,094	9,658	7,479	775	1,785	51,227
Product 5	945	3,398	3,472	4,585	3,453	8,476	8,118	5,796	2,920	4,840	4,717	2,211	52,931
Product 6	781	6,982	7,018	1,885	4,336	6,394	6,989	2,038	8,336	5,546	9,805	1,250	61,360
Product 7	997	7,267	5,006	6,692	8,388	9,072	8,968	5,923	7,618	1,683	4,311	3,304	69,229
Product 8	253	4,100	6,328	3,807	7,850	1,213	5,253	3,934	4,261	4,933	2,931	3,685	48,548
Product 9	310	2,467	5,349	7,142	2,343	2,712	4,629	3,961	1,250	2,278	7,167	8,470	48,078
Product 10	544	2,783	1,642	1,582	2,456	5,584	1,255	7,915	2,343	1,012	869	5,882	33,867
Product 11	781	8,626	6,938	5,200	8,197	6,542	5,955	1,775	2,211	4,688	2,309	5,472	58,694
Product 12	278	6,720	4,754	3,556	2,535	4,100	4,740	7,047	9,284	4,445	5,633	7,557	60,649
Product 13	736	3,248	7,295	4,344	2,076	8,372	1,846	1,264	3,741	7,764	8,649	2,249	51,584
Product 14	991	5,004	6,873	7,009	8,399	4,204	8,290	2,695	1,417	6,003	9,688	4,852	65,425
Product 15	659	8,499	1,404	1,749	5,999	4,398	2,211	1,167	9,495	4,916	489	5,015	46,001
Product 16	203	5,359	8,656	4,240	2,690	2,211	4,893	1,264	7,469	7,903	4,367	1,210	50,465
Product 17	73	5,814	2,773	4,464	2,067	8,424	1,337	1,404	7,711	5,579	4,398	6,824	50,868
Product 18	183	1,422	1,572	5,771	6,611	9,131	9,121	1,237	9,969	2,604	9,375	1,350	58,346
Product 19	153	2,938	5,923	9,180	7,783	1,542	2,123	5,953	1,336	4,121	1,542	1,153	43,747
Product 20	968	3,310	4,472	3,065	4,700	6,384	9,079	6,995	1,542	965	7,584	5,922	54,986
Total	$10,590	$92,911	$93,954	$99,096	$99,790	$98,444	$96,136	$81,889	$99,503	$96,023	$99,742	$91,362	$1,059,440

Sheet1   **Highlight Cells**   Top5a   Top5b   Data Bars   Combine ...

Figure 9-22 We created two conditions—one to flag high values and one to flag low values. These guys had a rough January.

You'll find the SalesByProduct.xlsx file with the other examples on the companion website.

This procedure is essentially the same for all the highlight cells and top/bottom rules, but several of these rules deserve additional comment:

- **Between**   This is obvious perhaps, but although the Greater Than, Less Than, and Equal To rules require you to type a single number criterion, the Between rule requires two criteria.

- **Text That Contains**   When you choose this rule, cells containing any form of the text string you type as a criterion are highlighted (entering "and" highlights cells containing sand, Andrew, and so on).

- **A Date Occurring**   This rule always uses the current date as the point of reference. The "occurring" options are all relative to this: Yesterday, Last Week, Next Month, and so on.

- **Duplicate Values**   This rule actually has two options, highlighting either duplicate or unique values.

The highlight cells rules are the only ones that operate independently of other cells. That is, each cell is evaluated against criteria individually and formatted accordingly. All other conditional formats depend entirely on the rest of the cell values formatted using the same condition. For example, Figure 9-23 shows the same top/bottom rule applied to two different selected regions. (In this case, we specified the top five.)

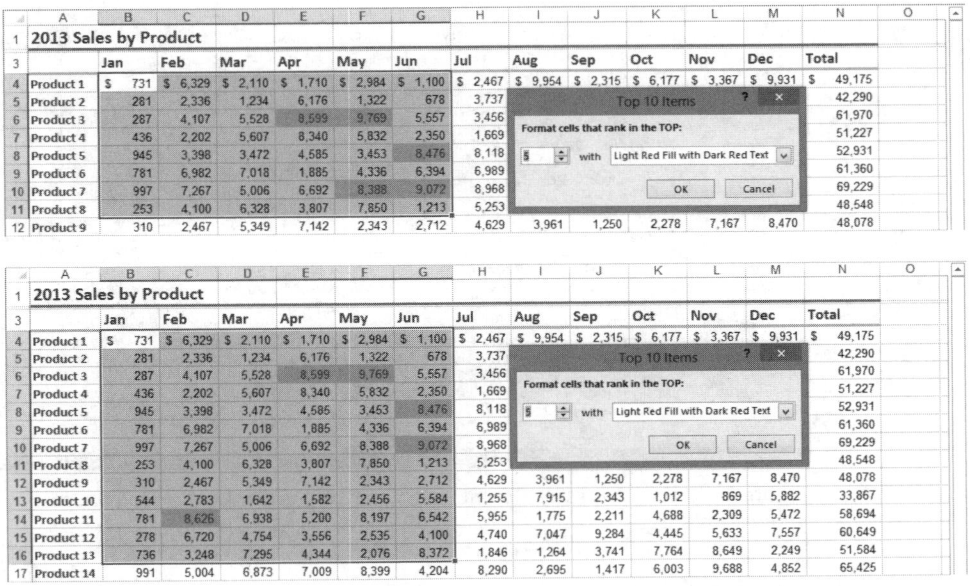

Figure 9-23 We used the same top/bottom rule on two different selections, with different results.

As you can see in Figure 9-23, cell F10 drops out of the top five, and cell C14 is added to the top five when we select a different range of cells. Excel uses all the values in the selected cell range to determine which cells to format. For data bars, color scales, and icon sets, Excel actually applies formatting to every cell in the selected range but adjusts the color, size, or icon based on each cell's value relative to the whole.

Data bars are a unique type of conditional format because each cell actually contains the same color (actually, a gradation of color), but the size of the colored area varies in each cell to reflect the cell's value relative to the other selected cells. Figure 9-24 shows a live preview of the orange data bar.

All these conditional formats are pretty flashy, and they definitely help identify relative values in a range, but you can begin to see that too much conditional formatting can become counterproductive. As with any flashy feature, it's easy to love it a little too much, so make sure you're serving the purpose of your worksheet. Figure 9-25 shows what might be considered a more judicious application of conditional formatting using highlight cells and data bars.

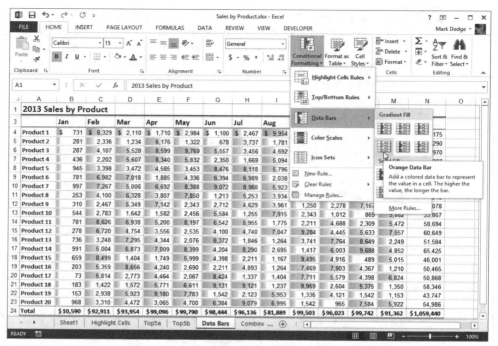

Figure 9-24 You can rest the pointer on items on the Data Bars menu to see a live preview on your worksheet.

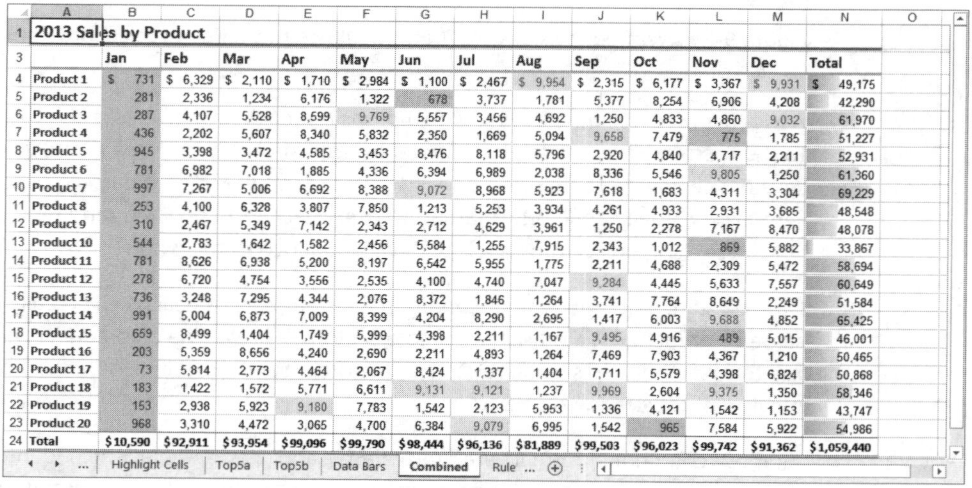

Figure 9-25 We used highlighted cells in the body of this table and data bars in the Totals column.

Creating conditional formatting rules

Excel provides a nice variety of conditional formatting options, but you can always create your own as well. You might have noticed the New Rule command at the bottom of the Conditional Formatting menu and the ubiquitous More Rules command on each submenu. These all do essentially the same task—display the New Formatting Rule dialog box shown in Figure 9-26.

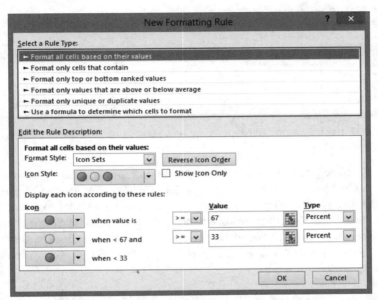

Figure 9-26 Use the New Formatting Rule dialog box to construct your own conditional formats.

All these commands open the same dialog box, but based on the menu or submenu where you clicked the command, a different rule type is selected when it opens. Each rule type displays a different set of rule-description criteria below it. To display the dialog box in Figure 9-26, we clicked Conditional Formatting on the Home tab, then Icon Sets, and then the More Rules command. Each format style has a different set of controls for creating conditional formatting rules.

The first rule type—Format All Cells Based On Their Values—contains all the controls for creating data bars, color scales, and icon sets. The rule description controls for the second rule type—Format Only Cells That Contain, shown in Figure 9-27—is what you use to create highlight cells rules. The controls for the remaining rule types are similar to this one.

We discuss the last rule type, Use A Formula To Determine Which Cells To Format, in "Creating conditional formatting formulas" later in this chapter.

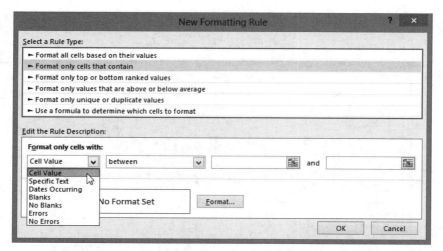

Figure 9-27 Use the second rule type in the New Formatting Rule dialog box to create your own highlight cells rules.

Use the Edit The Rule Description area to define your formats. This area changes depending on the rule selected. With Format Only Cells That Contain selected, the first drop-down list in this area (shown in Figure 9-27) allows you to define rules for highlighting Cell Value, Specific Text, Dates Occurring (relative to now), Blanks, No Blanks, Errors, or No Errors. Then select an operator (Between, Not Between, Equal To, Not Equal To, Greater Than, Less Than, Greater Than Or Equal To, Less Than Or Equal To) and type comparison values in the remaining text boxes.

After you establish the rule description criteria, click the Format button. An abbreviated version of the Format Cells dialog box appears, containing only Number, Font, Border, and Fill tabs. Specify any combination of formats you want to apply when your rule is triggered. When you finish, click OK to return to the New Formatting Rule dialog box, and click OK again to save your new rule. You can create as many rules as you want; next, we'll discuss how to work with them.

Managing conditional formatting rules

You can apply as many conditional formats as you think are necessary—using three or more per table is not uncommon. But it is also not uncommon for you to tweak some of the numbers or adjust some of the formatting. To do so, click Home, Conditional Formatting, Manage Rules to display a Conditional Formatting Rules Manager dialog box similar to the one shown in Figure 9-28.

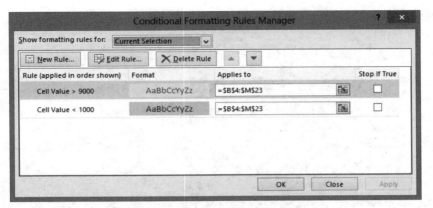

Figure 9-28 Use the Conditional Formatting Rules Manager dialog box to tweak any rules that have been applied in a workbook.

You can use the Show Formatting Rules For drop-down list at the top of the dialog box to choose where to look in the current workbook for rules: each worksheet in the current workbook is listed here, or you can choose This Worksheet or Current Selection (the default). As you can see in Figure 9-28, you can create, edit, and delete rules by using corresponding buttons. When you click New Rule, the now-familiar New Formatting Rule dialog box appears. When you click Edit Rule, a similar dialog box appears (Edit Formatting Rule) with the criteria for the selected rule displayed.

Excel applies the rules listed in the Conditional Formatting Rules Manager dialog box in the order in which they appear in the Rule list—new rules are added to the top of the list and are processed first. Use the two arrow buttons next to Delete Rule to move a selected rule up or down in the precedence list. The Applies To box contains the address of the cell range to which the rule is applied. If you want to change the cell range, click the Collapse button at the right end of the Applies To text box to collapse the dialog box, letting you see the worksheet, as shown in Figure 9-29. When you do so, you can drag to select the cell range you want and insert the range address in the text box. To restore the dialog box to its original size, click the Collapse (now Expand) button again.

The Stop If True check box is present in this dialog box only for backward compatibility. Previous versions of Excel cannot recognize multiple conditional formatting rules; instead, they apply the rule that occurs last in precedence. If you need to share files with older versions, you need to choose which conditional formatting rule you prefer. Select the Stop If True check box for the last rule in the list if you want Excel to use the previous rule; select the Stop If True check box for the last two rules to use the third-to-last rule, and so on.

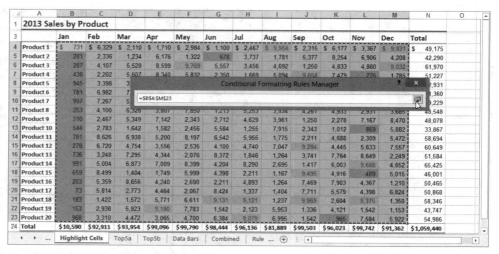

Figure 9-29 Click the Collapse button in the Applies To text box to minimize the dialog box and allow direct selection of the cell range you want.

> **Note**
>
> When two (or more) conditional rules are true for a particular cell but they are both set to apply a similar format, such as font color, the rule that is higher in the Conditional Formatting Rules Manager dialog box's list of precedence wins. Try to make multiple conditions compatible by having each rule apply a different type of format, such as the first rule applying cell color, the second applying font color, and the third applying bold formatting. In addition, conditional formats override manual formats when the condition in the cell is true.

Copying, clearing, and finding conditional formats

You can copy and paste conditionally formatted cells and use the Fill features or the Format Painter button to copy cells you have conditionally formatted. When you do, the conditional rules travel with the copied cells, and a new rule is created that references the new location in the workbook.

To remove conditional formatting rules, click Home, Conditional Formatting, Clear Rules, and then click Clear Rules From Selected Cells or Clear Rules From Entire Sheet to clear all the corresponding rules. If your conditions have been applied to a table or a PivotTable, additional corresponding commands are available.

You can use two commands on the Find & Select menu on the Home tab to locate cells on the current worksheet that conditional formats are applied to. The Conditional Formatting command locates and selects all the cells on the current worksheet to which conditional formats are applied. If conditional formatting exists in more than one cell region on the worksheet, using this command selects all the regions. This makes it easy to edit all the rules using the Conditional Formatting Rules Manager dialog box (shown earlier in Figure 9-28). You can also use the Go To Special command on the Find & Select menu to get a little more specific. Clicking this command displays the Go To Special dialog box, shown in Figure 9-30.

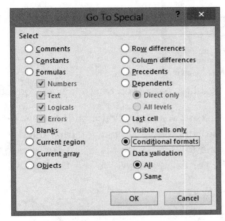

Figure 9-30 Use the Go To Special dialog box to locate all conditional formats or just matching ones.

When you select the Conditional Formats option, two additional options—All and Same— become available. Selecting All is the same as using the Conditional Formatting command on the Find & Select menu to select all conditionally formatted cells and regions. If you use the Same option, however, Go To Special finds only cells that are formatted using the same condition that exists in the selected cell. Before clicking the Go To Special command, select a cell containing the conditional format you want to locate.

Creating conditional formatting formulas

The last rule type in the New Formatting Rule dialog box shown in Figure 9-26 offers the ability to create your own conditional formatting formulas. When you select the rule type labeled Use A Formula To Determine Which Cells To Format, the dialog box looks similar to the one shown in Figure 9-31.

Figure 9-31 Use the last rule type in the list to create your own conditional formatting formulas.

You can create formulas to perform tasks such as identifying dates that fall on specific days of the week, specifying particular values, or doing anything you can't quite accomplish using the built-in conditional formatting tools. For example, using our worksheet example, we typed the following formula in the Format Values Where This Formula Is True text box in the New Formatting Rule dialog box:

=IF(ISERROR(B4),0)=0

Then we clicked the Format button and selected a color on the Fill tab. The formula applies the selected fill color to any cell that generates an error value. (The cell reference B4 is the relative reference of the upper-left cell of the range to which the format is applied.) When you use this technique, you can type any formula that results in the logical values TRUE (1) or FALSE (0). For example, you could use a logical formula such as =N4>AVERAGE($N$4:$N$37), which combines relative and absolute references to apply formatting to a cell when the value it contains is less than the average of the specified range. When you use relative references in this situation, the formatting formulas adjust in each cell where you apply or copy them, just as regular cell formulas do.

For more information, see "Using cell references in formulas" in Chapter 12 and "Understanding logical functions" in Chapter 14, "Everyday functions." Also, see other topics in Chapter 14 and Chapter 15, "Formatting and calculating date and time."

Formatting in depth

The formatting features in Excel control the display characteristics of numbers and text. Be sure to keep in mind the difference between underlying and displayed worksheet values. Formats do not affect the underlying numeric or text values in cells. For example, if you type a number with six decimal places in a cell that is formatted with two decimal places, Excel displays the number with only two decimal places. However, the underlying value isn't changed, and Excel uses the underlying value in calculations.

> **Note**
>
> When you copy a cell or range of cells, you copy both its contents and its formatting. If you then paste this information into another cell or range, the formatting of the source cells normally replaces any existing formatting. For more information about copying and pasting, see Chapter 8.

Most of your formatting needs should be quickly and easily fulfilled using buttons and controls located on the Home tab on the ribbon, but for more options, you can employ the Format Cells dialog box. To display the Format Cells dialog box, press Ctrl+1. Alternatively, click one of the dialog box launchers adjacent to the titles of the Font, Alignment, and Number groups on the Home tab. Clicking a dialog box launcher also activates the corresponding tab. Figure 9-32 shows the Format Cells dialog box.

Throughout the following sections, we'll discuss formatting options available directly on the ribbon, but we'll go into more depth by employing the Format Cells dialog box.

Formatting individual characters

If you select a cell and apply formats, the entire contents of the cell receive the formats. However, you can also apply formatting to individual text characters within cells (but not numeric values or formulas). Select individual characters or words inside a cell, and apply the attributes you want. When you are finished, press Enter to see the results, an example of which is shown in Figure 9-33.

For more examples of formatting individual characters, see "Using fonts" later in this chapter.

Chapter 9

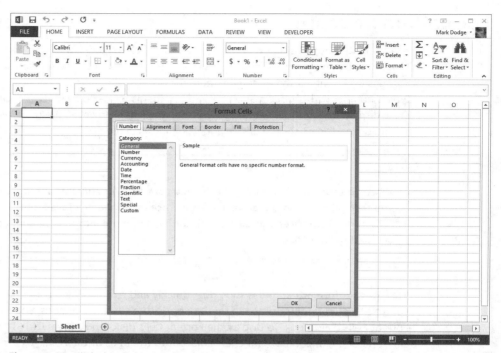

Figure 9-32 Click the dialog box launcher in the Number group to display the Number tab of the Format Cells dialog box.

Figure 9-33 You can format individual characters within a cell.

Formatting as you type

You can include special formatting characters—such as dollar signs, percent signs, commas, or fractions—to format numbers as you type them. When you type numeric-entry characters that represent a format Excel recognizes, Excel applies that format to the cell on the fly. The following list describes some of the more common special formatting characters:

- If you type **$45.00** in a cell, Excel interprets your entry as the value 45 formatted as currency with two decimal places. Only the value 45 appears in the formula bar after you press Enter, but the formatted value, $45.00, appears in the cell.

- If you type **1 3/8** (with a single space between 1 and 3), 1 3/8 appears in the cell and 1.375 appears in the formula bar. However, if you type **3/8**, then 8-Mar appears in the cell, because date formats take precedence over fraction formats. Assuming you make the entry in the year 2013, then 3/8/2013 appears in the formula bar. To display 3/8 in the cell as a fraction so that 0.375 appears in the formula bar, you must type **0 3/8** (with a space between 0 and 3). Of course, you can always type **.375** and then apply the Fraction format. For information about typing dates and a complete listing of date and time formats, see "Entering dates and times" in Chapter 14.

- If you type **23%** in a cell, Excel applies the no-decimal percentage format to the cell, and 23% appears in the formula bar. Nevertheless, Excel uses the 0.23 decimal value for calculations.

- If you type **123,456** in a cell, Excel applies the comma format without decimal places. If you type **123,456.00**, Excel formats the cell with the comma format including two decimal places.

> **Note**
>
> Leading zeros are almost always dropped, unless you create or use a format specifically designed to preserve them. For example, when you type **0123** in a cell, Excel displays the value 123, dropping the leading zero. Excel provides custom formats for a couple of commonly needed leading-zero applications—namely, ZIP codes and Social Security numbers—on the Number tab, Special category of the Format Cells dialog box. For more information, see "Using the special formats" later in this chapter. For information about creating your own formats, see "Creating custom number formats" later in this chapter.

Understanding the General format

The General format is the default format for all cells. Although it is not just a number format, it is nonetheless always the first number format category listed. Unless you specifically change the format of a cell, Excel displays any text or numbers you type in the General format. Except in the cases listed next, the General format displays exactly what you type. For example, if you type **123.45**, the cell displays 123.45. Here are the four exceptions:

- The General format abbreviates numbers too long to display in a cell. For example, if you type **12345678901234** (an integer) into a standard-width cell, Excel displays 1.23457E+13.

- Long decimal values are also rounded or displayed in scientific notation. Thus, if you type **123456.7812345** in a standard-width cell, the General format displays

123456.8. The actual typed values are preserved and used in all calculations, regard-less of the display format.

- The General format does not display trailing zeros. For example, if you type **123.0**, Excel displays 123.

- A decimal fraction typed without a number to the left of the decimal point is dis-played with a zero. For example, if you type **.123**, Excel displays 0.123.

Formatting numbers

The second option in the drop-down list displayed in the Number group on the Home tab is called, helpfully, *Number*. When you use the drop-down list, selecting Number applies a default number format, with two decimal places and comma separators. For example, if you apply the Number format with a cell selected containing 1234.556, the cell displays the number as 1,234.56. Excel rounds the decimal value to two places in the process, which does not change the actual value in the cell, just the displayed value.

> **Note**
>
> **The Comma Style button in the Number group on the Home tab applies the same for-mat as does the Number format in the drop-down list.**

In the Format Cells dialog box, the Number category contains additional options, letting you display numbers in integer, fixed-decimal, and punctuated formats, as shown in Fig-ure 9-34. It is essentially the General format with additional control over displayed decimal places, thousand separators, and negative numbers. You can use this category to format any numbers that do not fall into any of the other categories.

Follow these guidelines when using the Number category:

- Select the number of decimal places to display (0 to 30) by typing or scrolling to the value in the Decimal Places box.

- Select the Use 1000 Separator (,) check box to add commas between hundreds and thousands, and so on.

- Select an example in the Negative Numbers list to display negative numbers pre-ceded by a minus sign, in red, in parentheses, or in both red and parentheses.

> **Note**
>
> When formatting numbers, always select a cell containing a number before opening the Format Cells dialog box so that you can see the actual results in the Sample area.

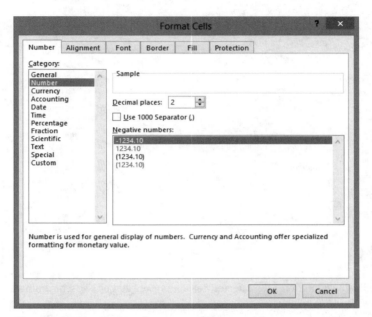

Figure 9-34 Use the Number category for general-purpose, noncurrency numeric formatting.

Using Currency formats

The quickest way to apply currency formatting is by clicking Currency in the Number drop-down list in the Number group on the Home tab, as shown in Figure 9-35. The Currency format is similar to the Number format that precedes it in the drop-down list, except it also includes the default currency symbol for your locale. Notice that most of the commands listed here display little previews showing you what the contents of the active cell will look like if you click that command.

> **Note**
>
> Despite the button's appearance, clicking the $ button on the Home tab actually applies a two-decimal Accounting format, which is similar to, but a little different from, the Currency format. We'll discuss Accounting formats in the next section.

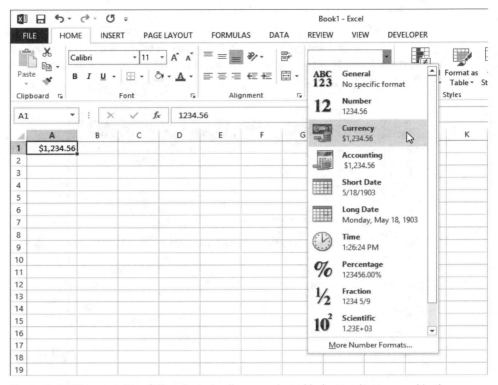

Figure 9-35 The contents of the selected cell are previewed below each command in the Number drop-down list.

For additional currency formatting options, select the Currency category in the Format Cells dialog box, which offers a similar set of options as the Number category (refer to Figure 9-34) but adds a drop-down list of worldwide currency symbols. In addition to clicking the dialog box launcher in the Number group on the Home tab to display the Format Cells dialog box, you can also select the More Number Formats command at the bottom of the Number drop-down list shown in Figure 9-35.

Using the decimal buttons

You can change the number of displayed decimal places in any selected cell or range at any time using two buttons—Increase Decimal and Decrease Decimal—in the Number group on the Home tab:

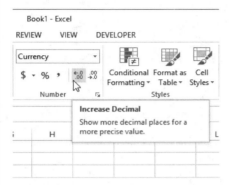

The Increase Decimal button displays an arrow pointing to the left, and the Decrease Decimal button displays an arrow pointing to the right, which might seem backward to those of us in the left-to-right/smaller-to-larger world of Western culture, but of course these buttons address what happens only on the right side of the decimal point. Each click adds or subtracts one decimal place from the displayed value. Interestingly, although you can specify up to 30 decimal places using the Format Cells dialog box, you can increase the number of decimal places to a maximum of 127, one click at a time, using the Increase Decimal button.

Using Accounting formats

The most-often-used Accounting format is directly available on the Home tab on the ribbon, using the Accounting Number Format button in the Number group. Clicking this button applies a standard two-decimal-place format with comma separators and currency symbols to the selected cells. Clicking the arrow button adjacent to the Accounting Number Format button displays a menu providing access to a few additional currency symbols, as shown in Figure 9-36.

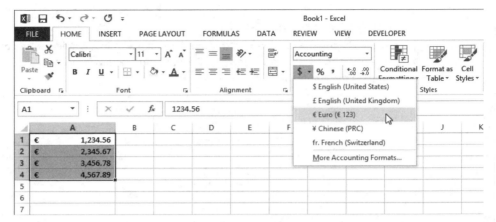

Figure 9-36 The $ button applies a standard Accounting format and offers a few optional currency symbols.

The Accounting formats address the needs of accounting professionals, but they benefit the rest of us as well. When you use one of these formats with the Single Accounting or Double Accounting font formats (to add underlines to your numbers), you can easily create profit and loss (P&L) statements, balance sheets, and other schedules that conform to generally accepted accounting principles (GAAP). The Accounting formats correspond roughly to the Currency format in appearance—you can display numbers with or without your choice of currency symbols and specify the number of decimal places. However, the two formats have some distinct differences. The rules governing the Accounting formats are as follows:

- The Accounting format displays every currency symbol flush with the left side of the cell and displays numbers flush with the right side, as shown in Figure 9-36. The result is that all the currency symbols in the same column are vertically aligned, which looks much cleaner than Currency formats.

- In the Accounting format, negative values are always displayed in parentheses and always in black—displaying numbers in red is not an option.

- The Accounting format includes a space equivalent to the width of a parenthesis on the right side of the cell so that numbers line up evenly in columns of mixed positive and negative values.

- The Accounting format displays zero values as dashes. The spacing of the dashes depends on whether you select decimal places. If you include two decimal places, the dashes line up under the decimal point.

- Finally, the Accounting format is the only built-in format that includes formatting criteria for text. It includes spaces equivalent to the width of a parenthesis on each side of text so that it too lines up evenly with the numbers in a column.

Typically, when creating a GAAP-friendly worksheet of currency values, you would use currency symbols only in the top row and in the totals row at the bottom of each column of numbers. This makes good sense because using dollar signs with every number would make for a much busier table. The middle of the table is then formatted using a compatible format without currency symbols, as shown in Figure 9-37.

	A	B	C	D	E	F	G	H	I	J	K	L	M	N	O
1	2013 Sales by Product														
3		Jan	Feb	Mar	Apr	May	Jun	Jul	Aug	Sep	Oct	Nov	Dec	Total	
4	Product 1	$ 731	$ 6,329	$ 2,110	$ 1,710	$ 2,984	$ 1,100	$ 2,467	$ 9,954	$ 2,315	$ 6,177	$ 3,367	$ 9,931	$ 49,175	
5	Product 2	281	2,336	1,234	6,176	1,322	678	3,737	1,781	5,377	8,254	6,906	4,208	42,290	
6	Product 3	287	4,107	5,528	8,599	9,769	5,557	3,456	4,692	1,250	4,833	4,860	9,032	61,970	
7	Product 4	436	2,202	5,607	8,340	5,832	2,350	1,669	5,094	9,658	7,479	775	1,785	51,227	
8	Product 5	945	3,398	3,472	4,585	3,453	8,476	8,118	5,796	2,920	4,840	4,717	2,211	52,931	
9	Product 6	781	6,982	7,018	1,885	4,336	6,394	6,989	2,038	8,336	5,546	9,805	1,250	61,360	
10	Product 7	997	7,267	5,006	6,692	8,388	9,072	8,968	5,923	7,618	1,683	4,311	3,304	69,229	
11	Product 8	253	4,100	6,328	3,807	7,850	1,213	5,253	3,934	4,261	4,933	2,931	3,685	48,548	
12	Product 9	310	2,467	5,349	7,142	2,343	2,712	4,629	3,961	1,250	2,278	7,167	8,470	48,078	
13	Product 10	544	2,783	1,642	1,582	2,456	5,584	1,255	7,915	2,343	1,012	869	5,882	33,867	
14	Product 11	781	8,626	6,938	5,200	8,197	6,542	5,955	1,775	2,211	4,688	2,309	5,472	58,694	
15	Product 12	278	6,720	4,754	3,556	2,535	4,100	4,740	7,047	9,284	4,445	5,633	7,557	60,649	
16	Product 13	736	3,248	7,295	4,344	2,076	8,372	1,846	1,264	3,741	7,764	8,649	2,249	51,584	
17	Product 14	991	5,004	6,873	7,009	8,399	4,204	8,290	2,695	1,417	6,003	9,688	4,852	65,425	
18	Product 15	659	8,499	1,404	1,749	5,999	4,398	2,211	1,167	9,495	4,916	489	5,015	46,001	
19	Product 16	203	5,359	8,656	4,240	2,690	2,211	4,893	1,264	7,469	7,903	4,367	1,210	50,465	
20	Product 17	73	5,814	2,773	4,464	2,067	8,424	1,337	1,404	7,711	5,579	4,398	6,824	50,868	
21	Product 18	183	1,422	1,572	5,771	6,611	9,131	9,121	1,237	9,969	2,604	9,375	1,350	58,346	
22	Product 19	153	2,938	5,923	9,180	7,783	1,542	2,123	5,953	1,336	1,542	1,153	43,747	
23	Product 20	968	3,310	4,472	3,065	4,700	6,384	9,079	6,995	1,542	965	7,584	5,922	54,986	
24	Total	$10,590	$92,911	$93,954	$99,096	$99,790	$98,444	$96,136	$81,889	$99,503	$96,023	$99,742	$91,362	$1,059,440	
25															

Figure 9-37 It is standard practice to use currency symbols only in the top and bottom rows of a table.

Luckily, Excel makes it easy for you to format this way by using buttons in the Number group on the Home tab. Despite seemingly incompatible button names, both the Accounting Number Format button and the Comma Style button apply Accounting formats adhering to the rules described earlier. So, to format the numeric entries in the table shown in Figure 9-37, select the first and last rows of numbers, click the Accounting Number Format button, then select all the cells containing numbers in between, and click the Comma Style button. (We then selected all the numeric cells in the table and clicked the Decrease Decimal button twice to hide all the decimal values. We also hid worksheet gridlines, by clearing the Gridlines option on the View tab, to simplify the appearance.)

Using accounting underlines

Generally accepted accounting principles specify the proper usage of single and double underlines in tables. The Underline button on the Home tab includes a menu letting you select single or double underlines, but unfortunately these do not rise to the accepted standard. But fear not—Excel provides two accounting-specific underline formats in a drop-down list of the same name on the Font tab in the Format Cells dialog box. These differ from their regular counterparts in two ways. First, accounting underlines are applied to the entire width of the cell (minus a parenthesis-sized space on each side), whereas regular underlines are applied only under the actual characters in a cell. If the cell contains a text entry that extends beyond the cell border, the accounting underlines stop at the cell border. Second, the accounting underline formats appear near the bottom of cells, unlike regular underlines, which are applied much closer to the numbers or text in the cell, resulting in annoying lines through commas and the descenders of letters like *g* and *p*. Of course, you can also apply single-line and double-line cell borders instead of underline formats, which is the approach used when you add a totals row to a table using the Totals Row option on the Table Tools Design tab.

For information about font formats, see "Using fonts" later in this chapter. For information about tables, see "Formatting tables" earlier in this chapter.

Formatting percentages

Not surprisingly, using the Percentage format displays numbers as percentages. The decimal point of the formatted number, in effect, moves two places to the right, and a percent sign appears at the end of the number. For example, if you choose a percentage format without decimal places, the entry **0.1234** is displayed as 12%; if you select two decimal places, the entry **0.1234** is displayed as 12.34%. Remember that you can always adjust the number of displayed decimal places using the Increase Decimal and Decrease Decimal buttons.

An interesting (and helpful) quirk about percentage formats is that they behave differently depending on whether you type a number and then apply the format or type a number in a previously formatted cell. For example, Figure 9-38 shows two cells formatted as percentages. We typed the same number—**22.33**—in each cell, but only cell A1 was previously formatted with the Percentage format; we clicked the Percent Style button *after* typing the value in cell A2.

As you can see, it makes a world of difference which way you do this. So, why is this behavior helpful? For example, if a worksheet contains a displayed value of 12% and you need to change it to 13%, typing **13** in the cell would seem to make sense, even though this is technically wrong. It is not particularly intuitive to type **.13** (including the leading decimal point). Usability studies show that most people would type **13** in this situation, which would logically result in a displayed value of 1300% (if not for the quirky behavior), so Excel assumes that you want to display 13%. If you apply the Percentage format to a range of cells that already contain values (or formulas that result in values), check all the cells afterward to make sure you get the intended results.

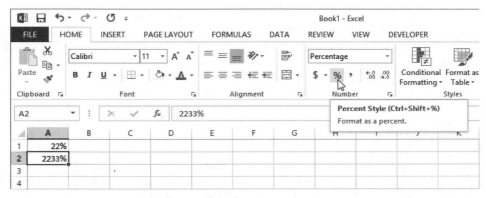

Figure 9-38 When using percentages, it makes a difference whether you format before or after typing values.

Formatting fractions

The formats in the Fraction category in the Format Cells dialog box, shown in Figure 9-39, display fractional numbers as actual fractions rather than as decimal values. As with all number formats, the underlying value does not change despite the displayed value of the fraction.

You can generate some wild, nonstandard fractions unless you apply constraints using options in the Format Cells dialog box. Here is how Excel applies different fraction formats:

- The Up To One Digit (single-digit) fraction format displays 123.456 as 123 1/2, rounding the display to the nearest value that can be represented as a single-digit fraction.

- The Up To Two Digits (double-digit) fraction format uses the additional precision allowed by the format and displays 123.456 as 123 26/57.

- The Up To Three Digits (triple-digit) fraction format displays 123.456 as the even more precise 123 57/125.

- The remaining six fraction formats specify the exact denominator you want by rounding to the nearest equivalent—for example, displaying 123.456 using the As Sixteenths format, or 123 7/16.

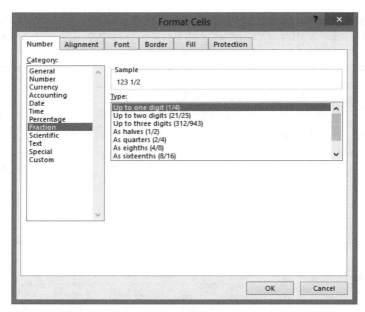

Figure 9-39 Excel provides many fraction-formatting options.

You can also apply fraction formatting on the fly by typing fractional values in a specific way. Type a number (or a zero), type a space, and then type the fraction, as in **123 1/2**. For more details, see "Formatting as you type" earlier in this chapter.

Formatting Scientific (exponential) values

The Scientific format displays numbers in exponential notation. For example, a two-decimal Scientific format (the default) displays the number 98765432198 as 9.88E+10 in a standard-width cell. The number 9.88E+10 is 9.88 times 10 to the 10th power. The symbol E stands for *exponent*, a synonym here for 10 to the *n*th power. The expression *"10 to the 10th power"* means 10 times itself 10 times, or 10,000,000,000. Multiplying this value by 9.88 gives you 98,800,000,000, an approximation of 98,765,432,198. Increasing the number of decimal places (the only option available for this format) increases the precision and will likely require a wider cell to accommodate the displayed value.

You can also use the Scientific format to display very small numbers. For example, in a standard-width cell this format displays 0.000000009 as 9.00E–09, which equates to 9 times 10 to the negative 9th power. The expression *"10 to the negative 9th power"* means 1 divided by 10 to the 9th power, 1 divided by 10 nine times, or 0.000000001. Multiplying this number by nine results in our original number, 0.000000009.

Understanding the Text format

Applying the Text format to a cell indicates that the entry in the cell is to be treated as text, even if it's a number. For example, a numeric value is ordinarily right-aligned in its cell. If you apply the Text format to the cell, however, the value is left-aligned as if it were a text entry. For all practical purposes, a numeric constant formatted as text is still considered a number because Excel is capable of recognizing its numeric value anyway.

Using the Special formats

The four Special formats shown in Figure 9-40 are a result of many requests from users. These generally noncalculated numbers include two ZIP code formats, a phone number format (complete with the area code in parentheses), and a Social Security number format. Using each of these Special formats, you can quickly type numbers without having to type the punctuation characters.

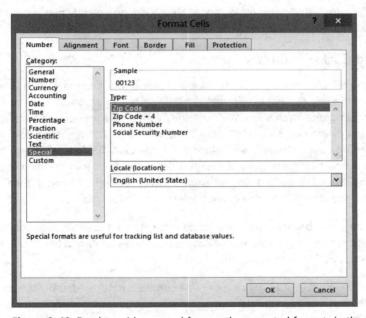

Figure 9-40 Excel provides several frequently requested formats in the Special category.

The following are guidelines for using the Special formats:

- **Zip Code and Zip Code +4**   Leading zeros are retained to correctly display the code, as in 04321. In most other number formats, if you type **04321**, Excel drops the zero and displays 4321.

- **Phone Number**   Excel applies parentheses around the area code and dashes between the digits, making it much easier to type many numbers at the same time because you don't have to move your hand from the keypad. Furthermore, the numbers you type remain numbers instead of becoming text entries, which they would be if you typed parentheses or dashes in the cell.

- **Social Security Number**   Excel places dashes after the third and fifth numbers. For example, if you type **123456789**, Excel displays 123-45-6789.

- **Locale**   This drop-down list lets you select from more than 120 locations with unique formats. For example, if you select Vietnamese, only two Special formats are available: Metro Phone Number and Suburb Phone Number.

Creating Custom number formats

Most of the number formats you need are available through commands and buttons on the ribbon, but you can use the Format Cells dialog box to accomplish minor feats of formatting that might surprise you. We'll use the Custom category on the Number tab in the Format Cells dialog box, shown in Figure 9-41, to create custom number formats using special formatting codes. (To quickly display the Format Cells dialog box, press Ctrl+1.) Excel adds new formats to the bottom of the list of formatting codes in the Type list, which also includes built-in formats. To delete a custom format, select the format in the Format Cells dialog box, and click Delete. You cannot delete built-in formats.

Creating new number formats   The quickest way to start creating a custom format is to use one of the built-in formats as a starting point. Here's an easy way to build on an existing format, as well as to see what the codes in the Type list mean:

1. Type a number (or, in the case of our example, a date), and apply the built-in format that most closely resembles the custom format you want to create. Leave this cell selected.

2. On the Number tab in the Format Cells dialog box, select the Custom category. The format you selected is highlighted in the Type list, representing the code equivalent of the format you want to modify, as shown in Figure 9-41.

Figure 9-41 Use the Custom category to create new formats using special codes.

3. Edit the contents of the Type text box, using the codes listed in Table 9-1. The built-in format isn't affected, and the new format is added to the bottom of the Type list.

For example, to create a format that displays the date and time with the longest available format for day, month, and year, start by typing a date in a cell, and then select it. In the Custom category in the Format Cells dialog box, edit the format in the Type text box to read *dddd, mmmm dd, yyyy – hh:mm AM/PM* (including spaces and commas), and then click OK. Figure 9-42 shows the result.

> **Note**
>
> Saving the workbook saves your new formats, but to carry special formats from one workbook to another, you must copy and paste a cell with the Custom format. For easy access to special formats, consider saving them in one workbook.

Chapter 9

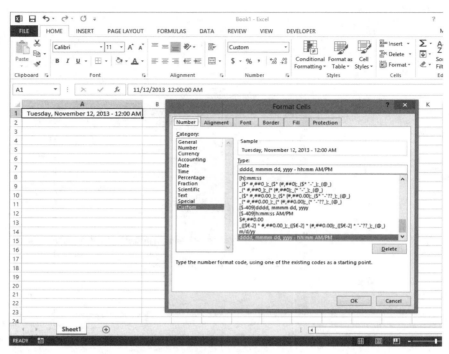

Figure 9-42 We created a custom format by typing codes in the Type text box.

You can create any number format using the codes in Table 9-1.

TABLE 9-1 Custom format symbols

Symbol	Meaning
0	**Digit placeholder.** This symbol ensures that a specified number of digits appear on each side of the decimal point. For example, if the format is 0.000, the value .987 is displayed as 0.987. If the format is 0.0000, the value .987 is displayed as 0.9870. If a number has more digits to the right of the decimal point than the number of zeros specified in the format, the number displayed in the cell is rounded. For example, if the format is *0.00*, the value .987 is displayed as 0.99; if the format is *0.0*, .987 is rounded to 1.0.
?	**Digit placeholder.** This symbol follows the same rules as the 0 placeholder, except that space is left for insignificant zeros on either side of the decimal point. This placeholder aligns numbers on the decimal points. For example, 1.4 and 1.45 would line up on the decimal point if both were formatted as *0.??*.
#	**Digit placeholder.** This symbol works like 0, except that extra zeros do not appear if the number has fewer digits on either side of the decimal point than # placeholders specified in the format. This symbol shows Excel where to display commas or other separating symbols. The format #,###, for example, tells Excel to display a comma after every third digit to the left of the decimal point.

Symbol	Meaning
.	**Decimal point.** This symbol determines how many digits (0 or #) appear to the right and left of the decimal point. If the format contains only # placeholders to the left of this symbol, Excel begins numbers less than 1 with a decimal point. To avoid this, use 0 as the first digit placeholder to the left of the decimal point instead of #. If you want Excel to include commas and display at least one digit to the left of the decimal point in all cases, specify the format #,##0.
%	**Percentage indicator.** This symbol multiplies the entry by 100 and inserts the % character.
/	**Fraction format character.** This symbol displays the fractional part of a number in a nondecimal format. The number of digit placeholders that surround this character determines the accuracy of the display. For example, the decimal fraction 0.269 when formatted with # ?/? is displayed as 1/4, but when formatted with # ???/??? is displayed as 46/171.
,	**Thousands separator.** If the format contains a comma surrounded by #, 0, or ? placeholders, Excel uses commas to separate hundreds from thousands, thousands from millions, and so on. In addition, the comma acts as a rounding and scaling agent. Use one comma at the end of a format to tell Excel to round a number and display it in thousands; use two commas to tell Excel to round to the nearest million. For example, the format code #,###,###, would round 4567890 to 4,568, whereas the format code #,###,###,, would round it to 5.
E– E+ e– e+	**Scientific format characters.** If a format contains one 0 or # to the right of an E–, E+, e–, or e+, Excel displays the number in scientific notation and inserts E or e in the displayed value. The number of 0 or # placeholders to the right of the E or e determines the minimum number of digits in the exponent. Use E– or e– to place a negative sign by negative exponents; use E+ or e+ to place a negative sign by negative exponents and a positive sign by positive exponents.
$ – + / ( ) space	**Standard formatting characters.** Typing any of these symbols adds the actual corresponding character directly to your format.
\	**Literal demarcation character.** Precede each character you want to display in the cell—except for : $ – + / ( ) and space—with a backslash. (Excel does not display the backslash.) For example, the format code #,##0 \D;–#,##0 \C displays positive numbers followed by a space and a D and displays negative numbers followed by a space and a C. To insert several characters, use the quotation-mark technique described in the "Text" table entry.
_	**Underscore.** This code leaves space equal to the width of the next character. For example, _) leaves a space equal to the width of the close parenthesis. Use this formatting character for alignment purposes.
"Text"	**Literal character string.** This formatting code works like the backslash technique except that all text can be included within one set of double quotation marks without using a separate demarcation character for each literal character.
*	**Repetition initiator.** This code repeats the next character in the format enough times to fill the column width. Use only one asterisk in the format.
@	**Text placeholder.** If the cell contains text, this placeholder inserts that text in the format where the @ appears. For example, the format code "This is a" @ displays "This is a debit" in a cell containing the word *debit*.

Table 9-2 lists the built-in formats and indicates how these codes relate to the other categories on the Number tab. (This table does not list date and time codes, which are covered in Chapter 15.)

TABLE 9-2 Built-in custom format codes

Category	Custom format codes
0	Digit
General	No specific format
Number	0
	0.00
	#,##0
	#,##0.00
	#,##0_);(#,##0)
	#,##0_);[Red](#,##0)
	#,##0.00_);(#,##0.00)
	#,##0.00_);[Red](#,##0.00)
Currency	$#,##0_);($#,##0)
	$#,##0_);[Red]($#,##0)
	$#,##0.00_);($#,##0.00)
	$#,##0.00_);[Red]($#,##0.00)
Percentage	0%
	0.00%
Scientific	0.00E+00
	##0.0E+0
Fraction	# ?/?
	# ??/??
Date	(See Chapter 15.)
Time	(See Chapter 15.)
Text	@
Accounting	_($* #,##0_);_($* (#,##0);_($* "-"_);_(@_)
	_(* #,##0_);_(* (#,##0);_(* "-"_);_(@_)
	_($* #,##0.00_);_($* (#,##0.00);_($* "-"??_);_(@_)
	_(* #,##0.00_);_(* (#,##0.00);_(* "-"??_);_(@_)

Creating four-part formats Within each custom format definition, you can specify completely different formats for positive, negative, zero, and text values. You can create custom formats with as many as four parts, separating the portions by semicolons—positive number; negative number; zero; text. Figure 9-43 shows how three different formats are constructed using codes.

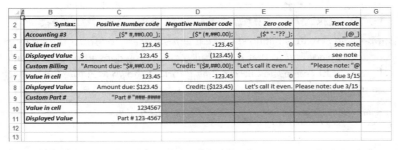

	B	C	D	E	F	G
2	Syntax:	*Positive Number code*	*Negative Number code*	*Zero code*	*Text code*	
3	*Accounting #3*	_($* #,##0.00_);	_($* (#,##0.00);	_($* "-"??_);	_(@_)	
4	*Value in cell*	123.45	-123.45	0	see note	
5	*Displayed Value*	$ 123.45	$ (123.45)	$ -	see note	
6	*Custom Billing*	"Amount due: "$#,##0.00_);	"Credit: "($#,##0.00);	"Let's call it even.";	"Please note: "@	
7	*Value in cell*	123.45	-123.45	0	due 3/15	
8	*Displayed Value*	Amount due: $123.45	Credit: ($123.45)	Let's call it even.	Please note: due 3/15	
9	*Custom Part #*	"Part # "###-####				
10	*Value in cell*	1234567				
11	*Displayed Value*	Part # 123-4567				
12						
13						

Figure 9-43 You can create your own four-part formats.

You'll find the FormattingNumbers.xlsx file with the other examples on the companion website. It contains many of the custom formatting code examples described in this section.

Among the built-in formats, only the Accounting formats use all four parts, as shown in Figure 9-43, which breaks down each part of the third Accounting format in Table 9-2. The following are some guidelines for creating multipart formats:

- If your custom format includes only one part, Excel applies that format to positive, negative, and zero values.

- If your custom format includes two parts, the first part applies to positive and zero values, and the second part applies only to negative values.

- If your custom format has three parts, the third part controls the display of zero values.

- The fourth and last element in a four-way format controls text-value formatting. Any formats with three or fewer elements have no effect on text entries.

> **Note**
>
> If you prefer, you can suppress the display of all zero values in a worksheet, including the displayed values of formulas with a zero result. Click the File tab, Options, and then click the Advanced category. In the Display Options For This Worksheet area, clear the Show A Zero In Cells That Have Zero Value check box.

Adding color to formats   You can also use the Number formats to change the color of selected cell entries. For example, you might use color to distinguish categories of information or to make totals stand out. You can even create formats that assign different colors to specific numeric ranges so that, for example, all values greater than or less than a specified value appear in a different color.

Create custom billing and part number formats

Suppose you create a billing statement and you want to format the totals in the Amount Due column so that they display differently depending on the value in each cell. You might create the Custom Billing format shown in Figure 9-43, which was created using the following code:

```
"Amount due: "$#,##0.00_);"Credit: "($#,##0.00);"Let's call it even. ";"Please note: "@
```

Suppose you're creating an inventory worksheet and you want all the entries in a particular column to appear in the format *Part # XXX-XXXX*, shown as the *Custom Part #* format in Figure 9-43, which was created using the following code:

```
"Part # "###-####
```

Using this code lets you type your part numbers as actual numbers rather than as text entries, which happens if you include any non-numeric characters, including dashes. This way, you can sort your part numbers properly and otherwise manipulate them as numeric data.

Note

You can create codes that assign different colors based on the value in the cell, but an easier way is built into Excel: You can use the Conditional Formatting menu on the Home tab on the ribbon. For more information, see "Formatting conditionally" earlier in this chapter.

To change the color of an entry, type the name of the new color in brackets in front of each segment of code. For example, if you want to apply a blue Currency format with two decimal places, edit the *$#,##0.00_);($#,##0.00)* format as follows:

```
[Blue]$#,##0.00_);($#,##0.00)
```

When you apply this format to a worksheet, positive and zero values appear in blue, and text and negative values appear as usual, in black. The following simple four-part format code displays positive values in blue, negative values in red, zero values in yellow, and text in green (with no additional number formatting specified):

```
[Blue];[Red];[Yellow];[Green]
```

You can specify the following color names in your formats: Black, Blue, Cyan, Green, Magenta, Red, White, and Yellow. You can also specify a color as COLOR*n*, where *n* is a number in the range 1 through 16. Excel selects the corresponding color from your worksheet's current 16-color palette.

> **Note**
>
> If you define colors that are not among your system's repertoire of solids, Excel produces them by mixing dots from solid colors. Such blended colors, which are said to be *dithered*, work well for shading. But for text and lines, Excel always uses the nearest solid color rather than a dithered color.

TROUBLESHOOTING

Decimal points in my Currency formats don't line up

Sometimes when you use Currency formats with trailing characters, such as the French Canadian dollar (23.45 $), you want to use the GAAP practice of using currency symbols only at the top and bottom of a column of numbers. The numbers between should not display any currency symbols, so how do you make all the decimal points line up properly?

You can create a custom format code to apply to the noncurrency format numbers in the middle of the column. An underscore character (_) in the format code tells Excel to leave a space that is equal in width to the character that follows it. For example, the code _$ leaves a space equal to the width of the dollar sign. Thus, the following code does the trick for you:

```
#,##0.00 _$;[Red]#,##0.00 _$
```

Make sure you add a space between the zeros and the underscores to properly line the numbers up with the built-in French Canadian dollar format.

Using custom format conditional operators   You can create custom formats that are variable. To do so, you can add a conditional operator to the first two parts of the standard four-part custom format. This, in effect, replaces the positive/negative formats with either/or formats. The third format becomes the default format for values that don't match the other two conditions (the "else" format). You can use the conditional operators <, >, =, <=, >=, and <> with any number to define a format.

For example, suppose you are tracking accounts receivable balances. To display accounts with balances of more than $50,000 in blue, negative values in parentheses and in red, and all other values in the default color, create this format:

```
[Blue][>50000]$#,## 0.00_);[Red][<0]($# ,##0.00);$#,##0.00_)
```

Using these conditional operators can also be a powerful aid if you need to scale numbers. For example, if your company produces a product that requires a few milliliters of a compound for each unit and you make thousands of units every day, you need to convert from milliliters to liters and kiloliters when you budget the use of this compound. Excel can make this conversion with the following numeric format:

```
[>999999]#,##0,," kl";[>999]##," L";#" ml"
```

The following table shows the effects of this format on various worksheet entries:

Entry	Display
72	72 ml
7286957	7 kl
7632	8 L

As you can see, using a combination of conditional formats, the thousands separator, and text with spaces within quotation marks can improve both the readability and the effectiveness of your worksheet—and without increasing the number of formulas.

The hidden number format

To hide values in a worksheet, assign a null format to them. To create a null format, type only the semicolon separator for that portion of the format. For example, to hide negative and zero values only, use this format:

```
$#,##0.00;;
```

To hide all entries in a cell, use this format:

```
;;;
```

The null format hides the cell contents in the worksheet, but the entry is still visible in the formula bar and accessible via reference in formulas. To hide the cell contents so that they don't appear in the worksheet or the formula bar, use the worksheet and cell protection features. For more information, see "Protecting worksheets" in Chapter 6, "How to work a worksheet."

Aligning data in cells

The Alignment group on the Home tab on the ribbon, shown in Figure 9-44, contains the most useful tools for positioning data within cells. For more precise control and additional options, click the dialog box launcher adjacent to the title of the Alignment group to display the Format Cells dialog box shown in Figure 9-45.

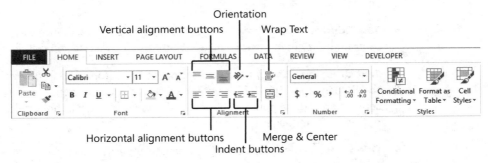

Figure 9-44 Excel can address most of your alignment needs via tools on the ribbon.

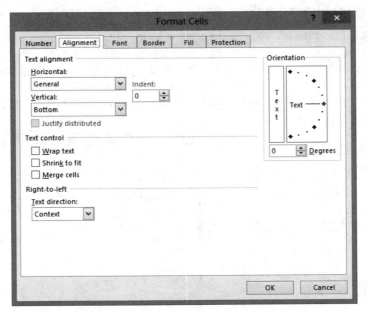

Figure 9-45 Alignment means a lot more than just right, left, or justified.

The Alignment tab in the Format Cells dialog box includes the following options:

- **Horizontal**   These options control the right or left alignment within the cell. The General option, the default for Horizontal alignment, right-aligns numeric values and left-aligns text values.

- **Vertical**   These options control the top-to-bottom position of cell contents within cells.

- **Text Control**   These three check boxes wrap text in cells, reduce the size of cell contents until they fit in the current cell width, and merge selected cells into one.

- **Text Direction**   The options in this drop-down list format individual cells for right-to-left languages. The default option is Context, which responds to the regional settings on your computer. (This feature is applicable only if support is available for right-to-left languages.)

- **Orientation**   These controls let you precisely specify the angle of text within a cell, from vertical to horizontal and anywhere in between.

Aligning text horizontally

The Align Left, Center, and Align Right buttons on the ribbon correspond to three of the options in the Horizontal drop-down list on the Alignment tab in the Format Cells dialog box: Left (Indent), Center, and Right (Indent). These options align the contents of the selected cells, overriding the default cell alignment. Figure 9-46 shows the Horizontal alignment options in action, all of which we'll discuss in detail in the following sections.

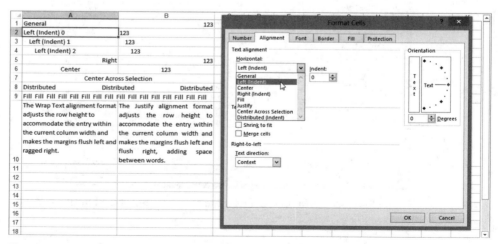

Figure 9-46 Use the Horizontal alignment options to control the placement of text from left to right.

Indenting cell contents   The Increase Indent button simultaneously applies left alignment to the selected cells and indents the contents by the width of one character. (One character width is approximately the width of the capital *X* in the Normal cell style.) Each click increments the amount of indentation by one. The adjacent Decrease Indent button does just the opposite, decreasing the indentation by one character width with each click.

In the Format Cells dialog box, the corresponding options are Left (Indent) and Right (Indent), shown in Figure 9-46. These are linked to the adjacent Indent control, whose displayed value is normally zero—the standard left-alignment setting. Each time you increase this value by one, the entry in the cell begins one character width to the right. For example, in Figure 9-46, row 2 is formatted with no left indent, row 3 with a left indent of 1, and row 4 with a left indent of 2. The maximum indent value you can use is 250.

Distributing cell contents   Using the Distributed (Indent) option in the Horizontal drop-down list, you can position text fragments contained in a cell with equal spacing within the cell. For example, in Figure 9-46, we first merged cells A8:B8 into one cell, then typed the word **Distributed** three times in the merged cell, and then applied the Distributed (Indent) horizontal alignment. The result shows that Excel expanded the spaces between words in equal amounts to justify the contents within the cell.

To learn about merging, see "Merging and unmerging cells" later in this chapter.

Centering text across columns   The Center Across Selection option in the Horizontal text alignment drop-down list centers text from one cell across all selected blank cells to the right or to the next cell in the selection that contains text. For example, in Figure 9-46, we applied the Center Across Selection format to cells A7:B7. The centered text is actually in cell A7.

Filling cells with characters   The Fill option in the Horizontal alignment drop-down list repeats your cell entry to fill the width of the column. For example, in Figure 9-46, cells A9:B9 contain the single word *Fill* and a space character, with the Fill alignment format applied. Only the first cell in the selected range needs to contain text. Excel repeats the text to fill the range. Like the other Format commands, the Fill option affects only the appearance, not the underlying contents, of the cell.

CAUTION

Because the Fill option affects numeric values as well as text, it can cause a number to look like something it isn't. For example, if you apply the Fill option to a ten-character-wide cell that displays 3, the cell appears to contain the number 3333333333.

Chapter 9

Center Across Selection vs. Merge & Center

Although the result might look similar to that of the Merge & Center button on the Home tab, the Center Across Selection alignment option does not merge cells. When you use Center Across Selection, the text from the leftmost cell remains in its cell but is displayed centered across the entire selected range. Notice in the following figure that the selection shading shows that cells A1 and B1 are still two separate cells. The Merge & Center button creates a single cell in place of all the selected cells. Although Merge & Center merges rows and columns of cells, Center Across Selection works only on rows.

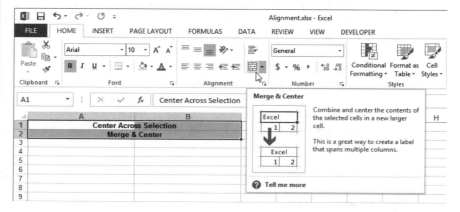

In the preceding figure, the text "Center Across Selection" actually spans two active cells, while the text "Merge & Center" is in a single cell that was created by selecting cells A2:B2 and clicking the Merge & Center button. Either method allows you to change column widths; the centering readjusts automatically. If you type anything in cell B1, the centered text "retreats" to cell A1; if you subsequently clear cell B1, the text is re-centered across the two cells until you clear the format from both cells. You cannot type anything in cell B2 because it essentially no longer exists after being merged with cell A2. For more information, see "Merging and unmerging cells" later in this chapter.

Wrapping text in cells   If you type a label that's too wide for the active cell, Excel extends the label past the cell border and into adjacent cells—provided those cells are empty. If you click the Wrap Text button on the Home tab (or the Wrap Text option on the Alignment tab in the Format Cells dialog box), Excel displays your label entirely within the active cell. To accommodate it, Excel increases the height of the row in which the cell is located and then wraps the text onto additional lines within the same cell. As shown in Figure 9-46, cell A10 contains a multiline label formatted with the Wrap Text option.

Justifying text in cells   The Alignment tab in the Format Cells dialog box provides two justify options—one in the Horizontal drop-down list and one in the Vertical drop-down list. The Horizontal Justify option not only forces text in the active cell to align flush with the right margin, as shown in cell B10 in Figure 9-46, but also wraps text within the cell and adjusts the row height accordingly.

> **Note**
>
> Do not confuse the Horizontal Justify option with the Justify command (on the Fill menu in the Editing group on the Home tab), which redistributes a text entry into as many cells as necessary below the selected cell by dividing the text into separate chunks. For more information about the Justify command on the Fill menu, see "Distributing long entries using the Justify command" in Chapter 8.

The Vertical Justify option performs essentially the same task as its Horizontal counterpart, except it adjusts cell entries relative to the top and bottom of the cell rather than the sides, as shown in cell E3 of Figure 9-47.

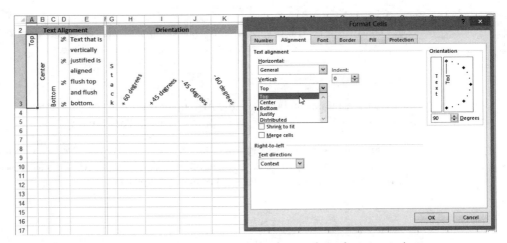

Figure 9-47 Use the Vertical options to control placement of text from top to bottom.

The Justify Distributed option becomes available only when you select one of the Distributed options in either the Horizontal drop-down list or the Vertical drop-down list. It combines the effect of the Justify option with that of the Distributed option not only by wrapping text in the cell and forcing it to align flush right but also by spacing the contents of the cell as evenly as possible within each wrapped line of text.

Aligning text vertically

The Top Align, Middle Align, and Bottom Align buttons on the Home tab control the vertical placement of cell contents and fulfill most of your needs in this regard. The Vertical drop-down list on the Alignment tab in the Format Cells dialog box includes two additional alignment options—Justify and Distributed—which are similar to the corresponding Horizontal alignment options. Cells A3:C3 in Figure 9-47 show examples of the first three alignment options. As noted earlier, cell E3 shows the Justify option in action. We formatted cell D3, containing the percent signs, using the Distributed option.

The options in the Vertical drop-down list create the following effects:

- **Top, Center, and Bottom**   These options force cell contents to align to each respective location within a cell. The default vertical cell orientation in new worksheets is Bottom.

- **Justify**   This option expands the space between lines so that text entries align flush with the top and bottom of the cell.

- **Distributed**   This option spreads the contents of the cell evenly from top to bottom, making the spaces between lines as close to equal as possible.

Controlling text orientation

Clicking the Orientation button in the Alignment group on the Home tab displays the menu shown in Figure 9-48, offering common orientation options.

The Orientation area on the Alignment tab in the Format Cells dialog box contains additional controls, which you can use to change the angle of cell contents to read at any angle from 90 degrees counterclockwise to 90 degrees clockwise.

Chapter 9

> **Note**
>
> Interestingly, as you experiment with orientation, you won't see a Horizontal option on the Orientation button's menu. This means that you need to use either the Format Cells dialog box or the Undo command (Ctrl+Z) to restore cells to their default orientation.

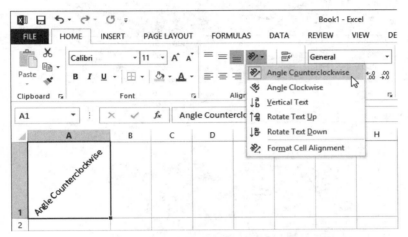

Figure 9-48 Use the Orientation menu to rotate or stack text in a cell.

Excel automatically adjusts the height of the row to accommodate vertical orientation unless you manually set the row height either before or after changing text orientation. Cell G3 in Figure 9-47 shows what happens when you click the tall, skinny Text button on the left side of the Orientation area. Although the button is labeled Text, you can also apply this "stacked letters" effect to numbers and formulas.

You can use the angle controls to rotate text to any point in a 180-degree arc. You can use either the Degrees box at the bottom or the large dial above it to adjust text rotation. To use the dial, click and drag the Text pointer to the angle you want; the number of degrees appears in the spinner below. You also can click the small up and down arrows in the Degrees box to increment the angle one degree at a time from horizontal (zero), or you can highlight the number displayed in the Degrees box and type a number from –90 through 90. Cells H3:K3 in Figure 9-47 show some examples of rotated text.

A cool application of angled text

Many times the label at the top of a column is much wider than the data stored in it. You can use the Wrap Text option to make a multiple-word label narrower, but sometimes that's not enough. Vertical text is an option, but it can be difficult to read and takes a lot of vertical space. Try using rotated text and cell borders:

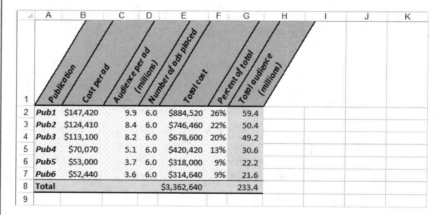

	A	B	C	D	E	F	G	H	I
	Publication	Cost per ad	Audience per ad (millions)	Number of ads placed	Total cost	Percent of total	Total audience (millions)		
1									
2	Pub1	$147,420	9.9	6.0	$884,520	26%	59.4		
3	Pub2	$124,410	8.4	6.0	$746,460	22%	50.4		
4	Pub3	$113,100	8.2	6.0	$678,600	20%	49.2		
5	Pub4	$70,070	5.1	6.0	$420,420	13%	30.6		
6	Pub5	$53,000	3.7	6.0	$318,000	9%	22.2		
7	Pub6	$52,440	3.6	6.0	$314,640	9%	21.6		
8	Total				$3,362,640		233.4		
9									

Here's how to do it:

1. Select the cells you want to format, and click the dialog box launcher in the Font group on the Home tab to display the Format Cells dialog box.

2. Click the Border tab, and apply vertical borders to the left, right, and middle of the range.

3. Click the Alignment tab, and use the Orientation controls to select the angle you want. (It's usually best to select a positive angle from 30 to 60 degrees.)

4. In the Horizontal Text Alignment drop-down list, select Center and then click OK. Excel rotates the left and right borders along with the text.

5. Drag down the bottom border of the row 1 header (the line between 1 and 2) to make it deep enough to accommodate the labels without wrapping.

6. Select all the active columns, and double-click any one of the lines between the selected column headers (for example, the line between the column letters C and D) to shrink all the columns to their smallest possible width.

Using the Angle Counterclockwise command on the Orientation button's menu (in the Alignment group on the Home tab) rotates the text to +45 degrees for you, but because we wanted to apply borders and alignment options as well, using the Format Cells dialog box was a more efficient method.

You'll find the Angled Text.xlsx file with the other examples on the companion Web site.

For more about cell borders, see "Customizing borders" later in this chapter. For more about row heights, see "Changing row heights" later in this chapter.

Shrinking text to fit in cells

The Shrink To Fit check box on the Alignment tab in the Format Cells dialog box reduces the size of the font in the selected cell until the contents can be completely displayed in the cell. This is useful when you have a worksheet in which adjusting the column width to allow a particular cell entry to be visible has undesirable effects on the rest of the worksheet or where angled text, vertical text, and wrapped text aren't feasible solutions. In Figure 9-49, we typed the same text in cells A1 and A2 (and increased the font size for readability) and applied the Shrink To Fit option to cell A2.

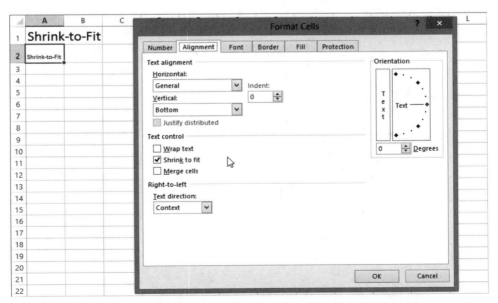

Figure 9-49 The Shrink To Fit alignment option reduces the font size until the cell contents fit within the cell.

The Shrink To Fit format is dynamic and readjusts if you change the column width, either increasing or decreasing the font size as needed. The assigned size of the font does not change; therefore, no matter how wide you make the column, the font will not expand beyond the assigned size.

The Shrink To Fit option can be a good way to solve a problem, but keep in mind that this option reduces the font to as small a size as necessary. If the cell is narrow enough and the cell contents long enough, the result might be too small to read.

Using fonts

The term *font* refers to a typeface (such as Calibri), along with its attributes (such as point size and color). The Font group on the Home tab on the ribbon, shown in Figure 9-50, is the easiest way to apply general font formatting to selected cells. Here are a few facts about the controls in the Font group:

- The Font, Font Size, Underline, Borders, Fill Color, and Font Color buttons all include arrows to their right, which you can click to display a menu or gallery with additional options.

- The appearance of the Font Color, Fill Color, and Borders buttons changes to reflect the last-used option. This lets you apply the same option again by clicking the button, without using the menu or gallery.

- The Bold and Italic buttons are toggles; click once to apply the format, and click again to remove it.

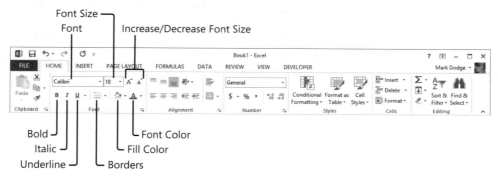

Figure 9-50 The Font group contains font-formatting controls, as well as border and fill controls.

For more extensive control over fonts, use the Font tab in the Format Cells dialog box. To specify a font, select the cell or range, click the dialog box launcher in the Font group, and then click the Font tab, shown in Figure 9-51.

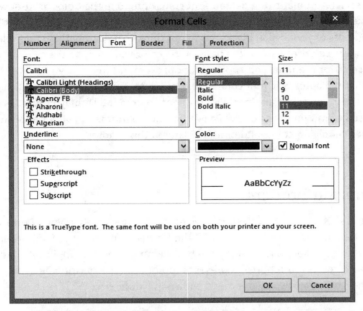

Figure 9-51 On the Font tab, you can assign fonts, character styles, sizes, colors, and effects to your cell entries.

> **Note**
>
> You can also press Ctrl+1 to display the Format Cells dialog box.

The numbers in the Size list show the point sizes at which Excel can optimally print the selected font, but you can type any number in the text box at the top of the list—even fractional point sizes up to two decimal places. Unless you preset it, Excel adjusts the row height as needed to accommodate the largest point size in the row. The available font styles vary depending on the font you select in the Font list. Most fonts offer italic, bold, and bold italic styles. To reset the selected cells to the font and size defined as the Normal cell style, select the Normal Font check box.

For more information about using cell styles, see "Formatting with cell styles" earlier in this chapter.

INSIDE OUT   Automatic font color isn't really automatic

If you select Automatic (the default font color option) in the Color drop-down list (or use its equivalent in the Font group on the Home tab on the ribbon), Excel displays the contents of your cell in black. You might think that Automatic should select an appropriate color for text on the basis of the color you apply to the cell, but this isn't the case. If, for example, you apply a black background to a cell, you might think, logically, that the automatic font color would be white. This isn't so; Automatic is always black unless you select another Window Font color in the Display Properties dialog box (accessed from Windows Control Panel). For more information about applying colors to cells, see "Applying colors and patterns" later in this chapter.

Customizing borders

Borders and shading can be effective devices for defining areas in your worksheet or for drawing attention to important cells, and the Borders button in the Font group on the Home tab is the easiest way to apply them. Clicking this button applies the last-used border format and displays a thumbnail representation of it on the button. Click the arrow to the right of the button to display the menu shown in Figure 9-52.

Note
As does the image displayed on the button, the button name also reflects the last-used border format when you rest the pointer on the button to display a ScreenTip.

The most-often-used border options are represented on the Borders menu, but for more precise control, click the More Borders command on the menu to display the Border tab in the Format Cells dialog box, shown in Figure 9-53. (As always, the dialog box launcher next to the Font group opens the dialog box as well.) If you have more than one cell selected when you open the dialog box, the Border preview area includes tick marks in the middle and at the corners, as shown in Figure 9-53.

Note
A solid gray line in the preview area means that the format applies to some but not all of the selected cells.

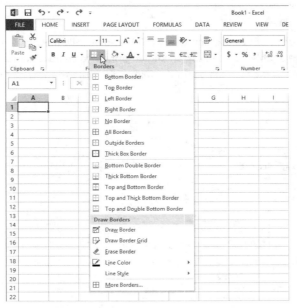

Figure 9-52 Click the arrow next to the Borders button to display the Borders menu.

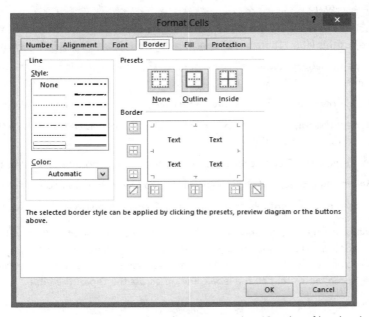

Figure 9-53 Using the Border tab, you can assign 13 styles of borders in 70 colors.

Chapter 9

An angled border trick

Sometimes you might want to use that pesky cell that generally remains empty in the upper-left corner of a table. You can use an angled border to create dual-label corner cells (we expanded the formula bar in the following figure to show all the text in cell A3):

A3	▾	:	×	✓	*fx*			Exam # Student				

◢	A	B	C	D	E	F	G	H	I
1	**First Quarter Exam Scores**								
2									
3	**Exam #** / **Student**	*1*	*2*	*3*	*4*	***Average***			
4	Kirwan	87	90	79	96	88.00			
5	Krieger	92	94	94	97	94.25			
6	Madigan	96	95	95	80	91.50			
7	Oliveira	85	87	87	88	86.75			
8	Mueller	81	88	88	85	85.50			
9									

Here's how to do it:

1. Select the cell you want to format, and type about 10 space characters. You can adjust this later. (There are 20 spaces before the Exam # label in the example.)

2. Type the label you want to correspond to the column labels across the top of the table.

3. Hold down the Alt key, and press Enter twice to create two line breaks in the cell.

4. Type the second label, which corresponds to the row labels down the left side of the table, and press Enter.

5. With the cell selected, click the More Borders command on the Borders menu.

6. Select a line style, and click the upper-left to lower-right angled border button.

7. Click the Alignment tab, select the Wrap Text check box, and then click OK.

You will probably need to fine-tune a bit by adjusting the column width and row height and by adding or removing space characters before the first label. In the example, we also selected cells B3:F3 and then clicked the Top Align button in the Alignment group on the Home tab so that all the labels line up across the top of the table.

For more information about alignment, see "Aligning data in cells" earlier in this chapter. For more about entering line breaks and tabs in cells, see "Formula-bar formatting" in Chapter 12.

You'll find the Angled Borders.xlsx file with the other examples on the companion website.

To apply borders, you can click the preview area where you want the border to appear, or you can click the buttons located around the preview area. An additional preset button, Inside, becomes active only when you have more than one cell selected. If you click the Outline button, borders are applied only to the outside edge of the entire selection. The None preset removes all border formats from the selection.

> ## Note
>
> Borders often make a greater visual impact on your screen when you remove worksheet gridlines. Click the View tab on the ribbon, and clear the Gridlines check box in the Show/Hide group to remove gridlines from your worksheet. For more information about gridlines, see "Controlling other elements of the Excel interface" in Chapter 3.

The default, or Automatic, color for borders is black. To select a line style, click the type of line you want to use in the Line area, and then click any of the buttons in the Border area or click the preview box directly to apply that style in the selected location. (The first finely dotted line in the Style area is a solid hairline when printed.) To remove a border, click the corresponding button—or the line in the preview window—without selecting another style.

By using the commands in the Draw Borders group at the bottom of the Borders menu (shown in Figure 9-52), you can create complex borders quickly and easily. When you click Draw Border, you enter *border-drawing mode*, which persists until you click Draw Border again or press Esc. After you activate this mode, you can drag to create lines and boxes along cell gridlines, as shown in Figure 9-54. If you click Draw Border Grid, not only are borders drawn along the boundaries of the selected cells, but they're also drawn along all the gridlines in the selection rectangle, as shown at the bottom of Figure 9-54.

If you make selections in the Line Color and Line Style galleries at the bottom of the Borders menu prior to using either Draw Border command, the borders you draw reflect your color and style selections. Clicking Erase Border predictably activates the opposite of border-drawing mode: *border-erasing mode*. Dragging while in erase mode removes all borders within the selection rectangle.

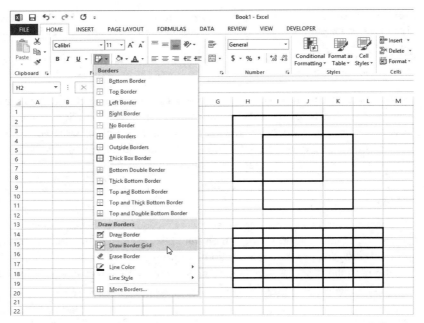

Figure 9-54 We created two boxes using the Draw Border command and another using the Draw Border Grid command.

Applying colors and patterns

The Fill Color button in the Font group on the Home tab offers colors you can apply to selected cells. Click the button's arrow to display the options shown in Figure 9-55.

If you want to do more than just fill cells with color, the Fill tab in the Format Cells dialog box provides additional control. (Click the dialog box launcher in the Font group on the ribbon to display the Format Cells dialog box.) The main feature of the Fill tab is a palette of colors, mimicking the palette available on the ribbon. A feature not available on the ribbon is the Pattern Style drop-down palette, shown in Figure 9-56. You use this palette to select a pattern for selected cells and the Pattern Color drop-down palette above it to choose a color.

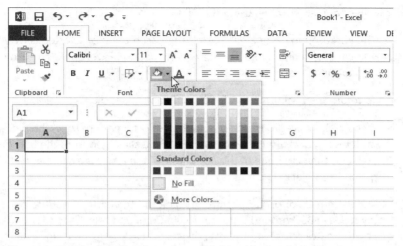

Figure 9-55 Use the Fill Color palette to add color to cells.

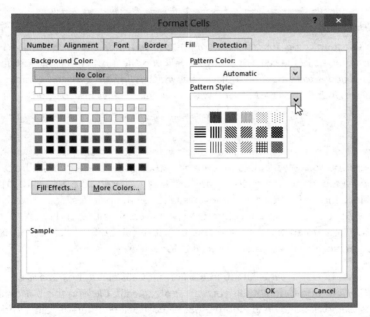

Figure 9-56 Using the Fill tab, you can select colors and patterns for cell backgrounds.

Follow these guidelines when using the Fill tab:

- The Background Color area controls the background of selected cells. When you choose a color and do not select any pattern, Excel applies a solid colored background.

- To return the background color to its default state, click No Color.

- If you pick a background color and then select a pattern style, the pattern is overlaid on the solid background. For example, if you select red from the Background Color area and then click one of the dot patterns, the result is a cell that has a red background and black dots.

- The Pattern Color options control the color of the pattern, not the cell. For example, if you leave Background Color set to No Color and select a red for Pattern Color and any dot pattern for Pattern Style, the cell is displayed with a white background with red dots.

> **Note**
>
> When selecting colors for cell backgrounds, select one on which you can easily read any text or numbers in the cell. For example, yellow is the most visible background color you can choose to complement black text, which is why you see this combination on road signs. A dark blue background with black text—that's not so good.

The More Colors button on the Fill tab displays the Colors dialog box shown in Figure 9-57, where you can select colors that are not otherwise represented on the color palettes. The Standard tab in the Colors dialog box displays a stylized color wheel using the current theme colors, most of which are already available on the palettes. The Custom tab shown in Figure 9-57 lets you pinpoint colors, use specific color values, and switch between the default RGB (red, green, blue) color model or HSL, a color model defined by hue, saturation, and luminosity values instead of RGB color values.

The Fill Effects button on the Fill tab in the Format Cells dialog box opens up another world of possibility, offering gradient fills you can apply to cells. Clicking this button displays the Fill Effects dialog box shown in Figure 9-58. You can select different colors and shading styles, but this version of the Fill Effects dialog box offers only two-color effects. The One Color and Preset options are not available. Note that Fill Effects gradient fills are static, unlike data bars, which are conditional gradient fills that respond to cell values and interact with adjacent cells by applying proportional amounts of fill to each cell.

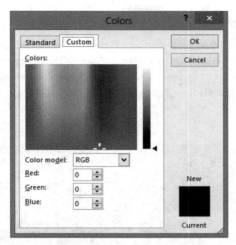

Figure 9-57 Click the More Colors button on the Fill tab in the Format Cells dialog box to select the colors you need.

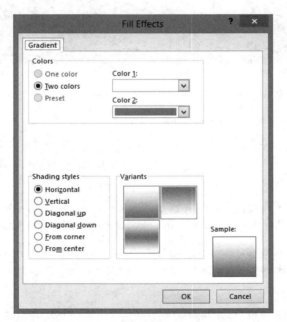

Figure 9-58 Click the Fill Effects button on the Fill tab in the Format Cells dialog box to use gradient fills in cells.

For more about gradients, see "Filling an area with a color gradient" in Chapter 20, "Formatting charts." For more about data bars, see "Formatting conditionally" earlier in this chapter.

Chapter 9

Adding graphic backgrounds to worksheets

Adding background images to worksheets is easy. Click the Page Layout tab on the ribbon, and click the Background button. A standard Windows file-management dialog box appears, from which you can open most types of image files, located anywhere on your computer or network. Excel then applies the graphic image to the background of the active worksheet, as shown in Figure 9-59.

Figure 9-59 Add a background graphic to any worksheet.

Here are some tips for working with background images:

- The example in Figure 9-59 is a cover sheet for a large workbook; be careful when using backgrounds behind data. It can be difficult to read cell entries with the wrong background applied.

- You might want to turn off the display of gridlines, as shown in Figure 9-59. To do so, clear the Gridlines View check box, which is also located on the Page Layout tab.

- If you don't like the way the background looks with your data, click the Background button again, whose name changes to Delete Background when a background is present.

- The graphic image is tiled in the background of your worksheet, which means the image is repeated as necessary to fill the worksheet.

- Cells to which you have assigned a color or pattern override the graphic background.

- Backgrounds are preserved when you save the workbook as a webpage.

Controlling the size of cells

The primary methods you use to control the size of cells are adjusting the row height and changing the column width. In addition, you can adjust the size of cells by merging several cells into one or by unmerging previously merged cells. The Format menu, located in the Cells group on the Home tab, is the central command location for cell sizing, as shown in Figure 9-60.

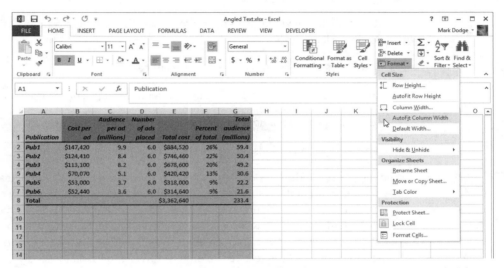

Figure 9-60 You can use the Cell Size commands on the Format menu to manage row height and column width.

Here are the options you can use:

- **Column Width and Row Height**   These two commands display a dialog box where you can type a different value to be applied to selected cells. Column width is limited to 255, and row height can be up to 409. The default column width for Excel is 8.43 characters; however, this does not mean each cell in your worksheet can display 8.43 characters. Because Excel uses proportionally spaced fonts (such as Arial) as well as fixed-pitch fonts (such as Courier), different characters can take up different amounts of space. A default-width column, for example, can display about eight numerals in most 10-point fixed-pitch fonts.

- **AutoFit Row Height**   This command adjusts the row height in selected cells by adjusting them to accommodate the tallest item in the row. (Row height is usually self-adjusting based on font size.)

- **AutoFit Column Width** This command adjusts column widths in selected cells by adjusting them to accommodate the widest entry in the column.

- **Default Width** This command displays a dialog box where you can change the starting column width for all selected worksheets in the current workbook. This has no effect on columns whose width you have previously specified.

Changing column widths

If the standard column width isn't enough to display the complete contents of a cell, one of the following will occur:

- Text that is too long runs over into adjacent cells.

- Long text entries are truncated at the border if the adjacent cell isn't empty.

- Long numbers appear in scientific notation (for example, 1.23E+12).

- A series of number signs (#) appears if you assign a numeric format.

To change column widths using the mouse, drag the lines between column headings. As you drag, the width of the column and the number of pixels appear in a ScreenTip, as shown in Figure 9-61. This figure also illustrates how to change the width of multiple columns at the same time: drag to select column headings; alternatively, hold down Ctrl, and click headings to select nonadjacent columns. Then, when you drag the line to the right of any selected column, all the selected column widths change simultaneously.

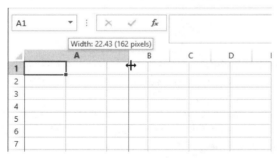

Figure 9-61 The pointer looks like a double-headed arrow when you adjust column width or row height with the mouse.

Note

Depending on the font you are using, characters that appear to fit within a column on your screen might not fit when you print the worksheet. You can preview your output before printing by pressing Ctrl+P to display the Print screen in Backstage view, where you can see an image of the worksheet as it will look when printed. For information about print preview, see Chapter 11, "Printing and presenting."

Tricks for tailoring cells

Here are a few methods you can use to speed up your cell-sizing chores:

- When you select a number of rows or columns, you can tailor all of them to fit their contents—essentially the same as using one of the AutoFit commands—by double-clicking any line to the right of a selected column header or any line below a selected row header. Doing so automatically snaps all the selected cells to accommodate the widest or tallest displayed values.

- To tailor all the cells in the worksheet at once, first click the gray square at the intersection of the row and column headers to select the entire worksheet (or press Ctrl+A). Then double-click any line in the row header to autofit all rows, and double-click any line in the column header to autofit all columns.

- To change the widths of all the columns in the current worksheet, select any entire row by clicking a row heading (or pressing Shift+Spacebar), and then click the Column Width command on the Format menu on the Home tab.

- To change the height of all of the rows in the current worksheet, select any entire column by clicking a column heading (or pressing Ctrl+Spacebar), and then click the Row Height command on the Format menu on the Home tab.

Changing row heights

The height of a row always changes dynamically to accommodate the largest font used in that row. Thus, you don't usually need to worry about characters being too tall to fit in a row. Adjusting row height is the same as adjusting column width—just drag one of the lines between row headings.

To restore the default height of one or more rows, select any cell in those rows and click AutoFit Row Height on the Format menu on the Home tab. Unlike column width, you cannot define a standard row height. The AutoFit command serves the same function, returning empty rows to the standard height needed to accommodate the default font and fitting row heights to accommodate the tallest entry. When you create or edit a multiline text entry using the Wrap Text button or the Justify option on the Alignment tab in the Format Cells dialog box, Excel automatically adjusts the row height to accommodate it.

For more information, see "Wrapping text in cells" and "Justifying text in cells" earlier in this chapter.

Hiding a column or row

If you want to hide information within a worksheet, you can hide entire columns or rows. To do so, select any cell in the row or column you want to hide. Then, on the Format menu on the Home tab, click Hide & Unhide, and then click Hide Rows or Hide Columns. This sets the width of the column to zero. You can also hide rows and columns by dragging the line between headings up or to the left until the height or width is zero. When a row or column's width is set to 0, Excel skips over it when you move the active cell, and the column letter or row number disappears. For example, if you hide column C, the column heading line reads A, B, D, and so on.

To redisplay a hidden row or column, drag to select the headings on both sides, and click Unhide Rows or Unhide Columns on the Hide & Unhide menu. Selecting the Hidden check box on the Protection tab of the Format Cells dialog box hides only formulas in the formula bar.

Merging and unmerging cells

The spreadsheet grid is arguably the most versatile type of document, and the ability to merge cells makes it all the more versatile. Select the cells you want to merge, and click the arrow to the right of the Merge & Center button in the Alignment group on the Home tab to display the menu shown in Figure 9-62.

CAUTION!

When you merge several cells that contain data, only the data in the uppermost, leftmost cell is preserved. Excel overwrites data in subsidiary cells. Copy any data you need to another location before merging.

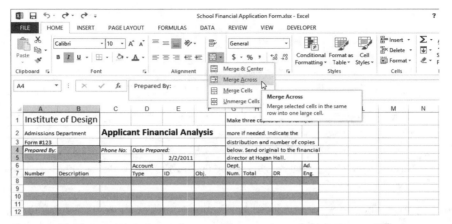

Figure 9-62 The Merge & Center button offers a variety of merge commands.

When you merge cells, you end up with a single cell that comprises the original cells. If in the worksheet shown in Figure 9-63, you select cells A4:B5 and click the Merge Across command, the result would be two merged cells, A4 and A5, each spanning two columns. Here are the differences between the Merge & Center commands:

- **Merge & Center**   This command consolidates all selected cells—both rows and columns—into one big cell and centers the contents across the newly merged cell.

- **Merge Across**   This command consolidates each row of selected cells into one wide cell per row.

- **Merge Cells**   This command consolidates all selected cells into one big cell, but it does not center the contents.

- **Unmerge Cells**   This command returns a merged cell to its original component cells and places its contents in the upper-leftmost cell. Clicking the Merge & Center button (not the Merge & Center command) when a merged cell is selected has the same effect, like a toggle "turning off" the merge.

Figure 9-63 shows the same worksheet shown in Figure 9-62 after merging cells A1:B3, C1:F3, G1:J5, A4:B4, A5:B5, D4:F4, D5:F5, D6:E6, A6:A7, B6:C7, F6:F7, G6:G7, H6:H7, I6:I7, and J6:J7. We had to shuffle some of the text, *before* merging so that we wouldn't lose it to the merging process. For example, the text in the original range G1:J5 was unevenly spaced because of the different row heights needed to accommodate the text in cells A1 and C2. To eliminate this problem, we used the Merge Cells command on the range A1:B3, we used the Merge & Center command on the ranges C1:F3 and G1:J5, and then we reentered the text.

Chapter 9

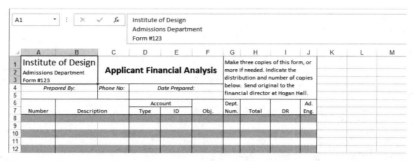

Figure 9-63 Most of the cells in the top five rows of this worksheet, and a couple in the sixth row, are merged in various combinations.

You'll find the School Financial Application Form.xlsx file with the other examples on the companion website.

When you merge cells, the new *big cell* uses the address of the cell in the upper-left corner, as shown in Figure 9-63. Cell A1 is selected, as you can see in the Name box. (In the figure, we also expanded the formula bar to show the three rows of text in the merged cell.) The headings for rows 1, 2, and 3 and columns A and B are highlighted, which would ordinarily indicate that the range A1:B3 is selected. For all practical purposes, however, cells A2:A3 and B1:B3 no longer exist. The other merged cells, or the subsidiary cells, act like blank cells when referred to in formulas and return zero (or an error value, depending on the type of formula).

> **Note**
>
> In Figure 9-63, the information in the formula bar is on three lines. To enter line breaks within a cell, press Alt+Enter. For more information, see "Formula-bar formatting" in Chapter 12.

Merging cells obviously has interesting implications, considering that it seems to violate the grid—one of the defining attributes of spreadsheet design. That's not as bad as it sounds, but keep in mind these tips:

- If you select a range to merge and any single cell contains text, a value, or a formula, the contents are relocated to the new big cell.

- If you select a range of cells to merge and more than one cell contains text or values, only the contents of the uppermost, leftmost cell are relocated to the new big cell. Contents of subsidiary cells are deleted; therefore, if you want to preserve data in subsidiary cells, make sure you add it to the upper-left cell or relocate it.

- Formulas adjust automatically. A formula that refers to a subsidiary cell in a merged range changes to refer to the address of the new big cell. If a merged range of cells contains a formula, relative references adjust. For more about references, see "Using cell references in formulas" in Chapter 12.

- You can copy, delete, cut and paste, or click and drag big cells as you would any other cell. When you copy or move a big cell, it replaces the same number of cells at the destination. The original location of a cut or deleted big cell returns to individual cells.

- You can drag the fill handle of a big cell as you can drag the fill handle of regular cells. When you do so, the big cell is replicated, in both size and content, replacing all regular cells in its path. For more about using the fill handle, see "Filling and creating data series" in Chapter 8.

- If you merge cells containing border formatting other than along any outer edge of the selected range, border formats are erased.

Using template files to store formatting

A *template* is a model that can serve as the basis for new worksheets. A template can include both data and formatting information. Template files are great timesavers. They're also an ideal way to ensure a consistent look among reports, invoices, and other documents you tend to create repeatedly. Figure 9-64 shows an example of a template for an expense report. This worksheet would make a good template because expense reports are used repeatedly, but each time you want to start with a fresh, clean copy.

	A	B	C	D	E	F	G	H	I	J
1	**Expense Report**						*For period ending:*		*3/31/2013*	
2		Sun	Mon	Tue	Wed	Thu	Fri	Sat	Total	
3	Date								0	
4	Place								0	
5	Air Fare								0	
6	Meals								0	
7	Taxi								0	
8	Tips								0	
9	Supplies								0	
10	Car Rental								0	
11	Parking								0	
12	Tolls								0	
13	Lodging								0	
14	Telephone								0	
15	Miscellaneous								0	
16	**Total**	0	0	0	0	0	0	0	0	
17										
18										

Figure 9-64 This template file serves as the basis for creating new expense reports.

You'll find the Expense Report.xltx file with the other examples on the companion website.

The advantages to using templates are standardization and protection. It is difficult to over-write the original accidentally, because when you save a new template-based workbook for the first time, you must supply a new name for it. This way you can repeatedly create new workbooks with the same appearance without worrying about overwriting the original.

The first time you create a template, you might need to specify a location in which to save your template files. This is typically C:\Users\Public Documents\My Templates (in Windows 7, it's C:\Users\<*your name*>\AppData\Roaming\Microsoft\Templates).

To create a template file for the first time, follow these steps:

1. Click the File tab, and click Options.

2. Click the Save category.

3. In the Default Personal Templates Location box, enter a path to the folder you want to use and then click OK.

4. Open the workbook you want to use as a template.

5. Click the File tab, Save As, choose a location, and supply a file name.

6. Choose Excel Template (*.xltx) from the Save As Type drop-down list, and click Save.

When you choose the Excel Template format in the Save As dialog box, Excel automatically switches to the Default Personal Templates folder that you specified and saves your new template there. This is the location that ensures that your template is always available when you click the New command on the File tab and click the Personal category.

When you create a new document by clicking the File tab, New and then selecting one of the many templates available, a fresh copy of the workbook is created, and the copy is given a temporary name consisting of the original file name plus a number. If the template file is named Expenses, for example, the working copy is named Expenses1.

INSIDE OUT   Full disclosure

Windows tries to keep secrets from you—for your own good, of course. But fearless readers of this book need no such accommodation, so here are a couple of actions you can take to make life a little easier. First, let's show hidden files and folders. If you go looking, the Templates folders described in this chapter can be hard to find (particularly in Windows 7) because they might be in locations Windows likes to keep hidden from view. To make them more findable, open the Windows Control Panel, Appearance And Personalization, Folder Options; then, on the View tab, select Show Hidden Files, Folders, And Drives. Second, let's display all the file extensions. The old-style MS-DOS extensions used to be three characters in length and now can be four, such as .xltx for templates and .xlsx for regular workbooks. These might be "retro," but they are also still helpful, letting you tell at a glance in which format a file is saved. To make extensions visible, clear the Hide Extensions For Known File Types check box, which is also on the View tab in the Folder Options dialog box.

PART 4

Adding graphics and printing

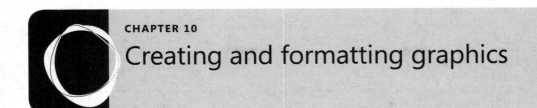

Creating and formatting graphics

MICROSOFT EXCEL 2013 gives you the tools to create a variety of graphic objects— boxes, lines, circles, ovals, arcs, freeform polygons, text boxes, buttons, and a wide assortment of complex predefined shapes, clip art, and SmartArt graphics. If you already have graphics created in other programs, Excel imports those graphics as well. Throughout this chapter, you'll learn how to add graphics to worksheets, but you can use many of the same kinds of effects also when you're creating charts. First we discuss creating and inserting various kinds of graphic objects, and then we cover formatting and working with them.

Most of your adventures with graphics begin by using the buttons and menus found on the Insert tab on the ribbon, shown in Figure 10-1.

For more information about charts, see Part 6, "Creating charts."

Figure 10-1 The Insert tab contains most of the drawing tools.

Users of Excel 2010 will notice a few new tools on the Insert tab in Excel 2013—namely, Recommended PivotTables in the Tables group, Online Pictures in the Illustrations group, Apps For Office in the Apps group, Recommended Charts and PivotChart in the Charts group, PowerView in the new Reports group, and Timeline in the Filters group.

For more about the Recommended Charts feature, see Chapter 19, "Designing charts." Timelines are discussed in Chapter 22, "Managing information in tables." Recommended PivotTables and PivotCharts are discussed in Chapter 23, "Analyzing data with PivotTable reports." You'll find more about Power View in Chapter 24, "Using PowerPivot."

Using the Shapes tools

The Excel graphics tool chest contains many of the powerful capabilities of dedicated illustration programs. Using only the tools in the Shapes gallery, you can create lines, rectangles, and ovals; smooth and freeform curves; linked objects using connectors; basic and not-so-basic shapes, such as pentagons and lightning bolts; a variety of straight, curved, three-dimensional (3-D), and multiheaded arrows; stars, emblems, and banners; and even a variety of callouts. Click the Shapes button to display the gallery shown in Figure 10-2.

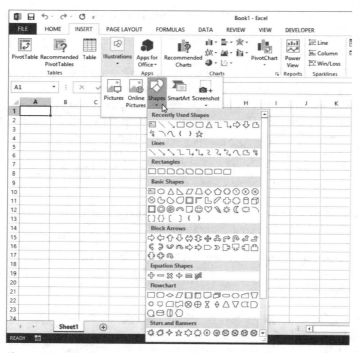

Figure 10-2 The Shapes gallery provides a wealth of graphics options.

> **Note**
>
> If your screen is wide enough, you'll see the Shapes button on the ribbon. Otherwise, as shown in Figure 10-2, the Illustrations group becomes a button that when clicked, displays a "sub-ribbon" of buttons, including the Shapes button. You'll notice this behavior with most other ribbon groups as well, providing better visibility than commands on a menu. It also makes the ribbon more touchscreen-friendly.

If you have ever used a drawing program, such as Paint or Adobe Illustrator, you already know how to create lines, arrows, ovals, and rectangles. In Excel, as in graphics programs, click the tool you want, and then drag the pointer to create the object. When you drag a simple box shape using the Rectangle tool, for example, Excel displays *Rectangle 1* in the Name box at the left end of the formula bar. Excel refers to new graphic objects by category and numbers them in the order in which you create them.

Objects you create appear to float over the worksheet or chart in a separate layer. Objects are separate from the worksheet or chart, and you can group and format them as discrete items. Here are a few more important facts you should know about using the drawing tools:

- Excel enters *drawing mode* when you click a Shapes tool and exits drawing mode when you finish drawing an object. You can cancel drawing mode by clicking the same tool again.

- Formatting you apply to underlying worksheet cells has no effect on objects.

- When you move the pointer over an object, the pointer changes to a four-headed move arrow. You can then select the object or move it elsewhere by dragging.

- After you select an object, you can stretch and resize it by dragging the handles that appear on its perimeter.

- If you drag a center handle, you change the object's height or width.

- When you select a graphic object in Excel, one or more new tabs appear on the ribbon, depending on the type of object you select. Figure 10-3 shows the Format tab under Drawing Tools. These tabs offer additional formatting and effects you can apply to selected objects.

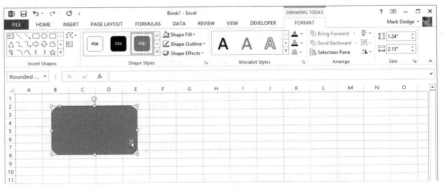

Figure 10-3 A new Drawing Tools tab appears on the ribbon when you select a graphics object.

Drawing constrained objects

The word *constrain* has a somewhat negative connotation, but in computer lingo, a constraint is usually a good thing. If you apply a constraint to an object you draw, for example, you force the object to adhere to a specific angle or proportion. Using constraints is the easiest way to create perfect circles and squares. For example, you can hold down Shift (and sometimes Ctrl) while creating objects to constrain them, as Figure 10-4 illustrates.

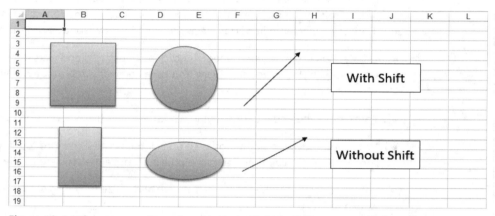

Figure 10-4 When you create or size objects, hold down Shift to constrain them.

The key you use to constrain your object depends on the type of constraint you want to cause. The following lists describe the types of constraints created using each method.

Holding down the Shift key causes the following constraints:

- The Line and Arrow tools draw perfectly horizontal or vertical lines or diagonal lines constrained to exact 15-degree increments (0°, 15°, 30°, 45°, 90°, and so on).

- The Rectangle tool draws perfect squares.

- The Oval tool draws perfect circles.

- Other shapes are drawn to predefined, roughly symmetrical constraints. Shapes come in many different forms, so the effect of the Shift key varies considerably depending on the shape.

Holding down the Ctrl key causes the following constraints:

- When you drag to create rectangles, ovals, text boxes, and AutoShapes, the object is centered on the point at which you click. Objects grow out from the center point as you drag.

- When you drag a handle to resize a previously drawn object, the object remains centered on its original center point and resizes equally in all directions.

- When you drag an object to move it, holding down Ctrl creates a copy of the object, leaving the original in place.

- You can use Ctrl+Shift to create symmetrical objects such as squares, circles, and stars that are centered on the point you click.

Holding down the Alt key also causes a constraint. You can hold down Alt while creating objects to use the gridlines on a worksheet as a drawing grid. The edges of your objects are then forced to follow the gridlines. Note, however, that if you use Shift and Alt together to draw a square or a circle aligned to the grid, Excel does its best, but the result might not be perfect because the default height and width of the cells on a worksheet might not provide an ideal grid for perfect squares or circles.

INSIDE OUT   Selecting objects

When you work with objects, it's almost as if another program with a transparent desktop is floating over the worksheet—as if the objects you draw are in another dimension. In a sense, they are. What goes on in the grid of Excel has little to do with what goes on in the drawing layer, although you do have opportunities to create interaction between objects and worksheets using macros and formulas.

When you are working in cells, you can click any graphic object to select it and then click the worksheet to select cells. You can hop back and forth between the object and worksheet, no problem. But they are still parallel universes, which becomes apparent when you try to select multiple items. For example, you can drag to select a range of cells, but you cannot drag a selection rectangle around a group of objects to select them; instead, you end up selecting a cell in that "other dimension" as soon as you click. You can press Ctrl and click to add nonadjacent cells to a selection on the worksheet, and this method works similarly with objects. In fact, you can select an object, hold down either Shift or Ctrl, and click additional objects to add them to the selection—either method accomplishes the same result. You can also press Ctrl+A to "select all" in either the worksheet or the object layer. If you do so with a cell selected, all cells are selected; if you do so with an object selected, all objects are selected. But you can't select cells and objects together, which you might want to do when you're copying a portion of a worksheet to another location and want to copy adjacent objects as well. You can actually accomplish this by selecting the underlying cells and pasting them in the new location. The objects might not be selected, but they are usually linked to a cell location. Unless you specify otherwise, objects travel with their underlying cells if you move or copy them. For more information, see "Positioning objects" later in this chapter.

Chapter 10

Drawing freehand lines and polygons

The tools in the Shapes gallery are extremely easy to use. Just click a tool, and then click and drag to create the object on the worksheet. We'll use the following tools in this discussion:

- **Curve**   Draws smoothly curved lines between clicked points.

- **Freeform**   Draws combined freehand lines and straight lines.

- **Scribble**   Draws unconstrained lines. (However, when you release the mouse button, the resulting line is smoothed somewhat.)

The Freeform and Curve tools are different from the others in that when you release the mouse button, you're not done drawing. To finish drawing using either of these tools, you must click the starting point to close the loop and create a solid object or double-click where you want the line to end to create a line. Figure 10-5 shows a few objects created using these tools.

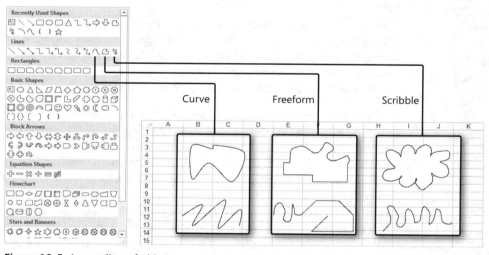

Figure 10-5 A sampling of objects created using the Curve, Freeform, and Scribble tools.

For example, if you click the Freeform tool in the Lines section of the Shapes gallery and then click anywhere on the worksheet or chart to begin drawing, the line remains anchored to the point you clicked. If you release the mouse button, the line remains "attached," stretching from the anchor point to the crosshairs pointer like a rubber band. If you stretch the line and click again, you create a segment that is anchored between the first and second point. You can continue this as long as you want, creating additional segments with each new anchor point. If you drag, you create a curved freehand line. By combining these methods, you can create a hybrid object with both straight and curved lines. If you click the beginning of the line, you create a solid object, or you can double-click at any time to finish drawing.

Adjusting freehand shapes with the Edit Points command

Drawing an attractive freehand line or polygon shape with a mouse can be challenging. If you have difficulty dragging the shape you want, use the Edit Points command, which changes a line or polygon created with the Scribble, Curve, or Freeform tool into a series of points you can drag to reshape the object.

To adjust a scribbled, curved, or freeform shape, right-click the object and then click Edit Points on the shortcut menu. (The Edit Points command also appears on the Edit Shape menu in the Insert Shapes group on the Drawing Tools Format contextual tab, which appears when you select an object.) After you click Edit Points, a new set of handles appears on the object, following its curves and corners. You can then drag as many of the handles as necessary to new positions. For example, we used the Freeform button to create the shape on the left in Figure 10-6. The shape on the right is the same freeform polygon after we clicked Edit Points and dragged one of the new points.

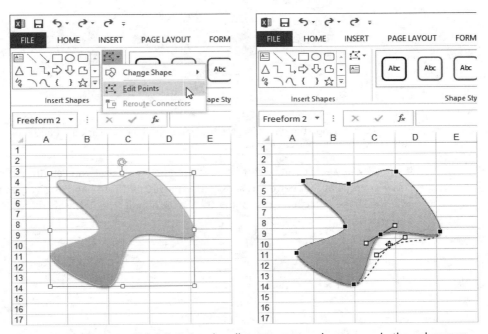

Figure 10-6 When you click Edit Points, handles appear at each vertex, as in the polygon on the right.

After you click Edit Points, you can add or delete any of the handles on an object. If you want to clean up your drawing by eliminating some of the points, press the Ctrl key and then click each handle you want to delete. If you want to add points, press Ctrl and click anywhere on a line where you want a handle to appear.

Working with curves

When you edit the points for an object you created using the Scribble, Curve, or Freeform tool, you can fine-tune the curves even further by using commands on the shortcut menu that appears when you right-click any edit point, as shown in Figure 10-7.

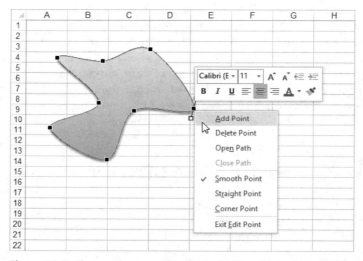

Figure 10-7 Change the type of a selected edit point by right-clicking it and then clicking commands on the shortcut menu.

If you click any edit point, *vertex handles* become visible that you can drag to modify the curve or angle at that vertex, as shown in Figure 10-8. These handles give you total control over the shape of a curve. The longer the vertex handle, the flatter the curve in the direction you drag.

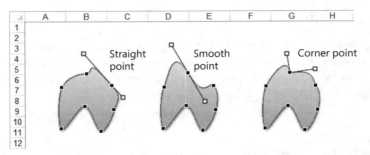

Figure 10-8 Change the shape of freeform objects by dragging the vertex handles that appear when you click a point.

Excel offers three types of points. You can right-click any existing point and change it to a different type of point by using the corresponding command on the shortcut menu:

- **Straight Point**   Creates a gradual transition between the lines flowing out from either side, which can be unequal, and displays vertex handles when selected. You can drag each vertex handle separately. The longer the vertex handle, the more gradual the curve on that side of the point.

- **Smooth Point**   Lines flowing out from either side of a smooth point are equally curved and display vertex handles of equal length when you select them. Drag a vertex handle, and the opposite handle moves equally in the opposite direction, creating an equal curve on either side of the point.

- **Corner Point**   Creates an abrupt transition between the lines flowing out from either side, and displays vertex handles when selected that can be dragged separately. The Scribble button always creates corner points.

Working with text boxes

Click the Text Box button in the Text group on the Insert tab to add notes, headings, legends, and other text to your worksheets and charts to give them more impact or to clarify the data you're presenting.

Click the Text Box button, point to a location on your worksheet, and drag to create a box. A blinking pointer appears in the box, indicating that you can begin typing. After you finish, you can select and format text using the same commands you use for text in cells. When you select a text box, drag any of its eight perimeter handles to resize it.

> **Note**
>
> If you click the Spelling command with a single cell selected, all the text on the current worksheet is checked, including text in text boxes. If you click Spelling while a text box (or any object) is selected, only the text contained in that text box (or object) is checked.

Adding text to other shapes

The Text Box button is quick and easy to use, but if you want to add graphic assistance to your message, you can add text to two-dimensional shapes created by using the Shapes gallery on the Insert tab, as shown in Figure 10-9, including banners, arrows, boxes, and just about any shape except lines and connectors.

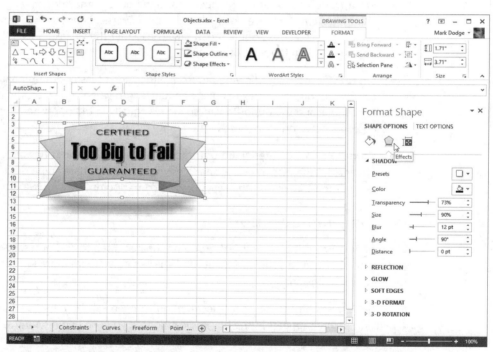

Figure 10-9 Text boxes are only one of the many graphic objects that can display text.

To create one of these custom text boxes, just draw the shape you want and then start typing. Resize the object as needed, and give the shape and its text the look you want by using the Drawing Tools Format tab, which appears on the ribbon when you select a shape.

If you click the dialog box launcher in the Shape Styles group on the Drawing Tools Format tab, the Format Shape task pane appears, as shown in Figure 10-9, docked to the right side of the Excel window. (You can also display the task pane by right-clicking a shape and clicking the Format Shape command on the shortcut menu.) The three icons in the task pane under Shape Options display different groups of options:

- The **Fill & Line** (paint bucket) icon displays color, weight, and fill options.

- The **Effects** icon (pentagon) displays object formatting tools.

- The **Size & Properties** icon (four-headed arrow) icon displays options for controlling object dimensions, plus display and editing options.

The phantom text toolbar

In Excel 2013 (and 2010), when you select some of the text you typed in an object, you'll notice that a ghostly toolbar appears nearby. When you move the pointer closer to the phantom image, it begins to appear more distinct, as shown here:

Curiously, when you move the pointer away, the toolbar gets more ghostly, and if you stay away too long, it does not reappear. Just reselect some text in the object, and the toolbar reappears. As soon as you click one of the tools, the toolbar "unghosts" completely, allowing you to use the tools as much as needed.

Working with shapes

The Shapes gallery on the Insert tab offers dozens of predrawn shapes you can use to add effective visual communication to your worksheets. Most shapes display a yellow, diamond-shaped handle somewhere on the perimeter. If you drag this handle, you can control a specific dimension of the shape (that varies based on the shape you selected), as Figure 10-10 illustrates.

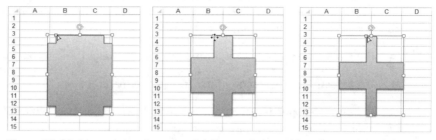

Figure 10-10 Many shapes have special diamond-shaped handles you can drag to control a specific feature of the shape.

In addition to the diamond handle, all two-dimensional objects in Excel display a panhandle you drag to rotate the object, as shown in Figure 10-11.

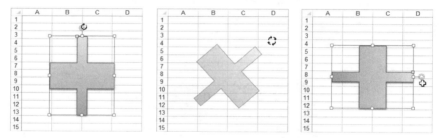

Figure 10-11 Drag the panhandle of any two-dimensional object to rotate it.

Create linked objects

You can create a link from a text box—or any other shape containing text—to a cell to display that cell's contents in the text box. First draw a text box. With the text box selected, type an equal sign in the formula bar and then type a cell reference or defined name. For example, suppose cell D3 contains a formula that returns the value $123.45. When you type **=$D$3** in the formula bar while you have the text box selected, the value $123.45 appears in the text box. When you link a text box in this way, you cannot type additional text into it. To remove the link, select the text box and delete the reference formula in the formula bar. For more about formulas and the formula bar, see Chapter 12, "Building formulas."

Using connectors and callouts

Most shapes are easy to use and somewhat self-explanatory. Connectors and callouts, however, have some special qualities that bear mentioning. If you ever spent time creating drawings using simple lines and boxes, you know what a problem it can be when you need to reposition any of the objects. You usually end up spending as much time fine-tuning the drawing as you spent drawing it in the first place. *Connectors*, which are special kinds of lines that are "sticky" on both ends, can help. You use them when you want to connect shapes with lines that remain attached and stretch, making it easier to reposition objects later with a minimum of tweaking.

The connector tools are the six tools located in the middle of the Lines group in the Shapes gallery, as shown in Figure 10-12. After you click one of these tools, special points appear when you rest the pointer on any existing shape. These are *connection points*, and if you click one of them, the connector line attaches to that point. The second click attaches the other end of the connector line to a point on another object and completes the connector line.

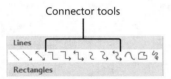

Figure 10-12 The connector tools appear in the Lines group in the Shapes gallery.

As Figure 10-13 shows, the resulting connector line stays attached to the two points even when you move the shapes. You don't have to attach connectors to anything. For example, you can connect one end to a shape and leave the other end free to create your own custom callout.

Connectors are particularly useful for creating flow charts. First, sketch your ideas using connectors with the Flowchart tools in the Shapes gallery. You can move flow charts as you work, and the connector lines reroute themselves as necessary.

You can also use SmartArt graphics to create flow charts and other types of diagrams. For more information, see "Creating SmartArt" later in this chapter.

Callouts are special text boxes with connector lines already attached. You can use them to add labels to important information or to describe important items. The most familiar type of callout is the kind you see in comics. Excel includes several of these balloon callouts, shown in Figure 10-14, with additional text formatting applied. Note that in this type of callout, the tip of the balloon pointer is the sticky point.

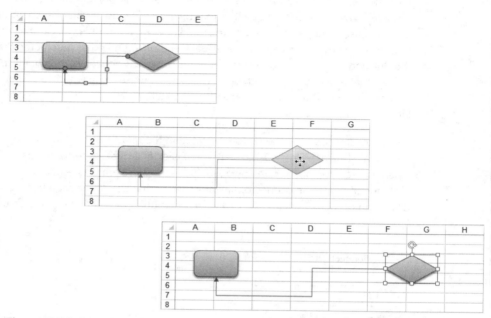

Figure 10-13 Connector lines remain attached to the points where you place them, even when you drag the shape to a new location.

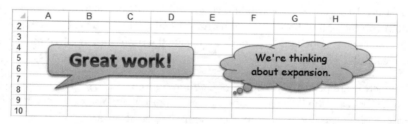

Figure 10-14 Callouts help you describe important items or call attention to important messages.

After drawing a callout, you can immediately begin typing the text you want in the callout. Then drag the diamond-shaped handle to move the tip of the callout indicator to the location you want.

Create a drawing grid

If you want a little help lining things up on screen, you can create a "graph paper" in Excel. Because drawings exist essentially on a layer floating above the worksheet, you can use the worksheet grid as a background for guidance. Starting with a new blank workbook, click the box at the intersection of the row and column headings. This selects the entire worksheet. Drag any line between column letters to the left until its width is 2.14 (20 pixels).

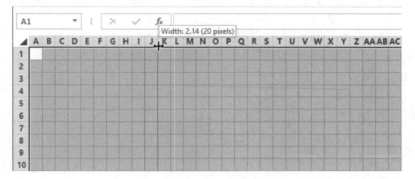

Excel helpfully includes the pixel count in the label that pops up when you drag to change the column width or row height. If you changed the default font or row height, just make sure the column width pixels match the row height pixels to ensure that every cell in the workbook is a tiny square. (Note that the New Sheet button will still add normal worksheets, so if you need more graph-paper tabs, right-click the Sheet1 tab, click Move Or Copy, and select Create A Copy.) Finally, click the File tab, click Save As, and select Excel Template in the Save As Type list so that you never run out of paper.

See "Tools to help you position objects on the worksheet" later in this chapter for information about using the Snap To Grid option to help with your drawings.

Chapter 10

Creating WordArt

The WordArt button on the Insert tab opens a gallery containing a number of fancy text styles you can employ to create impressive logos and headings. After you click the effect you want in the gallery, a new WordArt object appears on the worksheet. You can then type your text and modify the WordArt object, as shown in Figure 10-15. Notice that selected WordArt objects display the same handles as shapes, including the free rotate panhandle.

The Shape Styles group and the WordArt Styles group contain controls you use to change the look of the WordArt object. These groups appear on the Drawing Tools Format tab, a hidden tab that appears on the ribbon when you select a WordArt object, as shown in Figure 10-15.

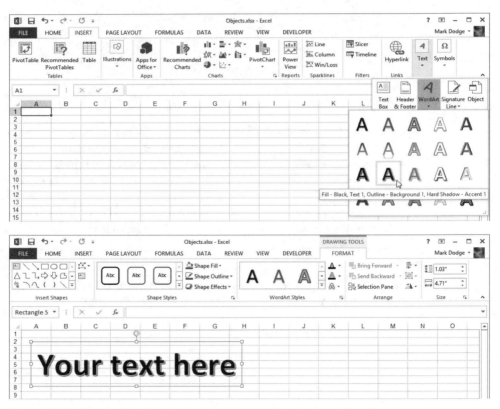

Figure 10-15 Use the WordArt button to create stunning logos and headings.

The WordArt Styles gallery on the Drawing Tools Format tab displays a selection of WordArt effects. This gallery is similar to the one displayed by clicking the WordArt button on the Insert tab, except that instead of creating a new WordArt object, you can use the

WordArt Styles gallery to modify an existing WordArt object. You can select styles that apply only to selected text in the object (or only to the word containing the active pointer), or you can select styles that apply to all the text in the object. The Clear WordArt command at the bottom of the gallery does not remove the object or the text, just the fancy formatting, resulting in a WordArt object of the same dimensions but formatted as plain text.

The Text Effects button displays a menu containing options for special effects you can apply to your WordArt object, as shown in Figure 10-16.

As with most galleries in Excel, you can rest the pointer on an icon for one of options in the Text Effects menu to see a live preview of how the effect will look if you apply it to the selected WordArt object. The same behavior is exhibited by the gallery in the Shape Styles group, although the results might not be what you expect. Applying shape styles does not change the look of the text but instead adds lines, colors, and fills to the area behind the text.

The rest of the controls on the Format tab under Drawing Tools apply to other objects as well as WordArt, and they are described in "Formatting objects that contain text" and in "Positioning objects" later in this chapter.

Figure 10-16 The Text Effects menu offers advanced formatting effects.

Creating SmartArt

The SmartArt button in the Illustrations group on the Insert tab represents a significant set of features. SmartArt graphics are prepackaged sets of graphic objects designed to address a variety of presentation tasks, such as creating timelines and decision trees, illustrating procedural steps and relationships, and creating organizational charts.

When you click the SmartArt button, the Choose A SmartArt Graphic dialog box shown in Figure 10-17 appears.

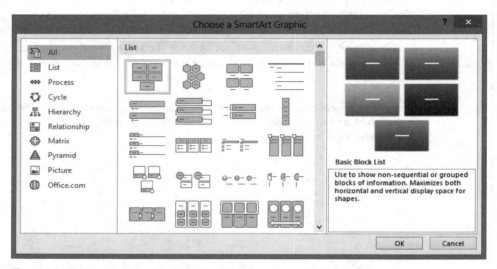

Figure 10-17 SmartArt graphics help you illustrate conceptual information.

The categories on the left represent conceptual approaches you can select to narrow the SmartArt graphics available in the main area of the dialog box:

- **List**   Creates a list of information that does not need to be in any particular order

- **Process**   Illustrates sequential steps to achieve a goal

- **Cycle**   Describes processes that are cyclical rather than goal oriented

- **Hierarchy**   Creates organizational charts or decision trees

- **Relationship**   Shows connections

- **Matrix**   Illustrates relationships that are interdependent

- **Pyramid**   Shows relationships that are proportional in size or importance

- **Picture**   Allows you to add your own pictures to predesigned graphics

- **Office.com**   Offers additional graphics available on the Office website

After you select a SmartArt graphic in the dialog box, click OK to add it to your worksheet, as shown in Figure 10-18. After inserting the graphic, we clicked the Text Pane button in the Create Graphic group on the SmartArt Tools Design tab that appears automatically after you insert the graphic.

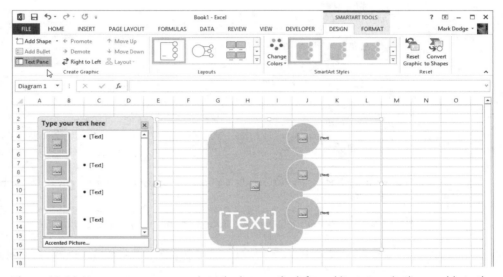

Figure 10-18 You can type your text into the box on the left, and it appears in the graphic to the right.

A SmartArt graphic comprises several components: the text pane with its Name box at the bottom displaying the currently active item; the SmartArt graphic; and the border surrounding the SmartArt like a picture frame. When you select a SmartArt graphic, several things appear: the text pane (if activated), the border, and two tabs on the ribbon under SmartArt Tools: Design and Format. The text pane makes organizing large charts and diagrams a lot easier and lets you easily perform editing tasks such as indenting bullet lists and rearranging hierarchical items. You also can click a "Text" placeholder and type directly in the graphic, if you prefer to hide the text pane.

The graphic shown inserted in Figure 10-18 is from the Picture category, which you can use to add not only your own text, but your own images as well. When you click one of the picture icons in either the graphic or the text pane, the Insert Pictures dialog box appears, as shown in Figure 10-19.

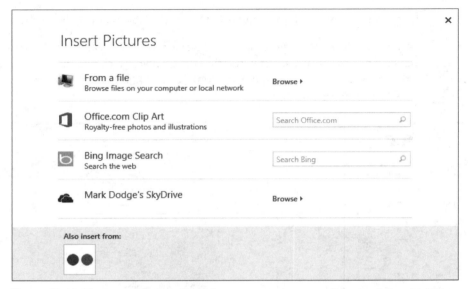

Figure 10-19 The Insert Pictures dialog box appears when you click any of the picture icons in a SmartArt graphic.

Here's more information about working with the text pane and the border:

- Resize the graphic by dragging any of the eight dotted handles on the border.

- Move the graphic by dragging the border; the text pane follows.

- Enter text directly into the graphic's items by clicking and typing.

- Redisplay a closed text pane by clicking the tiny arrow handle in the center of the left border, or by clicking the Text Pane button on the Design tab under SmartArt Tools.

- Click any photo icon to display the Insert Pictures dialog box. Selecting any inserted image displays the Picture Tools tab on the ribbon, which appears only when an image is selected.

If you change your mind about your original SmartArt selection, you can use the Layouts gallery on the Design tab under SmartArt Tools to switch to a different arrangement within the same SmartArt category without having to start from scratch. Or click the More Layouts command at the bottom of the Layouts gallery to switch to a different SmartArt category. The SmartArt Styles gallery offers different treatments within each category, as shown in

Figure 10-20. Both of these galleries exhibit live preview functionality: just rest the pointer on each thumbnail to quickly view your graphic in each style.

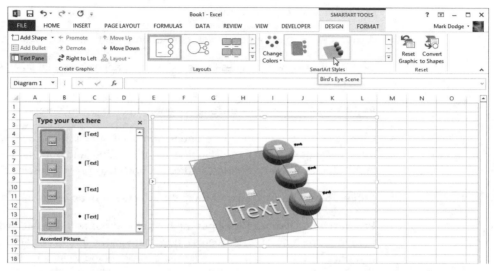

Figure 10-20 Use the SmartArt Styles group on the Design tab under SmartArt Tools to add graphic interest to your SmartArt.

> **Note**
>
> The Layouts and SmartArt Styles galleries share a clever design feature with a number of other galleries on the ribbon. The top two arrows on the right side of the gallery allow you to scroll up and down through the available styles without obscuring the worksheet; clicking the bottom arrow button displays the entire gallery.

The buttons in the Create Graphic group on the Design tab under SmartArt Tools offer ways to modify your graphic, and how they work depends on the particular graphic you're using. For example, the Add Bullet button works perfectly in most List graphics but not so well in the graphic shown in Figure 10-20. Experimentation is inevitable and rewarding. You can always press Ctrl+Z to undo any changes or click the Reset Graphic button on the Design tab under SmartArt Tools, in the Reset group.

Here is some more information about buttons in the Create Graphic and Reset categories on the SmartArt Tools Design tab:

- **Add Shape**   Inserts another shape similar to those already in the selected graphic. Clicking the arrow displays a menu of commands you use to choose where to put the new shape: above, below, after, or before the active shape. The Add Assistant command applies only to Hierarchical Organization Chart graphics; it adds a box outside the hierarchy that is typically used for administrative assistants or other positions outside the normal chain of command.

- **Add Bullet**   Creates a new bullet item subordinate to the active bullet.

- **Text Pane**   Displays or hides the text pane that appears when a SmartArt graphic is selected.

- **Right To Left**   Flips the horizontal orientation of applicable graphics.

- **Layout**   Controls the horizontal orientation of an organization chart. Menu commands include Standard, Left Hanging, Right Hanging, and Both (left *and* right hanging). This is available only when an organization chart graphic is selected.

- **Move Up and Move Down**   Moves the selected item up or down in the bullet list.

- **Promote and Demote**   Changes the hierarchical position of a selected bullet. Promoting to the highest level creates a new shape in the SmartArt graphic. Similarly, demoting a top-level bullet removes the corresponding shape in the graphic and adds its text as subordinate to the previous bullet. In organization chart graphics only, these buttons move the selected shape up or down the hierarchy and do not add or remove shapes from the graphic.

- **Reset Graphic**   Restores the selected graphic to its default, inserted form.

- **Convert To Shapes**   Changes selected SmartArt into regular graphic shapes. For example, if you convert the object as shown in Figure 10-20, the result is a group of individual objects that look identical, and are editable, but do not display the SmartArt tabs and controls when selected; instead, the Drawing Tools Format tab appears.

We discuss the controls available on the Format tab under SmartArt Tools in "Formatting graphics" later in this chapter. For more about the Drawing Tools Format tab, see "Using drawing tools" later in this chapter.

Inserting other graphics

Although the Excel graphics toolbox is overflowing with ways to create impressive objects from scratch, you can also employ several methods to insert ready-made graphics from other programs, to insert pictures, and to insert other types of graphic content onto your worksheets.

Inserting online pictures and clip art

If you don't have the time or inclination to take appropriate photographs or to create your own artwork, you can instantly call on the talents of numerous professional photographers and illustrators by clicking the Online Pictures button in the Illustrations group on the Insert tab. When you do so, a dialog box similar to the one shown in Figure 10-19 appears, offering Bing Image Search, SkyDrive, and Office.com Clip Art search boxes. Enter a search term and press Enter to display a set of results, as shown in Figure 10-21. We entered the term *businessmen* in the Clip Art search box, which resulted in a huge list of clip art and stock photography available for free on Office.com. (Note that you need the SkyDrive client installed on your computer for SkyDrive to appear as an option.)

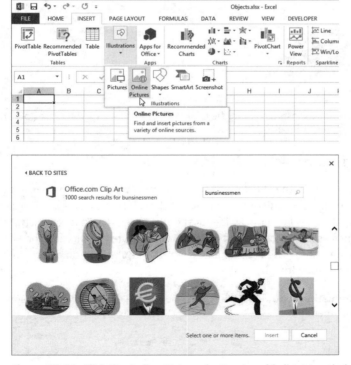

Figure 10-21 Click the Online Pictures button to add clip art and photos to your worksheets.

> **Note**
>
> **The Microsoft Clip Organizer is no longer available in Excel 2013.**

Figure 10-22 shows a piece of clip art inserted on the worksheet, which was accomplished by searching for Office.com Clip Art using the dialog box shown in Figure 10-23. Clip art or pictures that you insert this way are treated as pictures in Excel. When you select an inserted picture, the Picture Tools Format tab appears, and as shown in Figure 10-22, pointing to styles in the Picture Styles gallery gives you a live preview of that style in the selected image on the worksheet. We'll discuss the Picture Tools Format tab in "Using picture tools" later in this chapter.

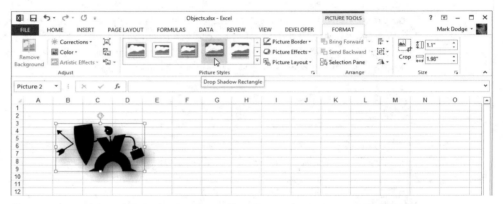

Figure 10-22 Objects inserted using the Online Pictures button, even pieces of clip art, are considered pictures in Excel 2013.

Inserting pictures

The Pictures button in the Illustrations group on the Insert tab lets you insert graphics that have been saved in a variety of file formats. Clicking Pictures displays the dialog box shown in Figure 10-23 that is functionally identical to the Open dialog box, which you can use to find image files in any location to which your computer has access. The File Type drop-down list to the right of the File Name text box lets you zero in on a particular file type but is set to All Pictures by default.

For more information about the Open dialog box, see "Opening files" in Chapter 2, "Exploring Excel fundamentals."

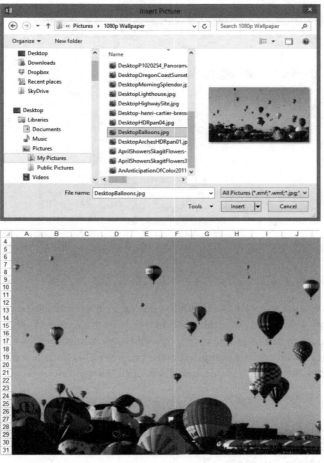

Figure 10-23 Images copied from other programs can usually be pasted in more than one format using Paste Special.

Good old copy and paste still works

After all is said and done, sometimes the classics are the best and easiest solutions. You can paste pictures into Excel from other programs that produce files compatible with the Clipboard. Simply copy the image in the source program; then, on the Home tab in Excel, click the Paste menu, and then click Paste Special, which allows you to select from several options; the options available depend on the type of picture you are working with.

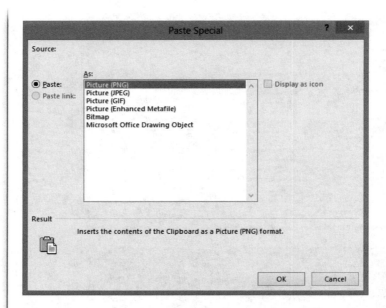

If the program used to create the graphic you want to import into Excel supports linking, you might also be able to establish a link between the source file and the graphic, allowing the graphic to be automatically updated in your workbook whenever you make changes to the original using the source program. The Paste Link option becomes available in the Paste Special dialog box if and when linking is possible.

For more information about linking, see Chapter 31, "Linking, hyperlinking, and embedding."

Inserting other objects

The Object button, which is located on the Insert tab in the Text group, gives you direct access to other programs you can use to create objects. The difference between inserting a picture and inserting an object is that a picture is always static and cannot be directly edited, whereas an inserted object retains a connection to its source program and is said to be *embedded* on a worksheet. You can open an embedded object for editing by double-clicking it.

When you click the Object button, a dialog box appears with two tabs: Create New and Create From File. The Create New tab, shown in Figure 10-24, starts the program selected in the Object Type list, allowing you to create the object directly in the program. The contents of this list vary depending on the configuration of your system and the programs you have installed.

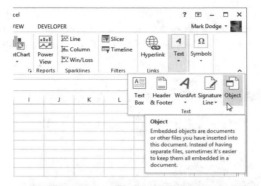

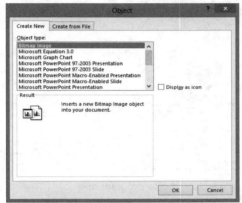

Figure 10-24 You can use the Create New tab of the Object dialog box to simultaneously insert an object and start the program used to create it.

When you select an item in the Object Type list, a small frame is inserted in the current worksheet at the location of the active cell, and the program needed to create or edit that object type is started. For example, if you select Bitmap Image in the Object Type list, Paint starts, and you can begin creating a new image, as you can see in Figure 10-25. When you are finished editing, close the object-editing program, and your new object appears on the worksheet.

Figure 10-26 shows the Create From File tab in the Object dialog box. You can use this tab to insert an existing file as an embedded object rather than create a new object with the Create New tab. Again, the object types you can embed depend on the programs installed on your computer.

Although the Link To File check box on the Create From File tab isn't selected by default, you can still open the object in its source program by double-clicking it. If you do select the Link To File check box, the object is updated automatically whenever the source file changes. Selecting the Display As Icon check box embeds the selected file in your workbook as an icon. This option is particularly convenient if an embedded object is long, large, or more easily viewed in its source program. However, if you distribute the workbook to other users, be sure the same program is available on their computers, or they will not be able to open the embedded icon for viewing.

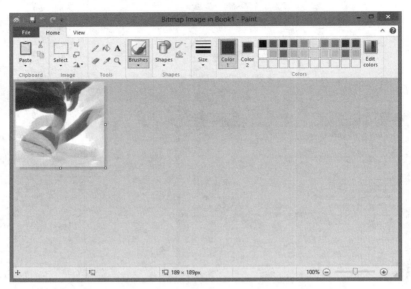

Figure 10-25 When you insert an object, the source program opens.

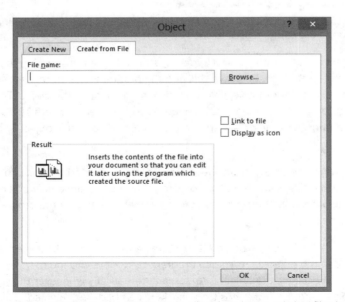

Figure 10-26 Use the Create From File tab to insert existing files into your workbooks.

To make changes to any embedded object, double-click the object. The source program starts, and the object file opens, allowing you to make modifications.

Formatting graphics

After you create or insert a graphic object, Excel provides plenty of powerful tools you can use to modify it. Most of these tools are on hidden ribbon tabs that appear only when an object is selected. Three types of hidden tabs exist, depending on the object you select: SmartArt Tools, Drawing Tools, or Picture Tools appear on a menu bar above the new tabs. All three types include a Format tab; SmartArt Tools includes an additional tab, Design, which is discussed in "Creating SmartArt" earlier in this chapter. The controls available on the Format tab change depending on the type of object selected.

Using picture tools

When you select an inserted picture or piece of clip art, you can use the Format tab under Picture Tools to make some rather extreme adjustments to the image. Although the source program that created an imported picture probably offers more options, you can do a surprising amount of formatting within Excel as well. All the basics are there, including tools for rotating and aligning images, adding borders, and cropping, but Excel now includes some surprisingly advanced formatting tools as well. Take a look at the largest group on the Format tab, Picture Styles, shown in Figure 10-27.

As Figure 10-27 shows, simply resting the pointer on a thumbnail in the Picture Styles gallery temporarily displays the selected picture using that style. The same functionality applies to most other galleries available on the Format tab.

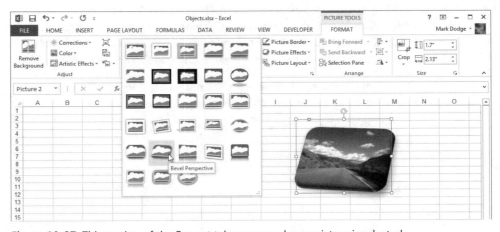

Figure 10-27 This version of the Format tab appears when a picture is selected.

Making adjustments to your images

The Adjust group on the Format tab hides a powerful collection of menus. They replace the relatively pedestrian Brightness, Contrast, and Recolor commands found in versions of Excel prior to 2010, and they also offer a robust arsenal of special controls and artistic effects. For example, the Corrections menu, shown in Figure 10-28, displays actual thumbnail representations of the selected picture and gives you an immediate idea of where you need to go, rather than using the trial-and-Undo method.

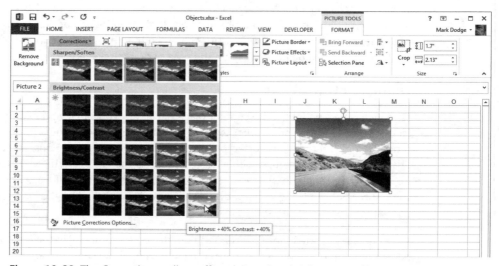

Figure 10-28 The Corrections gallery offers sharpening, brightness, and contrast adjustments.

The Brightness/Contrast thumbnail matrix displays 25 examples of the selected image in 0%, 20%, and 40% applications of brightness and contrast, as well as 25% and 50% applications of sharpening. For more control, click Picture Corrections Options at the bottom of the gallery to display the Format Picture task pane, as shown in Figure 10-29.

The Format Picture task pane controls pretty much everything you can do with pictures, including fill and line color, shadows, special effects, rotation, cropping, and sizing. Note that different picture types might cause some options to become active or disabled.

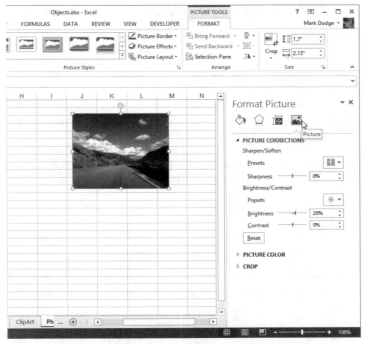

Figure 10-29 The Format Picture task pane contains all the available fine-tuning controls for the selected image.

Here is a quick rundown of the controls available in the Format Picture task pane and what they do. Clicking one of the four icons visible in Figure 10-29 displays a different set of controls; the figure shows the controls available in the Picture category. Note that if there is a corresponding menu or gallery on the ribbon, its options are duplicated here as well:

- **Fill & Line** (the paint bucket icon)

  - **Fill** Controls the color and nature of the fill (solid, gradient, picture, texture, pattern), if any.

  - **Line** Controls the color, size, transparency, and many other attributes of the line (solid or gradient), if any.

- **Effects** (the pentagon icon)

  - **Shadow** Controls a shadow's color, transparency, size, angle, distance from the object, and amount of "blur" you want it to exhibit. It includes presets.

  - **Reflection** Controls transparency, size, distance, and amount of blur for these shadowlike mirror images. It includes presets.

Chapter 10

○ **Glow** Includes presets and controls for color, size, and transparency.

○ **Soft Edges** Includes presets and a control for size.

○ **3-D Format** Offers options for type of bevel, color, depth, size, and options for surface material and lighting effects.

○ **3-D Rotation** Offers precise control of the orientation of the selected 3-D object in three dimensions, as well as distance from "ground." It includes presets.

○ **Artistic Effects** Duplicates the gallery of the same name on the ribbon, offering only an additional Reset button.

● **Size & Properties** (the "measuring" icon)

○ **Size** Provides control over the size and (non-3-D) rotation of the image, and a Reset button.

○ **Properties** Controls how the image reacts to changes in the underlying worksheet (Move But Don't Size With Cells being the default) and whether the object is locked or can be printed.

○ **Text Box** Controls margins, alignment, and wrapping of objects containing text, and whether the object automatically scales to fit its text contents.

○ **Alt Text** This is an accessibility feature provided for images that end up on the web. Use it to enter descriptive text for the visually impaired.

● **Picture** (the "sun and mountains" icon)

○ **Picture Corrections** Provides precision control of brightness, contrast, and sharpening. It includes presets.

○ **Picture Color** Controls the color saturation and "tone" (a.k.a. *color temperature*), ranging from very cool to very warm. It includes presets.

○ **Crop** Offers precise control of not only the cropping dimensions, but also the exact position of the picture on the worksheet.

Color is the next command in the Adjust group on the Picture Tools Format tab. It displays the gallery shown in Figure 10-30.

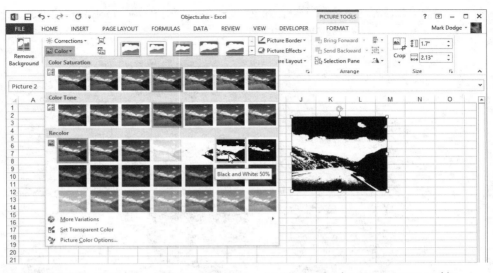

Figure 10-30 The Color menu offers control over saturation and color temperature, and it reveals a lot of nifty presets.

Here is an explanation of the options available on the Color menu:

- The Color menu's Color Saturation options give you an idea of the range available between no color at all (a.k.a. *grayscale*) and 400% color saturation.

- Color Tone is the same as color temperature and shows you a range of options between fairly cool (4,700 degrees Kelvin) and very warm (11,200 degrees Kelvin).

- The Recolor options essentially remove the color from the image (desaturate) and then add another color as a transparent overlay, much like a hand-tinted, black-and-white photograph. One of the more popular applications of this technique is Sepia, which is offered here, as well as several options without the added color, such as Black And White and Grayscale.

- At the bottom of the Color menu, More Variations offers a standard color palette if you want to select a color not represented in the menu as the overlay color. For more control, click Picture Color Options to display the Format Picture task pane.

- At the bottom of the Color menu on the Picture Tools Format tab is the Set Transparent Color command. Click the command, and then click anywhere in the image to essentially remove that color, leaving a see-through hole in the image. This is similar to removing the background (discussed next) except that it works only on a single color at a time.

Chapter 10

Clicking the Remove Background button in the Picture Tools Format tab's Adjust group displays the Background Removal tab, shown in Figure 10-31, which normally remains hidden.

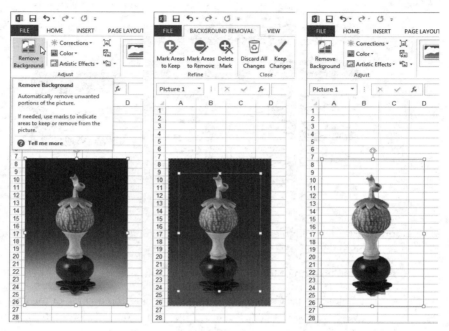

Figure 10-31 The Remove Background button works well on some images.

When you first click the Remove Background button, the image appears with selection handles inside its frame and, as Figure 10-31 shows, shaded areas that represent areas specified for removal. The selection handles indicate where the image will be cropped. The shaded areas are selected around the periphery of the image and are based on predominant, common, adjacent colors and—to some extent—lines and textures. You can drag the selection handles to include more or less of the image in the result, and the shaded areas might change when you do this. If the automatic selection doesn't quite get it right, you can use the Mark Areas To Keep and Mark Areas To Remove buttons, which do pretty much what they indicate. When you mark an area, you might find that an area has a lot more colors than it appeared to at first, so trial and error is helpful here. The Undo and Redo buttons work beautifully. In Figure 10-31, we simply dragged the bottom of the selection rectangle a bit, to include the entire finial, and the automatic background selection algorithms worked pretty well for this image.

The remaining menu in the Picture Tools Format tab's Adjust group is Artistic Effects, which includes a number of textures, screens, and various other types of distortions and manipulations. The very nice Pencil Grayscale effect is shown in Figure 10-32.

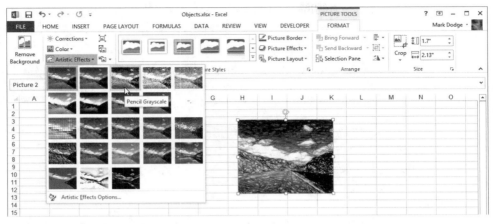

Figure 10-32 The Artistic Effects gallery includes some very interesting ones.

The second of the three buttons on the right side of the Picture Tools Format tab's Adjust group, Change Picture, allows you to swap the underlying image with another one by opening the Insert Picture dialog box. When you use Change Picture, any formatting you applied is not affected. The new image simply appears in place with all the same options applied. The last button on the right side of the Picture Tools Format tab's Adjust group, Reset Picture, does exactly what you think—reverts the image to its original inserted condition. It is actually a menu containing two options: Reset Picture and Reset Picture & Size. You can use these options to choose to keep the size (or not). The first button in this group of three—Compress Pictures—is discussed in "Applying compression to pictures" later in this chapter.

For more detail about many of the effects mentioned here, see "Using advanced object formatting effects" later in this chapter.

Using drawing tools

When you select any type of object other than pictures or embedded objects, the Format tab under Drawing Tools appears, containing controls similar to ones on the Format tab under Picture Tools and a couple of new ones, too, as you can see in Figure 10-33.

Here are details about the formatting controls on the Format tab under Drawing Tools that are different from those on the Format tab under Picture Tools:

- **Shape Fill**   This is a standard color palette you use to select colors, textures, gradients, and even pictures to fill the selected shape.

- **Shape Outline**   This is a standard palette that controls the outline of the selected shape, including its color, line weight, and line style, including options for dashed lines and arrows.

- **Shape Effects**   Displays a menu of special effects you can apply to the selected picture, including the Shadow, Reflection, Glow, Soft Edges, Bevel, and 3-D Rotation options, as shown in Figure 10-34.

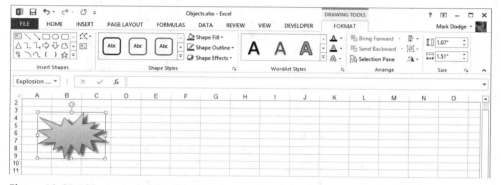

Figure 10-33 This version of the Format tab appears when any shape, text box, or WordArt object is selected.

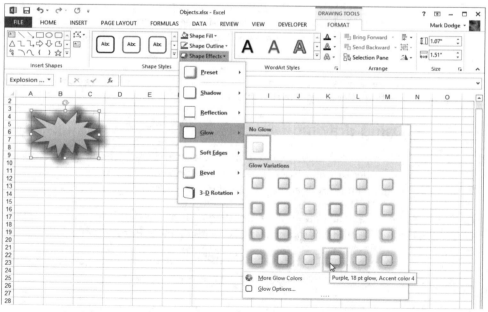

Figure 10-34 The Shape Effects menu offers numerous visual enhancements for your objects.

The Format tab under Drawing Tools and the Format tab under Picture Tools contain groups covered elsewhere in this book. For more about the Insert Shapes group, see "Using the Shapes tools" earlier in this chapter. To read about the WordArt group, see "Creating WordArt" earlier in this chapter. For information about the Arrange group, see "Positioning objects" later in this chapter.

Using SmartArt tools

When you select a SmartArt graphic, the Format tab under SmartArt Tools appears, containing controls similar to the two other versions of the Format tab (Picture Tools and Drawing Tools) and a few new ones, as you can see in Figure 10-35.

Figure 10-35 The SmartArt Tools Format tab offers a few unique controls.

You can click the Edit In 2-D button in the Shapes group to "flatten" a selected object with 3-D formatting applied. This does not eliminate 3-D formatting, it just suspends it and speeds up the redrawing of the object. The Larger and Smaller buttons are used to scale individually selected objects in a group by a preset amount, which is more precise than dragging selection handles and makes it easier to scale multiple objects by identical amounts.

On this version of the Format tab, the Arrange button has a menu with some familiar controls—Align, Group, Rotate, Bring Forward, and Send Backward—and one unfamiliar one, Selection Pane. Clicking the latter button opens a task pane with a list of all the objects on the worksheet. Clicking an item in the list selects the corresponding object. If you are working with multiple objects, especially if they are in close proximity or stacked, using the Selection pane can be very handy. For more information about the Selection Pane option, see "Working with graphic objects" later in this chapter.

Formatting text in graphics

Most of what you can do with text in cells applies to text in graphics as well. You can use the tools in the Font group on the Home tab to accomplish most of what you need to do in either cells or text-capable objects. You can also apply the advanced formatting options available in the WordArt Styles group on the Format tab that appears when an object is selected. However, you can employ a few additional text-formatting options using the Font dialog box when working with text in objects.

To see what we're talking about, click Shapes on the Insert tab, draw any kind of two-dimensional object, such as a rectangle, and then type some text. Drag through the text you just typed to select it, right-click the selected text, and finally click Font to display the Font dialog box, shown in Figure 10-36.

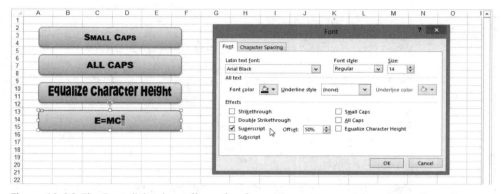

Figure 10-36 The Font dialog box offers a few formatting options not found elsewhere.

> **Note**
>
> You can also display the Font dialog box by selecting any text-capable object and clicking the dialog box launcher in the Font group on the Home tab.

The Font dialog box shares many of the same controls found in the Format Cells dialog box that you use to format text in cells. The Font dialog box additionally offers the following options, several of which are illustrated in Figure 10-36:

- **Double Strikethrough**   This effect draws two lines through the middle of the selected text.

- **Offset**   When the Superscript or Subscript effect is turned on, Offset offers precise control over the distance of the selected text from the baseline.

- **Small Caps**   This effect changes lowercase characters in selected text to small capital letters. Text typed as capital letters is unaffected.

- **All Caps**   This effect changes all the selected lowercase characters into capital letters.

- **Equalize Character Height**   This effect changes the size of each selected character so that they all occupy the same amount of vertical space. Characters with descenders are moved above the baseline.

- **Character Spacing** On the Character Spacing tab in the Font dialog box, you can use this effect to expand or condense the space between characters of selected text by a specified number of points, as shown in Figure 10-37.

- **Kerning** This effect applies special spacing rules to correct problematic character pairs and lets you specify a font size above which kerning is applied.

In Figure 10-37, the first text box is formatted as usual; kerning was applied to the second text box. The effect is subtle, but you can see that the spacing between each letter pair in the second box is a little tighter. Kerning is particularly noticeable when applied to large display fonts and logos.

Figure 10-37 Adjust the space between letters in graphic objects using the Character Spacing tab.

> **Note**
>
> Chapter 9, "Worksheet formatting techniques," discusses the overall formatting features of Excel; we discuss text formatting in depth in "Using fonts" in Chapter 9.

Applying compression to pictures

You can choose to optimize the storage of your inserted pictures to decrease the amount of disk space they consume. Clicking the Compress Pictures button on the Format tab under Picture Tools (which appears only when a picture is selected) displays a dialog box of the same name, as shown in Figure 10-38.

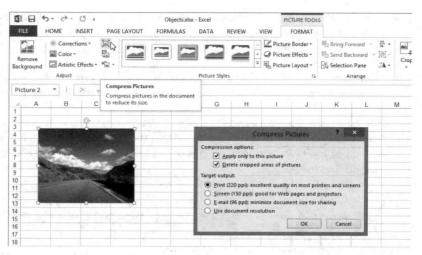

Figure 10-38 Apply compression settings to any imported picture.

Here are details about the options in the Compress Pictures dialog box:

- **Apply Only To This Picture** Ordinarily, all the images in your workbook are compressed at once. Select this check box to compress only the currently selected images.

- **Delete Cropped Areas Of Pictures** This discards any nonvisible portions of pictures you have cropped using the options in the Size group on the Format tab under Picture Tools. This is the default setting and is not reversible.

- **Target Output options** Use these options to specify the number of dots per inch (dpi) to suit your output requirements: print, screen, email, or the default resolution of the encapsulating document. (Document resolution options, if any, are available by clicking the File tab, Print, Printer Properties, and then clicking the Advanced button.)

Using advanced object formatting effects

Most of the formatting controls you need for graphics are right up front on the ribbon—the dashboard of Excel. The ribbon offers easy access to buttons and galleries as well as live preview functionality. However, a few additional options are not available on the ribbon. To access them, right-click any drawn object or shape, and click Format Shape to display the Format Shape task pane.

The categories available in the Format Shape task pane are always the same, no matter what type of object you select. However, the options available in each category change based on the object type. For example, the settings in the Text Box category are unavailable when you select a picture.

Much of what you find in the Format Shape task pane is self-explanatory, but we'll hit the high points for you in the following sections, which also serve to describe some of the inner workings of equivalent ribbon-based controls.

Formatting fills and lines

The Fill & Line (paint bucket) icon in the Format Shape task pane displays the Fill and Line categories. Options you select in the Fill category can change the controls displayed in the task pane, as shown in Figure 10-39.

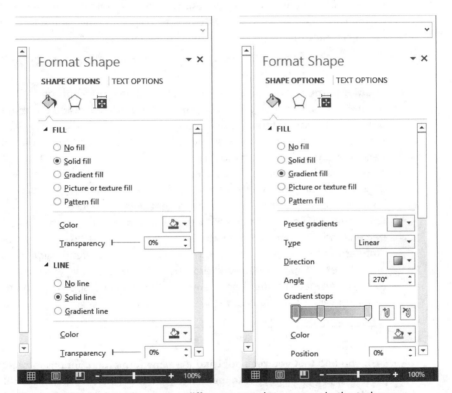

Figure 10-39 Each option causes different controls to appear in the task pane.

For example, you can see the differences between the controls available when the Solid Fill and Gradient Fill options are selected. As always, any changes you make in the task pane are reflected immediately in the selected object:

● **Gradient Fill**   Gradient Fill is the third option in the Fill category in the Format Shape task pane; a gradient fill consists of two or more colors, cross-fading from light to dark. You can choose from a number of presets in the Preset Gradients drop-down list, or you can customize your own. In the Type drop-down list, select from

Linear, Rectangular, Radial, or Path, which follows the contours of the selected object. You can select a fill direction for any gradient type except Path. You can specify an angle—the point from which the gradient emanates—from 0 to 359.9 degrees. The Direction settings are presets of the Angle setting; both settings are applicable only to linear gradients.

> **Note**
>
> The controls used most often in the Fill & Line, Effects, and Size & Properties categories in the Format Shape task pane are available directly on the ribbon. On the Format tab under Drawing Tools, which appears when you select a graphic object, click the Shape Fill or Shape Outline menu.

- **Gradient Stops** You can create complex, nonlinear gradients using the Gradient Stops controls, which let you specify up to 10 intervals of gradation using varying amounts of color and transparency. To get an idea how this works, select any of the more colorful samples in the Preset Gradients list and then look at the Gradient Stops bar. For example, the first preset, named Light Gradient – Accent 1, has four gradient stops. All are set to the same color, but each has different settings for Position, Transparency, and Brightness—the controls below the Gradient Stops slider. The Position control determines where along the gradient path the selected stop comes into play. For example, if you want to create a three-color gradient, you can add stops at 50 percent and 100 percent for a fairly even gradient or at 10 percent and 80 percent to emphasize the middle color. You can also use the Transparency slider to add varying amounts of transparency to each gradient stop. For example, you could set a shape to be 0 percent transparent on one end of the scale and 80 percent on the other end, revealing varying amounts of the worksheet below the shape.

> **Note**
>
> If you find that you keep applying the same formatting options to objects you create, you can easily make these hard-earned formats the default for all new objects you create. Right-click any object that's formatted the way you like, and click Set As Default Shape. The command name might change, depending on the object you select. Note that you must right-click the border of a text box, not the text area, to display the Set As Default Shape command.

- **Picture Or Texture Fill**   Selecting the Picture Or Texture Fill option in the Fill category in the Format Shape task pane reveals a different set of controls. You can select one of the preset textures in the Texture palette, or you can import an image from a file on disk, a piece of clip art, or even the current contents of the Clipboard by clicking the appropriate Insert Picture From button. Selecting the Tile Picture As Texture option repeats an image as needed to fill the selected shape; if this option is not selected, a single instance of an image is placed in the center of the selected shape. You can use the Offset option to specify a distance (in points) to offset the image from the edges of the shape, and use the Scale options to control the size of the image.

- **Line options**   The Line options in the Format Shape task pane don't contain any surprises; these categories are where you control the formatting of lines and arrows. You can create gradient lines and compound lines; you can specify different styles of dashed lines and arrowheads; you can add square, round, or flat caps to the end of lines; you can specify a percentage of transparency to solid lines; and you can specify round, bevel, or miter intersections where lines meet.

Applying shadows

Clicking the Effects icon in the Format Shape task pane displays categories you use to apply various special effects, including shadows. Clicking the Shadows category in the Format Shape task pane adds depth to any graphic object. In Figure 10-40, we created a shape, right-clicked it, and then clicked Format Shape. We then clicked the Effects icon and then clicked the Shadow category and applied shadow effects. When you click the Presets button, options appear for a number of built-in shadow configurations. After you apply a shadow effect, you can modify it using the sliders in the task pane.

> **Note**
>
> The same shadow presets in the Format Shape task pane are available on the ribbon; on the Format tab under Drawing Tools, which appears when a graphic object is selected, you can find the shadow presets by clicking the Shape Effects button and then clicking Shadow.

Chapter 10

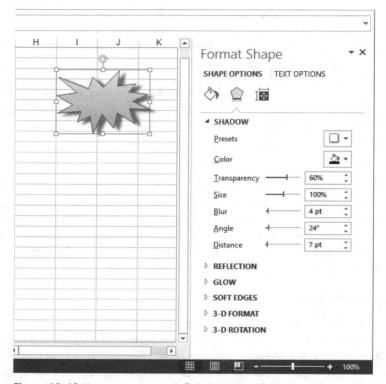

Figure 10-40 You can create an infinite number of shadow effects using the Format Shape task pane.

Applying 3-D effects

There are two categories in the Effects category of the Format Shape task pane that apply and control three-dimensional attributes of a selected object: 3-D Format and 3-D Rotation. Click the 3-D Format category to apply three-dimensional effects to the selected shape. If you apply one of the Bevel presets, several formats are applied to the selected object: color and amount of depth and contour, material, and lighting type. In Figure 10-41, we created a shape and applied the Convex preset from the Top Bevel palette.

> **Note**
>
> The controls used most often in the 3-D Format and 3-D Rotation categories in the Format Shape task pane are available directly on the ribbon. On the Format tab under Drawing Tools, which appears when you select a graphic object, click the Shape Effects button, and then click commands on the Bevel menu and the 3-D Rotation menu.

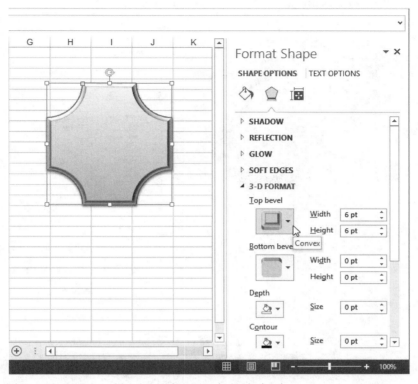

Figure 10-41 Start with a basic shape, and give it depth.

With the controls in the 3-D Rotation category in the Format Shape task pane, you can control the attitude of the selected shape in all three dimensions. We'll describe the controls in the both 3-D categories in the Format Shape task pane in detail.

- **Top Bevel and Bottom Bevel (in the 3-D Format category)**   Controls the amount of *extrusion* applied to the selected shape, giving it the appearance of having a beveled edge. You can create extrusions on both sides; the Top Bevel drop-down list controls the front of the shape, and the Bottom Bevel drop-down list controls the back, as shown in Figure 10-42. (To see the results of the Bottom Bevel settings, you must rotate the shape using controls in the 3-D Rotation category.) The Width settings control the width of the beveled edge, and the Height settings control the distance the bevel is extruded from the surface of the shape.

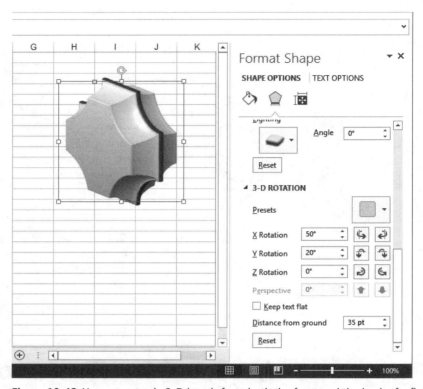

Figure 10-42 You can extrude 3-D bevels from both the front and the back of a flat shape.

- **Depth (in the 3-D Format category)**   Controls the thickness and color of the shape itself—not any extrusions you apply with the Bevel controls. (To see the results of the Depth settings, you must rotate the shape using controls in the 3-D Rotation category.)

- **Contour (in the 3-D Format category)**   Controls the size and color of a raised border applied to the perimeter of the selected shape.

- **Material (in the 3-D Format category)**   Contains options for surface treatment and lighting effects. Materials include surfaces such as plastic and metal, translucent, and special effects such as soft edge and wireframe. Choose from lighting effects such as Three-Point, Sunset, and Chilly, and choose the angle from which the light originates.

- **Rotation (in the 3-D Rotation category)**   Contains controls to adjust the position of the selected object in three-dimensional space. The x-axis is horizontal, the y-axis is vertical, and the z-axis is front to back.

- **Perspective (in the 3-D Rotation category)**   Controls the amount of foreshortening applied to a shape, if applicable. *Foreshortening* makes shapes that are closer look larger. You use this control to make shapes appear to tilt forward or backward. It is easiest to start by clicking one of the Perspective options in the Presets drop-down list; then you can change the angle of foreshortening using the Perspective controls.

- **Keep Text Flat (in the 3-D Rotation category)**   Prevents any text typed in a shape from rotating along with the shape, effectively separating the text from the shape.

Formatting objects that contain text

In addition to objects you create with the Text Box button in the Text group on the Insert tab, many of the objects you can create in Excel are de facto text boxes. Figure 10-43 shows two objects, one created with the Text Box tool and another created with one of the Star tools in the Shapes gallery. Both objects are subject to the influence of the Text Box controls in the Text Options pane of the Format Shape task pane, as are most two-dimensional shapes and even WordArt and SmartArt objects.

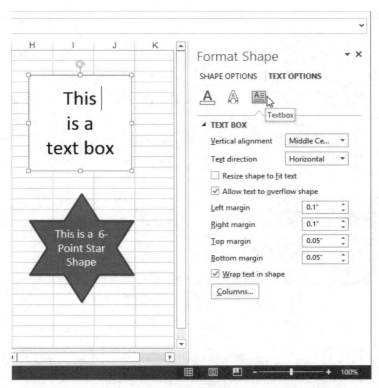

Figure 10-43 The Text Box category of the Format Shape task pane offers controls not found on the ribbon.

> **Note**
>
> The controls used most often in the Text Box category of the Format Shape task pane are available directly on the ribbon. On the Home tab, use the buttons in the Font and Alignment groups. For more information, see the following topics in Chapter 9: "Using fonts" and "Aligning data in cells." See "Working with text boxes" earlier in this chapter and, for advanced font formatting, see "Formatting text in graphics" earlier in this chapter.

The Allow Text To Overflow Shape check box is normally selected; if you clear this check box, text too large to fit the shape is truncated. If you select the Resize Shape To Fit Text check box, the object shrinks (or expands) to fit the text it contains as it's typed and formatted. The Margin settings add or decrease the amount of space between the edge of a shape and the text it contains. The Columns button displays a dialog box you can use to create columns of text within any text-capable object, as shown on the left in Figure 10-44.

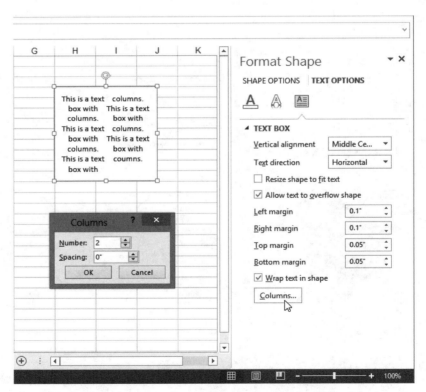

Figure 10-44 You can create columnar text boxes using the Columns button.

Selecting text or shapes

You have two ways to select objects containing text: you can select either the text area or the entire object. When you select the text area, you can edit it; when you select the object, you can move it. You tell the difference by looking at the object's border. When you click a shape created using the Text Box tool in the Text group on the Insert tab, the border is a dashed line at first, indicating the text area is ready for editing. Click the border of the box, and the border changes to a solid line, indicating the object is now selected:

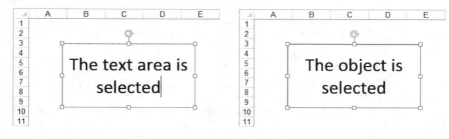

For shapes other than text boxes, selection depends on whether the shape contains text: click near the text, and the text area is selected; otherwise, the shape is selected. If a shape other than a text box doesn't contain text, you can't activate the text area, but you don't need to do so—just start typing after you select the object to create a text area.

Formatting embedded objects

A few object types—those inserted using the Object button in the Text group—are called *embedded objects*, which typically launch another application when double-clicked. To apply formatting to an embedded object, right-click it and then click the Format Object command. When you do so, a dialog box like the one shown in Figure 10-45 appears. Depending on the type of object selected, some of the options available in this dialog box have no effect.

For more information about embedded objects, see "Inserting other objects" earlier in this chapter.

In Figure 10-45, we used the Colors And Lines tab in the Format Object dialog box to apply a gradient fill to an embedded Microsoft Equation Editor 3.0 object and added 75 percent transparency and a 3-point border. In general, the options available in this dialog box are self-explanatory and similar to options found elsewhere.

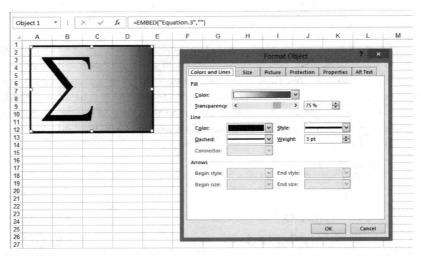

Figure 10-45 Your formatting options for embedded objects are in a dialog box instead of a task pane.

Working with graphic objects

In addition to all the nifty formatting options for graphics that are built into Excel, there are also tools you can use to select and arrange graphic objects, group and hide them, move them around, and protect them.

Selecting and grouping objects

Sometimes you'll find it convenient to move, resize, or even reformat more than one object at a time. If you create a logo using multiple objects, for example, you want to move the objects as a single unit, preserving their positions relative to one another. For these purposes, Excel includes the Group button, located in the Arrange group on the Page Layout tab. This button is a menu containing the Group, Ungroup, and Regroup commands, and it remains inactive unless more than one object is selected. (The Group button can also be found on the Drawing Tools Format tab that appears when an object is selected.)

> **Note**
>
> You can select multiple objects by holding down Shift and clicking individual objects. You can select all the objects on the current worksheet by clicking one to select it and then pressing Ctrl+A (Select All). You can also select all objects by clicking Home, Find & Select, Go To Special, and then selecting the Objects option.

After you select a group of objects, you can lock them together by using the Group button on the Page Layout tab or by right-clicking any of the selected objects, clicking Group, and then clicking one of the Group commands, as shown in Figure 10-46.

When you group objects, the sets of handles around each selected object are replaced by a single set of handles for the entire group, as shown in Figure 10-46. After you group the objects, you can manipulate the set of objects as a single object. You can resize, move, and apply formatting to them as a group. When you apply formatting, however, the separate objects might behave differently, especially if you have grouped different kinds of objects with different formats. It's best to apply formatting before you group objects, unless the objects are similar.

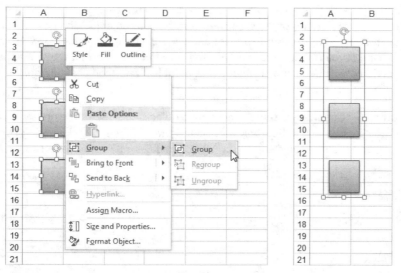

Figure 10-46 Select a group of objects, right-click any one of them, and then click Group to lock them together.

To ungroup a set of objects, select the group, right-click, and then click Group, Ungroup. You can use the Regroup command to reconstitute the group of objects you most recently ungrouped. This is handy, for example, if you ungrouped a set of objects to make changes to one or more of them. Rather than selecting them again and clicking Group, just click Regroup.

> **Note**
>
> Unlike with other objects, when you click an object containing text and a dotted border appears around it, the text area—not the object—is selected. To select the object, click the border; when the border appears as a solid line, the object is selected. If you want to move an object containing text while its text area is active, you can drag it by its border.

Positioning objects

Think of the objects on a worksheet as stacked on top of each other. Each new object you draw is placed on top of the stack. If necessary, you can adjust the position of objects in the stack by using the Bring Forward and Send Backward buttons in the Arrange group on the Page Layout tab, or better yet, on the Drawing Tools Format tab that appears when you select an object. (You can also right-click an object and then use the equivalent commands on the shortcut menu.)

Figure 10-47 shows two sets of ungrouped objects. The set on the right was originally just like the set on the left, but then we selected the banner and clicked Bring Forward, Bring To Front, and then we selected the star and clicked Send Backward, Send To Back.

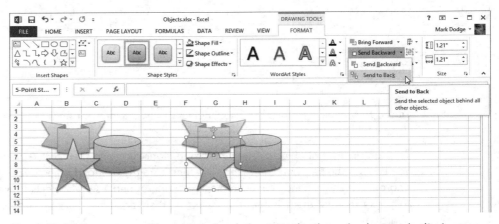

Figure 10-47 You can reposition objects in relation to each other using buttons in the Arrange group.

As you can see in Figure 10-47, the Send Backward button is both a menu and a button—clicking the main part of the button issues the Send Backward command, while clicking its arrow displays a short menu. The same is true for the Bring Forward button. The Bring Forward and Send Backward commands move the object one step at a time through the stack, while the Bring To Front and Send To Back commands move the object all the way forward or back with a single click.

If you need to work with multiple objects on a worksheet, you can gain a little more control using the Selection pane. Click the Selection Pane button in the Arrange group on the Page Layout tab to display a task pane like the one shown in Figure 10-48.

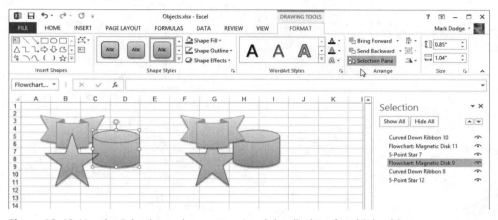

Figure 10-48 Use the Selection task pane to control the display of multiple objects.

You can use the buttons at the top of the Selection task pane to show and hide all objects on the worksheet and to move selected objects up and down in the object stack. You can click the little eyeball icon to the right of an object name to hide that object; click again to unhide it. You can also edit the names of the objects by simply clicking the name once to select it and then clicking it again to edit its text. Note that any hidden objects continue to appear on the list in the Selection pane, which is one of the only ways you can tell they are there.

> **Note**
> The Selection Pane button is also available on the Format tabs under both Drawing Tools and Picture Tools; these tabs appear when you select a picture, a shape, WordArt, a text box, or clip art.

You can change the relationship of objects to the underlying worksheet by using the options in the Size & Properties category in the Format Shape task pane. To do so, right-click an object, click Format Shape, click the Size & Properties (four-headed arrow) icon in the Shape Options pane and click Properties to display the task pane as shown in Figure 10-49.

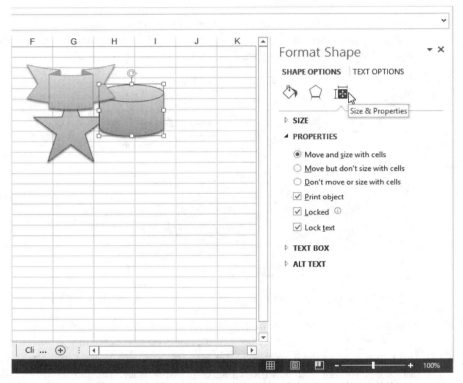

Figure 10-49 You can control how objects respond to changes on the worksheet.

> **Note**
>
> The Format Shape task pane is also available by clicking the dialog box launcher in the Size group on the Drawing Tools Format tab that appears when an object is selected.

The default option is Move And Size With Cells, meaning that if you do anything to change the size or shape of the underlying cells, the object adjusts accordingly. An underlying cell is any cell whose right or bottom border is between the upper-left corner and the lower-right corner of the object. Here are some facts you need to know about these options:

- If you insert columns or rows to the left of an object formatted with the Move And Size With Cells option, the object moves accordingly.

- If you insert columns or rows between the first and last cells underlying an object formatted with the Move And Size With Cells option, the object stretches to accommodate the insertion.

- If you select the Move But Don't Size With Cells option and then insert or delete columns or rows, the object moves but retains its shape and proportion.

- If you select the Don't Move Or Size With Cells option, the object floats above the worksheet and isn't affected by any changes you make to the underlying cells.

- The Print Object check box is ordinarily selected. If you clear it, the selected object isn't printed when you print the worksheet.

> **Note**
>
> In addition to moving and sizing objects with cells, Excel lets you control what happens when you cut, copy, or sort cells to which objects are attached. Click the File tab, click Options, select the Advanced category, and in the Cut, Copy, And Paste group, select or clear the Cut, Copy, And Sort Inserted Objects With Their Parent Cells check box.

The Size category in the Format Shape task pane offers precise control over the height, width, angle of rotation, scale, and cropping of the selected object. You can perform these tasks directly by dragging, but you might find it helpful to display the task pane if you want to resize objects proportionally using the Lock Aspect Ratio option.

Chapter 10

What is alt text?

You'll notice that the Size and Properties categories in the Shape Options pane of the Format Shape task pane include an Alt Text category. If you click it, you'll see Title and Description fields for adding text to the selected object, known in web parlance as *alt text*. (Also notice that in Figure 10-45, the Format Object dialog box includes an Alt Text tab that does the same job for embedded objects.)

When you save an Excel document as a webpage, graphics are converted to their web-based equivalents. In HTML, the language of the web, alternative text is added to images for four reasons. First, alt text appears in the browser while an image is loading, which is helpful for large images over slow connections. Second, when you rest the pointer on an image containing alt text in your browser, the text appears in a tiny pop-up window. Third, alt text is used by text-reading software commonly used by the visually impaired, allowing them to hear a description of the image. And fourth, web search engines index the alt text attached to images along with all the other "visible" text on your website. If you're planning to save your workbook in HTML format, you should add alternative text to all your graphics. For more information see Chapter 27, "Working in the cloud."

Tools to help you position objects on the worksheet

It's great to be able to create cool graphics with Excel, but the free-floating nature of graphic objects sometimes makes it hard to maintain a semblance of order on your worksheet. The Align button, in the Arrange group on the Drawing Tools Format tab, contains commands you can use to straighten up your worksheet, as shown in Figure 10-50.

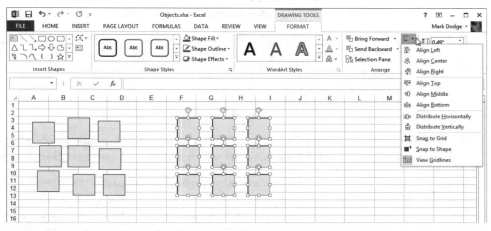

Figure 10-50 Use the Align commands to straighten up objects.

> **Note**
> You can also find the Align button menu in the Arrange group on the Page Layout tab.

Suppose you have a number of objects that you want to be evenly spaced, like the randomly spaced boxes shown on the left in Figure 10-50. You can start by selecting the top row of objects, using the Align Top command to line them up, and then selecting Distribute Horizontally to space them evenly. Then you can use the other alignment and distribution commands to position the rest of the objects to your liking. Here are some key points to remember about using these object-positioning commands:

- **Snap To Grid**   Uses the columns and rows of the worksheet to align objects. Preexisting objects don't line up with the grid when you choose this command, but as soon as you create or drag an object, it snaps to the nearest column and row borders. The Snap To Grid command is a toggle—that is, you click once to turn it on and click again to turn it off.

- **Snap To Shape**   Turns on the Snap To Grid command when you choose it, activating its functionality. It adds to the spreadsheet grid virtual gridlines tangent to the edges of any existing objects, making it easy to align objects to the grid or to one another. If you turn off the Snap To Grid command, the Snap To Shape command is turned off as well. The Snap To Shape command is also a toggle.

- **The Align and Distribute commands**   Arrange the selected objects relative to each other. These buttons are available only when you select two or more objects.

  - **Align Left/Right/Top/Bottom**   Lines up the edges of all selected objects with the corresponding edge of the leftmost, rightmost, top, or bottom object selected.

  - **Align Center**   Lines up the centers of objects along a vertical axis, and finds the average common centerline of all selected objects.

  - **Align Middle**   Lines up the centers of objects along a horizontal axis, and finds the average common centerline of all selected objects.

  - **Distribute Horizontally/Vertically**   Calculates the total amount of space between the selected objects and divides the space as equally as possible among them. The first and last objects (leftmost and rightmost or top and bottom) do not move—all the objects in between are adjusted as necessary.

> **Note**
> You can use the arrow keys on your keyboard to nudge selected objects 1 pixel at a time. If the Snap To Grid command is turned on, pressing an arrow key moves the selected object to the next gridline in that direction.

Protecting objects

Objects are ordinarily prevented from being selected, moved, formatted, or sized when you apply protection to a worksheet (Review tab, Protect Sheet). You can change this before applying sheet protection. To do so, right-click the object, click the Format Shape (or Format Picture) command to display the Format Shape task pane, click the Size & Properties icon (the four-headed arrow), and then select or clear the Locked check box in the Properties category. You can also select the Lock Text check box in the Properties category, which is available only when you select a text-capable object, to protect an object's text contents. Newly drawn objects are assigned Locked status. Remember, to activate worksheet security and protection, you must also click Protect Sheet on the Review tab. For more information about protection, see "Protecting worksheets" in Chapter 6, "How to work a worksheet."

Controlling the display of objects

You might want to suppress the display of objects in a workbook for security reasons or to simply speed up scrolling on an older computer. To do so, click the File tab, click Options, and select the Advanced category. In the Display Options For This Workbook area, the For Objects, Show All option is ordinarily selected. Selecting the Nothing (Hide Objects) option prevents both their display and printing. Note that hiding objects in this way removes all traces of them. If, before hiding all the objects, you first display the Selection pane, you can see a list of the hidden objects on the active sheet. If you want to hide individual objects rather than all of them, use the Selection pane. For more information about the Selection pane, see the discussion surrounding Figure 10-48 earlier in this chapter.

Although you cannot directly modify objects when they are hidden, some actions still change them. If you select anything other than Don't Move Or Size With Cells in the Format Shape task pane, hidden objects still respond to adjustments made to the column width or row height of underlying cells.

More tricks with graphic objects

But wait, there's more! We'll describe a few features that are hard to classify with the other graphics features. You can essentially turn any graphic object into a button by assigning a macro to it. In addition, you can take pictures of your worksheets and use those pictures in Excel workbooks (or even in other programs); they can appear as static bitmaps or dynamic windows that display what is happening in other areas of the workbook or in other workbooks.

Assigning macros to objects

You can attach a macro to any object, which lets you activate the macro by clicking the object. To attach a macro to an object, do the following:

1. Right-click the object, and click the Assign Macro command.

2. When the Assign Macro dialog box appears (shown in Figure 10-51), assign a macro to the object by clicking New to create a new macro using the Visual Basic Editor, by clicking Record to create a new macro by example, or by selecting an existing macro from the list.

For more information about macros, see Chapter 28, "Recording macros."

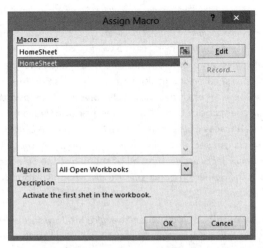

Figure 10-51 Assigning macros to objects turns them into buttons.

INSIDE OUT   Grouped objects and macros

Assigning macros to objects is a cool way to create some crazy-looking "buttons." You can also assign macros to grouped objects or to individual objects that you subsequently group, but you can't do both. For example, say you assign macros to two objects and then group the objects. You can click each object to run each macro, just as if they were ungrouped. But if you assign another macro to the grouped object, the new macro overrides the existing macros.

Creating screenshots or pictures of your worksheets

Excel provides several tools for taking pictures of your worksheets as well as other things on your computer screen. The Screenshot menu on the Insert tab allows you to capture almost anything on your computer screen. And you can use the Copy As Picture command or the Picture, Link, or Camera buttons to take pictures of your worksheets.

Taking screenshots

The Screenshot menu on the Insert tab performs a function that usually requires a separate program for many people (including authors of software books!). With it, you can take a snapshot of anything and everything that appears on your computer screen, with one notable exception: the current Excel window. If you want to take a picture of any part of a workbook, you'll need to open another workbook and take the screenshot from there.

There are two ways to use the Screenshot feature; you can capture any full window with a single click, or you can drag to select a specific area of the screen to capture. Click the Screenshot button on the Insert tab to display the menu shown in Figure 10-52.

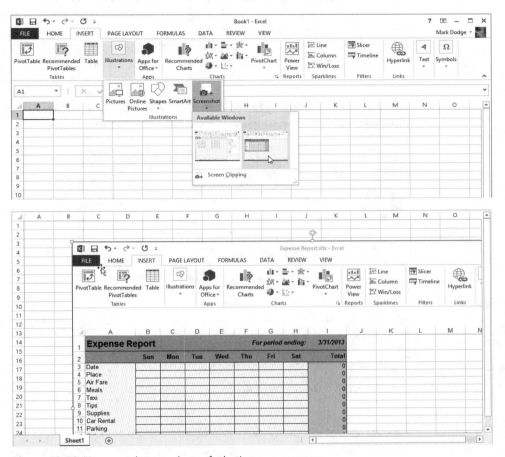

Figure 10-52 You can take snapshots of what's on your screen.

The Available Windows area of the Screenshot menu shows thumbnails of every window that is open on your computer, including applications, webpages, and so on. If one of these windows is what you are after, simply click its thumbnail to immediately insert an image of it onto the active worksheet. If you instead click Screen Clipping, the active instance of Excel minimizes itself and then you can drag to select any part of the screen you want, including any other open Excel windows. As soon as you are done selecting the area to shoot, the image is inserted onto the worksheet, as shown at the bottom of Figure 10-52. The inserted screenshot is considered a picture, and the Picture Tools Format tab appears when you select it.

Copying cells as a picture

The Copy As Picture command is located on the menu that appears when you click the little arrow next to the Copy button on the Home tab. It creates a graphic image of the selected area of the worksheet. After using the Copy As Picture command, you can paste what you copied into any Excel worksheet or into a document from any program that accepts Clipboard images. One reason to use this feature is to insert a worksheet image into another program that does not offer paste options. To avoid pasting an embedded link into the other program, use Copy As Picture to ensure that the image remains static.

Before clicking the Copy As Picture command, select the cells, object, or chart you want to copy. When you click the command, the dialog box in Figure 10-53 appears.

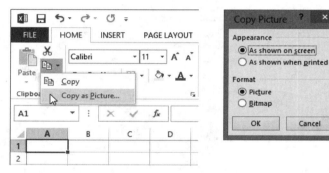

Figure 10-53 Use the Copy As Picture command to create static images of selected areas of your worksheets.

The options in the Copy Picture dialog box are as follows:

- **As Shown On Screen**   Reproduces the selection at the moment you take the picture.

- **As Shown When Printed**   Reproduces the selection according to the settings in the Page Setup dialog box that control the printing of gridlines and row and column headings.

- **Picture**   Copies the picture in a format that can be displayed on monitors with different resolutions. This is useful if the picture will be viewed on different computers.

- **Bitmap**   Copies the picture in a format that looks best when the display resolution is the same as the screen from which it was copied.

After you copy an image to the Clipboard, you can paste the image anywhere you want—into another location on the worksheet, another worksheet, or a document from another program.

Pasting cells as a picture

Where the Screenshot button allows you to take pictures of anything on your computer screen except the current Excel window, there are two Paste options buttons that take pictures of nothing but Excel. The Paste menu on the Home tab offers two picture options. The Linked Picture button creates a *linked image* (essentially using the As Shown When Printed option instead of the As Shown On Screen option).

Figure 10-54 shows the Northwind Sales Summary worksheet on the left. We selected the range F3:F16, pressed Ctrl+C to copy, activated Book2, selected cell D3, and then clicked the Linked Picture button on the Home tab's Paste menu. Excel inserts the picture of the worksheet cells as shown on the right in Figure 10-54.

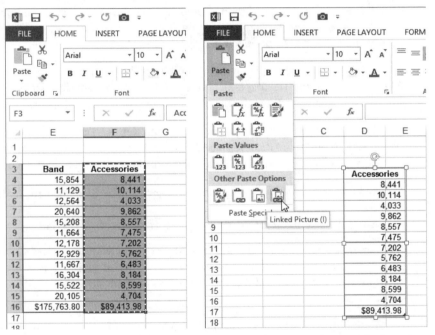

Figure 10-54 Use the Linked Picture button to create dynamic images of selected areas of your worksheets.

The image is dynamically linked to the cells originally selected, not to their contents. As a result, the pasted image changes dynamically whenever the contents of the original cells change. This way, you can create "activity monitors" on a summary sheet, showing you the contents of remote cells in real time.

> **Note**
>
> **Any graphic objects that happen to be within or overlapping the selected range also are displayed in the linked picture.**

When you select the linked picture, the formula bar displays a reference formula, as shown in Figure 10-54. After you create the picture, you can edit the formula and the picture changes accordingly. You can even change the references and link to a different worksheet or workbook. The link between the source and destination documents has another distinctive and useful characteristic. Suppose you close the Northwind Sales worksheet shown on the left in Figure 10-54. If you then double-click the embedded image in Book2, Northwind Sales opens automatically, with the pictured range selected. You can use it in this way to quickly create "buttons" for opening supporting workbooks.

After you paste the linked picture, you can change its size and proportions by dragging its selection handles and treating it just like any other graphic object. Changes in shape, size, and formatting do not affect the dynamic updating of the data displayed in the picture.

The Picture button on the Home tab's Paste menu does essentially the same thing as the Linked Picture button, minus the linking formula, so you can't change it after you paste, and there is no connection to the source if you paste it into a different document.

For more information about linking formulas, see "Formula fundamentals" in Chapter 12.

Creating linked images of cells using the Camera button

The Camera button offers a slightly faster way of doing what the Linked Picture button does. With the Camera button, the cells are linked, pasted as shown on screen (rather than as shown when printed), and the image changes dynamically if the contents of the original cells change.

When using the Linked Picture button, you select the destination before you click; when using the Camera button, you select the destination after you click. If you select the same range (F3:F16) as we did in the worksheet shown in Figure 10-54, click the Camera button, and the pointer changes from a plus sign to crosshairs. Then just click where you want the upper-left corner of the picture to appear, and Excel embeds the picture just as shown on the right in Figure 10-54. The Camera button represents a one-less-click advantage over the equivalent procedure using the Linked Picture button, which might be significant if you have a lot of repetitive work to do.

> ## Note
>
> The Camera button is not normally available on any tab or toolbar. You can add it to the ribbon if you create a custom group, but the quickest and easiest way to begin using the Camera button is to add it to the Quick Access Toolbar, as shown in Figure 10-55. To do so, click the File tab, Options, Quick Access Toolbar. In the Choose Commands From drop-down list, select Commands Not In The Ribbon, select Camera in the list, and then click the Add button.
>
>
>
> **Figure 10-55** Add the Camera button to the Quick Access Toolbar to quickly create dynamically linked worksheet images.

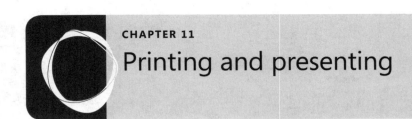

M ICROSOFT EXCEL makes it easy for you to produce polished, professional-looking reports. In this chapter, we explain how to define the layout of your printed pages, control page breaks, and preview your pages for printing.

Controlling the appearance of your pages

The options used most often to affect the appearance of your printed pages are available on the Page Layout tab on the ribbon, shown in Figure 11-1. This is the central control panel for setting up paper sizes, margins, and page orientation, as well as for working with page breaks, print areas, and other printing options. For even more control over the page layout, click the dialog box launcher in the Page Setup group on the Page Layout tab to display the Page Setup dialog box, also shown in Figure 11-1.

The Print category of the File tab (also known as the Backstage view) now includes the most-often-used options as well, and it provides some visual feedback about what all these things actually do. A print preview is displayed on the right side of the screen and dynamically displays the settings you select from the options on the left side. Click the File tab, and then click Print to display a screen similar to the one shown in Figure 11-2.

Setting page options

The settings you use most frequently are duplicated in several places. Most of what you need is on the Page Layout tab of the ribbon, in the Print category on the File tab, and, of course, in the Page Setup dialog box. These settings control page orientation, scaling, paper size, print quality, and page numbering.

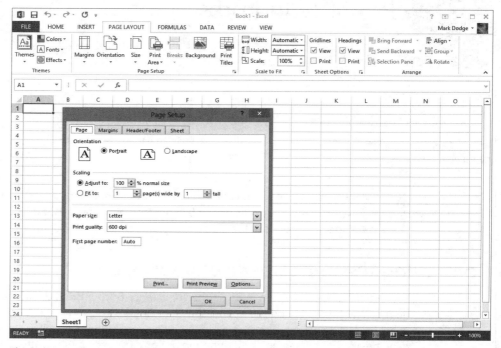

Figure 11-1 The Page Layout tab on the ribbon and the Page Setup dialog box control most printing options.

Printing wide or tall

The Orientation button on the Page Layout tab offers two options: Portrait and Landscape. These options determine whether Excel prints your worksheet vertically (Portrait) or horizontally (Landscape). Portrait, the default setting, offers more room for rows but less room for columns. Select Landscape if you have more columns but fewer rows on each page. You can also find these options on the Page tab in the Page Setup dialog box and in the Print category on the File tab.

Specifying paper size and print quality

The Size button on the Page Layout tab includes options for nearly every size of paper available (not just the sizes supported by your printer). You can additionally control the dimensions of your printout by clicking the Size button and then clicking More Paper Sizes (or clicking the dialog box launcher in the Page Setup group) to display the Page tab in the Page Setup dialog box. The same options are duplicated in the Print category on the File tab.

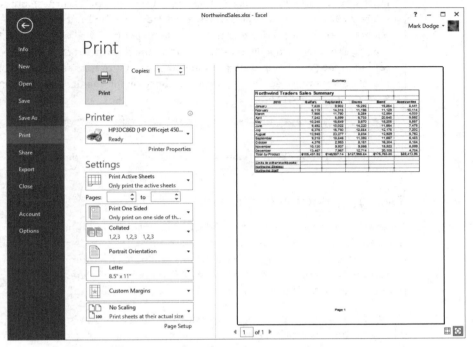

Figure 11-2 Click the File tab, and then click Print to display the most popular printing options, as well as Print Preview, in Backstage view.

On the Page tab of the Page Setup dialog box shown in Figure 11-1, the Print Quality drop-down list shows the quality options available for your printer. A laser printer, for example, might offer print-quality settings of 600 dots per inch (dpi), 300 dpi, and 150 dpi. Higher dpi settings look better, but they cause a page to take longer to print. If the Print Quality drop-down list is not available, you might be able to adjust these settings—and more—using your printer driver's dialog box, which you can access by clicking the Options button on the Page tab in the Page Setup dialog box. You can also access the printer driver dialog box by clicking Printer Properties in the Print category on the File tab.

Chapter 11

AutoLetter/A4 paper resizing

Excel includes help for folks who routinely share work across international borders. In much of the world, the standard paper size is Letter (8.5 by 11 inches), but A4 paper (210 by 297 millimeters) is also widely used. Now you can print worksheets set for A4 paper on printers loaded with standard Letter paper (and vice versa), and Excel adjusts the page setup accordingly. Excel does this on the fly, without changing the page size setting in the Page Setup dialog box. If you want to turn this feature off, click the File tab, click Options, select the Advanced category, and in the General group clear the Scale Content For A4 Or 8.5 × 11" Paper Sizes check box.

For more information about printer drivers, see "Setting printer driver options" later in this chapter.

Setting a reduction (scaling) ratio

There are several ways to specify a reduction or enlargement ratio for your printouts. Using the Scale To Fit group on the Page Layout tab, you can override the default size of your printouts in one of two ways: by specifying a scaling factor (from 10 percent through 400 percent) or by fitting the printout to a specified number of pages. Excel always scales in both the horizontal and vertical dimensions.

The Width and Height controls on the Page Layout tab, shown in Figure 11-1, normally display Automatic, which means the worksheet prints at full size on as many pages as necessary. In these drop-down lists, select a number of pages to constrain the printout. For example, choosing 2 Pages in the Width list (and leaving Height set to Automatic) scales the print area of the worksheet so that it spans two pages at its widest point, filling as many pages in length as necessary. Choosing 2 Pages in the Height list (and leaving Width set to Automatic) scales the print area of the worksheet so that it is only two pages long, filling as many pages in width as necessary.

The Fit To options in the Page Setup dialog box give you more precise control over scaling. These mirror the Height and Width controls on the Page Layout tab. To return to a full-size printout, select the Adjust To option and type **100** in the % Normal Size box.

You can also use the Scaling options in the File tab's Print category. You can use the Print category, shown in Figure 11-3, to specify scaling and other options on the fly just before you send the worksheet to the printer.

Figure 11-3 Click the File tab, click Print, and use the Scaling options to quickly tailor your printouts.

Setting the first page number

If you want to control the numbering of pages in your printout's header or footer—an essential tool when printing multipage worksheets—use the First Page Number box on the Page tab in the Page Setup dialog box. You can type any starting number, including 0 or negative numbers. By default, this option is set to Auto.

Working in Page Layout view

Page Layout view is similar to the large thumbnail representation of the worksheet that appears in the Print category on the File tab; you can see what a printout will look like. The difference is, not only can you see the page as it will print, but Excel is fully functional in Page Layout view, so you can make changes and see the results immediately. Click the Page Layout button on the View tab, shown in Figure 11-4. This might become your preferred working environment, if you don't mind the slight slowdown in performance that comes with a more graphically intensive interface.

Chapter 11

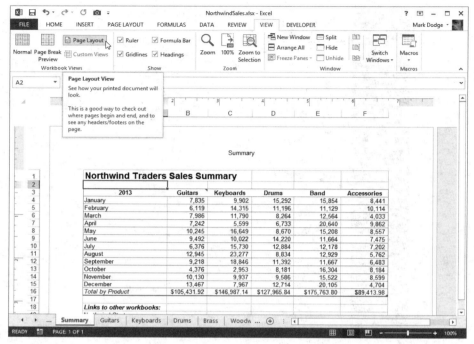

Figure 11-4 Page Layout view is not just a preview; it's a fully functional working environment.

In Page Layout view, you can do the following:

- Drag the edge between the shaded and white areas on the rulers to adjust margins.

- Drag lines between row and column headers to adjust row height and column width.

- Refer to the rulers to see the actual dimensions of your data relative to the printed page.

- Click the Page Layout tab and change settings in the Page Setup group to see the changes immediately reflected on your screen.

- Click and type directly in headers and footers.

- Click other tabs on the ribbon to zoom, apply formatting, and add formulas, graphics, charts, and other elements. Note, however, that Page Layout view can be set separately on each sheet, so switching to another sheet might also switch you back to Normal view.

In fact, we couldn't find anything you can't do in Page Layout view. Page Layout view is applied per worksheet; you can specify a different view for each open worksheet, and the settings are saved with the workbook.

> **Note**
>
> You can also use the three tiny buttons at the bottom of the screen next to the Zoom slider (which you can see in the lower-right corner in Figure 11-4) to change the view. The first button activates Normal view, the second activates Page Layout view, and the third activates Page Break Preview. For more about Page Break Preview, see "Adjusting page breaks" later in this chapter.

Setting margins

You can adjust the margins of your printouts to allow the maximum amount of data to fit on a page, to customize the amount of space available for headers and footers, or to accommodate special requirements, such as three-hole-punched paper and company logos. The Margins button on the Page Layout tab, shown in Figure 11-5, provides three settings that should meet most of your needs: Normal, Wide, and Narrow. These settings refer to the size of the margins, not the size of the printed area. For example, to fit more data on a page, use the Narrow setting. Note that when you apply your own margin settings, the Last Custom Setting command appears as the first item on the Margins menu, as Figure 11-5 shows. This command does not appear unless you specify your own margin settings. These commands also appear in the Print category on the File tab.

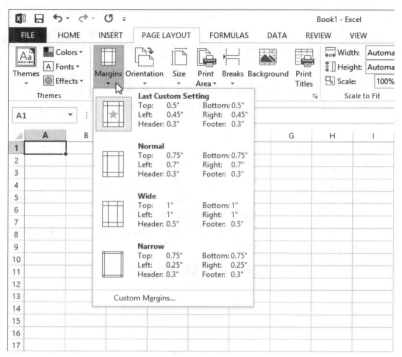

Figure 11-5 Click the Margins button on the Page Layout tab to select a basic margin setting.

The Margins tab in the Page Setup dialog box offers precise control over the top, bottom, left, and right margins of your printed worksheets. You can display the Margins tab, shown in Figure 11-6, by clicking the Margins button and then clicking Custom Margins.

When you click in any of the text boxes on the Margins tab, the corresponding margin line is highlighted in the sample page in the middle of the dialog box, showing you where the selected margin will appear.

If you want a header or footer to appear on each page, the top and bottom margins need to be large enough to accommodate them. For more information about setting up a header and footer, see "Creating a header and footer" next.

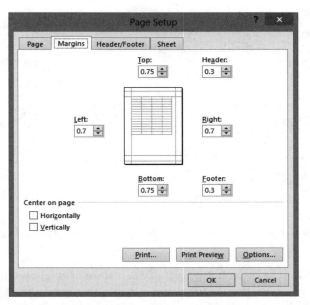

Figure 11-6 You can specify precise margin settings on the Margins tab in the Page Setup dialog box.

Centering your work on the page

Excel aligns worksheets to the upper-left corner of the printed page by default. If you want Excel to center your printout on the page vertically, horizontally, or both, use the Center On Page check boxes on the Margins tab in the Page Setup dialog box, shown in Figure 11-6.

Creating a header and footer

The easiest way to create headers and footers is to click the Insert tab, and then, in the Text group, click Header & Footer. This simultaneously displays the Header & Footer Tools Design tab, switches the worksheet to Page Layout view, and activates the header for editing, as shown in Figure 11-7.

Chapter 11

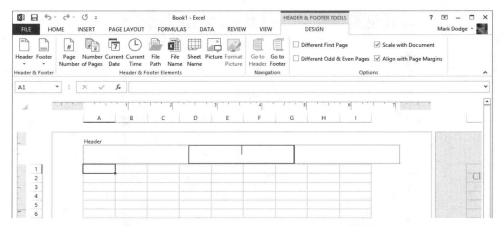

Figure 11-7 Click the Header & Footer button on the Insert tab to display the Header & Footer Tools Design tab.

Both the Header and Footer areas in Page Layout view consist of edit boxes in three sections—left, center, and right—that are formatted with the corresponding justification (that is, the contents of the box on the right are right-justified). Use these edit boxes to insert and format headers and footers using buttons on the Header & Footer Tools Design tab:

- **Header & Footer group**   These buttons display menus of predesigned headers and footers, shown as they appear when printed. For example, if you click Page 1 Of ? on the Header menu, the proper code is inserted in the header. If you then click the inserted information in the header, you can see the underlying code—much like a formula in a cell—that produces the result: *Page &[Page] of &[Pages]*. You don't really need to know these codes; buttons are available to create them for you.

- **Page Number**   Inserts the page number in the selected section.

- **Number Of Pages**   Inserts the total number of pages in the selected section; typically used in conjunction with the page number in a "Page X of Y" construction.

- **Current Date**   Inserts the date of printing.

- **Current Time**   Inserts the time of printing.

- **File Path**   Inserts the folder path and file name of the workbook.

- **File Name**   Inserts only the file name of the current workbook.

- **Sheet Name**   Inserts the name of the current worksheet.

- **Picture**   Displays the Insert Picture dialog box. (See "Adding pictures to headers and footers" later in this chapter.)

- **Format Picture**   Displays the Format Picture dialog box, which you use to adjust the settings of an inserted picture.

- **Navigation group**   The Go To Header and Go To Footer buttons are simply quick ways to jump between the corresponding edit boxes at the top and bottom of the page.

- **Different First Page**   Specifies a different header and footer for the first page only.

- **Different Odd & Even Pages**   Specifies different headers and footers for even and odd pages; typically used to create balanced two-page spreads when you print a worksheet double-sided.

- **Scale With Document**   Selected by default; clear this check box if you want headers and footers to remain unchanged even if you enlarge or shrink the rest of the document.

- **Align With Page Margins**   Selected by default; clear this check box if you want the headers and footers to remain fixed, unaffected by changes to the margins.

> **Note**
> By default, Excel prints footers .3 inch from the bottom edge and headers .3 inch from the top edge, but you can change this on the Margins tab in the Page Setup dialog box.

Excel uses codes to represent dynamic data in your headers and footers, such as the current time represented by *&[Time]*. Fortunately, you don't have to learn these codes to create headers and footers. Click the edit box where you want the information to appear, and then click the appropriate buttons to add the information to your header or footer. Here are some things to remember about editing headers and footers:

- To include text in a header or footer, just click a text box and start typing. You need to add spaces between text and inserted code elements, as well as between adjacent code elements.

- An ampersand (&) always precedes a code element, so never insert anything between the ampersand and its code. To include an actual ampersand in your header or footer, type two ampersands.

Chapter 11

- To apply formatting, use the small, ghostly toolbar that appears when you select text in an edit box. Or, because the worksheet is in Page Layout view, you can click the Home tab and use the formatting tools in the Font group as well as the editing tools in the Clipboard group.

- As in cells, if you enter more information in any of the header or footer edit boxes than can be displayed, the information spills over into adjacent edit boxes. Yes, you can enter too much data, actually causing text to overlap, but you'll see it immediately because you are working in Page Layout view.

- To remove header or footer information, click the None option at the top of the Header or Footer button menu, or simply delete the contents of the corresponding edit boxes in Page Layout view.

Using the header/footer controls

The Page Setup dialog box contains the old-school interface for Excel's header and footer features. It offers all the same controls as are available on the ribbon's Header & Footer Tools Design tab (which appears only when a header or footer is active). Click the Page Layout tab, click the dialog box launcher in the Page Setup group to display the Page Setup dialog box, and then click the Header/Footer tab, as shown in Figure 11-8.

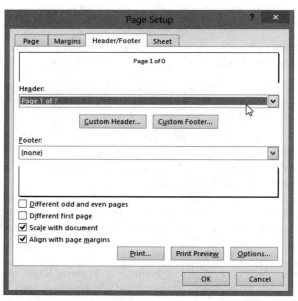

Figure 11-8 The Header/Footer tab contains controls similar to those on the Header & Footer Tools Design tab.

The drop-down lists that appear immediately under the words Header and Footer offer the same lists of predefined options as the eponymous buttons on the Header & Footer Tools Design tab. And the check-box options in the dialog box mirror the ones in the Options group on the tab. The three buttons at the bottom of the dialog box are really the only things that offer a little added value here. The Print button takes you directly to the Print screen in Backstage view, and the Print Preview button actually takes you to the same place, because Print Preview now appears in Backstage view as well. The Options button takes you directly to your printer's Properties dialog box. Click the Custom Header button to display a dialog box similar to the one shown in Figure 11-9.

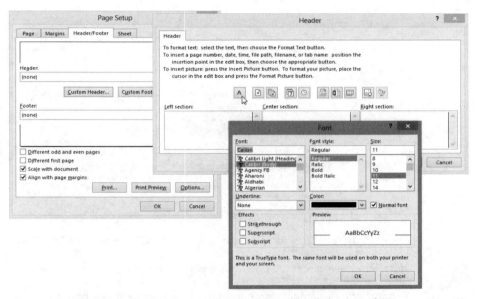

Figure 11-9 The Custom Header button displays the Header dialog box; the Format Text (A) button displays the Font dialog box.

The Header (and identical Footer) dialog box does almost all the things that the Header & Footer Tools Design tab does. The only difference here is the addition of the Format Text button (the first button on the left), which displays the Font dialog box shown in Figure 11-9.

Adding pictures to headers and footers

You can add pictures to custom headers and footers by using the Picture and Format Picture buttons on the Header & Footer Tools Design tab that appears when a header is active (as shown in Figure 11-7). For example, you can insert pictures to add company logos or banners to your documents. Click the Picture button to access the Insert Picture dialog box (a version of the standard Open dialog box), which you use to locate the picture you want to insert. When you insert the picture, Excel includes the code *&[Picture]*, and the image is displayed in the edit box. (Unlike with other header and footer codes, you can't just type this code—you have to use the Picture button.)

After you insert a picture, click the Format Picture button to specify the size, brightness, and contrast of the picture and to rotate, scale, or crop the picture. (You can't directly manipulate header or footer pictures—you must use the Format Picture button.) It might take some trial and error to obtain the result you want, adjusting the size of the picture as well as the top or bottom margins to accommodate it. Figure 11-10 shows a sample of a picture used in a header, with the worksheet displayed in Page Layout view.

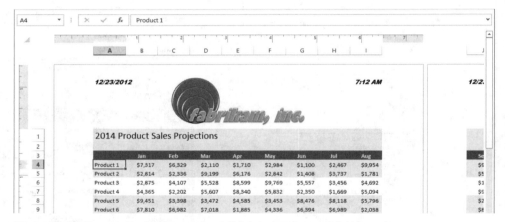

Figure 11-10 You can insert pictures from disk into headers and footers.

You'll find the Fabrikam.xlsx file with the other examples on the companion website.

To arrive at the example shown in Figure 11-10, we did the following:

- In the left section, we added the date and changed the font to 10-point, italic Arial Black.

- In the center section, we inserted a picture; then we clicked Format Picture and reduced its size.

- In the right section, we added the time and changed the font to 10-point, italic Arial Black.

- We clicked the Page Layout tab and clicked the dialog box launcher button in the Page Setup group to display the Page Setup dialog box.

- We selected both the Vertically and Horizontally check boxes below Center On Page on the Margins tab in the Page Setup dialog box.

- We dragged the top margin down using the side ruler in Page Layout view enough to accommodate the graphic.

Setting worksheet options

Clicking the dialog box launcher in the Page Setup group on the Page Layout tab displays the Page Setup dialog box. Click the Sheet tab, shown in Figure 11-11, to access settings specific to the active worksheet. You can specify different worksheet options for each worksheet in a workbook. (You can also display the Sheet tab by clicking the Print Titles button on the Page Layout tab.)

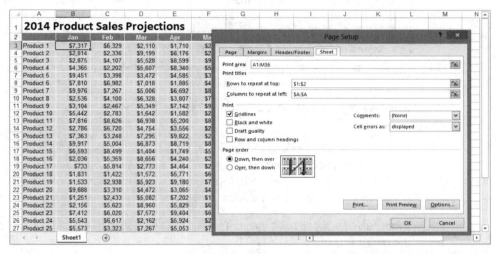

Figure 11-11 The Sheet tab in the Page Setup dialog box stores the print area and print titles data.

You'll find the 2014Projections.xlsx file with the other examples on the companion website.

Specifying the area to be printed

If you do not specify an area to print, Excel prints the entire active area of the selected worksheet or worksheets. If you don't want to print the entire worksheet, you can specify an area to print by using the Print Area button on the Page Layout tab. First, select the range or ranges you want to print, click Print Area on the Page Layout tab, and then click Set Print Area. To clear this setting, click the Print Area button and click Clear Print Area. You can specify a print area setting for each worksheet, and the settings are saved with the workbook.

The print area settings are stored in the first box on the Sheet tab in the Page Setup dialog box, which you can also use to set or edit the print area. To do so, click the Print Titles button on the Page Layout tab (a quick way to display the Page Setup dialog box). Click in the Print Area box, and then drag to select the cells on the worksheet you want to include. When you do this, the dialog box collapses so that you can see more of the worksheet, and Excel inserts the cell range reference of the area you select in the Print Area box, as shown in Figure 11-11. You can select multiple nonadjacent cell ranges by selecting a range, typing a comma, and then selecting the next range. Each range you select prints on a separate page.

> **Note**
>
> To remove a print area definition, you can return to the Page Setup dialog box and delete the cell references. You can also use the Define Name dialog box to do this by pressing Ctrl+F3 and deleting the name Print_Area. For more information, see "Naming cells and cell ranges" in Chapter 12, "Building formulas."

Specifying rows and columns to print on every page

On most worksheets, the column and row labels that identify your data appear in only the first couple of columns and top few rows. When Excel breaks up a large report into pages, those important column and row labels might appear only on the first page of the printout. You use the Print Titles feature to force Excel to print the contents of one or more columns, one or more rows, or a combination of columns and rows on every page of a report.

Suppose you want to print the contents of column A and rows 1 and 2 on all the pages of the report shown in Figure 11-11:

1. Click the Print Titles button on the Page Layout tab to display the Page Setup dialog box, open to the Sheet tab.

2. Click in the Rows To Repeat At Top text box, and then select the headings for the first two rows. (To select multiple contiguous row headings, drag through them.)

3. Click in the Columns To Repeat At Left text box, and then select the column A heading (or any cell in column A).

4. Click OK.

Figure 11-12 shows the result in Page Layout view. Notice that the column containing the product numbers appears on both pages displayed in Page Layout view. If you did not use print titles, the first column on the second page of the printout would display the August totals column instead of the product numbers. You can specify separate print titles for each worksheet in your workbook. Excel remembers the titles for each worksheet.

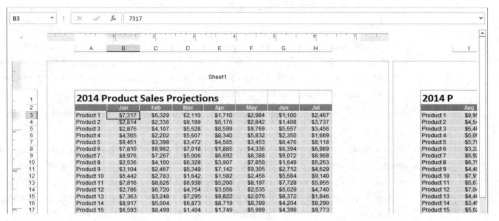

Figure 11-12 We defined print titles and used Page Layout view to see the results.

> **Note**
>
> To remove your print title definitions, you can return to the Page Setup dialog box and delete the cell references. You can also use the Define Name dialog box to do this by pressing Ctrl+F3 and deleting the name Print_Titles. For more information, see "Naming cells and cell ranges" in Chapter 12.

Printing gridlines and headings

By default, Excel does not print gridlines or row and column headings, regardless of whether they are displayed on your worksheet. If you want to print gridlines or headings, select the corresponding Print check box in the Sheet Options group on the Page Layout tab. You can also select the Gridlines or Row And Column Headings check box on the Sheet tab in the Page Setup dialog box (which you can see in Figure 11-11).

Printing comments and errors

Comments are annotations you create by clicking New Comment on the Review tab on the ribbon. To be sure the comments in your worksheet are included with your printout, select one of the Comments options on the Sheet tab in the Page Setup dialog box (which is shown in Figure 11-11). If you select At End Of Sheet from the drop-down list, Excel adds a page to the end of the printout and prints all your notes together, starting on that page. If you select As Displayed On Sheet, Excel prints the comments as pop-up windows wherever they are located on a worksheet. The latter option might cause the comments to obscure worksheet data.

> **Note**
> You can display all comments on the worksheet by clicking the Show All Comments button on the Review tab on the ribbon. This gives you an idea of how the worksheet will look when printed if you select the As Displayed On Sheet option in the Comments drop-down list on the Sheet tab of the Page Setup dialog box.

The drop-down list cryptically labeled Cell Errors As on the Sheet tab in the Page Setup dialog box gives you options for how error codes displayed on the worksheet should be printed. Ordinarily, error codes such as #NAME? are printed just as they appear on your screen, but you can change this so that cells containing error codes print as blank cells or with a double hyphen (--) or #NA displayed instead of the error code.

For more about creating comments, see "Adding comments to cells" in Chapter 8, "Worksheet editing techniques." For more about error codes, see "Understanding error values" in Chapter 12.

Printing drafts

If your printer offers a draft-quality mode, you can obtain a quicker, though less attractive, printout by selecting the Draft Quality check box on the Sheet tab in the Page Setup dialog box. This option has no effect if your printer has no draft-quality mode.

Translating screen colors to black and white

If you assigned colors and patterns to your worksheet, but you want to see what it will look like when it's printed on a black-and-white printer, select the Black And White check box on the Sheet tab in the Page Setup dialog box, which tells Excel to use only black and white when printing and previewing. You can see the results by clicking the Print Preview button in the Page Setup dialog box, which is just a handy way of getting to the Print screen in Backstage view—the same place you go by clicking the File tab on the ribbon and clicking Print.

Setting the printing order of large print ranges

When you print a large report, Excel breaks the report into page-size sections based on the current margin and page-size settings. If the print range is both too wide and too deep to fit on a single page, Excel ordinarily works in "down and then over" order. For example, suppose your print range measures 120 rows by 20 columns and that Excel can fit 40 rows and 10 columns on a page. Excel prints the first 40 rows and first 10 columns on page 1, the second 40 rows and first 10 columns on page 2, and so on, until it prints all the rows and starts at the top of the next 10 columns. If you prefer to have Excel print each horizontal chunk before moving to the next vertical chunk, select the Over, Then Down option on the Sheet tab in the Page Setup dialog box.

Controlling what and where to print

Click the File tab, and then click Print to display the Print screen in Backstage view, shown in Figure 11-13. Click the big Print button at the top of the screen to send the current worksheet immediately to the printer. But there are other things you might want to do first.

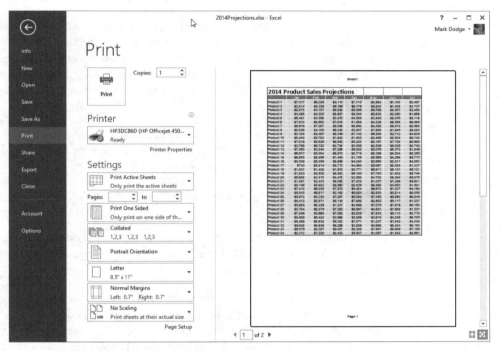

Figure 11-13 Click the File tab on the ribbon, and then click Print to tell Excel what you want to print and how many copies you want.

Setting printer driver options

Occasionally while working in Excel, you might need to set options that only your printer driver provides. For example, you might need to switch from automatic to manual paper feed or from one paper tray to another. You can do this by clicking either the Printer Properties link below the Printer button on the File tab's Print screen (which you can see in Figure 11-13) or the Options button in the Page Setup dialog box (shown in Figure 11-11) to open the Properties dialog box for the selected printer.

The File tab's Print screen contains these options for specifying what, where, and how you want Excel to print. Each large rectangle you see in Figure 11-13 is actually a menu, and collectively the following options are represented:

- **Print**   Click the big Print button when you're ready to send your job to the printer.

- **Copies**   Enter the number of copies you want. You can specify up to 32,767 copies.

- **Printer**   Displays the name of your default printer. To use a different printer, click to display a list of available printers, and then select the printer you want to use.

- **Sheet**   The default Print Active Sheets option prints the active worksheet (or a set of grouped worksheets). Print Entire Workbook, predictably, prints all the sheets in the workbook, and Print Selection prints only the selected cells. If you have defined a print area on any or all of the specified worksheets, Excel prints only those ranges. For more information about selecting a group of worksheets, see "Editing multiple worksheets" in Chapter 8.

- **Ignore Print Area**   If you defined print areas on the worksheet or worksheets specified for printing, select this item at the bottom of the Print Sheets menu box to disregard them. It is a toggle; click it again to turn it off.

- **Pages**   Specify an exact page or range of pages to print in the active worksheet or worksheets.

- **Print One Sided**   If your printer supports double-sided printing, select Print One Sided or one of two Print On Both Sides options: Flip Pages On The Long Edge, or Flip Pages On The Short Edge.

- **Collated**   If your worksheet is more than one page long and you plan to print multiple copies, Excel collates the copies for you. For example, instead of printing five copies of page 1 followed by five copies of page 2, Excel prints page 1 and page 2 together, prints the next set, and so on. Collated copies are more convenient but might take longer to print. Or you can select Uncollated.

- **Orientation**   Select Portrait or Landscape.

- **Page Size**   Select the size of the paper you're using. Letter 8½ x 11in is the default. Click More Paper Sizes to display the Page Setup dialog box.

- **Margins**   Select Normal, Wide, or Narrow, or select Last Custom Setting, which offers the last margin settings you specified. Click Custom Margins to display the Page Setup dialog box.

- **Scaling**   Shrink your worksheet to fit your output paper. Select Fit Sheet On One Page, Fit All Columns On One Page, Fit All Rows On One Page, or the default No Scaling. For more precise control, click Custom Scaling Options to display the Page Setup dialog box.

Printing immediately

Click the Quick Print button on the Quick Access Toolbar to print the active sheet immediately using the current settings. If the Quick Print button is not visible, click the arrow to the right of the Quick Access Toolbar to display the Customize Quick Access Toolbar menu, and click Quick Print to add the button to the toolbar.

For more information, see "Using the Quick Access Toolbar" in Chapter 2, "Explore Excel fundamentals."

Adjusting page breaks

Breaking pages across printed sheets of paper is often challenging using word-processing programs, and it can be even more challenging when planning the printing strategy for large spreadsheet models. Excel helps you adjust the positions of page breaks by offering a couple of approaches: the Breaks button on the Page Layout tab on the ribbon, and the Page Break Preview button on the View tab.

Using Page Break Preview

Clicking the Page Break Preview button results in a view of your worksheet like the one shown in Figure 11-14. You can move page breaks by dragging them. You can even edit your worksheet while in Page Break Preview mode. Page Break Preview mode zooms out to give you a bird's-eye view of the entire worksheet, but you can use the Zoom controls in the lower-right corner of the screen to adjust the zoom percentage.

Using Page Break Preview lets you see both the positions of your page breaks and the page numbers Excel will use when you print. Default page breaks—the ones Excel proposes to use if you don't intervene—appear as heavy dashed lines. If you're not happy with the position of a default break, drag the line where you want it. Your page break then becomes a manual page break and appears as a solid line. To exit Page Break Preview, click either the Normal button or the Page Layout button on the View tab.

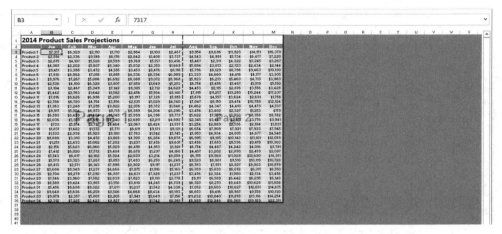

Figure 11-14 Page Break Preview shows default page breaks with heavy dashed lines that you can reposition by dragging them.

> **Note**
>
> After you apply any page setup options, Excel displays dashed lines in Normal view wherever a page break will occur. If you'd rather not see these lines, click the File tab, click Options, select the Advanced category, and in the Display Options For This Worksheet section clear the Show Page Breaks check box. Note that you cannot change this option while Page Break Preview is active.

If you attempt to extend the dimensions of a page beyond the maximum width or depth specified for the current page setup, Excel scales the worksheet to make it fit. You can see the adjusted Scale percentage value in the Scale To Fit group on the Page Layout tab on the ribbon.

If, after trying different page breaks, you want to revert to the automatic page breaks (heavy dashed lines), drag the manual page breaks (solid lines) to the left past the row headers or up past the column headers. After you remove all manual page breaks, the automatic breaks reappear in their default locations.

Inserting and removing manual page breaks

Spreadsheet pagination can be problematic, given that rows and columns of numbers often don't fit into the 8.5-by-11-inch world of printing. This is why Excel provides yet another method you can use to manually adjust page breaks. To add a page break in Normal view, select any cell in the row directly beneath or in the column directly to the right of where you want the break to occur, click the Breaks button on the Page Layout tab, and then click Insert Page Break. Excel applies page breaks both horizontally and vertically unless the selected cell is in the first row or column. To remove a break, select a cell in the row below a horizontal break or in the column to the right of a vertical break, click the Breaks button, and then click either Remove Page Break or Reset All Page Breaks.

TROUBLESHOOTING

My manual page breaks don't work very well

Selecting the Fit To option on the Page tab of the Page Setup dialog box can cause Excel to override manual page breaks. (Click the dialog box launcher button in the Page Setup group on the Page Layout tab to display the Page Setup dialog box.) The Fit To controls apply reduction sufficient to fit the entire print area onto a specific number of pages. To derail this override, switch to the Adjust To option. This sets the worksheet to print according to your manual page breaks.

If you prefer the compressed Fit To "look" but still want to control page breaks, you can define the print area by using multiple nonadjacent ranges—one range per page. Excel automatically prints each nonadjacent range as a separate page. Select the first range you want to print, hold down Ctrl, and select the next range. Select as many ranges (pages) as you want. Click the Print Area button on the Page Layout tab, and then click Set Print Area.

Using Print Preview

The Print Preview feature gives you a glimpse of your worksheets the way they will look on paper. To access Print Preview, use one of the following methods:

- Click the File tab, Print.

- Click the Print Preview button in the Page Setup dialog box.

Print Preview is incorporated into Backstage view (also known as the File tab). Clicking the File tab and then clicking Print not only displays most of the available printing controls, but also includes the Print Preview window, as shown in Figure 11-15.

Chapter 11

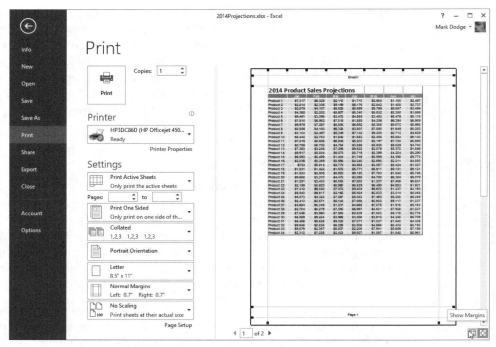

Figure 11-15 Click the Show Margins button to display lines and handles you can use to adjust margins and column widths.

> **Note**
>
> Although Page Layout view is generally better for helping you visualize your printed pages, it still displays your entire worksheet. Even if you specify smaller areas to print by using the Print Area button or the equivalent settings in the Page Setup dialog box, Page Layout view displays everything, and it indicates your defined print areas using dotted lines. Print Preview displays only what will be printed and nothing more, including page breaks, margins, and formatting.

If you're not satisfied with the appearance of your worksheet, you can access some helpful page layout settings without leaving the Print screen:

- The Show Margins button in the lower-right corner of the screen displays lines and handles you can use to change the margins and column widths, as shown in Figure 11-15.

- You can move forward or backward a page at a time by clicking the Next Page and Previous Page buttons (the arrows adjacent to the page number edit box at the bottom of the screen).

- Click the Zoom To Page button to display the page at the same size you see in Normal view, as shown in Figure 11-16. Click Zoom To Page again to return to the normal Print Preview whole-page view.

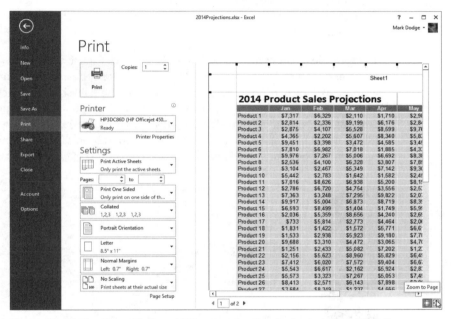

Figure 11-16 The Zoom To Page button toggles the display between the full-page preview and normal size.

After you click the Show Margins button, you can adjust a margin by dragging one of the dotted lines. To adjust a column's width, drag the column handle. (The Show Margins button is a toggle—click it again to turn it off.) You can change printing options in the Settings area to the left of the Print Preview display, and the results appear in the preview area.

Creating portable documents

A portable document file format lets you create a representation of "electronic paper" that displays your data on the screen as it would look when printed. One of the benefits of portable document formats is that you can share documents you do not want others to modify. Both the Microsoft XPS (XML Paper Specification) format and Adobe PDF (Portable Document Format) files require free software for viewing, and they promise cross-platform

Chapter 11

consistency and format compatibility regardless of the software and fonts available on your computer.

The two available portable document formats, PDF and XPS, provide portability, allow you to search a file's content, and let you preview the files in applications that support them, such as Windows Internet Explorer and Adobe Reader. Worksheets you save in XPS format are also viewable using a stand-alone XPS viewer, which might be necessary, depending upon the version of Windows you are using. Adobe's PDF, the format that gave birth (and an acronym) to the term "portable document format," has the advantage of being ubiquitous.

To save a file in either format, click the File tab, click Export, click Create PDF/XPS Document, and then click the Create PDF/XPS button that appears on the right side of the window, as shown in Figure 11-17. When you do, the Publish As PDF Or XPS dialog box appears, displaying two self-explanatory Optimize For options—Standard and Minimum Size—at the bottom of the dialog box, as shown in Figure 11-18. The Open File After Publishing check box causes the resulting file to open as soon as Excel finishes saving it; the file opens in Adobe Reader (PDF) or in your Web browser (XPS).

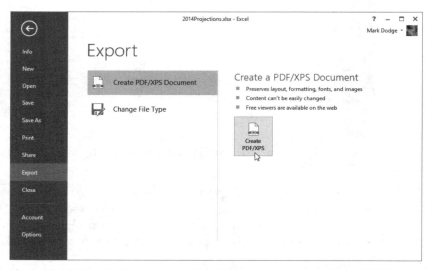

Figure 11-17 Use the Export screen in Backstage view to create PDF or XPS documents.

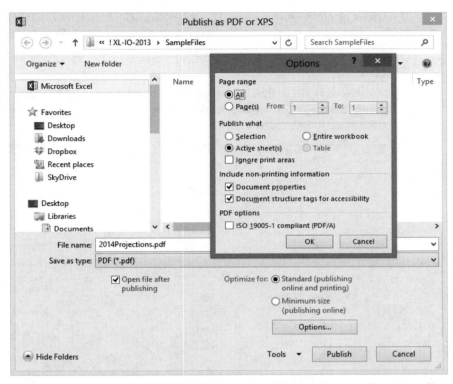

Figure 11-18 The Publish As PDF Or XPS dialog box offers options specific to these file types.

> **Note**
>
> If you don't have Adobe Reader, visit *www.adobe.com/reader/* for a free download. And if you are using an older version of Windows and can't see your XPS documents, visit *search.microsoft.com*, search on XPS Viewer, click the Downloads link, and select the XML Paper Specification Essentials Pack to display the page where you can download the viewer.

Click the Options button to display the dialog box also shown in Figure 11-18, where you can specify what to publish, including a specific page range, only the selected cells, the active table, or the entire workbook. You can use the nonprinting information options to specify whether to include document properties and *structure tags*. Structure tags are alternative text tags containing explanations of what each item does and are attached, for accessibility purposes, to visible structural elements of the document.

Chapter 11

If you save an entire multisheet workbook in XPS or PDF format, the resulting document displays each sheet as a separate image on a single page—scroll down to see them all.

> **Note**
>
> You can save as XPS or PDF, but you cannot open an XPS or a PDF document in Excel. To make changes, open the original Excel workbook, make your changes, and use Export again to save a new copy.

PART 5

Creating formulas and performing data analysis

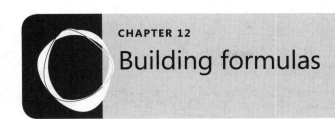

F ORMULAS are the heart and soul of a spreadsheet, and Microsoft Excel offers a rich environment in which to build complex formulas. Armed with a few mathematical operators and rules for cell entry, you can turn a worksheet into a powerful calculator. In this chapter, we cover the basics and then look more closely at using functions, defining names, building structured references, working with arrays, creating linking formulas, and constructing conditional tests.

Formula fundamentals

A lot of this section will seem elementary to experienced Excel users, but it is important information for anyone who is just arriving at the party. And even experienced users might find something useful here that they didn't know about.

All formulas in Excel begin with an equal sign.

This is the most fundamental fact of all. The equal sign tells Excel that the succeeding characters constitute a formula. If you omit the equal sign, Excel might interpret the entry as text. To show how formulas work, we'll walk you through some rudimentary ones. Begin by selecting blank cell A10. Then type **=10+5**, and press the Enter key. The value *15* appears in cell A10. Now select cell A10, and the formula bar displays the formula you just typed. What appears in the cell is the displayed value; what appears in the formula bar is the underlying value, which in this case is a formula.

Understanding the precedence of operators

Operators are symbols that represent specific mathematical operations, including the plus sign (+), minus sign (–), division sign (/), and multiplication sign (*). When performing these operations in a formula, Excel follows certain rules of precedence:

- Excel processes expressions within parentheses first.

- Excel performs multiplication and division before addition and subtraction.

- Excel calculates consecutive operators with the same level of precedence from left to right.

Type some formulas to see how these rules apply. Select an empty cell, and type **=4+12/6**. Press Enter, and you see the value *6*. Excel first divides 12 by 6 and then adds the result (2) to 4. Then select another empty cell, and type **=(4+12)/6**. Press Enter, and you see the value *2.666667*. This demonstrates how you can change the order of precedence by using parentheses. The formulas in Table 12-1 contain the same values and operators, but note the different results caused by the placement of parentheses.

TABLE 12-1 Placement of parentheses

Formula	Result
=3*6+12/4–2	19
=(3*6)+12/(4–2)	24
=3*(6+12)/4–2	11.5
=(3*6+12)/4–2	5.5
=3*(6+12/(4–2))	36

If you do not include a closing parenthesis for each opening parenthesis in a formula, Excel displays the message "Microsoft Excel found an error in this formula" and provides a suggested solution. If the suggestion matches what you had in mind, simply press Enter, and Excel completes the formula for you.

When you type a closing parenthesis, Excel briefly displays the pair of parentheses in bold. This feature is handy when you are typing a long formula and are not sure which pairs of parentheses go together.

> **Note**
>
> If you are unsure of the order in which Excel will process a sequence of operators, use parentheses even if the parentheses aren't necessary. Parentheses also make your formulas easier to read and interpret, which is helpful if you or someone else needs to change them later.

Using cell references in formulas

A cell reference identifies a cell or group of cells in a workbook. When you include cell references in a formula, the formula is said to be *linked* to the referenced cells. The resulting value of the formula depends on the values in the referenced cells and changes automatically when the values in the referenced cells change.

To see cell referencing at work, select cell A1, and type the formula **=10*2**. Now select cell A2, and type the formula **=A1**. The value in both cells is *20*. If at any time you change the value in cell A1, the value in cell A2 changes also. Now select cell A3, and type **=A1+A2**. Excel returns the value *40*. Cell references are especially helpful when you create complex formulas.

Entering cell references by clicking

When you start a formula by typing an equal sign into a cell, you activate *Enter mode*. If you then click another cell, you don't select it; instead, the cell's reference is inserted in the formula. You can save time and increase accuracy when you enter cell references this way. For example, to enter references to cells A9 and A10 in a formula in cell B10, do the following:

1. Select cell B10, and type an equal sign.

2. Click cell A9, and type a plus sign.

3. Click cell A10, and press Enter.

When you click each cell, a marquee surrounds the cell, and Excel inserts a reference to the cell in cell B10. After you finish entering a formula, be sure to press Enter. If you do not press Enter but select another cell, Excel assumes you want to include that cell reference in the formula as well.

The active cell does not have to be visible in the current window for you to enter a value in that cell. You can scroll through the worksheet without changing the active cell and click cells in remote areas of your worksheet, in other worksheets, or in other workbooks as you build a formula. The formula bar displays the contents of the active cell no matter which area of the worksheet is currently visible.

> **Note**
> If you scroll through your worksheet and the active cell is no longer visible, you can display it by pressing Ctrl+Backspace. You can return to the upper-left corner of the worksheet by pressing Ctrl+Home.

Understanding relative, absolute, and mixed references

Relative references—the type we've used so far in the sample formulas—refer to cells by their position in relation to the cell that contains the formula, such as "the cell two rows above this cell." A relative reference to cell A1, for example, looks like this: =A1.

Absolute references refer to cells by their fixed position in the worksheet, such as "the cell located at the intersection of column A and row 2." An absolute reference to cell A1 looks like this: =$A$1.

Mixed references contain a relative reference and an absolute reference, such as "the cell located in column A and two rows above this cell." A mixed reference to cell A1 looks like this: =$A1 or =A$1.

Dollar signs in a cell reference indicate its *absoluteness*. If the dollar sign precedes only the letter (A, for example), the column coordinate is absolute and the row is relative. If the dollar sign precedes only the number (1, for example), the column coordinate is relative and the row is absolute.

Absolute and mixed references are important when you begin copying formulas from one location to another in your worksheet. When you copy and paste, relative references adjust automatically, but absolute references do not. For information about copying cell references, see "How copying affects cell references" later in this chapter.

While you are entering or editing a formula, press F4 to change reference types quickly. The following steps show how:

1. Select cell A1, and type **=B1+B2** (but do not press Enter).

2. Press F4 to change the reference nearest the flashing pointer to absolute. The formula becomes =B1+$B$2.

3. Press F4 again to change the reference to mixed (relative column coordinate and absolute row coordinate). The formula becomes =B1+B$2.

4. Press F4 again to reverse the mixed reference (absolute column coordinate and relative row coordinate). The formula becomes =B1+$B2.

5. Press F4 again to return to the original relative reference.

When you use this technique to change reference types, click the formula bar to activate it. Then, before pressing F4, click in the cell reference you want to change or drag to select one or more cell references in the formula to change all the selected references at the same time.

Creating references to other worksheets in the same workbook

You can refer to cells in other worksheets within the same workbook just as easily as you refer to cells in the same worksheet. For example, to enter a reference to cell A9 in Sheet2 into cell B10 in Sheet1, do this:

1. Select cell B10 in Sheet1, and type an equal sign.

2. Click the Sheet2 tab.

3. Click cell A9, and then press Enter.

After you press Enter, Sheet1 once again becomes the active sheet. Select cell B10, and you can see that it contains the formula =Sheet2!A9.

The worksheet portion of the reference is separated from the cell portion by an exclamation point. Note also that the cell reference is relative, which is the default when you select cells to create references to other worksheets.

Creating references to worksheets in other workbooks

You can refer to cells in worksheets in separate workbooks in the same way you refer to cells in other worksheets within the same workbook. These references are called *external references*. For example, to enter a reference to Book2 in Book1, follow these steps:

1. Create a new workbook—Book2—by clicking the File tab, clicking New, and double-clicking Blank Workbook.

2. Click the View tab, click Arrange All, select the Vertical option, and click OK.

3. Select cell A1 in Sheet1 of Book1, and type an equal sign.

4. Click anywhere in the Book2 window to make the workbook active.

5. Click the Sheet2 tab at the bottom of the Book2 window.

6. Click cell A2. Before pressing Enter to lock in the formula, your screen should look similar to Figure 12-1. Note that when you click to enter references to cells in external workbooks, the inserted references are absolute.

7. Press Enter to lock in the reference.

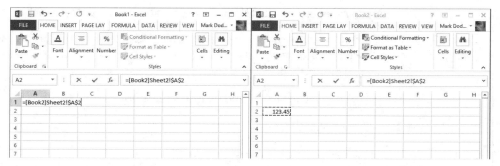

Figure 12-1 Enter external references easily by clicking the cell to which you want to refer.

Understanding the row-column reference style

In the regular A1 reference style, rows are numbered and columns are designated by letters. In the R1C1 reference style, both rows and columns are numbered. The cell reference R1C1 means *row 1, column 1*; therefore, R1C1 and A1 refer to the same cell. Although the R1C1 reference style isn't widely used anymore, it was the standard in some classic spreadsheet programs, such as Microsoft Multiplan.

To turn on the R1C1 reference style, click the File tab, click Options, select the Formulas category, select the R1C1 Reference Style check box, and then click OK. The column headers change from letters to numbers, and the cell references in all your formulas automatically change to R1C1 format. For example, cell M10 becomes R10C13, and cell XFD1048576, the last cell in your worksheet, becomes R1048576C16384.

In R1C1 notation, a relative cell reference is displayed in terms of its relationship to the cell that contains the formula rather than by its actual coordinates. This can be helpful when you are more interested in the relative position of a cell than in its absolute position. For example, suppose you want to enter in cell R10C2 (B10) a formula that adds cells R1C1 (A1) and R1C2 (B1). After selecting cell R10C2, type an equal sign, select cell R1C1, type a plus sign, select cell R1C2, and then press Enter. When you select cell R10C2, the formula =R[−9]C[−1]+R[−9]C appears in the formula bar. Negative row and column numbers indicate that the referenced cell is above or to the left of the formula cell; positive numbers indicate that the referenced cell is below or to the right of the formula cell. The brackets indicate relative references. This formula reads, "Add the cell nine rows up and one column to the left to the cell nine rows up in the same column."

A relative reference to another cell must include brackets. Otherwise, Excel assumes you're using absolute references. For example, if you select the entire formula we created in the previous paragraph in the formula bar and press F4, the formula changes to =R1C1+R1C2 using absolute references.

How copying affects cell references

One of the handiest benefits of using references is the ability to copy and paste formulas. But you need to understand what happens to your references after you paste so that you can create formulas with references that operate the way you want them to operate.

Copying relative references   When you copy a cell containing a formula with relative cell references, Excel changes the references automatically relative to the position of the cell where you paste the formula. Referring to Figure 12-2, suppose you type the formula **=AVERAGE(B4:E4)** in cell F4. This formula averages the values in columns B through E.

F4	▼	⋮	✕	✓	*fx*	=AVERAGE(B4:E4)		
◢	A	B	C	D	E	F	G	H
1	**First Quarter Exam Scores**							
2								
3	Student	Exam 1	Exam 2	Exam 3	Exam 4	Average		
4	Krieger, Doris	87	90	79	96	88.00		
5	Oliveira, Manuel	92	94	94	97			
6	Kodeda, Adam	96	95	95	80			
7	Lange, Michael	85	87	87	88			
8	Taylor, Maurice	81	88	88	85			
9								
10								

Figure 12-2 Cell F4 contains relative references to the cells to its left.

You'll find the Exams.xlsx file with the other examples on the companion website.

You want to include this calculation for the remaining rows as well. Instead of typing a new formula in each cell in column F, select cell F4 and press Ctrl+C to copy it (or click the Copy button in the Clipboard group on the Home tab). Then select cells F5:F8, click the arrow next to the Paste button on the Home tab, click Paste Special, and then select the Formulas And Number Formats option (to preserve the cell and border formatting). Figure 12-3 shows the results. Because the formula in cell F4 contains a relative reference, Excel adjusts the references in each copy of the formula. As a result, each copy of the formula calculates the average of the cells in the corresponding row. For example, cell F5 contains the formula =AVERAGE(B5:E5).

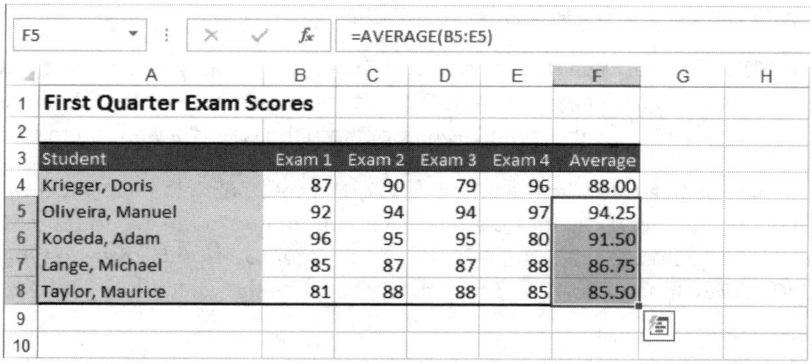

Figure 12-3 We copied the relative references from cell F4 to cells F5:F8.

Copying absolute references If you want cell references to remain the same when you copy them, use absolute references. For example, in the worksheet on the left in Figure 12-4, cell B2 contains the hourly rate at which employees are to be paid and cell C5 contains the relative reference formula =B2*B5. Suppose you copy the formula in C5 to the range C6:C8. The worksheet on the right in Figure 12-4 shows what happens: you get erroneous results. The formulas in cells C6:C8 should refer to cell B2, but they don't. For example, cell C8 contains the incorrect formula =B5*B8.

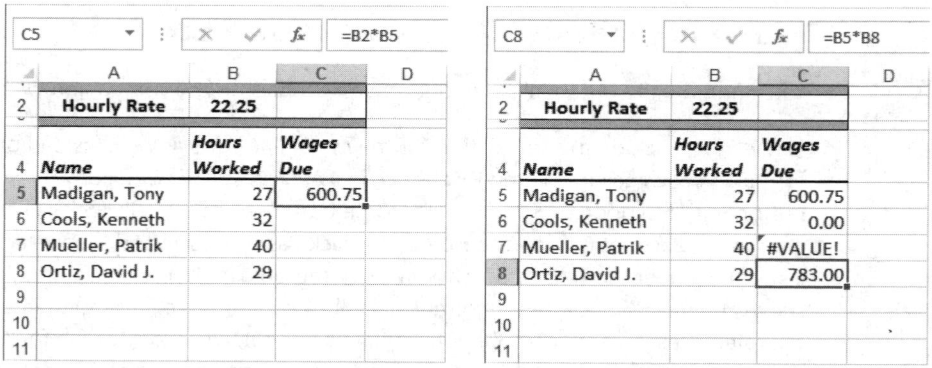

Figure 12-4 The formula in cell C5 contains relative references. We copied the relative formula in cell C5 to cells C6:C8, producing incorrect results.

You'll find the Wages.xlsx file with the other examples on the companion website.

Because the reference to cell B2 in the original formula is relative, it changes as you copy the formula to the other cells. To correctly apply the wage rate in cell B2 to all the calculations, you must change the reference to cell B2 to an absolute reference before you copy the formula.

To change the reference style, click the formula bar, click the reference to cell B2, and then press F4. The result is the following formula: =$B$2*B5.

When you copy this modified formula to cells C6:C8, Excel adjusts the second cell reference within each formula but not the first. In Figure 12-5, cell C8 now contains the correct formula: =$B$2*B8.

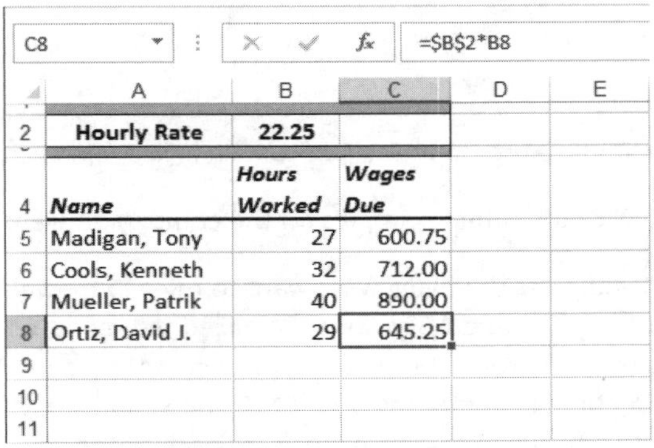

| C8 | ▾ | ⋮ | ✕ | ✓ | *fx* | =$B$2*B8 | |

◢	A	B	C	D	E
2	**Hourly Rate**	22.25			
		Hours	*Wages*		
4	*Name*	*Worked*	*Due*		
5	Madigan, Tony	27	600.75		
6	Cools, Kenneth	32	712.00		
7	Mueller, Patrik	40	890.00		
8	Ortiz, David J.	29	645.25		
9					
10					
11					

Figure 12-5 We created an absolute reference to cell B2 before copying the formula.

Copying mixed references   You can use mixed references in your formulas to anchor a portion of a cell reference. (In a mixed reference, one portion is absolute, and the other is relative.) When you copy a mixed reference, Excel anchors the absolute portion and adjusts the relative portion to reflect the location of the cell to which you copy the formula.

To create a mixed reference, you can press the F4 key to cycle through the four combinations of absolute and relative references—for example, from B2 to $B$2 to B$2 to $B2.

The loan payment table in Figure 12-6 uses mixed references (and an absolute reference). You need to enter only one formula in cell C6 and then copy it down and across to fill the table. Cell C6 contains the formula = –PMT($B6,$C$3,C$5) to calculate annual payments on a loan. We copied this formula to all the cells in the range C6:F10 to calculate payments using three additional loan amounts and four additional interest rates.

C6	▾	⋮	✕	✓	*fx*	=-PMT($B6,$C$3,C$5)

◢	A	B	C	D	E	F	G	H
1								
2		**Loan Payment Calculator**						
3		*Years:*	15					
4				**Loan Amount**				
5		*Rate:*	$ 10,000	$ 20,000	$ 30,000	$ 40,000		
6		3.00%	838	1,675	2,513	3,351		
7		3.50%	868	1,737	2,605	3,473		
8		4.00%	899	1,799	2,698	3,598		
9		4.50%	931	1,862	2,793	3,725		
10		5.00%	963	1,927	2,890	3,854		
11								
12								

Figure 12-6 This loan payment table uses formulas that contain mixed references.

You'll find the Loan.xlsx file with the other examples on the companion website.

The first cell reference, $B6, indicates that we always want to refer to the values in column B but the row reference (Rate) can change. Similarly, the mixed reference, C$5, indicates we always want to refer to the values in row 5 but the column reference (Loan Amount) can change. For example, cell E8 contains the formula = −PMT($B8,$C$3,E$5). Without mixed references, we would have to edit the formulas manually in each of the cells in the range C6:F10.

TROUBLESHOOTING

Inserted cells are not included in formulas

If you have a SUM formula at the bottom of a row of numbers and then insert new rows between the numbers and the formula, the range reference in the SUM function doesn't include the new cells. Unfortunately, you can't do much about this. This is an age-old worksheet problem, but Excel attempts to correct it for you automatically. Although the range reference in the SUM formula does not change when you insert the new rows, it adjusts as you type new values in the inserted cells. The only caveat is that you must enter the new values one at a time, starting with the cell directly below the column of numbers. If you enter values in the middle of a group of newly inserted rows or columns, the range reference remains unaffected. For more information about the SUM function, see "Using the SUM function" in Chapter 14, "Everyday functions."

Editing formulas

You edit formulas the same way you edit text entries: click in the cell or formula bar, click or drag to select characters, press Backspace or Delete or start typing. To replace a cell reference, highlight it and click the new cell you want the formula to use; Excel enters a relative reference automatically. You can also just click to place the insertion point where in the formula you want to insert a reference. To include cell B1 in the formula =A1+A3, place the insertion point between A1 and the plus sign, type another plus sign, and then click cell B1. Excel inserts the reference and the formula becomes =A1+B1+A3.

Understanding reference syntax

So far, we have used the default worksheet and workbook names for the examples in this book. When you save a workbook, you must give it a permanent name. If you create a formula first and then save the workbook with a new name, Excel adjusts the formula accordingly. For example, if you save Book2 as *Sales.xlsx*, Excel changes the remote reference formula =[Book2]Sheet2!$A$2 to =[Sales.xlsx]Sheet2!$A$2. And if you rename Sheet2 of Sales.xlsx to *February*, Excel changes the reference to =[Sales.xlsx]February!$A$2. If the referenced workbook is closed, Excel displays the full path to the folder where the workbook is stored in the reference, as shown in the example ='C:\Work\[Sales.xlsx]February'!$A$2.

In the preceding example, note that apostrophes surround the workbook and worksheet portion of the reference. Excel adds the apostrophes around the path when you close the workbook. If you type a new reference to a closed workbook, however, you must add the apostrophes yourself. To avoid typing errors, it is best to work with the linked workbooks open and click cells to enter references so that Excel inserts them in the correct syntax for you.

Using numeric text in formulas

The seemingly oxymoronic term *numeric text* refers to an entry that is not strictly numbers but includes both numbers and a few specific text characters. You can perform mathematical operations on numeric text values as long as the numeric string uses only the following characters in very specific ways:

0 1 2 3 4 5 6 7 8 9 . + – E e

In addition, you can use the forward slash (/) character in fractions. You can also use the following five number-formatting characters:

$, % ( )

You must enclose numeric text strings in quotation marks. For example, if you type the formula **=$1234+$123**, Excel displays an error message. (The error message also offers to correct the error for you by removing the dollar signs.) But the formula ="$1234"+"$123" produces the result *1357* (ignoring the dollar signs). When Excel performs the addition, it automatically translates numeric text entries into numeric values.

For more information about number-formatting characters, see "Formatting as you type" in Chapter 9, "Worksheet formatting techniques."

About text values

The term *text value* refers to any entry that is neither a number nor a numeric text value (as explained in the previous section); Excel treats the entry as text only. You can refer to and manipulate text values by using formulas. For example, if cell A1 contains the text *First* and you type the formula **=A1** in cell A10, cell A10 displays *First*.

For more information about manipulating text with formulas, see "Understanding text functions" in Chapter 14.

You can use the & (ampersand) operator to *concatenate*, or join, several text values. Extending the preceding example, if cell A2 contains the text *Quarter* and you type the formula **=A1&A2** in cell A3, then cell A3 displays *FirstQuarter*. To include a space between the two strings, change the formula to =A1&" "&A2. This formula uses two concatenation operators and a *literal string*, or *string constant* (in this case, a space enclosed in quotation marks).

You can use the & operator to concatenate strings of numeric values as well. For example, if cell A3 contains the numeric value *867* and cell A4 contains the numeric value *5309*, the formula =A3&A4 produces the string *8675309*. This string is left-aligned in the cell because it's considered a text value. (Remember, you can use numeric text values to perform any mathematical operation as long as the numeric string contains only the numeric characters listed in the previous section.)

Finally, you can use the & operator to concatenate a text value and a numeric value. For example, if cell A1 contains the text *January* and cell A3 contains the numeric value *2009*, the formula =A1&A3 produces the string *January2009*.

INSIDE OUT   Practical concatenation

Depending on the kind of work you do, the text manipulation prowess of Excel might turn out to be the most important skill you learn in this book. If you deal with a lot of mailing lists, for example, you probably use a word-processing application such as Microsoft Word. But you might find that Excel has the tools you've been wishing for, and it just might become your text-manipulation application of choice.

Suppose you have a database of names in which the first and last names are stored in separate columns. This example shows you how to generate lists of full names:

We created the full names listed in columns D and E using formulas like the one visible in the formula bar. For example, the formula in cell D2 is =B2&" "&A2, which concatenates and reverses the contents of the cells in columns A and B and adds a space character in between. The formula in cell E2 (=A2&", "&B2) reverses the position of the first and last names and adds a comma before the space character. For another nifty—and related—trick, see the sidebar "Practical text manipulation" in Chapter 14. And for an even niftier related feature that is new in Excel 2013, see "Automatic parsing and concatenation using Flash Fill" in Chapter 8, "Worksheet editing techniques."

You'll find the Concatenation.xlsx file with the other examples on the companion website.

Understanding error values

An *error value* is the result of a formula that Excel can't resolve. Table 12-2 describes the seven error values.

TABLE 12-2 Error values

Error value	Cause
#DIV/0!	You attempted to divide a number by zero. This error usually occurs when you create a formula with a divisor that refers to a blank cell.
#NAME?	You typed a name that doesn't exist in a formula. You might have mistyped the name or typed a deleted name. Excel also displays this error value if you do not enclose a text string in quotation marks.
#VALUE	You entered a mathematical formula that refers to a text entry.
#REF!	You deleted a range of cells whose references are included in a formula.
#N/A	No information is available for the calculation you want to perform. When building a model, you can type **#N/A** in a cell to show you are awaiting data. Any formulas that reference cells containing the #N/A value return #N/A.
#NUM!	You provided an invalid argument to a worksheet function. #NUM! can indicate also that the result of a formula is too large or too small to be represented in the worksheet.
#NULL!	You included a space between two ranges in a formula to indicate an intersection, but the ranges have no common cells.

Using functions: A preview

In simplest terms, a *function* is a predefined formula. Many Excel functions are shorthand versions of frequently used formulas. For example, compare =A1+A2+A3+A4+A5+A6+A7+A8+A9+A10 with =SUM(A1:A10). The SUM function makes the formula shorter, easier to read, and easier to create. Most Excel functions perform much more complex calculations, like the PMT function, which lets you calculate a loan payment at a given interest rate and principal amount.

All functions consist of a function name followed by a set of *arguments* enclosed in parentheses. (In the preceding example, A1:A10 is the argument in the SUM function.) If you omit a closing parenthesis when you enter a function, Excel adds the parenthesis after you press Enter—as long as it's obvious where the parenthesis is supposed to go. (Relying on this feature can produce unpredictable results; for accuracy, always verify your parentheses.)

For more information about functions, see Chapter 13, "Using functions." For more about the SUM function, see Chapter 14.

Using the Sum button

No surprise—the SUM function is used more often than any other function. To make this function more accessible, Excel includes the Sum button (which may be labeled AutoSum, depending on your screen resolution and window size) on the Home tab on the ribbon, which inserts the SUM function into a cell. (The ScreenTip that appears when you rest the pointer over this button says *Sum*. On the Formulas tab, the button includes the label *Auto-Sum*, which also appears on the Home tab if your screen is wide enough.)

> **Note**
> You can quickly enter a SUM function in the selected cell by pressing Alt+=.

To see how this works, do the following:

1. Enter a column of numbers, like we did in Figure 12-7.

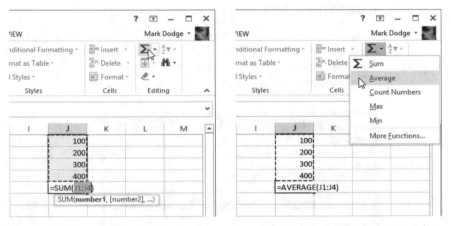

Figure 12-7 Use the Sum button to add a summary formula in a cell adjacent to columns or rows of numbers.

2. Select the cell below the column of numbers, and click the Sum button in the Editing group on the Home tab. The button inserts the entire formula for you and suggests a range to sum.

3. Check the selection. If the suggested range is incorrect, simply drag through the correct range.

4. Press Enter.

The Sum button includes a menu that appears when you click the arrow next to the button, as shown in Figure 12-7, offering popular alternative functions you can choose instead. The More Functions command opens the Insert Function dialog box, where you can access any Excel function. If you select a contiguous cell range that is adjacent to rows or columns of numbers before clicking the Sum button, Excel enters a SUM function in each cell.

> ### Note
>
> Get a quick sum by selecting the cells you want to sum and then looking at the status bar, where Excel automatically displays the sum, average, and count (the total number of cells containing entries) of the selected range. Right-click the status bar to add more readouts for the minimum, maximum, and numerical counts. For more information, see "Quick totals on the status bar" in Chapter 2, "Exploring Excel fundamentals."

For more information, see "Using the SUM function" in Chapter 14.

Inserting a function

When you want to use a built-in function, click the Insert Function button on the Formulas tab on the ribbon (or the little *fx* icon located on the formula bar). When you do, the Insert Function dialog box shown in Figure 12-8 appears. For all the details about using the Insert Function dialog box, see "Inserting functions" in Chapter 13.

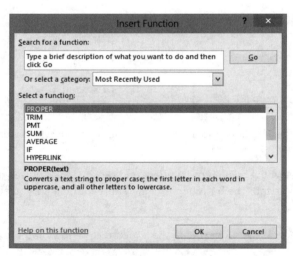

Figure 12-8 The Insert Function dialog box gives you access to all the built-in functions in Excel.

Using Formula AutoComplete

Excel makes creating formulas a little easier with a feature called *Formula AutoComplete*. Figure 12-9 illustrates what happens when you type an equal sign followed by the letter *S*—Excel lists all functions that begin with that letter. Formula AutoComplete also provides lists of defined names and function arguments, as well as special codes and names used in structured references and Cube functions. These lists appear automatically in the appropriate places as you enter a formula.

For more about defined names, see "Using names in formulas" later in this chapter; for more about structured references, see "Using structured references" later in this chapter.

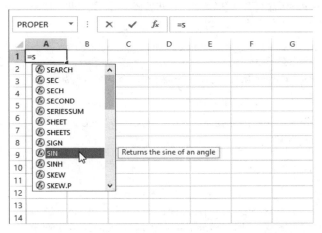

Figure 12-9 When you start to type a function, Excel lists all the functions that begin with the letter or letters you first type.

You can just keep typing your formula, or you can click any of the items in the Auto-Complete list to see a pop-up description of what that function does. Scroll down the list to see more functions; to insert one of the functions into your formula, double-click it. As you type additional characters, the list narrows further. For example, typing **=si** in the example shown in Figure 12-9 would narrow the AutoComplete list to three functions: SIGN, SIN, and SINH. Formula AutoComplete also works within nested formulas. For example, if you start typing a formula such as **=SUM(SIN(A4),S** into a cell, the AutoComplete list appears and readjusts its contents for each letter you type in the formula.

Working with formulas

We've covered most of the basics you need to know about how formulas and references work. In the following sections, we'll dig deeper, covering how to use defined names, inter-sections, structured references, and three-dimensional (3-D) formulas.

Naming cells and cell ranges

If you find yourself repeatedly typing cryptic cell addresses, such as **Sheet3!A1:AJ51**, into formulas, here's a better approach. Assign a short, memorable name to any cell or range and then use that name instead of the cryptogram in formulas. Naming cells has no effect on either their displayed values or their underlying values—you are just assigning nick-names you can use when creating formulas.

Each workbook contains its own set of names. After you define names on any worksheet, those names become available to every other worksheet in the workbook. You can also define worksheet-level names that are available only on the worksheet in which they are defined.

For more information about worksheet-level names, see "Workbook-wide vs. worksheet-only names" later in this chapter.

Using names in formulas

When you use the name of a cell or a range in a formula, the result is the same as using the cell or range address. For example, suppose you type the formula **=C1+C2** in cell C3. If you assign the name *Roger* to cell C1 and the name *Terry* to cell C2, the formula =Roger+Terry has the same result and is easier to read.

The easiest way to define a name follows:

1. Select a cell.

2. Click the Name box on the left end of the formula bar, as shown in Figure 12-10.

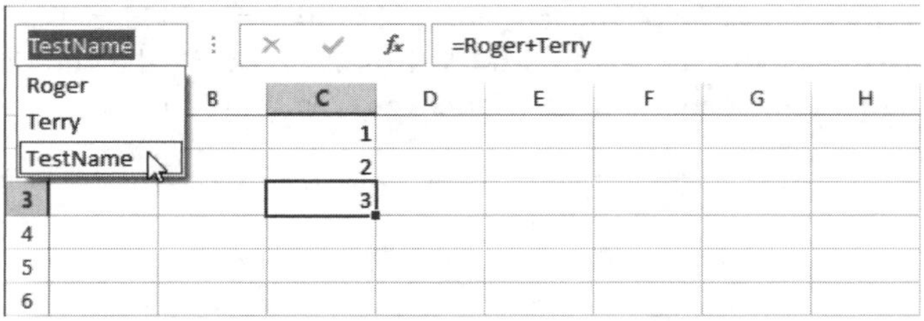

Figure 12-10 Use the Name box on the formula bar to quickly assign names to cells and ranges.

3. Type a name for the cell or range, and then press Enter. We used **TestName** in this example.

Keep the following in mind when using names in formulas:

- The Name box usually displays the address of the selected cell. If you named the selected cell or range, the name takes precedence over the address, and Excel displays it in the Name box.

- When you define a name for a range of cells, the range name does not appear in the Name box unless you select the same range.

- When you click the Name box and select a name, the cell selection switches to the named cells.

- If you type a name in the Name box that you already defined, Excel switches the selection to the named range instead of redefining the name.

- When you define a name, the stored definition is an absolute cell reference that includes the worksheet name. For example, when you define the name TestName for cell C3 in Sheet1, the actual name definition is recorded as Sheet1!$C$3.

For more information about absolute references, see "Understanding relative, absolute, and mixed references" earlier in this chapter.

Defining and managing names

Instead of coming up with new names for cells and ranges, you can simply use existing text labels to create names. Click the Define Name button on the Formulas tab on the ribbon to display the New Name dialog box shown in Figure 12-11. In this example, we selected cells B4:E4 before clicking the Define Name button, and Excel correctly surmised that the label *Region_1* was the most likely name candidate for that range. If you are happy using the adjacent label as a name, just press Enter to define the name, or you can first add a note in the Comment box if you want to provide some helpful documentation.

You can, of course, define a name without first selecting a cell or range on the worksheet. For example, in the New Name dialog box, type **Test2** in the Name text box, and then type **=D20** in the Refers To text box. Click OK to add the name, which also closes the New Name dialog box. To see a list of the names you defined, click the Name Manager button on the Formulas tab. The Name Manager dialog box appears, as shown in Figure 12-12.

Chapter 12

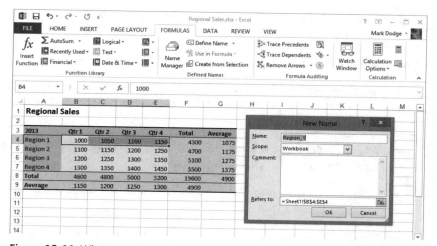

Figure 12-11 When you click Define Name on the Formulas tab, Excel suggests any label in an adjacent cell in the same row or column as a name.

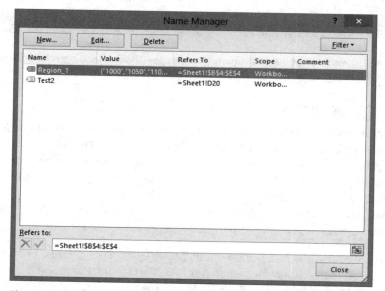

Figure 12-12 The Name Manager dialog box provides central control over all the names in a workbook.

The Name Manager dialog box lists all the names along with their values and locations. You'll see that the Refers To text box shows the definition of the name we just added, =Sheet1!D20. Excel adds the worksheet reference for you, but note that the cell reference stays relative, while the Region_1 definition created by Excel uses absolute references (indicated by the dollar signs in the Refers To definition). In fact, after defining the name Test2 using a relative reference, if you click a different cell before you open the Name Manager dialog box, the Refers To reference will not be the same as the one you typed because Excel adjusts it relative to the active cell. Also, if you do not enter an equal sign preceding the reference, Excel interprets the definition as text. For example, if you type **D20** instead of **=D20**, the Refers To text box displays the text constant ="D20" as the definition of the name Test2.

When you work with tables created using the new table features in Excel, some names are created automatically and others are implied. If this sounds intriguing, see "Using structured references" later in this chapter.

Editing names

Although you can edit name references directly using the Refers To text box in the Name Manager dialog box, it is preferable to click the Edit button at the top of the dialog box. Doing so opens the Edit Name dialog box, which is otherwise the same as the New Name dialog box shown in Figure 12-11 and offers additional opportunities to change the name and to add a comment.

In the Edit Name dialog box, you can change cell references in the Refers To text box either by typing or by selecting cells on the worksheet. When you click OK in the Edit Name dialog box, the Name Manager dialog box reappears, displaying the updated name definition. Clicking the New button in the Name Manager dialog box (as you might predict) displays the New Name dialog box; clicking the Delete button removes all selected names from the list in the Name Manager dialog box. Keep in mind that when you delete a name, any formula in the worksheet referring to that name returns the error value *#NAME?*.

Rules for naming

The following rules apply when you name cells and ranges in Excel:

- You must begin all names with a letter, a backslash (\), or an underscore (_). You cannot use any other symbol.

- You can also use numbers, periods, and underscore characters.

- You cannot use spaces; Excel translates blank spaces in labels to underscores in defined names.

- You can't use names that resemble cell references (for example, AB$5 or R1C7).

- You can use single letters, with the exception of the letters *R* and *C* (uppercase and lowercase), as names.

A name can contain 255 characters. Excel does not distinguish between uppercase and lowercase characters in names. For example, if you create the name Tax and then create the name TAX in the same workbook, the second name overwrites the first.

Workbook-wide vs. worksheet-only names

Names in Excel usually function on a workbook-wide basis. That is, a name you define on any worksheet is available for use in formulas on any other worksheet. But you can also create names whose scope is limited to the worksheet—that is, names that are available only on the worksheet in which you define them. You might want to do this if, for example, you have a number of worksheets doing similar jobs in the same workbook and you want to use the same names to accomplish similar tasks on each worksheet. To define a worksheet-only name, click the Scope drop-down list in the New Name dialog box, and select the name of the worksheet to which you want to limit the scope of the name.

TROUBLESHOOTING

My old worksheet-level names have changed

In versions of Excel prior to 2007, you created worksheet-level names by preceding the name (not the cell reference) with the name of the worksheet, followed by an exclamation point. This no longer works, and it's easier now anyway, using the Scope options in the New Name dialog box. If you have existing worksheet-level names in workbooks you created using previous versions of Excel, they will still work after you import the workbooks into Excel 2010 or 2013, but Excel modifies the name by removing the old designation (the worksheet name and exclamation point) and adds the Scope designation instead.

For example, to define TestSheetName as a worksheet-only name in Sheet1, select the range you want, click the Define Name button on the Formulas tab, type **TestSheetName** in the Name text box, and then select Sheet1 from the Scope drop-down list, as shown in Figure 12-13.

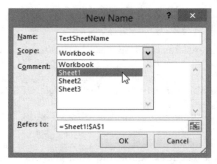

Figure 12-13 Use the Scope drop-down list to specify a worksheet to which you want to restrict a name's usage.

The following are some additional facts to keep in mind when working with worksheet-only and workbook-level names:

- Worksheet-only names do not appear in the Name box on the formula bar in work⌐ sheets other than the one in which you define them.

- When you select a cell or range to which you have assigned a worksheet-only name, the name appears in the Name box on the formula bar, but you have no way of knowing its scope. You can consider adding clues for your own benefit, such as including the word *Sheet* as part of all worksheet-only names when you define them.

- If a worksheet contains a duplicate workbook-level and worksheet-only name, the worksheet-level name takes precedence over the workbook-level name on the work-sheet where it lives, rendering the workbook-level version of the name useless on that worksheet.

- You can use a worksheet-only name in formulas on other worksheets by preceding the name with the name of the worksheet followed by an exclamation point. For example, you could type the formula **=Sheet1!TestSheetName** in a cell on Sheet3.

- You can't change the scope of an existing name.

Creating names semiautomatically

You can click the Create From Selection button on the Formulas tab to name several adja-cent cells or ranges at once, using row labels, column labels, or both. When you select this command, Excel displays the Create Names From Selection dialog box shown in Figure 12-14.

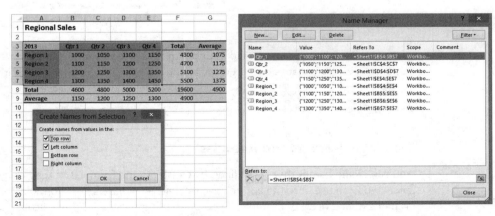

Figure 12-14 Use the Create Names From Selection dialog box to name several cells or ranges at once using labels.

Excel assumes that labels included in the selection are the names for each range. For example, Figure 12-14 shows that with A3:E7 selected, the Top Row and Left Column options in the Create Names From Selection dialog box are automatically selected, creating a set of names for each quarter and each region. Note that when using Create From Selection, you need to select the labels as well as the data. When you click the Name Manager button, you'll see the names you just created listed in the dialog box.

Selecting cells while a dialog box is open

The Refers To text boxes in the New Name and Name Manager dialog boxes (and many other text boxes in other dialog boxes) contain a *collapse dialog button*, located on the right side of the edit box. These edit boxes, when active, allow you to navigate and select cells on the worksheet. Most of the time, Excel complains loudly (ding!) when you click outside a dialog box. For example, after you click the Refers To text box, you can click outside the dialog box to select any other worksheet tab, drag scroll bars, switch workbooks, or make another workbook active. In addition, if you click the collapse dialog button, sure enough, the dialog box collapses, letting you see more of the worksheet, as shown here:

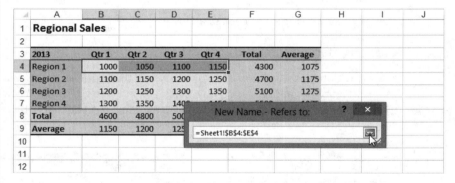

You can drag the collapsed dialog box around the screen using its title bar. When you finish, click the collapse dialog button again, and the dialog box returns to its original size.

Naming constants and formulas

You can create names that are defined by constants and formulas instead of by cell references. You can use absolute and relative references, numbers, text, formulas, and functions as name definitions. For example, if you often use the value *8.3%* to calculate sales tax, you can click the Define Name button, type the name **Tax** in the Name box, and then type **8.3%** (or **.083**) in the Refers To text box. Then you can use the name Tax in a formula, such as **=Price+(Price*Tax)**, to calculate the cost of items with 8.3 percent sales tax. Note that named constants and formulas do not appear in the Name box on the formula bar, but they do appear in the Name Manager dialog box.

You can also enter a formula in the Refers To text box. For example, you might define the name Price with a formula such as =Sheet1!A1*190%. If you define this named formula while cell B1 is selected, you can then type **=Price** in cell B1, and the defined formula takes care of the calculation for you. Because the reference in the named formula is relative, you can then type **=Price** in any cell in your workbook to calculate a price using the value in the cell directly to the left. If you type a formula in the Refers To text box that refers to a cell or range in a worksheet, Excel updates the formula whenever the value in the cell changes.

Using relative references in named formulas

When you create a named formula that contains relative references, such as =Sheet1!B22+1.2%, Excel interprets the position of the cells referenced in the Refers To text box as relative to the cell that is active when you define the name. Later, when you use such a name in a formula, the named formula uses whatever cell is in the same relative position. For example, if cell B21 is the active cell when you define the name Fees as =Sheet1!B22+1.2%, the name Fees always refers to the cell in the same column and one row below the cell in which the formula is currently located.

Creating three-dimensional names

You can create three-dimensional names, which use 3-D references as their definitions. For example, suppose you have a 13-worksheet workbook containing one identical worksheet for each month plus one summary sheet. You can define a 3-D name you can use to summarize totals from each monthly worksheet. To do so, follow these steps:

1. Select cell B5 in Sheet1 (the summary sheet).

2. Click the Define Name button.

3. Type **Three_D** (or any name you choose) in the Name box, and type **=Sheet2:Sheet13!B5** in the Refers To text box.

4. Press Enter (or click OK).

Now you can use the name Three_D in formulas that contain any of the following functions: SUM, AVERAGE, AVERAGEA, COUNT, COUNTA, MIN, MINA, MAX, MAXA, PRODUCT, STDEV, STDEVA, STDEVP, STDEVPA, VAR, VARA, VARP, and VARPA. For example, the formula =MAX(Three_D) returns the largest value in the three-dimensional range named Three_D. Because you used relative references in step 3, the definition of the range Three_D changes as you select different cells in the worksheet. For example, if you select cell C3 and display the Name Manager dialog box, =Sheet2:Sheet13!C3 appears in the Refers To text box.

> For more information on three-dimensional references, see "Creating three-dimensional formulas" later in this chapter.

Inserting names in formulas

After you define one or more names in your worksheet, you can insert those names in formulas by using one of several methods. First, if you know at least the first letter of the name you want to use, you can simply start typing to display the Formula AutoComplete drop-down list containing all the names beginning with that letter (along with any built-in functions that begin with that letter), as shown in Figure 12-15. To enter one of the names in your formula, double-click it.

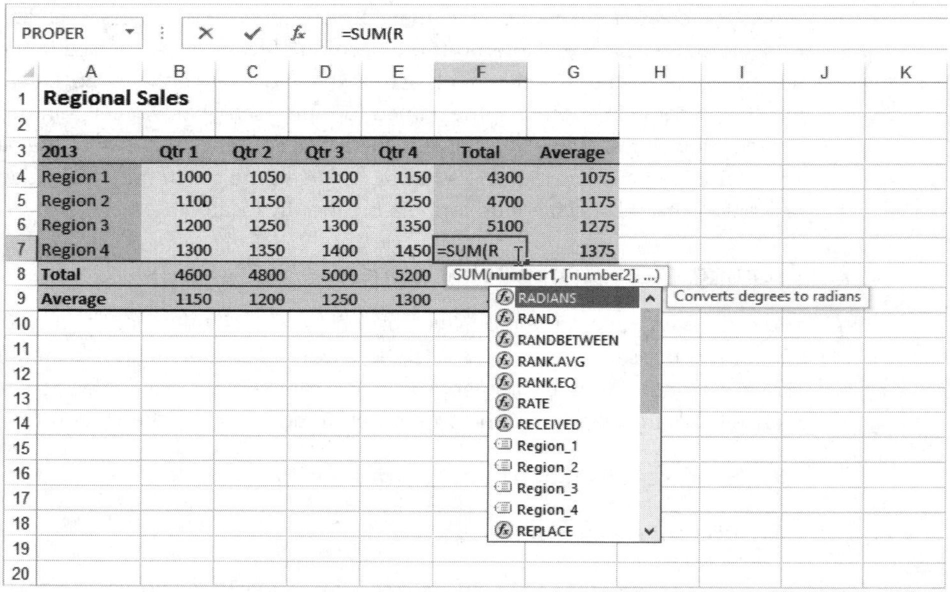

Figure 12-15 Names you define appear in the Formula AutoComplete list when you type a formula.

> For more information, see "Using Formula AutoComplete" earlier in this chapter.

You can also find a list of all the names relevant to the current worksheet when you click the Use In Formula button on the Formulas tab, which you can click while you're in the process of entering a formula, as shown in Figure 12-16.

Clicking the Paste Names command at the bottom of the Use In Formula menu displays the Paste Name dialog box shown in Figure 12-17. If you do this in Edit mode (while you are editing in a cell, as in Figure 12-16), the dialog box appears as shown in Figure 12-17.

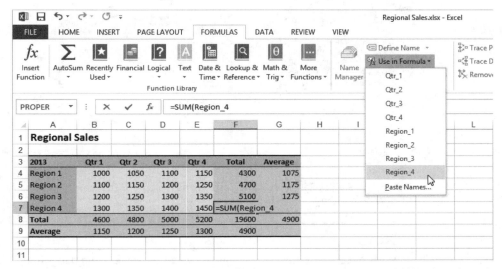

Figure 12-16 Click the Use In Formula button, and then select a name to enter it in the selected cell.

Figure 12-17 The Paste Name dialog box does the same job as the Use In Formula menu.

Creating a list of names

In large worksheet models, it's easy to accumulate a long list of defined names. To keep a record of all the names used, you can paste a list of defined names in your worksheet by clicking Paste List in the Paste Name dialog box, as shown in Figure 12-18. (When you open the Paste Name dialog box, the Paste List button is visible only if you are in Ready mode, not Edit mode. You cannot be editing a cell, as shown in Figure 12-16, when you click the Paste Names command.) Excel pastes the list in your worksheet beginning at the active cell. Worksheet-only names appear in the list only when you click Paste List on the worksheet where they live. Paste List is really the only useful feature in the Paste Name dialog box, given the superior methods of using names described in the previous section.

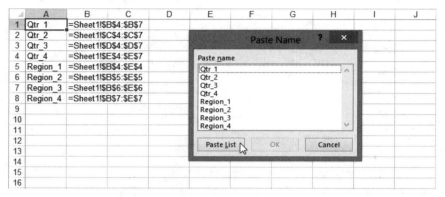

Figure 12-18 Click Paste List in the Paste Name dialog box to create a list of names and references starting at the active cell.

> **Note**
> When Excel pastes the list of names, it overwrites any existing data without asking for permission first. If you inadvertently overwrite data, press Ctrl+Z to undo it.

Replacing references with names

You can replace cell references with their corresponding names all at once by using the Apply Names command, which you access by clicking the arrow next to the Define Name button on the Formulas tab on the ribbon. When you do so, Excel locates all cell and range references for which you have defined names and replaces them with the appropriate name. If you select a single cell before you click the Apply Names command, Excel applies names throughout the active worksheet; if you select a range of cells first, Excel applies names to only the selected cells.

Figure 12-19 shows the Apply Names dialog box, which lists all the cell and range names you defined. Select each name you want to apply, and then click OK.

Excel ordinarily does not apply the column or row name if either is superfluous. For example, Figure 12-19 shows a worksheet after we applied names using the default options in the Apply Names dialog box. Cell D17 contained the formula =D5. Because D17 is in the same column as the referenced cell, only the row name was needed, thanks to implicit intersection, resulting in the formula =Region_2. In the figure, cell I17 is selected, and the formula bar shows it contains the formula =Region_2 Qtr_3, which before names were applied also contained the formula =D5. But because cell I17 isn't in the same row or column as any of the defined ranges, applying names normally results in an error value. Applying names works well in tables where your named ranges intersect, but to apply names in cells outside the table, you can force row and column names to be included in formulas by clearing the Omit Column Name If Same Column and Omit Row Name If Same Row check boxes.

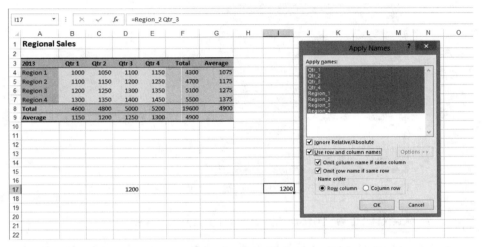

Figure 12-19 Use the Apply Names dialog box to substitute names for cell and range references in your formulas. Click Options to display all the options shown here.

The Name Order options control the order in which row and column components appear. For example, if we apply names using the Column Row option, the formula in cell I17 in Figure 12-19 becomes =Qtr_3 Region_2.

For more information about implicit intersection, see "Getting explicit about intersections" later in this chapter.

Select the Ignore Relative/Absolute check box to replace references with names regardless of the reference type. In general, leave this check box selected. Most name definitions use absolute references (the default when you define and create names), and most formulas use relative references (the default when you paste cell and range references in the formula bar). If you clear this check box, absolute, relative, and mixed references are replaced with name definitions only if the definitions use the same reference style.

Selecting the Use Row And Column Names check box is necessary if you want to apply names in intersection cases, as we showed in the examples. If you define names for individual cells, however, you can clear the Use Row And Column Names check box to apply names to only specific cell references in formulas.

Using Go To with names

When you click the Find & Select button on the Home tab and click Go To (or press F5), any names you defined appear in the Go To list, as shown in Figure 12-20. Select a name, and click OK to jump to the range to which the name refers. Note that names defined with constants or formulas do not appear in the Go To dialog box.

Figure 12-20 Use the Go To dialog box to quickly select a cell or range by name.

Getting explicit about intersections

In the worksheet in Figure 12-19, if you type the formula **=Qtr_1*4** in cell I4, Excel assumes you want to use only one value in the Qtr_1 range B4:B7—the one in the same row as the formula that contains the reference. This is called *implicit intersection*. Because the formula is in row 4, Excel uses the value in cell B4. If you type the same formula in cells I5, I6, and I7, each cell in that range contains the formula =Qtr_1*4, but at I5 the formula refers to cell B5, at I6 it refers to cell B6, and so on.

Explicit intersection refers to a specific cell with the help of the intersection operator. The *intersection operator* is the space character that appears when you press the Spacebar. If you type the formula **=Qtr_1 Region_1** at any location on the same worksheet, the space between the names tells Excel that you want to refer to the value at the intersection of the range labeled Qtr 1 and the range labeled Region 1, which is cell B4.

Creating three-dimensional formulas

You can use references to perform calculations on cells that span a range of worksheets in a workbook. These are called *3-D references*. Suppose you set up 12 worksheets in the same workbook—one for each month—with a year-to-date summary sheet on top. If all the monthly worksheets are laid out identically, you could use 3-D reference formulas to summarize the monthly data on the summary sheet. For example, the formula

=SUM(Sheet2:Sheet13!B5) adds all the values in cell B5 on all the worksheets between and including Sheet2 and Sheet13.

You can also use 3-D names in formulas. For more information, see "Creating three-dimensional names" earlier in this chapter.

To construct this three-dimensional formula, follow these steps:

1. In cell B5 of Sheet1, type **=SUM(**.

2. Click the Sheet2 tab, and select cell B5.

3. Click the tab-scrolling button for scrolling right (located to the left of the worksheet tabs) until the Sheet13 tab is visible.

4. Hold down the Shift key, and click the Sheet13 tab. All the tabs from Sheet2 through Sheet13 turn white, indicating they are selected for inclusion in the reference you are constructing.

5. Type a closing parenthesis, and then press Enter.

For more information about group editing, see "Editing multiple worksheets" in Chapter 8.

You can use the following functions with 3-D references: SUM, AVERAGE, AVERAGEA, COUNT, COUNTA, MIN, MINA, MAX, MAXA, PRODUCT, STDEV, STDEVA, STDEVP, STDEVPA, VAR, VARA, VARP, and VARPA.

Formula-bar formatting

You can enter spaces and line breaks in a formula to make it easier to read in the formula bar without affecting the calculation of the formula. To enter a line break, press Alt+Enter. Figure 12-21 shows a formula that contains line breaks. To see the complete formula in the formula bar, click the Expand Formula Bar button (the one with the chevron) at the right end of the formula bar.

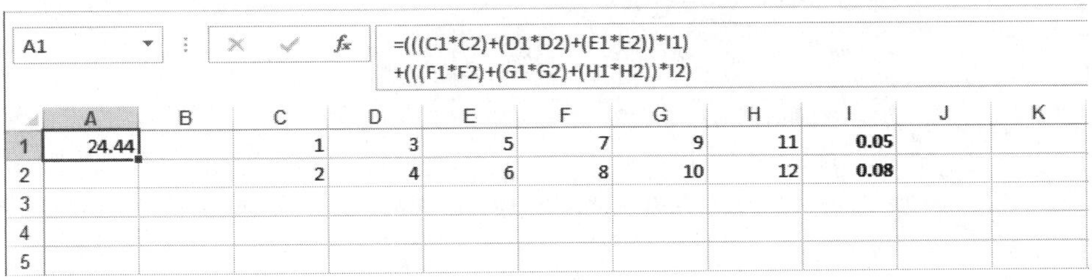

Figure 12-21 You can enter line breaks in a formula to make it more readable.

Using structured references

Creating names to define cells and ranges makes complex formulas easier to create and easier to read, and *structured references* offer similar advantages—and much more—whenever you create formulas in tables or formulas that refer to data in tables. Structured references are dynamic; formulas that use them automatically adjust to any changes you make to the table.

Structured references are created automatically when you create a table using the Table button in the Tables group on the Insert tab. Excel recognizes distinct areas of the table structure as separate components you can refer to by using *specifiers* that are either predefined or derived from the table. Figure 12-22 shows a modified version of the Regional Sales worksheet that we converted to a table. We'll refer to this table as we discuss structured references.

> **For more information about creating tables, see Chapter 22, "Managing information in tables."**

When you refer to data in tables by using formulas created through direct manipulation—that is, when you click or drag to insert cell or range references in formulas—Excel creates structured references automatically in most cases. (If a structured reference is not applicable, Excel inserts cell references instead.) Excel builds structured references using the table name and the column labels. (Excel automatically assigns a name to the table when you create one, as shown in Figure 12-22.) You can also type structured references by following strict syntax guidelines that we'll explain later in this section.

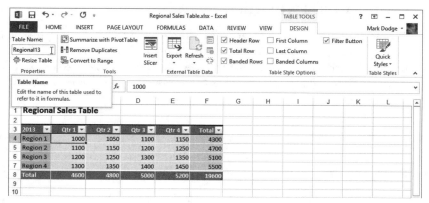

Figure 12-22 We created this table to illustrate the power of structured references.

> **Note**
>
> The capability to create structured references automatically is an option that is ordinarily turned on. To disable this feature, click the File tab, Options, and then in the Formulas category clear the Use Table Names In Formulas check box.

All Excel tables contain the following areas of interest, as far as structured references are concerned:

- **The table**   Excel automatically applies a table name when you create a table, which appears in the Table Name text box in the Properties group on the Table Tools Design tab that appears when you select a table. Excel named our table Table3 in this example, but we changed it to Regional13 by typing in the Table Name text box, as shown in Figure 12-22. The table name actually refers to all the data in the table, excluding the header and total rows.

- **Individual columns of data**   Excel uses your column headers in *column specifiers*, which refer to the data in each column, excluding the header and the total row. A *calculated column* is a column of formulas inside the table structure, such as F4:F7 in our example, which, again, does not include the header or total rows.

- **Special items**   These are specific areas of a table, including the total row, the header row, and other areas specified by using *special item specifiers*—fixed codes that are used in structured references to zero in on specific cells or ranges in a table. We'll explain these later in this section.

For details about calculated columns in tables, see Chapter 22.

> ## No more natural-language formulas
>
> In previous versions of Excel, you could use adjacent labels instead of cell references when creating formulas, which was like using names without actually having to define them. This was called the *natural-language formulas* feature, but it was riddled with problems and was replaced a couple of versions ago with structured references, which work much better. When you open an older workbook containing natural-language formulas, an error message appears letting you know that these formulas will be converted. This mandatory conversion has little effect on your worksheets other than changing some of the underlying formulas. Excel correctly identifies the offending labels and replaces them for you with the correct cell references. If you still want your formulas to be more readable, you can then rebuild them using names or structured references.

Let's look at an example of a structured reference formula. Figure 12-23 shows a SUM formula that we created by first typing **=SUM(**, clicking cell B4, typing another comma, and finally clicking cell C4. Because the data we want to use resides within a table and our formula is positioned in one of the same rows, Excel automatically uses structured references when we use the mouse pointer to select cells while building formulas.

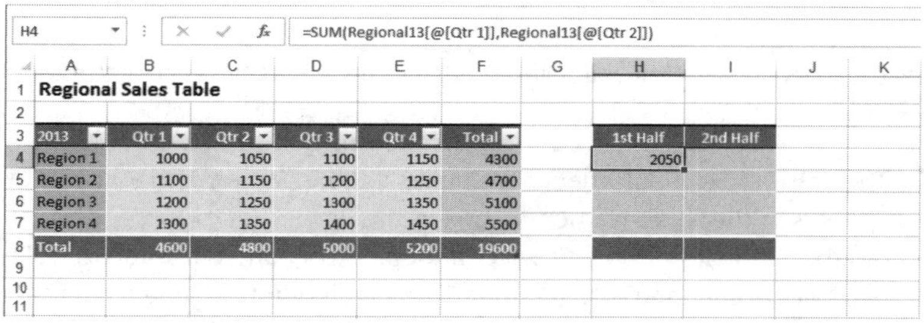

Figure 12-23 We created the formula in cell H4 by clicking to select cells in the table.

The result shown in the formula bar appears to be much more complex than necessary because we could just type **=SUM(B4:C4)** to produce the same result in this worksheet. But the structured formula is still quite easy to create using the mouse, and it has the distinct advantage of being able to automatically adjust after even the most radical changes to the table, which ordinary formulas are not nearly as good at accommodating.

Let's examine a little more closely the structured reference contained within the parentheses of the SUM function shown in Figure 12-23. The entire reference string shown here is equivalent to the expression (B4,C4), which combines the cells on both sides of the comma. The portion of the reference string in bold represents a single, complete structured reference:

`Regional13[@[Qtr 1]],Regional13[@[Qtr 2]])`

Here's how the reference string breaks down:

- The first item, Regional13, is the table specifier, which is followed by an opening bracket. Just like parentheses in functions, brackets in structured references always come in pairs. The table name is a little bit like a function, in that it always includes a pair of brackets that enclose the rest of the reference's components. This tells Excel that everything within the brackets applies to the Regional13 table.

- The second item, @, tells Excel that the following reference components apply only to those portions of the table that fall in the current row. (Obviously, this doesn't work if the formula is located above or below the table.) This represents an application of implicit intersection. (See "Getting explicit about intersections" earlier in this chapter.)

- The third item, [Qtr 1], is a column specifier. In our example, this corresponds to the range B4:B7. However, because it follows the @ specifier, only cells in the range that happen to be in the same row as the formula are included, or cell B4 in the example.

- The second reference follows the second comma in the string and is essentially the same as the first, specifying the other end of the range, or cell C4 in the example.

Understanding structured reference syntax

Here are some of the general rules governing the creation of structured references:

- Table-naming rules are the same as those for defined names. See "Naming cells and cell ranges" earlier in this chapter.

- You must enclose all specifiers in matching brackets.

- To make structured references easier to read, you can add a single space character in any or all of the following locations:

    ○ After the first opening (left) bracket (but not in subsequent opening brackets)

    ○ Before the last closing (right) bracket (but not in subsequent closing brackets)

    ○ After a comma

- Column headers are always treated as text strings in structured references, even if the column header is a number.

- You cannot use formulas in brackets.

- You need to use double brackets in column header specifiers that contain one of the following special characters: tab, line feed, carriage return, comma, colon, period, opening bracket, closing bracket, pound sign, single quotation mark, double quotation mark, left brace, right brace, dollar sign, caret, ampersand, asterisk, plus sign, equal sign, minus sign, greater-than symbol, less-than symbol, and division sign—for example, Sales[[$Canadian]]. Space characters are permitted.

Using operators with column specifiers

You can use three *reference operators* with column specifiers in structured references—a colon (:), which is the range operator; a comma (,), which is the union operator; and a space character ( ), which is the intersection operator.

For example, the following formula calculates the average combined sales for quarters 1 and 4 using a comma (the union operator) between the two structured references:

```
=AVERAGE(Regional3[Qtr 1],Regional3[Qtr 4])
```

The following formula calculates the average sales for quarters 2 and 3 by using colons (the range operator) to specify contiguous ranges of cells in each of the two structured references within the parentheses and by using a space character (the intersection operator) between the two structured references, which combines only the cells that overlap (Qtr 2 and Qtr 3):

```
=AVERAGE(Regional13[[Qtr 1]:[Qtr 3]] Regional13[[Qtr 2]:[Qtr 4]])
```

About the special item specifiers

Excel provides five special codes you can use with your structured references that refer to specific parts of a table. You already saw the special item specifier @ used in previous examples. Here are all five special item specifiers:

- **@**   This specifier identifies cells at the intersection created in conjunction with column specifiers; you cannot use it with any of the other special item specifiers in this list.

- **[#Totals]**   This refers to cells in the total row (if one exists) and returns a null value if there is no total row.

- **[#Headers]**   This refers only to cells in the header row.

- **[#Data]**   This refers only to cells in the data area between the header row and the total row.

- **[#All]**   This refers to the entire table, including the header row and the total row.

Are your references qualified?

Two kinds of structured references exist: *qualified* and *unqualified*. Generally, you can use unqualified references in formulas you construct within a table because the formulas are insulated from errors that could be introduced by inserting, deleting, or moving cells by virtue of the robust infrastructure of the table. When you build formulas outside the protective structure of a table, it is advisable to use qualified references to protect against such errors. Here is an example of an unqualified reference that works only within a table, followed by a qualified reference that produces the same result outside the table:

```
=[Qtr 1]/[Total]

=Regional13[@[Qtr 1]]/Regional13[@Total]]
```

Using Formula AutoComplete with structured references

As you enter your formulas, the Formula AutoComplete feature is there to help you along by displaying lists of applicable functions, defined names, and structured reference specifiers as you type. For example, Figure 12-24 shows a formula being constructed using a SUM function, along with an AutoComplete drop-down list displaying all defined items that begin with the opening bracket character (also called a *display trigger* in AutoComplete parlance) that you just typed in the formula. Notice that the list includes all the column specifiers for the table, as well as all the special item specifiers, all of which begin with a bracket.

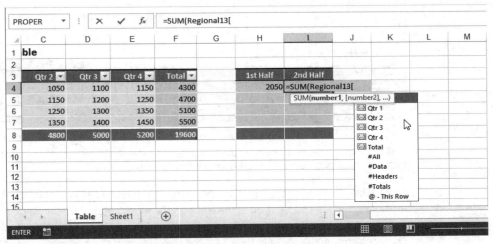

Figure 12-24 Structured reference specifiers appear in the AutoComplete drop-down list if they are applicable for a formula.

To enter one of the items in the list in the formula, double-click it. The Formula Auto-Complete list will most likely open more than once as you type formulas, offering any and all options that begin with the entered letters or display triggers. For example, the Auto-Complete list appeared after we typed **=S** with a list of all the items beginning with that letter and again after typing the **R** in Regional13.

For more information, see "Using Formula AutoComplete" earlier in this chapter.

Filling and copying structured references

As a rule, structured references do not adjust like relative cell references when you copy or fill them—the reference remains the same. The exceptions to this rule occur with column specifiers when you use the fill handle to copy fully qualified structured references outside the table structure. For example, in the worksheet shown in Figure 12-25, we dragged the fill handle to copy the % of Total formula in cell K4 to the right, and the column specifiers in the formulas adjusted accordingly.

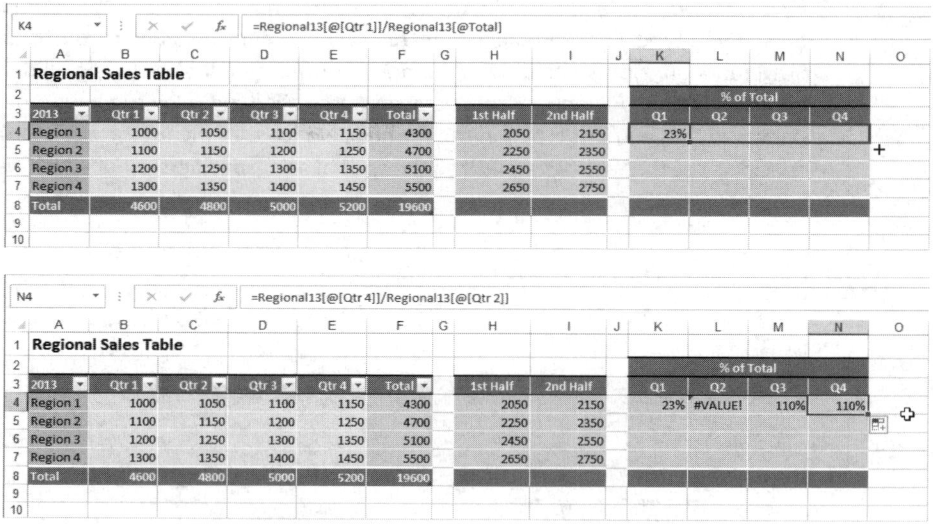

Figure 12-25 You can drag the fill handle to extend structured reference formulas into adjacent cells, but they behave a little bit differently from regular formulas.

The results illustrate some interesting structured-reference behavior. Notice that the first formula shown in cell K4 divides the value in the Qtr 1 column by the value in the Total column. After we filled to the right, the resulting formula in cell N4 divides the value in the Qtr 4 column by the value in the Qtr 2 column. How did this happen?

As far as filling cells is concerned, tables act like little traps—you can check in, but you can't check out. The formula shown at the top in Figure 12-25 has two column specifiers: Qtr 1 and Total. When we filled to the right, the Qtr 1 reference extended the way we wanted—to Qtr 2, Qtr 3, and Qtr 4 in each cell to the right. However, the Total reference, instead of extending to the right (G4, H4, I4) like a regular series fill would, "wrapped" around the table (2013, Qtr 1 and Qtr 2), resulting in the formula displayed in cell N4 at the bottom of Figure 12-25. This is interesting behavior, and we're sure people will figure out ways to put it to good use.

For more information about using the fill handle, see "Filling cells and creating data series" in Chapter 8.

What we need is a way to "lock" the Total column reference, but Excel doesn't offer any way to create "absolute" column specifiers, as it does with cell references. We can, however, substitute a cell reference for the entire Total reference, as shown in Figure 12-26. We used a mixed reference in this case, specifying the absolute column $F but letting the row number adjust so that we could fill down as well.

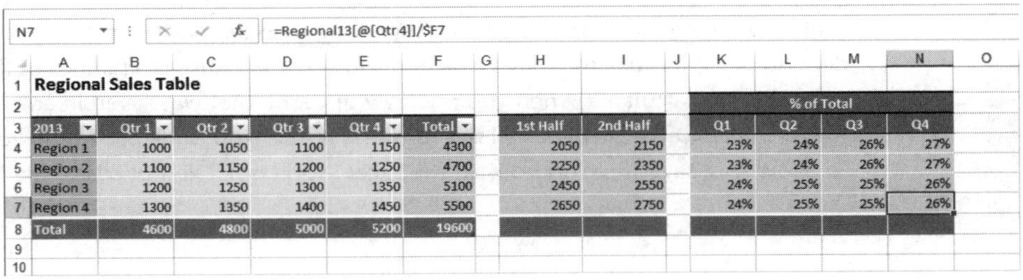

Figure 12-26 We replaced the second structured reference with a mixed cell reference to make filling these formulas work properly.

Note that if we were to select cell H4 in Figure 12-26 and drag the fill handle down, the formulas in each cell would not appear to adjust at all, yet they would work perfectly. (The formula in cell H4 appears in Figure 12-23.) This is because explicit intersection, the built-in behavior of column specifiers, and the functionality of the @ specifier eliminate the need to adjust row references.

> **Note**
> When you drag the fill handle to the right in a cell containing a structured-reference formula, pressing Ctrl prevents the column specifiers from adjusting as they usually would and instead copies the formula to the right without adjustment.

Worksheet calculation

When you change the value in any of the cells to which a formula refers, Excel updates the displayed values of the formula as well. This updating process is called *recalculation*, and it affects only cells containing references to cells that have changed. By default, Excel recalculates whenever you make changes to a cell. If a large number of cells must be recalculated, the word *Calculating* appears in the status bar, along with a percentage-of-progress meter if the process is going to take a particularly long time. You can interrupt the recalculation process simply by doing something, such as using commands or making cell entries; Excel pauses and then resumes the recalculation when you finish.

INSIDE OUT Legacy recalc

When you open an Excel 2010 or 2013 workbook, Excel recalculates only formulas that depend on cell values that have changed. However, because of changes in the way Excel 2010/2013 recalculates, when you open a workbook that was saved in an earlier Excel file format, Excel recalculates all the formulas in the workbook each time you open it. To avoid this, save the workbook in the Excel Workbook (.xlsx or .xlsm) file format.

Recalculating manually

There are various reasons why you might want to prevent Excel from recalculating each time you enter data in a cell, but computer speed, which used to be one of the top reasons, really isn't much of an issue anymore (unless your computer is very old). Nevertheless, you can switch from automatic to manual recalculation, and Excel will recalculate only when you tell it to. To set manual recalculation, click the Calculation Options button on the Formulas tab on the ribbon and then choose the Manual option. You can also click the File tab, Options, and then select the Formulas category to display the additional options shown in Figure 12-27.

Here are a few facts to remember about calculation options:

- With worksheet recalculation set to Manual, the status bar displays the word *Calculate* if you make a change; click it to initiate recalculation immediately.

- The Recalculate Workbook Before Saving check box helps make sure the most current values are stored on disk.

- To turn off automatic recalculation only for data tables, select the Automatic Except For Data Tables option. For more information, see "Using data tables" in Chapter 18, "Performing a what-if analysis."

- To recalculate all open workbooks, click the Calculate Now button in the Calculation group on the Formulas tab, or press F9.

- To calculate only the active worksheet in a workbook, click the Calculate Sheet button in the Calculation group on the Formulas tab, or press Shift+F9.

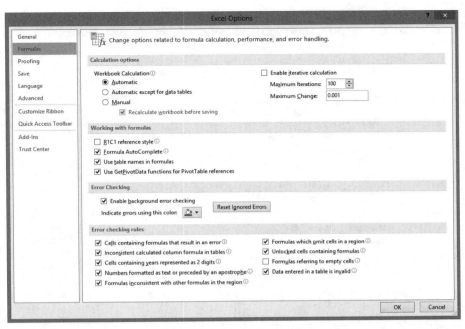

Figure 12-27 The Formulas category in the Excel Options dialog box controls worksheet calculation and iteration.

Multithreaded calculation

If you have a computer with a multicore processor, perhaps with additional hyperthreading, Excel takes full advantage of the additional power by dividing the workload among available processors. Click the File tab, Options, Advanced category, and look in the Formulas area. Excel automatically detects additional processors and displays the total number adjacent to the Use All Processors On This Computer option. The number of processors also appears in the status bar next to the word *Calculating*, if you have enough formulas to slow the calculation process sufficiently for it to appear. You can turn this option off to reserve some of your computer's processing bandwidth for other programs you need to run simultaneously.

Calculating part of a formula

You might want to see the result of just one part of a complex formula if, for example, you are tracking down a discrepancy. To change only part of a formula to a value, select the part you want to change and press F9. You also can use this technique to change selected cell references in formulas to their values. Figure 12-28 shows an example.

If you're just verifying your figures, press the Esc key to discard the edited formula. Otherwise, if you press Enter, you replace the selected portion of the formula.

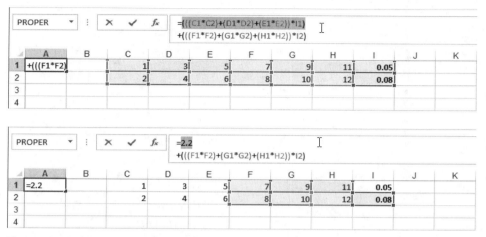

Figure 12-28 Select any part of a formula, and press F9 to convert it to its resulting value.

> **Note**
>
> You also can click the Evaluate Formula button on the Formulas tab to troubleshoot your workbook models. For more information, see "Evaluating and auditing formulas" in Chapter 8.

Working with circular references

A *circular reference* is a formula that depends on its own value. The most obvious type is a formula that contains a reference to the same cell in which it's entered. For example, if you type **=C1-A1** in cell A1, Excel displays the error message shown in Figure 12-29. After you click OK, Excel opens the Help dialog box, which displays a pertinent topic.

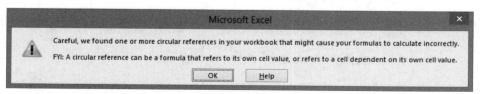

Figure 12-29 This error message appears when you attempt to enter a formula that contains a circular reference.

If a circular-reference warning surprises you, this usually means you made an error in a formula. If the error isn't obvious, verify the cells that the formula refers to by using the built-in, formula-auditing features. For details, see "Auditing and documenting worksheets" in Chapter 8.

When a circular reference is present in the current worksheet, the status bar displays the text *Circular References* followed by the cell address, indicating the location of the circular reference on the current worksheet. If *Circular References* appears without a cell address, the circular reference is located on another worksheet.

As you can see in Figure 12-30, when you click the arrow next to the Error Checking button on the Formulas tab and click Circular References, any circular references that exist on the current worksheet are listed on a menu (which appears only if a circular reference is present). Click the reference listed on this menu to activate the offending cell.

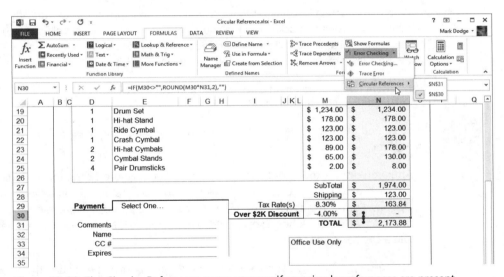

Figure 12-30 The Circular References menu appears if any circular references are present.

You can resolve many circular references. Some circular formulas are useful or even essential, such as the set of circular references shown in Figure 12-31. These formulas are circular because the formula in cell N30 depends on the value in N31, and the formula in N31 depends on the value in N30.

Figure 12-31 illustrates a circular reference scenario called *convergence*: the difference between results decreases with each iterative calculation. In the opposite process, called *divergence*, the difference between results increases with each calculation.

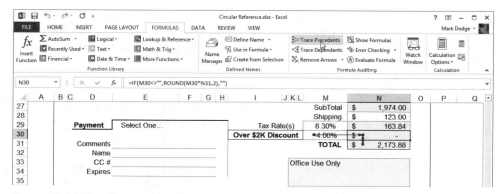

Figure 12-31 The discount formula in cell N30 is circular because it depends on the total, which in turn depends on the discount value in N30.

When Excel detects a circular reference, tracer arrows appear on the worksheet. To draw additional arrows to track down the source of an unintentional circular reference, select the offending cell and then click Trace Precedents on the Formulas tab to draw tracer arrows to the next level of precedent cells, as shown in Figure 12-31.

> **For more information about tracer arrows and other auditing features, see "Auditing and documenting worksheets" in Chapter 8.**

You'll find the Circular Reference.xlsx file with the other examples on the companion website.

After you dismiss the error message shown earlier in Figure 12-29, the formula will not resolve until you allow Excel to recalculate in controlled steps. To do so, click the File tab, Options, Formulas category, and in the Calculation Options section, select the Enable Iterative Calculation check box. Excel recalculates all the cells in any open worksheets that contain a circular reference.

If necessary, the recalculation repeats the number of times specified in the Maximum Iterations box (100 is the default). Each time Excel recalculates the formulas, the results in the cells get closer to the correct values. If necessary, Excel continues until the difference between iterations is less than the number typed in the Maximum Change text box (0.001 is the default). Thus, using the default settings, Excel recalculates either a maximum of 100 times or until the values change less than 0.001 between iterations, whichever comes first.

If the word *Calculate* appears in the status bar after the iterations are finished, more iterations are possible. You can accept the current result, increase the number of iterations, or lower the Maximum Change threshold. Excel does not repeat the "Cannot Resolve Circular Reference" error message if it fails to resolve the reference. You must determine when the answer is close enough. Excel can perform iterations in seconds, but in complex circular situations, you might want to set the Calculation option to Manual; otherwise, Excel recalculates the circular references every time you make a cell entry.

The Solver add-in, a "what-if" analysis tool, offers more control and precision when working with complex iterative calculations. For details, see "Using the Solver" in Chapter 18.

Understanding the precision of numeric values

Here are three interesting facts about numeric precision in Excel:

- Excel stores numbers with as much as 15-digit accuracy and converts any digits after the fifteenth to zeros.

- Excel drops any digits after the fifteenth in a decimal fraction.

- Excel uses scientific notation to display numbers that are too long for their cells.

TROUBLESHOOTING

Rounded values in my worksheet don't add up

Your worksheet can appear erroneous if you use rounded values. For example, if you use cell formatting to display numbers in currency format with two decimal places, Excel displays the value *10.006* as the rounded value $10.01. If you add 10.006 and 10.006, the correct result is 20.012. If all these numbers are formatted as currency, however, the worksheet displays the rounded values *$10.01* and *$10.01*, and the rounded value of the result is *$20.01*. The result is correct, as far as rounding goes, but its appearance might be unacceptable for a particular purpose, such as a presentation or an audit.

You can correct this problem by changing the currency format, or you can click the File tab, Options, Advanced category. In the When Calculating This Workbook area, select the Set Precision As Displayed check box. However, you should select this check box only with extreme caution because it permanently changes the underlying values in your worksheet to their displayed values. For example, if a cell containing the value *10.006* is formatted as currency, selecting the Set Precision As Displayed check box permanently changes the value to *10.01*. For more information, see "Formatting numbers" in Chapter 9.

Table 12-3 contains examples of how Excel treats integers and decimal fractions longer than 15 digits when they are typed in cells with the default column width of 8.43 characters.

TABLE 12-3 Examples of numeric precision

Typed entry	Displayed value	Stored value
123456789012345678	1.23457E+17	123456789012345000
1.23456789012345678	1.234568	1.23456789012345
1234567890.12345678	1234567890	1234567890.12345
123456789012345.678	1.23457E+14	123456789012345

Excel can calculate positive values as large as 9.99E+307 and approximately as small as 1.00E–307. If a formula results in a value outside this range, Excel stores the number as text and assigns a #NUM! error value to the formula cell.

Using arrays

Arrays are familiar concepts to computer programmers. Simply defined, an array is a collection of items. Excel is one of the few applications that facilitate array operations, in which items that are part of an array can be individually or collectively addressed in simple mathematical terms. Here is some basic array terminology you should know:

- An *array formula* acts on two or more sets of values, called *array arguments*, to return either a single result or multiple results.

- An *array range* is a block of cells that share a common array formula.

- An *array constant* is a specially organized list of constant values you can use as arguments in array formulas.

Arrays perform calculations in a way unlike anything else. You can use them for worksheet security, alarm monitors, linear regression tables, and much more.

One-dimensional arrays

The easiest way to learn about arrays is to look at a few examples. For instance, you can calculate the averages shown in Figure 12-32 by entering a single array formula.

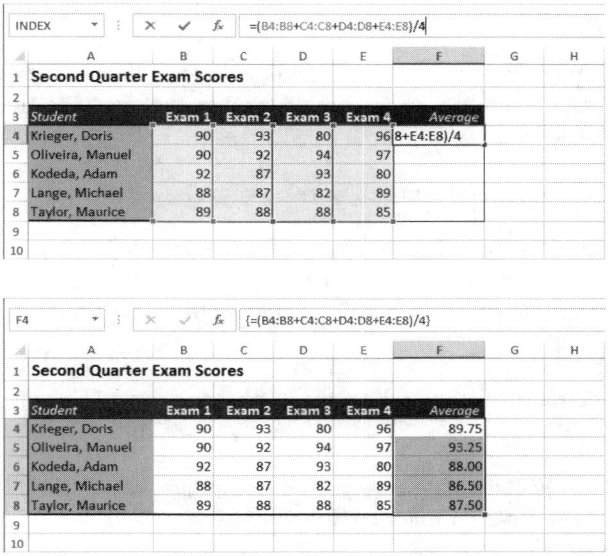

Figure 12-32 We entered a single array formula in the selected range F4:F8.

You'll find the Arrays.xlsx file with the other examples on the companion website.

This particular example might be used to help protect the formulas from tampering because modifying individual formulas in cells that are part of an array is impossible. To enter this formula, do the following:

1. Select the range F4:F8.

2. Type the formula in the formula bar, as shown in Figure 12-32.

3. Press Ctrl+Shift+Enter.

The resulting single array formula exists in five cells at once. Although the array formula seems to be five separate formulas, you can't make changes to any one formula without selecting the entire formula—that is, the entire array range F4:F8.

You can identify an array formula by looking at the formula bar. If the active cell contains an array formula, the entire formula, including the equal sign, is enclosed in curly braces— { }—in the formula bar, as you can see in Figure 12-32.

Chapter 12

Array formula rules

To enter an array formula, first select the cell or range that will contain the results. If the formula produces multiple results, you must select a range the same size and shape as the range or ranges on which you perform your calculations.

Follow these guidelines when entering and working with array formulas:

- Press Ctrl+Shift+Enter to lock in an array formula. Excel then places a set of curly braces around the formula in the formula bar to indicate that it's an array formula. Don't type the braces; if you do, Excel interprets your entry as text.

- You can't edit, clear, or move individual cells in an array range, and you can't insert or delete cells. You must treat the cells in the array range as a single unit and edit them all at once.

- To edit an array, select the entire array, click the formula bar, and edit the formula. Then press Ctrl+Shift+Enter to lock in the formula.

- To clear an array, select the entire array and press Delete.

- To select an entire array, click any cell in the array and press Ctrl+/.

- To move an array range, you must select the entire array and either cut and paste the selection or drag the selection to a new location.

- You can't cut, clear, or edit part of an array, but you can assign different formats to individual cells in the array. You can also copy cells from an array range and paste them in another area of your worksheet.

Two-dimensional arrays

In the preceding example, the array formula resulted in a vertical, one-dimensional array. You also can create arrays that include two or more columns and rows, otherwise known as *two-dimensional arrays*. Figure 12-33 shows an example.

To enter a two-dimensional array, do the following:

1. Select a range to contain your array.

2. Type your formula in the formula bar, and press Ctrl+Shift+Enter.

> **Note**
> Unfortunately, you can't create three-dimensional arrays across multiple worksheets in workbooks.

| B10 | ▼ | : | × | ✓ | *fx* | {=RANK(B4:E8,B4:E8)} | |

▲	A	B	C	D	E	F	G
1	**Second Quarter Exam Scores**						
2							
3	*Student*	Exam 1	Exam 2	Exam 3	Exam 4	*Average*	
4	Krieger, Doris	90	93	80	96	89.75	
5	Oliveira, Manuel	90	92	94	97	93.25	
6	Kodeda, Adam	92	87	93	80	88.00	
7	Lange, Michael	88	87	82	89	86.50	
8	Taylor, Maurice	89	88	88	85	87.50	
9			All Exams			*Student Average*	
10		8	4	19	2	2.00	
11		8	6	3	1	1.00	
12	**Score Rankings**	6	15	4	19	3.00	
13		12	15	18	10	5.00	
14		10	12	12	17	4.00	
15							
16							

Figure 12-33 We used a two-dimensional array formula in B10:E14 to compute the rank of each exam score. A similar one-dimensional array appears in F10:F14.

Single-cell array formulas

You can perform calculations on a vast collection of values within a single cell by using an array formula that produces a single value as a result. For example, you can create a simple single-cell array formula to multiply the values in a range of cells by the values in an adjacent range, as shown in Figure 12-34.

| B2 | ▼ | : | × | ✓ | *fx* | {=SUM(B5:B8*C5:C8)} | |

▲	A	B	C	D	E
2	**Total Wages**	3,715.75			
4	*Name*	*Hours Worked*	*Hourly Rate*		
5	Madigan, Tony	27.0	22.25		
6	Cools, Kenneth	32.0	31.50		
7	Mueller, Patrik	40.0	28.75		
8	Masters, Steve	29.0	33.00		
9					
10					

Figure 12-34 To calculate total wages paid, we used a single-cell array formula in B2 to multiply hours worked by wages due for each employee individually.

In the example shown in Figure 12-34, you must enter the formula as an array formula (by pressing Ctrl+Shift+Enter); entering it as a regular formula results in a #VALUE error. Our example shows a tiny worksheet, but an array formula like this can make fast work of giant tables.

Using array constants

An array constant is a specially organized list of values you can use as arguments in your array formulas. Array constants can consist of numbers, text, or logical values. Although Excel adds braces for you when you enter array formulas, you must type braces around array constants and separate their elements with commas and semicolons. Commas indicate values in separate columns, and semicolons indicate values in separate rows. The formula in Figure 12-35, for example, performs nine computations in one cell.

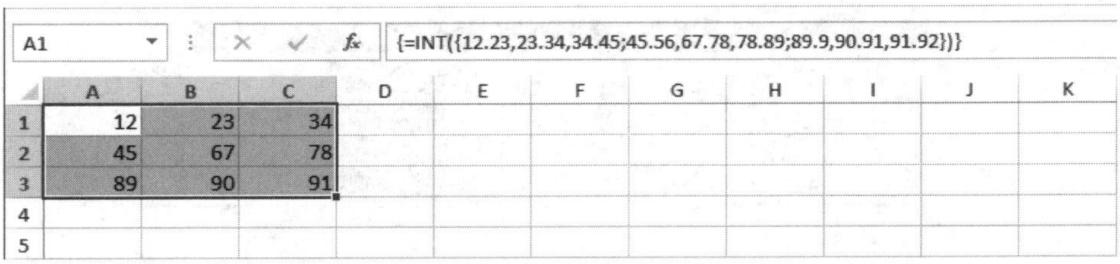

Figure 12-35 An array constant is the argument for this array formula.

A single-cell array formula application

Suppose you want the total number of items in a table that satisfy two criteria. You want to know how many transactions of more than $1,000 occurred after a specified date. You could add a column to the table containing an IF function to find each transaction that satisfies these criteria and then total the results of that column. A simpler way to do this is to use a single array formula like this one:

=SUM((A1:A100>41275)*(C1:C100>999))

The *41275* in the formula is the serial date value for January 1, 2013. Enter the formula by pressing Ctrl+Shift+Enter. Each item in the first parenthetical expression evaluates to either a *1* (TRUE) or a *0* (FALSE), depending on the date; each item in the second parenthetical expression evaluates also to either a *1* or a *0*, depending on whether its value is greater than 999. The formula then multiplies the 1s and 0s, and when both evaluate to TRUE, the resulting value is *1*. The SUM function adds the 1s and gives you the total. You can add more criteria by adding more parenthetical elements to the formula; any expression that evaluates to FALSE (0) eliminates that transaction because anything multiplied by 0 is 0.

You could enhance this formula in several ways. For example, replace the serial date number with the DATEVALUE function so that you can use "1/1/2013" as an argument instead of having to find the date value yourself. Even better, use cell references as arguments to each element so that you can type variable criteria in cells rather than editing the formula. For information about the DATEVALUE function, see Chapter 15, "Formatting and calculating date and time."

To enter a formula using an array constant, follow these steps:

1. Select a range of cells the size you need to contain the result. In Figure 12-35, the argument to the INT function contains three groups (separated by semicolons) of three values (separated by commas), which produces a three-row, three-column range.

2. Enter an equal sign to begin the formula and, optionally, a function name and opening parenthesis.

3. Type the array argument enclosed in braces to indicate that the enclosed values make up an array constant. If you entered a function, type its closing parenthesis.

4. Press Ctrl+Shift+Enter. The resulting array formula contains two sets of curly braces— one set encloses the array constant, and the other encloses the entire array formula.

When entering array constants, remember that commas between array elements place those elements in separate columns, and semicolons between array elements place those elements in separate rows.

Understanding array expansion

When you use arrays as arguments in a formula, all your arrays should have the same dimensions. If the dimensions of your array arguments or array ranges do not match, Excel often expands the arguments for you. For example, to multiply all the values in cells A1:B5 by 10, you can use either of the following array formulas: { =A1:B5*10} or { ={ 1,2;3,4;5,6;7,8;9,10}*10}.

Note that neither of these two formulas are balanced; ten values are on the left side of the multiplication operator, but only one is on the right. Excel expands the second argument to match the size and shape of the first. In the preceding example, the first formula is equivalent to { =A1:B5*{ 10,10;10,10;10,10;10,10;10,10} }, and the second is equivalent to { ={ 1,2;3,4;5,6;7,8;9,10}*{ 10,10;10,10;10,10;10,10;10,10} }.

When you work with two or more sets of multivalue arrays, each set must have the same number of rows as the argument with the greatest number of rows, and each must have the same number of columns as the argument with the greatest number of columns.

Linking workbooks

Creating dynamic links between workbooks using external reference formulas provides a number of advantages. For example, you could break a large, complex company budget model into more manageable departmental models. Then you could link all the departmental workbooks (supporting workbooks) to a master budget workbook (a dependent workbook). In addition to creating more manageable and flexible models, linked workbooks can save recalculation time and memory.

The following sections discuss some special considerations you should be aware of when working with workbooks linked by external reference formulas. For more information about external references, see "Creating references to other worksheets in the same workbook" and "Creating references to worksheets in other workbooks," both of which appear earlier in this chapter.

Saving linked workbooks

When you create a set of linked workbooks, you should save the supporting workbooks before you save the dependent workbooks. For example, suppose you created and saved a workbook named Actual that details your company's actual (as opposed to budgeted) expenditures. Now suppose you have another active workbook in which you are modeling budgeted expenditures, as yet unsaved and still named Book1. Then you create linking formulas in Actual that depend on totals in your budget workbook (Book1, still unsaved). If you save Book1 as Budget while the Actual workbook is still open, all references to Book1 in the Actual workbook change automatically to Budget. For example, if Actual contains the reference =[Book1]Sheet1!$A$1, the reference changes to ='[Budget.xlsx]Sheet1'!$A$1.

Great, but what if that doesn't happen? If you try to close the dependent Actual workbook before you save the supporting Book1 (Budget) workbook, you see the "Save Actual with references to unsaved documents?" warning. Suppose you ignore it and click OK to save and close the workbook. When you then save Book1 as Budget, Excel doesn't update the references to Book1 in the Actual workbook because it isn't open; the formulas continue to reference Book1.

When you reopen Actual, Excel displays the security warning in Figure 12-36, alerting you that links are present that cannot be updated (because Book1 does not exist). Click the Edit Links button to display the dialog box shown in Figure 12-37.

Excel is, of course, unable to find Book1. You need to click the Change Source button to locate the Actual workbook so that Excel can reestablish the links.

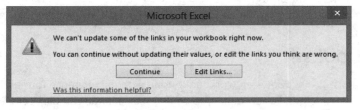

Figure 12-36 If an external link cannot be found, Excel requires your intervention.

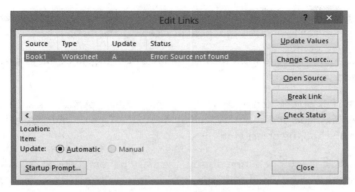

Figure 12-37 Use the Edit Links dialog box to manage all your external links.

Opening a dependent workbook

When you save a workbook that contains dependent formulas, Excel stores the most recent results of those formulas. If you open and edit the supporting workbook after closing the dependent workbook, the values of edited cells in the supporting workbook might be different. When you open the dependent workbook again, the workbook contains the old values of the external references in the dependent formulas, and Excel displays a security warning, alerting you that automatic links are present. If you click the Update button, Excel searches for the supporting workbook. If it finds the workbook, Excel does not open it, but reads the supporting values and updates the dependent formulas in the dependent workbook. However, If Excel can't find the supporting workbook, it displays the error message shown in Figure 12-36, because the file referred to in the formula (Book1) no longer exists. Click the Edit Links button to display the dialog box shown in Figure 12-37.

Editing links

You can open supporting workbooks, as well as specify different supporting workbooks, when you click the Edit Links button, located in the Connections group on the Data tab on the ribbon. When you do so, you'll see a dialog box like the one shown in Figure 12-37. Here is some helpful information about using the Edit Links dialog box:

- An *A* in the Update column indicates a link that is updated automatically.

- An *M* in the Update column indicates a manual link that isn't updated until you click Update Values.

- Click Open Source to open the supporting workbook.

- Click Change Source to select a different supporting workbook.

- Click Break Link to convert all existing external references in formulas to their current values. You can't undo this action, so proceed with caution.

- Click Update Values to fetch the latest figures from the supporting workbook without having to open it.

- You can link objects and documents created in other applications, such as Word, to Excel worksheets and charts. When you do so, the Type column displays the application name and the object type.

Clicking the Startup Prompt button displays the Startup Prompt dialog box shown in Figure 12-38. You can use this dialog box to specify how links are handled whenever the workbook is opened.

Figure 12-38 The Startup Prompt dialog box lets you customize the startup behavior of external links.

Ordinarily, Excel displays a security alert when you open a workbook containing linking formulas, which individual Excel users can choose to suppress on their computers. If you prefer to suppress the security alert for the current workbook, you can do so by selecting either Don't Display The Alert And Don't Update Automatic Links or Don't Display The Alert And Update Links in the Startup Prompt dialog box.

> **Note**
>
> To change the default behavior of disabling automatic links, click the File tab, Options, Advanced category, and then in the General section clear the Ask To Update Automatic Links option.

Copying, cutting, and pasting in linked workbooks

You can use relative or absolute references to cells in other workbooks as you do in a single workbook. Relative and absolute references to cells in supporting workbooks respond to the Copy, Cut, and Paste commands and buttons in much the same way as do references to cells in the same workbook.

For example, suppose you type the formula **=[Form2.xlsx]Sheet1!F1** in cell A1 on Sheet1 of Form1 and then use Copy and Paste to copy this formula to cell B1. The formula in cell B1 becomes =[Form2.xlsx]Sheet1!G1. The original formula changes when you copy it to cell B1 because the reference to cell F1 is relative. However, if the formula in cell A1 of Form1 contained an absolute reference, such as =[Form2.xlsx]Sheet1!$F$1, the reference in the copied formula would not change.

Copying and pasting between workbooks

When you copy a dependent formula from one workbook to another and that formula includes a relative reference to a third workbook, Excel adjusts the reference to reflect the new position of the formula on the worksheet grid. For example, suppose that cell A1 in Form1 contains the formula =[Form2.xlsx]Sheet1!A1. If you copy and paste that formula into cell B5 in Form3, the result is the formula =[Form2.xlsx]Sheet1!B5. Excel adjusts the formula to reflect its new relative position. If, on the other hand, you copy a formula that contains an absolute reference to another workbook, the formula remains the same after you paste.

Even if you copy a dependent formula to the workbook to which the formula refers, it's still a dependent formula. For example, if you copy the formula =[Form2.xlsx]Sheet1!$A$1 from cell A1 of Form1 to cell A3 on Sheet1 of Form2, the resulting formula is essentially the same, except that the book reference isn't necessary because the formula is in the same workbook. As a result, the formula becomes =Sheet1!$A$1.

Cutting and pasting between workbooks

Excel does not adjust the relative references in a formula when you cut it from one workbook and paste it in another, as it does when you copy a formula. For example, suppose that cell A1 on Sheet1 of Form1 contains the formula =[Form2.xlsx]Sheet1!A1. If you cut rather than copy that formula and paste it into cell B5 of Form3, the references do not change.

Creating conditional tests

A conditional test formula compares two numbers, functions, formulas, labels, or logical values. You can use conditional tests to flag values that fall outside a given threshold, for example. You can use simple mathematical and logical operators to construct logical formulas, or you can use an assortment of built-in functions. For information about using conditional test functions, see "Understanding logical functions" in Chapter 14.

You might also be able to satisfy some of your conditional curiosities by using the conditional formatting feature in Excel. For details, see "Formatting conditionally" in Chapter 9.

Each of the following formulas performs a rudimentary conditional test:

```
=A1>A2
=5-3<5*2
=AVERAGE(B1:B6)=SUM(6,7,8)
=C2="Female"
=COUNT(A1:A10)=COUNT(B1:B10)
=LEN(A1)=10
```

Every conditional test must include at least one logical operator, which defines the relationship between elements of the conditional test. For example, in the conditional test A1>A2, the greater than (>) logical operator compares the values in cells A1 and A2. Table 12-4 lists the six logical operators.

TABLE 12-4 Logical operators

Operator	Definition
=	Equal to
>	Greater than
<	Less than
> =	Greater than or equal to
< =	Less than or equal to
< >	Not equal to

The result of a conditional test is either the logical value TRUE (1) or the logical value FALSE (0). For example, the conditional test =A1=10 returns TRUE if the value in A1 equals *10* or FALSE if A1 contains any other value.

Using conditional functions

Often, you need to total some, but not all, numbers in a range or count items that conform to specific criteria. You can easily construct these kinds of conditional formulas by using the SUMIF, SUMIFS, COUNTIF, and COUNTIFS functions.

Versions of Excel prior to the 2010 release included the Conditional Sum Wizard, an add-in that helped construct the necessary array formulas using the SUM and IF functions. The formula visible in the formula bar of the background worksheet in Figure 12-39 shows just such a legacy formula that was originally created by the wizard. This approach, and this formula, still works just fine, in case you still have some of these wizard-generated models in your workbooks. The Conditional Sum Wizard is history in 2013, but there is a somewhat easier method of arriving at the same result. The worksheet in the foreground of Figure 12-39 shows a similar task accomplished with SUMIF functions.

For details on these functions, see "The SUMIF, SUMIFS, and COUNTIF functions" and "Understanding logical functions," both of which are in Chapter 14.

| G4 | ▾ | : | × | ✓ | *fx* | {=SUM(IF($A$4:$A$19=F4,$D$4:$D$19,0))} |

	A	B	C	D	E	F	G	H
1	**Northwind Traders**							
2	Jan-14		Transactions					
3	Name	Units	Location	Sales		Salesperson	Total Sales	
4	Kirwan, Yvette	12.00	1	5,130.00		Kirwan, Yvette	14,753.00	
5	Krieger, Doris	4.00	1	5,745.00		Krieger, Doris	5,745.00	
6	Madigan, Tony	6.00	2	4,836.00		Madigan, Tony	12,732.00	
7	Gibbins, Phil	9.00	1	5,243.00		Hedlund, Magnus	17,724.00	
8	Hedlund, Magnus	14.00	3	7,164.00		Cools, Kenneth	3,985.00	
9	Cools, Kenneth	18.00	2	2,655.00		Oliveira, Manuel	2,334.00	
10	Hedlund, Magnus	12.00	2	4,081.00				
11	Kirwan, Yvette	4.00	3	5,646.00				
12	Madigan,							
13	Gibbins, P							

| G4 | ▾ | : | × | ✓ | *fx* | =SUMIF($A$4:$A$19,F4,$D$4:$D$19) |

	A	B	C	D	E	F	G	H
1	**Northwind Traders**							
2	Feb-14		Transactions					
3	Name	Units	Location	Sales		Salesperson	Total Sales	
4	Kirwan, Yvette	3.00	2	4,366.00		Kirwan, Yvette	19,800.00	
5	Krieger, Doris	6.00	2	7,813.00		Krieger, Doris	7,813.00	
6	Madigan, Tony	9.00	1	3,514.00		Madigan, Tony	10,574.00	
7	Gibbins, Phil	13.00	2	3,715.00		Hedlund, Magnus	18,077.00	
8	Hedlund, Magnus	8.00	2	8,055.00		Cools, Kenneth	8,489.00	
9	Cools, Kenneth	12.00	1	6,154.00		Oliveira, Manuel	8,761.00	
10	Hedlund, Magnus	14.00	3	7,235.00				
11	Kirwan, Yvette	8.00	3	5,034.00				
12	Madigan, Tony	7.00	3	1,035.00				
13	Gibbins, Phil	19.00	1	7,675.00				

Figure 12-39 Conditional sum formulas are easily created using the SUMIF function.

You'll find the NorthwindTransactions.xlsx file with the other examples on the companion website.

You can use the SUMIF function to collect a total of items in a range that match a given criterion. In Figure 12-39, the salesperson's name is used as the criterion to collect sales totals (of course, correct spelling and punctuation is key). If you want to be even more selective, you can use the SUMIFS function, which allows you to specify up to 127 separate sets of criteria. Figure 12-40 shows a SUMIFS function in the formula bar that uses two criteria: salesperson and location. For each criterion, there are two arguments in the formula: one defines the range of cells containing the values from which you want to gather totals, and the other specifies the criterion identifying values you want to include.

As you might imagine, the COUNTIF and COUNTIFS functions operate similarly to their SUM-family brethren, but instead of adding values together, they count *instances*. For example, Figure 12-41 shows a worksheet displaying the number of times each salesperson worked at each store location. The result cells in the Worked At Location area each contain a COUNTIFS function that looks at both the salesperson and the location, and they return not a total but a tally of the number of times this combination occurs.

CAUTION

If a label in the column of criteria includes an invisible space character at the end of the text string, Excel excludes it from the total, even if all the instances are otherwise identical.

I4   fx   =SUMIFS($D$4:$D$19,$A$4:$A$19,$F4,$C$4:$C$19,I$3)

Northwind Traders

Name	Units	Location	Sales	Salesperson	Total Sales	1	2	3
Mar-14		Transactions					Sales by Location	
Kirwan, Yvette	12.00	1	8,873.00	Kirwan, Yvette	21,294.00	19,944.00	1,350.00	-
Krieger, Doris	11.00	2	5,409.00	Krieger, Doris	5,409.00	-	5,409.00	-
Madigan, Tony	9.00	3	7,080.00	Madigan, Tony	20,631.00	-	-	20,631.00
Gibbins, Phil	11.00	3	1,928.00	Hedlund, Magnus	21,049.00	-	21,049.00	-
Hedlund, Magnus	9.00	2	6,095.00	Cools, Kenneth	11,545.00	11,545.00		-
Cools, Kenneth	15.00	1	7,201.00	Oliveira, Manuel	4,125.00	-	4,125.00	-
Hedlund, Magnus	14.00	2	6,887.00	TOTAL		31,489.00	31,933.00	20,631.00
Kirwan, Yvette	8.00	1	5,831.00					
Madigan, Tony	12.00	3	8,538.00					
Gibbins, Phil	11.00	2	5,598.00					
Hedlund, Magnus	19.00	2	8,067.00					
Kirwan, Yvette	9.00	1	5,240.00					
Madigan, Tony	12.00	3	5,013.00					
Oliveira, Manuel	8.00	2	4,125.00					
Kirwan, Yvette	15.00	2	1,350.00					
Cools, Kenneth	8.00	1	4,344.00					
TOTAL			91,579.00					

Figure 12-40 You can use the SUMIFS function to specify up to 127 sets of criteria.

I4   fx   =COUNTIFS($A$4:$A$19,$F4,$C$4:$C$19,I$3)

Northwind Traders

Name	Units	Location	Sales	Salesperson	Total Sales	1	2	3
Apr-14		Transactions					Worked at location	
Kirwan, Yvette	12.00	1	8,003.00	Kirwan, Yvette	17,928.00	3	1	
Krieger, Doris	11.00	2	4,875.00	Krieger, Doris	4,875.00		1	
Madigan, Tony	9.00	3	6,196.00	Madigan, Tony	18,025.00			3
Gibbins, Phil	11.00	3	1,073.00	Hedlund, Magnus	18,724.00		3	
Hedlund, Magnus	9.00	2	5,387.00	Cools, Kenneth	9,992.00	2		
Cools, Kenneth	15.00	1	6,267.00	Oliveira, Manuel	3,548.00		1	
Hedlund, Magnus	14.00	2	6,039.00					
Kirwan, Yvette	8.00	1	4,845.00					
Madigan, Tony	12.00	3	7,812.00					
Gibbins, Phil	11.00	2	4,888.00					
Hedlund, Magnus	19.00	2	7,298.00					
Kirwan, Yvette	9.00	1	4,417.00					
Madigan, Tony	12.00	3	4,017.00					
Oliveira, Manuel	8.00	2	3,548.00					
Kirwan, Yvette	15.00	2	663.00					
Cools, Kenneth	8.00	1	3,725.00					
TOTAL			79,053.00					

Figure 12-41 With the COUNTIFS function, you can use multiple criteria to tally the number of times the specified condition occurs.

Using lookup functions

You can create formulas using the INDEX and MATCH functions that pinpoint specific values in tables of data. Typically, a lookup formula includes two MATCH functions: one to identify a row, and one to indentify a column. The INDEX function takes these values and returns the contents of the cell at the specified location.

Versions of Excel prior to the 2010 release included the Lookup Wizard, an add-in that helps to construct the necessary formulas using the INDEX and MATCH functions. These formulas still work perfectly, in case you still have some of these wizard-generated models in your workbooks.

For details about the INDEX and MATCH functions, see "Understanding lookup and reference functions" in Chapter 14.

As you can see in the formula bar in Figure 12-42, there are two MATCH functions at work within the INDEX function; the first locates the row, and the second locates the column. They do so using the values in cells P5 and Q5, respectively, containing column and row criteria you specify. The INDEX function then takes these criteria and returns the value found at the intersection of the designated row and column.

R5			f_x	=INDEX($A$3:$M$37, MATCH(P5,$A$3:$A$37,), MATCH(Q5,$A$3:$M$3,))						
	A	B	C	D	M	N	O	P	Q	R	S
1	**2014 Product Sales Projections**										
3	Column1	Jan	Feb	Mar	Dec	Total		Fetch a Specific Product & Month			
4	Product 1	$7,317	$6,329	$2,110	$16,379	$86,119		row	column	result	
5	Product 2	$2,814	$2,336	$9,199	$7,220	$57,476		Product 25	Mar	$7,267	
6	Product 3	$2,875	$4,107	$5,528	$3,267	$58,503					
7	Product 4	$4,365	$2,202	$5,607	$2,144	$45,772					
8	Product 5	$9,451	$3,398	$3,472	$10,130	$83,266					
9	Product 6	$7,810	$6,982	$7,018	$3,935	$61,937					
10	Product 7	$9,976	$7,267	$5,006	$3,963	$81,645					
11	Product 8	$2,536	$4,100	$6,328	$5,550	$60,289					
12	Product 9	$3,104	$2,467	$5,349	$3,428	$51,136					
13	Product 10	$5,442	$2,783	$1,642	$17,237	$93,532					
14	Product 11	$7,816	$8,626	$6,938	$1,758	$68,768					
15	Product 12	$2,786	$6,720	$4,754	$12,124	$77,713					
16	Product 13	$7,363	$3,248	$7,295	$4,537	$62,251					
17	Product 14	$9,917	$5,004	$6,873	$179	$62,022					

Sheet1   READY   100%

Figure 12-42 Locate values in tables using the INDEX and MATCH functions.

You'll find the Lookup Functions.xlsx file with the other examples on the companion website.

In the previous three figures, you'll notice a mixture of relative and absolute references in the formulas. (A row number or column letter preceded by a dollar sign is an absolute reference.) These are generally used to allow the copying of formulas to other locations while maintaining the proper relationships. For details, see "Understanding relative, absolute, and mixed references" back near the beginning of this chapter.

Using functions

WORKSHEET FUNCTIONS are special tools that perform complex calculations quickly and easily. They work like the special keys on sophisticated calculators that compute square roots, logarithms, and statistical evaluations—except Microsoft Excel has hundreds of these special functions. Some functions, such as SIN and FACT, are the equivalent of lengthy mathematical formulas you would otherwise have to create by hand. Other functions, such as IF and VLOOKUP, can't be otherwise duplicated by formulas. When none of the built-in functions is quite what you need, you can create custom functions, as explained in Chapter 29, "Creating custom functions."

Using the built-in function reference in Excel

While preparing this book, we had to make some tough choices. Fully describing each of the hundreds of worksheet functions would fill an entire book—or two, perhaps. To provide the greatest benefit, we had to decide which functions to focus on and which to mention only briefly. Admittedly, we tend to devote more ink to financial, information, and lookup functions than we do to engineering or trigonometric functions. We think this makes sense for the majority of our readers. If you need more information about functions that we do not cover in great detail, Excel offers several built-in resources:

- **The Help system**   The Excel Help system includes a detailed description of each worksheet function. Just press F1 or click a question-mark icon to display the Excel Help window, and then type a function name in the Search text box to find all the relevant Help topics. You can also type **Excel functions** in the Search box and then click either the Excel Functions (By Category) or Excel Functions (Alphabetical) Help topic. For example, clicking Excel Functions (By Category) displays the information shown in Figure 13-1.

  For more information, see "Using the Help system" in Chapter 2, "Exploring Excel fundamentals."

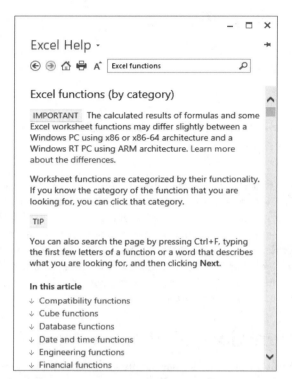

Figure 13-1 The Help system includes a comprehensive function reference.

- **The Insert Function dialog box** You can use this dialog box, shown in Figure 13-2, to browse through the entire list of functions if you're not sure which function you need. To display the Insert Function dialog box, click the tiny Insert Function button on the formula bar (or the extra-large Insert Function button on the Formulas tab).

- **The Function Arguments dialog box** This dialog box, shown in Figure 13-3, provides details about the selected function. Required arguments appear as separate text boxes in the middle of the dialog box. Notice also the link to the relevant Help topic at the bottom of the dialog box. To display the Function Arguments dialog box, click the Insert Function button on the formula bar, select a function, and click OK. You can also click the Insert Function button while you are in the process of entering a formula—*after* you type a valid function name and an open parenthesis—to display the Function Arguments dialog box.

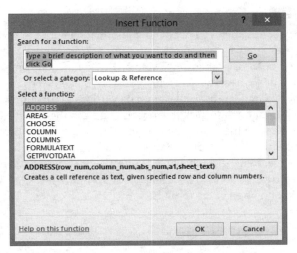

Figure 13-2 The Insert Function dialog box provides assistance with using functions.

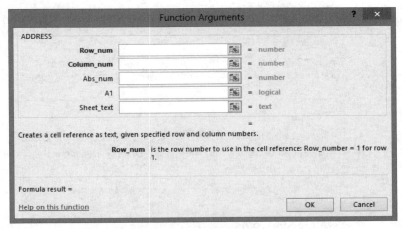

Figure 13-3 The Function Arguments dialog box provides assistance with entering function arguments.

> **Note**
>
> Drag the Function Arguments dialog box around the screen if you need to see the cells behind it. For maximum viewing, make the dialog box smaller by clicking one of the collapse dialog buttons on the right side of the argument boxes.

- **Function ScreenTips** These little pop-up descriptions appear below selected formulas. They are useful if you need more information about the syntax of a function as you type a formula; you can get help without even leaving the cell. After you type the required open parenthesis following any valid function name, the appropriate ScreenTip appears, as shown in Figure 13-4. The ScreenTip shows you the correct function syntax and any available alternate versions of the function (also shown in Figure 13-4). You can also click the function name in the ScreenTip to display the relevant topic from the Help system. If you click an argument name in the ScreenTip, the corresponding section of the formula is highlighted for you, making it easy to identify each argument. As shown in Figure 13-4, we clicked the *row_num* argument in the ScreenTip, resulting in the selection of the entire MATCH function (which calculates the row number) in the formula.

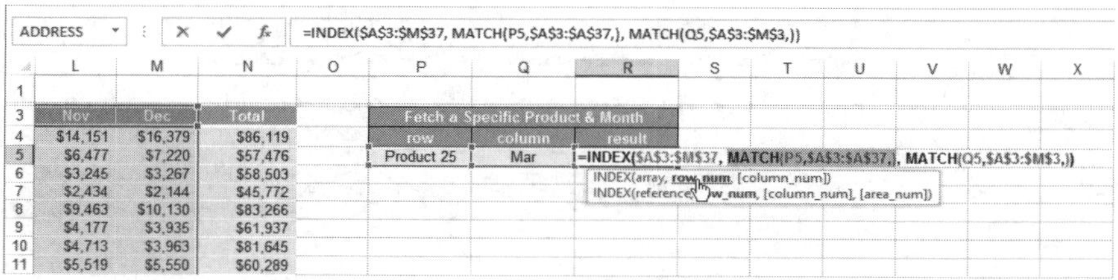

Figure 13-4 Click an argument name in the function ScreenTip that appears when you click an existing function to highlight the corresponding argument in the cell.

> **Note**
>
> To turn off function ScreenTips, click the File tab, click Options, select the Advanced category, and then in the Display area clear the Show Function Screen-Tips check box.

- **Formula AutoComplete** As you type a formula, Excel provides pop-up lists that offer function names and defined names that match the letters you are typing in the formula. For example, if you type **=S** in a cell, Excel displays a scrolling list of all functions (and defined names, if any) that begin with the letter *S*, which you can then double-click to insert in your formula.

  For details, see "Using Formula AutoComplete" and "Naming cells and cell ranges," both in Chapter 12, "Building formulas."

Exploring the syntax of functions

Worksheet functions have two parts: the name of the function and the arguments that follow. Function names—such as SUM and AVERAGE—describe the operation the function performs. Arguments specify the values or cells to be used by the function. For example, the function ROUND has the following syntax: =ROUND(*number, num_digits*), as in the formula =ROUND(M30,2). The M30 part is a cell reference entered as the *number* argument—the value to be rounded. The 2 part is the *num_digits* argument. The result of this function is a number (whatever the value in cell M30 happens to be) rounded to two decimal places.

Parentheses surround function arguments. The opening parenthesis must appear immediately after the name of the function. If you add a space or some other character between the name and the opening parenthesis, the error value #NAME? appears in the cell.

> **Note**
>
> A few functions—such as PI, TRUE, and NOW—have no arguments. (You usually nest these functions in other formulas.) Even though they have no arguments, you must place an empty set of parentheses after them, as in =NOW( ), so that Excel knows they are functions and not defined names.

When you use more than one argument in a function, you separate the arguments with commas. For example, the formula =PRODUCT(C1,C2,C5) tells Excel to multiply the numbers in cells C1, C2, and C5. Some functions, such as PRODUCT and SUM, take an unspecified number of arguments. You can use as many as 255 arguments in a function, as long as the total length of the formula does not exceed 8,192 characters. However, you can use a single argument or a range that refers to any number of cells in your worksheet in a formula. For example, the function =SUM(A1:A5,C2:C10,D3:D17) has only three arguments, but it actually totals the values in 29 cells. (The first argument, A1:A5, refers to the range of five cells from A1 through A5, and so on.) The referenced cells, in turn, can also contain formulas that refer to more cells or ranges.

Expressions as arguments

You can use combinations of functions to create an expression that Excel evaluates to a single value and then interprets as an argument. For example, in the formula =SUM(SIN(A1*PI( )),2*COS(A2*PI( ))) the comma separates two complex expressions that Excel evaluates and uses as the arguments of the SUM function.

Types of arguments

In the examples presented so far, all the arguments have been cell or range references. You can also use numbers, text, logical values, range names, arrays, and error values as arguments.

Numeric values

The arguments to a function can be numeric. For example, the SUM function in the formula =SUM(327,209,176) adds the numbers 327, 209, and 176. Usually, however, you type the numbers you want to use in cells in a worksheet and then use references to those cells as arguments to your functions.

Text values

You can also use text as an argument to a function. For example, in the formula =TEXT(NOW( ),"*mmm d, yyyy*"), the second argument to the TEXT function, *mmm d, yyyy*, is a text argument specifically recognized by Excel. It specifies a pattern for converting the serial date value returned by NOW into a text string. Text arguments can be text strings enclosed in quotation marks or references to cells that contain text.

For more about text functions, see "Understanding text functions" in Chapter 14, "Everyday functions."

Logical values

The arguments to a few functions specify only that an option is set or not set; you can use the logical values TRUE to set an option and FALSE to specify that the option isn't set. A logical expression returns the value TRUE or FALSE (which evaluates to 1 and 0, respectively) to the worksheet or the formula containing the expression. For example, the first argument of the IF function in the formula =IF(A1=TRUE,"Future ", "Past ")&"History" is a logical expression that uses the value in cell A1. If the value in A1 is TRUE (or 1), the expression A1=TRUE evaluates to TRUE, the IF function returns Future, and the formula returns the text Future History to the worksheet.

For more about logical functions, see "Understanding logical functions" in Chapter 14.

Named references

You can use a defined name as an argument to a function. For example, if you click the Formulas tab on the ribbon and use the Define Name button to assign the name QtrlyIncome to the range C3:C6, you can use the formula =SUM(QtrlyIncome) to total the numbers in cells C3, C4, C5, and C6.

For more about names, see "Naming cells and cell ranges" in Chapter 12.

Arrays

You can use an array as an argument in a function. Some functions, such as TREND and TRANSPOSE, require array arguments; other functions don't require array arguments but do accept them. Arrays can consist of numbers, text, or logical values.

For more about arrays, see "Using arrays" in Chapter 12.

Mixed argument types

You can mix argument types within a function. For example, the formula =AVERAGE(Group1,A3,5*3) uses a defined name (Group1), a cell reference (A3), and a numeric expression (5*3) to arrive at a single value. All three are acceptable.

Inserting functions

The easiest way to locate and insert built-in functions is by clicking the Insert Function button. This button has two versions—one is the little *fx* button that appears on the formula bar, and the other is located in the Function Library group on the Formulas tab on the ribbon. In either location, when you click Insert Function, the dialog box shown in Figure 13-2 appears. If you're not sure what function you need, type a description of what you are trying to do in the Search text box. For example, if you type **how many cells contain values** and then click the Go button, the Insert Function dialog box returns a list of recommended functions, similar to the list shown in Figure 13-5.

You can also select a function category from the Or Select A Category drop-down list to filter the list. Function categories include Financial, Date & Time, Lookup & Reference, Text, and more. The Recommended category keeps track of any functions returned as a result of using the Search text box. When you select a function, the syntax and a brief description appear at the bottom of the dialog box. You can obtain help on a function selected in the Select A Function list by clicking the Help On This Function link at the bottom of the dialog box.

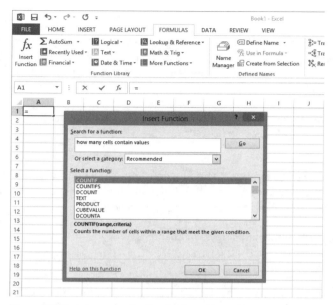

Figure 13-5 Ask a question in the Search text box, and Excel suggests some functions you can try.

When you select a function and click OK, Excel enters an equal sign to start a formula in the active cell, inserts the function name and a set of parentheses, and displays the Function Arguments dialog box, shown in Figure 13-3. The Function Arguments dialog box contains one text box for each argument of the selected function. If the function accepts a variable number of arguments (such as SUM), the dialog box gets bigger as you type additional arguments. A description of the argument whose text box currently contains the insertion point appears near the bottom of the dialog box. To the right of each argument text box, a display area shows the current value of the argument. This display is handy when you are using references or defined names because the value of each argument is calculated for you. The current value of the function (Formula Result) appears at the bottom of the dialog box.

Some functions, such as INDEX, have more than one form. When you select such a function from the Insert Function dialog box, Excel presents the Select Arguments dialog box, shown in Figure 13-6, in which you select the form you want to use.

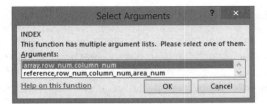

Figure 13-6 If a function has more than one form, the Select Arguments dialog box appears.

You can also use the Function Library group on the Formulas tab on the ribbon to insert functions. Each of the categories listed in the Insert Function dialog box has a button or menu in the Function Library group. For example, clicking the More Functions button reveals a menu containing additional categories of functions, as shown in Figure 13-7. When you click one of the functions listed on any of these menus, Excel inserts the selected function in the formula bar, and the Function Arguments dialog box appears.

Figure 13-7 The Function Library group on the Formulas tab provides direct access to the built-in functions in Excel.

TROUBLESHOOTING

I get a #NAME? error

You might get the #NAME? error for a few reasons, but one of the more common ones is that you typed the function name incorrectly. Here's a good habit to acquire if you type functions: use lowercase letters. When you press Enter, Excel converts the name of the function to uppercase letters if you typed it correctly. If the letters don't change to uppercase, you probably typed the name of the function incorrectly. If you're not sure of the exact name or if you continue to get an error, perhaps it's time to consult Help or use the Insert Function dialog box.

Inserting references and names

As you can with any other formula, you can insert cell references and defined names into your functions easily by using the mouse. For example, to enter a function in cell C11 that averages the cells in the range C2:C10, select cell C11, type **=average(**, and then select the range C2:C10. A marquee appears around the selected cells, and a reference to the selected range appears in the formula. Then type the closing parenthesis. If you define named ranges, constants, or formulas in your worksheets, you can insert them in your formulas. To do this, click the Formulas tab, click the Use In Formula button in the Defined Names group, and then select the name you want to use. When you click the name, it appears at the insertion point in the formula.

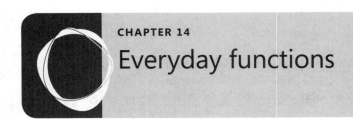

Everyday functions

T HIS CHAPTER describes some of the more useful functions Microsoft Excel has to offer. To keep this book from threatening the structural integrity of your bookshelf, we had to make some hard choices about which functions to highlight. Therefore, this chapter (along with Chapters 15, 16, and 17) by no means represents a comprehensive reference. For complete information about all the built-in functions, you can use a number of on-screen tools, which are covered in "Using the built-in function reference in Excel" in Chapter 13, "Using functions." Appendix C, "Function reference," lists every function available in Excel, along with the basic information you need to put each one to use, and it includes cross-references to any information available in this and other chapters.

For more information, see Chapter 15, "Formatting and calculating date and time," Chapter 16, "Functions for financial analysis," and Chapter 17, "Functions for analyzing statistics."

Understanding mathematical functions

Most of the work you do in Excel probably involves at least a few mathematical functions. The most popular among these is the SUM function, but Excel is capable of calculating just about anything. In the next sections, we discuss some of the most used (and most useful) mathematical functions in Excel.

Using the SUM function

The SUM function totals a series of numbers. It takes the form =SUM(*number1*, *number2*, ...). The *number* arguments are a series of as many as 30 entries that can be numbers, formulas, ranges, or cell references that result in numbers. SUM ignores arguments that refer to text values, logical values, or blank cells.

The Sum button

Because SUM is such a commonly used function, Excel provides the Sum button on the Home tab on the ribbon, as well as the AutoSum button on the Formulas tab. In addition to

SUM, these buttons include a menu of other commonly used functions. If you select a cell and click the Sum button, Excel creates a SUM formula and guesses which cells you want to total. To enter SUM formulas in a range of cells, select the cells before clicking Sum.

The SUMIF, SUMIFS, and COUNTIF functions

The SUMIF function is similar to SUM, but it first tests each cell using a specified conditional test before adding it to the total. This function takes the arguments (*range, criteria, sum_range*). The *range* argument specifies the range you want to test, the *criteria* argument specifies the conditional test to be performed on each cell in the range, and the *sum_range* argument specifies the cells to be totaled. For example, if you have a worksheet with a column of month names defined using the range name Months and an adjacent column of numbers named Sales, use the formula =SUMIF(Months, "June", Sales) to return the value in the Sales cell that is adjacent to the label June. Alternatively, you can use a conditional test formula such as =SUMIF(Sales, ">=999", Sales) to return the total of all sales figures that are more than $999.

The SUMIFS function does similar work to that of the SUMIF function, except you can specify up to 127 different ranges to sum, each with their own criteria. Note that in this function, the *sum_range* argument is in the first position instead of the third position: (*sum_range, criteria_range1, criteria1, criteria_range2, criteria2, ...*). The sum range and each criteria range must all be the same size and shape. Using a similar example to the one we used for the SUMIF function, suppose we also created defined names for cell ranges Months, Totals, Product1, Product2, and so on. The formula =SUMIFS(Totals, Product3, "<=124", Months, "June") returns the total sales for the month of June when sales of Product3 were less than or equal to $124.

Similarly, COUNTIF counts the cells that match specified criteria and takes the arguments (*range, criteria*). Using the same example, you can find the number of months in which total sales fell to less than $600 by using a conditional test, as in the formula =COUNTIF(Totals, "<600").

For more information about conditional tests, see "Creating conditional tests" in Chapter 12, "Building formulas." For more about using range names, see "Naming cells and cell ranges" in Chapter 12.

Using selected mathematical functions

Excel has over 60 built-in math and trigonometry functions; the following sections brush only the surface, covering a few of the more useful or misunderstood functions. You can access them directly by clicking the Math & Trig button on the Formulas tab on the ribbon.

The AGGREGATE function

The AGGREGATE function, new in Excel 2013, returns an aggregate of a range or array by applying one of 19 functions, and it offers the option to ignore hidden rows, error values, or both. This function is designed for use on columns of data; it is not intended for use with rows, or ranges of data that are arranged horizontally.

When used with lists and ranges, the AGGREGATE function takes the arguments *(function_num, options, ref1, ref2, ...)*, where *function_num* is a number from 1 to 19 indicating the function you want to apply to the selected range, as shown in Table 14-1; *options* is an optional number from 1 to 7 indicating specific instructions for ignoring particular values, as shown in Table 14-2; and *ref1*, *ref2*, and the like are the cells or ranges you want to aggregate.

TABLE 14-1 AGGREGATE function numbers

Argument	Description
1	AVERAGE
2	COUNT
3	COUNTA
4	MAX
5	MIN
6	PRODUCT
7	STDEV
8	STDEV.P
9	SUM
10	VAR.S
11	VAR.P
12	MEDIAN
13	MODE.SNGL
14	LARGE *(ref2 required)*
15	SMALL *(ref2 required)*
16	PERCENTILE.INC *(ref2 required)*
17	QUARTILE.INC *(ref2 required)*
18	PERCENTILE.EXC *(ref2 required)*
19	QUARTILE.EXC *(ref2 required)*

A *ref2* argument is required for functions 14 through 19, as indicated in Table 14-1. When used with arrays, the AGGREGATE function takes the arguments *(function_num, options, array, k)*, where *array* is the array of values you want to aggregate and, depending on the function, *k* is a number indicating the percentile, quartile, or *k*th largest or *k*th smallest value you want to find.

TABLE 14-2 AGGREGATE options

Argument	Description
0 or omitted	Ignore nested SUBTOTAL and AGGREGATE functions
1	Ignore hidden rows, nested SUBTOTAL and AGGREGATE functions
2	Ignore error values, nested SUBTOTAL and AGGREGATE functions
3	Ignore hidden rows, error values, nested SUBTOTAL and AGGREGATE functions
4	Ignore nothing
5	Ignore hidden rows
6	Ignore error values
7	Ignore hidden rows and error values

The PRODUCT and SUMPRODUCT functions

The PRODUCT function multiplies all its arguments and can take as many as 255 arguments that are text or logical values; the function ignores blank cells.

You can use the SUMPRODUCT function to multiply the value in each cell in one range by the corresponding cell in another range of equal size and then add the results. You can include up to 255 arrays as arguments, but each array must have the same dimensions. (Non-numeric entries are treated as zero.) For example, the following formulas are essentially the same:

```
=SUMPRODUCT(A1:A4, B1:B4)
```

```
{=SUM(A1:A4*B1:B4)}
```

The only difference between them is that you must enter the SUM formula as an array by pressing Ctrl+Shift+Enter.

For more information about arrays, see "Using arrays" in Chapter 12.

The MOD function

The MOD function returns the remainder of a division operation (modulus). It takes the arguments (*number, divisor*). The result of the MOD function is the remainder produced when *number* is divided by *divisor*. For example, the function =MOD(9, 4) returns *1*, the remainder that results from dividing 9 by 4.

A MOD example

Here's a practical use of the MOD function that you can ponder:

1. Select a range of cells such as B5:F16, click Conditional Formatting on the Home tab on the ribbon, and then click New Rule.

2. Select the Use A Formula To Determine Which Cells To Format option in the Select A Rule Type list.

3. In the text box, type the formula =**MOD(ROW(), 2)=0**.

4. Click the Format button, and select a color on the Fill tab to create a format that applies the selected color to every other row. Note that if you select a single cell in an odd-numbered row before creating this formatting formula, nothing seems to happen, but if you copy or apply the format to other rows, you'll see the result. Click OK to accept the format, and then click OK to apply the formatting.

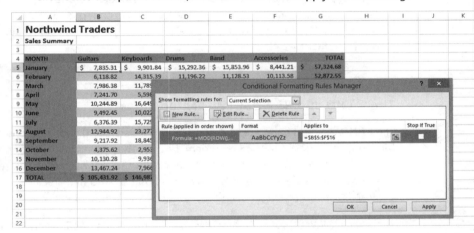

We clicked the Conditional Formatting button and clicked Manage Rules to display the dialog box shown in the preceding figure. The MOD formula identifies the current row number using the ROW function, divides it by 2, and if there is a remainder (indicating an odd-numbered row), it returns FALSE because the formula also contains the conditional test =0. If MOD returns anything but 0 as a remainder, the condition returns FALSE. Therefore, Excel applies formatting only when the formula returns TRUE (in even-numbered rows). For more information about conditional formatting, see "Formatting conditionally" in Chapter 9, "Worksheet formatting techniques." You can also achieve similar results (with additional functionality) by converting the cell range into a table and using the table formatting features. For more information, see Chapter 22, "Managing information in tables."

The COMBIN function

The COMBIN function determines the number of possible combinations, or groups, that can be taken from a pool of items. It takes the arguments (*number, number_chosen*), where *number* is the total number of items in the pool and *number_chosen* is the number of items you want to group in each combination. For example, to determine how many different 11-player football teams you can create from a pool of 17 players, type the formula **=COMBIN(17, 11)**. The result indicates that you could create 12,376 teams.

Try your luck

The COMBIN function can help you figure out just how slim a chance you have of drawing the elusive ace-high straight flush in a game of five-card stud. You express the number of 5-card combinations by using the formula =COMBIN(52, 5), resulting in 2,598,960. That's not too bad when you consider the odds of winning the lottery. For a lotto game in which you select 6 numbers out of a total of 49, the formula **=COMBIN(49, 6)** reveals that there are 13,983,816 possibilities. You'd better keep your day job either way.

The RAND and RANDBETWEEN functions

The RAND function generates a random number between 0 and 1. It's one of the few Excel functions that doesn't take an argument, but you must still type a pair of parentheses after the function name. The result of a RAND function changes each time you recalculate your worksheet. This is called a *volatile* function. If you use automatic recalculation, the value of the RAND function changes each time you make a worksheet entry.

The RANDBETWEEN function provides more control than RAND. With RANDBETWEEN, you can specify a range of numbers within which to generate random integer values. The arguments (*bottom, top*) represent the smallest and largest integers that the function should use. The values for these arguments are inclusive. For example, the formula =RANDBETWEEN(123, 456) can return any integer from 123 up to and including 456.

Using the rounding functions

Excel includes several functions devoted to the seemingly narrow task of rounding numbers by a specified amount.

The ROUND, ROUNDDOWN, and ROUNDUP functions

The ROUND function rounds a value to a specified number of decimal places. Digits to the right of the decimal point that are less than 5 are rounded down, and digits greater than or equal to 5 are rounded up. It takes the arguments (*number, num_digits*). If *num_digits* is a positive number, then *number* is rounded to the specified number of decimal points; if *num_digits* is negative, the function rounds to the left of the decimal point; if *num_digits* is 0, the function rounds to the nearest integer. For example, the formula =ROUND(123.4567, −2) returns *100*, and the formula =ROUND(123.4567, 3) returns *123.457*. The ROUNDDOWN and ROUNDUP functions take the same form as ROUND. As their names imply, they always round down or up, respectively.

> **CAUTION!**
>
> Don't confuse the rounding functions with rounded number formats, such as the one applied when you click the Accounting Number Format button in the Number group on the Home tab. When you format the contents of a cell to a specified number of decimal places, you change only the display of the number in the cell; you don't change the cell's value. When performing calculations, Excel always uses the underlying value, not the displayed value. Conversely, the rounding functions permanently change the underlying values.

The EVEN and ODD functions

The EVEN function rounds a number up to the nearest even integer. The ODD function rounds a number up to the nearest odd integer. Negative numbers are correspondingly rounded down. For example, the formula =EVEN(22.4) returns *24*, and the formula =ODD(−4) returns *−5*.

The FLOOR and CEILING functions

The FLOOR function rounds a number down to its nearest given multiple, and the CEILING function rounds a number up to its nearest given multiple. These functions take the arguments (*number, multiple*). For example, the formula =FLOOR(23.4, 0.5) returns *23*, and the formula =CEILING(5, 1.5) returns *6*, the nearest multiple of 1.5. The FLOOR.PRECISE and CEILING.PRECISE functions round numbers down or up to the nearest integer or multiple of significance. Both take the arguments (*number, significance*). For example, the formula =FLOOR.PRECISE(23.4, 4) returns *20*, which is the nearest integer below 23.4 that is a multiple of 4. Most of the time, you see no difference in results between the regular and precise versions of these functions, unless your arguments are negative numbers. The precise versions always round up, regardless of the number's sign.

Using the flexible MROUND function

Suppose you want to round a number to a multiple of something other than 10—for example, rounding numbers to sixteenths so that when formatted as fractions they never appear with a denominator larger than 16. The MROUND function rounds any number to a multiple you specify.

The function takes the form =MROUND(*number*, *multiple*). For example, typing the formula =**MROUND(A1, .0625)** rounds the number displayed in cell A1 in increments of one-sixteenth. The function rounds up if the remainder after dividing *number* by *multiple* is at least half the value of *multiple*. If you want to apply this to an existing formula, just wrap the MROUND formula around it by replacing A1 (in the example) with your formula.

The INT function

The INT function rounds numbers down to the nearest integer. For example, the formulas

=INT(100.01)

=INT(100.99999999)

both return the value 100, even though the number 100.99999999 is essentially equal to 101. When a number is negative, INT also rounds that number down to the next integer. If each of the numbers in these examples were negative, the resulting value would be *–101*.

AVERAGE vs. AVG

Some other spreadsheet programs use the AVG statistical function to compute averages. In some previous versions of Excel, typing the formula =**AVG(2, 4, 5, 8)** results in a #NAME? error. Excel now accepts AVG, although when you type the function, an error dialog box appears, asking whether you want to change the function to AVERAGE. That's still kind of rude, but it works. Presumably, one reason why Excel doesn't just change AVG to AVERAGE for you is to remind you to start using the correct function name.

When you use this function, Excel ignores cells containing text, logical values, or empty cells, but it includes cells containing a zero value. You can also choose the AVERAGEA function, which operates in the same way as AVERAGE, except it includes text and logical values in the calculation.

The TRUNC function

The TRUNC function truncates everything to the right of the decimal point in a number, regardless of its sign. It takes the arguments (*number, num_digits*). If *num_digits* isn't specified, it's set to 0. Otherwise, TRUNC truncates everything after the specified number of digits to the right of the decimal point. For example, the formula =TRUNC(13.978) returns the value *13*; the formula =TRUNC(13.978, 1) returns the value *13.9*.

Understanding text functions

Text functions in Excel are some of the most useful word-processing and data-management tools you'll find anywhere—they perform tasks that word-processing programs can't. These functions are conveniently listed for you when you click the Text button on the Formulas tab on the ribbon.

You can use the TRIM and CLEAN functions to remove extra spaces and nonprinting characters, which is great for cleaning up imported data—a task that ranges from difficult to impossible using search and replace. The UPPER, LOWER, and PROPER functions change the case of words, sentences, and paragraphs with no retyping. You might find yourself copying text from other documents into Excel just so that you can apply these functions. After using text functions, select the cells containing the formulas, press Ctrl+C to copy, click the Paste button on the Home tab, and then click Paste Values to convert the formulas to their resulting (text) values. You can then copy the edited text into the original document.

In the following sections, we discuss the most useful Excel text functions.

Using selected text functions

Text functions convert numeric entries, as well as *numeric text* entries, into text strings so that you can manipulate the text strings themselves. Numeric text is a type of numeric entry that provides a few specific text characters in addition to numeric characters. For details, see "Using numeric text in formulas" in Chapter 12.

The TEXT function

The TEXT function converts a number into a text string with a specified format. Its arguments are (*value, format_text*), where *value* represents any number, formula, or cell reference; and *format_text* is the format for displaying the resulting string. For example, the formula =TEXT(98/4, "0.00") returns the text string *24.50*. You can use any Excel formatting symbol ($, #, 0, and so on) except the asterisk (*) to specify the format you want, but you can't use the General format.

> For information about formatting symbols and codes, see Table 9-1, "Custom format symbols," and Table 9-2, "Built-in custom format codes," both in Chapter 9.

The DOLLAR function

Like the TEXT function, the DOLLAR function converts a number into a string. DOLLAR, however, formats the resulting string as currency with the number of decimal places you specify. The arguments (*number, decimals*) specify a number or reference and the number of decimal places you want. For example, the formula =DOLLAR(45.899, 2) returns the text string *$45.90*. Notice that Excel rounds the number when necessary.

If you omit *decimals*, Excel uses two decimal places. If you add a comma after the first argument but omit the second argument, Excel uses zero decimal places. If you use a negative number for *decimals*, Excel rounds to the left of the decimal point.

The LEN function

The LEN function returns the number of characters in an entry. The single argument can be a number, a string enclosed in double quotation marks, or a reference to a cell. Trailing zeros are ignored. For example, the formula =LEN("Test") returns *4*.

The LEN function returns the length of the displayed text or value, not the length of the underlying cell contents. For example, suppose cell A10 contains the formula =A1+A2+A3+A4+A5+A6+A7+A8 and its result is the value 25. The formula =LEN(A10) returns the value *2*, which indicates the length of the resulting value, *25*. The cell referenced as the argument of the LEN function can contain another string function. For example, if cell A1 contains the function =REPT("–*", 75), which enters the two-character hyphen and asterisk string 75 times in a cell, the formula =LEN(A1) returns the value *150*.

The ASCII functions: CHAR and CODE

Every computer uses numeric codes to represent characters. The most prevalent system of numeric codes is ASCII, or American Standard Code for Information Interchange. ASCII uses a number from 0 to 127 (or to 255 in some systems) to represent each number, letter, and symbol.

The CHAR and CODE functions deal with these ASCII codes. The CHAR function returns the character that corresponds to an ASCII code number; the CODE function returns the ASCII code number for the first character of its argument. For example, the formula =CHAR(83) returns the text *S*. The formula =CODE("S") returns the ASCII code *83*. If you type a literal character as the text argument, be sure to enclose the character in quotation marks; otherwise, Excel returns the #NAME? error value.

> **Note**
>
> If you use certain ASCII symbols often, you can use the ASCII code number with the CHAR function to create a symbol without using the Symbol button on the Insert tab on the ribbon. For example, to create a registered trademark symbol (®), just type =CHAR(174).

The cleanup functions: TRIM and CLEAN

Leading and trailing blank characters often prevent you from correctly sorting entries in a worksheet or a database. If you use string functions to manipulate text in your worksheet, extra spaces can prevent your formulas from working correctly. The TRIM function eliminates leading, trailing, and extra blank characters from a string, leaving only single spaces between words.

The CLEAN function is similar to TRIM, except it operates only on nonprintable characters, such as tabs and program-specific codes. CLEAN is especially useful if you import data from another program or operating system, because the translation process often introduces nonprintable characters that appear as symbols or boxes. You can use CLEAN to remove these characters from the data.

The EXACT function

The EXACT function is a conditional function that determines whether two strings match exactly. The function ignores formatting, but it is case sensitive, so uppercase letters are considered different from lowercase letters. If both strings are identical, the function returns TRUE. Both arguments must be literal strings enclosed in quotation marks, references to cells that contain text, numeric values, or formulas that evaluate to numeric values. For example, if cell A5 and cell A6 on your worksheet both contain the text *Totals*, the formula =EXACT(A5, A6) returns TRUE.

For information about comparing strings, see "Creating conditional tests" in Chapter 12.

The case functions: UPPER, LOWER, and PROPER

Three functions manipulate the case of characters in text strings. The UPPER and LOWER functions convert text strings to all uppercase or all lowercase letters. The PROPER function capitalizes the first letter in each word, capitalizes any other letters in the text string that do not follow another letter, and converts all other letters to lowercase. For example, if cell A1 contains the text *mark Dodge*, you can type the formula **=UPPER(A1)** to return *MARK DODGE*. Similarly, the formula =LOWER(A1) returns *mark dodge*, and **=PROPER(A1)** returns *Mark Dodge*.

Unexpected results can occur when the text contains an apostrophe, however. For example, if cell A1 contains the text *it wasn't bad*, the PROPER function converts it to *It Wasn'T Bad*.

Using the substring text functions

The following functions locate and return portions of a text string or assemble larger strings from smaller ones: FIND, SEARCH, RIGHT, LEFT, MID, REPLACE, SUBSTITUTE, and CONCATENATE.

The FIND and SEARCH functions

You use the FIND and SEARCH functions to locate the position of a substring within a string. Both functions return the position in the string of the character you specify. (Excel counts blank spaces and punctuation marks as characters.) These two functions work the same way, except FIND is case sensitive and SEARCH allows wildcards. Both functions take the same arguments: (*find_text, within_text, start_num*). The optional *start_num* argument is helpful when *within_text* contains more than one occurrence of *find_text*. If you omit *start_num*, Excel reports the first match it locates. For example, to locate the *p* in the string *A Night at the Opera*, you type the formula **=FIND("p", "A Night at the Opera")**. The formula returns *17*, because *p* is the 17th character in the string.

If you're not sure of the character sequence you're searching for, you can use the SEARCH function and include wildcards in your *find_text* string. Suppose you used the names Smith and Smyth in your worksheet. To determine whether either name is in cell A1, type the formula **=SEARCH("Sm?th", A1)**. If cell A1 contains the text *John Smith* or *John Smyth*, the SEARCH function returns the value *6*—the starting point of the string *Sm?th*.

If you're not sure of the number of characters, use the * wildcard. For example, to find the position of Allan or Alan within the text (if any) stored in cell A1, type the formula **=SEARCH("A*an", A1)** (which would also return the word *American*).

> **Note**
> You might notice the presence of several text functions that look similar to others but end in "B," such as FINDB, LEFTB, LENB, REPLACEB, and so on. These functions perform similar tasks to their "non-B" counterparts, but they are included specifically for use with double-byte character sets, such as Japanese, Chinese, and Korean.

The RIGHT and LEFT functions

The RIGHT function returns the rightmost series of characters from a specified string; the LEFT function returns the leftmost series of characters. These functions take the same arguments: (*text, num_chars*). The *num_chars* argument indicates the number of characters to extract from the *text* argument.

> ### Practical text manipulation
>
> Excel excels at text manipulation. If you deal with a lot of mailing lists, for example, here is a trick you might find useful, and it serves as a good example as well. Suppose you import a database of addresses in which the first and last names are stored together in the same cell. This example shows you a formula you can use to parse them into separate columns:
>
>
>
> The formulas in columns C and D use the SEARCH function to locate the space character. The function assigns it a number based on its position in the cell. Inside the RIGHT function shown in this figure, the number is subtracted from the total number of characters in the cell, provided by the LEN function. This returns everything to the right of the space. The formula you can't see in cell C2 doesn't require the LEN function: =LEFT(A2,SEARCH(" ",A2)). You might want to use the TRIM function on column A first to be sure there are no extra spaces. For a related text-manipulation trick, see "Practical concatenation" in Chapter 12. And for an even better trick that is new in Excel 2013, see "Automatic parsing and concatenation using Flash Fill" in Chapter 8, "Worksheet editing techniques."

 You'll find the Text.xlsx file with the other examples on the companion website.

These functions count blank spaces in the *text* argument as characters; if *text* contains leading or trailing blank characters, you might want to use a TRIM function within the RIGHT or LEFT function to ensure the expected result. For example, suppose you type **This is a test** in cell A1 on your worksheet. The formula =RIGHT(A1, 4) returns the word *test*.

The MID function

You can use the MID function to extract a series of characters from a text string. This function takes the arguments (*text, start_num, num_chars*). For example, if cell A1 contains the text *This Is A Long Text Entry*, you can type the formula **=MID(A1, 11, 9)** to extract the characters *Long Text* from the entry in cell A1.

The REPLACE and SUBSTITUTE functions

The REPLACE and SUBSTITUTE functions substitute new text for old text. The REPLACE function replaces one string of characters with another string of characters and takes the arguments (*old_text, start_num, num_chars, new_text*). Suppose cell A1 contains the text *Eric Miller, CEO*. To replace the first four characters with the string *Geof*, type the formula **=REPLACE(A1, 1, 4, "Geof")**. The result is *Geof Miller, CEO*.

With the SUBSTITUTE function, you specify the text to replace. The function takes the arguments (*text, old_text, new_text, instance_num*). Suppose cell A1 contains the text *Mandy* and you want to place it in cell A2 but change it to *Randy*. Type **=SUBSTITUTE(A1, "M", "R")** in cell A2.

The *instance_num* argument optionally replaces only the specified occurrence of *old_text*. For example, if cell A1 contains the text *through the hoop*, the *4* in the formula =SUBSTITUTE(A1, "h", "l", 4) tells Excel to substitute an *l* for the fourth *h* found in cell A1. If you don't include *instance_num*, Excel changes all occurrences of *old_text* to *new_text*.

> **Note**
>
> You can create an array formula using the SUBSTITUTE function to count the number of occurrences of a text string in a range of cells. Use the formula =SUM(LEN(<range>)–LEN(SUBSTITUTE(<range>, "text", "")))/LEN("text") to count the number of times *text* appears in <range>. Type the formula, and press Ctrl+Shift+Enter.

The CONCATENATE function

To assemble strings from as many as 255 smaller strings or references, the CONCATENATE function is the function equivalent of the *&* character. For example, if cell B4 contains the text *Salt*, the formula =CONCATENATE(B4, " of the Earth") returns *Salt of the Earth*. Note that we included a leading space character in the *text* argument; otherwise, the result would be *Saltof the Earth*. You could also specify the space character as a separate argument, as in the formula =CONCATENATE(B4, " ", "of the Earth").

TROUBLESHOOTING

Concatenated dates become serial numbers

If you try to concatenate the contents of a cell formatted as a date, the result is probably not what you expect. Because a date in Excel is only a serial number, what you usually see is a formatted representation of the date. But when you concatenate the contents of a date-formatted cell, you get the unformatted version of the date. To avoid this problem, use the TEXT function to convert the serial number to a recognizable form. For example, suppose cell A1 contains the text *Today's Date is*, and cell A2 contains the function =NOW() and is formatted to display the date in *dd/mm/yyyy* format. Despite the cell's formatting, the formula =CONCATENATE(A1, " ", A2) results in the value *Today's Date is 41573* (or whatever the current date serial number happens to be). To remedy this problem, use the TEXT function as follows:

=CONCATENATE(A1, " ", TEXT(A2, "dd/mm/yyyy")).

This version returns the value *Today's Date is 10/26/2013* (or whatever today's date happens to be). Note that the formula includes a space character (" ") as a separate argument between the two cell reference arguments.

Understanding logical functions

You use logical functions to test for specific conditions. These functions are often called *logical operators* in discussions of Boolean logic, which is named after George Boole, the British mathematician. You might have run across logical operators in *set theory*, which is used for teaching logical concepts in high school. You use logical operators to arrive at one of two conclusions: TRUE or FALSE. We discuss the most useful logical functions in the following sections. You can access the logical functions by clicking the Logical button on the Formulas tab on the ribbon.

Using selected logical functions

Excel has a rich set of logical functions. Most logical functions use conditional tests to determine whether a specified condition is TRUE or FALSE.

For more information about conditional tests, see "Creating conditional tests" in Chapter 12.

The IF function

The IF function returns values according to supplied conditional tests. It takes the arguments (*logical_test, value_if_true, value_if_false*). For example, the formula =IF(A6<22, 5, 10) returns *5* if the value in cell A6 is less than 22; otherwise, it returns *10*. You can nest other functions within an IF function. For example, the formula =IF(SUM(A1:A10)>0, SUM(A1:A10), 0) returns the sum of A1 through A10 if the sum is greater than 0; otherwise, it returns *0*.

You can also use text arguments to return nothing instead of zero if the result is false. For example, the formula =IF(SUM(A1:A10)>0, SUM(A1:A10), " ") returns a null string (" ") if the conditional test is false. The *logical_test* argument can also consist of text. For example, the formula =IF(A1="Test", 100, 200) returns the value *100* if cell A1 contains the string *Test*; it returns *200* if A1 contains any other entry. The match between the two text entries must be exact except for case.

INSIDE OUT   Streamline formulas using the SUMIF function

If you find yourself frequently using the IF function to perform conditional tests on individual rows or columns and then use the SUM function to total the results, the SUMIF function might make your work a little easier. With SUMIF, you can add specific values in a range according to a criterion you supply. For example, you can type the formula =**SUMIF(C12:C27, "Yes", A12:A27)** to find the total of all numbers in A12:A27 in which the cell in the same row in column C contains the word *Yes*. This performs all the calculations you need in one cell and eliminates having to create a column of IF formulas. For more information about SUMIF, see "The SUMIF, SUMIFS, and COUNTIF functions" later in this chapter.

The AND, OR, and NOT functions

These three functions help you develop compound conditional tests. They work with the logical operators =, >, <, >=, <=, and <>. The AND and OR functions can each have as many as 255 logical arguments. The NOT function takes only one argument. Arguments can be conditional tests, arrays, or references to cells that contain logical values.

Suppose you want Excel to return the text *Pass* only if a student has an average score greater than 75 and fewer than five unexcused absences. In Figure 14-1, we typed the formula =**IF(AND(G4<5,F4>75), "Pass", "Fail")**. This fails the student in row 5 because of the five absences. If you use OR instead of AND in the formula shown in Figure 14-1, all students would pass.

H4	▼	:	×	✓	*fx*	=IF(AND(G4<5,F4>75),"Pass","Fail")			

◢	A	B	C	D	E	F	G	H	I
1	**Math Exam Scores**								
2	Ms. Martins								
3	*Student*	**Exam 1**	**Exam 2**	**Exam 3**	**Exam 4**	*Average*	*Absences*	*Pass/Fail*	
4	Krieger, Doris	87	90	79	96	88.00	2	Pass	
5	Oliveira, Manuel	92	94	94	97	94.25	5	Fail	
6	Kodeda, Adam	96	95	95	80	91.50	0	Pass	
7	Lange, Michael	85	87	87	88	86.75	4	Pass	
8	Taylor, Maurice	81	88	88	85	85.50	1	Pass	
9									
10									

Figure 14-1 You can create complex conditional tests using the AND function.

You'll find the And Or Not.xlsx file with the other examples on the companion website.

The OR function returns the logical value TRUE if any one of the conditional tests is true; the AND function returns the logical value TRUE only if all the conditional tests are true.

Because the NOT function negates a condition, you usually use it with other functions. NOT instructs Excel to return the logical value TRUE if the argument is false or the logical value FALSE if the argument is true. For example, the formula =IF(NOT(A1=2), "Go", " ") tells Excel to return the text *Go* if the value of cell A1 is anything but *2*.

Nested IF functions

Sometimes you can't resolve a logical problem using only logical operators and the AND, OR, and NOT functions. In these cases, you can nest IF functions to create a hierarchy of tests. For example, the formula =IF(A1=100, "Always", IF(AND(A1>=80, A1<100), "Usually", IF(AND(A1>=60, A1<80), "Sometimes", "Who cares?"))) states, in plain language, the following: If the value is *100*, return *Always*; if the value is from *80* through *99*, return *Usually*; if the value is from *60* through *79*, return *Sometimes*; or if none of these conditions is true, return *Who cares?*. You can create formulas containing up to 64 levels of nested functions.

Other uses for conditional functions

You can use all the conditional functions described in this section as stand-alone formulas. Although you usually use functions such as AND, OR, NOT, ISERROR, ISNA, and ISREF within an IF function, you can also use formulas, such as =AND(A1>A2, A2<A3), to perform simple conditional tests. This formula returns the logical value TRUE if the value in A1 is greater than the value in A2 and the value in A2 is less than the value in A3. You might use this type of formula to assign TRUE and FALSE values to a range of numeric database cells and then use the TRUE and FALSE conditions as selection criteria for printing a specialized report.

Chapter 14

Understanding information functions

The information functions can be considered the internal monitoring system in Excel. Although they perform no specific calculations, you can use them to find out about elements of the Excel interface and then use that information elsewhere. We discuss the most useful of these functions in the following sections. You can find these functions by clicking the More Functions button on the Formulas tab on the ribbon and then clicking Information.

Using selected information functions

With information functions, you can gather information about the contents of cells, their formatting, and the computing environment and also perform conditional tests for the presence of specific types of values.

The TYPE and ERROR.TYPE functions

The TYPE function determines whether a cell contains text, a number, a logical value, an array, or an error value. The result is a code for the type of entry in the referenced cell: *1* for a number (or a blank cell), *2* for text, *4* for a logical value (TRUE or FALSE), *16* for an error value, and *64* for an array. For example, if cell A1 contains the number *100*, the formula =TYPE(A1) returns *1*. If A1 contains the text Microsoft Excel, the formula returns *2*.

Like the TYPE function, the ERROR.TYPE function detects the contents of a cell, except it detects different types of error values. The result is a code for the type of error value in the referenced cell: *1* for #NULL!, *2* for #DIV/0!, *3* for #VALUE!, *4* for #REF!, *5* for #NAME!, *6* for #NUM!, and *7* for #N/A. Any other value in the referenced cell returns the error value #N/A. For example, if cell A1 contains a formula that displays the error value #NAME!, the formula =ERROR.TYPE(A1) returns *5*. If A1 contains the text Microsoft Excel, the formula returns #N/A.

The COUNTBLANK function

The COUNTBLANK function counts the number of empty cells in the specified range, which is its only argument. This function is tricky because formulas that evaluate to null text strings, such as =" ", or to zero might seem empty, but they aren't and therefore aren't counted.

Using the IS information functions

You can use the ISBLANK, ISERR, ISERROR, ISEVEN, ISFORMULA, ISLOGICAL, ISNA, ISNON-TEXT, ISNUMBER, ISODD, ISREF, and ISTEXT functions to determine whether a referenced cell or range contains the corresponding type of value.

All the IS information functions take a single argument. For example, the ISBLANK function takes the form =ISBLANK(*value*). The *value* argument is a reference to a cell. If *value* refers to a blank cell, the function returns the logical value TRUE; otherwise, it returns FALSE. Note that when you type numeric values as text, such as **="21"**, the IS functions, unlike other functions, do not recognize them as numbers. Therefore, the formula =ISNUMBER("21") returns FALSE.

TROUBLESHOOTING

My IS function returns unexpected results

Although you can use a cell range (rather than a single cell) as the argument to any IS function, the result might not be what you expect. For example, you might think the ISBLANK function returns TRUE if the referenced range is empty or FALSE if the range contains any values. Instead, the function's behavior depends on where the range is in relation to the cell containing the formula. If the argument refers to a range that intersects the row or column containing the formula, ISBLANK uses implicit intersection to arrive at the result. In other words, the function looks at only one cell in the referenced range and only if it happens to be in the same row or column as the cell containing the function. The function ignores the rest of the range. If the range shares neither a row nor a column with the formula, the result is always FALSE. For more about intersection, see "Getting explicit about intersections" in Chapter 12.

An ISERR example

You can use ISERR to avoid getting error values as formula results. For example, suppose you want to call attention to cells containing a particular character string, such as 12A, resulting in the word *Yes* appearing in the cell containing the formula. If the string isn't found, you want the cell to remain empty. You can use the IF and FIND functions to perform this task, but if the value isn't found, you get a #VALUE! error rather than a blank cell.

To solve this problem, add an ISERR function to the formula. The FIND function returns the position at which a substring is found within a larger string. If the substring isn't there, FIND returns #VALUE!. The solution is to add an ISERR function, such as =IF(ISERR(FIND("12A", A1)), " ", "Yes"). Because you're not interested in the error, which is simply a by-product of the calculation, this traps the error, leaving only the results in which you are interested.

Understanding lookup and reference functions

Lookup and reference functions help you use your own worksheet tables as sources of information to be used elsewhere in formulas. You can use three primary functions to look up information stored in a list or a table or to manipulate references: LOOKUP, VLOOKUP, and HLOOKUP. Some powerful lookup and reference functions in addition to these three are available; we describe many of them in the following sections. You can find a list of all these functions by clicking the Lookup & Reference button on the Formulas tab on the ribbon.

Using selected lookup and reference functions

VLOOKUP and HLOOKUP are nearly identical functions that look up information stored in tables you have constructed. VLOOKUP and HLOOKUP operate in either vertical or horizontal orientation (respectively), but LOOKUP works either way.

When you look up information in a table, you usually use a row index and a column index to locate a particular cell. Excel derives the first index by finding the largest value in the first column or row that is less than or equal to a lookup value you supply, and then it uses a row number or column number argument as the other index. You need to make sure the table is sorted by the row or column containing the lookup values first, or you will get unexpected results.

You can create powerful lookup formulas by using conditional tests. For more information, see "Creating conditional tests" in Chapter 12.

These functions take the following forms:

```
=VLOOKUP(lookup_value, table_array, col_index_num, range_lookup)
```

```
=HLOOKUP(lookup_value, table_array, row_index_num, range_lookup)
```

Table 14-3 lists LOOKUP function arguments and their descriptions. The LOOKUP function takes two forms. The first is called the *vector form*, and the second is called the *array form*:

```
=LOOKUP(lookup_value, lookup_vector, result_vector)
```

```
=LOOKUP(lookup_value, array)
```

The difference between the lookup functions is the type of table each function uses: VLOOKUP works only with vertical tables (tables arranged in columns); HLOOKUP works only with horizontal tables (tables arranged in rows). You can use the array form of LOOKUP with either horizontal tables or vertical tables, and you can use the vector form with single rows or columns of data.

TABLE 14-3 LOOKUP function arguments

Argument	Description
lookup_value	The value, cell reference, or text (enclosed in quotation marks) you want to find in a table or a range.
table_array	A cell range or name that defines the table in which to look.
row_index_num *col_index_num*	The row or column number in the table from which to select the result, counted relative to the table (not according to the actual row and column numbers).
range_lookup	A logical value that determines whether the function matches *lookup_value* exactly or approximately. Type **FALSE** to match *lookup_value* exactly. The default is TRUE, which finds the closest match.
lookup_vector	A one-row or one-column range that contains numbers, text, or logical values.
result_vector	A one-row or one-column range that must be the same size as *lookup_vector*.
array	A range containing numbers, text, or logical values to compare with *lookup_value*.

The array form of LOOKUP determines whether to search horizontally or vertically based on the shape of the table defined in the *array* argument. If the table has more columns than rows, LOOKUP searches the first row for *lookup_value*; if the table has more rows than columns, LOOKUP searches the first column for *lookup_value*. LOOKUP always returns the last value in the row or column containing the *lookup_value* argument, or you can specify a row or column number using VLOOKUP or HLOOKUP.

The VLOOKUP and HLOOKUP functions

For the VLOOKUP and HLOOKUP functions, whether Excel considers a lookup table to be vertical or horizontal depends on where the comparison values (the first index) are located. If the values are in the leftmost column of the table, the table is vertical; if they are in the first row of the table, the table is horizontal. (In contrast, LOOKUP uses the shape of the table to determine whether to use the first row or column as the comparison values.) The comparison values can be numbers or text, but they *must* be sorted in ascending order. No comparison value should be used more than once in a table.

The *index_num* argument (sometimes called the *offset*) provides the second index and tells the lookup function which column or row of the table to look in for the function's result. The first column or row in the table has an index number of 1; therefore, the *index_num* argument must be greater than or equal to 1 and must never be greater than the number of rows or columns in the table. For example, if a vertical table is three columns wide, the index number can't be greater than 3. If any value does not meet these rules, the function returns an error value.

You can use the VLOOKUP function to retrieve information from the table in Figure 14-2.

C1			✕	✓	*fx*	=VLOOKUP(41,A3:C7,3)		
	A	B	C	D	E	F	G	
1			14					
2								
3	10	17.98	5					
4	20	5.89	8					
5	30	5.59	11					
6	40	23.78	14					
7	50	6.79	17					
8								
9								

Figure 14-2 VLOOKUP returns a value in the same row as the lookup value.

You'll find the Lookup.xlsx file with the other examples on the companion website.

Remember that these lookup functions usually search for the greatest comparison value that is less than or equal to the lookup value, not for an exact match between the comparison values and the lookup value. If all the comparison values in the first row or column of the table range are greater than the lookup value, the function returns the #N/A error value. If all the comparison values are less than the lookup value, however, the function returns the value that corresponds to the last (largest) comparison value in the table, which might not be what you want. If you require an exact match, type **FALSE** as the *range_lookup* argument.

The worksheet in Figure 14-3 shows an example of a horizontal lookup table using the HLOOKUP function.

A1			✕	✓	*fx*	=HLOOKUP(6,B2:E7,3)		
	A	B	C	D	E	F	G	
1	101							
2		3	6	10	16			
3		5	100	99	1			
4		10	101	98	2			
5		25	105	95	3			
6		30	110	94	2			
7		35	125	90	1			
8								
9								

Figure 14-3 HLOOKUP returns a value in the same column as the lookup value.

The LOOKUP function

The LOOKUP function is similar to VLOOKUP and HLOOKUP, follows the same rules, and is available in the same two forms, *vector* and *array*, whose arguments are described in Table 14-3.

Like HLOOKUP and VLOOKUP, the vector form of LOOKUP searches for the largest comparison value that isn't greater than the lookup value. It then selects the result from the corresponding position in the specified result range. The *lookup_vector* and *result_vector* arguments are often adjacent ranges, but they don't have to be when you use LOOKUP. They can be in separate areas of the worksheet, and one range can be horizontal and the other vertical. The only requirement is that they must have the same number of elements.

For example, consider the worksheet in Figure 14-4, where the ranges are not parallel. Both the *lookup_vector* argument, A1:A5, and the *result_vector* argument, D6:H6, have five elements. The *lookup_value* argument, 3, matches the entry in the third cell of the *lookup_vector* argument, making the result of the formula the entry in the third cell of the result range: 300.

The *array form* of LOOKUP is similar to VLOOKUP and HLOOKUP, but it works with either a horizontal table or a vertical table, using the dimensions of the table to figure out the location of the comparison values. If the table is taller than it is wide or the table is square, the function treats it as a vertical table and assumes that the comparison values are in the leftmost column. If the table is wider than it is tall, the function views the table as horizontal and assumes that the comparison values are in the first row of the table. The result is always in the last row or column of the specified table; you can't specify column or row numbers.

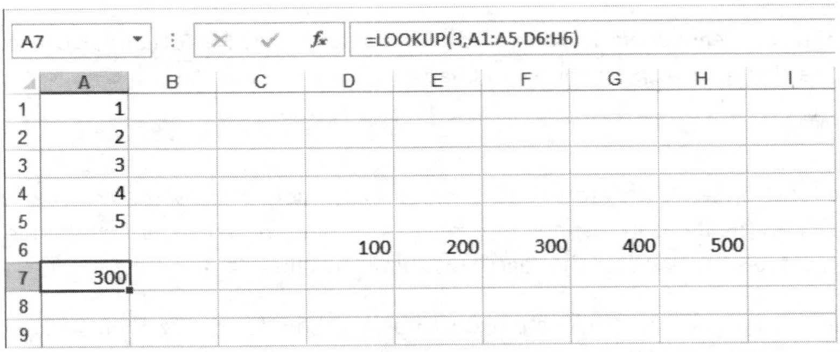

Figure 14-4 The vector form of the LOOKUP function can retrieve information from a nonparallel cell range.

Because HLOOKUP and VLOOKUP are more predictable and controllable, you'll generally find using them preferable to using LOOKUP.

The ADDRESS function

The ADDRESS function provides a handy way to build a cell reference by using numbers typed into the formula or using values in referenced cells. It takes the arguments (*row_num, column_num, abs_num, a1, sheet_text*). For example, the formula =ADDRESS(1, 1, 1, TRUE, "Data Sheet") results in the reference 'Data Sheet'v!$A$1.

The CHOOSE function

You use the CHOOSE function to retrieve an item from a list of values. The function takes the arguments (*index_num, value 1, value 2, ...*) and can include up to 254 values. The *index_num* argument is the position in the list you want to return; it must be positive and can't exceed the number of elements in the list. The function returns the value of the element in the list that occupies the position indicated by *index_num*. For example, the formula =CHOOSE(2, 6, 1, 8, 9, 3) returns the value *1*, because *1* is the second item in the list. (The *index_num* value isn't counted as part of the list.) You can use individual cell references for the list, but you can't specify ranges. You might be tempted to create a formula such as =CHOOSE(A10, C1:C5) to take the place of the longer function in the preceding example. If you do, however, the result is a #VALUE! error value.

The MATCH function

The MATCH function is closely related to the CHOOSE function. However, where CHOOSE returns the item that occupies the position in a list specified by the *index_num* argument, MATCH returns the position of the item in the list that most closely matches a lookup value.

> **Note**
> You can create powerful lookup formulas by using the MATCH and INDEX functions. See "Using lookup functions" in Chapter 12.

This function takes the arguments (*lookup_value, lookup_array, match_type*), where *lookup_value* and the items in the *lookup_array* can be numeric values or text strings, and *match_type* defines the rules for the search, as shown in Table 14-4.

When you use MATCH to locate text strings, you should specify a *match_type* argument of 0 (an exact match). You can then use the wildcards * and ? in the *lookup_value* argument.

TABLE 14-4 MATCH function arguments

match_type	Description
1 (or omitted)	Finds the largest value in the specified range (which must be sorted in ascending order) that is less than or equal to *lookup_value*. If no items in the range meet these criteria, the function returns #N/A.
0	Finds the first value in the specified range (no sorting necessary) that is equal to *lookup_value*. If no items in the range match, the function returns #N/A.
−1	Finds the smallest value in the specified range (which must be sorted in descending order) that is greater than or equal to *lookup_value*. If no items in the range meet these criteria, the function returns #N/A.

The INDEX function

The INDEX function has two forms: an *array form,* which returns a value, and a *reference form,* which returns a cell reference. The forms of these functions are as follows:

```
=INDEX(array, row_num, column_num)
```

```
=INDEX(reference, row_num, column_num, area_num)
```

The array form works only with an array argument; it returns the value of the result, not the cell reference. The result is the value at the position in *array* indicated by *row_num* and *column_num*. For example, the formula

```
=INDEX({10,20,30;40,50,60} , 1, 2)
```

returns the value *20,* because *20* is the value in the cell in the second column and first row of the array.

> **Note**
>
> Each form of the INDEX function offers an advantageous feature. Using the reference form of the function, you can use multiple, nonadjacent areas of the worksheet as the *reference* lookup range. Using the array form of the function, you can get a range of cells, rather than a single cell, as a result.

The reference form returns a cell address instead of a value and is useful when you want to perform operations on a cell (such as changing the cell's width) rather than on its value. This function can be confusing, however, because if an INDEX function is nested in another function, that function can use the value in the cell whose address is returned by INDEX. Furthermore, the reference form of INDEX doesn't display its result as an address; it displays the value or values at that cell address. Remember that the result is an address, even if it doesn't look like one.

Here are a few guidelines to keep in mind when using the INDEX function:

- If you type **0** as the *row_num* or *column_num* argument, INDEX returns a reference for the entire row or column, respectively.

- The *reference* argument can be one or more ranges, which are called *areas*. Each area must be rectangular and can contain numbers, text, or formulas. If the areas are not adjacent, you must enclose the *reference* argument in parentheses.

- You need the *area_num* argument only if you include more than one area in *reference*. The *area_num* argument identifies the area to which the *row_num* and *column_num* arguments will be applied. The first area specified in *reference* is designated *area 1*, the second *area 2*, and so on.

Let's consider some examples to see how all this works. Figure 14-5 shows an example of an INDEX function. The formula in cell A1 uses the row coordinate in cell A2 and the column coordinate in cell A3 to return the contents of the cell in the third row and second column of the specified range.

	A	B	C	D	E	F	G
				=INDEX(C3:E6,A2,A3)			
1	700						
2	3						
3	2		100	500	9000		
4			200	600	1100		
5			300	700	1200		
6			400	800	1300		
7							
8							

Figure 14-5 Use the INDEX function to retrieve the address or value in a cell where information is located.

The following example is a bit trickier: Using the same worksheet as in Figure 14-5, the formula =INDEX(C3:E6, 0, 2) displays the #VALUE! error value because the *row_num* argument of 0 returns a reference to the entire column specified by the *column_num* argument of *2*, or the range D3:D6. Excel can't display a range as the result. However, try nesting this formula in another function as follows: =SUM(INDEX(C3:E6, 0, 2)). The result is *2600*, the sum of the values in D3:D6. This illustrates the utility of obtaining a reference as a result.

Now we'll show how the INDEX function works with multiple ranges in the *reference* argument. (When you're using more than one range, you must enclose the argument in parentheses.) For example, in the formula =INDEX((A1:C5,D6:F10), 1, 1, 2), the *reference* range comprises two areas: A1:C5 and D6:F10. The *area_num* argument (2) tells INDEX to work on the second of these areas. This formula returns the address D6, which is the cell in the first column and first row of the range D6:F10. The displayed result is the value in that cell.

The INDIRECT function

The INDIRECT function returns the contents of a cell by using its reference. It takes the arguments (*ref_text, a1*), where *ref_text* is an A1-style or R1C1-style reference or a cell name. The *a1* argument is a logical value indicating which type of reference you're using. If *a1* is FALSE, Excel interprets *ref_text* as R1C1 format; if *a1* is TRUE or omitted, Excel interprets *ref_text* as A1 format. For example, if cell C6 on your worksheet contains the text value *B3* and cell B3 contains the value *2.888*, the formula =INDIRECT(C6) returns the value *2.888*. If your worksheet is set to display R1C1-style references and cell R6C3 contains the text reference R3C2 and cell R3C2 contains the value *2.888*, then the formula =INDIRECT(R6C3, FALSE) also returns the value *2.888*.

For information about A1-style and R1C1-style references, see "Understanding the row-column reference style" in Chapter 12.

The ROW and COLUMN functions

The result of the ROW and COLUMN functions is the row or column number, respectively, of the cell or range referred to by the function's single argument. For example, the formula =ROW(H5) returns the result *5*. The formula =COLUMN(C5) returns the result *3* because column C is the third column on the worksheet.

If you omit the argument, the result is the row or column number of the cell that contains the function. If the argument is a range or a range name and you enter the function as an array by pressing Ctrl+Shift+Enter, the result of the function is an array that consists of the row or column numbers of each row or column in the range. For example, suppose you select cells B1:B10, type the formula **=ROW(A1:A10)**, and then press Ctrl+Shift+Enter to enter the formula in all cells in the range B1:B10. That range will contain the array result {1;2;3;4;5;6;7;8;9;10}, the row numbers of each cell in the argument.

The ROWS and COLUMNS functions

The ROWS and COLUMNS functions return the number of rows or columns, respectively, referenced by the function's single argument in a reference or an array. The argument is an array constant, a range reference, or a range name. For example, the result of the formula =ROWS({100,200,300;1000,2000,3000}) is *2* because the array consists of two rows (separated by a semicolon). The formula =ROWS(A1:A10) returns *10* because the range A1:A10 contains ten rows. And the formula =COLUMNS(A1:C10) returns *3* because the range A1:C10 contains three columns.

The AREAS function

You can use the AREAS function to determine the number of areas in a reference. *Areas* refer to individual cell or range references, not regions. The single argument to this function can be a cell reference, a range reference, or several range references. If you use several range references, you must enclose them in a set of parentheses so that Excel doesn't misinterpret the commas that separate the ranges. (Although this function takes only one argument, Excel still interprets unenclosed commas as argument separators.) For example, suppose you assign the name *Test* to the group of ranges A1:C5,D6,E7:G10. The function =AREAS(Test) returns *3*, the number of areas in the group.

The TRANSPOSE function

The TRANSPOSE function changes the horizontal or vertical orientation of an array. It takes a single argument, *array*. If the argument refers to a vertically oriented range, the resulting array is horizontal. If the range is horizontal, the resulting array is vertical. The first row of a horizontal array becomes the first column of the vertical array result, and vice versa. You must type the TRANSPOSE function as an array formula in a range that has the same number of rows and columns as the *array* argument has columns and rows, respectively.

> ## Note
> For quick and easy transposition, select the range you want to transpose, press Ctrl+C to copy the range, click the cell where you want the upper-left corner of the transposed range to begin, click the Paste button on the Home tab, and then click the Transpose button.

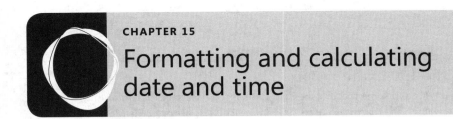

Formatting and calculating date and time

YOU CAN use date and time values to stamp documents and to perform date and time arithmetic. Creating a production schedule or a monthly billing system is relatively easy with Microsoft Excel. Although Excel uses numeric values to count each nanosecond, starting from the beginning of the twentieth century, you can use formatting to display those numbers in whatever form you want.

Understanding how Excel records dates and times

Excel assigns serial values to days, hours, minutes, and seconds, which makes it possible for you to perform sophisticated date and time arithmetic. The basic unit of time in Excel is the day. Each day is represented by a serial date value. The base date, represented by the serial value *1*, is Sunday, January 1, 1900. When you enter a date in your worksheet, Excel records the date as a serial value that represents the number of days between the base date and the specified date. For example, Excel represents the date January 1, 2014, by the serial value *41640*, representing the number of days between the base date—January 1, 1900— and January 1, 2014.

The time of day is a decimal value that represents the portion of a day that has passed since the day began—midnight—to the specified time. Therefore, Excel represents noon by the value 0.5 because the difference between midnight and noon is exactly half a day. Excel represents the time/date combination 12:59:54 PM, January 1, 2014, by the serial value *41640.54159* because January 1, 2014, is day 41640 (counting January 1, 1900, as day 1), and the interval between midnight and 12:59:54 PM amounts to .54159 of a whole day.

> ### Note
> You can see the serial value of a formatted date by selecting the cell containing the date and pressing Ctrl+Shift+tilde (~). Or click the Number Format drop-down list on the Home tab and select the General format. Either way, to return the cell to its date format, press Ctrl+Z.

Using the 1904 date system

Whereas all PCs and some Macintoshes use 1900 as the base year for computing serial date values, the Macintosh used 1904 for much of its history. (The Macintosh debuted in 1984 with Apple's legendary Orwellian TV ad that aired only once, during the Super Bowl.) Or maybe it was because 1900 was not a leap year. (It's a long story about the programming of calendar systems and the calculation of leap years...Bing it.) If you transfer documents between Excel for the Macintosh and Excel for Windows, the proper date system for the worksheet is automatically set for you. When the date system changes, existing serial date values display different dates, but the underlying values do not change. But if you change date systems after you start entering dates in a worksheet, all your dates will be off by four years.

You can change the base date (the date that corresponds to the serial value *1*) from January 1, 1900 to January 2, 1904. Click the File tab, click Options, select the Advanced category, and then select the Use 1904 Date System check box in the When Calculating This Workbook area.

When you select this check box, the serial date values in your worksheet remain the same, but the display of all dates changes so that the serial values of any dates you enter on your Excel for Windows worksheets match corresponding serial values from Excel for the Macintosh worksheets. If you transfer information into Excel for Windows from a worksheet created in Excel for the Macintosh, selecting this option ensures that Excel evaluates the serial date values correctly. In this book, we use the 1900 date system.

Entering dates and times

Although Excel records dates and times as serial date values, you don't have to type them that way. You can manipulate dates and times in your worksheet formulas just as you manipulate other types of values. You enter date values in formats that Excel automatically applies. To enter date values in this way, type the date in one of the following formats: m/d/yy, d-mmm-yy, d-mmm, or mmm-yy. (You can also type four-digit years for any of these formats.)

> **Note**
> You can change the default date, time, currency, and numbering settings through the
> Clock, Language, And Region item in Windows Control Panel (or Date, Time, Language,
> And Regional Options in Windows XP). These settings determine how Excel interprets
> your date entries. For example, with regional options set to Italian, typing a date in
> d/m/yy format results in a properly displayed date, but if you type the same date with
> regional options set to English, the entry is interpreted as text.

If your entry doesn't match any of the built-in date or time formats, Excel picks the format
that's most similar to your entry. For example, if you type **1 dec**, you see the formatted
entry 1-Dec in the cell. In the formula bar, the entry appears as 12/1/2013 (if the current
year is 2013) so that you can edit the date more easily.

You can also type times in a time format. Select a cell, and type the time in one of the following forms: h:mm AM/PM, h:mm:ss AM/PM, h:mm, h:mm:ss, or the combined date and
time format, m/d/yy h:mm. Notice that you must separate the hours, minutes, and seconds
of the time entries by colons.

**For more information about custom formats, see "Creating your own date and time formats"
later in this chapter.**

If you don't include AM, PM, A, or P with the time, Excel uses the 24-hour (military) time
convention. In other words, Excel always assumes that the entry 3:00 means 3:00 AM, unless
you specifically enter **PM**.

You can enter the current date in a cell or formula by holding down Ctrl and pressing
the semicolon (;) key. This enters the date stamp in the short-date format currently set in
Control Panel. Enter the current time in a cell or formula by holding down Ctrl+Shift and
pressing the colon (:) key. This enters the time stamp in h:mm AM/PM format. (Of course,
the colon and semicolon occupy the same key—the Shift key changes the entry to a time
stamp.)

INSIDE OUT The magic crossover date

December 31, 2029, is the default magic crossover date—that is, the last day Excel assumes is in the future if you enter the year using only two digits. For example, if you type **12/31/29** in a cell, Excel assumes you mean the year 2029. If, however, you type **1/1/30** in a cell, Excel interprets it to mean January 1, 1930. (Perhaps this would be better characterized as a cross*under* date.)

You can change this magic date, but not from Excel; instead you use Windows Control Panel. (Therefore, changing this setting also affects any other applications that need to interpret past or future date entries.) In Windows, open Control Panel and click Clock, Language, And Region (or Regional And Language Options in Windows XP). Next, click Region, and then click the Additional Settings button. (In Windows 7, click Region And Language, and then Additional Settings. In Windows Vista, click Regional And Language Options, and then Customize This Format. In Windows XP, click the Customize button on the Regional Options tab.) Finally, click the Date tab, and change the last date (2029) to the value of your choice. Of course, you're still limited to a 100-year span; if you change the last date that Windows recognizes as being in the future, the corresponding beginning date—January 1, 1900—changes accordingly. If you need to enter century-spanning dates, you should get into the habit of typing the full four-digit year to avoid surprises.

Entering a series of dates

You can create an evenly spaced series of dates in a row or column in several ways, but the job is especially easy when you use the fill handle. Suppose you want to create a series of dates in row 1. The series begins with March 1, 2011, and the dates must be exactly one month apart.

If you type **3/1/2014** in cell A1 and drag the fill handle to the right, Excel extends the series of dates incrementally by days, as shown in Figure 15-1. After you drag, Excel displays an option button adjacent to the selection. Click the button to display a menu, shown in Figure 15-1, that provides a number of AutoFill options; select Fill Months to convert the day series into a month series.

If you drag the fill handle by right-clicking it, a shortcut menu that is similar to the options menu appears. You can use this shortcut menu to select a fill command before performing any fill action. If what you want to do isn't represented on the menu, click the Series command to display the Series dialog box.

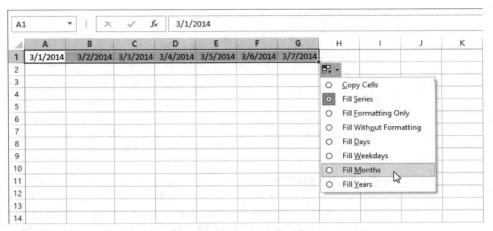

Figure 15-1 After you drag the fill handle to extend a date series, use the options menu to adjust the series.

You can use the Series command to tend to a series of dates with a bit more flexibility than with the fill handle. To use this approach, type the starting date, select the range of cells you want to fill (including the starting date), click the Fill button in the Editing group on the Home tab, and click Series to display the Series dialog box shown in Figure 15-2.

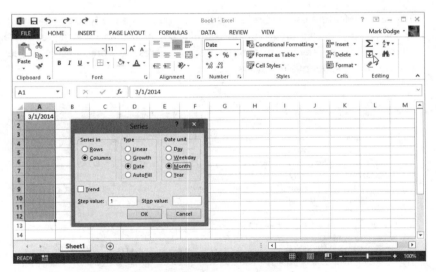

Figure 15-2 Use the Series dialog box to create date series.

Chapter 15

When extending a series of dates, remember the following:

- You can use the Series In options to choose whether to extend the selected date across the current row or down the current column.

- You can use the Step Value option to specify the interval between cells. For example, by typing **2** in the Step Value text box and selecting Month in the Date Unit area, you can create a series of dates occurring every other month. By typing a negative number in the Step Value text box, you can create a series that decreases (goes backward in time).

- You can use the Stop Value text box to set an ending date for the series. Using this method, you can use the Series command without having to figure out how many cells to select in advance. For example, to enter a series of dates that extends from 3/1/2014 through 2/1/2015, type **3/1/2014** in a cell. Then select only that cell, display the Series dialog box, select the Columns option, and type **2/1/2015** in the Stop Value text box. Excel extends a series of dates following the original cell.

For more information about AutoFill and the Series command, see "Filling cells and creating data series" in Chapter 8, "Worksheet editing techniques."

Extending an existing date series

The AutoFill feature uses the selected cells to determine the type of series you intend to create when you drag the fill handle. AutoFill copies text and nonsequential values and increments sequential numeric values. Because dates are stored as serial values, AutoFill extends them sequentially, as illustrated in Figure 15-3.

	A	B	C	D	E	F	G	H
1	**Selected Values**		**Resulting Series**					
2								
3	9:00	10:00	11:00	12:00	13:00	14:00	15:00	
4	2013	2014	2015	2016	2017	2018	2019	
5	1/1/2013	2/1/2013	3/1/2013	4/1/2013	5/1/2013	6/1/2013	7/1/2013	
6	1/1/2013	3/1/2013	5/1/2013	7/1/2013	9/1/2013	11/1/2013	1/1/2014	
7	1-Jan	2-Jan	3-Jan	4-Jan	5-Jan	6-Jan	7-Jan	
8	Dec-13	Dec-14	Dec-15	Dec-16	Dec-17	Dec-18	Dec-19	
9	Dec-13	Dec-15	Dec-17	Dec-19	Dec-21	Dec-23	Dec-25	
10	Product 1	Product 2	Product 3	Product 4	Product 5	Product 6	Product 7	
11	Sat	Mon	Wed	Fri	Sun	Tue	Thu	
12	1 1/2	2 3/4	4	5 1/4	6 1/2	7 3/4	9	
13								

Figure 15-3 Starting with the values in the Selected Values area, we created the values to the right by dragging the fill handle.

When you use the fill handle to extend the value in a single selected cell, Excel assumes you want to increment the numeric value in each cell. (If you want to copy the cell instead, hold down Ctrl while dragging the fill handle.) Notice in Figure 15-3 that the entries in rows 7 through 11 contain text values. AutoFill recognizes text entries for days and months and extends them as though they were numeric values. In addition, when a cell contains a mixed text and numeric entry (as in row 10), AutoFill copies the text portion if it's not the name of a month or day and extends the numeric portion if it occurs at either end of the entry.

Formatting dates and times

After you type a date or time in a cell, you can use the Number Format drop-down list on the Home tab on the ribbon to change its format to one of the popular date and time formats, or you can click More Number Formats at the bottom of the list to select any of the built-in formats. In the Format Cells dialog box, select the Date or Time category to display the list of available formats in the Type box on the right. A preview of the format appears in the Sample box in the upper-right corner, as shown in Figure 15-4.

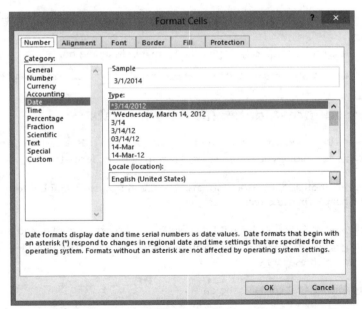

Figure 15-4 Use the Number tab in the Format Cells dialog box to apply date and time formats to cells.

Chapter 15

> **Note**
>
> At the top of the list of date and time formats are several types that begin with an asterisk (*). These formats respond to changes in the settings available on the Date and Time tabs in the Customize Regional Options dialog box, which you access by opening Windows Control Panel, clicking Regional And Language Options, and then clicking the Customize button on the Formats tab. All other formats are not affected by these Control Panel settings.

Most of the date and time formats are easy to understand, but a few special formats exist:

- The 13:30 and 13:30:55 time formats use the 24-hour (military) time convention.

- The 30:55.2 time format displays only minutes and seconds; Excel displays a fraction of a second as a decimal value.

- The 37:30:55 time format displays elapsed time.

> **Note**
>
> You can press Ctrl+1 to quickly display the Format Cells dialog box.

Creating your own date and time formats

To supplement the standard date and time formats, you can create custom formats by using the same technique you use to create custom numeric formats.

For more information about custom formats, see "Creating custom number formats" in Chapter 9, "Worksheet formatting techniques."

For example, you can create a format that displays all the available date and time information. The entry 2/24/14 would appear as Tuesday, February 24, 2014 0:00:00.0. To create this format, follow these steps:

1. Select the cell that contains the date.

2. Press Ctrl+1 to display the Format Cells dialog box, and if necessary click the Number tab.

3. Select the Custom category.

4. Highlight the entry in the text box at the top of the Type list, and type the following custom format code: **dddd mmmm dd, yyyy h:mm:ss.0**

5. Click OK. Excel stores the new format in the Type list for the Custom category and displays the date using the new format in the selected cell.

You can use the same procedure to display only a portion of the date or the time information available. For example, if you create the format *mmmm*, Excel displays the date 2/24/2014 as simply *February*.

Table 15-1 shows the formatting codes you can use to create custom date and time formats. Be sure to keep two facts in mind. First, Excel assumes that *m* means months, but if you type the code **m** immediately after an **h**, or the code **mm** immediately after an **hh**, Excel displays minutes instead of months. Second, if you include one of the codes AM/PM, am/pm, A/P, or a/p in a time format, Excel uses the 12-hour time convention; if you omit these codes, Excel uses the 24-hour (military) time convention.

TABLE 15-1 Codes for creating custom date and time formats

Code	Display
General	Number in General (serial value) format.
d	Day number without leading zero (1–31).
dd	Day number with leading zero (01–31).
ddd	Day-of-week abbreviation (Sun–Sat).
dddd	Complete day-of-week name (Sunday–Saturday).
m	Month number without leading zero (1–12).
mm	Month number with leading zero (01–12).
mmm	Month name abbreviation (Jan–Dec).
mmmm	Complete month name (January–December).
yy	Last two digits of year number (00–99).
yyyy	Complete four-digit year number (1900–2078).
h	Hour without leading zero (0–23).
hh	Hour with leading zero (00–23).
m	Minute without leading zero (0–59).
mm	Minute with leading zero (00–59).
s	Second without leading zero (0–59).
ss	Second with leading zero (00–59).
s.0	Second and tenths of a second without leading zero.
s.00	Second without leading zero and hundredths of a second without leading zero.

Code	Display
ss.0	Second without leading zero and tenths of a second with leading zero.
ss.00	Second and hundredths of a second with leading zero.
AM/PM	Time in AM/PM notation.
am/pm	Time in am/pm notation.
A/P	Time in A/P notation.
a/p	Time in a/p notation.
[ ]	Brackets display the absolute elapsed time when used to enclose a time code, as in *[h]*. You can use brackets only around the first component of the code.

After you add a custom date or time format to the Type list, you can apply it to any date or time entry. Select the Custom category, select the format you entered from the Type list (new custom formats appear at the bottom of the list), and click OK to apply the format.

Measuring elapsed time

You can enclose time codes in brackets, as listed at the bottom of Table 15-1, to display more than 24 hours, more than 60 minutes, or more than 60 seconds in a time value. The brackets must always appear around the first code in the format. Excel provides one built-in elapsed-time code, [h]:mm:ss, in the Custom category Type list. Other valid codes for measuring elapsed time include [mm]:ss and [ss].

Bracketed codes have no effect if you use them in any position of the format other than first. For example, if you use the code h:[mm]:ss, Excel ignores the brackets and displays the time using the regular h:mm:ss format.

> **Note**
>
> One format in the Time category on the Number tab in the Format Cells dialog box represents elapsed time: 37:30:55. This is the same as the [h]:mm:ss format in the Custom category.

Suppose you want to determine the elapsed time between two dates. Type the following values into cells A1 and A2, respectively:

11/23/14 13:32

11/25/14 23:59

And type the following formula into cell A3:

=A2–A1

If you use the Custom category on the Number tab of the Format Cells dialog box (press Ctrl+1) to apply the built-in format **[h]:mm:ss** to cell A3, the result of the formula is 58:27:00—the total elapsed time between the two dates, as shown in Figure 15-5. If you apply the standard **h:mm:ss** format to cell A3 instead, the result is 10:27:00—the difference between the two times of day. Without the elapsed-time-format code brackets [ ], Excel ignores the difference in dates.

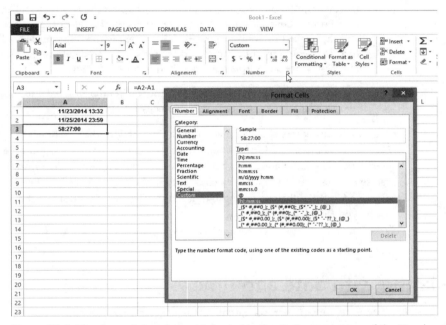

Figure 15-5 The elapsed-time format is buried in the Custom category of the Number tab in the Format Cells dialog box.

Chapter 15

TROUBLESHOOTING

I can't enter a number of hours greater than 9,999

Suppose you have a worksheet in which you keep a running total of flying time for pilots, using the time formats in Excel. Whenever you try to enter a number of hours greater than 9,999 (which isn't uncommon), Excel treats the entry as text. What's wrong?

Nothing is wrong—that's just a built-in limitation of Excel. Here are a couple of ways to work with this limitation:

- Use an elapsed-time format. In the Cells group on the Home tab, click Format, click Format Cells, click the Number tab if necessary, select the Custom category, and then select [h]:mm:ss in the Type list to apply the built-in, elapsed-time format. If you don't need to record seconds, you can delete :ss. Elapsed-time formats can store and display an unlimited number of hours.

- If you need to enter more than 9,999 hours at a time, you have to break it into two smaller chunks and type it in two cells.

You should also know that when you type a time greater than 24 hours (even 24:01), Excel adds a date in the formula bar. Unless the number of hours typed exceeds a year's worth, the date Excel adds is sometime in 1900; you just have to live with that. You can select the year in the formula bar and type the correct year, but then the year is displayed in the cell along with the time. Otherwise, the date doesn't show in the cell unless you format it accordingly.

Calculating with date and time

Because Excel records dates as serial date values, you can use dates in formulas and functions as you would any other value. Suppose you want to find the date that falls exactly 200 days after July 4, 2014. If cell A1 contains the entry 7/4/14, you can type the following formula to compute the date 200 days later: **=A1+200**, which results in *1/20/15* (or the serial date value *42024*).

As another example, suppose you want to find the number of weeks between October 31, 2003, and May 13, 2013. Type the formula **=(("5/13/13")–("10/31/03"))/7**, which returns 497 weeks.

You can also use times in formulas and functions, but the results of time arithmetic are not as easy to understand as the results of date arithmetic. For example, you can determine how much time has elapsed between 8:22 AM and 10:45 PM by typing the formula **="22:45"–"8:22"**. The result is *.599306*, which can be formatted using a 24-hour time format (one that doesn't include AM/PM) to display *14:23*. Excel displays the result relative to midnight.

Suppose you want to determine the time that is 2 hours, 23 minutes, and 17 seconds after 12:35:23 PM. The formula =("12:35:23 PM")+("2:23:17") returns the correct answer, *.624074*, which can be formatted as *14:58:40*. In this formula, *2:23:17* represents not an absolute time (2:23:17 AM) but an interval of time (2 hours, 23 minutes, and 17 seconds). This format is perfectly acceptable to Excel.

TROUBLESHOOTING

Excel displays my time as

Usually, a cell full of number signs means the cell isn't wide enough to show its displayed contents. But Excel can't display negative numbers as dates or times. If the result of a date or time calculation is negative and you attempt to display this result in a date or time format, you will see a cell full of number signs, no matter how much you widen the cell. This typically happens when you subtract a later time of day from an earlier time of day. You can work around the problem by converting the result to elapsed hours. To do that, multiply the result by 24 and display it in a numeric format, not a date or time format.

Working with date and time functions

Using the Excel date and time functions, you can perform worksheet calculations quickly and accurately. For example, if you use your worksheet to calculate your company's monthly payroll, you might use the HOUR function to determine the number of hours worked each day and the WEEKDAY function to determine whether employees should be paid at the standard rate (for Monday through Friday) or at the overtime rate (for Saturdays and Sundays).

In the following sections, we explore a few of the most useful date and time functions in detail. You can access all 20 of the date and time functions available in Excel by clicking the Date & Time button on the Formulas tab on the ribbon.

Using the TODAY and NOW functions

You can type **=TODAY( )** in a cell or a formula to insert the serial value of the current date. If you type the function in a cell with the General format (which is the default), Excel displays the resulting value in mm/dd/yyyy format. Although this function takes no arguments, you must remember to include the empty parentheses. (Remember that *arguments* are variables that supply the values a function needs to perform its calculations. You place arguments between the parentheses for functions that require them.)

Similarly, you can type **=NOW( )** in a cell or formula to insert the current date and time. This function also takes no arguments. The result of the function is a serial date and time value that includes an integer (the date) and a decimal value (the time). Excel doesn't update the value of NOW continuously. If the value of a cell that contains the NOW function isn't current, you can update the value by recalculating the worksheet. (You recalculate the worksheet by making a new entry or by pressing F9.) Excel also updates the NOW function whenever you open or print the worksheet.

The NOW function is an example of a *volatile* function—that is, a function whose calculated value is subject to change. Any time you open a worksheet that contains one or more NOW functions, Excel prompts you to save changes when you close the worksheet, regardless of whether you made any, because the current value of NOW has changed since the last time you used the worksheet. (Another example of a volatile function is RAND.)

For more about the RAND function, see "The RAND and RANDBETWEEN functions" in Chapter 14, "Everyday functions."

Using the WEEKDAY function

The WEEKDAY function returns the day of the week for a specific date and takes the arguments (*serial_number, return_type*). The *serial_number* argument can be a serial date value, a reference to a cell that contains either a date function or a serial date value, or text such as 1/27/14 or January 27, 2014. If you use text, be sure to enclose the text in quotation marks. The function returns a number that represents the day of the week on which the specified date falls. The optional *return_type* argument determines the way the result is displayed. Table 15-2 lists the available return types.

TABLE 15-2 Return type codes

If *return_type* is	WEEKDAY returns
1 or omitted	A number from 1 through 7, where 1 is Sunday and 7 is Saturday
2	A number from 1 through 7, where 1 is Monday and 7 is Sunday
3	A number from 0 through 6, where 0 is Monday and 6 is Sunday

Note

You might want to format a cell containing the WEEKDAY function with a custom day-of-the-week format, such as dddd. By applying this custom format, you can use the result of the WEEKDAY function in other functions and still have a meaningful display on the screen.

Using the YEAR, MONTH, and DAY functions

The YEAR, MONTH, and DAY functions return the value of the year, month, and day portions of a serial date value. All three take a single argument, which can be a serial date value, a reference to a cell that contains either a date function or a serial date value, or a text date enclosed in quotation marks. For example, if cell A1 contains the date 3/25/2014, the formula =YEAR(A1) returns the value *2014*, the formula =MONTH(A1) returns the value *3*, and the formula =DAY(A1) returns the value *25*.

Using the HOUR, MINUTE, and SECOND functions

Just as the YEAR, MONTH, and DAY functions extract the value of the year, month, and day portions of a serial date value, the HOUR, MINUTE, and SECOND functions extract the value of the hour, minute, and second portions of a serial time value. For example, if cell B1 contains the time 12:15:35 PM, the formula =HOUR(B1) returns the value *12*, the formula =MINUTE(B1) returns the value *15*, and the formula =SECOND(B1) returns the value *35*.

Using the DATEVALUE and TIMEVALUE functions

The DATEVALUE function translates a date into a serial value. You must type the single argument as text, using any date from 1/1/1900 to 12/31/9999, and you must add quotation marks around the text. You can enter the argument using any of the built-in date formats; however, if you type the date without a year, Excel uses the current year from your computer's internal clock. For example, the formula =DATEVALUE("December 31, 2014") returns the serial value *42004*.

Similarly, the TIMEVALUE function translates a time into a decimal value. You must type its single argument as text. You can use any of the built-in time formats, but you must add quotation marks around the text. For example, the formula =TIMEVALUE("4:30 PM") returns the decimal value *0.6875*.

Working with specialized date functions

Excel includes a set of specialized date functions that perform operations such as calculations for the maturity dates of securities, for payroll, and for work schedules.

Using the EDATE and EOMONTH functions

You can use the EDATE function to calculate the exact date that occurs an indicated number of months before or after a given date. It takes the arguments (*start_date, months*), where *start_date* is the date you want to use as a starting point and *months* is an integer value that indicates the number of months before or after the start date. If the *months* argument is positive, the function returns a date after the start date; if the *months* argument is negative, the function returns a date before the start date. For example, to find the date that falls exactly 23 months after June 12, 2014, type the formula **=EDATE("6/12/2014", 23)**, which returns the value *42502*, or May 12, 2016.

The EOMONTH function returns a date that is an indicated number of months before or after a given date. Although EOMONTH is similar to EDATE and takes the same arguments, the value returned is always rounded up to the last day of the month. For example, to calculate the serial date value that is the last day of the month 23 months after June 12, 2014, type the formula **=EOMONTH("6/12/2014", 23)**, which returns *42521*, or May 31, 2016.

Using the YEARFRAC function

The YEARFRAC function calculates a decimal number that represents the portion of a year that falls between two given dates. This function takes the arguments (*start_date*, *end_date*, *basis*), where *start_date* and *end_date* specify the period of time you want to convert to a fractional year. The *basis* argument is the type of day count you want to use, as described in Table 15-3.

For example, to determine what fraction of a year is represented from 4/12/10 to 12/15/10, you can type the formula **=YEARFRAC("4/12/14", "12/15/14")**. This formula returns *0.675* based on the default 30-day month and 360-day year.

TABLE 15-3 Basis codes

If *basis* is	YEARFRAC returns
0 (or omitted)	30/360, or 30 days per month and 360 days per year, as established in the United States by the National Association of Security Dealers (NASD)
1	Actual/actual, or the actual number of days in the month(s)/actual days in the year
2	Actual/360
3	Actual/365
4	European 30/360

Using the WORKDAY, NETWORKDAYS, WORKDAY.INTL, and NETWORKDAYS.INTL functions

The WORKDAY and NETWORKDAYS functions are invaluable for anyone who calculates payroll and benefits or determines work schedules. Both functions return values based on working days, excluding weekend days. In addition, you can choose whether to include holidays and specify the exact dates. The .INTL forms of these two functions include an additional argument you can use to specify exactly what constitutes a weekend.

The WORKDAY function returns the date that is an indicated number of working days before or after a given date. This function takes the arguments (*start_date*, *days*, *holidays*), where *start_date* is the date you want the function to count from and *days* is the number of workdays before or after the start date, excluding weekends and holidays. Use a positive value for *days* to count forward from the start date; use a negative value to count backward. The optional *holidays* argument can be an array or a reference to a cell range that contains any dates you want to exclude from the calculation. If you leave *holidays* blank, the function counts all weekdays from the start date. For example, to determine the date that is 100 working days, not counting holidays, from the current date, type the formula **=WORKDAY(NOW( ),100)**.

Similarly, the NETWORKDAYS function calculates the number of working days between two given dates. It takes the arguments (*start_date*, *end_date*, *holidays*). For example, to determine the number of working days from January 15, 2014 to June 30, 2014, type the formula **=NETWORKDAYS("1/15/14", "6/30/14")**, which results in a value of *119*.

The WORKDAY.INTL and NETWORKDAYS.INTL functions work the same way as their non-INTL counterparts, but each includes an additional *weekend* argument. These functions use the form (*start_date*, *days*, *weekend*, *holidays*), where *weekend* is a number indicating which days you want to omit, as shown in Table 15-4.

TABLE 15-4 INTL weekend codes

If *weekend* is	The weekend days omitted are
1 or omitted	Saturday, Sunday
2	Sunday, Monday
3	Monday, Tuesday
4	Tuesday, Wednesday
5	Wednesday, Thursday
6	Thursday, Friday
7	Friday, Saturday
11	Sunday only
12	Monday only
13	Tuesday only
14	Wednesday only
15	Thursday only
16	Friday only
17	Saturday only

There are two ways to specify the *weekend* argument. The first is to enter one of the numbers shown in Table 15-4, which are codes that specify days you want to omit. The other method is to enter a 7-digit numeric text string with which you specify individual days of the week (starting with Monday) that you want to include and exclude; a zero (0) indicates a workday, and a one (1) indicates a nonwork (weekend) day. For example, the string **"0010100"** specifies Wednesdays and Fridays as your "weekend" days.

For example, the formula =NETWORKDAYS.INTL("1/1/14","2/21/15","0010100") returns the value *297*, the number of working days between January 1, 2014 and February 21, 2015, skipping all Wednesdays and Fridays.

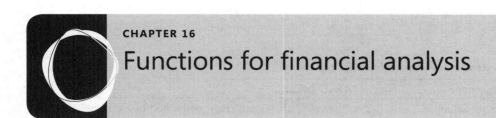

Functions for financial analysis

W ITH THE financial functions provided with Microsoft Excel, you can perform common business calculations, such as net present value and future value, without building long and complex formulas. These functions are the heart of spreadsheets—the word *spreadsheet* itself refers to the seemingly antiquated system of using special grid paper to track financial information. Functions have taken the place of the old 10-key calculator sequences (*algorithms*) used by accounting professionals before computers revolutionized the discipline.

The financial functions built into Excel fall into three major categories: investments, depreciation, and securities. The functions included within each category accept similar arguments. To streamline this chapter, we first define the common arguments and then discuss their implementation in the individual functions. Excel offers more than 50 financial functions, and in this chapter we touch on most of them, with special emphasis on those most often used, needed, or misunderstood. For complete information about all the built-in functions that Excel has to offer, you can use the onscreen tools covered in "Using the built-in function reference in Excel" in Chapter 13, "Using functions."

Calculating investments

The functions we discuss in this section are used when working with cash flows. All of the functions for calculating investments are available on the Formulas tab, in the Function Library group's Financial drop-down list.

Table 16-1 lists the arguments used in functions dedicated to calculating investments.

TABLE 16-1 Investment function arguments

Argument	Description
Future value	The value of an investment at the end of the term (0 if omitted).
value1, value2, ... value n	Periodic payments (*inflows*) when individual amounts differ.
Number of periods	Term of investment.
Payment	Periodic payments when individual amounts are the same.
Type	When payment is to be made (0 if omitted); 0 = at end of period; 1 = at beginning of period.
Period	Number of an individual periodic payment.
Present value	Value of investment today.
Rate	Discount rate or interest rate.
Guess	A starting interest rate for iterative calculations (10 percent if omitted).
Finance rate	The rate at which you borrow money to purchase an investment.
Reinvestment rate	The rate at which you reinvest cash received from an investment.

The PV function

Present value (PV) is one of the most common methods for measuring the attractiveness of a long-term investment. *Present value* is the current value of the investment. It's determined by discounting the inflows (payments received) from the investment back to the present time. If the present value of the inflows is greater than the cost of the investment, the investment is a good one.

The PV function computes the present value of a series of equal periodic payments or of a lump-sum payment. (A series of equal payments is often called an *ordinary annuity*.) This function takes the arguments *rate, number of periods, payment, future value,* and *type*; for definitions of these arguments, see Table 16-1. To compute the present value of a series of payments, type a value for the *payment* argument; to compute the present value of a lump-sum payment, type a value for the *future value* argument. For an investment with both a series of payments and a lump-sum payment, use both arguments.

Here's a real-world example of how this function works: Suppose you are presented with an investment opportunity that returns $1,000 each year over the next five years. To receive this annuity, you must invest $4,000. Are you willing to pay $4,000 today to earn $5,000 over the next five years? To decide whether this investment is acceptable, you need to determine the present value of the stream of $1,000 payments you will receive.

Assuming you could invest your money in a five-year CD money-market account at 2.1 percent, we'll use 2.1 percent as the discount rate of the investment. (Because this discount rate is a sort of hurdle over which an investment must leap before it becomes attractive to you, it's often called the *hurdle rate*.) To determine the present value of this investment, use the formula =PV(2.1%, 5, 1000), which returns the value –4699.81, meaning you should be willing to spend $4699.81 now to receive $5,000 over the next five years. (Negative values indicate money going out; positive values indicate money coming in.) Because your investment is only $4,000, you can surmise that this is an excellent investment.

Suppose you're offered $5,000 at the end of five years instead of $1,000 for each of the next five years. Is the investment still as attractive? To find out, use the formula =PV(2.1%, 5,, 5000). (Include a comma as a placeholder for the unused *payment* argument.) This formula returns the present value –4506.52, which means that at a hurdle rate of 2.1 percent, you should be willing to spend $4,506.52 to receive $5,000 in five years. Although the proposal might not be as attractive under these terms, it's still acceptable because your investment is only $4,000. However, it also makes a guaranteed 2.1 percent CD look a bit more attractive by comparison.

The NPV function

The NPV function calculates the net present value, which is another common method for determining the profitability of an investment. In general, any investment that yields a net present value greater than zero is considered profitable. This function takes the arguments *rate*, *value1*, *value2*, and so on; for definitions of these arguments, see Table 16-1. You can use as many as 254 separate inflow values as arguments, but you can include any number of values by using an array as an argument.

NPV differs from PV in two important respects. Whereas PV assumes constant inflow values, NPV allows variable payments. The other major difference is that PV allows payments and receipts to occur at either the beginning or the end of the period, whereas NPV assumes that all payments and receipts are evenly distributed and that they occur at the end of each period. If the cost of the investment must be paid up front, you should not include the cost as one of the function's inflow arguments but should subtract it from the result of the function. On the other hand, if the cost must be paid at the end of the first period, you should include it as a negative first inflow argument. Let's consider an example to help clarify this distinction.

Suppose you are contemplating an investment on which you expect to incur a loss of $85,000 at the end of the first year, followed by gains of $95,000; $140,000; and $185,000 at the ends of the second, third, and fourth years. You will invest $250,000 up front, and the hurdle rate is 8 percent. To evaluate this investment, use the formula =NPV(8%, –85000, 95000, 140000, 185000) –250000.

The result, −139.48, tells you not to expect a net profit from this investment. Note that the negative values in this formula indicate the money you spend on your investment. (You can use the Goal Seek command to determine what initial cost or interest rate would justify the investment. For more information about this command, see "Using the Goal Seek command" in Chapter 18, "Performing a what-if analysis.")

This formula does not include the up-front cost of the investment as an argument for the NPV function. However, if you fund the initial $250,000 investment at the end of the first year instead of at the beginning, the formula is =NPV(8%,(−250000–85000), 95000, 140000, 185000). The result, $18,379.04, suggests that this might be a profitable investment.

The FV function

The FV function determines the future value of an investment and is essentially the opposite of present value, computing the value at some future date of an investment that makes payments as a lump sum or as a series of equal periodic payments. This function takes the arguments *rate*, *number of periods*, *payment*, *present value*, and *type*; for definitions of these arguments, see Table 16-1. Use the *payment* argument to compute the future value of a series of payments and the *present value* argument to compute the future value of a lump-sum payment.

Suppose you're thinking about starting an IRA. You plan to deposit $5,000 in the IRA at the beginning of each year, and you expect the average rate of return to be 3 percent per year for the entire term. Assuming you're now 30 years old, how much money will your account accumulate by the time you're 65? Use the formula =FV(3%, 35, −5000,, 1) to learn that your IRA balance will be $311,379.72 at the end of 35 years.

Now assume you started an IRA account three years ago and have already accumulated $12,500 in your account. Use the formula =FV(3%, 35, −5000, −12500, 1) to learn that your IRA will grow to $346,553.00 at the end of 35 years.

In both of these examples, the *type* argument is 1 because payments occur at the beginning of the period. Including this argument is particularly important in financial calculations that span many years. If you omit the *type* argument (1) in the preceding formula, Excel assumes you add money to your account at the end of each year and returns the value $337,483.69—a difference of $9,069.31.

The PMT function

The PMT function computes the periodic payment required to amortize a loan over a specified number of periods. This function takes the arguments *rate*, *number of periods*, *present value*, *future value*, and *type*; for definitions of these arguments, see Table 16-1.

Suppose you want to take out a 30-year mortgage for $300,000. Assuming an interest rate of 3.2 percent, what will your monthly payments be? First, divide the 3.2 percent interest rate by 12 to arrive at a monthly rate (2.66 percent). Next, convert the number of periods into months by multiplying 30 by 12 (360). You can include these computations as arguments by using the formula =PMT((3.2%/12), (30*12), 300000) to compute the monthly mortgage payment, which turns out to be –$1,297.40. (The result is negative because it's a cost to you.)

TROUBLESHOOTING

The PMT function produces unrealistic results

Sometimes you might find that the PMT function seems to produce unrealistic results—such as payments that are excessively large. As you should with all functions used for calculating investments, make sure you are using the same units for both the *rate* and *nper* (*number of periods*) arguments. If, for example, you type **3%** for the rate, you must type the *nper* argument in years because 3 percent is an annual rate. If you type **3%** for the rate and **360** as the term, Excel returns the payment required to amortize a loan at either 3 percent per month for 30 years or 3 percent per year for 360 years! You can resolve your problem by dividing 3 percent by 12 (which is the standard way of expressing a loan) or typing **30** for *nper*, indicating the term in years. Note, however, that these two options are not equivalent—they yield very different results because of the way interest is calculated. You should use the same units your lender uses, which is probably the annual interest rate divided by 12 and *nper* expressed in months.

The IPMT function

The IPMT function computes the interest part of an individual payment made to repay an amount over a specified time period with constant periodic payments and a constant interest rate. This function takes the arguments *rate, period, number of periods, present value, future value,* and *type*; for definitions of these arguments, see Table 16-1.

Suppose you borrow $200,000 for 30 years at 3 percent interest. The formula =IPMT((3/12)%, 1, 360, 200000) tells you that the interest component of the payment due for the first month is an even –$500.00. The formula =IPMT((3/12)%, 360, 360, 200000) tells you that the interest component of the final payment of the same loan is –$2.10.

The PPMT function

The PPMT function is similar to the IPMT function, except it computes the principal component of an individual payment when a loan is repaid over a specified time with constant periodic payments and a constant interest rate. If you compute both IPMT and PPMT for the same period, you can add the results to obtain the total payment. The PPMT function takes the arguments *rate*, *period*, *number of periods*, *present value*, *future value*, and *type*; for definitions of these arguments, see Table 16-1.

If you borrow $200,000 for 30 years at 3 percent interest, the formula =PPMT((3/12)%, 1, 360, 200000) tells you that the principal component of the payment for the first month of the loan is –$343.21. The formula =PPMT((3/12)%, 360, 360, 200000) tells you that the principal component of the final payment of the same loan is –$841.11.

The NPER function

The NPER function computes the number of periods required to amortize a loan, given a specified periodic payment. This function takes the arguments *rate*, *payment*, *present value*, *future value*, and *type*; for definitions of these arguments, see Table 16-1.

Suppose you can afford mortgage payments of $2,000 per month and you want to know how long it will take to pay off a $300,000 loan at 3 percent interest. The formula =NPER((3/12)%, –2000, 300000) tells you that your mortgage payments will extend over 188 months.

If the payment is too small to amortize the loan at the indicated rate of interest, the function returns an error value. The monthly payment must be at least equal to the period interest rate times the principal amount; otherwise, the loan will never be amortized. For example, the formula =NPER((3/12)%, –500, 300000) returns the #NUM! error value. In this case, the monthly payment must be at least $751 to amortize the loan (although it would take more than 220 years worth of payments at that amount).

The RATE function

The RATE function determines the rate of return of an investment that generates a series of equal periodic payments or a single lump-sum payment. This function takes the arguments *number of periods*, *payment*, *present value*, *future value*, *type*, and *guess*; for definitions of these arguments, see Table 16-1. You use either the *payment* argument to compute the rate for a series of equal periodic payments or the *future value* argument to compute the rate of a lump-sum payment.

Suppose you're considering an investment that will pay you four annual $1,000 payments. The investment costs $3,000. To determine the actual annual rate of return on your investment, type the formula **=RATE(4, 1000, −3000)**. This formula returns 13 percent, an excellent rate of return on this investment.

> **Note**
>
> The RATE function uses *iteration* to compute the rate of return. The function begins by computing the net present value of the investment at the *guess* rate. If that first net present value is greater than zero, the function selects a higher rate and repeats the net present value calculation; if the first net present value is less than zero, the function selects a lower rate for the second iteration. RATE continues this process until it arrives at the correct rate of return or until it has gone through 20 iterations. For more information about iteration, see "Working with circular references" in Chapter 12, "Building formulas."

If you receive the #NUM! error value when you enter the RATE function, Excel probably cannot calculate the rate within 20 iterations. Try typing a different *guess* rate to give the function a running start. A rate from 10 percent through 100 percent usually works.

The IRR function

The IRR function determines the internal rate of return of an investment, which is the rate that causes the net present value of the investment to equal zero. In other words, the internal rate of return is the rate that causes the present value of the inflows from an investment to equal the cost of the investment.

Internal rate of return, like net present value, compares one investment opportunity with another. An attractive investment is one whose net present value, discounted at the appropriate hurdle rate, is greater than zero. Turn that equation around, and you can see that the discount rate required to generate a net present value of zero must be greater than the hurdle rate. Thus, an attractive investment is one for which the discount rate required to yield a net present value of zero—that is, the internal rate of return—is greater than the hurdle rate.

The IRR function takes the arguments *values* and *guess*. (For definitions of these arguments, see Table 16-1.) The *values* argument is an array or a reference to a range of cells that contain numbers. Only one *values* argument is allowed, and it must include at least one positive and one negative value. IRR ignores text, logical values, and blank cells. IRR assumes that transactions occur at the end of a period and returns the equivalent interest rate for that period's length. The *guess* argument is optional, but if you receive the #NUM! error value, try including a *guess* to help Excel reach the answer.

Chapter 16

Suppose you agree to buy an income property for $350,000 and rent it. Over the next ten years, you expect to receive net rental income starting at $40,000 the first year, increasing by $1,000 per year. You can set up a simple worksheet that contains your investment and income information. Type the 11 values, starting with the initial investment amount, in cells A1:A11 on the worksheet. (Be sure to type the initial $350,000 investment in cell A1 as a negative value.) Then the formula =IRR(A1:A11) returns the internal rate of return of 4.46 percent. If the hurdle rate is 3.5 percent, you can consider this property to be a good investment.

The MIRR function

The MIRR function calculates the modified internal rate of return of an investment. The difference from the IRR function is that MIRR takes into account the cost of the money you borrow to finance the investment. MIRR assumes that you'll reinvest the cash the investment generates and that transactions occur at the end of a period. It then returns the equivalent interest rate for that period's length.

The MIRR function takes the arguments *values*, *finance rate*, and *reinvestment rate*. (For definitions of these arguments, see Table 16-1.) The *values* argument must be an array or a reference to a range of cells that contain numbers. This argument represents a series of payments and income occurring at regular periods. You must include at least one positive value and one negative value in the *values* argument.

Suppose you borrow $120,000 at 3 percent interest to acquire an investment that will return increasing amounts of income over five years. If cells A1 through A6 contain the values −120000, 22000, 24000, 28000, 31000, and 33000, representing the initial investment (as a negative value) and the subsequent cash inflows from that investment, the formula =MIRR(A1:A6, 3%, 2%) returns a modified internal rate of return of 4 percent.

Calculating depreciation

Depreciation has an enormous effect on the bottom line of any business, and accurately calculating depreciation is crucial if you want to avoid triggering a detailed scrutiny of your financial records. These functions help you precisely determine the depreciation of an asset for a specific period. Table 16-2 lists the common arguments used in these functions. All of the functions for calculating depreciation are available on the Formulas tab, in the Function Library group's Financial drop-down list.

TABLE 16-2 Depreciation function arguments

Argument	Description
Cost	Initial cost of the asset
Life	Length of time the asset will be depreciated
Period	Individual time period to be computed
Salvage	Asset's remaining value after it has been fully depreciated

The SLN function

The SLN function determines the straight-line depreciation for an asset for a single period. This depreciation method assumes that the depreciation is uniform throughout the useful life of the asset. The cost or basis of the asset, less its estimated salvage value, is deductible in equal amounts over the life of the asset. This function takes the arguments *cost*, *salvage*, and *life*. (For definitions of these arguments, see Table 16-2.)

Suppose you want to determine the annual depreciation for a machine that costs $8,000 new, has a life of 10 years, and has a salvage value of $500. The formula =SLN(8000, 500, 10) tells you that each year's straight-line depreciation is $750.

The DDB and DB functions

The DDB (double declining balance) function computes an asset's depreciation at an accelerated rate—more in the early periods and less later. Using this method, depreciation is computed as a percentage of the net book value of the asset (the cost of the asset less any prior years' depreciation).

The function takes the arguments *cost*, *salvage*, *life*, *period*, and *factor*. All DDB arguments must be positive numbers, and you must use the same time units for life and period; that is, if you express life in months, period must also be in months. The *factor* argument is optional and has a default value of 2, which indicates the normal double declining balance method. Using 3 for the *factor* argument specifies the triple declining balance method. For other argument definitions, see Table 16-2.

Suppose you want to calculate the depreciation of a machine that costs $5,000 new and has a life of five years (60 months) and a salvage value of $100. The formula =DDB(5000, 100, 60, 1) tells you that the double declining balance depreciation for the first month is $166.67. (Note that *life* is expressed in months.) The formula =DDB(5000, 100, 5, 1) tells you that the double declining balance depreciation for the first year is $2,000.00. (Note that *life* is expressed in years.)

The DB (declining balance) function is similar to the DDB function except it uses the fixed declining balance method of depreciation and can calculate depreciation for a particular period in the asset's life. It takes the arguments *cost, salvage, life, period*, and *month*. The *life* and *period* arguments must use the same units. The optional *month* argument is the number of months depreciated in the first year, which is 12—a full year—if it's omitted. For example, to calculate the real depreciation for the first period on a $1,000,000 item with a salvage value of $100,000, a life of six years, and seven months in the first year, use the formula =DB(1000000, 100000, 6, 1, 7), which returns $186,083.33.

The VDB function

The VDB (variable declining balance) function calculates the depreciation of an asset for any complete or partial period, using either the double declining balance or another accelerated-depreciation factor you specify.

This function takes the arguments *cost, salvage, life, start, end, factor*, and *no switch*). The *start* argument is the period after which depreciation will be calculated, and *end* is the last period for which depreciation will be calculated. These arguments determine the depreciation for any length of time during the life of the asset. The *life, start*, and *end* arguments must all use the same units (days, months, or years). The optional *factor* argument is the rate at which the balance declines. If you omit *factor*, Excel assumes that the argument is 2 and uses the double declining balance method. The optional *no switch* argument is a value that specifies whether to switch to straight-line depreciation when the straight-line depreciation is greater than the declining balance. If you omit *no switch* or type **0 (FALSE)**, Excel switches to straight-line depreciation; to prevent the switch, type **1 (TRUE)**. For other argument definitions, see Table 16-2.

Suppose you purchased a $15,000 asset at the end of the first quarter of the current year and that this asset will have a salvage value of $2,000 after five years. To determine the depreciation of this asset next year (the fourth to seventh quarters of its use), use the formula =VDB(15000, 2000, 20, 3, 7). The depreciation for this period is $3,760.55. The units used here are quarters. Notice that the *start* argument is 3, not 4, because we are jumping over the first three periods to start in the fourth.

The SYD function

The SYD function computes an asset's depreciation for a specific time with the sum-of-the-years'-digits method. The SYD function takes the arguments *cost, salvage, life*, and *period*. (For definitions of these arguments, see Table 16-2.) You must use the same units for *life* and *period*. Using the sum-of-the-years'-digits method, Excel calculates depreciation on the cost of the item less its salvage value. Like the double declining balance method, the sum-of-the-years'-digits method is an accelerated depreciation method.

Suppose you want to determine the depreciation of a machine that costs $15,000 and has a life of three years and a salvage value of $1,250. The formula =SYD(15000, 1250, 3, 3) tells you that the sum-of-the-years'-digits depreciation for the third year is $2,291.67.

Analyzing securities

The Financial button on the Formulas tab includes a group of functions designed for specific tasks related to computing and analyzing various types of securities.

> **Note**
>
> In older versions of Excel, these functions were part of the Analysis Toolpak add-in, but Microsoft fully integrated these functions back in Excel 2007. As a result, the functions might produce slightly different results, but Microsoft says they're so insignificantly different that the results are nonetheless "equally correct" (Microsoft's words). Although its worksheet functions have been integrated into Excel, the Analysis Toolpak is still available as an add-in with sophisticated data-analysis tools. For more information, see "Installing the Analysis Toolpak" in Chapter 17, "Functions for analyzing statistics."

Many of these functions share similar arguments. We'll describe the most common ones in Table 16-3 to avoid revisiting the same information in the function discussions that follow.

TABLE 16-3 Security-analysis function arguments

Argument	Description
Basis	Day count basis of the security. If omitted, defaults to 0, indicating U.S. (NASD) 30/360 basis. Other basis values include 1 = actual/actual, 2 = actual/360, 3 = actual/365, and 4 = European 30/360.
Coupon	The security's annual coupon rate.
Frequency	Number of coupon payments made per year: 1 = annual, 2 = semiannual, 4 = quarterly.
Investment	Amount of investment in the security.
Issue	Issue date of the security.
Maturity	Maturity date of the security, which must be greater than the settlement date.
Par	Par value (face value) of the security; $1,000 if omitted.
Price	Price of the security.
Rate	Interest rate of the security at the issue date, which must be greater than or equal to zero.
Redemption	Value of the security at redemption.
Settlement	Settlement date of the security (the day you have to pay for it), which must be greater than the issue date.
Yield	Annual yield of the security, which must be greater than or equal to zero.

Chapter 16

You can type dates by using any of the following: the date's serial number, the date enclosed in quotation marks, or a reference to a cell that contains a date. For example, you can type the date June 30, 2013, as the serial date value *41455*, as *6/30/13*, or as a reference to a cell containing this date. If the security-analysis function results in a #NUM! error value, be sure the dates are in the correct form and that they meet the criteria described in Table 16-3.

For more information about serial date values, see "Understanding how Excel records dates and times" in Chapter 15, "Formatting and calculating date and time."

The DOLLARDE and DOLLARFR functions

One of this pair of functions converts fractional pricing of securities to decimals, and the other converts decimals to fractions. The DOLLARDE function takes the arguments *fractional dollar* and *fraction*, and the DOLLARFR function takes the arguments *decimal dollar* and *fraction*). The *fractional dollar* argument is the value you want to convert expressed as an integer, followed by a decimal point and the numerator of the fraction you want to convert. The *decimal dollar* argument is the value you want to convert expressed as a decimal. The *fraction* argument is an integer indicating the denominator you want to use in the conversion. For the DOLLARFR function, *fraction* is the unit that the function should use when converting the decimal value, effectively rounding the decimal number to the nearest half, quarter, eighth, sixteenth, thirty-second, and so on.

For example, the formula =DOLLARDE(1.03, 32) translates as 1+3/32, which is equivalent to 1.09375. On the other hand, the formula =DOLLARFR(1.09375, 32) returns the result 1.03.

The ACCRINT and ACCRINTM functions

The ACCRINT function returns the interest accrued by a security that pays interest on a periodic basis. This function takes the arguments *issue, first interest, settlement, rate, par, frequency, basis,* and *calculation method,* in which *first interest* indicates the date on which interest is first accrued and *calculation method* is a logical value (1 or TRUE; 0 or FALSE). The default value of TRUE for *calculation method* returns the total accrued interest; a value of FALSE returns the interest accrued after the *first interest* date. For other argument definitions, see Table 16-3. For example, suppose a U.S. Treasury bond has an issue date of March 1, 2014; a settlement date of April 1, 2014; a first interest date of September 1, 2014; a 1.7 percent coupon rate with semiannual frequency; a par value of $1,000; and a basis of 30/360. The accrued interest formula is =ACCRINT("3/1/14", "9/1/14", "4/1/14", 0.017, 1000, 2, 0), which returns 1.4167, indicating that $1.42 accrues from March 1, 2014, to April 1, 2014.

Similarly, the ACCRINTM function returns the interest accrued by a maturity security (a type of security not only with a rhyming name but that also pays interest at maturity).

This function takes the arguments *issue*, *settlement*, *rate*, *par*, and *basis*. Using the preceding example with a maturity date of July 31, 2018, the accrued interest formula is =ACCRINTM("3/1/14", "7/31/18", 0.017, 1000, 0), which returns 75.0833, indicating that the $1,000 bond will pay $75.08 interest on July 31, 2018.

The INTRATE and RECEIVED functions

The INTRATE function calculates the rate of interest, or discount rate, for a fully invested security. This function takes the arguments *settlement*, *maturity*, *investment*, *redemption*, and *basis*; for argument definitions, see Table 16-3. For example, suppose a bond has a settlement date of March 31, 2014, and a maturity date of September 30, 2014. A $1,000,000 investment in this bond will have a redemption value of $1,024,324, using the default 30/360 basis. The bond's discount rate formula is =INTRATE("3/31/14", "9/30/14", 1000000, 1024324, 0), which returns 0.048648, or 4.86 percent.

Similarly, the RECEIVED function calculates the amount received at maturity for a fully invested security and takes the arguments *settlement*, *maturity*, *investment*, *discount*, and *basis*. Using the preceding example with a 5.5 percent discount rate, the formula =RECEIVED("3/31/14", "9/30/14", 1000000, 0.055, 0) returns the mature value $1,028,277.63.

The PRICE, PRICEDISC, and PRICEMAT functions

The PRICE function calculates the price per $100 of face value of a security that pays interest on a periodic basis. This function takes the arguments *settlement*, *maturity*, *rate*, *yield*, *redemption*, *frequency*, and *basis*; for argument definitions, see Table 16-3. For example, suppose a bond's settlement date is March 31, 2014; its maturity date is July 31, 2014; and the interest rate is 5.75 percent, with semiannual frequency. The security's annual yield is 6.50 percent, its redemption value is $100, and it is calculated using the standard 30/360 basis. The bond price formula is =PRICE("3/31/14", "7/31/14", 0.0575, 0.065, 100, 2, 0), which returns $99.73498.

Similarly, the PRICEDISC function returns the price per $100 of face value of a security that is discounted instead of paying periodic interest. This function takes the arguments *settlement*, *maturity*, *discount*, *redemption*, and *basis*. Using the preceding example with the addition of a discount amount of 7.5 percent, the formula =PRICEDISC("3/31/14", "7/31/14", 0.075, 100, 0) returns a price of $97.50.

Finally, the PRICEMAT function returns the price per $100 of face value of a security that pays its interest at the maturity date. This function takes the arguments *settlement*, *maturity*, *issue*, *rate*, *yield*, and *basis*). Using the preceding example with a settlement date of July 31, 2014; an issue date of March 1, 2014; and the maturity date changed to July 31, 2015. The formula =PRICEMAT("7/31/14", "7/31/15", "3/1/14", 0.0575, 0.065, 0) returns $99.15.

The DISC function

The DISC function calculates the discount rate for a security and takes the arguments *settlement*, *maturity*, *price*, *redemption*, and *basis*. (For argument definitions, see Table 16-3.) For example, suppose a bond has a settlement date of June 15, 2014; has a maturity date of December 31, 2014; has a price of $96.875; has a $100 redemption value; and uses the standard 30/360 basis. The bond discount rate formula =DISC("6/15/14", "12/31/14", 96.875, 100, 0) returns 0.057398, or 5.74 percent.

The YIELD, YIELDDISC, and YIELDMAT functions

The YIELD function determines the annual yield for a security that pays interest on a periodic basis and takes the arguments *settlement*, *maturity*, *rate*, *price*, *redemption*, *frequency*, and *basis*; for definitions of these arguments, see Table 16-3. For example, suppose a bond has a settlement date of February 15, 2014; has a maturity date of December 1, 2014; has a coupon rate of 3.75 percent with semiannual frequency; has a price of $99.2345; has a $100 redemption value; and uses the standard 30/360 basis. The annual bond yield formula =YIELD("2/15/14", "12/1/14", 0.0375, 99.2345, 100, 2, 0) returns 0.047363, or 4.74 percent.

The YIELDDISC function, on the other hand, calculates the annual yield for a discounted security. It takes the arguments *settlement*, *maturity*, *price*, *redemption*, and *basis*. Using the preceding example but changing the price to $97.00, the bond yield formula =YIELDDISC("2/15/14", "12/1/14", 97, 100, 0) returns 0.03893, or 3.89 percent.

The YIELDMAT function calculates the annual yield for a security that pays its interest at maturity. This function takes the arguments *settlement*, *maturity*, *issue*, *rate*, *price*, and *basis*. Using the arguments from the YIELD example but adding an issue date of January 1, 2014, and changing the price to $99.2345, the yield-at-maturity formula =YIELDMAT("2/15/14", "12/1/14", "1/1/14", 0.0375, 99.2345, 0) returns 0.04728, or 4.73 percent.

The TBILLEQ, TBILLPRICE, and TBILLYIELD functions

The TBILLEQ function calculates the bond-equivalent yield for a U.S. Treasury bill. It takes the arguments *settlement*, *maturity*, and *discount*. (For argument definitions, see Table 16-3.) For example, suppose a U.S. Treasury bill has a settlement date of February 1, 2014; a maturity date of July 1, 2014; and a discount rate of 0.86 percent. The formula for calculating the bond yield that is equivalent to the yield of a U.S. Treasury bill is =TBILLEQ("2/1/14", "7/1/14", 0.0086), which returns 0.008751, or .88 percent.

You use the TBILLPRICE function to calculate the price per $100 of face value for a U.S. Treasury bill. This function takes the arguments *settlement*, *maturity*, and *discount*. Using the preceding example, the formula to calculate the price per $100 of face value, =TBILLPRICE("2/1/14", "7/1/14", 0.0086), returns 99.6417, or $99.64.

Finally, the TBILLYIELD function calculates a U.S. Treasury bill's yield. It takes the arguments *settlement*, *maturity*, and *price*. Using the preceding example with its precise result, 99.6417, the yield formula =TBILLYIELD("2/1/14", "7/1/14", 99.6417) returns the yield 0.00863, or 0.86 percent.

The COUPDAYBS, COUPDAYS, COUPDAYSNC, COUPNCD, COUPNUM, and COUPPCD functions

This group of functions performs calculations related to bond coupons. For all the sample formulas in this section, we use as our example a bond with a settlement date of March 1, 2014, and a maturity date of December 1, 2014. Its coupons are payable semiannually, using the actual/actual basis (that is, a *basis* argument of 1). All these functions take the arguments *settlement*, *maturity*, *frequency*, and *basis*. (For definitions of these arguments, see Table 16-3.)

The COUPDAYBS function calculates the number of days from the beginning of the coupon period to the settlement date. Using our sample data, the formula =COUPDAYBS("3/1/14", "12/1/14", 2, 1) returns 90.

The COUPDAYS function calculates the number of days in the coupon period that contains the settlement date. Using our sample data, the formula =COUPDAYS("3/1/14", "12/1/14", 2, 1) returns 182.

The COUPDAYSNC function calculates the number of days from the settlement date to the next coupon date. Using our sample data, the formula =COUPDAYSNC("3/1/14", "12/1/14", 2, 1) returns 92.

The COUPNCD function calculates the next coupon date after the settlement date. Using our sample data, the formula =COUPNCD("3/1/14", "12/1/14", 2, 1) returns 41791, or June 1, 2014.

The COUPNUM function calculates the number of coupons payable between the settlement date and the maturity date and rounds the result to the nearest whole coupon. Using our sample data, the formula =COUPNUM("3/1/14", "12/1/14", 2, 1) returns 2.

The COUPPCD function calculates the coupon date before the settlement date. Using our sample data, the formula =COUPPCD("3/1/14", "12/1/14", 2, 1) returns 41609, or December 1, 2013.

The DURATION and MDURATION functions

The DURATION function calculates the annual duration for a security whose interest payments are made on a periodic basis. *Duration* is the weighted average of the present value of the bond's cash flow and measures how a bond's price responds to changes in the yield.

This function takes the arguments *settlement*, *maturity*, *coupon*, *yield*, *frequency*, and *basis*. For argument definitions, see Table 16-3.

For example, suppose a bond has a settlement date of January 1, 2010; has a maturity date of December 31, 2015; has a semiannual coupon rate of 8.5 percent; has a yield of 9.5 percent; and uses the default 30/360 basis. The resulting formula, =DURATION("1/1/10", "12/31/15", 0.085, 0.095, 2, 0), returns a duration of 4.7871.

The MDURATION function calculates the annual modified duration for a security with interest payments made on a periodic basis, adjusted for market yield per number of coupon payments per year. This function takes the arguments *settlement*, *maturity*, *coupon*, *yield*, *frequency*, and *basis*. Using the values from the DURATION formula, the modified duration formula is =MDURATION("1/1/10", "12/31/15", 0.085, 0.095, 2, 0) and returns a value of 4.57.

Using the Euro Currency Tools add-in

You might find that the Euro Currency Tools add-in can make life simpler if you routinely work with various European currencies. To install this add-in, click the File tab, click Options, select the Add-Ins category, and click the Go button to display the Add-Ins dialog box. Select the Euro Currency Tools check box, and then click OK.

To see what this add-in provides, click the Formulas tab on the ribbon. A Solutions group is added on the right side of the Formulas tab and includes the Euro Conversion command, the Euro Formatting command, and a drop-down menu offering an option for converting to or from euros to each individual European currency.

Clicking the Euro Formatting button applies a standard currency number format with a Euro symbol instead of a dollar sign. You can select any conversion option listed in the drop-down list and see what the value in the selected cell would be if converted to the selected currency. The result, which you can also select and copy, appears in a box to the right of the Euro Conversion button that does not appear until you select a conversion option from the list.

If you need to convert the values in a worksheet full of cells (or just one cell) from one European Union member currency to another, use the Euro Conversion button, which displays the Euro Conversion dialog box. Options in this dialog box work as follows:

- The Source Range box, when selected, lets you drag to select the range you want to convert. You can select a matching range for the results using the Destination Range box, but you need to select only one cell, which becomes the upper-left corner of the resulting range.

- The From and To boxes in the Currency Conversion area select the European Union member currency of the source range and destination range, respectively.

- You use the Output Format list to select a format for the resulting values: the corresponding currency format; the International Standardization Organization (ISO) format, which uses the appropriate three-letter ISO code instead of currency symbols; or None, if you prefer unformatted numbers.

Clicking the Advanced button displays the Advanced Euro Options dialog box, which contains the following options:

- **Convert To Values Only**   Converts all numbers and formulas in the source range to raw values, which is the default option.

- **Prompt To Convert Formulas**   Displays a dialog box during the conversion process in which you can specify conversion options for each formula, including three that are not available in the Advanced Euro Options dialog box. You can copy the original formula instead of creating a conversion formula in the destination cell, you can choose to leave the cell blank, or you can edit each formula individually.

- **Link New Formulas To Original Data**   Pastes formulas instead of values in the destination range for any corresponding source range cells that contain formulas. These new formulas use the EUROCONVERT function with the same references used in the source formulas, creating conversion formulas that update dynamically.

- **Output Full Precision**   Controls the rounding of numbers. Usually, based on European Union rules, Excel calculates converted currency values with a rounding factor that uses six significant digits of precision. To suppress this rounding factor, select the Output Full Precision check box.

- **Set Triangulation Precision To**   Determines the number of significant digits of precision, from 3 through 15, to be used in the intermediate calculations (which are performed in euros) when converting between two European Union member currencies.

> **Note**
>
> The membership of the European Union is subject to change. If a member country's currency isn't available in any of the Euro Currency Tools, visit the Microsoft Office Update website (*office.microsoft.com*), or click the Help button to look for an updated version of the add-in.

Chapter 16

Functions for analyzing statistics

Microsoft Excel provides a wide range of features that can help you perform statistical analyses of your data. A number of functions that assist in simple analysis tasks—such as AVERAGE, MEDIAN, and MODE—are built into the program. If the built-in statistical functions aren't enough, you can turn to the Analysis Toolpak, an add-in that provides a collection of tools that augment the built-in analytical capabilities of Excel. You can use these tools to create histograms and rank-and-percentile tables, extract samples from a data set, perform regression analysis, generate special random-number sets, apply Fourier and other transformations to your data, and more. In this chapter, we explore the most important statistical-analysis functions that are built into Excel, as well as those included with the Analysis Toolpak.

Analyzing distributions of data

In statistics, a collection of measurements is called a *distribution*. Excel has several methods you can use to analyze distributions: built-in statistical functions, the sample and population statistical functions, and the rank-and-percentile functions together with the Rank And Percentile tool.

> **Note**
> You can also analyze distributions using the Descriptive Statistics and Histogram tools, both of which are included in the Analysis Toolpak add-in. For more information, see "Using the Analysis Toolpak data analysis tools" later in this chapter.

Using built-in statistical functions

You use the built-in statistical functions to analyze a group (or population) of measurements. In the following sections, the discussion is limited to the most commonly used statistical functions. To quickly access these functions, click the More Functions button on the Formulas tab on the ribbon and then click Statistical to display a menu of statistical functions.

> **Note**
>
> Excel also offers the advanced statistical functions LINEST, LOGEST, TREND, and GROWTH, which operate on arrays. For more information, see "Understanding linear and exponential regression" later in this chapter.

The AVERAGE functions

The AVERAGE and AVERAGEA functions compute the arithmetic mean, or average, of the numbers in a range by summing a series of numeric values and then dividing the result by the number of values. These functions take the arguments *number1*, *number2*, and so on, and they can include up to 255 arguments. The AVERAGE function ignores blank cells and cells containing logical and text values, but the AVERAGEA function includes them. For example, to calculate the average of the values in cells B4 through B15, you could use the formula =(B4+B5+B6+B7+B8+B9+B10+B11+B12+B13+B14+B15)/12, but it's obviously more efficient to use =AVERAGE(B4:B15).

For more information about this function, see the sidebar "AVERAGE vs. AVG" in Chapter 14, "Everyday functions." Also, see "The AGGREGATE function" in Chapter 14, which you can also use to apply this function with options to ignore hidden rows and error values.

The AVERAGEIF function takes the arguments *range*, *criteria*, and *average_range*, where *range* represents the cells to average; *criteria* is a number, expression, cell reference, or text used to select the cells within *range* to include; and *average_range* is an optional argument specifying an alternate range of cells to evaluate. For example, the formula =AVERAGEIF(sales,">20",A2:C30) averages all cells in the range A2:C30 with values greater than 20. If the third argument is omitted, the formula performs the same operation on the named range *sales* instead. The *average_range* criterion becomes useful when you want to select cells on the basis of the contents of one row or column and actually perform the calculation on numbers contained in adjacent rows or columns.

The AVERAGEIFS function is similar to the AVERAGEIF function, but it allows you to specify multiple criteria. This function takes the arguments *average_range*, *criteria_range1*, *criteria1*, *criteria_range2*, *criteria2*, and so on, where *average_range* specifies the cell range you want to average, *criteria_range* specifies the cells containing the values you want to compare, and *criteria* is a value, expression, cell reference, or text defining the cells within *average_range* that you want to include. You can add up to 127 sets of *criteria_range* and *criteria* arguments. This function is useful for finding the average sale prices of particular automobile models on an online auction site, where you limit the results to include specific features, such as number of doors, transmission type, interior options, and other such details.

> ## What are "compatibility" functions?
>
> Excel has a number of functions with a "mid-period" in the Insert Function dialog box and on the Formulas tab's Function Reference menus. Most of these functions are on the More Functions menu's Statistical menu, including BETA.DIST and STDEV.P, among many others. Most of these represent refinements to, or clarifications of, existing functionality. For example, the STDEV.S and STDEV.P functions are identical in functionality to the old STDEV and STDEVP functions. Other functions now have two forms where there used to be only one, such as RANK, which has been replaced by RANK.AVG and RANK.EQ, which simply treat multiple results differently. The Compatibility menu on the More Functions menu lists all the functions that have been replaced by their "mid-period" forms. And yes, you can still use the old ones.

The MEDIAN, MODE.SNGL, MODE.MULT, MAX, MIN, and COUNT functions

These functions all take the same arguments, essentially just a cell range or a list of numbers separated by commas, such as *number1*, *number2*, and so on. They can accept up to 255 arguments and ignore text, error values, and logical values. Here's a brief description of each:

- **MEDIAN** Computes the median of a set of numbers. The median is the number in the middle of the set; that is, an equal number of values are higher and lower than the median. If the numbers specified include an even number of values, the value returned is the average of the two that lie in the middle of the set.

- **MODE.SNGL** Determines which value occurs most frequently in a set of numbers. If no number occurs more than once, MODE.SNGL returns the #N/A error value.

- **MODE.MULT** Determines which values occur most frequently in a set of numbers, and returns a vertical array of them. You must select enough cells to contain the results before entering the formula as an array. For more information, see "Using arrays" in Chapter 12, "Building formulas."

- **MAX** Returns the largest value in a range.

- **MIN** Returns the smallest value in a range.

- **COUNT** Tells you how many cells in a given range contain numbers, including dates and formulas that evaluate to numbers.

> ## The A functions
>
> Excel includes a set of functions that give you more flexibility when you're calculating data sets that include text or logical values. These functions are AVERAGEA, COUNTA, MAXA, MINA, STDEVA, STDEVPA, VARA, and VARPA, all of which accept a series of up to 255 arguments as (*value1, value2, ...*).
>
> Ordinarily, the non-A versions of these functions ignore cells containing text values. For example, if a range of 10 cells contains one text value, AVERAGE ignores that cell and divides by 9 to arrive at the average, whereas AVERAGEA considers the text value part of the range and divides by 10. This is helpful if you want to include all referenced cells in your calculations, especially if you use formulas that return text flags, such as "none," if a certain condition is met. For more information about STDEVA, STDEVPA, VARA, and VARPA, see "Using sample and population statistical functions" later in this chapter.

You can also use the AGGREGATE function to apply these functions with options to ignore hidden rows and error values. For more information, see "The AGGREGATE function" in Chapter 14.

Using functions that analyze rank and percentile

Excel includes several sets of functions that extract rank and percentile information from a set of input values: PERCENTRANK, PERCENTILE, QUARTILE, SMALL, LARGE, and RANK.

You can also use the AGGREGATE function to apply these functions with options to ignore hidden rows and error values. For more information, see "The AGGREGATE function" in Chapter 14.

The PERCENTRANK functions

The PERCENTRANK.INC and PERCENTRANK.EXC functions return a ranking for any item (aka *member*) of a data set as a percentage. The .INC (inclusive) form of this function includes the entire data set, and the .EXC (exclusive) form eliminates rankings of 0% and 100%. We used PERCENTRANK.INC to create the percentile ranking in column E in Figure 17-1. These functions are meant to replace the old PERCENTRANK function, which you can still use and is equivalent to the .INC form.

You can find the SAT Scores.xlsx file with the other examples on the companion website.

Both forms of the PERCENTRANK function take the arguments *array*, *x*, and *significance*. The *array* argument specifies the input range (which is $D$2:$D$1001, in our example), and *x* specifies the value whose rank you want to obtain. The *significance* argument, which is optional, indicates the number of digits of precision you want; if this argument is omitted, results are rounded to three digits (*0.xxx* or *xx.x%*).

| E2 | ▾ | : | ✕ | ✓ | *fx* | =PERCENTRANK.INC($D$2:$D$1001,D2,4) |

◢	A	B	C	D	E	F	G	H	I
1	Student ID	Verbal	Math	Total	Percentile				
2	722-4499	418	518	936	3%				
3	605-3475	465	557	1022	34%				
4	546-3500	463	549	1012	27%				
5	655-8550	466	587	1053	55%				
6	812-6448	520	544	1064	62%				
7	814-6503	470	537	1007	24%				
8	332-3453	533	549	1082	73%				

Figure 17-1 The PERCENTRANK.INC function determines where a value stands in a population.

The PERCENTILE and QUARTILE functions

You use the PERCENTILE.INC and PERCENTILE.EXC functions to find the member of a data set that stands at a specified percentile rank; they both take the arguments *array*, and *k*. The .INC (inclusive) form of this function includes the entire data set, and the .EXC (exclusive) form eliminates rankings of 0% and 100%. You must express the percentile *k* as a decimal fraction from 0 to 1. For example, to find out which score in the worksheet partially shown in Figure 17-1 represents the 86th percentile, you can use the formula =PERCENTILE.INC($D$2:$D$1001, 0.86).

You can also use the AGGREGATE function to apply these functions with options to ignore hidden rows and error values. For more information, see "The AGGREGATE function" in Chapter 14.

The QUARTILE functions, which take the arguments *array*, and *quart*, work much like the PERCENTILE functions, except they return the values at the lowest, 25th, median, 75th, or highest percentile in the input set. The *array* argument specifies the input range. The *quart* argument specifies the value to be returned, as shown in Table 17-1.

TABLE 17-1 The *quart* argument

quart	Returns
0	Lowest value
1	25th-percentile value
2	Median (50th-percentile) value
3	75th-percentile value
4	Highest value

INSIDE OUT   Use MIN, MEDIAN, and MAX

QUARTILE is a powerful function, but if you don't need the 25th or 75th percentile values, you will get faster results using other functions, particularly when working with large data sets. Use the MIN function instead of QUARTILE(*array*, 0), the MEDIAN function instead of QUARTILE(*array*, 2), and the MAX function instead of QUARTILE(*array*, 4).

The SMALL and LARGE functions

The SMALL and LARGE functions return the *k*th smallest and *k*th largest values in an input range; both take the arguments *array* and *k*, where *k* is the position from the largest or smallest value to the value in the array you want to find. For example, to find the 15th highest score in the worksheet partially shown in Figure 17-1, you can use the formula =LARGE($D$2:$D$1001, 15).

The RANK functions

The RANK.AVG and RANK.EQ functions return the ranked position of a particular value within a set of values; both take the arguments *number*, *ref*, and *order*. If more than one value in the set has the same rank, the .AVG form of the function returns their average, while the .EQ form returns the higher value. The *number* argument is the number for which you want to find the rank, *ref* is the range containing the data set, and *order* (an optional argument) ranks the number as if it were in a ranking list in an ascending or descending (the default) order. For example, to find out where the score 1200 falls in the data set in Figure 17-1, you can use the formula =RANK.AVG(1200, $D$2:$D$1001).

Using sample and population statistical functions

Variance and standard deviation are statistical measurements of the dispersion of a group, or population, of values. The standard deviation is the square root of the variance. As a rule, about 68 percent of a normally distributed population falls within one standard deviation of the mean, and about 95 percent falls within two standard deviations. A large standard deviation indicates that the population is widely dispersed from the mean; a small standard deviation indicates that the population is tightly packed around the mean.

The VAR and STDEV function families compute the variance and standard deviation of the numbers in a range of cells. Before you make these calculations, you must determine whether those values represent the total population or only a representative sample of that population. The VAR.S and STDEV.S functions assume that the values represent only a sample of the total population, while the VAR.P and STDEV.P functions assume that the values represent the total population. The A versions—VARA, VARPA, STDEVA, and STDEVPA— include numeric text entries and logical values in their calculations, while the others do not.

Calculating sample statistics: VAR.S and STDEV.S

The VAR.S and STDEV.S functions compute variance and standard deviation, assuming that their arguments represent only a sample of the total population. These functions take the arguments *number1*, *number2*, and so on, and they accept up to 255 arguments. The worksheet in Figure 17-2 shows exam scores for five students and assumes that the scores in cells B4:E8 represent only a part of the total population.

I4	▾	:	✕	✓	*fx*	=VAR.S(B4:E8)					

◢	A	B	C	D	E	F	G	H	I	J
1	First Quarter Exam Scores									
2										
3	*Student*		Exam 1	Exam 2	Exam 3	Exam 4	*Average*		Overall Average	89.20
4	Krieger, Doris		87	90	79	96	88.00		Variance	30.80
5	Oliveira, Manuel		92	94	94	97	94.25		Standard Deviation	5.55
6	Kodeda, Adam		96	95	95	80	91.50			
7	Lange, Michael		85	87	87	88	86.75			
8	Taylor, Maurice		81	88	88	85	85.50			
9										
10										

Figure 17-2 Here, the VAR.S and STDEV.S functions measure the dispersion of sample exam scores.

You can find the VAR.xlsx file with the other examples on the companion website.

The formula in cell I4 =VAR.S(B4:E8) calculates the variance for this sample group of test scores. The formula in cell I5 =STDEV.S(B4:E8) calculates the standard deviation.

Assuming that the test scores in the example are normally distributed, you can deduce that about 68 percent of the students (the general-rule percentage) achieved scores from 83.65 (the average 89.20 minus the standard deviation 5.55) to 94.75 (89.20 plus 5.55).

You can also use the AGGREGATE function to apply the VAR.S function with options to ignore hidden rows and error values. For more information, see "The AGGREGATE function" in Chapter 14.

Calculating total population statistics: VAR.P and STDEV.P

If the numbers you're analyzing represent an entire population rather than a sample, use the VAR.P and STDEV.P functions to calculate variance and standard deviation. These functions take the arguments *number1*, *number2*, and so on, and they accept up to 255 arguments.

Assuming that cells B4:E8 in the worksheet shown in Figure 17-2 represent the total population, you can calculate the variance and standard deviation with the formulas =VAR.P(B4:E8) and =STDEV.P(B4:E8). The VAR.P function returns 29.26, and the STDEV.P function returns 5.41.

> **Note**
>
> The STDEV.S, STDEV.P, VAR.S, and VAR.P functions do not include text values or logical values in their calculations. If you want to include these values, use the A versions: STDEVA, STDEVPA, VARA, and VARPA. For more information, see "The A functions" earlier in this chapter.

You can also use the AGGREGATE function to apply these functions with options to ignore hidden rows and error values. For more information, see "The AGGREGATE function" in Chapter 14.

Understanding linear and exponential regression

Excel includes several array functions for performing linear regression (LINEST, TREND, FORECAST, SLOPE, and STEYX) and for performing exponential regression (LOGEST and GROWTH). You enter these functions as array formulas, and they produce array results. You can use each of these functions with one or several independent variables. The following list defines the different types of regression:

- **Linear regression** Produces the slope of a line that best fits a single set of data. Based on a year's worth of sales figures, for example, linear regression can tell you the projected sales for March of the following year by giving you the slope and y-intercept (that is, the point where the line crosses the y-axis) of the line that best fits the sales data. By following the line forward in time, you can estimate future sales, if you can safely assume that growth will remain linear.

- **Exponential regression**   Produces an exponential curve that best fits a set of data that you suspect does not change linearly with time. For example, a series of measurements of population growth is nearly always better represented by an exponential curve than by a line.

- **Multiple regression**   Is the analysis of more than one set of data, which often produces a more realistic projection. You can perform both linear and exponential multiple-regression analyses. For example, suppose you want to project the appropriate price for a house in your area based on square footage, number of bathrooms, lot size, and age. Using a multiple-regression formula, you can estimate a price by using a database of information about existing houses.

Regressing into the future?

The concept of *regression* might sound strange because the term is usually associated with movement backward, whereas in the world of statistics, regression is often used to predict the future. Simply put, *regression* is a statistical technique that finds a mathematical expression that best describes a set of data.

Often businesses try to predict the future using sales and percent-of-sales projections that are based on history. A simple percent-of-sales technique identifies assets and liabilities that vary along with sales, determines the proportion of each, and assigns them percentages. Although using percent-of-sales forecasting is often sufficient for slow or steady short-term growth, the technique loses accuracy as growth accelerates.

Regression analysis uses more sophisticated equations to analyze larger sets of data and translates them into coordinates on a line or curve. In the not-so-distant past, regression analysis was not widely used because of the large volume of calculations involved. Since spreadsheet applications such as Excel began offering built-in regression functions, the use of regression analysis has become more widespread.

Calculating linear regression

The equation $y = mx + b$ algebraically describes a straight line for a set of data with one independent variable, where x is the independent variable, y is the dependent variable, m represents the slope of the line, and b represents the y-intercept. If a line represents a number of independent variables in a multiple-regression analysis to an expected result, the equation of the regression line takes the form

$$y = m_1 x_1 + m_2 x_2 + \ldots + m_n x_n + b$$

in which y is the dependent variable, x_1 through x_n are n independent variables, m_1 through m_n are the coefficients of each independent variable, and b is a constant.

The LINEST function

The LINEST function returns the values of m_1 through m_n and the value of b, given a known set of values for y and a known set of values for each independent variable. This function takes the form =LINEST(*known_y's, known_x's, const, stats*).

The *known_y's* argument is the set of y-values you already know. This argument can be a single column, a single row, or a rectangular range of cells. If *known_y's* is a single column, each column in the *known_x's* argument is considered an independent variable. Similarly, if *known_y's* is a single row, each row in the *known_x's* argument is considered an independent variable. If *known_y's* is a rectangular range, you can use only one independent variable; *known_x's* in this case should be a range of the same size and shape as *known_y's*. If you omit the *known_x's* argument, Excel uses the sequence 1, 2, 3, 4, and so on.

The *const* and *stats* arguments are optional. If either is included, it must be a logical constant—either TRUE or FALSE. (You can substitute *1* for TRUE and *0* for FALSE.) The default settings for *const* and *stats* are TRUE and FALSE, respectively. If you set *const* to FALSE, Excel forces *b* (the last term in the straight-line equation) to be *0*. If you set *stats* to TRUE, the array returned by LINEST includes the following validation statistics:

se_1 through se_n	Standard error values for each coefficient
se_b	Standard error value for the constant b
r^2	Coefficient of determination
se_y	Standard error value for y
F	F statistic
D_f	Degrees of freedom
ss_{reg}	Regression sum of squares
ss_{resid}	Residual sum of squares

Before creating a formula using LINEST, you must select a range large enough to hold the result array returned by the function. If you omit the *stats* argument (or set it explicitly to FALSE), the result array encompasses one cell for each of your independent variables and one cell for *b*. If you include the validation statistics, the result array looks like the following example. After selecting a range to contain the result array, type the function, and then press Ctrl+Shift+Enter to enter the function in each cell of the result array.

M_n	M_{n-1}	...	m_2	m_1	b
se_n	se_{n-1}	...	se_2	se_1	se_b
r^2	se_y				
F	D_f				
ss_{reg}	ss_{resid}				

Note that, with or without validation statistics, the coefficients and standard error values for your independent variables are returned in the opposite order from your input data. For example, if you have four independent variables organized in four columns, LINEST evaluates the leftmost column as x_1, but it returns m_1 in the fourth column of the result array.

Figure 17-3 shows a simple example of the use of LINEST with one independent variable. The entries in column B of this worksheet represent monthly product demand. The numbers in column A represent the months in the period. Suppose you want to compute the slope and y-intercept of the regression line that best describes the relationship between the demand and the months. In other words, you want to describe the trend of the data. To do this, select the range F6:G6, type the formula =**LINEST(B2:B19, A2:A19)**, and press Ctrl+Shift+Enter. The resulting number in cell F6 is 20.613, the slope of the regression line; the number in cell G6 is 4002.065, the y-intercept of the line.

F6		:	×	✓	f_x	{=LINEST(B2:B19,A2:A19)}			
	A	B	C	D	E	F	G	H	I
1	Month	Demand, thousands	Trend						
2	1	4039	4022.67836						
3	2	4057	4043.29137						
4	3	4052	4063.90437						
5	4	4094	4084.51737			Linear Estimation			
6	5	4104	4105.13037			20.613003	4002.0654		
7	6	4110	4125.74338						

Figure 17-3 The LINEST function computes the slope and y-intercept of a regression line.

You can find the Analysis.xlsx file with the other examples on the companion website.

The LINEST and LOGEST functions return only the y-axis coordinates used for calculating lines and curves. The difference between them is that LINEST projects a straight line and LOGEST projects an exponential curve.

INSIDE OUT   A real (estate) regression application

One often-used regression model is sometimes known as the Competitive Market Analysis (CMA). Realtors use CMAs to arrive at an estimated selling price for a home, basing the price on historical sales data for comparable homes in the area. Here is a sample Excel-based version of this tool, called the Home Price Estimator:

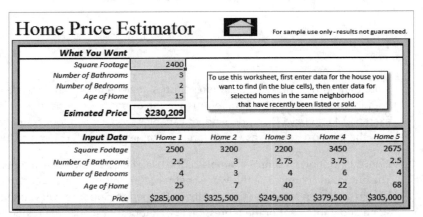

This is a simple application that uses the LINEST function to analyze the statistics in the Input Data area and generate an array of results based on similar statistics you enter in the What You Want area. The LINEST array is actually located in hidden rows below the visible area of the worksheet, as shown next. The first row of values in the LINEST data array is used by the Estimated Price formula to extrapolate an estimated value. Usually in this workbook, row and column headings are hidden, rows 25 through 37 are hidden, worksheet protection is turned on, and cells are locked with data entry allowed only in the designated input areas.

Although you can use real estate listing prices to arrive at an estimated price, it is better to use actual sale prices, if you can get them. And of course, this is only one tool and it only works with five variables; there are always many other variables to consider. No guarantees.

You can find the Home Price Estimator.xlsx file with the other examples on the companion website.

The TREND function

LINEST returns a mathematical description of the straight line that best fits known data. TREND finds points that lie along that line and that fall into the unknown category. You can use the numbers returned by TREND to plot a trendline—a straight line that helps make sense of actual data. You can also use TREND to *extrapolate*, or make intelligent guesses about, future data based on the tendencies exhibited by known data. (Be careful. Although you can use TREND to plot the straight line that best fits the known data, TREND can't tell you whether that line is a good predictor of the future. Validation statistics returned by LINEST can help you make that assessment.) The TREND function takes the form =TREND(*known_y's, known_x's, new_x's, const*).

The first two arguments represent the known values of your dependent and independent variables. As in LINEST, the *known_y's* argument can be a single column, single row, or rectangular range. The *known_x's* argument also follows the pattern described for LINEST. The third and fourth arguments are optional. If you omit *new_x's*, the TREND function considers *new_x's* to be identical to *known_x's*. If you include *const*, the value of that argument must be TRUE or FALSE (or *1* or *0*). If *const* is TRUE, TREND forces *b* to be *0*.

To calculate the trendline data points that best fit your known data, simply omit the third and fourth arguments from this function. The results array will be the same size as the *known_x's* range. In Figure 17-4, we used TREND to find the value of each point on the regression line that describes the data set from the example in Figure 17-3. To create these values, we selected the range C2:C19 and entered **=TREND(B2:B19, A2:A19)** as an array formula using Ctrl+Shift+Enter.

To extrapolate from existing data, you must supply a range for *new_x's*. You can supply as many or as few cells for *new_x's* as you want. The result array will be the same size as the *new_x's* range. In Figure 17-5, we used TREND to calculate demand for the 19th, 20th, and 21st months. To arrive at these values, we typed **19** through **21** in A21:A23, selected C21:C23, and entered **=TREND(B2:B19, A2:A19, A21:A23)** as an array formula by pressing Ctrl+Shift+Enter.

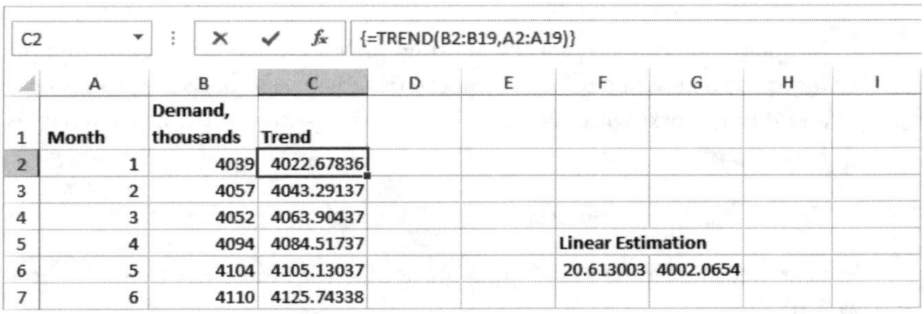

Figure 17-4 The TREND function creates a data series that can be plotted as a line on a chart.

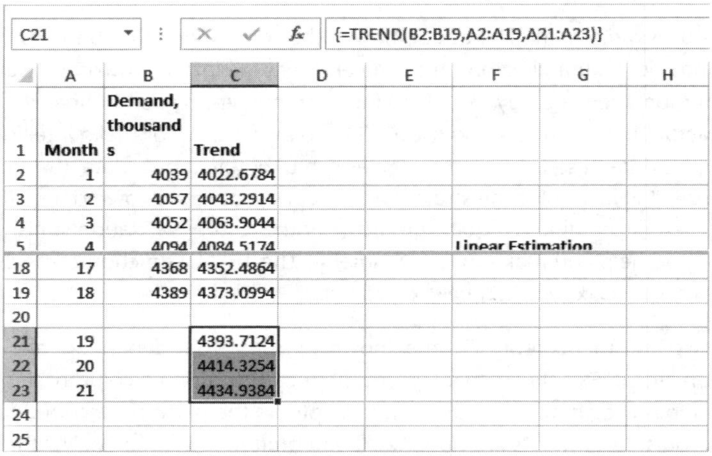

Figure 17-5 TREND can predict the sales figures for months 19, 20, and 21.

The FORECAST function

The FORECAST function is similar to TREND, except it returns a single point along a line rather than returning an array that defines the line. This function takes the form =FORECAST(x, known_y's, known_x's).

The x argument is the data point for which you want to extrapolate a value. For example, instead of using TREND, you can use the FORECAST function to extrapolate the value in cell C23 in Figure 17-5 by using the formula =FORECAST(21, B2:B19, A2:A19), where the x argument refers to the 21st data point on the regression line. You can use this function if you want to calculate any point in the future.

The SLOPE function

The SLOPE function returns the slope of the linear-regression line. The slope is defined as the vertical distance divided by the horizontal distance between any two points on the regression line. Its value is the same as the first number in the array returned by the LINEST function. In other words, SLOPE calculates the trajectory of the line used by the FORECAST and TREND functions to calculate the values of data points. The SLOPE function takes the form =SLOPE(*known_y's, known_x's*).

To find the slope of the regression line that describes the data set from the example shown in Figure 17-5, you can use =SLOPE(B2:B19, A2:A19), which returns a value of 20.613.

The STEYX function

The STEYX function calculates the standard error of a regression, a measure of the amount of error accrued in predicting a *y* for each given *x*. This function takes the form =STEYX(*known_y's, known_x's*). If you apply this function to the worksheet shown in Figure 17-5, the formula =STEYX(B2:B19, A2:A19) returns a standard error value of 12.96562.

Calculating exponential regression

Unlike linear regression, which plots values along a straight line, exponential regression describes a curve by calculating the array of values needed to plot it. The equation that describes an exponential regression curve is as follows:

$$y = b * m_1^{x1} * m_2^{x2} * \ldots * m_n^{xn}$$

If you have only one independent variable, the equation is as follows:

$$y = b * m^x$$

The LOGEST function

The LOGEST function works like LINEST, except you use it to analyze data that is nonlinear, and it returns the coordinates of an exponential curve instead of a straight line. LOGEST returns coefficient values for each independent variable plus a value for the constant *b*. This function takes the form =LOGEST(*known_y's, known_x's, const, stats*).

LOGEST accepts the same arguments as the LINEST function and returns a result array in the same fashion. If you set the optional *stats* argument to TRUE, the function also returns validation statistics. For more information about the LOGEST function's underlying equations and its arguments, see "The LINEST function" earlier in this chapter.

> **Note**
>
> The LINEST and LOGEST functions return only the y-axis coordinates used for calculating lines and curves. The difference between them is that LINEST projects a straight line and LOGEST projects an exponential curve. You must be careful to match the appropriate function to the analysis at hand. The LINEST function might be more appropriate for sales projections, and the LOGEST function might be more suited to applications such as statistical analyses or population trends.

The GROWTH function

Where the LOGEST function returns a mathematical description of the exponential regression curve that best fits a set of known data, the GROWTH function finds points that lie along that curve. The GROWTH function works like its linear counterpart, TREND, and takes the form =GROWTH(*known_y's, known_x's, new_x's, const*). For more information about the GROWTH function's arguments, see "The TREND function" earlier in this chapter.

Using the Analysis Toolpak data analysis tools

The Analysis Toolpak add-in is part of the deal when you purchase Excel, although you might not know it. *Add-ins* are little packages of tools that more or less seamlessly integrate into the user interface of Excel. However, they require you to install them first. The following sections discuss the installation of—and the tools included with—the Analysis Toolpak.

Installing the Analysis Toolpak

To see whether you have the Analysis Toolpak installed, click the Data tab on the ribbon. If the Data Analysis button is there, you're good to go. If not, click the File tab, click Options, and select the Add-Ins category. Click the Go button at the bottom of the dialog box to display the Add-Ins dialog box. In the Add-Ins dialog box, select the Analysis Toolpak check box, and then click OK to install it. You can also select the Analysis Toolpak—VBA check box if you want the Toolpak functions to be available for programmatic usage, but this add-in is not necessary for our purposes.

When you click the Data Analysis button on the Data tab, the Data Analysis dialog box appears, as shown in Figure 17-6.

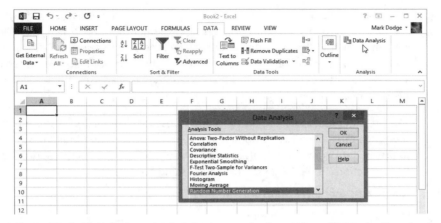

Figure 17-6 Click the Data Analysis button on the Data tab to display the Data Analysis dialog box.

Using the Descriptive Statistics tool

The Descriptive Statistics tool provides a table of statistics that shows the general tendencies and variability for one or more sets of input values. For each variable in the input range, this tool's output range includes a detailed list of statistics, as shown in Figure 17-7. To use the Descriptive Statistics tool, click the Data Analysis button on the Data tab on the ribbon, select Descriptive Statistics, and click OK. The Descriptive Statistics dialog box shown in Figure 17-7 appears.

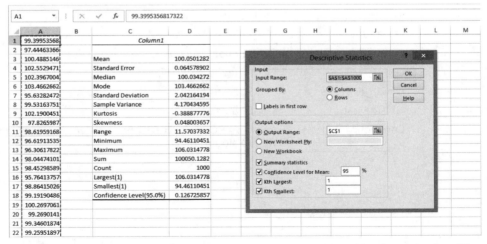

Figure 17-7 We used the Descriptive Statistics tool to generate this table of statistics describing the column of 1,000 values contained in column A.

Chapter 17

The Descriptive Statistics tool requires an input range that consists of one or more variables and an output range. You must also indicate whether the variables are to be arranged by column or by row. If you include a row of labels, be sure to select the Labels In First Row check box. Excel then uses the labels to identify the variables in its output table. Select the Summary Statistics check box only if you want the detailed output table shown in Figure 17-7; otherwise, leave this check box clear.

Like the other tools in the Analysis Toolpak, Descriptive Statistics creates a table of constants. If a table of constants doesn't suit your needs, you can obtain most of the same statistical data from other Analysis Toolpak tools or from formulas that use the Excel worksheet functions. Table 17-2 lists the statistics and formulas.

TABLE 17-2 Descriptive Statistics formulas

Statistic	Formula
Mean	=AVERAGE(*number1, number2, ...*)
Standard error	Similar to =STEYX(*known_y's, known_x's*) but uses ± distribution rather than the standard distribution
Median	=MEDIAN(*number1, number2, ...*)
Mode	=MODE.SNGL(*number1, number2, ...*)
Standard deviation	=STDEV.S(*number1, number2, ...*)
Variance	=VAR.S(*number1, number2, ...*)
Kurtosis	=KURT(*number1, number2, ...*)
Skewness	=SKEW(*number1, number2, ...*)
Range	=MAX(*number1, number2*) – MIN(*number1, number2, ...*)
Minimum	=MIN(*number1, number2, ...*)
Maximum	=MAX(*number1, number2, ...*)
Sum	=SUM(*number1, number2, ...*)
Count	=COUNT(*value1, value2, ...*)
*k*th largest	=LARGE(*array, k*)
*k*th smallest	=SMALL(*array, k*)
Confidence	Similar to =CONFIDENCE(*alpha, standard_dev, size*) but uses a different algorithm

Creating histograms

A *histogram* is a chart (usually a simple column chart) that takes a collection of measure-ments and plots the number of measurements (called the *frequency*) that fall within each of several intervals (called *bins*).

To demonstrate how the Histogram tool works, we'll use a table of 1,000 test scores. (The input range must contain numeric data only.) To see a breakdown of the total scores at 50-point intervals, begin by setting up the distribution bins shown in column F of Figure 17-8.

	D2			×	✓	fx	=B2+C2			
	A	B	C	D	E	F	G	H		
1	Student ID	Verbal	Math	Total		Bins				
2	722-4499	418	518	936		600				
3	605-3475	465	557	1022		650				
4	546-3500	463	549	1012		700				
5	655-8550	466	587	1053		750				
6	812-6448	520	544	1064		800				
7	814-6503	470	537	1007		850				
8	332-3453	533	549	1082		900				
9	55-0476	476	570	1046		950				
10	745-0539	468	548	1016		1000				
11	675-1544	441	562	1003		1050				
12	836-6513	570	560	1130		1100				
13	146-4509	503	554	1057		1150				
14	45-9450	551	556	1107		1200				
15	924-3538	498	562	1060		1250				
16	664-9559	466	525	991		1300				
17	596-5425	414	549	963		1350				
18	914-1483	497	545	1042		1400				
19	266-3469	581	519	1100		1450				
20	116-2492	402	568	970		1500				

Figure 17-8 Column F contains the distribution bins.

The distribution bins don't have to be equally spaced like the ones in Figure 17-8 are, but they must be in ascending order. Click the Data Analysis button on the Data tab, select the Histogram tool, and then click OK. Figure 17-9 shows the Histogram dialog box.

The Histogram tool can take three items of information: the location of the data (in this case, $D$2:$D$1001), the location of the bins ($F$2:$F$23), and the upper-left cell of the range where you want the analysis to appear ($G$1). After you click OK, Excel pastes the analysis report in columns G and H, as shown in Figure 17-10.

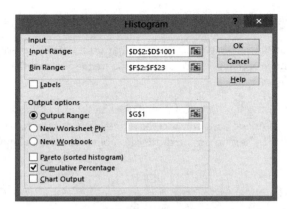

Figure 17-9 This dialog box appears after you select the Histogram tool in the Data Analysis dialog box.

	A	B	C	D	E	F	G	H	I	J
	D2	▾ : ✕ ✓ *fx*	=B2+C2							
1	Student ID	Verbal	Math	Total		Bins	Bin	Frequency	Cumulative %	
2	722-4499	418	518	936		600	600	0	0.00%	
3	605-3475	465	557	1022		650	650	0	0.00%	
4	546-3500	463	549	1012		700	700	0	0.00%	
5	655-8550	466	587	1053		750	750	0	0.00%	
6	812-6448	520	544	1064		800	800	0	0.00%	
7	814-6503	470	537	1007		850	850	0	0.00%	
8	332-3453	533	549	1082		900	900	3	0.30%	
9	55-0476	476	570	1046		950	950	48	5.10%	
10	745-0539	468	548	1016		1000	1000	155	20.60%	
11	675-1544	441	562	1003		1050	1050	329	53.50%	
12	836-6513	570	560	1130		1100	1100	291	82.60%	
13	146-4509	503	554	1057		1150	1150	150	97.60%	
14	45-9450	551	556	1107		1200	1200	23	99.90%	
15	924-3538	498	562	1060		1250	1250	1	100.00%	
16	664-9559	466	525	991		1300	1300	0	100.00%	
17	596-5425	414	549	963		1350	1350	0	100.00%	
18	914-1483	497	545	1042		1400	1400	0	100.00%	
19	266-3469	581	519	1100		1450	1450	0	100.00%	
20	116-2492	402	568	970		1500	1500	0	100.00%	
21	524-5404	488	539	1027		1550	1550	0	100.00%	
22	883-4501	547	536	1083		1600	1600	0	100.00%	
23	275-2453	456	567	1023		1650	1650	0	100.00%	
24	475-1532	536	559	1095			More	0	100.00%	
25	864-9444	546	551	1097						

Figure 17-10 The Frequency column shows a fairly tight distribution of test scores.

> **Note**
>
> We created our own distribution bins for this model, but you can let the Histogram tool determine the divisions for you. Leave the Bin Range box blank to create evenly distributed bin intervals with the minimum and maximum values in the input range as beginning and ending points. The number of intervals is equal to the square root of the number of input values.

Here are a few facts to keep in mind when using the Histogram tool:

- In the Frequency column, the histogram reports the number of input values that are equal to or greater than the bin value but less than the next bin value.

- The last value in the table reports the number of input values equal to or greater than the last bin value.

- Select the Pareto check box in the Histogram dialog box to sort the output in descending order.

- Select the Cumulative Percentage option to add a column showing the percentage of total input values accounted for at each bin level, as shown in Figure 17-10.

- If you select the Chart Output option in the Histogram dialog box, the Histogram tool simultaneously generates a chart and places it on the worksheet.

  For everything you need to know about charts, see Part 6, "Creating charts."

INSIDE OUT   Beware of bin formulas

Notice that the Histogram tool duplicates your column of bin values in its Bin column, which is convenient if you place the output somewhere else in your workbook. But because the Histogram tool copies the bin values, it's best if the bin range contains numeric constants rather than formulas. If you do use formulas, be sure they don't include relative references; otherwise, when the Histogram tool copies the range, the formulas might produce unwanted results.

Analyzing distribution with the FREQUENCY function

It's easy to use the Histogram tool to generate a new frequency distribution table whenever you change the input values, but the Histogram tool generates static numbers (numeric constants). If you'd rather create formulas linked to the input values, you can use the built-in FREQUENCY array function, which calculates the number of times specified values occur in a population and takes the arguments *data_array* and *bins_array*. Figure 17-11 shows the FREQUENCY function applied to the data shown in Figure 17-8.

To use the FREQUENCY function, set up a column of bin values, just as you would with the Histogram tool, and then select the entire range where you want the output to appear, which in our example is G2:G21—the cells in column G that are directly adjacent to the bin values in column F. (This range must be a column because FREQUENCY can't use a row or multicolumn range as its output range.) Next, type the formula, specifying the input range as the first argument and the bin range as the second. Press Ctrl+Shift+Enter to lock in the array formula. For more information about arrays, see "Using arrays" in Chapter 12.

G2			f_x	{=FREQUENCY(D2:D1001,F2:F20)}				
	A	B	C	D	E	F	G	H	I
1	Student ID	Verbal	Math	Total		Bins			
2	722-4499	418	518	936		600	0		
3	605-3475	465	557	1022		650	0		
4	546-3500	463	549	1012		700	0		
5	655-8550	466	587	1053		750	0		
6	812-6448	520	544	1064		800	0		
7	814-6503	470	537	1007		850	0		
8	332-3453	533	549	1082		900	3		
9	55-0476	476	570	1046		950	48		
10	745-0539	468	548	1016		1000	155		
11	675-1544	441	562	1003		1050	329		
12	836-6513	570	560	1130		1100	291		
13	146-4509	503	554	1057		1150	150		
14	45-9450	551	556	1107		1200	23		
15	924-3538	498	562	1060		1250	1		
16	664-9559	466	525	991		1300	0		
17	596-5425	414	549	963		1350	0		
18	914-1483	497	545	1042		1400	0		
19	266-3469	581	519	1100		1450	0		
20	116-2492	402	568	970		1500	0		
21	524-5404	488	539	1027		1550	0		
22	883-4501	547	536	1083					
23	275-2453	456	567	1023					

Figure 17-11 Use the FREQUENCY function to link the distribution analysis to the input data.

Using the Rank And Percentile tool

Suppose you want to rank the scores shown in Figure 17-8. You could rank them by sorting the data in descending order, with the best score at the top and the worst score at the bottom of the column. To find the rank of any score, you might want to create an ascending series of numbers beside the sorted scores, with *1* beside the best score and *1,000* beside the worst.

The Rank And Percentile tool not only performs these tasks for you but also creates percentile figures for each value in your input range. To use this tool, click the Data Analysis button on the Data tab, select Rank And Percentile, and then click OK. Figure 17-12 shows the Rank And Percentile dialog box.

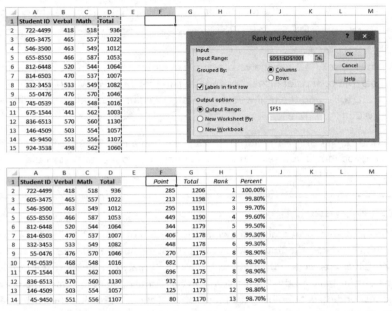

Figure 17-12 Use the Rank And Percentile tool to generate an output table like the one shown in the lower figure.

> **Note**
>
> If the Data Analysis button does not appear on the Data tab, see "Installing the Analysis Toolpak" earlier in this chapter.

Here's how to read the output of the Rank And Percentile tool, shown at the bottom of Figure 17-12. The first row of the output table (F2:I2) tells us that the 285th item in the input range is a total score of 1,206, which ranks first and is better than 100 percent of the other scores. Here are some hints to remember when using the Rank And Percentile tool:

- It's best to select the Labels In First Row check box in the Rank And Percentile dialog box and then include the column heading in the input range. This way, the second column in the output table uses the same label, as shown in Figure 17-12. If you do not include the label in the input range, the output column is labeled Column1.

> **Note**
>
> If you select the Labels In First Row option but do not actually include the cell containing the label in your input range, the first value in the input range becomes the title. For example, if the input range in Figure 17-12 were $D$2:$D$1001, the resulting label in column G would be 936 instead of Total.

- In Figure 17-12, we analyzed a single column of data, but we could analyze the Verbal, Math, and Total columns together. In that case, we would specify the input range B1:D1001, and the tool would generate 12 columns of output, four for each input column.

- You can also have the output table placed on a new worksheet or workbook, which is a good idea if you select multiple columns of input data that would result in a large output table.

Correlating tables

The input and output tables shown at the bottom of Figure 17-12 share a common column of data—the Total column—and the same number of rows. But because the two tables are sorted differently, the rows don't match. The easiest solution is to sort the output table by the Point column; in this context, *Point* indicates the position of the corresponding data point in the input range. Therefore, sorting the output table by the Point column puts it in the same order as the input table:

	A	B	C	D	E	F	G	H	I	J	K
1	Student ID	Verbal	Math	Total		Point	Total	Rank	Percent		
2	722-4499	418	518	936		1	936	972	2.70%		
3	605-3475	465	557	1022		2	1022	657	33.90%		
4	546-3500	463	549	1012		3	1012	726	26.60%		
5	655-8550	466	587	1053		4	1053	447	54.60%		
6	812-6448	520	544	1064		5	1064	379	61.70%		
7	814-6503	470	537	1007		6	1007	756	23.80%		
8	332-3453	533	549	1082		7	1082	270	72.60%		
9	55-0476	476	570	1046		8	1046	502	49.50%		
10	745-0539	468	548	1016		9	1016	693	29.90%		
11	675-1544	441	562	1003		10	1003	779	21.30%		
12	836-6513	570	560	1130		11	1130	61	93.70%		
13	146-4509	503	554	1057		12	1057	419	57.60%		
14	45-9450	551	556	1107		13	1107	140	85.50%		

If you want to add information from the output table to the existing input table, you can delete the Point column (because the Point column simply indicates the row number), the Total column (because the input table already has a Total column), and the blank column in the output table, creating a single, correlated table.

Generating random numbers

The built-in random-number function, RAND, generates a uniform distribution of random real numbers from 0 to 1. In other words, all values from 0 to 1 share the same probability of being returned by a set of formulas based on the RAND function. Because the sample is relatively small, the distribution is by no means perfectly uniform. Nevertheless, repeated tests demonstrate that the RAND function doesn't favor any position within its spectrum of distribution. For more information, see "The RAND and RANDBETWEEN functions" in Chapter 14.

TROUBLESHOOTING

Random numbers keep changing

The RAND function is one of Excel's *volatile* functions—that is, it recalculates every time the worksheet recalculates, which happens when you open the worksheet as well as every time you make an entry or edit data in a cell. If you want to generate a set of random numbers and then "freeze" them, select all the RAND formulas in your worksheet, and then press Ctrl+C to copy them. Click the Paste button on the Home tab on the ribbon, and click Paste Values to replace the volatile formulas with fixed values. Or, instead of using the RAND function, use the Random Number Generation tool (described next), which produces constants instead of formulas.

The Random Number Generation tool creates sets of random numbers that are not uniformly distributed. You can then use the Histogram tool to sort and plot the results for Monte Carlo decision analysis and other kinds of simulations. Six distribution types are available: Uniform, Normal, Bernoulli, Binomial, Poisson, and Discrete (user-defined). In addition, you can select Patterned in the Distribution list to create nonrandom numbers at specified intervals. Click the Data Analysis button on the Data tab, select Random Number Generation, and then click OK to display a dialog box like the one shown in Figure 17-13.

Here are a few important points about using the Random Number Generation tool:

- In the Number Of Variables and Number Of Random Numbers text boxes, you indicate how many columns of numbers you want and how many numbers you want in each column. For example, if you want 10 columns of 100 numbers each, specify **10** in the Number Of Variables text box and **100** in the Number Of Random Numbers text box.

- You can also specify a seed value. However, each time you generate a random-number set with a particular distribution type and use the same seed value, you get the same sequence of numbers; therefore, you should specify a seed value only if you need to be able to reproduce a random-number sequence.

- The parameters shown directly below the Distribution list change depending on the type of distribution you select. As Figure 17-13 shows, when you select Uniform in the Distribution list, you can specify the beginning and ending points of the distribution in the Between and And text boxes.

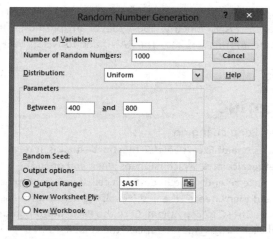

Figure 17-13 The Parameters area in the Random Number Generation dialog box changes to reflect the distribution type you select.

Distributing random numbers uniformly

This option asks you to specify two numbers between which (and including) to generate a set of random numbers. It works much the same way as the RANDBETWEEN function, generating an evenly distributed set of real numbers. You can use this option as a more convenient alternative to RAND if you want endpoints other than 0 and 1 or if you want sets of numbers to be based on the same seed value.

Distributing random numbers normally

Normal distribution has the following characteristics:

- One particular value, the mean, is more likely to occur than any other value.

- Values greater than the mean are as likely to occur as values less than it.

- Values close to the mean are more likely to occur than values distant from the mean.

To generate normally distributed random numbers, you specify two parameters: the mean and the standard deviation. The standard deviation is the average absolute difference between the random numbers and the mean. (Approximately 68 percent of the values in a normal distribution fall within one standard deviation of the mean.)

Generating random numbers using Bernoulli distribution

The Bernoulli Distribution option simulates the probability of success of a number of trials, given that all trials have an equal probability of succeeding and that the success of one trial has no impact on the success of subsequent trials. (Note that success in this context has no value implication. In other words, you can use this distribution to simulate failure as readily as success.) All values in the Bernoulli distribution's output are either 0 or 1.

The probability that each cell will return a 1 is given by the distribution's sole parameter—P Value—for which you supply a number from 0 to 1. For example, if you want a sequence of 100 random Bernoulli values whose most likely sum is 27, you define a 100-cell output range and specify a P Value of 0.27.

Generating random numbers using binomial distribution

The Binomial Distribution option simulates the number of successes in a fixed number of trials, given a specified probability rate. As with the Bernoulli Distribution option, the trials are assumed to be independent; that is, the outcome of one has no effect on any other. To generate binomially distributed numbers, you specify Number Of Trials and the P Value (probability) that any trial will succeed. (Again, success in this context has no value implication. In other words, you can use this distribution to simulate failure as readily as success.)

For example, suppose you make 10 sales presentations a week, you close the sale 20 percent of the time, and you would like to know what your success rate might be over the next year. Type **50** (for 50 working weeks in the year) in the Number Of Random Numbers text box, **0.2** in the P Value text box, and **10** in the Number Of Trials text box to learn that you can expect to make no sales four weeks in the coming year.

Generating random numbers using Poisson distribution

The Poisson Distribution option simulates the number of times an event occurs within a particular time span, given a certain probability of occurrence. The occurrences are assumed to be independent; that is, each occurrence has no effect on the likelihood of others.

The Poisson Distribution option takes a single parameter, Lambda, which represents the expected outcome of an individual occurrence. For example, suppose you receive an average of 10 service calls a day. You want to know how often you can expect to get 18 or more service calls in a day over a year. To get this information, type **260** (52 weeks times 5 days) in the Number Of Random Numbers box and **10** in the Lambda box (the expected average). You can then use the COUNTIF function to count the number of times 18 shows up in the output range. For more information, see "The SUMIF, SUMIFS, and COUNTIF functions" in Chapter 14.

Generating random numbers using discrete distribution

Use the Discrete Distribution option to create a custom distribution pattern by specifying a table of possible outcomes along with the probability associated with each outcome. The probability values must be from 0 to 1, and the sum of the probabilities in the table must equal 1. To use the Discrete Distribution option, specify the possible outcomes and their probabilities as a two-column range whose reference is the only parameter used by this option.

For example, you could create a custom distribution pattern to examine random snow-shovel sales patterns based on a two-column input range: Month Number and Probability of Snow.

Generating semi-random numbers using patterned distribution

Selecting Patterned in the Distribution list in the Random Number Generation dialog box generates numbers that are both random and part nonrandom. Selecting the Patterned option displays the dialog box shown in Figure 17-14.

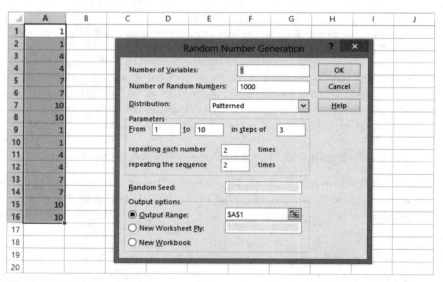

Figure 17-14 The Patterned option in the Distribution list creates an arithmetic series with operational repetitions.

You can think of the Patterned option as a fancy Fill Series command. It creates one or more arithmetic series with optional internal repetitions. For example, to create the series shown in Figure 17-14, complete the dialog box as shown, requesting two sequences of the numbers 1 through 10, using a step interval of 3 and repeating each number twice within each cycle.

For more information, see "Filling cells and creating data series" in Chapter 8, "Worksheet editing techniques."

If the step interval takes the series beyond the specified upper value, the output range includes the upper value because the last interval is truncated. For example, if you specify a step interval of 4 and the numbers 1 through 10, Excel creates the series 1, 5, 9, and 10.

Sampling a population of numbers

The Sampling tool extracts a subset of numbers from a larger group (or population) of numbers. From an input range, you can sample a specified number of values at random or at every *n*th value. The Sampling tool copies the extracted numbers to an output range you specify. Click the Data Analysis button on the Data tab, select Sampling, and then click OK to display the Sampling dialog box shown in Figure 17-15.

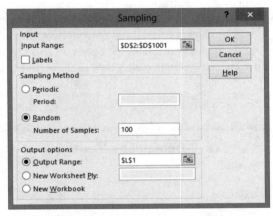

Figure 17-15 The Sampling tool extracts a random or periodic subset from a numeric population.

The values in the input range must be numeric. They can include blank values and dates, provided you type the dates as numbers, not text. For example, to simplify a chart of daily commodity prices, you can use the Sampling tool to extract every *n*th data point and then create a new plot from the extracted data.

> ## Note
> To perform the equivalent of sampling from a range containing text values, set up a series of ascending integers beginning at 1 in a column alongside the text values, and then use the Sampling tool to extract numbers from this series. Then you can assemble a list of sampled text values by using the resulting numbers as arguments to the INDEX function. For more information, see "The INDEX function" in Chapter 14.

Calculating moving averages

A *moving average* is a forecasting technique that simplifies trend analysis by smoothing fluctuations that occur in measurements taken over time. These fluctuations can be caused by random noise that is often a by-product of the measurement technique. For example, measurements of the height of a growing child vary with the accuracy of the ruler and whether the child is standing straight or slouching. You can take a series of measurements, however, and smooth them over time, resulting in a curve that reflects the child's actual growth rate. Fluctuations in measurements can result from other temporary conditions that introduce bias. Monthly sales, for example, might vary with the number of working days in the month or the absence of a star salesperson who is on vacation.

Suppose you created the 18-month demand curve shown in Figure 17-16. To generate a less noisy trendline from this data, you can plot a six-month moving average. The first point in the moving average line is the average of the first six monthly figures (January through June 2014). The next point averages the figures for the second through seventh months (February through July 2014), and so on. You can use the Moving Average tool to perform this analysis for you. Click the Data Analysis button on the Data tab, select Moving Average, and then click OK to display the Moving Average dialog box, as shown in Figure 17-17.

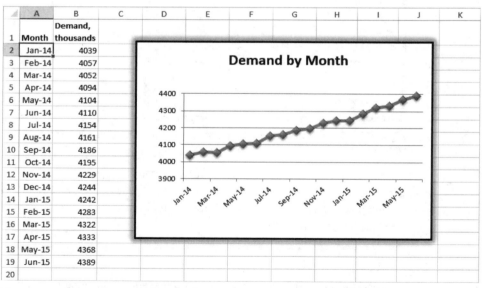

Figure 17-16 We'll use this 18-month demand curve to demonstrate the Moving Average tool.

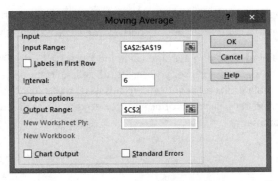

Figure 17-17 The Moving Average tool helps smooth out bumpy curves to reveal the trend.

The Moving Average tool requires three pieces of information: the input range containing the data you want to analyze, the output range where the averaged data will appear, and the interval over which the data is averaged. To determine a three-month moving average, for example, specify an interval of 3.

Figure 17-18 shows a six-month moving average superimposed over the original demand curve chart shown in Figure 17-17. The Moving Average tool produced the data in column C, which the Moving Average tool used to create the straighter plot line in the chart. Notice that the first five cells in the tool's output range contain #N/A error values. Where the interval is *n*, you will always have *n*−1 #N/A error values at the beginning of the output. Including those values in a chart presents no problem because Excel leaves the first area of the plot line blank.

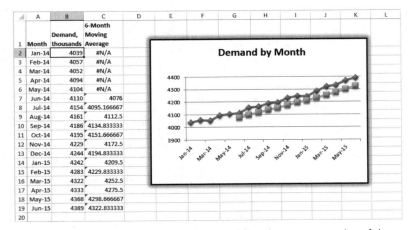

Figure 17-18 The Moving Average tool provides a better perspective of the overall trend.

In Figure 17-18, we applied some judicious formatting to the rather plain chart generated by the Moving Average tool. To learn more about charts, see Part 6, "Creating charts."

Notice that each cell containing a moving average value in Figure 17-18 displays a flag in its upper-left corner. This is an error flag; after you select the cell, an option menu appears that alerts you that the formula omits adjacent cells. In this case, that's okay. To remove the flags, select all the flagged cells, click the option button to display its menu, and then choose the Ignore Error command.

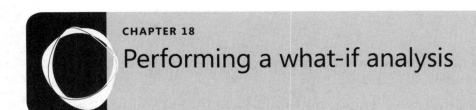

Performing a what-if analysis

O NE OF THE most important financial questions is "What if?"; spreadsheet software was literally created to answer that question, taking the tedium out of the complicated calculations necessary to do so. Instead of starting your calculations from the beginning every time your assumptions change, you can change just a few variables and instantly see the effect. Excel offers a number of advanced what-if features, which we discuss in this chapter.

Using data tables

A data table, or sensitivity table, summarizes the impact of one or two variables on formulas that use those variables. You can click the What-If Analysis button in the Data Tools group on the Data tab and then click Data Table to create two kinds of data tables: tables based on a single input variable that test the variable's impact on more than one formula, and tables based on two input variables that test their impact on a single formula.

> **Note**
>
> Some of the most powerful tools Excel offers for performing a what-if analysis are not covered in this chapter because they are awesome enough to have chapters of their own. Take a look at Chapter 23, "Analyzing data with PivotTable reports," for a comprehensive look at PivotTables and see Chapter 24, "An introduction to PowerPivot," for coverage of PowerPivot, introduced in Excel 2010 and enhanced in Excel 2013. These tools give you superhuman powers over mass quantities of data, providing easy access to giant databases and allowing you to slice and dice the data any way you like.

Data tables based on one input variable

Suppose you're considering buying a house that requires you to take on a 30-year, $200,000 mortgage, and you need to calculate monthly payments on the loan for several interest rates. A one-variable data table, such as the one shown in Figure 18-1, can give you the information you need.

You can find the Goal Seek.xlsx file with the other examples on the companion website.

To create this table, type the interest rates you want to test, as shown in cells B3:B9 in Figure 18-1. This is the *input range* because it contains the input values you want to test. Type the loan amount in a cell outside the data table area. We typed **$200,000** in cell C1. By doing this, you can easily change the loan amount to test various scenarios. Enter the formula that uses the input variable. In this case, type the formula **=PMT(A2/12, 360, C1)** in cell C2. In this formula, *A2/12* is the monthly interest rate, *360* is the term of the loan in months, and *C1* refers to the cell containing the loan principal.

C2		⋮	✕	✓	f_x	=PMT(A2/12,360,C1)		
	A	B	C	D	E	F	G	H
1		Loan Amount:	$200,000.00					
2			(555.56)					
3		2.0%						
4		2.5%						
5		3.0%						
6		3.5%						
7		4.0%						
8		4.5%						
9		5.0%						
10								
11								

Figure 18-1 Begin building the data table by typing the interest rates, loan amount, and PMT function in the worksheet, as shown on the Data Table tab of the Goal Seek.xlsx workbook.

Note

Notice that the formula in cell C2 refers to cell A2, which is blank. Because A2 is blank, the function returns a spurious result: the payment required to amortize the loan at an interest rate of 0 percent. This is a data table quirk, if you will. Cell A2 is a placeholder through which Excel feeds the values in the input range to create the data table. You need to designate a blank cell for this purpose. Because Excel never changes the underlying value of this cell, this placeholder cell can be anywhere, as long as it is outside the data table.

After you enter the inputs and the formula, select the data table—the smallest rectangular block that includes the formula and all the values in the input range. In this case, select the range B2:C9. On the Data tab, in the Data Tools group, click the What-If Analysis button and then click Data Table.

In the Data Table dialog box, shown in Figure 18-2, specify the location of the input cell in the Row Input Cell or Column Input Cell box. The *input cell* is the placeholder cell referred to by the table formula—in this example, A2. If the input values are arranged in a row, type the input cell reference in the Row Input Cell box. If the values in the input range are arranged in a column, as in our example, use the Column Input Cell box.

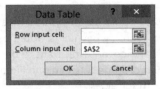

Figure 18-2 Use the Data Table dialog box to specify the input cell.

After you click OK, Excel enters the results of the table formula (one result for each input value) in the available cells of the data table range. In this example, Excel enters six results in the range C3:C9, as shown in Figure 18-3, with a little formatting we added for easier reading.

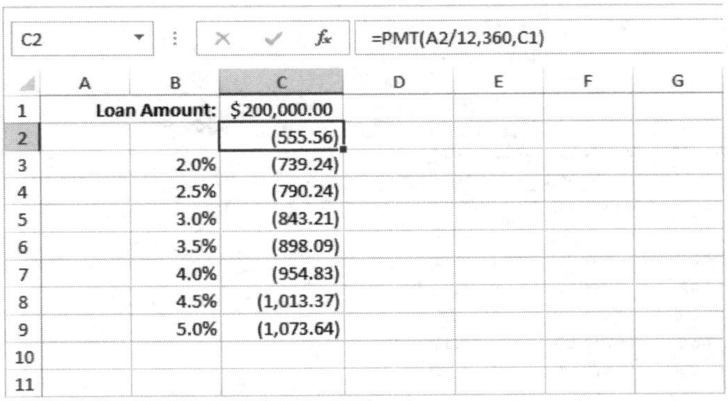

	A	B	C	D	E	F	G
		C2			=PMT(A2/12,360,C1)		
1		Loan Amount:	$200,000.00				
2			(555.56)				
3		2.0%	(739.24)				
4		2.5%	(790.24)				
5		3.0%	(843.21)				
6		3.5%	(898.09)				
7		4.0%	(954.83)				
8		4.5%	(1,013.37)				
9		5.0%	(1,073.64)				
10							
11							

Figure 18-3 The monthly loan payments for each interest rate now appear in the data table, as shown on the Data Table2 tab of the Goal Seek.xlsx workbook.

When you create this data table, Excel enters the array formula { =TABLE(,A2)} in each cell in the *results range* C3:C9. In the sample data table, the formula computes the results of the PMT function by using each of the interest rates in column B. After you build the table, you can change the loan amount or any of the interest rate values to see the results immediately.

> **Note**
> The TABLE function is an internal function, meaning that you can't select it in the Insert Function dialog box or type it manually.

Single-variable tables with more than one formula

When you create a single-variable data table, you can include as many output formulas as you want. If your input range is in a column, type the second output formula directly to the right of the first one, the third to the right of the second, and so on. You can use different formulas for different columns, but they must all use the same input cell.

Suppose you're thinking about buying a house that would require you to take out a $180,000 mortgage. You want to know what your monthly payments would be on that mortgage at each of the interest rates in the input range, and you want to be able to compare these payments with those for the $200,000 mortgage calculated in Figure 18-3. You can expand the table in Figure 18-3 to include both formulas.

To add a formula to the data table, type the new formula in cell D2. For this example, we typed **=PMT(A2/12, 360, D1)**. This formula must also refer to cell A2, the same input cell as in the first formula. Then type **$180,000** in cell D1, and select the table range B2:D9. Then click the What-If Analysis button on the Data tab, and click Data Table. Finally, type the same input cell reference ($A$2) in the Column Input Cell box and click OK. Figure 18-4 shows the result.

D2			⁝	✕	✓	f_x	=PMT(A2/12,360,D1)		
	A	B		C		D	E	F	G
1		Loan Amount:		$200,000.00		$180,000.00			
2				(555.56)		(500.00)			
3		2.0%		(739.24)		(665.32)			
4		2.5%		(790.24)		(711.22)			
5		3.0%		(843.21)		(758.89)			
6		3.5%		(898.09)		(808.28)			
7		4.0%		(954.83)		(859.35)			
8		4.5%		(1,013.37)		(912.03)			
9		5.0%		(1,073.64)		(966.28)			
10									
11									

Figure 18-4 This data table computes the monthly payments on two different loan amounts at various interest rates, as shown on the Data Table3 tab of the Goal Seek.xlsx workbook.

Data tables based on two input variables

Suppose you want to build a data table that computes the monthly payment on a $200,000 mortgage, but this time you want to vary not only the interest rate but also the term of the loan. You want to know what effect changing the interest rate and the term have on your monthly payment.

To create this table, you can again type seven interest rates in cells B3:B9. Then type the second set of input values—the loan terms, in months—in a row above and to the right of the first set, as shown in Figure 18-5.

B2		▾	:	×	✓	*fx*	=PMT(A2/12,B1,I2)				

◢	A	B	C	D	E	F	G	H	I	J
1					Months				Loan Amount	
2	◈	#NUM!	180	240	300	360			$ 200,000.00	
3		2.0%								
4		2.5%								
5		3.0%								
6	Rates	3.5%								
7		4.0%								
8		4.5%								
9		5.0%								
10										
11										

Figure 18-5 Cell B2 contains the formula for this two-variable table, as shown on the Data Table4 tab of the Goal Seek.xlsx workbook.

After you type the loan amount in a cell outside the table area (cell I2 in this example), you can create the table formula. Because this is a two-variable table, you must type the formula in the cell at the intersection of the row and column that contain the sets of input values—cell B2, in this example. Although you can include as many formulas as you want in a single-variable data table, you can include only one output formula in a two-variable table. The formula for the table in this example is =PMT(A2/12, B1, I2).

You'll notice immediately that the formula in cell B2 returns an error value because of the two blank placeholder cells, A2 and B1. As you'll see, this spurious result does not affect the performance of the table.

Finally, select the data table—the smallest rectangular block that includes all the input values and the table formula. In this example, the table range is B2:F9. Click the What-If Analysis button on the Data tab, click Data Table, and finally specify the (empty) input cells. Because this is a two-variable table, you must define two input cells. For this example, type the reference for the first input cell, **$B$1**, in the Row Input Cell box, and then type the reference for the second input cell, **$A$2**, in the Column Input Cell box. Figure 18-6 shows the result.

C3	▼	:	×	✓	*fx*	{=TABLE(B1,A2)}					

◢	A	B	C	D	E	F	G	H	I	J
1					Months				Loan Amount	
2		#NUM!	180	240	300	360			$ 200,000.00	
3		2.0%	(1,287.02)	(1,011.77)	(847.71)	(739.24)				
4		2.5%	(1,333.58)	(1,059.81)	(897.23)	(790.24)				
5		3.0%	(1,381.16)	(1,109.20)	(948.42)	(843.21)				
6	Rates	3.5%	(1,429.77)	(1,159.92)	(1,001.25)	(898.09)				
7		4.0%	(1,479.38)	(1,211.96)	(1,055.67)	(954.83)				
8		4.5%	(1,529.99)	(1,265.30)	(1,111.66)	(1,013.37)				
9		5.0%	(1,581.59)	(1,319.91)	(1,169.18)	(1,073.64)				
10										
11										

Figure 18-6 This data table calculates monthly payments using various interest rates and terms.

TROUBLESHOOTING

The results in my two-input data table are wrong

Be careful not to reverse the input cells in a two-variable table. If you do, Excel uses the input values in the wrong place in the table formula, which creates a set of meaningless results. For example, if you reverse the input cells in the example shown in Figure 18-6, Excel uses the values in the input range C2:F2 as interest rates and the values in the input range B3:B9 as terms, resulting in monthly payments in the $20 million range!

To be sure you're using the correct input cells, look at the formula. In our example, =PMT(A2/12, B1, I2), A2 appears in the first argument, which is *rate*. Because the rates are arranged in a column, A2 is the column input cell.

Editing tables

Although you can edit the input values or formulas in the left column or top row of a table, you can't edit the contents of any individual cell in the results range because the data table is an array. If you make a mistake when you set up a data table, you must select all the results, press the Delete key, and then recompute the table.

You can copy the table results to a different part of the worksheet. You might want to do this to save the table's current results before you change the table formula or variables. In Figure 18-7, we copied the values from C3:F9 to C11:F17. When you do this, the copied values are constants, not array formulas. Excel automatically changes the results of the table from a set of array formulas to their numeric values if you copy the results out of the table range.

| C11 | ▼ | ⋮ | ✕ | ✓ | *fx* | -1287.01740111545 | | | | |

▲	A	B	C	D	E	F	G	H	I	J
1					**Months**				**Loan Amount**	
2		#NUM!	180	240	300	360			$ 200,000.00	
3		2.0%	(1,287.02)	(1,011.77)	(847.71)	(739.24)				
4		2.5%	(1,333.58)	(1,059.81)	(897.23)	(790.24)				
5		3.0%	(1,381.16)	(1,109.20)	(948.42)	(843.21)				
6	**Rates**	3.5%	(1,429.77)	(1,159.92)	(1,001.25)	(898.09)				
7		4.0%	(1,479.38)	(1,211.96)	(1,055.67)	(954.83)				
8		4.5%	(1,529.99)	(1,265.30)	(1,111.66)	(1,013.37)				
9		5.0%	(1,581.59)	(1,319.91)	(1,169.18)	(1,073.64)				
10										
11			(1,287.02)	(1,011.77)	(847.71)	(739.24)				
12			(1,333.58)	(1,059.81)	(897.23)	(790.24)				
13			(1,381.16)	(1,109.20)	(948.42)	(843.21)				
14			(1,429.77)	(1,159.92)	(1,001.25)	(898.09)				
15			(1,479.38)	(1,211.96)	(1,055.67)	(954.83)				
16			(1,529.99)	(1,265.30)	(1,111.66)	(1,013.37)				
17			(1,581.59)	(1,319.91)	(1,169.18)	(1,073.64)				
18										
19										

Figure 18-7 Copying the results of the TABLE function to another part of the worksheet transfers the numeric values, not the formulas used to compute them, as shown on the Data Table5 tab of the Goal Seek.xlsx workbook.

Using the Scenario Manager

To model more complicated problems than data tables can handle—those involving as many as 32 variables—you can call on the services of the Scenario Manager by clicking the What-If Analysis button in the Data Tools group on the Data tab and then clicking Scenario Manager. A *scenario* is a named combination of values assigned to one or more variable cells in a what-if model. The worksheet in Figure 18-8 is a what-if model set up so that you can type variable figures and watch the effect on dependent computed values. The Scenario Manager records, tracks, and applies combinations of variable values.

You can find the Revenue Scenarios.xlsm file with the other examples on the companion website.

Here are some of the tasks you can do with the Scenario Manager:

- Create multiple scenarios for a single what-if model, each with its own sets of variables. You can create as many scenarios as your model requires.

- Distribute a what-if model to other members of your group so that they can add their own scenarios. Then you can collect the multiple versions and merge the scenarios into a single worksheet.

- Track changes made to scenarios with the version-control features of the Scenario Manager. You can use this feature to record the date and the user name each time a scenario is added or modified.

- Print reports detailing all the changing cells and result cells.

- Password-protect scenarios from modification, and even hide them from view.

- Examine relationships between scenarios created by multiple users by using Scenario Summary and PivotTable reports. For more about PivotTables, see Chapter 23.

	A	B	C	D	E	F
1		Revenue	Name	Total per week	Total per year	
2		Revenues per Customer Visit	Revenue	34.78		
3		Direct Costs per Customer Visit	DirCosts	30.12		
4		Gross Profit per Customer Visit	GrossProfitVisit	4.66		
5		Average Customer Visits	AvgCustVisits	33,759		
6		Gross Profit		157,317	8,180,481	
7		Overhead				
8			Payroll		3,494,046	
9			Facilities		1,635,511	
10			Depreciation		453,305	
11			Advertising		291,647	
12			Supplies		496,944	
13			Other		1,295,828	
14		Subtotal			7,667,281	
15						
16		Operating Profit			513,200	
17						

Figure 18-8 We'll use the Scenario Manager to model the effects of changing values in D2:D3, D5, and E8:E13 of this worksheet.

Imagine that you manage a grocery store whose profit picture is modeled by the worksheet in Figure 18-8. The numbers in D2:D5 and E8:E13 are historic averages; column C contains the range names applied to the relevant cells in columns D and E. You're interested in testing the impact of changes in these cells on the bottom line in cell E16.

> **Note**
>
> Cell references are OK, but before you begin using the Scenario Manager, you should name the cells you plan to use for your variables, as well as any cells containing formulas whose values depend on your variable cells. This step isn't required, but it makes the scenario reports, as well as some of the dialog boxes, more intelligible. For more information, see "Naming cells and cell ranges" in Chapter 12, "Building formulas."

Defining scenarios

We created different sets of assumptions for the model shown in Figure 18-8 and saved each one as a different scenario using the dialog boxes in Figure 18-9, resulting in the list of Advertising.xlsx workbook scenarios shown later in this chapter in Figure 18-12. To define a scenario, follow these steps:

1. On the Data tab, click the What-If Analysis button and then click Scenario Manager.

2. In the Scenario Manager dialog box, shown in Figure 18-9, click Add. (Note that the sample file already contains defined scenarios, so this dialog box might look different.)

Figure 18-9 Use the Scenario Manager to define and store different sets of assumptions you can retrieve at any time.

3. In the Add Scenario dialog box, shown in Figure 18-9, type **Starting Values** as the Scenario Name.

> **Note**
>
> It's a good idea to define the values you begin with as a scenario before chang-ing any of them. You can name this scenario something like Starting Values or Last Year, as in our example. If you don't name the starting scenario, you'll lose your original what-if assumptions when you display the new changing cell values on your worksheet.

4. In the Changing Cells box, type or select the cells you plan to vary. For this example, click cell D2, then hold down Ctrl and click cell D3, then click cell D5, and then drag to select E8:E13. (Select nonadjacent cells and ranges by pressing the Ctrl key before selecting the cells or by separating their references or names with commas, as shown in Figure 18-10.)

Chapter 18

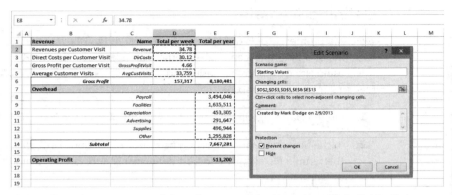

Figure 18-10 Here we entered the references of the changing cells individually by selecting cells and ranges, separating each reference from the next with a comma.

> **Note**
>
> The Prevent Changes check box in the Add Scenario dialog box is selected by default. As you might expect, it protects the selected scenario from modification, but only after you click Protect Worksheet on the Review tab. Similarly, clicking the Hide check box removes the selected scenario from the list of scenarios offered in the Scenario Manager dialog box, but only if worksheet protection has been activated.

5. Click OK to create the first Starting Values scenario. The Scenario Values dialog box appears, displaying a box for each changing cell. If you named the changing cells, the names appear adjacent to the boxes, as shown in Figure 18-11; otherwise, the references of the changing cells appear.

6. To complete a scenario, edit these values; however, for this example, leave the values as they are, and just click OK.

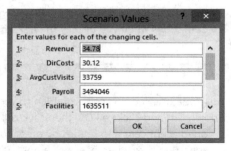

Figure 18-11 Because we previously named each changing cell, the names appear in the Scenario Values dialog box.

> **Note**
>
> In each text box in the Scenario Values dialog box, you can type either a constant or a formula. For example, to increase the value of the first variable in Figure 18-11, click in front of the value in the first variable's box, and type **=1.1*** to create a formula that multiplies the current value by 1.1. (Note that although you can type formulas in the Scenario Values dialog box, Excel alerts you that the formulas are converted to their resulting values after you click OK.)

7. To create another scenario, click Add to return to the Add Scenario dialog box.

Browsing your scenarios

Select a scenario name in the Scenario Manager dialog box, and click Show. The Scenario Manager replaces the variable values currently on the worksheet with the values you specified when you created the scenario. In Figure 18-12, the example worksheet has a scenario showing average customer visits increased by 5 percent and revenues per customer visit decreased by 5 percent.

The Scenario Manager dialog box remains on the screen after you click the Show button so that you can look at the results of other scenarios without returning to the worksheet. If you click Close or press Esc to close the Scenario Manager dialog box, the values from the last scenario you browsed remain on the worksheet. (This is a good reason to create a starting values scenario, as mentioned earlier.)

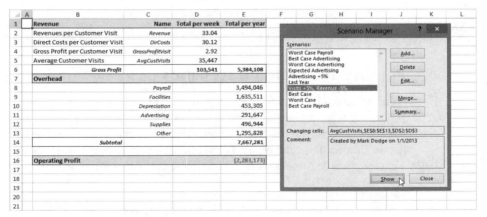

Figure 18-12 Clicking Show replaces your current worksheet values with the values of a specified scenario.

Adding, editing, and deleting scenarios

Excel saves scenarios with all other data when you save the workbook. Each worksheet in a workbook can contain its own set of scenarios. In the Scenario Manager dialog box, you add new scenarios by clicking Add, and you edit existing scenarios by clicking Edit, which displays the Edit Scenario dialog box (which is functionally the same as the Add Scenario dialog box shown in Figure 18-9). You can change the name of the selected scenario, add or remove changing cells, or add comments in the Edit Scenario dialog box.

Tracking changes

If someone edits a scenario, Excel adds a Modified By entry to the Comment box in the Scenario Manager dialog box, beneath the Created By entry that appears when you first add a scenario. Each time a scenario is modified, Excel adds the name of the user and the date of modification. This information is particularly helpful if you route your what-if models to others and then merge their scenarios into a single what-if model, as discussed in the following section.

INSIDE OUT   Comment modifications

When you edit scenarios, you can modify the contents of the Comment box; those modifications persist in all dialog boxes, including the creation and modification dates. You might not want to permit users to modify the comments if you really want to track changes or prevent tampering. If you don't want these comments modified, make sure you take advantage of the preventative measures discussed in "Protecting worksheets" in Chapter 6, "How to work a worksheet."

Routing and merging scenarios

If part of your job is to develop what-if models or projections for your company, you probably spend a lot of time gathering information about trends and market forces that might affect the company in the future. Often, you need input from several people, each of whom knows about a particular aspect of the business, such as payroll costs or sales trends. Excel includes a scenario-merging feature to make this sort of information gathering easier.

For example, suppose you want to distribute a what-if model to your coworkers: Vicki has expertise about customer trends, Max knows the payroll story, and Regina keeps track of advertising. You can distribute individually named copies of the workbook to each person, and after your coworkers add their what-if scenarios and return the workbook or workbooks, you can merge the scenarios into a master worksheet. Simply open all the workbooks containing the scenarios you want, open the worksheet where you want the result to go, and click Merge in the Scenario Manager dialog box. When you do, a dialog box like the one in Figure 18-13 appears.

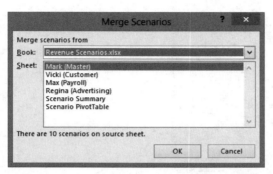

Figure 18-13 Clicking Merge in the Scenario Manager dialog box displays the Merge Scenarios dialog box, with which you can import scenarios from any worksheet in any open workbook.

INSIDE OUT   Request only the data you need

Merging scenarios works best if the basic structure of all the worksheets is identical. Although this uniformity isn't a strict requirement, merging scenarios from worksheets that are laid out differently can cause changing cell values to appear in unexpected locations. For this reason, and because it's generally difficult to ascertain the skill level of everyone contributing data, you might try a different approach. Distribute a questionnaire requesting only the data you need, use external cell references to link the requested data with the appropriate locations on your master worksheet, and create the scenarios yourself.

In the Merge Scenarios dialog box, you select the workbook and worksheet from which you want to merge scenarios. As shown in Figure 18-13, if you select a worksheet in the Sheet list, a message at the bottom of the dialog box tells you how many scenarios exist on that worksheet. When you click OK, the scenarios on that worksheet are copied to the active worksheet. After merging all the scenarios from your coworkers, the Scenario Manager dialog box for this example looks like the one shown in Figure 18-14.

Notice in Figure 18-14 that the Comment box displays the name of the creator and modifier of the selected scenario. If the Scenarios list includes similarly named scenarios, Excel appends a creator name, date, or number to the name. You can use the Edit button to rename the scenarios if you want.

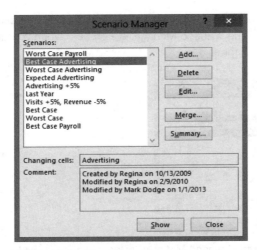

Figure 18-14 The merged scenarios are now available on the same worksheet.

Each group of scenarios provided by the coworkers uses different changing cells. Vicki's scenarios change the values in cells D2, D3, and D5; Max's scenarios change only the value in E8; and Regina's scenarios change only the value in E11. You can display these different scenarios together and watch how the combinations affect the bottom line.

Creating scenario reports

The Revenue Scenarios workbook with its merged scenarios has become a somewhat complex what-if model. However, you can create models that are far more complex, using as many scenarios as you want (or as many as your computer can handle) and up to 32 variables per scenario. The Scenario Manager summary reports help you keep track of the possibilities, and PivotTable reports give you additional what-if functionality by allowing you to manipulate the elements of the report. However, although you can create as many scenarios as you like, the Scenario Summary report displays only the first 251 of them.

Clicking Summary in the Scenario Manager dialog box displays the dialog box shown in Figure 18-15. Use it to create reports that show the values that each scenario assigns to each changing cell.

At the bottom of the dialog box, you identify result cells that you want to appear in the report, separated by commas. You want cells that are dependent on the most changing cells—in this case, the Operating Profit value in cell E16, as well as cell E6, the yearly Gross Profit value.

Figure 18-15 Use the Scenario Summary dialog box to specify the type of report and the result cells you want to see.

The Scenario Summary report

The Scenario Summary is a fully formatted report placed on a new worksheet, as shown in Figure 18-16. Notice that all the changing cells are shaded in gray. The shading indicates cells that change in the scenario named at the top of the column.

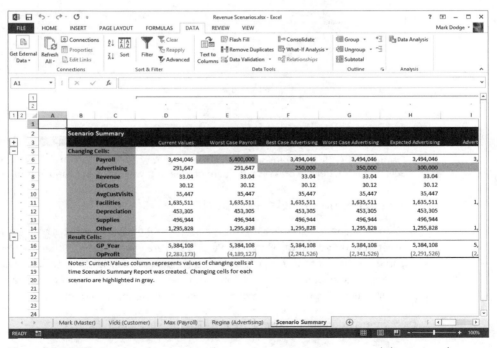

Figure 18-16 The Scenario Summary option creates a report on a new worksheet named Scenario Summary.

Chapter 18

Notice also that outlining symbols appear above and to the left of the summary report, allowing you to show and hide details. As you can see in Figure 18-17, clicking the outline plus sign symbol displays hidden data—the contents of the Comment box in the Scenario Manager dialog box, including the creation and modification dates of each scenario.

For information about working with worksheet outlines, see "Outlining worksheets" in Chapter 8.

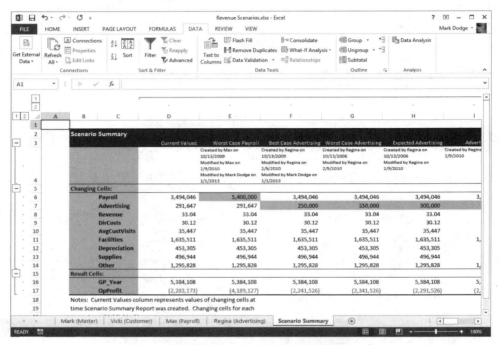

Figure 18-17 Click the plus sign icon adjacent to row 3 to display comments entered in the Scenario Manager dialog box, which are hidden in row 4 of the Scenario Summary report.

The Scenario PivotTable report

Like the Scenario Summary report, the Scenario PivotTable report is created as a new worksheet in your workbook. However, PivotTables are what-if tools in their own right that allow you to use direct mouse-manipulation techniques to mix and match different scenarios in the report and watch the effects on result cells. Figure 18-18 shows a Scenario PivotTable report created from a version of the Revenue Scenarios workbook.

For information about how to use PivotTables, see Chapter 23.

Use Scenario Summary reports

PivotTables are powerful analysis tools best suited to complex what-if models that include scenarios with different sets of changing cells created by different people. The more one-dimensional your what-if model is, the less useful a PivotTable becomes. PivotTables take longer to create and consume more memory than summary reports. If you create all the scenarios yourself and use the same set of changing cells in each, you might find using the Scenario Summary reports easier given that you don't need the advantages offered by the PivotTable.

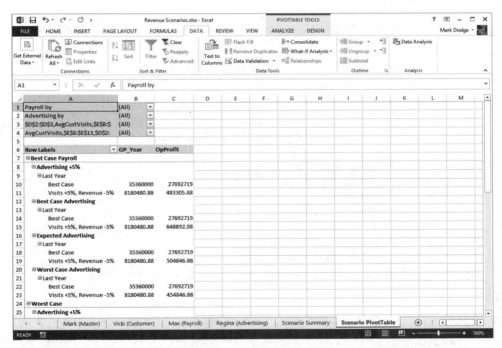

Figure 18-18 The Scenario PivotTable report manipulates the actual data in the report.

Using the Goal Seek command

By clicking the What-If Analysis button on the Data tab and then clicking Goal Seek, you can compute an unknown value that produces the result you want. For example, suppose you want to know the maximum 30-year mortgage you can afford if the interest rate is 3.5 percent and if you must limit your monthly payments to $2,000. To use the Goal Seek command to answer this question, first set up the problem using trial values. For example, in the mortgage problem shown in Figure 18-19, a $500,000 mortgage would require monthly payments in excess of the $2,000 target.

	A	B	C	D	E	F	G	H	I
	Payment	▼ : × ✓ fx	=PMT(Interest/12,Term*12,Principal)						
1	Principal	$500,000.00							
2	Interest	3.50%							
3	Term	30							
4	Payment	$ (2,245.22)							
5									
6									
7									
8									

Figure 18-19 Use the Goal Seek command to find the maximum mortgage you can borrow if you want to keep your payments under a certain limit.

Here's how to perform goal seeking on this problem:

1. Select the formula cell—in this case, B4—to make it the active cell.

2. On the Data tab, click the What-If Analysis button and then click Goal Seek to display the Goal Seek dialog box shown in Figure 18-20.

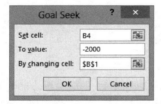

Figure 18-20 To use goal seeking, complete the Goal Seek dialog box.

3. Accept the value in the Set Cell box (making sure it specifies the cell containing the formula). By default, Excel enters the cell you selected before clicking What-If Analysis on the Data tab. In the To Value box, type the maximum value you want as the result of the formula—in this case, **–2000**. (You type a negative number because payments represent cash spent rather than received.)

4. In the By Changing Cell box, type the reference or click the cell on the worksheet whose value is unknown—in this case, cell B1 (the Principal value). Alternatively, if you assigned a name, such as Principal, to the changing cell, you can type that name in the By Changing Cell box.

5. Click OK, or press Enter. Excel displays the Goal Seek Status dialog box shown in Figure 18-21. The answer you are looking for appears in the cell specified in the By Changing Cell box.

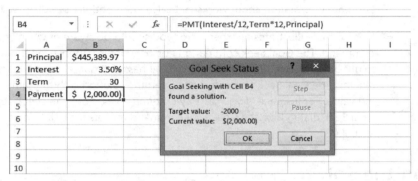

Figure 18-21 The Goal Seek Status dialog box informs you when Excel finds a solution.

6. To enter this value on the worksheet, click OK in the Goal Seek Status dialog box. To restore the value that was in the changing cell before you used the Goal Seek command, click Cancel.

Excel uses an iterative technique to perform goal seeking. It tries one value after another for the variable cell specified in the By Changing Cell box until it arrives at the solution you requested. Excel solves the mortgage problem we just looked at quickly. Other problems might take longer, and some might not be solvable at all.

While Excel is working on a complex goal-seeking problem, you can click Pause in the Goal Seek Status dialog box to interrupt the calculation, and then click Step to display the result of each successive iteration. A Continue button appears in the dialog box if you are solving a problem in this stepwise fashion. To resume full-speed goal seeking, click Continue.

Precision and multiple solutions

Suppose you enter the formula =A2^2 in cell A1 of a blank worksheet (the caret symbol indicates that the number following it is an exponent) and then use the Goal Seek command to find the value of A2 that will make A1 equal to 4. (In other words, in the Goal Seek dialog box, type **$A$1** in the Set Cell box, **4** in the To Value box, and **$A$2** in the By Changing Cell box.) The result might be surprising. Excel seems to be telling you that the closest value it can find to the square root of 4 is 2.000023.

By default, the Goal Seek command stops when it has either performed 100 iterations (trial solutions) or found an answer that comes to within 0.001 of your specified target value. If you need greater precision than this, you can change the default limits by clicking the File tab, clicking Options, selecting the Formulas category, and then changing the Maximum Iterations value to a number greater than 100, setting the Maximum Change value to a number less than 0.001, or both.

For more information about worksheet calculation options, see Chapter 12.

This example illustrates another factor you should be aware of when you use the Goal Seek command. The Goal Seek command finds only one solution, even though your problem might have several. In this case, the value 4 has two square roots: +2 and −2. In situations like this, the Goal Seek command gives you the solution with the same sign as the start-ing value. For instance, if you start by entering a value of −1 in cell A2 before opening the Goal Seek dialog box, the Goal Seek command reports the solution as −1.999917, instead of +2.000023.

Using the Solver

The Goal Seek command is handy for problems that involve an exact target value that depends on a single unknown value. For problems that are more complex, you should use the Solver add-in. The Solver can handle problems that involve many variable cells and can help you find combinations of variables that maximize or minimize a target cell. It also specifies one or more constraints—conditions that must be met for the solution to be valid.

> **Note**
>
> The Solver is an add-in. If the Solver button does not appear on the Data tab on the ribbon, click the File tab, Options, Add-Ins category, and then click the Go button. Select the Solver Add-In check box, and then click OK to install it.

As an example of the kind of problem that the Solver can tackle, imagine you are plan-ning an advertising campaign for a new product. Your total budget for print advertising is $12,000,000; you want to expose your ads at least 800 million times to potential readers; and you've decided to place ads in six publications—we'll call them Pub1 through Pub6. Each publication reaches a different number of readers and charges a different rate per page. Your job is to reach the readership target at the lowest possible cost with the follow-ing additional constraints:

- At least six advertisements should run in each publication.

- No more than a third of your advertising dollars should be spent on any one publication.

● Your total cost for placing advertisements in Pub3 and Pub4 must not exceed $7,500,000.

Figure 18-22 shows one way to lay out the problem.

	A	B	C	D	E	F	G	H
1	Publication	Cost per ad	Audience per ad (millions)	Number of ads placed	Total cost	Percent of total	Total audience (millions)	
2	Pub1	$147,420	9.9	6.0	$884,520	26%	59	
3	Pub2	$124,410	8.4	6.0	$746,460	22%	50	
4	Pub3	$113,100	8.2	6.0	$678,600	20%	49	
5	Pub4	$70,070	5.1	6.0	$420,420	13%	31	
6	Pub5	$53,000	3.7	6.0	$318,000	9%	22	
7	Pub6	$52,440	3.6	6.0	$314,640	9%	22	
8	Total				$3,362,640		233	
9	Total Pub3 + Pub4				$1,099,020			
10								
11			Constraints:		Total advertising budget		$12,000,000	
12					Total budget for Pub3 + Pub4		$7,500,000	
13					Minimum total audience (millions)		800	
14					Maximum % of budget spent on any publication		33.30%	
15					Maximum number of ads per publication		6	
16								

Figure 18-22 You can use the Solver to determine how many advertisements to place in each publication to meet your objectives at the lowest possible cost.

You can find the Advertising.xlsx file with the other examples on the companion website.

> **Note**
>
> This section merely introduces the Solver. A complete treatment of this powerful tool is beyond the scope of this book. For more details, including an explanation of the Solver error messages, see the Help system. For background material about optimization, we recommend *Financial Models Using Simulation and Optimization II: Investment* by Wayne L. Winston (Palisade Corporation, 2008). Also, visit Frontline Systems' Solver website at *www.solver.com* for information about purchasing a more sophisticated version.

You might be able to work out this problem yourself by substituting many alternatives for the values currently in D2:D7, keeping your eye on the constraints and noting the impact of your changes on the total expenditure figure in E8. In fact, that's what the Solver does for you—but it does it more rapidly, and it uses some analytic techniques to home in on the optimal solution without having to try every conceivable alternative.

On the Data tab, click the Solver button to display the dialog box shown in Figure 18-23. To complete this dialog box, you must give the Solver three sets of information: your *objective* (minimizing total expenditure); your *variable cells* (the number of advertisements you will place in each publication); and your *constraints* (the conditions summarized at the bottom of the worksheet in Figure 18-22).

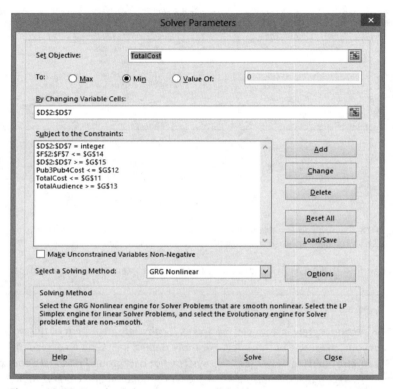

Figure 18-23 Use the Solver Parameters dialog box to set up your problem.

Stating the objective

In the Set Objective box, you indicate the goal that you want Solver to achieve. In this example, you want to minimize your total cost—the value in cell E8—so you specify your objective by typing **E8** in the Set Objective box (or by clicking the cell). In this example, because you want the Solver to set your objective to its lowest possible value, also select the Min option.

> **Note**
> It's a good idea to name all the important cells of your model before you put the Solver to work. If you don't name the cells, the Solver constructs names to use in its reports based on the nearest column-heading and row-heading text, but these constructed names don't appear in the Solver dialog boxes. For more information, see "Naming cells and cell ranges" in Chapter 12.

You don't have to specify an objective. If you leave the Set Objective box blank, click Options, and then select the Show Iteration Results check box, you can use the Solver to step through some or all the combinations of variable cells that meet your constraints. You then receive an answer that solves the constraints but isn't necessarily the optimal solution.

For more information about the Show Iteration Results option, see "Viewing iteration results" later in this chapter.

Specifying variable cells

The next step is to tell the Solver which cells to change. In our example, the cells whose values can be adjusted are those that specify the number of advertisements to be placed in each publication, or cells D2:D7. You can specify up to 200 variable cells, and they can be nonadjacent (unlike our example). When you enter nonadjacent cell references or named ranges, separate them with commas.

Specifying constraints

The last step, specifying constraints, is optional. To specify a constraint, click Add in the Solver Parameters dialog box and complete the Add Constraint dialog box. Figure 18-24 shows how you express the constraint that total advertising expenditures (the value in cell E8 in the model) must be less than or equal to the total budget (the value in cell G11).

Figure 18-24 Click Add in the Solver Parameters dialog box to add constraints.

Figure 18-25 shows how the Solver Parameters dialog box looks after we have specified all our constraints.

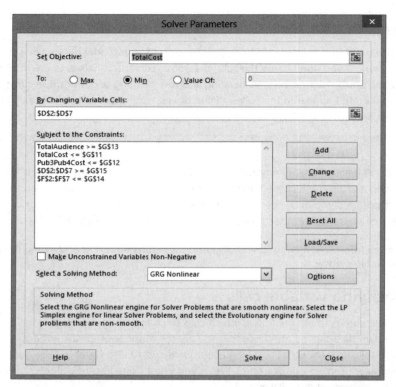

Figure 18-25 The Solver lists the constraints and uses defined cell and range names whenever possible.

Notice that two of the constraints have range references on the left side of the comparison operator. The expression $D$2:$D$7>=$G$15 stipulates that the value of each cell in D2:D7 must be 6 or greater, and the expression $F$2:$F$7<=$G$14 stipulates that the value of each cell in F2:F7 must be no greater than 33.30 percent. Each of these expressions is a shortcut way of stating six separate constraints. If you use this kind of shortcut, the constraint value on the right side of the comparison operator must be a single cell reference, a range of the same dimensions as the range on the left side, or a constant value. We could have entered constant values as constraints, but this way we can change the numbers on the spreadsheet (where we can see them) and rerun the Solver.

After completing the Solver Parameters dialog box, click Solve. In the advertisement campaign example, the Solver succeeds in finding an optimal value for the objective cell while meeting all the constraints and displays the dialog box shown in Figure 18-26. The values displayed on your worksheet at that time result in the optimal solution. You can leave these values in the worksheet by selecting the Keep Solver Solution option and clicking OK, or you can restore the original values by selecting the Restore Original Values option and clicking OK (or by clicking Cancel). You also have the option of assigning the solution values to a named scenario.

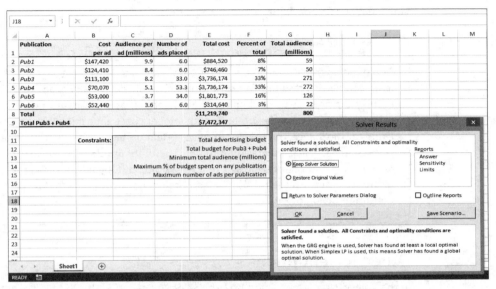

Figure 18-26 When the Solver succeeds, it presents the Solver Results dialog box.

Specifying integer constraints

Notice that in Figure 18-26, the Solver arrived at 53.3 for the number of ads placed in Pub4. Unfortunately, because it's not possible to run three-tenths of an advertisement, the solution isn't practical.

To stipulate that your ad-placement variables be restricted to whole numbers, start the Solver and click the Add button in the Solver Parameters dialog box. In the Add Constraint dialog box, select the cell reference that holds your ad placement numbers—D2:D7. Click the list in the middle of the dialog box, and select *int*. The Solver inserts the word *integer* in the Constraint box, as shown in Figure 18-27. Click OK to return to the Solver Parameters dialog box.

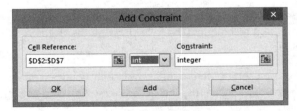

Figure 18-27 To specify an integer constraint, select the item labeled *int*.

Note that when Excel converts numbers to integers, the program effectively rounds down; the decimal portion of the number is truncated. The integer solution shows that by placing 53 ads in Pub4, you can buy an additional ad in Pub5. For a very small increase in budget, you can reach an additional two million readers.

Determine whether you need integer constraints

Adding integer constraints to a Solver problem can geometrically increase the problem's complexity, resulting in possibly unacceptable delays. The example discussed in this chapter is relatively simple and does not take an inordinate amount of time to solve, but a more complex problem with integer constraints might pose more of a challenge for the Solver. The Solver can solve certain problems only by using integer constraints. In particular, integer solutions are useful for problems in which variables can assume only two values, such as 1 or 0 (yes or no), but if you're looking for "yes or no" results, you can also use the bin (binary) option in the list in the middle of the Change Constraint dialog box.

Other Solver options

In the Solver Parameters dialog box, the Select A Solving Method drop-down list offers three options: GRG Nonlinear (the default), Simplex LP, and Evolutionary. Simply put, here are the differences:

- **GRG Nonlinear**   The default solving method is optimized for "smooth nonlinear" problems involving points along a curved (but smooth) line.

- **Simplex LP**   This method works best for linear problems that can be defined as points along a straight line.

- **Evolutionary**   This option works best when your model involves "non-smooth," or random, discontinuous elements that would not plot along either a straight or curved line.

Click the Options button in the Solver Parameters dialog box to display the Options dialog box shown in Figure 18-28, which contains many additional settings. It's best to leave the options on the GRG Nonlinear and Evolutionary tabs at their default settings—unless you understand linear optimization techniques. The following options on the All Methods tab warrant some explanation:

- The Constraint Precision setting determines how closely you want values in the constraint cells to match your constraints. The closer this setting is to the value 1, the lower the precision is. If you specify a setting that is less than the default 0.000001, it results in a longer solution time.

- The Max Time and Iterations boxes tell the Solver, in effect, how hard to work on the solution. If the Solver reaches either the time limit or the number of iterations limit before finding a solution, calculation stops, and Excel asks you whether you want to continue. The default settings are usually sufficient for solving most problems, but if you don't reach a solution with these settings, you can try adjusting them.

- The Integer Optimality (%) setting represents a percentage of error allowed for the solution of integer-only constraints.

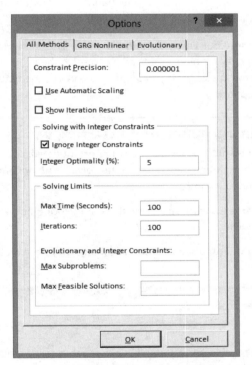

Figure 18-28 Fine-tune your optimization problems using the Solver Options dialog box.

This section only scratches the surface of optimization theory. There is extensive reading available on the subject. For evidence, type **nonlinear optimization** into your browser's Search box and scan the results. You can also click the Help button at the bottom of the Solver Parameters dialog box to display the Excel Help topic on the Solver.

Linear models

A linear optimization problem is one in which the value of the target cell is a linear function of each variable cell; that is, if you plot X Y (scatter) charts of the target cell's value against all meaningful values of each variable cell, your charts are straight lines. If some of your plots produce curves instead of straight lines, the problem is nonlinear.

In the Solver Parameters dialog box, you can use the Simplex LP option in the Select A Solving Method drop-down list only for what-if models in which all the relationships are linear. Models that use simple addition and subtraction and worksheet functions such as SUM are linear in nature. However, most models are nonlinear. They are generated by multiplying changing cells by other changing cells, by using exponentiation or growth factors, or by using nonlinear worksheet functions, such as PMT.

Linear problems can be solved more quickly by using the Simplex LP option. However, if you select this option for a nonlinear problem and then try to solve the problem, the Solver Results dialog box displays an error message. If you are not sure about the nature of your model, it's best not to use this option.

The importance of using appropriate starting values

If your problem is nonlinear, you must be aware of one important detail: Your choice of starting values can affect the solution generated by the Solver. With nonlinear problems, you should always do the following:

- Set your variable cells to reasonable approximations of their optimal values before running the problem.

- Test alternative starting values to see what impact, if any, they have on the Solver solution.

Viewing iteration results

If you're interested in exploring many combinations of your variable cells, rather than only the combination that produces the optimal result, click Options in the Solver Parameters dialog box and select the Show Iteration Results check box. When you do, the Show Trial Solution dialog box appears after each iteration, which you use to save the scenario and then either stop the trial or continue with the next iteration.

Be aware that if you use Show Iteration Results, the Solver pauses for solutions that do not meet all your constraints, as well as for suboptimal solutions that do.

Saving and reusing the Solver parameters

If you save a workbook after using the Solver, Excel saves all the values you typed in the Solver dialog boxes along with your worksheet data. You do not need to retype the parameters of the problem if you want to continue working with it during a later Excel session.

Each worksheet in a workbook can store one set of Solver parameter values. To store more than one set of Solver parameters with a given worksheet, you must use the Save Model option. To use this option, follow these steps:

1. Click the Solver button on the Data tab.

2. Click the Load/Save button. Excel prompts you for a cell or range in which to store the Solver parameters on the worksheet.

3. Specify a blank cell by clicking it or typing its reference, and then click Save. The Solver pastes the model beginning at the indicated cell and inserts formulas in as many of the cells below it as necessary. (Be sure that the cells below the indicated cell do not contain data.)

4. To reuse the saved parameters, click Load/Save in the Solver Parameters dialog box, specify the range in which you stored the Solver parameters, and then click Load.

You'll find it easiest to save and reuse Solver parameters if you assign a name to each save-model range immediately after you use the Save Model option. You can then specify that name when you use the Load Model option.

> For more information about naming, see "Naming cells and cell ranges" in Chapter 12.

Assigning the Solver results to named scenarios

An even better way to save your Solver parameters is to save them as named scenarios using the Scenario Manager. As you might have noticed, the Solver Results dialog box includes a Save Scenario button (shown in Figure 18-26). Click this button to assign a scenario name to the current values of your variable cells. This option provides an excellent way to explore and perform further what-if analyses on a variety of possible outcomes.

> For more information about scenarios, see "Using the Scenario Manager" earlier in this chapter.

Generating reports

In addition to inserting optimal values in your problem's variable cells, the Solver can summarize its results in three reports: Sensitivity, Answer, and Limits. To generate one or more reports, select the names of the reports in the Solver Results dialog box. Select the reports you want, and then click OK. Each report is saved on a separate worksheet in the current workbook.

The Sensitivity report

The Sensitivity report provides information about how sensitive your target cell is to changes in your constraints. This report has two sections: one for your variable cells and one for your constraints. The right column in each section provides the sensitivity information.

Each changing cell and constraint cell appears in a separate row. The Changing Cell area includes a Reduced Gradient value that indicates how the target cell would be affected by a one-unit increase in the corresponding changing cell. Similarly, the Lagrange Multiplier column in the Constraints area indicates how the target cell would be affected by a one-unit increase in the corresponding constraint value.

The Answer report

The Answer report lists the target cell, the variable cells, and the constraints. This report also includes information about the status of and slack value for each constraint. The status can be Binding, Not Binding, or Not Satisfied. The *slack value* is the difference between the solution value of the constraint cells and the number that appears on the right side of the constraint formula. A binding constraint is one for which the slack value is 0. A nonbinding constraint is a constraint that was satisfied with a nonzero slack value.

> **Note**
>
> If you select the Assume Linear Model option in the Solver Options dialog box, the Answer report is the only report that the Solver produces for you. (The Limits and Sensitivity reports are not meaningful.)

The Limits report

The Limits report tells you how much you can increase or decrease the values of your variable cells without breaking the constraints of your problem. For each variable cell, this report lists the optimal value as well as the lowest and highest values you can use without violating constraints.

TROUBLESHOOTING

The Solver can't solve my problem

The Solver is powerful but not miraculous. It might not be able to solve every problem you give it. This is not always because the problem cannot be solved; sometimes it is because you need to provide better starting parameters. If the Solver can't find the optimal solution to your problem, it presents an unsuccessful completion message in the Solver Results dialog box. The most common unsuccessful completion messages are the following:

- **Solver could not find a feasible solution**   The Solver is unable to find a solution that satisfies all your constraints. This can happen if the constraints are logically conflicting or if not all the constraints can be satisfied (for example, if you insist that your advertising campaign reach 800 million readers on a $1 million budget). In some cases, the Solver also returns this message if the starting values of your variable cells are too far from their optimal values. If you think your constraints are logically consistent and your problem is solvable, try changing your starting values and rerunning the Solver.

- **The maximum iteration limit was reached; continue anyway?**   To avoid tying up your computer indefinitely with an unsolvable problem, the Solver is designed to pause and present this message after it has performed its default number of iterations without arriving at a solution. If you see this message, you can resume the search for a solution by clicking Continue, or you can quit by clicking Stop. If you click Continue, the Solver begins solving again and does not stop until it finds a solution, gives up, or reaches its maximum time limit. If your problems frequently exceed the iteration limit, you can increase the default iteration setting by clicking the Solver button on the Data tab, clicking the Options button, and typing a new value in the Iterations box.

- **The maximum time limit was reached; continue anyway?**   This message is similar to the iteration-limit message. The Solver is designed to pause after a default time period has elapsed. You can increase this default by choosing the Solver command, clicking Options, and modifying the Max Time value.

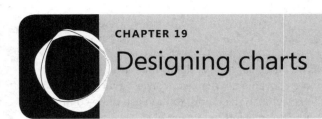

WHEN you create a chart in Microsoft Excel, two new tabs appear on the ribbon under the heading Chart Tools. The first of these tabs, Design, offers options related to the structure of the chart—the type of chart, the presence or absence of various chart elements, the location of the chart, and other similar matters. The second new tab, Format, is concerned with the appearance of the chart.

The current chapter and the one that follows adhere more or less to this framework, although the distinction between structure and appearance is by no means hard and fast. We'll look first at design issues, and then follow in Chapter 20, "Formatting charts," with matters of format and style. The third chapter in this section—Chapter 21, "Using sparklines"—looks at *sparklines*, miniature charts that you can use to depict data graphically within the confines of single worksheet cells.

Selecting data for your chart

The first step in creating a chart is to select some data. If you're plotting all the cells in a contiguous block of cells, you don't have to select the entire block; select any cell within the block, and Excel knows what to do. If, on the other hand, you want to plot only certain rows and columns within the range, you need to select those rows and columns explicitly.

Under some conditions, it's advantageous to set up your source data as a table (by selecting a cell within it and pressing Ctrl+T or Ctrl+L) before creating a chart from it:

- If you plot data in a table and subsequently add new rows or columns to the table, Excel automatically incorporates those rows or columns into the chart.

- If you want your chart to focus on particular rows of data within a large block, a table can make that process more convenient. When you convert a range to a table, Excel adds filter controls to each column in the range. You can use these controls to hide the rows in which you're not currently interested. For example, you can set up a chart that plots the most recent month's numbers in a table of time-related data or the rows that have the top 10 values in some column of interest. Note, however, that when you change or remove the filter, Excel adjusts the chart so that it plots the visible rows. To make a permanent plot of particular rows in a range, select those rows explicitly without filtering the range. (You can plot noncontiguous rows by holding down Ctrl while you select each one.)

- If you want your source data and chart to have consistent or complementary formatting characteristics, you can achieve that more easily using table styles and chart styles.

For information about tables, see Chapter 22, "Managing information in tables." For information about chart styles, see "Choosing a chart style" later in this chapter.

Creating a new chart

When you have selected the data you want to chart, click the Insert tab. The Charts group on the ribbon appears in the center of the ribbon, presenting you with an assortment of chart-type buttons. You can go straight to the options for creating a particular kind of chart by clicking that chart-type button. For example, if you know you want a column chart, you can click the Column Chart button to see a set of options related to that chart type:

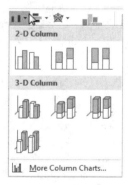

The gallery that unfolds presents a set of subtype options—various kinds of stacked and unstacked two-dimensional column charts, for example, as well as a selection of three-dimensional possibilities—and you can see still more choices by clicking the More... button at the bottom of the gallery.

In many cases, you will find it simpler to skip this gallery and click Recommended Charts instead. Microsoft made that item the largest button in the Charts group; you can't miss it. The Insert Chart dialog box that appears when you click Recommended Charts presents a gallery of potentially suitable chart types and provides a preview of what your data will look like in each of these offerings:

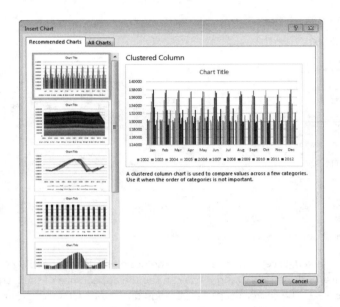

Scroll through the options on the left side of this dialog box until you find one that's right for your data. Of course, Excel won't always understand your data well enough to provide suitable options in the Recommended Charts gallery; if you don't find what you need there, click on the All Charts tab in the Insert Chart dialog box to see the full range of chart type options.

When you click OK, Excel plants a chart object on your worksheet, as shown in Figure 19-1. A *chart object* is a graphic element that lies atop your worksheet in its own window. You can drag any part of the object's perimeter to move it or drag one of the handles in the corners or midpoints of the sides to change the object's size. As you'll see, you also have the option of turning the chart object into a separate chart sheet.

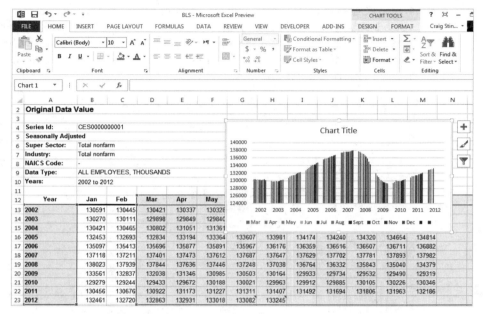

Figure 19-1 A chart object floats atop your worksheet.

With your chart selected, Excel adds two tabs to the ribbon under the heading Chart Tools and selects the first of these tabs, Design. You can see the appearance of the Design tab at the top of Figure 19-1. The centerpiece of the Design tab, the Chart Styles group, provides lots of alternatives for the basic appearance of your chart. If the ones you see immediately on the ribbon don't give you the look you require, click the arrow in the lower right corner of the group to see an expanded set:

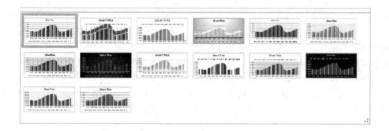

Notice that you do not have to actually select one of these items to see its effect; simply hover the mouse over a choice and Excel will give you a preview.

> **Note**
>
> The ribbon presents a different set of options, including an Analyze tab, if the selected chart is a PivotChart. Because PivotCharts are inextricably connected with PivotTables, we discuss them separately in Chapter 23, "Analyzing data with PivotTable reports." See "Creating PivotCharts" in Chapter 23.

The buttons on the Design tab, from Add Chart Element on the left to Move Chart on the right, focus on basic structural issues relating to your chart. You can use them, among other tasks, to add, format, or remove titles, legends, or axes; to swap rows and columns; or to remove particular values from the chart. The Format tab, shown next, lets you do such things as add arrows, shapes, and descriptive text.

Notice that when a chart object is selected, Excel displays three customizing buttons next to the upper right corner of the chart:

These buttons—Chart Elements, Chart Styles, and Chart Filters—are new in Excel 2013 and offer some alternatives to the ribbon for common chart-formatting tasks. They're handy, particularly if you like to work with the ribbon out of sight. If you don't see the buttons when a chart object appears to be selected, click the chart again; the buttons sometimes disappear when you move a chart, even though the chart remains selected, but they'll reappear when you click.

Changing the chart type

If you didn't get the chart type you were expecting, select the chart and click Change Chart Type on the Design tab of the ribbon. The Change Chart Type dialog box, shown next, provides access to all the chart types that Excel can create.

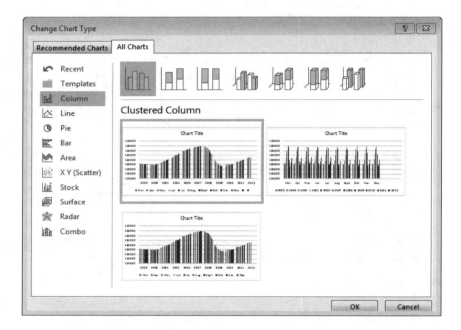

The row of buttons across the top of this dialog box represent subtypes of the selected type; in the figure just shown, for example, the button on the left end of that row offers clustered-column options; the next one to the right presents stacked columns, and so on. Hover your mouse over any of the charts shown in the main part of the dialog box to obtain a magnified view.

Using a combo chart type

A *combo chart* is one in which one or more data series are plotted in a chart type different from that of the remaining series. Combo charts are particularly useful when one of the series is qualitatively different from the others. In the following clustered column chart, for example, the series labeled *Average* is different in kind from the other series, each of which represents an individual person:

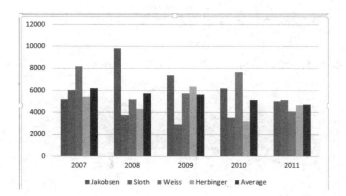

Plotting the Average series as a line instead of a column improves the readability of the chart, allowing you to see at a glance who is and isn't above average:

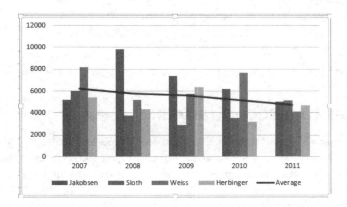

With some data sets, Excel will recognize that a combo chart is appropriate and will propose it in the Recommended Charts gallery. If that doesn't happen, however, you can always change a single-type chart to a combo at any time. Select the chart, click Change Chart Type, and then choose Combo in the list of chart types at the left side of the dialog box. Select one of the chart pictures at the top of the dialog box, above the preview window, and then work with the options in the bottom of the dialog box to get the combination of types that you want. In the following dialog box, for example, you can see that Excel has correctly intuited that the Average series should be a line, but it has incorrectly proposed to plot Herbinger as a line as well.

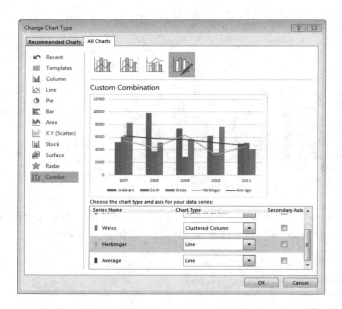

You can fix that by selecting Clustered Column in the drop-down list next to Herbinger.

Assigning a series to a secondary axis

A secondary value axis makes it possible to compare data series that fall within divergent ranges. The secondary axis, positioned at the right, can have a completely different scale from the primary axis. You can assign as many series as you like to the secondary axis.

In the following chart, for example, the Cost Per Square Foot numbers are so small in comparison with the Median Square Footage numbers that no useful comparisons can be made:

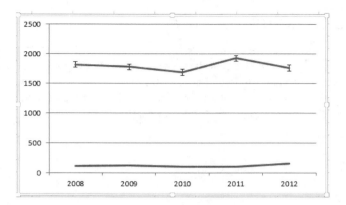

Plotting the two series on separate axes provides more useful information. To move a series to another axis, you can right-click it, choose Format Data Series, and then choose Secondary Axis in the task pane that appears. Alternatively, you can select any part of the chart, click Change Chart Type, select Combo, and then work with the options at the bottom of the Change Chart Type dialog box. As the following illustrates, the Change Chart Type dialog box lets you see the effect of your customization before you click OK:

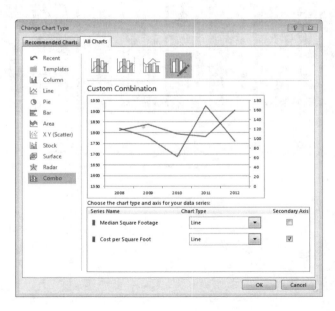

Switching rows and columns

Most of the time when you present a block of data to Excel for charting, the program fig-ures out correctly how to organize that data—which labels to assign to the horizontal axis and which to put in the chart's legend. Because this might not always be the case, however, the program offers a Switch Row/Column button in the Data group of the Design tab. Clicking that button, for example, transforms this chart:

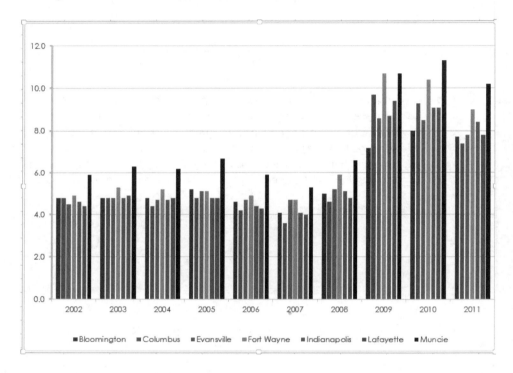

into this one:

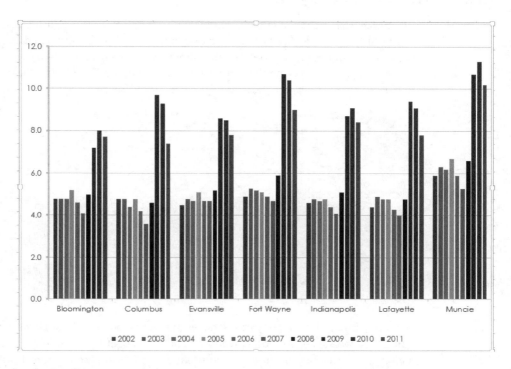

In the first example, each data cluster represents a year, and the various column colors (identified in the legend) represent cities. In the second example, this orientation is reversed.

Choosing a chart layout

What Excel calls a chart *layout* is a combination of choices affecting such elements as the chart's title, legend, axes, axis titles, and gridlines. Each of the program's chart types comes with an assortment of packaged layout options. With the chart selected, you can see the available layouts by clicking the Quick Layout button in the Chart Layouts group of the ribbon. Here, for example, are the layouts provided for a line chart:

Don't be dismayed by the tiny boxes; hover the mouse, and Excel will preview your selection on the worksheet. And don't worry if none of the built-in layouts gives you the combination and positioning of chart elements that you're looking for. You can always tailor those elements with individual formatting commands.

Choosing a chart style

A chart *style* is a combination of foreground and background colors designed to coordinate with cell styles, shape styles, and table styles to give your workbook a consistent, professional, and high-impact appearance. To apply a chart style, select the chart and then click Design under Chart Tools on the ribbon. The Chart Styles group shows you a half-dozen or more choices, depending on your screen resolution. To see more, click the arrow at the lower right corner of the group.

Chart styles let you do such things as apply attractive gradient fills to your chart backgrounds, add photorealistic highlighting to bar and column markers, switch line-chart markers from fat to svelte, and so on. The best way to see the wealth of possibilities is to select a chart, open the gallery, and experiment.

Note that cell styles, table styles, and chart styles are all components of the current theme. That is, when you change the theme applied to your workbook (by clicking Page Layout on the ribbon and opening the Themes gallery at the left side of the ribbon), your available cell styles, table styles, and chart styles all change as well. Also, be aware that theme changes on your computer do not affect the appearance of your chart on someone else's computer; if your chart is full of pink, it might still look green to your coworker.

For more information about themes, see "Formatting with themes" in Chapter 9, "Worksheet formatting techniques." For more information about cell styles, see "Formatting with cell styles" in Chapter 9. For more information about table styles, see "Customizing table styles" in Chapter 22.

Moving the chart to a separate chart sheet

If you don't need to have your chart next to the numbers from which it is derived, you might consider putting it on its own chart sheet. A *chart sheet* is a separate, special-purpose sheet that gives the maximum amount of screen area to your graph. To move your chart from a worksheet to a chart sheet, right-click on the chart border or the plot area and choose Move Chart (or select the chart and then click Move Chart on the Design tab). In the dialog box that appears, select New Sheet, supply a name for the chart sheet or accept the default name, and then click OK. If you decide to move the chart back to the worksheet, repeat this process, select Object In, select the name of the worksheet you want to move the chart to, and then click OK.

INSIDE OUT   Press F11 to move a chart

You can move a chart object to a chart sheet by selecting the chart and pressing F11. The only disadvantage to this approach is that you don't get to name the chart sheet. But you can always do that later by double-clicking the sheet tab and changing the default name to something of your choosing. You can even create a chart on a chart sheet directly from data—by selecting a cell or range and pressing F11. Here the one disadvantage is that Excel uses the current default chart type, which might not be what you want. But you can always switch to a different type by selecting the chart on the chart sheet and clicking Change Chart Type.

Adding, editing, and removing a chart title

If your chart doesn't already have a title, you can add one by selecting the chart and doing either of the following:

- Click the Chart Elements button next to the upper right corner of your chart, and then select the Chart Title check box. Excel displays a title with default text, centered above the plot area. To display the title near the top of the chart but within the plot area, click the arrow that appears when you hover the mouse over Chart Title in the Chart Elements list, and then choose Centered Overlay on the submenu that appears.

- Click the Design tab, click Add Chart Element, click Chart Title, and then select either Above Chart or Centered Overlay. Excel displays a title with default text, in the position you selected.

If you selected Above Chart, Excel positions the title above the plot area, in some cases shrinking the plot area just enough to make room for the title. If you selected Centered Overlay, Excel centers the title near the top of the chart without adjusting the plot area. This option gives you a little more room for your vertical axis, gridlines, and chart markers, but in some cases it might make the title or the markers hard to read. The title is a floating text object in any case; you can select it and drag it anywhere within the chart area.

To edit a chart title, select it and type. When you press Enter, your text replaces the current title. To use the value of a worksheet cell as the title, type an equal sign, point to the cell, and press Enter. If that's awkward to do—for example, if the text you want to cite is not in sight—type a worksheet-qualified reference to the cell in question. To grab the text from cell A4 on Sheet1, for example, you could type **=sheet1!A4**. Note that the formula must include the sheet name, even if the text is on the same sheet as the chart.

To make the title text bold or italic, you can select the title and press Ctrl+B or Ctrl+I. For more elaborate font changes—for example, to choose a different typeface or size—select the title, right-click, and then choose Font from the shortcut menu.

To change the appearance of individual words or characters in a title, select the title and then click within the title to get an insertion point. Select the text you want to format, and then choose Font. (To select a particular word, double-click that word.) If for any reason you're having trouble getting the insertion point, right-click the title and choose Edit Text.

Excel will automatically break a long title into two centered lines. If you don't like where the break comes, or if you want to break a short title into multiple lines, position the insertion pointer where you want a line break and then press Shift+Enter.

To delete a title, simply select it and press the Delete key.

> **Note**
>
> Additional options for customizing chart titles are available via the Format Chart Title task pane. To display the task pane, choose More Options on the Chart Title submenu, or click Add Chart Element on the ribbon, choose Chart Title, and then choose More Title Options. We discuss these additional options in Chapter 21 in the following sections: "Formatting lines and borders," "Formatting areas," and "Formatting text."

Adding, editing, and removing a legend

The steps for adding, editing, and removing a legend are essentially the same as those for working with a chart title. For details, see the previous discussion.

You can choose to position a legend at the top, left side, right side, or bottom of the chart area. Like the chart title, the legend is a floating text object; you can drag it to any suitable location within the chart area.

Excel uses either column headings or row headings within your chart's data block as default legend text. (If there are no such headings, it uses dummy text, such as "Series 1" and "Series 2.") You can change the legend text by editing the column or row headings. If by chance you want something in the legend different from what you have on the worksheet, select the chart, click the Design tab on the ribbon, and then click Select Data. Suppose, for example, that your data block uses spelled-out month names, but using those names makes for a bulky, two-line legend. The foregoing steps would take you to the Select Data Source dialog box, shown next:

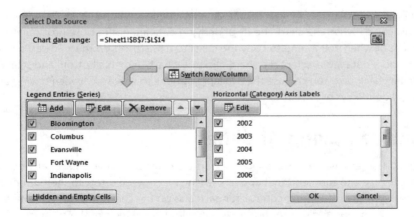

Here you could select month names, click Edit, and supply the shortened versions you prefer.

Adding and positioning data labels

You can add data labels to all series in a chart by selecting the chart, clicking the Chart Elements button, and selecting the Data Labels check box. The submenu includes a set of positioning options geared to the type of chart. With some charts, you might find a Best Fit option; as Figure 19-2 shows, this option can be handy on pie charts with narrow slices.

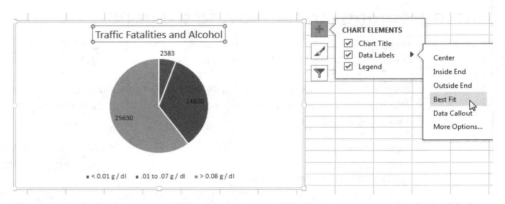

Figure 19-2 If you choose Best Fit for this chart's data labels, Excel doesn't try to fit the label *2383* into the narrow slice but displays it outside the pie instead.

Adding a data table

A *data table* is a copy of your source data included within the chart. Data tables are useful particularly when the chart and its underlying data are not in close proximity on the worksheet or when you intend to copy the chart to a Microsoft Word or PowerPoint document. To add a data table, select the chart, click the Chart Elements button, and select the Data Table check box. You can use the available options to choose between having and not having legend keys with your table.

Adding and removing gridlines

To add or remove gridlines, click the Chart Elements button and select or clear the Gridlines check box. The submenu that appears when you click the arrow to the right of the Gridlines check box gives you finer control; for each axis on the chart, you can select either major gridlines, minor gridlines, or both. Excel previews the effects of these choices as you hover the mouse pointer over the check boxes.

Be aware that major gridlines in certain kinds of three-dimensional charts can make data points appear to have less than their true value. In the following illustration, for example, the data points have exact integer values from 1 to 10, but the gridlines, in combination with the three-dimensional perspective, make each point appear somewhat smaller.

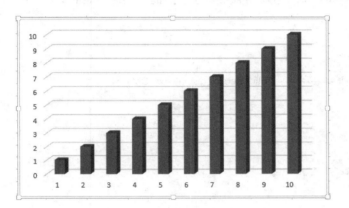

Adding and editing axis titles

To add axis titles to a chart, select the chart, click the Chart Elements button, and select the Axis Titles check box. To add or delete a title for a particular axis only, click the arrow to the right of the Axis Titles check box and then clear or select the check box for the axis in question.

Excel initially uses default text for axis titles. You can edit that text in the same manner that you edit chart title text; for details, see "Adding, editing, and removing a chart title" earlier in this chapter.

Working with axes

To display or suppress one or more chart axes, select the chart and click the Chart Elements button. You can make all the axes disappear or reappear by clearing or selecting the Axes check box. To manipulate a particular axis, click the arrow to the right of Axes in the Chart Elements list.

If you're an Excel veteran, you might have seen the terms *category axis* and *value axis* in some older versions of the product. Excel now uses the more commonplace descriptions *horizontal* and *vertical*. It's worthwhile understanding why the older terms were used, however. A value axis is one that is scaled numerically. Value axes are generally vertical (except in bar charts, which are essentially column charts rotated 90 degrees), but in an X Y (scatter) chart, both the vertical and horizontal axes are value axes. A category axis is delineated either by labels that have no numeric significance or by dates.

Changing the scale of a value axis

The easiest way to manipulate the scale of a value axis is to double-click it. That brings up the Format Axis task pane, shown in Figure 19-3. (The values exemplified in Figure 19-3 are derived from the chart shown in Figure 19-1 earlier in this chapter.)

Figure 19-3 Double-clicking an axis displays its formatting task pane, in which, among other things, you can adjust the axis's scale.

By entering new values in the Minimum and Maximum text boxes, you can override Excel's default choice of axis boundaries.

Changing the positions of tick marks and gridlines

The Major and Minor boxes below the heading Units determine the spacing between tick marks—and hence between gridlines. If your axis labels or your gridlines are too close together, type new values in those boxes. The Minor Units value is relevant only if you choose to display minor tick marks.

Changing the point where axes intersect

By default, axes intersect at the minimum value on the vertical axis scale. You can move the intersection to a different point by typing a new value in the box next to Axis Value, below the heading Horizontal Axis Crosses. You can also move the intersection to the highest point on the value axis by selecting Maximum Axis Value. On a typical chart with a vertical value axis and a horizontal category axis, that would put the category axis at the top of the chart (unless you also select Values In Reverse Order).

Reversing the value-axis scale

You can turn the value-axis scale upside down so that the higher values appear near the bottom of the chart. You might find this option convenient if all your chart values are negative and you're interested primarily in their absolute value. To invert the scale, select Values In Reverse Order.

Using logarithmic scaling

To use logarithmic scaling, select the Logarithmic Scale check box. If you want to use a base other than 10, type that base in the box to the right.

In a logarithmic scale, the lowest value is 1. You cannot plot negative and 0 values. If you apply logarithmic scaling to a chart that includes negative or 0 values, Excel displays an error message and removes the points that it cannot plot. You can restore those points by returning to linear scaling.

Applying a scaling factor

To facilitate the plotting of large numbers, Excel lets you scale your value axis in units ranging from hundreds to trillions. When you choose one of these options, you might also want to ensure that the Show Display Units Label On Chart check box is selected so that it will be clear that a scaling factor has been applied.

Changing the display format of a value axis

By default, Excel displays numbers on the value axis in the same format as the worksheet cells from which those numbers are derived. If you want something different, you can go back to the worksheet and change the format there. Alternatively, you can click Number in the Format Axis task pane, and then open the Category drop-down menu. The options available there are the same as those for formatting worksheet numbers; for details, see "Formatting in depth" in Chapter 9.

For more about formatting value axes, see "Formatting axes," in Chapter 20.

Changing the scale of a category axis

Excel recognizes two kinds of category axes—those that have ordinary text labels and those whose labels are dates. If the axis labels are dates, Excel ordinarily applies time-scaling to it; that is, it spaces the labels and data according to their temporal positions. To take a simple

Chapter 19

example, if you plot a column chart for dates at the beginning of April, May, August, and September, Excel gives you something that looks like this:

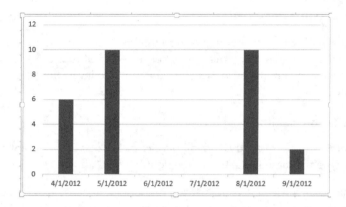

The markers for August and September are moved to the positions they would occupy if data for June and July were included—and, in fact, Excel creates labels for the missing dates, perhaps on the assumption that you will supply the missing data later. Excel will also sort the chart in chronological order in the event that the worksheet data is not sorted.

Ordinarily, Excel knows whether an axis should be time-scaled or not and proceeds accordingly. As the following illustration shows, Excel's default Axis Type option is Automatically Select Based On Data:

There might be occasions when you want to override Excel's decision and convert a date axis to a text axis. In the preceding example, if you don't intend ever to fill in the missing months, you might prefer an evenly spaced, text-based chart, which would look like this:

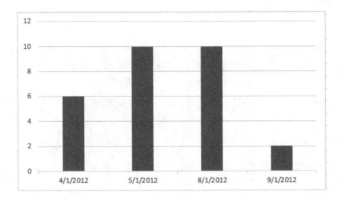

To convert a date-scaled category axis to a text-based one, display the Format Axis task pane (double-click the axis to get there) and choose Text Axis.

Changing the beginning and end points on a date axis

By default, Excel makes your earliest time value the minimum point on the scale and the latest time value the maximum. By specifying different values for those boundary parameters, you can zoom in on a subset of your data. For example, if your chart plots monthly information from January through December, you can focus on the third quarter by changing the Minimum value to 7/1 of the year in question and the Maximum value to 9/30. Furthermore, if you want to stress that the future is unknown, you can extend the maximum to a date beyond the date of your last data point. Excel then compresses the plot into the left side of the chart, leaving space on the right.

To change the end points of a time-scaled chart, use the Bounds section of the Format Axis task pane:

The Major setting under Units determines the spacing of major tick marks, axis labels, and major gridlines. To move labels and gridlines farther apart, increase the Major value. The Minor setting under Units determines the spacing of minor tick marks and minor gridlines.

> **Note**
>
> On a time-scaled chart, Excel plots data in chronological order even if it's not sorted by date on the worksheet. We don't recommend randomizing your data, but it's interesting to know that the Excel charting engine doesn't object.

Changing the base unit

On charts with date axes, Excel can plot data points only at intervals of the base unit. The available base units are Days, Months, and Years. Excel decides what base unit to use according to the smallest difference in value between points in your source data. In other words, the program usually knows what to do and usually gets it right. You might occasionally find it convenient to overrule, however.

For example, Figure 19-4 plots daily price data using the automatically determined base unit of Days. Switching the base unit to Months or Years (Figures 19-5 and 19-6, respectively) turns the simple daily line chart into an open-high-low-close chart that shows the variation of prices over larger time intervals.

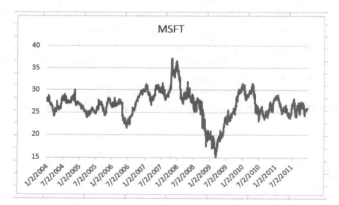

Figure 19-4 With the base unit set to its automatically determined value, Days, Excel generates a simple line chart of daily prices.

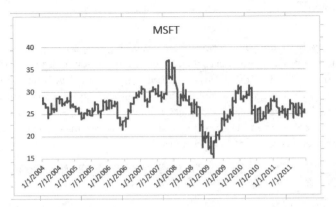

Figure 19-5 Changing the base unit to Months creates a monthly open-high-low-close chart.

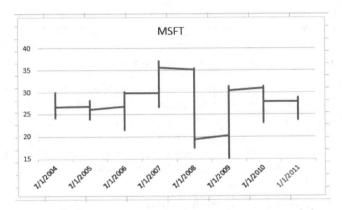

Figure 19-6 Switching the base unit to Years creates yearly bars.

Unfortunately, Excel offers only three base unit choices—Days, Months, and Years. Thus, if your data provides, say, hourly price points, you will get a daily chart regardless. If you prefer an ordinary line chart showing hourly price progressions, your recourse is to turn off date scaling in favor of a text category axis.

> ### Note
>
> Fiddling with the base unit value is not the only way to get open-high-low-close charts! Excel offers four types of stock charts, including open-high-low-close candlesticks. To see the choices, click the Insert tab on the ribbon and then click Other Charts. The stock charts, listed in the gallery under the heading Stock, require you to set up your data in columns—for example, with separate columns for Open, High, Low, and Close. The methods described in this chapter are useful to know about when your data is not arrayed as required for the built-in stock chart types.

Modifying a chart's data

The simplest way to add new data points to an existing series on a chart is to make the chart's source range a table (select any cell within the range, and press Ctrl+T; for more information, see "Creating a table," in Chapter 22) and then add new rows to the table. Excel incorporates these rows into the chart without requiring you to do anything further.

If you add a new column immediately to the right of a table, Excel expands the table to include the column. If you've created a chart from such a table, the new column becomes a new data series. That might or might not be desirable, depending on the contents of the new column. If you find yourself with an unwanted new series, you can delete it by selecting the series on the chart and pressing the Delete key. Alternatively, you can use the Filter button to remove it. (See "Filtering chart data," later in this chapter.)

Using the mouse to add data points

If you choose not to make your source data a table, you can still use your mouse to add data points to an existing chart series. Figure 19-7 shows a candlestick chart that plots data through May 2. Notice that because the chart area is selected, Excel draws two rectangles around the source data. The first rectangle, in column A, outlines the range that the chart is using for its category axis labels. The second, encompassing columns B through E, outlines the four data series. Excel uses magenta for the first rectangle and blue for the second to help you distinguish between the two.

	A	B	C	D	E
1	Date	Open	High	Low	Settle
731	4/8	548.5	557.0	547.5	556.5
732	4/9	555.0	555.5	546.0	546.7
733	4/10	547.5	551.5	545.5	549.2
734	4/11	553.5	557.0	548.0	556.2
735	4/12	555.0	556.0	549.5	551.8
736	4/15	546.5	549.5	545.0	548.0
737	4/16	548.0	550.5	523.0	529.2
738	4/17	530.0	533.5	528.0	530.5
739	4/18	532.5	532.5	525.0	526.7
740	4/19	525.0	529.5	523.0	525.7
741	4/22	527.0	534.0	527.0	532.5
742	4/23	533.0	535.5	531.0	531.5
743	4/24	530.5	532.5	528.5	529.2
744	4/25	531.0	540.0	530.5	536.5
745	4/26	537.0	537.0	525.5	526.2
746	4/29	533.0	534.5	525.0	525.5
747	4/30	524.0	533.0	524.0	529.1
748	5/1	536.0	545.0	535.0	542.5
749	5/2	543.0	543.5	534.0	542.0
750	5/3	543.5	553.0	537.5	547.0
751	5/6	546.0	551.5	545.5	549.0
752	5/7	548.0	555.0	546.0	551.5
753	5/8	551.5	555.0	545.5	546.5
754	5/9	547.0	548.0	543.5	544.7
755	5/10	545.0	546.5	536.0	537.5

Figure 19-7 When you select the chart area, Excel outlines the source data on your worksheet. You can drag a fill handle to alter the source range.

To extend the chart so that it includes the data in rows 750 through 755, drag the fill handle in the bottom right corner of either rectangle. Be sure to drag the fill handle, not the bottom of the rectangle, if you intend to add data. Dragging the edge of the rectangle moves the data selection without changing its size. Dragging the bottom down five rows in Figure 19-7, for example, would move both the start date and the end date forward.

Filtering chart data

The Filter button to the right of a chart provides an easy way to suppress the display of particular series or categories items on that chart. In Figure 19-8, for example, you can remove certain cities or years from the chart by clearing their associated check boxes. The Filter button also gives you an easy way to focus attention on a particular element of the chart without actually changing the chart. When you hover the mouse over an item, as we have hovered over Bloomington in the figure, Excel displays the rest of the chart in pale colors so that your attention is drawn to a particular data series. As soon as you move your mouse from the item you're hovering over, the chart resumes its normal appearance.

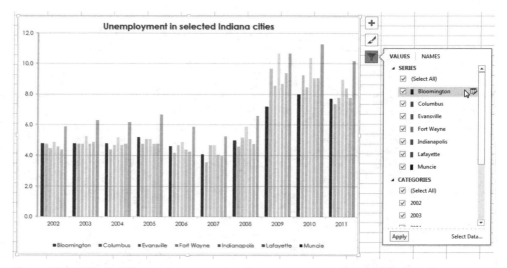

Figure 19-8 With the Filter button you can easily remove a particular series from a chart or simply highlight a series temporarily.

Plotting noncontiguous source ranges

There might be times when the data you want to plot does not lie in a contiguous block of cells. Suppose, for example, that from the following table you want to generate a column chart that compares Petra Chvojkova with Andrej Koklic, omitting the other five salespersons:

	A	B	C
1	Salesperson	2011 Sales	2012 Sales
2	Berg, Karen	1876	1163
3	Chvojkova, Petra	5394	3291
4	Egelund-Mueller, Anja	8679	5534
5	Faisandier, Antoine	5316	3329
6	Koklic, Andrej	5391	2968
7	Nesseth, Jorun	8444	6502
8	Zulechner, Markus	9148	4757
9			

The simplest way to do this is to use the filter control next to the Salesperson heading to restrict the table to Chvojkova and Koklic. Excel responds by hiding rows 2, 4, 5, 7, and 8, and any chart generated from the table will plot only the visible rows. If you don't have filter controls, you can accomplish the same feat by manually hiding the rows you want to omit using the Format command in the Cells group of the Home tab.

You can also plot noncontiguous data by pressing Ctrl and selecting the rows or columns you want to plot. In this example, you could hold down Ctrl, select rows 1, 3, and 5, and then click the appropriate command in the Charts group on the Insert tab. If you use this method, be sure to include the header row (row 1 in this example) in your selection so that Excel can provide appropriate labels for your chart series.

Changing the way Excel plots empty and hidden cells

Excel ordinarily plots empty cells as gaps—that is, it doesn't plot them. It also omits cells in hidden rows and columns. As Figure 19-9 shows, you can change both defaults if you want. The alternatives for empty cells are to plot them as zeros or to fill the gap with a straight line. The latter option is available only in line and X Y (scatter) charts.

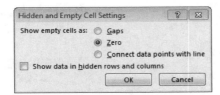

Figure 19-9 By default, Excel omits missing data in a source range and ignores data in hidden rows and columns.

Hidden and empty cell settings are chart-specific. To modify the behavior for a particular chart, right-click the chart and click Select Data. Then click Hidden And Empty Cells.

Adding moving averages and other trendlines

A *trendline* is a line that describes the general tendency of a data series. It can be a moving average, linear-regression line, or line generated by one of various kinds of nonlinear, curve-fitting methods.

To plot a trendline for a particular series, click on any chart marker for the series and then click the Chart Elements button. If you select the Trendline check box, Excel will use the default trendline type. To see additional options, click the arrow to the right of Trendline. The submenu will offer Linear, Exponential, Two Period Moving Average, and More Options. Clicking More Options opens the Format Trendline task pane, shown in Figure 19-10. (If you don't see the set of options shown in Figure 19-10, click the third button beneath the heading Trendline Options.)

Figure 19-10 Using the Format Trendline task pane, you can add six types of trendlines to a data series.

To specify the type of trendline or moving average you want, select one of the six options at the top of the task pane. If you choose Polynomial, indicate the highest power (from 2 through 6) for the independent variable in the adjacent Order text box. If you select Moving Average, indicate the number of periods Excel should use in its calculations.

After you choose the type of trendline you want, you can use the Trendline Name area of the task pane to customize the name that appears in the chart's legend. Options under Forecast (not available for moving averages) let you extrapolate the trendline. If you're adding a linear, polynomial, or exponential trendline, you can also select the Set Intercept check box to use a y intercept and then specify the y-intercept value in the box on the right. Select the Display Equation On Chart and Display R-Squared Value On Chart check boxes to display the regression equation and R-squared value on the chart.

Adding error bars

When you plot statistical or experimental data, it's often helpful to indicate the confidence level of your data. The error-bar feature makes this easy. To add error bars to a data series in an area, bar, column, line, or X Y (scatter) chart, select the series, click the Chart Elements button, and then click the arrow next to Error Bars. As with trendlines, you can see the full set of available options by choosing More Options. Figure 19-11 shows the Format Error Bars task pane that appears.

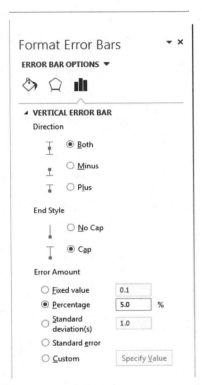

Figure 19-11 You can customize error bars for direction, style, and amount.

Formatting charts

I N CHAPTER 19, "Designing charts," you saw the basic procedures for setting up a chart in Excel, as well as those for adding titles, axes, gridlines, data labels, and so on. As you'll recall, when you create and select a chart object, Excel adds a Chart Tools heading to the ribbon, with two tabs—labeled Design and Format—subordinate to that new heading. Virtually all of the procedures described in Chapter 19 are accessible via the Design tab—although, as always in Excel, there are alternative ways to get the job done that don't involve a trip to the ribbon.

In this chapter, we look at issues of style and appearance, aspects of the charting interface that are accessible via the Format tab, and associated formatting task panes.

Formatting charts with the Chart Styles gallery

Before you get too involved with the kinds of formatting procedures described later in this chapter, however, be sure to familiarize yourself with the Chart Styles gallery, located in the middle of the Design tab when a chart is selected. The gallery typically offers a dozen or more combinations of structural details and formatting choices tailored to the selected graph; click the arrow in the lower right corner of the gallery to see the entire set of offerings. You can preview the effect of each style on your chart by passing your mouse through the gallery. Here's what the gallery might look like for a simple line chart:

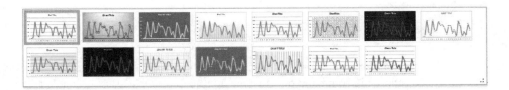

Some of the styles have gridlines, while others do not; some have compound lines, some have data labels, and some have background colors. (If you want a background color but don't like what the gallery offers, experiment with the Change Colors command, just to the left of the gallery on the ribbon.) Even if you don't find exactly what you want in the gallery, it will at least give you a sense of the styling possibilities and might give you a jumping-off point from which you can refine your stylistic preferences.

Selecting chart elements

Just as creating a chart begins with selecting data, applying formatting begins with select-ing a chart element—the title, series, area, legend, or whatever you want to format. An Excel chart consists of many separate elements, each of which can be formatted inde-pendently. You can see the names of all these components by selecting the chart, clicking the Format tab, and then opening the Chart Objects list, the drop-down list that appears directly under the left corner of the ribbon. Figure 20-1 shows what the Chart Objects list might look like for a three-dimensional area chart.

Figure 20-1 The Chart Objects list enumerates the elements of the current chart that you can format.

You can format an object by selecting it in the Chart Objects list and then clicking Format Selection, the command directly beneath the Chart Objects list on the left side of the rib-bon. Alternatively, and more simply, you can just double-click the part of the chart you want to format. Or you can right-click the object and choose the formatting command that appears at the bottom of the shortcut menu. All of these methods result in the arrival of the appropriate formatting task pane.

The Chart Objects list doesn't explicitly list all the elements you can format. Specifically, it doesn't allow you to select individual points in a data series, individual data labels, or individual series names in a legend. You can select and format these items separately from their companions, however. To do so, click the item in question twice (slowly—not a double-click). The first click selects the set, and the second selects the member. After you refine your selection to an individual item, the Chart Objects list confirms your selection; handles do as well.

Repositioning chart elements with the mouse

You can move the chart title, axis titles, data labels, and legend by dragging them with the mouse. You can also use your mouse to explode a pie slice or doughnut bite. Note, in particular, that you can adjust the positions of individual data labels without moving an entire series of labels; in addition, although Excel creates legends in certain fixed positions, you're free to drag them anywhere you like, even to the middle of the chart.

Unfortunately, although you can move data labels at will, you have no such freedom with the tick-mark labels that appear along your axes. You can rotate these, but you cannot pick them up and drop them elsewhere. In addition, you cannot do anything with individual axis labels; you can modify them only as a group. Therefore, if you want to change the color of a particular label or move it inside the plot area, you're out of luck. You need to create individual text annotations to serve as axis labels.

For information about rotating axis labels, see "Changing the rotation of axis labels" later in this chapter. For information about adding text annotations, see "Adding arrows, shapes, and text" later in this chapter.

Formatting lines and borders

Excel uses lines for axes, line charts, and trendlines. It also uses lines to create borders around a variety of chart elements—the chart area, plot area, titles, legends, markers on bar and column charts, and so on. Not all of these borders appear by default (for example, chart titles are borderless by default), but all are available if you want them. You can also add lines to annotate charts (as discussed in "Adding arrows, shapes, and text," later in this chapter), and the same formatting commands that are available for borders and chart lines are also available for annotative lines.

Most of the formatting options are the same for all the various kinds of lines and borders. You can color them, fatten them, change them from solid to dotted or dashed, and so on.

(You can also delete them.) Series lines in line charts have a couple of additional options. You can add arrowheads to their beginnings and endings, and you can smooth the lines so that the series becomes a sequence of curves instead of straight line segments. As Figure 20-2 shows, a smoothed line, with or without an arrowhead, can emphasize direction while playing down the exact positions of intermediate data points.

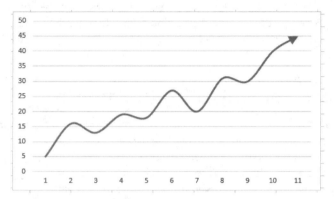

Figure 20-2 In addition to the formatting options available for other kinds of lines, a series line can be smoothed and capped with an arrowhead.

To format a line, or to add a border to an object that doesn't currently have one, begin by displaying the object's formatting task pane. As mentioned, often the simplest way to do that is to double-click the object you're interested in. To add a border to a chart title, for example, you can start by double-clicking the title. (Alternatively, right-click the title and choose Format Chart Title.)

As Figure 20-3 shows, a formatting task pane is a tabbed dialog box, offering several sets of options under various textual and iconic headings. In the case of the Format Chart Title task pane, for example, the headings appear directly under the main heading. The one you want is the one on the left labeled Title Options, not the one that says Text Options. Directly below are some iconic headings. Again, to perform line formatting, the one you want is on the left—the icon that looks like a tipped paint bucket, whose formal name (which appears as a ScreenTip if you hover the mouse over it) is Fill & Line.

The word *Automatic* in formatting task panes, as elsewhere in Excel, is equivalent to *default*. It means, "Let Excel decide." In the Border section of the Format Chart Title task pane, shown in Figure 20-3, the Automatic choice is equivalent to No Line, because Excel, by default, does not draw a border around chart titles. (Don't let the redundancy get on your nerves; there are contexts in which the effect of Automatic varies depending on circumstances.)

Click here
and here
to get to
line-formatting
options

Figure 20-3 The various formatting task panes in Excel cram a lot of options into a compact space; click headings at the top of the pane to get to the options you need.

If you want a border for a title, you can choose Solid Line or Gradient Line. *Solid* here does not mean "unbroken"; it means "of a single color." The Gradient Line option—more commonly used for areas than for lines—lets you apply multiple colors with smooth transitions. The procedures for creating gradient lines are essentially the same as for areas; for more information about creating gradients, see "Filling an area with a color gradient" later in this chapter.

The options most likely to be of interest for line formatting include Color, Width, Compound Type, and Dash Type. As the following illustrations show, the Compound Type drop-down list offers four alternatives to a simple line, and the Dash Type drop-down list lets you chop your line in seven different fashions. Regardless of what you select or don't select in these two drop-down lists, you can vary the weight of your line via the Width drop-down list.

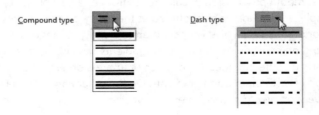

Formatting areas

Excel provides a rich set of options for formatting the background areas of your charts—including the plot area, the chart area, and the walls and floors of three-dimensional charts. You can also apply these formatting options to legends, to the background areas of titles and data labels, and to certain kinds of chart markers—including columns, bars, pyramids, cones, cylinders, areas, bubbles, pie slices, and doughnut bites. These options are all available via the Fill section of the formatting task pane. Shown here is the pane as it might appear for the chart area with a solid fill selected:

Choosing a solid fill

To fill an area with a solid color, simply choose Solid Fill and open the color picker, which is the drop-down list next to the Color heading. When you choose Solid Fill, the Transparency control also becomes available. For a discussion of the uses of transparency, see "Making areas transparent" later in this chapter.

Filling an area with a color gradient

A *color gradient* is a smooth progression of color tones from one part of an area to another—for example, a transition from bright red at the top of a column marker to black at the bottom. Color gradients can give your chart areas a classy, professional appearance. Of course, depending on how you use them, color gradients can also be distracting. If you're creating charts that are intended to convince or impress others, it's probably a good idea to exercise a bit of restraint in using gradients. On the other hand, if flamboyance is your style, Excel gives you plenty of ways to express yourself.

As Figure 20-4 shows, the formatting task pane presents several new controls when you choose Gradient Fill. The sheer range of possibilities can seem a little overwhelming at first. The best way to familiarize yourself with the options is to experiment. Create a chart, move it to a separate chart sheet (or enlarge it on the worksheet), select the plot area (because it's the largest area of the chart), and then try out the various controls to see what they do.

Figure 20-4 With Gradient Fill selected, the task pane expands, presenting options that let you select colors, angles, directions, transparency, and more.

A good place to start is with the Preset Gradients drop-down list. Click there to reveal a gallery of 30 tasteful gradients. Then move on to the Type, Direction, Angle, and Gradient Stops controls.

A gradient stop is a boundary between colors. You can have as many stops and colors as you want. To add a stop, click either on the slider or on the first of the two icons directly to the right of the slider. To remove a stop, click the second icon to the right of the slider. To specify a color for a gradient stop, select it and then open the color picker, directly below the Gradient Stops control.

Filling an area with a texture or picture

If you don't care for solids or gradients, why not fill your background areas or data markers with textures or pictures? You can use images in a wide variety of supported formats, paste an item from your clip art library (or from the Office.com clip art library), or use one of the 24 texture images supplied by Excel. The texture images evoke familiar materials, such as oak, marble, and cloth. For example, Figure 20-5 shows a fish-fossil texture applied to a chart's plot area, with a clip art image applied to the column markers.

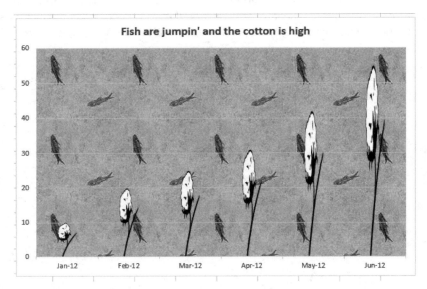

Figure 20-5 A fish-fossil texture is applied to the plot area of this chart, and a clip art image is applied to the column markers.

To apply a texture or picture, choose Picture Or Texture Fill in the task pane for the chart element you have selected. Open the Texture drop-down list to choose from the texture gallery, or click the File, Clipboard, or Online button to apply a picture. Excel stretches pictures to fit unless you also select one of the Stack options. If you're using a bitmapped image, the stretching is likely to produce distortion unless the size of the picture is exactly that of the area you're formatting. To avoid distortion, you can shrink the image by moving it away from the left, right, top, and bottom borders of the area—in other words, by setting margins. To do that, set nonzero values in the various Offset text boxes.

Making areas transparent

A default chart displayed on a white worksheet has a solid white background. Note that this is not the same as having no fill; a chart area with no fill is transparent, which allows the underlying worksheet gridlines to shine through.

Making the chart area transparent can be useful at times. If you want to create a worksheet display that minimizes the chart apparatus and simply shows a small graphic to support a set of numbers, using the No Fill option is good way to get there. (A sparkline can serve this purpose as well, of course, but sparklines—described in the previous chapter—are available only in a small number of chart types.) Eliminate the border around the chart area (as discussed in "Formatting lines and borders" earlier in this chapter), get rid of any chart elements you don't want (the title, legend, or whatever), and assign the No Fill option to your chart and plot areas. Figure 20-6 shows an example of a chart reduced to basics in this way.

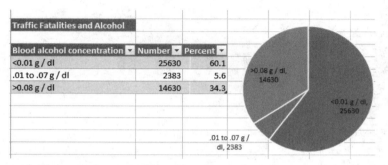

Figure 20-6 Less is sometimes more. Applying No Fill to this chart's chart area eliminates distraction.

Formatting text

The simplest way to carry out most formatting tasks for chart titles, axis titles, axis labels, and other chart text is to select the text and then use the familiar commands in the Font group of the Home tab. You can change the font, size, and color of chart text this way, for example. You can format particular words in a title by selecting them, just as you might do with ordinary worksheet text, and you can employ the standard keyboard shortcuts, such as Ctrl+B for bold or Ctrl+I for italic. Note, however, that you cannot format individual axis labels in this manner; formatting directives in that context apply to the entire set of labels.

Using WordArt

When any text element on your chart is selected, Excel makes the WordArt Styles group on the Format tab available. For information about using WordArt, see "Creating WordArt," in Chapter 10, "Creating and formatting graphics." In addition to a gallery of readymade WordArt styles, the WordArt Styles group offers three commands—Text Fill, Text Outline, and Text Effects—that you can use to dress up your chart text. If you're interested in adding some visual flair to chart titles and other textual elements, be sure to experiment with these commands.

Changing the rotation of axis labels

If you create a chart with labels on the horizontal axis that will overlap if displayed horizontally, Excel ordinarily angles the labels, like this:

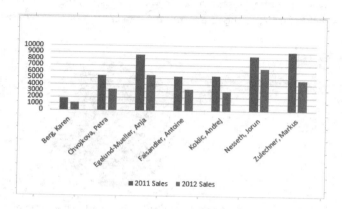

If you widen the chart, the program reverts to a horizontal label display—in some cases, breaking labels onto two lines:

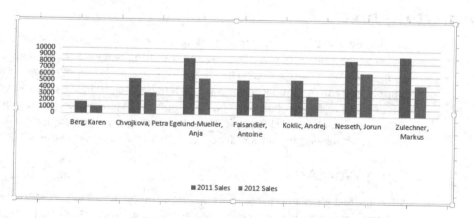

Although this "automatic" behavior suits most users fine in most circumstances, you can override it. To change the rotation explicitly, select the axis labels and then click the Orientation tool in the Alignment group of the Home tab:

For more precise control, double-click the axis labels to display the Format Axis task pane. Click the Size And Properties icon (the third icon from the left under the heading Axis Options), and specify an angle in the Custom Angle text box:

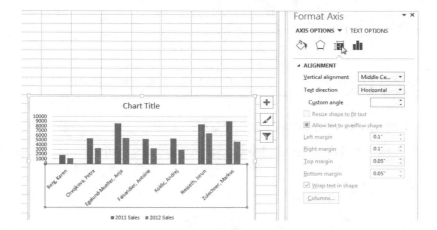

To make your labels angle in from the left, as they are shown in the figure here, specify a negative angle. To make them come in from the other side, specify a positive angle. Note that the Text Direction box might say Horizontal even for angled labels like the one shown in this figure. That is a small bug that you can easily ignore.

Changing the interval between axis labels

Occasionally, Excel crams labels together in unsightly ways. In Figure 20-7, for example, the labels along the depth axis overlap one another pointlessly. Making the chart larger will alleviate the crowding, of course, but if that's not convenient, you can simply ask Excel to display fewer labels. In this example, it's clear that the labels represent a sequence of months from January to December, so displaying every other or every third label would be adequate. To suppress some of the labels, double-click the axis, click the fourth icon in the array of icons under the heading Axis Options, expand the Labels heading, and then specify a number other than 1 in the Specify Interval Unit text box.

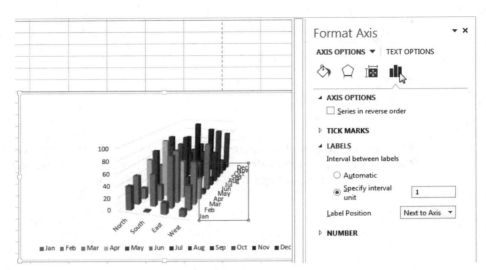

Figure 20-7 You can reduce crowding along this axis by specifying a number greater than 1 in the Specify Interval Unit box.

Changing the position of axis labels

By default, Excel displays axis labels adjacent to axes. Sometimes that's not ideal:

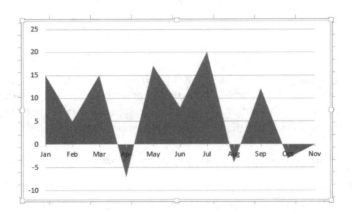

When the chart includes both negative and positive values, as this one does, Excel draws the horizontal axis appropriately at the 0 point of the vertical axis, but it's not smart enough to move the axis labels away from the negative values. You can fix this by double-clicking the axis, choosing the fourth icon under the heading Axis Options in the Format Axis task pane, and then choosing Low in the Label Position drop-down list. The result looks like this:

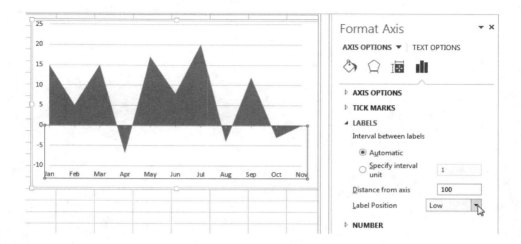

Changing the numeric format used by axis labels

When you first create a chart, Excel links the numeric format of your value-axis labels to that of the source data. Create a chart from data with the Currency format, for example, and Excel applies the Currency format to the labels on your value axis. Change the format of the source data, and the labels stay in step.

You can override this linkage by applying a specific numeric format to your axis labels. To do this, double-click the axis, click the Axis Options icon (the fourth icon under the heading Axis Options in the Format Axis task pane), open the Category drop-down list (under the heading Number), and choose the format you want. Additional options might appear when you do this. For example, if you choose the Currency format, the task pane will expand to give you options regarding the currency symbol, number of decimal places, and handling of negative values.

After you explicitly format your axis labels, Excel no longer copies formatting changes from the source data to the chart. To relink the format of your axis labels with that of the source data, revisit the task pane and select the Linked To Source check box.

Adding arrows, shapes, and text

The Insert Shapes group on the Format tab offers arrows and shapes you can deploy to annotate your charts. Here you'll also find a Text Box tool you can use for adding free text remarks. All of these features work the same way in charts as they do on the worksheet grid; for details, see Chapter 10.

Using sparklines

THE charting features introduced in Chapter 19, "Designing charts," create graphic objects that can be moved and sized independently from the worksheet. They reside in a *graphics layer* that lies atop the worksheet grid. In contrast to these familiar chart objects, *sparklines*, a feature that was introduced in Microsoft Excel 2010, are graphic representations of data that live within worksheet cells. Described by their inventor, Edward Tufte, as "intense, simple, word-sized graphics," sparklines are ideal for situations in which simplicity and spatial economy matter more than graphic elaboration.

Figure 21-1 provides an example. Each sparkline in cells C3:C11 is a graphic summary of the monthly data in D3:J11. A glance at the sparklines tells us that Tony Madigan's numbers rose steadily through the first five months; that Gisli Olafsson's began flat and then picked up for a while; that Geert Camelbeke's began high and then dropped; and that the others' varied randomly. Gleaning this much information from a direct inspection of the numbers would be laborious.

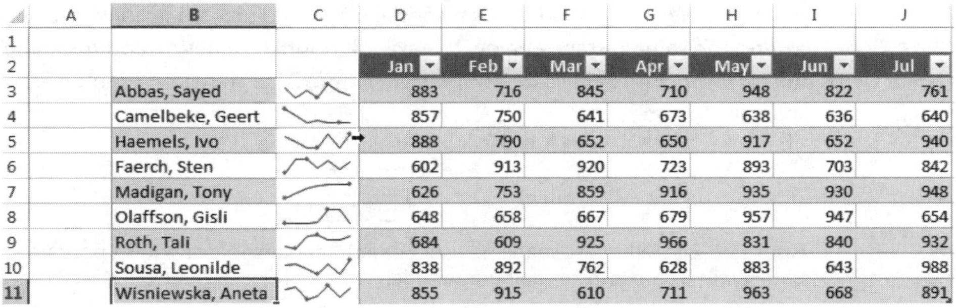

⊿	A	B	C	D	E	F	G	H	I	J
1										
2				Jan ▾	Feb ▾	Mar ▾	Apr ▾	May ▾	Jun ▾	Jul ▾
3		Abbas, Sayed		883	716	845	710	948	822	761
4		Camelbeke, Geert		857	750	641	673	638	636	640
5		Haemels, Ivo		888	790	652	650	917	652	940
6		Faerch, Sten		602	913	920	723	893	703	842
7		Madigan, Tony		626	753	859	916	935	930	948
8		Olaffson, Gisli		648	658	667	679	957	947	654
9		Roth, Tali		684	609	925	966	831	840	932
10		Sousa, Leonilde		838	892	762	628	883	643	988
11		Wisniewska, Aneta		855	915	610	711	963	668	891

Figure 21-1 Sparklines, such as those in column C of this example, let you implant miniature line or column charts within worksheet cells.

Creating sparklines

To create a sparkline, select the cell where you want the sparkline to appear and then click the Insert tab. The Sparklines group appears, more or less in the center of the Insert tab:

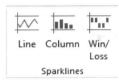

Choose a chart type from the three offerings here, and then fill out the ensuing dialog box:

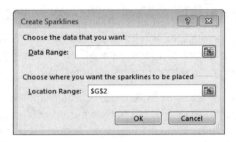

In the Data Range field, point to the cell or cells whose data you want to plot; in the Location Range field, enter the location of the new sparkline.

The first two options, Line and Column, are self-explanatory. The third choice might not be obvious. A Win/Loss sparkline is a special kind of column chart in which all negative values extend the same distance below the axis, all positive values extend the same distance above the axis, and zero values are not plotted. Figure 21-2 shows an example of a Win/Loss sparkline.

Figure 21-2 A Win/Loss sparkline uses column markers to distinguish positive and negative values, without regard to their magnitude.

You can use a Win/Loss sparkline to show which divisions or time periods generated profit and which did not, to depict a sports team's won-lost record through the course of a season, and to present other data sets in which the direction of an outcome is more important than its magnitude.

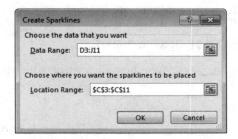

Creating groups of sparklines

It often makes sense to create groups of related sparklines—such as the ones in column C in Figure 21-1. You can do this in either of two ways. The first is to create one member of the group—say, the sparkline in cell C3 in Figure 21-1. After you do that, you can simply drag the fill handle to generate the remainder of the set. Excel copies the sparkline attributes of the first cell to the rest of the range, just as it would replicate a worksheet formula or a set of formatting parameters.

The second way to create a set of related sparklines is to specify the entire block at once. To set up the sparklines in Figure 21-1, for example, you could fill out the Create Sparklines dialog box like this:

Whichever way you create the related sparklines, Excel treats the set as a group. When you select any cell within the group, Excel draws a blue rectangle around the entire group, and any formatting changes you make are applied to the whole set. If this is not what you want—for example, if you need to change the weight or color of a particular sparkline within the group—select any member of the group and then click Ungroup. If you change your mind, select the entire set and click Group.

Expanding a set of sparklines

The monthly figures in Figure 21-1 extend from January through July. What do you do when the August numbers arrive? The simplest way to expand the sparklines is to make the original data set a table. (Select a cell and press Ctrl+T. For more information, see "Creating a table" in Chapter 22, "Managing information in tables.") When you add new columns to the right edge of a table, the new columns join the table, and formulas and charts that reference the table automatically incorporate the new data.

Customizing sparklines

When you select one or more cells that contain sparklines, Excel displays a new Design tab under the heading Sparkline Tools:

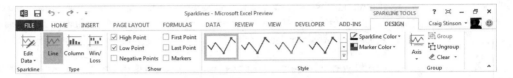

You can use this tab to customize the color (and, in the case of line sparklines, the weight) of chart markers, to emphasize particular points in a sparkline, to switch a sparkline from one chart type to another, and to modify a sparkline's axes.

Changing the sparkline color and weight

You can change the color of a sparkline by choosing from the gallery in the Style group:

Click here to expand the gallery

If you don't find the color you want, click Sparkline Color and choose from the array of theme colors and standard colors that appears. If those options still don't meet your needs, click Sparkline Color and then click More Colors. To change the weight of a line sparkline—that is, to make the line thicker or thinner—click Sparkline Color and then Weight.

Emphasizing particular points

You can use the check boxes in the Show group to draw attention to particular points in a sparkline—the highest or lowest point, the first or last point, or any points with negative values. If you select High Point, for example, Excel plants a marker on the high point of a line sparkline or uses a contrasting color to draw the highest column in a column sparkline. You can select as many or as few of the check boxes in the Show group as you need or want to, and you can use the Marker Color drop-down list to tailor the colors of various marker types individually.

In keeping with its minimalist approach to graphic communication, Excel draws sparklines by default without axes. (You can add a horizontal axis if you want; see the following section.) If your data includes negative as well as positive numbers and you don't want to add a horizontal axis, you'll probably need to mark the negative points.

For sparklines that traverse a wide range of data points, marking the high and low values can be illuminating. In the following example, the high and low markers make it clear that the low price in this 12-month data series occurred near the beginning of the date range and the high point occurred near the end:

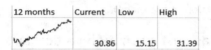

Customizing axes

Sparklines appear by default without axes. You can add a horizontal axis (but not a vertical axis) by clicking Axis (in the Group group) and choosing Show Axis:

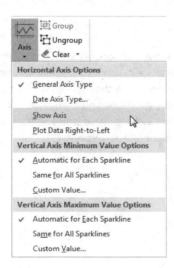

Note that if your sparkline's data range lies entirely above or below zero and you use default scaling for the vertical axis, you will not see a horizontal axis even if you choose Show Axis. To adjust the default vertical-axis scaling, see the following section.

Setting minimum and maximum values for the vertical axis

By default, Excel scales a sparkline's vertical axis so that the minimum and maximum values are just below and above the data range. These default scale settings are called *Automatic* and are designed to make the sparkline fit snugly within the vertical confines of its cell. (This scaling behavior differs from the default scaling of independent—that is, nonspark-line—charts.) In some circumstances, you might want to override the automatic scaling. In column sparklines, for example, the lowest value might be barely visible if the axis mini-mum is set to Automatic:

To change the vertical-axis scaling, click Axis and then choose Custom Value (in either the Minimum Value or Maximum Value section of the menu).

Plotting a group of sparklines against a common vertical axis

Although formatting attributes for a sparkline within a group are applied to all members of the group, scaling calculations are performed individually. That enables each sparkline within a group to fit well within its cell. If you prefer to see a set of sparklines plotted along a common axis, click Axis and then choose Same For All Sparklines (in either the Minimum Value or Maximum Value section of the menu).

Using a time-scaled horizontal axis

Excel ordinarily plots sparkline points evenly across the horizontal axis. If your data is asso-ciated with dates and the dates are not evenly spaced, you might prefer a time-scaled axis. With time scaling, points are plotted according to where they fall along the time axis. To switch from ordinary scaling to time-axis scaling, click Axis and then choose Date Axis Type. In the ensuing dialog box, specify the range that includes your dates. To cancel time-axis scaling, return to the same menu and choose General Axis Type.

Adding text to sparklines

Because sparklines are meant to be simple, Excel doesn't offer titling or annotation options. However, nothing precludes you from adding worksheet data to a cell that contains a sparkline. In the following example, the sparkline cell includes the text MSFT 2009:

You might need to adjust the alignment of text (for example, change the vertical alignment from Bottom to Top) to keep the verbal message distinct from the graphic.

Removing sparklines

Because sparklines are kin to cell formats, the action of removing them is called *clearing*. To clear a sparkline or a group of sparklines, on the Sparkline Tools Design tab, click Clear and then choose Clear Selected Sparklines or Clear Selected Sparkline Groups.

PART 7

Managing databases and tables

Managing information in tables

MICROSOFT EXCEL 2013 offers an extensive set of features for managing information in tables. You'll find these features invaluable for almost any kind of tabular work—whether it's a simple list of names and phone numbers or something much more complex, such as a list of transactions that includes tax or discount calculations, subtotals, and totals.

If you are coming to Excel 2013 from a version prior to Excel 2007, here are some advances in table management you will enjoy:

- **Autoexpansion**   If you add a row directly below the last row of a table or add a column directly to the right of a table, the table expands to incorporate the new row or column. All table styles, conditional formatting, calculations, and data validation rules extend to the new row or column. Charts based on data from the table also are similarly updated. Likewise, if you add a new column adjacent to the table, the column is automatically incorporated into the table definition.

- **Structured referencing**   Formulas that reference elements of a table can use column names and other tags in place of ordinary cell addresses. This kind of referencing, exemplified in Figure 22-1, makes table calculations self-documenting and enhances reliability.

- **Filtering improvements**   It's easier now to filter a table so that you see only the rows in which you're currently interested. You can filter on multiple criteria or on icon sets applied via conditional formatting. You can also use filters based on dynamic date definitions, such as last week or the current quarter.

- **Formula replication**   If you add a column that performs calculations based on table data (a column such as the one that generates total scores in Figure 22-1), Excel automatically replicates the calculation formula throughout the column.

- **Removal of duplicate data**   A simple command lets you highlight and (optionally) remove duplicate rows from a table.

- **Table styles**   Excel 2013 comes with a large library of styles you can use to apply gorgeous and consistent formatting to your tables. The styles are intelligent and dynamic. If you use a style that adds banding to a table (displaying alternate rows in contrasting colors), the banding adjusts correctly to changes in sorting, filtering, and table dimensions. You can also create your own table styles or customize any of the existing styles.

E2	▾	:	✕	✓	*fx*	=SUM(SATScores[@[Critical Reading]:[Math]])	

	A	B	C	D	E	F
1	Student ▾	Critical Readir ▾	Writing ▾	Math ▾	Total ▾	
2	Aaberg, Jesper	418	695	518	1631	
3	Aalling, Lene	465	632	557	1654	
4	Abbas, Syed	463	740	549	1752	
5	Abola, Lina	466	486	587	1539	
6	Abrus, Luka	520	694	544	1758	
7	Abu-Dayah, Ahmad	470	602	537	1609	
8	Adalsteinsson, Gudmundur	533	716	549	1798	
9	Adolphi, Stephan	476	793	570	1839	
10	Agarwal, Manoj	468	631	548	1647	
11	Agarwal, Nupur	441	792	562	1795	
12	Alad, Hatim	570	792	560	1922	
13	Akın, Çigdem	503	788	554	1845	
14	Alboni, Ezio	551	791	556	1898	
15	Alexieva-Bosseva, Diliana	498	653	562	1713	
16	Allen, Tony	466	556	525	1547	
17	Almosnino, Gilead	414	699	549	1662	
18	Alverca, Luis	497	466	545	1508	
19	Alverca, Luis	581	451	519	1551	
20	Alwan, Antonio	402	617	568	1587	
21	Ambrus, Zsolt	488	400	539	1427	
22	Amireh, Kamil	547	438	536	1521	
23	Amitai, Zwie	456	619	567	1642	
24	Anand, Deepak	536	409	559	1504	
25	Anashkin, Oleg	546	514	551	1611	
26	Andersen, Elizabeth A.	485	604	558	1647	
27	Andersen, Erik	539	505	558	1602	
28	Andersen, Erik	401	794	551	1746	
29	Andersen, Erik	495	633	555	1683	
30	Andersen, Erik	538	570	510	1618	
31	Andersen, Henriette Thaulow	410	507	528	1445	
32	Andersen, Thomas	555	657	547	1759	
33	Andrade, Diogo	504	756	566	1826	
34	Andrade, Diogo	512	765	571	1848	
35	Antebi, Roy	382	791	536	1709	
36	Arndt, Torsten	420	681	525	1626	

Figure 22-1 Structured referencing, exemplified by the formula in E2, makes calculations easier to understand and less prone to error.

How to organize a table

In a sense, you can call anything you put in a contiguous block of spreadsheet cells a *table*, but in Excel the term has a more specific meaning. It refers to a block of data organized so that each row refers to an item (such as a person in an address list, a sale in a transaction log, or a product in a product catalog) and each column contains one piece of information about that item (for example, the postal code of a contact, the date of a sale, or the catalog number of a product). In addition, for a block of data to become a table, you have to designate it as such. (See "Creating a table," next.)

Typically, the worksheet range defined as a table should have the following characteristics:

- The top row should consist of labels, with each label describing the contents of the column beneath it. Each label should be unique. (The labels row is not mandatory, but if you omit it, Excel generates one for you by using default column names.)

- Each column should contain the same kind of information.

- Each category of information you want to be able to sort by, search on, or otherwise manipulate individually should occupy a separate column.

Creating a table

After you have some data in a worksheet range, you can designate that range as a table by selecting any cell within it and pressing Ctrl+T or Ctrl+L. That's the easy way. If you want to work a little harder, you can click Table in the Tables group on the Insert tab. Either way, start by selecting a single cell anywhere in the table range before issuing the command. Excel figures out the dimensions of the table for you and asks for confirmation in the Create Table dialog box:

Unless the program has made some kind of mistake, you can click OK to create your table. If you select more than one cell but less than the entire range before pressing Ctrl+T, Excel tries to create a table out of the specific cells you selected.

> **Note**
>
> Many features of Excel tables do not work if your workbook is opened in Compatibility mode. You must convert a workbook you have saved with the Excel 97–2003 Workbook file type to an Excel 2013 workbook to get the new functionality. See "File formats" in Chapter 2, "Exploring Excel fundamentals," for details about converting a Compatibility-mode workbook to native Excel format.

Overwriting default headers

Notice that, in addition to recognizing the size of the table, Excel figures out whether the top row of your range is a header row—a row of column labels. If your range does not include such a row or if, for some reason, you choose to clear the My Table Has Headers check box in the Create Table dialog box, Excel creates a header row for you using labels such as Column 1, Column 2, and so on. Default headers like these are both uninformative and unattractive; it's far better to set up your own descriptive headers before creating the table. But if you omit this step, you can always override the defaults later by selecting the header cells and typing over them, just as if they were ordinary worksheet cells. (They're not quite ordinary data, actually; Excel won't let you delete them, and if you try to clear a header, you'll just get the default back.)

Turning a table back into an ordinary range

If the need arises to turn a table back into an ordinary worksheet range, select any cell or block of cells within the table. Then click Convert To Range in the Tools group on the Table Tools Design tab. Click Yes to answer the confirmation prompt. Note that after you change a table into a regular range, the formatting turns into regular cell formatting. This can cause unexpected behavior if you ever turn the range back into a table. See "Formatting tables," later in this chapter, for details about managing table and cell formatting.

INSIDE OUT   Check the ribbon

An easy way to tell whether a range is a table is to select a cell in the range and look at the ribbon. If you see a Table Tools tab, the current list has been converted to a table.

Naming a table

When you designate a range as a table, Excel assigns a name to that table and displays the name in the Properties group on the Table Tools Design tab:

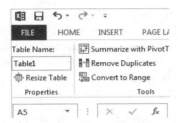

As this example shows, Excel uses default names (Table1, Table2, and so on) unless you supply your own names. Does the name matter? Perhaps. Formulas that take advantage of structured referencing use the table name, and a descriptive name serves the purpose of self-documentation better than a default name. For example, in the formula

=SUM(Scores[Math])

the word *Scores* is the table's name. (The formula sums the values from the Math column of the Scores table.)

Giving a meaningful name to a table is particularly useful when you have multiple tables on a single worksheet and formulas that refer to the tables. By using names for the tables, you can instantly tell when looking at a formula which table it is referencing.

It's definitely worthwhile to assign an intelligible name to your table if you think you might record or write, at some point, a macro that references the table. That way, your macro code will be easier to understand (easier for you and easier for anyone else who sees your code). Moreover, if you record a macro that references Table1 and you subsequently name the table SurveyData, your macro will no longer perform as expected and will cause you considerable vexation. It's best to form the habit of naming objects when you create them.

To change a table's current name (default or otherwise), select a cell within the table and click the Table Tools Design tab. Then type the new name in the Table Name box in the Properties group.

Expanding a table

To add a new row to the end of a table, go to the bottom-right cell of the table (ignoring the total row, if there is one) and press the Tab key. Excel extends the table for you, no questions asked, copying all formatting and formulas in the process. When you get to the last column in the new row, press Tab to create yet another new row. Thus, after you have created the stub of a table, you can expand it downward simply by typing in the usual way and pressing Tab between cells (or, at any rate, at the end of each row).

Selecting rows and columns within a table

Excel makes it easy to select rows and columns within a table. If you rest the pointer on the left edge of the first cell in a row, the pointer changes to a solid arrow. Click once, and you've selected the row. If your table happens to begin in column A of the worksheet, be sure you rest the pointer inside the first cell rather than on the worksheet frame. On the frame, the pointer also changes to a solid arrow, but clicking here will select the entire worksheet row.

To select a column, rest the pointer near the top of the column's heading and then click. Clicking once selects the column's data, excluding the header and the total (if you have displayed the total row). Clicking a second time selects the entire column—header, data, and total.

To select the entire table, rest the pointer on the top-left corner of the first column's header. When you see the pointer turn down and to the right, click. Click once for the data only or twice for everything—data, headers, and totals.

Selecting with the keyboard is even easier, particularly with a large table when the top and left edges are out of sight. Pressing Shift+Spacebar selects the current row, regardless of which cell is selected. Pressing Ctrl+Spacebar selects the current column's data, omitting the header and total. Pressing Shift+Ctrl+Spacebar or Ctrl+A selects all the table's data.

Multiple key presses expand the selection predictably: Pressing Shift+Spacebar twice selects the entire current worksheet row. Pressing Ctrl+Spacebar twice selects the current table column, with the header and total. Pressing Ctrl+Spacebar three times selects the entire current worksheet column. Pressing Shift+Ctrl+Spacebar or Ctrl+A twice gets the entire table—headers and totals included. Pressing that combination a third time selects all gazillion cells of the worksheet.

Note that pressing Tab creates a new table row above the total row, if your table has a total row. The total row simply moves down one row to accommodate your new data, and Excel updates the formulas appropriately. (For more about the total row, see "Adding totals to a table" later in this chapter.) If you don't have a total row in your table, you can also extend the table by typing in the blank row below the bottom row of the table. Pressing Tab to extend the table works whether you have a total row or not.

Automatic expansion works for columns as well as rows. If you type in any row of the column directly to the right of a table, Excel expands the table to include the new column. If the new data is a formula, the formula is replicated throughout the column.

If you don't want the table to automatically expand or automatically fill columns with formulas, you can turn off these options. Click File, and then click Options. Select the Proofing category, and click AutoCorrect Options. In the AutoCorrect dialog box, shown in Figure 22-2, click the AutoFormat As You Type tab. Clear the Include New Rows And Columns In Table check box to prevent Excel from expanding the table, and clear the Fill Formulas In Tables To Create Calculated Columns check box to prevent Excel from filling entire columns with identical formulas.

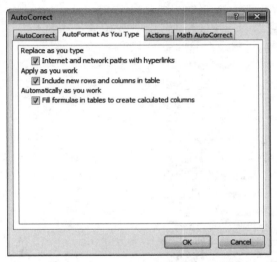

Figure 22-2 Use the AutoCorrect dialog box to control table expansion.

If you're not currently using a total row in your table, you'll find a minuscule handle in the bottom-right corner of the cell occupying the bottom-right corner of your table. This handle gives you yet another way to expand your table. Usually, it's easier just to add data and let Excel expand the table. But if you want to add several new rows or columns all at once, the handle is a good way to do it.

Chapter 22

Adding totals to a table

To add a total row to your table, select any cell within the table and then select the Total Row check box in the Table Style Options group on the Table Tools Design tab. You can toggle the row on or off by selecting or clearing this check box. Figure 22-3 shows an example of a total row.

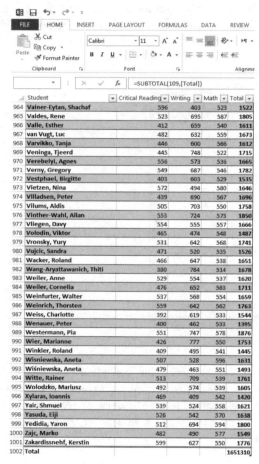

Figure 22-3 The total row uses the SUBTOTAL function to perform summary calculations.

By default, the total row applies the SUBTOTAL function, with a *Function_num* argument of 109, to the rightmost column of the table. (Using 109 in the *Function_num* argument creates a sum that ignores all rows hidden by filters.) That generates a sum in the bottom-right corner—which might not be what you want. In Figure 22-3, for example, it would make more sense to show an average in that cell than a sum. It would also be useful to calculate averages in the Critical Reading, Writing, and Math columns, as well as in the Total column. All that is easy to do. When you click the small arrow at the right edge of a total row cell, a list of alternative functions appears:

1000	Zajc, Marko		482	490	577	1549	
1001	Zakardissnehf, Kerstin		599	627	550	1776	
1002	Total					1651310	▼
1003						None	
1004						Average	
1005						Count	
1006						Count Numb	
1006						Max	
1006						Min	
1007						Sum	
1008						StdDev	
						Var	
						More Functi	

You can make the same list appear in any other total row cell (not just the rightmost) by selecting the cell and clicking the arrow that appears. You can also type directly over any of the total row cells. Here's how you might make the total row look if you wanted to replace the sums with averages:

999	Yedidia, Yaron		512	694	594	1800
1000	Zajc, Marko		482	490	577	1549
1001	Zakardissnehf, Kerstin		599	627	550	1776
1002	Averages		497.062	605.426	548.822	1651.31

Here are a few more points to note about the total row:

- The total row does not limit you to the commonplace aggregation functions. With the help of the More Functions command in the list, you can create any kind of formulas you want.

- Because the choices in the list—AVERAGE, COUNT, COUNT NUMBERS, and so on—generate formulas based on the SUBTOTAL function (using arguments in the 101–111 range), they ignore rows that are hidden by filters. If you want to aggregate based on all rows except those you manually hide, subtract 100 from the first argument function. For example, change SUBTOTAL(101,column) to SUBTOTAL(1,column). If you want aggregate calculations based on all rows, ignoring the column filter settings, change the formulas to standard aggregate functions. For example, substitute SUM(column) for SUBTOTAL(109,column).

- After you customize the formulas in the total row, turning the total row off and then back on retains your customized formulas. If you frequently toggle the total row off and on, consider putting the command on your Quick Access Toolbar. (Click on the Design tab under Table Tools, right-click the Total Row check box, and select Add To Quick Access Toolbar.)

Chapter 22

Sorting tables and other ranges

Excel provides numerous ways to sort worksheet ranges. You can use the same techniques to sort both tables and ranges that you have not defined as tables. (We'll call the latter *lists*.)

You can sort by column or row, in ascending or descending order, and with capitalization considered or ignored. (When you sort by row, your rows are rearranged and the columns remain in the same order. When you sort by column, the opposite kind of rearrangement occurs.) You can even define custom sorting sequences so that, for example, your company's division names always appear in a particular order, regardless of their alphabetic sequence. Excel 2013 can sort by as many fields as you want, not just the three-at-a-time limit of some previous versions. And you can sort by using the format of the cells, not just the value. Sorting a table is essentially the same as sorting a simple list in the worksheet. Having headings at the top of the range is helpful but not necessary.

Sorting on a single column

To sort on a single column—the Last Name column in Figure 22-4, for example—select one cell anywhere within that column. Then click either the Sort A To Z button in the Sort & Filter group on the Data tab (to arrange the column in ascending numeric or alphabetic order) or the Sort Z To A button (to do the opposite). Excel sorts in the order you want on the column in which the selection resides. If you don't want to switch to the Data tab on the ribbon, right-click a cell and then click the appropriate sort command on the Sort menu.

You'll find the Staff.xlsx file with the other examples on the companion website.

When you click one of the Sort buttons, Excel assumes you want to sort the rows. If you're sorting a table, the table definition determines whether the first row holds headers (and should not be sorted) or data (and should be sorted). If you're sorting a list, Excel guesses whether the first row includes headers or not. If the quick command version doesn't meet your needs, you need to use the Sort dialog box.

To use the Sort dialog box, click the Sort button in the Sort & Filter group on the Data tab. (It's also available when you right-click a cell in the range you want to sort.) If this is the first time you've sorted the current range, the Sort dialog box, shown in Figure 22-5, appears. If you've sorted the range before, the dialog box displays the sort parameters you last used.

If your data includes a header row that should remain in place while the other rows are sorted, Excel usually recognizes that fact and selects the My Data Has Headers check box. If Excel, for some reason, fails to notice a header row or if it detects a header row when one isn't really there, you can correct it before clicking OK.

Figure 22-4 One easy way to sort on a single column is to right-click a cell in the column and choose Sort.

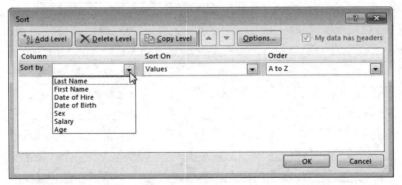

Figure 22-5 In the Sort dialog box, you can specify the field to sort by, the order to sort by, and whether to sort on values, colors, or icons.

Sorting on more than one column

You can sort on as many columns as you want. To sort on more than one column, click the Add Level button in the Sort dialog box. For example, to sort the staff list shown in Figure 22-4 first in descending order by salary and then in ascending order by last name, you fill out the dialog box as shown in Figure 22-6. Excel then rearranges the list as shown in Figure 22-7.

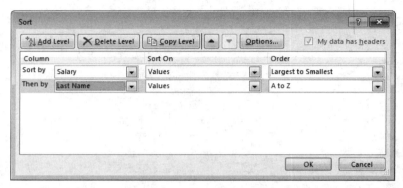

Figure 22-6 To sort on two or more levels, click Add Level and fill out the expanded dialog box.

	A	B	C	D	E	F	G
	Last Name	First Name	Date of Hire	Date of Birth	Sex	Salary	Age
2	Aaberg	Jesper	1/12/92	5/28/64	M	100000	48
3	Aalling	Lene	4/21/99	11/24/77	F	100000	34
4	Camelbeke	Geert	11/17/77	3/31/74	M	100000	38
5	Casqueiro	Joao	11/1/95	6/2/70	M	100000	42
6	Eremenko	Alexei	7/31/90	9/19/61	F	100000	51
7	Klimov	Sergey	6/30/75	6/16/77	M	100000	35
8	Kupkova	Helena	11/20/74	10/17/49	M	100000	63
9	Adalsteinsson	Gudmundur	7/4/89	3/26/59	M	99000	53
10	Klco	Rene	7/23/94	2/28/61	M	99000	51
11	Kurmann	Benno	3/27/91	7/20/64	M	99000	48
12	Levitan	Michal	3/11/97	8/1/67	F	99000	45
13	Balazs	Erzsebet	7/12/99	9/20/54	M	98000	58
14	Junca	David	12/4/97	7/30/75	M	98000	37
15	Abola	Lina	11/22/07	9/2/75	M	97000	37
16	Buschmann	Monika	3/30/81	4/18/51	F	97000	61
17	Gazit	Inbar	5/5/84	6/13/71	M	97000	41
18	Haemels	Ivo	3/5/97	7/18/68	M	97000	44
19	Hanif	Kerim	6/23/00	3/7/64	F	97000	48
20	Johannsen	Jens	6/17/74	11/29/62	M	96000	49
21	Kirwan	Yvette	7/24/83	5/30/70	M	96000	42
22	Fonteneau	Karl	4/26/95	6/7/76	F	95000	36
23	Kirilov	Stanimir	5/3/80	9/22/75	M	95000	37
24	Bento	Paula	7/8/89	5/14/55	M	94000	57
25	Blaauboer	Nils	9/12/92	4/15/70	M	94000	42
26	Casqueiro	Joao	4/17/90	11/8/67	F	94000	45
27	Ersan	Ebru	9/8/76	6/26/61	F	94000	51
28	Garghentini	Davide	6/24/88	10/22/71	M	94000	41
29	Gibbins	Phil	1/26/93	12/3/76	F	94000	35
30	Khoury	Soohad Michael	3/19/99	11/26/49	M	94000	62
31	Komashinsky	Ivan	1/23/75	10/22/56	F	94000	56

Figure 22-7 The rows are now arranged in descending order by salary, with rows of common salary sorted in ascending order by last name.

Sorting only part of a list

If you sort a table, Excel always sorts the entire table, regardless of how many cells within the table you initially select.

In a regular range, if you select a single cell before sorting, Excel scans the area surrounding the selected cell, highlights the entire contiguous range of cells, and assumes you want to sort that entire range. If you want to sort only part of a range, start by selecting only those rows and columns you want to sort. Then click Data, Sort. To sort rows 10 through 20 in Figure 22-4, for example, you start by selecting A10:G20. If you select one column from something that appears to be a list, Excel asks you whether you really do want to sort just that one column or whether you want to expand the selection to include the entire list. Most of the time, you'll probably want to sort the entire list, so either convert the list to a table or be sure to select only a single cell before you sort the list.

You can't specify a sort range in the Sort dialog box. You must select the range before you open the dialog box. The dialog box doesn't indicate the range Excel is about to sort. Check your worksheet immediately after a sort, and use the Undo command if you don't like what you get.

Sorting by column

Thus far, our examples have involved sorting by row—leaving the columns alone. You also can sort by column, leaving the order of the rows alone. If you turned a list into a table, you cannot sort by column. This makes sense because a table is always row oriented. You're more likely to use horizontal sorting with a grid, which doesn't function as a table anyway.

To sort by column, follow these steps:

1. Select the range you want to sort—excluding any row headings that shouldn't be sorted.

2. Click the Sort button in the Sort & Filter group on the Data tab.

3. Click the Options button in the Sort dialog box, and then select the Sort Left To Right option in the Sort Options dialog box that is displayed, as shown in Figure 22-8.

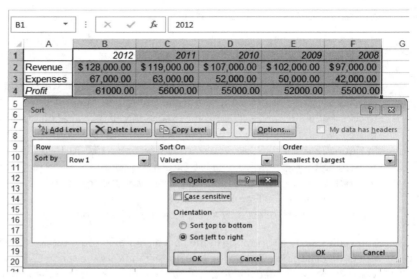

Figure 22-8 Use the Sort Left To Right option to reorder the years into an ascending sequence.

4. Click OK to return to the main part of the Sort dialog box.

5. Select the row you want to sort by and the direction of the sort. Add rows to sort by if you need them.

6. Click OK.

Figure 22-9 shows the result of this left-to-right sort.

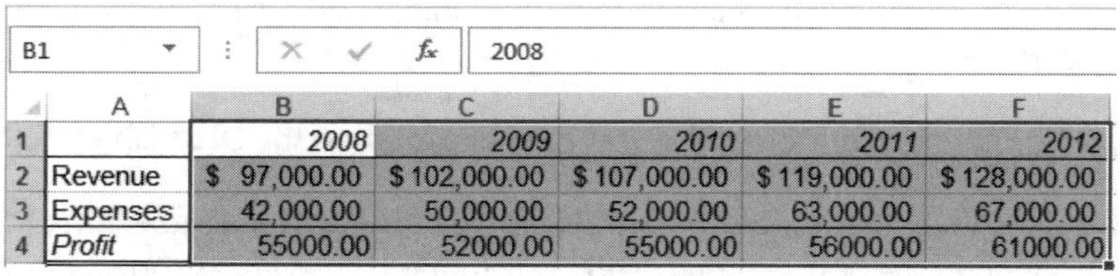

▲	A	B	C	D	E	F
1		2008	2009	2010	2011	2012
2	Revenue	$ 97,000.00	$ 102,000.00	$ 107,000.00	$ 119,000.00	$ 128,000.00
3	Expenses	42,000.00	50,000.00	52,000.00	63,000.00	67,000.00
4	Profit	55000.00	52000.00	55000.00	56000.00	61000.00

Figure 22-9 The lateral sort specified in Figure 22-8 generates this rearrangement of the data.

Excel doesn't recognize row headings in column-oriented sorts, so it's best to select the range you want to sort, rather than just a single cell, when you're sorting laterally. If you select only one cell, Excel proposes to sort all the contiguous cells, including the labels in your first column.

Sorting cells that contain formulas

You need to exercise caution when sorting cells that contain formulas with cell references. If you sort by row, references to other cells in the same row will be correct after the sort, but references to cells in other rows of the list will no longer be correct.

Similarly, if you sort by column, references to other cells in the same columns will be correct after the sort, but references to cells in other columns will be broken. With either kind of sort, relative references to cells outside the list will be broken by the sort. Relative references from cells outside the sort range will keep referring to the same cells as before—even if the contents of the cell are moved by the sort.

Figure 22-10 demonstrates the hazards of sorting a range that contains formulas. Row 5 of the worksheet calculates the year-to-year change in profit using relative-reference formulas. Cell C5, for example, uses the formula =C4–B4 to calculate the difference between the 2007 profits and the 2006 profits. Each of the other formulas also references the cell directly to its left.

If you include row 5 in the sort range, the formulas get sorted along with the other columns. Each formula in row 5 still references the cell to the left, but B5 now shows an error because B4 tries to subtract the text *Profit* from the number 61,000.

If, on the other hand, you exclude row 5 from the sort range, the formulas keep working, but the meaning of the calculation is different. When the columns are sorted by row 1 in ascending order, the formulas in row 5 give the change from the *preceding* year. After you sort the columns by row 1 in descending order, the formulas in row 5 give the change from the *following* year. Both before and after the sort, the formulas give the change from the previous column.

Sorting is different from cutting and pasting cells. If you pick up each column and move it to its new location, Excel updates the formulas appropriately after each move. If you do it by clicking Sort on the Data tab, Excel doesn't adjust the references.

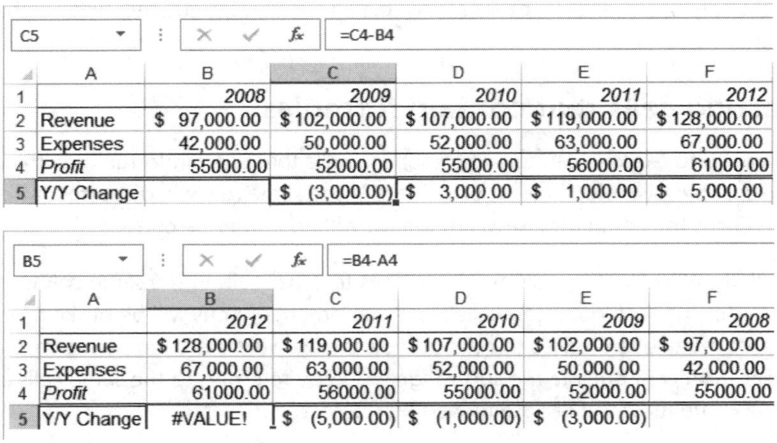
C5 =C4-B4

	A	B	C	D	E	F
1		2008	2009	2010	2011	2012
2	Revenue	$ 97,000.00	$ 102,000.00	$ 107,000.00	$ 119,000.00	$ 128,000.00
3	Expenses	42,000.00	50,000.00	52,000.00	63,000.00	67,000.00
4	Profit	55000.00	52000.00	55000.00	56000.00	61000.00
5	Y/Y Change		$ (3,000.00)	$ 3,000.00	$ 1,000.00	$ 5,000.00

B5 =B4-A4

	A	B	C	D	E	F
1		2012	2011	2010	2009	2008
2	Revenue	$ 128,000.00	$ 119,000.00	$ 107,000.00	$ 102,000.00	$ 97,000.00
3	Expenses	67,000.00	63,000.00	52,000.00	50,000.00	42,000.00
4	Profit	61000.00	56000.00	55000.00	52000.00	55000.00
5	Y/Y Change	#VALUE!	$ (5,000.00)	$ (1,000.00)	$ (3,000.00)	

Figure 22-10 Sorting the columns of the worksheet from the order shown in the top table to the order shown in the bottom table breaks the formulas in row 5.

To avoid the problems associated with sorting ranges containing formulas, observe the following rules:

- In formulas that reference cells outside the sort range, use only absolute references.
- When sorting by row, avoid formulas that reference cells in other rows. If you must use such formulas, reference cells by name, not by address.
- When sorting by column, avoid formulas that reference cells in other columns. If you must use such formulas, reference cells by name, not by address.
- Cells outside the sort range can make relative references to cells inside the sort range, but they always reference the cell location, not the sorted contents. To exclude the cells from the sort range, insert a blank row or column to separate them from the sorted range.

Understanding the default sorting sequence in Excel

To avoid surprises, you should understand the following points about the way Excel sorts:

- Excel sorts cells according to their underlying values, not their current number formats. This means, for example, that Excel places a date cell formatted as November 16, 2012 ahead of a date cell formatted as 12/27/2012 (because the first date has a lower numeric value). If you type the two dates as text, Excel reverses their order.

- Excel sorts numeric values ahead of text values. The value 98052 is sorted ahead of the value 1 Microsoft Way, because the former is a number and the latter is text.

- Logical values are sorted after text, and FALSE is sorted before TRUE.

- Error values (#DIV/0!, #NAME?, #VALUE, #REF!, #N/A, #NUM!, and #NULL!) are sorted after logical values. Excel regards all error values as equivalent; that is, it leaves them in the order it finds them.

- Blanks are placed last, in both ascending and descending sorts.

- An apostrophe wins over a hyphen, which wins over a space, and all three come before letters and numbers. This means they are essentially ignored unless they are the only difference between entries.

- The sort order for text depends on many factors, including your current locale settings. If knowing the exact sort order is important for you, type the formula =**CHAR(ROW())** in cell A1. It returns a blank because the first character in the ANSI character set is not printable. Copy the formula down 255 rows. Convert the formula to values and sort it. That sort shows you the order Excel is using.

Sorting months, weekdays, or custom lists

Excel ordinarily sorts text in alphabetical order, but it can sort on the basis of any of its custom lists if you want it to do so. The program includes four custom lists by default (Sun, Mon, Tues, ...; Sunday, Monday, Tuesday, ...; Jan, Feb, Mar, ...; and January, February, March, ...). If you have a column consisting of these day or month labels, you can sort them in their proper chronological order. If you created other custom lists, you can sort text fields in the order of those lists as well.

For information about creating and using custom lists, see "Creating custom lists" in Chapter 8, "Worksheet editing techniques."

To sort on the basis of a custom list, simply select Custom List in the Order list in the Sort dialog box. The four default custom lists appear there, along with any others you have created.

You can use a custom list for any sort field you want. You could sort a column of month names using one custom list and a separate column of day names using a separate custom list, all within one sort operation.

Performing a case-sensitive sort

Usually when Excel sorts text, it disregards case variants entirely. In other words, the program regards the letter *A* as equivalent to the letter *a*. You can change this behavior by clicking Options in the Sort dialog box and then selecting the Case Sensitive check box.

If you're familiar with the standard character-encoding systems used by Windows (ANSI or Unicode), you might suppose that selecting the Case Sensitive check box would cause Excel to sort all capital letters before all lowercase letters. That, after all, is how those character-encoding systems are constructed. (The capital alphabet occupies the range 65 through 90—decimal notation)—and the lowercase alphabet resides at 97 through 122.) However, selecting the Case Sensitive check box does not cause Excel to perform a "straight" ANSI or Unicode sort. Instead, it makes the program put lowercase variants ahead of capital variants *of the same letter*.

For example, suppose the range A1:A4 holds the following four text values:

Pine
pine
tree
Tree

If you perform a default (not case-sensitive) ascending sort on these four cells, their order remains unchanged because *p* comes before *t* and Excel disregards the variation in case. If you sort again after selecting the Case Sensitive check box, the order becomes

pine
Pine
tree
Tree

because *p* now comes before *P* and *t* comes before *T*. In a conventional ANSI sort, you'd get

Pine
Tree
pine
tree

because all capitals come before all lowercase letters.

Filtering a list or table

Filtering a list or table means hiding all the rows except those that meet specified criteria. Excel provides two filtering methods: Simple, which uses lists on the header row, and Advanced, which uses a separate criteria range. The Advanced method can filter in place or extract a subset to another part of the worksheet. You can use both methods with tables and also with standard lists—as long as the lists have header rows.

Using filters

When you create a table, Excel adds filters to the header row automatically. To turn header row filters on or off, first select any cell in your table and then click the Filter button in the Sort & Filter group on the Data tab. When you turn on the filter, Excel displays small arrows next to each of the column headings. Clicking the arrow next to any heading reveals a list of the column's unique values, which you can use to specify filtering criteria.

INSIDE OUT   Display arrows for selected columns

Sometimes, you want to apply filtering criteria to only one or two of your columns. If you're working with a standard list—not a table—select only the column headings you want to use as filters (the columns must be adjacent to one another), and then click the Filter button. This makes it clear which columns you are using for filtering.

Let's look at an example. Suppose that from the list shown in Figure 22-4 you'd like to see only rows where the age is 34. To generate this subset, first make sure the filter arrows appear next to the column headings. If they don't, click the Filter button in the Sort & Filter group on the Data tab. Then click the small arrow next to the Age heading. Clear the Select All check box, select the 34 check box, and finally click OK. The result looks like Figure 22-11.

	A	B	C	D	E	F	G
1	Last Name ↓	First Name ▾	Date of Hire ▾	Date of Birth ▾	Sex ▾	Salary ↓	Age ▾
3	Aalling	Lene	4/21/99	11/24/77	F	100000	34
51	Anand	Deepak	1/6/97	6/2/78	M	88000	34
56	Andersen	Erik	1/12/99	9/24/78	M	86000	34
86	Banai	Yossi	2/19/75	10/13/78	M	82000	34
89	Bankov	Martin	1/14/85	7/24/78	M	81000	34
118	Berg	Anne-Jorun	7/27/81	2/19/78	F	74000	34
125	Lohndorf-Larsen	Lars	3/11/87	2/19/78	M	74000	34
192	Dryml	Jan	10/15/75	1/16/78	M	57000	34
197	Dunton	Bryn Paul	8/10/87	4/5/78	M	57000	34
240	Freitas	Victor	3/17/91	1/28/78	M	48000	34
253	Krieger	Doris	8/27/81	7/28/78	F	45000	34
260	Leoni	Alessandro	9/18/92	11/1/78	M	44000	34
281	Lang	Ingelise	1/29/85	11/16/77	F	41000	34
303	Gufler	Hans	1/16/94	2/3/78	M	36000	34
360	**Average**					**65,214**	**34**

Figure 22-11 Use the filter lists to display only rows in which the age is 34.

From the gaps in the row numbers shown in Figure 22-11, you can tell that Excel has hidden the rows that didn't meet the filtering criterion. To remind you that you have filtered your list, Excel also displays the filtered row numbers in a contrasting color.

Determining how many rows pass the filter

Immediately after you add a new filter, Excel displays the number of rows that meet your criteria on the status bar. This information is ephemeral, however. Fortunately, you can use the SUBTOTAL function to arrive at this number. The easiest way to add the SUBTOTAL function is to turn the list into a table. Press Ctrl+T, and click OK. Even if you change the table back to a range, you want it to be a table long enough to create SUBTOTAL formulas in a total row. After the list is a table, select the Total Row check box on the Design tab to create a total row with a default SUBTOTAL function. The default function displays a sum. To change it to a count, select any cell in the total row and click the small arrow. Click Count. Otherwise, you can create the SUBTOTAL function yourself.

Removing a filter

To remove a filter from a single column, click the small arrow to the right of the column heading and then click Clear Filter From Column. To remove all filters currently in effect, click the Clear button in the Sort & Filter group on the Data tab. To remove the filter arrows, click the Filter button in the Sort & Filter group on the Data tab. This removes the arrows from the header row cells. Converting a table to an ordinary range does automatically turn off the filters, but you can click the Filter button on the Data tab to turn the filters back on without turning the range back into an explicit table.

Using filter criteria in more than one column

You can specify filter criteria for your list in as many columns as you want. Filter your list on one column, filter the resulting list on another column, and repeat the process as many times as you want. Each successive application of a filter refines the list further so that the result includes only rows that meet all your criteria.

> **Note**
>
> Basic filter operations always show only the rows that satisfy the criteria for *all* the filtered columns. If you want to see rows that pass either the filter for one column or the filter for another, you need to use the Advanced Filter command.

Using a filter to find the top or bottom *n* items

You can use a filter to find the top or bottom *n* items in a numeric column or items that make up the top or bottom *n* percent of a column's total. Click the arrow for the column, click Number Filters, and then click Top 10. The dialog box shown in Figure 22-12 appears.

Figure 22-12 Use the Top 10 AutoFilter dialog box to zero in on the top or bottom *n* list elements.

The Top 10 AutoFilter dialog box has three boxes. In the first, you can select either Top or Bottom. In the second, you can specify any number from 1 to 500. In the third, you can select either Items or Percent.

Using a filter to display blank entries

If a column contains blank cells, you find a Blanks check box at the bottom of its filter list. (You open this list by clicking the small arrow to the right of the column header.) If you want to locate rows in which a particular column has no entry, select the Blanks check box as your criterion.

Using filters to select dates

Dates can often be frustrating to filter because you usually want to filter based on some kind of grouping. You don't just want March 13, 2012. You want all of March. Also, when filtering by dates, you often want to filter by dates that are relative to the present date. For example, you want to see the orders from last month, the plan for next year, or the invoices so far this year. Excel includes filter capabilities to make all these tasks simple.

If the column you are filtering by contains dates, the selection list automatically groups the dates into months and years. Click the small arrow for a column that contains dates, and you now see a list of years. You can then expand the years to see months:

To see individual dates for a month, expand the month heading.

In addition, clicking the Date Filters command in the Filter list gives you many date-specific options, including many that compare the date to the current day—such as Next Month or Last Month.

Using filters to specify more complex criteria

The example in Figure 22-11 used a single equality comparison for its criterion. That is, you asked Excel to display only rows in which the Age field was equal to a particular value, 34. Each data type column has a specialized list of the functions most common to that data type:

- Number filters include comparisons such as Greater Than, Between, and even Above Average.

- Date filters include comparisons such as Yesterday, Next Year, and All Dates In Quarter 1 (regardless of year).

- Text filters include comparisons such as Begins With and Contains.

These data type–specific filtering options can handle most of your basic needs.

Using custom filters to specify complex relationships

If you want to get even more complex, you can use the Custom Filter command. To access this command, click the small arrow to the right of a column heading, click the data type–specific menu (such as Number Filters or Date Filters), and then click Custom Filter. The Custom AutoFilter dialog box shown in Figure 22-13 appears. For numeric and date fields, the Custom Filter command is most useful when you use the Or option with two nonequal comparisons in the same column—for example, all the age values less than 25 or greater than 65. For text columns, the Custom Filter command lets you create *between* ranges and lets you use sophisticated wildcard comparisons. For example, you might create a filter to find names with *A* as the first letter and *e* as the third letter.

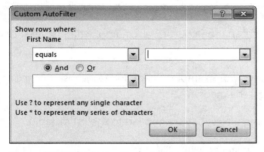

Figure 22-13 Use the Custom AutoFilter dialog box to apply more complex filter criteria to a single column.

You can enter one or two criteria in the Custom AutoFilter dialog box, and you can select from a full range of Excel relational operators. The list boxes on the left side of the dialog box provide a selection of relationships (Equals, Does Not Equal, Is Greater Than, and so on), and the list boxes on the right let you select the values that appear in your list. You can, of course, type directly in the boxes on the right, if you prefer that to fishing through the list for a value.

Suppose you want to see all the people on your Staff list with salaries greater than or equal to $90,000, as well as all those with salaries less than or equal to $30,000. After displaying the Custom AutoFilter dialog box for the Salary column, select Is Greater Than Or Equal To in the top-left box and type **90000** in the top-right box. Select the Or option, select Is Less Than Or Equal To in the bottom-left box, and type **30000** in the bottom-right box. If you neglect to select the Or option, you ask Excel for the names of employees who made both 90,000 or more and 30,000 or less, and you get an empty list.

Finding an alphabetical range of text values   To find all the text values in a column that fall within a particular range of letters, use the Custom AutoFilter dialog box and specify two criteria joined by And. For example, to find all last names beginning with B, C, or D, filter the Last Name column, and specify Is Greater Than Or Equal To B and Is Less Than E in the Custom AutoFilter dialog box.

Using wildcards in custom criteria The Custom AutoFilter dialog box accepts two kinds of wildcard characters. You can use the asterisk (*) to represent any sequence of characters or the question mark (?) to represent any single character. For example, to find all last names starting with B, you can specify Is Equal To B* in the Custom AutoFilter dialog box. To include a literal question mark or asterisk in a filter, precede the ? or * with a tilde (~).

Using the Advanced Filter command

In contrast to the Filter command, the Advanced Filter command lets you do the following:

- Specify criteria involving two or more columns and the conjunction OR.

- Specify three or more criteria for a particular column, where at least one OR conjunction is involved.

- Specify computed criteria (for example, all employees whose salaries are more than 25 percent greater than the median salary).

- See in printable form the filters that are applied to the list or table.

In addition, you can use the Advanced Filter command to extract rows from the range and place copies of those rows in another part of the current worksheet. As with a regular filter, you can use Advanced Filter whether you turn the list into a table or not. Some features—such as showing totals at the bottom—are much easier if you turn the list into a table.

TROUBLESHOOTING

I can't extract to a separate worksheet

You cannot extract rows from a list and place them on a separate worksheet. Your criteria range can be on a different worksheet, but the range you extract cannot. After you extract a set of rows, you can, of course, copy or move it to another location.

Specifying a criteria range

The Advanced Filter command, unlike the standard filter, requires that you specify filtering criteria in a worksheet range separate from your list or table. Because entire rows are hidden when the filter is executed, it's inadvisable to put the criteria range *alongside* the list. Instead, put it above the list or on a separate worksheet. A criteria range must consist of at least two rows. Type one or more column headings in the top row, and type your filtering criteria in the second and subsequent rows. With the exception of computed criteria, you must spell the headings in your criteria range exactly like those in your list. (Capitalization and formatting don't have to match, but spelling does.) To ensure accuracy, the best way to create these headings is by selecting the column headings in your list and then using the Copy and Paste commands.

Keep in mind that a criteria range does not have to include headings for every column in the list. Columns that are not involved in the selection process don't have to be part of the criteria range.

An example using two columns joined by OR

Figure 22-14 shows a list of homes for sale. (The underscored items in column A are hyperlinks to pictures of the houses.) Suppose you're interested in homes with a lot size (column H) of more than two acres. You'll also consider homes on smaller lots if they're in the elementary-school district U (column O). To filter the list so that homes meeting either criterion are shown, begin by creating the criteria range shown in Figure 22-15. We created this criteria range above the list in three newly inserted rows.

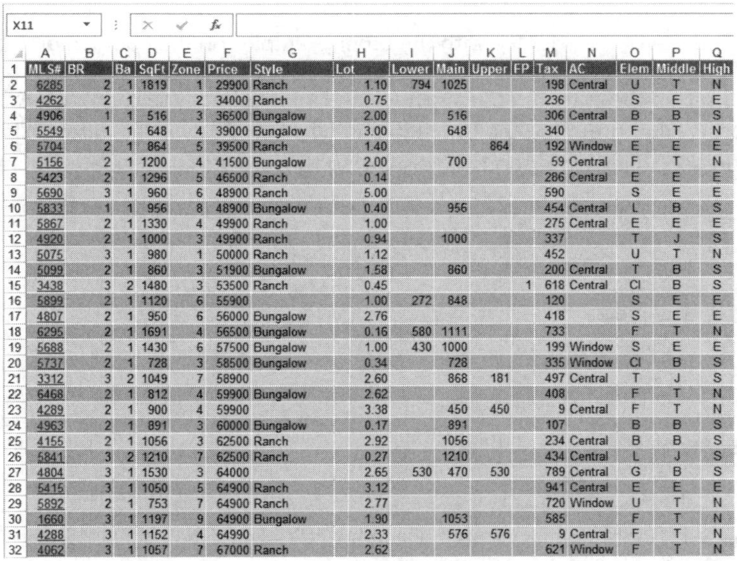

Figure 22-14 Use the Advanced Filter command to locate homes within this list that meet specific criteria.

S3

	A	B	C	D	E	F	G	H	I	J	K	L	M	N	O	P	Q
1	Elem	Lot															
2	U																
3		>2															
4																	
5																	
6	MLS#	BR	Ba	SqFt	Zone	Price	Style	Lot	Lower	Main	Upper	FP	Tax	AC	Elem	Middle	High
7	6285	2	1	1819	1	29900	Ranch	1.10	794	1025			198	Central	U	T	N
8	4262	2	1			34000	Ranch	0.75					236		S	E	E
9	4906	1	1	516	3	36500	Bungalow	2.00		516			306	Central	B	B	S
10	5549	1	1	648	4	39000	Bungalow	3.00		648			340		F	T	N
11	5704	2	1	864	5	39500	Ranch	1.40			864		192	Window	E	E	E
12	5156	2	1	1200	4	41500	Bungalow	2.00		700			59	Central	F	T	N
13	5423	2	1	1296	5	46500	Ranch	0.14					286	Central	E	E	E
14	5690	3	1	960	6	48900	Ranch	5.00					590		S	E	E
15	5833	1	1	956	8	48900	Bungalow	0.40		956			454	Central	L	B	S
16	5867	2	1	1330	4	49900	Ranch	1.00					275	Central	E	E	E
17	4920	2	1	1000	3	49900	Ranch	0.94		1000			337		T	J	S
18	5075	3	1	980	1	50000	Ranch	1.12					452		U	T	N
19	5099	2	1	860	3	51900	Bungalow	1.58		860			200	Central	T	B	S
20	3438	3	2	1480	3	53500	Ranch	0.45				1	618	Central	Cl	B	S
21	5899	2	1	1120	6	55900		1.00	272	848			120		S	E	E
22	4807	2	1	950	6	56000	Bungalow	2.76					418		S	E	E
23	6295	2	1	1691	4	56500	Bungalow	0.16	580	1111			733		F	T	N
24	5688	2	1	1430	6	57500	Bungalow	1.00	430	1000			199	Window	S	E	E
25	5737	2	1	728	3	58500	Bungalow	0.34		728			335	Window	Cl	B	S
26	3312	3	2	1049	7	58900		2.60		868	181		497	Central	T	J	S
27	6468	2	1	812	4	59900	Bungalow	2.62					408		F	T	N
28	4289	2	1	900	4	59900		3.38		450	450		9	Central	F	T	N
29	4963	2	1	891	3	60000	Bungalow	0.17		891			107		B	B	S
30	4155	2	1	1056	3	62500	Ranch	2.92		1056			234	Central	B	B	S
31	5841	3	2	1210	7	62500	Ranch	0.27		1210			434	Central	L	J	S
32	4804	3	1	1530	3	64000		2.65	530	470	530		789	Central	G	B	S

Figure 22-15 The criteria range in A1:B3 filters the list to show homes that are on lots greater than two acres or within elementary-school district U.

You'll find the Homes.xlsx file with the other examples on the companion website.

Having set up the criteria range as shown in Figure 22-15, you then click Advanced Filter in the Sort & Filter group on the Data tab and fill out the Advanced Filter dialog box as shown in Figure 22-16. Excel responds by displaying the filtered list shown in Figure 22-17.

Figure 22-16 In the Advanced Filter dialog box, click Filter The List, In-Place and specify the address of your list and your criteria ranges.

Elem	Lot
U	
	>2

MLS#	BR	Ba	SqFt	Zone	Price	Style	Lot	Lower	Main	Upper	FP	Tax	AC	Elem	Middle	High
6285	2	1	1819	1	29900	Ranch	1.10	794	1025			198	Central	U	T	N
5549	1	1	648	4	39000	Bungalow	3.00		648			340		F	T	N
5690	3	1	960	6	48900	Ranch	5.00					590		S	E	E
5075	3	1	980	1	50000	Ranch	1.12					452		U	T	N
4807	2	1	950	6	56000	Bungalow	2.76					418		S	E	E
3312	3	2	1049	7	58900		2.60		868	181		497	Central	T	J	S
6468	2	1	812	4	59900	Bungalow	2.62					408		F	T	N
4289	2	1	900	4	59900		3.38		450	450		9	Central	F	T	N
4155	2	1	1056	3	62500	Ranch	2.92		1056			234	Central	B	B	S
4804	3	1	1530	3	64000		2.65	530	470	530		789	Central	G	B	S
5415	3	1	1050	5	64900	Ranch	3.12					941	Central	E	E	E
5892	2	1	753	7	64900	Ranch	2.77					720	Window	U	T	N
4288	3	1	1152	4	64990		2.33		576	576		9	Central	F	T	N
4062	3	1	1057	7	67000	Ranch	2.62					621	Window	F	T	N
5078	4	1	1998	5	68000		2.95	768	462	768	1		Central	E	E	E
4285	3	2	1100	3	69000	Ranch	2.41		1100			550	Central	H	T	N
4267	4	1	1008	5	69900	Ranch	2.48		1008			498	Central	E	E	E
5734	2	1	750	10	69900		0.14		750			717	Window	U	T	N
	3	2	1112	3	69900	Ranch	2.21		1112		1	525	Central	G	B	S
2479	3	1	1225	4	69950	Ranch	3.50		1225			642	Central	H	B	N
6446	2	1	1627	3	73900	Bungalow	4.27	469	1158			465	Central	L	B	S
4630	3	2	1740	5	73900	Bi-level	3.38	732	1008			740	Window	E	E	E
4446	3	1	960	10	75000	Ranch	0.32		960			334		U	T	N
3800	3	2	1124	3	75000	Ranch	3.21		1124			728	Central	Cl	B	S
6278	3	2	1533	5	75000	Bi-level	2.35	525	1008			775		E	E	E
4603	2	2	1910	7	75500	Townhouse	3.10	750	600	560	1	1584	Central	Ch	J	S
3963	3	2	1440	3	75900	Townhouse	2.06		720	720		644	Central	H	B	S

Figure 22-17 Excel responds with a list filtered to show just the homes in which you're interested.

Like a standard filter, the Advanced Filter command hides all rows that don't pass the filter. It also displays the qualifying row numbers in a contrasting color. As with a regular filter, it's worth making the list into a table if you want to add a total row. On the total row, you can easily add a COUNT function to see how many rows passed the filter.

In Figure 22-15, notice that we specified the two criteria on separate lines. This tells Excel to find rows that meet either criterion. If you put the two criteria on the same line, you ask for just those rows that meet both criteria. In other words, criteria on the same line are joined by AND, and criteria on separate lines are joined by OR. You can put as many separate criteria as you like in a criteria range.

We specified both criteria as simple text values. The value U under the Elem heading tells Excel to get any rows with Elem values that begin with the letter *U*. (In other words, there's an implied asterisk wildcard after the U.) If you want the filter to allow only values that match the letter *U* exactly, type **="U"**. This clumsy formulation causes the cell to display =U and has the effect of removing the implied asterisk wildcard.

A value of >2 under the Lot heading tells Excel to get rows with Lot values greater than 2. You can use any of the relational operators >, <, >=, or <= in a numeric criterion. If you want an exact match (all lot sizes of exactly 2 acres, for example), type the number without an operator.

Be aware that a blank cell in a criteria range means "accept any value for this column." If you accidentally include a blank row in the criteria range, you get an unfiltered list.

> ### Note
>
> As long as your criteria range is on the same worksheet as your list, Excel assigns the name Criteria to it immediately after you use it. You can use this behavior as a navigational tool. If you need to return to a criteria range to edit it, you can get there by pressing F5 and selecting Criteria in the Go To dialog box.

An example using three ORs on a column

Now let's suppose you want to filter the list to show all houses in three elementary-school districts—U, F, and T. You include only the Elem field in the criteria range and type the letters **U**, **F**, and **T** on three separate rows immediately below the heading. The Advanced Filter command then generates the list shown in Figure 22-18.

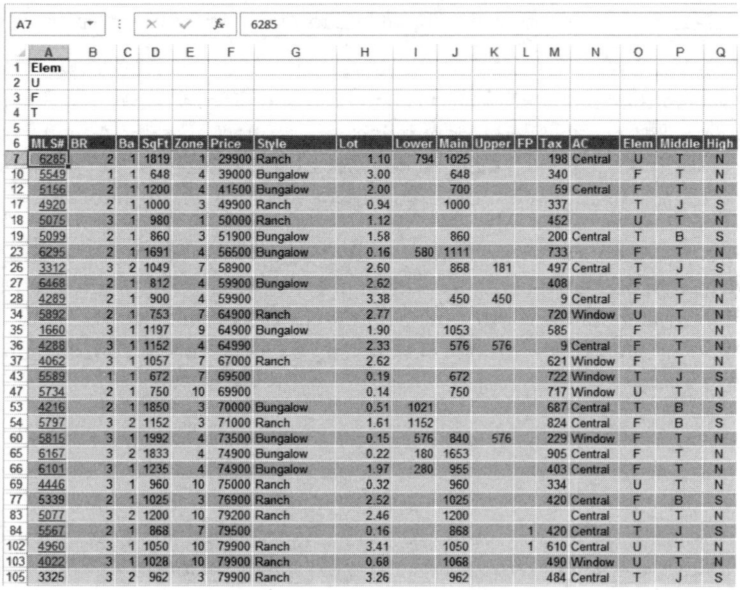

Figure 22-18 Using the criteria range in cells A1:A4 reduces the list to houses in elementary-school districts U, F, and T.

An example using both OR and AND

If you want to see all houses in middle-school district T or J that are at least 2,000 square feet, you set up the criteria range as in Figure 22-19. The criterion >=2000 appears in two places, cells B2 and B3, because for each of the middle-school districts (T and J), you want to see houses only of 2,000 square feet or more.

	A	B	C	D	E	F	G	H	I	J	K	L	M	N	O	P	Q
1	Middle	SqFt															
2	T	>=2000															
3	J	>=2000															
4																	
5																	
6	MLS#	BR	Ba	SqFt	Zone	Price	Style	Lot	Lower	Main	Upper	FP	Tax	AC	Elem	Middle	High
93	5372	3	2	2214	10	79900	Ranch	5.00	756	1458			2247	Central	M	T	N
112	6299	4	2	3256	7	83000		3.08	1268	1548	440		562	Central	T	J	S
119	3881	3	3	3207	4	84700	Contemporary	3.39	1125	1125	957		1200	Central	A	T	N
146	4836	3	2	2000	4	89900	Bi-level	2.24	960	1040			892	Central	A	T	N
167	4342	3	2	2016	7	93900	Ranch	0.32	1008	1008			720	Central	L	J	S
168	4924	3	1	2164	4	94000	Ranch	0.44	1082	1082			788	Central	F	T	N
175	6330	3	1	2136	4	96000	Bungalow	1.38	680	1456			518		F	T	N
177	5047	6	2	2632	4	96900	Quad level	0.45	632	684	632		1330	Central	A	T	N
192	5900	3	2	2018	10	99900		0.41	684	614	720	1	1161	Central	M	T	N
193	6279	3	3	3202	3	99900		0.80	1136	1136	930	2	1407	Central	G	T	N
196	5164	3	1	3007	4	99900	Ranch	5.00	1314	1693			1141	Central	A	T	N
200	4717	3	1	2520	4	99900		1.77	480	1500	540	1	943	Central	A	T	N
219	5702	4	2	2100	4	107000		0.57	1550	550		1	936	Central	A	T	N
237	5281	3	1	2400	7	109900	Bungalow	1.31		1200			552	Central	R	J	N

Figure 22-19 To display 2,000-square-foot houses in middle-school districts T and J, repeat the >=2000 criterion in each line of the criteria range.

> ## Note
>
> Each time you use the Advanced Filter command, Excel reexamines the entire list rather than only the rows that passed the most recent filter. Therefore, you don't have to use the Clear command before changing the filter. If you want to refine a filter set—that is, filter the filtrate—add your new criteria to the previous criteria range and filter again.

Applying multiple criteria to the same column

To apply two or more criteria to the same column, repeat the column in your criteria range. For example, to retrieve rows with Price values from $50,000 to $90,000, your criteria range would look like the following:

Price	Price
>=50000	<=90000

To exclude rows with prices in this range but admit everything else, you'd set up this criteria range:

Price	Price
<=50000	>=90000

Using computed criteria

Computed criteria involve any test other than a simple comparison of a column's value to a constant. Asking Excel to find houses with prices less than $200,000 does not require a computed criterion. Asking for houses with prices less than the median price of all houses in the list does.

When setting up a computed criterion, observe these rules:

- The column heading above a computed criterion must not be a copy of a column heading in the list. This heading can be blank, or it can be anything you want—other than a heading that already appears in the list.

- References to cells outside the list should be absolute.

- References to cells inside the list should be relative—unless you're referencing all the cells in a column.

Let's look at some examples. The next three sections explore referencing cells within the list, referencing a cell outside the list, and referencing all rows in a column.

Referencing cells within the list In cell A2 of Figure 22-20, we used the formula =F7/D7<50 to find all houses with prices per square foot less than $50. Notice that the heading above the criterion (at cell A1) is not a copy of any heading in the list and that the formula uses relative references to fetch values from within the list. F7 and D7 are the relevant values from the first row of the unfiltered list. Excel therefore begins by dividing F7 by D7 and comparing the result to 50. Because the references are relative, it continues by dividing F8 by D8, dividing F9 by D9, and so on.

The criterion formula in A2 returns TRUE because the result of that initial calculation (involving F7 and D7) is TRUE. It doesn't make any difference what that criterion formula returns, however; in fact, as you'll see, it can even return an error value.

In some rows of the unfiltered list, the SqFt column is blank. Dividing by a blank cell always returns the #DIV/0! error constant. This is not a problem. When Excel looks at a row with a blank SqFt value, it compares #DIV/0! with 50, and the result of that comparison is #DIV/0! Because the comparison doesn't yield a TRUE result, the row containing the blank SqFt value is excluded from the filter set—which is, presumably, the outcome you want.

A2			fx	=F7/D7<50												
Price per sqft < 50																
TRUE																
MLS#	**BR**	**Ba**	**SqFt**	**Zone**	**Price**	**Style**	**Lot**	**Lower**	**Main**	**Upper**	**FP**	**Tax**	**AC**	**Elem**	**Middle**	**High**
6285	2	1	1819	1	29900	Ranch	1.10	794	1025			198	Central	U	T	N
5704	2	1	864	5	39500	Ranch	1.40			864		192	Window	E	E	E
5156	2	1	1200	4	41500	Bungalow	2.00		700			59	Central	F	T	N
5423	2	1	1296	5	46500	Ranch	0.14					286	Central	E	E	E
5867	2	1	1330	4	49900	Ranch	1.00					275	Central	E	E	E
4920	2	1	1000	3	49900	Ranch	0.94		1000			337		T	J	S
3438	3	2	1480	3	53500	Ranch	0.45				1	618	Central	CI	B	S
5899	2	1	1120	6	55900		1.00	272	848			120		S	E	E
6295	2	1	1691	4	56500	Bungalow	0.16	580	1111			733		F	T	N
5688	2	1	1430	6	57500	Bungalow	1.00	430	1000			199	Window	S	E	E
4804	3	1	1530	2	64000		2.65	530	470	530		789	Central	G	B	S
5078	4	1	1998	5	68000		2.95	768	462	768	1		Central	E	E	E
5208	3	2	1926	7	69900	Ranch	1.29	963	963			388		E	E	E
4216	2	1	1850	3	70000	Bungalow	0.51	1021				687	Central	T	B	S
2297	2	2	1576	10	72000	Ranch	0.20	645	931			439	Central	R	J	N
4682	2	2	1846	7	73000		1.00	182	936	728		337	Central	R	J	S
5815	3	1	1992	4	73500	Bungalow	0.15	576	840	576		229	Window	F	T	N
6446	2	1	1627	3	73900	Bungalow	4.27	469	1158			465	Central	L	B	S
4630	3	2	1740	5	73900	Bi-level	3.38	732	1008			740	Window	E	E	E
5760	3	3	1700	7	74000	Townhouse	0.36	550	600	550		1022	Central	Ch	B	S
6167	3	2	1833	4	74900	Bungalow	0.22	180	1653			905	Central	F	T	N
3682	3	2	1815	3	74900	Ranch	0.27		1815		1	339	Central	CI	B	S
6278	3	2	1533	5	75000	Bi-level	2.35	525	1008			775		E	E	E
4603	2	2	1910	7	75500	Townhouse	3.10	750	600	560	1	1584	Central	Ch	J	S
6202	3	1	1632	7	79900	Ranch	0.33	662	970			397	Window	L	B	S
5282	3	1	1752	6	79900		2.69		960	792		889	Central	E	E	E
5372	3	2	2214	10	79900	Ranch	5.00	756	1458			2247	Central	M	T	N
1502	3	2	1883	5	80000	Bi-level	0.40	875	1008			817	Central	E	E	E
6299	4	2	3256	7	83000		3.08	1268	1548	440		562	Central	T	J	S

Figure 22-20 The criterion in A2 returns all houses with prices per square foot less than $50.

If you assign names to the columns of your list, you can use those names instead of first-row cell references in your computed criterion. In other words, with the names SqFt and Price assigned to the appropriate columns, the formula at A2 reads =Price/SqFt<50.

Referencing a cell outside the list   The criterion formula in A2 of Figure 22-21 compares prices against the median price, which is stored outside the list, in H1. (The median is calculated with the formula =MEDIAN(price), where *price* is a name assigned to all cells in the Price column.) The reference to H1 is absolute. If it were not, Excel would compare the price in the first row of the list to H1, the price in the second row to H2, and so on—not what you want.

Chapter 22

| G7 | ▼ | : | × | ✓ | fx | Ranch |

	A	B	C	D	E	F	G	H	I	J	K	L	M	N	O	P	Q
1	Median price						Median	85500									
2	FALSE																
3																	
4																	
5																	
6	MLS#	BR	Ba	SqFt	Zone	Price	Style	Lot	Lower	Main	Upper	FP	Tax	AC	Elem	Middle	High
124	5924	3	1	1320	3	85900	Ranch	2.59		1320		1	760	Window	Cl	B	S
125	4111	3	1	1123	7	86500	Ranch	2.65		1123		1	351	Central	U	T	N
126	4762	2	1	1260	3	86900	Ranch	0.81					568	Central	B	B	S
127	5321	3	2	1750	4	87200	Ranch	1.98		1750				Central	E	E	E
128	5810	3	2	1409	7	87500	Ranch	0.32		1409			411	Central	G	B	S
129	5698	3	2	1488	4	87500	Ranch	0.22	480	1008			251	Central	E	E	E
130	5596	4	2	1430	3	87900		0.29	474	434	522		823	Central	G	B	S
131	3003	3	2	1316	3	87900	Bi-level	0.22	500	816			810	Central	G	B	S
132	4723	3	2	1040	4	88900	Ranch	3.01	1040					Central	A	T	N
133	4724	3	2	1040	4	88900	Ranch	0.41	1040					Central	A	T	N
134	4720	3	2	1040	4	88900	Ranch	2.97	1040					Central	A	T	N
135	6111	3	2	1275	3	88900		0.82	700	575			720	Central	G	B	S
136	2965	3	2	1200	3	88900	Ranch	2.42				1	722	Central	H	T	N
137	6318	3	1	1325	5	89500	Ranch	0.62		1325		1	765	Window	E	E	E
138	6397	3	3	2053	3	89500	Bi-level	0.49	1008	1045			1267	Central	G	B	S
139	4706	3	2	1560	5	89500	Ranch	1.00		1560		1	441		S	E	E
140	4199	3	2	1600	3	89500	Ranch	0.35	600	1000			604	Central	B	B	S
141	2320	3	1	1179	4	89500	Ranch	0.19			1179		1155	Central	A	T	N
142	3933	3	1	1450	7	89900	Ranch	0.40		1450		1	973	Central	U	J	N
143	5006	3	2	1240	3	89900	Ranch	0.26		1240			713	Central	H	B	N
144	4806	3	3	1520	4	89900	Townhouse	1.38	760	760			1511	Central	A	T	N
145	4833	3	1	1008	7	89900	Ranch	0.42		1008			417	Window	L	J	S
146	4836	3	2	2000	4	89900	Bi-level	2.24	960	1040			892	Central	A	T	N
147	3779	3	2	1560	7	89900	Bi-level	0.72	560	1000			1232	Central	T	B	S
148	5332	2	2	1824	10	89900	Ranch	0.63	910	914			751	Central	U	T	N
149		3	2	1500	5	89900	Bi-level	0.20	750	750			1006	Central	E	E	E
150	6265	2	1	800	7	89900	Ranch	2.80		800			518	Central	T	B	S
151	4001	3	2	1680	5	89900	Ranch	1.00		1680			544	Central	E	E	E

Figure 22-21 The criterion in A2 uses an absolute reference because the referenced cell, H1, lies outside the list.

Referencing all rows in a column   If you change the formula in A2 of Figure 22-21 to =F6>MEDIAN($F$7:$F$239), you get the same set of rows as shown in Figure 22-21. In this case, the MEDIAN function references cells within the list, but the reference has to be absolute. Otherwise, Excel looks at F7:F239, then at F8:F240, and so on. (You could drop the absolute reference to column F and make the row references absolute. If you use the F4 shortcut to create the absolute references, however, it's just as easy to make the whole reference absolute.)

Extracting filtered rows

The Advanced Filter dialog box includes an option for copying the selected rows to another worksheet location instead of displaying a filtered list. To copy rows rather than display them, select the Copy To Another Location option in the Advanced Filter dialog box and supply the name or address of the range where you want the information to appear in the Copy To text box.

The easiest way to specify the Copy To range is to click a blank cell in your worksheet where you want the range to start. Be sure the cell has plenty of blank space below and to the right of it. Excel then copies your list's column headings and all the rows that meet the Advanced Filter criteria to the range that begins with the cell you specified. Be careful, though; any data already stored in the selected range will be overwritten. Alternatively, if you specify a range of cells, Excel copies the rows that pass the filter but stops when the range is full.

If you put the extract range to the side of the source list, be careful not to filter the source list. Filtering the source list hides entire rows, which will hide rows from your extract range as well. Be sure to turn off any in-place filters in the source list or put the extract range *below* the source range. The extract range has to be on the same worksheet as the source list, but after you extract the list, you can move it to a different worksheet.

> **Note**
>
> When you specify a Copy To range in the Advanced Filter dialog box, Excel assigns the name Extract to that range. You can use this name as a navigational aid. For example, when you need to return to the range to change column headings, select Extract from the Name box to the left of the formula bar.

To copy only certain columns of your list to a new location, create copies of the headings for those columns. Then specify the headings (not only the first cell, but the entire set of copied headings) as your Copy To range. Be sure not to select a blank row under the extract headings, or you will get only a single row from the filter.

The Unique Records Only check box

The Unique Records Only check box in the Advanced Filter dialog box adds a filter to whatever you specify in your criteria range. It eliminates rows that are duplicates in every respect (not just duplicates in the columns that you happen to be extracting, but duplicates in all columns). The Unique Records Only check box works only in conjunction with the Copy To Another Location option; this option is particularly useful when you are extracting only some of the columns. For example, you could extract only the Price and Style columns. By using the Unique Records Only check box, you would get a list of unique Price/Style combinations from the list.

Removing duplicate records

In some earlier versions of Excel, one reason for using the Unique Records Only check box was to eliminate duplicates from a list. That task is much easier now because a special command simply removes duplicate rows from the list. You can use this command in two ways. One way is just to remove all the duplicate rows—in case there happen to be any. The other way is to select specific columns that you will force to be unique. When you select specific columns, Excel chooses the values from all the other columns that happen to be in the first unique combination.

To remove complete row duplicates, select a single cell within the list or table, and click the Remove Duplicates command in the Data Tools group on the Data tab. In the Remove Duplicates dialog box, leave all the check boxes for the columns selected and click OK. Excel tells you how many duplicates it found and how many rows are left.

To remove partial-row duplicates, you probably want to start by making a copy of the list, because real information is destroyed in the process. Next, you should sort the list for any columns you don't want to include. For example, if you want only one row for each home style, but you want that row to be the most expensive home, sort the list in descending order by Price before you execute the Remove Duplicates command.

After you sort the list, select a single cell and click Remove Duplicates. Click the Unselect All button to clear all the check boxes, and then select the check boxes for the few columns in which you want distinct values. For example, you might select only the Style column. Then click OK. You end up with a list that contains only the first row for each style—the most expensive, if you sorted the list first.

Using formulas with tables

Excel formulas are extremely powerful and useful. They can also be cryptic. What exactly does a formula such as =TODAY()–D2 actually mean? Without looking at the worksheet, it's impossible to tell. But what if the formula looked like =TODAY()–[Date of Birth] instead? Just by looking at the formula, you can tell that it calculates the current age in days.

In an Excel table, you can create meaningful formulas in a simple, unambiguous way. One of the most common uses of a formula in a table is to perform a calculation that looks only at values from other rows of the same table. This type of formula is extraordinarily easy.

For example, using traditional formulas to calculate the (approximate) age in years of each staff member, you would use a formula such as the one in cell G2 in Figure 22-22.

After you change the list to a table, you can edit the formula, and Excel adjusts the reference for you. Just select a cell with the formula, select the cell in the formula with the traditional single-cell reference, and then click the cell you are referring to (in this case, cell D2). Excel automatically replaces the cell address with the name of the table column, as you can see in Figure 22-23.

When you enter the formula in the cell, Excel automatically copies the formula to the entire Age column, replacing all the existing formulas.

G2
=INT((TODAY()-D2)/365.25)

	A	B	C	D	E	F	G
1	Last Name	First Name	Date of Hire	Date of Birth	Sex	Salary	Age
2	Aaberg	Jesper	1/12/92	5/28/64	M	100000	48
3	Aalling	Lene	4/21/99	11/24/77	F	100000	34
4	Abbas	Syed	2/16/96	4/18/64	F	92000	48
5	Abola	Lina	11/22/07	9/2/75	M	97000	37
6	Abrus	Luka	3/19/88	10/21/54	M	93000	58
7	Abu-Dayah	Ahmad	7/13/84	2/28/54	M	33000	58
8	Adalsteinsson	Gudmundur	7/4/89	3/26/59	M	99000	53
9	Adolphi	Stephan	8/26/75	12/3/69	M	92000	42
10	Agarwal	Nupur	2/22/95	4/4/57	M	92000	55
11	Agarwal	Manoj	8/1/99	8/14/68	M	92000	44
12	Aiad	Hatim	6/24/85	10/16/62	M	91000	50
13	Akın	Çigdem	2/18/95	8/28/55	F	91000	57
14	Alboni	Ezio	12/11/96	1/9/60	M	91000	52
15	Alexieva-Bosseva	Diliana	12/20/90	8/31/71	M	91000	41
16	Allen	Tony	6/22/92	6/20/63	M	90000	49
17	Almosnino	Gilead	3/9/90	9/21/75	M	90000	37
18	Alverca	Luis	9/15/92	8/31/77	M	89000	35
19	Alverca	Luis	9/21/00	8/3/71	F	89000	41
20	Alwan	Antonio	1/2/86	5/14/68	M	89000	44
21	Ambrus	Zsolt	12/27/87	9/26/51	M	89000	61
22	Amireh	Kamil	11/6/86	3/14/76	M	87000	36
23	Amitai	Zwie	6/29/77	1/12/76	F	89000	36
24	Anand	Deepak	1/6/97	6/2/78	M	88000	34
25	Anashkin	Oleg	9/23/00	6/15/69	M	88000	43
26	Andersen	Erik	11/8/99	4/11/52	F	87000	60
27	Andersen	Elizabeth A.	2/19/92	3/18/76	F	86000	36
28	Andersen	Erik	1/12/99	9/24/78	M	86000	34
29	Andersen	Erik	5/12/99	3/15/65	M	86000	47
30	Andersen	Thomas	8/11/98	3/9/65	M	86000	47
31	Andersen	Erik	6/11/77	3/17/66	M	86000	46
32	Andersen	Henriette Thaulow	5/10/98	3/31/56	M	86000	56

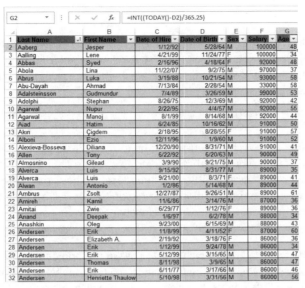

Figure 22-22 The formula in cell G2 uses an ordinary cell reference to D2.

G2
=INT((TODAY()-[@[Date of Birth]])/365.25)

	A	B	C	D	E	F	G
1	Last Name	First Name	Date of Hire	Date of Birth	Sex	Salary	Age
2	Aaberg	Jesper	1/12/92	5/28/64	M	100000	48
3	Aalling	Lene	4/21/99	11/24/77	F	100000	34
4	Abbas	Syed	2/16/96	4/18/64	F	92000	48
5	Abola	Lina	11/22/07	9/2/75	M	97000	37
6	Abrus	Luka	3/19/88	10/21/54	M	93000	58
7	Abu-Dayah	Ahmad	7/13/84	2/28/54	M	33000	58
8	Adalsteinsson	Gudmundur	7/4/89	3/26/59	M	99000	53
9	Adolphi	Stephan	8/26/75	12/3/69	M	92000	42
10	Agarwal	Nupur	2/22/95	4/4/57	M	92000	55
11	Agarwal	Manoj	8/1/99	8/14/68	M	92000	44
12	Aiad	Hatim	6/24/85	10/16/62	M	91000	50
13	Akın	Çigdem	2/18/95	8/28/55	F	91000	57
14	Alboni	Ezio	12/11/96	1/9/60	M	91000	52
15	Alexieva-Bosseva	Diliana	12/20/90	8/31/71	M	91000	41
16	Allen	Tony	6/22/92	6/20/63	M	90000	49
17	Almosnino	Gilead	3/9/90	9/21/75	M	90000	37
18	Alverca	Luis	9/15/92	8/31/77	M	89000	35
19	Alverca	Luis	9/21/00	8/3/71	F	89000	41
20	Alwan	Antonio	1/2/86	5/14/68	M	89000	44
21	Ambrus	Zsolt	12/27/87	9/26/51	M	89000	61
22	Amireh	Kamil	11/6/86	3/14/76	M	87000	36
23	Amitai	Zwie	6/29/77	1/12/76	F	89000	36
24	Anand	Deepak	1/6/97	6/2/78	M	88000	34
25	Anashkin	Oleg	9/23/00	6/15/69	M	88000	43
26	Andersen	Erik	11/8/99	4/11/52	F	87000	60
27	Andersen	Elizabeth A.	2/19/92	3/18/76	F	86000	36
28	Andersen	Erik	1/12/99	9/24/78	M	86000	34
29	Andersen	Erik	5/12/99	3/15/65	M	86000	47
30	Andersen	Thomas	8/11/98	3/9/65	M	86000	47
31	Andersen	Erik	6/11/77	3/17/66	M	86000	46
32	Andersen	Henriette Thaulow	5/10/98	3/31/56	M	86000	56
33	Andrade	Diogo	11/25/96	9/23/73	M	86000	39

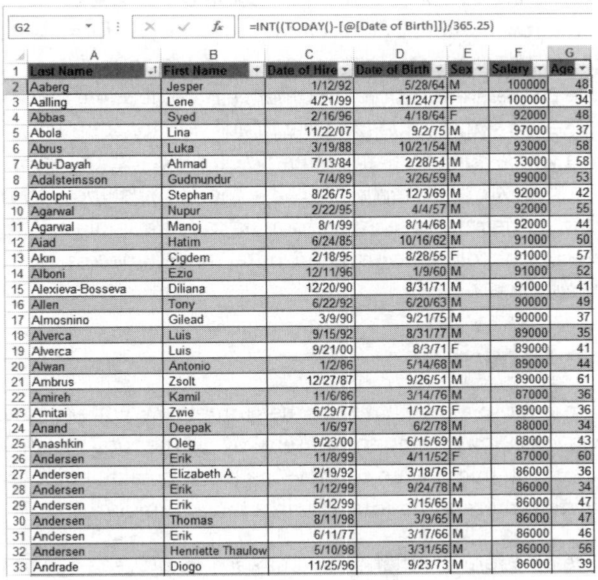

Figure 22-23 By turning the list into a table and editing the formula, you can turn the formula in G2 into something easier to read.

Chapter 22

> **Note**
>
> Excel automatically replaces all the formulas only if they are all equivalent. If you created an exception formula somewhere in the list, Excel puts the formula into only the one cell, but it adds an AutoCorrect icon that asks whether you want to replace all the formulas in the column with the new formula.

You might wonder about a few characteristics of the formula. First, why did Excel put brackets around the name of the column so that it shows up as [Date of Birth]? Well, Excel needs something around the name because otherwise the spaces in the name could make it hard to tell where the name ends. Simple parentheses wouldn't work well because they are used in formulas to show calculation order. (Brackets are what Microsoft Access 2010 uses to identify column names, and it works pretty well in that application, too.)

Second, how does the formula know which row to use? In the original formula in cell G2, the reference was D2. When you copy the formula to cell G3, the reference changes to D3. The reference might be a little cryptic, but it's pretty clear which column and row it refers to. The reference [Date of Birth] tells which column, but how does Excel know which row? Notice in the traditional reference that the row number in the reference (for example, B2) is always the same as the row number of the cell that contains the formula (for example, G2). The people on the Excel team noticed that in many, many formulas—and especially in formulas in tables—the cell references point to other cells in the *same row*. So they created a rule. If the formula needs a single value (and the minus sign for subtraction needs a single value) and you give it a whole column as the reference, it picks just the value from the current row. This is called *implicit intersection* because the formula *implicitly* uses the current row to *intersect* the range reference in the formula to get a single cell. (Excel can also implicitly intersect the current column with a horizontal range if necessary, but tables don't have horizontally named rows.)

Referencing the total row

Sometimes you need to refer to a row that's not the current row. For example, a common calculation in a table involves comparing the current row to the total row. If your table includes sales by regions, you might want to show the percent each region is of the total. Excel has a special way to represent the total row in a table formula.

As an example, we'll create a formula that compares each employee's age to the average staff age. To begin, add a total row to the table and change the formula for the Age column in the total row to Average. Next, type a new heading directly to the right of the table in the headers row. Excel responds by creating a new column for the table. For the new column's header, type something like **Versus Avg**. After the new, formatted column appears in the table, select any cell in the column. Type an equal sign to start the formula, and click the Age column for the current row. The formula will say =[@Age], showing that it recognizes the Age column. Then type a minus sign (–), and click the cell for the Age column in the total row. (As a keyboard shortcut, press the Left Arrow key to get to the Age column, and then press Ctrl+Down Arrow to jump to the bottom of the table—the total row.) The formula now says =[@Age]–TStaff[[#Totals],[Age]]. When you press Enter, Excel inserts the formula into all the cells of the column. You can now apply a number format to the column. The result looks like the worksheet in Figure 22-24.

H329			fx	=[@Age]-TStaff[[#Totals],[Age]]			
	A	B	C	D	E	F	G	H

#	Last Name	First Name	Date of Hire	Date of Birth	Sex	Salary	Age	Versus Avg
329	Kretowicz	Marcin	9/26/77	8/31/60	M	39000	52	3.3
330	Krieger	Doris	8/27/81	7/28/78	F	45000	34	-14.7
331	Krschne	Peter	4/8/78	7/31/62	F	76000	50	1.3
332	Kuhlmann	Lone	10/18/88	4/2/56	M	76000	56	7.3
333	Kulikov	Evgeny	9/20/00	1/7/66	M	76000	46	-2.7
334	Kupkova	Helena	11/20/74	10/17/49	M	100000	63	14.3
335	Kurmann	Benno	3/27/91	7/20/64	M	99000	48	-0.7
336	Kurmann	Benno	5/25/82	12/23/64	M	39000	47	-1.7
337	Lacerda	Carlos	5/3/88	3/5/68	M	39000	44	-4.7
338	Lacerda	Carlos	6/22/80	1/24/72	M	39000	40	-8.7
339	Lang	Ingelise	1/29/85	11/16/77	F	41000	34	-14.7
340	Lange	Michael	4/11/92	11/1/72	M	39000	40	-8.7
341	Langhorn	Carl	5/12/86	4/3/70	M	42000	42	-6.7
342	Langvad-Nielsen	Anders	7/19/96	7/5/58	M	42000	54	5.3
343	Larsen	Henrik	11/7/92	3/4/54	F	42000	58	9.3
344	Larsen	Henrik	12/20/87	6/3/53	M	42000	59	10.3
345	Larsson	Katarina	9/18/88	8/24/62	M	42000	50	1.3
346	Lassila	Tiina	7/17/84	6/4/51	M	43000	61	12.3
347	Lazecky	Petr	1/17/00	3/12/60	M	43000	52	3.3
348	Lee	Soo Jung	12/28/86	11/21/55	M	43000	56	7.3
349	Lee	Soo Jung	8/26/77	6/17/53	M	43000	59	10.3
350	Leeissarapong	Sombat	4/4/87	5/26/73	F	43000	39	-9.7
351	Lembeck	Roman	12/12/78	8/31/74	M	43000	38	-10.7
352	Lengyel	Attila	11/30/77	7/12/60	M	73000	52	3.3
353	Leoni	Alessandro	9/18/92	11/1/78	M	44000	34	-14.7
354	Lertpiriyasuwat	Kitti	8/20/98	11/18/51	F	43000	60	11.3
355	Letzen	Johan	10/28/00	10/4/62	M	73000	50	1.3
356	Levitan	Michal	3/11/97	8/1/67	F	99000	45	-3.7
357	Lidman	Anna	2/2/80	8/14/65	F	25000	47	-1.7
358	Lielbriedis	Aleksandrs	6/13/82	3/26/74	F	74000	38	-10.7
359	Lohndorf-Larsen	Lars	3/11/87	2/19/78	M	74000	34	-14.7
360	Average						49	

Figure 22-24 This formula uses structured referencing to compare the current row to the total row.

The syntax is a little bit scary, but once you get the hang of it, it's not too bad. The first part simply references the Age column in the current row. (For an explanation of what the @ is doing in that reference, see the next section.) The second part is a little trickier. In the reference TStaff[[#Totals],[Age]], TStaff is an arbitrary name assigned to the table. (See "Naming a table" earlier in this chapter.) [#Totals] is a special structured-reference tag that Excel automatically applies to the total row of the table. You can't use the [#Totals] tag without first giving the name of the table. (Excel wouldn't know which table you meant if you omitted this.) So the full reference has three parts: the name of the table (followed by square brackets), the special structured-reference tag [#Totals], and then the column name [Age]. The [#Totals] tag and the table column name are separated by a comma.

A structured reference is harder to write than it is to read. Fortunately, Excel automatically creates the structured-reference formula for you as you create new formulas that reference elements of a table.

Chapter 22

Explicitly referencing the current row

Implicit intersection lets you use column names in table formulas. It's a great feature and makes formulas much easier to understand and to write. The only time implicit intersection can be a problem is when you use a function that can accept a whole range but you want it to apply to only the current row. Implicit intersection kicks in only when the formula requires a single value—which is typical of arithmetic operations. But functions such as SUM can work just fine with a whole range. Suppose that you want to sum the scores for different parts of a test—but only for the current student. One way to do this is to select each cell separately and use the plus (+) sign to add them. In this way, implicit intersection will work.

But if you have a lot of columns, using a range is easier. Fortunately, Excel has a special structured-reference tag, @, that *explicitly* limits the range to the current row. And Excel automatically adds that special tag when you create a formula that uses a function such as SUM over multiple columns of the current row. Figure 22-25 shows the formula Excel generates when you create a sum of multiple columns in the current row.

E2	▾	:	✕	✓	*fx*	=SUM(SATScores[@[Critical Reading]:[Math]])		

	A	B	C	D	E	F
1	Student ▾	Critical Readin ▾	Writing ▾	Math ▾	Total ▾	
2	Aaberg, Jesper	418	695	518	1631	
3	Aalling, Lene	465	632	557	1654	
4	Abbas, Syed	463	740	549	1752	
5	Abola, Lina	466	486	587	1539	
6	Abrus, Luka	520	694	544	1758	
7	Abu-Dayah, Ahmad	470	602	537	1609	
8	Adalsteinsson, Gudmundur	533	716	549	1798	
9	Adolphi, Stephan	476	793	570	1839	
10	Agarwal, Manoj	468	631	548	1647	
11	Agarwal, Nupur	441	792	562	1795	
12	Aiad, Hatim	570	792	560	1922	
13	Akın, Çigdem	503	788	554	1845	
14	Alboni, Ezio	551	791	556	1898	
15	Alexieva-Bosseva, Diliana	498	653	562	1713	
16	Allen, Tony	466	556	525	1547	
17	Almosnino, Gilead	414	699	549	1662	
18	Alverca, Luis	497	466	545	1508	
19	Alverca, Luis	581	451	519	1551	
20	Alwan, Antonio	402	617	568	1587	
21	Ambrus, Zsolt	488	400	539	1427	
22	Amireh, Kamil	547	438	536	1521	
23	Amitai, Zwie	456	619	567	1642	

Figure 22-25 The @ tag tells Excel to total values from the current row only.

The formula =SUM(SATScores[@[Critical Reading]:[Math]]) includes the standard SUM function. The reference follows the same pattern that is used for referring to the total row. There's the name of the table, followed by brackets. Within the brackets is the special structured-reference tag @. Finally, there is the part that specifies the column. In this case, you're specifying a range of columns, so the formula uses the range (:) operator between two table column names.

Referencing parts of a table

In addition to the @ tag, whose explicit meaning changes depending on the cell containing the formula, Excel has four structured-reference tags for other parts of the table. Table 22-1 lists the tags along with their meanings.

TABLE 22-1 Some additional structured-reference tags

Tag	Meaning
#Data	The data region of the table, excluding the header and total rows. If you refer to the table with no qualifier, this is what you get.
#Totals	The total row (if there is one).
#Headers	The header row (if there is one).
#All	The entire table, including headers, data, and totals.

These names are all row oriented. #Totals and #Headers reference single rows, but #Data and #All include all rows. If you combine any of these with a column name, you get the intersection. If you combine multiple row-oriented names, you get the union. For example, [#Headers],[#Data] results in everything except the totals.

Table 22-2 provides some examples of formulas that use the COUNTA function with structured-reference tags. Because each formula returns the total number of cells in a range, you can see how the different tags interact with one another. (All formulas reference a table named Staff.)

You can use the pointer to generate almost all of these combinations while constructing a formula. To select the #Data portion of the table, rest the pointer on the top-left corner of the table until it changes to a black arrow that points down and to the right and then click once. To select the #All portion of the table, rest the pointer on the same place, but double-click. To select a column's #Data area, rest the pointer on the top of the column until it turns into a black arrow that points down, and then click once. To select the #All area for the column, rest the pointer on the same place, but double-click. To select the #Header and #Data combination, you have to manually edit the formula.

TABLE 22-2 Some formulas that combine structured-reference tags

Formula	Description
=COUNTA(Staff)	Number of data cells in the table body
=COUNTA(Staff[Salary])	Number of data cells in the Salary column
=COUNTA(Staff[#Headers])	Number of cells in the header row
=COUNTA(Staff[#Totals])	Number of cells in the total row
=COUNTA(Staff[#Data])	Number of data cells in the table (same as referencing the table name alone)
=COUNTA(Staff[[#Data],[Salary]])	Same as referencing the column name alone
=COUNTA(Staff[#All])	Number of cells in the entire table, including the header and total row
=COUNTA(Staff[[#All],[Salary]])	Number of cells in one column, including the header and total row
=COUNTA(Staff[[#Headers],[#Data]])	Number of cells in the table, including headers but excluding the total row
=COUNTA(Staff[[#Headers],[#Data],[Salary]])	Number of cells in one column, including headers but excluding the total row

When you get used to the brackets, structured references are much more meaningful than simple cell addresses. And if you change the size of a table, the structured names automatically adjust. If you change the label in a column heading, any formulas that reference that column are automatically adjusted.

> **Note**
>
> How structured-reference tags work is a lot more detailed, especially when you include special characters such as & or [in the heading for a column. The details are described in the Help topic "Using structured references with Excel tables." To find the topic, search for *Structured References*.

Formatting tables

It is easy to make a table look really good. Just select any cell in the table, click the Design tab under Table Tools, and then select a style. The styles have several elements, and you can turn elements on or off at will. To see the full range of elements for the built-in styles, select all the check boxes in the Table Style Options group before selecting a style. The table in Figure 22-26 uses one of the Dark styles—Table Style Dark 6—because it shows the different elements quite clearly.

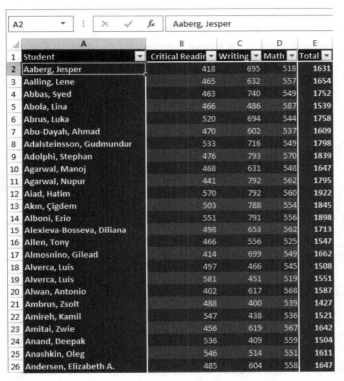

Figure 22-26 This example shows a Dark style, with all six of the Table Style Options selected.

As you clear different check boxes in the Table Style Options group, the appearance of the previews in the Table Styles list change accordingly. The Header Row and Total Row options are different from the other options in that turning them on or off actually changes the structure of the table, not just the format. If you want to have a header row or a total row but don't want a special format for it, you can customize the style, as explained in the next section.

The Banded Rows and Banded Columns options make every other row or column change color. Including both tends to make the table a little busy. By default, the style definitions alternate one row (or column) dark with one row (or column) light. You can customize the number of rows (or columns) in each band. The First Column and Last Column options are like the Header Row and Total Row options but for columns. Many times, as in Figure 22-26, the first column contains names or some other unique label and looks better with a distinct format. It is also often common—again, Figure 22-26 is an example—to have a total column at the right that deserves its own format.

Chapter 22

In terms of formatting priority, the header row and total row have priority over any of the columnar formats. Next come the column formats—the First Column, Last Column, and Banded Columns options take precedence over Banded Rows. In cases such as our example, where you can still see banding on the rows even though the Banded Columns option is selected, one of the column bands has no format applied, which lets the lowly row banding show.

> **Note**
>
> **If you do not see any changes when you apply a table style, you might have already applied cell formatting to the cells. If that's the case, right-click the Table Styles group on the ribbon and click Apply And Clear Formatting. If the format still doesn't work properly—for example, if the font does not change when you change styles—your workbook might have a customized Normal cell style. Make sure the Normal cell font is set to use the current theme's Body font.**

Using themes to change style appearance

Styles are designed to be used with themes. A theme specifies two fonts: Heading and Body. Excel tables use the Body font for all the cells styled with the Table Styles list. Built-in Excel table styles also take advantage of the background/text colors and accent colors defined in a theme. This means you can easily change the look of a table by switching the theme or by changing the font or the colors of the current theme. Excel tables don't use the Effects component of a theme.

To dramatically change the look of a table by switching to a new theme, select any cell in the table and then click the small arrow below the Themes button in the Themes group on the Page Layout tab. As you rest the pointer on the different themes, you can see the change in the table. Click the theme you like.

To change the color scheme of the current theme without changing the font, click the arrow to the right of the Colors button in the Themes group and then select a new color scheme. To select a new font without changing the colors, click the arrow to the right of the Fonts button in the Themes group. Remember that Excel tables use only the Body font style.

> **Note**
>
> Technically, Excel table styles use the font from the cell style named Normal, and the default font for the Normal cell style is the Body font. If you change the Normal style to use a font that is not assigned to the heading or the totals, the font does not change when you switch themes. If you want the Excel table styles to automatically use the Heading font rather than the Body font, change the Normal style to use the current Heading font. Changing the Normal style affects all unformatted cells in the workbook and also the row and column heading labels.

Customizing table styles

You can easily create your own style by cloning one of the built-in styles and then modifying its settings. To clone a style, on the Design tab under Table Tools, right-click any style and click Duplicate. The Modify Table Style dialog box, shown in Figure 22-27, appears. With this dialog box, you can format individual elements of the style.

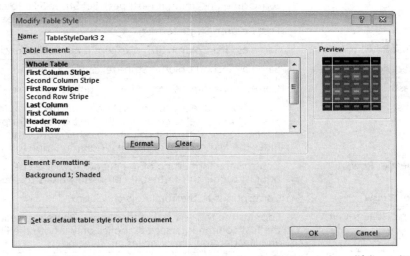

Figure 22-27 You can create your own styles by duplicating and modifying existing ones.

Most of the configurable elements relate directly to the check boxes in the Table Style Options group on the Design tab. If an item in the list is bold, that element has a custom format. If the item is not bold, the format of the "next layer down" applies. So, for example, if you clear the formatting for Header Row, the First Column and Last Column formats will apply to the first and last cells of the header row. (Even if you clear the formatting for header and total rows, a default underlying style consists of the underlying table format plus a bold font; you can't clear that underlying style.)

When you select a modified style element—that is, one that is bold—you can see a brief description of what is different about the element, including the font style, the font theme color, the border definition, and whether there is a background shading. Table 22-3 describes the table style elements.

TABLE 22-3 The elements of a table style

Element	Description
Whole Table	Underlying style that applies to everything.
First Column Stripe	Applies only when the Banded Columns check box is selected. Formats the first column and then alternates with the Second Column Stripe format. Set Stripe Size to control how many columns will have this format before cycling to the Second Column Stripe format.
Second Column Stripe	Applies only when the Banded Columns check box is selected. Formats the alternate columns with the First Column Stripe format. Leave this element unformatted to show the underlying formatting (including row stripes). Set Stripe Size to control how many columns will have this format before cycling back to the First Column Stripe format.
First Row Stripe	Same as First Column Stripe, except it applies to row banding.
Second Row Stripe	Same as Second Column Stripe, except it applies to row banding.
Last Column	Corresponds directly to the Last Column check box.
First Column	Corresponds directly to the First Column check box. Whether First Column is selected or not, the First Column Stripe format applies to the same first column. In other words, this format hides the first column of the First Column Stripe format.
Header Row	Controls the formatting of the header row. The check box does not just toggle this format; it completely hides the header row.
Total Row	Corresponds to the Total Row check box.
First Header Cell	Formats the top-left cell of the table—where the header row and the first column intersect. It applies only if both the First Column and Header Row check boxes are selected.
Last Header Cell	Formats the top-right cell of the table if both the Header Row and Last Column check boxes are selected.
First Total Cell	Formats the bottom-left cell of the table if both the Total Row and First Column check boxes are selected.
Last Total Cell	Formats the bottom-right cell of the table if both the Total Row and Last Column check boxes are selected.

After you create your customized style, it appears at the top of the gallery of styles. You can modify and delete only the styles you've created. After you create a style, you might need to click that style to apply it to the table.

To modify a table style element, right-click the custom style and click Modify (if you're not already in the Modify Table Style dialog box). Select the element you want to modify, and click Format. Click on the tab for the element you want to modify—for example, to change the cell background, click on the Fill tab. Select one of the theme colors, and click OK. Then select another element, or click OK to accept the format changes.

When you modify a table style, you cannot choose the font. The table style always uses the font from the Normal cell style (which defaults to the Body theme font). You can set the font style, size, and effects. When you modify a table style, it's a good idea to choose theme colors—or their tones and tints—and not a custom color. If you choose a custom color, the color won't change when you switch to a new theme.

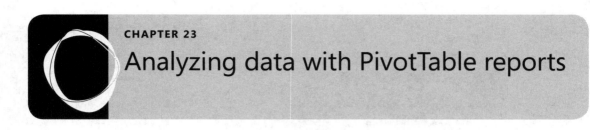

Analyzing data with PivotTable reports

A PivotTable report is a special kind of table that summarizes information from selected fields of a data source. The source can be a Microsoft Excel list or table, a relational database file, or an online analytical processing (OLAP) cube. When you create a PivotTable, you specify which fields you're interested in, how you want the table organized, and what kinds of calculations you want the table to perform. After you build the table, you can rearrange it to view your data from alternative perspectives. This ability to *pivot* the dimensions of your table—for example, to transpose column headings to row positions—gives the PivotTable its name and its analytical power.

Introducing PivotTables

PivotTables are linked to the data from which they're derived. If the PivotTable is based on external data (data stored outside Excel), you can choose to have it refreshed at regular time intervals, or you can refresh it whenever you want.

Figure 23-1 shows Books.xlsx, a list of sales figures for a small publishing firm. The list is organized by year, quarter, category, distribution channel, units sold, and sales receipts. The data spans a period of eight quarters (2011 and 2012). The firm publishes six categories of fiction (mystery, western, romance, sci fi, young adult, and children) and uses three distribution channels—domestic, international, and mail order. It's difficult to get useful summary information by looking at a list like this, even though the list itself is well organized.

You'll find the Books.xlsx file with the other examples on the companion website.

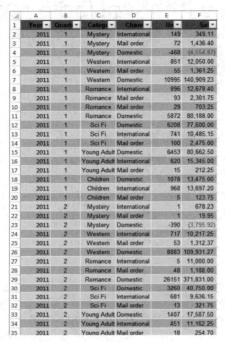

	A	B	C	D	E	F
1	Year	Quart	Categ	Chan	Un	Sal
2	2011	1	Mystery	International	149	349.11
3	2011	1	Mystery	Mail order	72	1,436.40
4	2011	1	Mystery	Domestic	-468	(4,554.87)
5	2011	1	Western	International	851	12,050.00
6	2011	1	Western	Mail order	55	1,361.25
7	2011	1	Western	Domestic	10995	140,909.23
8	2011	1	Romance	International	896	12,678.40
9	2011	1	Romance	Mail order	93	2,301.75
10	2011	1	Romance	Mail order	29	703.25
11	2011	1	Romance	Domestic	5872	80,188.00
12	2011	1	Sci Fi	Domestic	6208	77,600.00
13	2011	1	Sci Fi	International	741	10,485.15
14	2011	1	Sci Fi	Mail order	100	2,475.00
15	2011	1	Young Adult	Domestic	6453	80,662.50
16	2011	1	Young Adult	International	620	15,345.00
17	2011	1	Young Adult	Mail order	15	212.25
18	2011	1	Children	Domestic	1078	13,475.00
19	2011	1	Children	International	968	13,697.20
20	2011	1	Children	Mail order	5	123.75
21	2011	2	Mystery	International	1	678.23
22	2011	2	Mystery	Mail order	1	19.95
23	2011	2	Mystery	Domestic	-390	(3,795.92)
24	2011	2	Western	International	717	10,217.25
25	2011	2	Western	Mail order	53	1,312.37
26	2011	2	Western	Domestic	8883	109,931.27
27	2011	2	Romance	International	5	11,000.00
28	2011	2	Romance	Mail order	48	1,188.00
29	2011	2	Romance	Domestic	26151	371,831.00
30	2011	2	Sci Fi	Domestic	3260	40,750.00
31	2011	2	Sci Fi	International	681	9,636.15
32	2011	2	Sci Fi	Mail order	13	321.75
33	2011	2	Young Adult	Domestic	1407	17,587.50
34	2011	2	Young Adult	International	451	11,162.25
35	2011	2	Young Adult	Mail order	18	254.70

Figure 23-1 It's difficult to see the bottom line in a flat list like this; turning the list into a PivotTable will help.

Figures 23-2 through 23-4 show several ways you can transform this flat table into Pivot-Tables that show summary information at a glance.

The example on the left in Figure 23-2 breaks the data down first by category, second by distribution channel, and finally by year, with the total sales at each level displayed in column B. Looking at this table, you can see (among many other details) that the Children category generated domestic sales of $363,222, with more revenue in 2011 than in 2012.

In the example on the right in Figure 23-2, the per-category data is broken out first by year and then by distribution channel. The data is the same; only the perspective is different.

Both the PivotTables shown in Figure 23-2 are single-axis tables. That is, we generated a set of row labels (Children, Mystery, Romance, and so on) and set up outline entries below these labels. (And, by default, Excel displays outline controls next to all the headings, so you can collapse or expand the headings to suit your needs.)

	A	B	C
3	Row Labels ▾	Sum of Sales	
4	⊟Children	420838	
5	⊟Domestic	363222	
6	2011	198675	
7	2012	164547	
8	⊟International	43879	
9	2011	24423	
10	2012	19456	
11	⊟Mail order	13736	
12	2011	6089	
13	2012	7648	
14	⊟Mystery	89346	
15	⊟Domestic	103749	
16	2011	105564	
17	2012	-1815	
18	⊟International	-21474	
19	2011	4274	
20	2012	-25749	
21	⊟Mail order	7072	
22	2011	1825	
23	2012	5247	
24	⊟Romance	928462	
25	⊟Domestic	837227	
26	2011	779354	
27	2012	57873	
28	⊟International	81707	
29	2011	31369	
30	2012	50338	
31	⊟Mail order	9528	
32	2011	7999	
33	2012	1530	
34	⊟Sci Fi	1107382	
35	⊟Domestic	1042637	
36	2011	144225	
37	2012	898412	
38	⊟International	55044	
39	2011	37738	

	A	B	C
3	Row Labels ▾	Sum of Sales	
4	⊟Children	420838	
5	⊟2011	229186	
6	Domestic	198675	
7	International	24423	
8	Mail order	6089	
9	⊟2012	191651	
10	Domestic	164547	
11	International	19456	
12	Mail order	7648	
13	⊟Mystery	89346	
14	⊟2011	111663	
15	Domestic	105564	
16	International	4274	
17	Mail order	1825	
18	⊟2012	-22317	
19	Domestic	-1815	
20	International	-25749	
21	Mail order	5247	
22	⊟Romance	928462	
23	⊟2011	818721	
24	Domestic	779354	
25	International	31369	
26	Mail order	7999	
27	⊟2012	109740	
28	Domestic	57873	
29	International	50338	
30	Mail order	1530	
31	⊟Sci Fi	1107382	
32	⊟2011	187977	
33	Domestic	144225	
34	International	37738	
35	Mail order	6014	
36	⊟2012	919405	
37	Domestic	898412	
38	International	17305	
39	Mail order	3688	

Figure 23-2 These two PivotTables provide summary views of the information in Figure 23-1.

Figure 23-3 shows a more elaborate PivotTable that uses two axes. Along the row axis, we have categories broken out by distribution channel. Along the column axis, we have years (2011 and 2012), and we added the quarterly detail (not included in the Figure 23-2 examples) so that we can see how each category in each channel did each quarter of each year. With four dimensions (category, distribution channel, year, and quarter) and two axes (row and column), we have a lot of choices about how to arrange the furniture. Figure 23-3 shows only one of many possible permutations.

Figure 23-4 presents a different view. Now the distribution channels are arrayed by themselves along the column axis, while the row axis offers years broken out by quarters. The category, meanwhile, has been moved to what you might think of as a page axis. The data has been filtered to show the numbers for a single category, Mystery, but by using the filter control at the right edge of cell B1, you could switch the table to a different category (or combination of categories). Filtering the Category dimension by one category after another is like flipping through a stack of index cards.

Chapter 23

Sum of Sales	Column Labels ▼				2011 Total	2012				2012 Total	Grand Total
	2011										
Row Labels ▼	1	2	3	4		1	2	3	4		
⊟ Children	27296	127512	38560	35819	229186	104136	19036	81070	-12590	191651	420838
Domestic	13475	118400	34500	32300	198675	88650	13713	77321	-15136	164547	363222
International	13697	7231	2377	1118	24423	13060	4259	1274	863	19456	43879
Mail order	124	1881	1683	2401	6089	2426	1064	2475	1683	7648	13736
⊟ Mystery	-2769	-3098	-877	118408	111663	-34001	-1154	11704	1134	-22317	89346
Domestic	-4555	-3796	-1331	115245	105564	-488	-677	-148	-502	-1815	103749
International	349	678	134	3113	4274	-34770	-2153	11154	21	-25749	-21474
Mail order	1436	20	319	50	1825	1257	1676	698	1616	5247	7072
⊟ Romance	95871	384019	168786	170045	818721	10310	8225	97226	-6020	109740	928462
Domestic	80188	371831	159791	167544	779354	3040	6424	75852	-27443	57873	837227
International	12678	11000	7040	651	31369	6976	1683	20864	20815	50338	81707
Mail order	3005	1188	1955	1850	7999	293	117	510	608	1530	9528
⊟ Sci Fi	90560	50708	32761	13948	187977	317670	83354	317403	200977	919405	1107382
Domestic	77600	40750	23950	1925	144225	310755	81264	308188	198205	898412	1042637
International	10485	9636	7202	10414	37738	5802	1571	8547	1387	17305	55044
Mail order	2475	322	1609	1609	6014	1114	520	668	1386	3688	9702
⊟ Western	154320	121461	95300	98612	469692	-45293	-19679	64900	-23962	-24034	445659
Domestic	140909	109931	93317	97381	441538	-48616	-30774	45443	-28204	-62150	379388
International	12050	10217	1073	472	23812	3206	10873	19181	1891	35151	58963
Mail order	1361	1312	910	758	4342	117	223	275	2351	2966	7308
⊟ Young Adult	96220	29004	51030	135710	311964	92810	232973	275384	112398	713565	1025528
Domestic	80663	17588	32213	113863	244325	85088	224169	268213	103116	680585	924910
International	15345	11162	18761	21805	67073	7500	8462	6500	8583	31044	98117
Mail order	212	255	57	42	566	223	342	671	566	1935	2501
Grand Total	461498	709606	385559	572540	2129204	445631	322755	847686	271939	1888011	4017215

Figure 23-3 In this PivotTable, we arranged the data along two axes—rows and columns.

Category	Mystery ▼			
Sum of Sales	Column Labels ▼			
Row Labels ▼	Domestic	International	Mail order	Grand Total
⊟ 2011	105564	4274	1825	111663
1	-4555	349	1436	-2769
2	-3796	678	20	-3098
3	-1331	134	319	-877
4	115245	3113	50	118408
⊟ 2012	-1815	-25749	5247	-22317
1	-488	-34770	1257	-34001
2	-677	-2153	1676	-1154
3	-148	11154	698	11704
4	-502	21	1616	1134
Grand Total	103749	-21474	7072	89346

Figure 23-4 This PivotTable presents a filtered view, confining the report to a single category.

None of these tables required more than a few clicks to generate.

Creating a PivotTable

You can create a PivotTable from either an Excel range or an external data source. If you're working from an Excel range, your data should meet the criteria for a well-constructed list. That is, it should have column labels at the top (the headings become field names in the PivotTable), each column should contain a particular kind of data item, and you should not have any blank rows within the range. If the range includes summary formulas (totals, subtotals, or averages, for example), you should omit them from the PivotTable; the PivotTable performs its own summary calculations.

For information about connecting to and querying external data sources, see Chapter 25, "Working with external data."

The source range on your Excel worksheet can be a table (as described in Chapter 22, "Managing information in tables") or an ordinary list. Starting from a table has the advantage of allowing for expansion. When you create a PivotTable from a table, Excel references your source data by its table name (either a default name, such as Table1, or the name you assign to the table). If you add rows to a table, the table dimensions automatically adjust to encompass the new data, and hence your PivotTable stays in sync with the expanded source data.

To create a PivotTable, select a single cell within the source data and do one of the following:

- Click the Insert tab, and then click PivotTable or Recommended PivotTables in the Tables group.

- If your source data is a table and you're currently displaying the Design tab under Table Tools, click Summarize With PivotTable in the Tools group.

If you click Recommended PivotTables, Excel presents a half-dozen or more plausible ways to summarize your data in a PivotTable, as shown next.

Chapter 23

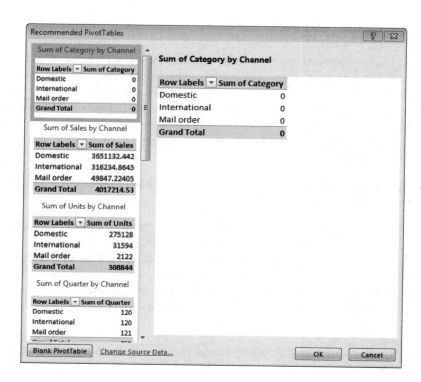

One of the options in the Recommended PivotTables dialog box might be just what you're looking for—or close enough to it to serve as a starting point. If not, go back to the ribbon and click PivotTable or Summarize With PivotTable. The Create PivotTable dialog box appears:

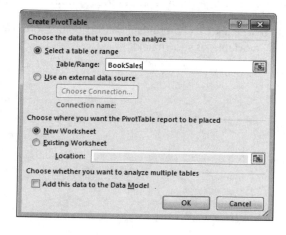

By default, your PivotTable arrives on a new worksheet, and that's generally a good arrangement. If you want it elsewhere, specify where in the Location box. After you click OK, Excel generates a blank table layout on the left side of the worksheet and displays the PivotTable Fields pane on the right. (See Figure 23-5.) The PivotTable Fields pane is docked at the right by default. You can make it wider or narrower by dragging the split bar on its left edge. You can also undock it or drag it across the worksheet and dock it on the left.

> **Note**
>
> If you want to work with only a subset of items in a field, you can filter the field before you add it to the table. If your data source is large, and particularly if the source is external, you can save some time by filtering in advance. (You can also filter fields after you create the table, of course.) To filter a field before you add it to the table, select the field name in the PivotTable Fields pane, and then click the arrow on the right. For more details, see "Filtering PivotTable fields" later in this chapter.

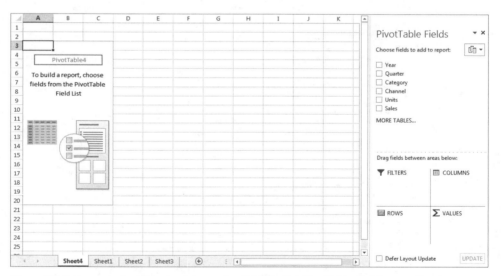

Figure 23-5 As you select the check boxes for fields in the PivotTable Fields pane, Excel populates the table layout at the left side of the worksheet.

To put some fields and data on that blank layout, begin by selecting the check boxes for those fields in the Choose Fields To Add To Report area of the PivotTable Fields pane. As you select fields, Excel positions them in the four boxes at the bottom of the pane. These four boxes represent the various components of the table. The Rows and Columns boxes hold the fields that appear on the row and column axes. The Filters box holds the field (or fields) you want to use to filter the table (comparable to the Category field in Figure 23-4), and the Values box holds the field (or fields) you want to use for calculations—the data you're summarizing (your sales, for example).

Initially, Excel puts selected fields in default table locations that depend on their data types. Most likely, you'll want some arrangement other than the one you get by default. That's not a problem, because you can move fields from one location to another easily; just drag them between the various boxes at the bottom of the PivotTable Fields pane. Let's look at an example.

To create the table shown in Figure 23-3, you need to put the Category and Channel fields in the Rows box, the Year and Quarter fields in the Columns box, and the Sales field in the Values box. When you select the check boxes for Category and Channel, Excel drops those fields in the Rows box (because they are text fields). When you select the check box for Sales, that one goes straight to the Values box (because it's a numeric field). These are excellent guesses on the part of Excel—in fact, just what you want. As you select field headings, Excel begins creating your PivotTable—as Figure 23-6 shows.

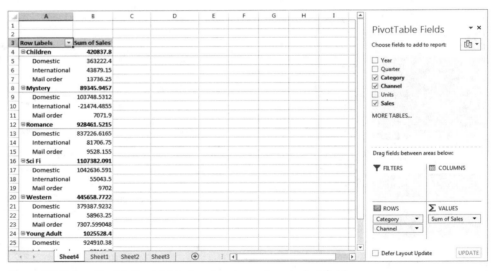

Figure 23-6 Excel builds the table, piece by piece, as you select fields.

So far, so good. The numeric formats aren't right, but you can fix that easily enough.

What remains to be done is to put the Year and Quarter fields into the Columns box. Unfortunately, if you simply select the respective check boxes, Excel drops these fields in the Values box because the fields are numbers and the program has a predilection for adding numbers. This (as you can see in Figure 23-7) is definitely not what you want.

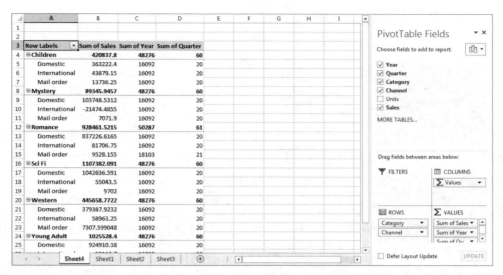

Figure 23-7 By default, Excel puts all numeric fields, including years and quarters, in the Values box. You can fix that by dragging field headings to the appropriate locations.

The solution is simple: Select the check boxes for the Year and Quarter fields, and then drag the Sum Of Quarter and Sum Of Year headings from the Values box to the Columns box. (Alternatively, you can make sure your field headings go where you want them by dragging them directly from the Choose Fields To Add To Report box to the appropriate boxes below, disregarding the defaults.)

Rearranging PivotTable fields

To pivot, or rearrange, a PivotTable, drag one or more field headings from one part of the PivotTable Fields pane to another. For example, if you use the mouse to change this configuration of the PivotTable Fields pane:

Drag fields between areas below:

▼ FILTERS	▦ COLUMNS
	Year ▼
	Quarter ▼

▦ ROWS	∑ VALUES
Category ▼	Sum of Sales ▼
Channel ▼	

☐ Defer Layout Update   UPDATE

to this one:

you can change the table from the form shown in Figure 23-3 earlier in this chapter to this:

▲	A	B	C	D	E	F	G	H
1								
2								
3	Sum of Sales	Column Labels ▼						
4		⊟Children			Children Total	⊟Mystery		N
5	Row Labels ▼	Domestic	International	Mail order		Domestic	International	Mail order
6	⊟2011	198675	24422.9	6088.5	229186.4	105563.53	4274.42	1825.05
7	1	13475	13697.2	123.75	27295.95	-4554.87	349.11	1436.4
8	2	118400	7230.65	1881	127511.65	-3795.92	678.23	19.95
9	3	34500	2377.2	1683	38560.2	-1330.68	134.08	319.2
10	4	32300	1117.85	2400.75	35818.6	115245	3113	49.5
11	⊟2012	164547.4	19456.25	7647.75	191651.4	-1814.9988	-25748.9055	5246.85
12	1	88650	13060.45	2425.5	104135.95	-487.6488	-34770.4655	1256.85
13	2	13712.5	4259.15	1064.25	19035.9	-677.29	-2152.97	1675.8
14	3	77321	1273.5	2475	81069.5	-147.57	11153.51	698.25
15	4	-15136.1	863.15	1683	-12589.95	-502.49	21.02	1615.95
16	Grand Total	363222.4	43879.15	13736.25	420837.8	103748.5312	-21474.4855	7071.9

> **Note**
>
> If you don't see the PivotTable Fields pane, select a cell in the PivotTable. (The pane disappears when your selection is not within the table.) If you still don't see it, click the Analyze tab under PivotTable Tools on the ribbon, and then click Field List. This button is a handy way to toggle the field list in and out of view, letting you reduce distraction when you don't need to do any field rearrangement.

To rearrange fields within the same axis—for example, to put Year before Quarter or Channel before Category in Figure 23-3, you can drag field headings from one place to another within the same area of the PivotTable Fields pane. Often, it's simpler to click the arrow to the right of the field heading you want to move. (For example, you might click the arrow to the right of Channel in the Rows box.) The menu that appears includes easy-to-use positioning commands:

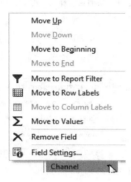

INSIDE OUT   Pivot your tables the Excel 2003 way if you prefer

Earlier versions of Excel let you move fields around by dragging them directly on the table, instead of requiring you to work with the PivotTable Fields pane. If you prefer that way of working, right-click any cell in the PivotTable, and click PivotTable Options. In the PivotTable Options dialog box, click the Display tab. Then select the Classic PivotTable Layout (Enables Dragging Of Fields In The Grid) check box. Note, however, that this option also changes the appearance of your table from the compact, outline-style presentation of Excel 2013 to the more space-consuming, tabular style of earlier versions.

Refreshing a PivotTable

Because users often generate PivotTables from large volumes of data (and, in many cases, that data resides on external servers), Excel doesn't automatically update PivotTables when their source data changes. To refresh a PivotTable, right-click any cell within it and click Refresh. Alternatively, under PivotTable Tools, click the Analyze tab, and then click Refresh in the Data group. If you prefer keyboard shortcuts, press Alt+F5.

To ensure that your PivotTable is up to date whenever you open the file, right-click any cell in the table, choose PivotTable Options from the shortcut menu, and click the Data tab in the PivotTable Options dialog box. Select the Refresh Data When Opening The File check box, and then click OK.

Changing the numeric format of PivotTable data

As Figure 23-6 shows, Excel initially displays numeric PivotTable data in the General format, regardless of how it's formatted in your source range. To fix that, right-click a cell in the field you want to change and then click Number Format.

Choosing report layout options

PivotTables, by default, use a compact layout that indents inner fields on the row axis beneath their outer fields. If you prefer, you can select from two alternative layouts, called Outline and Tabular. To switch from one layout to another, select a cell within the table, click the Design tab under PivotTable Tools, click Report Layout in the Layout group, and then click one of the displayed layouts (Show In Compact Form, Show In Outline Form, or Show In Tabular Form). Figure 23-8 compares the three layout options.

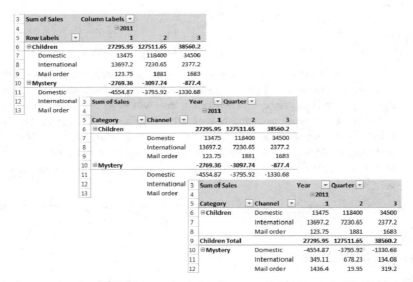

Figure 23-8 Excel offers three PivotTable layout options: Compact (top left), Outline (center), and Tabular (bottom right).

Note that the layout options affect the row axis only. For example, the outline form simply indents the distribution channels below each category of book.

Formatting a PivotTable

The Design tab that appears on the ribbon under PivotTable Tools when you select any part of a PivotTable includes a large selection of professionally designed PivotTable styles. These styles work just like—and, in fact, are similar to—the styles available with ordinary tables. By choosing from the PivotTable Styles gallery, you can ensure that your PivotTable looks good and uses colors consistent with the rest of your workbook. You can customize the built-in style choices by selecting or clearing the check boxes in the PivotTable Style Options group, and you can add your own designs by clicking New PivotTable Style at the bottom of the PivotTable Styles gallery. To display the PivotTable Styles gallery, click the More button at the bottom of the scroll bar. (This button is a small arrow with a line above it.) For more information about using and customizing built-in styles, see "Formatting tables" in Chapter 22.

Customizing the display of empty or error cells

Empty cells in a PivotTable are usually displayed as empty cells. If you prefer, you can have your PivotTable display something else—a text value such as NA, perhaps—in cells that would otherwise be empty. To do this, right-click any cell in the PivotTable and click Pivot-Table Options. On the Layout & Format tab in the PivotTable Options dialog box, select the For Empty Cells Show check box, and in the text box type the text or value that you want to see.

If a worksheet formula references a cell containing an error value, that formula returns the same error value. This is usually true in PivotTables as well. Error values in your source data propagate themselves into the PivotTable. If you prefer, you can have error values generate blank cells or text values. To customize this aspect of PivotTable behavior, right-click any cell in the PivotTable, and click PivotTable Options. On the Layout & Format tab in the Pivot-Table Options dialog box, select the For Error Values Show check box. Then, in the text box, type what you want to see.

Merging and centering field labels

When you have two or more fields stacked either on the column axis or on the row axis of a PivotTable, centering the outer labels over the inner ones can sometimes improve the table's readability. Just right-click a PivotTable cell, click PivotTable Options, and then select the Merge And Center Cells With Labels check box on the Layout & Format tab in the PivotTable Options dialog box. With this option, you can change this kind of presentation:

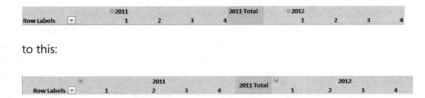

to this:

Hiding outline controls

You'll probably find outline controls useful in some contexts and not in others. They're great when you have large or complex PivotTables and you want to be able to switch quickly from details to overview. But if you find them to be cluttering the picture instead of enhancing it, you can banish them: select a PivotTable cell, click the Analyze tab under PivotTable Tools, and then click +/– Buttons in the Show group.

> **Note**
>
> With outline controls suppressed, you can still expand and collapse field headings. Select a heading in the field you're interested in, click the Analyze tab under PivotTable Tools on the ribbon, and then click Expand Entire Field or Collapse Entire Field in the Active Field group.

Hiding the Row Labels and Column Labels headings

The headings Row Labels and Column Labels that Excel displays near the upper-left corner of your PivotTable can prove distracting at times. You can suppress them by selecting a PivotTable cell, clicking the Analyze tab under PivotTable Tools, and then clicking Field Headers in the Show group. Note, however, that removing these labels also removes their associated filter controls—and you might want those controls from time to time. (See "Filtering PivotTable fields" later in this chapter.) The Field Headers command is a toggle. Click it again to restore the headings—and the filter controls.

> **Note**
>
> You can change the name of a PivotTable field or an item within a field by selecting any occurrence of it and typing the name you want. When you change one occurrence, all occurrences in the table change.

Displaying totals and subtotals

By default, Excel generates grand totals for all outer fields in your PivotTable by using the same summary function as the body of the table. In Figure 23-3, for example, row 30 displays grand totals for each quarter of each year, as well as for the years themselves. Column L, meanwhile, displays per-category totals by channel. The intersection of column L and row 30 displays the grandest of totals, the sum of all sales for the period covered by the table. Because the body of the table uses the SUM function, all these grand totals use that function as well.

To remove grand totals from a PivotTable, right-click any cell in the table and click Pivot-Table Options. On the Totals & Filters tab in the PivotTable Options dialog box, clear the Show Grand Totals For Rows check box, the Show Grand Totals For Columns check box, or both check boxes.

Naturally, PivotTables are not restricted to calculating sums. For other calculation options, see "Changing PivotTable calculations" later in this chapter.

Customizing subtotals

By default, Excel creates subtotals for all but the innermost fields. For example, in Figure 23-3, cell B6 displays the sum of cells B7:B9 (the Children subtotal for Quarter 1 of 2011), cell C10 displays the sum of cells C11:C13 (the Mystery subtotal for Quarter 2 of 2011), and so on. Columns F and K display yearly subtotals. The innermost fields, Channel (for the row axis) and Quarter (for the column axis), do not have subtotals.

To find options affecting all subtotals, select a cell in the PivotTable, click the Design tab under PivotTable Tools, and then click Subtotals on the left edge of the ribbon:

You can use this menu to turn subtotaling off altogether or to move row-axis subtotals from their default position above the detail items to a position below.

To customize subtotals for a particular field, right-click an item in the field, and then click Field Settings. (Alternatively, select an item in the field, click the Analyze tab under Pivot-Table Tools, and then click Field Settings in the Active Field group.) Figure 23-9 shows the Field Settings dialog box for the Category field in our PivotTable example.

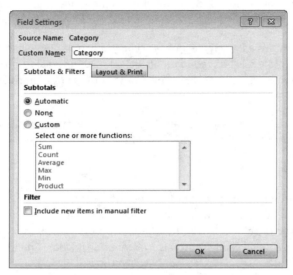

Figure 23-9   In the Field Settings dialog box, you can override the default subtotaling behavior for a particular field.

The Automatic option on the Subtotals & Filters tab in this dialog box means—as Automatic means throughout Excel—that you're letting the program decide what to do. In other words, this option gives you the default behavior. You can turn off subtotals for the selected field by selecting None. Selecting Custom lets you change the default subtotal calculation, such as from Sum to Average. And, as the text above the function list suggests, you're not limited to one function. You can select as many as you need by holding down Ctrl while you click. Figure 23-10 shows a PivotTable with four subtotaling calculations applied to the Category field. (Note that when you have multiple subtotals for a field, Excel moves them below the detail.)

	Sum of Sales	Column Labels							
3				2011			2011 Total		2012	
4										
5	Row Labels	1	2	3	4		1	2	3
6	⊟Children								
7	Domestic	13475	118400	34500	32300	198675	88650	13712.5	77321
8	International	13697.2	7230.65	2377.2	1117.85	24422.9	13060.45	4259.15	1273.5
9	Mail order	123.75	1881	1683	2400.75	6088.5	2425.5	1064.25	2475
10	Children Sum	27295.95	127511.65	38560.2	35818.6	229186.4	104135.95	19035.9	81069.5
11	Children Average	9098.65	42503.88333	12853.4	11939.53333	19098.86667	34711.98333	6345.3	27023.16667
12	Children Max	13697.2	118400	34500	32300	118400	88650	13712.5	77321
13	Children Min	123.75	1881	1683	1117.85	123.75	2425.5	1064.25	1273.5
14	⊟Mystery								
15	Domestic	-4554.87	-3795.92	-1330.68	115245	105563.53	-487.6488	-677.29	-147.57
16	International	349.11	678.23	134.08	3113	4274.42	-34770.4655	-2152.97	11153.51
17	Mail order	1436.4	19.95	319.2	49.5	1825.05	1256.85	1675.8	698.25
18	Mystery Sum	-2769.36	-3097.74	-877.4	118407.5	111663	-34001.2643	-1154.46	11704.19
19	Mystery Average	-923.12	-1032.58	-292.4666667	39469.16667	9305.25	-11333.75477	-384.82	3901.396667
20	Mystery Max	1436.4	678.23	319.2	115245	115245	1256.85	1675.8	11153.51
21	Mystery Min	-4554.87	-3795.92	-1330.68	49.5	-4554.87	-34770.4655	-2152.97	-147.57
22	⊟Romance								
23	Domestic	80188	371831	159791	167543.71	779353.71	3040.226488	6424.37	75851.56
24	International	12678.4	11000	7039.5	650.9	31368.8	6975.95	1683	20864.25
25	Mail order	3005	1188	1955.25	1850.29	7998.54	293.475	117.39	510.3

Figure 23-10 You can generate subtotals using more than one summary function; this table uses four for the Category field.

By using the Field Settings dialog box, you can also generate subtotals for innermost fields—subtotals that Excel usually does not display. Such inner subtotals appear at the bottom of the table (just above the grand total row) or at the right side of the table (just to the left of the grand total column). Figure 23-11 shows an example of inner-field subtotaling.

10	⊟Mystery									
11	Domestic	-4554.87	-3795.92	-1330.68	115245	105563.53	-487.6488	-677.29	-147.57	-502.49
12	International	349.11	678.23	134.08	3113	4274.42	-34770.4655	-2152.97	11153.51	21.02
13	Mail order	1436.4	19.95	319.2	49.5	1825.05	1256.85	1675.8	698.25	1615.95
14	⊟Romance									
15	Domestic	80188	371831	159791	167543.71	779353.71	3040.226488	6424.37	75851.56	-27443.25
16	International	12678.4	11000	7039.5	650.9	31368.8	6975.95	1683	20864.25	20814.75
17	Mail order	3005	1188	1955.25	1850.29	7998.54	293.475	117.39	510.3	608.45
18	⊟Sci Fi									
19	Domestic	77600	40750	23950	1925	144225	310755.0007	81264	308188	198204.59
20	International	10485.15	9636.15	7202.35	10414.4	37738.05	5801.5	1570.65	8546.6	1386.7
21	Mail order	2475	321.75	1608.75	1608.75	6014.25	1113.75	519.75	668.25	1386
22	⊟Western									
23	Domestic	140909.23	109931.27	93316.82	97381.05	441538.37	-48615.73684	-30774.07	45443.15	-28203.79
24	International	12050	10217.25	1073	472	23812.25	3206.25	10872.75	19181	1891
25	Mail order	1361.25	1312.37	909.68	758.47	4341.77	116.5790476	222.56	275.44	2351.25
26	⊟Young Adult									
27	Domestic	80662.5	17587.5	32212.5	113862.5	244325	85087.5	224168.95	268212.86	103116.07
28	International	15345	11162.25	18760.5	21804.75	67072.5	7499.5	8461.7	6500	8583
29	Mail order	212.25	254.7	56.6	42.45	566	222.75	342.45	670.81	699.31
30	Domestic Sum	388279.86	654703.85	342439.64	528257.26	1913680.61	438429.3416	294118.46	774869	230035.03
31	International Sum	64604.86	49924.53	36586.63	37572.9	188688.92	1773.1845	24694.28	67518.86	33559.62
32	Mail order Sum	8613.65	4977.77	6532.48	6710.21	26834.11	5428.904048	3942.2	5298.05	8343.96
33	Grand Total	461498.37	709606.15	385558.75	572540.37	2129203.64	445631.4301	322754.94	847685.91	271938.61

Figure 23-11 Subtotals for Channel, an inner field, appear in rows 30–32 of this table.

Sorting PivotTable fields

You can sort a PivotTable field either by its own items (for example, alphabetizing the categories in Figure 23-11) or on the basis of values in the body of the table (for example, sorting categories in descending order of sales totals so that the best-selling categories appear at the top). To sort a field, right-click any item in that field and then click Sort. On the menu that appears, you can specify how you want to sort (for example, A to Z or Z to A in the case of a text column). If you want to sort the field by values in the body of the table, click More Sort Options. You'll see a dialog box similar to the one shown here (with the name of the field you selected in the title of the dialog box).

To sort by values in the table body instead of by items in the selected field, open the Ascending or Descending list. The list will include the available value fields.

> **Note**
> To ensure that Excel retains your sort specification when you update your PivotTable, click More Options, which is shown in the preceding dialog box. Then select Sort Automatically Every Time The Report Is Updated.

Filtering PivotTable fields

Filtering a field lets you focus your table on a subset of items in that field. You can filter on the basis of the field's own content (only the Children and Young Adult categories, for example) or on the basis of values associated with the field (for example, the three categories with the best overall sales). You can apply filters in a variety of ways.

Filtering with the Report Filter axis

Figure 23-4, earlier in this chapter, shows a PivotTable in which one field, Category, appears on the Report Filter axis. To create this table, we simply dragged the Category field in the PivotTable Fields pane to the Filters area below the fields list. With the table arranged in this manner, you can focus on one category at a time.

When you put a field heading in the Filters area, the table initially aggregates all values of the field and displays the heading (All) next to the field name—like this:

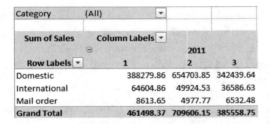

To filter the report so that it shows a particular field value, click the drop-down arrow next to the field name and select a value:

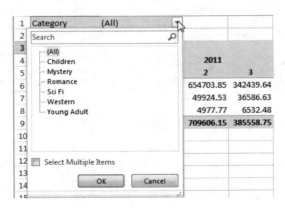

To select two or more field values, select the Select Multiple Items check box. Note, however, that if you filter on multiple field values, the indication next to the field name, above the table, does not tell you which values you're looking at. It simply says (Multiple Items):

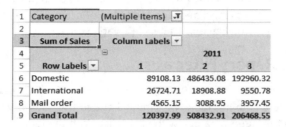

1	Category	(Multiple Items)		
2				
3	**Sum of Sales**	**Column Labels**		
4			2011	
5	**Row Labels**	1	2	3
6	Domestic	89108.13	486435.08	192960.32
7	International	26724.71	18908.88	9550.78
8	Mail order	4565.15	3088.95	3957.45
9	**Grand Total**	120397.99	508432.91	206468.55

If you want to see at a glance which items have been selected, it's better to filter with a slicer; that feature is described next.

Filtering with slicers

A slicer is an independently movable and formattable window containing buttons for each item in a field. You can use the buttons to filter your PivotTable. Figure 23-12 presents an example. Here, we selected three members of the Category field—Children, Romance, and Young Adult. Because these field items appear in a contrasting color in the slicer, you can see at a glance how the table has been filtered.

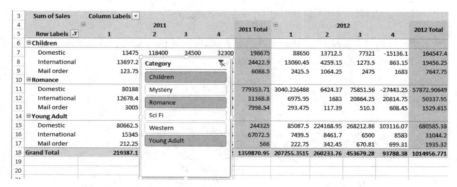

Figure 23-12 A slicer makes it easy to see how the table has been filtered.

To use a slicer, select any cell in your PivotTable, click Insert Slicer in the Sort & Filter group on the PivotTable Tools Analyze tab, and then click Insert Slicer. The Insert Slicers dialog box presents a check box for each field in your table. Select a field, and then click OK. You can select multiple fields to create more than one slicer. Figure 23-13 shows a table filtered by two slicers.

	Sum of Sales	Column Labels ▾										
			2011			2011 Total		2012				2012 Total
	Row Labels ▾	1	2	3	4		1	2	3	4	
	⊟Children										
	Domestic	13475	118400	34500	32300	198675	88650	13712.5	77321	-15136.1	164547.4
	Mail order	123.75						1064.25	2475	1683	7647.75
	⊟Romance										
	Domestic	80188						5424.37	75851.56	-27443.25	57872.90649
	Mail order	3005						117.39	510.3	608.45	1529.615
	⊟Young Adult										
	Domestic	80662.5						4168.95	268212.86	103116.07	680585.38
	Mail order	212.25						342.45	670.81	699.31	1935.32
	Grand Total	177666.5						829.91	425041.53	63527.48	914118.3715

Category: Children, Mystery, Romance, Sci Fi, Western, Young Adult

Channel: Domestic, International, Mail order

Figure 23-13 You can use multiple slicers to filter in more complex ways.

Connecting a slicer to multiple PivotTables

A single slicer can slice many tables. If you create multiple PivotTables to show a common set of data in different perspectives, you might find it convenient to set up slicers that are linked to all the related tables. To connect an existing slicer to another PivotTable, select the slicer. Then click Report Connections in the Slicer group on the Slicer Tools Options tab. The Report Connections dialog box displays the name of the selected slicer and a check box for each available PivotTable, as shown here.

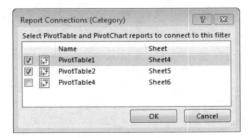

Select the tables you want to slice, and click OK.

Formatting slicers

You can style your slicers by using the same techniques you use to style a PivotTable or an ordinary table. Select a slicer, click the Slicer Tools Options tab, and then take your pick of styles from the Slicer Styles gallery. As with styles elsewhere in Excel, the available choices are keyed to your current workbook theme, so your slicer uses colors that are consistent with the rest of your workbook. For more information about using and customizing built-in styles, see "Formatting tables" in Chapter 22.

Filtering in the PivotTable Fields pane

If you're working with a large external data source and you need only a subset of the data, you can save yourself some time by setting up a filter in the PivotTable Fields pane before you execute the query and create your PivotTable. To filter in the PivotTable Fields pane, select the heading for the field you want to filter and then click the arrow to the right of the field heading. The dialog box that appears includes check boxes for each unique item in the selected field:

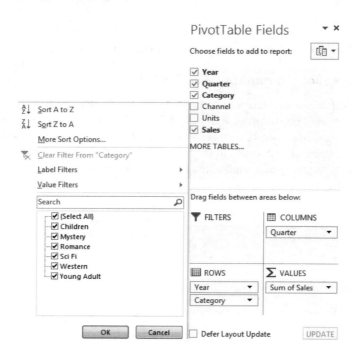

You can use the check boxes to select one or more particular items in your selected field. If your field is more complex than the example here, you might want to click Label Filters, in response to which Excel presents many additional filtering options:

The options that appear on this menu are tailored for the data type of the selected field. If your field holds dates instead of text, for example, you see these options like these:

To filter a field on the basis of values associated with that field, click the arrow next to the field heading in the PivotTable Fields pane and then click Value Filters on the menu that appears. For example, to filter the PivotTable in Figure 23-3 so that it shows only the three categories with the highest total sales, click the arrow next to Category and then click Value Filters to see the following menu.

Then click Top 10 to display the Top 10 Filter dialog box:

Replace the 10 with a 3, and then click OK. As Figure 23-14 shows, the result is a table showing the categories with the three highest grand total values in each of the three distribution types.

	2011				2011 Total	2012				2012 Total	Grand Total
Sum of Sales / Column Labels											
Row Labels	1	2	3	4		1	2	3	4		
Domestic	238450.5	430168.5	215953.5	283331.21	1167903.71	398882.7272	311857.32	652252.42	273877.41	1636869.877	2804773.587
Romance	80188	371831	159791	167543.71	779353.71	3040.226488	6424.37	75851.56	-27443.25	57872.90649	837226.6165
Sci Fi	77600	40750	23950	1925	144225	310755.0007	81264	308188	198204.59	898411.5907	1042636.591
Young Adult	80662.5	17587.5	32212.5	113862.5	244325	85087.5	224168.95	268212.86	103116.07	680585.38	924910.38
International	40073.4	32379.5	26873	22927.65	122253.55	17681.7	21017.45	46545.25	31288.75	116533.15	238786.7
Romance	12678.4	11000	7039.5	650.9	31368.8	6975.95	1683	20864.25	20814.75	50337.95	81706.75
Western	12050	10217.25	1073	472	23812.25	3206.25	10872.75	19181	1891	35151	58963.25
Young Adult	15345	11162.25	18760.5	21804.75	67072.5	7499.5	8461.7	6500	8583	31044.2	98116.7
Mail order	5603.75	3390.75	5247	5859.79	20101.29	3832.725	1701.39	3653.55	3677.45	12865.115	32966.405
Children	123.75	1881	1683	2400.75	6088.5	2425.5	1064.25	2475	1683	7647.75	13736.25
Romance	3005	1188	1955.25	1850.29	7998.54	293.475	117.39	510.3	608.45	1529.615	9528.155
Sci Fi	2475	321.75	1608.75	1608.75	6014.25	1113.75	519.75	668.25	1386	3687.75	9702
Grand Total	284127.65	465938.75	248073.5	312118.65	1310258.55	420397.1522	334576.16	702451.22	308843.61	1766268.142	3076526.692

Figure 23-14 This table has been filtered to show only the three best-selling categories; the rankings are based on values in the Grand Total column.

Changing PivotTable calculations

By default, Excel populates the Values area of your PivotTable by applying the SUM function to any numeric field you put there or by applying the COUNT function to any nonnumeric field. But you can choose from many alternative forms of calculation, and you can add your own calculated fields to the table.

Using a different summary function

To switch to a different summary function, right-click any cell in the Values area of your PivotTable and then click Value Field Settings. (Alternatively, click the Analyze tab under PivotTable Tools, and then click Field Settings in the Active Field group.) Excel displays the Value Field Settings dialog box, shown in Figure 23-15. Select the function you want from the Summarize Value Field By list, and then click OK.

Excel fills in the Custom Name line in this dialog box according to your selection in the Summarize Value Field By list. If you switch from SUM to AVERAGE, for example, the Custom Name line changes to include the word *Average*. You can type whatever you like there, though.

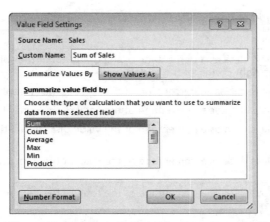

Figure 23-15 Using this dialog box, you can change the function applied to a field in the Values area of your PivotTable.

Applying multiple summary functions to the same field

You can apply as many summary functions as you want to a value field. To use a second or subsequent function with a field that's already in the Values area of your PivotTable, drag another copy of the field in the PivotTable Fields pane to the Values box. Then select a Values area cell, return to the Value Field Settings dialog box, and select the function you want to use. The available functions are SUM, COUNT, AVERAGE, MAX, MIN, PRODUCT, COUNT NUMBERS, STDDEV, STDDEVP, VAR, and VARP.

Using custom calculations

In addition to offering the standard summary functions enumerated in the previous paragraph, Excel offers a set of custom calculations. With these, you can have each item in the Values area of your table report its value as a percentage of the total values in the same row or column, create running totals, or show each value as a percentage of some base value.

To apply a custom calculation, right-click a cell in the Values area and then click Value Field Settings. Click the Show Values As tab in the Value Field Settings dialog box. Then select a calculation from the Show Values As list. Table 23-1 lists the available options.

TABLE 23-1 Custom calculation options

Option	Result
% Grand Total	Displays data as a percentage of the grand total (the value in the lower-right corner of the table)
% Of Column Total	Displays data as a percentage of the total of the current column
% Of Row Total	Displays data as a percentage of the total of the current row
% Of	Displays data as a percentage of the value of a specified base field and base item
% Of Parent Row Total	Displays data as a percentage of the total of the item's parent row
% Of Parent Column Total	Displays data as a percentage of the total of the item's parent column
% Of Parent Total	Displays data as a percentage of the parent's grand total
Difference From	Displays data as a difference from a specified base field and base item
% Difference From	Displays data as a percentage difference from a specified base field and base item
Running Total In	Displays data as a running total
% Running Total In	Displays running totals as percentages
Rank Smallest To Largest	Displays ordinal numbers to indicate items' rankings, from smallest to largest
Rank Largest To Smallest	Displays ordinal numbers to indicate items' rankings, from largest to smallest
Index	Uses this formula: ((Value in cell) * Grand Total of Grand Totals)) / ((Grand Row Total) * (Grand Column Total))

When you select a calculation in the Show Values As list, the Base Field and Base Item boxes display choices that are relevant to your calculation. For example, if you select Difference From in our books example, the Base Field box displays Quarter, Category, Channel, and so on. If you select Quarter in this list, the Base Item box presents the four quarters, along with the self-explanatory items Previous and Next.

Figure 23-16 shows a PivotTable using the Rank Largest To Smallest option. Note that displaying data in this way is completely separate from sorting the data.

	A	B	C	D	E	F	G	H	I	J	K	L
3	Sum of Sales	Column Labels ▼										
4			⊟2011			2011 Total	⊟2012				2012 Total	Grand Total
5	Row Labels ▼		1	2	3	4		1	2	3	4	
6	⊟Domestic											
7	Children		5 2 3 5			4	2 3 3 4				3	5
8	Mystery		6 6 6 2			6	5 5 6 3				5	6
9	Romance		3 1 1 1			1	4 4 4 5				4	3
10	Sci Fi		4 4 5 6			5	1 2 1 1				1	1
11	Western		1 3 2 4			2	6 6 5 6				6	4
12	Young Adult		2 5 4 3			3	3 1 2 2				2	2
13	⊟International											
14	Children		2 5 4 4			4	1 3 6 5				4	5
15	Mystery		6 6 6 3			6	6 6 3 6				6	6
16	Romance		3 2 3 5			3	3 4 1 1				1	2
17	Sci Fi		5 4 2 2			2	4 5 4 4				5	4
18	Western		4 3 5 6			5	5 1 2 3				2	3
19	Young Adult		1 1 1 1			1	2 2 5 2				3	1
20	⊟Mail order											
21	Children		6 1 2 1			2	1 2 1 2				1	1
22	Mystery		3 6 5 5			5	2 1 2 3				2	5
23	Romance		1 3 1 2			1	4 6 5 6				6	3
24	Sci Fi		2 4 3 3			3	3 3 4 4				3	2
25	Western		4 2 4 4			4	6 5 6 1				4	4
26	Young Adult		5 5 6 6			6	5 4 3 5				5	6
27	Grand Total											

Figure 23-16 Using the custom calculation Rank Largest To Smallest generates ordinal numbers that indicate the sales rankings.

Using calculated fields and items

In case custom calculations don't meet all your analytical needs, Excel lets you add calculated fields and calculated items to your PivotTables. A *calculated field* is a new field, derived from calculations performed on existing fields in your table. A *calculated item* is a new item in an existing field, derived from calculations performed on other items that are already in the field. After you create a custom field or item, Excel makes it available to your table as though it were part of your data source.

Custom fields and items can apply arithmetic operations to any data already in your PivotTable (including data generated by other custom fields or items), but they cannot reference worksheet data outside the PivotTable.

Creating a calculated field

To create a calculated field, select any cell in the PivotTable. Then click the Analyze tab under PivotTable Tools, and click Field, Items, & Sets in the Calculations group. On the Fields, Items, & Sets menu, click Calculated Field. Figure 23-17 shows the Insert Calculated Field dialog box.

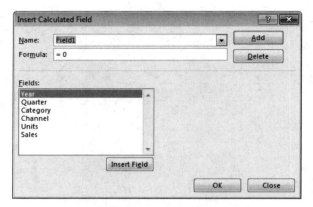

Figure 23-17 Create a calculated field in this dialog box.

Type a name for your calculated field in the Name box, and then type a formula in the Formula box. To enter a field in the formula, select it from the Fields list and click Insert Field. Figure 23-18 shows an example of a calculated field.

Figure 23-18 This calculated field multiplies an existing field by a constant.

Creating a calculated item

To create a calculated item for a field, select any existing item in the field or the field heading. Then click the Analyze tab under PivotTable Tools, and click Fields, Items, & Sets in the Calculations group. On the Fields, Items, & Sets menu, click Calculated Item. Excel displays a dialog box comparable to the one in Figure 23-19.

Figure 23-19 Use this dialog box to create a calculated item for a field.

To create a calculated item, type a unique name for the item in the Name box and then enter a formula in the Formula box. You can select from the Fields and Items lists and click Insert Field and Insert Item to enter field and item names in the formula.

> **Note**
>
> **You cannot create calculated items in fields that have custom subtotals.**

Figure 23-20 shows an example of a calculated item. In this case, the new item represents domestic sales divided by the sum of international and mail order sales.

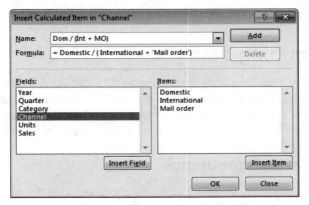

Figure 23-20 This calculated item appears by default whenever you include the Channel field in the PivotTable.

Chapter 23

Displaying a list of calculated fields and items

To display a list of your calculated fields and items, along with their formulas, click the Analyze tab under PivotTable Tools and then click Fields, Items, & Sets in the Calculations group. On the Fields, Items, & Sets menu, click List Formulas. Excel displays the list on a new worksheet, as shown in Figure 23-21.

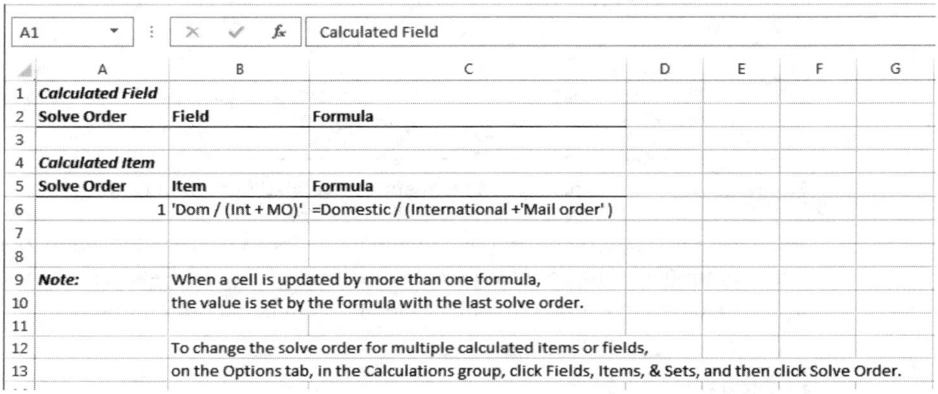

Figure 23-21 Excel lists calculated fields and items on a new worksheet.

As the note in Figure 23-21 indicates, you need to be careful when a cell in your table is affected by more than one calculated field or item. In such cases, the value is set by the formula that's executed last. The Solve Order information in the list of calculated fields and items tells you which formula that is. If you need to change the solve order, select the worksheet that contains the PivotTable, click the Analyze tab under PivotTable Tools, and then click Fields, Items, & Sets in the Calculations group. Then click Solve Order.

Grouping and ungrouping data

PivotTables group inner field items under each outer field heading and, if requested, create subtotals for each group of inner field items. You might find it convenient to group items in additional ways—for example, to collect monthly items into quarterly groups or sets of numbers into larger numeric categories. Excel provides several options for grouping items.

Creating ad hoc item groupings

Suppose that after looking at Figure 23-3 you decide you'd like to see the domestic and international sales figures grouped into a category called *Retail*. To create this group, select the Domestic and International items anywhere in the table. Then click the Analyze tab under PivotTable Tools, click Group, and then choose Group Selection. Excel creates a new heading called *Group1*:

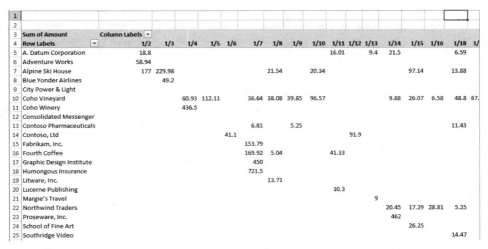

	Column Labels										
Sum of Sales	⊟2011				2011 Total	⊟2012				2012 Total	Grand To
Row Labels	1	2	3	4		1	2	3	4		
⊟**Children**	27295.95	127511.65	38560.2	35818.6	229186.4	104135.95	19035.9	81069.5	-12589.95	191651.4	4208:
⊟**Group1**											
Domestic	13475	118400	34500	32300	198675	88650	13712.5	77321	-15136.1	164547.4	3632:
International	13697.2	7230.65	2377.2	1117.85	24422.9	13060.45	4259.15	1273.5	863.15	19456.25	4387!
⊟**Mail order**											
Mail order	123.75	1881	1683	2400.75	6088.5	2425.5	1064.25	2475	1683	7647.75	1373(
⊟**Mystery**	-2769.36	-3097.74	-877.4	118407.5	111663	-34001.2643	-1154.46	11704.19	1134.48	-22317.0543	89345.9
⊟**Group1**											
Domestic	-4554.87	-3795.92	-1330.68	115245	105563.53	-487.6488	-677.29	-147.57	-502.49	-1814.9988	103748.5
International	349.11	678.23	134.08	3113	4274.42	-34770.4655	-2152.97	11153.51	21.02	-25748.9055	-21474.4
⊟**Mail order**											
Mail order	1436.4	19.95	319.2	49.5	1825.05	1256.85	1675.8	698.25	1615.95	5246.85	70!
⊟**Romance**	95871.4	384019	168785.75	170044.9	818721.05	10309.65149	8224.76	97226.11	-6020.05	109740.4715	928461.5
⊟**Group1**											
Domestic	80188	371831	159791	167543.71	779353.71	3040.226488	6424.37	75851.56	-27443.25	57872.90649	837226.6
International	12678.4	11000	7039.5	650.9	31368.8	6975.95	1683	20864.25	20814.75	50337.95	81700
⊟**Mail order**											
Mail order	3005	1188	1955.25	1850.29	7998.54	293.475	117.39	510.3	608.45	1529.615	9528.
⊟**Sci Fi**	90560.15	50707.9	32761.1	13948.15	187977.3	317670.2507	83354.4	317402.85	200977.29	919404.7907	1107382.
⊟**Group1**											

Sum of Sales

Grouping items in date or time ranges

Figure 23-22 shows a PivotTable that summarizes daily transactions by payee. As you can see, the data in this table is extremely sparse. Most intersections between a day item and a payee item are blank.

Sum of Amount	Column Labels																
Row Labels	1/2	1/3	1/4	1/5	1/6	1/7	1/8	1/9	1/10	1/11	1/12	1/13	1/14	1/15	1/16	1/18	1/
A. Datum Corporation	18.8									16.01		9.4	21.5			6.59	
Adventure Works	58.94																
Alpine Ski House	177	229.98				21.54		20.34						97.14		13.88	
Blue Yonder Airlines		49.2															
City Power & Light																	
Coho Vineyard			60.93	112.11		36.64	38.08	39.85	96.57				9.88	26.07	6.58	48.8	67.
Coho Winery			436.5														
Consolidated Messenger																	
Contoso Pharmaceuticals						6.81	5.25									11.43	
Contoso, Ltd					41.1						91.9						
Fabrikam, Inc.						153.79											
Fourth Coffee						169.92	5.04		41.33								
Graphic Design Institute						450											
Humongous Insurance						721.5											
Litware, Inc.						13.71											
Lucerne Publishing									30.3								
Margie's Travel													9				
Northwind Traders													20.45	17.29	28.81	5.25	
Proseware, Inc.													462				
School of Fine Art													26.25				
Southridge Video																14.47	

Figure 23-22 To make the data in this table more meaningful, you can group the date field.

You'll find the Transactions.xlsx file with the other examples on the companion website.

To make this kind of table more meaningful, you can group the date field. To do this, select an item in the field. Then click the Analyze tab under PivotTable Tools, Click Group, and choose Group Field. Excel responds by displaying the Grouping dialog box, shown in Figure 23-23.

Figure 23-23 Excel gives you lots of ways to group by date.

Excel gives you a great deal of flexibility in the way your date and time fields are grouped. In the By list, you can choose any common time interval, from seconds to years, and if the standard intervals don't meet your needs, you can select an arbitrary number of days. You can also select multiple items to create two or more groupings at the same time; the results of grouping by both Quarter and Month are shown in Figure 23-24.

Sum of Amount	Column Labels													Grand Total
	Qtr1			Qtr2			Qtr3			Qtr4				
Row Labels	Jan	Feb	Mar	Apr	May	Jun	Jul	Aug	Sep	Oct	Nov	Dec		
A. Datum Corporation	114.87	72.19	193.49	89.42	377.46	121.04	15.98	18.91	121.91	199.06	40.54	161.42		1526.29
Adventure Works	58.94	248.91	75.32		75.61	32	14.66	165.45	234.31	792.2	984.4	57.13		2738.93
Alpine Ski House	1093.01	684.44	1433.42	1288.59	1098.2	1261.47	771.93	701.06	803.66	1331.2	785.71	689.21		11941.9
Blue Yonder Airlines	49.2	189.95	31.48	41.13	136.67	49.74	24.22	230.94	194.05	18.43	80.77	18.14		1064.72
City Power & Light		16.79		24.68			24.52	28.52	109.8		15.73	25.15		245.19
Coho Vineyard	630.53	427.69	694.55	939.71	710.46	681.21	777.2	572.13	917.39	483.68	861.11	999.64		8695.3
Coho Winery	436.5	6		11.7	20.84		22.05		232.75		10.95	28		768.79
Consolidated Messenger		26.24		173.9				83.54	156.45	47.95		43.74		531.82
Contoso Pharmaceuticals	46.97	212	461.12	57.17		219.17	125.56	357.7	521.91	510.76	619.46	388.7		3520.52
Contoso, Ltd	133	76.04	87.2	237.16	233.31	177.03	127.1	42.25	273.4	322.9	416.14	46.81		2172.34
Fabrikam, Inc.	368.59	17.83			22.97	13.46	37.62	33.12	60.83		142.52	70		766.94
Fourth Coffee	326.88	316.82	617.08	408.44	319.48	399.52	393.93	974.65	391.25	797.83	605.86	333.77		5885.51
Graphic Design Institute	450	56			16.92			15.5	278			27.95		844.37
Humongous Insurance	721.5	83			164.71		48	995		12.59		363.49		2388.29
Litware, Inc.	13.71	105.5			14.85			15		37.7		10.97		197.73
Lucerne Publishing	35.55	80.35	60.69	23.6	74.9	30.9	5.25	25.47	28.85	125.09	320.97	152.58		964.2
Margie's Travel	9	84	9	9	9	9		24.5	9	32.08		120		314.58
Northwind Traders	71.8	23.07	138.89		395		52.18	18		38.28	6.02	121.73		864.97
Proseware, Inc.	462		3.76		73.66			4.95	628.75	134.9	36.6	15.39		1360.01
School of Fine Art	26.25	26.25	41.24	26.25	42.49	26.25		146.25	599.81	239.48		291.83		1466.1

Figure 23-24 In this table, daily data is grouped by months and then by quarters.

Displaying the details behind a data value

If you double-click any PivotTable value that represents a summary calculation, Excel displays the details behind that calculation on a new worksheet. For example, Figure 23-24 informs us that we spent $681.21 at Coho Vineyard during the month of June. Double-clicking that cell reveals the details:

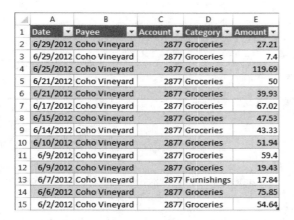

	A	B	C	D	E
1	Date	Payee	Account	Category	Amount
2	6/29/2012	Coho Vineyard	2877	Groceries	27.21
3	6/29/2012	Coho Vineyard	2877	Groceries	7.4
4	6/25/2012	Coho Vineyard	2877	Groceries	119.69
5	6/21/2012	Coho Vineyard	2877	Groceries	50
6	6/21/2012	Coho Vineyard	2877	Groceries	39.93
7	6/17/2012	Coho Vineyard	2877	Groceries	67.02
8	6/15/2012	Coho Vineyard	2877	Groceries	47.53
9	6/14/2012	Coho Vineyard	2877	Groceries	43.33
10	6/10/2012	Coho Vineyard	2877	Groceries	51.94
11	6/9/2012	Coho Vineyard	2877	Groceries	59.4
12	6/9/2012	Coho Vineyard	2877	Groceries	19.43
13	6/7/2012	Coho Vineyard	2877	Furnishings	17.84
14	6/6/2012	Coho Vineyard	2877	Groceries	75.85
15	6/2/2012	Coho Vineyard	2877	Groceries	54.64

Creating PivotCharts

PivotCharts, like PivotTables, summarize tabular information and allow for easy transposition of fields and axes. They're a great way to study or present elements of your data set.

You can create a PivotChart directly from your source data by selecting a cell in the original data range, clicking the Insert tab, and then clicking PivotChart in the Charts group. After you specify or confirm your data source and indicate where you want the new PivotChart to reside (in a location on the existing worksheet or on a new worksheet), Excel presents both a blank PivotChart layout and the PivotTable Fields task pane. (See Figure 23-25.) As you work with the task pane, Excel creates a new PivotTable at the same time it creates the PivotChart.

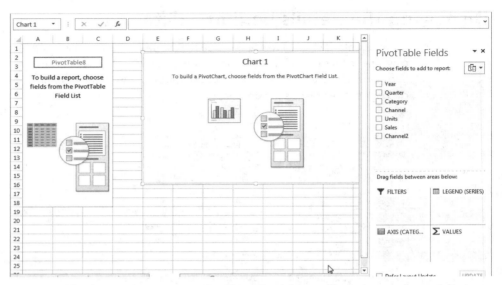

Figure 23-25 When you create a new PivotChart, Excel draws a blank chart canvas and displays the PivotTable Fields task pane.

Figure 23-26 shows a simple PivotChart created from this chapter's Books table. Because charts are generally most effective when applied to a modest amount of data, we used the Filters box to restrict the presentation to a single category (Children).

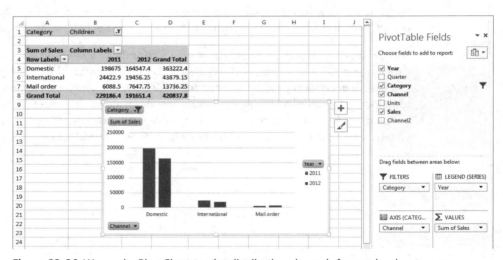

Figure 23-26 We used a PivotChart to plot distribution channels for one book category.

When you select a PivotChart, Excel adds a new set of tabs to the ribbon, under Pivot-Chart Tools. With these tabs, you can manipulate and format your PivotChart the same way you do an ordinary chart. While the chart is selected, changes in the four boxes below the field list reflect the fact that you're working with a chart instead of a table: the Rows box becomes the Axis (Category) box, and the Columns box becomes the Legend (Series) box. You can pivot the chart the same way you would pivot a PivotTable—by dragging field names from one box to another. You can also change the filter applied to the chart by manipulating the drop-down lists that appear alongside the chart axes and above the legend.

A PivotChart and its associated PivotTable are inextricably linked. Changes to one are immediately reflected in the other.

In Figures 23-25 and 23-26, we created a PivotChart directly from the source data. You can also create one from an existing PivotTable. Select any cell in the PivotTable, click the Analyze tab under PivotTable Tools, and then click PivotChart in the Tools group.

Moving beyond PivotTables

As powerful as the Excel PivotTable feature is, it is not without limitations. The most crucial limitation is that native PivotTables can analyze data from only one table at a time. To move beyond this limitation, Excel includes an add-in called PowerPivot. That is the subject of Chapter 24, "Using PowerPivot."

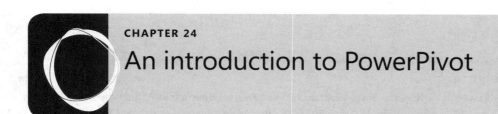

MICROSOFT POWERPIVOT for Microsoft Excel 2013 is an add-in aimed at providing self-service business intelligence (BI). This is a real revolution in the world of data analysis, because it gives you all the power needed to perform complex data analysis without requiring the intervention of BI technicians. PowerPivot implements a fast, powerful, in-memory database that can organize data, detect interesting relationships, and provide the fastest way to browse information.

Some of the most interesting features of PowerPivot are

- The ability to organize tables for the PivotTable tool in a relational way, freeing up the analyst from the need to import data as Excel sheets before analyzing them.

- The availability of a fast, space-saving columnar database that can handle huge amounts of data without the limitations of Excel sheets.

- DAX, a powerful programming language that defines complex expressions on top of the relational database. DAX makes it possible to define surprisingly rich expressions, compared to those in standard Excel.

- The ability to integrate different sources of data—such as databases, Excel sheets, data sources available on the Internet—and virtually any kind of data.

- Amazingly fast in-memory processing of complex queries over the whole database.

PowerPivot is complex and elaborate, and the current chapter provides only a cursory introduction to the subject. For complete information about all of PowerPivot's features, see *Microsoft Excel 2013: Building Data Models with PowerPivot* by Alberto Ferrari and Marco Russo (Microsoft Press, 2013).

> **Note**
>
> As of this writing, the PowerPivot and Power View features are included only with specific configurations of Office 2013. The PowerPivot feature, which was available in all versions of Excel 2010, is available only in Office 2013 Professional Plus, SharePoint 2013 Enterprise Edition, SharePoint Online 2013 Plan 2, and the E3 or E4 editions of Office 365. The Power View feature, new in Excel 2013, is included with the same versions as PowerPivot. Happily, the Excel Data Model is supported in all configurations of Excel 2013. The variety of available configurations may change, however, so stay tuned.

Using a PivotTable on an Excel table

Excel's native PivotTable feature, described in Chapter 23, "Analyzing data with PivotTable reports," provides an easy and convenient way to browse data that you collect into Excel sheets. However, it's helpful to recall the main features of the PivotTable to compare that tool with PowerPivot.

Let us suppose you have a standard Excel table, imported from a query run against a database that contains all the data you want to analyze. To get this data, you probably asked your IT department to provide some means to access the database and a specific query, in order to retrieve the information. Your Excel sheet would look like the one in Figure 24-1. Because the table contains raw data, it is very difficult to analyze.

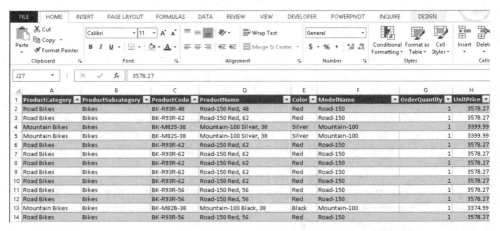

Figure 24-1 Here you can see some sample data we used to create a new PivotTable.

Having all the data available in a sheet, you can then choose to insert a PivotTable. The wizard prompts you for the table to use as the source of the pivot and for where to put the Pivot-Table, and then it provides the standard Excel PivotTable interface shown in Figure 24-2.

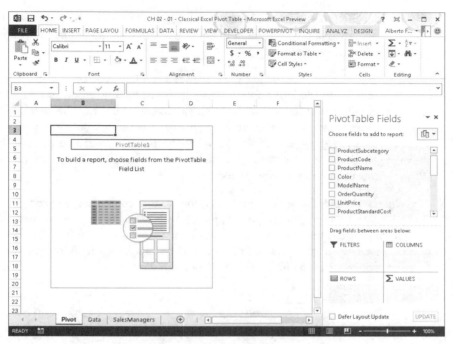

Figure 24-2 This is the standard PivotTable interface in Excel.

From here, you can choose to take, for example, the year and put it on the columns and put the product category on the rows, displaying the sales amount in the intersection of rows and columns. After properly formatting your numbers, you get a nice report (as shown in Figure 24-3) showing how each category performed over time.

One of the best characteristics of the PivotTable tool is its ease of use. Excel analyzes the source table, detects numeric values, and provides you the ability to display their total slicing data over all other columns. By default, totals are aggregated using the SUM function, because this is what is normally needed. If you want a different aggregation function, you can choose it using the various PivotTable options.

As easy as they are to use, PivotTables have some limitations:

- PivotTables can analyze information coming from only a single table stored in an Excel sheet. If you have different tables, containing different information, there is no easy way to correlate information coming from them.

- It is not always easy to get the source data into a format that is suitable for analysis. In the previous example, you saw a table that is extracted from a SQL query run against the AdventureWorks database and that you build to analyze data. The skills needed to build such a query are somewhat technical, and this often raises the problem of asking your IT department to develop such queries before you even start the analysis process.

- Because only one table can be analyzed at a time, you often end up building the queries needed for a specific analysis, and, if for any reason you want to perform a different analysis, you need to build different queries. If, for example, you have a query that returns sales at the month level, you cannot use it to perform a further analysis at the "day of week" level; to do that, you need a new query. This in turn might involve the need to contact IT again and can become expensive if IT charges for the amount of work it does.

When PivotTables are not enough, as is the case for companies with complex data models, it is common to start a complete BI project with products like SQL Server Analysis Services, which provides the same pivoting features on complex data structures known as OLAP cubes. OLAP cubes are the definitive solution to BI requirements, but they are expensive and require a strong effort from the IT department.

Sum of SalesAmount	Column Labels				
Row Labels	2005	2006	2007	2008	Grand Total
Bike Racks			16,440.00	22,920.00	39,360.00
Bike Stands			18,921.00	20,670.00	39,591.00
Bottles and Cages			23,280.27	33,517.92	56,798.19
Caps			7,956.15	11,731.95	19,688.10
Cleaners			3,044.85	4,173.75	7,218.60
Fenders			19,408.34	27,211.24	46,619.58
Gloves			14,228.69	20,792.01	35,020.70
Helmets			92,583.54	132,752.06	225,335.60
Hydration Packs			16,771.95	23,535.72	40,307.67
Jerseys			70,370.46	102,580.22	172,950.68
Mountain Bikes	585,973.27	1,562,456.76	3,989,638.48	3,814,691.06	9,952,759.56
Road Bikes	2,680,400.39	4,967,886.77	3,952,029.21	2,920,267.67	14,520,584.04
Shorts			30,445.65	40,874.16	71,319.81
Socks			2,229.52	2,876.80	5,106.32
Tires and Tubes			103,259.76	142,269.56	245,529.32
Touring Bikes			1,417,434.93	2,427,366.12	3,844,801.05
Vests			13,017.50	22,669.50	35,687.00
Grand Total	**3,266,373.66**	**6,530,343.53**	**9,791,060.30**	**9,770,899.74**	**29,358,677.22**

Figure 24-3 This figure shows an example of a report with the PivotTable tool.

Using PowerPivot in Office 2013

To let you analyze more complex data, Microsoft introduced *self-service BI*. The goal of this technology is to let you build complex data structures and analyze them with PivotTables, removing the current limitations of the PivotTable. PowerPivot is the primary tool available from Microsoft to handle self-service BI, along with its companion Power View, which we will discuss later in this chapter.

You can use PowerPivot to analyze data without contacting IT to produce complex queries. Furthermore, it removes the limitation that a PivotTable can analyze only a single table, because you can query more tables at the same time, producing reports that easily integrate information coming from different sources.

> ## Working with the AdventureWorks sample database
>
> To provide examples, we will use the AdventureWorks database throughout this book. We chose AdventureWorks because it is a well-known database, is freely available on the web, and contains sample data you can easily use for complex analysis. The database contains information about Adventure Works Cycles, which is a fictitious large, multinational company that manufactures and sells metal and composite bicycles to North American, European, and Asian commercial markets.
>
> You can download the AdventureWorks database from *http://www.codeplex.com/ SqlServerSamples*, where you will find different versions of the database, depending on the release of SQL Server you have installed. The companion website includes an Excel workbook that you can use to follow the demos in this chapter. Thus, you will be able to follow most of the examples even if you do not have access to a database.

 You'll find the Access version of AdventureWorks, Adventureworks.accdb, on the companion website.

The first version of PowerPivot for Excel was initially released as an add-in for Excel 2010. PowerPivot is a powerful columnar database that does not work with classic Excel tables. It works with data stored inside its proprietary database and can be queried using the DAX language or a PivotTable. Although this information seems to be just a curiosity about the history of PowerPivot, it is in reality very important. For PowerPivot to work, the data should not be stored inside Excel tables; instead, it needs to be stored inside the PowerPivot database.

At the beginning, the PowerPivot database was somewhat separated from Office, meaning that all of its features were available only to users who decided to download and install the add-in. If an Excel workbook containing PowerPivot data was opened on a PC where the add-in was not installed, it simply did not work, even if the data contained in Excel sheets was always visible.

In Office 2013, PowerPivot comes pre-installed and needs only to be activated. Moreover, in Office 2013, the PowerPivot engine is fully integrated in Excel and starts to work even before being activated.

To start using PowerPivot, you are going to take the easy way: you will create PowerPivot tables without even activating the add-in. This happens smoothly as soon as you activate the following advanced features of Excel for the analysis of data:

- Power View reports

- Relationships between tables

- PivotTables spanning more than one table

Adding information to the Excel table

Let's start making the analysis slightly more complex. The dataset provided by our Excel table contains information about product categories. Assume that, at AdventureWorks, each product category is assigned to a salesperson and this information is not stored in the database, so you don't have the option to modify the original query to grab this information. Because you are an Excel power user, you can fill another Excel table with this information, like the one shown in Figure 24-4.

Category	SalesManager	Office
Bike Racks	Maurizio	Redmond
Bike Stands	Maurizio	Redmond
Bottles and Cages	Maurizio	Redmond
Caps	Maurizio	Redmond
Cleaners	Alberto	Seattle
Fenders	Alberto	Seattle
Gloves	Alberto	Seattle
Helmets	Alberto	Seattle
Hydration Packs	Alberto	Seattle
Jerseys	Marco	Redmond
Mountain Bikes	Marco	Redmond
Road Bikes	Marco	Redmond
Shorts	Marco	Redmond
Socks	Marco	Redmond
Tires and Tubes	Marco	Redmond
Touring Bikes	Louis	Seattle
Vests	Louis	Seattle

Figure 24-4 The SalesManager Excel table will prove useful to show the performance of managers, instead of categories.

You'll find the Classic PivotTable.xlsx file with the other examples on the companion website.

To use this new information in the PivotTable, you need to bring over the SalesManager column from the original data model. As you already know, VLOOKUP is your best friend here. Add a column to our original table with this formula:

```
=VLOOKUP([@ProductCategory],SalesManagers,2)
```

You will end up with a new dataset, which now contains the sales manager, as you can see in Figure 24-5.

| B2 | ▼ | ⋮ | ✕ | ✓ | *fx* | =VLOOKUP([@ProductCategory],SalesManagers,2) |

▲	A	B	C	D
1	**ProductCategory** ▼	**SalesManager** ▼	**ProductSubca** ▼	**ProductCode** ▼
2	Road Bikes	Marco	Bikes	BK-R93R-48
3	Road Bikes	Marco	Bikes	BK-R93R-62
4	Mountain Bikes	Marco	Bikes	BK-M82S-38
5	Mountain Bikes	Marco	Bikes	BK-M82S-38
6	Road Bikes	Marco	Bikes	BK-R93R-62
7	Road Bikes	Marco	Bikes	BK-R93R-62
8	Road Bikes	Marco	Bikes	BK-R93R-62
9	Road Bikes	Marco	Bikes	BK-R93R-62
10	Road Bikes	Marco	Bikes	BK-R93R-62
11	Road Bikes	Marco	Bikes	BK-R93R-56
12	Road Bikes	Marco	Bikes	BK-R93R-56
13	Mountain Bikes	Marco	Bikes	BK-M82B-38
14	Road Bikes	Marco	Bikes	BK-R93R-56
15	Mountain Bikes	Marco	Bikes	BK-M82B-44

Figure 24-5 Using VLOOKUP, you were able to bring the sales manager into the original table.

With the new dataset, the PivotTable can be easily modified by adding the SalesManager data to the rows, resulting in the desired report, as you can see in Figure 24-6.

Sum of SalesAmount	Column Labels ▼				
Row Labels ▼	2005	2006	2007	2008	**Grand Total**
⊟**Alberto**			**146,037.37**	**208,464.78**	**354,502.15**
Cleaners			3,044.85	4,173.75	7,218.60
Fenders			19,408.34	27,211.24	46,619.58
Gloves			14,228.69	20,792.01	35,020.70
Helmets			92,583.54	132,752.06	225,335.60
Hydration Packs			16,771.95	23,535.72	40,307.67
⊟**Louis**			**1,430,452.43**	**2,450,035.62**	**3,880,488.05**
Touring Bikes			1,417,434.93	2,427,366.12	3,844,801.05
Vests			13,017.50	22,669.50	35,687.00
⊟**Marco**	**3,266,373.66**	**6,530,343.53**	**8,147,973.08**	**7,023,559.47**	**24,968,249.73**
Jerseys			70,370.46	102,580.22	172,950.68
Mountain Bikes	585,973.27	1,562,456.76	3,989,638.48	3,814,691.06	9,952,759.56
Road Bikes	2,680,400.39	4,967,886.77	3,952,029.21	2,920,267.67	14,520,584.04
Shorts			30,445.65	40,874.16	71,319.81
Socks			2,229.52	2,876.80	5,106.32
Tires and Tubes			103,259.76	142,269.56	245,529.32
⊟**Maurizio**			**66,597.42**	**88,839.87**	**155,437.29**
Bike Racks			16,440.00	22,920.00	39,360.00
Bike Stands			18,921.00	20,670.00	39,591.00
Bottles and Cages			23,280.27	33,517.92	56,798.19
Caps			7,956.15	11,731.95	19,688.10
Grand Total	**3,266,373.66**	**6,530,343.53**	**9,791,060.30**	**9,770,899.74**	**29,358,677.22**

Figure 24-6 The SalesManager column is now visible in the PivotTable.

This technique works fine, but if you now want to slice data using the Office column from the SalesManager table, you need to repeat the operation of using VLOOKUP to put the Office column in the original table. Even if, in this specific example, it does not mean a huge amount of work, it is better to move to the next level and learn some of the new features available with the Excel 2013 data model.

Creating a data model with many tables

Instead of using VLOOKUP to populate a single dataset, as you did in the previous example, you want to add the SalesManager table to the PivotTable so that you can use all of its columns. You are moving from a classical single table analysis to a more advanced multitable one. Doing so is easy. If you look at the bottom of the PivotTable Fields list in the right pane, you see the More Tables option. (See Figure 24-7.)

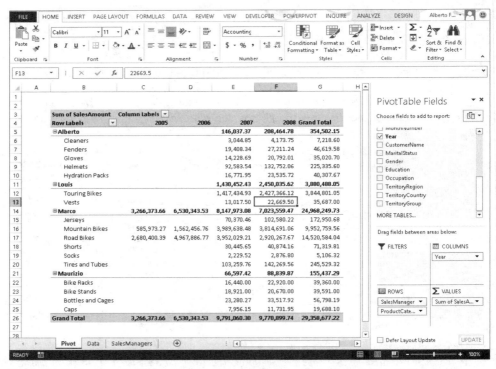

Figure 24-7 The More Tables option lets you add more tables to a single PivotTable report.

If you click it, you will see an information message that asks you to confirm whether you want to proceed with creating a new PivotTable. The Create A New PivotTable message box appears, shown in Figure 24-8. It contains useful information about what is happening, because it speaks about something new: the data model.

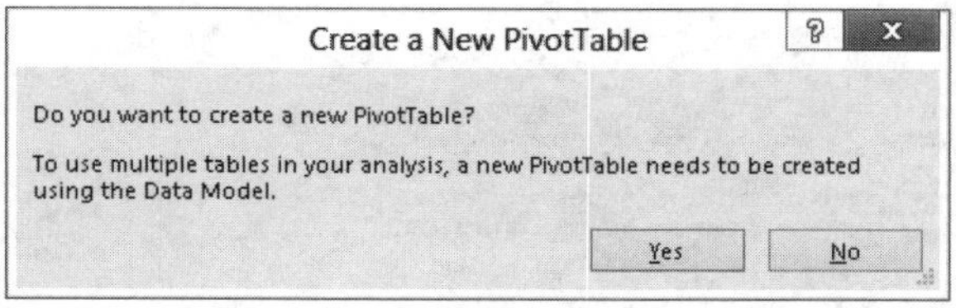

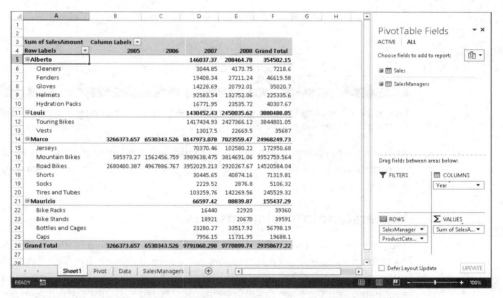

Figure 24-8 As simple as it is, this confirmation window contains a lot of useful information.

If you simply click Yes, Excel creates a new PivotTable with a structure that is identical to the current one but with more tables. You can see the result in Figure 24-9, where the Pivot-Table Fields list now contains two tables: Sales and SalesManagers.

Figure 24-9 The new PivotTable contains two tables in the PivotTable Fields list.

You can now remove the SalesManager and the ProductCategory fields from the row axis; then, after expanding the SalesManagers table, you add the Office field to the row axis. The result is *not* what you would expect. In fact, as you can see in Figure 24-10, it seems that all of the offices (two, in our example) have exactly the same amount of sales, which you know is false. The PivotTable also seems to detect that something is wrong because the following warning appears in the PivotTable Fields list: "Relationships between tables may be needed." The warning appears with an inviting Create button.

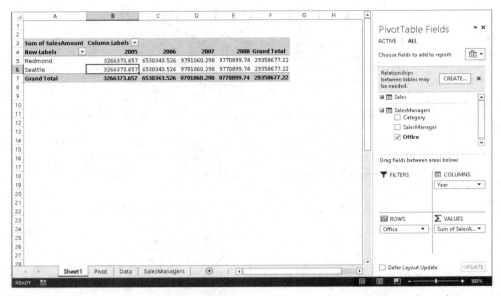

Figure 24-10 Adding the Office column to the PivotTable produces incorrect results and a warning about relationships.

As you might imagine, creating the relationship is the key to making the PivotTable show correct values. However, before doing that, you'll find that it is worth learning better what a *relationship* is.

Understanding relationships

You now have two tables: Sales and SalesManagers. Each sale is about a product, and the product has a category. Each category has a sales manager, and the relationship between categories and sales managers is stored in the SalesManagers table. To bring the sales manager name into the Sales table, you previously used VLOOKUP, which searched for the category name in the SalesManagers table and, after finding the category, grabbed the sales manager name.

In more technical terms, you can say that there is a relationship between the Sales and the SalesManagers tables, based on the Category column. To be more precise, the relationship is defined by the following:

- **Source table**   The source table from where the relationship starts. In our example, it is the Sales table, which contains only the ProductCategory column.

- **Foreign key column**   The column in the source table that contains the value you need to search. In our example, the column is ProductCategory, which contains the category of the product, which you used as the first parameter of VLOOKUP.

- **Related table**   The table that contains the values you want to look for. In our example, the related table is the SalesManagers table, which contains both the product category and the sales manager name, along with that manager's office.

- **Related column**   The column, in the related table, containing the value that should match the foreign key column. In our example, the column is Category, in the Sales-Managers table.

You can think of a relationship as a sort of automatic VLOOKUP. In fact, the parameters of a relationship are similar to the parameters of VLOOKUP. The only information missing is the value of the column you want to retrieve because, once a relationship is in place, you can use it retrieve any of the columns in the related table, without the need to specify which ones you are interested in (unlike VLOOKUP, which retrieved only a single column from the related table).

With this new information, you can now click the Create button and create the relationship, filling the boxes with the values shown in Figure 24-11.

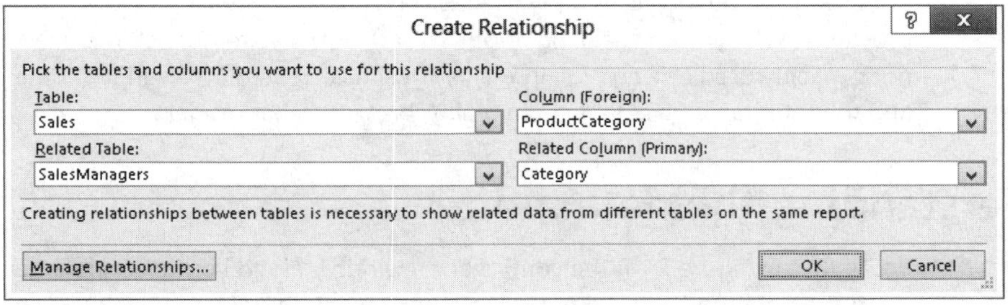

| Create Relationship | ? | x |

Pick the tables and columns you want to use for this relationship

Table:	Column (Foreign):
Sales	ProductCategory
Related Table:	Related Column (Primary):
SalesManagers	Category

Creating relationships between tables is necessary to show related data from different tables on the same report.

| Manage Relationships... | OK | Cancel |

Figure 24-11 This figure shows the correct parameters to enter to create the relationship.

After you click OK, Excel creates the relationship and updates the content of the PivotTable, which now shows correct values sliced by office. In Figure 24-12, you can see the result, where we put even the SalesManager column from the SalesManagers table on the rows.

Relationships play an important role in PowerPivot, and when you create more complex scenarios, they will be the key to creating interesting data models. For now, it is enough to think of a relationship as a way to tie together two tables, using a column common to both. If for a specific row the two columns share the same value, we say that the relationship has a match and the two rows are tied together.

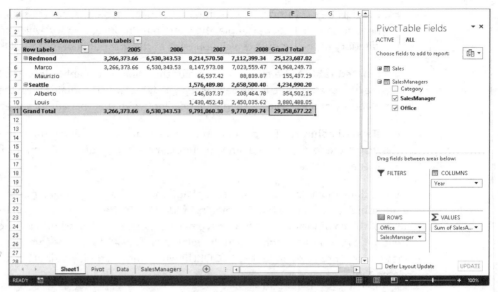

Figure 24-12 The PivotTable shows correct results once the relationship is set.

But...wait! Did we say that relationships are important for PowerPivot? Right now, you have not used PowerPivot, you simply used Excel features to create a PivotTable on more than one table. Why are we speaking about PowerPivot? The reason is simple: even if you have not explicitly used PowerPivot, in reality Excel has created a PowerPivot data model for you and the multitable PivotTable is, in reality, browsing that model.

Understanding the data model

Recall that in Figure 24-8 the confirmation window asked you to create a new PivotTable using the data model. It did not explain what a data model is and why it is needed to show more than one table in the PivotTable, but it was clear that the new PivotTable would use the data model. You need to understand better what the data model is before diving into more advanced topics.

Excel tables are exactly what their name suggests: tables. You can have hundreds of tables in an Excel workbook, but each table is separated from the others, and this is the reason why you can create a PivotTable only over a single table. Adding more than one table to a PivotTable is meaningless, because the tables share nothing. The key to turning a set of tables into a data model is the existence of relationships. If many tables are tied together by relationships, it is useful to show them all together inside a PivotTable, because filtering a table has the side effect of filtering other, related, tables.

In our example, putting a filter on the Office column of the SalesManagers table had the side effect of placing a filter on the Sales table. In fact, rows containing information about the Seattle office showed only values derived from categories that are handled by Seattle personnel. The reason the Sales table is filtered by Office is that each sale is pertinent to a sales manager who works in an office. The relationship between the two tables makes this mechanism work. Thus, you now know the following:

- A set of tables is nothing but a set of separate tables.

- A set of tables with relationships between them is a data model.

Excel 2013 introduced the concept of *data model* as one of the tools available to users to analyze data. Each Excel table can belong to the data model; a table is automatically added to the data model as soon as a relationship is defined on the table, either as the source or as the target of the relationship.

All this seems fine, but what does PowerPivot share with this description of a data model? The data model in Excel is, in reality, a PowerPivot data model. Whenever you add a table to the data model, in reality you are adding the table to the PowerPivot data model.

The PowerPivot data model and the Excel tables are two distinct entities. If you add an Excel table to the data model, you are not transforming the Excel table into a PowerPivot one. What happens instead is that the data in the Excel table is copied into a PowerPivot table. The two tables are thereby linked, so if you update the original Excel table and refresh the PivotTable, the updates are brought to the PowerPivot data model. But, from the point of view of storage, the data is really duplicated; the original table in Excel exists alongside a copy in PowerPivot.

Querying the data model

In the previous section of this chapter, you learned that, by creating relationships between tables, you can create a PowerPivot data model inside your Excel workbook. After the data model has been created for the first time, it can be queried with many PivotTables, without the need to add more tables to the same model. In this section, you learn how to perform this convenient operation.

When you create a new PivotTable, Excel prompts you with the Create PivotTable dialog box, shown in Figure 24-13.

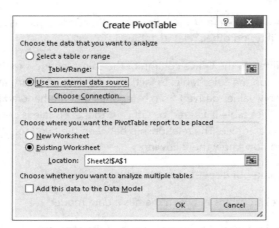

Figure 24-13 The Create PivotTable dialog box prompts you for the parameters of a new PivotTable.

Instead of choosing a range, which you are probably used to doing, you select the Use An External Data Source option and then click Choose Connection. The Existing Connections dialog box is displayed, which shows the external connections that can be used. On the Tables tab, shown in Figure 24-14, you can see both the Excel tables and the data model listed.

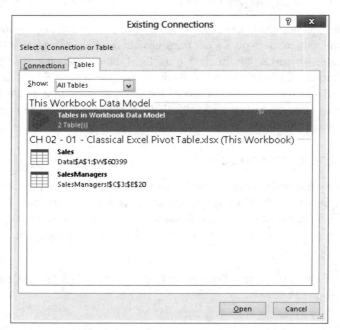

Figure 24-14 The list of external tables contains the Workbook data model, which is the PowerPivot data model.

Selecting the Workbook data model and confirming everything up to the end of the Pivot-Table creation process leads you to a new PivotTable connected to the same data model we previously created, based on our original Excel tables.

The PowerPivot add-in

In the previous sections of this chapter, you learned that the new features of Excel 2013 require you to create a PowerPivot data model to work with and that this data model can be created without your having enabled the PowerPivot add-in, which comes pre-installed but disabled. Once the data model has been created, you can query it with a PivotTable (or, as you'll see, with Power View). If, on the other hand, you want to look at the data model, Excel does not offer a way to analyze it or simply look at its content. To see the data model, you need to enable the PowerPivot add-in.

To enable the PowerPivot add-in, you need to open the Excel options, select Add-Ins, and then choose COM Add-Ins from the Manage list at the bottom of the window, as shown in Figure 24-15.

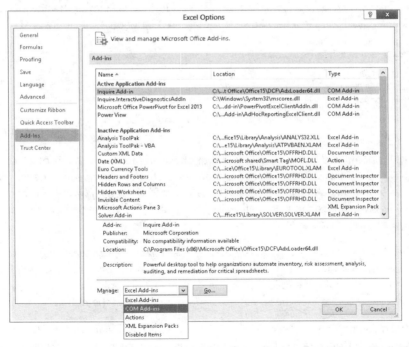

Figure 24-15 You need to enable the PowerPivot add-in to use the new PowerPivot features.

After you select COM Add-Ins, click Go to open the list of COM add-ins available, which you can see in Figure 24-16.

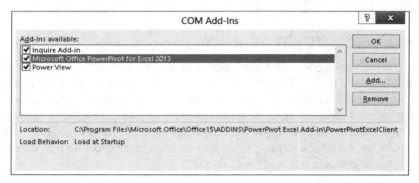

Figure 24-16 In the list of COM add-ins, you can enable or disable the PowerPivot add-in.

To enable the PowerPivot add-in, you simply select the Microsoft Office PowerPivot For Excel 2013 check box and then click OK. While you are here, if you have not already done so, you should enable the Power View add-in as well. After the PowerPivot add-in is enabled, you will see a new PowerPivot tab on the ribbon. (See Figure 24-17.)

Figure 24-17 The PowerPivot tab on the ribbon appears as soon as you enable the PowerPivot add-in.

At this point, you can use a wide number of exciting functions, many of which are beyond the scope of this chapter. For now, we are interested only in opening the PowerPivot window and taking a quick tour of the data model. To open the PowerPivot window, you need to click the Manage button on the ribbon, which opens the main PowerPivot window, as you can see in Figure 24-18.

The PowerPivot window opens by default in the data view, showing the content of the tables in the model. You can browse the rows and, at the bottom of the window, you can see the tabs of the tables loaded in the data model. To look at the data model, you need to click the Diagram View button at the upper-right edge of the ribbon.

When you do this, the PowerPivot window switches from data view to diagram view, which is shown in Figure 24-19. The diagram view is a convenient way of visualizing the data model because, instead of focusing on the content of the tables, it shows the structure of the relationships, making it easier to have a graphical representation of relationships.

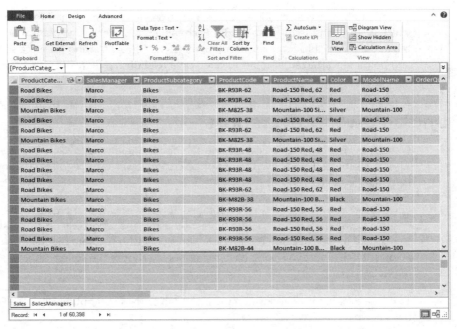

Figure 24-18 The PowerPivot window is the main window you use to access PowerPivot advanced features.

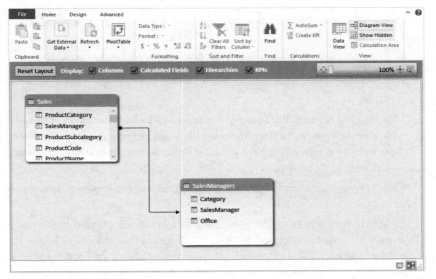

Figure 24-19 Use the diagram view to focus on the relationship structure of the data model.

The diagram view is a canonical "boxes and arrows" representation of the relational model, which is stored inside the data model. Each table is represented with a box and, if two tables are linked through a relationship, there is an arrow starting from the source table and pointing to the target table. Clicking on a relationship highlights the columns that are part of that relationship.

Creating a Power View report

Power View is a great graphical analysis tool that is integrated in Excel 2013 as an add-in. After it is activated, you have the option to create Power View reports based on the Power-Pivot data model.

Power View does not work with Excel tables; it works only with the data model. Thus, if you create a Power View report, all the tables you use in the report will be automatically added to the data model. Because Power View works only with the data model, when you create a Power View report you don't have the option to choose the source of data—it is the data model by default.

To create a Power View report, on the Insert tab of the Excel ribbon, click the Power View button, which is shown in Figure 24-20.

Figure 24-20 Click the Power View button to create a new Power View report.

> **Note**
>
> Power View requires the Silverlight component to be installed on your system. If you have never installed Silverlight, Power View will prompt you to do so, directing you to the website where you can download it. Once Silverlight is installed, Power View will work fine.

You will create a simple report using the same workbook created in this chapter. The Power View environment is designed to be simple: most of the features of Power View require a single mouse click to be activated, and you don't have all the configuration options available in classic Excel charts. The major benefit of Power View is that you can use it to create beautiful reports with minimum effort.

When the Power View report is opened, you will see an empty canvas on the left of your window and the list of tables in the data model in the right panel, which resembles the PivotTable Fields list. To start creating your first report, expand the Sales table and select the ProductCategory column. You will see the list of categories in a new table on the canvas. Then, when you select the SalesAmount column, Power View adds the total sales amount to each row of the table, showing the total sales for each category. At this point, your Excel window will look like Figure 24-21.

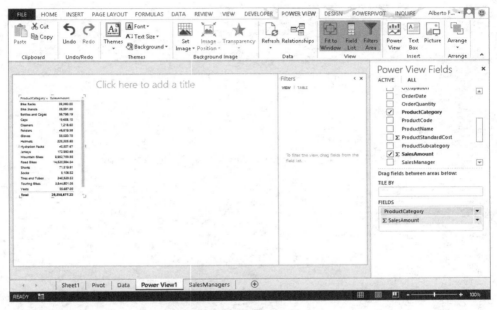

Figure 24-21 The Power View report with categories and sales.

The idea of Power View is to start with data and decide only later the format you want to use for it. Let us say, for example, you are interested in creating a report that shows the total sales for each category (which we already did) and, beside that, a report that shows the sales divided by geographical area.

You now want to create a new table containing the country in which the sale took place, along with the total sales amount. This can be done easily by clicking in the empty area of the Power View canvas and then selecting the TerritoryCountry column first and the Sales-Amount column next. At this point, your report should look like the one in Figure 24-22.

Although the data is there, it is not very appealing. The tabular representation of information is not amazing; you need a way to show the same information with charts. Let us start with the geography data. It would be much better to show the sales on a map. To perform this operation, simply select the table containing the TerritoryCountry column and, on the

Design tab of the ribbon, click the Map button, which is shown in Figure 24-23. The table is transformed into a map, where the total sales data is shown with the size of the points on the map.

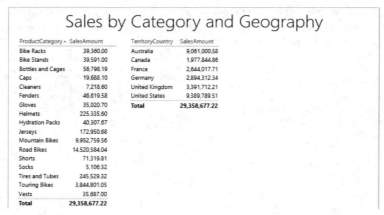

Figure 24-22 The Power View report shows tabular data by default.

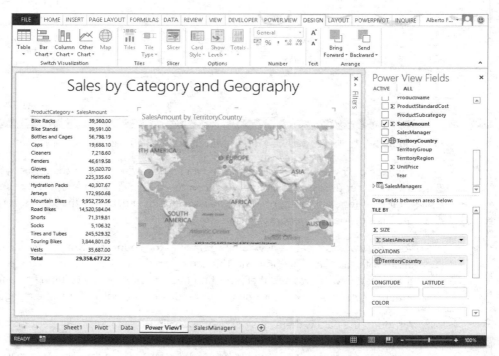

Figure 24-23 The Map button transforms the tabular representation into a map.

At this point, you can follow the same procedure to transform the categories table into a column chart, resize it, and put it below the map. The chart, at this point, looks like the one in Figure 24-24.

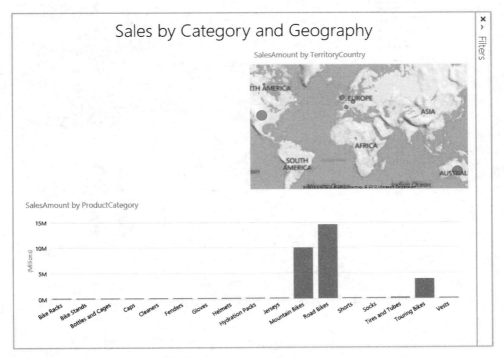

Figure 24-24 The categories table is now a column chart.

Now you can click on an empty space of the report and, following the same steps, add two tables: one with the Office column from the SalesManagers table, and another one with the SalesManager column from the same table. As you might have noticed, you need to click an empty space to create a new table because, if you have a table already selected, the columns on which you click will be added to the selected table.

The chart, at this point, has two tables, one map, and a column chart, as you can see in Figure 24-25.

Finally, you can convert the last two tables into slicers, by clicking the Slicer button on the Design tab of ribbon. Converting a table into a slicer lets you use it to filter the report. As soon as you click on a row of a slicer, the full report shows data using that slicer as a filter. In Figure 24-26, you can now see the final report, where we selected the Seattle office and Alberto as the sales manager.

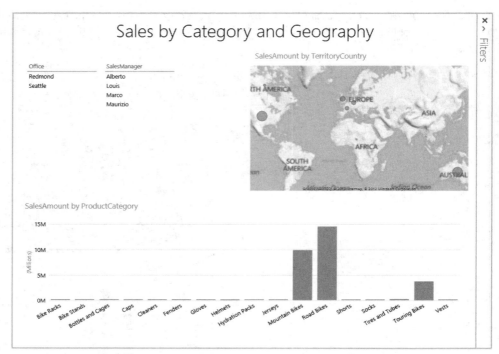

Figure 24-25 The report now includes two tables, a map, and a column chart.

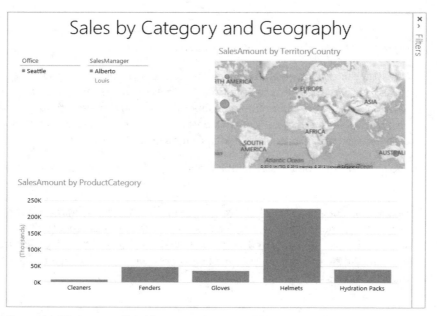

Figure 24-26 A report like this one can be created in a matter of a few seconds.

Creating beautiful graphical views of data is really simple with Power View. Remember that simplicity is the leitmotif of Power View. Do not even try to search inside the charting capabilities of Power View for the richness and complexity of Excel charts. Excel lets you create any type of chart, by giving you thousands of different options. Power View goes in the opposite direction: a few mouse click are always enough to build beautiful charts. However, if you need lots of configurability, Power View is not the tool to use.

Loading data from external sources

In the preceding examples, you loaded data in Excel and then created the PowerPivot data model. You have already seen that the PowerPivot storage is different from that used by Excel. Thus, by following this way of creating the data model, you effectively use more than twice the space needed to work with your data.

You use more than twice the space because the PowerPivot data model uses xVelocity storage, which is highly compressed, when data is loaded in memory, whereas Excel does not compress data for its tables in memory and uses a less efficient compression technique when data is stored on disk. Moreover, PowerPivot is capable of storing hundreds of millions of rows in memory, while Excel still has the limitation of one million rows for a table. Thus, by using the technique of loading data first in Excel and only later in the data model, you are not making good use of resources and you are hitting the limits of Excel long before you hit the limits of PowerPivot.

One of the most interesting features of PowerPivot is its capability of loading data directly inside the data model. Doing this, you load data only once and in its best format: highly compressed.

To load data directly into the data model, open the PowerPivot window by clicking the PowerPivot tab on the ribbon and then clicking the Manage button. After the PowerPivot window opens, on the Home tab, click the Get External Data button and then click the From Database button, as shown in Figure 24-27.

There are a lot of different drivers that you can use to load data from different databases. For this demo, you'll use the SQL Server connection. In the drop-down list of databases, click From SQL Server.

At this point, PowerPivot opens the Table Import Wizard, which guides you through the full process of data loading. The first page of the wizard (shown in Figure 24-28) prompts you for the connection parameters. In the Server Name box, type the name of the server that hosts the database (in the example, Demo), and in the Database Name box, type the database name (in the example, AdventureWorks DW2012).

Figure 24-27 Click the From Database button to load data directly into the PowerPivot data model.

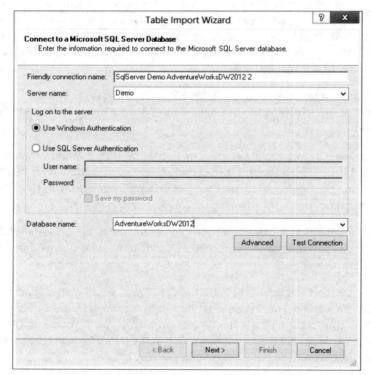

Figure 24-28 The Table Import Wizard guides you through the process of loading data into the data model.

Clicking Next takes you to the Choose How To Import The Data page of the wizard, where you need to decide whether you want to load from a list of tables or from a query. (See Figure 24-29.)

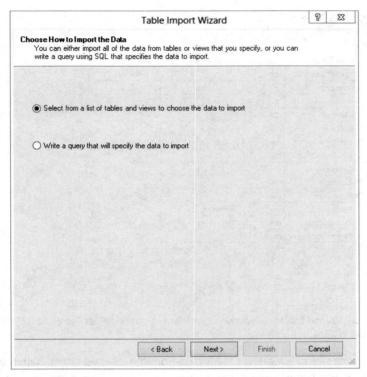

Figure 24-29 On the Choose How To Import The Data page, you can choose to load data from tables or to write an SQL query

Loading from a query is slightly more complex because you need to know the SQL language. Thus, for this small example, click the Select From A List Of Tables And Views To Choose The Data To Import option. The wizard shows the Select Tables And Views page, which contains a list of all the tables available in the database, as you can see in Figure 24-30.

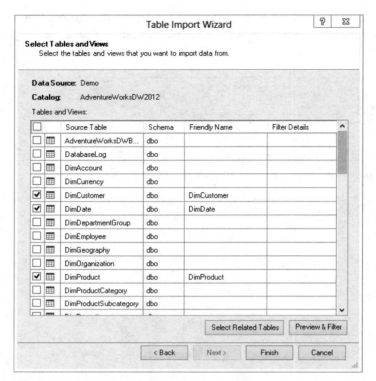

Figure 24-30 To load tables, select their check boxes on the Select Tables And Views page of the Table Import Wizard.

When you click Finish, PowerPivot loads data from the selected tables in memory. When it finishes, it shows a summary report and returns you to the PowerPivot window, which now displays all the data in the data model.

Note that, when PowerPivot loads tables from a server, it not only loads the data but also performs an extra step. It analyzes any existing relationship in the database. If an existing relationship can be loaded, PowerPivot automatically creates it.

In the example, we loaded four tables: DimProduct, DimCustomer, FactInternetSales, and DimDate. If you switch to the diagram view right after loading these four tables, as shown in Figure 24-31, you'll notice that several relationships were automatically created during the loading procedure because PowerPivot detected their presence in the database.

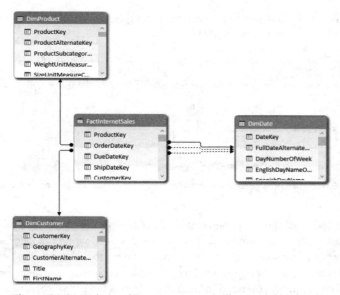

Figure 24-31 Relationships are automatically created in the data model if they are present in the source database.

Using the DAX language

DAX, an acronym for Data eXpression Language, is the language of PowerPivot. Designed to be easy to learn for Excel users, it offers many functions that share both their name and behavior with counterparts in Excel. However, it is not identical to the Excel language because the two languages work on completely different data structures.

In this introduction to DAX, we'll show you how to use DAX in a simple way. You'll create the two kinds of formulas that exist in the PowerPivot data model: calculated columns and calculated fields. Both calculations can be created only by using the PowerPivot add-in; there is no way to create calculated columns or calculated fields with the default Excel user interface.

Creating a calculated column

Calculated columns are columns stored in the data model that can extend the content of a table. They are similar to new columns defined with formulas in an Excel table.

Let's start with the PivotTable shown earlier, in which you aggregated the sales amount and divided it by color and year. If you are interested in profitability, the sales amount is only one part of the equation; you need to take into account at least the product cost to determine the profit margin. To do that, add the TotalProductCost column from the

FactInternetSales table to the values area. Doing this gives you a PivotTable with both values side by side, as shown in Figure 24-32.

Column Labels				
	2005		2006		2007
Row Labels	Sum of SalesAmount	Sum of TotalProductCost	Sum of SalesAmount	Sum of TotalProductCost	Sum of SalesAmount
Black	345815.493	195784.9111	1728251.554	1001103.186	3851090.661
Blue					860380.78
Multi					42099.32
NA					184354.22
Red	2634959.004	1598361.906	3935630.74	2397388.037	953203.05
Silver	285599.16	160620.9696	720397.3572	396577.3682	2044406.894
White					2229.52
Yellow			146063.875	88424.7832	1853295.853
Grand Total	**3266373.657**	**1954767.787**	**6530343.526**	**3883493.375**	**9791060.298**

Figure 24-32 By default, new values are shown side by side, making the report sometimes hard to read.

Depending on the kind of report you want to build, having the two fields side by side can be good or bad. In this example, the table is not easy to read when the fields are positioned in this way. It would be much better to show them one on top of the other, better resembling the subtraction operation you need to carry out. To position the fields on the rows instead of on the columns, you need to drag the Σ Values field from the Columns area of the PivotTable (which is shown in Figure 24-33) to the Rows area.

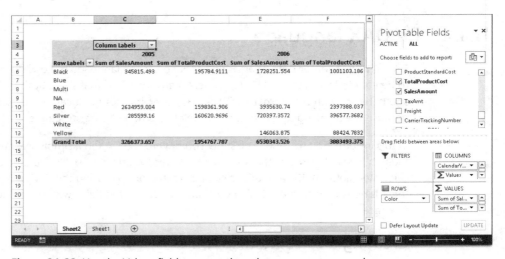

Figure 24-33 Use the Values field to move the values on rows or on columns.

In Figure 24-34, you can see the resulting PivotTable, which is much easier to read.

Even though the report shows both values, you're still missing the most important one: the gross margin, which is computed by subtracting the total product cost from the sales amount. If you were working in an Excel worksheet, this would be easy to compute, but doing it inside a PivotTable is more of a challenge. PivotTables are good at showing aggregates of columns from tables; the problem is that you do not have a column in the FactInternetSales table that contains the gross margin.

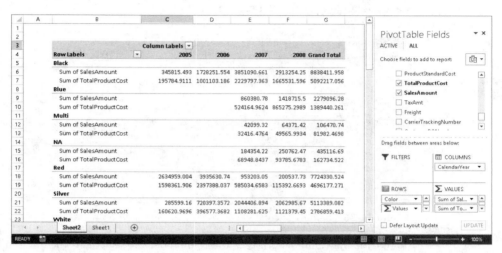

Figure 24-34 Showing the measures one on top of the other makes the report easier to read.

It is time to start using DAX. Using DAX, you can add a column to the FactInternetSales table with the desired computation. First, go back to the PowerPivot window, click Data View, and move to the FactInternetSales table using the tabs at the bottom of the window. On the Design tab of the ribbon, click the Add button, as shown in Figure 24-35.

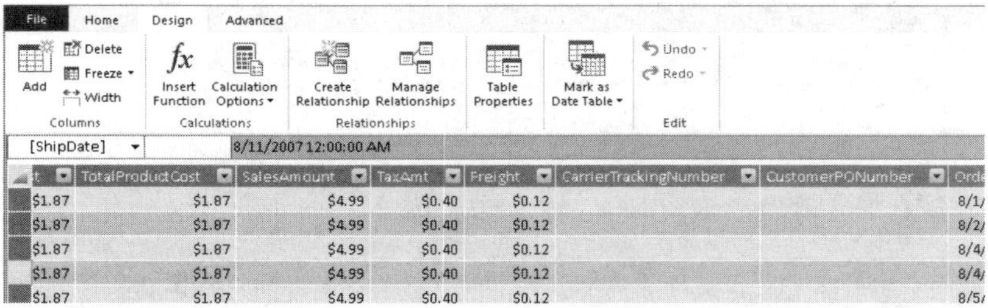

Figure 24-35 Click the Add button to create a new calculated column in the PowerPivot window.

The new column you are adding does not belong to the source database; rather, it is a column created to satisfy your reporting needs. At this point, you can write a DAX expression in the formula bar. In this case, the expression is a simple one:

```
=FactInternetSales[SalesAmount] - FactInternetSales[TotalProductCost]
```

Even if you don't know DAX, the meaning of this expression is easy to figure out: you subtract the product cost from the sales amount. Once you confirm the expression, PowerPivot computes the values and adds them to a new column, which is named, by default, CalculatedColumn1. You can see the result in Figure 24-36.

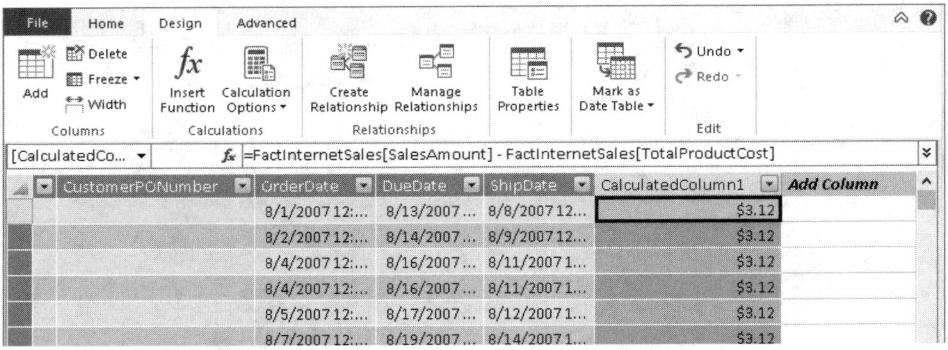

Figure 24-36 The new calculated column is added as the rightmost one with a default name.

To rename the column, right-click the column header, select Rename Column, and type the new name of the column. In this example, it is GrossMargin. If, at this point, you go back to the PivotTable and expand the columns of FactInternetSales, you will see, at the bottom, the new calculated column GrossMargin. Simply clicking on it is enough to add it to the PivotTable and show the new column in the report, as you can see in Figure 24-37.

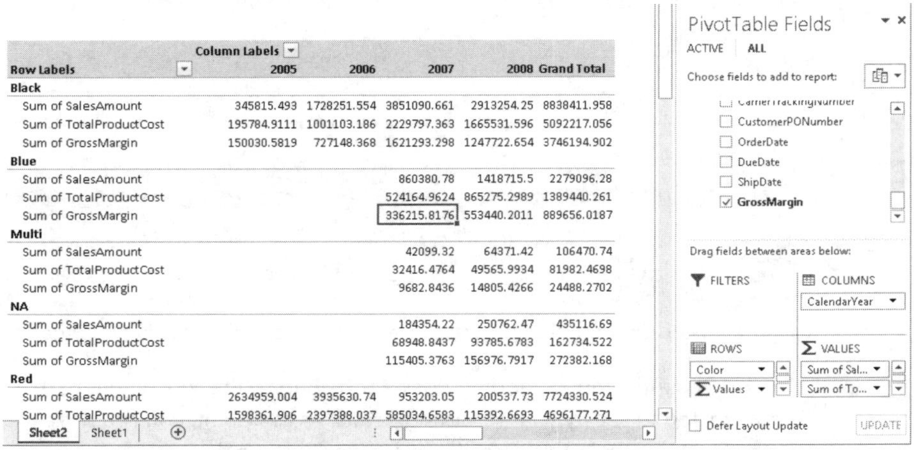

Figure 24-37 Once a calculated column has been added to the data model, it appears in the PivotTable Fields list.

Creating a calculated field

As you saw in the previous section, calculated columns are useful whenever you want to perform a calculation for each row of a table and then aggregate its value in a PivotTable. But some formulas cannot be computed on a row-by-row basis. Such formulas should be computed at the aggregate level.

If you want to compute the gross margin not as a value but as a percentage of the sales amount, you can create a simple calculated column containing this expression:

```
GrossMarginPct = FactInternetSales[GrossMargin] / FactInternetSales[SalesAmount]
```

This calculation works fine at the row level, giving you the percentage of margin for a single row. Nevertheless, when it comes to computing it at the aggregate level, the expression no longer works. In fact, if you add this column to the model and then put it in a PivotTable, you will get the result shown in Figure 24-38.

Row Labels	Column Labels	2005	2006	2007	2008	Grand Total
Black						
Sum of SalesAmount		345815.493	1728251.554	3851090.661	2913254.25	8838411.958
Sum of TotalProductCost		195784.9111	1001103.186	2229797.363	1665531.596	5092217.056
Sum of GrossMargin		150030.5819	727148.368	1621293.298	1247722.654	3746194.902
Sum of GrossMarginPct		65.53332736	360.6291298	2137.918725	2440.121774	5004.202956
Blue						
Sum of SalesAmount				860380.78	1418715.5	2279096.28
Sum of TotalProductCost				524164.9624	865275.2989	1389440.261
Sum of GrossMargin				336215.8176	553440.2011	889656.0187
Sum of GrossMarginPct				854.3894099	1313.157337	2167.546747

Figure 24-38 GrossMarginPct is not computed correctly at the aggregate level.

The result is clearly wrong. The problem here is that you're performing the sum of all the percentages and not the percentage on the sums. Calculated columns will not help. For such a calculation, you need calculated fields.

A calculated field is a DAX expression that is not computed on a row-by-row basis for each table; instead, it is computed at the aggregate level. To create a new calculated field, click the PowerPivot tab of the ribbon and then click the Calculated Fields button, as shown in Figure 24-39.

Figure 24-39 Click the Calculated Fields button on the PowerPivot tab of the ribbon to create calculated fields.

When you select New Calculated Field, the Calculated Field dialog box appears (shown in Figure 24-40) in which you can create the DAX formula, give the new field a name, create a format string and, in general, set all the properties of the new field.

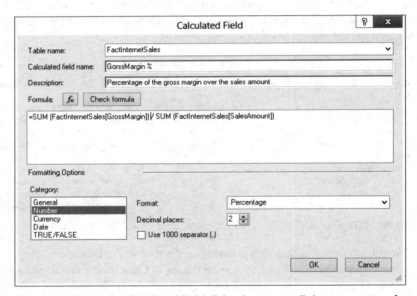

Figure 24-40 Use the Calculated Field dialog box to set all the parameters of a calculated field.

In the example, the formula used for the calculated field is the following:

```
=SUM ( FactInternetSales[GrossMargin] ) / SUM ( FactInternetSales[SalesAmount] )
```

In the calculated field, you can set the number format. In the example, we used Percentage as the number format so that numbers will show as percentages. When you click OK, the calculated field is added to the PowerPivot data model and is available in the PivotTable. You can add it to the PivotTable by clicking it. You obtain the result shown in Figure 24-41, where GrossMargin% is displayed in the PivotTable Fields list on the right.

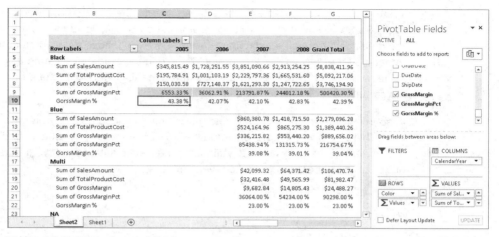

Figure 24-41 The calculated field computes the correct value working at the aggregate level.

Calculated fields are very useful because they let you create complex expressions, store them inside the PowerPivot data model, and then use them in any PivotTable. In fact, the calculated field is not local to the PivotTable in which it is being created; it belongs to the data model and will be available in any PivotTable or report you create on your data model.

Refreshing the PowerPivot data model

You've seen how the PowerPivot data model can load tables from a database without using Excel as an intermediate step. Because the database content is dynamic in nature, you will want to refresh the content of your data model to reflect the newly added or updated rows in the database tables.

To refresh the content of the data model, from inside the PowerPivot window, click the Refresh button on the Home tab of the PowerPivot ribbon, as shown in Figure 24-42.

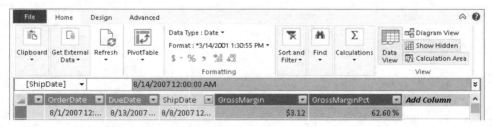

Figure 24-42 Click the Refresh button in the PowerPivot window to reload the content from the database.

You have the option to refresh all the tables or only the one that is currently shown in the PowerPivot window. If you select, for example, Refresh All, PowerPivot starts fetching all the data again from all the databases from where you loaded data, and it automatically updates all the calculated columns you defined in the model. Calculated fields do not need to be recomputed because they are not stored in the PowerPivot data model; instead, they are calculated on the fly as needed.

Keep in mind that refreshing the data model means reloading everything from the database. There is no way to load only updated rows. Whenever you issue a refresh command, the content of the tables is read again from the source databases. If your data model is a huge one, this operation can take several minutes.

Working with external data

Microsoft Excel 2013 is a superb tool for analyzing data, but before you can do any analysis, you have to get the data into Excel. In many cases, the information you need resides somewhere "outside"—on a server, on a website, in an XML file, or perhaps in a database program such as Oracle or Microsoft Access. Excel 2013 supports a wide variety of data formats, including SQL Server (and SQL Server Analysis Services), Access, dBase, FoxPro, Oracle, Paradox, and various kinds of text files. We'll look at some techniques for retrieving external data in this chapter.

Using and reusing Office Data Connections

An Office Data Connection (.odc) file is a small XML file that records information about how a workbook connects to an external data source. Such information can include the location and type of the external data, a query specification (if the connection is designed to retrieve a subset of the external source), and details about how to log on to the external server. ODC files are designed to facilitate the reuse of external connections.

Often the simplest way to import data from an external source is to execute an ODC file—a connection that you or someone else has already established. To see what connections are available, click the Data tab on the ribbon, and then click Existing Connections. A dialog box comparable to the one shown in Figure 25-1 appears.

In Figure 25-1, the Show list, at the top of the dialog box, is set to display all available connection files. You can use this list to restrict the dialog box to connections that are already open on your computer (if any), connections that are already in use in the current workbook, or connections that are available on your network. If a connection file that you're looking for doesn't appear in the Existing Connections dialog box, click Browse For More and use Windows Explorer to navigate to it.

Figure 25-1 The Existing Connections dialog box lists connection files that are already established for you.

To open a connection file, double-click it in the Existing Connections dialog box. The Import Data dialog box, shown in Figure 25-2, appears. In this dialog box, you indicate where you want the data to go and whether you want an ordinary table or a PivotTable.

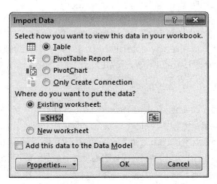

Figure 25-2 By default, Excel renders imported data as a table. By using the Import Data dialog box, you can create a PivotTable or PivotChart instead.

Setting refresh options

To specify how you want the data refreshed, you can click Properties in the Import Data dialog box. (See Figure 25-2.). Alternatively, after the table (or PivotTable) has been created, select a cell within it, click the Data tab, and then click Properties. In the External Data Properties dialog box that appears, click the Connection Properties button (to the right of the Name box), as shown next.

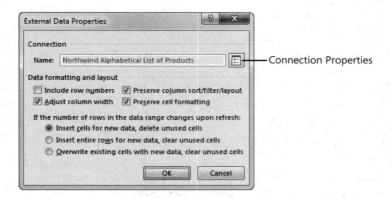

Connection Properties

These steps bring you to the Connection Properties dialog box, shown in Figure 25-3. Your refresh options appear on the Usage tab in this dialog box.

The check boxes in the Refresh Control area in this dialog box are not mutually exclusive. You can have Excel refresh your data whenever you open the file as well as at regular time intervals. The Enable Background Refresh check box, selected by default, means you can do other work in Excel while the refresh is in progress. Note that this option is not available with online analytical processing (OLAP) queries.

If you select the Refresh Data When Opening The File check box, an additional option to remove the data from your worksheet when you close the file becomes available. You might as well select this check box because Excel is going to refresh the data when you reopen the file anyway.

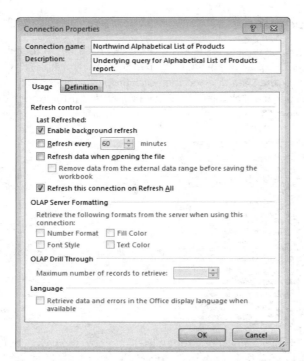

Figure 25-3 You can set your connection to refresh the imported data at regular time intervals.

Requiring or not requiring a password to refresh

If connecting to your external data requires a password, Excel, by default, requires that you supply the password again whenever you refresh. If that's a burdensome obligation, click the Definition tab in the Connection Properties dialog box. Then select the Save Password check box.

Refreshing on demand

In addition to requesting a refresh at regular time intervals, you can refresh the data whenever the need arises. Right-click a cell within the table, and then click Refresh. Alternatively, click the Data tab, click the arrow next to Refresh All, and then click Refresh. (Or simply click Refresh All; this refreshes all connections open in the current workbook.)

Opening an entire Access table in Excel

To import an entire table created in Access (as opposed to a specific set of records from that table), click the Data tab, and then click From Access in the Get External Data group. Windows launches a search for files with the extensions .mdb, .mde, .accdb, and .accde. When you find the Access file you're looking for, select it, and then click Open. If your database has more than one table, you're presented with the Select Table dialog box, which is shown in Figure 25-4. (Drag the lower-right corner of the Select Table dialog box if you need to see more of the Description column.)

> **Note**
>
> You can download the Northwind sample database from *http://office.microsoft.com/ en-us/templates/desktop-northwind-2007-sample-database-TC001228997.aspx*.

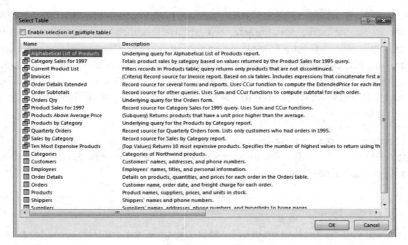

Figure 25-4 When you click the From Access command to open an Access file, the Select Table dialog box asks you to choose which table you want to import.

For information about importing selected records from an Access (or other) database using Microsoft Query, see "Using Microsoft Query to import data" later in this chapter.

The Select Table dialog box actually lists not only tables from your Access file but certain views as well. (The items shown in Figure 25-4, for example, are all views from the Northwind database that Microsoft supplies as a sample file with Access.) If you open any Access view in Excel, you get all the records currently displayed by Access in that view. If you open a table, you import all the records in that table. In either case, the data you import becomes a table or a PivotTable in Excel, depending on how you complete the Import Data dialog box. (See Figure 25-2.)

You can set refresh parameters for your imported Access data the same way as for any other data connection. For details, see "Setting refresh options" earlier in this chapter.

> **Note**
>
> You can also import an Access table by clicking the File tab, clicking Open, and then selecting Access Databases from the list next to the File Name box. (The resulting table or PivotTable behaves as though you used the From Access command on the ribbon.) You cannot save an Excel range as an Access table, however.

Working with data in text files

Excel can read data in fixed-width as well as delimited text files. (A *delimited file* is one that uses some particular character or combination of characters to mark the boundaries between fields. A *fixed-width file* is one that uses space characters—as many as necessary—to achieve field alignment.) You can open a text file (by clicking File, and then Open) or import it (by clicking the Data tab and then clicking From Text in the Get External Data group). If you want to be able to maintain a refreshable link to the source file, you need to do the latter.

When you open a comma-separated-values (.csv) file, Excel parses the data immediately into columns. If you open or import any other kind of text file, Excel presents the Text Import Wizard, described next.

> **Note**
>
> When you ask Excel to open or import a text file, the program looks for files with the extensions .prn, .txt, and .csv. If you want a file with a different extension, select All Files in the list to the right of the File Name box. Excel determines a file's type by its content, so it doesn't matter what the extension is.

Using the Text Import Wizard

With the Text Import Wizard, you can show Excel how to parse your text file. You get to tell the program what character or character combination (if any) is used to delimit columns, what kind of data appears in each column, and what character set or language was used to create the original file. You can also use the Text Import Wizard to exclude one or more rows at the top of your file—an option that's particularly useful if your file begins with some kind of nontabular descriptive information.

The first page of the wizard, shown in Figure 25-5, presents a preview of the data that Excel is about to import. It also indicates the best estimation of whether you're importing a delimited file or a fixed-width file. You'll find that the wizard is usually correct with this first guess—but if it's mistaken, you can set it straight. (If you're not sure, just go to the second page. When you get there, you'll know whether the program was wrong, and you can return to the first page to fix the problem.)

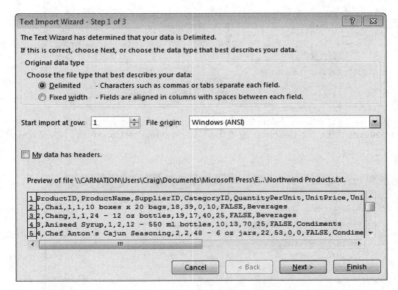

Figure 25-5 You can use the Text Import Wizard to tell Excel how to parse your text file.

While you're still on the first page of the wizard, use the Start Import At Row text box to eliminate any header rows that you can live without in Excel. Header rows make it hard for Excel to parse your file correctly, so you can help the program (and yourself) by lopping them off here. Click Next.

The second page of the Text Import Wizard looks something like Figure 25-6 or Figure 25-7, depending on whether your file is delimited or fixed-width. In both cases, the vertical lines in the Data Preview section show how Excel proposes to split your file into columns. The Data Preview section regrettably shows a paltry five rows at a time and 65 characters per row. You cannot make it show more, but you can look at other parts of the file by using the scroll bars.

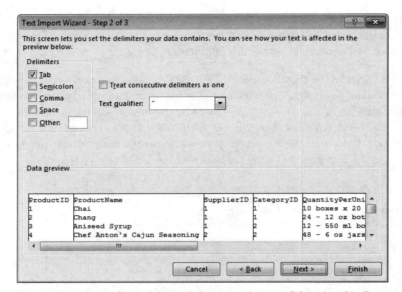

Figure 25-6 If your file is delimited, the second page of the wizard indicates what character Excel believes to be the delimiter, and the Data Preview section shows how Excel will parse your file.

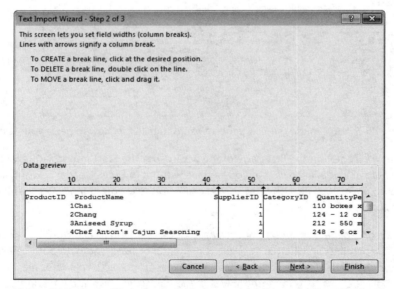

Figure 25-7 If your file is fixed-width, be sure to look at the Data Preview box; you can fix any mistakes by manipulating the vertical bars.

If your file is delimited, the second page of the wizard gives you the opportunity to specify the delimiting character for your text file. Note that Excel defaults to treating the Tab character as the delimiter; you will need to fix this if your file is otherwise delimited. In Figure 25-6, for example, we indicated that the file in question is tab-delimited. You can also select more than one check box to indicate that your file is delimited by multiple characters. If you select two or more check boxes, Excel breaks to a new column whenever it sees any of your choices.

A separate check box lets you stipulate that Excel should regard consecutive delimiting characters as a single delimiter. This option sometimes saves the day with tab-delimited files. The original creator of the file might occasionally have used two or more tabs to skip to the next column when the current column's contents were short. That strategy could disrupt your alignment in Excel unless you tell the program to treat consecutive delimiters as a single delimiter.

Excel is much more likely to introduce errors when trying to parse a fixed-width file. If you have a choice between opening a fixed-width file and an equivalent delimited file, by all means go with the latter.

To fix parsing errors, drag the vertical lines to the left or right to reposition the column breaks. To create a column break where one doesn't yet exist, click once at the appropriate place. To remove a column break that shouldn't be there at all, double-click it. When you are finished, click Next.

The third page of the wizard, shown in Figure 25-8, lets you specify the data type of each column. Your choices are limited to General (which treats text as text, numbers as numbers, and dates in recognizable formats as dates), Text (which treats everything as text), Date, and Do Not Import Column (Skip). Excel initially assigns the General description to all columns, but you'll probably want to override that presumption in some cases. For example, if your file happens to have a text field that begins with a hyphen, Excel will regard the hyphen as a minus sign and attempt to turn your text into a formula. You can avoid errors by indicating that the field is Text.

The third page also includes an Advanced button. By clicking it, you can change the way the wizard handles commas and periods in numeric data. By default, Excel uses the settings specified in the Regional And Language Options item of Control Panel. If your text file was created under other assumptions, you'll need to make some adjustments in the Advanced Text Import Settings dialog box. Click OK, click Finish, and then click OK to import the text file.

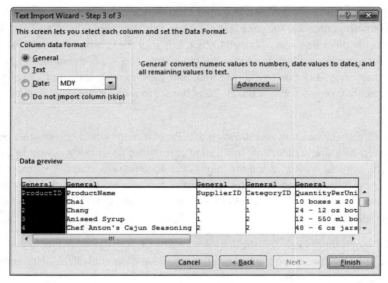

Figure 25-8 You can use the third page of the wizard to control the data type of each column.

Parsing Clipboard text

Occasionally, when working with text data, you might find long text strings you need to break into separate columns. This can happen, for example, if you paste text into Excel from the Clipboard. To parse such data, select it, click the Data tab, and then click Text To Columns in the Data Tools group.

Working with XML files

Excel can open, import, and export XML data in any structure. To open a list that has been saved in XML, click File, Open—just as you would to open an ordinary Excel workbook. With the Open dialog box set to display all Excel files, your XML files are included. But if you have trouble finding the file you want (because of all the other Excel files in the same folder), select XML Files in the list beside the File Name box.

When you open your file, Excel presents the Open XML dialog box, shown in Figure 25-9.

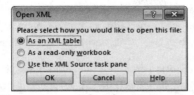

Figure 25-9 When you open an XML data file, Excel presents this dialog box. Choose the first option to open all elements of the XML structure or the third option to work only with particular elements.

As Figure 25-10 shows, the result of opening an XML file using the As An XML Table option is a table that presents each element of the source file, in order, as a table column. All records in the source file are included in the resulting list.

	OrderID	CustomerID	EmployeeID	OrderDate	RequiredDate	ShippedDate	ShipVia	Freight	ShipNam
2	10248	WILMK	5	7/4/1996 0:00	8/1/1996 0:00	7/16/1996 0:00	3	32.38	Vins et a
3	10249	TRADH	6	7/5/1996 0:00	8/16/1996 0:00	7/10/1996 0:00	1	11.61	Toms Sp
4	10250	HANAR	4	7/8/1996 0:00	8/5/1996 0:00	7/12/1996 0:00	2	65.83	Hanari C
5	10251	VICTE	3	7/8/1996 0:00	8/5/1996 0:00	7/15/1996 0:00	1	41.34	Victuaill
6	10252	SUPRD	4	7/9/1996 0:00	8/6/1996 0:00	7/11/1996 0:00	2	51.3	Suprême
7	10253	HANAR	3	7/10/1996 0:00	7/24/1996 0:00	7/16/1996 0:00	2	58.17	Hanari C
8	10254	CHOPS	5	7/11/1996 0:00	8/8/1996 0:00	7/23/1996 0:00	2	22.98	Chop-su
9	10255	RICSU	9	7/12/1996 0:00	8/9/1996 0:00	7/15/1996 0:00	3	148.33	Richter S
10	10256	WELLI	3	7/15/1996 0:00	8/12/1996 0:00	7/17/1996 0:00	2	13.97	Wellingt
11	10257	HILAA	4	7/16/1996 0:00	8/13/1996 0:00	7/22/1996 0:00	3	81.91	HILARIÓ
12	10258	ERNSH	1	7/17/1996 0:00	8/14/1996 0:00	7/23/1996 0:00	1	140.51	Ernst Ha
13	10259	CENTC	4	7/18/1996 0:00	8/15/1996 0:00	7/25/1996 0:00	3	3.25	Centro c
14	10260	OLDWO	4	7/19/1996 0:00	8/16/1996 0:00	7/29/1996 0:00	1	55.09	Ottilies
15	10261	QUEDE	4	7/19/1996 0:00	8/16/1996 0:00	7/30/1996 0:00	2	3.05	Que Deli
16	10262	RATTC	8	7/22/1996 0:00	8/19/1996 0:00	7/25/1996 0:00	3	48.29	Rattlesn
17	10263	ERNSH	9	7/23/1996 0:00	8/20/1996 0:00	7/31/1996 0:00	3	146.06	Ernst Ha
18	10264	FOLKO	6	7/24/1996 0:00	8/21/1996 0:00	8/23/1996 0:00	3	3.67	Folk och
19	10265	BLONP	2	7/25/1996 0:00	8/22/1996 0:00	8/12/1996 0:00	1	55.28	Blondel
20	10266	WARTH	3	7/26/1996 0:00	9/6/1996 0:00	7/31/1996 0:00	3	25.73	Wartian
21	10267	FRANK	4	7/29/1996 0:00	8/26/1996 0:00	8/6/1996 0:00	1	208.58	Franken
22	10268	GROSR	8	7/30/1996 0:00	8/27/1996 0:00	8/2/1996 0:00	3	66.29	GROSELL
23	10269	WHITC	5	7/31/1996 0:00	8/14/1996 0:00	8/9/1996 0:00	1	4.56	White Cl
24	10270	WARTH	1	8/1/1996 0:00	8/29/1996 0:00	8/2/1996 0:00	1	136.54	Wartian
25	10271	SPLIR	6	8/1/1996 0:00	8/29/1996 0:00	8/30/1996 0:00	2	4.54	Split Rail
26	10272	RATTC	6	8/2/1996 0:00	8/30/1996 0:00	8/6/1996 0:00	2	98.03	Rattlesn

XML Source

XML maps in this workbook:

dataroot_Map

- dataroot
  - Orders
    - OrderID (10
    - CustomerID (
    - EmployeeID (
    - OrderDate (
    - RequiredDat
    - ShippedDate
    - ShipVia (3)
    - Freight (32.3
    - ShipName (V
    - ShipAddress
    - ShipCity (Re

To map repeating elements, drag the elements from the tree onto the worksheet where you want the data headings to appear.

To import XML data, right click an XML mapped cell, point to XML, and then click Import.

Options | XML Maps...

Verify Map for Export...

Figure 25-10 Each element of the opened XML file maps to a column in the resulting XML table.

TROUBLESHOOTING

Excel reports a problem with the specified XML or schema source

When you open an XML file, Excel looks for an associated schema file, which defines the structure of the XML data. If it doesn't find one, or if it finds errors in the associated schema file, Excel displays an error message. If you click OK, Excel infers the structure from the data it sees. In many cases, especially with files that are not particularly complex, this works out fine. You can forget about the error message after you click OK. If Excel can't infer the structure of your file, you need to fix the schema (or provide one).

After Excel opens the XML file, it can display an XML Source task pane, which shows how the elements of the source file map to columns in the table. If the task pane isn't visible and you want to see it, right-click a cell in the table, click XML, and then click XML Source.

Opening an XML file by the method just described creates a new workbook. If you want to create an XML table on an existing worksheet, click the Data tab, click From Other Sources (in the Get External Data group), and click From XML Data Import. After you select your file in the ensuing dialog box, Excel asks you where to put the incoming data.

You can refresh an XML table the same way you would an imported text or Access table. For details, see "Setting refresh options" earlier in this chapter.

Creating an ad hoc mapping of XML elements to table columns

Opening an XML file using the As An XML Table option (as shown in Figure 25-9) might be fine for a relatively simple XML structure. But if your structure is not simple, it's likely you'll be interested in only certain portions of the XML data. In such cases, it's usually more effective to open the file using the third option, Use The XML Source Task Pane. When you do this, Excel presents the XML structure in the XML Source task pane without creating a table—as shown in Figure 25-11.

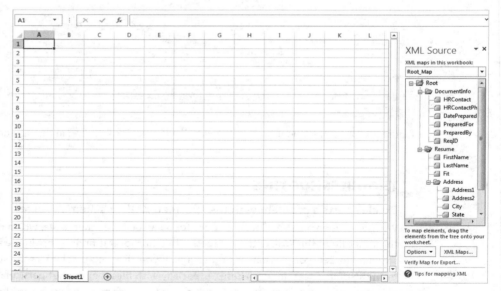

Figure 25-11 When you open an XML file using the XML Source task pane to map elements to table columns, no data appears until you drag XML elements from the task pane to the worksheet and then refresh.

In the example shown in Figure 25-11, the data file consists of ratings and contact data for a set of job applicants, along with contact information about the human-resources person who conducted each interview. If you're reviewing this data, you might be interested in only the HRContact field from the DocumentInfo element, the LastName and FirstName fields from the Resume element, and perhaps some additional fields pertaining to individual applicants. To create a table on your worksheet that displays only the fields you care about, you can Ctrl+click the headings of interest in the XML Source task pane and then drag the selected set onto the worksheet. (Excel calls this process of associating XML elements with table headings *mapping*.) The result might look like Figure 25-12.

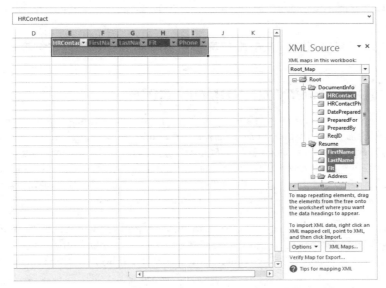

Figure 25-12 You can drag headings from the XML Source task pane to the worksheet to create a table showing only particular columns.

To populate the table after you structure it, click a cell in the table header row, click the Data tab (or Design tab), and then click Refresh All. (If you have other tables open and you want to refresh only this one, click the small arrow beneath Refresh All, and then click Refresh.)

Importing XML data using an existing XML structure

Populating the table by clicking Refresh All, as just described, brings in data from the file whose structure you imported into the XML Source task pane. As an alternative, you can right-click a cell in the table header, click XML, and then click Import. You're then prompted for the name of an XML data file.

The Import command lets you bring in records from any file whose structure is reflected in the XML Source task pane. Importing is particularly useful when you have a number of identically structured XML files. For example, if each member of your human-resources staff created a separate file of interviewee data with each file built on the same XML schema, you could examine each one in turn with the help of the Import command.

> **Note**
>
> If you perform successive imports of two or more identically structured files, each import replaces the previous one. If instead you want to import several files at once, use the Import procedure as described, and then Ctrl+click each file you want to import.

Using Microsoft Query to import data

If you don't have a connection already set up for the data you need, you can create one with the help of Microsoft Query, a versatile querying tool included with Microsoft Office 2013. Query generates statements in SQL and passes those statements to the data source while shielding you from the need to master SQL. If your query is relatively simple, you might not need to interact directly with Query; instead, you can formulate your request by means of a four-step wizard that acts as a front end to Query.

The first step in creating a query is to form a connection to the data source. Click the Data tab, click From Other Sources in the Get External Data group, and then click From Microsoft Query. The Choose Data Source dialog box, shown in Figure 25-13, appears.

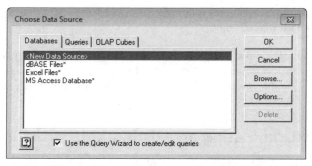

Figure 25-13 The first step in using Microsoft Query is to choose a data source.

You can query a separate Excel file (extracting particular records from a table in that file), a dBase file, or an Access file by selecting one of the options on the Databases tab. To edit an existing query (a .dqy file that has already been created), click the Queries tab. To work with OLAP data, click the OLAP Cubes tab. Otherwise, click New Data Source, and click OK. If you click New Data Source and click OK, the Create New Data Source dialog box prompts you to supply a name for the new query, identify the driver for the type of database you are going to query, supply logon information for your connection to the external source, and select the table in the external database you want to use. Click OK to save your changes.

In the following sections, we assume for the sake of simplicity that you're going to work with an Access file. After double-clicking MS Access Database in the Choose Data Source dialog box (or selecting that entry and clicking OK), you will see a Select Database dialog box:

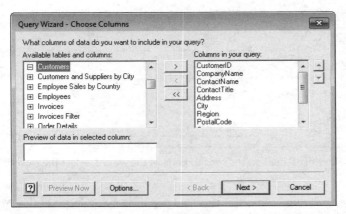

We'll choose the file Northwind.mdb for this example. After we double-click that file in the Select Database dialog box, the opening page of the Query Wizard, shown in Figure 25-14, appears.

Figure 25-14 The Query Wizard, a friendly front end to Microsoft Query, begins by asking you to choose the columns of data you want to include in your query.

Choosing tables and fields (columns)

On the first page of the wizard, you see a list of tables on the left and selected fields (Query refers to them as *columns*) on the right. Outline controls (plus signs and minus signs) appear to the left of table names. Your job is to pick the particular fields, from one or more tables, that you want to include in your query.

To add a field to your query, click the plus sign beside the name of the table it belongs to. This expands the table to reveal its fields. Then select the field, and click the right arrow button to add that field to your query. (To add all fields from a given table, you can select the table name and click the right arrow button.)

If you add fields from a second or subsequent table to your query, Query performs a join operation on the selected tables if it can. Query joins related tables when it recognizes a primary key field in one table and a field with the same data type (and typically, but not necessarily, the same field name) in the other table. For an example of a query that involves two joined tables, see "Working directly with Microsoft Query" later in this chapter.

Filtering records

After specifying tables and fields and clicking Next, you arrive at the Query Wizard – Filter Data page, shown in Figure 25-15. Here you can specify one or more filter criteria. This is an optional page; if you skip it, Query returns all records from the selected tables.

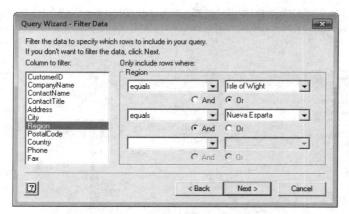

Figure 25-15 Filters, specified on the second page of the wizard, select the records that meet your criteria.

A filter criterion has three components: a field name, relationship, and value. You can specify as many as three criteria for each field, connected by And or Or. The list at the left side of the wizard page includes the names of all your selected fields. The lists in the center include available relationships, and the lists at the right include all the available values for the selected field. Figure 25-15 shows how the second page of the wizard looks if you want to see only records in which the Region field equaled either Isle Of Wight or Nueva Esparta.

INSIDE OUT   For more relationships, use Microsoft Query directly

The Query Wizard offers a long list of relational operators for building filtering criteria. If you use Microsoft Query directly, four additional relationships are available: Is One Of, Is Not One Of, Is Between, and Is Not Between. These additional operators work with two or more values—something the wizard doesn't accommodate. For example, Is Between and Is Not Between both require two values. Is One Of and Is Not One Of can use a list of values. For more information, see "Working directly with Microsoft Query" later in this chapter.

TROUBLESHOOTING

The Query Wizard won't let me get rid of a filter

The Query Wizard is a little clumsy when it comes to letting you remove filters. It doesn't have a Delete button. To get rid of a criterion, open its relationship list and select the blank entry at the top of the list.

If you filter on two or more different fields, you'll find that when you select the second or third field, the wizard removes the previous criterion from view. You can tell that you applied a criterion to a field, however, by looking at the left window on the page. Filtered fields appear there in bold.

Note

Because the wizard accepts up to three criteria per field, you can use it to generate some pretty marvelous filters. But it's a whole lot easier to see what you're doing if you use the full Query interface for multifield filtering. For details, see "Working directly with Microsoft Query" later in this chapter.

Sorting records

After you finish filtering and click Next, the wizard presents its Query Wizard – Sort Order page, shown in Figure 25-16. Sorting is optional, of course. If you decline, Query returns records in the order in which they're stored in the external database field.

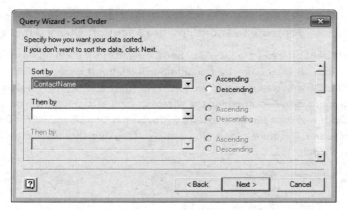

Figure 25-16 Use the Sort Order page to arrange the records that are returned to Excel.

To sort, begin by clicking the Sort By list. There you'll find the name of each field in the table you're querying. Select a field, and then select the Ascending or Descending option to the right of the list. You can sort on as many fields as you want. To remove a sort item, select the blank entry at the top of the list. In Figure 25-16, we asked for records sorted in ascending order by ContactName. Click Next.

Saving the query or moving to Microsoft Query

The Save Query button, on the final page of the wizard (shown in Figure 25-17), lets you name and save your query as a DQY file. The resulting DQY file encapsulates all the selections you made in the construction of your query—your choice of tables and fields, your filters, and your sorting specifications. Note that this is different from the ODC file you might have made earlier. An ODC file records information required to achieve a connection with an external data source; a DQY file records query specifications.

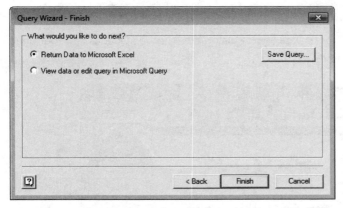

Figure 25-17 Save the query if you want, and indicate whether you want to return directly to Excel or go on to the full Microsoft Query for further processing.

Working directly with Microsoft Query

The Query Wizard is an ideal tool for creating relatively simple queries, but it doesn't provide access to all the power of Microsoft Query. You need to work directly with Query if your query uses criteria involving calculations (other than simple comparisons) or if you want to create a query that prompts the user for one or more parameters when run. Query, but not the Query Wizard, also lets you do the following:

- Filter on the basis of fields you don't intend to import into Excel—that is, fields that are not included in the *result set*, the records that meet your current criteria.

- Filter using Is One Of, Is Not One Of, Is Between, or Is Not Between.

- Limit the result set to unique entries.

- Perform aggregate calculations, such as totals or averages.

- Create your own joins between tables.

- Edit a query's SQL code.

Getting to Query

If you already stored the query you want to edit in a DQY file, you can open it in Microsoft Query as follows:

1. Click the Data tab, and then click From Other Sources.

2. On the menu that appears, click From Microsoft Query.

3. In the Choose Data Source dialog box, click the Queries tab. Your query should appear there:

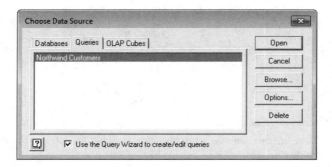

If you just finished creating your query in the Query Wizard and want to open it in Microsoft Query for further editing, select View Data Or Edit Query In Microsoft Query on the final page of the wizard (shown in Figure 25-17), and click Finish.

Figure 25-18 shows Microsoft Query with a query against three tables from Northwind.mdb. The tables are Products, Categories, and Suppliers. The Products table is joined to the Categories table in the CategoryID field and to the Suppliers table in the SupplierID field. The query shows selected fields from these tables, revealing products by category and supplier (CompanyName), along with some price and inventory information.

Note that the Query window is divided horizontally into two panes—an upper pane for tables and a lower one for data. The tables pane shows a window for each table that's currently involved in the query. The data pane shows the result set—the collection of records that meet the criteria. (At the moment, we haven't defined any filters, so all records in the three tables are included.)

Shortly, you'll see that Query can also accommodate a third pane, in which you specify filtering criteria. All these panes, as well as the individual table windows, are independently sizeable and movable. We bumped the data pane down a bit from its default position to make more room for the Suppliers and Products tables, and we stretched the windows in which those tables are displayed so that we won't have to scroll to see all their fields. Query seldom gives you an ideal window layout when it starts, but you can manipulate it to get the view you need.

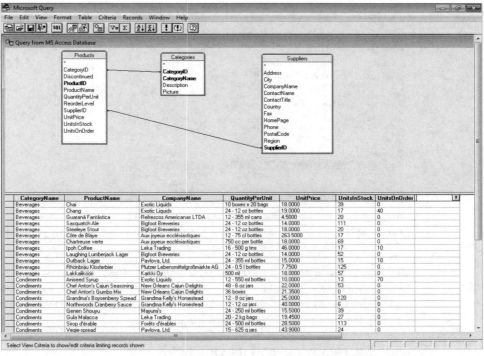

Figure 25-18 We're using Query to edit a query against three tables in Northwind.mdb.

Adding and removing tables

To add a table to the data pane, click Table and then click Add Tables. The Add Tables dialog box lists all the tables available in the data source you're using. To add a table, select it and click Add. You can add as many as you like before closing the Add Tables dialog box. To remove a table, select it in the table pane and then click Table, Remove Table.

Working with joins

If Query doesn't already have your tables joined appropriately, you can create your own joins by dragging. If you click a field in one table and then drag to a field in another, Query creates a join based on those fields and draws a line to indicate that it has done so. You can create, inspect, and modify joins by double-clicking any join line or by clicking Table, Joins. Figure 25-19 shows the Joins dialog box for the query shown in Figure 25-18.

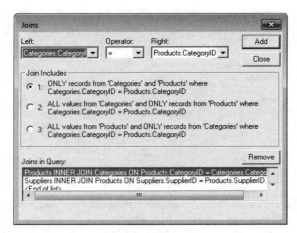

Figure 25-19 The Joins dialog box tells you exactly how your tables are joined and lets you modify the joins or create new ones.

If you're not sure what's joined to what or what the effect of a join is, you should visit the Joins dialog box. The Join Includes area in the dialog box provides a pretty clear description of what's happening. By working with the Left, Operator, and Right fields, you can also modify the ways in which your tables are joined.

Adding, removing, and moving fields

To add a field to your data pane, double-click it in a table window. To add all fields to the data pane from a table, double-click the asterisk at the top of the table window.

To remove a field, select its heading (this action selects the entire field) and press Delete. To move a field from its current location, first select its heading and then drag it to the position you want.

INSIDE OUT   Hide selected fields without removing them from the query

If you find yourself scrolling horizontally a lot but don't want to rearrange your fields, you can temporarily hide fields you don't need to see. Select a field, and then click Format, Hide Columns. To redisplay a hidden field, click Format, Show Columns; select the field in the Show Columns dialog box; and then click Show.

Renaming fields

By default, Query uses the names of your fields as field headings. If these field names are short and cryptic, you might want to supply different headings.

Select the column you want to change, and then click Records, Edit Column. In the Edit Column dialog box, type a new heading in the Column Heading box, and then click OK.

Sorting the result set

Query initially displays records in the order in which they are stored in the external data source. You can change their order by clicking Records, Sort. Figure 25-20 shows the Sort dialog box with the CategoryName field selected. (The dialog box, like others in Query, qualifies field names with the tables to which they belong; it says Categories.CategoryName because the CategoryName field is part of the Categories table.)

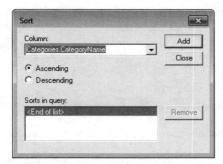

Figure 25-20 The Sort dialog box displays the current sort order and lets you add fields from a list.

The Sorts In Query section in the dialog box indicates what sort specification, if any, is currently in effect. In Figure 25-20, the list is empty, indicating that the result set is currently unsorted. The Column list at the top of the dialog box lists all the table fields available for sorting. When you add a field to the Sorts In Query list, Query performs the sort immediately but leaves the dialog box open in case you want to sort on additional fields. You can sort on as many as you please.

For multiple-field sorts, sort first on the most important sort field. Then sort on your secondary field, and so on. Figure 25-21 shows the result set sorted first by Suppliers.CompanyName and then by Products.ProductName. (The Asc abbreviation in the Sorts In Query list indicates ascending sorts.) The records now are alphabetized by supplier, with records of a common supplier alphabetized by product name.

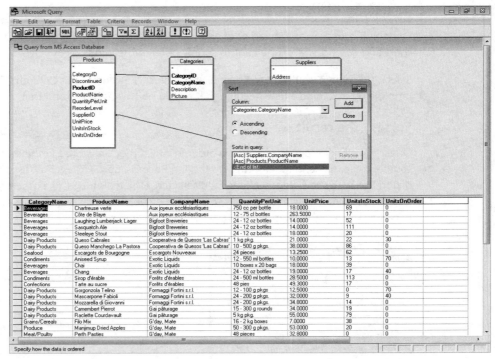

Figure 25-21 We sorted first by the supplier's company name and then by product name.

When you click Add in the Sort dialog box, Query adds your new sort field above the currently selected field in the Sorts In Query list. If you accidentally add a field in the wrong order, select it and click Remove. Then add the field in the correct position.

You also can sort with the toolbar. The Sort icons on the Query toolbar work differently from the Sort command on the ribbon in Excel. You can add a sort to the current list by holding down the Ctrl key when you click a Sort icon. If you do not hold down Ctrl, clicking a Sort icon replaces the current sort with the new one.

Filtering the result set

Query provides a variety of methods by which you can filter the result set so that it includes only the records in which you're interested. As with the Query Wizard, you create a filter by specifying one or more criteria—conditions that particular fields must meet.

Creating exact-match criteria   The simplest kind of criterion is one in which you stipulate that a field must exactly equal some value. Query makes it extremely easy to create such criteria:

1. Select a field value that meets your exact-match criterion.

2. Click the Criteria Equals button on the toolbar.

For example, suppose you want to filter the result set shown in Figure 25-21 to include only records in which the CompanyName field is Bigfoot Breweries. To do this, select any record with the CompanyName field that already equals Bigfoot Breweries and click the Criteria Equals button. Query responds by displaying the criteria pane (if it's not already displayed) and applying the new filter to the table, as shown in Figure 25-22.

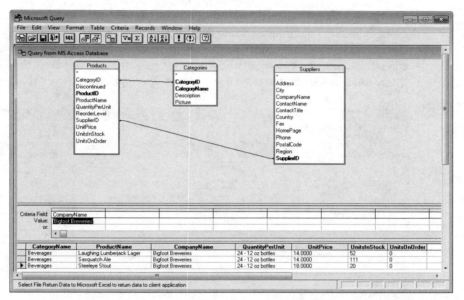

Figure 25-22 When you click the Criteria Equals button, Query displays the criteria pane and applies the filter to the result set.

If you used the Advanced Filter command (see "Using the Advanced Filter command" in Chapter 22, "Managing information in tables"), you'll notice that the criteria pane in Query looks a lot like a criteria range in an Excel worksheet. Field headings appear in the top row, and criteria are stated in subsequent rows. Although you can type new criteria or edit existing ones directly in the criteria pane, it's not necessary because the Query menu commands take care of entering information in the criteria pane for you. In fact, you don't need to have the criteria pane on your screen at all.

> **Note**
>
> To remove the criteria pane, click the Show/Hide Criteria button on the toolbar in Query or click View, Criteria. To remove the tables pane, click Show/Hide Tables or click View, Tables.

Using multiple exact-match criteria   To generate a query that uses exact-match criteria in two or more fields, repeat the process just described for the second and each subsequent criterion. For example, to filter the result set in Figure 25-21 to show only records with CompanyName equal to Exotic Liquids and CategoryName equal to Beverages, select Exotic Liquids in the CompanyName field, click Criteria Equals, select Beverages in the CategoryName field, and click Criteria Equals again. As Figure 25-23 shows, the criteria pane then shows the two criteria on the same line. Just as with an Excel criteria range, Query treats criteria on the same line as if they are connected by the AND operator.

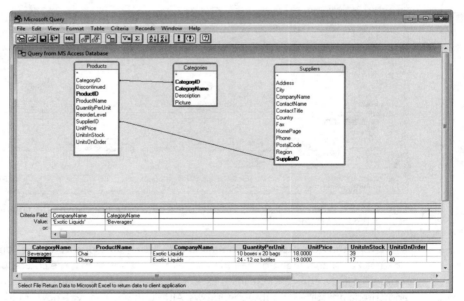

Figure 25-23 When you use the Criteria Equals button in two separate fields, the filter in Query admits only records that meet both criteria.

Automatic Query vs. manual query

By default, Query updates the result set every time you add a new field to the data pane, rearrange the order of the existing fields in the data pane, change a sort specification, or change a filter criterion. (If you're working in the criteria pane, the query is executed as soon as you click away from the current criteria-pane call.) In response to these actions, Query creates a new SQL statement and executes that statement against your data source. (You can see the SQL code—and edit it, if you are inclined—by clicking the View SQL button on the toolbar.) If your data source is particularly large or you're working on a slow network, Automatic Query can cause annoying delays. You can turn off the Automatic Query feature so that Query executes the current SQL statement only when you ask it to do so.

You can determine whether Automatic Query is on by verifying whether the Auto Query button on the toolbar is selected (has a "pushed in" appearance). To turn the feature off, click the Auto Query button or click Records, Automatic Query.

To execute the current query in manual mode, click the Query Now button or click Records, Query Now.

Using menu commands to specify exact-match criteria   If you'd rather use menu commands than toolbar buttons, you can specify an exact-match criterion as follows:

1. Click Criteria, Add Criteria. You'll see a dialog box similar to the one shown in Figure 25-24.

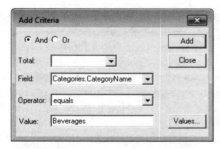

Figure 25-24 The Add Criteria dialog box lets you select fields, comparison operators, and values.

In the Add Criteria dialog box, you can construct your criteria by selecting options from various lists. For example, you can select a field from the Field list and then select an operator, such as Is Greater Than, in the Operator list. You can also enter a value in the Value text box by typing it or clicking the Values button and selecting from the list.

> **Note**
>
> For comparison criteria that don't involve computed fields, be sure the Total field in the Add Criteria dialog box is blank, as it is in Figure 25-24. For more information about the Total field, see "Filtering on calculated fields" later in this chapter.

2. After you fill out the Field, Operator, and Value fields, click Add.

   Query responds by creating the appropriate entry in the criteria pane and, if Automatic Query is on, executing the new query. The Add Criteria dialog box remains open so you can specify more criteria.

3. To add another criterion, select the And option or the Or option at the top of the dialog box and then type the information as before.

4. When you finish typing criteria, click Close.

Filtering on fields that are not in the result set   Your filter criteria can be based on fields that are not currently displayed in the result set. The Field list in the Add Criteria dialog box includes all fields in all active tables, not only the fields you plan to return to Excel.

Limiting the result set to unique entries   To limit the result set to unique entries, click View, Query Properties. In the Query Properties dialog box, select Unique Values Only. You can make this selection before or after you create your filter.

Comparing fields   Your comparison criteria can compare the value in one field to that in another. For example, to display records where UnitsInStock is less than ReorderLevel, you fill out the Add Criteria dialog box as shown in Figure 25-25. Note that you have to type a field name in the Value box.

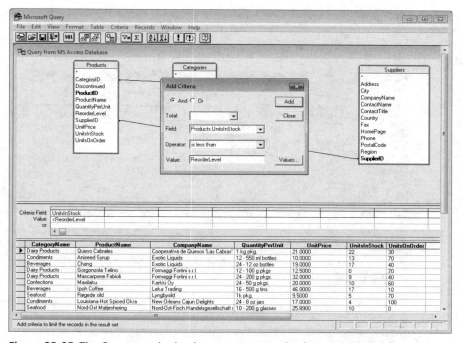

Figure 25-25 The Operator criterion here returns records where units in stock are below the reorder level.

Performing aggregate calculations

You can analyze your results thoroughly after you get the data back onto the Excel worksheet. If you prefer, however, you can have Query do some of the calculating for you. With Query, you can make aggregate calculations (sums, averages, counts, and so on) the basis of filtering criteria.

Query refers to all calculations as totals, although summing values is only one of the options available. The aggregate functions that are common to all database drivers are AVG (average), COUNT, MIN (minimum), and MAX (maximum). Your driver might support additional functions.

Cycling through the totals   One way to perform aggregate calculations is by clicking the Cycle Through Totals button on the toolbar in Query. For example, to find the total of the UnitsOnOrder field, follow these steps:

1. Display only the UnitsOnOrder field in the data pane, and remove all filtering criteria from the criteria pane.

2. Select the UnitsOnOrder field, and click the Cycle Through Totals button.

As Figure 25-26 shows, Query responds by displaying the total in the data pane.

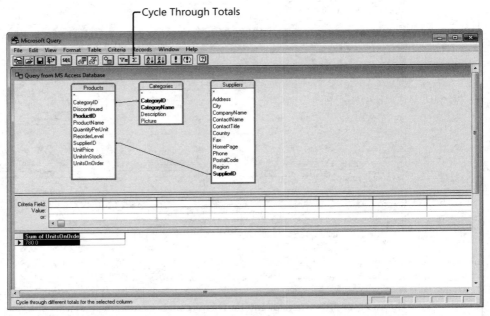

Figure 25-26 We used the Cycle Through Totals button to calculate the total units on order.

Cycling through the functions In the previous example, clicking Cycle Through Totals a second time changes the aggregate function from SUM to AVG, and the number shown in the data pane changes accordingly. Successive clicks on the Cycle Through Totals button result in the count, the minimum, and the maximum. One more click returns the result set to its unaggregated state.

> **Note**
>
> Not all the aggregate functions are available for every field type.

Using menu commands If you prefer menus to tools, you can use the Edit Column command:

1. Click Records, Edit Column. (Alternatively, double-click the field heading.)

2. In the Edit Column dialog box (shown in Figure 25-27), select the function you want from the Total list.

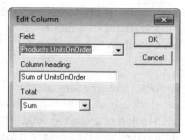

Figure 25-27 Instead of clicking Cycle Through Totals, you can click Records, Edit Column.

Aggregating groups of records   In addition to grand totals, you can also calculate totals for groups of records. For example, to find out how many units are on order for each supplier company, do the following:

1.   In the data pane, display the CompanyName field followed by the UnitsOnOrder field.

2.   Select the UnitsOnOrder field, and click Cycle Through Totals.

As Figure 25-28 shows, Query displays one record for each company and shows the total units on order for each.

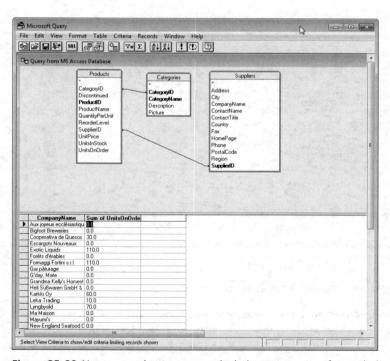

Figure 25-28 You can apply aggregate calculations to groups of records; here, we calculated the total units on order per company.

Using more than one aggregate field You can add as many aggregate fields to your result set as you need. To display both sums and averages for a numeric field, for example, you can drag that field to the data pane twice. Click the Cycle Through Totals button to apply the function you want to each copy of the field.

Filtering on calculated fields A field that performs an aggregate calculation is called a *calculated field*. You can use calculated fields as the basis for filtering criteria. To base a criterion on a calculated field in the Add Criteria dialog box, use the Total list to select the function you want. (If you're entering the criterion directly in the criteria pane, type the function name and enclose the field name in parentheses.) Figure 25-29 shows a criterion that returns the names of companies for which the total number of products on order is greater than 20.

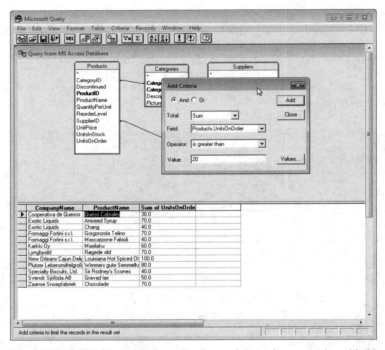

Figure 25-29 We filtered the supplier list to show only companies with 20 or more products on order.

Creating a parameter-based query

A *parameter-based query* is one in which a filter criterion is based on a value supplied by the user at the time the query is executed. To create such a query, first turn the Automatic Query feature off by clicking the Auto Query button on the toolbar. Then specify a criterion in the usual way—either by using the Add Criteria dialog box or by typing values directly in the criteria pane. Instead of typing a value, though, type a left bracket character, a prompt of your choosing, and a right bracket character. (The prompt must not be identical to the field name, although it can include the field name.) When you execute the query, either in Query or in Excel, a dialog box containing your prompt appears. Figure 25-30 shows a parameter-based query.

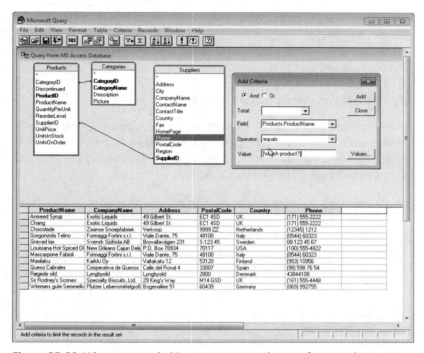

Figure 25-30 When executed, this query prompts the user for a product name.

Saving a query

To store your query specification in a reusable DQY file, click File, Save. This step is optional. If you do not save the query, you can still refresh it from the data range that it creates on your Excel worksheet. You have to re-create it if you want to use it in another workbook, however.

Returning the result set to Excel

To return your data to Excel, click File, Return Data To Microsoft Excel. The Import Data dialog box (shown earlier in Figure 25-2) appears, asking you where and how you want the data returned.

Using a web query to return Internet data

Web queries let you grab specific information—such as stock prices, sports scores, or your company's current sales data—from the Internet or an intranet. You can set up queries to prompt you for the data you want (for stock ticker symbols, for example) or to get the same information every time they're executed. The Excel graphical interface for creating web queries lets you build a query by pointing to the data you want. You can refresh the query at any time or at regular intervals, and you can save the query in an IQY file for reuse in other worksheets. You do not need to understand how the target web page is built to construct a query to it.

Using an existing web query

To run an existing web query—one of the samples supplied with Excel or one that you or someone else has set up—click the Data tab and then click Existing Connections. As Figure 25-31 shows, web queries are identified in the Existing Connections dialog box by a pair of intersecting blue rectangles and a globe.

Figure 25-31 Web queries are marked by intersecting rectangles and a globe.

When you double-click a web query, Excel prompts you to specify a location for the incoming web data. Depending on how the query is set up, it might also prompt you for parameters. For example, when you double-click the MSN MoneyCentral Investor Stock Quotes query, after you indicate where you want the data to go, you see the following dialog box, which prompts you to supply one or more stock symbols:

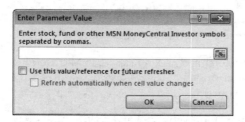

To supply parameters via the Enter Parameter Value dialog box, simply type in the box. If you prefer, you can point to a worksheet range containing your parameters. If you specify a multicell range, Excel parses the range moving across and then down.

If you use a worksheet range to feed parameters to your web query, you can also stipulate that the query be refreshed automatically any time the worksheet range changes. To do this, select both check boxes.

Figure 25-32 shows an example of data returned by a web query. Note that this query is set up to return the names of market indexes as hyperlinks. Clicking a hyperlink takes you to a relevant page in the MSN MoneyCentral Investor website.

	A	B	C	D	E	F	G	H	I	J	K	L	M	N	O	P
1	**Stock Quotes Provided by MSN Money**															
2	Click here to visit MSN Money															
3				Last	Previous Close	High	Low	Volume	Change	% Change	52 Wk High	52 Wk Low	Market Cap	EPS	P/E Ratio	# Shares Out
4	Dow Jones Industrial Average Index	Chart	News	13104.14	12938.11	13109.13	12883.89	145,738,333	166.03	1.28%	13661.87	12035.09				
5	NASDAQ Composite Index	Chart	News	3019.51	2960.31	3021.41	2953.52	1,558,749,454	59.2	2.00%	3196.93	2627.23				
6	NASDAQ Transport Index	Chart	News	2280.92	2243.54	2280.92	2241.82	0	37.38	1.67%	2452.45	2027.5				
7	Dow Jones Utility Average Index	Chart	News	453.09	446.7	453.5	443.69	14,136,741	6.39	1.43%	499.82	435.57				
8	$DAX (Invalid symbol)	???	???	???	???	???	???	???	???	???	???	???	???	???	???	???
9	FTSE 100 Index	Chart	News	5897.81	5925.37	5925.43	5873.43	0	-27.56	-0.47%						
10	$HSI (Invalid symbol)	???	???	???	???	???	???	???	???	???	???	???	???	???	???	???
11	INTERACTIVE WEEK INTERNET INDEX	Chart	News	327	327	327.91	319.73	0	0	0.00%	336.24	281.62				
12	NASDAQ Composite Index	Chart	News	3019.51	2960.31	3021.41	2953.52	1,558,749,454	59.2	2.00%	3196.93	2627.23				
13	$NI225 (Invalid symbol)	???	???	???	???	???	???	???	???	???	???	???	???	???	???	???
14	$CAC (Invalid symbol)	???	???	???	???	???	???	???	???	???	???	???	???	???	???	???
15	$SOX.X (Invalid symbol)	???	???	???	???	???	???	???	???	???	???	???	???	???	???	???
16	S&P 500 Insurance (Industry Group)	Chart	News	199.72	196.98	199.78	196.08	0	2.74	1.39%	206.42	169.07				
17	S&P 100 Index	Chart	News	646.61	636.17	646.91	633.93	0	10.44	1.64%	677.02	570.69				
18	S&P 500 Index	Chart	News	1426.19	1402.43	1426.74	1398.11	0	23.76	1.69%	1474.51	1257.46				
19	$STI (Invalid symbol)	???	???	???	???	???	???	???	???	???	???	???	???	???	???	???
20	$AOI (Invalid symbol)	???	???	???	???	???	???	???	???	???	???	???	???	???	???	???
21	Toronto SE 300 Composite Index	Chart	News	12433.53	12316.12	12457.33	12289.66	99,702,015	117.41	0.95%	12788.63	11209.55				
22																
23	Symbol Lookup			MSN Money Home			Microsoft Office Tools on the Web									
24	Find stocks, mutual funds, options, indices, and currencies.			Discover MSN Money's tools, columns, and more!			Get the latest from Microsoft Office									
25																
26	Terms of Use. © 2013 Microsoft Corporation and/or its suppliers. All rights reserved.															

Figure 25-32 Data returned by this web query includes hyperlinks to the MSN MoneyCentral Investor site.

Creating your own web query

Excel provides three easy ways to construct a web query:

- Clicking the Data tab and then clicking From Web

- Copying and pasting information from your web browser

- Right-clicking in Internet Explorer and clicking Export To Microsoft Excel

Using the From Web command

To create a web query by using the From Web command, follow these steps:

1. Click the Data tab, and then click From Web. The New Web Query form that appears is a specialized web browser, and your home page appears initially in its window.

2. If you know the URL of the website you want to query, you can type or paste it into the Address field.

3. Click Go; your site appears in the main window, as Figure 25-33 shows.

Figure 25-33 We displayed the site we want to query in the New Web Query form.

Yellow boxes with arrows appear along the left edge of the window. Each of these boxes represents a section of the website that you can import into Excel. As you rest your pointer on any of these yellow boxes, a thick bounding rectangle indicates the section of the site you will be importing if you select the yellow box. You can select any or all of the yellow boxes.

After making your selections, you can click Import to transform your selection into a query. But before you do so, you might want to save the query (making it a reusable IQY file) or explore the menu of options. To save the query in its current form, click the Save Query command, directly to the left of the word Options on the toolbar in the New Web Query form. To set options, click Options. Figure 25-34 shows the Web Query Options dialog box.

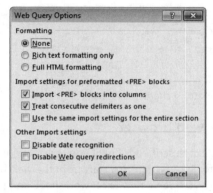

Figure 25-34 In addition to offering other features, the Web Query Options dialog box lets you control how much of the website's formatting Excel should preserve.

In the Formatting area of the dialog box, select None to import the data as plain text. Select Rich Text Formatting Only to preserve hyperlinks and merged cells in the web data. Select Full HTML Formatting to retrieve as much as possible of the original website's formatting. Figure 25-35 shows a website queried with full HTML formatting. Note the inclusion of hyperlinks in the downloaded data.

	A	B	C	D	E	F	G	H	I
1		Back	June	July	Aug	Sept	Oct	Nov	
2	**Data Series**	Data	2012	2012	2012	2012	2012	2012	
3	Labor Force Data								
4	Civilian Labor Force (1)	Jump to page with historical data	3,180.90	3,159.90	3,141.10	3,142.50	3,149.90	(P) 3,150.2	
5	Employment (1)	Jump to page with historical data	2,926.20	2,900.40	2,881.10	2,886.10	2,898.00	(P) 2,898.0	
6	Unemployment (1)	Jump to page with historical data	254.7	259.5	260	256.4	251.9	(P) 252.2	
7	Unemployment Rate (2)	Jump to page with historical data	8	8.2	8.3	8.2	8	(P) 8.0	
8	Nonfarm Wage and Salary Employment								
9	Total Nonfarm (3)	Jump to page with historical data	2,878.90	2,887.10	2,902.20	2,900.00	2,905.00	(P) 2,895.9	
10	**12-month % change**	Jump to page with historical data	2	2.1	2.6	2.3	2.5	(P) 2.1	
11	Mining and Logging (3)	Jump to page with historical data	6.7	6.7	6.7	6.6	6.5	(P) 6.5	
12	**12-month % change**	Jump to page with historical data	0	-1.5	-1.5	-2.9	-4.4	(P) -4.4	
13	Construction (3)	Jump to page with historical data	125.5	128.4	131.1	130.8	129.9	(P) 123.7	
14	**12-month % change**	Jump to page with historical data	6.7	8.3	9.1	4.6	5.7	(P) -0.6	
15	Manufacturing (3)	Jump to page with historical data	487.7	488	487.2	485.5	488.6	(P) 488.9	
16	**12-month % change**	Jump to page with historical data	5.3	4.9	5.1	4.1	4.2	(P) 4.7	
17	Trade, Transportation, and Utilities (3)	Jump to page with historical data	552.3	551.7	553	555.3	557.5	(P) 562.3	
18	**12-month % change**	Jump to page with historical data	0.3	0.5	0.9	1.7	2	(P) 2.7	
19	Information (3)	Jump to page with historical data	34	34.3	34.3	34.4	34.7	(P) 34.5	
20	**12-month % change**	Jump to page with historical data	0	-0.3	0.6	1.2	2.7	(P) 1.8	
21	Financial Activities (3)	Jump to page with historical data	131.5	130.1	128.3	128.5	127.8	(P) 126.7	
22	**12-month % change**	Jump to page with historical data	-0.2	-0.9	-2.1	-1.9	-1.9	(P) -2.2	
23	Professional & Business Services (3)	Jump to page with historical data	300	301.2	299	295.7	293.8	(P) 288.6	
24	**12-month % change**	Jump to page with historical data	5.4	5.9	4.8	2.6	2.1	(P) 0.1	

Sheet1 Sheet4 Sheet3 Sheet5 **Sheet7**

Figure 25-35 Because we queried this site using full HTML formatting, the downloaded data includes active hyperlinks and other formatting characteristics.

Copying and pasting from the web browser

The method for creating a web query just described is fine if you're starting in Excel and you know the address of the target site. But you can also start from the web browser. Select the data you want, press Ctrl+C to copy it, open a new Excel worksheet, and press Ctrl+V. You'll see an options button near the lower-right corner of the pasted data. Open the menu, shown here, and click Refreshable Web Query. Your data selection will appear in the New Web Query form.

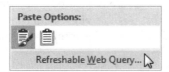

Exporting from Internet Explorer to Excel

If your web browser is Internet Explorer, you can also create a web query by right-clicking a webpage and clicking Export To Microsoft Excel. (If you don't see this command, you probably already have something selected in Internet Explorer. Clear your selection, and try again.) The Export To Microsoft Excel command begins by creating a new instance of Excel. (It does this to avoid overwriting Excel data you might already be working with.) If you right-clicked something that Internet Explorer recognizes as an HTML table, it transfers that table directly onto Sheet1!A1 as a new web query. If you clicked anywhere other than an HTML table, the command opens the New Web Query form.

PART 8
Using Excel collaboratively

Collaborating on a network or by email

N THE DISTANT PAST, if you wanted to share your worksheets with other people, you copied everything onto floppy disks, carried them down the hall (or flipped them over the partition), and handed them to the person who wanted them. This system (still effective, if you happen to have a machine with a diskette drive) was known affectionately as *sneakernet*. The lucky few who worked for large companies might have been connected to a network. These days, even people who work at home have networks, and everyone can take advantage of the Internet. Microsoft Excel 2013 makes it easier than ever to get connected and provides easy-to-use tools that can help foster the synergy that is the hallmark of effective collaboration.

Saving and retrieving files over a network

When you click File, Save As, the Places list on the left side of the Save As screen provides access to all the remote and local resources you need. To save to a location on your local area network, click Computer. If the networked folder you're looking for is one you used recently, it will probably appear in the Recent Folders list, on the right side of the screen. If not, click Browse. That will take you to a familiar-looking Save As dialog box, in which you can navigate to the desired folder. The process for opening a networked file is similar. When you click File, Open, recently used workbooks appear in a list on the right side of the screen. If the one you want isn't there, click Computer in the places list, and then use the Recent Folders list or the Browse button to locate your workbook.

For information about basic file-management tasks in Excel, see "Exploring file-management fundamentals" in Chapter 2, "Exploring Excel fundamentals."

When you try to open a file that resides on a network drive while another user has the file open, Excel 2013 displays a dialog box you can use to open the file in read-only mode.

Figure 26-1 shows the File In Use dialog box that appears when you attempt to open a busy file.

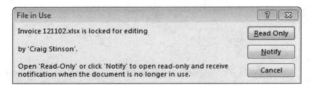

Figure 26-1 The File In Use dialog box appears when you try to open a busy file.

If you click Notify in the File In Use dialog box, Excel opens your file in read-only mode. To save your file while in read-only mode, you will of course have to supply a new file name. Your file will then acquire read/write status under the new name. However, if you don't save and the file becomes available, Excel alerts you with the File Now Available dialog box shown in Figure 26-2. At this point, you can click Read-Write to assume full control of the file under its original name.

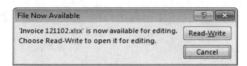

Figure 26-2 The File Now Available dialog box alerts you when the file is no longer in use.

Sharing workbooks on a network

It has always been possible to share Excel files on a network. You just had to be sure you coordinated your efforts to avoid having more than one person open a file at the same time. With recent versions of Excel, however, two or more people can work on the same workbook simultaneously. In Excel 2013, click the Review tab, and then click Share Workbook in the Changes group on the ribbon to open the Share Workbook dialog box shown in Figure 26-3.

To share the workbook, select the Allow Changes By More Than One User At The Same Time check box. When you click OK, Excel displays a confirmation prompt and then saves the workbook. This step is necessary because the workbook must be saved as "sharable" before another user can open it. After you save the workbook, [Shared] appears in the title bar whenever anyone opens the workbook, and it remains until you turn off sharing.

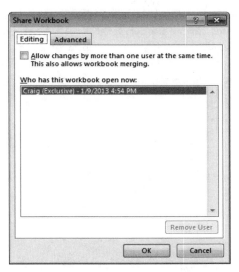

Figure 26-3 Select the Allow Changes By More Than One User At The Same Time check box to share the workbook.

TROUBLESHOOTING

Excel won't let me share the workbook

You will get an error message if you try to share a workbook that contains tables or XML maps, or one in which privacy has been enabled. To make the workbook sharable, you first have to remove the offending features. Fortunately, the error message that appears when you try to share provides explicit instructions about how to accomplish the feature removal.

Note

To change the name users see in the Share Workbook dialog box when they work with a shared file, click the File tab and then click Options to open the Excel Options dialog box. In the General category, edit the User Name box.

Of course, there are inherent risks when people work in the same file at the same time. Conflicts can arise when several people are making changes that affect the same cells.

When someone saves changes, Excel not only saves the workbook but also updates it if other users save any changes. A dialog box informs you that Excel has incorporated your changes. After you save, Excel outlines changes that have been made by other people with a colored border and adds a special cell comment to explain who did what when. When you point to the cell, a comment box displays this information, as shown in Figure 26-4.

	A	B	C	D	E	F
1	**Expenses**					
2	Space	$2,100.00				
3	Union labor	$ 900.00				
4	Rights	$1,400.00				
5	Sets	$ 500.00				
6	Costumes	$ 500.00				
7	Props	$ 175.00				
8	Choreographer	$ -				
9	Stage manager	$ 250.00				
10	Lighting	$ 250.00				
11	Progams/tickets	$ 300.00				
12	**Total**	$6,375.00				

> Kathy, 1/11/2013 2:53 PM:
> Changed cell B5 from ' $375.00 ' to ' $500.00 '.

Figure 26-4 Excel attaches a comment to identify cells changed by others in a shared workbook.

Note

When a shared file has been edited by another user, the triangular comment indicators specifying changed cells appear in the upper-left corner of the cell instead of in the upper-right corner, as they do for standard cell comments.

Note

Change tracking, which determines whether outlines and comment boxes appear in your worksheet, is turned on separately. You can control change tracking by clicking the Review tab, clicking Track Changes, and then clicking Highlight Changes. In the Highlight Changes dialog box, select the Track Changes While Editing check box. Be sure this check box is selected before you save the worksheet for sharing if you want to track and review changes later. For more information, see "Tracking changes" later in this chapter.

When you save a shared file, Excel looks for conflicts and determines whether any mediation is necessary. Usually, a dialog box appears after you save the file to inform you that Excel has incorporated changes made by other users. However, if others' changes involve any of the same cells you changed, the mediator arrives in the form of the Resolve Conflicts dialog box shown in Figure 26-5.

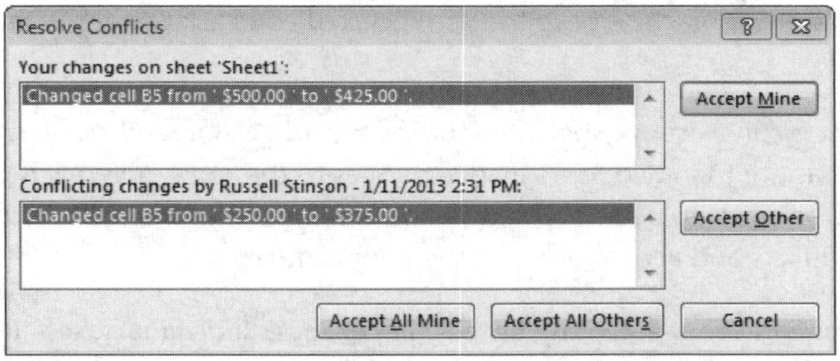

Figure 26-5 If more than one person changes the same cells, the last person to save changes might get to decide which ones to keep.

What you can and can't do with a shared workbook

You can edit shared workbooks using Excel 97 and newer versions only. Older versions, such as Microsoft Excel 7 for Windows 95, don't support shared editing.

When you open a workbook for sharing, you can type text and numbers; change cell formatting; edit formulas; and copy, paste, and move data by dragging. You can insert columns and rows, but you can't insert blocks of cells. You can't merge cells, insert charts or other objects, create hyperlinks, assign passwords, insert automatic subtotals, create outlines, or create data tables or PivotTables. You can't do anything with macros except run them, although you can record macros if you store them in a separate, unshared workbook. The Conditional Formatting, Scenarios, and Data Validation commands are not available for a workbook in shared mode (although you can still see their effects). Most of the buttons on the Drawing toolbar aren't available either. Also note that multiple users cannot edit a workbook stored on a SharePoint site.

Note

When setting up a multiuser workbook, establish some working guidelines and design the workbook for maximum safety. For example, each person could have a separate named worksheet in the workbook, with each worksheet reflecting a specific area of responsibility. Then you could create a separate consolidation worksheet that pulls together all the relevant data from the personal worksheets to present it in the necessary format. For more information, see "Consolidating worksheets" in Chapter 8, "Worksheet editing techniques."

For each conflict identified, the Resolve Conflicts dialog box specifies the cells involved and lets you decide whose changes to keep. You can resolve conflicts individually or use the buttons at the bottom of the dialog box to accept all the changes entered by you or others. You must resolve the conflicts to save the workbook. If you click Cancel, Excel will not save the workbook.

Note that conflicts can exist only between the last saved version and the version you are trying to save. If more than two users made changes to the same cells, each person who saves the workbook gets to decide who wins the conflict of the moment. You can, however, revisit all the conflicts and accept or reject them individually later.

For more information about accepting or rejecting changes individually, see "Reviewing changes" later in this chapter.

Using advanced sharing options

You can change some aspects of the default behavior of shared workbooks. To do so, click the Review tab and then click Share Workbook to open the Share Workbook dialog box. Click the Advanced tab, shown in Figure 26-6. (The options on this tab are not available if you haven't selected the Allow Changes By More Than One User At The Same Time check box on the Editing tab.) Each shared workbook user can set these options individually. Use the first area on the Advanced tab to specify the length of time you want to keep track of changes or whether you want to track them at all. Excel keeps the change history for only the number of days you specify. If you need to track changes but are unsure how long you want to track them, set a high number (such as 999 days).

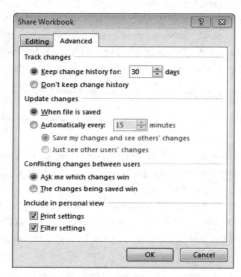

Figure 26-6 Use the Advanced tab to determine the way Excel handles changes.

Turning off change tracking detracts from your ability to merge workbooks. For more information, see "Combining changes made to multiple workbooks" later in this chapter.

In the Update Changes area, select when you want updates to occur. Ordinarily, when a user saves a file, Excel saves the changes and also updates the copy of the workbook with any changes made by others. The Automatically Every option is handy, letting you specify how often updates occur automatically. When you choose automatic updating, the usual procedure is as described previously: Excel saves your changes and incorporates changes made by others into your copy. You also can select the Just See Other Users' Changes option, which gives you the ability to hold your changes back until you decide to save them, while at the same time updating your file at regular intervals with any changes recorded by others. This is a good workbook-management technique, particularly if your team includes users who aren't in the habit of regularly saving their changes.

As mentioned previously, when conflicts arise, the Resolve Conflicts dialog box shown in Figure 26-5 appears. However, if you select The Changes Being Saved Win in the Conflicting Changes Between Users area on the Advanced tab in the Share Workbook dialog box, Excel essentially resolves all conflicts in favor of the last user to issue the Save command. Click OK to dismiss the Resolve Conflicts dialog box and return to the Share Workbook dialog box.

With the Include In Personal View check boxes, you can change the print settings and any views set with the Filter or Advanced Filter command on the Data tab. With these check boxes selected, each person who has a shared workbook open can have different print and filter settings, which are recalled the next time that person opens the shared workbook.

INSIDE OUT   Password-protect workbooks before you share

You can use the standard Excel password-protection options with shared workbooks, but you must apply the password before sharing. Click the File tab, click Save As, and then click Browse. In the file-management dialog box that appears, click the small arrow next to Tools, and then click the General Options command. In the File Sharing area, you can type a password for opening the workbook and another password for modifying the workbook. Click OK to save your changes. Then you can disseminate the necessary passwords to members of your workgroup. For more information about file protection, see "Protecting files" in Chapter 2.

Tracking changes

Change tracking in Excel is closely linked with shared workbooks. To turn on change track-ing, click the Review tab, click Track Changes, and then click Highlight Changes to display the dialog box shown in Figure 26-7. In the Highlight Changes dialog box, select the Track Changes While Editing check box, which puts your workbook into shared mode and saves it, just as if you had clicked the Share Workbook command. Even if you select the Don't Keep Change History option on the Advanced tab in the Share Workbook dialog box, shown in Figure 26-6, you can still turn on change tracking by using the Track Changes commands.

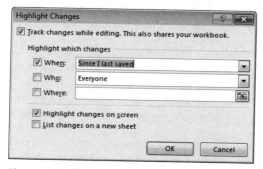

Figure 26-7 Use the Highlight Changes command to show what's been done in a shared workbook.

INSIDE OUT   Track changes without sharing

You don't have to share a workbook to track the changes you make. Just turn on change tracking and save the workbook in an unshared folder on your own hard disk instead of in a shared network location.

You control which changes you want Excel to highlight. Use the When list to select whether you want to see all the changes made since the workbook was first shared, only changes you haven't yet reviewed, changes made since the last time you saved, or changes made since a date you specify. The Who options include Everyone, Everyone But Me, and the name of every individual who has made changes to the shared workbook. If you want, you can type a specific cell or range in the Where box. If you select the check box next to the Where option, you can drag to select the cells directly on the worksheet while the dialog box is still open.

Ordinarily, the changes are highlighted on the screen with cell borders and cell comments are attached. Clear the Highlight Changes On Screen check box to turn off this option. You can also create a history worksheet detailing all the changes made. To do so, select the List Changes On A New Sheet check box (which is unavailable until you have actually made some changes). The resulting worksheet is inserted after the last worksheet in the workbook, as shown in Figure 26-8.

	A	B	C	D	E	F	G	H	I	J	K
1	Action Number ▾	Date ▾	Time ▾	Who ▾	Change ▾	Sheet ▾	Range ▾	New Value ▾	Old Value ▾	Action Type ▾	Losing Action ▾
2	1	1/11/2013	2:52 PM	Craig	Cell Change	Sheet1	B5	$400.00	$375.00		
3	2	1/11/2013	2:53 PM	Kathy	Cell Change	Sheet1	B5	$500.00	$375.00	Won	1
4											
5	The history ends with the changes saved on 1/11/2013 at 2:53 PM.										
6											

Figure 26-8 You can choose to create a history worksheet detailing the changes made to a shared workbook.

> **Note**
>
> Formatting changes aren't recorded in the change history.

The history worksheet is a special locked worksheet that can be displayed only when a worksheet is in shared mode. The worksheet disappears when you turn off change tracking. If you subsequently restart a shared workbook session, the history starts fresh, and any changes recorded in previous sharing sessions are lost.

> **Note**
>
> To preserve the change history, copy the contents of the locked history worksheet before you discontinue the sharing session, and then paste them into another worksheet. You can also copy the worksheet.

Protecting the change history

If you want to ensure that Excel records every change made during a sharing session, click the Review tab and then click Protect Shared Workbook. (The command is labeled Protect And Share Workbook if the workbook is not already shared.) The Protect Shared Workbook dialog box, shown in Figure 26-9, appears.

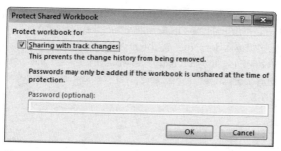

Figure 26-9 You can ensure that change tracking is protected in a shared workbook.

If you select the Sharing With Track Changes check box and then click OK, no one in your workgroup can directly turn off change tracking for the shared workbook. However, anyone can turn off the protection by turning off sharing for the workbook. To eliminate this possibility, you can type a password in the Protect Shared Workbook dialog box. But you must do this when the workbook is not in shared mode. Anyone who tries to turn off protection must type the identical, case-sensitive password.

> **Note**
>
> Successfully typing a password to turn off sharing protection not only turns off protection but also removes the workbook from sharing. Note that this isn't the case unless the workbook has a password. When you remove a workbook from sharing, you cut off anyone else who has the workbook open, and Excel erases the change history.

Reviewing changes

You can decide at any time to go through each change that users have made to the shared workbook, provided that you selected the Track Changes While Editing check box in the Highlight Changes dialog box when you first saved the worksheet for sharing. Clicking the Review tab and then clicking Track Changes, Accept/Reject Changes on the ribbon saves the workbook and displays the Select Changes To Accept Or Reject dialog box shown in Figure 26-10. The When, Who, and Where lists are similar to those in the Highlight Changes dialog box, except that in the When list the only options available are Not Yet Reviewed and Since Date.

When you click OK, the Accept Or Reject Changes dialog box shown in Figure 26-11 appears and, on the worksheet, Excel highlights the first change that meets the criteria you specified in the Select Changes To Accept Or Reject dialog box. (If the cell in question has been changed more than once, Excel lists each change for that cell in the dialog box, and you can select one to accept.) The dialog box describes the change, who made it, and the time it was made. At this point, you can accept or reject the change, or you can accept or reject all changes. After you accept or reject all the changes, you cannot review them again. You can, however, still display the history worksheet.

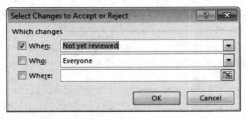

Figure 26-10 Use the Select Changes To Accept Or Reject dialog box to specify which changes you want to review.

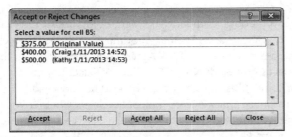

Figure 26-11 Each change is highlighted and described, and you can accept or reject it.

Canceling the shared workbook session

You can discontinue the sharing session at any time by clearing the Allow Changes By More Than One User At The Same Time check box on the Editing tab in the Share Workbook dialog box. (Anyone else using the shared workbook can also do this; no one "owns" the right to enable or disable sharing.) Doing this has several effects. First, the change history is lost. If you subsequently start a new sharing session, the history starts fresh. Second, any other users who still have the shared workbook open won't be able to save their changes to the same file. They'll be in read-only mode, but Excel won't inform them of that until they attempt to save, at which time the Save As dialog box appears. Even if you turn sharing off and then turn it back on while another person still has the file open, the person won't be able to share the file until he closes or reopens it.

You can click the Remove User button on the Editing tab in the Share Workbook dialog box if you want to disconnect someone from the sharing session manually. Doing this maintains the change history for the master workbook. You'll probably want to warn the person you're disconnecting, of course.

Chapter 26

Combining changes made to multiple workbooks

Another way to share a workbook is to make a separate copy of the workbook for each person in your workgroup. This is a good option if not everyone in your group has access to the same network server, if some users need to work on the workbook when they are on the road, or if no network or Internet file-sharing options are available to you. In this scenario, after all the distributed copies have been updated with each person's changes, someone collects the copies and merges everyone's work into a master workbook.

You can merge workbooks that are created equal—that is, a set of workbooks created from the same master. When you merge workbooks, all changes made to the merged workbooks are merged into the master workbook. Merging workbooks, like change tracking, is closely linked with the shared workbooks feature; you can merge only workbooks that have been saved with sharing turned on.

The command to merge workbooks, Compare And Merge Workbooks, is well hidden, but you can easily add it to the Quick Access Toolbar. Click the File tab, and then click Options. In the Excel Options dialog box, select the Quick Access Toolbar category. In the Choose Commands From list, select Commands Not In The Ribbon. Select Compare And Merge Workbooks in the list of commands, and then click the Add button to add it to the Quick Access Toolbar. In the Customize Quick Access Toolbar list, select whether you want to add the Compare And Merge Workbooks command to the Quick Access Toolbar for all workbooks or just for a specific workbook.

For more information about customizing the Quick Access Toolbar, see "Customizing the Quick Access Toolbar" in Chapter 3, "Custom-tailoring the Excel workspace."

The following procedure explains how to set up your workbooks for distribution and eventual merging:

1. Open the workbook you want to distribute.

2. Click the Review tab, and then click Share Workbook.

3. On the Editing tab in the Share Workbook dialog box, select the Allow Changes By More Than One User At The Same Time check box.

4. Click the Advanced tab. In the Keep Change History For box, specify a sufficient number of days for all the members of your workgroup to finish their edits and for you to merge the workbooks. If you are unsure about how long to specify, type a large number, such as 999. If this time limit is exceeded, you will not be able to merge workbooks.

5. Click OK to save the workbook in shared mode.

6. Click the File tab, and then click Save As. Save additional copies of the workbook under different names—one for each person in your distribution list. Save one to use as a master workbook. Because you turned on sharing, each copy also is in shared mode.

7. Distribute the copies to the members of your group.

After you prepare, distribute, and collect the edited workbooks, you are ready to merge by following these steps:

1. Open the workbook you want to use as the master workbook. All the changes made to the other workbooks will be replicated in the master workbook. You must have saved the master workbook from the original shared workbook, just as the workbooks you distributed were.

2. Be sure the other workbooks you want to merge aren't open, and then click Compare And Merge Workbooks on the Quick Access Toolbar to display the Select Files To Merge Into Current Workbook dialog box shown in Figure 26-12.

3. Select the files you want to merge.

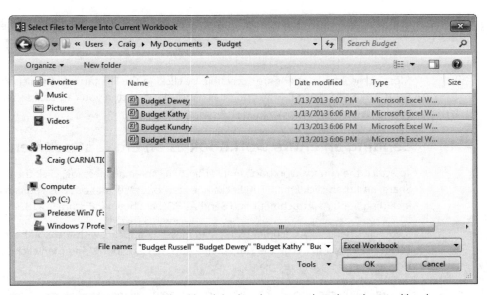

Figure 26-12 When the master workbook is already open, select the other workbooks to merge.

> **Note**
> Merging workbooks combines all changes from a set of workbooks. Consolidation, on
> the other hand, combines values only from a set of worksheets. (These worksheets can
> be in different workbooks.) The Consolidate command can assemble information from
> as many as 255 supporting worksheets into a single master worksheet. For more infor-
> mation about the Consolidate command, see "Consolidating worksheets" in Chapter 8.

Excel merges the workbooks you select in the Select Files To Merge Into Current Workbook
dialog box one by one, in the order in which they appear in the dialog box. Excel takes all
the changes made to the merged workbooks and makes them in the master workbook.
You can accept and reject changes and display the history worksheet just as you can with
shared workbooks, as described in "Tracking changes" earlier in this chapter.

Distributing workbooks and worksheets by email

Provided you have Microsoft Outlook or another compatible email program installed on
your system, Excel offers a variety of ways to distribute your work to others via email. Specifically, you can do the following:

- You can send an entire workbook as an attachment to an email message.

- You can send a workbook out for review.

Most of the email options are accessible by clicking the File tab and then clicking Save &
Send. The Send Using E-Mail option also includes a button you can click to send your work
to an Internet fax service.

Sending an entire workbook as an email attachment

To attach the current workbook in its entirety to an email message, click the File tab, click
Share, and then click Email. The Backstage view offers several options you can choose from,
including Send As Attachment and Send As PDF, as shown in Figure 26-13.

If you click Send As Attachment, an email message appears with the workbook attached.
Select the recipients, type the subject line and message body, and then click Send to send
the workbook to your recipients.

Naturally, you can also attach a workbook to an email message by working directly in
Microsoft Outlook or another email program. For example, create a new message in
Outlook and click the Attach File button on the Message tab, which has the same effect as
the procedure described previously.

Figure 26-13 Excel's Backstage view offers a number of options for sending a workbook in email.

Sending a worksheet, chart, or range by email

To send one or more worksheets from a workbook but not the entire workbook, copy the worksheets to a new workbook. To do so, select the worksheets, right-click one of the selected sheet tabs, and click Move Or Copy. The Move Or Copy dialog box appears, as shown in Figure 26-14. Select (New Book) in the Move Selected Sheets To Book list, and select the Create A Copy check box.

Figure 26-14 Use the Move Or Copy dialog box to create a workbook that contains only the worksheets you want to email to the recipient.

To send a range or chart from a worksheet, simply copy the selection in Excel and then paste it into the body of an Outlook message.

Sending a workbook for review

In previous versions of Excel, the Send For Review command provided an easy way to circulate a workbook for comments and changes by members of your workgroup. When you use this command, Excel attaches the document to an email message and uses "Please review [file name]" as the default subject for your message. To use this command in Excel 2013, you need to add it to your Quick Access Toolbar from the list of commands not on the ribbon. (See "Customizing the Quick Access Toolbar" in Chapter 2.)

Ideally, you should use the Send For Review command with workbooks you have set up for sharing. If you apply this command to a workbook that isn't shared, Excel prompts you to save a shared version. You don't have to share (you can use this command as an alternative way to send any document as an attachment), but your recipients will be able to carry out their reviewing duties more efficiently using a shared workbook.

Working in the cloud

C LOUD COMPUTING—the use of Internet-hosted applications and storage for sharing, backup, and portability—has become, for most of us, an indispensable feature of our daily work lives. Storage is abundant and cheap (often free), the apps are getting better all the time, and the convenience afforded by the cloud is irresistible. In this chapter, we look at the two cloud-computing components that are freely available to all users of Microsoft Excel 2013: Microsoft SkyDrive and the Office Web Apps.

Using SkyDrive

SkyDrive is a service you can use to store data securely on a Microsoft server, synchronize the server copies of files with copies stored locally on your computer, share files with specific people, and more. Microsoft gives you 7 gigabytes (GBs) of storage for free; you can buy more storage at reasonable rates (for example, an additional 25 GBs for $10 per year).

To use SkyDrive, you need a Microsoft account. That sounds more ominous than it is; you simply need to choose a login name and password and then provide some information that Microsoft can use to help you reset the password if you subsequently forget it. If you don't already have a Microsoft account, you'll be prompted for these details the first time you go to SkyDrive. If you do already have an account, you might be asked to sign in.

Microsoft also offers a free SkyDrive application. The SkyDrive app creates a folder on your local computer and synchronizes that folder with the web-based SkyDrive folder. When you save a workbook or other document to the local SkyDrive folder, the application automatically copies the file to the cloud; any additions, changes, or deletions you make to files in the online folder are similarly copied back to the local SkyDrive folder. (If you don't want global synchronization, you can specify particular subfolders to be synchronized and leave the rest unsynchronized.) All this back and forth between ground-based and cloud-based storage happens unobtrusively in the background.

If you use the SkyDrive application on multiple computers, tablets, or mobile phones, all devices on which it is installed synchronize with the mother ship and with each other. So you can save a file to the SkyDrive folder on Device A and have that file be more or less instantaneously available on Devices B and C as well—and so on.

> **Note**
>
> The synchronization capability of the SkyDrive application replaces a similar set of services offered previously by Windows Live Mesh. Windows Live Mesh was retired officially on February 13, 2013. For information about migrating from Windows Live Mesh to SkyDrive, see *http://windows.microsoft.com/en-US/skydrive/mesh-users*.

Working with the SkyDrive application

As a user of Microsoft Office 2013, you probably already have the SkyDrive app installed on your system. In Windows Explorer or File Explorer, you will find a SkyDrive folder in your user profile. (See Figure 27-1.)

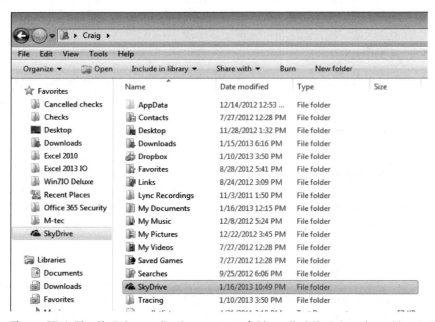

Figure 27-1 The SkyDrive application creates a folder called SkyDrive, alongside My Documents, My Pictures, and the other subfolders of your user profile.

If you do not have the SkyDrive application installed, you can download it for free from *http://windows.microsoft.com/en-US/skydrive/download*. You can also find links on that webpage for downloading the SkyDrive app to Windows Phone, iOS, and Android devices.

Using the SkyDrive notification icon

With the SkyDrive application installed, Windows adds a SkyDrive icon to the operating system's notification area. You can click that icon to see your system's synchronization status:

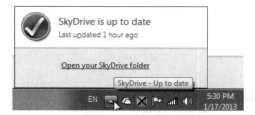

Clicking the Open Your SkyDrive Folder link in this information box takes you to the local SkyDrive folder in File Explorer or Windows Explorer.

> **Note**
>
> The SkyDrive icon in your notification area might be hidden. If so, click the Show Hidden Icons button (the upward-pointing triangle) at the left edge of the notification area and click Customize. In the list that appears, find Microsoft SkyDrive. Then open the drop-down list in the Behaviors column and select Show Icon And Notifications. Click OK to save the change.

Specifying which folders to synchronize

By default, the SkyDrive application synchronizes everything in your SkyDrive folder. If that's not convenient for some reason, right-click the SkyDrive icon in the notification area. Doing so summons a small menu:

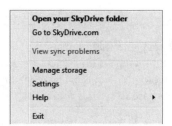

Commands at the top of this menu let you navigate to your local SkyDrive folder, open the web-based SkyDrive folder (at SkyDrive.com), diagnose synchronization issues (if there are any), and check the amount of web-based storage you have consumed. (You can also use the Manage Storage command to purchase additional storage.) To restrict synchronization to particular folders, click the Settings command. Then click the Choose Folders tab and click Choose Folders. The Sync Only What You Want screen appears, as shown next.

Clicking Choose Folders To Sync reveals the subfolder tree for your SkyDrive folder, allowing you to make your wishes known.

Saving workbooks to and retrieving them from SkyDrive

When you click File, Save As in Excel 2013, the first item that appears in your Places list is
your SkyDrive. (See Figure 27-2.) Selecting that item makes it easy to save your document
to the cloud. The file goes first to the SkyDrive folder on your local system, and then the
SkyDrive application synchronizes it to the web-based SkyDrive folder.

The SkyDrive folder appears in a comparable place of honor in the Places list when you
click File, Open. Opening a file from this location retrieves the synchronized copy from your
local SkyDrive folder.

Working with your cloud-based SkyDrive

You can open your SkyDrive on the web by directing your browser to *skydrive.com*. You can
also get there by right-clicking the SkyDrive icon in your notification area and clicking Go
To SkyDrive.com. Figure 27-3 shows a sample SkyDrive webpage.

Figure 27-2 The Save As command encourages you to save your files to your SkyDrive folder, from whence they will be synchronized with your cloud-based SkyDrive.

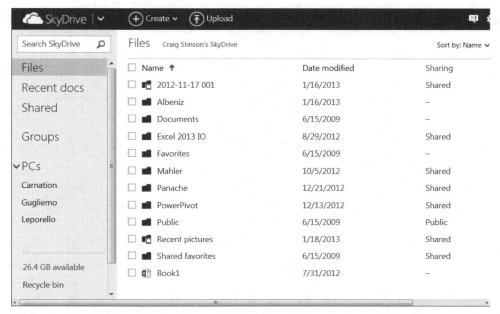

Figure 27-3 The cloud-based SkyDrive interface offers two display options: list and tiles. The list option is shown here.

Chapter 27

The web-based interface is simple and discoverable. Along the top is a command bar; its offerings change depending on what's selected below. In the upper-left corner is a handy Search box. Near the upper-right corner is a Sort By drop-down list. In Figure 27-3, the SkyDrive contents are sorted by name in ascending order, but you can switch to sorting by Date Modified, Date Created, or Size:

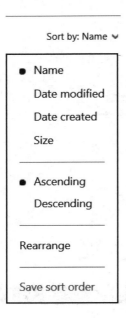

To the right of the Sort By drop-down list (not shown in Figure 27-3) are three buttons:

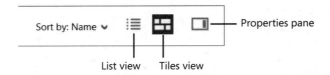

The first two let you switch between the list view and tiles view. The third opens a properties pane for the current selection. You'll probably find the tiles view more useful for picture folders than for folders containing Excel workbooks. Like live tiles in Windows 8, picture folders in SkyDrive's tiles view change at regular intervals to keep you entertained. Figure 27-4 shows SkyDrive in the tiles view.

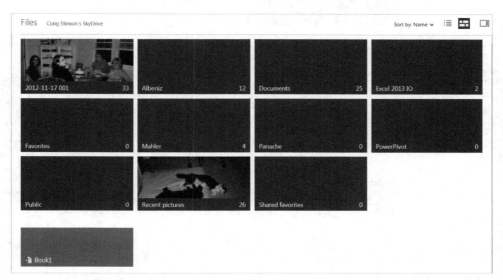

Figure 27-4 Tiles view is handier for picture folders than for folders containing Excel documents.

The properties pane, shown in Figure 27-5, lets you see at a glance all the important information about a selected folder or file, including its dates, size, and sharing details. If you know you've shared a folder or file, but you can't remember with whom, the properties pane is the place to go. The properties pane button is a toggle; clicking it a second time makes the pane disappear.

Figure 27-5 The properties pane reveals important details about a selected file or folder.

Uploading, downloading, and managing files and folders

To upload a file or folder to SkyDrive, click the Upload button on the command bar. A self-explanatory Upload window appears:

Upload

Drop files here or select them from your computer.

Close

Downloading is similarly straightforward. Select the check box for the item you want to download, and then click the Download button. Your browser will ask you to confirm the action.

To create a new folder in SkyDrive, click the Create button. The following options appear:

Here you can click Folder to create a folder or one of the other options to create a new document in one of the Office Web Apps. (The Office Web Apps are discussed later in this chapter.)

For other file-management tasks, including deletions, select an item's check box and click Manage on the command bar. The following options appear:

The one item here that might not be self-explanatory is Version History. Clicking this opens the selected document in its Office Web App, with available versions of the document listed in a pane at the left side of the window.

Opening documents

To open a document in the associated Office Web App, simply click its name. To download it to your computer and open it in the native Office application, select the check box beside it and click Open. The following menu appears:

Click Open In Excel (or Open In Word, for a Word document, and so on) to open a local copy of the document.

Sharing folders and documents

To share a folder or a file, select its check box and then click Sharing. The window shown in Figure 27-6 appears.

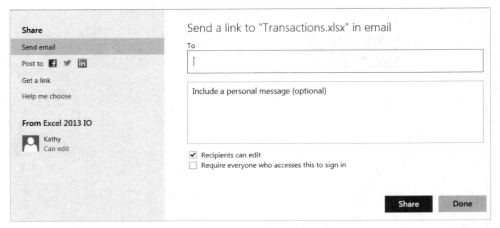

Figure 27-6 SkyDrive gives you three ways to share a file or folder: via email, by posting to a social networking site, or by means of an embeddable hyperlink.

In the left pane of this window you'll find options for sharing the item via email, via a social networking site, or by means of an HTML link. The Send Email option simply sends the selected recipient or recipients a link they can use to connect with the shared item. The Post To option lets you post the selected item on a social networking site you have linked to your Microsoft account. (If you have not yet linked any sites to your Microsoft account, you'll be prompted to do so and informed about both Microsoft's privacy policies and those of the selected social networking site.) The Get A Link option is useful for sharing an item with people whose email addresses you might not know. The system generates an HTML link you can embed, for example, in your company's website or intranet.

The default permissions setting for a shared item is Can Edit, which means that those with whom you share can do whatever they want with your item. To make the share read-only, clear the Recipients Can Edit check box.

To remove sharing privileges for a particular user, follow these steps:

1. Select the check box associated with the folder or document.

2. Display the properties pane.

3. In the properties pane, click Share. (Expand the Sharing heading if you don't see Share.)

4. On the left side of the Share window, click the name of the person whose permissions you want to change.

5. Clear the Can Edit check box to change the permissions to read-only, or click Remove Permissions to cancel the sharing completely for this person.

Opening recent documents in SkyDrive

The Recent Docs item, on the left side of the SkyDrive window, works just like its counterpart in Windows: It provides quick access to folders and files you've recently worked with. If you have a lot of material stored on SkyDrive or you have a complex tree of folders and subfolders, you'll find Recent Docs particularly useful.

Seeing and accessing items others have shared with you

To see and use the files and folders other users have shared with you, click Shared, on the left side of the SkyDrive window. As Figure 27-7 shows, the resulting window, in the list view, shows the source of each shared item, its size, and the date on which it was shared.

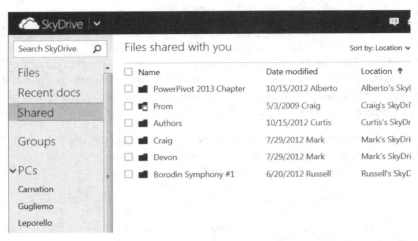

Figure 27-7 Clicking Shared provides a list or tiled display of all the items that have been shared with you.

Fetching files from remote computers

File sharing and synchronization are not all that SkyDrive can do. You can also use it to access any of your computer's files remotely. If you have the SkyDrive application installed on a computer, you can access that computer from anywhere by logging on to *skydrive.com*. In the left pane of the SkyDrive window under the heading PCs, you'll find a list of computers where you have the SkyDrive application installed. Select a computer in that list to browse or open files on that computer. (See Figure 27-8.)

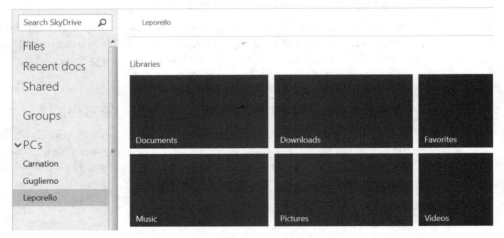

Figure 27-8 You can use SkyDrive to browse any file stored on a PC that has the SkyDrive application installed.

This "fetch" feature is enabled by default. If you find it unavailable, right-click the SkyDrive notification icon and click Settings. The Microsoft SkyDrive dialog box appears:

To enable the fetch feature, on the Settings tab of this dialog box, select the check box labeled Let Me Use SkyDrive To Fetch Any Of My Files On This PC. Note that the feature must be enabled separately on each computer to which you want remote access, and that the feature does not work with Macs.

Using Microsoft Office Web Apps

The Office Web Apps are scaled-down versions of Excel, Word, PowerPoint, and OneNote that can be run for free by anyone with an Internet connection. They're ideal for sharing documents with users who do not have Microsoft Office. They're also great for working with your own files—or creating new ones—when you're using a device without Office.

To open a workbook in the Excel Web App, simply click it in a SkyDrive file list. To create a new workbook, click Create in SkyDrive and then Excel Workbook. Figure 27-9 shows an Excel workbook in the Web App.

The Excel Web App displays your workbook in an environment that's much like the desktop environment but with a somewhat reduced feature set. One of the most striking differences is that there is no Save command. Changes you make are saved immediately. If you are concerned that you might inadvertently change the document, you can click the View tab and then switch from Editing View to Reading View; the latter, as its name suggests, presents the workbook in read-only mode. You can also click File, Save As to create a copy of the file in the same online folder as the original.

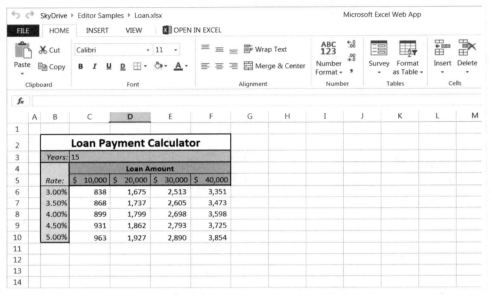

Figure 27-9 The Excel Web App lets you view and edit workbooks much as you would in the full desktop version of Excel.

If you find yourself constrained by the Web App environment, you can click Open In Excel to send a copy back to your desktop. Because this action entails opening a program on your computer and downloading a file to that program, you'll be prompted for permission:

If your workbook is shared, others with read-write permissions might have the workbook open at the same time as you. In the lower-right corner of the window you will find an indication of how many people are editing. If it says "1 person editing," that person is, of course, you. If two or more are editing, you can click the arrow to the right of this indicator to see who's at work:

If someone else opens a file while you're already working on it, an alert box pops up to let you know.

How the Web App handles unsupported features

Certain features in Excel workbooks are not supported by the Web App. These include macros, protected sheets, custom properties linked to cells, comments, and shapes. You also cannot open Excel files stored in XLS format (as opposed to the newer XLSX) or files that were shared in the desktop version of Excel. If you open a file containing certain problematic features, such as macros, you will see a dialog box similar to this:

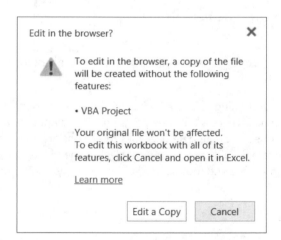

This Edit In The Browser dialog box offers to create a copy of your document with the unsupported features removed, allowing you to edit that copy in the Web App. If that is not satisfactory, you can click Cancel and then use SkyDrive to open the file for editing in the desktop version of Excel.

If the unsupported features are simply objects that cannot be displayed in the Web App, you will still see an Edit In The Browser dialog box, similar to the previous illustration. In this case, clicking Cancel will open the document in the Web App, but you will see the following banner atop the workbook:

With other kinds of unsupported features that cannot be removed, you will instead see an Open In Excel dialog box:

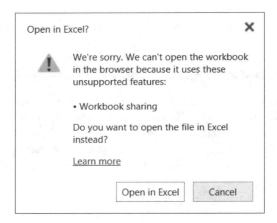

In this case, your only editing option is to open the document in the desktop version of Excel.

One of the great things about running software in the cloud is that you don't personally have to do anything to upgrade. There is only one program, and it's updated at the web server rather than being pushed out in update packages to millions of individual workstations. So, cloud-based software should remain more stable, in general. And it's possible that Office Web Apps will become more and more useful as time goes by, and that some of the issues just described will one day disappear.

PART 9

Automating Excel

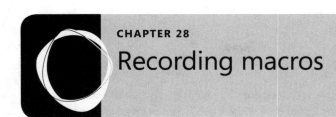

Recording macros

A MACRO is a set of instructions that tells Microsoft Excel 2013 (or another application) to perform one or more actions for you. Macros in Excel 2013 are like computer programs, but they run completely within Excel. You can use them to automate tedious or frequently repeated tasks.

Macros can carry out sequences of actions much more quickly than you can yourself. For example, you can create a macro that enters a series of dates across one row of a worksheet, centers the date in each cell, and then applies a border format to the row. Or you can create a macro that defines a combination of print settings—margins, orientation, scaling, headers, and footers—that you want to use in many documents. Macros are great for any task you do repeatedly.

You can create a macro in two ways: you can record it, or you can build it by typing instructions in a module. Either way, your instructions are encoded in the programming language Microsoft Visual Basic for Applications (VBA). (You can also combine the two approaches.)

Even if you're not a programmer and have no intention of becoming one, macros can be a useful addition to your Excel toolkit. Thanks to the macro recorder, you don't have to understand all the ins and outs of VBA to create effective and time-saving macros. And if you're curious about VBA and want to learn to do more with macros than is possible with the recorder alone, you will find the recorder to be an excellent learning tool. You can get a great start on acquiring VBA expertise by examining the code that the recorder generates.

Configuring macro security

Macros execute code, and code can serve evil ends as well as good ones. If your system is permitted to run all macros, regardless of their source, you might inadvertently run a macro that damages your system in some way. Because VBA macros included in Microsoft Office documents (typically attached to email messages) have occasionally served as virus vectors in recent years, Microsoft no longer permits VBA code to run by default. You have to take steps to enable macro execution.

Like other security configuration settings, the settings that permit or deny macro execution are in the Trust Center. To get there, click File, Options. In the Excel Options dialog box, select the Trust Center category, and then click Trust Center Settings.

For more information about the Trust Center, see "The Trust Center" in Chapter 4, "Security and privacy."

How you configure macro security depends on how you expect to use macros, the degree to which you are concerned about potentially malicious macro code, and perhaps the security policies of your organization. If your organization's IT staff has disabled access to the Trust Center and also macro execution, this discussion is moot (unless you can convince someone to relax the rules). Assuming that's not the case, your first stop in the Trust Center should be the Macro Settings category, where you will see something like the following:

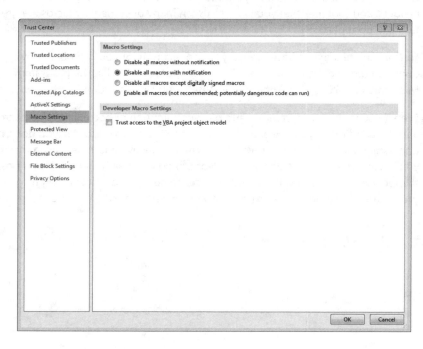

The four options in the Macro Settings area of this dialog box determine how Excel handles macro code in files that are not stored in a trusted location. The default setting disallows such macros but causes a notification bar to appear whenever you open a file that contains a proscribed macro. The notification bar looks like this:

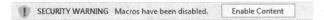

If you know for sure that whatever macros the file might contain are benign, you can over-rule the security cop by clicking Enable Content. If you use macros regularly, however, you probably don't want to deal with the notification bar every time you open a workbook containing macros. You might instead be tempted to change the Macro Settings option in the Trust Center to Enable All Macros (Not Recommended; Potentially Dangerous Code Can Run). As the parenthetical comment suggests, however, this is not an ideal approach to macro security.

A better approach is to designate the folders you use regularly—as well as those from which you are likely to open macro-laden files created by trustworthy others—as trusted locations. Excel permits all macro content to run in files stored in such locations. To config-ure a trusted location, return to the Trust Center and select the Trusted Locations category. You see a list comparable to the following:

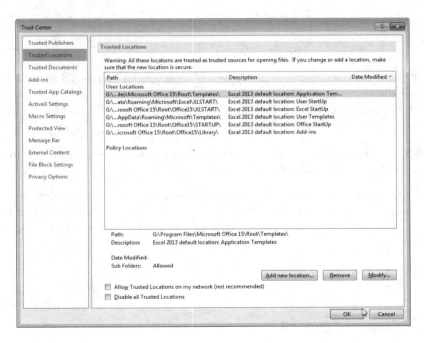

The top area in this dialog box lists trusted locations you create, as well as those provided as defaults by the Microsoft Office Setup program. Below that list, under the heading Policy Locations, you might see additional trusted locations established by your IT staff. To set up a new trusted location, click Add New Location. In the dialog box that appears, you can specify the path of the new location, indicate whether you also want to trust subfolders in that location, and add a description of the location. Excel provides a date and time stamp for you.

By using the trusted-locations mechanism, you can create no-questions-asked zones for the macros you create and use, without disabling the defenses Excel uses against external threats. If you leave in place the default Macro Settings option—Disable All Macros With Notification—Excel will inform you if you happen to open a file from a nontrusted location that contains a macro. When that occurs, you can make a judgment call about whether to allow the banned content.

Having configured the security options to your satisfaction, you still have one more decision to make before you can begin creating your own macros. The Excel default workbook format (.xlsx) does not support macros. To save a workbook containing one or more macros, you need to use one of the following formats:

- Excel Macro-Enabled Workbook (.xlsm)

- Excel Binary Workbook (.xlsb)

- Excel 97–2003 Workbook (.xls)

If you plan to use macros regularly, or even occasionally, you should consider changing the default to one of these macro-supporting formats. To do this, return to the Excel Options dialog box, select the Save category, and select a format in the Save Files In This Format drop-down list.

For more information about file format options, see "Understanding the "XL" formats" in Chapter 2, "Exploring Excel fundamentals."

If you prefer not to change the default file format to Excel Macro-Enabled Workbook, you can always save in that format on a case-by-case basis when you create a file that uses a macro. Excel warns you when you try to save a file with macros in a non-macro-enabled format.

Using the macro recorder

To see how the recorder works, try creating a simple macro that inserts a company name and address in a worksheet. Follow these steps:

1. On the View tab, in the Macros group, click Macros and then Record Macro. Excel displays the Record Macro dialog box shown in Figure 28-1.

2. Assign a name to the macro. You can accept the suggestion (Macro1) or type your own name. Let's use **CompanyAddress**. (The macro recorder doesn't permit space characters.)

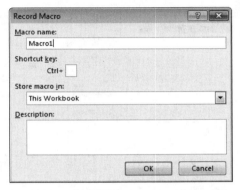

Figure 28-1 In the Record Macro dialog box, you must provide a name for the macro and indicate where the macro should be stored. The Shortcut Key and Description fields are optional.

3. Assign a key combination to the macro by typing a letter in the text box. If possible, use something related to the purpose of the macro so that you'll remember it later. Let's use uppercase A. (The recorder distinguishes capital letters from lowercase ones.)

4. Accept the default of This Workbook for Store Macro In. (We'll discuss the Personal Macro Workbook option later in this chapter.)

5. Type a description for the macro in the Description box. **Enter company address** will do nicely.

6. To begin recording, click OK. A Stop Recording button appears on the status bar.

7. Select A6, and type **Coho Winery**. In A7, type **3012 West Beaujolais St.**, and in A8, type **Walla Walla, WA 98765**.

8. Click Stop Recording on the status bar.

Chapter 28

To test the new macro, clear the worksheet and then press Ctrl+Shift+A. Excel runs the macro and performs the sequence of actions in the same way you recorded them.

If you forget the keyboard shortcut for a macro, or if you didn't bother to assign one, you can run your macro by clicking Macros and then View Macros in the Macros group on the View tab. In the Macro dialog box that appears, shown in Figure 28-2, you can select a macro and run it. You can also click the Edit button in the Macro dialog box to visit (and alter) the code, or click the Options button to assign the shortcut you neglected to assign earlier.

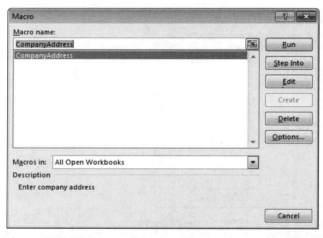

Figure 28-2 The Macro dialog box lets you run macros without keyboard shortcuts.

Recording with relative references

The macro you just recorded has one serious fault (other than it doesn't create your company address): it always does its business in cells A6:A8. It would be considerably more valuable if you could use it anywhere.

By default, the macro recorder records absolute references. That is, if you're in A6 when you record a cell entry, the action will play back in A6. To make it record relative references instead, click Macros and then Use Relative References in the Macros group on the View tab.

The Use Relative References button is a toggle. If you're using relative references and you click this button again, the recorder returns to absolute referencing. You can toggle between the two modes as often as you like while you are recording—which means your recorded macros can contain whatever combination of absolute and relative references suits your purposes.

CAUTION

When clicked, the Use Relative References command does not change to say Use Absolute References, as you might expect. To avoid disappointment, be sure to verify the state of this toggle when you begin recording.

What to do when the macro recorder does not give you what you expect

The most likely reason a recorded macro might not generate the expected result is that it was recorded in the wrong relative/absolute state. If output from your macro does not appear in the worksheet location where you want it, consider the possibility that you recorded it with absolute instead of relative references, and try recording it again.

A second common cause for disappointment is that the macro recorder records completed actions only. An example will illustrate: Suppose you want to record a macro that places a full date and time stamp in the current cell. You know you can press Ctrl+; to generate the current date and Ctrl+: to generate the current time. But you want the date and the time in the same cell, and Excel has no keyboard shortcut for that. A macro can help.

One way to achieve the date and time stamp (without a macro) is to type **=NOW()** and then press F9 before pressing Enter. The NOW function returns the full date and time, and pressing F9 before pressing Enter converts the formula to its calculated result.

You might suppose you could turn on the macro recorder, set references to relative, and then record exactly those steps: =NOW(),F9. Unfortunately, the result of your work would be a macro that always entered the date and time of its creation, not the current date and time. That's because the macro recorder sees a sequence such as this as a single action, even though it might seem like two separate steps to you.

The solution to this problem is to find another way to carry out the action that really does involve discrete steps. You can accomplish that by typing the formula, pressing Enter, selecting the cell in which you typed the formula, copying it to the Clipboard, and then using the Paste Special command and selecting Values in the Paste Special dialog box. That's the long way around when you want to convert a formula to its result immediately, but it works for the macro recorder.

Further troubleshooting of recorded macros requires a rudimentary understanding of VBA. If you like the convenience and enhanced productivity that macros afford, you will probably find it worthwhile to look at the code that the macro recorder generates and learn a bit about how that code works. If you're new to VBA, the following sections will help you get started.

Chapter 28

Introducing the Visual Basic Editor

When you click OK in the Record Macro dialog box, Excel creates a container, called a *module*, for the new VBA code, storing the module in the active workbook. As you carry out the actions for the recorder to record, Excel transcribes those actions into the new module.

The module doesn't appear with the other worksheets and chart sheets in the workbook. To view it, press Alt+F11. This takes you to the Visual Basic Editor. In the upper-left corner of the Visual Basic Editor, you'll find a small window known as the Project Explorer:

Yours will look different depending on how you've named the current workbook and what other workbooks happen to be open. In any case, you should see the entry Modules with an outline control (a plus sign) beside it. Click the outline control, and then double-click the entry Module1 that appears. To the right of the Project Explorer, you will see the Code window for Module1, which is displayed in Figure 28-3.

As you can see, a module looks like a window you might see in a word processor. The menu bar above the module includes menus for editing, debugging, and running VBA code. In the module, you can review, type, copy, move, insert, and delete VBA statements and comments, just as you might manipulate text in a word processor. From the Visual Basic Editor, you can switch back to your workbook by clicking the Excel icon at the left edge of the toolbar. From there, you can return to the Visual Basic Editor by pressing Alt+F11.

The Visual Basic Editor is a big place, full of interesting details, but for now we'll focus only on the code we recorded. The first and last lines act as the beginning point and the end point for the macro. A *Sub* statement starts the macro and names it, and an *End Sub* statement ends it. You'll notice that special VBA terms, called *keywords*, appear in dark blue. (You can view and change the colors assigned to various elements of a macro by clicking Tools, Options in the Visual Basic Editor and then clicking the Editor Format tab.)

Below the *Sub* statement are two comment lines, displayed in green. (If you type a description for your macro in the Record Macro dialog box, you'll find an additional comment line.) Comment lines begin with the apostrophe character and are ignored when you run the macro. Their only purpose is to help you (or anyone else looking at your code) understand what you've done and why.

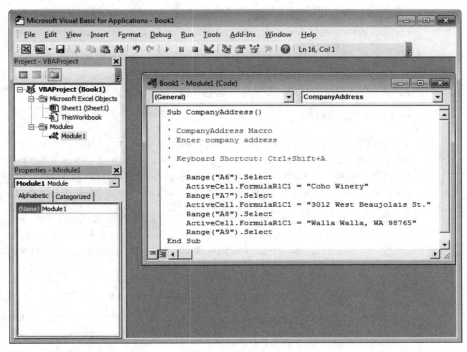

Figure 28-3 Excel stores the VBA code for each action you record in a module. You can inspect and edit it in the Visual Basic Editor.

The statements following the comments are the meat of the macro—the code that does the (presumably) useful work. Our simple macro includes four lines that select cells and three lines that enter data.

Learning the basics of Visual Basic

You can get detailed information about a keyword by selecting the word and pressing F1. For example, if you click anywhere within the keyword *Sub* and press F1, the Visual Basic Editor presents a Help screen containing an entry for the *Sub* statement. Many Help topics for VBA keywords include one or more examples of the keyword as you might use it in working code. You can copy this code, paste it into a module, and edit the resulting text to meet your needs.

Objects, methods, and properties

To VBA, every item in the Excel environment is an object rather than an abstract set of data structures or an arrangement of pixels on the screen. Objects can contain other objects. At the top of the hierarchy, the largest object within the Excel object model is the Excel application. Objects contained within this largest container include *workbooks*. Workbooks contain worksheets and chart sheets, worksheets contain ranges (and can also contain chart objects), and so on.

The first executable statement in the *CompanyAddress* macro after the *Sub* statement is the following:

```
Range("A6").Select
```

This line illustrates an important characteristic of VBA code. The syntax of many statements specifies first an object and then an action. An object can be a range, a worksheet, a graphic object, a workbook, or any of the more than 100 types of objects in Excel. Here, we specify a *Range* object (the absolute cell reference A6) and an action (*Select*).

The behaviors, or sets of actions, that an object "knows" how to perform, are called the *methods* of the object. Methods are like verbs. To understand this concept, imagine you are programming a robotic dog through VBA. To cause the dog to bark, you might use the following statement:

```
Dog.Bark
```

Robotic dogs, however, are (or ought to be) capable of more than just barking. For example, you might want the dog to understand the following statements:

```
Dog.Sit
Dog.RollOver
Dog.Fetch
```

The tricks your robodog can perform—such as barking, rolling over, and fetching—are its methods. The list of methods an object can perform depends on the object. A *Range* object, for example, supports almost 80 different methods you can use to copy and paste cells, sort, add formatting, and so on.

Like objects in the real world, objects in VBA also have properties. If you think of objects as the nouns of VBA and methods as the verbs, properties are the adjectives. A property is a quality, characteristic, or attribute of an object, such as its color or pattern. Characteristics such as your robodog's color, the number of spots on its back, the length of its tail, and the volume of its bark are among its properties.

You set a property by following the name of the property with an equal sign and a value. Continuing the robotic dog example, you could set the length of the dog's tail with the following:

```
Dog.TailLength = 10
```

Here, *TailLength* is a property of the *Dog* object.

For example, the following executable statement in our *CompanyAddress* macro

```
ActiveCell.FormulaR1C1 = "Coho Winery"
```

changes one of the properties, *FormulaR1C1*, of the active cell, setting that property to the value *Coho Winery*.

The remaining statements in the *CompanyAddress* macro consist of two more cell-selection and text-entry couplets. The macro selects cells A7 and A8 and enters text in each cell. (The last line, which selects cell A9, is there only because Excel moves the selection down a row by default after you type something in a cell.)

The Object Browser

You can view the various types of objects, methods, and properties available to Excel by clicking View, Object Browser (or pressing F2) in the Visual Basic Editor. The window displayed on the right of the screen, as shown in Figure 28-4, appears.

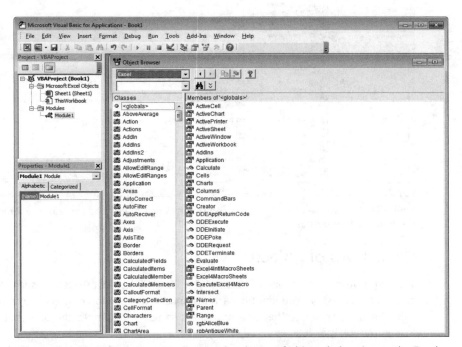

Figure 28-4 The Object Browser displays the classes of objects belonging to the Excel application.

On the left is a list of the various classes of objects available to Excel. You can think of a *class* as a template or description for a type of object; a specific chart, for example, would be an object that is an instance of the *Chart* class. In VBA, classes belong to a project or library. As shown in Figure 28-4, the Object Browser lists the object classes belonging to the library Excel.

If you scroll down the classes and select a class—the *Range* class, for example—the right pane of the Object Browser lists the properties and methods (called the *members* of the class) belonging to that object. Figure 28-5 shows the members of the *Range* class.

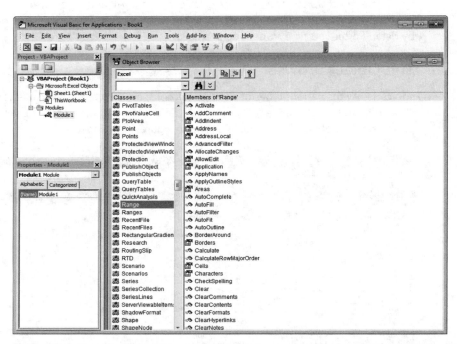

Figure 28-5 Here the Object Browser shows the *Range* object and some of the *Range* object's methods and properties.

Collections of objects

You can have more than one instance of the same VBA object. Together, such instances comprise a *collection*. You identify each instance in a collection of objects by either its index value (its position within the collection) or its name. For example, the collection of all sheets in a workbook is as follows:

```
Sheets()
```

In addition, a specific instance of a sheet—the third one in the collection—is as follows:

```
Sheets(3)
```

If the third sheet were named Summary, you could also identify it as follows:

```
Sheets("Summary")
```

In VBA, each item in a collection has its own index, but the index numbers for an entire collection are not necessarily consecutive. If you delete one instance of an object in a collection, VBA might not renumber the index values of the remaining instances. For example, if you delete Sheets(3) from a collection of 12 sheets in a workbook, you don't have any guarantee that VBA will renumber Sheets(4) through Sheets(12) to fill the gap.

In other programming languages, you might use a *For...Next* construction such as the following to repeat an operation many times:

```
For n = 1 to 12 ' Activate each sheet
    Sheets(n).Activate
Next n
```

If you run this code in a VBA macro after deleting Sheets(3), VBA displays an error message and stops the macro because Sheets(3) no longer exists. To allow for nonconsecutive indexes, VBA offers *For Each...Next*, a control structure that applies a series of statements to each item in a collection regardless of the index numbers. For example, suppose you'd like to label each sheet in the active workbook by typing the text **Sheet 1**, **Sheet 2**, and so on in cell A1 of each sheet. Because you won't, in general, know how many sheets any given workbook contains, you might use the following VBA code:

```
Sub EnterSheetNum()
    n = 0
    for Each Sheet In Sheets()
        n = n + 1
        Sheet.Activate
        Range("A1").Select
        ActiveCell.FormulaR1C1 = "Sheet" + Str(n)
    Next
End Sub
```

The *Str* function in VBA converts a numeric value to a text value so that you can concatenate the word *Sheet* with the appropriate number.

Manipulating an object's properties without selecting the object

The code just listed activates each sheet in turn, selects cell A1 on that sheet, and finally assigns a new value to that cell's *FormulaR1C1* property. This sequence of steps mimics the steps you would follow if you were working manually. In VBA, everything but the last step in the sequence is unnecessary. That is, you can replace the following instructions

```
Sheet.Activate
Range("A1").Select
ActiveCell.FormulaR1C1 = "Sheet" + Str(n)
```

with a single instruction:

```
Sheet.Range("A1").FormulaR1C1 = "Sheet" + Str(n)
```

The benefit of this change is that it enables the macro to run faster, because Excel is no longer required to activate sheets and select cells.

Naming arguments to methods

Many methods in VBA have *arguments*, words that act like adverbs, allowing you to specify options for an action to be performed. Arguments for our mythical robodog's *wag* method, for example, might include *WagRate* (the number of wags per second), *WagTime* (the duration of wagging in seconds), and *WagArc* (the number of degrees of arc in each wag). You can use either of two syntaxes to specify arguments.

In the first syntax, which is often called the *by-name* syntax, you name each argument you use, in any order. For example, the following statement wags the tail three times per second for an hour, over an arc of 180 degrees. (It also assumes that our particular robodog is a member of a collection of such creatures and is named Fido.)

```
Robodogs("Fido").Tail.Wag _
    WagRate := 3, _
    WagTime := 3600, _
    WagArc := 180
```

You assign a value to an argument by using a colon and an equal sign, and you separate arguments with commas.

> **Note**
>
> An underscore character at the end of a line tells VBA that the line after the underscore is part of the same statement. Using this symbol breaks a statement over multiple lines; in this case, it makes the list of supplied arguments easier to read. You must always precede the underscore with a space character.

In the second syntax, which is often called the *by-position* syntax, you type arguments in a prescribed order. For example, the preceding statement expressed in the by-position syntax looks like this:

```
Robodogs("Fido").Tail.Wag(3,3600,100)
```

Notice that the list of arguments is surrounded by parentheses. The by-position syntax isn't as easy to read as the by-name syntax because you have to remember the order of arguments, and when you review the code later, you won't have the argument names to refresh your memory about their settings.

> **Note**
>
> The macro recorder records arguments by position rather than by name. This can make it more difficult to understand recorded macros than macros created manually, in which you've named the arguments.

Adding code to or editing recorded macros

Suppose you record a macro that enters a series of labels, sets their font, and then draws a border around them. Then you discover that you forgot a step or recorded a step incorrectly—you chose the wrong border format, for example. What do you do?

To add code to an existing macro, you can record actions in a temporary macro and then transfer the code to the macro you want to change. For example, to add to the *Company-Address* macro a step that sets the font options for the company's name to 14-point Cambria Bold Italic, follow these steps:

1. Switch to the worksheet containing the address you typed earlier, and select cell A6, which contains the name of the company.

2. Turn on the macro recorder. In the Record Macro dialog box, type the name **MacroTemp**, and then click OK.

3. Press Ctrl+1 (which is the fastest way to get to the Format Cells dialog box, assuming the current selection is a cell).

4. Click the Font tab, and then select 14-point Cambria Bold Italic. Click OK to apply the formats.

5. Click the Stop Recording button.

6. Click Macros and then View Macros in the Macros group on the View tab. In the Macro dialog box, select MacroTemp and click Edit. A window appears containing the original macro you recorded plus the *MacroTemp* macro, as shown in Figure 28-6.

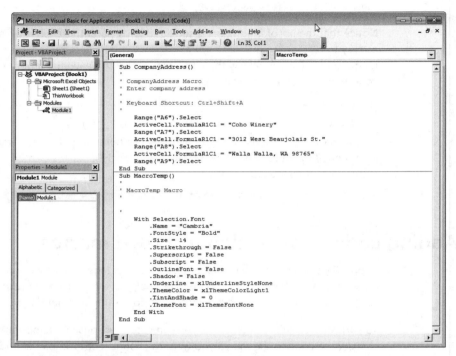

Figure 28-6 The *MacroTemp* macro contains the formatting code you recorded.

7. Select all the code inside the *MacroTemp* macro—from the line beginning with *With* through the line beginning with *End With*—and then press Ctrl+C to copy it.

8. Scroll up to display the *CompanyAddress* macro.

9. Click at the beginning of the line that contains this statement:

```
Range("A7").Select
```

10. Press Enter to create a blank line. Then position the insertion point at the beginning of the blank line.

11. Press Ctrl+V to paste.

12. Scroll down, and delete the entire *MacroTemp* macro, from the *Sub* statement to the *End Sub* statement.

The *CompanyAddress* macro now looks like this (with the comment lines removed):

```
Sub CompanyAddress()
    Range("A6").Select
    ActiveCell.FormulaR1C1 = "Coho Winery"
    With Selection.Font
        .Name = "Cambria"
        .FontStyle = "Bold Italic"
        .Size = 14
        .Strikethrough = False
        .Superscript = False
        .Subscript = False
        .OutlineFont = False
        .Shadow = False
        .Underline = xlUnderlineStyleNone
        .ThemeColor = 2
        .TintAndShade = 0
        .ThemeFont = xlThemeFontMajor
    End With
    Range("A7").Select
    ActiveCell.FormulaR1C1 = "3012 West Beaujolais St."
    Range("A8").Select
    ActiveCell.FormulaR1C1 = "Walla Walla, WA 98765"
    Range("A9").Select
End Sub
```

To test the macro, return to Excel, clear the company name and address you typed earlier when you recorded the macro, and then press Ctrl+Shift+A.

The *With* and *End With* statements that the macro recorder created when you recorded *MacroTemp* (the statements you subsequently copied into *CompanyAddress*) specify a group of properties belonging to an object—in this case, the font of the current selection. The *With...End With* construct provides a kind of shorthand for a series of VBA statements that would otherwise look like this, for example:

```
Selection.Font.Name = "Cambria"
Selection.Font.FontStyle = "Bold Italic"
Selection.Font.Size = 14
```

In the *CompanyAddress* macro, the *ActiveCell* object and the *Selection* object both refer to the same range on the worksheet, cell A6. Because you can apply a series of font-formatting options to an entire range, Excel records the action with *Selection* rather than with *ActiveCell*. Enclosing the property assignments within the *With...End With* structure simplifies the code and also makes it run faster.

Chapter 28

Using subroutines in macros

Suppose you're creating a complex macro and you discover that, among other things, you want the macro to perform a task you already recorded under a different name. Or suppose you discover that a task you recorded as part of a macro is something you want to use by itself—or in an entirely different macro. In our *CompanyAddress* macro, for example, it might be convenient if we could quickly and easily apply the font formats of the company name to other items in a worksheet.

With VBA, you can divide large macros into a series of smaller macros, and you can easily string together a series of small macros to create one large macro. A macro procedure that is used by another macro is called a *subroutine*. Subroutines can simplify your macros because you have to write only one set of instructions rather than repeat the instructions over and over. To use a subroutine in another macro, you call the subroutine by using its name in the other macro.

To demonstrate, let's split the *CompanyAddress* macro into two parts by following these steps:

1. Click Macros and then View Macros in the Macros group on the View tab. In the Macro dialog box, select CompanyAddress and click Edit. Then select the statements that format the font of the company's name:

    ```
    With Selection.Font
        .Name = "Cambria"
        .FontStyle = "Bold Italic"
        .Size = 14
        .Strikethrough = False
        .Superscript = False
        .Subscript = False
        .OutlineFont = False
        .Shadow = False
        .Underline = xlUnderlineStyleNone
        .ThemeColor = xlThemeColorLight1
        .TintAndShade = 0
        .ThemeFont = xlThemeFontMajor
    End With
    ```

2. Click Edit, Cut (or press Ctrl+X).

3. Click after the *End Sub* statement at the end of the *CompanyAddress* macro, and type **Sub CompanyFont()**. Press Enter.

4. The Visual Basic Editor types an *End Sub* statement for you. In the blank line between the *Sub* and *End Sub* statements, click Edit, Paste (or press Ctrl+V) to insert the font-formatting code.

You've created a new *CompanyFont* macro by moving the formatting code from the *CompanyAddress* macro to the new *CompanyFont* macro. As mentioned, to run one macro from another, you must use the name of the second macro in the first. To update the *CompanyAddress* macro so that it uses the *CompanyFont* macro, add the following statement at the top of the *CompanyAddress* macro:

```
CompanyFont
```

The two macros should now look like the ones in the following listing:

```
Sub CompanyAddress()
    Range("A6").Select
    ActiveCell.FormulaR1C1 = "Coho Winery"
    CompanyFont
    Range("A7").Select
    ActiveCell.FormulaR1C1 = "3012 West Beaujolais St."
    Range("A8").Select
    ActiveCell.FormulaR1C1 = "Walla Walla, WA 98765"
    Range("A9").Select
End Sub

Sub CompanyFont()
    With Selection.Font
        .Name = "Cambria"
        .FontStyle = "Bold Italic"
        .Size = 14
        .Strikethrough = False
        .Superscript = False
        .Subscript = False
        .OutlineFont = False
        .Shadow = False
        .Underline = xlUnderlineStyleNone
        .ThemeColor = xlThemeColorLight1
        .TintAndShade = 0
        .ThemeFont = xlThemeFontMajor
    End With
End Sub
```

When you activate the *CompanyAddress* macro by pressing Ctrl+Shift+A, Excel runs the first statement in the macro, which selects cell A6. The macro then calls the *CompanyFont* macro, which switches execution to the first line of the *CompanyFont* subroutine. When Excel reaches the *End Sub* statement at the end of *CompanyFont*, it returns to the statement in *CompanyAddress* immediately after the one that called *CompanyFont* and continues until it reaches the *End Sub* statement at the end of *CompanyAddress*.

Using the Personal Macro Workbook

When you recorded the *CompanyAddress* macro earlier in this chapter, you placed the macro in a module that belonged to the active workbook. A macro you place in a module is available only when you open the workbook containing the module.

To make a macro available at all times, store it in the Personal Macro Workbook. This workbook is ordinarily hidden; you can unhide it by clicking Unhide in the Window group on the View tab and then selecting Personal in the Unhide dialog box. If the Unhide command is unavailable, you have not yet created a Personal Macro Workbook. To create one, begin recording a macro, as described earlier in this chapter, and then select Personal Macro Workbook in the Store Macro In drop-down list in the Record Macro dialog box. Excel creates the Personal Macro Workbook (Personal.xlsb) and makes it available each time you start Excel. It's a good place to record macros that you want to be able to use in any workbook.

Going on from here

In this chapter, you learned how to create macros with the help of the macro recorder. As you learn more about VBA, you'll notice that the macro recorder often creates more code for a task than you really need. In our *CompanyFont* macro, for example, the following lines that the recorder generated are unnecessary because all you wanted to do was set the font name, point size, and style:

```
.Strikethrough = False
.Superscript = False
.Subscript = False
.OutlineFont = False
.Shadow = False
.Underline = xlUnderlineStyleNone
.ThemeColor = xlThemeColorLight1
.TintAndShade = 0
.ThemeFont = xlThemeFontMajor
```

The recorder added these lines because it didn't (and couldn't) know they weren't necessary. You can remove them without changing the functionality of the macro.

Earlier in the chapter, you saw that it is possible, using VBA, to change an object's property settings (a cell's font formats, for example) without selecting the object. Nevertheless, the recorder always selects objects before taking actions that affect those objects. It does so because it must mimic everything you do when you create the recording. As you acquire more proficiency with VBA, you'll learn ways to edit the recorder's code to make it more efficient.

As you improve your expertise in VBA, you will probably find yourself creating most of your code directly in the Visual Basic Editor, bypassing the recorder altogether. Chances are, though, you'll still return to the recorder now and then. The Excel object model includes so many objects, methods, properties, and arguments that it's difficult to try to remember them all. When you can't remember what property, object, or method is required in a certain programming situation, one of the easiest ways to get the information you need is by turning on the macro recorder, working through by hand the actions you want to program, and then seeing what code the recorder generates.

Chapter 28

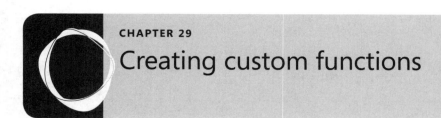

CHAPTER 29

Creating custom functions

A LTHOUGH Microsoft Excel 2013 includes a multitude of built-in worksheet functions, chances are that it doesn't have a function for every type of calculation you perform. The designers of Excel couldn't possibly anticipate every calculation need of every user. But they do provide you with the ability to create custom functions. In the same way that a macro lets you encapsulate a sequence of actions and then execute that sequence with a single command, a *custom function* lets you encapsulate a sequence of calculations so that you can perform those calculations with a single formula.

Custom functions, like macros, use the Visual Basic for Applications (VBA) programming language. They differ from macros in two significant ways. First, they use *function* procedures instead of *sub* procedures. That is, they start with a *Function* statement instead of a *Sub* statement and end with *End Function* instead of *End Sub*. Second, they perform calculations instead of taking actions. Certain kinds of statements (such as statements that select and format ranges) are excluded from custom functions. In this chapter, you'll learn how to create and use custom functions.

Creating a simple custom function

Suppose your company offers a quantity discount of 10 percent on the sale of a product when an order is for 100 units or more. In the following paragraphs, you'll build a function to calculate this discount.

The worksheet in Figure 29-1 shows an order form that lists each item, the quantity, the price, the discount (if any), and the resulting extended price.

You'll find the TreeOrders.xlsm file with the other examples on the companion website. You can use this file for reference or to practice creating your own custom functions.

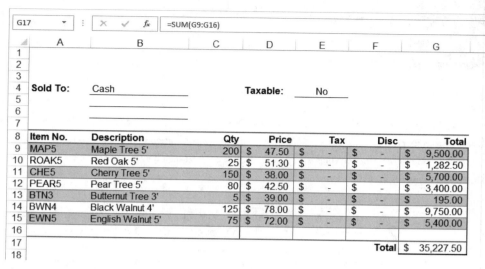

Figure 29-1 In column F, we want to calculate the discount for each item ordered.

To create a custom DISCOUNT function in this workbook, follow these steps:

1. Press Alt+F11 to open the Visual Basic Editor, and then click Insert, Module. A new module appears, as shown in Figure 29-2.

2. In the new module, type the following code. To make the code more readable, use the Tab key to indent lines. (The indentation is for your benefit only and is optional. The code runs with or without indentation.) After you type an indented line, the Visual Basic Editor assumes your next line should be similarly indented. To move out (that is, to the left) one tab character, press Shift+Tab.

```
Function Discount(quantity, price)
    If quantity >=100 Then
        Discount = quantity * price * 0.1
    Else
        Discount = 0
    End If
    Discount = Application.Round(Discount, 2)
End Function
```

3. After you create the function in the Microsoft Visual Basic for Applications window, be sure to save the file as an Excel Macro-Enabled Workbook. Then close the Microsoft Visual Basic for Applications window to return to Excel.

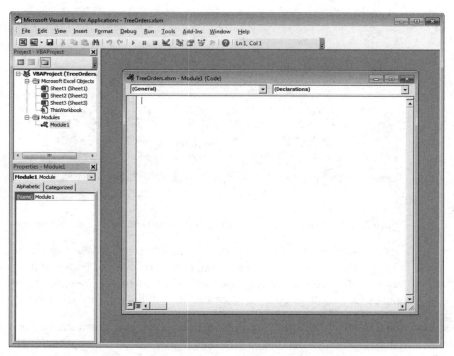

Figure 29-2 Clicking Insert, Module adds a new module to the workbook.

Using custom functions

Now you're ready to use the new DISCOUNT function. Press Alt+F11 to switch to the worksheet shown in Figure 29-1. Select cell F9, and type the following:

=DISCOUNT(C9,D9)

Excel calculates the 10 percent discount on 200 units at $47.50 per unit and returns $950.00.

The first line of your VBA code, *Function Discount(quantity, price)*, indicates that the DISCOUNT function requires two arguments, quantity and price. When you call the function in a worksheet cell, you must include these two arguments. In the formula =DISCOUNT(C9,D9), *C9* is the quantity argument and *D9* is the price argument. Now you can copy the DISCOUNT formula to F10:F15 to get the worksheet shown in Figure 29-3.

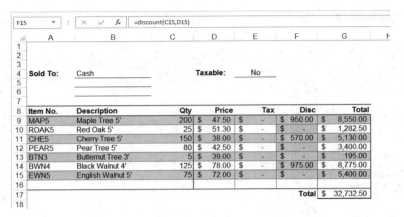

Figure 29-3 This worksheet shows the result of the DISCOUNT custom function.

Let's consider how Excel interprets this function procedure. When you press Enter, Excel looks for the name *DISCOUNT* in the current workbook and finds that it is a procedure in Module1. The argument names enclosed in parentheses—*quantity* and *price*—are place-holders for the values on which the calculation of the discount is based.

The *If* statement in the following block of code examines the quantity argument and determines whether the number of items sold is greater than or equal to 100:

```
If quantity >= 100 Then
    Discount = quantity * price * 0.1
Else
    Discount = 0
End If
```

If the number of items sold is greater than or equal to 100, VBA executes the following statement, which multiplies the *quantity* value by the *price* value and then multiplies the result by 0.1:

```
Discount = quantity * price * 0.1
```

The result is stored as the variable *Discount*. A VBA statement that stores a value in a variable is called an *assignment statement* because it evaluates the expression on the right side of the equal sign and assigns the result to the variable name on the left. Because the variable *Discount* has the same name as the function procedure, the value stored in the variable is returned to the worksheet formula that called the DISCOUNT function.

If *quantity* is less than *100*, VBA executes the following statement:

```
Discount = 0
```

Finally, the following statement rounds the value assigned to the *Discount* variable to two decimal places:

```
Discount = Application.Round(Discount, 2)
```

VBA has no ROUND function, but Excel does. Therefore, to use ROUND in this statement, you tell VBA to look for the *Round* method (function) in the *Application* object (Excel). You do that by adding the word *Application* before the word *Round*. Use this syntax whenever you need to access an Excel function from a VBA module.

Understanding custom function rules

A custom function must start with a *Function* statement and end with an *End Function* statement. In addition to the function name, the *Function* statement usually specifies one or more arguments. You can, however, create a function with no arguments. Excel includes several built-in functions—RAND and NOW, for example—that don't use arguments. As you'll see later in this chapter, you can also create functions with optional arguments, which are arguments you can either include or omit when you call the function.

Following the *Function* statement, a function procedure includes one or more VBA statements that make decisions and perform calculations using the arguments passed to the function. Finally, somewhere in the function procedure, you must include a statement that assigns a value to a variable with the same name as the function. This value is returned to the formula that calls the function.

Using VBA keywords in custom functions

The number of VBA keywords you can use in custom functions is smaller than the number you can use in macros. Custom functions are not allowed to do anything other than return a value to a formula in a worksheet or to an expression used in another VBA macro or function. For example, custom functions cannot resize windows, edit a formula in a cell, or change the font, color, or pattern options for the text in a cell. If you include "action" code of this kind in a function procedure, the function returns the #VALUE! error.

The one action a function procedure can do (apart from performing calculations) is display a dialog box. You can use an *InputBox* statement in a custom function as a means of getting input from the user executing the function. You can use a *MsgBox* statement as a means of conveying information to the user. You can also use custom dialog boxes—also called *UserForms*—but that's a subject beyond the scope of this introduction.

Chapter 29

Documenting macros and custom functions

Even simple macros and custom functions can be difficult to read. You can make them easier to understand by typing explanatory text in the form of comments. You add comments by preceding the explanatory text with an apostrophe. For example, Figure 29-4 shows the DISCOUNT function with comments. Adding comments like these makes it easier for you or others to maintain your VBA code as time passes. If you need to make a change to the code in the future, you'll have an easier time understanding what you (or someone else) did originally.

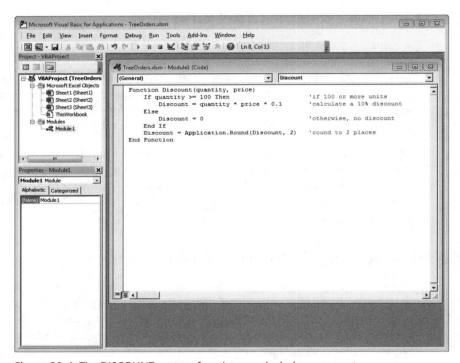

Figure 29-4 The DISCOUNT custom function now includes comments.

An apostrophe tells Excel to ignore everything to the right on the same line, so you can create comments either on lines by themselves or on the right side of lines containing VBA code. You might begin a relatively long block of code with a comment that explains its overall purpose and then use inline comments to document individual statements.

Another way to document your macros and custom functions is to give them descriptive names. For example, rather than name a macro *Labels*, you could name it *MonthLabels* to describe more specifically the purpose the macro serves. Using descriptive names for macros and custom functions is especially helpful when you've created many procedures, particularly if you create procedures that have similar but not identical purposes.

How you document your macros and custom functions is a matter of personal preference. What's important is to adopt some method of documentation and use it consistently.

Creating custom functions with optional arguments

Some of the built-in Excel functions let you omit certain arguments. For example, if you omit the *type* and *future value* arguments from the PV function, Excel still computes the result because those arguments are optional. Your custom functions can also use optional arguments.

For example, suppose you want to create a custom function called *RightTriangle* that uses the Pythagorean theorem to compute the length of any side of a right triangle given the lengths of the other two sides. The equation that expresses the Pythagorean theorem is $a^2 + b^2 = c^2$, in which a and b are the short sides and c is the hypotenuse. Given any two sides, you can use this equation to solve for the third side.

In a general-purpose *RightTriangle* function, you want to accept three arguments (one for each side of the triangle) but make each argument optional so that the user of the function can supply any two arguments and the function will solve for the third argument. The following code does the trick:

```
Function RightTriangle(Optional side1, Optional side2, _
    Optional hypotenuse)
    If Not (IsMissing(side1)) And Not (IsMissing(side2)) Then
        RightTriangle = Sqr(side1 ^ 2 + side2 ^ 2)
    Else
        If Not (IsMissing(side1)) And Not (IsMissing(hypotenuse)) Then
            RightTriangle = Sqr(hypotenuse ^ 2 - side1 ^ 2)
        Else
            If Not (IsMissing(side2)) And Not (IsMissing(hypotenuse)) Then
                RightTriangle = Sqr(hypotenuse ^ 2 - side2 ^ 2)
            Else
                RightTriangle = "Please supply two arguments."
            End If
        End If
    End If
End Function
```

After you create the function in the Microsoft Visual Basic for Applications window, be sure to save the file as an Excel Macro-Enabled Workbook. Then close the Microsoft Visual Basic for Applications window to return to Excel.

The first statement names the custom function and the optional arguments *side1*, *side2*, and *hypotenuse*. The next block of code contains a series of *If* statements that use the VBA *IsMissing* function to test whether each possible pair of arguments has been supplied. If *side1* is not missing and *side2* is not missing, Excel computes the square root of the sum of the squares of the two short sides and returns the length of the hypotenuse to the worksheet.

If fewer than two arguments are supplied, the following statement returns a text string to the worksheet:

```
RightTriangle = "Please supply two arguments."
```

Now let's see what happens when you use this custom function in a worksheet formula. The formula =RightTriangle(3,4) returns 5. The *hypotenuse* argument is omitted, so the function returns the square root of (3^2 + 4^2). You could also write the formula =RightTriangle(3,4,); however, the second comma is not necessary. The formula =RightTriangle (,4,5) returns 3 because the *side1* argument is omitted. The formula =RightTriangle(4,,5) also returns 3.

The function as written has at least two flaws. First, if the user supplies all three arguments, the function behaves as though the third argument were omitted. You might prefer to have it return an error message. Second, the function accepts negative and zero arguments even though triangles cannot have sides of negative or zero length.

You can eliminate the first of these defects by adding the following *If...End If* block immediately after the *Function* statement:

```
If Not (IsMissing(side1)) And Not (IsMissing(side2)) And _
    Not (IsMissing(hypotenuse)) Then
    RightTriangle = "Please supply only two arguments."
    Exit Function
End If
```

Note that this block includes an *Exit Function* statement. This saves the function the trouble of searching for missing arguments when it has already discovered that none are missing.

You can use a similar *If...End If* construction to look for arguments less than or equal to zero and return an appropriate error message and exit the function if any are found. Note that other kinds of inappropriate arguments (text, for example) cause the function to return one of the built-in error constants. If you call the function and offer a text argument, the function returns #VALUE! because it attempts to perform arithmetic operations on a nonarithmetic value.

How much error trapping you add to your custom functions depends, of course, on how much work you want to do and how you plan to use the function. If you're writing a function for your personal use, you might not need to deal with every conceivable aberrant use. If you write the function for others, you'll probably want to eliminate all possibility of error—or at least try to do so.

Making your custom functions available anywhere

To use a custom function, the workbook containing the module in which you created the function must be open. If that workbook is not open, you get a #NAME? error when you try to use the function. Even with the workbook open, if you use the function in a different workbook, you must precede the function name with the name of the workbook in which the function resides. For example, if you create a function named DISCOUNT in a workbook named Personal.xlsb and you call that function from another workbook, you must type **=personal.xlsb!discount()**, not simply **=discount()**.

You can save yourself some keystrokes (and possibly some typing errors) by selecting your custom functions from the Insert Function dialog box. Your custom functions appear in the User Defined category:

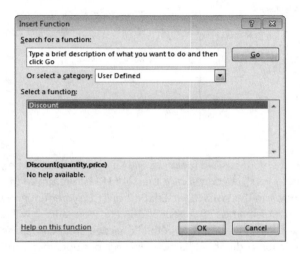

An easier way to make your custom functions available at all times is to store them in a separate workbook and then save that workbook as an add-in. You can then make the add-in available whenever you run Excel. Here's how to do this:

1. After you create the functions you need, click File, Save As.

2. In the Save As dialog box, open the Save As Type drop-down list and select Excel Add-In. Save the workbook under a recognizable name—such as Myfunctions—in the AddIns folder. (The Save As dialog box will propose that folder, so all you need to do is accept the default location.)

3. After you save the workbook, click File, Options.

4. In the Excel Options dialog box, click the Add-Ins category.

5. In the Manage drop-down list, select Excel Add-Ins. Then click the Go button.

6. In the Add-Ins dialog box, select the check box beside the name you used to save your workbook.

After you follow these steps, your custom functions will be available each time you run Excel. If you want to add to your function library, press Alt+F11 to return to the Visual Basic Editor. As Figure 29-5 shows, in the Visual Basic Editor Project Explorer under a VBAProject heading, you will see a module named after your add-in file. (Your add-in will have the extension .xlam.) Double-clicking that module in the Project Explorer causes the Visual Basic Editor to display your function code. To add a new function, position your insertion point after the *End Function* statement that terminates the last function in the Code window and begin typing. You can create as many functions as you need in this manner, and they will always be available in the User Defined category in the Insert Function dialog box.

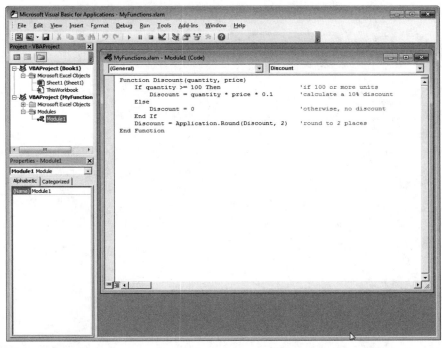

Figure 29-5 If you save your custom functions as an add-in, the code for those functions is available in a module in the Visual Basic Editor, and you can add more functions as the need arises.

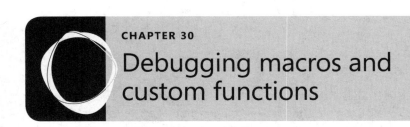

F YOU made it through the previous two chapters, you now have at least a smattering of Microsoft Visual Basic for Applications (VBA) at your command—as well as, we hope, an appetite for learning more. The best ways to acquire more expertise in this versatile programming language are to read a book on the subject, such as *Microsoft Visual Basic 2010 Step by Step* by Michael Halvorson (Microsoft Press, 2010), and to experiment. As you do your everyday work in Microsoft Excel 2013, look for chores that are ripe for automating. When you come across something macro-worthy, record your actions. Then inspect the code generated by the macro recorder. Be sure you understand what the recorder has given you (read the Help text for any statements you don't understand), and see whether you can find ways to make the code more efficient. Eliminate statements that appear unnecessary, and then see whether the code still does what you expect it to do. Look for statements that select ranges or other objects, and see whether you can make your code perform the essential tasks without first selecting those objects.

As you experiment and create larger, more complex macros and functions, you will undoubtedly produce some code that either doesn't run at all or doesn't give you the results you want. Missteps of this kind are an inevitable aspect of programming. Fortunately, the VBA language and the Visual Basic Editor provide tools to help you trap errors and root out bugs. These tools are the subject of this chapter.

In this chapter, you'll look at two kinds of error-catching tools: those that help you at design time, when you're creating or editing code, and those that work at run time, while the code is running.

Using design-time tools

The Visual Basic Editor design-time error-handling tools let you correct mistakes in VBA syntax and catch misspellings of variable names. They also let you follow the "flow" of a macro or function (seeing each line of code as it is executed) and monitor the values of variables during the course of a procedure's execution.

Catching syntax errors

If you type a worksheet formula incorrectly in Excel, Excel alerts you to the error and refuses to accept the entry. The VBA compiler (the system component that converts your English-like VBA code into the machine language that actually executes the macro on your computer) ordinarily performs the same service for you if you type a VBA expression incorrectly. If you omit a required parenthesis, for example, the compiler beeps as soon as you press Enter. It also presents an error message and displays the offending line of code in a contrasting color (red, by default).

Certain kinds of syntax errors don't become apparent to the compiler until you attempt to run your code. For example, if you write the following

```
With Selection.Border
    .Weight = xlThin
    .LineStyle = xlAutomatic
```

and attempt to run this code without including an *End With* statement, you see this error message:

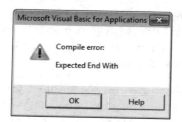

Your procedure halts, and you are now in break mode. (You can tell you're in break mode by the appearance of the word break in brackets in the Visual Basic Editor title bar. The line the compiler was attempting to execute will be highlighted—in yellow, by default.) Break mode lets you fix your code and then continue running it. For example, if you omit an *End With* statement, you can add that statement while in break mode and then press F5 (or select Run, Continue) to go on with the show. If you want to exit from break mode rather than continue with the execution of your procedure, select Run, Reset.

If you don't like having the compiler complain about obvious syntax errors the moment you commit them, you can turn off that functionality. In the Visual Basic Editor window, click Tools, Options, click the Editor tab (shown in Figure 30-1), and clear the Auto Syntax Check check box. With automatic syntax checking turned off, your syntax errors will still be flagged when you try to run your code.

You'll find the files used in this chapter's examples, Breakpoints.xlsm and LakhsCrores.xlsm, with the other examples on the companion website.

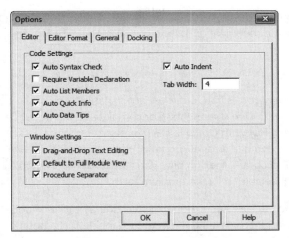

Figure 30-1 Clear the Auto Syntax Check check box if you don't want to know about syntax errors until you run your code.

> **Note**
>
> You can also use the Options dialog box to change the color that the Visual Basic Editor uses to highlight syntax errors. If you don't like red, click the Editor Format tab, select Syntax Error Text in the Code Colors list, and then select a different color.

Auto Syntax Check is on by default. So are three other "auto" options: Auto List Members, Auto Quick Info, and Auto Data Tips. These options are all useful, and you should leave them on, especially if you're relatively new to VBA. Auto List Members and Auto Quick Info help you complete a line of VBA code by displaying available options at the current insertion point or the names of arguments required by the function you're currently entering. Auto Data Tips is relevant only in break mode. If you rest your pointer on a variable name in break mode, the Auto Data Tips feature displays the current value of that variable as a ScreenTip.

Catching misspelled variable names

The VBA compiler doesn't care about the capitalization style of your variable names. *MyVar*, *myVar*, and *myvar* are identical names as far as the compiler is concerned. (If you're inconsistent about the capitalization of a variable name, the Visual Basic Editor adjusts all instances of that variable to make them the same.) If you change the spelling of a variable name in mid-program, however, the compiler creates a new variable, and havoc for your program ensues. An error in programming introduced by a misspelled variable can be especially treacherous because the program might appear to behave normally.

You can virtually eliminate the possibility of having inconsistently spelled variable names in a module by adding a single statement at the top of that module (before any *Sub* or *Function* statement):

```
Option Explicit
```

The *Option Explicit* statement forces you to declare any variables used in the current module. You declare variables with *Dim* statements. (For complete details about *Dim*, type **Dim** in a module and then press F1.) With *Option Explicit* in place, if you use a variable without first declaring it, you get a compile error at run time. If you accidentally misspell a variable name somewhere in your program, the compiler flags the misspelled variable as an undeclared variable, and you'll be able to fix the problem forthwith.

You can add *Option Explicit* to every new module you create by clicking Tools, Options, going to the Editor tab, and then selecting the Require Variable Declaration check box. This option is off by default, but it's good programming practice to turn it on. *Option Explicit* does more for you than eliminate misspelled variable names. By forcing you to declare your variables, it also encourages you to think ahead as you work.

Stepping through code

The Visual Basic Editor step commands cause the compiler to execute either a single instruction or a limited set of instructions and then pause in break mode, highlighting the next instruction that will be executed. Execution is suspended until you take another action—such as issuing another step command, resuming normal execution, or terminating execution. By issuing step commands repeatedly, you can follow the procedure's execution path. You can see, for example, which way the program branches when it comes to an *If* statement or which of the alternative paths it takes when it encounters a *Select Case* structure. (A *Select Case* structure causes the program to execute one of a set of alternative statements, depending on the value of a particular variable. For details, type **case** in a module and press F1.) You can also examine the values of variables at each step along the way.

> **Note**
> You can monitor the value of variables by displaying the Watch Window or the Quick Watch dialog box or by resting your pointer on particular variables while in break mode. For information about using the Watch Window, see "Using the Watch Window to monitor variable values and object properties," later in this chapter.

You have four step commands at your disposal. You'll find these commands—and their keyboard shortcuts—on the Debug menu:

- **Step Into**   Executes the next instruction only.

- **Step Over**   Works like Step Into unless the next instruction is a call to another procedure (that is, a subroutine). In that case, Step Into executes the entire called procedure as a unit.

- **Step Out**   Executes the remaining steps of the current procedure.

- **Run To Cursor**   Executes everything up to the current cursor position.

You can run an entire procedure one step at a time by repeatedly pressing F8 (the keyboard shortcut for Debug, Step Into). To begin stepping through a procedure at a particular instruction, move your cursor to that instruction, and press Ctrl+F8 (the shortcut for Debug, Run To Cursor). Alternatively, you can force the compiler to enter break mode when it reaches a particular instruction, and then you can use any of the step commands.

Setting breakpoints with the Toggle Breakpoint command

A *breakpoint* is an instruction that causes the compiler to halt execution and enter break mode. The simplest way to set a breakpoint is to put your cursor where you want the breakpoint and then click Debug, Toggle Breakpoint (or press F9). Click this command sequence a second time to clear a breakpoint. You can set as many breakpoints in a procedure as you like using this method. The Toggle Breakpoint command sets an unconditional breakpoint—one that always occurs when execution arrives at the breakpoint. To set a conditional breakpoint—one that takes effect under a specified condition only—see the next section.

As Figure 30-2 shows, the Visual Basic Editor highlights a line where you set a breakpoint in a contrasting color and displays a large bullet in the left margin of the Code window. To customize the highlighting color, click Tools, Options. Click the Editor Format tab, and then select Breakpoint Text.

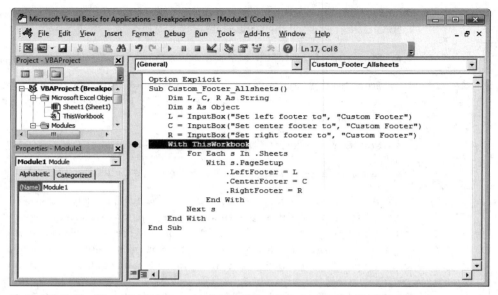

Figure 30-2 The Visual Basic Editor uses highlighting to mark breakpoint lines.

Setting conditional breakpoints using *Debug.Assert*

With the *Assert* method of the *Debug* object, you can cause the VBA compiler to enter break mode only if a particular expression generates a FALSE result. Figure 30-3 provides a simple example.

The *Debug.Assert* statement in this otherwise useless bit of code asserts that *x* is less than *9*. As long as that assertion is true, the procedure runs. When it becomes false, the compiler enters break mode. As the Watch Window in Figure 30-3 shows, the compiler enters break mode when *x* is equal to *9*. (We'll discuss the Watch Window next.)

> **Note**
>
> You can also use the Watch Window to set conditional breakpoints. See "Setting conditional breakpoints with the Watch Window," later in this chapter.

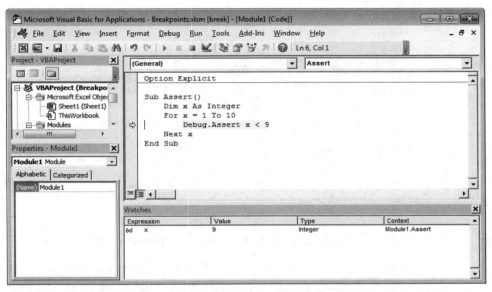

Figure 30-3 This *Debug.Assert* statement puts the compiler in break mode when the value of *x* equals *9* or greater.

Using the Watch Window to monitor variable values and object properties

The Watch Window shows the current values of selected variables or expressions and the current property settings for selected objects. You can use the Watch Window to monitor the status of variables and objects as you step through a procedure.

To display the Watch Window, click View, Watch Window. (To close the window, click its Close button.) To add a variable or object to the Watch Window, you can select it in the Code window and drag it to the Watch Window. You can add expressions, such as *a + 1*, to the Watch Window in this manner. Alternatively, you can add something to the Watch Window by clicking Debug, Add Watch. In the Expression text box in the Add Watch dialog box (shown in Figure 30-4), type a variable name or other valid VBA expression.

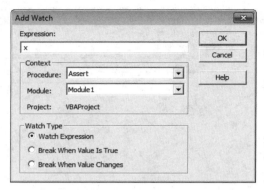

Figure 30-4 You can use the Add Watch dialog box to add a watch variable or to set a conditional breakpoint.

Setting conditional breakpoints with the Watch Window

As Figure 30-4 shows, you can use the Add Watch dialog box to set a conditional breakpoint. Click Debug, Add Watch; specify the name of a variable or a VBA expression; and then select either Break When Value Is True or Break When Value Changes. Selecting Break When Value Is True for an expression is comparable to using a *Debug.Assert* statement to set a conditional breakpoint. The difference is that *Debug.Assert* causes a break when an expression becomes false, and Break When Value Is True does the opposite.

Using Quick Watch to monitor a variable or add a watch item

In break mode, you can select any variable name or expression in your code and click Debug, Quick Watch (or press Shift+F9) to see the current value of the selected item. If you decide you want to monitor that item continuously, you can click Add in the Quick Watch dialog box. The Visual Basic Editor then adds the item to the Watch Window.

Using the Immediate window

While in break mode or before running a procedure, you can execute any VBA statement in the Immediate window. (If the Immediate window isn't visible, click View, Immediate Window, or press Ctrl+G.) For example, you can discover the value of a variable x by typing **Print x** in the Immediate window. (As a shortcut, you can type **?x**. The question mark character is a synonym for *Print* in VBA.)

You can also use the Immediate window to monitor an action in a procedure while that procedure is running. You do this by inserting *Debug.Print* statements into the procedure. The statement *Debug.Print x*, for example, displays the current value of x in the Immediate window.

The Immediate window can be a handy place to test VBA statements while you're still wrestling with the syntax of this programming language. If you're not sure a particular statement will have the effect you intend, you can try it in the Immediate window and see what happens.

Dealing with run-time errors

In many cases, run-time errors are caused by factors outside your control. For example, suppose you write the following macro to format the numbers in a selected range using the Indian system of *lakhs* and *crores*. (The crore is a unit equal to ten million in the Indian numbering system, while the lakh is equal to 100,000.)

```
Sub LakhsCrores()
    Dim cell As Object
    For Each cell In Selection
        If Abs(cell.Value) > 10000000 Then
            cell.NumberFormat = "#"","""##"","""##"",""""###"
        ElseIf Abs(cell.Value) > 100000 Then
            cell.NumberFormat = "##"","""##"",""""###"
        End If
    Next cell
End Sub
```

This macro works fine if the person who runs it selects a range containing numbers before running the macro. But if the user selects something else—a chart embedded on the worksheet, for example—VBA displays an error message:

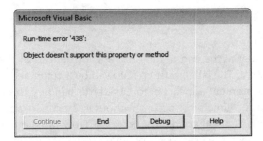

The macro generates a run-time error and enters break mode because the *For Each* statement has to be applied to a collection or an array, and a chart object is neither. (A range is a collection of cells, so *For Each* does work with a range.) Even though you can figure out easily enough what the error message means and what you have to do about it (try again with a range selected), the message still might be annoying. If you intend for this macro to be used by someone else, it's definitely impolite to let that other user see such a message.

You can trap an error such as this—that is, shield yourself and others from VBA's run-time error messages—by means of an *On Error GoTo* statement. The statement must appear before the code that might cause a run-time error, and it has the following syntax, in which *label* is a name that identifies an error-handling section elsewhere in your procedure:

```
On Error GoTo label
```

If a run-time error occurs, the *On Error GoTo* statement transfers execution to the error-handling code. In the case of your *LakhsCrores* procedure, the macro complete with error handling might look like this:

```
Sub LakhsCrores()
    'Catch run-time error caused by inappropriate selection
    On Error GoTo ErrorHandler
    Dim cell As Object
    For Each cell In Selection
        If Abs(cell.Value) > 10000000 Then
            cell.NumberFormat = "#"","""##"","""##"",""###"
        ElseIf Abs(cell.Value) > 100000 Then
            cell.NumberFormat = "##"","""##"",""###"
        End If
    Next cell

    'Exit Sub statement keeps execution from entering
    'error handler if no error occurs
    Exit Sub


    'Error Handler
ErrorHandler:
    MsgBox "Please select a worksheet range."
End Sub
```

Notice that the error handler goes at the end of the program, introduced by the label that appears in the *On Error* statement. The label must be followed by a colon and must appear on a line by itself. An *Exit Sub* statement appears before the error handler. This statement terminates the macro when no run-time error occurs; without it, execution would continue into the error handler regardless of whether an error occurred. Now when the user runs the macro after selecting a chart object, the user sees a polite message box instead of a rude run-time error message.

The macro still has a problem, however. The code works fine when the selected range includes numbers, text, or blank cells. However, if it includes a cell containing an Excel error constant, such as #NA, a different run-time error occurs: error 13, Type Mismatch. The message box generated by the error handler shown previously would not be appropriate for this kind of error.

How do you make your code show one message for a nonrange selection and another for a range that includes one or more error values? You use the *Number* property of the *Err* object. This property is always set to the most recent run-time error number (or 0, if no procedure is running or if no error has occurred). You can handle both run-time errors (438 and 13) with the following code, for example:

```
ErrorHandler:
If Err.Number=438 Then
    MsgBox "Please select a worksheet range."
ElseIf Err.Number = 13 Then
    MsgBox "Please select a range without error values."
Else
    MsgBox "Sorry! Unknown error!"
End If
```

This isn't particularly elegant, but at least you have all your bases more or less covered.

The foregoing error-handler examples assume your program should terminate when a run-time error occurs. The purpose of the error handler is to prevent the jolting VBA message from showing up—and to provide the user with a simple explanation of what went wrong.

In some cases, you'll want your procedure to continue running after a run-time error occurs. In such a case, your error handler needs to return VBA to the appropriate instruction so that it can continue executing your program. Use either a *Resume* statement or a *Resume Next* statement to do this. A *Resume* statement causes VBA to re-execute the line that caused the error. A *Resume Next* statement causes VBA to continue at the line after the line that caused the error.

By combining *On Error* with *Resume Next*, you can tell VBA to ignore any run-time errors that might occur and go to the next statement. If you're sure you've anticipated the kinds of run-time errors that might occur with your program, *On Error Resume Next* can often be the simplest and most effective way to deal with potential mishaps. In the *LakhsCrores* macro, for example, you can write the following:

```
Sub LakhsCrores()
    'Tell VBA to ignore all run-time errors
    On Error Resume Next

    Dim cell As Object
    For Each cell In Selection
        If Abs(cell.Value) > 10000000 Then
            cell.NumberFormat = "#"","""##"",""""##"",""""###"
        ElseIf Abs(cell.Value) > 100000 Then
            cell.NumberFormat = "##"",""""##"",""""###"
        End If
    Next cell
Exit Sub
```

With this code, if the user selects a chart and runs the macro, VBA ignores the run-time error, the program moves on to the *For Each* block, and nothing happens—because nothing can happen. If the user selects a range containing one or more error values, the program skips over those cells it can't format and formats the ones it can. In all cases, neither an error message nor a message box appears, and all is well. This solution works for this particular macro.

Of course, when you use *On Error Resume Next*, you've disabled the VBA run-time checking altogether. You should do this only when you're sure you've thought of everything that could possibly go awry—and the best way to arrive at that serene certainty is to test, test again, and then test some more.

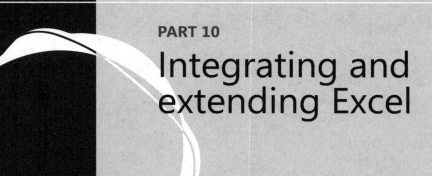

PART 10

Integrating and extending Excel

Linking, hyperlinking, and embedding

WORKBOOKS seldom live in isolation. The material you manipulate in a Microsoft Excel 2013 document is related to other material elsewhere—on the Internet, on a file server, in another workbook, or perhaps in your collection of digital photographs. This chapter surveys some of the ways you can connect the pieces in Excel.

Linking and embedding with OLE technology

Microsoft long ago stopped using the term *object linking and embedding* (OLE) to describe its technology for creating *compound* documents—that is, documents that integrate data from multiple applications. But the technology is still there. Part of the reason that OLE has disappeared from Microsoft's formal vocabulary is that linking and embedding capabilities are nearly universal in major Windows applications now, and it ostensibly works so well that you seldom have to think about what you're doing. Nevertheless, you should understand the general differences between embedding and linking, know when it's appropriate to use one form of integration as opposed to the other, and know how to fix matters in the event that a link becomes broken.

Embedding vs. linking

When you embed another application's data in Excel, your workbook stores a complete copy of the source data. Because you have a complete copy (a paragraph from Microsoft Word, for example, or a voice annotation created in a sound-recording program), that information remains intact even if the source is destroyed or becomes otherwise unavailable. But the embedded copy is independent of the source. The source might change, but the embedded copy does not.

When you link your Excel workbook to external data, the workbook records a pointer to the source of that data; if the source data changes, your workbook changes accordingly. Whether it changes automatically to match the source or only when you request an update depends on options that you set. In any event, your Excel document retains a connection to the source.

Excel displays information that you link or embed if it is in a text or graphic format that Excel recognizes. You can also choose to display a linked item as an icon rather than as the actual text or graphic. When you double-click the icon, Excel *renders* the information (plays the sound clip or video, for example), as long as an application capable of rendering it is available.

Because embedding typically stores more information in your Excel document than linking does, embedding tends to generate larger files. If minimizing file size matters, you should favor linking over embedding. You should also link if you need Excel to update your workbook automatically when the source data changes. On the other hand, if you need to take a document that is linked to a file on a remote computer on the road with you, you'll want to embed the file instead. Otherwise, Excel won't be able to find the linked file when you're offline.

Embedding vs. static pasting

What's the difference between embedding something and doing an ordinary paste from the Clipboard? If you paste text into Excel from Notepad—an application that doesn't support embedding—it arrives as if you typed it directly in the active worksheet cell. (If the text spans multiple lines, Excel delivers each new line to a new cell in the current column.) What you paste, in other words, becomes ordinary worksheet data.

If you embed text from Word (or another word processor that supports embedding), the text appears to land in the cell that is active when you perform the embedding, but in fact it floats above the worksheet cells in an object layer. Excel displays the text in an opaque rectangle that's initially aligned with the active cell; you can drag the rectangle to reposition the embedded object.

To embed text copied from Word, click the arrow under the Paste button on the Home tab, click Paste Special, and choose Microsoft Word Document Object, as shown in Figure 31-1. As Figure 31-2 shows, when you select the embedded text object (we dragged it away from the edge to show the bounding box), the word *Object*, followed by a number, appears in the Name box in the upper-left corner; handles appear on the object's bounding rectangle (you can use these to change the size of the rectangle); and an EMBED formula appears in the formula line. You can't do much with this formula because EMBED isn't a worksheet function, but it is helpful to identify the program from which the embedded data originated.

More important, perhaps, if you double-click the embedded object, you can edit it using the application that created it. If you double-click the Word object in Figure 31-2, for example, Excel displays a thick border around the embedded object. The Excel ribbon is replaced by the Word ribbon, leaving you with a kind of hybrid user interface. At this point, you are essentially working in Word, although the Excel context remains visible. When you finish using Word to edit the object, you can click outside it (back on the worksheet), and the Word paraphernalia disappears.

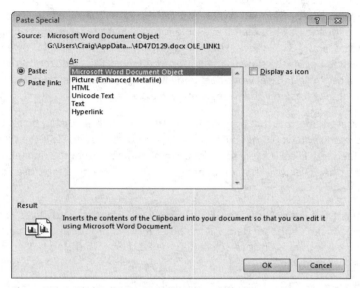

Figure 31-1 The Paste Special dialog box offers several formats you can use for linking or embedding.

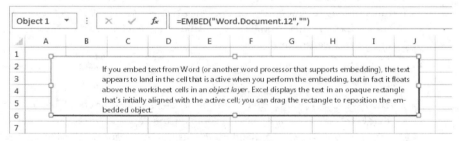

Figure 31-2 Embedding text creates a movable object whose source is identified by an EMBED formula.

This kind of object editing is called *editing in place*. Not all applications that support embedding offer it. If you double-click an embedded object from an application that doesn't support editing in place, Excel launches a regular copy of that application (although it might include a command on the application's File menu for updating your Excel document with the changes you make).

In cases where embedding and static pasting are both options, you should favor embedding if you want to retain the ability to edit the material in its native application—or if you want to be able to apply object-formatting commands to the incoming material.

Embedding and linking from the Clipboard

When you copy data to the Clipboard, the source application typically posts the data to the Clipboard in a variety of formats. When you use the Paste Special command in Excel, the Paste Special dialog box lists all the available formats that the receiving application knows how to use, as Figure 31-1 shows. For example, if you copy a Microsoft PowerPoint 2013 slide, PowerPoint posts the slide to the Clipboard in more than a dozen formats. If you right-click a cell in your Excel worksheet and click the Paste Special command, the Paste Special dialog box lists only the formats that Excel can accept.

In many cases, the format that appears first in the Paste Special dialog box is the default format—the one you would get by clicking Paste or pressing Ctrl+V. If the Clipboard data can be embedded, Excel is likely to make the embedding format the default. If you need to be certain, however, you shouldn't depend on these generalizations; use Paste Special instead of Paste.

If the format listed in the Paste Special dialog box includes the word *Object*, choosing that format embeds the Clipboard data. All the other formats produce a static paste. If you're not sure what a format is or does, select it in the Paste Special dialog box and read the descriptive text below the format list.

As Figure 31-1 shows, the Paste Special dialog box includes two options, Paste and Paste Link. To link your source data, select Paste Link. Excel renders your source data in whatever format you select and also creates a link to the source. In this case, instead of the EMBED formula used with embedded text (as shown in Figure 31-2), Excel creates an external-reference formula that is similar to the kind of formula created if you reference a cell in an external Excel workbook.

> **Note**
>
> The Paste Link option in the Paste Special dialog box is not available for all the formats that Excel can paste. If it's not available for the data and format you want, try linking by means of the Object command on the Insert tab. For more information, see "Embedding and linking with the Object command" later in this chapter.

As mentioned, if you embed or link a format that Excel cannot render, the incoming data is represented by an icon. In some cases, you can also ask for some iconic representation of data that Excel can render. Displaying an icon instead of the rendered data is an excellent choice if you want the user of your Excel document to have access to external information but not be distracted by it. The icon takes up little space on your worksheet, and you can add text beside it to explain its purpose. (An even better choice is a hyperlink; see "Linking with hyperlinks," later in this chapter.)

Embedding and linking with the Object command

By clicking Object, in the Text group on the Insert tab, you can embed an object that doesn't exist as Clipboard data. As Figure 31-3 shows, the Object dialog box has two tabs: Create New and Create From File. By using the Create New tab, you can create an object from scratch and then embed it. Using the Create From File tab, you can embed or link an entire file.

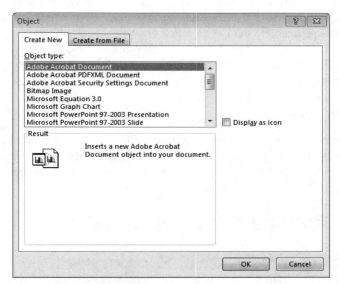

Figure 31-3 By clicking the Object command on the Insert tab, you can create embeddable objects or link or embed entire files.

The list on the Create New tab includes document types that are probably familiar, such as Bitmap Image and Microsoft Office PowerPoint 97–2003 Presentation, as well as the names of OLE server applications on your system—applications that might or might not be familiar. If you select a document type and click OK, Excel launches the application associated with that document type. If the application in question supports editing in place, the Excel user interface is replaced by that of the application, and you can create your object in a window that appears on your Excel worksheet. If the application does not support editing in place, the full application appears in a separate window. After you create your object, you can send the new object to your Excel worksheet by means of a command (such as Update Document) on the application's File menu.

Some of the items on the Create New tab represent OLE server applications whose sole purpose is to create embeddable objects. If you select Microsoft Equation 3.0, for example, the Microsoft Equation Editor appears, which you use to create and embed a mathematical, chemical, or other technical expression as an object on your Excel worksheet.

On the Create From File tab in the Object dialog box, you can type the name of a file or use the Browse button to locate it. To embed the file, click OK. To create a link to it, select the Link To File check box. To display an embedded or linked object as an icon, select the Display As Icon check box.

Using the Create From File tab in the Object dialog box, you can embed any file in your Excel document or link to the file. If you embed a file type that's not listed on the Create New tab, the resulting formula references the Windows Packager application. Packager is a *wrapper* that encapsulates the embedded file. When you double-click the object on your worksheet, Packager executes the file, an action equivalent to double-clicking it in Windows Explorer or File Explorer. If the file is not associated with an application, a Run With dialog box appears. In the Run With dialog box, you can select an application with which to open the file.

Managing links

If an Excel workbook includes links to other documents, you can use the Edit Links command (in the Connections group on the Data tab) to summon the dialog box shown in Figure 31-4. The Edit Links dialog box lists all the links in the current file, including links created by formula references to cells in other worksheets.

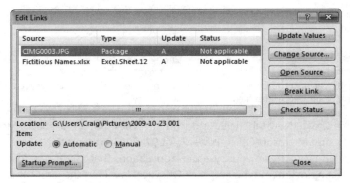

Figure 31-4 To update, alter, or sever a link, click the Data tab and then click Edit Links in the Connections group.

Choosing automatic or manual update

The Automatic and Manual options, near the bottom of the Edit Links dialog box, control the manner in which your links are updated. If you select Automatic (the only choice available for links to other Excel documents), your link is updated whenever the source changes. This automatic updating occurs instantaneously with some source applications and takes a while with others. Theoretically, you don't need to concern yourself with refreshing the link; Windows performs that duty for you. If you find that the updating occurs more frequently than you want it to (or if the process intrudes on your concentration in any way), you might want to switch from Automatic to Manual. With updating set to Manual, you can force an update by returning to the Edit Links dialog box and clicking Update Values.

Fixing broken links

If Excel tries to update a link and can't find the source file, it presents an error message. This kind of problem occurs most commonly when a file to which you've defined a link is renamed, relocated, or removed. If the source has been renamed or moved and you know its current identity and whereabouts, you can often fix the problem by editing the link formula. Alternatively, revisit the Edit Links dialog box (click Edit Links on the Data tab), and then click the Change Source button to display the dialog box shown in Figure 31-5. Unfortunately, the Change Links dialog box does not include a file browser, so you need to type or edit the file specification manually.

Figure 31-5 The Change Links dialog box requires you to manually type in a new link address.

Linking with hyperlinks

Hyperlinks in Excel look and function like text hyperlinks in webpages. That is, a hyperlink can be a simple word or phrase, underlined and colored to distinguish it from other text in your workbook. After you click such a link, the color ordinarily changes, indicating that you've visited the link's target.

Just as links on webpages can be attached to graphics as well as to text, so can they in Excel. You can assign them to drawn objects or charts, as well as to ordinary worksheet cells.

Here's a short inventory of useful tasks you can perform with hyperlinks in Excel:

- **Link to websites**   You'll find the ability to link to webpages particularly useful if you use Excel to generate material on the web. When you post your Excel document to your web server, you can already have the appropriate links to related pages in place.

- **Link to other documents**   Let's say you're a realtor with a worksheet that summarizes your current listings portfolio. You have pictures of each house, but the pictures don't fit neatly into worksheet cells. Create hyperlinks to the pictures instead. You can assign the hyperlinks to cells containing the multiple listing service (MLS) numbers or street addresses. Or suppose you're looking for a way to catalog your digital photo collection. Although you can use file and folder names to describe photo contents, dates, or locations, Excel limits how much information you can supply in a file name. Consider setting up an Excel table instead, with hyperlinks from descriptive information to individual photo files.

- **Link to a document that doesn't yet exist**   Excel creates the document when you click the link.

- **Link to another place in the current document**   Perhaps you built a complete worksheet for someone else to use. You can help that person navigate your document by supplying a table of hyperlinks.

- **Link to an e-message**   You can create a contact list in Excel and link each name to the person's email address. When you click the link, Excel launches your default email program, with the message already addressed.

- **Link to a network path**   You can make it easy for yourself or other users of your workbooks to connect to a file-server location by entering a Universal Naming Convention (UNC) path to that location in a worksheet cell. Excel recognizes the address as a network path and creates a hyperlink. Clicking the hyperlink opens the network folder in Windows Explorer or File Explorer.

Creating a hyperlink in a cell

You can create a hyperlink in a cell by clicking the Insert tab and then clicking Hyperlink. But if you're linking to a website and you already know the site's URL, you can type the URL directly in the cell. If the URL begins with *www*, Excel assumes it's an HTTP (website) URL and creates a hyperlink for you. If the URL doesn't begin with *www*, you need to include the prefix *http://*. (If the URL uses some other prefix, such as *ftp://*, you must, of course, type that.)

As mentioned, you can use the same technique to create a hyperlink to a network path. If the cell contents look like *servername**sharename*, Excel creates a link to the folder *sharename* on the server *servername*.

TROUBLESHOOTING

Excel doesn't turn my URLs into hyperlinks

Excel turns obvious URLs into hyperlinks by default. If it doesn't perform this service for you, click the File tab and then click Options. In the Excel Options dialog box, select the Proofing category, and then click AutoCorrect Options. In the AutoCorrect dialog box, click the AutoFormat As You Type tab. Finally, select the Internet And Network Paths With Hyperlinks check box. Click OK to save your changes.

Turning ordinary text into a hyperlink

To turn text other than a URL or a network path into a hyperlink, select the cell that contains the text. Then click the Insert tab, and click Hyperlink. (Alternatively, and more simply, press Ctrl+K.) The Insert Hyperlink dialog box shown in Figure 31-6 appears.

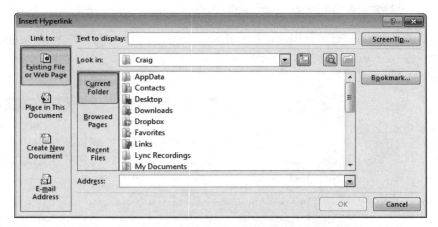

Figure 31-6 You can use the Insert Hyperlink dialog box to link to a file or webpage.

Follow these steps to create a hyperlink in a worksheet cell:

1. In the Address box, type the target of the link (the place to which you're taken when you click the link).

2. In the Text To Display box, type the text for the hyperlink. Excel displays this text underlined in your worksheet cell. (Unless you start with an empty cell, this box might already be filled in correctly when you get to the Insert Hyperlink dialog box.)

3. Click ScreenTip to supply the tip that appears when your pointer rests on the cell. This might be a friendly name for a website or a description of a file's contents. Click

OK to save the tip. If you omit this step, Excel uses a default tip that identifies the target of the link. Click OK to close the Insert Hyperlink dialog box.

> **Note**
>
> Because PivotTable cells move when a PivotTable report is rearranged, you cannot assign a hyperlink to a cell within a PivotTable.

Linking to a website or local file

To create a link to a website or a document in your own file storage, supply the URL or file name in the Address box in the Insert Hyperlink dialog box. If the site or document in which you're interested is one you visited recently, the dialog box makes this process easy. The most recently used (MRU) list that appears when you click the arrow next to the Address box is identical to the one maintained by Internet Explorer. If you don't find what you're looking for in this list, click the Browsed Pages button to reveal information from the Internet Explorer History bar, which is sorted so that the sites you visited most recently appear at the top of the list. As Figure 31-7 shows, the Browsed Pages list (like the Internet Explorer History bar) also includes the names of files you recently opened.

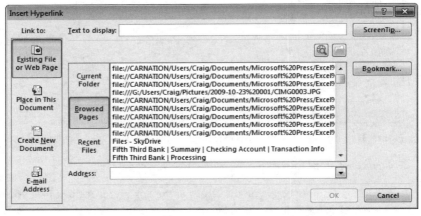

Figure 31-7 Clicking the Browsed Pages button reveals the names of sites you recently visited and files you recently opened.

If you don't find your site via the Address list or Browsed Pages—or if you're not sure you've found the right site—click the Browse The Web button (next to the folder icon above the Browsed Pages list). This action launches your web browser. Use the browser to navigate to the page you want. When you return to Excel, the Insert Hyperlink dialog box will contain the address of that site.

Note that if you're linking to a website from your desktop, the Address box must include the appropriate protocol prefix (*http://* or *ftp://*, for example). If you're creating a link that will be used on a website, a target address that isn't fully qualified is assumed to be relative to the current page.

If you're linking to a local document, as opposed to a webpage, you'll probably find that document most easily by clicking the Recent Files button. As Figure 31-8 shows, the Recent Files list includes only files from local (and local area network) storage. If the file you want doesn't appear in the list, click the Browse For File button (above the upper-right corner of the Recent Files list).

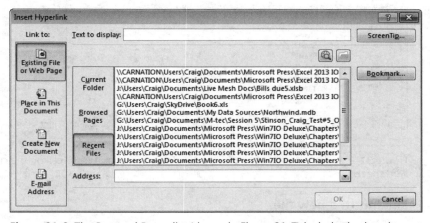

Figure 31-8 The Browsed Pages list (shown in Figure 31-7) includes both webpages and local documents. To filter out the webpages, click Recent Files.

TROUBLESHOOTING

I don't want that hyperlink

Sometimes a URL is just a URL, and you don't want to launch your browser every time you click it. Right-click the cell in question, and click Remove Hyperlink.

Note

If you're linking to an Excel file, you can also click the Bookmark button in the Insert Hyperlink dialog box to specify a location within that file. You can specify a worksheet name or a named cell or range. Unfortunately, you can't use the Bookmark button to link to a bookmark in a Word document.

Linking to a location in the current document

To link to a location in the current document, click Place In This Document in the Insert Hyperlink dialog box. As Figure 31-9 shows, you can link to any worksheet or to a named cell or range. If you select a worksheet name, use the Type The Cell Reference box to identify the cell on that worksheet to which you want to link. Excel links to A1 by default.

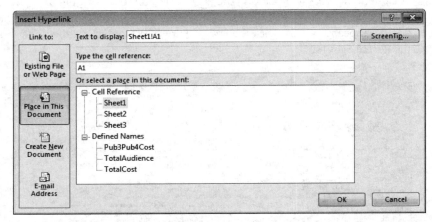

Figure 31-9 You can create a link to any worksheet, named range, or cell on the current worksheet.

Linking to a new file

To create a link to a new file, click Create New Document in the navigation bar at the left side of the Insert Hyperlink dialog box. As Figure 31-10 shows, the dialog box then changes to reveal a pair of option buttons. With one, you create the file immediately; with the other, you create the file the first time you click the hyperlink.

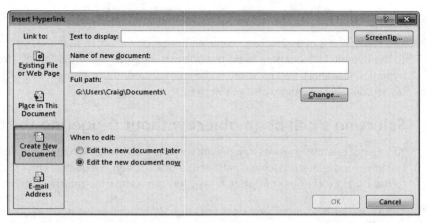

Figure 31-10 You can link to a file that doesn't yet exist and create it either immediately or the first time you click the hyperlink.

Linking to an email message

By clicking the E-Mail Address button in the navigation bar at the left side of the Insert Hyperlink dialog box, you can create a hyperlink that opens your email program and fills out a new message. Figure 31-11 shows how the Insert Hyperlink dialog box appears after you click E-Mail Address. If you use this feature occasionally, the Recently Used E-Mail Addresses portion of the dialog box will list previous addresses, and you can resend to a former recipient by selecting from the list. If the address you want isn't there, you have to type it in the E-Mail Address box; Excel won't open your Contacts folder for you.

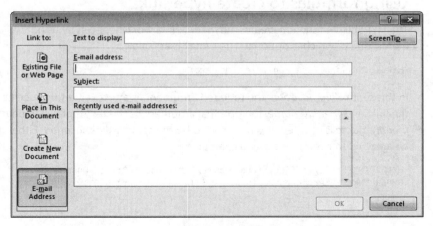

Figure 31-11 You can use this form of the Insert Hyperlink dialog box to create a mailto: link.

Assigning a hyperlink to a shape, image, or chart

You can assign a hyperlink to a shape, an image, or a chart so that clicking the object jumps to the hyperlinked location. To do this, select the object, and press Ctrl+K. (To assign a hyperlink to a chart, you must select the chart area, and the easiest way to do this is to click just inside the outer perimeter of the chart.)

Selecting a cell or an object without triggering the hyperlink

To select a cell that contains a hyperlink without activating the hyperlink, click the cell and hold the mouse button down a half second or so. When the pointer changes from a hand to the usual Excel pointer (a white cross), you can release the mouse button.

This click-and-hold procedure does not work for hyperlinks assigned to graphic objects or charts. To select one of these without zooming off to the link target, hold down the Ctrl key while you click.

Editing or deleting a hyperlink

If you right-click a cell containing a hyperlink, the shortcut menu that appears includes both an Edit Hyperlink command and a Remove Hyperlink command. If you right-click a graphic object or chart that has a hyperlink attached, typically you'll see no such thing. To edit or delete a hyperlink in this case, press Ctrl, select the object in question and then press Ctrl+K. This keyboard shortcut takes you to the Edit Hyperlink dialog box, which includes a handy Remove Link button (only if a link is present). Click the button, and the link is gone.

Using formulas to create hyperlinks

The HYPERLINK function creates a hyperlink in a worksheet cell by using two text arguments, one of which is optional. The syntax is as follows:

```
=HYPERLINK(link_location,friendly_name)
```

In this syntax, *link_location*, the required argument, is a text value that specifies the target of the link, and *friendly_name*, the optional argument, is the text that will appear in the cell. If *friendly_name* is omitted, it is assumed to be the same as *link_location*. Either argument can be a cell reference. Here are two examples:

```
=HYPERLINK(http://office.microsoft.com,"Microsoft Office Online")
=HYPERLINK("\\Cervantes\Rocinante\myfile.xlsx\Sheet2!B29")
```

The first example displays the text *Microsoft Office Online* as a hyperlink that connects to *http://office.microsoft.com*. Note that you must include the *http://* prefix in *the link_location* argument. The second example creates a hyperlink that takes you to cell B29 on Sheet2 of Myfile.xlsx, stored on the Rocinante share on the server named Cervantes.

INSIDE OUT   Create dynamic links with the HYPERLINK function

The most likely use for the HYPERLINK function is to construct a link target from text in another cell. For example, if you want a set of links to jump to different servers at different times, you could type the current server name in a cell and then build HYPER-LINK formulas with absolute references to that cell. By changing the cell contents, you could then update all the HYPERLINK formulas at once.

Using Excel data in Word documents

TS MANY presentation features notwithstanding, Microsoft Excel 2013 is at heart an analytical tool. When it comes time to organize Excel data and present it in the context of a larger textual report, you need another Microsoft Office 2013 stalwart—Microsoft Word 2013. Naturally, Word is designed to work hand-in-hand with Excel, so you can easily do your analysis in Excel and transfer the results to Word when you need to incorporate tables and charts into a report.

In this chapter, we survey the few points you need to know when incorporating Excel tables and charts into Word. You'll also see how you can use contact lists stored in Excel to generate form letters, mailing labels, and envelopes in Word.

Using Excel tables in Word documents

You can create tables directly in Word, of course, but if your tables consist of more than a few rows or columns, you'll probably find it simpler to build them in Excel and then transfer them to your Word documents. You can use either of the following methods to move a worksheet range from Excel into Word:

- Copy the Excel data to the Clipboard, and then use Paste or Paste Special in Word to paste the table in the format of your choice, with or without a link to the source data.

- On the Insert tab in Word, click Object. The Object command in Word works just like its counterpart in Excel. (See "Embedding and linking with the Object command" in Chapter 31, "Linking, hyperlinking, and embedding.")

Pasting an Excel table from the Clipboard

If you copy an Excel worksheet range to the Clipboard and then paste that range into Word (using either the Paste command or its keyboard shortcut, Ctrl+V), the options menu that appears below the lower-right corner of the pasted data, shown in Figure 32-1, provides quick access to the formatting options you're most likely to want. These options are as follows:

- **Keep Source Formatting**   Word receives the data as a block of HTML and creates a table, preserving the fonts, alignment properties, numeric formatting, text color, and shading of your original. In most but not all cases, this option (the default) is an adequate way to create a table in Word that matches the appearance of your Excel data. After you perform the paste, if you click the pasted data, a Table Tools tab appears on the ribbon in Word, and you can use commands on the Design and Layout tabs to alter the appearance of the table in Word.

- **Use Destination Styles**   The data becomes a table in Word, but Word formats it as if you created the table directly in Word.

- **Link & Keep Source Formatting**   Same as Keep Source Formatting but adds a link.

- **Link & Use Destination Styles**   Same as Use Destination Styles but adds a link.

- **Picture**   Word turns the pasted table into a picture and makes picture-formatting functionality available. You might choose this format if you want to add some pizzazz to your numbers—for example, shadows, reflections, borders with rounded corners, and so on.

- **Keep Text Only**   If you select this option, Word does not create a table. Instead, it simply pastes each cell's contents in the current default font, separating cells with single tab characters. You might find this option useful if you're simply copying a single column from Excel. Where multiple columns are involved, the Keep Text Only choice sometimes produces a misaligned hash in Word.

The options menu provides two Link commands to link your Word table (in either Excel format or Word format) to its source in Excel. These are equivalent to selecting Paste Special and selecting the Paste Link option. We discuss these options later in this chapter. (See "Paste-linking an Excel table into Word.")

CAUTION

Don't close your Excel document before pasting. If you copy data from Excel to the Clipboard and then close the Excel document, your options for pasting into Word are considerably diminished. The default paste format changes from HTML to rich-text format (RTF), and the options to link your Word document to its source in Excel disappear.

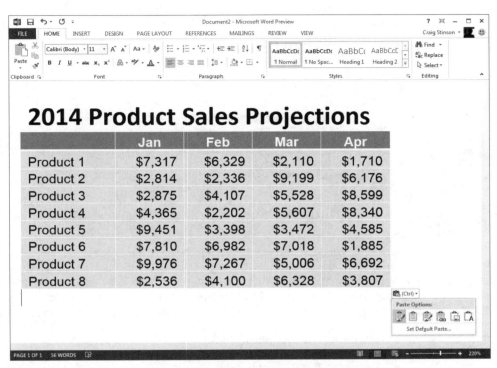

Figure 32-1 Immediately after you paste Excel cells into Word, an options menu gives you access to the formatting options you're most likely to need.

Using Paste Special to control the format of your table

The options menu that appears when you paste Excel data includes only the most commonly used formatting options. These will probably meet your needs in most cases. However, you sometimes might find the HTML badly rendered in Word. This has been known to happen, for example, when pasting from documents in older Excel file formats, but most of these problems appear to have been solved in later versions. If your Excel table (or any other pasted data) does arrive with formatting distortions in Word, all is not lost. Erase the pasted data in Word, and then try again using the Paste Special command in Word. (On the Home tab in Word, click the small arrow below Paste, and then click Paste Special.) Figure 32-2 shows the Paste Special dialog box as it appears when your Excel document is still open. (If you close the Excel document, fewer options are available.)

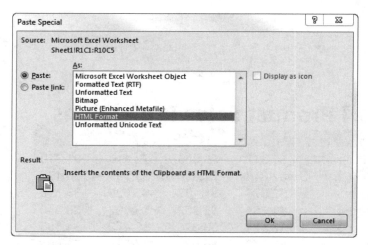

Figure 32-2 Word can paste an Excel range in any of these formats.

With almost any of the formats displayed in the Paste Special dialog box, you can either paste or paste-link. We'll look at the latter operation later in this chapter. (See "Paste-linking an Excel table into Word.") First, we'll describe the available paste formats:

- Microsoft Excel Worksheet Object

- Formatted Text (RTF) and HTML Format

- Unformatted Text and Unformatted Unicode Text

- Bitmap and Picture (Enhanced Metafile)

Using the Microsoft Excel Worksheet Object format

Pasting using the Worksheet Object format provides a completely faithful replication of the appearance of your Excel table—including any graphical elements that happened to be within your Excel selection. It also lets you edit the pasted table using Excel commands and features rather than Word ones. For example, if you want to apply a custom numeric format to your data after pasting it as an object into Word, you can do that by double-clicking the object. When you do this, the user interface of Word temporarily merges with Excel, as shown in Figure 32-3. After you edit the object and click any other part of the Word document, the Excel ribbon is replaced by the Word ribbon, and the worksheet column and row headings disappear.

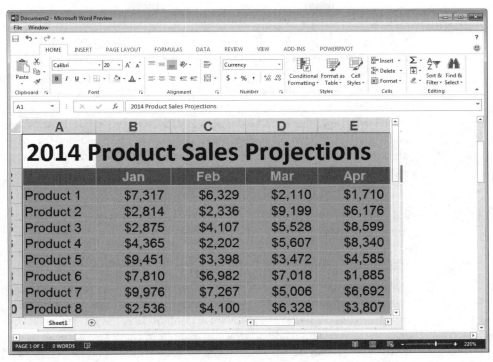

Figure 32-3 When you double-click an embedded Excel object, the Word ribbon is temporarily replaced by the Excel ribbon, letting you use Excel formatting and editing features to modify the object.

> **Note**
>
> **When you double-click an embedded Excel object that includes graphical elements, Word might truncate those elements temporarily. When you return to the regular Word interface, however, Word will fully restore your graphical elements.**

An important peculiarity to note about Excel objects embedded in Word documents is that Excel embeds the entire workbook, not only the selection you copied to the Clipboard. The sheet tab at the bottom of the Excel object shown in Figure 32-3 illustrates this point. Although the editing window that appears in Word when you double-click the Excel object has the same dimensions as the original selection in Excel, you can scroll to any part of the current worksheet and even switch to another worksheet in the same workbook. When you return to Word (by clicking away from the embedded object), Word treats any scrolling you do as an edit to the embedded object. If you switch from Sheet1 to Sheet2 while you're editing, you'll see Sheet2 when you return to your Word document.

Using RTF and HTML formats

The RTF and HTML formats preserve the font and numeric formatting of your Excel selection. They differ in the way they preserve that formatting. RTF (Rich Text Format) is a method of encoding formatting information that has been available for a long time in Microsoft Office and other kinds of documents. HTML (HyperText Markup Language) is the newer, default format for pasting into Word (the format you get if you press Ctrl+V), and it's the language that renders webpages in your browser. Both formats generate tables in Word, maintaining the cell alignment you had in Excel and allowing for manipulation via the Table commands in Word. Neither format includes graphical elements that are part of your Excel selection.

HTML is more likely than RTF to render the formatting of your Excel selection accurately. But you might want to experiment to see which format suits your purposes more effectively. If you don't like the results you get, undo it and try again with a different format.

Using Unformatted Text and Unformatted Unicode Text

Use Unformatted Text and Unformatted Unicode Text when you do not want your Clipboard data to become a table in Word. Both formats transfer data from the Clipboard as though you had typed it in your Word document. They use tab characters between the columns of your original Excel selection and return characters at the ends of lines. Ordinarily, the result is that data that was aligned neatly in Excel is no longer aligned in Word. Use the Unicode format if your data includes characters outside the regular ANSI range—for example, characters from non-Latin alphabets. Otherwise, it doesn't matter which of these two formats you use.

Using Bitmap and Picture (Enhanced Metafile)

The Bitmap and Picture (Enhanced Metafile) formats produce more or less faithful graphical representations of your original Excel selection (including any graphical elements associated with it). Because the results are pictures, not tables, you can modify them with the picture-formatting features in Word.

Of the available picture formats, Bitmap usually provides the most faithful replication of original appearances—at the cost of additional file size. Experiment to see which works best for you.

Paste-linking an Excel table into Word

You can paste-link any of the formats shown in Figure 32-2 and described in the preceding sections by selecting Paste Link in the Paste Special dialog box. When you do this, Word creates a field that references the source of your Excel data. The field is a code (comparable to an external-reference formula in Excel) that tells the application how to update the data if you request a manual update. The code also tells the application how to locate the data for editing if you double-click the linked information in your Word document. You can see the code by clicking the File tab in Word, clicking Options, selecting the Advanced category, and then selecting the Show Field Codes Instead Of Their Values check box, located in the Show Document Content section. Figure 32-4 shows the cryptic result, which you probably don't want to leave like this in your Word document.

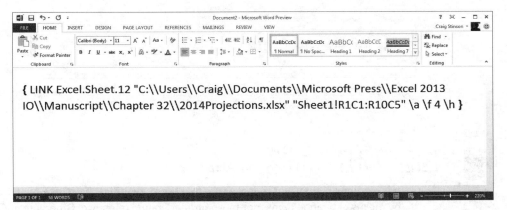

Figure 32-4 The Show Field Codes Instead Of Their Values option hides the objects while revealing the underlying links.

Links from Excel into Word are automatic by default, which means that anytime the Excel source is changed, the Word document is automatically adjusted. You can switch to manual linking by going to the Links dialog box shown in Figure 32-5. To get there, right-click the Excel table in the Word document, click Linked Worksheet Object, and then click Links.

If you're using manual updating, you can also force an update by clicking Update Now in the Links dialog box. A simpler way to update your table is to select it and press F9.

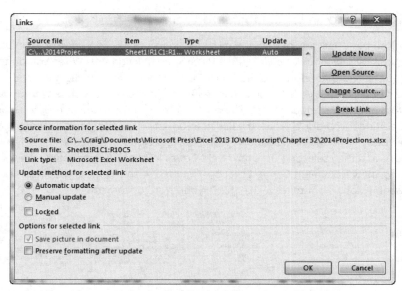

Figure 32-5 In the Links dialog box in Word, you can switch between manual and automatic updating, modify the link specifications, or break the connection.

INSIDE OUT   Link to named ranges

It is extremely important to make sure that Word identifies the source of an Excel link by means of a range name, not by an ordinary range reference. Otherwise, if the source table changes location for any reason (for example, if someone inserts or deletes a few rows), the link will no longer reference the original table. At best, you'll have a blank table in your Word document. At worst, you'll have the wrong table.

If the worksheet range has a name at the time you copy it to the Clipboard, Word will reference it by name when you perform your paste-link. If the worksheet range is not named, Word will reference it by cell address using R1C1 notation. If you subsequently assign a name to the range in Excel and perform a manual update, Word will continue to reference it by address, not by name. If you inadvertently linked to a range address instead of a range name, the simplest way to fix the problem is to remove the linked data, be sure the source range is named, and then re-create the link.

Linking with hyperlinks

An alternative way to create a link between a Word document and an Excel document is to use a hyperlink. With an Excel range on the Clipboard, you can click the Home tab in Word, click the arrow below the Paste command, and then click Paste Special. The Paste Special dialog box displays the usual list of formats, but the Word Hyperlink option appears only if you select the Paste Link option, as Figure 32-6 shows.

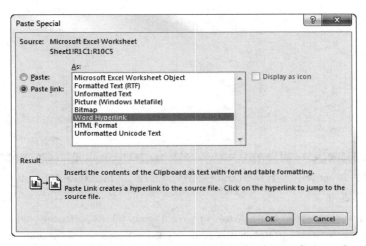

Figure 32-6 Word Hyperlink appears as an option in Word's Paste Special dialog box only if you select the Paste Link option.

After you paste in Word Hyperlink format, every character in the pasted range is underlined like a hyperlink; Ctrl+click any part of it to take you to the source data. The principal disadvantage of using hyperlinks instead of paste-linking is that hyperlinks don't get updated when the source changes. A hyperlink can make it easy for you or another user to find your way back to the data source, but it provides no assurance that your Word document is faithful to the source.

Using the Object command

The Clipboard methods just described are fine for importing existing Excel tables into Word documents. If you're creating a table from scratch, you have the option of using an alternative method—by clicking the Object command on the Insert tab in Word. When you do this, the Object dialog box appears. On the Create New tab, select Microsoft Excel Worksheet (you might need to scroll down the list a bit) and then click OK. Word displays a window into a blank Excel worksheet, as Figure 32-7 shows.

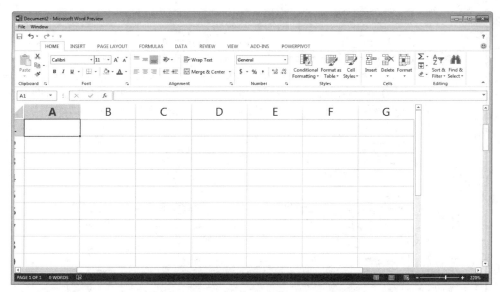

Figure 32-7 When you select Microsoft Excel Worksheet on the Create New tab in the Object dialog box in Word, a window into Excel appears in your Word document.

Here you can create your table by taking advantage of all the formatting and calculation tools in Excel. When your table is ready for inclusion in your Word document, click outside the Excel window. The result is an Excel object embedded in your Word file—exactly what you get if you create the table initially in Excel, copy it to the Clipboard, and then choose Microsoft Excel Worksheet Object from the Paste Special dialog box in Word.

INSIDE OUT Resizing the embedded object

The table that Word embeds using the Object command has the same row and column dimensions as the Excel window in which you create the table. That is, empty cells are embedded along with populated ones. If you have to scroll to populate certain cells, some of your Excel table will not be embedded. You might need to adjust the size of the Excel window so that it includes all the rows and columns you want to see in Word. As long as the Excel window is active (you can still see the Excel ribbon commands), dragging the handles of the embedded object resizes the worksheet object, increasing or decreasing the number of rows and columns visible. However, if you drag the object handles when Excel controls are not visible (you are back to editing in Word), dragging the handles stretches or shrinks the size of the image rather than adding or subtracting rows and columns.

Using Excel charts in Word documents

To create a quick chart from scratch in Word, click Chart in the Illustrations group on the Insert tab on the ribbon. All 2007, 2010, and 2013 Office applications share a common charting engine, so—provided you're working with a recent Word document format (as opposed to a Word 97–2003 document)—you're greeted by the same Insert Chart dialog box you see in Excel, as shown in Figure 32-8.

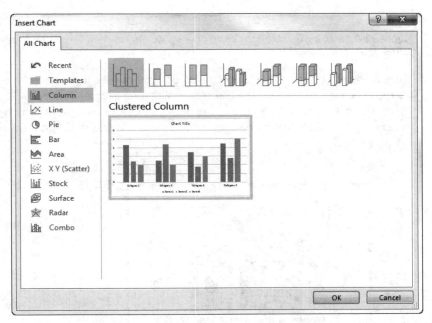

Figure 32-8 The Chart button on Word's Insert tab displays the same interface used in Excel and other Office applications.

After you select a chart type from this gallery and click OK, Excel creates a worksheet titled Chart In Microsoft Word containing dummy data values for your chart, as shown in Figure 32-9. Edit the values in the worksheet, and then close the worksheet window. Your chart now appears in your Word document.

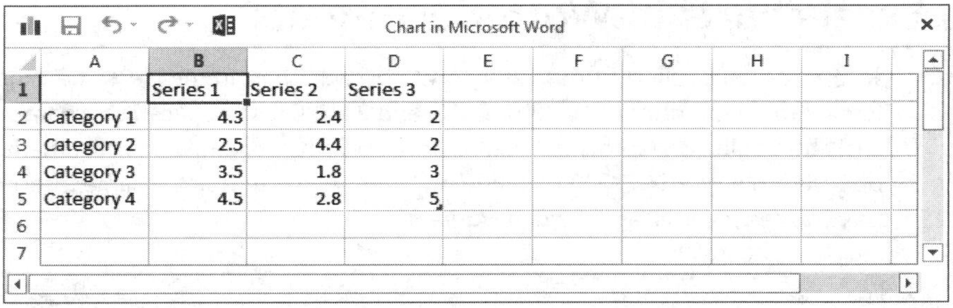

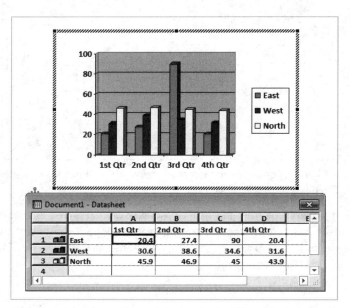

| ⏹ 🔲 ↶ ⤷ ⬛ | | Chart in Microsoft Word | | | | | | | ✕ |

◢	A	B	C	D	E	F	G	H	I
1		Series 1	Series 2	Series 3					
2	Category 1	4.3	2.4	2					
3	Category 2	2.5	4.4	2					
4	Category 3	3.5	1.8	3					
5	Category 4	4.5	2.8	5					
6									
7									

Figure 32-9 Inserting a chart from Word opens a dummy table in Excel used to specify the values you want to display.

There is another option in the Object dialog box you can use to create a chart in Word: Microsoft Graph Chart. This is the charting engine used in older versions of Microsoft Office, and it does not offer all the added benefits of the latest Office charting engine. Instead, the Microsoft Graph Chart option summons a Microsoft Graph window, as shown in Figure 32-10.

Figure 32-10 Microsoft Graph is the classic Office charting engine.

Microsoft Graph is a more awkward environment for creating a chart, and we don't recommend it. Instead of using Microsoft Graph, you're better off creating a chart in Excel and then transferring it to your Word document via the Clipboard.

If you paste an Excel chart into a Word 2013 document, the chart arrives (by default) as a chart, not a picture, and because Excel 2013 and Word 2013 use a common charting engine, all the formatting tools available to you in Excel are also available in Word. With the chart selected in your Word document, two new tabs—Design and Format—appear on the ribbon under Chart Tools, as shown in Figure 32-11. Using these tabs, you can work with the chart in Word exactly as you would in Excel. The chart, by default, will be linked to its source data. With the chart selected, the Design tab includes an Edit Data command and a Refresh Data command. You can use these to return to and modify the source or to per-form a manual update, ensuring that your chart reflects the current numbers in Excel.

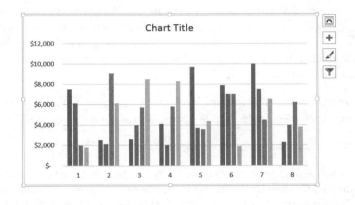

Figure 32-11 Two Chart Tools tabs appear in Word when an embedded chart is selected.

If you prefer, you can paste the chart as a picture by using the Picture command on the options menu that appears right after you paste. If you do this, your chart is no longer linked to the source, but you have the Word picture-formatting tools available for adding shadows, borders, and other visual effects.

Using Excel to supply mail-merge data to Word

Microsoft Word includes a mail-merge feature that facilitates the batch creation of letters, email messages, envelopes, mailing labels, and directories. You can use Excel ranges (as well as many other types of data sources) to supply names, addresses, phone numbers, and other information for mail-merge use.

Before you merge data from Excel into the mail-merge feature in Word, be sure your Excel worksheet is well structured for this purpose. Your table should meet the following criteria:

- Each cell in the first row should be a field name, such as Title, Salutation, First Name, Middle Name, Last Name, Address, and so on.

- Each field name should be unique.

- Every piece of information that you want to manipulate separately in your merge document should be recorded in a separate field. In a form letter, for example, you probably want to work with first and last names separately so that you can use both of them in an address block but then use the last name only (with a salutation or title) at the beginning of the letter. Therefore, your Excel table should have separate fields for first and last names.

- Each row should provide information about a particular item. In a mailing list, for example, each row should include information about a particular recipient.

- Your table should have no blank rows.

See "Practical text manipulation" in Chapter 14, "Everyday functions," for a trick you can use to parse combined first and last names into separate cells. "Practical concatenation" in Chapter 12, Building formulas," shows the opposite trick: combining names stored in separate cells into a single cell.

To use the mail-merge feature, follow these steps:

1. On the Mailings tab in Word, click the Start Mail Merge command, and then click Step By Step Mail Merge Wizard.

2. The Mail Merge task pane appears and consists of six steps. If you're going to create a mail-merge letter or email message, the third step is the one that involves Excel. When you get there, the Mail Merge task pane will look like the one shown in Figure 32-12.

Figure 32-12 The Step By Step Mail Merge Wizard command in Word displays the Mail Merge task pane to guide you through the process.

3. To use an Excel table as your data source, select Use An Existing List. Then click Browse. When you browse to your Excel file and click Open, the Select Table dialog box that appears (shown in Figure 32-13) displays an entry for each worksheet. Specify the worksheet that contains the records you want to merge, and then click OK.

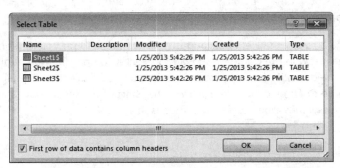

Figure 32-13 In the Select Table dialog box, select the worksheet that contains the records you want to merge.

4. The Mail Merge Recipients dialog box appears (shown in Figure 32-14), letting you sort and filter the data source. Initially, the check box to the left of each record is selected, which means all records will be included in your merge. To remove particular items, clear their check boxes.

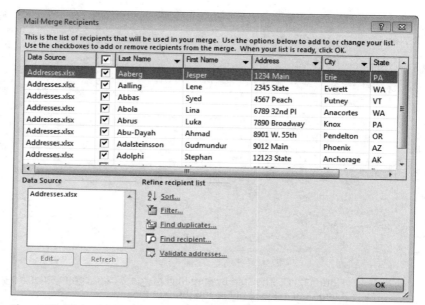

Figure 32-14 In the Mail Merge Recipients dialog box, you can filter and sort the data source.

5. You can use the arrows to the right of each field name for easy filtering. These function like their counterparts in an Excel table. For formulaic filtering—for example, to restrict the list to ZIP codes greater than 90000—click the arrow next to any field (it doesn't matter which), click Advanced, and then fill out the Filter And Sort dialog box shown in Figure 32-15.

Click the arrow in the Field box, and then select the field for your filtering criterion. Next, click the arrow in the Comparison field to select a comparison operation, and in the Compare To field specify a comparison value. If you need more than one filtering criterion, select And or Or by clicking the arrow at the start of the second line and then continue with more field names, operators, and comparison values.

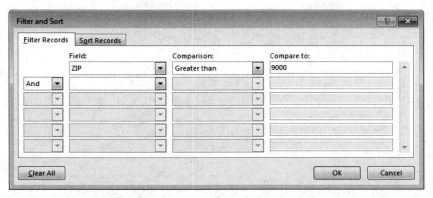

Figure 32-15 We used the Filter And Sort dialog box to limit our list to ZIP codes that start with 9.

You can use the Sort Records tab to change the order in which your data will be fed to the mail-merge mechanism. If you're sorting by one field only, however, you'll find it simpler to click the field heading in the Mail Merge Recipients dialog box (shown in Figure 32-14). Click a heading to generate an ascending sort by that heading; a second click turns it into a descending sort.

When you have your data as you want it, click OK to return to the Mail Merge task pane. In the remaining steps, you can create your merge document (the document that uses your data records), preview the results, and then carry out the merge.

Chapter 32

Appendixes

Menu-to-ribbon command reference

THIS APPENDIX lists the menu commands and major toolbar buttons from Microsoft Excel 2003 and shows you where to find the equivalent functionality in Microsoft Excel 2013. In most cases, Microsoft has relocated commands to the ribbon. In other cases, Excel 2013 has new and better features that replace old functionality using new nomenclature and renamed or repositioned commands. Also, Microsoft has removed a few Excel 2003 commands from Excel 2013. We organized this appendix to reflect the Excel 2003 menu structure, including buttons from the Standard and Formatting toolbars, which are usually displayed in Excel 2003.

Excel 2003 File menu

Excel 2003 File menu command	Excel 2013 location and command
File menu	File tab
New	File tab, New
Open	File tab, Open
Close	File tab, Close
Save	File, Save (also, Quick Access Toolbar, Save button)
Save As	File tab, Save As
Save As Web Page	File tab, Save As, Browse, Save As Type: Web Page
Save Workspace	Removed in 2013
File Search	Removed in 2010
Permission, Unrestricted Access	Review tab, Changes group, Protect Workbook command; clear the Structure and Windows check boxes under Protect Workbook For

Excel 2003 File menu command	Excel 2013 location and command
Permission, Do Not Distribute	Removed in 2010
Permission, Restrict Permission As	Review tab, Changes group, Track Changes, Highlight Changes; then specify Who, When, and Where
Check Out	Removed in 2010
Check In	Removed in 2010
Version History	File tab, Info, Manage Versions
Web Page Preview	Removed in 2010
Page Setup	Page Layout tab, Page Setup group, Page Setup dialog box launcher
Print Area, Set Print Area	Page Layout tab, Page Setup group, Print Area command, Set Print Area command
Print Area, Clear Print Area	Page Layout tab, Page Setup group, Print Area command, Clear Print Area command
Print Preview	File tab, Print
Print	File tab, Print, Print button
Send To, Mail Recipient	File tab, Share, Email
Send To, Original Sender	Removed in 2010
Send To, Mail Recipient (For Review)	You must add a button to the ribbon or the Quick Access Toolbar for this command: File tab, Options, Customize Ribbon or Quick Access Toolbar, All Commands, Send For Review
Send To, Mail Recipient (As Attachment)	File tab, Share, Email, Send As Attachment
Send To, Routing Recipient	Removed in 2010
Send To, Exchange Folder	Removed in 2010
Send To, Online Meeting Participant	Removed in 2010
Send To, Recipient Using Internet Fax Service	File tab, Share, Email, Send As Internet Fax
Properties	File tab, Info
Most Recently Used Documents	File tab, Open
Exit	Removed (click the Window Close button in the upper-right corner of the Excel window)
Sign Out	Removed in 2010

Excel 2003 Edit menu

Excel 2003 Edit menu command	Excel 2013 location and command
Undo	Quick Access Toolbar, Undo
Redo	Quick Access Toolbar, Redo
Cut	Home tab, Clipboard group, Cut
Copy	Home tab, Clipboard group, Copy
Office Clipboard	Home tab, Clipboard group, Clipboard dialog box launcher
Paste	Home tab, Clipboard group, Paste button
Paste Special	Home tab, Clipboard group, Paste button menu, Paste Special
Paste As Hyperlink	Home tab, Clipboard group, Paste button menu, Paste Link
Fill, Down	Home tab, Editing group, Fill, Down
Fill, Right	Home tab, Editing group, Fill, Right
Fill, Up	Home tab, Editing group, Fill, Up
Fill, Left	Home tab, Editing group, Fill, Left
Fill, Across Worksheets	Home tab, Editing group, Fill, Across Worksheets
Fill, Series	Home tab, Editing group, Fill, Series
Fill, Justify	Home tab, Editing group, Fill, Justify
Clear, All	Home tab, Editing group, Clear, Clear All
Clear, Formats	Home tab, Editing group, Clear, Clear Formats
Clear, Contents	Home tab, Editing group, Clear, Clear Contents
Clear, Comments	Home tab, Editing group, Clear, Clear Comments
Delete	Home tab, Cells group, Delete button
Delete Sheet	Home tab, Cells group, Delete button menu, Delete Sheet command
Move Or Copy Sheet	Home tab, Cells group, Format, Move Or Copy Sheet
Find	Home tab, Editing group, Find & Select, Find
Replace	Home tab, Editing group, Find & Select, Replace
Go To	Home tab, Editing group, Find & Select, Go To
Links	Data tab, Connections group, Edit Links
Object	Select an object to see its associated drawing tools
Clear, Series	Removed in 2010

Excel 2003 View menu

Excel 2003 View menu command	Excel 2013 location and command
Normal	View tab, Workbook Views group, Normal
Page Break Preview	View tab, Workbook Views group, Page Break Preview
Task Pane	In some ribbon groups, dialog box launchers display a task pane instead of a dialog box—for example, Home tab, Clipboard group, Clipboard dialog box launcher.
Toolbars, Standard	The commands from the Standard toolbar are now available on the Home tab and the File tab.
Toolbars, Formatting	The commands from the Formatting toolbar are on the Home tab.
Toolbars, Borders	The commands from the Borders toolbar are on the Home tab, Font group, Borders command.
Toolbars, Chart	The commands from the Chart toolbar are available on the Chart Tools tabs when you insert or select a chart.
Toolbars, Control Toolbox	The commands from the Control Toolbox are on the Developer tab. To display the Developer tab, click the File tab, click Options, click Customize Ribbon, and select the Developer check box in the Customize The Ribbon list.
Toolbars, Drawing	The commands from the Drawing toolbar are available on the Drawing Tools tabs when you select or insert a shape.
Toolbars, External Data	The commands from the External Data toolbar are on the Data tab.
Toolbars, Forms	The commands from the Forms toolbar are available on the Developer tab. To display the Developer tab, click the File tab, click Options, click Customize Ribbon, and select the Developer check box in the Customize The Ribbon list.
Toolbars, Formula Auditing	The commands from the Formula Auditing toolbar are on the Formulas tab, Formula Auditing group.
Toolbars, List	The majority of these commands are available on the Table Tools tabs when you select a cell in an Excel table.
Toolbars, Picture	The commands from the Picture toolbar are available on the Picture Tools tabs when you insert or select a picture.
Toolbars, PivotTable	The commands from the PivotTable toolbar are available on the PivotTable Tools tabs when you insert or select a cell in a PivotTable.
Toolbars, Protection	The commands from the Protection toolbar are available on the Review tab, Changes group.
Toolbars, Reviewing	The commands from the Reviewing toolbar are available on the Review tab.

Excel 2003 View menu command	Excel 2013 location and command
Toolbars, Task Pane	In some groups, dialog box launchers display a task pane instead of a dialog box—for example, Home tab, Clipboard group, dialog box launcher.
Toolbars, Text To Speech	Removed in 2010
Toolbars, Visual Basic	The commands from the Microsoft Visual Basic toolbar are available on the Developer tab. To display the Developer tab, click the File tab, click Options, click Customize Ribbon, and then select the Developer check box in the Customize The Ribbon list.
Toolbars, Watch Window	The commands from the Watch Window toolbar are available on the Formulas tab, Formula Auditing group, Watch Window.
Toolbars, Web	Some of the commands from the Web toolbar are available in the Options dialog box. Click the File tab, click Options, select the Customize category, and click All Commands in the Choose Commands From list.
Toolbars, WordArt	The commands from the WordArt toolbar are available on the Drawing Tools tabs when you insert or select WordArt.
Toolbars, Customize	Click the File tab, click Options, and then select the Customize Ribbon or Quick Access Toolbar category.
Formula Bar	View tab, Show group, and select the Formula Bar check box
Status Bar	Removed in 2010. The status bar is always visible.
Header And Footer	Insert tab, Text group, Header & Footer
Comments	Review tab, Comments group, Show All Comments
Custom Views	View tab, Workbook Views group, Custom Views
Full Screen	Click the Ribbon Display Options button in the upper-right corner of the Excel window and click Auto-Hide the Ribbon
Zoom	View tab, Zoom group, Zoom
Sized With Window	Removed in 2010
Chart Window	Removed in 2010

Appendix A

Excel 2003 Insert menu

Excel 2003 Insert menu command	Excel 2013 location and command
Menu	Home tab, Cells group, Insert button menu
Rows	Home tab, Cells group, Insert button menu, Insert Sheet Rows
Columns	Home tab, Cells group, Insert button menu, Insert Sheet Columns
Worksheet	Home tab, Cells group, Insert button menu, Insert Sheet
Chart	Insert tab, Charts group
Symbol	Insert tab, Symbols group, Symbol
Page Break	Page Layout tab, Page Setup group, Breaks, Insert Page Break
Reset All Page Breaks	Page Layout tab, Page Setup group, Breaks, Reset All Page Breaks
Function	Formulas tab, Function Library group, Insert Function
Name, Define	Formulas tab, Defined Names group, Name Manager
Name, Paste	Formulas tab, Defined Names group, Use In Formula, Paste Names
Name, Create	Formulas tab, Defined Names group, Create From Selection
Name, Apply	Formulas tab, Defined Names group, Define Name, Apply Names
Name, Label	Formulas tab, Defined Names group, Define Name
Comment	Review tab, Comments group, New Comment
Ink Annotations	Review tab, Ink, Show Ink
Picture, Clip Art	Insert tab, Illustrations group, Online Pictures, Office.com Clip Art
Picture, From File	Insert tab, Illustrations group, Picture
Picture, From Scanner Or Camera	Removed in 2010
Picture, Ink Drawing And Writing	Removed in 2013
Picture, AutoShapes	Insert tab, Illustrations group, Shapes
Picture, WordArt	Insert tab, Text group, WordArt
Picture, Organization Chart	Insert tab, Illustrations group, SmartArt
Diagram	Insert tab, Illustrations group, SmartArt
Object	Insert tab, Text group, Object
Hyperlink	Insert tab, Links group, Hyperlink

Excel 2003 Format menu

Excel 2003 Format menu command	Excel 2013 location and command
Cells	Home tab, Cells group, Format, Format Cells
Row, Height	Home tab, Cells group, Format, Row Height
Row, AutoFit	Home tab, Cells group, Format, AutoFit Row Height
Row, Hide	Home tab, Cells group, Format, Hide & Unhide, Hide Rows
Row, Unhide	Home tab, Cells group, Format, Hide & Unhide, Unhide Rows
Column, Width	Home tab, Cells group, Format, Column Width
Column, AutoFit Selection	Home tab, Cells group, Format, AutoFit Column Width
Column, Hide	Home tab, Cells group, Format, Hide & Unhide, Hide Columns
Column, Unhide	Home tab, Cells group, Format, Hide & Unhide, Unhide Columns
Column, Standard Width	Home tab, Cells group, Format, Default Width
Sheet, Rename	Home tab, Cells group, Format, Rename Sheet
Sheet, Hide	Home tab, Cells group, Format, Hide & Unhide, Hide Sheet
Sheet, Unhide	Home tab, Cells group, Format, Hide & Unhide, Unhide Sheet
Sheet, Background	Page Layout tab, Page Setup group, Background
Sheet, Tab Color	Home tab, Cells group, Format, Tab Color
AutoFormat	Home tab, Styles group, Format As Table
Conditional Formatting	Home tab, Styles group, Conditional Formatting
Style	Home tab, Styles group, Cell Styles

Excel 2003 Tools menu

Excel 2003 Tools menu command	Excel 2013 location and command
Spelling	Review tab, Proofing group, Spelling command
Research	Review tab, Proofing group, Research command
Error Checking	Formulas tab, Formula Auditing group, Error Checking
Speech, Show Text To Speech Toolbar	Removed in 2010
Speech	Removed in 2010

Appendix A

Excel 2003 Tools menu command	Excel 2013 location and command
Shared Workspace	Removed in 2013
Share Workbook	Review tab, Changes group, Share Workbook
Track Changes, Highlight Changes	Review tab, Changes group, Track Changes, Highlight Changes
Track Changes, Accept Or Reject Changes	Review tab, Changes group, Track Changes, Accept/Reject Changes
Compare And Merge Workbooks	You must add a button to the ribbon or the Quick Access Toolbar for this command: File tab, Options, Customize Ribbon or Quick Access Toolbar, All Commands, Compare And Merge Workbooks
Protection, Protect Sheet	Review tab, Changes group, Protect Sheet command
	Home tab, Cells group, Format command, Protect Sheet command
Protection, Allow Users To Edit Ranges	Review tab, Changes group, Allow Users To Edit Ranges
Protection, Protect Workbook	Review tab, Changes group, Protect Workbook
Protection, Protect And Share Workbook	Review tab, Changes group, Protect And Share Workbook
Online Collaboration, Meet Now	Removed in 2010
Online Collaboration, Schedule Meeting	Removed in 2010
Online Collaboration, Web Discussions	Removed in 2010
Online Collaboration, End Review	Removed in 2010
Goal Seek	Data tab, Data Tools group, What-If Analysis command, Goal Seek
Scenarios	Data tab, Data Tools group, What-If Analysis command, Scenario Manager
Formula Auditing, Trace Precedents	Formulas tab, Formula Auditing group, Trace Precedents
Formula Auditing, Trace Dependents	Formulas tab, Formula Auditing group, Trace Dependents
Formula Auditing, Trace Error	Formulas tab, Formula Auditing group, Error Checking, Trace Error
Formula Auditing, Remove All Arrows	Formulas tab, Formula Auditing group, Remove Arrows
Formula Auditing, Evaluate Formula	Formulas tab, Formula Auditing group, Evaluate Formula
Formula Auditing, Hide Watch Window	Formulas tab, Formula Auditing group, Watch Window

Excel 2003 Tools menu command	Excel 2013 location and command
Formula Auditing, Formula Auditing Mode	Formulas tab, Formula Auditing group, Show Formulas
Formula Auditing, Show Formula Auditing Toolbar	Formulas tab, Formula Auditing group
Macro, Macros	Developer tab, Code group, Macros command
	View tab, Macros group, Macros command
Macro, Record New Macro	Developer tab, Code group, Record Macro command
	View tab, Macros group, Macros, Record Macro
Macro, Security	Developer tab, Code group, Macro Security
Macro, Visual Basic Editor	Developer tab, Code group, Visual Basic
Macro, Microsoft Script Editor	Removed in 2010
Add-Ins	File tab, Options, Add-Ins category
AutoCorrect Options	File tab, Options, Proofing category, AutoCorrect Options
Customize	File tab, Options, Customize Ribbon
Show Signatures	File tab, Info
Options	File tab, Options

Excel 2003 Data menu

Excel 2003 Data menu command	Excel 2013 location and command
Sort	Data tab, Sort & Filter group, Sort
Filter	Data tab, Sort & Filter group, Filter
Filter, AutoFilter	Home tab, Editing group, Sort & Filter, Filter
Filter, Show All	Data tab, Sort & Filter group, Clear
	Home tab, Editing group, Sort & Filter, Clear
Filter, Advanced Filter	Data tab, Sort & Filter group, Advanced
Form	You must add a button to the ribbon or the Quick Access Toolbar for this command: File tab, Options, Customize Ribbon or Quick Access Toolbar, All Commands, Form
Subtotals	Data tab, Outline group, Subtotal
Validation	Data tab, Data Tools group, Data Validation
Table	Data tab, Data Tools group, What-If Analysis, Data Table
Text To Columns	Data tab, Data Tools group, Text To Columns
Consolidate	Data tab, Data Tools group, Consolidate

Excel 2003 Data menu command	Excel 2013 location and command
Group And Outline, Hide Detail	Data tab, Outline group, Hide Detail
Group And Outline, Show Detail	Data tab, Outline group, Show Detail
Group And Outline, Group	Data tab, Outline group, Group
	PivotTable Tools Options tab, Group
Group And Outline, Ungroup	Data tab, Outline group, Ungroup
	PivotTable Tools Options tab, Group, Ungroup
Group And Outline, Auto Outline	Data tab, Outline group, Group button menu, Auto Outline
Group And Outline, Clear Outline	Data tab, Outline group, Ungroup button menu, Clear Outline
Group And Outline, Settings	Data tab, Outline group, dialog box launcher
PivotTable And PivotChart Report	Insert tab, Tables group, PivotTable
Import External Data, Import Data	Data tab, Get External Data group
Import External Data, New Web Query	Data tab, Get External Data group, From Web
Import External Data, New Database Query	Data tab, Get External Data group, From Other Sources, From Microsoft Query
Import External Data, Edit Query	You must add a button to the ribbon or the Quick Access Toolbar for this command: File tab, Options, Customize Ribbon or Quick Access Toolbar, All Commands, Edit Query
Import External Data, Data Range Properties	Data tab, Connections group, Properties
	Table Tools Design tab, External Table Data, Properties
Import External Data, Parameters	You must add a button to the ribbon or the Quick Access Toolbar for this command: File tab, Options, Customize Ribbon or Quick Access Toolbar, All Commands, Parameters
List, Create List	Insert tab, Tables group, Table
List, Resize List	Table Tools Design tab, Properties, Resize Table
List, Total Row	Table Tools Design tab, Table Style Options group, Total Row check box
List, Convert To Range	Table Tools Design tab, Tools group, Convert To Range
List, Publish List	Table Tools Design tab, External Table Data group, Export command, Export Table To SharePoint List
List, View List On Server	Table Tools Design tab, External Table Data group, Open In Browser
List, Unlink List	Table Tools Design tab, External Table Data group, Unlink

Excel 2003 Data menu command	Excel 2013 location and command
List, Synchronize List	You must add a button to the ribbon or the Quick Access Toolbar for this command: File tab, Options, Customize Ribbon or Quick Access Toolbar, All Commands, Synchronize List
List, Discard Changes And Refresh	You must add a button to the ribbon or the Quick Access Toolbar for this command: File tab, Options, Customize Ribbon or Quick Access Toolbar, All Commands, Discard Changes And Refresh
List, Hide Border Of Inactive Lists	Removed in 2010
XML, Import	Developer tab, XML group, Import
XML, Export	Developer tab, XML group, Export
XML, Refresh XML Data	Developer tab, XML group, Refresh Data
XML, XML Source	Developer tab, XML group, Source
XML, XML Map Properties	Developer tab, XML group, Map Properties
XML, Edit Query	Removed in 2010
XML, XML Expansion Packs	Developer tab, XML group, Expansion Packs
Refresh Data	PivotChart Tools Analyze tab, Data group, Refresh
	PivotTable Tools Analyze tab, Data group, Refresh
	Table Tools Design tab, External Table Data group, Refresh
	Data tab, Connections group, Refresh All

Excel 2003 Chart menu

Excel 2003 Chart menu command	Excel 2013 location and command
Chart Type	Chart Tools Design tab, Type group, Change Chart Type
Select Data	Chart Tools Design tab, Data group, Select Data
Source Data	PivotChart Tools Design tab, Data group, Select Data
Chart Options	Chart Tools Layout tab
Location	Chart Tools Design tab, Location group, Move Chart
	PivotChart Tools Design tab, Location group, Move Chart
Add Data	Chart Tools Design tab, Data group, Select Data
Add Trendline	Chart Tools Design tab, Chart Layouts group, Add Chart Element, Trendline
3-D View	Chart Tools Design tab, Change Chart Type, and then choose a 3-D chart style

Excel 2003 Window menu

Excel 2003 Window menu command	Excel 2013 location and command
New Window	View tab, Window group, New Window
Arrange All	View tab, Window group, Arrange All
Compare Side By Side With	View tab, Window group, View Side By Side
Hide	View tab, Window group, Hide
Unhide	View tab, Window group, Unhide
Split	View tab, Window group, Split
Freeze Panes	View tab, Window group, Freeze Panes
Currently Open Workbooks	View tab, Window group, Switch Windows

Excel 2003 Help menu

Excel 2003 Help menu command	Excel 2013 location and command
Menu	The Help button (?) in the upper-right corner of the Excel window
Microsoft Office Online	The Help button
Contact Us	Removed in 2013
Check For Updates	Removed in 2013
Detect And Repair	Removed in 2010
Activate Product	File tab, Account
About Microsoft Office Excel	File tab, Account
Show The Office Assistant	Removed in 2010

Excel 2003 Standard toolbar

Excel 2003 Standard toolbar command	Excel 2013 location and command
New	File tab, New, Blank Workbook
Open	File tab, Open
Save	Quick Access Toolbar, Save
	File tab, Save

Excel 2003 Standard toolbar command	Excel 2013 location and command
Permission	Review tab, Changes group, Track Changes, Highlight Changes; then select Track Changes While Editing and specify Who, When, and Where.
Email	File tab, Share, Email
Print	File tab, Print, Print
Print Preview	File tab, Print
Spelling	Review tab, Proofing group, Spelling
Research	Review tab, Proofing group, Research
Cut	Home tab, Clipboard group, Cut
Copy	Home tab, Clipboard group, Copy
Paste	Home tab, Clipboard group, Paste
Format Painter	Home tab, Clipboard group, Format Painter
Undo	Quick Access Toolbar, Undo
Redo	Quick Access Toolbar, Redo
Ink Annotations	Review tab, Show Ink
Hyperlink	Insert tab, Links group, Hyperlink
AutoSum	Home tab, Editing group, AutoSum
	Formulas tab, Function Library group, AutoSum
Sort Ascending	Data tab, Sort & Filter group, Sort A To Z
Sort Descending	Data tab, Sort & Filter group, Sort Z To A
Chart Wizard	Insert tab, Charts group; click one of the chart types
Drawing	These commands are available on the Drawing Tools tabs when you insert or select a shape.
Zoom	View tab, Zoom group, Zoom command
Microsoft Excel Help	Click the Help button (?) in the upper-right corner of the Excel window.
PivotTable And PivotChart Report	Insert tab, Tables group, PivotTable
Comment	Review tab, Comments group, New Comment
AutoFilter	This functionality is now added when you create a table. Otherwise, you must add a button to the ribbon or the Quick Access Toolbar for this command: File tab, Options, Customize Ribbon or Quick Access Toolbar, All Commands, AutoFilter

Appendix A

Excel 2003 Formatting toolbar

Excel 2003 Formatting toolbar command	Excel 2013 location and command
Font	Home tab, Font group, Font
Font Size	Home tab, Font group, Font Size
Bold	Home tab, Font group, Bold
Italic	Home tab, Font group, Italic
Underline	Home tab, Font group, Underline
Align Left	Home tab, Alignment group, Align Left
Center	Home tab, Alignment group, Center
Align Right	Home tab, Alignment group, Align Right
Merge And Center	Home tab, Alignment group, Merge & Center
Currency Style	Home tab, Number group, Accounting Number Format
Percent Style	Home tab, Number group, Percent Style
Comma Style	Home tab, Number group, Comma Style
Increase Decimal	Home tab, Number group, Increase Decimal
Decrease Decimal	Home tab, Number group, Decrease Decimal
Decrease Indent	Home tab, Alignment group, Decrease Indent
Increase Indent	Home tab, Alignment group, Increase Indent
Borders	Home tab, Font group, Borders
Fill Color	Home tab, Font group, Fill Color
Font Color	Home tab, Font group, Font Color
Chart, Chart Type	Chart Tools Design tab, Type group, Change Chart Type
Chart, Source Data	Chart Tools Design tab, Data group, Select Data
	PivotChart Tools Design tab, Data group, Select Data
Chart, Chart Options	Chart Tools Layout tab
Chart, Location	Chart Tools Design tab, Location group, Move Chart
	PivotChart Tools Design tab, Location group, Move Chart
Chart, Add Data	Chart Tools Design tab, Data group, Select Data
Chart, Add Trendline	Chart Tools Layout tab, Chart Layouts group, Add Chart Element, Trendline
Chart, 3-D View	Chart Tools Layout tab, Change Chart Type, and then select a 3-D chart

Excel 2003 Formatting toolbar command	Excel 2013 location and command
AutoFormat	Home tab, Styles group, Format As Table
Cells	Home tab, Cells group, Format
Increase Font Size	Home tab, Font group, Increase Font Size
Decrease Font Size	Home tab, Font group, Decrease Font Size
Text Direction	Home tab, Alignment group, Orientation

THIS APPENDIX lists keyboard-accessible commands and controls in Microsoft Excel. Besides being an essential accessibility table, it also provides a glimpse into the depth and breadth of the features available. The first five tables in this appendix list keyboard shortcuts according to the keys found on most keyboards. The rest of the tables in this appendix list keyboard shortcuts according to task.

Shortcuts by key: Function keys

Press	To
F1	Display the Help window.
Ctrl+F1	Show/hide the ribbon.
Alt+F1	Insert a chart as an object.
Shift+Alt+F1	Insert a new worksheet.
Ctrl+Alt+F1	Insert a Microsoft Excel 4 macro worksheet.

Press	To
F2	Activate cell editing mode. (*Edit* is displayed in the status bar.)
Shift+F2	Insert/edit a comment.
Alt+F2	Display the Save As dialog box.
Ctrl+F2	Display Print Preview on the Print tab in Backstage view.
Shift+Alt+F2	Save.
Ctrl+Alt+F2	Display the Open dialog box.
Shift+Ctrl+Alt+F2	Display the Print tab in Backstage view.
F3	Display the Paste Name dialog box (only if a name is defined).
Shift+F3	Display the Insert Function dialog box.
Ctrl+F3	Display the Name Manager dialog box.
Shift+Ctrl+F3	Display the Create Names From Selection dialog box.
Ctrl+Alt+F3	Display the New Name dialog box.
F4	Repeat the last command or action; also, when editing a cell reference, pressing F4 cycles through the four relative/absolute reference combinations.
Shift+F4	Find the next instance of the most recent search.
Ctrl+F4	Close the workbook.
Alt+F4	Close the application.
Shift+Ctrl+F4	Find the previous instance of the most recent search.
Shift+Alt+F4	Close the application.
Ctrl+Alt+F4	Close the application.
Shift+Ctrl+Alt+F4	Close the application.
F5	Display the Go To dialog box.
Shift+F5	Display the Find And Replace dialog box.
Ctrl+F5	Restore the selected window size.
F6	Switch the active location among the ribbon (activating shortcut key labels), the task pane (if present), split window panes (if present), and the Zoom controls.
Shift+F6	Same as F6, in reverse order.
Ctrl+F6	Move to the next workbook.
Shift+Ctrl+F6	Move to the previous workbook.
F7	Check spelling.
Ctrl+F7	Move the window.
F8	Extend Selection mode.
Shift+F8	Add to Selection mode.

Press	To
Alt+F8	Display the Effects dialog box.
F9	Calculate all, or when a portion of a formula is selected, calculate the selected portion.
Shift+F9	Calculate the active worksheet.
Ctrl+F9	Minimize the active window.
Ctrl+Alt+F9	Calculate all worksheets in all open workbooks, regardless of whether they have changed since the last calculation.
Ctrl+Shift+Alt+F9	Recheck dependent formulas, and then calculate all cells in all open workbooks, including cells not marked as needing to be calculated.
F10	Display shortcut key labels.
Shift+F10	Activate shortcut (context) menus.
Ctrl+F10	Toggle the maximized/restored window.
Alt+Shift+F10	Display the menu of the Error Checking button.
F11	Insert a chart on a new worksheet.
Shift+F11	Create a new worksheet.
Alt+F11	Show the Visual Basic Editor.
F12	Display the Save As dialog box.
Shift+F12	Save.
Ctrl+F12	Display the Open dialog box.
Shift+Ctrl+F12	Display the Print tab in Backstage view.

Shortcuts by key: Control and navigation keys

Press	To
Backspace	Edit and clear.
Shift+Backspace	Collapse the selection to the active cell.
Ctrl+Backspace	Show the active cell.
Alt+Backspace	Undo.
Delete	Clear.
Shift+Delete	Cut.
Ctrl+Delete	Clear.
End	Toggle End mode.
Shift+End	Toggle End mode (and extend when you press Shift+an arrow key).
Ctrl+End	Select the last cell in the worksheet.

Press	To
Shift+Ctrl+End	Extend the selection to the last active cell in the worksheet.
Esc	Cancel (edit, copy, cut, dialog boxes, and so on).
Shift+Esc	Cancel (edit, copy, cut, dialog boxes, and so on).
Ctrl+Esc	Display the Windows Start menu.
Shift+Ctrl+Esc	Display the Windows Task Manager.
Enter	Enter the value, and move down.
Shift+Enter	Enter the value, and move up.
Ctrl+Enter	Fill the value in the edited cell into all selected cells.
Alt+Enter	Redo.
Shift+Ctrl+Enter	Fill the value in the edited cell into all selected cells.
Home	Select the first cell in the row.
Shift+Home	Extend the selection to the first cell in the row.
Ctrl+Home	Select the first cell in the window (or pane).
Shift+Ctrl+Home	Extend the selection to the first cell in the window or pane.
Insert	Toggle Overwrite mode in Edit mode.
Shift+Insert	Paste.
Ctrl+Insert	Copy.
Down Arrow	Move down one cell.
Shift+Down Arrow	Extend the selection down one cell.
Ctrl+Down Arrow	Select the last cell in the region down.
Alt+Down Arrow	Open the list (AutoComplete, Filter, Pick From List, or Validation).
Shift+Ctrl+Down Arrow	Extend the selection down to the last cell in the current region or the first cell in the next region.
Left Arrow	Move left one cell.
Shift+Left Arrow	Extend the selection left one cell.
Ctrl+Left Arrow	Select the leftmost cell in the current region or the rightmost cell in the next region.
Shift+Ctrl+Left Arrow	Extend the selection left to the last cell in the current region or the first cell in the next region.
Shift+Alt+Left Arrow	Ungroup.
Ctrl+Alt+Left Arrow	Move the active cell to the upper-left cell of the selection.
Right Arrow	Move right one cell.

Press	To
Shift+Right Arrow	Extend the selection right one cell.
Ctrl+Right Arrow	Select the last cell to the right in the current region or the first cell in the next region.
Shift+Ctrl+Right Arrow	Extend the selection to the right, to the last cell in the current region, or to the first cell in the next region.
Shift+Alt+Right Arrow	Group.
Ctrl+Alt+Right Arrow	Move the active cell to the next nonadjacent region within the selection.
Up Arrow	Move up one cell.
Shift+Up Arrow	Extend the selection up one cell.
Ctrl+Up Arrow	Select the cell at the top of the region.
Shift+Ctrl+Up Arrow	Extend the selection up to the end of the region.
Page Down	Scroll down one page.
Shift+Page Down	Extend the selection down one page.
Ctrl+Page Down	Move to the next worksheet.
Alt+Page Down	Scroll one page right.
Shift+Ctrl+Page Down	Extend the selection one worksheet down.
Shift+Alt+Page Down	Extend the selection one page right.
Page Up	Scroll up one page.
Shift+Page Up	Extend the selection one page up.
Ctrl+Page Up	Move to the previous worksheet.
Alt+Page Up	Scroll one page left.
Shift+Ctrl+Page Up	Extend the selection one worksheet up.
Shift+Alt+Page Up	Extend the selection one page left.
Return	Enter the value, and move down.
Shift+Return	Enter the value, and move up.
Ctrl+Return	Fill the value in the edited cell into all selected cells and do not move.
Alt+Return	Redo.
Shift+Ctrl+Return	Fill the value in the edited cell into all selected cells and do not move.
Shift+Spacebar	Select row.
Ctrl+Spacebar	Select column.

Press	To
Shift+Ctrl+Spacebar	Select all.
Tab	Move to the next cell to the right.
Shift+Tab	Move to the next cell to the left.
Ctrl+Tab	Move to the next window.
Alt+Tab	Move to the next application.
Shift+Ctrl+Tab	Move to the previous window.
Shift+Alt+Tab	Indent.
Ctrl+Alt+Tab	Outdent.

Shortcuts by key: Numeric keys

Press	To
Ctrl+0	Hide the selected column.
Ctrl+1	Display the Format Cells dialog box.
Shift+Ctrl+1	Apply the two-decimal-place Number format with the thousands separator.
Ctrl+2	Toggle bold formatting.
Shift+Ctrl+2	Apply the Time (AM/PM) format.
Ctrl+3	Toggle italic formatting.
Shift+Ctrl+3	Apply the Date format.
Ctrl+4	Toggle underline formatting.
Shift+Ctrl+4	Apply the Currency format.
Ctrl+5	Toggle strikethrough formatting.
Shift+Ctrl+5	Apply the Percentage format.
Ctrl+6	Toggle the display of objects (between Show, Hide, and Show Placeholders).
Shift+Ctrl+6	Apply the two-place exponential Scientific format.
Shift+Ctrl+7	Apply the Outline border format.
Ctrl+8	Toggle the outline symbol display.
Shift+Ctrl+8	Select the current region.
Ctrl+9	Hide the selected row.
Shift+Ctrl+9	Show the row.

Shortcuts by key: Symbol keys and keypad

Press	To
Ctrl+' (apostrophe)	Copy the underlying value (entered value or exact formula) of the cell above, and edit.
Alt+' (apostrophe)	Display the Style dialog box.
Shift+Ctrl+' (apostrophe)	Copy the displayed value in the cell above and edit.
Ctrl+Hyphen	Display the Delete dialog box.
Shift+Ctrl+Hyphen	Remove all the borders.
Shift+Ctrl+Comma	Fill down.
Ctrl+Period	Rotate the active cell through the corners of the selection.
Shift+Ctrl+Period	Fill right.
Ctrl+/ (slash)	Select array.
Ctrl+; (semicolon)	Insert the current date.
Shift+Ctrl+; (semicolon)	Insert the current time.
Ctrl+[(open bracket)	Select the direct precedent cells.
Shift+Ctrl+[(open bracket)	Select all the precedent cells.
Ctrl+] (close bracket)	Select the directly dependent cells.
Shift+Ctrl+] (close bracket)	Select all the dependent cells.
Ctrl+Shift+{ (open brace)	Select all the cells directly or indirectly referenced by formulas in the selection.
Ctrl+Shift+} (close brace)	Select cells that contain formulas that directly or indirectly reference the active cell.
Ctrl+` (accent grave)	Toggle the display of all formulas.
Shift+Ctrl+` (accent grave)	Apply the General format.
Ctrl+= (equal sign)	Calculate now.
Alt+= (equal sign)	AutoSum.
Shift+Ctrl+= (equal sign)	Display the Insert dialog box.
Ctrl+Add (keypad)	Display the Insert dialog box.
Ctrl+Decimal (keypad)	Rotate the active cell through the corners of the selection.
Ctrl+Divide (keypad)	Select the array.
Ctrl+Multiply (keypad)	Select the current region.
Ctrl+Subtract (keypad)	Display the Delete dialog box.

Appendix B

Shortcuts by key: Letter keys

Press	To
Ctrl+A	Select the current region or select all.
Shift+Ctrl+A	Insert arguments in the formula.
Ctrl+B	Apply bold formatting.
Ctrl+C	Copy.
Ctrl+D	Fill down.
Ctrl+F	Display the Find And Replace dialog box, Find tab.
Shift+Ctrl+F	Display the Format Cells dialog box, Font tab.
Ctrl+G	Display the Go To dialog box.
Ctrl+H	Display the Find And Replace dialog box, Replace tab.
Ctrl+I	Apply italic formatting.
Ctrl+K	Display the Insert Hyperlink dialog box.
Ctrl+L	Display the Create Table dialog box.
Shift+Ctrl+L	Toggle AutoFilter.
Ctrl+N	Create a new workbook.
Ctrl+O	Display the Open dialog box.
Shift+Ctrl+O	Select the first cell containing a comment.
Ctrl+P	Display the Print window.
Shift+Ctrl+P	Display the Format Cells dialog box, Font tab.
Ctrl+R	Fill right.
Ctrl+S	Save the workbook.
Ctrl+T	Display the Create Table dialog box.
Shift+Ctrl+T	Toggle the total row (when the table is selected).
Ctrl+U	Toggle the underline format.
Ctrl+V	Paste.
Ctrl+Alt+V	Display the Paste Special dialog box.
Ctrl+W	Close the window.
Ctrl+X	Cut.
Ctrl+Y	Redo.
Ctrl+Z	Undo.

Shortcuts by task: Insert charts

Press	To
F11	Create a chart of the data in the current range on a new worksheet.
Alt+F1	Create an embedded chart of the data in the current range on the current worksheet.
Down Arrow	Select the previous group of elements in a chart.
Up Arrow	Select the next group of elements in a chart.
Right Arrow	Select the next element within a group.
Left Arrow	Select the previous element within a group.

Shortcuts by task: Work in dialog box text boxes

Press	To
Home	Move to the beginning of the entry.
End	Move to the end of the entry.
Left Arrow or Right Arrow	Move one character to the left or right.
Ctrl+Left Arrow	Move one word to the left.
Ctrl+Right Arrow	Move one word to the right.
Shift+Left Arrow	Select or deselect one character to the left.
Shift+Right Arrow	Select or deselect one character to the right.
Ctrl+Shift+Left Arrow	Select or deselect one word to the left.
Ctrl+Shift+Right Arrow	Select or deselect one word to the right.
Shift+Home	Select from the insertion point to the beginning of the entry.
Shift+End	Select from the insertion point to the end of the entry.

Shortcuts by task: Work in dialog boxes

Press	To
Tab	Move to the next option or option group.
Shift+Tab	Move to the previous option or option group.
Ctrl+Tab or Ctrl+Page Down	Switch to the next tab in a dialog box.
Ctrl+Shift+Tab or Ctrl+Page Up	Switch to the previous tab in a dialog box.
Arrow keys	Move between options in an open list or between options in a group of options.
Spacebar	Perform the action for the selected button, or select or clear the selected check box.

Press	To
First letter of an option	Open the list if it is closed, and in a list, move to that option in the list.
Alt+the underlined letter in an option	Select an option, or select or clear a check box.
Alt+Down Arrow	Open the selected drop-down list.
Enter	Perform the action for the default button in the dialog box (the button with the bold outline, often the OK button).
Esc	Cancel the command, and close the dialog box.

Shortcuts by task: Edit data

Press	To
F2	Edit the active cell and position the insertion point at the end of the cell contents.
Alt+Enter	Start a new line in the same cell.
Backspace	Edit the active cell and then clear it, or delete the preceding character in the active cell as you edit cell contents.
Delete	Delete the character to the right of the insertion point, or delete the selection.
Ctrl+Delete	Delete text to the end of the line.
F7	Start the spelling checker.
Shift+F2	Edit a cell comment.
Enter	Complete a cell entry, and select the next cell below.
Ctrl+X	Cut the selected cells.
Ctrl+Z	Undo the last action.
Esc	Cancel a cell entry.

Shortcuts by task: Work with formulas

Press	To
= (equal sign)	Start a formula.
F2	Move the insertion point into the formula bar when editing in a cell is turned off.
Backspace	In the formula bar, delete one character to the left.
Enter	Complete a cell entry from the cell or formula bar.
Ctrl+Shift+Enter	Enter a formula as an array formula.
Esc	Cancel an entry in the cell or formula bar.

Press	To
Shift+F3	Display the Insert Function dialog box.
Ctrl+A	When the insertion point is to the right of a function name in a formula, display the Function Arguments dialog box.
Ctrl+Shift+A	When the insertion point is to the right of a function name in a formula, insert the argument names and parentheses.
F3	Display the Paste Name dialog box.
Alt+= (equal sign)	Insert an AutoSum formula.
Ctrl+Shift+" (quotation mark)	Copy the displayed value from the cell above the active cell and activate it for editing.
Ctrl+' (apostrophe)	Copy the underlying value (the entered value or the exact formula) from the cell above the active cell into the active cell.
Ctrl+` (accent grave)	Alternate between displaying cell values and displaying formulas.
F9	Calculate all worksheets in all open workbooks, or when a portion of a formula is selected, calculate the selected portion.
Shift+F9	Calculate the active worksheet.
Ctrl+Alt+F9	Calculate all worksheets in all open workbooks, regardless of whether they have changed since the last calculation.

Shortcuts by task: Enter data

Press	To
Enter	Complete a cell entry and select the cell below.
Alt+Enter	Start a new line in the same cell.
Ctrl+Enter	Fill the selected cell range with the current entry.
Shift+Enter	Complete a cell entry, and select the previous cell above.
Tab	Complete a cell entry, and select the next cell to the right.
Shift+Tab	Complete a cell entry, and select the previous cell to the left.
Esc	Cancel a cell entry.
Arrow keys	Move one character up, down, left, or right.
Home	Move to the beginning of the line.
F4 or Ctrl+Y	Repeat the last action.
Ctrl+Shift+F3	Create names from row and column labels.
Ctrl+D	Fill down.

Press	To
Ctrl+R	Fill to the right.
Ctrl+F3	Display the Name Manager dialog box.
Ctrl+K	Display the Insert Hyperlink dialog box.
Ctrl+; (semicolon)	Enter the date.
Ctrl+Shift+: (colon)	Enter the time.
Alt+Down Arrow	Display a drop-down list of the values in the current column of a table, if your insertion point is in the cell containing the column name.
Ctrl+Z	Undo the last action.

Shortcuts by task: Select cells

Press	To
F8	Turn on or off Extend mode. In Extend mode, *EXT* appears on the status bar, and the arrow keys extend the selection.
Shift+F8	Add another range of cells to the selection, or use the arrow keys to move to the start of the range you want to add, and then press F8 and the arrow keys to select the next range.
Shift+arrow key	Extend the selection by one cell.
Ctrl+Shift+arrow key	Extend the selection to the last nonblank cell in the same column or row as the active cell.
Shift+Home	Extend the selection to the beginning of the row.
Ctrl+Shift+Home	Extend the selection to the beginning of the worksheet.
Ctrl+Shift+End	Extend the selection to the last used cell on the worksheet (lower-right corner).
Shift+Page Down	Extend the selection down one screen.
Shift+Page Up	Extend the selection up one screen.
End, Shift+arrow key	Extend the selection in the direction of the arrow key to the last cell in the current region or the first cell in the next region.
End, Shift+Home	Extend the selection to the intersection of the lowest used row and the rightmost used column.
End, Shift+Enter	Extend the selection to the right to the current row of the last used column. This key sequence does not work if you have turned on transition navigation keys (File tab, Options, Advanced category, Lotus Compatibility section).
Scroll Lock+Shift+Home	Extend the selection to the cell in the upper-left corner of the window.
Scroll Lock+Shift+End	Extend the selection to the cell in the lower-right corner of the window.

Shortcuts by task: Filter tables

Press	To
Alt+Down Arrow	In the cell that contains the arrow, display the Filter list for the current column.
Down Arrow	Select the next item in the Filter list.
Up Arrow	Select the previous item in the Filter list.
Enter	Filter the list based on the item selected from the Filter list.

Shortcuts by task: Work with borders

Press	To
Alt+T	Apply or remove the top border.
Alt+B	Apply or remove the bottom border.
Alt+L	Apply or remove the left border.
Alt+R	Apply or remove the right border.
Alt+H	If cells in multiple rows are selected, apply or remove the horizontal divider.
Alt+V	If cells in multiple columns are selected, apply or remove the vertical divider.
Alt+D	Apply or remove the downward diagonal border.
Alt+U	Apply or remove the upward diagonal border.

Shortcuts by task: Format data

Press	To
Alt+' (apostrophe)	Display the Style dialog box.
Ctrl+1	Display the Format Cells dialog box. (Note that you must use the 1 key on the keyboard, not on the keypad.)
Ctrl+Shift+~ (tilde)	Apply the General number format.
Ctrl+Shift+$	Apply the Currency format with two decimal places (negative numbers in parentheses).
Ctrl+Shift+%	Apply the Percentage format with no decimal places.
Ctrl+Shift+^ (caret)	Apply the exponential number format with two decimal places.
Ctrl+Shift+# (pound)	Apply the Date format with the day, month, and year.
Ctrl+Shift+@	Apply the Time format with the hour and minute and AM or PM.
Ctrl+Shift+! (exclamation point)	Apply the Number format with two decimal places, thousands separator, and minus sign (–) for negative values.

Appendix B

Press	To
Ctrl+B	Apply or remove bold formatting.
Ctrl+I	Apply or remove italic formatting.
Ctrl+U	Apply or remove underlining.
Ctrl+5	Apply or remove strikethrough.
Ctrl+9	Hide the selected rows.
Ctrl+Shift+((opening parenthesis)	Unhide any hidden rows within the selection.
Ctrl+0 (zero)	Hide the selected columns.
Ctrl+Shift+& (ampersand)	Apply the outline border to the selected cells.
Ctrl+Shift+_ (underscore)	Remove the outline border from the selected cells.

Shortcuts by task: Work with Help

Press	To
F1	Display the Microsoft Excel Help window.
Tab or Shift+Tab	Select the next or previous hidden text or hyperlink.
Enter	Perform the action for the selected hidden text or hyperlink.
Alt+F4	Close the Help window.
Alt+Left Arrow	Go to the previous Help topic.
Alt+Right Arrow	Go to the next Help topic.
Up Arrow or Down Arrow	Scroll toward the beginning or end of a Help topic.
Page Up or Page Down	Scroll toward the beginning or end of a Help topic a screen at a time.
Home or End	Go to the beginning or end of a Help topic.
Ctrl+P	Print the current Help topic.
Ctrl+A	Select the entire Help topic.
Ctrl+C	Copy the selected items to the Clipboard.

Shortcuts by task: Insert, delete, and copy cells

Press	To
Ctrl+C	Copy the selected items to the Clipboard.
Ctrl+X	Cut the selected cells.
Ctrl+V	Paste copied cells.
Ctrl+Alt+V	Display the Paste Special dialog box.
Delete	Clear the contents of the selected cells.

Ctrl+Hyphen	Display the Delete dialog box.
Ctrl+Shift+Plus Sign	Display the Insert dialog box.

Shortcuts by task: Work with macros

Press	To
Alt+F8	Display the Macro dialog box.
Alt+F11	Display the Visual Basic Editor. After the editor is open, acts as a toggle, switching the display between the main Excel window and the editor.
Ctrl+F11	Insert a Microsoft Excel 4 macro worksheet.

Shortcuts by task: Work with the ribbon

Press	To
F10 or Alt	Display shortcut key labels (pressing Alt toggles on and off), and activate the ribbon.
Alt, Tab or Alt, Shift+Tab	Select the next or previous item on the ribbon.
Enter	Open the selected menu or perform the action for the selected button or command.
Shift+F10	Display the shortcut menu for the selected item.
Alt+Spacebar	Display the Control menu for the Excel window.
Down Arrow or Up Arrow	When a menu or submenu is open, select the next or previous command.
Left Arrow or Right Arrow	Select the menu to the left or right. When a submenu is open, switch between the main menu and the submenu. When the ribbon is active, select the next or previous tab.
Esc	Close an open menu. When a submenu is open, close only the submenu.

Shortcuts by task: Move and scroll in End mode

Press	To
End	Turn on or off End mode. (*End Mode* appears on the status bar.)
End+arrow key	Move in the direction of the arrow key to the last cell in the current region or the first cell in the next region.
End+Home	Move to the intersection of the lowest used row and the rightmost used column.
End+Enter	Move to the rightmost cell in the current row of the last used column.

Shortcuts by task: Move and scroll in worksheets

Press	To
Arrow keys	Move one cell up, down, left, or right.
Ctrl+arrow key	Move to the edge of the current data region.
Home	Move to the beginning of the row.
Ctrl+Home	Move to the beginning of the worksheet.
Ctrl+End	Move to the last cell on the worksheet: the cell in the lowest used row of the rightmost used column.
Page Down	Move down one screen.
Ctrl+Page Down	Select the next worksheet in the workbook.
Ctrl+Page Up	Select the previous worksheet in the workbook.
Page Up	Move up one screen.
Alt+Page Down	Move one screen to the right.
Alt+Page Up	Move one screen to the left.
Ctrl+Backspace	Scroll to display the active cell.
F5	Display the Go To dialog box.
Shift+F5	Display the Find And Replace dialog box.
Shift+F4	Repeat the last Find action (same as Find Next).
Tab	Move between unlocked cells on a protected worksheet.

Shortcuts by task: Move within a selected range

Press	To
Enter	Move one cell at a time from top to bottom within the selected range.
Shift+Enter	Move one cell at a time from bottom to top within the selected range.
Tab	Move from left to right one cell at a time within the selected range. If cells in a single column are selected, move down.
Shift+Tab	Move from right to left one cell at a time within the selected range. If cells in a single column are selected, move up.
Ctrl+Period	Move clockwise to the next corner of the selected range.
Ctrl+Alt+Right Arrow	In nonadjacent selections, switch to the next selection to the right.
Ctrl+Alt+Left Arrow	Switch to the next nonadjacent selection to the left.

Shortcuts by task: Print

Press	To
Ctrl+P or Ctrl+Shift+F12	Display the Print dialog box.
Alt+F, then press P	Open the Print/Print Preview screen in Backstage view.

Shortcuts by task: Work in Backstage view

Press	To
Alt+F	Activate the File tab, a.k.a. Backstage view, and display keyboard command labels; press the labeled key to activate that screen in Backstage view. (For example, press P to activate the Print screen.)
Tab	Activate the next item in Backstage view (for example, controls on the Print screen).
Arrow keys	Select any available options/pages for the selected item.
Enter	Display the selected menu, or activate the selected command or option.
Esc	Close Backstage view and return to the worksheet.

Shortcuts by task: Select cells, rows, columns, and objects

Press	To
Ctrl+Spacebar	Select the entire column.
Shift+Spacebar	Select the entire row.
Ctrl+A	Select the entire worksheet.
Shift+Backspace	With multiple cells selected, select only the active cell.
Ctrl+Shift+Spacebar	Select the entire worksheet. With an object selected, select all the objects on a worksheet.
Ctrl+6	Toggle the display of objects.

Shortcuts by task: Select cells with special characteristics

Press	To
Ctrl+Shift+* (asterisk)	Select the current region around the active cell (the data area enclosed by blank rows and blank columns). In a PivotTable, select the entire PivotTable.
Ctrl+/ (slash)	Select the array containing the active cell.
Ctrl+Shift+O (the letter O)	Select all cells that contain comments.
Ctrl+[(opening bracket)	Select all cells directly referenced by formulas in the selection.
Ctrl+Shift+{ (opening brace)	Select all cells directly or indirectly referenced by formulas in the selection.
Ctrl+] (closing bracket)	Select cells that contain formulas that directly reference the active cell.
Ctrl+Shift+} (closing brace)	Select cells that contain formulas that directly or indirectly reference the active cell.

Shortcuts by task: Work with outlines

Press	To
Alt+Shift+Right Arrow	Display the Group dialog box.
Alt+Shift+Left Arrow	Display the Ungroup dialog box.
Ctrl+8	Display or hide the outline symbols.
Ctrl+9	Hide the selected rows.
Ctrl+Shift+((opening parenthesis)	Unhide any hidden rows within the selection.
Ctrl+0 (zero)	Hide the selected columns.

Shortcuts by task: Work with options menus

Press	To
Down Arrow	Select the next item on an options menu.
Up Arrow	Select the previous item on an options menu.
Enter	Perform the action for the selected item on an options menu.
Esc	Close the options menu or message.

Shortcuts by task: Work with task panes

Press	To
F6	Move between ribbon and task pane or panes, in the program window. (You might need to press F6 more than once.)
Tab or Shift+Tab	When a task pane is active, select the next or previous item in the task pane.
Down Arrow or Up Arrow	Move among choices on a selected submenu, or move among certain options in a group of options.
Spacebar or Enter	Open the selected menu, or perform the action assigned to the selected button.
Home or End	When a menu or submenu is visible, select the first or last command on the menu or submenu.
Page Up or Page Down	Scroll up or down in the selected task pane.

Shortcuts by task: Navigate Windows

Press	To
Mouse wheel	Activate the next tab when the pointer is hovering over the ribbon.
Alt+Tab	Switch to the next program.
Alt+Shift+Tab	Switch to the previous program.
Ctrl+Esc	Display the Windows Start menu.
Ctrl+W or Ctrl+F4	Close the selected workbook window.
Ctrl+F6	Switch to the next open workbook.
Ctrl+Shift+F6	Switch to the previous open workbook.
Ctrl+F9	Minimize a window to an icon.
Ctrl+F10	Maximize or restore the selected window.
Print Screen	Copy a picture of the screen to the Clipboard.
Alt+Print Screen	Copy a picture of the selected window to the Clipboard.

Shortcuts by task: Work with worksheets

Press	To
Shift+F11 or Alt+Shift+F1	Insert a new worksheet.
Ctrl+Page Down	Move to the next worksheet in the workbook.
Ctrl+Page Up	Move to the previous worksheet in the workbook.
Shift+Ctrl+Page Down	Select the current and next worksheets. To cancel selection of multiple worksheets, press Ctrl+Page Down; to select a different worksheet, press Ctrl+Page Up.
Shift+Ctrl+Page Up	Select the current and previous worksheets.
Alt+O, H, R	Rename the current worksheet.
Alt+E, M	Move or copy the current worksheet.
Alt+E, L	Delete the current worksheet.

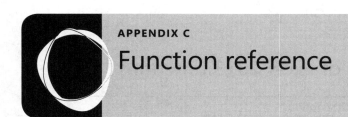

APPENDIX C

Function reference

THIS APPENDIX lists the worksheet functions available in Microsoft Excel 2013 in alphabetical order. We include a description of the function, the function syntax, and a description of each argument.

You must type all function arguments in the order shown, and you should not add any spaces between or within arguments. Although Excel now generally accepts spaces in functions for readability, when you use spaces within a text argument or a reference argument, you must still enclose the entire argument in quotation marks. Arguments displayed in bold are required, and those in regular type are optional.

> **Note**
>
> The underlying algorithms for the following functions were modified for increased accuracy for the 2010 release of Excel, with minimal visible changes, but some have additional arguments. Also, some of these functions now have additional forms; refer to the reference table for more information.
>
> *Statistical distribution functions:*
> BINOM.DIST, CHISQ.DIST (CHIDIST), CHISQ.INV (CHIINV), CRITBINOM, EXPON.DIST, F.DIST, F.INV, GAMMA.DIST, GAMMA.INV, HYPGEOM.DIST, LOGNORM.DIST, LOGNORM.INV (LOGINV), NEGBINOM.DIST, NORM.DIST, NORM.INV, NORM.S.DIST, NORM.S.INV, POISSON.DIST, T.DIST, T.INV, and WEIBULL.DIST
>
> *Financial functions:*
> CUMIPMT, CUMPRINC, IPMT, IRR, PMT, and PPMT
>
> *Other functions:*
> ASINH, CEILING, CONVERT, ERF, ERFC, FLOOR, GAMMALN, GEOMEAN, MOD, RAND, STDEV.S, and VAR.S

Alphabetical list of Excel 2013 functions

Function	Description
ABS	Returns the absolute value of a number. Takes the form =ABS(**number**). If a number is negative, this function simply removes the sign, making it a positive number.
ACCRINT	Returns the interest accrued by a security that pays interest on a periodic basis. Takes the form =ACCRINT(**issue**, **first_ interest**, **settlement**, **rate**, par, **frequency**, basis, calc_ method), where *issue* is the issue date of the security, *first_interest* is the date of the initial interest payment, *settlement* is the day you pay for the security, *rate* is the interest rate of the security at the issue date, *par* is the par value of the security, *frequency* is the number of coupon payments made per year (1 = annual, 2 = semiannual, 4 = quarterly), *basis* is the day-count basis of the security (if 0 or omitted = 30/360, if 1 = actual/actual, if 2 = actual/360, if 3 = actual/365, if 4 = European 30/360), and calc_method, if TRUE (1), calculates the accrued interest from issue date to settlement date, and if FALSE (0), calculates the interest accrued between first_interest and settlement. See "Analyzing securities" in Chapter 16.
ACCRINTM	Returns the interest accrued by a maturity security that pays interest at maturity. Takes the form =ACCRINTM(**issue**, **settlement**, **rate**, par, basis), where *issue* is the issue date of the security, *settlement* is the security's settlement (maturity) date, *rate* is the interest rate of the security at the issue date, *par* is the par value of the security, and *basis* is the day-count basis of the security (if 0 or omitted = 30/360, if 1 = actual/ actual, if 2 = actual/360, if 3 = actual/365, if 4 = European 30/360). See "Analyzing securities" in Chapter 16.
ACOS	Returns the arccosine (inverse cosine) of a number in radians. Takes the form =ACOS(**number**), where *number* is the cosine of an angle.
ACOSH	Returns the inverse hyperbolic cosine of a number. Takes the form =ACOSH(**number**), where *number* must be >=1.
ACOT	Returns the arccotangent (inverse cotangent) of a number. Takes the form =ACOT(**number**), where *number* must be a real number.
ACOTH	Returns the inverse hyperbolic arccotangent of a number. Takes the form =ACOTH(**number**), where *number* must be greater than 1.

Function	Description
ADDRESS	Builds references from numbers. Takes the form =ADDRESS(**row_num**, **column_num**, abs_num, a1, sheet_text), where *row_num* and *column_num* designate the row and column values for the address; *abs_num* determines whether the resulting address uses absolute references (1), mixed (2 means absolute row, relative column; 3 means relative row, absolute column), or relative (4); *a1* is a logical value (if TRUE, the resulting address is in A1 format; if FALSE, the resulting address is in R1C1 format); and *sheet_text* specifies the name of the sheet. See "Using selected lookup and reference functions" in Chapter 14.
AGGREGATE	Returns an aggregate of a range or array by applying one of 19 aggregation functions with options to ignore hidden rows, error values, or both. For lists and ranges, it takes the form =AGGREGATE(**function_num, options, ref1**, ref2, ...). For arrays, it takes the form =AGGREGATE(**function_num, options, array**, k) Function numbers: 1 AVERAGE, 2 COUNT, 3 COUNTA, 4 MAX, 5 MIN, 6 PRODUCT, 7 STDEV.S, 8 STDEV.P, 9 SUM, 10 VAR.S, 11 VAR.P, 12 MEDIAN, 13 MODE.SNGL, 14 LARGE, 15 SMALL, 16 PERCENTILE.INC, 17 QUARTILE.INC, 18 PERCENTILE.EXC, 19 QUARTILE.EXC. Options: 0 or omitted: Ignore nested SUBTOTAL and AGGREGATE functions; 1 Ignore hidden rows, nested SUBTOTAL and AGGREGATE functions; 2 Ignore error values, nested SUBTOTAL and AGGREGATE functions; 3 Ignore hidden rows, error values, nested SUBTOTAL and AGGREGATE functions; 4 Ignore nothing; 5 Ignore hidden rows; 6 Ignore error values; 7 Ignore hidden rows and error values. For arrays, the following functions require a Ref2 argument: LARGE(array,k), SMALL(array,k), PERCENTILE.INC(array,k), QUARTILE.INC(array,quart), PERCENTILE.EXC(array,k), QUARTILE.EXC(array,quart).
AMORDEGRC	Returns the depreciation for each accounting period (French accounting system only), including any partial period. Takes the form =AMORDEGRC(**cost**, **date_purchased**, **first_period**, **salvage**, **period**, **rate**, basis), where *cost* is the cost of the asset, *date_purchased* is the date of the purchase, *first_period* is the date of the end of the first period, *salvage* is the salvage value at the end of the life of the asset, *period* is the period for which you want to calculate depreciation, *rate* is the rate of depreciation, and *basis* is the year *basis* to be used (0 = 360 days, 1 = actual, 3 = 365 days, 4 = European 360 days). This function is similar to AMORLINC, except a depreciation coefficient is applied depending on the asset life (1.5 if 3–4 years, 2 if 5–6 years, 2.5 if greater than 6 years).
AMORLINC	Returns the depreciation for each accounting period (French accounting system only), including any partial period. See AMORDEGRC for syntax and arguments.

Appendix C

Function	Description
AND	Helps develop compound conditional test formulas in conjunction with the simple logical operators =, >, <, >=, <=, and <>. The AND function can have as many as 30 arguments and takes the form =AND(**logical1**, logical2, ...), where each *logical* can be conditional tests, arrays, or references to cells that contain logical values. See "Using selected logical functions" in Chapter 14.
ARABIC	Converts a Roman numeral to an Arabic numeral. Takes the form =ARABIC(**text**), where *text* is a valid Roman numeral, or a reference to a cell containing one. Also, see the ROMAN function.
AREAS	Returns the number of areas in a reference (a cell or block of cells). Takes the form =AREAS(**reference**), where *reference* can be a cell reference, a range reference, or several range references enclosed in parentheses. See "Using selected lookup and reference functions" in Chapter 14.
ASC	Changes text in double-byte character set languages to single-byte characters. Takes the form =ASC(**text**), where *text* is either text or a reference to a cell containing text. Has no effect on single-byte characters.
ASIN	Returns the arcsine of a number in radians. Takes the form =ASIN(**number**), where *number* is the sine of the angle you want and must be from -1 to 1.
ASINH	Returns the inverse hyperbolic sine of a number. Takes the form =ASINH(**number**).
ATAN	Returns the arctangent of a number. Takes the form =ATAN(**number**), where *number* is the tangent of an angle.
ATAN2	Returns the arctangent of the specified x and y coordinates in radians. Takes the form =ATAN2(**x_num**, **y_num**), where *x_num* is the x coordinate of the point, and *y_num* is the y coordinate of the point. A positive result represents a counterclockwise angle from the x axis; a negative result represents a clockwise angle.
ATANH	Returns the inverse hyperbolic tangent of a number. Takes the form =ATANH(**number**), where *number* must be between (not including) -1 and 1.
AVEDEV	Returns the average of the absolute deviations of data points from their mean. Takes the form =AVEDEV(**number1**, number2, ...), where the numbers can be names, arrays, or references that resolve to numbers. Accepts up to 30 arguments.

Function	Description
AVERAGE	Returns the arithmetic mean of the specified numbers. Takes the form =AVERAGE(**number1**, number2, ...), where the numbers can be names, arrays, or references that resolve to numbers. Cells containing text, logical values, or empty cells are ignored, but cells containing a zero value are included. See "Using built-in statistical functions" in Chapter 17.
AVERAGEA	Acts like AVERAGE except text and logical values are included in the calculation. See "Using built-in statistical functions" in Chapter 17.
AVERAGEIF	Finds the arithmetic mean cells in the specified range that meet a given criteria. Takes the form =AVERAGEIF(**range**, **criteria**, average_range), where *range* is the cells to evaluate; *criteria* is an expression, cell reference, or number used to define which cells to average; and *average_range* is the actual cells to average. Excel uses the upper-left cell of *average_range* as the beginning and the lower-left cell of either *average_range* or *range* (whichever is larger) to determine the size of the cell range to be used. If *average_range* is omitted, *range* is used.
AVERAGEIFS	Acts like AVERAGEIF, but accepts multiple criteria. Takes the form =AVERAGEIFS(**average_range**, **criteria_range1**, **criteria1**, criteria_range2, criteria2, ...).
BAHTTEXT	Converts a number to Thai text, and adds the suffix *Baht*. Takes the form =BAHTTEXT(**number**), where *number* can be a reference to a cell containing a number or a formula that resolves to a number.
BASE	Converts a number into a text representation with the given base (radix). Takes the form =BASE(**number**, **radix**, min_length), where *number* is an integer $>= 0$ and $<2^{53}$; *radix* is the base that you want to convert the number into, which must be an integer $>=2$ and $<=36$. *min_length* is the optional minimum length of the returned string, which adds leading zeros if necessary to achieve the minimum length.
BESSELI	Returns the modified Bessel function, which is equivalent to the Bessel function evaluated for imaginary arguments. Takes the form =BESSELI(**x**, **n**), where *x* is the value at which to evaluate the function, and *n* is the order of the Bessel function.
BESSELJ	Returns the Bessel function using the form =BESSELJ(**x**, **n**), where *x* is the value at which to evaluate the function, and *n* is the order of the Bessel function.
BESSELK	Returns the modified Bessel function, which is equivalent to the Bessel function evaluated for imaginary arguments. Takes the form =BESSELK(**x**, **n**), where *x* is the value at which to evaluate the function, and *n* is the order of the Bessel function.

Function	Description
BESSELY	Returns the Bessel function (also called the Weber or Neumann function). Takes the form =BESSELY(**x**, **n**), where x is the value at which to evaluate the function, and n is the order of the function.
BETA.DIST	Returns the cumulative beta probability density function. Takes the form =BETA.DIST(**x**, **alpha**, **beta**, **cumulative**, A, B), where x is the value between A and B at which to evaluate the function, *alpha* is a parameter to the distribution, *beta* is a parameter to the distribution, A is an optional lower bound to the interval of x, and B is an optional upper bound to the interval of x. If *cumulative* is TRUE, BETA.DIST returns the cumulative distribution function; otherwise, it returns the probability density function. The old form of this function is BETADIST, which is still supported as a Compatibility Function.
BETA.INV	Returns the inverse of the cumulative beta probability density function. Takes the form =BETA.INV(**probability**, **alpha**, **beta**, A, B), where *probability* is a probability associated with the beta distribution. For additional argument descriptions, see BETA.DIST. The old form of this function is BETAINV, which is still supported as a Compatibility Function.
BIN2DEC	Converts a binary number to decimal. Takes the form =BIN2DEC(**number**), where *number* is the binary integer you want to convert.
BIN2HEX	Converts a binary number to hexadecimal. Takes the form =BIN2HEX(**number**, **places**), where *number* is the binary integer you want to convert and *places* is the number of characters to use. *Places* is useful for padding the return value with leading zeros.
BIN2OCT	Converts a binary number to octal. Takes the form =BIN2DEC(**number**, places), where *number* is the binary integer you want to convert, and *places* is the number of characters to use. *Places* is useful for padding the return value with leading zeros.
BINOMDIST	Supported as a Compatibility Function. See the new forms BINOM.DIST and BINOM.DIST.RANGE.
BINOM.DIST	Returns the individual term binomial distribution probability. Takes the form =BINOM.DIST(**number_s**, **trials**, **probability_s**, **cumulative**), where *number_s* is the number of successes in trials, *trials* is the number of independent trials, *probability_s* is the probability of success on each trial, and *cumulative* is a logical value that determines the form of the function. If *cumulative* is TRUE, BINOM.DIST returns the probability that there are at most *number_s* successes; if *cumulative* is FALSE, BINOM.DIST returns the probability that there are *number_s* successes. The old form of this function is BINOMDIST, which is still supported as a Compatibility Function.

Function	Description
BINOM.DIST.RANGE	Returns the probability of a trial result using a binomial distribution. Takes the form =BINOM.DIST.RANGE(**trials**, **probability_s**, **number_s**, number_s2), where *trials* is the number of independent trials and must be >= 0; *probability_s* is probability of success in each trial and must be >=0 and <=1; *number_s* is the number of successes in trials and must be >=0 and <= Trials; optionally, *Number_s2* returns the probability that the number of successful trials will fall between *Number_s* and *number_s2* and must be >=*Number_s* and <=*Trials*.
BINOM.INV	Returns the smallest value for which the cumulative binomial distribution is greater than or equal to a criterion value. Takes the form =BINOM.INV(**trials**, **probability_s**, **alpha**), where *trials* is the number of Bernoulli trials, *probability_s* is the probability of a success on each trial, and *alpha* is the criterion value. The old form of this function is CRITBINOM, which is still supported as a Compatibility Function.
BITAND	Compares the representations of two numbers in binary form, returning a number indicating the bit positions that do not match. Takes the form =BITAND(**number1**, **number2**), where both *numbers* must be in decimal form and >=0.
BITLSHIFT	Returns a number that has been shifted to the left by a specified number of bits by adding zeros to the right of the number in binary form. Takes the form =BITLSHIFT(**number**, **shift_amount**), where *number* is an integer >= 0 and *Shift_amount* is an integer.
BITOR	Compares the representations of two numbers in binary form, returning a number indicating the bit positions that match. Takes the form =BITOR(**number1**, **number2**), where both *numbers* must be in decimal form and >=0.
BITRSHIFT	Returns a number that has been shifted to the right by a specified number of bits by removing digits to the right of the number in binary form. Takes the form =BITRSHIFT(**number**, **shift_amount**), where *number* is an integer >= 0 and *Shift_amount* is an integer.
BITXOR	Compares the representations of two numbers in binary form, returning a number indicating the result of an "exclusive OR" of its arguments. Takes the form =BITXOR(**number1**, **number2**), where *number1* and *number2* must be in decimal form and >=0.
CEILING	Rounds a number to the nearest given multiple of significance. Takes the form =CEILING(**number**, **significance**), where *number* and *significance* must be numeric and have the same sign. If they have different signs, Excel returns the #NUM! error value. See "Using the rounding functions" in Chapter 14.

Function	Description
CEILING.MATH	Rounds a number up to the nearest integer or the nearest multiple of significance. Takes the form =CEILING.MATH(**number**, significance, mode), where *number* must be less than 9.99E+307 and greater than –2.229E–308; optionally, *significance* is the multiple to which *number* should be rounded; optionally, *mode* indicates how negative numbers are handled and has no effect on positives. A mode of 1 rounds toward zero, and a mode of –1 rounds away from zero. This function replaces the CEILING.PRECISE function.
CELL	Returns information about the contents, location, or formatting of a cell. Takes the form =CELL(**info_type**, reference), where *info_type* specifies the type of information you want and *reference* is the cell you want information about. The *info_type* argument can be any of the following: *address*, *col* (column #), *color*, *contents*, *filename*, *format*, *parentheses*, *prefix*, *protect*, *row*, *type*, or *width*. See Excel's Help for a table of *format* codes returned.
CHAR	Returns the character that corresponds to an ASCII code number. Takes the form =CHAR(**number**), where *number* accepts ASCII codes with or without leading zeros. See "Using selected text functions" in Chapter 14.
CHIDIST	Supported as a Compatibility Function. See the new forms CHISQ.DIST and CHISQ.DIST.RT.
CHISQ.DIST	Returns the chi-squared distribution. Takes the form =CHISQ.DIST(**X, deg_freedom, cumulative**), where *X* is the value at which you want to evaluate the distribution and *deg_freedom* is the number of degrees of freedom. If *cumulative* is TRUE, CHISQ.DIST returns the cumulative distribution function, otherwise, it returns the probability density function. The old form of this function is CHIDIST, which is still supported as a Compatibility Function.
CHISQ.DIST.RT	Returns the right-tailed probability of the chi-squared distribution. Takes the form =CHISQ.DIST.RT(**X, deg_freedom**), where *X* is the value at which you want to evaluate the distribution and *deg_freedom* is the number of degrees of freedom. The old form of this function is CHIDIST, which is still supported as a Compatibility Function.
CHIINV	Supported as a Compatibility Function. See the new forms CHISQ.INV and CHISQ.INV.RT.
CHISQ.INV	Returns the inverse of the left-tailed probability of the chi-squared distribution. Takes the form =CHISQ.INV(**probability, deg_freedom**), where *probability* is a probability associated with the chi-squared distribution and *deg_freedom* is the number of degrees of freedom. The old form of this function is CHIINV, which is still supported as a Compatibility Function.

Function	Description
CHISQ.INV.RT	Returns the inverse of the right-tailed probability of the chi-squared distribution. Takes the form =CHISQ.INV.RT(**probability, deg_freedom**), where *probability* is a probability associated with the chi-squared distribution and *deg_freedom* is the number of degrees of freedom. The old form of this function is CHIINV, which is still supported as a Compatibility Function.
CHITEST	Supported as a Compatibility Function. See the new form CHISQ.TEST.
CHISQ.TEST	Returns the test for independence. Takes the form =CHISQ.TEST(**actual_range, expected_range**), where *actual_range* is the range of data that contains observations to test against expected values and *expected_range* is the range of data that contains the ratio of the product of row totals and column totals to the grand total. The old form of this function is CHITEST, which is still supported as a Compatibility Function.
CHOOSE	Retrieves an item from a list of values. Takes the form =CHOOSE(**index_num, value1**, value2, ...), where *index_num* is the position in the list of the item you want to look up and the *value* arguments are the elements of the list, which can be values or cell references. Returns the value of the element of the list that occupies the position indicated by *index_num*. See "Using selected lookup and reference functions" in Chapter 14.
CLEAN	Removes nonprintable characters such as tabs and program-specific codes from a string. Takes the form =CLEAN(**text**). See "Using selected text functions" in Chapter 14.
CODE	Returns the ASCII code number for the first character of its argument. Takes the form =CODE(**text**). See "Using selected text functions" in Chapter 14.
COLUMN	Returns the column number of the referenced cell or range. Takes the form =COLUMN(reference). If *reference* is omitted, the result is the column number of the cell containing the function. If *reference* is a range or a name and the function is entered as an array (by pressing Ctrl+Shift+Enter), the result is an array of the numbers of each of the columns in the range. See "Using selected lookup and reference functions" in Chapter 14.
COLUMNS	Returns the number of columns in a reference or an array. Takes the form =COLUMNS(**array**), where *array* is an array constant, a range reference, or a range name. See "Using selected lookup and reference functions" in Chapter 14.

Appendix C

Function	Description
COMBIN	Determines the number of possible group combinations that can be derived from a pool of items. Takes the form =COMBIN(**number**, **number_chosen**), where *number* is the total items in the pool and *number_chosen* is the number of items you want in each group. See "Using selected mathematical functions" in Chapter 14.
COMBINA	Determines the number of possible group combinations, including repetitions, that can be derived from a pool of items. Takes the form =COMBINA(**number**, **number_chosen**), where *number* is the total items in the pool and *number_chosen* is the number of items you want in each group.
COMPLEX	Converts real and imaginary coefficients into a complex number of the form $x + yi$ or $x + yj$. Takes the form =COMPLEX(**real_num**, **i_num**, suffix), where *real_num* is the real coefficient of the complex number, *i_num* is the imaginary coefficient of the complex number, and *suffix* is the suffix for the imaginary component of the complex number. If omitted, *suffix* is assumed to be *i*.
CONCATENATE	Assembles larger strings from smaller strings. Takes the form =CONCATENATE(**text1**, **text2**, ...), and accepts up to 30 arguments, which can be text, numbers, or cell references. See "Using the substring text functions" in Chapter 14.
CONFIDENCE	Supported as a Compatibility Function. See the new forms CONFIDENCE.NORM and CONFIDENCE.T.
CONFIDENCE.NORM	Returns the confidence interval for a population mean using a normal distribution. Takes the form =CONFIDENCE.NORM(**alpha**, **standard_dev**, **size**), where *alpha* is the significance level used to compute the confidence level (an *alpha* of 0.1 indicates a 90 percent confidence level), *standard_dev* is the population standard deviation for the data range and is assumed to be known, and *size* is the sample size. The old form of this function is CONFIDENCE, which is still supported as a Compatibility Function.
CONFIDENCE.T	Returns the confidence interval for a population mean using a Student's *t* distribution. Takes the form =CONFIDENCE.T(**alpha**, **standard_dev**, **size**), where *alpha* is the significance level used to compute the confidence level (an *alpha* of 0.1 indicates a 90 percent confidence level), *standard_dev* is the population standard deviation for the data range and is assumed to be known, and *size* is the sample size. The old form of this function is CONFIDENCE, which is still supported as a Compatibility Function.

Function	Description
CONVERT	Converts a number from one measurement system to another. Takes the form =CONVERT(**number, from_unit, to_unit**), where *number* is the value to convert, *from_unit* is the units for *number*, and *to_unit* is the units for the result. See Excel's Help for a table of unit codes.
CORREL	Returns the correlation coefficient of the *array1* and *array2* cell ranges. Takes the form =CORREL(**array1, array2**), where arrays are ranges of cells containing values.
COS	Returns the cosine of an angle and is the complement of the SIN function. Takes the form =COS(**number**), where *number* is the angle in radians.
COSH	Returns the hyperbolic cosine of a number. Takes the form =COSH(**number**), where *number* is any real number.
COT	Returns the cotangent of an angle in radians. Takes the form =COT(**number**), where *number* is any real number.
COTH	Returns the hyperbolic cotangent of an angle in radians. Takes the form =COTH(**number**), where *number* is any real number.
COUNT	Tells you how many cells in a given range contain numbers, including dates and formulas that evaluate to numbers. Takes the form =COUNT(**number1**, number2, ...), and accepts up to 30 arguments, ignoring text, error values, and logical values. See "Using built-in statistical functions" in Chapter 17.
COUNTA	Acts like COUNT except text and logical values are included in the calculation. Takes the form =COUNT(**value1**, value2, ...). See "Using built-in statistical functions" in Chapter 17.
COUNTBLANK	Counts empty cells in a specified range. Takes the form =COUNTBLANK(**range**). See "Using selected lookup and reference functions" in Chapter 14.
COUNTIF	Counts only cells that match specified criteria. Takes the form =COUNTIF(**range, criteria**), where *range* is the range you want to test and *criteria* is the logical test to be performed on each cell. See "Using built-in statistical functions" in Chapter 17.
COUNTIFS	Acts like COUNTIF but accepts multiple criteria, taking the form =COUNTIFS(**range1, criteria1**, range2, criteria2, ...).

Function	Description
COUPDAYBS	Calculates the number of days from the beginning of the coupon period to the settlement date. Takes the form =COUPDAYBS(**settlement**, **maturity**, **frequency**, basis), where *settlement* is the day you pay for the security, *maturity* is the maturity date of the security, *frequency* is the number of coupon payments made per year (1 = annual, 2 = semiannual, 4 = quarterly), and *basis* is the day-count basis of the security (if 0 or omitted = 30/360, if 1 = actual/actual, if 2 = actual/360, if 3 = actual/365, if 4 = European 30/360). See "Analyzing securities" in Chapter 16.
COUPDAYS	Calculates the number of days in the coupon period that contains the settlement date. Takes the form =COUPDAYS(**settlement**, **maturity**, **frequency**, basis). See COUPDAYBS for argument definitions. See "Analyzing securities" in Chapter 16.
COUPDAYSNC	Calculates the number of days from the settlement date to the next coupon date. Takes the form =COUPDAYSNC(**settlement**, **maturity**, **frequency**, basis). See COUPDAYBS for argument definitions. See "Analyzing securities" in Chapter 16.
COUPNCD	Calculates the next coupon date after the settlement date. Takes the form =COUPNCD(**settlement**, **maturity**, **frequency**, basis). See COUPDAYBS for argument definitions. See "Analyzing securities" in Chapter 16.
COUPNUM	Calculates the number of coupons payable between the settlement date and the maturity date, and rounds the result to the nearest whole coupon. Takes the form =COUPNUM(**settlement**, **maturity**, **frequency**, basis). See COUPDAYBS for argument definitions. See "Analyzing securities" in Chapter 16.
COUPPCD	Calculates the coupon date previous to the settlement date. Takes the form =COUPPCD(**settlement**, **maturity**, **frequency**, basis). See COUPDAYBS for argument definitions. See "Analyzing securities" in Chapter 16.
COVAR	Supported as a Compatibility Function. See the new forms COVARIANCE.P and COVARIANCE.S.
COVARIANCE.P	Returns population covariance, the average of the products of deviations for each data point pair in two data sets. Takes the form =COVARIANCE.P(**array1**, **array2**), where *array* values are cell ranges containing integers. The old form of this function is COVAR, which is still supported as a Compatibility Function.

Function	Description
COVARIANCE.S	Returns sample covariance, the average of the products of deviations for each data point pair in two data sets. Takes the form =COVARIANCE.S(**array1**, **array2**), where the *array* values are cell ranges containing integers. The old form of this function is COVAR, which is still supported as a Compatibility Function.
CRITBINOM	See BINOM.INV
CSC	Returns the cosecant of an angle in radians. Takes the form =CSC(**number**), where *number* is any real number.
CSCH	Returns the hyperbolic cosecant of an angle in radians. Takes the form =CSCH(**number**), where *number* is any real number.
CUBEKPIMEMBER	Returns a key performance indicator (KPI) property and the name of the KPI. Takes the form =CUBEKPIMEMBER(**connection**, **kpi_name**, **kpi_property**, caption), where *connection* is a text string indicating the name of the cube connection, *kpi_name* is the text name of the KPI, and *kpi_property* is the component of the KPI that is returned (one of *KPIValue, KPIGoal, KPIStatus, KPITrend, KPIWeight*, or *KPICurrentTimeMember*). This function is supported only when Excel is connected to a Microsoft SQL Server 2005 Analysis Services (or later) data source. Cube functions are used with online analytical processing (OLAP) databases, where data structures called *cubes* are used to draw multidimensional relationships among data sets.
CUBEMEMBER	Returns a member or tuple from the cube. Takes the form =CUBEMEMBER(**connection**, **member_expression**, caption), where *connection* is a text string indicating the name of the cube connection, *member_expression* is a text string of a multidimensional expression (MDX) that evaluates to a unique number in the cube, and *caption* is a text string to display in the cell instead of the defined caption from the cube. Cube functions are used with online analytical processing (OLAP) databases, where data structures called *cubes* are used to draw multidimensional relationships among data sets.
CUBEMEMBERPROPERTY	Returns the value of a member property from the cube. Takes the form =CUBEMEMBERPROPERTY(**connection**, **member_expression**, **property**), where *connection* is a text string indicating the name of the cube connection, *member_expression* is a text string of a multidimensional expression (MDX) that evaluates to a unique number in the cube, and *property* is a text string of the property name or a reference to a cell containing a property name. Cube functions are used with online analytical processing (OLAP) databases, where data structures called *cubes* are used to draw multidimensional relationships among data sets.

Function	Description
CUBERANKEDMEMBER	Returns the *N*th (ranked) member in a set. Takes the form =CUBERANKEDMEMBER(**connection**, **set_expression**, **rank**, caption), where *connection* is a text string indicating the name of the cube connection; *set_expression* is a text string indicating a set expression, the CUBESET function, or a reference to a cell containing the CUBESET function; *rank* is an integer specifying the top value to return (1 = top value, 2 = second value, and so on); and *caption* is a text string to be displayed in the cell instead of the caption supplied by the cube. Cube functions are used with online analytical processing (OLAP) databases, where data structures called *cubes* are used to draw multidimensional relationships among data sets.
CUBESET	Returns a calculated set of members or tuples from the cube database. Takes the form =CUBESET(**connection**, **set_ expression**, caption, sort_order, sort_by), where *connection* is a text string indicating the name of the cube connection, *set_ expression* is a text string that returns a set of members or is a reference to a cell range containing a set of members or tuples, *caption* is a text string to be displayed in the cell instead of the caption supplied by the cube, *sort_by* is a text string indicating the value in the set by which you want to sort the results, and *sort_order* is a number specifying the type of sort (0 = none, 1 = ascending, 2 = descending, 3 = alpha ascending, 4 = alpha descending, 5 = natural ascending, and 6 = natural descending). Cube functions are used with online analytical processing (OLAP) databases, where data structures called *cubes* are used to draw multidimensional relationships among data sets.
CUBESETCOUNT	Returns the number of items in a set. Takes the form =CUBESETCOUNT(**set**), where *set* is a text string of an expression that evaluates to a set defined by the CUBESET function, the CUBESET function itself, or a reference to a cell containing a CUBESET function. Cube functions are used with online analytical processing (OLAP) databases, where data structures called *cubes* are used to draw multidimensional relationships among data sets.
CUBEVALUE	Returns an aggregated value from a cube. Takes the form =CUBEVALUE(**connection**, **member_expression1**, member_ expression2, ...), where *connection* is a text string indicating the name of the cube connection and *member_expression* is a text string of a multidimensional expression (MDX) that evaluates to a unique number in the cube. Cube functions are used with online analytical processing (OLAP) databases, where data structures called *cubes* are used to draw multidimensional relationships among data sets.

Function	Description
CUMIPMT	Returns the cumulative interest paid on a loan between *start_period* and *end_period*. Takes the form =CUMIPMT(**rate**, **nper**, **pv**, **start_period**, **end_period**, **type**), where *rate* is the interest rate, *nper* is the total number of payment periods, *pv* is the present value, and *start_period* is the first period in the calculation. Payment periods are numbered beginning with 1; *end_period* is the last period in the calculation, and *type* is the timing of the payment.
CUMPRINC	Returns the cumulative principal paid on a loan between *start_period* and *end_period*. Takes the form =CUMPRINC(**rate**, **nper**, **pv**, **start_period**, **end_period**, **type**). For argument descriptions, see CUMIPMT.
DATE	Returns the serial number that represents a particular date. Takes the form =DATE(**year**, **month**, **day**), where *year* can be one to four digits from 1 to 9999, *month* is a number representing the month of the year, and *day* is a number representing the day of the month.
DATEVALUE	Translates a date into a serial value. Takes the form =DATEVALUE(**date_text**), where *date_text* represents a date entered as text in quotation marks. See "Working with date and time functions" in Chapter 15.
DAVERAGE	Averages the values in a column in a table or database that match conditions you specify. Takes the form =DAVERAGE(**database**, **field**, **criteria**), where *database* is the range of cells that make up the table or database and the first row of the table contains labels for each column, *field* indicates which column is used in the function (by label name or by position), and *criteria* is the range of cells that contain the conditions you specify.
DAY	Returns the value of the day portion of a serial date/time value. Takes the form =DAY(**serial_number**), where *serial_number* can be a date value, a reference, or text in date format enclosed in quotation marks. See "Working with date and time functions" in Chapter 15.
DAYS	Returns the number of days between two dates. Takes the form =DAYS(**end_date**, **start_date**), where both arguments are serial date values or references to cells containing valid date values.
DAYS360	Returns the number of days between two dates based on a 360-day year (12 months of 30 days each), which is used in some accounting calculations. Takes the form =DAYS360(**start_date**, **end_date**, method), where *start_date* and *end_date* are the two dates between which you want to know the number of days, and *method* is a logical value that specifies whether to use the U.S. or European method in the calculation. If *method* is FALSE or omitted, the function uses the U.S. (NASD) method; if *method* is TRUE, the function uses the European method.

Function	Description
DB	Computes fixed declining balance depreciation for a particular period in the asset's life. Takes the form =DB(**cost**, **salvage**, **life**, **period**, month), where *cost* is the initial asset cost, *salvage* is the remaining value after the asset is fully depreciated, *life* is the length of depreciation time, *period* is the individual period to be computed, and *month* is the number of months depreciated in the first year. (If omitted, it is assumed to be 12.) See "Calculating depreciation" in Chapter 16.
DCOUNT	Counts the cells that contain numbers in a column in a table or database that match conditions you specify. Takes the form =DCOUNT(**database**, **field**, **criteria**), where *database* is the range of cells that make up the table or database, *field* indicates which column is used in the function, and *criteria* is the range of cells that contain the conditions you specify.
DCOUNTA	Acts like DCOUNT, except it also includes cells containing text, logical values, and error values. See DCOUNT for arguments.
DDB	Computes double-declining balance depreciation. Takes the form =DDB(**cost**, **salvage**, **life**, period, factor), where *cost* is the initial asset cost, *salvage* is the remaining value after the asset is fully depreciated, *life* is the length of depreciation time, *period* is the individual period to be computed, and *factor* indicates the method used (2 or omitted indicates double-declining balance, and 3 indicates triple-declining balance). See "Calculating depreciation" in Chapter 16.
DECIMAL	Converts numeric text to a decimal number in a given base. Takes the form =DECIMAL(**text**, **radix**), where *text* is the numeric text you want to convert and *radix* is an integer specifying a base from 2 to 36.
DEC2BIN	Converts a decimal number to binary. Takes the form =DEC2BIN(**number**, places), where *number* is the decimal integer you want to convert and *places* is the number of characters to use. *Places* is useful for padding the return value with leading zeros.
DEC2HEX	Converts a decimal number to hexadecimal. Takes the same form and arguments as DEC2BIN.
DEC2OCT	Converts a decimal number to octal. Takes the same form and arguments as DEC2BIN.
DEGREES	Converts radians to degrees. Takes the form =DEGREES(**angle**), where *angle* represents an angle measured in radians.

Function	Description
DELTA	Tests whether two values are equal. Takes the form =DELTA(**number1**, **number2**), where *number1* is the first number and *number2* is the second number (which, if omitted, is assumed to be zero). Returns 1 if *number1* equals *number2*; otherwise, returns 0.
DEVSQ	Returns the sum of squares of deviations of data points from their sample mean. Takes the form =DEVSQ(**number1**, **number2**, ...), where the numbers can be names, arrays, or references that resolve to numbers. Accepts up to 30 arguments.
DGET	Extracts a single value from a column in a table or database that matches conditions you specify. Takes the form =DGET(**database**, **field**, **criteria**), where *database* is the range of cells that make up the table or database, *field* indicates which column is used in the function, and *criteria* is the range of cells that contain the conditions you specify.
DISC	Calculates the discount rate for a security. Takes the form =DISC(**settlement**, **maturity**, **price**, **redemption**, **basis**), where *settlement* is the day you pay for the security, *maturity* is the maturity date of the security, *price* is the security's price per $100 of face value, *redemption* is the value of the security at redemption, and *basis* is the day-count basis of the security (if 0 or omitted = 30/360, if 1 = actual/actual, if 2 = actual/360, if 3 = actual/365, if 4 = European 30/360). See "Analyzing securities" in Chapter 16.
DMAX	Returns the largest number in a column in a table or database that matches conditions you specify. Takes the form =DMAX(**database**, **field**, **criteria**), where *database* is a range that makes up the table or database, *field* indicates which column is used in the function, and *criteria* is the range of cells that contain the conditions you specify.
DMIN	Returns the smallest number in a column in a table or database that matches conditions you specify. Takes the same form and arguments as DMAX.
DOLLAR	Converts a number into a string formatted as currency with the specified number of decimal places. Takes the form =DOLLAR(**number**, decimals). If you omit *decimals*, the result is rounded to two decimal places. If you use a negative number for *decimals*, the result is rounded to the left of the decimal point. See "Using selected text functions" in Chapter 14.

Function	Description
DOLLARDE	Converts the familiar fractional pricing of securities to decimals. Takes the form =DOLLARDE(**fractional dollar**, **fraction**), where *fractional dollar* is the value you want to convert expressed as an integer followed by a decimal point and the numerator of the fraction you want, and *fraction* is an integer indicating the denominator to be used. See "Analyzing securities" in Chapter 16.
DOLLARFR	Converts a security price expressed in decimals to fractions. Takes the form =DOLLARFR(**decimal_dollar**, **fraction**), where *decimal_dollar* is the value you want to convert expressed as a decimal and *fraction* is an integer indicating the denominator of the fraction you want. See "Analyzing securities" in Chapter 16.
DPRODUCT	Multiplies the values in a column in a table or database that match conditions you specify. Takes the form =DPRODUCT(**database**, **field**, **criteria**), where *database* is a range that makes up the table or database, *field* indicates which column is used in the function, and *criteria* is the range of cells that contain the conditions you specify.
DSTDEV	Estimates the standard deviation of a population based on a sample, using the numbers in a column in a table or database that match conditions you specify. Takes the same form and arguments as DPRODUCT.
DSTDEVP	Calculates the standard deviation of a population based on the entire population, using the numbers in a column in a table or database that match conditions you specify. Takes the same form and arguments as DPRODUCT.
DSUM	Adds the numbers in a column in a table or database that match conditions you specify. Takes the same form and arguments as DPRODUCT.
DURATION	Calculates the weighted average of the present value of a bond's cash flows for a security whose interest payments are made on a periodic basis. Takes the form =DURATION(**settlement**, **maturity**, **coupon**, **yield**, **frequency**, basis), where *settlement* is the day you pay for the security, *maturity* is the maturity date of the security, *coupon* is the security's annual coupon rate, *yield* is the annual yield of the security, *frequency* is the number of coupon payments made per year (1 = annual, 2 = semiannual, 4 = quarterly), and *basis* is the day-count basis of the security (if 0 or omitted = 30/360, if 1 = actual/actual, if 2 = actual/360, if 3 = actual/365, if 4 = European 30/360). See "Analyzing securities" in Chapter 16.

Function	Description
DVAR	Estimates the variance of a population based on a sample, using the numbers in a column in a table or database that match conditions you specify. Takes the form =DVAR(**database**, **field**, **criteria**), where *database* is the range of cells that make up the table or database, *field* indicates which column is used in the function, and *criteria* is the range of cells that contain the conditions you specify.
DVARP	Calculates the variance of a population based on the entire population, using the numbers in a column in a table or database that match conditions you specify. Takes the same form and arguments as DVAR.
EDATE	Returns the exact date that falls an indicated number of months before or after a given date. Takes the form =EDATE(**start_date**, **months**), where *start_date* is the date to calculate from and *months* is the number of months before (negative) or after (positive) the start date. See "Working with specialized date functions" in Chapter 15.
EFFECT	Returns the effective interest rate. Takes the form =EFFECT(**nominal_rate**, **npery**), where *nominal_rate* is the annual interest rate and *npery* is the number of annual compounding periods.
ENCODEURL	Returns a specified string to be encoded as a Universal Resource Locator (URL) for web use. Takes the form =ENCODEURL(**text**).
EOMONTH	Returns a date that falls on the last day of the month an indicated number of months before or after a given date. Takes the form =EOMONTH(**start_date**, **months**), where *start_date* is the date to calculate from and *months* is the number of months before (negative) or after (positive) the start date. See "Working with specialized date functions" in Chapter 15.
ERF	Returns the error function integrated between *lower_limit* and *upper_limit*. Takes the form =ERF(**lower_limit**, upper_limit), where *lower_limit* is the lower bound and *upper_limit* is the upper bound. If *upper_limit* is omitted, ERF integrates between zero and *lower_limit*.
ERF.PRECISE	Returns the error function. Takes the form =ERF.PRECISE(**x**), where *x* is the lower bound.
ERFC	Returns the complementary ERF function integrated between *x* and infinity. Takes the form =ERFC(**x**), where *x* is the lower bound for integrating ERF.
ERFC.PRECISE	Returns the precise complementary ERF function integrated between *x* and infinity. Takes the form =ERFC.PRECISE(**x**), where *x* is the lower bound for integrating ERF.

Function	Description
ERROR.TYPE	Detects the type of error value in a referenced cell. Takes the form =ERROR.TYPE(**error_val**), and returns a code designating the type of error value in the referenced cell: 1 (#NULL!), 2 (#DIV/0!), 3 (#VALUE!), 4 (#REF!), 5 (#NAME!), 6 (#NUM!), and 7 (#N/A). Any other value in the referenced cell returns the error value #N/A. See "Using selected lookup and reference functions" in Chapter 14.
EUROCONVERT	Converts a number to euros—or converts any EU member currency to euros or any other member currency. Takes the form =EUROCONVERT(**number**, **source**, **target**, full_ precision, triangulation_precision), where *number* is the value you want to convert, *source* is the ISO country code for the source currency, *target* is the ISO country code for the currency to which you want to convert, *full_precision* is a logical value that displays all significant digits when TRUE and uses a currency-specific rounding factor when FALSE, and *triangulation_precision* is an integer equal to or greater than 3 that specifies the number of significant digits to use when converting from one EU member currency to another. This function is installed with the Euro Currency Tools add-in. See Excel's Help for tables of ISO codes and rounding factors.
EVEN	Rounds a number up to the nearest even integer. Takes the form =EVEN(**number**). Negative numbers are correspondingly rounded down. See "Using the rounding functions" in Chapter 14.
EXACT	Determines whether two strings match exactly, including uppercase and lowercase letters but not including formatting differences. Takes the form =EXACT(**text1**, **text2**), where both arguments must be either literal strings enclosed in quotation marks or references to cells that contain text. See "Using selected text functions" in Chapter 14.
EXP	Computes the value of the constant e (approx. 2.71828183) raised to the power specified by its argument. Takes the form =EXP(**number**). The EXP function is the inverse of the LN function.
EXPON.DIST	Returns exponential distribution. Takes the form =EXPON.DIST(**x**, **lambda**, **cumulative**), where x is the value of the function, *lambda* is the parameter value, and *cumulative* is a logical value that indicates which form of the exponential function to provide. (If *cumulative* is TRUE, EXPON.DIST returns the cumulative distribution function; if *cumulative* is FALSE, it returns the probability density function.) The old form of this function is EXPONDIST, which is still supported as a Compatibility Function.
FACT	Returns the factorial of a number. Takes the form =FACT(**number**), where *number* is a positive integer.

Function	Description
FACTDOUBLE	Returns the double factorial of a number. Takes the form =FACTDOUBLE(**number**), where *number* is a positive integer.
FALSE	Represents an alternative for the logical condition FALSE. The FALSE function accepts no arguments and takes the form =FALSE(). See "Using selected logical functions" in Chapter 14.
F.DIST	Returns the F probability distribution. Takes the form =F.DIST(**x**, **deg_freedom1**, **deg_freedom2**, **cumulative**), where *x* is the value at which to evaluate the function, *deg_freedom1* is the numerator degrees of freedom, and *deg_freedom2* is the denominator. If *cumulative* is TRUE, F.DIST returns the cumulative distribution function; otherwise, it returns the probability density function. The old form of this function is FDIST, which is still supported as a Compatibility Function.
F.DIST.RT	Returns the right-tailed F probability distribution. Takes the form =F.DIST.RT(**x**, **degrees_freedom1**, **degrees_freedom2**), where *x* is the value at which to evaluate the function, *degrees_freedom1* is the numerator degrees of freedom, and *degrees_freedom2* is the denominator. The old form of this function is FDIST, which is still supported as a Compatibility Function.
FIND	Returns the position of specified text within a string. Takes the form =FIND(**find_text**, **within_text**, start_num), where *find_text* is the text you want to find (case sensitive) and *within_text* indicates where to look. Both arguments accept either literal text enclosed in quotation marks or cell references. The optional *start_num* specifies the character position in *within_text* where you want to begin the search. You get a #VALUE! error value if *find_text* isn't contained in *within_text*, if *start_num* isn't greater than zero, or if *start_num* is greater than the number of characters in *within_text* or greater than the position of the last occurrence of *find_text*. See "Using the substring text functions" in Chapter 14.
FINDB	Returns the position of specified text within a string based on the number of bytes each character uses from the first character of *within_text*. Takes the form =FINDB(**find_text**, **within_text**, start_num), and takes the same arguments as FIND. This function is for use with double-byte character sets, such as Chinese, Japanese, and Korean.
F.INV	Returns the inverse of the F probability distribution. Takes the form =F.INV(**probability**, **deg_freedom1**, **deg_freedom2**), where *probability* is a probability associated with the F cumulative distribution, *degrees_freedom1* is the numerator degrees of freedom, and *degrees_freedom2* is the denominator degrees of freedom. The old form of this function is FINV, which is still supported as a Compatibility Function.

Function	Description
F.INV.RT	Returns the inverse of the right-tailed F probability distribution. Takes the form =F.INV.RT(**probability**, **deg_ freedom1**, **deg_freedom2**), where *probability* is a probability associated with the F cumulative distribution, *degrees_ freedom1* is the numerator degrees of freedom, and *degrees_ freedom2* is the denominator degrees of freedom. The old form of this function is FINV, which is still supported as a Compatibility Function.
FILTERXML	Returns data from XML content using a specified XPath expression. Takes the form =FILTERXML(**xml**, **xpath**), where *xml* is a valid XML string and *xpath* is a valid Xpath expression.
FISHER	Returns the Fisher transformation at *x*. Takes the form =FISHER(**x**), where *x* is a value between −1 and 1 (not inclusive).
FISHERINV	Returns the inverse of the Fisher transformation. Takes the form =FISHERINV(**y**), where *y* is any numeric value.
FIXED	Rounds a number to the specified number of decimals, formats the number in decimal format using a period and commas, and returns the result as text. Takes the form =FIXED(**number**, decimals, no_commas), where *number* is the number you want to round and convert to text, *decimals* is the number of digits to the right of the decimal point (2 if omitted), and *no_commas* is a logical value (if TRUE, prevents commas; if FALSE or omitted, includes commas).
FLOOR	Rounds a number down to the nearest given multiple. Takes the form =FLOOR(**number**, **significance**), where *number* and *significance* must be numeric and have the same sign. If they have different signs, Excel returns the #NUM! error value. See "Using the rounding functions" in Chapter 14.
FLOOR.MATH	Rounds a number down to the nearest integer or the nearest multiple of significance. Takes the form =FLOOR.MATH(**number**, significance, mode), where *number* is the number to be rounded down; optionally, *significance* is the multiple to which number should be rounded; optionally, *mode* indicates how negative numbers are handled and has no effect on positives. A mode of 1 rounds up toward zero, and a mode of −1 rounds down away from zero. This function replaces the old FLOOR.PRECISE function.
FORECAST	Returns a single point along a trend line. Takes the form =FORECAST(**x**, **known_y's**, **known_x's**). For arguments and usage details, see "The FORECAST function" in Chapter 17.
FORMULATEXT	Returns a formula as displayed in the formula bar, as a text string. Takes the form =FORMULATEXT(**reference**), where *reference* is a cell or range reference.

Function	Description
FREQUENCY	Returns the number of times that values occur within a population. Takes the form =FREQUENCY(**data_array**, **bins_array**). For usage and argument details, see "Analyzing distribution with the FREQUENCY function" in Chapter 17.
F.TEST	Returns the result of an F-test, the one-tailed probability that the variances in *array1* and *array2* are not significantly different. Takes the form =F.TEST(**array1**, **array2**). The old form of this function is FTEST, which is still supported for compatibility.
FV	Computes the value at a future date of an investment based on periodic, constant payments and a constant interest rate. Takes the form =FV(**rate**, **nper**, **payment**, pv, type), where *rate* is the interest rate, *nper* is the term (periods) of the investment, *payment* is the amount of each periodic payment when individual amounts are the same, *pv* is the investment value today, and *type* indicates when payments are made (0 or omitted = at end of period, 1 = at beginning of period). See "Calculating investments" in Chapter 16.
FVSCHEDULE	Returns the future value of an initial principal after applying a series of variable compound interest rates. Takes the form =FVSCHEDULE(**principal**, **schedule**), where *principal* is the present value and *schedule* is an array of interest rates to apply.
GAMMA	Supported as a Compatibility Function. See the new form GAMMA.DIST.
GAMMA.DIST	Returns the gamma distribution. Takes the form =GAMMA.DIST(**x**, **alpha**, **beta**, **cumulative**), where x is the value at which you want to evaluate the distribution, *alpha* is a parameter to the distribution, and *beta* is a parameter to the distribution. If *cumulative* is TRUE, GAMMA.DIST returns the cumulative distribution function; otherwise, it returns the probability density function. The old form of this function is GAMMADIST, which is still supported as a Compatibility Function.
GAMMA.INV	Returns the inverse of the gamma cumulative distribution. Takes the form =GAMMA.INV(**probability**, **alpha**, **beta**), where *probability* is the probability associated with the gamma distribution, *alpha* is a parameter to the distribution, and *beta* is a parameter to the distribution. The old form of this function is GAMMAINV, which is still supported as a Compatibility Function.
GAMMALN	Returns the natural logarithm of the gamma function. Takes the form =GAMMALN(**x**), where x is a positive value.
GAMMALN.PRECISE	Returns the natural logarithm of the gamma function. Takes the form =GAMMALN.PRECISE(**x**), where x is a positive value.

Function	Description
GAUSS	Returns the percent probability that a member of a normal population will fall between the mean and *z* standard deviations from the mean. Takes the form =GAUSS(**z**), where *z* is the number of standard deviations to use.
GCD	Returns the greatest common divisor of two or more integers (the largest integer that divides both *number1* and *number2* without a remainder). Takes the form =GCD(**number1**, number2, ...), where the numbers are 1 to 30 positive integer values.
GEOMEAN	Returns the geometric mean of an array or range of positive data. Takes the form =GEOMEAN(**number1**, number2, ...), where the numbers are 1 to 30 positive integer values.
GESTEP	Returns 1 if *number* is greater than or equal to *step*; otherwise, returns 0 (zero). Takes the form =GESTEP(**number**, step), where *number* is the value to test against *step* and *step* is the threshold value (zero if omitted).
GETPIVOTDATA	Returns data stored in a PivotTable report. Takes the form =GETPIVOTDATA(**data_field**, **pivot_table**, field1, item1, field2, item2, ...), where *data_field* is the name, in quotation marks, for the data field that contains the data you want retrieved; *pivot_table* is a reference to a cell in the PivotTable report that contains the data you want to retrieve; and *fieldx* and *itemx* are 1 to 14 pairs of field names and item names that describe the data you want to retrieve.
GROWTH	Returns values of points that lie along an exponential growth trend line. Takes the form =GROWTH(**known_y's**, known_x's, new_x's, const). For arguments and usage details, see "The GROWTH function" in Chapter 17.
HARMEAN	Returns the harmonic mean of a data set. Takes the form =HARMEAN(**number1**, number2, ...), where the numbers are 1 to 30 positive values.
HEX2BIN	Converts a hexadecimal number to binary. Takes the form =HEX2BIN(**number**, places), where *number* is the hexadecimal number you want to convert and *places* is the number of characters to use. (It's useful for padding the return value with leading zeros.)
HEX2DEC	Converts a hexadecimal number to decimal. Takes the form =HEX2DEC(**number**), where *number* is the hexadecimal number you want to convert.
HEX2OCT	Converts a hexadecimal number to octal. Takes the form =HEX2OCT(**number**, places), where *number* is the hexadecimal number you want to convert and *places* is the number of characters to use. (It's useful for padding the return value with leading zeros.)

Function	Description
HLOOKUP	Looks for a specified value in the top row in a table, and returns the value in the same column and a specified row. Takes the form =HLOOKUP(**lookup_value**, **table_array**, **row_index_num**, range_lookup), where *lookup_value* is the value to look for; *table_array* is the range containing the lookup and result values sorted in alphabetical order by the top row; *row_index_num* is the row number containing the value you want to find; and *range_lookup* is a logical value, which, if FALSE, forces an exact match. See "Using selected lookup and reference functions" in Chapter 14.
HOUR	Returns the hour portion of a serial date/time value. Takes the form =HOUR(**serial_number**), where *serial_number* can be a time/date value, a reference, or text in time/date format enclosed in quotation marks. See "Working with date and time functions" in Chapter 15.
HYPERLINK	Creates a shortcut or jump that opens a document stored on a network server, an intranet, or the Internet. When you click the cell that contains the HYPERLINK function, Excel opens the file stored at *link_location*. Takes the form =HYPERLINK(**link_location**, friendly_name), where *link_location* is the path and file name to the document to be opened and *friendly_name* is the jump text or numeric value that is displayed in the cell.
HYPGEOM.DIST	Returns the hypergeometric distribution (the probability of a given number of sample successes, given the size of the sample and population and the number of population successes). Takes the form =HYPGEOM.DIST(**sample_s**, **number_sample**, **population_s**, **number_pop**, **cumulative**), where *sample_s* is the number of successes in the sample, *number_sample* is the size of the sample, *population_s* is the number of successes in the population, and *number_pop* is the population size. If *cumulative* is TRUE, HYPGEOM.DIST returns the cumulative distribution function; otherwise, it returns the probability density function. The old form of this function is HYPGEOMDIST, which is still supported as a Compatibility Function.
IF	Returns values based on supplied conditional tests. Takes the form =IF(**logical_test**, **value_if_true**, value_if_false). You can nest up to seven additional functions within an IF function. If you use text arguments, the match must be exact except for case. See "Using selected logical functions" in Chapter 14.
IFERROR	Returns a specified value when a formula evaluates to an error. Takes the form =IFERROR(**value**, **value_if_error**), where *value* refers to the formula you want to check and *value_if_error* is the value you want to display if *value* returns an error.

Appendix C

Function	Description
IFNA	Returns a specified value when a formula evaluates to #N/A. Takes the form =IFNA(**value**, **value_if_na**), where *value* refers to the argument you want to check and *value_if_na* is the value you want to display if *value* returns #N/A.
IMABS	Returns the absolute value (modulus) of a complex number in *x* + *yi* or *x* + *yj* text format. Takes the form =IMABS(**inumber**), where *inumber* is a complex number for which you want the absolute value.
IMAGINARY	Returns the imaginary coefficient of a complex number in *x* + *yi* or *x* + *yj* text format. Takes the form =IMAGINARY(**inumber**), where *inumber* is a complex number for which you want the imaginary coefficient.
IMARGUMENT	Returns the argument theta, an angle expressed in radians. Takes the form =IMARGUMENT(**inumber**), where *inumber* is a complex number for which you want the argument theta.
IMCONJUGATE	Returns the complex conjugate of a complex number in *x* + *yi* or *x* + *yj* text format. Takes the form =IMCONJUGATE(**inumber**), where *inumber* is a complex number for which you want the conjugate.
IMCOS	Returns the cosine of a complex number in *x* + *yi* or *x* + *yj* text format. Takes the form =IMCOS(**inumber**), where *inumber* is a complex number for which you want the cosine.
IMCOSH	Returns the hyperbolic cosine of a complex number in *x* + *yi* or *x* + *yj* text format. Takes the form =IMCOSH(**inumber**), where *inumber* is a complex number for which you want the hyperbolic cosine.
IMCOT	Returns the cotangent of a complex number in *x* + *yi* or *x* + *yj* text format. Takes the form =IMCOT(**inumber**), where *inumber* is a complex number for which you want the cotangent.
IMCSC	Returns the cosecant of a complex number in *x* + *yi* or *x* + *yj* text format. Takes the form =IMCSC(**inumber**), where *inumber* is a complex number for which you want the cosecant.
IMCSCH	Returns the hyperbolic cosecant of a complex number in *x* + *yi* or *x* + *yj* text format. Takes the form =IMCSCH(**inumber**), where *inumber* is a complex number for which you want the hyperbolic cosecant.
IMDIV	Returns the quotient of two complex numbers in *x* + *yi* or *x* + *yj* text format. Takes the form =IMDIV(**inumber1**, **inumber2**), where *inumber1* is the complex numerator or dividend and *inumber2* is the complex denominator or divisor.

Function	Description
IMEXP	Returns the exponential of a complex number in $x + yi$ or $x + yj$ text format. Takes the form =IMEXP(**inumber**), where *inumber* is a complex number for which you want the exponential.
IMLN	Returns the natural logarithm of a complex number in $x + yi$ or $x + yj$ text format. Takes the form =IMLN(**inumber**), where *inumber* is a complex number for which you want the natural logarithm.
IMLOG10	Returns the common logarithm (base 10) of a complex number in $x + yi$ or $x + yj$ text format. Takes the form =IMLOG10(**inumber**), where *inumber* is a complex number for which you want the common logarithm.
IMLOG2	Returns the base-2 logarithm of a complex number in $x + yi$ or $x + yj$ text format. Takes the form =IMLOG2(**inumber**), where *inumber* is a complex number for which you want the base-2 logarithm.
IMPOWER	Returns a complex number in $x + yi$ or $x + yj$ text format raised to a power. Takes the form =IMPOWER(**inumber, number**), where *inumber* is a complex number you want to raise to a power and *number* is the power to which you want to raise the complex number.
IMPRODUCT	Returns the product of 2 to 29 complex numbers in $x + yi$ or $x + yj$ text format. Takes the form =IMPRODUCT(**inumber1**, inumber2, ...). The *inumbers* are 1 to 29 complex numbers to multiply.
IMREAL	Returns the real coefficient of a complex number in $x + yi$ or $x + yj$ text format. Takes the form =IMREAL(**inumber**), where *inumber* is a complex number for which you want the real coefficient.
IMSEC	Returns the secant of a complex number in $x + yi$ or $x + yj$ text format. Takes the form =IMSEC(**inumber**), where *inumber* is a complex number for which you want the secant.
IMSECH	Returns the hyperbolic secant of a complex number in $x + yi$ or $x + yj$ text format. Takes the form =IMSECH(**inumber**), where *inumber* is a complex number for which you want the hyperbolic secant.
IMSIN	Returns the sine of a complex number in $x + yi$ or $x + yj$ text format. Takes the form =IMSIN(**inumber**), where *inumber* is a complex number for which you want the sine.
IMSINH	Returns the hyperbolic sine of a complex number in $x + yi$ or $x + yj$ text format. Takes the form =IMSINH(**inumber**), where *inumber* is a complex number for which you want the hyperbolic sine.

Function	Description
IMSQRT	Returns the square root of a complex number in $x + yi$ or $x + yj$ text format. Takes the form =IMSQRT(**inumber**), where *inumber* is a complex number for which you want the square root.
IMSUB	Returns the difference of two complex numbers in $x + yi$ or $x + yj$ text format. Takes the form =IMSUB(**inumber1**, **inumber2**), where *inumber1* is the complex number from which to subtract *inumber2* and *inumber2* is the complex number to subtract from *inumber1*.
IMSUM	Returns the sum of two or more complex numbers in $x + yi$ or $x + yj$ text format. Takes the form =IMSUM(**inumber1**, inumber2, ...), where the *inumbers* are 1 to 29 complex numbers to add.
IMTAN	Returns the tangent of a complex number in $x + yi$ or $x + yj$ text format. Takes the form =IMTAN(**inumber**), where *inumber* is a complex number for which you want the tangent.
INDEX	Returns a value or values, or a reference to a cell or range, using one of two forms: *array*: =INDEX(**array**, row_num, column_num) or *reference:* =INDEX(**reference**, row_num, column_num, area_num). The array form works only with array arguments and returns the resulting values located at the intersection of *row_num* and *column_num*. The reference form returns a cell address using similar arguments, where *reference* can be one or more ranges (areas) and *area_num* is needed only if more than one area is included in *reference*. See "Using selected lookup and reference functions" in Chapter 14.
INDIRECT	Returns the contents of a cell using its reference. Takes the form =INDIRECT(**ref_text**, **a1**), where *ref_text* is a reference or a name and *a1* is a logical value indicating the type of reference used in *ref_text*. (FALSE indicates R1C1 format, and TRUE or omitted indicates A1 format.) See "Using selected lookup and reference functions" in Chapter 14.
INFO	Returns information about the current operating environment. Takes the form =INFO(**type_text**), where *type_text* is text specifying what type of information you want returned. Information types include *directory*, *memavail*, *memused*, *numfile*, *origin*, *osversion*, *recalc*, *release*, *system*, and *totmem*. See Excel's Help for more information.
INT	Rounds numbers down to the nearest integer. Takes the form =INT(**number**). When *number* is negative, INT also rounds that number down to the nearest integer. See "Using the rounding functions" in Chapter 14.

Function	Description
INTERCEPT	Calculates the point at which a line intersects the *y* axis by using existing *x* values and *y* values. Takes the form =INTERCEPT(**known_y's**, **known_x's**), where *known_y's* is the dependent set of observations or data and *known_x's* is the independent set of observations or data.
INTRATE	Calculates the rate of interest (discount rate) for a fully invested security. Takes the form =INTRATE(**settlement**, **maturity**, **investment**, **redemption**, basis), where *settlement* is the day you pay for the security, *maturity* is the maturity date of the security, *investment* is the amount invested in the security, *redemption* is the amount to be received at maturity, and *basis* is the day-count basis of the security (if 0 or omitted = 30/360, if 1 = actual/actual; if 2 = actual/360, if 3 = actual/365; if 4 = European 30/360). See "Analyzing securities" in Chapter 16.
IPMT	Computes the interest portion of an individual payment made to repay an amount over a specified time period with constant periodic payments and a constant interest rate. Takes the form =IPMT(**rate**, **period**, **nper**, **pv**, fv, type), where *rate* is the interest rate, *period* is the number of an individual periodic payment, *nper* is the term (periods) of the investment, *pv* is the investment value today, *fv* is the investment value at the end of the term, and *type* indicates when payments are made (0 or omitted = at end of period, 1 = at beginning of period). See "Calculating investments" in Chapter 16.
IRR	Returns the rate that causes the present value of the inflows from an investment to exactly equal the cost of the investment. Takes the form =IRR(**values**, guess), where *values* is an array or a reference to a range of cells that contain numbers beginning with the cost expressed as a negative value and *guess* is an approximate interest rate (10 percent if omitted). See "Calculating investments" in Chapter 16.
ISBLANK	Returns TRUE if the referenced cell is empty; otherwise, returns FALSE. Uses the form =ISBLANK(**value**). See "Using the IS information functions" in Chapter 14.
ISERR	Returns TRUE if the value contains any error value except #N/A; otherwise, returns FALSE. Uses the form =ISERR(**value**). See "Using the IS information functions" in Chapter 14.
ISERROR	Returns TRUE if the value contains any error value (including #N/A); otherwise, returns FALSE. Uses the form =ISERROR(**value**). See "Using the IS information functions" in Chapter 14.
ISEVEN	Returns TRUE if the value is an even number; otherwise, returns FALSE. Uses the form =ISEVEN(**number**). See "Using the IS information functions" in Chapter 14.

Appendix C

Function	Description
ISFORMULA	Returns TRUE if the value is a formula; otherwise, returns FALSE. Uses the form =ISFORMULA(**reference**). See "Using the IS information functions" in Chapter 14.
ISLOGICAL	Returns TRUE if the value is a logical value; otherwise, returns FALSE. Uses the form =ISLOGICAL(**value**). See "Using the IS information functions" in Chapter 14.
ISNA	Returns TRUE if the value is the #N/A error value; otherwise, returns FALSE. Uses the form =ISNA(**value**). See "Using the IS information functions" in Chapter 14.
ISNONTEXT	Returns TRUE if the value is not text; otherwise, returns FALSE. Uses the form =ISNONTEXT(**value**). See "Using the IS information functions" in Chapter 14.
ISNUMBER	Returns TRUE if the value is a number; otherwise, returns FALSE. Uses the form =ISNUMBER(**value**). See "Using the IS information functions" in Chapter 14.
ISODD	Returns TRUE if the value is an odd number; otherwise, returns FALSE. Uses the form =ISODD(**number**). See "Using the IS information functions" in Chapter 14.
ISOWEEKNUM	Returns a number that indicates where the week falls numerically within a year, according to the European ISO standard, where the week containing the first Thursday of the year is the first week of the year. Takes the form =ISOWEEKNUM(**date**), where *date* is any valid date.
ISPMT	Calculates the interest paid during a specific period of an investment. Provided for Lotus 1-2-3 compatibility, and takes the form =ISPMT(**rate**, **per**, **nper**, **pv**), where *rate* is the interest rate for the investment, *per* is the period for which you want to find the interest, *nper* is the total number of payment periods for the investment, and *pv* is the present value of the investment (or the loan amount).
ISREF	Returns TRUE if the value is a reference; otherwise, returns FALSE. Uses the form =ISREF(**value**). See "Using the IS information functions" in Chapter 14.
ISTEXT	Returns TRUE if the value is text; otherwise, returns FALSE. Uses the form =ISTEXT(**value**). See "Using the IS information functions" in Chapter 14.
KURT	Returns the kurtosis of a data set (characterizes the relative "peakedness" or flatness of a distribution compared with the normal distribution). Takes the form =KURT(**number1**, number2, ...), and accepts up to 30 numeric arguments.
LARGE	Returns the *k*th largest value in an input range. Takes the form =LARGE(**array**, **k**), where *k* is the position from the largest value in *array* you want to find. See "Using functions that analyze rank and percentile" in Chapter 17.

Function	Description
LCM	Returns the least common multiple of integers (the smallest positive integer that is a multiple of all arguments). Takes the form =LCM(**number1**, number2, ...), and accepts up to 29 numeric integer arguments.
LEFT	Returns the leftmost series of characters from a string. Takes the form =LEFT(**text**, num_chars), where *num_chars* indicates how many characters you want to extract from the string (1 if omitted). See "Using the substring text functions" in Chapter 14.
LEFTB	Returns the leftmost series of characters from a string, based on the specified number of bytes. Takes the form =LEFT(**text**, num_bytes), where *num_bytes* indicates how many characters you want to extract from the *text* string, based on bytes. This function is for use with double-byte character sets such as Chinese, Japanese, and Korean.
LEN	Returns the number of displayed characters in an entry. Takes the form =LEN(**text**), where *text* is a number, a string enclosed in quotation marks, or a reference to a cell. Trailing zeros are ignored, but spaces are counted. See "Using selected text functions" in Chapter 14.
LENB	Returns the number of characters in an entry, expressed in bytes. Takes the form =LENB(**text**). It is otherwise identical to the LEN function. This function is intended for use with double-byte characters.
LINEST	Calculates the statistics for a line using the least squares method to arrive at a slope that best describes the given data. Takes the form LINEST(**known_y's**, known_x's, const, stats). For arguments and usage details, see "The LINEST function" in Chapter 17.
LN	Returns the natural (base e) logarithm of the positive number referred to by its argument. Takes the form =LN(**number**). LN is the inverse of the EXP function.
LOG	Returns the logarithm of a positive number using a specified base. Takes the form =LOG(**number**, base). If you don't include the base argument, Excel assumes the base is 10.
LOG10	Returns the base-10 logarithm of a number. Takes the form =LOG10(**number**), where *number* is a positive real number.
LOGEST	Returns statistics describing known data in terms of an exponential curve. Takes the form =LOGEST(**known_y's**, known_x's, const, stats). For arguments and usage details, see "The LOGEST function" in Chapter 17.

Appendix C

Function	Description
LOGNORM.DIST	Returns the cumulative lognormal distribution of *x*, where ln(*x*) is usually distributed with parameters *mean* and *standard_dev*. Takes the form =LOGNORMDIST(*x*, **mean**, **standard_dev**, **cumulative**), where *x* is the value at which to evaluate the function, *mean* is the mean of ln(*x*), and *standard_dev* is the standard deviation of ln(*x*). If *cumulative* is TRUE, LOGNORM.DIST returns the cumulative distribution function; otherwise, it returns the probability density function. The old form of this function is LOGNORMDIST, which is still supported as a Compatibility Function.
LOGNORM.INV	Returns the inverse of the lognormal cumulative distribution function of *x*, where ln(*x*) is usually distributed with parameters *mean* and *standard_dev*. Takes the form =LOGINV(**probability**, **mean**, **standard_dev**), where *probability* is a probability associated with the lognormal distribution, *mean* is the mean of ln(*x*), and *standard_dev* is the standard deviation of ln(*x*). The old form of this function is LOGINV, which is still supported as a Compatibility Function.
LOOKUP	Looks for a specified value in a one-dimensional or two-dimensional range. Takes two forms, *vector* or *array*: =LOOKUP(**lookup_value**, **lookup_vector**, **result_vector**) or =LOOKUP(**lookup_value**, **array**), where *lookup_value* is the value to look for, *lookup_vector* is a one-row or one-column range containing the lookup values sorted in alphabetical order, *result_vector* is a range that contains the result values and must be identical in size to *lookup_vector*, and *array* is a two-dimensional range containing both lookup and result values. The array form of this function works like HLOOKUP if *array* is wider than it is tall or like VLOOKUP if *array* is taller than it is wide. See "Using selected lookup and reference functions" in Chapter 14.
LOWER	Converts a text string to all lowercase letters. Takes the form =LOWER(**text**). See "Using selected text functions" in Chapter 14.
MATCH	Returns the position in a list of the item that most closely matches a lookup value. Takes the form =MATCH(**lookup_value**, **lookup_array**, match_type), where *lookup_value* is the value or string to look up, *lookup_array* is the range that contains the sorted values to compare, and *match_type* defines the rules for the search (if 1 or omitted, finds, in a range sorted in ascending order, the largest value that is less than or equal to *lookup_value*; if 0, finds the value that is equal to *lookup_value*; if –1, finds, in a range sorted in descending order, the smallest value that is greater than or equal to *lookup_value*). See "Using selected lookup and reference functions" in Chapter 14.

Function	Description
MAX	Returns the largest value in a range. Takes the form =MAX(**number1**, number2, …), and accepts up to 30 arguments, ignoring text, error values, and logical values. See "Using built-in statistical functions" in Chapter 17.
MAXA	Acts like MAX except text and logical values are included in the calculation. See "Using built-in statistical functions" in Chapter 17.
MDETERM	Returns the matrix determinant of an array. Takes the form =MDETERM(**array**), where *array* is a numeric array with an equal number of rows and columns.
MDURATION	Calculates the annual modified duration for a security with interest payments made on a periodic basis, adjusted for market yield per number of coupon payments per year. Takes the form =MDURATION(**settlement**, **maturity**, **coupon**, **yield**, **frequency**, basis), where *settlement* is the day you pay for the security, *maturity* is the maturity date of the security, *coupon* is the security's annual coupon rate, *yield* is the annual yield of the security, *frequency* is the number of coupon payments made per year (1 = annual, 2 = semiannual, 4 = quarterly), and *basis* is the day-count basis of the security (if 0 or omitted = 30/360, if 1 = actual/actual, if 2 = actual/360, if 3 = actual/365, if 4 = European 30/360). See "Analyzing securities" in Chapter 16.
MEDIAN	Computes the median of a set of numbers. Takes the form =MEDIAN(**number1**, number2, …), and accepts up to 30 arguments, ignoring text, error values, and logical values. See "Using built-in statistical functions" in Chapter 17.
MID	Extracts a series of characters (substring) from a text string. Takes the form =MID(**text**, **start_num**, **num_chars**), where *text* is the string from which you want to extract the substring, *start_num* is the location in the string where the substring begins (counting from the left), and *num_chars* is the number of characters you want to extract. See "Using the substring text functions" in Chapter 14.
MIDB	Extracts a series of characters (substring) from a text string, based on the number of bytes you specify. Takes the form =MID(**text**, **start_num**, **num_bytes**), where *text* is the string from which you want to extract the substring, *start_num* is the location in the string where the substring begins (counting from the left), and *num_bytes* is the number of characters you want to extract, in bytes. This function is for use with double-byte characters.
MIN	Returns the smallest value in a range. Takes the form =MIN(**number1**, number2, …), and accepts up to 30 arguments, ignoring text, error values, and logical values. See "Using built-in statistical functions" in Chapter 17.

Appendix C

Function	Description
MINA	Acts like MIN except text and logical values are included in the calculation. See "Using built-in statistical functions" in Chapter 17.
MINUTE	Returns the minute portion of a serial date/time value. Takes the form =MINUTE(**serial_number**), where *serial_number* can be a time/date value, a reference, or text in time/date format enclosed in quotation marks. See "Working with date and time functions" in Chapter 15.
MINVERSE	Returns the inverse matrix for the matrix stored in an array. Takes the form =MINVERSE(**array**), where *array* is a numeric array with an equal number of rows and columns.
MIRR	Calculates the rate of return of an investment, taking into account the cost of borrowed money and assuming resulting cash inflows are reinvested. Takes the form =MIRR(**values**, **finance_rate**, **reinvestment_rate**), where *values* is an array or a reference to a range of cells that contain numbers beginning with the cost expressed as a negative value, *finance_rate* is the rate at which you borrow money, and *reinvestment_rate* is the rate at which you reinvest the returns. See "Calculating investments" in Chapter 16.
MMULT	See MODE.MULT
MOD	Returns the remainder of a division operation (modulus). Takes the form =MOD(**number**, **divisor**). If *number* is smaller than *divisor*, the result of the function equals *number*. If *number* is exactly divisible by *divisor*, the function returns 0. If *divisor* is 0, MOD returns the #DIV/0! error value. See "Using selected mathematical functions" in Chapter 14.
MODE.MULT	Returns a vertical array of the most frequently occurring values in a set of numbers. Takes the form =MODE.MULT(**number1**, number2, ...), and accepts up to 30 arguments, ignoring text, error values, and logical values. The old form of this function is MODE, which is still supported as a Compatibility Function. See "Using built-in statistical functions" in Chapter 17.
MODE.SNGL	Determines which value occurs most frequently in an array or range. Takes the form =MODE.SNGL(**number1**, number2, ...), and accepts up to 30 arguments, ignoring text, error values, and logical values. The old form of this function is LOGNORMDIST, which is still supported as a Compatibility Function. See "Using built-in statistical functions" in Chapter 17.

Function	Description
MONTH	Returns the value of the month portion of a serial date/time value. Takes the form =MONTH(**serial_number**), where *serial_number* can be a date value, a reference, or text in date format enclosed in quotation marks. See "Working with date and time functions" in Chapter 15.
MROUND	Rounds any number to a multiple you specify. Takes the form =MROUND(**number**, **multiple**), where *number* and *multiple* must both have the same sign. The function rounds up if the remainder after dividing *number* by *multiple* is at least half the value of *multiple*. See "Using the flexible MROUND function" in Chapter 14.
MULTINOMIAL	Returns the ratio of the factorial of a sum of values to the product of factorials. Takes the form =MULTINOMIAL(*num1*, *num2*, ...), where *nums* are up to 29 values for which you want to find the multinomial.
MUNIT	Returns a unit matrix of specified dimensions as an array. Takes the form =MUNIT(**dimension**), where *dimension* is an integer specifying the dimensions of the desired unit matrix.
N	Returns a value converted to a number. Takes the form =N(**value**), where *value* is the value you want to convert. This function is included for compatibility with other spreadsheet programs but is not necessary in Excel.
NA	Represents an alternative for the error value #N/A. The NA function accepts no arguments and takes the form =NA().
NEGBINOM.DIST	Returns the negative binomial distribution (the probability that there will be *number_f* failures before the *number_s*-th success, when the constant probability of a success is *probability_s*). Takes the form =NEGBINOM.DIST(**number_f**, **number_s**, **probability_s**, **cumulative**), where *number_f* is the number of failures, *number_s* is the threshold number of successes, and *probability_s* is the probability of a success. If *cumulative* is TRUE, NEGBINOM.DIST returns the cumulative distribution function; otherwise, it returns the probability density function. The old form of this function is NEGBINOMDIST, which is still supported as a Compatibility Function.
NETWORKDAYS	Returns the number of working days between two given dates. Takes the form =NETWORKDAYS(**start_date**, **end_date**, holidays), where *start_date* is the date you want to count from, *end_date* is the date you want to count to, and *holidays* is an array or reference containing any dates you want to exclude. See "Working with specialized date functions" in Chapter 15.

Appendix C

Function	Description
NETWORKDAYS.INTL	Returns the number of working days between two given dates, and allows you to indicate specific days as weekends. Takes the form =NETWORKDAYS.INTL(**start_date**, **end_date**, weekend, holidays), where *start_date* is the date you want to count from, *end_date* is the date you want to count to, *weekend* is a number indicating the weekend days you want to use, and *holidays* is an array or reference containing any dates you want to exclude. Weekend numbers: 1 or omitted, Sat-Sun; 2, Sun-Mon; 3 Mon-Tue; 4 Tue-Wed; 5 Wed-Thu; 6 Thu-Fri; 7 Fri-Sat; 11 Sun only; 12 Mon only; 13 Tue only; 14 Wed only; 15 Thu only; 16 Fri only; 17 Sat only. See "Working with specialized date functions" in Chapter 15.
NOMINAL	Returns the nominal annual interest rate. Takes the form =NOMINAL(**effect_rate**, **npery**), where *effect_rate* is the effective interest rate and *npery* is the number of compounding periods per year.
NORM.DIST	Returns the normal cumulative distribution for the specified mean and standard deviation. Takes the form =NORM.DIST(**x**, **mean**, **standard_dev**, **cumulative**), where *x* is the value for which you want the distribution, *mean* is the arithmetic mean of the distribution, *standard_dev* is the standard deviation of the distribution, and *cumulative* is a logical value that determines the form of the function. (If *cumulative* is TRUE, NORM.DIST returns the cumulative distribution function; if *cumulative* is FALSE, it returns the probability density function.) The old form of this function is NORMDIST, which is still supported as a Compatibility Function.
NORM.INV	Returns the inverse of the normal cumulative distribution for the specified mean and standard deviation. Takes the form =NORM.INV(**probability**, **mean**, **standard_dev**), where *probability* is a probability corresponding to the normal distribution, *mean* is the arithmetic mean of the distribution, and *standard_dev* is the standard deviation of the distribution. The old form of this function is NORMINV, which is still supported as a Compatibility Function.
NORMSDIST	Supported as a Compatibility Function. See the new form NORM.S.DIST.
NORM.S.DIST	Returns the standard normal cumulative distribution function. Takes the form =NORM.S.DIST(**z, cumulative**), where *z* is the value you want to use, and *cumulative*, if TRUE returns the cumulative distribution function, and if FALSE returns the probability mass function. The old form of this function is NORMSDIST, which is still supported as a Compatibility Function.

Function	Description
NORM.S.INV	Returns the inverse of the standard normal cumulative distribution (with a mean of zero and a standard deviation of one). Takes the form =NORM.S.INV(**probability**), where *probability* is a probability corresponding to the normal distribution. The old form of this function is NORMSINV, which is still supported as a Compatibility Function.
NOT	Helps develop compound conditional test formulas in conjunction with the simple logical operators =, >, <, >=, <=, and <>. The NOT function has only one argument and takes the form =NOT(**logical**), where *logical* can be a conditional test, an array, or a reference to a cell containing a logical value. See "Using selected logical functions" in Chapter 14.
NOW	Returns the serial value of the current date and time. Takes the form =NOW(), and accepts no arguments. See "Working with date and time functions" in Chapter 15.
NPER	Computes the number of periods required to amortize a loan, given a specified periodic payment. Takes the form =NPER(**rate**, **payment**, **present_value**, future_value, type), where *rate* is the interest rate, *payment* is the amount of each periodic payment when individual amounts are the same, *present_value* is the investment value today, *future_value* is the investment value at the end of the term, and *type* indicates when payments are made (0 or omitted = at end of period, 1 = at beginning of period). See "Calculating investments" in Chapter 16.
NPV	Determines the profitability of an investment. Takes the form =NPV(**rate**, **value1**, value2, ...), where *rate* is the interest rate and the values represent up to 29 payments (or any size array) when individual amounts differ. See "Calculating investments" in Chapter 16.
NUMBERVALUE	Converts text to a number. Takes the form =NUMBERVALUE(**text**, decimal_separator, group_separator), where *text* is the text you want to convert, *decimal_separator* is optionally the character you want to use to separate the integer and decimal, and *group_separator* is optionally the character you want to use to separate groups of numbers (to separate thousands from millions, for example).
OCT2BIN	Converts an octal number to binary. Takes the form =OCT2BIN(**number**, places), where *number* is the octal number you want to convert and *places* is the number of characters to use. (If omitted, OCT2BIN uses the minimum number of characters necessary.)
OCT2DEC	Converts an octal number to decimal. Takes the form =OCT2DEC(**number**), where *number* is the octal number you want to convert.

Function	Description
OCT2HEX	Converts an octal number to hexadecimal. Takes the form =OCT2HEX(**number**, places), where *number* is the octal number you want to convert and *places* is the number of characters to use. (If omitted, uses the minimum number of characters necessary.)
ODD	Rounds a number up to the nearest odd integer. Takes the form =ODD(**number**). Negative numbers are correspondingly rounded down. See "Using the rounding functions" in Chapter 14.
ODDFPRICE	Returns the price per $100 of face value for a security having an odd first period. Takes the form =ODDFPRICE(**settlement**, **maturity**, **issue**, **first_coupon**, **rate**, **yield**, **redemption**, **frequency**, basis), where *settlement* is the day you pay for the security, *maturity* is the maturity date of the security, *issue* is the issue date of the security, *first_coupon* is the security's first coupon due date as a serial date value, *rate* is the interest rate of the security at the issue date, *yield* is the annual yield of the security, *redemption* is the value of the security at redemption, *frequency* is the number of coupon payments made per year (1 = annual, 2 = semiannual, 4 = quarterly), and *basis* is the day-count basis of the security (if 0 or omitted = 30/360, if 1 = actual/actual, if 2 = actual/360, if 3 = actual/365, if 4 = European 30/360).
ODDFYIELD	Calculates the yield of a security that has an odd first period. Takes the form =ODDFYIELD(**settlement**, **maturity**, **issue**, **first_coupon**, **rate**, **price**, **redemption**, **frequency**, basis), where *price* is the security's price. See ODDFPRICE for additional argument definitions.
ODDLPRICE	Calculates the price per $100 face value of a security having an odd last coupon period. Takes the form =ODDLPRICE(**settlement**, **maturity**, **last_interest**, **rate**, **yield**, **redemption**, **frequency**, basis), where *last_interest* is the security's last coupon due date as a serial date value. See ODDFPRICE for additional argument definitions.
ODDLYIELD	Calculates the yield of a security that has an odd last period. Takes the form =ODDLYIELD(**settlement**, **maturity**, **last_interest**, **rate**, **price**, **redemption**, **frequency**, basis), where *last_interest* is the security's last coupon due date and *price* is the security's price. See ODDFPRICE for additional argument definitions.

Function	Description
OFFSET	Returns a reference of a specified height and width, located at a specified position relative to another specified reference. Takes the form =OFFSET(**reference**, **rows**, **cols**, height, width), where *reference* specifies the position from which the offset is calculated, *rows* and *cols* specify the vertical and horizontal distance from *reference*, and *height* and *width* specify the shape of the reference returned by the function. The *rows* and *cols* arguments can be positive or negative: Positive values specify offsets below and to the right of *reference*; negative values specify offsets above and to the left of *reference*.
OR	Helps develop compound conditional test formulas in conjunction with logical operators. Takes the form =OR(**logical1**, logical2, ...), where the *logical*s can be up to 30 conditional tests, arrays, or references to cells that contain logical values. See "Using selected logical functions" in Chapter 14.
PDURATION	Returns the number of periods an investment requires to reach a specific value. Takes the form =PDURATION(**rate**, **pv**, **fv**), where *rate* is the periodic rate of interest, *pv* is the investment's present value, and *fv* is the investment's desired future value.
PEARSON	Returns the Pearson product moment correlation coefficient, *r*, a dimensionless index that ranges from −1 to 1 (inclusive) and reflects the extent of a linear relationship between two data sets. This function takes the form =PEARSON(**array1**, **array2**), where *array1* is a set of independent values and *array2* is a set of dependent values.
PERCENTILE.INC PERCENTILE.EXC	Returns the member of an input range that is at a specified percentile ranking. Takes the form =PERCENTILE.INC(**array**, **k**), where *array* is the input range (inclusive or exclusive, depending on the form of the function used) and *k* is the rank you want to find. The old form of this function is PERCENTILE, which is still supported as a Compatibility Function. See "Using functions that analyze rank and percentile" in Chapter 17.
PERCENTRANK.INC PERCENTRANK.EXC	Returns a percentile ranking for any member of a data set. Takes the form =PERCENTRANK.INC(**array**, **x**, significance), where *array* specifies the input range (inclusive or exclusive, depending on the form of the function used), *x* specifies the value whose rank you want to obtain, and the optional *significance* indicates the number of digits of precision you want. If *significance* is omitted, results are rounded to three digits (0.xxx or xx.x%). The old form of this function is PERCENTRANK, which is still supported as a Compatibility Function. See "Using functions that analyze rank and percentile" in Chapter 17.

Function	Description
PERMUT	Returns the number of permutations for a given number of objects that can be selected from a larger group of objects. Takes the form =PERMUT(**number**, **number_chosen**), where *number* is an integer that describes the total number of objects you want to use and *number_chosen* is an integer that describes the number of objects you want in each permutation.
PERMUTATIONA	Returns the number of permutations, including repetitions, for a given number of objects that can be selected from a larger group of objects. Takes the form =PERMUTATIONA(**number**, **number_chosen**), where *number* is an integer that describes the total number of objects you want to use and *number_chosen* is an integer that describes the number of objects you want in each permutation.
PHI	Returns the density function value for a standard normal distribution. Takes the form =PHI(**x**), where *x* is the value you want to calculate.
PHONETIC	Extracts—in Japanese, Simplified or Traditional Chinese, and Korean—the phonetic (furigana) characters from a referenced cell or range. Takes the form =PHONETIC(**reference**), where *reference* denotes a single cell or range. If *reference* is a range, the function returns phonetic text only from the cell in the upper-left corner.
PI	Returns the value of pi, accurate to 14 decimal places (3.14159265358979). Takes the form =PI(), and accepts no arguments, but you must still type empty parentheses after the function name. To calculate the area of a circle, multiply the square of the circle's radius by the PI function.
PMT	Computes the periodic payment required to amortize a loan over a specified number of periods. Takes the form =PMT(**rate**, **nper**, **pv**, fv, type), where *rate* is the interest rate, *nper* is the term (periods) of the investment, *pv* is the investment value today, *fv* is the investment value at the end of the term, and *type* indicates when payments are made (0 or omitted = at end of period, 1 = at beginning of period). See "Calculating investments" in Chapter 16.
POISSON.DIST	Returns the Poisson distribution. Takes the form =POISSON.DIST(**x**, **mean**, **cumulative**), where *x* is the number of events, *mean* is the expected numeric value, and *cumulative* is a logical value that determines the form of the probability distribution returned. (If *cumulative* is TRUE, POISSON.DIST returns the cumulative Poisson probability that the number of random events occurring will be between *zero* and *x* inclusive; if *cumulative* is FALSE, it returns the Poisson probability mass function that the number of events occurring will be exactly *x*.) The old form of this function is POISSON, which is still supported as a Compatibility Function.

Function	Description
POWER	Returns the result of a number raised to a power. Takes the form =POWER(**number**, **power**), where *number* is the base number and *power* is the exponent to which the base number is raised.
PPMT	Computes the principal component of an individual payment made to repay a loan over a specified time period with constant periodic payments and a constant interest rate. Takes the form =PPMT(**rate**, **period**, **nper**, **pv**, fv, type), where *rate* is the interest rate, *period* is the number of an individual periodic payment, *nper* is the term (periods) of the investment, *pv* is the investment value today, *fv* is the investment value at the end of the term, and *type* indicates when payments are made (0 or omitted = at end of period, 1 = at beginning of period). See "Calculating investments" in Chapter 16.
PRICE	Calculates the price per $100 of a security that pays periodic interest. Takes the form =PRICE(**settlement**, **maturity**, **rate**, **yield**, **redemption**, **frequency**, basis), where *settlement* is the day you pay for the security, *maturity* is the maturity date of the security, *rate* is the interest rate of the security at the issue date, *yield* is the annual yield of the security, *redemption* is the value of the security at redemption, *frequency* is the number of coupon payments made per year (1 = annual, 2 = semiannual, 4 = quarterly), and *basis* is the day-count basis of the security (if 0 or omitted = 30/360, if 1 = actual/actual, if 2 = actual/360, if 3 = actual/365, if 4 = European 30/360). See "Analyzing securities" in Chapter 16.
PRICEDISC	Returns the price per $100 of a discounted security. Takes the form =PRICEDISC(**settlement**, **maturity**, **discount**, **redemption**, basis), where *settlement* is the day you pay for the security, *maturity* is the maturity date of the security, *discount* is the security's discount rate, *redemption* is the value of the security at redemption, and *basis* is the day-count basis of the security (if 0 or omitted = 30/360, if 1 = actual/actual, if 2 = actual/360, if 3 = actual/365, if 4 = European 30/360). See "Analyzing securities" in Chapter 16.
PRICEMAT	Returns the price per $100 of a security that pays interest at maturity. Takes the form =PRICEMAT(**settlement**, **maturity**, **issue**, **rate**, **yield**, basis), where *settlement* is the day you pay for the security, *maturity* is the maturity date of the security, *issue* is the issue date of the security, *rate* is the interest rate of the security at the issue date, *yield* is the annual yield of the security, and *basis* is the day-count basis of the security (if 0 or omitted = 30/360, if 1 = actual/actual, if 2 = actual/360, if 3 = actual/365, if 4 = European 30/360). See "Analyzing securities" in Chapter 16.

Appendix C

Function	Description
PROB	Returns the probability that values in a range are between two limits. Takes the form =PROB(**x_range**, **prob_range**, **lower_limit**, upper_limit), where *x_range* is the range of numeric values of *x* with which there are associated probabilities, *prob_range* is a set of probabilities associated with values in *x_range*, *lower_limit* is the lower bound on the value for which you want a probability, and *upper_limit* is the optional upper bound on the value for which you want a probability.
PRODUCT	Multiplies all the numbers referenced by its arguments. Takes the form =PRODUCT(**number1**, number2, ...), and accepts as many as 30 arguments. Text, logical values, and blank cells are ignored. See "Using selected mathematical functions" in Chapter 14.
PROPER	Capitalizes the first letter in each word and any other letters in a text string that do not follow another letter—all other letters are converted to lowercase. Takes the form =PROPER(**text**). See "Using selected text functions" in Chapter 14.
PV	Computes the present value of a series of equal periodic payments or a lump-sum payment. Takes the form =PV(**rate**, **nper**, **payment**, future_value, type), where *rate* is the interest rate, *nper* is the term (periods) of the investment, *payment* is the amount of each periodic payment when individual amounts are the same, *future_value* is the investment value at the end of the term, and *type* indicates when payments are made (0 or omitted = at end of period, 1 = at beginning of period). See "Calculating investments" in Chapter 16.
QUARTILE.INC QUARTILE.EXC	Returns the value in an input range (either inclusive or exclusive, depending on the form of the function used) that represents a specified quarter-percentile. Takes the form =QUARTILE.INC(**array**, **quart**). The old form of this function is QUARTILE, which is still supported as a Compatibility Function. For usage and argument details, see "The PERCENTILE and QUARTILE functions" in Chapter 17.
QUOTIENT	Returns the integer portion of a division. Takes the form =QUOTIENT(numerator, denominator), where *numerator* is the dividend and *denominator* is the divisor.
RADIANS	Converts degrees to radians. Takes the form =RADIANS(**angle**), where *angle* represents an angle measured in degrees.
RAND	Generates a random number between 0 and 1. Takes the form =RAND() with no arguments, but you must still type empty parentheses after the function name. The result changes with each sheet recalculation. See "Using selected mathematical functions" in Chapter 14.

Function	Description
RANDBETWEEN	Generates random integer values between a specified range of numbers. Takes the form =RANDBETWEEN(**bottom**, **top**), where *bottom* is the smallest integer you want to use and *top* is the largest, inclusive. See "Using selected mathematical functions" in Chapter 14.
RANK.AVG	Returns the ranked position of a particular number within a set of numbers. Takes the form =RANK.AVG(**number**, **ref**, order). If more than one value has the same rank, the function returns the average rank. The old form of this function is RANK, which is still supported as a Compatibility Function. For usage and argument details, see "The RANK functions" in Chapter 17.
RANK.EQ	Returns the ranked position of a particular number within a set of numbers. Takes the form =RANK.EQ(**number, ref**, order). If more than one value has the same rank, the function returns the top rank. The old form of this function is RANK, which is still supported as a Compatibility Function. For usage and argument details, see "The RANK functions" in Chapter 17.
RATE	Calculates the rate of return of an investment that generates a series of equal periodic payments or a single lump-sum payment. Takes the form =RATE(**nper**, **payment**, **present_value**, future_value, type, guess), where *nper* is the term (periods) of the investment, *payment* is the amount of each periodic payment when individual amounts are the same, *present_value* is the investment value today, *future_value* is the investment value at the end of the term, *type* indicates when payments are made (0 or omitted = at end of period, 1 = at beginning of period), and *guess* is an approximate interest rate (10 percent if omitted). See "Calculating investments" in Chapter 16.
RECEIVED	Calculates the amount received at maturity for a fully invested security. Takes the form =RECEIVED(**settlement, maturity, investment, discount**, basis), where *settlement* is the day you pay for the security, *maturity* is the maturity date of the security, *investment* is the amount invested in the security, *discount* is the security's discount rate, and *basis* is the day-count basis of the security (if 0 or omitted = 30/360, if 1 = actual/actual, if 2 = actual/360, if 3 = actual/365, if 4 = European 30/360). See "Analyzing securities" in Chapter 16.
REPLACE	Substitutes one string of characters with another string. Takes the form =REPLACE(**old_text, start_num, num_chars, new_text**), where *old_text* is the text string where you want to replace characters, *start_num* specifies the starting character to replace, *num_chars* specifies the number of characters to replace (counting from the left), and *new_text* specifies the text string to insert. See "Using the substring text functions" in Chapter 14.

Appendix C

Function	Description
REPLACEB	Substitutes one string of characters with another string. Takes the form =REPLACEB(**old_text**, **start_num**, **num_bytes**, **new_text**), where *old_text* is the text string in which you want to replace characters, *start_num* specifies the starting character to replace, *num_bytes* specifies the number of bytes to replace, and *new_text* specifies the text string to insert. This function is for use with double-byte characters.
REPT	Fills a cell with a string of characters repeated a specified number of times. Takes the form =REPT(**text**, **number_times**), where *text* specifies a string in double quotation marks and *number_times* specifies how many times to repeat *text*. The result of the function cannot exceed 32,767 characters.
RIGHT	Returns the rightmost series of characters from a string. Takes the form =RIGHT(**text**, num_chars), where *num_chars* indicates how many characters you want to extract from the *text* string (1, if omitted). Blank spaces count as characters. See "Using the substring text functions" in Chapter 14.
RIGHTB	Returns the rightmost series of characters from a string, based on the number of bytes you specify. Takes the form =RIGHTB(**text**, num_bytes), where *num_bytes* indicates how many characters you want to extract from the *text* string, based on bytes. This function is for use with double-byte characters.
ROMAN	Converts an Arabic numeral to Roman numerals, as text. Takes the form =ROMAN(**number**, form), where *number* is the Arabic numeral you want to convert and *form* is a number specifying the type of Roman numeral you want (1, 2, or 3 = more concise notation; 4 or FALSE = simplified notation; TRUE = classic notation). Also, see the ARABIC function.
ROUND	Rounds numbers to a specified number of decimal places. Takes the form =ROUND(**number**, **num_digits**), where *number* can be a number, a reference to a cell that contains a number, or a formula that results in a number; and *num_digits* can be any positive or negative integer and determines the number of decimal places. Use a negative *num_digits* to round to the left of the decimal; use zero to round to the nearest integer. See "Using the rounding functions" in Chapter 14.
ROUNDDOWN	Rounds numbers down to a specified number of decimal places. Takes the same form and arguments as ROUND. See "Using the rounding functions" in Chapter 14.
ROUNDUP	Rounds numbers up to a specified number of decimal places. Takes the same form and arguments as ROUND. See "Using the rounding functions" in Chapter 14.

Function	Description
ROW	Returns the row number of the referenced cell or range. Takes the form =ROW(reference). If *reference* is omitted, the result is the row number of the cell containing the function. If *reference* is a range or a name and the function is entered as an array (by pressing Ctrl+Shift+Enter), the result is an array of the numbers of each of the rows or columns in the range. See "Using selected lookup and reference functions" in Chapter 14.
ROWS	Returns the number of rows in a reference or an array. Takes the form =ROWS(**array**), where *array* is an array constant, a range reference, or a range name. See "Using selected lookup and reference functions" in Chapter 14.
RRI	Returns an equivalent interest rate for an investment based on its growth. Takes the form =RRI(**nper**, **pv**, **fv**), where *nper* is the number of periods, *pv* is the present value, and *fv* is the future value of the investment.
RSQ	Returns the square of the Pearson product moment correlation coefficient through data points in the arrays *known_y's* and *known_x's*. Takes the form =RSQ(**known_y's**, **known_x's**).
RTD	Returns real-time data from a program that supports COM automation. Takes the form =RTD(**progID**, server, topic1, topic2, ...), where *progID* is the program identifier (enclosed in quotation marks) for a registered COM automation add-in that has been installed on the local computer, *server* is the name of the server where the add-in should be run (if other than the local computer), and *topic* values are up to 28 parameters describing the real-time data you want.
SEARCH	Returns the position of specified text within a string. Takes the form =SEARCH(**find_text**, **within_text**, start_num), where *find_text* is the text you want to find, *within_text* indicates where to look, and *start_num* specifies the character position in *within_text* where you want to begin the search. See "Using the substring text functions" in Chapter 14.
SEARCHB	Returns the position of specified text within a string, expressed in bytes. Takes the form =SEARCHB(**find_text**, **within_text**, start_num), and is otherwise identical to SEARCH.
SEC	Returns the secant of an angle. Takes the form =SEC(**number**), where *number* is the angle for which you want the secant, expressed in radians, and must be less than 2^{27}. If *number* is in degrees, use the RADIANS function to convert it to radians.

Function	Description
SECH	Returns the hyperbolic secant of an angle. Takes the form =SECH(**number**), where *number* is the angle for which you want the hyperbolic secant, expressed in radians, and must be less than 2^{27}. If *number* is in degrees, use the RADIANS function to convert it to radians.
SECOND	Returns the seconds portion of a serial date/time value. Takes the form =SECOND(**serial_number**), where *serial_number* can be a time/date value, a reference, or text in time/date format enclosed in quotation marks. See "Working with date and time functions" in Chapter 15.
SERIESSUM	Returns the sum of a power series. Takes the form =SERIESSUM(**x**, **n**, **m**, **coefficients**), where *x* is the input value to the power series, *n* is the initial power to which you want to raise *x*, *m* is the step by which to increase *n* for each term in the series, and *coefficients* is a set of coefficients by which each successive power of *x* is multiplied. The number of values in coefficients determines the number of terms in the power series.
SHEET	Returns the sheet number of a referenced worksheet. Takes the form =SHEET(value), where *value* is either the name of a sheet or a reference from which you want to learn the sheet number. If *value* is omitted, returns the sheet on which the SHEET function resides.
SHEETS	Returns the number of sheets referenced. Takes the form =SHEETS(reference), where *reference* is a reference from which you want to learn the number of sheets. If *reference* is omitted, returns the number of sheets contained in the workbook in which the SHEETS function resides.
SIGN	Determines the sign of a number. Returns 1 if the number is positive, zero (0) if the number is 0, and −1 if the number is negative. Takes the form =SIGN(**number**), where *number* is any real number.
SIN	Returns the sine of an angle. The complement of the COS function, it takes the form =SIN(**number**), where *number* is the angle in radians.
SINH	Returns the hyperbolic sine of a number. Takes the form =SINH(**number**), where *number* is any real number.
SKEW	Returns the skew of a distribution (the degree of asymmetry of a distribution around its mean). Takes the form =SKEW(**number1**, number2, ...), and accepts up to 30 arguments.
SKEW.P	Returns the skew of a distribution (the degree of asymmetry of a distribution around its mean), based on a given population. Takes the form =SKEW.P(**number1**, number2, ...), and accepts up to 30 arguments.

Function	Description
SLN	Returns straight-line depreciation for an asset for a single period. Takes the form =SLN(**cost**, **salvage**, **life**), where *cost* is the initial asset cost, *salvage* is the remaining value after asset is fully depreciated, and *life* is the length of depreciation time. See "Calculating depreciation" in Chapter 16.
SLOPE	Returns the slope of a linear regression line. Takes the form =SLOPE(**known_y's**, **known_x's**). For arguments and usage details, see "The SLOPE function" in Chapter 17.
SMALL	Returns the *k*th smallest value in an input range. Takes the form =SMALL(**array**, **k**), where *k* is the position from the smallest value in *array* you want to find. See "Using functions that analyze rank and percentile" in Chapter 17.
SQRT	Returns the positive square root of a number. Takes the form =SQRT(**number**).
SQRTPI	Returns the square root of (number * pi). Takes the form =SQRTPI(**number**).
STANDARDIZE	Returns a normalized value from a distribution characterized by *mean* and *standard_dev*. Takes the form =STANDARDIZE(**x**, **mean**, **standard_dev**), where *x* is the value you want to normalize, *mean* is the arithmetic mean of the distribution, and *standard_dev* is the standard deviation of the distribution.
STDEV.S	Computes standard deviation, assuming that the arguments represent only a sample of the total population. Takes the form =STDEV.S(**number1**, number2, ...), and accepts up to 30 arguments. The old form of this function is STDEV, which is still supported as a Compatibility Function. See "Using sample and population statistical functions" in Chapter 17.
STDEVA	Acts like STDEV except text and logical values are included in the calculation. See "Using sample and population statistical functions" in Chapter 17.
STDEV.P	Computes the standard deviation, assuming that the arguments represent the total population. Takes the form =STDEV.P(**number1**, number2, ...). The old form of this function is STDEVP, which is still supported as a Compatibility Function. See "Using sample and population statistical functions" in Chapter 17.
STDEVPA	Acts like STDEV.P except that text and logical values are included in the calculation. See "Using sample and population statistical functions" in Chapter 17.
STEYX	Calculates the standard error of a regression. Takes the form =STEYX(**known_y's**, **known_x's**). For arguments and usage details, see "The SLOPE function" in Chapter 17.

Function	Description
SUBSTITUTE	Replaces specified text with new text within a specified string. Takes the form =SUBSTITUTE(**text**, **old_text**, **new_text**, instance_num), where *text* is the string you want to work on; *old_text* is the text to be replaced; *new_text* is the text to substitute; and *instance_num* is optional, indicating a specific occurrence of *old_text* within *text*. See "Using the substring text functions" in Chapter 14.
SUBTOTAL	Returns a subtotal in a table or database. Takes the form =SUBTOTAL(**function_num**, **ref1**, ref2, ...), where *function_num* is a number that specifies which function to use in calculating subtotals (1=AVERAGE, 2=COUNT, 3=COUNTA, 4=MAX, 5=MIN, 6=PRODUCT, 7=STDEV, 8=STDEVP, 9=SUM, 10=VAR, 11=VARP), and the *ref*s are 1 to 29 ranges or references for which you want the subtotal.
SUM	Totals a series of numbers. Takes the form =SUM(**num1**, num2, ...), where the *num*s (up to 30) can be numbers, formulas, ranges, or cell references. Ignores arguments that refer to text values, logical values, or blank cells. See "Using the SUM function" in Chapter 14.
SUMIF	Tests each cell in a range before adding it to the total. Takes the form =SUMIF(**range**, **criteria**, sum_range), where *range* is the range you want to test, *criteria* is the logical test to be performed on each cell, and *sum_range* specifies the cells to be totaled. See "Using built-in statistical functions" in Chapter 17.
SUMIFS	Tests each cell in a range using multiple criteria before adding it to the total. Takes the form =SUMIFS(**sum_range**, **criteria_range1**, **criteria1**, criteria_range2, criteria2, ...), where *sum_range* is the range containing values you want to sum; *criteria_rangeX* is a cell range containing data to be evaluated; and *criteriaX* is a cell range containing values, expressions, references, or text that define which cells will be added to the total.
SUMPRODUCT	Multiplies the value in each cell in a specified range by the corresponding cell in another equal-sized range and then adds the results. Takes the form =SUMPRODUCT(**array1**, **array2**, array3, ...), and can include up to 30 arrays. Nonnumeric entries are treated as zero. See "Using selected mathematical functions" in Chapter 14.
SUMSQ	Returns the sum of the squares of each specified value in a specified range. Takes the form =SUMSQ(**number1**, **number2**, ...), and accepts up to 30 arguments or a single array or array reference.
SUMX2MY2	Calculates the sum of the differences of the squares of the corresponding values in x and y. Takes the form =SUMX2MY2(**array_x**, **array_y**), where x and y are arrays that contain the same number of elements.

Function	Description
SUMX2PY2	Calculates the sum of the sum of the squares of the corresponding values in *x* and *y*. Takes the form =SUMX2PY2(**array_x**, **array_y**), where *x* and *y* are arrays that contain the same number of elements.
SUMXMY2	Calculates the sum of the squares of the differences of the corresponding values in *x* and *y*. Takes the form =SUMXMY2(**array_x**, **array_y**), where *x* and *y* are arrays that contain the same number of elements.
SYD	Computes depreciation for a specific time period with the sum-of-the-years'-digits method. Takes the form =SYD(**cost**, **salvage**, **life**, **period**), where *cost* is the initial asset cost, *salvage* is the remaining value after the asset is fully depreciated, *life* is the length of depreciation time, and *period* is the individual period to be computed. See "Calculating depreciation" in Chapter 16.
T	Returns the text referred to by *value*. Takes the form =T(**value**), where *value* is the value you want to test. This function is included for compatibility with other spreadsheet programs but is not necessary in Excel.
TAN	Returns the tangent of an angle. Takes the form =TAN(**number**), where *number* is the angle in radians.
TANH	Returns the hyperbolic tangent of a number. Takes the form =TANH(**number**), where *number* is any real number.
TBILLEQ	Calculates the bond-equivalent yield for a U.S. Treasury bill. Takes the form =TBILLEQ(**settlement**, **maturity**, **discount**), where *settlement* is the day you pay for the security, *maturity* is the maturity date of the security, and *discount* is the discount rate of the security. See "Analyzing securities" in Chapter 16.
TBILLPRICE	Calculates the price per $100 of face value for a U.S. Treasury bill. Takes the form =TBILLPRICE(**settlement**, **maturity**, **discount**), where *settlement* is the day you pay for the security, *maturity* is the maturity date of the security, and *discount* is the discount rate of the security. See "Analyzing securities" in Chapter 16.
TBILLYIELD	Calculates a U.S. Treasury bill's yield. Takes the form =TBILLYIELD(**settlement**, **maturity**, **price**), where *settlement* is the day you pay for the security, *maturity* is the maturity date of the security, and *price* is the security's price. See "Analyzing securities" in Chapter 16.
T.DIST.2T	Returns the two-tailed Student's *t* distribution. Takes the form =T.DIST.2T(**x**, **deg_freedom**), where *x* is the numeric value at which to evaluate the distribution, and *deg_freedom* is an integer indicating the number of degrees of freedom. The old form of this function is TDIST, which is still supported as a Compatibility Function.

Appendix C

Function	Description
T.DIST.RT	Returns the right-tailed Student's *t* distribution. This function takes the form =T.DIST.RT(**x**, **deg_freedom**), where *x* is the numeric value at which to evaluate the distribution and *deg_freedom* is an integer indicating the number of degrees of freedom. The old form of this function is TDIST, which is still supported as a Compatibility Function.
TEXT	Converts a number into a text string using a specified format. Takes the form =TEXT(**value**, **format_text**), where *value* can be any number, formula, or cell reference; and *format_text* specifies the format using built-in custom formatting symbols. See "Using selected text functions" in Chapter 14.
TIME	Returns the decimal number for a particular time. Takes the form =TIME(**hour**, **minute**, **second**), where *hour* is a number from 0 (zero) to 23 representing the hour, *minute* is a number from 0 to 59 representing the minute, and *second* is a number from 0 to 59 representing the second.
TIMEVALUE	Translates a time into a decimal value. Takes the form =TIMEVALUE(**time_text**), where *time_text* represents a time entered as text in quotation marks. See "Working with date and time functions" in Chapter 15.
T.INV	Returns the left-tailed inverse of the Student's *t* distribution as a function of the probability and the degrees of freedom. Takes the form =T.INV(**probability**, **deg_freedom**), where *probability* is the probability associated with the two-tailed Student's *t* distribution and *deg_freedom* is the number of degrees of freedom to characterize the distribution. The old form of this function is TINV, which is still supported as a Compatibility Function.
T.INV.2T	Returns the two-tailed inverse of the Student's *t* distribution. Takes the form =T.INV.2T(**probability**, **deg_freedom**), where *probability* is the probability associated with the two-tailed Student's *t* distribution and *deg_freedom* is the number of degrees of freedom to characterize the distribution. The old form of this function is TINV, which is still supported as a Compatibility Function.
T.TEST	Returns the probability associated with a Student's *t* test. Takes the form =T.TEST(**array1**, **array2**, **tails**, **type**), where *array1* is the first data set, *array2* is the second data set, *tails* specifies the number of distribution tails (if 1, uses the one-tailed distribution; if 2, uses the two-tailed distribution), and *type* is the kind of t-test to perform (1 = paired, 2 = two-sample equal variance, 3 = two-sample unequal variance). The old form of this function is TTEST, which is still supported as a Compatibility Function.

Function	Description
TODAY	Returns the serial value of the current date. Takes the form =TODAY(), and accepts no arguments. See "Working with date and time functions" in Chapter 15.
TRANSPOSE	Changes the horizontal or vertical orientation of an array. Takes the form =TRANSPOSE(**array**). If *array* is vertical, the result is horizontal, and vice versa. Must be entered as an array formula by pressing Ctrl+Shift+Enter, with a range selected with the same proportions as *array*. See "Using selected lookup and reference functions" in Chapter 14.
TREND	Returns values of points that lie along a linear trendline. Takes the form =TREND(**known_y's**, known_x's, new_x's, const). For arguments and usage details, see "The TREND function" in Chapter 17.
TRIM	Removes leading, trailing, and extra blank characters from a string, leaving single spaces between words. Takes the form =TRIM(**text**). See "Using selected text functions" in Chapter 14.
TRIMMEAN	Returns the mean of the interior of a data set (the mean taken by excluding a percentage of data points from the top and bottom tails of a data set). This function takes the form =TRIMMEAN(**array**, **percent**), where *array* is the array or range of values to trim and average and *percent* is the fractional number of data points to exclude from the calculation.
TRUE	Represents an alternative for the logical condition TRUE. The TRUE function accepts no arguments, and takes the form =TRUE(). See "Using selected logical functions" in Chapter 14.
TRUNC	Truncates everything to the right of the decimal point, regardless of its sign. Takes the form =TRUNC(**number**, num_digits). Truncates everything after the specified *num_digits* to the right of the decimal point. See "Using the rounding functions" in Chapter 14.
TYPE	Determines the type of value a cell contains. Takes the form =TYPE(**value**). The result is one of the following numeric codes: 1 (number), 2 (text), 4 (logical value), 16 (error value), or 64 (array). See "Using selected lookup and reference functions" in Chapter 14.
UNICHAR	Returns the Unicode character indicated by a given number. Takes the form =UNICHAR(**number**), where *number* is a valid Unicode character value.

Function	Description
UNICODE	Returns the Unicode number code that corresponds to the first character in a given text string. Takes the form =UNICODE(**text**), where *text* is a character (or string) for which you want the Unicode value (for the first character only).
UPPER	Converts a text string to all uppercase letters. Takes the form =UPPER(**text**). See "Using selected text functions" in Chapter 14.
VALUE	Converts a text string that represents a number to a number. Takes the form =VALUE(**text**), where *text* is the text enclosed in quotation marks or a reference to a cell containing the text you want to convert. This function is included for compatibility with other spreadsheet programs but is not necessary in Excel.
VARA	Acts like VAR.S except text and logical values are included in the calculation. See "Using sample and population statistical functions" in Chapter 17.
VAR.S	Computes variance, assuming that the arguments represent only a sample of the total population. Takes the form =VAR.S(**number1**, number2, ...), accepting up to 30 arguments. See "Using sample and population statistical functions" in Chapter 17. The old form of this function is VAR, which is still supported as a Compatibility Function.
VAR.P	Computes variance, assuming that the arguments represent the total population. Takes the form =VAR.P(**number1**, number2, ...). See "Using sample and population statistical functions" in Chapter 17. The old form of this function is VAR, which is still supported as a Compatibility Function.
VARPA	Acts like VAR.P except text and logical values are included in the calculation. See "Using sample and population statistical functions" in Chapter 17.
VDB	Calculates depreciation for any complete or partial period, using either double-declining balance or a specified accelerated-depreciation factor. Takes the form =VDB(**cost**, **salvage**, **life**, **start_period**, **end_period**, factor, no_switch), where *cost* is the initial asset cost, *salvage* is the remaining value after the asset is fully depreciated, *life* is the length of depreciation time, *start_period* is the period number after which depreciation begins, *end_period* is the last period calculated, *factor* is the rate at which the balance declines, and *no_switch* turns off the default switch to straight-line depreciation when it becomes greater than the declining balance. See "Calculating depreciation" in Chapter 16.

Function	Description
VLOOKUP	Looks for a specified value in the leftmost column in a table, and returns the value in the same row and a specified column. Takes the form =VLOOKUP(**lookup_value**, **table_array**, **col_index_num**, range_lookup), where *lookup_value* is the value to look for; *table_array* is the range containing the lookup and result values sorted in alphabetical order by the leftmost column; *col_index_num* is the column number containing the value you want to find; and *range_lookup* is a logical value, which, if FALSE, forces an exact match. See "Using selected lookup and reference functions" in Chapter 14.
WEBSERVICE	Returns data from an Internet-based or intranet-based web service. Takes the form =WEBSERVICE(**url**), where *url* is the valid Universal Resource Locator (URL) of the web service from which you want data.
WEEKDAY	Returns a number value representing the day of the week for a specified date. Takes the form =WEEKDAY(**serial_number**, return_type), where *serial_number* is a date value, a reference, or text in date form enclosed in quotation marks; and *return_type* determines the way the result is represented (if 1 or omitted, Sunday is day 1; if 2, Monday is day 1; if 3, Monday is day 0). See "Working with date and time functions" in Chapter 15.
WEEKNUM	Returns a number that indicates where the week falls numerically within a year. Takes the form =WEEKNUM(**serial_num**, return_type), where *serial_num* is a date within the week and *return_type* is a number that determines the day on which the week begins (1 or omitted = week begins on Sunday, 2 = week begins on Monday). See also ISOWEEKNUM.
WEIBULL.DIST	Returns the Weibull distribution. Takes the form =WEIBULL.DIST(**x**, **alpha**, **beta**, **cumulative**), where *x* is the value at which to evaluate the function, *alpha* is a parameter to the distribution, *beta* is a parameter to the distribution, and *cumulative* determines the form of the function. The old form of this function is WEIBULL, which is still supported as a Compatibility Function.
WORKDAY	Returns a date that is a specified number of working days before or after a given date. Takes the form =WORKDAY(**start_date**, **days**, holidays), where *start_date* is the date you want to count from; *days* is the number of workdays before or after the start date, excluding weekends and holidays; and *holidays* is an array or reference containing any dates you want to exclude. See "Working with specialized date functions" in Chapter 15.

Appendix C

Function	Description
WORKDAY.INTL	Returns a date that is a specified number of working days before or after a given date, and allows you to indicate specific days as weekends. Takes the form =WORKDAY.INTL(**start_date**, **days**, weekend, holidays), where *start_date* is the date you want to count from, *days* is the number of workdays before or after the start date (negative value indicates a past date), *weekend* is a number indicating the weekend days you want to use, and *holidays* is an array or reference containing any dates you want to exclude. Weekend numbers: 1 or omitted, Sat-Sun; 2 Sun-Mon; 3 Mon-Tue; 4 Tue-Wed; 5 Wed-Thu; 6 Thu-Fri; 7 Fri-Sat; 11 Sun only; 12 Mon only; 13 Tue only; 14 Wed only; 15 Thu only; 16 Fri only; 17 Sat only. See "Working with specialized date functions" in Chapter 15.
XIRR	Returns the internal rate of return for a schedule of cash flows that is not necessarily periodic. Takes the form =XIRR(**values**, **dates**, guess), where *values* is a series of cash flows that corresponds to a schedule of payments in dates, *dates* is a schedule of payment dates that corresponds to the cash flow payments, and *guess* is a number you think is close to the result.
XNPV	Returns the net present value for a schedule of cash flows that is not necessarily periodic. Takes the form =XNPV(**rate**, **values**, **dates**), where *rate* is the discount rate to apply to the cash flows, *values* is a series of cash flows that corresponds to a schedule of payments in dates, and *dates* is a schedule of payment dates that corresponds to the cash flow payments.
XOR	Returns an Exclusive OR of all arguments. Takes the form =XOR(**logical1**, logical2, ...), where *logical* values are 1 to 254 conditions you want to test.
YEAR	Returns the value of the year portion of a serial date/time value. Takes the form =YEAR(**serial_number**), where *serial_number* can be a date value, a reference, or text in date format enclosed in quotation marks. See "Working with date and time functions" in Chapter 15.
YEARFRAC	Returns a decimal number that represents the portion of a year that falls between two given dates. Takes the form =YEARFRAC(**start_date**, **end_date**, basis), where *start_date* and *end_date* specify the span you want to convert to a decimal, and *basis* is the type of day count (0 or omitted = 30/360, 1 = actual/actual, 2 = actual/360, 3 = actual/365, 4 = European 30/360). See "Working with specialized date functions" in Chapter 15.

Function	Description
YIELD	Determines the annual yield for a security that pays interest on a periodic basis. Takes the form =YIELD(**settlement, maturity, rate, price, redemption, frequency,** basis), where *settlement* is the day you pay for the security, *maturity* is the maturity date of the security, *rate* is the interest rate of the security at the issue date, *price* is the security's price, *redemption* is the value of the security at redemption, *frequency* is the number of coupon payments made per year (1 = annual, 2 = semiannual, 4 = quarterly), and *basis* is the day-count basis of the security (if 0 or omitted = 30/360, if 1 = actual/actual, if 2 = actual/360, if 3 = actual/365, if 4 = European 30/360). See "Analyzing securities" in Chapter 16.
YIELDDISC	Calculates the annual yield for a discounted security. Takes the form =YIELDDISC(**settlement, maturity, price, redemption,** basis), where *settlement* is the day you pay for the security, *maturity* is the maturity date of the security, *price* is the security's price, *redemption* is the value of the security at redemption, and *basis* is the day-count basis of the security (if 0 or omitted = 30/360, if 1 = actual/actual, if 2 = actual/360, if 3 = actual/365, if 4 = European 30/360). See "Analyzing securities" in Chapter 16.
YIELDMAT	Calculates the annual yield for a security that pays its interest at maturity. Takes the form =YIELDMAT(**settlement, maturity, issue, rate, price,** basis), where *settlement* is the day you pay for the security, *maturity* is the maturity date of the security, *issue* is the issue date of the security, *rate* is the interest rate of the security at the issue date, *price* is the security's price, and *basis* is the day-count basis of the security (if 0 or omitted = 30/360, if 1 = actual/actual, if 2 = actual/360, if 3 = actual/365, if 4 = European 30/360). See "Analyzing securities" in Chapter 16.
Z.TEST	Returns the two-tailed P-value of a Z-test (generates a standard score for x with respect to the data set and *array*, and returns the two-tailed probability for the normal distribution). This function takes the form =Z.TEST(**array, x,** sigma), where *array* is the array or range of data against which to test x, x is the value to test, and *sigma* is the known population's standard deviation. The old form of this function is ZTEST, which is still supported as a Compatibility Function.

Index to troubleshooting topics

Index

Symbols and numbers

` (accent grave), 1019
& (ampersand), 478–479
' (apostrophe), apostrophe ('),
* (asterisk). *See* asterisk (*)
@ (at symbol). *See* at symbol (@)
\ (backslash). *See* backslash (\)
^ (caret), 149–150
: (colon), 501–502
, (comma). *See* comma (,)
. (decimal point). *See* decimals
$ (dollar sign). *See* dollar sign ($)
= (equal sign). *See* equal sign (=)
> (greater than). *See* greater than (>)
######... (insufficient column space indicators), 147, 360, 577
< (less than), 522, 742–744
– (minus sign), 144–145. *See also* subtraction
(number sign), 332
% (percent sign). *See* percent sign (%)
+ (plus sign), 144–145, 467–468. *See also* addition
? (question mark). *See* question mark (?)
" (quotation marks), 478
; (semicolon), 1019
/ (slash). *See* slash (/)
_ (underscore character), 333, 926
{ } (curly braces), 513–514, 516
( ) parentheses. *See* parentheses ( )
... (ellipsis) buttons, 18, 25
1 through 9 keys, shortcut commands with, 1018
3-D controls for graphics formatting, 402, 407, 414–417
3-D names, 491–492
3-D references, 496–497
3-D View command, 2003 Chart menu, 1007
15-digit precision limit, 146
24-hour (military) time convention, 567, 572
64-bit Excel, 11
2003 menu commands, 2013 ribbon equivalents
   Chart menu, 1007
   Data menu, 1005–1007
   Edit menu, 999
   File menu, 997–998
   Format menu, 1003
   Formatting toolbar, 1010–1011
   Help menu, 1008
   Insert menu, 1002
   Standard toolbar, 1008–1009
   Tools menu, 1003–1005
   View menu, 1000–1001
   Window menu, 1008

A

A1 cell, jumping to, 19, 134
ABS function (absolute value), 1034
absolute references, 470, 474–475
accent grave (`), 1019
Access, Microsoft
   importing an entire table from, 843–844
   querying. *See* Microsoft Query
accessibility
   Accessibility Checker, 99
   Alt key for keyboard commands, 100
   cell value AutoComplete option, 100
   Ease Of Access options, 101
   gridline colors, 100
   MSAA, 99
   panning options, 100
   Provide Feedback With Sound option, 100
   ScreenTips options, 99–100
   scrolling options, 100
   worksheet tab color options, 100
   zooming options for, 100–101
Account command, 39–40
accounting
   Accounting formats, 323–326, 335, 543
   billing formats, custom, 336
   depreciation and amortization. *See* depreciation functions
   GAAP (generally accepted accounting principles), 326
   investments. *See* investment functions
   units for. *See* currency
ACCRINT functions, 594–595, 1034
accuracy, 15-digit standard, 511–512
ACOS function, 1034
ACOSH function, 1034
ACOT function, 1034
ACOTH function, 1034
Across Worksheets command, 230, 258
Activate Product command, 1008
active areas of worksheets, 20, 131
active cells
   definition of, 15
   fill handles, turning on, 131
   moving within a selection, 141
   selection of, 134

H

S

Protect Workbook command, 167, 169
Quick Access Toolbar customizations, attaching, 91–92
recent, opening, 57
recovering corrupted, 60–61
saving. *See* saving files
Select All Sheets command, 155
subsets of worksheets, new workbooks from, 893
summary information, adding to files, 54–56
tab split handles, 19
templates for. *See* templates
View Side By Side button, 176–178
windows on, 16
WORKDAY functions, 580–582, 1085–1086
worksheets
active areas of, 20
autofitting all rows or columns, 361
background graphics for, 358
cells of. *See* cells
columns of. *See* columns
components of, 15–16
copying, 157–158
creating new, 16
deleting, 154–156
designing. *See* designing worksheets
dragging, 157–158
freezing panes, 160–162
groups. *See* groups, worksheet
hiding, 170–171, 185
inserting new, 154–156
keyboard shortcuts for managing, 1032
keyboard shortcuts for navigation, 19
managing, 154–156, 1032
moving, 157–158
naming, 156
navigational controls, 18–20
New Sheet button, 154–155, 253–254
ranges of, selecting, 155
renaming, 156
rows of. *See* rows
scrolling techniques, 18–20
Select All Sheets command, 155
sets of. *See* workbooks
Sheet commands, 2003 Format menu, 1003
SHEET functions, 1078
sheet tab shortcut menu, 154–155, 157
splitting into panes, 159–160
tabs, 100, 156, 253
ungrouping, 256–257
Unhide button, 185
windows on, 16
Worksheet command, Insert menu, 1002
workspaces
deprecated in 2013, 20
worksheets of. *See* worksheets
Wrap Text button, 148
wrapping text, 342–344

X
XIRR function, 1086
XLAM file format, 50
XLK file extension, 53
XLS file format, 50, 909, 916
XLSB file format, 50, 916
XLSM files, 50, 916
XLStart folder, 59
XLSX file format, 14, 46, 49–51, 916
XLT file format, 51
XLTM file format, 50
XLTX file format, 50
XML file format
Excel 97-2003 Add-In format, 51
external data integration benefit, 14
FILTERXML function, 1054
importing data from, 848–852
increased capacity and speed from, 12
mapping XML elements, 851
multiple file imports, 852
schema files, 850
XML commands, 2003 Data menu, 1007
XML Source task pane, 850–852
XNPV function, 1086
XOR function, 1086
XPS files, 62, 461–464
xVelocity, 827

Y
YEAR functions, 579, 1086
YEARFRAC function, 580
YIELD functions, 596, 1087

Z
zero values
Accounting format display of, 324
#DIV/0! error value, 480
hiding display of, 98
suppressing display of, 335
ZIP codes, 329–330
Zoom On Roll With IntelliMouse option, 222
zooming
accessibility options for, 100–101
effect for multiple windows, 179–180
Fit Selection option, 162
selection enabled by, 135
status bar controls for, 38
wheel mouse, with, 18, 164
worksheet controls for, 162–163
Zoom command location, 1001
Zoom On Roll With IntelliMouse option, 222
Zoom To Selection option, 162–163
Z.TEST function, 1087

About the authors

Mark Dodge has been working with and writing about Microsoft software since 1989, and is co-author of over a dozen Microsoft Press books on Microsoft Excel. As a former senior technical writer at Microsoft, he created print, online, and multimedia documentation for all Microsoft Office programs. Mark is a lifelong jazz and rock musician, as well as an award-winning fine art photographer.

Craig Stinson, an industry journalist since 1981, was editor of *Softalk for the IBM Personal Computer*, one of the earliest machine-specific computer magazines. He is the author of more than 20 Microsoft Press books about Windows and Excel.

Microsoft

How To Download Your eBook

Thank you for purchasing this Microsoft Press® title. Your companion PDF eBook is ready to download from O'Reilly Media, official distributor of Microsoft Press titles.

To download your eBook, go to http://aka.ms/PressEbook
and follow the instructions.

Please note: You will be asked to create a free online account and enter the access code below.

Your access code:

> ## TGTQPNM

Microsoft Excel 2013 Inside Out

Your PDF eBook allows you to:

- Search the full text
- Print
- Copy and paste

Best yet, you will be notified about free updates to your eBook.

If you ever lose your eBook file, you can download it again just by logging in to your account.

Need help? Please contact:
mspbooksupport@oreilly.com
or call 800-889-8969.

What do you think of this book?

We want to hear from you!
To participate in a brief online survey, please visit:

microsoft.com/learning/booksurvey

Tell us how well this book meets your needs—what works effectively, and what we can do better. Your feedback will help us continually improve our books and learning resources for you.

Thank you in advance for your input!